Lecture Notes in Computer Science   8950

Commenced Publication in 1973
Founding and Former Series Editors:
Gerhard Goos, Juris Hartmanis, and Jan van Leeuwen

Rocco De Nicola   Rolf Hennicker (Eds.)

Software, Services, and Systems

Essays Dedicated to Martin Wirsing
on the Occasion of His Retirement from the Chair
of Programming and Software Engineering

Springer

Volume Editors

Rocco De Nicola
IMT - Institute for Advanced Studies
Piazza San Francesco 19, 55100 Lucca, Italy
E-mail: rocco.denicola@imtlucca.it

Rolf Hennicker
Ludwig-Maximilians-Universität München
Institut für Informatik
Oettingenstraße 67, 80538 München, Germany
E-mail: hennicke@pst.ifi.lmu.de

Cover illustration: Wassily Kandinsky, St. George III, 1911.
Source: Städtische Galerie im Lenbachhaus in Munich, Germany
(http://www.lenbachhaus.de/collection/the-blue-rider/).

Photograph on p. V: The photograph of the honoree was taken by Christoph Olesinski.
Used with permission.

ISSN 0302-9743   e-ISSN 1611-3349
ISBN 978-3-319-15544-9   e-ISBN 978-3-319-15545-6
DOI 10.1007/978-3-319-15545-6
Springer Cham Heidelberg New York Dordrecht London

Library of Congress Control Number: 2015930335

LNCS Sublibrary: SL 2 – Programming and Software Engineering

Typesetting: Camera-ready by author, data conversion by Scientific Publishing Services, Chennai, India

Printed on acid-free paper

Springer is part of Springer Science+Business Media (www.springer.com)

Martin Wirsing

Preface

This volume contains the 38 papers written by close collaborators and friends of Martin Wirsing on the occasion of the celebration of his retirement from the chair of Programming and Software Engineering at the Ludwig-Maximilians-Universität in Munich.

The volume is a reflection, with gratitude and admiration, on Martin's highly creative, remarkably fruitful, and intellectually generous life, which is thriving as strongly as ever. It is also a snapshot of research ideas that in many cases have been deeply influenced by Martin's work. In a sense, it is also a vantage point from which to foresee further developments to come: by Martin himself, and by many other people encouraged and stimulated by his friendship and example.

The book consists of six sections. The first section contains personal remembrance and expression of gratitude from Martin's friends. The remaining five sections comprise groups of papers corresponding to specific scientific interests of Martin and are ordered according to his scientific evolution:

– Logical and Algebraic Foundations
– Algebraic Specifications, Institutions, and Rewriting
– Foundations of Software Engineering
– Service-Oriented Systems
– Adaptive and Autonomic Systems

As book editors, we were helped by several reviewers, who gave comments on the submitted papers and suggestions for their improvement. We would like to thank all of them for their very professional and reliable help. In fact, each paper was reviewed by at least two colleagues and for a few papers we had a couple of rounds of interactions with authors and reviewers before we were sure that the standard of the published work was in line with what Martin deserves.

This volume was presented to Martin on March 6, 2015, during a two-day symposium held at the Institut für Informatik of Ludwig-Maximilians-Universität in Munich. During the symposium all papers were presented by one of the authors and we also had three invited talks from eminent scientists, whose friendship with Martin dates back many years. We thank Manfred Broy, José Meseguer, and Ugo Montanari for having accepted our invitation.

We would also like to thank the Programming and Software Technology group at the Institut für Informatik of LMU for the support in the organization of the symposium, and EU project ASCENS and LMU Munich for the financial and logistic support. We are grateful to Alfred Hofmann and to the Springer LNCS team for their support during the publication phase of this Festschrift and we take the occasion to acknowledge the excellent support provided by the conference management system EasyChair.

Our editorial activity made us further experience how much Martin is appreciated all around the world, and to witness the great esteem with which he is held in the scientific community. Congratulations Martin!

March 2015   Rocco De Nicola
                                                                       Rolf Hennicker

Organization

Reviewers

Arbab, Farhad
Baumeister, Hubert
ter Beek, Maurice H.
Bensalem, Saddek
Bergstra, Jan
Bicocchi, Nicola
Breu, Ruth
Bruni, Roberto
Bureš, Tomáš
Caires, Luis
Cengarle, María Victoria
Choppy, Christine
Combaz, Jacques
Corradini, Andrea
Ernst, Gidon
Fiadeiro, José Luiz
Futatsugi, Kokichi
Gadducci, Fabio
Gaina, Daniel
Gilmore, Stephen
Gnesi, Stefania
Hillston, Jane
Hofmann, Martin
Hussmann, Heinrich
Hölzl, Matthias
Klarl, Annabelle
Knapp, Alexander
Koch, Nora
Kuhlemann, Martin
Kurz, Alexander
Latella, Diego
Lengauer, Christian

Loreti, Michele
Majster-Cederbaum, Mila
Massink, Mieke
Mayer, Philip
Merz, Stephan
Meseguer, José
Montanari, Ugo
Mossakowski, Till
Möller, Bernhard
Nielson, Flemming
Nielson, Hanne Riis
Nipkow, Tobias
Ölveczky, Peter
Orejas, Fernando
Padawitz, Peter
Pattinson, Dirk
Pugliese, Rosario
Reus, Bernhard
Roggenbach, Markus
Sannella, Donald
Schröder, Lutz
Serbedzija, Nikola
Störrle, Harald
Talcott, Carolyn
Tarlecki, Andrzej
Tiezzi, Francesco
Tribastone, Mirco
Tůma, Petr
Tuosto, Emilio
Vandin, Andrea
Zambonelli, Franco
Zavattaro, Gianluigi

Table of Contents

A Homage to Martin Wirsing.. 1
  Rocco De Nicola and Rolf Hennicker

Homage from Friends

Ode to the PST 13
  Matthias Hölzl, Nora Koch, Philip Mayer, and Andreas Schroeder

From Formal Logic through Program Transformations to System
Dynamics: 40 Years of Meeting Points with Martin Wirsing 24
  Wolfgang Hesse

The Broad View: How to Spawn a Radical Organizational
Transformation 'En Passant' 27
  Heinrich Hussmann

Logical and Algebraic Foundations

Modal Satisfiability via SMT Solving 30
  Carlos Areces, Pascal Fontaine, and Stephan Merz

Division by Zero in Common Meadows 46
  Jan A. Bergstra and Alban Ponse

Logical Relations and Nondeterminism 62
  Martin Hofmann

Simplified Coalgebraic Trace Equivalence 75
  Alexander Kurz, Stefan Milius, Dirk Pattinson, and Lutz Schröder

Localized Operational Termination in General Logics 91
  Salvador Lucas and José Meseguer

Partial Valuation Structures for Qualitative Soft Constraints 115
  *Alexander Schiendorfer, Alexander Knapp, Jan-Philipp Steghöfer,
  Gerrit Anders, Florian Siefert, and Wolfgang Reif*

Algebraic Specifications, Institutions, and Rewriting

An Institution for Object-Z with Inheritance and Polymorphism 134
  *Hubert Baumeister, Mohamed Bettaz, Mourad Maouche,
  and M'hamed Mosteghanemi*

Abstract Constraint Data Types 155
  José Luiz Fiadeiro and Fernando Orejas

Generate & Check Method for Verifying Transition Systems
in CafeOBJ 171
  Kokichi Futatsugi

Institutions for OCL-Like Expression Languages 193
  Alexander Knapp and María Victoria Cengarle

Towards an Institutional Framework for Heterogeneous Formal
Development in UML — A Position Paper — 215
  Alexander Knapp, Till Mossakowski, and Markus Roggenbach

Formal Analysis of Leader Election in MANETs
Using Real-Time Maude 231
  Si Liu, Peter Csaba Ölveczky, and José Meseguer

The Foundational Legacy of ASL 253
  Donald Sannella and Andrzej Tarlecki

Soft Agents: Exploring Soft Constraints to Model Robust Adaptive
Distributed Cyber-Physical Agent Systems 273
  Carolyn Talcott, Farhad Arbab, and Maneesh Yadav

Foundations of Software Engineering

Structured Document Algebra in Action 291
  *Don Batory, Peter Höfner, Dominik Köppl, Bernhard Möller,
  and Andreas Zelend*

From EU Projects to a Family of Model Checkers:
From Kandinsky to KandISTI 312
  Maurice H. ter Beek, Stefania Gnesi, and Franco Mazzanti

Pragmatic Formal Specification of System Properties by Tables 329
  Manfred Broy

Formal Modelling for Cooking Assistance 355
  *Bernd Krieg-Brückner, Serge Autexier, Martin Rink,
  and Sidoine Ghomsi Nokam*

A Framework for Defining and Comparing Modelling Methods 377
  Gianna Reggio, Egidio Astesiano, and Christine Choppy

A Theory Agenda for Component-Based Design...................... 409
  Joseph Sifakis, Saddek Bensalem, Simon Bliudze, and Marius Bozga

Effective and Efficient Model Clone Detection 440
  Harald Störrle

Living Modeling of IT Architectures: Challenges and Solutions......... 458
  Thomas Trojer, Matthias Farwick, Martin Häusler, and Ruth Breu

Service-Oriented Systems

A Flow Analysis Approach for Service-Oriented Architectures 475
Bernhard Bauer, Melanie Langermeier, and Christian Saad

Service Composition for Collective Adaptive Systems 490
Stephen Gilmore, Jane Hillston, and Mirco Tribastone

The Evolution of Jolie: From Orchestrations
to Adaptable Choreographies 506
Ivan Lanese, Fabrizio Montesi, and Gianluigi Zavattaro

Stochastic Model Checking of the Stochastic Quality Calculus 522
Flemming Nielson, Hanne Riis Nielson, and Kebin Zeng

Adaptive and Autonomic Systems

Software-Intensive Systems for Smart Cities: From Ensembles
to Superorganisms 538
Nicola Bicocchi, Letizia Leonardi, and Franco Zambonelli

A White Box Perspective on Behavioural Adaptation 552
*Roberto Bruni, Andrea Corradini, Fabio Gadducci,
Alberto Lluch Lafuente, and Andrea Vandin*

Rule-Based Modeling and Static Analysis of Self-adaptive Systems
by Graph Transformation 582
*Antonio Bucchiarone, Hartmut Ehrig, Claudia Ermel,
Patrizio Pelliccione, and Olga Runge*

Formalization of Invariant Patterns
for the Invariant Refinement Method 602
*Tomáš Bureš, Ilias Gerostathopoulos, Jaroslav Keznikl,
František Plášil, and Petr Tůma*

On StocS: A Stochastic Extension of SCEL......................... 619
Diego Latella, Michele Loreti, Mieke Massink, and Valerio Senni

Programming Autonomic Systems with Multiple Constraint Stores 641
Ugo Montanari, Rosario Pugliese, and Francesco Tiezzi

Adaptive and Autonomous Systems and Their Impact on Us 662
Nikola Šerbedžija

The KnowLang Approach to Self-adaptation 676
Emil Vassev and Mike Hinchey

Author Index 693

A Homage to Martin Wirsing

Rocco De Nicola[1] and Rolf Hennicker[2]

[1] IMT Institute for Advanced Studies Lucca, Italy
[2] Ludwig-Maximilians-Universität München, Germany

1 Martin's Origins, Positions and Services

Martin Wirsing was born on Christmas Eve, December 24th, 1948, in Bayreuth, a Bavarian town which is famous for the annually celebrated Richard Wagner Festival. There he visited the Lerchenbühl School and the High-School "Christian Ernestinum" where he followed the humanistic branch focusing on Latin and Ancient Greek. After that, from 1968 to 1974, Martin studied Mathematics at University Paris 7 and at Ludwig-Maximilians-Universität in Munich. In 1971 he became Maitrise-en-Sciences Mathematiques at the University Paris 7 and, in 1974, he got the Diploma in Mathematics at LMU Munich.

After graduating Martin took up a position as a research and teaching assistant within the "Sonderforschungsbereich 49 für Programmiertechnik" at the Technical University of Munich where he stayed until 1983. This was a tremendously fruitful time and the beginning of Martin's extraordinary career. At TU Munich, Martin was a member of the CIP-group which was formed by Friedrich L. Bauer and Klaus Samelson to investigate new methods for program development with correctness-preserving program transformations. Martin's contributions were backed by his excellent knowledge in the field of Mathematical Logic. In 1976 Martin got his PhD degree with a thesis entitled "Das Entscheidungsproblem der Prädikatenlogik 1. Stufe mit Funktionszeichen in Herbrandformeln". His supervisor was Kurt Schütte, an important German logician and the chair of the Mathematical Logic group at LMU Munich. Schütte was a student of David Hilbert who became this way a scientific grandfather of Martin. Five years later, 1981, Martin went to the University of Edinburgh where he worked for half a year as a substitute for the chair of Rod Burstall. During that time he started a collaboration with Don Sannella and developed with him the foundations for a kernel algebraic specification language, called ASL, which was the topic of Martin's habilitation thesis a few years later. In Edinburgh Martin also met the first author of this foreword who had just arrived there as a PhD student not knowing that a close collaboration with Martin will follow 20 years later.

In 1983 Martin became professor at the University of Passau where he helped building up the newly founded Faculty for Mathematics and Informatics. Two years later, he got a chair of computer science with focus on programming languages. Martin staid in Passau till 1992. During that time he formed a highly recognised and successful research group which was involved in several national and international projects dealing with algebraic specifications, formal program

R. De Nicola and R. Hennicker (Eds.): Wirsing Festschrift, LNCS 8950, pp. 1–12, 2015.

development, reusability of software and object-oriented software engineering. Five doctoral theses and one habilitation treatise have been successfully completed under Martin's guidance in Passau. Martin served as dean and as vice-dean of the faculty, in both cases for a two year term. Between 1989 and 1992 he was additionally leading the research group "Programming Systems" of the Bavarian Research Center for Knowledge-based Systems and he was member of its board of directors.

The year 1992 brought Martin back to the town of his scientific origins. He took over the chair of the Research Unit for Programming and Software Technology (PST) at Ludwig-Maximilians-Universität in Munich. At that time Informatics was introduced as a Diploma course of studies at the Department of Informatics of LMU and, again, much of Martin's work was devoted to establish the new course and to help building up the department. Soon, he formed a strong research group at LMU which continuously changed over time resulting, until now, in 26 doctoral theses and three habilitations. Martin's PST group has participated in more than thirty national and international research projects which dealt with hot new topics like mobile systems, hypermedia applications, service-oriented architectures and autonomous, self-adaptive systems. Martin's ideas and his talents in organisation were also recognised and appreciated by the leading administrative institutions of LMU. From 1999 to 2001 he was dean of the Faculty for Mathematics and Informatics, from 2002 to 2004 he was member of LMU's senate, and from 2006 to 2007 he was director of the Institute for Informatics. In 2007 Martin became vice-chair of the senate and he filled this position until 2010. During that time he was also member of the University Council of LMU which is now the most successful university in German's excellence initiative. Since 2010 Martin is vice-president of LMU taking care of studies and teaching.

Also outside of LMU, Martin's advice in scientific and organisational issues was very much in demand by national and international scientific groups and organisations. It would go far beyond the scope of this foreword to mention all scientific boards and groups in which Martin was a valuable member, so we restrict ourselves to some selected ones. From 1999-2007 Martin was speaker of the Specification and Semantics group of the German Informatics Society GI, from 2006 to 2011 he was member of the scientific board of FIRST (Fraunhofer Institute for Computer Architecture and Software Technique), from 2007 to 2010 Martin served as chairman of the scientific board of INRIA (Institut National de Recherche en Informatique et Automatique, France), and from 2008 to 2011 he was coordinator of the advisory board of the IMT Institute for Advanced Studies in Lucca. Currently, Martin is member of the scientific committees of the University of Bordeaux, IMDEA Software Madrid, and the Institut Mines-Télécom. He is and was member of the editorial boards of several scientific journals and book series including Theoretical Computer Science, Journal of Computer Science and Technology, Journal of Software and Informatics, the AMAST Series in Computing, and the LNCS Transactions on Foundations for Mastering Change. Martin is also an active member of the IFIP Working Group 1.3 on Foundations of System Specification and an emeritus member of the Working Group 2.2 dealing with Formal Description of Programming Concepts. He was member of numerous program committees and chairman of many scientific meetings and conferences including WADT'83 and 2002, STACS'87 and 88, PLILP'91, AMAST'96, EDOC 2008, FASE 2009, and TGC 2010.

During his career Martin has also spent some long periods as visiting researcher/professor at many institutions, among the most renowned and influential ones. We would like to mention the Department of Computer Science of the University of Edinburgh - Scotland, Bell Labs at Murray Hill in New Jersey - USA, the Department of Computer and Information Science at University of Genoa - Italy, the Computer Science Laboratory of SRI in Stanford - USA and the IMDEA Software Institute in Madrid - Spain.

2 Martin's Research

Before we summarise Martin's research achievements, we want to pay tribute to his extraordinary personality as a researcher, colleague, and friend. Martin is always curious. He wants to understand new approaches and results, he is tireless in listening and asking questions, and he contributes with ideas, proposals and solutions. Martin has visions. His intuition leads him continuously to challenging new research directions which he pursues with great commitment and resilience for finding the right scientific paths and collaborations[1]. Martin is encouraging. He is open for the work of others and supports them with ideas and suggestions. And: Martin is always fair to colleagues and to students.

Martin Wirsing is the head of LMU's research group on Programming and Software Technology which consists of about 15 researchers and PhD students. He is the co-author and editor of more than 20 books and has published around 250 scientific papers. His research areas comprise:

1. Logic,
2. Algebraic Specification Techniques,
3. Software Development using Formal Mehods,
4. Semantics of Specification and Programming Languages,
5. Systematic Development of Service-Oriented Systems,
6. Engineering Adaptive and Autonomic Systems.

Martin's research ambition has always been to support the development of correct software. In the following, we try to sketch a picture of Martin's research by pointing to selected publications and projects being aware that our account is far from being complete.

2.1 Selected Publications

From the CIP-Project to Algebraic Specifications. Martin started his research career at the Technical University of Munich as a member of the CIP group founded

---

[1] Resilience and a strong will to win was also a distinguished quality of Martin when he was playing soccer or table tennis which was really unfortunate for his opponents.

by Friedrich L. Bauer and Klaus Samelson. CIP is an acronym for Computer-aided, Intuition-guided Programming. The objective of this project was to investigate a comprehensive program development methodology which involves correctness preserving program transformations using a multi-level (wide spectrum) programming language, called CIP-L. By exploiting his broad knowledge of mathematical logic and universal algebra, Martin contributed to this project by investigating theoretical foundations of CIP-L, in particular techniques for transforming functional, recursive programs into iterative programs [14]. A crucial issue for proving the correctness of such transformations was the formal treatment of programs and data structures. A promising approach for this purpose were abstract data types which appeared in the mid-seventies as a new research direction in the United States initiated by the PhD thesis of John Guttag in 1975. The CIP-group took up this idea and, in the following years, Martin did a lot of work on algebraic specifications, often in cooperation with Manfred Broy, considering, e.g., partial abstract types [8] and hierarchies of abstract data types [9]. Soon Martin became a key person in that area which is reflected by his article on algebraic specifications in the Handbook of Theoretical Computer Science [12]. An important part of program development concerns modular construction, stepwise refinement and observational abstraction. These aspects are incorporated in the algebraic specification language ASL [10,11] whose foundations as a kernel language with a model class semantics have been investigated together with Don Sannella during Martin's stay in Edinburgh in 1981.[2]

Software Development and Semantics. A prerequisite for proving the correctness of a program against a specification is the availability of a formal semantics for both the specification and the programming language at hand. Concerning the semantics of programming languages, a foundational study of a denotational semantics of nondeterministic and noncontinuous constructs has been worked out by Martin in an earlier paper with Broy and Gnatz in [20]. Much later, motivated by the success of Java and its concurrency mechanisms, Martin has worked on a structural operational semantics for multi-threaded Java which formalises precisely the Java specification [22]. This was the first formal semantics for multi-threaded Java which did not need any additional assumptions on the memory model. At that time, beginning of the nineties, object-oriented software engineering methods based on diagrammatic, semi-formal models as specifications became more and more popular. Martin was one of the first researchers to realise that diagrammatic notations, enhanced by formal annotations, would provide a promising tool for the production of correct software. At a time where UML

---

[2] Observational abstraction is obtained in ASL by relaxing the model class of a specification w.r.t. observational equivalence of algebras. Another, at a first glance, totally different looking approach is to relax the satisfaction relation w.r.t. observational equivalence between the elements of an algebra as suggested in a paper of Horst Reichel and in Goguen's Hidden Algebra. The second author of this foreword remembers well that after a dinner with Martin and Michel Bidoit, Martin raised the question whether the two different approaches couldn't been formally related. The outcome was the paper [13] which gave a positive answer to Martin's question.

was not yet on the table, Martin and Alexander Knapp extended the OOSE approach of Jacobson, which was built on use cases, class and interaction diagrams, to FOOSE, a "Formal Approach to Object-Oriented Software Engineering" [16] suitable for formal analysis and simulation. With the appearance of UML Martin was interested in extensions of UML which would allow formal reasoning. He has co-authored two papers [23,24] proposing a heterogeneous approach to the semantics of UML. Martin's idea was to provide a formal semantics for each of the different diagram types and to relate them by institution morphisms. Thus one can analyse the consistency between different models representing different views or different abstraction levels of a system. Later, in [25], Martin has worked on a translation of KLAIM specifications for distributed, asynchronously communicating systems into Maude. He has proved the correctness of the translation such that Maude's tools can be soundly used for analysis. This was the first implementation of KLAIM that has been proven to be correct.

Systems Engineering. Martin was always very much interested in new trends of software systems and software engineering. He worked in various projects (see below) for the Systematic Development of Mobile Systems, Service-Oriented Systems, Physiological Computing Systems, Hypermedia Applications, and Adaptive Autonomic Systems. His concern was always to support the different phases of the software lifecycle and to provide means for formal analysis and reasoning. In the field of mobile systems, Martin has contributed in [39] to an extension of UML class and activity diagrams that allows to model the migration of objects from one location to another. He has studied specification and refinement of mobile systems in [7] and [19]. Martin's work on service-oriented systems [26,27] led to a systematic development methodology using a service-oriented extension of UML, a transformation of UML models into a family of process calculi, and quantitative analysis methods with the stochastic process algebra PEPA. Martin has also worked on physiological computing [33,35] which deals with interactive systems deducing emotional states of human beings from physiological sensor inputs. In [32] Martin has presented together with Nora Koch a reference model for adaptive hypermedia applications which was highly recognised by the community. Martin's work on adaptive autonomous systems was carried out in the context of the still running ASCENS project. His vision about a systematic development of such systems is described in [36] incorporating the whole software lifecycle from requirements engineering to implementation in the language SCEL (Software Component Ensemble Language). It includes a quantitative analysis method using continuous-time Markov chains and ordinary differential equations.

In the last ten years Martin has also contributed to the field of soft constraints which are applicable in different areas like, e.g., Web services or optimisation of scheduling algorithms. During his visit at SRI International, in 2006, he has developed with Carolyn Talcott and colleagues a rewriting logic framework for soft constraints and has implemented a soft constraint solver in Maude [37].

This work has been extended in [38] to allow modelling of decision problems with multiple preference criteria.

References

(I) Logic
  1. M.: Das Entscheidungsproblem der Klasse von Formeln, die höchstens zwei Primformeln enthalten. Manuscripta Mathematica 22, 13–25 (1977)
  2. Wirsing, M.: Kleine unentscheidbare Klassen der Prädikatenlogik mit Identität und Funktionszeichen. Archiv für mathematische Logik und Grundlagenforschung 19(1-2), 97–109 (1978)
  3. Wirsing, M.: "Small" universal Post systems. Zeitschrift für mathematische Logik und Grundlagen der Mathematik 25, 559–564 (1979), Journal of Symbolic Logic 44, 476–477 (1979)
  4. Bauer, F.L., Wirsing, M.: Elementare Aussagenlogik, 228 p. Springer, Heidelberg (1991)
  5. Hennicker, R., Wirsing, M., Bidoit, M.: Proof systems for structured specifications with observability operators. Theoretical Computer Science 173, 393–443 (1997)
  6. Poernomo, I., Crossley, J., Wirsing, M.: Adapting Proofs-as-Programs: The Curry–Howard Protocol. Springer Monographs in Computer Science, 420 p. (2005)
  7. Merz, S., Wirsing, M., Zappe, J.: A Spatio-Temporal Logic for the Specification and Refinement of Mobile Systems. In: Pezzé, M. (ed.) FASE 2003. LNCS, vol. 2621, pp. 87–101. Springer, Heidelberg (2003)

(II) Algebraic Specification Techniques
  8. Broy, M., Wirsing, M.: Partial Abstract Types. Acta Informatica 18, 47–64 (1982)
  9. Broy, M., Dosch, W., Partsch, H., Pepper, P., Wirsing, M.: On Hierarchies of Abstract Data Types. Acta Informatica 20, 1–34 (1983)
  10. Sannella, D., Wirsing, M.: A Kernel Language for Algebraic Specification and Implementation. In: Karpinski, M. (ed.) Colloquium on Foundations of Computation Theory, Linkping (Schweden). LNCS, vol. 158, pp. 413–427. Springer, Heidelberg (1983)
  11. Wirsing, M.: Structured Algebraic Specifications: A Kernel Language. Theoretical Computer Science 43, 123–250 (1986)
  12. Wirsing, M.: Algebraic Specification. In: van Leeuwen, J. (ed.) Handbook of Theoretical Computer Science, pp. 675–788. North-Holland, Amsterdam (1990)
  13. Bidoit, M., Hennicker, R., Wirsing, M.: Behavioural and Abstractor Specifications. Science of Computer Programming 25, 149–186 (1995)

(III) Software Development using Formal Methods
  14. Bauer, F.L., Broy, M., Dosch, W., Gnatz, R., Krieg-Brückner, B., Laut, A., Luckmann, M., Matzner, T.A., Möller, B., Partsch, H., Pepper, P., Samelson, K., Steinbüggen, R., Wössner, H., Wirsing, M.: Programming in a Wide Spectrum Language: A Collection of Examples. Science of Computer Programming 1, 73–114 (1981)

15. Broy, M., Wirsing, M.: Correct Software: From Experiments to Applications. In: Jähnichen, S., Broy, M. (eds.) KORSO 1995. LNCS, vol. 1009, pp. 1–24. Springer, Heidelberg (1995)

16. Wirsing, M., Knapp, A.: A Formal Approach to Object-Oriented Software Engineering. Theo. Comp. Sci. 285, 519–560 (2002)

17. Reus, B., Wirsing, M., Hennicker, R.: A Hoare Calculus for Verifying Java Realizations of OCL-Constrained Design Models. In: Hussmann, H. (ed.) FASE 2001. LNCS, vol. 2029, pp. 300–317. Springer, Heidelberg (2001)

18. Wirsing, M., Baumeister, H., Knapp, A.: Property-Driven Development. In: Cuellar, J., Liu, Z. (eds.) Second IEEE Internat. Conf. on Software Engineering and Formal Methods, SEFM 2004, pp. 96–103. IEEE Computer Society, Beijing (2004)

19. Knapp, A., Merz, S., Wirsing, M., Zappe, J.: Specification and Refinement of Mobile Systems in MTLA and Mobile UML. Theoretical Computer Science 351(2), 184–202 (2006)

(IV) Semantics of Specification and Programming Languages

20. Broy, M., Gnatz, R., Wirsing, M.: Semantics of Nondeterministic and Noncontinuous Constructs. In: Bauer, F.L., Broy, M. (eds.) Program Construction. LNCS, vol. 69, pp. 553–592. Springer, Heidelberg (1979)

21. Broy, M., Pepper, P., Wirsing, M.: On the Algebraic Definition of Programming Languages. TOPLAS 9(1), 54–99 (1987)

22. Cenciarelli, P., Knapp, A., Reus, B., Wirsing, M.: An Event-Based Structural Operational Semantics of Multi-threaded Java. In: Alves-Foss, J. (ed.) Formal Syntax and Semantics of Java. LNCS, vol. 1523, pp. 157–200. Springer, Heidelberg (1999)

23. Cengarle, M.V., Knapp, A., Tarlecki, A., Wirsing, M.: A Heterogeneous Approach to UML Semantics. In: Degano, P., De Nicola, R., Meseguer, J. (eds.) Concurrency, Graphs and Models. LNCS, vol. 5065, pp. 383–402. Springer, Heidelberg (2008)

24. Boronat, A., Knapp, A., Meseguer, J., Wirsing, M.: What is a multi-modeling language? In: Corradini, A., Montanari, U. (eds.) WADT 2008. LNCS, vol. 5486, pp. 71–87. Springer, Heidelberg (2009)

25. Eckhardt, J., Mühlbauer, T., Meseguer, J., Wirsing, M.: Semantics, Distributed Implementation, and Formal Analysis of KLAIM Models in Maude. Science of Computer Programming, 51 p. (to appear, 2014)

(V) Systematic Development of Service-Oriented Systems

26. Wirsing, M., Clark, A., Gilmore, S., Hölzl, M., Knapp, A., Koch, N., Schroeder, A.: Semantic-Based Development of Service-Oriented Systems. In: Najm, E., Pradat-Peyre, J.-F., Donzeau-Gouge, V.V. (eds.) FORTE 2006. LNCS, vol. 4229, pp. 24–45. Springer, Heidelberg (2006)

27. Wirsing, M., De Nicola, R., Gilmore, S., Hölzl, M., Lucchi, R., Tribastone, M., Zavattaro, G.: SENSORIA Process Calculi for Service-Oriented Computing. In: Montanari, U., Sannella, D., Bruni, R. (eds.) TGC 2006. LNCS, vol. 4661, pp. 30–50. Springer, Heidelberg (2007)

28. Wirsing, M., Bocchi, L., Clark, A., Fiadeiro, J., Gilmore, S., Hölzl, M., Koch, N., Mayer, P., Pugliese, R., Schroeder, A.: Sensoria: Engineering for Service-Oriented Overlay Computers. In: di Nitto, E., Sassen, A.-M., Traverso, P., Zwegers, A. (eds.) At Your Service: Service Oriented Computing from an EU Perspective, pp. 159–182. MIT Press, Cambridge (2009)

29. van Riemsdijk, M.B., Wirsing, M.: Comparing Goal-Oriented and Procedural Service Orchestration. Journal on Multiagent and Grid Systems 6(2), 133–163 (2010)

30. Tribastone, M., Mayer, P., Wirsing, M.: Performance Prediction of Service-Oriented Systems with Layered Queueing Networks. In: Margaria, T., Steffen, B. (eds.) ISoLA 2010, Part II. LNCS, vol. 6416, pp. 51–65. Springer, Heidelberg (2010)

31. Wirsing, M., Hölzl, M. (eds.): SENSORIA. LNCS, vol. 6582. Springer, Heidelberg (2011)

(VI) Engineering Adaptive and Autonomic systems

32. Koch, N., Wirsing, M.: The munich reference model for adaptive hypermedia applications. In: De Bra, P., Brusilovsky, P., Conejo, R. (eds.) AH 2002. LNCS, vol. 2347, p. 213. Springer, Heidelberg (2002)

33. Wirsing, M., Bauer, S., Schroeder, A.: Modeling and Analyzing Adaptive User-Centric Systems in Real-Time Maude. In: Ölvecki, P.C. (ed.) Proc. of 1st International Workshop on Rewriting Techniques for Real-Time Systems, RTRTS 2010, Longyearbyen, Spitsbergen, Norway, April 6-9. EPTCS, vol. 36, pp. 1–25 (2010)

34. Schroeder, A., Bauer, S., Wirsing, M.: A Contract-Based Approach to Adaptivity. J. Log. Algebr. Program. 80(3-5), 180–193 (2011)

35. Schroeder, A., Wirsing, M.: Developing Physiological Computing Systems: Challenges and Solutions. In: Jähnichen, S., Küpper, A., Albayrak, S. (eds.) Software Engineering 2012. GI Lecture Notes in Informatics, vol. 198, pp. 21–36 (2012)

36. Wirsing, M., Hölzl, M., Tribastone, M., Zambonelli, F.: ASCENS: Engineering Autonomic Service-Component Ensembles. In: Beckert, B., Damiani, F., de Boer, F.S., Bonsangue, M.M. (eds.) FMCO 2011. LNCS, vol. 7542, pp. 1–24. Springer, Heidelberg (2012)

(VII) Miscellaneous

37. Wirsing, M., Denker, G., Talcott, C., Poggio, A., Briesemeister, L.: A Rewriting Logic Framework for Soft Constraints. In: Proc. 6th Int. Workshop on Rewriting Logic and its Applications (WRLA 2006), Vienna, Austria. Electronic Notes in Theoretical Computer Science (ENTCS), vol. 176, pp. 181–197 (2007)

38. Hölzl, M., Meier, M., Wirsing, M.: Which Soft Constraints do you Prefer? In: Proc. 7th Int. Workshop on Rewriting Logic and its Applications (WRLA 2008), Budapest, March 29-30. Electr. Notes Theor. Comput. Sci, vol. 238(3), pp. 189–205 (2009)

39. Baumeister, H., Koch, N., Kosiuczenko, P., Wirsing, M.: Extending Activity Diagrams to Model Mobile Systems. In: Akşit, M., Mezini, M., Unland, R. (eds.) NODe 2002. LNCS, vol. 2591, pp. 278–293. Springer, Heidelberg (2003)

2.2 Research Projects

Thanks to Martin's permanent curiousness about new developments and technologies, he was always very active in conceiving, planning, coordinating and running national and international projects. Most projects were funded by DFG (the German Research Society) or by European Union, some others were funded by the German Federal Ministry of Education and Research. The first project of Martin was run in Passau together with Manfred Broy. It was a DFG project in which a rapid prototyping tool for algebraic specifications has been developed which has attracted much attention. The next projects during Martin's stay in Passau were the European projects METEOR and DRAGON. The METEOR project investigated the use of algebraic methods, like data abstraction, structuring of specifications, and analysis of data structures for formally based software construction. The objective of the DRAGON project was the investigation of methods supporting software reusability. Since then, Martin has guided around 40 projects and he has been the coordinator of huge EU projects, like SENSORIA and ASCENS. In the following, we will list only the most important projects coordinated by Martin. More details on the projects run at PST in Munich are provided in the contribution to this Festschrift by the PST group, immediately following the current chapter.

1983-1985 Rapid Prototyping of Algebraic Specifications. Sponsor: DFG.
1983-1989 ESPRIT-Project METEOR: Development of a formally based programming environment tailored to industrial purposes. Sponsor: EU.
1987-1992 ESPRIT-Project DRAGON: Development of methods and tools for designing reusable software in the area of distributed real time applications. Sponsor: EU.
1990-1994 SPECTRUM: Development of an Algebraic Specification Language. Sponsor: DFG.
1991-1994 KORSO: Component-oriented formal software development. Sponsor: BMFT.
1995-1998 EPKfix: Methods and Tools for Efficient Design of Electronical Product Catalogues. Sponsor: BMFT.
2000-2002 CARUSO: Customer Care and Relationship Support Office. Sponsor: EU
2001-2004 InOpSys: View-Oriented Development of Software Components. Sponsor: DFG.

2002-2004 AGILE: Architectures for Mobility. Sponsor: EU.
2005-2010 SENSORIA: Software Engineering for Service-Oriented Overlay Computers. EU-funded Integrated Project. Sponsor: EU.
2005-2011 MAEWA I-II: Modellbasiertes Engineering adaptiver Rich-Internet-Applications. Sponsor: DFG.
2008-2011 REFLECT: Responsive Flexible Collaborating Ambient. EU-funded Specific Targeted Research Project. Sponsor: EU.
2010-2014 ASCENS: Autonomic Service-Component Ensembles. EU-funded Integrated Project. Sponsor EU.

3   Martin's Students

Under Martin's supervision up to now 31 PhD theses and four habilitation theses have been successfully completed at the University of Passau and at LMU in Munich. His PhD students and the post-doc researchers working in his group always profited from Martin's inspirations, stimulations and advices and they appreciated very much the constructive and friendly atmosphere in meetings and discussions with him. But Martin was (and is) also demanding and very clear with his goals and expectations about good work. Martin's international contacts and collaborations formed an excellent environment for his students. Also the many interesting projects Martin has guided brought new and challenging topics which provided the ground on which a new generation of doctoral theses has been accomplished. Eleven students of Martin are now professors or lecturers at national and international universities. Detailed impressions about the education at PST are described in the contribution of the PST group immediately following this chapter.

Habilitations

1. Peter Padawitz: Foundations of Specifications and Programming with Horn-Clauses, University of Passau, 1987.
2. Thomas Streicher: Investigations in Intensional Type Theory, LMU München, 1993.
3. Rolf Hennicker: Structured Specifications with Behavioural Operators: Semantics, Proof Methods and Applications, LMU München, 1997.
4. Thom Frühwirth: A Declarative Language for Constraint Systems: Theory and Practice of Constraint Handling Rules, LMU München, 1998.

Dissertations at University of Passau

1. Rolf Hennicker: Beobachtungsorientierte Spezifikationen, Passau, 1988.
2. Friederike Nickl: Algebraic Specification of Semantic Domain Constructions. Passau, 1988.
3. Alfons Geser: Termination Relative. Passau, 1990.

4. Ruth Breu: Specification and Design of Object-Oriented Programs. Passau, 1991.
5. Ulrich Fraus: Mechanizing Inductive Theorem Proving in Conditional Theories, Passau 1994.

Dissertations at LMU München

6. Maria Victoria Cengarle: Formal Specifications with Higher-Order Parameterization, 1994.
7. Luis Mandel: Constrained Lambda Calculus, 1995.
8. Michael Mehlich: Implementation of Combinator Specifications, 1995.
9. Bernhard Reus: Program Verification in Synthetic Domain Theory, 1995.
10. Andy Mück: Eine verifizierte Implementierung funktional-logischer Programmiersprachen, 1996.
11. Hannes Peterreins: Ein Gentzen-Kalkül für Strukturierte Algebraische Spezifikationen, 1996.
12. Weishi Zhang: Formal Description and Development of Graphical User Interfaces, 1996.
13. Dimitris Dranidis: A Formal Framework for the Design and Specification of Neural Networks, 1997.
14. Alexander Knapp: Formal Approach to Object-Oriented Software Engineering, 2000.
15. Nora Parcus de Koch: Software Engineering for Adaptive Hypermedia Systems: Reference Model, Modeling Techniques and Development Process, 2000.
16. Harald Störrle: Formal Approach to Object-Oriented Software Engineering, 2000.
17. Nataly Lyabakh: Design and Rigorous Prototyping of Object-Oriented Modeling with Syntropy, 2000.
18. Dirk Pattinson: Expressivity Results in the Modal Logic of Coalgebras, 2001.
19. Matthias Hölzl: Constraint Lambda Calculus, 2001.
20. Moritz Hammer: Verfeinerungstechniken fr visuelle Modellierungen reaktiver Systeme, 2004.
21. Philipp Meier: Agentenkomponenten: Ein komponenten-orientierter Ansatz zur (grafischen) Entwicklung von Multi-Agenten-Systemen, 2005.
22. Shiping Yang: Towards "Living Cooperative Information Systems for Virtual Organizations: Based on Peers, Foundet in Living Systems Theory", 2006.
23. Shadi Al-Dehni: Model Transformation For Validation Of Software Design, 2008.
24. Michael Barth: Entwicklung und Bewertung zeitkritischer Softwaremodelle: Simulationsbasierter Ansatz und Methodik, 2008.
25. Florian Mangold: Analyse von IT-Anwendungen mittels Zeitvariation, 2010.
26. Philip Mayer: MDD4SOA: Model-Driven Development for Service-Oriented Architectures, 2010.

27. Axel Rauschmayer: Connected Information Management, 2010.
28. Gefei Zhang: Aspect-Oriented State Machines, 2010.
29. Andreas Schroeder: Software Engineering Perspectives on Physiological Computing, 2011.
30. Partha Sampathkumaran: Computing the Cost of Business Processes, 2013.
31. Max Meier: Algorithmic Composition of Music in Real-Time with Soft Constraints, 2014.

Ode to the PST

Matthias Hölzl, Nora Koch, Philip Mayer, Andreas Schroeder
with Lenz Belzner, Marianne Busch, Anton Fasching, Annabelle Klarl,
Christian Kroiss, and Laith Raed

Programming & Software Engineering Group (PST)
Ludwig-Maximilians-University Munich, Germany
`first.last@ifi.lmu.de`

Thanks, sir; all the rest is mute.
    – William Shakespeare, *All's Well That Ends Well*

1   Welcome to the PST

1992! Internet in Germany was in its infancy, object oriented programming wasn't well-known yet, and even the European Union, which has funded so many of our research efforts lately, had not been formed.

Computing was certainly not mainstream when Martin Wirsing took the post of full professor at the Ludwig-Maximilians-Universität München in that year. The chair for Programming & Software Engineering (*Lehrstuhl für Programmierung und Softwaretechnik, PST*) was created along with his appointment. Indeed, the first *Diplom* course of studies in Computer Science (*Informatik*) at LMU had been created only the year before. The institute was still situated in the Leopoldstraße in Schwabing, only moving to the *Institute am Englischen Garten* in the Oettingenstraße in 1996 (Figure 1) — a beautiful location set right in the English Garden in Munich, five minutes away from one of the main tourist spots, the *Biergarten am Chinesischen Turm*. And with a history — the building was the site of the former *Radio Free Europe* [28], a radio station funded by the U.S. Government with its own history (including a bomb attack in 1981 on the very building where PST is now located).

Fast-forward to 2015, where all of us are pretty much dependent on the computers in our pockets — and where it is clear that computing has had, and will have in the future, a tremendous influence on our society and our way of life. It certainly has been an interesting time for computer scientists!

This development forms the framework for a personal story — 24 years in which Martin has headed the PST group at LMU; 24 years in which he has supervised over two dozen doctoral theses, participated in over nearly 40 research projects, and taught countless students; and 24 years in which he has organized a *tiresome* number of hikes in the Bavarian alps...

In this short expression of thanks/collection of travel notes/feeble summary attempt (delete to taste) we shall revisit the PST history in the fields of science and education (Section 2), research projects (Section 3), supervision of doctorates and habilitations (Section 4), and the PST as a fun place to work (Section 5). We invite you to come with us on this journey!

R. De Nicola and R. Hennicker (Eds.): Wirsing Festschrift, LNCS 8950, pp. 13–23, 2015.

Fig. 1. Institute am Englischen Garten

2   Science and Education

You would expect a certain affinity for mathematics and logic from somebody who started his scientific career with a dissertation called "Das Entscheidungsproblem der Prädikatenlogik 1. Stufe mit Funktionszeichen in Herbrandformeln" (The Decision Problem of First-Order Predicate Logic with Function Symbols in Herbrand Formulae) that was supervised by the eminent Munich logician Kurt Schütte. And indeed, Martin's desire to use algebraic and logical methods to improve the development of software has remained one of the constant factors throughout his career until today.

Before arriving at LMU, Martin had mostly worked in the areas of programming languages, abstract data types and algebraic specifications, and written the definitive handbook chapter on one of these areas [29]. However, recognizing the increasing importance of developing for large systems as well as the (at that time) emerging trend towards mobile computing, he successfully broadened the research areas pursued at PST in different directions: formal approaches to engineering object-oriented systems [34]; a reference model for multimedia and hypermedia applications [16]; global computing [5]; mobile systems and software agents [18,17,15]; physiological computing [27]; service-oriented computing [30]; and, in the last few years, software engineering for autonomic ensembles, i.e., distributed systems operating in open-ended, non-deterministic and non-predictable environments [11,33,13].

Martin also remained active in research areas closer to his academic roots. For example, he co-authored one of the first proposals for a formal semantics of multithreaded Java code [6,7], and a novel, heterogeneous approach to UML semantics [8]; he also co-developed an abstract framework for developing new systems of program synthesis by adapting proofs-as-programs to new contexts [20] and a system of soft constraints that can deal with lexicographic orders of preferences [10].

For the members of PST this offered many exciting possibilities to work in new and emerging areas of software engineering research. For many of us, the possibility to interact with colleagues working on a broad range of topics but centered around the common core of using formal techniques for software development was a particularly pleasant aspect of working in Martin's group. Not unsurprisingly, this also led to occasional exclamations of "We're supposed to be working on *what?*" invariably followed, after a short discussion, by "The deadline is *when?!?*"

Altogether, Martin's scientific work has so far resulted in more than 240 publications with almost 230 co-authors, which were cited more than 5300 times.

In addition to these more visible scientific activities, Martin's expertise and foresight were in high demand from other scientific institutions and the European Union: Among many other activities he was speaker of the section on "Specification and Semantics" of the German Gesellschaft für Informatik and president of INRIA's scientific advisory council; he has been the coordinator of the advisory board of the "Computer Science and Applications" research area of the Institute for Advanced Studies in Lucca, and last year he has joined the Comité Stratégique of the Université de Bordeaux.

Life at a university is not all about research, however. Teaching and administrative work play a large part as well, and in Martin's case they are more closely entwined than for most other professors: in addition to editing or authoring more than 15 scientific books, he has written two textbooks [2,12], and he was instrumental in establishing the Elite Graduate Program "Software Engineering" which is taught jointly by the University of Augsburg, the Technical University Munich and Ludwig-Maximilians-University Munich. Given his combination of scientific excellence, administrative skills and dedication to teaching, it is no wonder that he quickly became indispensable in LMU's boards: first as *Dekan* and, after a reorganization, as director of the faculty for Mathematics, Computer Science and Statistics, then as senator, as member of the *Hochschulrat*, and finally in his current position as vice-president of the LMU responsible for academic studies and teaching.

However, despite his calendar being filled to the brim Martin always managed to find time for discussions about PhD theses and organizational things, and provided an open ear to questions and suggestions.

3   Research Projects across Europe

Martin acted out his research interests in almost 40 German and European funded projects. He preferred those funding opportunities where he could introduce formal methods in the software engineering process in very different but always exciting and challenging domains, such as electronic product catalogues (EPK-fix) [24], architectures for mobility (AGILE) [1], service-oriented architectures (SENSORIA) [31], and adaptive and autonomous systems (ASCENS) [32].

In addition, due to his research excellence he was invited to participate in amazing projects like the Responsive Flexible Collaborating Ambient project (REFLECT) [26], in which psychologists, car engineers and software engineers developed a mood player that selects the music according to the users emotional state and a car assistance prototype which configured the vehicles performance according to the emotional, cognitive and physical drivers condition.

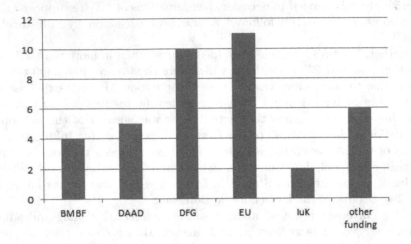

Fig. 2. Number of funded projects

Martin started with small budget German DFG and BMBF projects, such as SPECTRUM and KORSO to end up with the coordination of huge EU IP projects in the FET Proactive initiative like SENSORIA and ASCENS with budgets around eight million Euros (Figure 2). All of them addressing innovative issues like the modularization, reuse and correctness of specifications in the beginning of the nineties, and the behaviour of autonomic service-component ensembles twenty-five years later. Martin also supported non-funded projects of enthusiastic researchers; some of them curiously have male or female acronyms such as HUGO/RT (UML model translator for model checking, theorem proving, and code generation) [23], UWE (UML-based Web Engineering) [14], and HELENA (Handling massively distributed systems with ELaborate ENsemble Architectures) [9].

He managed and participated in EU projects of different types and challenges: Integrated Project (IP), Specific Targeted Research Project (STREP), Coordinated Action (CA) and Network of Excellence. Regarding personnel resources these projects funded the research activities from one PhD student to the work of more than 50 researchers belonging to a set of up to 18 partners. Martin created consortia with impressive experts of the computer science community, such as Marco Dorigo, Joseph Sifakis, Rocco De Nicola, Ugo Montanari, and Franco Zambonelli.

In his projects, Martin has collaborated with people from an amazing number of places — over 60 cities in 18 countries all over Europe, as the impressive map in Figure 3 shows!

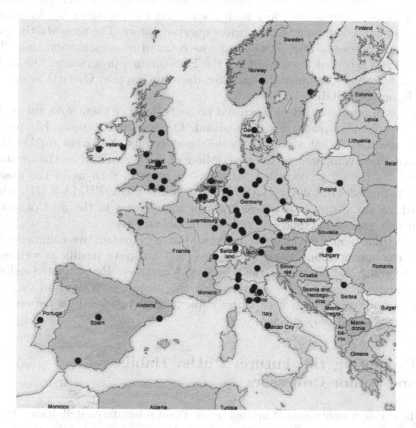

Fig. 3. Project Partners all over Europe

The first hurdle of every project is to get the proposal approved, which requires novelty and a perfectly written document. How did Martin achieve the high quality that characterized the proposals he submitted? On the one hand, he had a sixth sense regarding the team and partners he selected to work with, together with the ability to describe how these project members would complement each other. He managed not only to convince the European commission, the proposal reviewers but also the future partners about the complementary skills of them. And it worked! On the other hand, Martin's proposal management style was open for discussion and suggestions but each decision had to be thoroughly founded. He personally revised every detail and spent many nights in the production of successful proposals. We as the writing team learned from his precise feedback and new ideas about how to improve a proposal in long brainstorming meetings and several iterations. Very often these improvements took place during the last days and nights before the deadline!

Most of his proposals for EU funded projects were selected for the hearing in Brussels, where he was able to provide convincing arguments for getting the funding. We think he will remember quite well the ASCENS hearing presentation in Brussels, where some technical problems made him suffer a little bit. Hearing presentations are structured in a such a way that the presenter has assigned a fixed, very limited amount of time before questions start. The time Martin spent starting the notebook after it went off was counted as presentation time! The proposal was accepted anyway within the FP6 funding programme, the fourth in a row following Customer Care and Relationship Support Office (Caruso) [3], AGILE, and SENSORIA.

Successful proposals led to successful projects, most of them with the review mark "excellent" in each reporting period. On several occasions, EU project officers mentioned that the projects delivered results that went further than expected when compared to the description of work provided in the technical annexes. Successful projects led to follow-up projects such as in the case of the DFG-funded MAEWA I/MAEWA II [4] and PUMA/PUMA-2 [21], which allowed for interesting research results over many years in the field of model-driven web engineering, and program and model analysis.

Project meetings were characterized by Martin's constructive comments and strong recommendations to try to improve and integrate results as well as to promote collaboration among the teams and partners. He promoted cultural and culinary activities in conjunction with the project meetings and surprised us at every dinner speech with entirely unexpected relationships between the event location and project issues.

4   Promoting the Future: PhDs, Habils, and Junior Professors

Martin's achievements are not limited to his direct scientific contributions. Under his supervision, a total of so far 27 doctoral theses and four habilitation theses were successfully completed at the University of Passau and at the Ludwig-Maximilians-University of Munich. Of these doctoral students, 13 have remained in academia, and 14 have entered industry or civil service. All of the habilitands have stayed in academia.

His ideas and vision therefore are not only continuously refined and pursued in research, but have a significant impact in industry as well, ranging from product-oriented software companies (such as Celonis GmbH), consulting and software solutions companies (such as NTT DATA), to even game developer studios (such as EA Digital Illusions CE). Martin's scientific offspring in research are also distributed over the globe. While most of them can be found working in Germany (11 out of 16), some of them are pursuing their research in the UK, in Greece, Denmark, Austria, and Australia.

The area of contributions of the theses completed under Martin's supervision is very varied. They range from purely theoretical contributions in the domain of coalgebras [19] to the exploration of hands-on application domains such as connected information management [22] and the application of theoretical results to entirely different domains such as physiological computing [25]. The variety of theses topics is extremely broad, and shows that Martin has remained open and curious over the years, regularly willing to embrace and work on new topics. He is always ready to listen and discuss research topic proposals, even risky or exotic ones.

Even though the research topics feature a great variety, their scientific contributions are always formally founded: Each of the theses includes a clear, deep, and sound mathematical section. This formal work is one of the main pillars required for the scientifically sound and methodological development of the thesis. The mathematical treatment of the topic helps students with the development of a clear language, making the underlying concepts graspable and workable.

Martin's exceptional network of top researchers within and outside of Europe benefits PhD students as well. Martin has been providing and still is providing unique collaboration opportunities with top researchers to his doctoral students, such as Carolyn Talcott and José Meseguer at the SRI in California, USA, Rocco De Nicola at the IMT in Lucca, Italy, Ugo Montanari in Pisa, Italy, and Stefan Jähnichen in Berlin, Germany. There are also many collaborations with researchers working with those mentioned.

Throughout the whole research and writing process that encompasses a thesis project, Martin is unanimously found to be supportive and respectful, even in difficult times, when teaching duties grow overhead or paper deadlines seem infeasible. Instead of applying pressure, he always stays supportive and constructive, and aims at bringing each of his students to their full potential.

5   The Social Framework: It's a Group Thing!

Martin has always placed great emphasis on a relaxed and social atmosphere in the PST group. Our meeting room — equipped with an industry-strength automatic coffee dispenser, lovingly maintained by Anton Fasching — saw many rounds of discussions on research topics, and the two white boards were interchangingly filled with math, UML diagrams, algorithm sketches, and even code. On special occasions, such as a PhD defense, the meeting room would be transformed into a party location, filled with the smell of *Leberkäs*, the clinking of champagne glasses, and cheers to whomever was the focus of the event. In winter, we always had an advent wreath provided my Mrs. Wirsing.

The climax of each year, though, were the hut seminars (*Doktorandenseminare*). On these occasions, we traveled to a hut deep within the Bavarian alps for three days of talks, discussions, and socializing in the evening.

The first hut seminar took place in 2001 at the Dr. Erich Berger Hütte in Wildschönau, where we stayed until 2003. After a hiatus in 2004, the seminar was moved to Going (and the hut of the TV 1861 Ingolstadt), where it took place in 2004 and 2005. Since 2007, the location has been the *Alte Tanneralm* near Bayrischzell (Figure 4). Hard to get to, and even harder to leave (since the trail leads uphill), the hut was a perfect place for a retreat. Each year we took

Fig. 4. Alte Tanneralm

advantage of the location to go on a hike to one of the nearby mountains (with the Wendelstein being a popular choice in recent years).

The numbers of participants, semmeln, beer, and other drinks consumed fluctuated over the years. We can, however, empirically establish that the only thing rising in a monotone fashion is the amount of Marillenschnäpschen (Figure 5).

Due to the remote locations of the huts, each arrival felt like the *invasion of the geeks*: Power cables and strips were laid out, projectors installed, mobile Internet antennas positioned, and (since several huts coincided with world or European football championships) terrestrial TV receiving technology set up. For our screen we used a white bed sheet — and in at least one case, the weather even permitted us to do talks outside!

However, the hut seminars were not the only time in the year when we got together for social events. Each year has also seen a *Sommerfest*, which between 1997 and 2007 alternately took place at Krögers' and Wirsings', and after 2007, at Wirsings' — with honorable exceptions in 2003 (Faschings') and 2010 (Hennickers'). Martin proved on these occasions that opening a beer barrel poses no difficulties for him. It was also great to see many former members of the PST group show up for a talk about the "good old times".

Winter in Munich can get quite cold, and there have even been known cases of snow! What better way to get into the mood for Christmas than by doing a hike in the snow-covered parks of Munich, concluded with a dinner at a nice Wirtshaus. These now-famous *PST winter hikes* started in 1999 with a tour through the snow-covered Nymphenburger Park, ending in a christmas coffee at the Metzgerwirt. Over the years, we have added such illustrious locations as

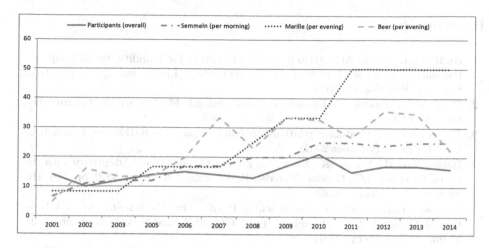

Fig. 5. Hut statistics

the Aumeister, the Asam Schlössel, and the Emmeramsmühle to the list. Again, honorable exceptions from these hikes were a visit to *Kloster Fürstenfeld* in 2004, followed up by a party at Matthias Hölzls place, and going bowling in 2006 at *Bavaria Bowling*. Thus, we can honestly claim that PST social activities not only covered summer, spring and autumn, but the winter as well.

Many of the PST group members have become good friends in their private lives as well, or continued doing research together long after they left the group. We believe that Martin has succeeded in establishing an atmosphere of mutual respect, trust, and having fun at work which had an impact above and beyond the immediate working environment of the PST.

6   Closing Words

With these notoriously incomplete journey notes, we have tried to give some insights into the activities at PST in the last 24 years. So much going on! We leave it to other authors in this *Festschrift* to cover the deep plunges into the formal and technical side of things for us.

With our closing words, we would like to thank Martin for the great atmosphere he has created at the PST. We wish him every success in his continuing career and private life, and we look forward to more Marillenschnäpschen at the next hut, which we have been pleased to learn will indeed take place!

Acknowledgements. We thank all contributors and colleagues for their insights and helpful material for this tour de force through PST history.

References

1. Andrade, L., et al.: AGILE: Software Architecture for Mobility. In: Wirsing, M., Pattinson, D., Hennicker, R. (eds.) WADT 2003. LNCS, vol. 2755, pp. 1–33. Springer, Heidelberg (2003)
2. Bauer, F.L., Wirsing, M.: Elementare Aussagenlogik. Mathematik für Informatiker. Springer (1991)
3. Baumeister, H.: Customer relationship management for SMEs. In: Proceedings E2002, Prague (October 2002)
4. Baumeister, H., Knapp, A., Koch, N., Zhang, G.: Modelling Adaptivity with Aspects. In: Lowe, D.G., Gaedke, M. (eds.) ICWE 2005. LNCS, vol. 3579, pp. 406–416. Springer, Heidelberg (2005)
5. Baumeister, H., Koch, N., Kosiuczenko, P., Stevens, P., Wirsing, M.: UML for Global Computing. In: Priami, C. (ed.) GC 2003. LNCS, vol. 2874, pp. 1–24. Springer, Heidelberg (2003)
6. Cenciarelli, P., Knapp, A., Reus, B., Wirsing, M.: From Sequential to Multi-Threaded Java: An Event-Based Operational Semantics. In: Johnson, M. (ed.) AMAST 1997. LNCS, vol. 1349, pp. 75–90. Springer, Heidelberg (1997)
7. Cenciarelli, P., Knapp, A., Reus, B., Wirsing, M.: An event-based structural operational semantics of multi-threaded java. In: Alves-Foss, J. (ed.) Formal Syntax and Semantics of Java. LNCS, vol. 1523, p. 157. Springer, Heidelberg (1999)
8. Cengarle, M.V., Knapp, A., Tarlecki, A., Wirsing, M.: A Heterogeneous Approach to UML Semantics. In: Degano, P., De Nicola, R., Meseguer, J. (eds.) Concurrency, Graphs and Models. LNCS, vol. 5065, pp. 383–402. Springer, Heidelberg (2008)
9. Hennicker, R., Klarl, A.: Foundations for Ensemble Modeling – The HELENA Approach. In: Iida, S., Meseguer, J., Ogata, K. (eds.) Specification, Algebra, and Software. LNCS, vol. 8373, pp. 359–381. Springer, Heidelberg (2014)
10. Hölzl, M., Meier, M., Wirsing, M.: Which soft constraints do you prefer? ENTCS 238(3), 189–205 (2009)
11. Hölzl, M., Rauschmayer, A., Wirsing, M.: Software engineering for ensembles. In: Wirsing, M., Banâtre, J.-P., Hölzl, M., Rauschmayer, A. (eds.) Soft-Ware Intensive Systems. LNCS, vol. 5380, pp. 45–63. Springer, Heidelberg (2008)
12. Hölzl, M.M., Raed, A., Wirsing, M.: Java kompakt - Eine Einführung in die Software-Entwicklung mit Java. eXamen.press. Springer (2013)
13. Hölzl, M., Wirsing, M.: Towards a system model for ensembles. In: Agha, G., Danvy, O., Meseguer, J. (eds.) Formal Modeling: Actors, Open Systems, Biological Systems. LNCS, vol. 7000, pp. 241–261. Springer, Heidelberg (2011)
14. Knapp, A., Koch, N., Wirsing, M., Zhang, G.: UWE - An Approach to Model-Driven Development of Web Applications. i-com, Oldenbourg 6(3), 5–12 (2007) (in German)
15. Knapp, A., Merz, S., Wirsing, M., Zappe, J.: Specification and Refinement of Mobile Systems in MTLA and Mobile UML. In: Theoretical Computer Science, pp. 184–202 (2006)
16. Koch, N., Wirsing, M.: The Munich Reference Model for Adaptive Hypermedia Applications. In: De Bra, P., Brusilovsky, P., Conejo, R. (eds.) AH 2002. LNCS, vol. 2347, pp. 213–222. Springer, Heidelberg (2002)
17. Meier, P., Wirsing, M.: Towards a Formal Specification for the AgentComponent. In: Ryan, M.D., Meyer, J.-J.C., Ehrich, H.-D. (eds.) Objects, Agents, and Features. LNCS, vol. 2975, pp. 175–188. Springer, Heidelberg (2004)

18. Merz, S., Wirsing, M., Zappe, J.: A Spatio-Temporal Logic for the Specification and Refinement of Mobile Systems. In: Pezzé, M. (ed.) FASE 2003. LNCS, vol. 2621, pp. 87–101. Springer, Heidelberg (2003)

19. Pattinson, D.: Expressivity Results in the Modal Logic of Coalgebras. PhD thesis, Ludwig-Maximilians-Universität München (2001)

20. Poernomo, I., Crossley, J., Wirsing, M.: Adapting Proofs-as-Programs: The Curry–Howard Protocol. Springer Monographs in Computer Science. Springer (2005)

21. PUMA/PUMA-2. Graduiertenkolleg Programm- Und Modell-Analyse, 2008-2012/2013-2017. https://puma.informatik.tu-muenchen.de.

22. Rauschmayer, A.: Connected Information Management. PhD thesis, Ludwig-Maximilians-Universität München (2010)

23. Schäfer, T., Knapp, A., Merz, S.: Model Checking UML State Machines and Collaborations. In: Stoller, S.D., Visser, W. (eds.) Proc. Wsh. Software Model Checking. Electr. Notes Theo. Comp. Sci., 13 pages (2001), http://www.elsevier.nl/locate/entcs/volume55.html

24. Schneeberger, J., Koch, N., Turk, A., Lutze, R., Wirsing, M., Fritzsche, H., Closhen, P.: EPK-fix: Software-Engineering und Werkzeuge für elektronische Produktkataloge. In: Informatik aktuell. Informatik 1997, Informatik als Innovationsmotor, 27. Jahrestagung der Gesellschaft für Informatik. Springer (September 1997)

25. Schroeder, A.: Software engineering perspectives on physiological computing. PhD thesis, Ludwig-Maximilians-Universität München (2011)

26. Schroeder, A., Bauer, S.S., Wirsing, M.: A contract-based approach to adaptivity. J. Log. Algebr. Program. 80(3-5), 180–193 (2011)

27. Filipović, I., O'Hearn, P., Rinetzky, N., Yang, H.: Abstraction for Concurrent Objects. In: Castagna, G. (ed.) ESOP 2009. LNCS, vol. 5502, pp. 252–266. Springer, Heidelberg (2009)

28. Wikipedia - The Free Encyclopedia. Radio Free Europe, http://en.wikipedia.org/wiki/Radio_Free_Europe/Radio_Liberty

29. Wirsing, M.: Algebraic specification. In: Handbook of Theoretical Computer Science (vol. B), pp. 675–788. MIT Press (1991)

30. Wirsing, M., Clark, A., Gilmore, S., Hölzl, M., Knapp, A., Koch, N., Schroeder, A.: Semantic-based development of service-oriented systems. In: Najm, E., Pradat-Peyre, J.-F., Donzeau-Gouge, V.V. (eds.) FORTE 2006. LNCS, vol. 4229, pp. 24–45. Springer, Heidelberg (2006)

31. Wirsing, M., Hölzl, M. (eds.): SENSORIA. LNCS, vol. 6582. Springer, Heidelberg (2011)

32. Wirsing, M., Hölzl, M., Tribastone, M., Zambonelli, F.: ASCENS: Engineering Autonomic Service-Component Ensembles. In: Beckert, B., Bonsangue, M.M. (eds.) FMCO 2011. LNCS, vol. 7542, pp. 1–24. Springer, Heidelberg (2012)

33. Wirsing, M., Hölzl, M., Tribastone, M., Zambonelli, F.: ASCENS: Engineering Autonomic Service-Component Ensembles. In: Beckert, B., Bonsangue, M.M. (eds.) FMCO 2011. LNCS, vol. 7542, pp. 1–24. Springer, Heidelberg (2012)

34. Wirsing, M., Knapp, A.: A formal approach to object-oriented software engineering. Theor. Comput. Sci. 285(2), 519–560 (2002)

From Formal Logic through Program Transformations to System Dynamics: 40 Years of Meeting Points with Martin Wirsing

Wolfgang Hesse

Ludwig-Maximilians-Universität München, Germany

My first meeting with Martin Wirsing is of rather virtual nature: We both have the same academic background and got our diplomas from the same institution, the Institute of Mathematical Logic of LMU Munich directed by Kurt Schütte. But we did not (yet) meet personally: While I worked on my diploma thesis on μ-recursive functions and the non-eliminability of some ugly functionals in intricate number theory, Martin entered the institute as a student and left it some years later having completed two theses (diploma and Ph.D.) on similarly mystical problems such as (un-)decidability of (sub-)classes of formulae in first-order predicate logic.

By 1970 Informatics was not yet known as a scientific discipline and at the Technical University of Munich Friedrich L. Bauer and Klaus Samelson just opened the first academic institute for that brand-new science. I got the chance to work there as a researcher in the new, growing and fascinating field of programming languages and compilers. Shortly later, Martin had the same idea and so we met in Bauer's and Samelson's group in 1974 – exactly 40 years back from now. ALGOL was the newest hit of (academic) programming at that time but the flavour of the year was ALGOL 68 – a gigantic tower of very useful but in their totality rather intricate and sophisticated language constructs. Our task was to build a compiler for that monster. This giant artefact saw the light of day as a modern dinosaur but nevertheless it served some generations of students for their first ALGOL 68 programming exercises.

Our boss F. L. Bauer was not happy with the universal language approach of ALGOL 68 (and even less happy with its inventor Aad van Wijngaarden) and he thought of new ways of programming – more exactly: of *developing software* – which was then discovered as a much more encompassing and challenging process requiring its own methodology and specialised tools. This was the starting point of a new branch of Informatics: *Software Engineering (SE)*.

F. L. Bauer's approach to developing software was that of *computer-aided, intuition-guided programming (CIP)* and thus Martin and I found ourselves working together on that topic in a large group of young and inspired colleagues. In the CIP group we had to deal with innovative ideas and concepts such as program transformations, logical and recursive programs, program verification and, last not least, with CIP-L, a completely new, multi-level Wide Spectrum Language. While I was struggling with L_0, the lowermost language level and its formal description and compiler, Martin was chosen to stroll in the high-level regions of

R. De Nicola and R. Hennicker (Eds.): Wirsing Festschrift, LNCS 8950, pp. 24–26, 2015.

transforming predicate-calculus program versions of the greatest common divisor (and similar problems) into tail-recursive ones and related transgressions.

In the late 1970ies, our professional ways took different directions. For me, working at the Munich-based software house *Softlab* offered the chance to deal with "real" Software Engineering tasks in an industrial environment whereas Martin got the chance to complete his academic career by a habilitation – which in turn opened him the door to be elected as a young professor and to build up a new Computer Science faculty at the just founded University of Passau.

In the late 1980ies and beginning 1990ies, we both found our final academic home – Martin at the LMU Munich and me at the University of Marburg. Software Engineering was the connecting link which brought us together from time to time – be it at SE conferences or in the new field of modelling, model transformations and modelling languages.

Starting with my own retirement in 2008/9, a new (and still continuing) period of close co-operation began. Now being located not only in academic but also in physical neighbourhood (close to the Chinese Tower in Munich's English Garden) we thought of opening a series of courses for bachelor and master students on a subject which has not only pure computer science but also many interdisciplinary aspects. Thus we started in 2010 our joint, combined lecture & seminar on *Modelling of dynamic and adaptive systems* – briefly: *ModaS*.

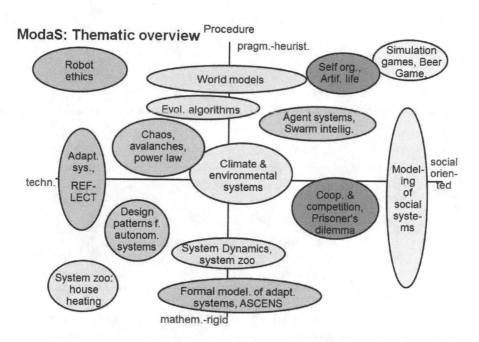

The graphic depicted above gives a short overview of the bunch of themes we are discussing with our students: Dynamic Systems encompasses the exciting plethora of computer-supported domains of modern human real life. Applications (following the horizontal axis of the diagram) range from more technical ones such as house heating, robots in households, industry and space, through chaotic or hardly predictable processes such as avalanches, earthquakes, weather and climate changes to social and economic problem areas such as cooperation & competition, self-organisation, artificial life and simulation games. Another dimension (depicted in vertical direction) concerns the procedural aspects of computer support – it ranges from mathematically rigid methods to pragmatic approaches containing a lot of heuristics. An example of the latter are Forrester's world models for assessing possible future states of man-kind, their environment and limits to growth.

It was – and still is – a great pleasure and stimulus for me to meet Martin, planning seminars and other events with him, discussing professional, political and private issues and – last not least – participate at his unforgettable garden parties and combined birthday & Christmas celebrations. I wish him many more years of energy, productivity and enjoyment. I wish us all many more opportunities to meet Martin, to work, to celebrate or just stay together with him.

The Broad View: How To Spawn a Radical Organizational Transformation 'En Passant'

Heinrich Hussmann

Ludwig-Maximilians-Universität München, Institut für Informatik, Germany
hussmann@ifi.lmu.de

Abstract. This short paper is a rather personal account on the process, which in the end led to the effect that the author moved from a scholar of an influential person to a colleague of him. It tries to tell the story how a new organizational backbone for the Institute of Informatics at LMU was created by predictive thinking, and it is a hommage to the ability to switch from technical detail to a very broad but nevertheless precise analysis of development opportunities for an organization.

1 Introduction

It may be the case that a mind being able to do deep theoretical analysis and to invent abstract concepts is also good in analyzing practical organizational weaknesses and in envisioning creative solutions for such practical problems. At least this appears to be the case for Martin Wirsing's way of approaching problems. In the lines below, a concrete story is told which is somehow a proof for this hypothesis.

The author of this paper is now professor for "Media Informatics" at Ludwig-Maximilians-Universität (LMU), and therefore a colleague of Martin Wirsing. Quite a number of years ago, the author used to be an academic scholar of Martin Wirsing in the area of Software Engineering, and the story also explains the path between the two positions.

2 The Broad View on Scientific Topics

When looking through the list of publications co-authored by Martin Wirsing, it is interesting to find, besides a large number of contributions to the theoretical side of software engineering, a quite broad selection of other topics, including for instance hypermedia, security, and e-learning. His research group has always kept a good balance between going into the depth of a specific issue and tackling a broader range of diverse topics. One group of topics which appears more often than others can be described by the catchword "multimedia".

An interesting time in this respect were the years around 1997/1998. During this time, I just had obtained my first position as a professor, in Software Engineering at the Technische Universität Dresden. From my work in industry

R. De Nicola and R. Hennicker (Eds.): Wirsing Festschrift, LNCS 8950, pp. 27–29, 2015.
© Springer International Publishing Switzerland 2015

during the preceding years I had developed some interest in multimedia technology. At the time, it came as a surprise to me to find that Martin Wirsing's group had worked on a project related to multimedia presentations of electronic product catalogues [1]. As a follow-up of this project, Martin Wirsing organized a workshop at the "GI-Jahrestagung" in Aachen, which was devoted to Software Engineering for Multimedia Systems [2], and I had the possibility to give a talk there. This was a first hint at an extension of my work focus to come.

3   The Broad View on Organizational Structures

Around the same time, the Institute for Informatics at Ludwig-Maximilians-Universität started an effort to better define the institute's profile, combined with an initiative to apply for further extension of the institute. This was a joint effort of all professors at the institute, but Martin Wirsing is said to have been quite influential within this initiative. The result was a "white book" [3] describing opportunities for further development of computer science at LMU. One very interesting passage of this books reads as follows (translated from the German original): "More and more, the demands of end users become foreground topics, users who neither have administrative nor technical background knowledge. Taking the more recent developments of computer science into account, ergonomic investigations in the following areas look promising: graphical-textual user interfaces, controlled languages, modeling and specification languages, modifiable reactive documents, query languages or information systems, new types of input devices, multimedia output, group work software for software development."

This visionary view on new topics finally led to a significant extension of the institute, in particular including a new professorship for "media informatics" inspired by the topics mentioned in the above quotation and by the vision of establishing interdisciplinary co-operations with other departments of LMU, like communication science and business administration. The study program "media informatics" was started in 2001/2002.

4   Finding Creative Solutions for Organizational Problems

At that time (from 2001 on), I was looking for possibilities to move back to Munich, and was applying for positions in software engineering. In fact, it was Martin Wirsing in person who brought to my attention that there was an open position at LMU in media informatics. I myself probably would not have applied for this position, which sounded far from software engineering. But by thinking further, a bridge between the two areas became apparent, which was mentioned already in the quote above: "ergonomic investigations". In fact, what was called "software ergonomics" was an established area of software engineering already at that time, and clearly it had to do with multimedia interfaces.

After the successful application and after becoming responsible for the area of "media informatics", I tried to define the area in a way which takes the link to ergonomics strongly into account, which meant to address the area of Human-Computer Interaction (HCI). This was a novel and nascent topic at that time, and it has developed itself with massive speed and force since then.

Looking back at the development from nowadays (2014), there has been a quite prosperous development for the Institute of Informatics. The "media informatics" program now has by far the highest number of enrolled students among the study programs offered by the department, higher than for traditional computer science. Education in human-computer interaction is an integral part of media informatics, and there is even a special professorship for Human-Computer Interaction, and a Master program bearing this title. The HCI group of LMU is well established in the international research community. During the last few years, it could be observed that several other universities with media informatics programs take a similar route in defining the profile for media informatics.

5 Conclusion

What can be learnt from this little story? Besides my personal thankfulness for having been pointed at such an interesting opportunity to change the focus of my professional activities, I would like to claim that the story shows successful application of scientific analysis to problems on the organizational meta level of a university. I think it takes a scientific mind with a broad perspective to see the opportunities for develop-ment at the right point in time. And what I admire most is that Martin managed to make this happen *en passant*, in parallel to his highly successful detailed work on very technical areas of his home discipline, formal methods and software engineering.

References

1. Knapp, A., et al.: EPK-fix: Methods and tools for engineering electronic product catalogues. In: Steinmetz, R. (ed.) IDMS 1997. LNCS, vol. 1309, pp. 199–209. Springer, Heidelberg (1997)
2. Wirsing, M., Schneeberger, J., Lutze, R.: Workshop: Software-Engineering für Multimedia-Systeme. In: Informatikâ 97 Informatik als Innovationsmotor, p. 631. Springer, Heidelberg (1997)
3. Bry, F., Clote, P., Hegering, H.-G., Kriegel, H.P., Kröger, F., Ludwig, T., Wirsing, M.: Weißbuch über Perspektiven in der Ludwig-Maximilians-Universität zum Anbruch des Informationszeitalters, Internal Document LMU (1998), http://epub.ub.uni-muenchen.de/

Modal Satisfiability via SMT Solving*

Carlos Areces[1], Pascal Fontaine[2,3], and Stephan Merz[2,3]

[1] Universidad Nacional de Córdoba & CONICET, Córdoba, Argentina
[2] Université de Lorraine, LORIA, UMR 7503, Vandœuvre-lès-Nancy, France
[3] INRIA, Villers-lès-Nancy, France

Abstract. Modal logics extend classical propositional logic, and they are robustly decidable. Whereas most existing decision procedures for modal logics are based on tableau constructions, we propose a framework for obtaining decision procedures by adding instantiation rules to standard SAT and SMT solvers. Soundness, completeness, and termination of the procedures can be proved in a uniform and elementary way for the basic modal logic and some extensions.

1 Introduction

Classical languages like first-order and second-order logic have been investigated in detail, and their model theory is well developed. Computationally though, they are lacking as their satisfiability problem is undecidable [9,25], and even their model checking problem is already PSPACE-complete [8]. This has motivated a search for computationally well-behaved fragments. For instance, early in the twentieth century, Löwenheim already gave a decision procedure for the satisfiability of first-order sentences with only unary predicates [17]. Many familiar fragments of first-order logic are defined by means of restrictions of the quantifier prefix of formulas in prenex normal forms, and their (un)decidability has been carefully charted [7]. Finite-variable (and in particular two-variable) fragments of first-order logic are yet another kind of fragments whose computational properties have been studied extensively, with decidability results going back to the early 1960s [23,14,15,20]. But even though many of these fragments have good computational properties, their meta-logical properties are often poor, and, in particular, they usually lack a good model theory that explains their computational properties.

Research efforts have been devoted to identify fragments of first-order or second-order logic that manage to combine good computational behavior with good meta-logical properties. One such effort takes (propositional) modal logic as its starting point [4,5]. Although modal logics are syntactically presented as an extension of propositional logic, there exist well-known translations through which modal languages may semantically be viewed as fragments of first-order languages. Modal fragments are

* This work was partly supported by grants ANPCyT-PICT-2008-306, ANPCyT-PICT-2010-688, ANPCyT-PICT-2012-712, the FP7-PEOPLE-2011-IRSES Project "Mobility between Europe and Argentina applying Logics to Systems" (MEALS), the project ANR-13-IS02-0001 of the Agence Nationale de la Recherche, the STIC AmSud MISMT, and the Laboratoire International Associé "INFINIS".

R. De Nicola and R. Hennicker (Eds.): Wirsing Festschrift, LNCS 8950, pp. 30–45, 2015.

computationally very well-behaved; their satisfiability and model checking problems are of reasonably low complexity, and they are so in a robust way [26,13]. The good computational behavior of modal fragments has been explained in terms of the tree model property, and generalizations thereof.

Broadly speaking, there are three general strategies for modal theorem proving: *(i)* develop purpose-built calculi and tools; *(ii)* translate modal problems into automata-theoretic problems, and use automata-theoretic methods to obtain answers; *(iii)* translate modal problems into first-order problems, and use general first-order tools. The advantage of indirect methods such as *(ii)* and *(iii)* is that they allow us to reuse well-developed and well-supported tools instead of having to develop new ones from scratch. In this paper we focus on the third option: translation-based theorem proving for modal logic, where modal formulas are translated into first-order formulas to be fed to first-order theorem provers. In particular, we will investigate the use of Satisfiability Modulo Theories (SMT) techniques [3,18] for reasoning in restricted first-order theories. We provide rules that constrain the instantiations of quantifiers in the translated formulas, and we show that these rules are sound, complete and terminating.

Outline. Section 2 introduces basic modal logic and explains the overall architecture of the SMT-based decision procedure. The precise rules are indicated in section 3, together with the proofs of soundness, completeness, and termination. Extensions of the procedure to global modalities and hybrid logic appear in section 4, and section 5 concludes the paper and discusses related work.

2   Background

2.1   Basic Modal Logic

The basic modal logic BML can be seen as an extension of propositional logic. Let $\mathcal{P}$ be a set of propositional symbols, the syntax of BML is defined as

$$\varphi \doteq p \mid \neg p \mid \varphi \wedge \varphi' \mid \varphi \vee \varphi \mid \Box \varphi \mid \Diamond \varphi,$$

where $p \in \mathcal{P}$. Observe that we assume formulas to be in negation normal form where negation is only applied to atomic propositions. Semantically, formulas of BML are interpreted over relational structures. Let $\mathcal{M} = \langle M, \cdot^{\mathcal{M}} \rangle$ be such that M is a non-empty set called the *domain* and $\cdot^{\mathcal{M}}$ is an *interpretation function* that assigns to each $p \in \mathcal{P}$ a subset $p^{\mathcal{M}}$ of M and introduces a relation $R^{\mathcal{M}} \subseteq M \times M$ ($R^{\mathcal{M}}$ is usually called the *accessibility relation* of $\mathcal{M}$). For a relational structure $\mathcal{M}$, we will often write $|\mathcal{M}|$ for the domain of $\mathcal{M}$, and if $w \in |\mathcal{M}|$ we will say that $\mathcal{M}, w$ is a pointed model. For a pointed model $\mathcal{M}, w$, the satisfaction relation for formulas in BML is defined by

$$
\begin{array}{lll}
\mathcal{M}, w \models p & \text{iff} & w \in p^{\mathcal{M}} \\
\mathcal{M}, w \models \neg p & \text{iff} & w \notin p^{\mathcal{M}} \\
\mathcal{M}, w \models \varphi \wedge \varphi' & \text{iff} & \mathcal{M}, w \models \varphi \text{ and } \mathcal{M}, w \models \varphi' \\
\mathcal{M}, w \models \varphi \vee \varphi' & \text{iff} & \mathcal{M}, w \models \varphi \text{ or } \mathcal{M}, w \models \varphi' \\
\mathcal{M}, w \models \Box \varphi & \text{iff} & \text{for all } (w, v) \in R^{\mathcal{M}} \text{ we have that } \mathcal{M}, v \models \varphi \\
\mathcal{M}, w \models \Diamond \varphi & \text{iff} & \text{for some } (w, v) \in R^{\mathcal{M}} \text{ we have that } \mathcal{M}, v \models \varphi.
\end{array}
$$

We say that φ is *satisfiable* if there is a pointed model $\mathcal{M}, w$ such that $\mathcal{M}, w \models \varphi$, otherwise φ is unsatisfiable. We define Mod(φ) as the set of pointed models of φ, formally, Mod(φ) = $\{\mathcal{M}, w \mid \mathcal{M}, w \models \varphi\}$ (we will use Mod(φ) for the set of models of φ also when φ is a propositional formula). For a set Σ of formulas, we let Mod(Σ) = $\bigcap_{\varphi \in \Sigma}$ Mod(φ). Finally, let Σ ∪ {φ} be a set of formulas, we say that φ is a consequence of Σ and we write Σ $\models$ φ if Mod(Σ) $\subseteq$ Mod(φ).

The definition above makes it clear that the semantics of basic modal logic is purely first-order. Actually, through *translation*, modal languages may be viewed as fragments of first-order languages. Our starting point is the relational translation ST, which translates modal formulas by transcribing their truth definitions as first-order formulas. Let φ be a modal formula and x a first-order variable; then $ST_x(\varphi)$ is defined as follows:

$$ST_x(p) \doteq P(x) \qquad\qquad\qquad ST_x(\neg p) \doteq \neg P(x) \qquad\qquad (1)$$

$$ST_x(\varphi \wedge \varphi') \doteq ST_x(\varphi) \wedge ST_x(\varphi') \qquad ST_x(\varphi \vee \varphi') \doteq ST_x(\varphi) \vee ST_x(\varphi') \qquad (2)$$

$$ST_x(\Box\varphi) \doteq \forall y : \neg R(x,y) \vee ST_y(\varphi) \qquad ST_x(\Diamond\varphi) \doteq \exists y : R(x,y) \wedge ST_y(\varphi). \quad (3)$$

In (1), P is a unary predicate symbol corresponding to the proposition letter p; in (3), the variable y is fresh. Observe how (3) reflects the truth definition of the modal operators. Also observe that $ST_x(\varphi)$ is a first-order formula in negation normal form whose only free variable is x, for any BML formula φ. ST is extended to sets of formulas in the obvious way, i.e., $ST_x(\Sigma) = \{ST_x(\varphi) : \varphi \in \Sigma\}$.

Proposition 1. *Let $\mathcal{M}, w$ be a pointed model, and φ a formula of BML then*

$$\mathcal{M}, w \models \varphi \quad iff \quad \mathcal{M}, g[x \mapsto w] \models ST_x(\varphi),$$

where, on the right-hand side, $\mathcal{M}$ is viewed as a first-order interpretation, g is an arbitrary assignment for $\mathcal{M}$, and $g[x \mapsto w]$ coincides with g but assigns w to x.

2.2 SMT Solving for Modal Satisfiability: Overall Setup

Starting from the relational translation of modal logic into first-order logic, we propose in this paper an SMT-based procedure for deciding the satisfiability of BML formulas. It consists of two cooperating modules, as illustrated in the schema below.

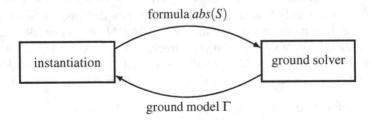

The procedure maintains a finite set S of first-order formulas. Initially, S is obtained by relational translation from the set of BML formulas whose satisfiability we wish to decide. New formulas can be added through instantiation, provided that the resulting set of formulas is equisatisfiable with the original one.

The *ground solver* is given a ground abstraction of the set S, denoted in the following by $abs(S)$, and it decides if $abs(S)$ is satisfiable. The solver is assumed to be sound, complete, and terminating for ground formulas; it includes a SAT solver and possibly other decision procedures. For example, the extension to hybrid logic of section 4.2 requires a decision procedure for quantifier-free formulas over the theory of uninterpreted function and predicate symbols with equality. The abstraction $abs(S)$ for BML is obtained by (consistently) mapping formulas φ in S that are either atomic or contain an outermost quantifier to fresh propositional symbols that we denote by $\boxed{\varphi}$, while preserving the Boolean structure of formulas in S. For example, consider the set

$$S = \{(\forall x : \neg R(c,x) \lor P(x)), \ R(c,d) \land \neg P(d)\}.$$

Its abstraction will be denoted as

$$abs(S) = \{\, \boxed{\forall x : \neg R(c,x) \lor P(x)}\,, \ \boxed{R(c,d)} \land \neg \boxed{P(d)}\,\}.$$

Conversely, given a set Γ of propositional formulas whose atoms are all of the form $\boxed{\varphi}$, we define $conc(\Gamma)$ to be the set of first-order formula obtained by "erasing the boxes". In particular, $conc(abs(S)) = S$.

If the ground solver finds $abs(S)$ to be unsatisfiable, then the procedure declares the original set of formulas unsatisfiable. Otherwise, it computes a set of literals Γ built from the atomic propositions in $abs(S)$ that corresponds to a model of $abs(S)$. Although Γ is a propositional model of $abs(S)$, a first-order model for $conc(\Gamma)$, or indeed for S, may not exist. For example, the set S above is unsatisfiable, but $abs(S)$ has the propositional model

$$\Gamma = \{\, \boxed{\forall x : \neg R(c,x) \lor P(x)}\,, \ \boxed{R(c,d)}\,, \neg \boxed{P(d)}\,\}.$$

In order to rule out models of $abs(S)$ that do not correspond to first-order models of S, the decision procedure also contains an *instantiation module* that computes refinements of $abs(S)$. More precisely, given a model Γ of $abs(S)$, the instantiation module may generate relevant instances of the quantified formulas that are abstracted in $abs(S)$. For the above example, the instantiation module should produce the formula

$$(\forall x : \neg R(c,x) \lor P(x)) \Rightarrow (\neg R(c,d) \lor P(d))$$

that will be added to S, yielding set S'. Note that Γ is no longer a model of $abs(S')$, and that in fact $abs(S')$ is unsatisfiable. We must ensure that only finitely many instances are generated over time, so that the feedback loop eventually terminates and the procedure outputs a verdict.

3   Decision Procedure for Basic Modal Logic

We now define instantiation rules for basic modal logic BML. We show that these rules are sound and complete. Moreover, only finitely many instantiations are created for each quantified formula, hence the procedure terminates.

3.1 Instantiation Rules

Recall from section 2.1 that formulas arising from the relational translation of basic
modal logic are built from unary predicate symbols $P(\_)$ that correspond to the proposition symbols in $\mathcal{P}$ and a single binary predicate symbol $R(\_,\_)$. Formulas are in negation normal form and contain exactly one free variable, representing the current point
of evaluation. Occurrences of quantifiers are restricted to the forms

$$\forall y : \neg R(x,y) \vee \varphi(y) \qquad \text{and} \qquad \exists y : R(x,y) \wedge \varphi(y)$$

where x is the variable designating the point of evaluation of the quantified formula,
and y is the only free variable in $\varphi(y)$.

The set of formulas given as input to the decision procedure is assumed to consist
of formulas of this form. We replace the unique free variable by a Skolem constant,
obtaining a closed set S^0 of formulas. The decision procedure will maintain a set of
formulas in this form, extended by formulas $(Qx : \psi(x)) \Rightarrow \chi$ where Q is a quantifier
and $\psi(x)$ and χ are formulas in negation normal form; χ has no free variables and $\psi(x)$
contains exactly the free variable x.

A *configuration* of the decision procedure is a triple $\langle S, \Theta_\exists, \Theta_\forall \rangle$ where

- S is a set of closed formulas as described above and
- the sets $\Theta_\exists$ and $\Theta_\forall$ contain information about instances that have already been
  produced and need not be created anew.

The initial configuration is $\langle S^0, \emptyset, \emptyset \rangle$. Given a configuration $\langle S, \Theta_\exists, \Theta_\forall \rangle$, the decision
procedure invokes the ground solver on the set $abs(S)$. If $abs(S)$ is unsatisfiable, the
procedure terminates, declaring S^0 unsatisfiable. Otherwise, the ground solver produces
a set of literals Γ that represents a model of $abs(S)$, and the decision procedure computes
a successor configuration by applying one of the following instantiation rules ($\exists$) or ($\forall$)
and continues. If no instantiation rule is applicable, the procedure terminates, declaring
S^0 satisfiable.

Rule ($\exists$). This rule instantiates existentially quantified formulas in S by fresh constants:

$$\langle S, \Theta_\exists, \Theta_\forall \rangle \xrightarrow{\Gamma} \langle S', \Theta_\exists', \Theta_\forall \rangle \quad \text{if there exists } \varepsilon \doteq \boxed{\exists y : R(c,y) \wedge \varphi(y)} \text{ s.t.}$$

- $\varepsilon \in \Gamma \setminus \Theta_\exists$ is an atom corresponding to an existentially quantified formula
  that appears in Γ but for which no instance has yet been created,
- d is a fresh constant,
- $S' = S \cup \{conc(\varepsilon) \Rightarrow (R(c,d) \wedge \varphi(d))\}$,
- $\Theta_\exists' = \Theta_\exists \cup \{\varepsilon\}$.

Rule ($\forall$). This rule instantiates universally quantified formulas in S for constants such
that the guard of the quantified formula appears in Γ:

$$\langle S, \Theta_\exists, \Theta_\forall \rangle \xrightarrow{\Gamma} \langle S', \Theta_\exists, \Theta'_\forall \rangle \quad \text{if there exist } \varepsilon \doteq \boxed{\forall y : \neg R(c,y) \vee \varphi(y)} \text{ and } d \text{ s.t.}$$

- $\varepsilon \in \Gamma$, $\boxed{R(c,d)} \in \Gamma$, $(\varepsilon, d) \notin \Theta_\forall$. In words, ε is an atom that corresponds to a universally quantified formula that appears in Γ, and d is a constant for which the guard of ε is asserted in Γ but for which ε has not yet been instantiated,
- $S' = S \cup \{conc(\varepsilon) \Rightarrow (\neg R(c,d) \vee \varphi(d))\}$,
- $\Theta'_\forall = \Theta_\forall \cup \{(\varepsilon, d)\}$.

The rules are natural, and they resemble the rules in a tableaux algorithm for the basic modal language, but implemented in the SMT setup. In particular, rule ($\exists$) uses fresh constants to denote unique witnesses for existential quantifiers. It can be understood as on-the-fly Skolemization of an outermost existential quantifier. Universal quantifiers are instantiated only for successors (via the accessibility relation) of the only constant that appears in the guard of the quantifier. These instantiations are guided by the propositional model Γ computed by the ground solver.

3.2 Soundness and Completeness

The soundness of the rules ($\exists$) and ($\forall$) is a consequence of the following two lemmas, whose proof is straightforward.

Lemma 2. *Assume that* $\langle S, \Theta_\exists, \Theta_\forall \rangle \xrightarrow{\Gamma} \langle S', \Theta'_\exists, \Theta'_\forall \rangle$ *according to rules* ($\exists$) *or* ($\forall$). *Then S and S' are equisatisfiable sets of first-order formulas.*

Lemma 3. *If $\mathcal{M}$ is a first-order model of S, then $abs(S)$ has a ground model Γ.*

Proof. Define Γ to be the set of literals built from the atomic formulas in $abs(S)$ such that $\boxed{\psi} \in \Gamma$ if $\mathcal{M} \models \psi$ and $\neg \boxed{\psi} \in \Gamma$ if $\mathcal{M} \not\models \psi$. A straightforward inductive proof shows that $\Gamma \models abs(S)$. $\qquad\square$

Theorem 4 (Soundness). *Assume that the procedure terminates with verdict "unsatisfiable". Then the initial set S^0 of formulas is unsatisfiable.*

Proof. The verdict "unsatisfiable" is based on a sequence of configurations

$$\langle S^0, \emptyset, \emptyset \rangle \xrightarrow{\Gamma^0} \langle S^1, \Theta_\exists^1, \Theta_\forall^1 \rangle \xrightarrow{\Gamma^1} \cdots \xrightarrow{\Gamma^{n-1}} \langle S^n, \Theta_\exists^n, \Theta_\forall^n \rangle$$

such that the ground solver finds $abs(S^n)$ to be unsatisfiable. By Lemma 3, it follows that S^n is unsatisfiable, and so is S^0, by iterating Lemma 2. $\qquad\square$

The completeness proof relies on the construction of a first-order model of the original set S^0 of formulas from a propositional model of a saturated set S^n in a configuration where no rules are applicable anymore.

Theorem 5 (Completeness). *Assume that the procedure terminates with verdict "satisfiable". Then the initial set S^0 of formulas is satisfiable.*

Proof. The verdict "satisfiable" is based on a sequence of configurations

$$\langle S^0, \emptyset, \emptyset \rangle \xrightarrow{\Gamma^0} \langle S^1, \Theta_\exists^1, \Theta_\forall^1 \rangle \xrightarrow{\Gamma^1} \cdots \xrightarrow{\Gamma^{n-1}} \langle S^n, \Theta_\exists^n, \Theta_\forall^n \rangle$$

such that the ground solver finds $abs(S^n)$ to be satisfiable, and no transition according to the rules $(\exists)$ or $(\forall)$ is possible. The ground solver produces a set Γ of literals that corresponds to a propositional model of $abs(S^n)$; more precisely, the propositional interpretation Γ^* that satisfies the atomic formulas $\boxed{\psi}$ iff $\boxed{\psi} \in \Gamma$ is a model of $abs(S^n)$.

Observe that the set S^n is a superset of S^0 obtained by adding formulas of the form

$$(\exists y : R(c,y) \wedge \varphi(y)) \Rightarrow \ldots \qquad \text{and} \qquad (\forall y : \neg R(c,y) \vee \varphi(y)) \Rightarrow \ldots$$

by applications of rules $(\exists)$ and $(\forall)$. We define a first-order interpretation $\mathcal{M}$ as follows. The universe $|\mathcal{M}|$ consists of the constants that appear in S^n: observe that this set is nonempty since S^0 contains precisely one constant and $S^0 \subseteq S^n$. For the predicate symbols $P(\_)$ that appear in S^n and any $a \in |\mathcal{M}|$, we define $a \in P^{\mathcal{M}}$ iff $\boxed{P(a)} \in \Gamma$. Similarly, for the relation symbol, we let $(a,b) \in R^{\mathcal{M}}$ iff $\boxed{R(a,b)} \in \Gamma$.

Step 1. We show that for every ground instance of every subformula ψ of a formula in S^0 for constants that appear in S^n, if $\Gamma^* \models abs(\psi)$ then $\mathcal{M} \models \psi$. The proof is by induction on ψ.

- For $\psi \doteq P(a)$ or $\psi \doteq R(a,b)$, if $\Gamma^* \models abs(\psi)$ then $abs(\psi) \in \Gamma$ and therefore $\mathcal{M} \models \psi$ by definition of $\mathcal{M}$. Similarly, if $\Gamma^* \models \neg abs(\psi)$ then $abs(\psi) \notin \Gamma$ and therefore $\mathcal{M} \models \neg\psi$, again by definition of $\mathcal{M}$.
- For conjunctions and disjunctions, the proof of the inductive step is immediate.
- Assume that $\psi \doteq \exists y : R(c,y) \wedge \varphi(y)$ is a ground instance of a subformula in S^0 and that $\Gamma^* \models abs(\psi)$, i.e. $\boxed{\psi} \in \Gamma$. Since rule $(\exists)$ cannot be applied, we must have $\boxed{\psi} \in \Theta_\exists$, and therefore S^n must contain

$$\psi \Rightarrow (R(c,d) \wedge \varphi(d))$$

  for some constant d, where the right-hand side of the implication is a ground instance of a subformula in S^0. Moreover, $abs(S^n)$ contains

$$\boxed{\psi} \Rightarrow abs(R(c,d) \wedge \varphi(d)).$$

  Since $\Gamma^* \models \boxed{\psi}$, it follows that $\Gamma^* \models abs(R(c,d) \wedge \varphi(d))$. Now, $\mathcal{M} \models R(c,d) \wedge \varphi(d)$ follows by induction hypothesis, and this proves $\mathcal{M} \models \psi$.
- Assume now that $\psi \doteq \forall y : \neg R(c,y) \vee \varphi(y)$ and that $\Gamma^* \models abs(\psi)$, i.e. $\boxed{\psi} \in \Gamma$. Moreover, assume that $\mathcal{M} \models R(c,d)$ for a constant $d \in |\mathcal{M}|$: we must show that $\mathcal{M} \models \varphi(d)$. By the definition of $\mathcal{M}$ and the assumption that $\mathcal{M} \models R(c,d)$ it follows

that $\boxed{R(c,d)} \in \Gamma$. Since rule ($\forall$) cannot be applied, we must have $(\boxed{\psi},d) \in \Theta_\forall$, and S^n, resp. $abs(S^n)$, contain the formulas

$$\psi \Rightarrow (\neg R(c,d) \vee \varphi(d)) \qquad \text{resp.} \qquad \boxed{\psi} \Rightarrow (\neg \boxed{R(c,d)} \vee abs(\varphi(d))).$$

where the right-hand side of the implication on the left is a ground instance of a subformula of S^0. Because $\Gamma^* \models abs(S^n)$, we can conclude that $\Gamma^* \models abs(\varphi(d))$, and therefore $\mathcal{M} \models \varphi(d)$ by induction hypothesis, and this suffices.

Step 2. Now suppose that formula φ appears in the original set S^0. Then φ is ground and $\Gamma^* \models abs(\varphi)$ because Γ^* is a model of $abs(S^n) \supseteq abs(S_0)$. By step 1, it follows that $\mathcal{M} \models \varphi$. Thus, $\mathcal{M}$ is a model of S^0, and this concludes the proof. □

Remark. Notice that the restriction to ground instances of (sub-)formulas of S^0 in the above proof is necessary: the model $\mathcal{M}$ need not satisfy all formulas in S^n. For example, consider a set S^0 containing the formula

$$\underbrace{(\exists x : R(a,x) \wedge P(x))}_{\varepsilon_1} \vee \underbrace{(\exists y : R(a,y) \wedge P(y) \wedge Q(y))}_{\varepsilon_2}$$

resulting from the translation of the modal formula $(\Diamond p) \vee \Diamond(p \wedge q)$. The saturation of S^0 by application of the instantiation rules may result in a set S^n containing the two implications

$$\varepsilon_1 \Rightarrow R(a,b) \wedge P(b) \quad \text{and} \quad \varepsilon_2 \Rightarrow R(a,c) \wedge P(c) \wedge Q(c)$$

for two constants b and c. A possible propositional model Γ of $abs(S^n)$ contains the literals

$$\neg \boxed{\varepsilon_1}, \ \neg \boxed{R(a,b)}, \ \neg \boxed{P(b)}, \ \boxed{\varepsilon_2}, \ \boxed{R(a,c)}, \ \boxed{P(c)}, \ \boxed{Q(c)}.$$

The corresponding first-order interpretation satisfies $R(a,c) \wedge P(c)$, hence it satisfies ε_1, but it does not satisfy $R(a,b)$ or $P(b)$. Therefore it is not a model of S^n.

Observe, however, that the formulas added by applications of rule ($\forall$) are first-order valid, and in particular true in the interpretation $\mathcal{M}$.

3.3 Termination

Finally, we show that the procedure must terminate because only finitely many constants can be introduced during any run of the procedure.

Theorem 6 (Termination). *For any finite set S^0, there cannot be an infinite transition sequence*

$$\langle S^0, \Theta_\exists^0, \Theta_\forall^0 \rangle \xrightarrow{\Gamma^0} \langle S^1, \Theta_\exists^1, \Theta_\forall^1 \rangle \xrightarrow{\Gamma^1} \dots$$

Proof. The key is to observe that only finitely many constants can be introduced in sets S^i by applications of rule ($\exists$), and that every constant can only give rise to finitely many applications of rule ($\forall$). We associate a depth ∂_c with every constant c that appears in sets S^i, as follows:

- S^0 contains only a single constant c whose depth ∂_c is 0.
- If $\langle S^{i+1}, \Theta_\exists^{i+1}, \Theta_\forall^{i+1} \rangle$ results from an application of rule ($\forall$) the set of constants is unchanged.
- If $\langle S^{i+1}, \Theta_\exists^{i+1}, \Theta_\forall^{i+1} \rangle$ introduces constant d through an application of rule ($\exists$) for formula $\exists y : R(c,y) \wedge \varphi(y)$, then $\partial_d = \partial_c + 1$.

We prove by induction that the set of constants c at depth $\partial_c = k$ is finite, for any $k \in \mathbb{N}$:

- The assertion is obvious for $k = 0$.
- Assuming there are only finitely many constants c at depth k, there can only be a finite set of formula instances $\exists y : R(c,y) \wedge \varphi(y)$ in the sets S^i for every such c since all these instances come from subformulas of the original set S^0 of formulas, of which there are only finitely many, and each of these instances can be used only once to generate a new constant by rule ($\exists$) because its abstraction is then added to $\Theta_\exists$. Therefore the set of constants of depth $k + 1$ is again finite.

Moreover, the depth of constants introduced in any set S^i is bounded by the maximal quantifier depth of any formula in S^0, since every instantiation removes a quantifier.

Hence, the set of constants that appear throughout the transition sequence is finite, and therefore the rule ($\exists$) can be applied only finitely often. Moreover, rule ($\forall$) can only be applied once per pair of universally quantified formula instance and constant. This proves termination.   □

The proof above is a recast of the standard termination proof used in tableau calculi. We now consider some extensions of the basic modal language. Interestingly, the proof requires only small changes. By comparison, the corresponding termination proof for, say, the basic hybrid logic is much more involved.

4   Extensions of the Basic Modal Logic

In this section, we consider some extensions of the basic modal logic to which we adapt the procedure described before.

4.1   Global Modalities

The relational translation for modal operators of BML gives rise to formulas where quantifiers are guarded by accessibility conditions (see definition clauses (3) on page 32). Global modalities [12] refer to arbitrary elements of the relational structure, which need not be related to the current point. The existential global modality is usually denoted by E and A is its univesal dual. Their semantics conditions are as follows

$$M, w \models \mathsf{A}\varphi \quad \text{iff} \quad \text{for all } v \in M \text{ we have that } M, v \models \varphi$$
$$M, w \models \mathsf{E}\varphi \quad \text{iff} \quad \text{for some } v \in M \text{ we have that } M, v \models \varphi.$$

Their relational translations introduces formulas

$$\forall y : \varphi(y) \quad \text{and} \quad \exists y : \varphi(y)$$

where y is again the only free variable; moreover, $\varphi(y)$ does not contain any constant.

We introduce two new rules (E) and (A) for these modalities. In these rules, $\varphi(y)$ denotes an unguarded formula that contains only y as free variable (and no constant).

Rule (E). This rule instantiates unguarded existentially quantified formulas in S by fresh constants:

$$\langle S, \Theta_{\exists}, \Theta_{\forall} \rangle \xrightarrow{\Gamma} \langle S', \Theta'_{\exists}, \Theta_{\forall} \rangle \quad \text{if there exists } \varepsilon \doteq \boxed{\exists y : \varphi(y)} \text{ s.t.}$$

- $\varepsilon \in \Gamma \setminus \Theta_{\exists}$ is an atom corresponding to an unguarded existentially quantified formula that appears in Γ but has not been handled yet,
- d is a fresh constant,
- $S' = S \cup \{conc(\varepsilon) \Rightarrow \varphi(d))\}$,
- $\Theta'_{\exists} = \Theta_{\exists} \cup \{\varepsilon\}$.

Rule (A). This rule instantiates unguarded universally quantified formulas in S for constants that have not yet been instantiated.

$$\langle S, \Theta_{\exists}, \Theta_{\forall} \rangle \xrightarrow{\Gamma} \langle S', \Theta_{\exists}, \Theta'_{\forall} \rangle \quad \text{if there exist } \varepsilon \doteq \boxed{\forall y : \varphi(y)} \text{ and } d \text{ s.t.}$$

- $\varepsilon \in \Gamma$, d is a constant in S, $(\varepsilon, d) \notin \Theta_{\forall}$. In words, ε is an atom corresponding to an unguarded universally quantified formula that appears in Γ, and d is a constant for which ε has not yet been instantiated,
- $S' = S \cup \{conc(\varepsilon) \Rightarrow \varphi(d)^A\}$,
- $\Theta'_{\forall} = \Theta_{\forall} \cup \{(\varepsilon, d)\}$.

Without additional precautions, the rule (A) may lead to the regeneration of copies of formulas for different constants that could make the procedure fail to terminate. For example, a subformula $\forall x : \exists y : R(x, y) \wedge P(y)$ that corresponds to the relational translation of the modal formula $A \Diamond p$ may lead to the generation of infinitely many copies of the formula $R(c, d) \wedge P(d)$ for different constants c and d.

In order to avoid the generation of redundant copies, we adopt a blocking rule similar to the one proposed by Schmidt and Tishkovsky [22]. The instantiated formula $\varphi(d)$ generated in the above rule has been decorated in order to remember that it is an instance of an unguarded universally quantifier. This decoration is understood to be distributed across the Boolean connectives that appear in φ. As a concrete example, consider the unguarded formula

$$\varepsilon \doteq \forall y : P(y) \vee (\exists z : R(y, z) \wedge Q(z))$$

that corresponds to the modal formula $A(p \vee \Diamond q)$. The application of rule (A) to this formula will introduce the implication

$$conc(\varepsilon) \Rightarrow P(y)^A \vee (\exists z : R(y, z) \wedge Q(z))^A.$$

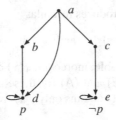

Fig. 1. Model for example formula with global modalities

The decorated formulas are not distinguished from undecorated ones, except that we add the following variant of the rule ($\exists$).

$$\langle S, \Theta_\exists, \Theta_\forall \rangle \xrightarrow{\Gamma} \langle S', \Theta'_\exists, \Theta_\forall \rangle \quad \text{if there exists } \varepsilon \doteq \boxed{(\exists y : R(c,y) \wedge \varphi(y))^A} \text{ s.t.}$$

- $\varepsilon \in \Gamma \setminus \Theta_\exists$ is an atom corresponding to an existentially quantified formula that appears in Γ but for which no instance has yet been created,
- if S contains the formula

$$(\exists y : R(a,y) \wedge \varphi(y))^A \Rightarrow (R(a,d) \wedge \varphi(d))$$

for some constants a and d, then

$$S' = S \cup \{conc(\varepsilon) \Rightarrow (R(c,d) \wedge \varphi(d))\}$$

for that constant d, otherwise S' is defined as above for a fresh constant d,
- $\Theta'_\exists = \Theta_\exists \cup \{\varepsilon\}$.

For the soundness proof, it is essential to notice that Lemma 2 carries over to the new rules. In particular, the above variant of the rule ($\exists$) ensures equisatisfiability of sets S and S' because the same successor satisfying $\varphi(d)$ may be chosen for any two diamond formulas in the scope of a global A modality. The completeness and termination proofs of section 3 carry over to the above rules in the obvious manner.

As a concrete example, the application of our rules to the modal formula

$$\Diamond\Box p \wedge \Diamond\Box\neg p \wedge A(\Diamond p \vee \Diamond\neg p)$$

may result in the model shown in figure 1. Its domain has five elements a, b, c, d, and e, with a corresponding to the root point satisfying the original formula. The proposition p is true at d and false at e. Note that every point has either d or e as a successor, ensuring that the subformula $A(\Diamond p \vee \Diamond\neg p)$ is satisfied.

4.2   Hybrid Logic

Hybrid languages [2] are modal languages that have special symbols to name individual points in models. Syntactically, these new symbols $i, j, k, \ldots$, often called nominals, are just another sort of propositional symbols[1]. For example, if i is a nominal and p and q are ordinary atomic propositions, then

$$\Box i \wedge \Diamond q \wedge \Diamond \neg q \quad \text{and} \quad \Box p \wedge \Diamond q \wedge \Diamond \neg q$$

are both well-formed formulas; but they have quite a different meaning. Actually, as we will now explain, the second formula is satisfiable whereas the first one is not. The difference comes from the interpretation that should be attributed to nominals. Because a nominal i represents a particular element in the model it should be true at a unique state. Formally, its interpretation $i^{\mathcal{M}}$ is a singleton set. For the left-hand formula above to be true at some point w, the first conjunct requires that at most one state (the one denoted by i) can be accessible from the evaluation point w. It is then impossible to satisfy both q and $\neg q$ at that unique successor, as required by the two other conjuncts. In contrast, the first conjunct of the right-hand formula just requires that all states accessible from w satisfy p, but does not restrict their multiplicity. Hence, some successor may satisfy q and another one $\neg q$.

Once we have names for states we can introduce, for each nominal i, an operator $@_i$ that allows us to jump to the point named by i. The formula $@_i \varphi$ (read "at i, φ") moves the point of evaluation to the state named by i and evaluates φ there: Intuitively, the $@_i$ operators internalize the satisfaction relation "$\models$" into the logical language:

$$\mathcal{M}, w \models @_i \varphi \quad \text{iff} \quad \mathcal{M}, u \models \varphi \text{ where } i^{\mathcal{M}} = \{u\}.$$

For this reason, these operators are usually called satisfaction operators.

We will now extend our calculus to handle the operators of the basic hybrid logic.

4.3   SMT-Based Decision Procedure for Hybrid Logic

The relational translation for basic modal logic extends to hybrid logic through the definitions

$$\mathsf{ST}_x(i) \doteq x = i$$
$$\mathsf{ST}_x(@_i \varphi) \doteq \mathsf{ST}_i(\varphi).$$

In particular, note that nominals are translated as constants of first-order logic. The relational translation still produces formulas with at most one free variable.

We now adapt our SMT-based decision procedure to hybrid logic, starting from the relational translation of the input set of hybrid logic formulas; if that translation has a (single) free variable, it is again replaced by a (Skolem) constant, otherwise the translation must contain a constant corresponding to a nominal. Because equality is now a central part of reasoning, we no longer produce propositional abstractions for use with a SAT solver, but rely on a ground SMT solver that includes a decision procedure for equality over uninterpreted predicate symbols. Accordingly, the abstraction preserves

---

[1] Propositional symbols and nominals are however handled quite differently while translating to first-order formulas, as we will see later.

all ground formulas of the forms $P(a)$, $R(a,b)$, and $a = n$, but quantified formulas that
arise from the translation of modal operators are still abstracted, as in

$$\forall x : \neg R(c,x) \vee (x = i \wedge \neg P(x))$$

that corresponds to asserting the formula $\square(i \wedge \neg p)$ of hybrid logic at world c.

The algorithm from section 3 remains essentially unchanged. However, ground models Γ are now not just propositional models of $abs(S)$, but consist of an arrangement of
the finite set C of constants in S given by an equivalence relation $\equiv$ whose set of equivalence classes we will denote by $[C]$, valuations $[\![P]\!] \subseteq [C]$ and $[\![R]\!] \subseteq [C] \times [C]$ that
indicate the extensions of the unary and binary predicates in Γ, as well as a set of atoms
$\boxed{\varphi}$ that correspond to abstracted subformulas in S that are true in Γ. The rules $(\exists)$ and
$(\forall)$ of section 3 remains basically the same, except that conditions $\psi \in \Gamma$ should be read
as $\Gamma \models \psi$, and that atomic formulas are no longer abstracted, as discussed above.

4.4   Soundness, Completeness, and Termination

The proof of soundness extends immediately the one of section 3.2.

Theorem 7 (Soundness for hybrid logic). *Assume that the procedure terminates with
verdict "unsatisfiable". Then the initial set S^0 of formulas is unsatisfiable.*

Proof. The analogues of lemmas 2 and 3 remain true for hybrid logic: for any transition
$\langle S, \Theta_\exists, \Theta_\forall \rangle \xrightarrow{\Gamma} \langle S', \Theta'_\exists, \Theta'_\forall \rangle$, we have that S and S' are equisatisfiable. Also, any first-
order model of S again gives rise to a model of $abs(S)$, hence unsatisfiability of $abs(S)$
implies unsatisfiability of S.

The soundness theorem is an immediate consequence of these two lemmas.   □

Completeness. The completeness proof is also analogous to the one in section 3.2:
whenever the procedure produces a ground model in a state where no instantiation rule
can be applied, then the set of formulas is satisfiable.

Theorem 8 (Completeness for hybrid logic). *Assume that the procedure terminates
with verdict "satisfiable". Then the initial set S^0 of formulas is satisfiable.*

Proof. Assume that the procedure terminates after a sequence of transitions

$$\langle S^0, \emptyset, \emptyset \rangle \xrightarrow{\Gamma^0} \langle S^1, \Theta_\exists^1, \Theta_\forall^1 \rangle \xrightarrow{\Gamma^1} \cdots \xrightarrow{\Gamma^{n-1}} \langle S^n, \Theta_\exists^n, \Theta_\forall^n \rangle$$

such that $abs(S^n)$ is satisfied by a ground model Γ, and no transition according to $(\exists)$ or
$(\forall)$ is possible. As before, S^0 is exactly the subset of S^n without the formulas added by
applications of rules $(\exists)$ and $(\forall)$. Let $\mathcal{M}$ be the first-order structure that corresponds to
Γ, i.e. the universe $|\mathcal{M}|$ is the set $[C]$ of equivalence classes of the constants in $abs(S^n)$,
and $\mathcal{M}$ interprets the unary and binary predicate symbols, as well as the abstracted
quantified formulas $\boxed{\varphi}$ that appear in $abs(S^n)$. We will prove that $\mathcal{M}$ is a model of S^0.

Step 1. We again prove that for every ground instance of every subformula ψ of a formula in S^0 for constants that appear in $abs(S^n)$, if $\mathcal{M} \models abs(\psi)$ then $\mathcal{M} \models \psi$.

- For literals ψ that are ground instances of subformulas in S^n (and a fortiori in S^0), we now have $abs(\psi) = \psi$, and therefore $\mathcal{M} \models abs(\psi)$ iff $\mathcal{M} \models \psi$. Note that this argument extends to ground instances of the new subformulas $x = i$ introduced by the translation from hybrid logic.
- For conjunctions and disjunctions, the proof of the inductive step is immediate.
- For ground instances ψ of quantified formulas of the forms $\exists y : R(c,y) \wedge \varphi(y)$ and $\forall y : \neg R(c,y) \vee \varphi(y)$, the arguments are exactly the same as in the proof of theorem 5, replacing $\boxed{\psi} \in \Gamma$ by $\mathcal{M} \models \boxed{\psi}$.

Step 2. For any formula $\varphi \in S^0$, we have that φ is ground and $\mathcal{M} \models abs(\varphi)$ because $\mathcal{M}$ is a model of $abs(S^n) \supseteq abs(S^0)$. By step 1, we conclude that $\mathcal{M} \models \varphi$.   □

Termination. The termination proof follows exactly the lines of that of Theorem 6, except that now S^0 may contain several constants, corresponding to nominals and to the Skolem constant for the world from which the model construction for S^0 starts. All these (finitely many) constants are assigned depth 0. The procedure applies the same rules as for the case of basic modal logic, and the structure of the formulas is essentially the same (up to the addition of atomic equalities), and therefore termination is ensured by the same argument.

The fact that the proofs of soundness, completeness, and termination carry over in a straightforward way from basic modal logic to hybrid logic is in marked contrast to the situation for tableau calculi. In particular, the proof of termination is highly non-trivial for tableaux for hybrid logic [6].

5   Conclusions and Related Work

We have presented an SMT-based decision procedure for modal logic and some of its extensions. It is based on combining a ground solver for propositional logic or quantifier-free first-order logic with a custom instantiation module that lazily produces instances of quantified formulas as directed by the ground solver. The procedure robustly extends from basic modal logic to hybrid logic, the main difference being the replacement of a SAT solver by an SMT solver for reasoning about equality. We have also adapted the procedure to take into account standard conditions on the accessibility relation, such as reflexivity, symmetry, and transitivity; for lack of space, these extensions will be described elsewhere. Further extensions, such as to the guarded fragment of predicate logic [1] that generalizes modal logic while retaining its good computational properties, are an interesting avenue for future work.

In principle, the instantiation procedure can be implemented using patterns and e-matching, which are provided by standard SMT solvers. However, one should not expect such a naive implementation to yield an efficient decision procedure for modal logics. In particular, without imposing further control, subsequent calls to the ground solver may result in completely different ground models. One way to obtain a decision procedure running in polynomial space is to impose a depth-first search strategy similar to modal tableaux, where instances corresponding to fully explored branches can be forgotten for the remainder of the exploration. This will imply for the SMT solver to forget instances in a smart way, and such a feature requires some careful engineering. Our preliminary experiments confirm that SMT solvers with trigger-based instantiation as currently implemented are off-the-shelf decision procedures for basic modal logic, but also show that forgetting instances is a required first step towards efficiency. More efficient translations from modal to first-order logic, such as the functional translation and its variants [19], may also help improving the performance without changing the basic setup of our procedure.

Whereas semantic tableaux remain state of the art decision procedures for modal and related logics, several authors proposed alternative methods. In particular, Hustadt and Schmidt [10,16,21] systematically explored techniques based on translations to first-order logic and the use of resolution and superposition provers. Our work starts from the same encodings in first-order languages but relies on ground decision procedures for suitable fragments of first-order logic. We believe that our proofs are more elementary, and we hope to obtain similarly efficient implementations by controlling repeated calls to the ground solver.

Sebastiani et al. [11,24] investigate the use of SAT solvers for modal and related logics. Their approach does not start from an encoding into first-order logic, but abstracts formulas with top-level modal connectives, similar to our abstractions of quantified formulas. When the set of abstracted formulas is found satisfiable, the SAT solver is launched again on sets of sub-problems derived from the formulas beneath the topmost modal operators. Whereas their decision procedure is very efficient for basic modal logic, it appears to fundamentally depend on the clean separation of truth conditions for worlds that correspond to distinct modal depths, and this condition is not satisfied for many extensions of modal logic, including hybrid logic.

Our small investigation into SMT-based decision procedures for modal and related logics owes in part to Martin Wirsing's interest in modal logic, as witnessed by Chapter 6 of [4]. Our work is being developed within an ongoing cooperation between teams located in Argentina and in Europe, which Martin actively fostered. For both reasons, we hope that this paper is a suitable contribution for the present volume, and we present Martin our sincere wishes for many more years of intellectual happiness in pursuing research at the interface of algebra, logic, and computer science.

References

1. Andréka, H., van Benthem, J., Németi, I.: Modal languages and bounded fragments of predicate logic. Journal of Philosophical Logic 27, 217–274 (1998)
2. Areces, C., ten Cate, B.: Hybrid logics. In: Blackburn, P., Wolter, F., van Benthem, J. (eds.) Handbook of Modal Logics, pp. 821–868. Elsevier (2006)
3. Barrett, C., Sebastiani, R., Seshia, S.A., Tinelli, C.: Satisfiability modulo theories. In: Biere, A., Heule, M.J.H., van Maaren, H., Walsh, T. (eds.) Handbook of Satisfiability. Frontiers in Artificial Intelligence and Applications, vol. 185, ch. 26, pp. 825–885. IOS Press (February 2009)
4. Bauer, F.L., Wirsing, M.: Elementare Aussagenlogik. Springer, Heidelberg (1991)

5. Blackburn, P., de Rijke, M., Venema, Y.: Modal Logic. Cambridge Tracts in Theoretical Computer Science, vol. 53. Cambridge University Press, Cambridge (2001)
6. Bolander, T., Blackburn, P.: Termination for hybrid tableaus. Journal of Logic and Computation 17(3), 517–554 (2007)
7. Börger, E., Grädel, E., Gurevich, Y.: The Classical Decision Problem. Springer, Berlin (1997) With an appendix by C. Allauzen, B. Durand
8. Chandra, A., Merlin, P.: Optimal implementation of conjunctive queries in relational databases. In: Proc. 9th ACM Symp. Theory of Computing, pp. 77–90 (1977)
9. Church, A.: A note on the Entscheidungsproblem. Journal of Symbolic Logic 1, 40–41 (1936)
10. Ganzinger, H., Hustadt, U., Meyer, C., Schmidt, R.A.: A resolution-based decision procedure for extensions of K4. In: Zakharyaschev, M., Segerberg, K., de Rijke, M., Wansing, H. (eds.) Advances in Modal Logic, pp. 225–246. CSLI Publications (1998)
11. Giunchiglia, F., Sebastiani, R.: Building decision procedures for modal logics from propositional decision procedures: The case study of modal K(m). Information and Computation 162(1-2), 158–178 (2000)
12. Goranko, V., Passy, S.: Using the universal modality: Gains and questions. Journal of Logic and Computation 2(1), 5–30 (1992)
13. Grädel, E.: Why are modal logics so robustly decidable? Bulletin EATCS 68, 90–103 (1999)
14. Grädel, E., Kolaitis, P., Vardi, M.: On the decision problem for two-variable first-order logic. Bulletin of Symbolc Logic 3, 53–69 (1997)
15. Grädel, E., Otto, M., Rosen, E.: Two-variable logic with counting is decidable. In: Proc. 12th Ann. IEEE Symp. Logic in Computer Science (LICS 1997), pp. 306–317. IEEE Comp. Soc. (1997)
16. Hustadt, U., de Nivelle, H., Schmidt, R.A.: Resolution-based methods for modal logics. Logic Journal of the IGPL 8(3), 265–292 (2000)
17. Löwenheim, L.: Über Möglichkeiten im Relativkalkül. Mathematische Annalen 76, 447–470 (1915)
18. Nieuwenhuis, R., Oliveras, A., Tinelli, C.: Solving SAT and SAT Modulo Theories: From an abstract Davis-Putnam-Logemann-Loveland procedure to DPLL(T). J. ACM 53(6), 937–977 (2006)
19. Ohlbach, H.J., Schmidt, R.A.: Functional translation and second-order frame properties of modal logics. Journal of Logic and Computation 7(5), 581–603 (1997)
20. Pacholsky, L., Szwast, W., Tendera, L.: Complexity of two-variable logic with counting. In: Proc. 12th Ann. IEEE Symp. Logic in Computer Science (LICS 1997), pp. 318–327 (1997)
21. Schmidt, R.A., Hustadt, U.: First-order resolution methods for modal logics. In: Voronkov, A., Weidenbach, C. (eds.) Programming Logics. LNCS, vol. 7797, pp. 345–391. Springer, Heidelberg (2013)
22. Schmidt, R.A., Tishkovsky, D.: Using tableau to decide description logics with full role negation and identity. ACM Trans. Comput. Log. 15(1) (2014)
23. Scott, D.: A decision method for validity of sentences in two variables. Journal of Symbolic Logic 27(377), 74 (1962)
24. Sebastiani, R., Tacchella, A.: SAT techniques for modal and description logics. In: Biere, A., Heule, M., van Maaren, H., Walsh, T. (eds.) Handbook of Satisfiability. Frontiers in Artificial Intelligence and Applications, vol. 185, pp. 781–824. IOS Press (2009)
25. Turing, A.: On computable numbers, with an application to the 'Entscheidungsproblem'. Proc. London Mathematical Society 2nd. series 42, 230–265 (1937)
26. Vardi, M.: Why is modal logic so robustly decidable? In: DIMACS Ser. Disc. Math. Theoret. Comp. Sci., vol. 31, pp. 149–184. AMS (1997)

Division by Zero in Common Meadows[*]

Jan A. Bergstra[**] and Alban Ponse

Section Theory of Computer Science
Informatics Institute, Faculty of Science
University of Amsterdam, The Netherlands
https://staff.fnwi.uva.nl/{j.a.bergstra/,a.ponse/}

Abstract. Common meadows are fields expanded with a total multiplicative inverse function. Division by zero produces an additional value denoted with "**a**" that propagates through all operations of the meadow signature (this additional value can be interpreted as an error element). We provide a basis theorem for so-called common cancellation meadows of characteristic zero, that is, common meadows of characteristic zero that admit a certain cancellation law.

Keywords: Meadow, common meadow, division by zero, additional value, abstract datatype.

1 Introduction

Elementary mathematics is uniformly taught around the world with a focus on natural numbers, integers, fractions, and fraction calculation. The mathematical basis of that part of mathematics seems to reside in the field of rational numbers. In elementary teaching material the incorporation of rational numbers in a field is usually not made explicit. This leaves open the possibility that some other abstract datatype or some alternative abstract datatype specification improves upon fields in providing a setting in which such parts of elementary mathematics can be formalized.

In this paper we will propose the signature for — and model class of — *common meadows* and we will provide a *loose* algebraic specification of common meadows by way of a set of equations. In the terminology of Broy and Wirsing [10,15], the semantics of a loose algebraic specification S is given by the class of all models of S, that is, the semantic approach is not restricted to the isomorphism class of initial algebras. For a loose specification it is expected that its

---

[*] This paper is dedicated to Martin Wirsing on the occasion of his emeritation; an earlier version appeared as report arXiv:1406.6878v1 [math.RA], 26 June 2014.

[**] Jan Bergstra expresses his great appreciation for Martin's work, and recalls many meetings and discussions over the years about datatypes and software engineering. Worth mentioning here is their 1981-paper *On the power of algebraic specifications* [3], written together with Manfred Broy and John Tucker, in which it was proven that every computable partial algebra has an equational hidden enrichment specification. The present paper proposes, however, a particular alternative to the conventional option to have a partial multiplicative inverse function.

R. De Nicola and R. Hennicker (Eds.): Wirsing Festschrift, LNCS 8950, pp. 46–61, 2015.
© Springer International Publishing Switzerland 2015

initial algebra is an important member of its model class, worth of independent investigation. In the case of common meadows this aspect is discussed in the last remark of Section 4 (Concluding remarks).

A common meadow (using inversive notation) is an extension of a field equipped with a multiplicative inverse function $(...)^{-1}$ and an additional element **a** that serves as the inverse of zero and propagates through all operations. It should be noticed that the use of the constant **a** is a matter of convenience only because it merely constitutes a derived constant with defining equation $\mathbf{a} = 0^{-1}$. This implies that all uses of **a** can be removed from the story of common meadows (a further comment on this can be found in Section 4).

The inverse function of a common meadow is not an involution because $(0^{-1})^{-1} = \mathbf{a}$. We will refer to meadows with zero-totalized inverse, that is, $0^{-1} = 0$, as *involutive meadows* because inverse becomes an involution. By default a "meadow" is assumed to be an involutive meadow.

The key distinction between meadows and fields, which we consider to be so important that it justifies a different name, is the presence of an operator symbol for inverse in the signature (inversive notation, see [4]) or for division (divisive notation, see [4]), where divisive notation x/y is defined as $x \cdot y^{-1}$. A major consequence is that fractions can be viewed as terms over the signature of (common) meadows. Another distinction between meadows and fields is that we do not require a meadow to satisfy the separation axiom $0 \neq 1$.

The paper is structured as follows: below we conclude this section with a brief introduction to some aspects of involutive meadows that will play a role later on, and a discussion on why common meadows can be preferred over involutive meadows. In Section 2 we formally define common meadows and present some elementary results. In Section 3 we define "common cancellation meadows" and provide a basis theorem for common cancellation meadows of characteristic zero, which we consider our main result. Section 4 contains some concluding remarks.

1.1 Common Meadows versus Involutive Meadows

Involutive meadows, where instead of choosing $1/0 = \mathbf{a}$, one calculates with $1/0 = 0$, constitute a different solution to the question how to deal with the value of $1/0$ once the design decision has been made to work with the signature of meadows, that is to include a function name for inverse or for division (or both) in an extension of the syntax of fields. Involutive meadows feature a definite advantage over common meadows in that, by avoiding an extension of the domain with an additional value, theoretical work is very close to classical algebra of fields. This conservation property, conserving the domain, of involutive meadows has proven helpful for the development of theory about involutive meadows in [2,1,6,4,9,8]. Earlier and comparable work on the equational theory of fields was done by Komori [12] and Ono [14]: in 1975, Komori introduced the name *desirable pseudo-field* for what was introduced as a "meadow" in [8].[1]

---

[1] [8] was published in 2007; the finding of [12,14] is mentioned in [4] (2011) and was found via Ono's 1983-paper [14].

Table 1. The set Md of axioms for (involutive) meadows

$(x + y) + z = x + (y + z)$	$x \cdot y = y \cdot x$
$x + y = y + x$	$1 \cdot x = x$
$x + 0 = x$	$x \cdot (y + z) = x \cdot y + x \cdot z$
$x + (-x) = 0$	$(x^{-1})^{-1} = x$
$(x \cdot y) \cdot z = x \cdot (y \cdot z)$	$x \cdot (x \cdot x^{-1}) = x$

An equational axiomatization Md of involutive meadows is given in Table 1, where $^{-1}$ binds stronger than $\cdot$, which in turn binds stronger than $+$. From the axioms in Md the following identities are derivable:

$$0 \cdot x = 0, \qquad\qquad 0^{-1} = 0,$$
$$x \cdot (-y) = -(x \cdot y), \qquad\qquad (-x)^{-1} = -(x^{-1}),$$
$$-(-x) = x, \qquad\qquad (x \cdot y)^{-1} = x^{-1} \cdot y^{-1}.$$

Involutive *cancellation meadows* are involutive meadows in which the following cancellation law holds:

$$(x \neq 0 \wedge x \cdot y = x \cdot z) \rightarrow y = z. \tag{CL}$$

Involutive cancellation meadows form an important subclass of involutive meadows: in [1, Thm.3.1] it is shown that the axioms in Table 1 constitute a complete axiomatization of the equational theory of involutive cancellation meadows. We will use a consequence of this result in Section 3.

A definite disadvantage of involutive meadows against common meadows is that $1/0 = 0$ is quite remote from common intuitions regarding the partiality of division.

1.2   Motivating a Preference for Common Meadows

Whether common meadows are to be preferred over involutive meadows depends on the applications one may have in mind. We envisage as an application area the development of alternative foundations of elementary mathematics from a perspective of abstract datatypes, term rewriting, and mathematical logic. For that objective we consider common meadows to be the preferred option over involutive meadows. At the same time it can be acknowledged that a systematic investigation of involutive meadows constitutes a necessary stage in the development of a theory of common meadows by facilitating in a simplified setting the determination of results which might be obtained about common meadows. Indeed each result about involutive meadows seems to suggest a (properly adapted) counterpart in the setting of common meadows, while proving or disproving such counterparts is not an obvious matter.

2   Common Meadows

In this section we formally define "common meadows" by fixing their signature and providing an equational axiomatization. Then, we consider some conditional equations that follow from this axiomatization. Finally, we discuss some conditional laws that can be used to define an important subclass of common meadows.

2.1   Meadow Signatures

The signature Σ_f^S of fields (and rings) contains a sort (domain) S, two constants 0, and 1, two two-place functions $+$ (addition) and $\cdot$ (multiplication) and the one-place function $-$ (minus) for the inverse of addition.

We write Σ_{md}^S for the signature of meadows in inversive notation:

$$\Sigma_{md}^S = \Sigma_f^S \cup \{_-^{-1} : S \to S\},$$

and we write $\Sigma_{md,\mathbf{a}}^S$ for the signature of meadows in inversive notation with an $\mathbf{a}$-totalized inverse operator:

$$\Sigma_{md,\mathbf{a}}^S = \Sigma_{md}^S \cup \{\mathbf{a} : S\}.$$

The interpretation of $\mathbf{a}$ is called the additional value and we write $\hat{\mathbf{a}}$ for this value. Application of any function to the additional value returns that same value.

When the name of the carrier is fixed it need not be mentioned explicitly in a signature. Thus, with this convention in mind, Σ_{md} represents Σ_{md}^S and so on. If we want to make explicit that we consider terms over some signature Σ with variables in set X, we write $\Sigma(X)$.

Given a field several meadow signatures and meadows can be connected with it. This will now be exemplified with the field $\mathbb{Q}$ of rational numbers. The following meadows are distinguished in this case:

$\mathbb{Q}_0$, the meadow of rational numbers with zero-totalized inverse: $\Sigma(\mathbb{Q}_0) = \Sigma_{md}^{\mathbb{Q}}$.
$\mathbb{Q}_{\mathbf{a}}$, the meadow of rational numbers with $\mathbf{a}$-totalized inverse: $\Sigma(\mathbb{Q}_{\mathbf{a}}) = \Sigma_{md,\mathbf{a}}^{\mathbb{Q}_{\mathbf{a}}}$.
    The additional value $\hat{\mathbf{a}}$ interpreting $\mathbf{a}$ has been taken outside $|\mathbb{Q}|$ so that $|\mathbb{Q}_{\hat{\mathbf{a}}}| = |\mathbb{Q}| \cup \{\hat{\mathbf{a}}\}$.

2.2   Axioms for Common Meadows

The axioms in Table 2 define the class (variety) of *common meadows*, where we adopt the convention that $_-^{-1}$ binds stronger than $\cdot$, which in turn binds stronger than $+$. Some comments: Axioms $(15)-(17)$ take care of $\mathbf{a}$'s propagation through all operations, and for the same reason, axioms (11) and (12) have their particular form. Axiom (4) is a variant of the common axiom on additional inverse, which also serves $\mathbf{a}$'s propagation. Axioms (13) and (14) are further identities needed for manipulation of $(\ldots)^{-1}$-expressions. Finally, axiom (10) is needed to reason with expressions of the form $0 \cdot t$.

The following proposition provides some typical identities for common meadows.

Table 2. Md_a, a set of axioms for common meadows

$$(x + y) + z = x + (y + z) \tag{1}$$
$$x + y = y + x \tag{2}$$
$$x + 0 = x \tag{3}$$
$$x + (-x) = 0 \cdot x \tag{4}$$
$$(x \cdot y) \cdot z = x \cdot (y \cdot z) \tag{5}$$
$$x \cdot y = y \cdot x \tag{6}$$
$$1 \cdot x = x \tag{7}$$
$$x \cdot (y + z) = x \cdot y + x \cdot z \tag{8}$$
$$-(-x) = x \tag{9}$$
$$0 \cdot (x \cdot x) = 0 \cdot x \tag{10}$$
$$(x^{-1})^{-1} = x + 0 \cdot x^{-1} \tag{11}$$
$$x \cdot x^{-1} = 1 + 0 \cdot x^{-1} \tag{12}$$
$$(x \cdot y)^{-1} = x^{-1} \cdot y^{-1} \tag{13}$$
$$1^{-1} = 1 \tag{14}$$
$$0^{-1} = a \tag{15}$$
$$x + a = a \tag{16}$$
$$x \cdot a = a \tag{17}$$

Proposition 2.2.1. *Equations that follow from* $\dot{M}d_a$ *(see Table 2):*

$$0 \cdot 0 = 0, \tag{e1}$$
$$-0 = 0, \tag{e2}$$
$$0 \cdot x = 0 \cdot (-x), \tag{e3}$$
$$0 \cdot (x \cdot y) = 0 \cdot (x + y), \tag{e4}$$
$$-(x \cdot y) = x \cdot (-y), \tag{e5}$$
$$(-1) \cdot x = -x, \tag{e6}$$
$$(-x)^{-1} = -(x^{-1}), \tag{e7}$$
$$(x \cdot x^{-1}) \cdot x^{-1} = x^{-1} \tag{e8}$$
$$-a = a, \tag{e9}$$
$$a^{-1} = a. \tag{e10}$$

Proof. Most derivations are trivial.

(e1). By axioms (3), (7), (8), (2) we find $x = (1 + 0) \cdot x = x + 0 \cdot x = 0 \cdot x + x$, hence $0 = 0 \cdot 0 + 0$, so by axiom (3), $0 = 0 \cdot 0$.

(e2). By axioms (3), (2), (4) and (e1) we find $-0 = (-0) + 0 = 0 + (-0) = 0 \cdot 0 = 0$.

(e3). By axioms (2), (4), (9) we find $0 \cdot x = x + (-x) = (-x) + --(-x) = 0 \cdot (-x)$.

(e4). First note $0 \cdot x + 0 \cdot x = (0+0) \cdot x = 0 \cdot x$. By axioms $(2) - (4)$, (6), (8), (10) we find $0 \cdot (x+y) = 0 \cdot ((x+y) \cdot (x+y)) = (0 \cdot x + 0 \cdot (x \cdot y)) + (0 \cdot y + 0 \cdot (x \cdot y)) = (0 + 0 \cdot y) \cdot x + (0 + 0 \cdot x) \cdot y = 0 \cdot (x \cdot y) + 0 \cdot (x \cdot y) = 0 \cdot (x \cdot y)$.

(e5). We give a detailed derivation:

$$
\begin{aligned}
-(x \cdot y) &= -(x \cdot y) + 0 \cdot -(x \cdot y) && \text{by } x = x + 0 \cdot x \\
&= -(x \cdot y) + 0 \cdot (x \cdot y) && \text{by (e3)} \\
&= -(x \cdot y) + x \cdot (0 \cdot y) && \text{by axioms (5) and (6)} \\
&= -(x \cdot y) + x \cdot (y + (-y)) && \text{by axiom (4)} \\
&= -(x \cdot y) + (x \cdot y + x \cdot (-y)) && \text{by axiom (8)} \\
&= (-(x \cdot y) + x \cdot y) + x \cdot (-y) && \text{by axiom (1)} \\
&= 0 \cdot (x \cdot y) + x \cdot (-y) && \text{by axioms (2) and (4)} \\
&= 0 \cdot (x \cdot -y) + x \cdot (-y) && \text{by axioms (6) and (5), and (e3)} \\
&= x \cdot (-y). && \text{by } x = 0 \cdot x + x
\end{aligned}
$$

Thus, with axiom (9) it follows that $(-x) \cdot (-y) = x \cdot y$.

(e6). From (e5) with $y = 1$ we find $-x = -(x \cdot 1) = x \cdot (-1) = (-1) \cdot x$.

(e7). By axiom (12), $(-1) \cdot (-1)^{-1} = 1 + 0 \cdot (-1)^{-1}$, hence $(-1)^{-1} = (-1) + 0 \cdot (-1) \cdot (-1)^{-1} = (-1) + 0 \cdot (-1)^{-1}$. Now derive $1 = ((-1) \cdot (-1))^{-1} = (-1)^{-1} \cdot (-1)^{-1} = (-1)^{-1} \cdot ((-1) + 0 \cdot (-1)^{-1}) = (-1) \cdot (-1)^{-1} + 0 \cdot (-1)^{-1}$. $(-1)^{-1} = (-1) \cdot (-1)^{-1} + 0 \cdot (1)^{-1} = (-1) \cdot (-1)^{-1}$, thus $(-1)^{-1} = -1$. Hence, $(-x)^{-1} = (-1 \cdot x)^{-1} = (-1)^{-1} \cdot x^{-1} = (-1) \cdot x^{-1} = -(x^{-1})$.

(e8). By axioms (12) and (10), $(x \cdot x^{-1}) \cdot x^{-1} = (1 + 0 \cdot x^{-1}) \cdot x^{-1} = x^{-1} + 0 \cdot x^{-1} = x^{-1}$.

(e9). By (e5) and axioms (6) and (17), $-\mathbf{a} = -(\mathbf{a} \cdot 1) = \mathbf{a} \cdot (-1) = \mathbf{a}$.

(e10). By axioms (11) and $(15) - (17)$, $\mathbf{a}^{-1} = (0^{-1})^{-1} = 0 + 0 \cdot \mathbf{a} = \mathbf{a}$. $\square$

The next proposition establishes a generalization of a familiar identity concerning the addition of fractions.

Proposition 2.2.2. $\mathrm{Md_a} \vdash x \cdot y^{-1} + u \cdot v^{-1} = (x \cdot v + u \cdot y) \cdot (y \cdot v)^{-1}$.

Proof. We first derive

$$
\begin{aligned}
x \cdot y \cdot y^{-1} &= x \cdot (1 + 0 \cdot y^{-1}) && \text{by axiom (12)} \\
&= x + 0 \cdot x \cdot y^{-1} && \\
&= x + 0 \cdot x + 0 \cdot y^{-1} && \text{by (e4)} \\
&= x + 0 \cdot y^{-1}. && \text{(18)}
\end{aligned}
$$

Hence,

$$
\begin{aligned}
(x \cdot v + u \cdot y) \cdot (y \cdot v)^{-1} &= x \cdot y^{-1} \cdot v \cdot v^{-1} + u \cdot v^{-1} \cdot y \cdot y^{-1} \\
&= (x \cdot y^{-1} + 0 \cdot v^{-1}) + (u \cdot v^{-1} + 0 \cdot y^{-1}) && \text{by (18)} \\
&= (x \cdot y^{-1} + 0 \cdot y^{-1}) + (u \cdot v^{-1} + 0 \cdot v^{-1}) \\
&= x \cdot y^{-1} + u \cdot v^{-1}.
\end{aligned}
$$

$\square$

We end this section with two more propositions that characterize typical properties of common meadows and that are used in the proof of Theorem 3.2.1. The first of these establishes that each (possibly open) term over $\Sigma_{md,a}$ has a simple representation in the syntax of meadows.

Proposition 2.2.3. *For each term t over $\Sigma_{md,a}(X)$ with variables in X there exist terms r_1, r_2 over $\Sigma_f(X)$ such that $\mathsf{Md_a} \vdash t = r_1 \cdot r_2^{-1}$ and $\mathsf{VAR}(t) = \mathsf{VAR}(r_1) \cup \mathsf{VAR}(r_2)$.*

Proof. By induction on the structure of t, where the $\mathsf{VAR}(t)$-property follows easily in each case.

If $t \in \{0, 1, x, \mathbf{a}\}$, this follows trivially (for the first three cases we need $1^{-1} = 1$).
Case $t \equiv t_1 + t_2$. By Proposition 2.2.2.
Case $t \equiv t_1 \cdot t_2$. Trivial.
Case $t \equiv -t_1$. By Proposition 2.2.1 (e5).
Case $t \equiv t_1^{-1}$. By induction there exist $r_i \in \Sigma_f(X)$ such that $\mathsf{Md_a} \vdash t_1 = r_1 \cdot r_2^{-1}$.
    Now derive $t_1^{-1} = r_1^{-1} \cdot (r_2^{-1})^{-1} = r_1^{-1} \cdot (r_2 + 0 \cdot r_2^{-1}) = r_2 \cdot r_1^{-1} + 0 \cdot r_1^{-1} + 0 \cdot r_2^{-1} = r_2 \cdot r_1^{-1} + 0 \cdot r_2^{-1}$ and apply Proposition 2.2.2.

□

The next proposition shows how a term of the form $0 \cdot t$ with t a (possibly open) term over $\Sigma_f(X)$ can be simplified (note that $0 \cdot x = 0$ is not valid, since $0 \cdot \mathbf{a} = \mathbf{a}$).

Proposition 2.2.4. *For each term t over $\Sigma_f(X)$, $\mathsf{Md_a} \vdash 0 \cdot t = 0 \cdot \sum_{x \in \mathsf{VAR}(t)} x$, where $\sum_{x \in \emptyset} x = 0$.*

Proof. By induction on the structure of t, where identity (e4) (Proposition 2.2.1) covers the multiplicative case.

□

2.3   Conditional Equations

We discuss a number of conditional equations that will turn out useful, and we start off with a few that follow directly from $\mathsf{Md_a}$.

Proposition 2.3.1. *Conditional equations that follow from $\mathsf{Md_a}$ (see Table 2):*

$$x \cdot y = 1 \rightarrow 0 \cdot y = 0, \tag{ce1}$$

$$x \cdot y = 1 \rightarrow x^{-1} = y, \tag{ce2}$$

$$0 \cdot x = 0 \cdot y \rightarrow 0 \cdot (x \cdot y) = 0 \cdot x, \tag{ce3}$$

$$0 \cdot x \cdot y = 0 \rightarrow 0 \cdot x = 0, \tag{ce4}$$

$$0 \cdot (x + y) = 0 \rightarrow 0 \cdot x = 0, \tag{ce5}$$

$$0 \cdot x^{-1} = 0 \rightarrow 0 \cdot x = 0, \tag{ce6}$$

$$0 \cdot x = \mathbf{a} \rightarrow x = \mathbf{a}. \tag{ce7}$$

Table 3. Some conditional laws for common meadows

$x \neq \mathbf{a} \;\rightarrow\; 0 \cdot x = 0$	Normal Value Law	(NVL)
$x^{-1} = \mathbf{a} \;\rightarrow\; 0 \cdot x = x$	Additional Value Law	(AVL)
$x \neq 0 \wedge x \neq \mathbf{a} \;\rightarrow\; x \cdot x^{-1} = 1$	Common Inverse Law	(CIL)

Proof. Most derivations are trivial.

(ce1). By axiom (10), $0 \cdot x \cdot y = 0 \cdot x \cdot y \cdot y = 0 \cdot x \cdot y + 0 \cdot y \cdot y = (0 \cdot x + 0 \cdot y) \cdot y$, and hence by assumption, $0 = 0 \cdot 1 = 0 \cdot x \cdot y = (0 \cdot x + 0 \cdot y) \cdot y = 0 \cdot x \cdot y + 0 \cdot y \cdot y = 0 + 0 \cdot y = 0 \cdot y$.

(ce2). By assumption and axioms (13) and (14), $x^{-1} \cdot y^{-1} = 1$, and thus by (ce1), $0 \cdot x^{-1} = 0$, so by axiom (12), $y = (1 + 0 \cdot x^{-1}) \cdot y = (x \cdot x^{-1}) \cdot y = (x \cdot y) \cdot x^{-1} = x^{-1}$.

(ce3). By assumption, identity (e4), and axiom (8), $0 \cdot (x \cdot y) = 0 \cdot x + 0 \cdot y = 0 \cdot x + 0 \cdot x = 0 \cdot x$.

(ce4). By assumption, $0 \cdot x = 0 \cdot x + 0 \cdot x \cdot y = x \cdot (0 + 0 \cdot y) = 0 \cdot (x \cdot y) = 0$.

(ce5). Apply identity (e4) to (ce4).

(ce6). By axiom (12) and assumption, $x \cdot x^{-1} = 1 + 0 \cdot x^{-1} = 1$, so by (ce1), $0 \cdot x = 0$.

(ce7). By $x = x + 0 \cdot x$ and assumption, $x = x + \mathbf{a} = \mathbf{a}$. $\qquad\square$

Note that (ce1) and (ce2) immediately imply

$$x \cdot y = 1 \rightarrow 0 \cdot x^{-1} = 0.$$

In Table 3 we define various conditional laws that we will use to single out certain classes of common meadows in Section 3: the Normal Value Law (NVL), the Additional Value Law (AVL), and the Common Inverse Law (CIL). Here we use the adjective "normal" to express that values different from $\mathbf{a}$ (more precisely, the interpretation of $\mathbf{a}$) are at stake. We conclude this section by interrelating these laws.

Proposition 2.3.2.

1. $\mathsf{Md_a} + \mathsf{NVL} \vdash (x \cdot y = \mathbf{a} \wedge x \neq \mathbf{a}) \rightarrow y = \mathbf{a}$,
2. $\mathsf{Md_a} + \mathsf{NVL} \vdash x^{-1} \neq \mathbf{a} \rightarrow 0 \cdot x = 0$,
3. $\mathsf{Md_a} + \mathsf{NVL} + \mathsf{AVL} \vdash \mathsf{CIL}$,
4. $\mathsf{Md_a} + \mathsf{CIL} \vdash \mathsf{NVL}$,
5. $\mathsf{Md_a} + \mathsf{CIL} \vdash \mathsf{AVL}$.

Proof.

1. By NVL, $x \neq \mathbf{a} \rightarrow 0 \cdot x = 0$, so $0 \cdot y = (0 \cdot x) \cdot y = 0 \cdot (x \cdot y) = 0 \cdot \mathbf{a} = \mathbf{a}$ and hence $y = (1 + 0) \cdot y = y + 0 \cdot y = y + \mathbf{a} = \mathbf{a}$.

2. By NVL, $0 \cdot x^{-1} = 0$ and hence by axiom (12), $x \cdot x^{-1} = 1$ and by (ce1), $0 \cdot x = 0$.

3. From $x \neq \mathbf{a}$ we find $0 \cdot x = 0$. There are two cases: $x^{-1} = \mathbf{a}$ which implies by AVL that $x = 0$ contradicting the assumptions of CIL, and $x^{-1} \neq \mathbf{a}$ which implies by NVL that $0 \cdot x^{-1} = 0$, and this implies $x \cdot x^{-1} = 1$ by axiom (12).

4. Assume that $x \neq \mathbf{a}$. If $x = 0$ then also $0 \cdot x = 0$. If $x \neq 0$ then by CIL, $0 = 0 \cdot 1 = 0 \cdot x \cdot x^{-1}$, so $0 \cdot x = 0$ by (ce1).

5. We distinguish three cases: $x = 0$, $x = \mathbf{a}$, and $x \neq 0 \wedge x \neq \mathbf{a}$. In the first two cases it immediately follows that $0 \cdot x = x$. In the last case it follows by CIL that $x \cdot x \cdot x^{-1} = x$, so $x^{-1} = \mathbf{a}$ implies $x = \mathbf{a}$, and thus $x = 0 \cdot x$.

$\square$

3   Models and Model Classes

In this section we define "common cancellation meadows" as common meadows that satisfy the so-called "inverse cancellation law", a law that is equivalent with the Common Inverse Law CIL. Then, we provide a basis theorem for common cancellation meadows of characteristic zero.

3.1   Common Cancellation Meadows

In [1, Thm.3.1] we prove a generic basis theorem that implies that the axioms in Table 1 constitute a complete axiomatization of the equational theory of the involutive cancellation meadows (over signature Σ_{md}). The cancellation law used in that result (that is, CL in Section 1.1) has various equivalent versions, and a particular one is $x \neq 0 \rightarrow x \cdot x^{-1} = 1$, a version that is close to CIL.

Below we define common cancellation meadows, using a cancellation law that is equivalent with CIL, but first we establish a correspondence between models of $\mathsf{Md_a} + \mathsf{NVL} + \mathsf{AVL}$ and involutive cancellation meadows.

Proposition 3.1.1.

1. *Every field can be extended with an additional value* $\hat{\mathbf{a}}$ *and subsequently it can be expanded with a constant* $\mathbf{a}$ *and an inverse function in such a way that the equations of common meadows as well as* NVL *and* AVL *are satisfied, where the interpretation of* $\mathbf{a}$ *is* $\hat{\mathbf{a}}$.

2. *A model of* $\mathsf{Md_a} + \mathsf{NVL} + \mathsf{AVL}$ *extends a field with an additional value* $\hat{\mathbf{a}}$ *(the interpretation of* $\mathbf{a}$*) and expands it with the* $\mathbf{a}$*-totalized inverse.*

Proof. Statement 1 follows immediately. To prove 2, consider the substructure of elements b of the domain that satisfy $0 \cdot b = 0$. Only $\hat{\mathbf{a}}$ is outside this subset. For b with $0 \cdot b = 0$ we must check that $0 \cdot b^{-1} = 0$ unless $b = 0$. To see this distinguish two cases: $b^{-1} = \mathbf{a}$ (which implies $b = 0$ with help of AVL), and $b^{-1} \neq \mathbf{a}$ which implies $0 \cdot b^{-1} = 0$ by NVL. $\square$

As a consequence, we find the following result.

Table 4. C_0, the set of axioms for meadows of characteristic zero and numerals

---

$$\underline{n+1} \cdot (\underline{n+1})^{-1} = 1 \qquad\qquad (n \in \mathbb{N}) \qquad\qquad (C_0)$$

$$\underline{0} = 0 \qquad\qquad \text{(axioms for}$$
$$\underline{1} = 1 \qquad\qquad \text{numerals,}$$
$$\underline{n+1} = \underline{n} + 1 \qquad\qquad n \in \mathbb{N} \text{ and } n \geq 1)$$

Theorem 3.1.2. *The models of* $\mathsf{Md_a} + \mathsf{NVL} + \mathsf{AVL}$ *that satisfy* $0 \neq 1$ *are in one-to-one correspondence with the involutive cancellation meadows satisfying* Md *(see Table 1).*

Proof. An involutive cancellation meadow can be expanded to a model of $\mathsf{Md_a} + \mathsf{NVL} + \mathsf{AVL}$ by extending its domain with a constant â in such a way that the equations of common meadows as well as NVL and AVL are satisfied, where the interpretation of $\mathbf{a}$ is â (cf. Proposition 3.1.1.1).

Conversely, given a model $\mathbb{M}$ of $\mathsf{Md_a} + \mathsf{NVL} + \mathsf{AVL}$, we construct a cancellation meadow $\mathbb{M}'$ as follows: $|\mathbb{M}'| = |\mathbb{M}| \setminus \{\hat{a}\}$ with â the interpretation of $\mathbf{a}$, and $0^{-1} = 0$ (by $0 \neq 1$, $|\mathbb{M}'|$ is non-empty). We find by NVL that $0 \cdot x = 0$ and by CIL (thus by $\mathsf{NVL} + \mathsf{AVL}$, cf. Proposition 2.3.2.3) that $x \neq 0 \to x \cdot x^{-1} = 1$, which shows that $\mathbb{M}'$ is a cancellation meadow. □

We define a *common cancellation meadow* as a common meadow that satisfies the following *inverse cancellation law* (ICL):

$$(x \neq 0 \wedge x \neq \mathbf{a} \wedge x^{-1} \cdot y = x^{-1} \cdot z) \to y = z. \qquad\qquad (\mathsf{ICL})$$

The class CCM of common cancellation meadows is axiomatized by $\mathsf{Md_a} + \mathsf{CIL}$ in Table 2 and Table 3, respectively. In combination with $\mathsf{Md_a}$, the laws ICL and CIL are equivalent: first, $\mathsf{Md_a} + \mathsf{ICL} \vdash \mathsf{CIL}$ because

$$(x \neq 0 \wedge x \neq \mathbf{a}) \overset{(e8)}{\to} (x \neq 0 \wedge x \neq \mathbf{a} \wedge x^{-1} \cdot x \cdot x^{-1} = x^{-1} \cdot 1) \overset{\mathsf{ICL}}{\to} x \cdot x^{-1} = 1.$$

Conversely, $\mathsf{Md_a} + \mathsf{CIL} \vdash \mathsf{ICL}$:

$$(x \neq 0 \wedge x \neq \mathbf{a} \wedge x^{-1} \cdot y = x^{-1} \cdot z) \to x \cdot x^{-1} \cdot y = x \cdot x^{-1} \cdot z \overset{\mathsf{CIL}}{\to} y = z.$$

3.2 A Basis Theorem For Common Cancellation Meadows of Characteristic Zero

As in our paper [2], we use numerals $\underline{n}$ and the axiom scheme C_0 defined in Table 4 to single out common cancellation meadows of characteristic zero. In this section we prove that $\mathsf{Md_a} + C_0$ constitutes an axiomatization for common cancellation meadows of characteristic zero. In [2, Cor.2.7] we prove that $\mathsf{Md} + C_0$ (for

Md see Table 1) constitutes an axiomatization for involutive cancellation meadows of characteristic zero. We define CCM_0 as the class of common cancellation meadows of characteristic zero.

We further write $\dfrac{t}{r}$ (and sometimes t/r in plain text) for $t \cdot r^{-1}$.

Theorem 3.2.1. $\mathrm{Md_a} + \mathrm{C_0}$ *is a basis for the equational theory of* CCM_0.

Proof. Soundness holds by definition of CCM_0.

Assume $\mathrm{CCM}_0 \models t = r$ and $\mathrm{CCM}_0 \models t = \mathbf{a}$. Then, by axioms $(15) - (17)$ and identities $(e9) - (e10)$, t and r are provably equal to $\mathbf{a}$, that is, $\mathrm{Md_a} \vdash t = r$.

Assume $\mathrm{CCM}_0 \models t = r$ and $\mathrm{CCM}_0 \not\models t = \mathbf{a}$. By Proposition 2.2.3 we can bring t in the form t_1/t_2 and r in the form r_1/r_2 with t_i, r_i terms over $\Sigma_f(X)$, thus

$$\mathrm{CCM}_0 \models \frac{t_1}{t_2} = \frac{r_1}{r_2}. \tag{19}$$

We will first argue that (19) implies that the following three equations are valid in CCM_0:

$$0 \cdot t_2^{-1} = 0 \cdot r_2^{-1}, \tag{20}$$

$$0 \cdot t_1 + 0 \cdot t_2 = 0 \cdot r_1 + 0 \cdot r_2, \tag{21}$$

$$t_2 \cdot r_2 \cdot (t_1 \cdot r_2 + (-r_1) \cdot t_2) + 0 \cdot t_2^{-1} + 0 \cdot r_2^{-1}$$
$$= 0 \cdot t_1 + 0 \cdot t_2^{-1} + 0 \cdot r_1 + 0 \cdot r_2^{-1}. \tag{22}$$

Ad (20). Assume this is not the case, then there exists a common cancellation meadow $\mathbb{M} \in \mathrm{CCM}_0$ and an interpretation of the variables in t_2 and r_2 such that one of t_2^{-1} and r_2^{-1} is interpreted as $\hat{\mathbf{a}}$ (the interpretation of $\mathbf{a}$), and the other is not. This contradicts (19).

Ad (21). This equation characterizes that t_1/t_2 and r_1/r_2 contain the same variables, and is related to Proposition 2.2.4. Assume this is not the case, say t_1 and/or t_2 contains a variable x that does not occur in r_1 and r_2. Since $\mathrm{CCM}_0 \not\models r_1/r_2 = \mathbf{a}$, there is an instance of r_i's variables, say $\overline{r_i}$ such that $\mathrm{CCM}_0 \models \overline{r_1}/\overline{r_2} \neq \mathbf{a}$. But then x can be instiantiated with $\mathbf{a}$, which contradicts (19).

Ad (22). It follows from (19) that in (22) both the lefthand-side and the righthand-side equal zero in all involutive cancellation meadows. By Theorem 3.1.2 we find $\mathrm{CCM} \models (22)$, and hence $\mathrm{CCM}_0 \models (22)$.

We now argue that $(20) - (22)$ are derivable from $\mathrm{Md_a} + \mathrm{C_0}$, and that from those (19) is derivable from $\mathrm{Md_a} + \mathrm{C_0}$.

Ad (20). The statement $\mathrm{CCM}_0 \models 0 \cdot t_2^{-1} = 0 \cdot r_2^{-1}$ implies that t_2 and r_2 have the same zeros in the algebraic closure $\overline{\mathbb{Q}}$ of $\mathbb{Q}$ (if this were not the case, then $\overline{\mathbb{Q}_\mathbf{a}} \not\models 0 \cdot t_2^{-1} = 0 \cdot r_2^{-1}$, but $\overline{\mathbb{Q}_\mathbf{a}} \in \mathrm{CCM}_0$). We may assume that the gcd of t_2's coefficients is 1, and similar for r_2: if not, then $t_2 = k \cdot t'$ with t' a polynomial with that property, and since k is a fixed numeral, we find $0 \cdot k = 0$ (also in fields with a characteristic that is a factor of k), and hence $0 \cdot t_2 = 0 \cdot t'$. We can apply [13, Cor.2.4 (Ch.IV)]: because t_2 and r_2 are polynomials in $\Sigma_f(\mathsf{VAR}(t_2, r_2))$ with the property that they have the same zeros and that the gcd of their coefficients is 1, they have equal factorization in primitive polynomials. So, in common cancellation meadows of characteristic zero (thus, models in $\mathrm{CCM_0}$), each such factor of t_2 is one of r_2, and vice versa. Application of axiom (10) (that is, $0 \cdot (x \cdot x) = 0 \cdot x$) then yields

$$\mathsf{Md_a} + \mathsf{C_0} \vdash 0 \cdot t_2^{-1} = 0 \cdot r_2^{-1}. \tag{23}$$

Ad (21). From Proposition 2.2.4 and validity of (21) it follows that

$$\mathsf{Md_a} \vdash 0 \cdot t_1 + 0 \cdot t_2 = 0 \cdot \sum\nolimits_{x \in \mathsf{VAR}(t_1/t_2)} x = 0 \cdot \sum\nolimits_{x \in \mathsf{VAR}(r_1/r_2)} x = 0 \cdot r_1 + 0 \cdot r_2. \tag{24}$$

Ad (22). We first derive

$$\begin{aligned}
\mathsf{Md_a} \vdash 0 \cdot t_1 + 0 \cdot t_2^{-1} &= 0 \cdot t_1 + 0 \cdot (1 + 0 \cdot t_2^{-1}) \\
&= 0 \cdot t_1 + 0 \cdot t_2 \cdot t_2^{-1} \qquad \text{with axiom (12)} \\
&= 0 \cdot t_1 + 0 \cdot t_2 + 0 \cdot t_2^{-1},
\end{aligned}$$

and in a similar way one derives $\mathsf{Md_a} \vdash 0 \cdot r_1 + 0 \cdot r_2^{-1} = 0 \cdot r_1 + 0 \cdot r_2 + 0 \cdot r_2^{-1}$. Hence, we find with (23) and (24) that

$$\begin{aligned}
\mathsf{Md_a} + \mathsf{C_0} \vdash 0 \cdot t_1 + 0 \cdot t_2^{-1} &= (0 \cdot t_1 + 0 \cdot t_2^{-1}) + (0 \cdot r_1 + 0 \cdot r_2^{-1}) \tag{25} \\
&= 0 \cdot r_1 + 0 \cdot r_2^{-1}. \tag{26}
\end{aligned}$$

From $\mathrm{CCM_0} \models (22)$ it follows from the completeness result on the class of involutive meadows of characteristic zero (see [2, Cor.2.7]) that $\mathsf{Md} + \mathsf{C_0} \vdash (22)$, and hence $\mathsf{Md_a} + \mathsf{C_0} \vdash (22)$.

We now show the derivability of $t_1/t_2 = r_1/r_2$. Multiplying both sides of (22) with $(t_2 \cdot r_2)^{-1} \cdot (t_2 \cdot r_2)^{-1}$ implies by (e8), $0 \cdot x + 0 \cdot x = 0 \cdot x$, and axiom (10) that

$$\mathsf{Md_a} + \mathsf{C_0} \vdash (t_2 \cdot r_2)^{-1} \cdot (t_1 \cdot r_2 + (-r_1) \cdot t_2) + 0 \cdot t_2^{-1} + 0 \cdot r_2^{-1} = \\ 0 \cdot t_1 + 0 \cdot t_2^{-1} + 0 \cdot r_1 + 0 \cdot r_2^{-1},$$

which implies by Proposition 2.2.2 that

$$\mathsf{Md_a} + \mathsf{C_0} \vdash \frac{t_1}{t_2} + \frac{-r_1}{r_2} + 0 \cdot t_2^{-1} + 0 \cdot r_2^{-1} = 0 \cdot t_1 + 0 \cdot t_2^{-1} + 0 \cdot r_1 + 0 \cdot r_2^{-1},$$

and thus

$$\mathsf{Md_a} + \mathsf{C_0} \vdash \frac{t_1}{t_2} + \frac{-r_1}{r_2} + 0 \cdot t_1 + 0 \cdot t_2^{-1} + 0 \cdot r_1 + 0 \cdot r_2^{-1} = \\ 0 \cdot t_1 + 0 \cdot t_2^{-1} + 0 \cdot r_1 + 0 \cdot r_2^{-1}, \tag{27}$$

and hence

$$
\begin{aligned}
\mathsf{Md_a} + \mathsf{C_0} \vdash \frac{t_1}{t_2} &= \frac{t_1}{t_2} + 0 \cdot t_1 + 0 \cdot t_2^{-1} \\
&= \frac{t_1}{t_2} + 0 \cdot t_1 + 0 \cdot t_2^{-1} + 0 \cdot r_1 + 0 \cdot r_2^{-1} && \text{by (25)} \\
&= \frac{t_1}{t_2} + (\frac{r_1}{r_2} + \frac{-r_1}{r_2}) + 0 \cdot t_1 + 0 \cdot t_2^{-1} + 0 \cdot r_1 + 0 \cdot r_2^{-1} \\
&= (\frac{t_1}{t_2} + \frac{-r_1}{r_2}) + \frac{r_1}{r_2} + 0 \cdot t_1 + 0 \cdot t_2^{-1} + 0 \cdot r_1 + 0 \cdot r_2^{-1} \\
&= \frac{r_1}{r_2} + 0 \cdot t_1 + 0 \cdot t_2^{-1} + 0 \cdot r_1 + 0 \cdot r_2^{-1} && \text{by (27)} \\
&= \frac{r_1}{r_2} + 0 \cdot r_1 + 0 \cdot r_2^{-1} && \text{by (26)} \\
&= \frac{r_1}{r_2}.
\end{aligned}
$$

$\square$

4   Concluding Remarks

Open Question. It is an open question whether there exists a basis result for the equational theory of CCM. We notice that in [5] a basis result for one-totalized non-involutive cancellation meadows is provided, where the multiplicative inverse of 0 is 1 and cancellation is defined as usual (that is, by the cancellation law CL in Section 1.1).

Common Intuitions and Related Work. Common meadows are motivated as being the most intuitive modelling of a totalized inverse function to the best of our knowledge. As stated in Section 1 (Introduction), the use of the constant $\mathbf{a}$ is a matter of convenience only because it merely constitutes a derived constant with defining equation $\mathbf{a} = 0^{-1}$, which implies that all uses of $\mathbf{a}$ can be removed.[2] We notice that considering $\mathbf{a} = 0^{-1}$ as an error-value supports the intuition for the equations of $\mathsf{Md_a}$.

As a variant of involutive and common meadows, *partial meadows* are defined in [4]. The specification method used in this paper is based on meadows and therefore it is more simple, but less general than the construction of Broy and Wirsing [10] for the specification of partial datatypes.

The construction of common meadows is related to the construction of *wheels* by Carlström [11]. However, we have not yet found a structural connection between both constructions which differ in quite important details. For instance, wheels are involutive whereas common meadows are non-involutive.

---

[2] We notice that $0 = 1 + (-1)$, from which it follows that 0 can also be considered a derived constant over a reduced signature. Nevertheless, the removal of 0 from the signature of fields is usually not considered helpful.

Quasi-Cancellation Meadows of Characteristic Zero. Following Theorem 3.2.1, a common meadow of characteristic zero can alternatively be defined as a structure that satisfies all equations true of all common cancellation meadows of characteristic zero. We write CM_0 for the class of all common meadows of characteristic zero.

With this alternative definition in mind, we define a *common quasi-cancellation meadow of characteristic zero* as a structure that satisfies all conditional equations which are true of all common cancellation meadows of characteristic zero. We write $CQCM_0$ for the class of all common quasi-cancellation meadows of characteristic zero.

It is easy to show that $CQCM_0$ is strictly larger than CCM_0. To see this one extends the signature of common meadows with a new constant c. Let $L_{ccm,0}$ be the set of conditional equations true of all structures in CCM_0. We consider the initial algebra of $L_{ccm,0}$ in the signature extended with c. Now neither $L_{ccm,0} \vdash c = \mathbf{a}$ can hold (because c might be interpreted as say 1), nor $L_{ccm,0} \vdash 0 \cdot c = 0$ can hold (otherwise $L_{ccm,0} \vdash 0 = 0 \cdot \mathbf{a} = \mathbf{a}$ would hold). For that reason in the initial algebra of $L_{ccm,0}$ in the extended signature interprets c as an entity e in such a way that neither $c = \mathbf{a}$ nor $0 \cdot c = 0$ is satisfied. For that reason c will be interpreted by a new entity that refutes CIL.

CM_0 is strictly larger than $CQCM_0$. To see this let $E_{ccm,0}$ denote the set of equations valid in all common cancellation meadows of characteristic zero. Again we add an extra constant b to the signature of common meadows. Consider the initial algebra I of $E_{ccm,0} + (b^{-1} = \mathbf{a})$ in the extended signature. In I the interpretation of b is a new object because it cannot be proven equal to 0 and not to $\mathbf{a}$ and not to any other closed term over the signature of common meadows. Now we transform $E_{ccm,0} + (b^{-1} = \mathbf{a})$ into its set of closed consequences $E_{ccm,0}^{cl,b}$ over the extended signature. We claim that $b = 0 \cdot b$ cannot be proven from $E_{ccm,0} + (b^{-1} = \mathbf{a})$. If that were the case at some stage in the derivation an $\mathbf{a}$ must appear from which it follows that $b = \mathbf{a}$ is provable as well, because $\mathbf{a}$ is propagated by all operations. But that cannot be the case as we have already concluded that b differs from $\mathbf{a}$ in the initial algebra I_0 of $E_{ccm,0}^{cl,b}$. Thus, $b \neq \mathbf{a} \rightarrow 0 \cdot b = 0$ (an instance of NVL) is not valid in I_0.

However, at this stage we do not know the answers to the following two questions:

- Is there a finite equational basis for the class CM_0 of common meadows of characteristic zero?
- Is there a finite conditional equational basis for the class $CQCM_0$ of common quasi-cancellation meadows of characteristic zero?

The Initial Common Meadow. In [7] we introduce *fracpairs* with a definition that is very close to that of the field of fractions of an integral domain. Fracpairs are defined over a commutative ring R that is *reduced*, i.e., R has no nonzero nilpotent elements. A fracpair over R is an expression $\frac{p}{q}$ with $p, q \in R$ (so $q = 0$ is allowed) modulo the equivalence generated by

$$\frac{x \cdot z}{y \cdot (z \cdot z)} = \frac{x}{y \cdot z}.$$

This rather simple equivalence appears to be a congruence with respect to the common meadow signature $\Sigma_{md,a}$ when adopting natural definitions: $0 = \frac{0}{1}$, $1 = \frac{1}{1}$, $\mathbf{a} = \frac{1}{0}$, $\left(\frac{p}{q}\right) + \left(\frac{r}{s}\right) = \frac{p \cdot s + r \cdot q}{q \cdot s}$, $\left(\frac{p}{q}\right) \cdot \left(\frac{r}{s}\right) = \frac{p \cdot r}{q \cdot s}$ $-\left(\frac{p}{q}\right) = \frac{-p}{q}$, and $\left(\frac{p}{q}\right)^{-1} = \frac{q \cdot q}{p \cdot q}$.

In [7] we prove that the initial common meadow is isomorphic to the initial algebra of fracpairs over the integers $\mathbb{Z}$. Moreover, we prove that the initial algebra of fracpairs over $\mathbb{Z}$ constitutes a homomorphic pre-image of the common meadow $\mathbb{Q}_\mathbf{a}$, and we define "rational fracpairs" over $\mathbb{Z}$ that constitute an initial algebra that is isomorphic to $\mathbb{Q}_\mathbf{a}$. Finally, we consider some term rewriting issues for meadows.

These results reinforce our idea that common meadows can be used in the development of alternative foundations of elementary (educational) mathematics from a perspective of abstract datatypes, term rewriting and mathematical logic.

Acknowledgement. We thank Bas Edixhoven (Leiden University) for helpful comments concerning the proof of Theorem 3.2.1, including his suggestion to use [13] as a reference for this proof. Furthermore, we thank the referees for valuable comments.

References

1. Bergstra, J.A., Bethke, I., Ponse, A.: Cancellation meadows: a generic basis theorem and some applications. The Computer Journal 56(1), 3–14 (2013)
2. Bergstra, J.A., Bethke, I., Ponse, A.: Equations for formally real meadows. arXiv:1310.5011v3 [math.RA, cs.LO], this version (v3) (February 11, 2014)
3. Bergstra, J.A., Broy, M., Tucker, J.V., Wirsing, M.: On the power of algebraic specifications. In: Gruska, J., Chytil, M.P. (eds.) MFCS 1981. LNCS, vol. 118, pp. 193–204. Springer, Heidelberg (1981)
4. Bergstra, J.A., Middelburg, C.A.: Inversive meadows and divisive meadows. Journal of Applied Logic 9(3), 203–220 (2011), doi:10.1016/j.jal.2011.03.001
5. Bergstra, J.A., Middelburg, C.A.: Division by zero in non-involutive meadows. arXiv:1406.2092v1 [math.RA] (June 9, 2014). To appear in Journal of Applied Logic 13(1), 1–12 (2015), doi:10.1016/j.jal.2014.10.001
6. Bergstra, J.A., Ponse, A.: Signed meadow valued probability mass functions. arXiv:1307.5173v1 [math.LO] (July 19, 2013)
7. Bergstra, J.A., Ponse, A.: Fracpairs: fractions over a reduced commutative ring. arXiv:1411.4410v1 [math.RA] (November 17, 2014)
8. Bergstra, J.A., Tucker, J.V.: The rational numbers as an abstract data type. Journal of the ACM 54(2), Article 7, 25 pages (2007)
9. Bethke, I., Rodenburg, P.H.: The initial meadows. Journal of Symbolic Logic 75(3), 888–895 (2010)
10. Broy, M., Wirsing, M.: On the algebraic specification of nondeterministic programming languages. In: Astesiano, E., Böhm, C. (eds.) CAAP 1981. LNCS, vol. 112, pp. 162–179. Springer, Heidelberg (1981)
11. Carlström, J.: Wheels – on division by zero. Mathematical Structures in Computer Science 14(01), 143–184 (2004), doi:10.1017/S0960129503004110
12. Komori, Y.: Free algebras over all fields and pseudo-fields. Report 10, pp. 9–15, Faculty of Science, Shizuoka University, Japan (1975)

13. Lang, S.: Algebra, 3rd edn. Graduate Texts in Mathematics, vol. 211. Springer (2002)
14. Ono, H.: Equational theories and universal theories of fields. Journal of the Mathematical Society of Japan 35(2), 289–306 (1983)
15. Wirsing, M.: Algebraic specifications. In: van Leeuwen, J. (ed.) Handbook of Theoretical Computer Science. Volume B: Formal models and semantics, pp. 675–788. North-Holland (1990)

Logical Relations and Nondeterminism

Martin Hofmann

LMU Munich, Germany

Abstract. The purpose of this article is to illustrate some technical difficulties encountered when trying to extend a logical relation to the Hoare powerdomain. We give a partial solution and some applications. Our vehicle is a simple call-by-value programming language with binary nondeterministic choice. We define both a big-step operational semantics and a denotational semantics using the Hoare powerdomain. Using our logical relation we then show equivalence of the two semantics in the sense of computational adequacy and some type-dependent program equivalences.

1 Introduction

The aim of this article is two-fold. On the one hand, I would like to express with it my thanks to my long time colleague, mentor, and personal friend Martin Wirsing; on the other hand, I would like to take this opportunity to explain some difficulties we [3] had encountered when trying to extend the well-established methods of denotational semantics and logical relations to nondeterminism.

To be precise, the difficulties occurred in the context of modelling concurrency, but the source of the problem rather appears to be the nondeterminism and so it seems reasonable to concentrate on this feature alone so as to bring out the salient features. In addition, Martin himself has written on nondeterminism in the context of algebraic specification [5,6].

Also from Martin's lecture notes on functional programming which I used as a basis for my own course on this topic I got the impression that he had and hopefully still has a certain fondness for denotational semantics. Indeed, what we do in this paper is essentially an exercise in classical denotational semantics, but the results achieved cannot to the best of our knowledge be found in the literature. This is probably due to the fact that a lot of work on logical relations has been done in the last five to ten years; a period in which the interest in domain theory and denotational semantics has somewhat declined in favour of syntactical methods.

We think that results like the ones presented here it will help to "refurbish" domain theory so as to become up-to-date with the most recent accomplishments in semantics.

2 Language

We use an untyped language with higher-order functions, recursion, and nondeterminism. For the sake of simplicity we do not include updatable references. The values and terms of the language are thus given by the following grammar.

$$v ::= x \mid n \mid \operatorname{rec} f\, x.t \mid x \operatorname{op} y$$
$$t ::= v \mid \operatorname{let} x = t_1 \operatorname{in} t_2 \mid v_1\, v_2 \mid \operatorname{if} v \operatorname{then} t_1 \operatorname{else} t_2 \mid {?}$$

R. De Nicola and R. Hennicker (Eds.): Wirsing Festschrift, LNCS 8950, pp. 62–74, 2015.

Here, x ranges over variables and $n \in \mathbb{Z}$ denotes an integer constant. The symbol op ranges over the usual binary operators including arithmetic and comparisons. We use 0 and 1 to represent boolean values false and true. More precisely, any nonzero integer is allowed as a representation of true thus equality on boolean values is nontrivial.

The syntactic category v represents *values*, i.e. expressions whose evaluation necessarily does not involve nondeterminism. The syntactic category t then represents arbitrary terms and includes the values. We only allow values in function applications and as arguments of binary operators. One can use the let-construct to generalise these to arbitrary terms. Thus, in examples, we may use $t_1 \; t_2$ as an abbreviation for the official construct let $x = t_1$ in let $y = t_2$ in $x \; y$. The use of this *let normal form* simplifies the definition of the semantics and the metatheory and also relieves one from having to specify the evaluation order of nested expressions.

The term rec $f \, x.t$ denotes a recursive function with body e and recursive calls made via f, we use $\lambda x.t$ as syntactic sugar in the case when f is not free in t. The construct ? returns a nondeterministically chosen value from $\{0, 1\}$. The other constructs, let, if, and application are self-explanatory.

2.1 Examples

The following term, henceforth denoted t_1 **or** t_2 nondeterministically decides whether to execute t_1 or t_2.

$$t_1 \text{ or } t_2 := \text{let } y = ? \text{ in if } y = 0 \text{ then } t_1 \text{ else } t_2$$

The following two functions have been considered by Sieber [11] who studied the full abstraction problem for a language akin to the one considered here.

$$f_1 := \lambda x.1 \text{ or } 2 \qquad f_2 := (\lambda x.1) \text{ or } (\lambda x.2)$$

He argues that these functions can be distinguished under call-by-value but are indistinguishable under call-by-name. In this paper, we focus exclusively on call-by-value; let us recall the distinguishing context. Putting $g := \lambda f.f \; 0 + f \; 0$ we have that $g \; f_1$ has possible outcomes $2, 3, 4$, whereas $g \; f_2$ has possible outcomes $2, 4$.

The function $h := \text{rec } x \; f.\text{let } y = ? \text{ in if } x = y \text{ then } x \text{ else } f \; x$ compares a nondeterministically chosen value with its input and if they agree returns the input and otherwise calls itself recursively. Thus, the only possible outcome of $h \; n$ is n, but $h \; n$ diverges on inputs different from 0, 1 and *may* even diverge on 0 and 1.

The following function yields a nondeterministically chosen natural number.

$$m := \text{rec } x \; f.\text{let } y = ? \text{ in if } y = 0 \text{ then } x \text{ else } f \; (x + 1)$$

Now, $m \; 0$ returns any number ≥ 0, but may also diverge.

3 Operational Semantics

We define the set of free variables $FV(t)$ of a term as usual, e.g. $FV(\text{let } y = 0 \text{ in } x + y) = \{x\}$ and $FV(\text{rec } x \; f.f \; x \; y) = \{y\}$. A term t is closed if $FV(t) = \emptyset$. If v is a closed value we define the substitution $t[v/x]$ of v for x in t in the usual way. Note that $FV(t[v/x]) = FV(t) \setminus \{x\}$.

We now define inductively a relation $t \longrightarrow v$ (big-step operational semantics) between closed terms and closed values which signifies that t may evaluate to v, i.e. that v is among the possible results of the nondeterministic evaluation of t. The defining rules are given in Figure 1.

The reader may check that the example functions evaluate as predicted. Consider, for example 1 **or** 2 = let y = ? in if $y = 0$ then 1 else 2. We have ? $\longrightarrow$ 0 and if $0 = 0$ then 1 else 2 $\longrightarrow$ 1, so 1 **or** 2 $\longrightarrow$ 1. But we also have ? $\longrightarrow$ 1 and if $1 = 0$ then 1 else 2 $\longrightarrow$ 2, so 1 **or** 2 $\longrightarrow$ 2.

Now consider $h\,0$ with h defined in Section 2.1. We have to evaluate

$$\text{let } y = ? \text{ in if } 0 = y \text{ then } 0 \text{ else } h\,0$$

Now, ? $\longrightarrow$ 0, so $h\,0 \longrightarrow 0$. We can also use the fact that ? $\longrightarrow$ 1. Then we must evaluate let $y = ?$ in if $0 = 1$ then x else $h\,0$ which evaluates to the same results as $h\,0$. We conclude that the only value v for which $h\,0 \longrightarrow v$ holds is $v = 0$. We note that

$$n \longrightarrow n \qquad \frac{n \text{ op } n' \longrightarrow n''}{n'' = n \text{ op } n'} \qquad \frac{? \to n}{n \in \{0,1\}}$$

$$\frac{\text{if } 0 \text{ then } t_1 \text{ else } t_2 \longrightarrow v}{t_1 \longrightarrow v} \qquad \frac{\text{if } 1 \text{ then } t_1 \text{ else } t_2 \longrightarrow v}{t_2 \longrightarrow v}$$

$$\frac{\text{let } x = t_1 \text{ in } t_2 \longrightarrow v}{t_1 \longrightarrow v_1 \quad t_2[v_1/x] \longrightarrow v} \qquad \frac{\text{rec } x\,f.t\,v_a \longrightarrow v}{t[v_a/x][\text{rec } x\,f.t/f] \longrightarrow v}$$

Fig. 1. Definition of big-step operational semantics

our operational semantics cannot tell the difference between h and, say, the function rec $x\,f.$if $x = 0 \vee x = 1$ then x else $f\,x$. It only considers the terminating computations, whether or not a nonterminating computation *may* happen or not is irrelevant.

If we want to make such distinctions, we could use a small step operational semantics, an abstract machine, or a big-step semantics with an extra judgement $t \uparrow$ describing the possibility of nontermination. We refrain from doing so in this paper.

4   Denotational Semantics

We now describe a denotational semantics of this language which is based on the Hoare powerdomain [9]. Just as our operational semantics, the Hoare powerdomain focuses on terminating computations and is oblivious to the possibility of nontermination. As in the case of the operational semantics it is possible to use other powerdomains that differentiate more finely. We begin by reviewing the necessary domain-theoretic background.

A *predomain* is an ω-cpo, *i.e.*, a partial order with suprema of ascending chains. A *domain* is a predomain with a least element, $\bot$. A function $f : A \to A'$ is *continuous* if it is monotone $x \le y \Rightarrow f(x) \le f(y)$ and preserves suprema of chains, *i.e.*, $f(\sup_i x_i) = \sup_i f(x_i)$. Any set is a predomain with the discrete order (flat predomain). If X is a set and A a predomain then any $f : X \to A$ is continuous. We denote a partial (continuous) function from set (predomain) A to set (predomain) B by $f : A \rightharpoonup B$. We write $f(a) \downarrow$ to mean that such a partial function f is defined on $a \in A$. We extend standard notation for application and composition to partial functions in the usual way. E.g. $f(g(a))$ denotes c if $g(a) = b$ and $f(b) = c$. On the other hand, $f(g(a))$ is always undefined when $g(a)$ is undefined.

If A, B are predomains the cartesian product $A \times B$ and the set of continuous functions $A \to B$ form themselves predomains (with the obvious componentwise and pointwise orders) and make the category of predomains cartesian closed. Likewise, the partial continuous functions $A \rightharpoonup B$ between predomains A, B form a domain.

A subset $U \subseteq A$ is *admissible* if whenever $(a_i)_i$ is an ascending chain in A such that $a_i \in U$ for all i, then $\sup_i a_i \in U$, too. If $f : X \times A \to A$ is continuous and A is a domain then one defines $f^\dagger(x) = \sup_i f_x^i(\bot)$ with $f_x(a) = f(x, a)$. One has, $f(x, f^\dagger(x)) = f^\dagger(x)$ and if $U \subseteq A$ is admissible and contains $\bot$ and $f : X \times U \to U$ then $f^\dagger : X \to U$, too. An element d of a predomain A is *compact* if whenever $d \le \sup_i a_i$ then $d \le a_i$ for some i. E.g. in the domain of partial functions from $\mathbb{N}$ to $\mathbb{N}$ the compact elements are precisely the finite functions. A partial continuous function $f : A \rightharpoonup A$ is a *retract* if whenever $f(a)$ is defined then $f(a) \le a$ and $f(f(a)) = f(a)$. In short: $f \le id_A$ and $f \circ f \le f$.

If A is a predomain the Hoare powerdomain $P(A)$ contains the subsets of A which are down-closed and admissible. That is to say, if $U \in P(A)$ then if $x \le y \in U$ then $x \in U$, too, and furthermore, if $x_i \in U$ for each i and $(x_i)_i$ forms a chain then $\sup_i x_i \in U$. Such subsets are also known as Scott-closed sets. We denote the down-closure of a set U by $\downarrow U$. The elements of $P(A)$ are ordered by set inclusion. The supremum of a chain of sets $(U_i)_i$ is given as the least Scott-closed set containing the union $\bigcup_i U_i$. We denote the least Scott-closed set comprising a set U by $U^\ddagger$. We can now define the predomain of values as the least solution of the following domain equation. $\mathbb{V} \simeq \mathbb{Z} + (\mathbb{V} \to P\mathbb{V})$

An environment is a finite map η from variables to values. The environments form themselves a predomain with the understanding that $\eta \le \eta'$ if $\mathrm{dom}(\eta) = \mathrm{dom}(\eta')$ and $\eta(x) \le \eta'(x)$ for all $x \in \mathrm{dom}(\eta)$. For each expression t of our metalanguage we can now define a continuous map $[\![t]\!]$ from environments to computations. We also define an auxiliary map $[\![v]\!]$ from environments to values for v a syntactic value. The defining equations are given in Figure 2.

5   Program Equivalences

The denotational semantics can directly validate some expected program equivalences that are more difficult to obtain directly from the operational semantics. An example is fixpoint unrolling which is at the basis of various loop optimisations: For any term t we have

$$\llbracket x \rrbracket \eta = \eta(x) \qquad \llbracket n \rrbracket \eta = \llbracket n \rrbracket \qquad \llbracket v \rrbracket \eta = \{\llbracket v \rrbracket\}^{\ddagger} \qquad \llbracket ? \rrbracket \eta = \{0, 1\}$$

$$\llbracket \mathtt{rec}\ f\ x.t \rrbracket \eta = g^{\dagger}\eta$$
$$\text{where } g(\eta, u) = \lambda d.\llbracket t \rrbracket \eta[f \mapsto u, x \mapsto d]$$
$$\llbracket \mathtt{let}\ x = t_1\ \mathtt{in}\ t_2 \rrbracket \eta = (\bigcup \{\llbracket t_2 \rrbracket \eta[x \mapsto a] \mid a \in \llbracket t_2 \rrbracket \eta\})^{\ddagger}$$
$$\llbracket \mathtt{if}\ v\ \mathtt{then}\ t_2\ \mathtt{else}\ t_3 \rrbracket \eta = \begin{cases} \llbracket t_2 \rrbracket \eta & \text{if } \llbracket v \rrbracket \eta \in \mathbb{Z} \setminus \{0\}1 \\ \llbracket t_3 \rrbracket \eta & \text{if } \llbracket v \rrbracket \eta = 0 \end{cases}$$

Fig. 2. Denotational semantics

$$\llbracket \mathtt{rec}\ x\ f.t \rrbracket \eta = \llbracket \lambda x.t[\mathtt{rec}\ x\ f.t/f] \rrbracket \eta$$

The proof of this is direct from the interpretation of recursive definition as least fixpoints and the following substitution lemma:

Lemma 1. *Let t be a term, v a value, and η an environment. We always have*

$$\llbracket t \rrbracket \eta[x \mapsto \llbracket v \rrbracket \eta] = \llbracket t[v/x] \rrbracket \eta$$

Another important equivalence is commutativity of `let` which is at the basis of all kinds of optimisations involving changes to the order of control flow. Of course, in general commutativity must be conditioned on the absence or noninterference of other side-effects.

$$\llbracket \mathtt{let}\ x_1 = t_1\ \mathtt{in}\ \mathtt{let}\ x_2 = t_2\ \mathtt{in}\ t_3 \rrbracket \eta = \llbracket \mathtt{let}\ x_2 = t_2\ \mathtt{in}\ \mathtt{let}\ x_1 = t_1\ \mathtt{in}\ t_3 \rrbracket \eta$$

There are also some inequations, for instance, we have the following rule about duplicate computation:

$$\llbracket \mathtt{let}\ x_1 = t_1\ \mathtt{in}\ \mathtt{let}\ x_2 = t_1\ \mathtt{in}\ t_2 \rrbracket \eta \sqsupseteq \llbracket \mathtt{let}\ x_1 = t_1\ \mathtt{in}\ t_2[x_1/x_2] \rrbracket \eta$$

Furthermore, semantic equality and inequality are clearly congruences with respect to all term formers for the obvious reason that the semantics is defined in a compositional fashion. Of course, similar equations can also be proved for the operational semantics in the sense of applicative bisimulation, contextual equivalence, or similar, but with a less direct route.

Other equations, however, only hold under additional assumptions that can conveniently be phrased as typing assertions.

For a simple example consider the term $t_1 := \lambda f.\lambda x.\mathtt{if}\ x\ \mathtt{then}\ f\ 0\ \mathtt{else}\ f\ 1$. If f "has type" `bool` $\to \alpha$ then we expect that t is equal to $\lambda f.f$. But of course, $\llbracket t \rrbracket \neq \llbracket \lambda f.f \rrbracket$ because the semantics does not know about types.

Perhaps more interesting is the following one. The terms $t_2 := \lambda x.x + 1$ and $t_3 := \lambda x.x + 8$ are equal when viewed at type $\mathbb{Z}_7 \to \mathbb{Z}_7$ when $\mathbb{Z}_7$ stands, as usual, for integers modulo 7. The term $t_4 := \lambda x.\mathtt{if}\ x = 0\ \mathtt{then}\ 1\ \mathtt{else}\ 0$ does not even *have* the type $\mathbb{Z}_7 \to \mathbb{Z}_7$.

A well-established method for proving such type-dependent equivalences consists of interpreting types as partial equivalence relations (PERs) on values. In order that these are compatible with the usual typing rules and become a congruence, the interpretation at function types is essentially forced: two pure functions will be related if they send related arguments to related results; in particular, a function is related to itself if it respects relatedness. In our case, functions do not return values, but sets of values. It is thus necessary to lift relatedness from values to sets of values. How exactly this should be done is the main technical contribution of this paper.

6   Lifting Predicates to Sets

Recall the definition of admissibility from Section 4.

Definition 1. *Let P be a subset of a predomain A. We define $Adm(P)$ as the least admissible superset of P.*

Proposition 1. *Let A, B be predomains and $P \subseteq A$ and $Q \subseteq B$. We have $Adm(P \times Q) = Adm(P) \times Adm(Q)$.*

Proof. The direction $\subseteq$ is obvious. For the other one, fix $b \in Adm(Q)$ and define $S \subseteq A$ by $S = \{a \mid (a, b) \in Adm(P \times Q)\}$. Since S is admissible and contains P, we have $Adm(P) \subseteq S$ and the claim follows.

In order to get compatibility of the admissible closure with function spaces and the powerdomain construction we need the following technical definition.

Definition 2. *A predomain A is* effectively algebraic *if there exists a family of retracts $r_i : A \to A$ such that*

- *$r_i \leq r_{i+1}$ holds for all i, so the r_i form a chain and for each $a \in A$,*
- *the image of each r_i is a finite subset of A,*
- *for each $a \in A$ one has $a = \sup_i r_i(a)$, i.e. $\sup_i r_i = id_A$,*
- *the elements of the form $r_i(a)$ for $a \in A$ are compact.*

We remark that effectively algebraic domains are also known as bifinite or SFP domains but those are usually presented in a different way. See e.g. Section 4.2 of [1].

Proposition 2. *If A and B are effectively algebraic so are $A \times B$ and $A \to B$ and PA.*

Proof. If r_i and r_i' are the retracts for A and B then the i-th retract for $A \times B$ sends (a, b) to $(r_i(a), r_i'(b))$. The one for $A \to B$ sends f to $r_i' \circ f \circ r_i$ and the i-th retract for $P(A)$ sends U to $\downarrow\{r_i(a) \mid a \in U\}$.

Most of the required properties are obvious from the definition; we verify that a function of the form $r_i' \circ f \circ r_i$ is compact: suppose that $r_i' \circ f \circ r_i \leq \sup_i f_i$. Since $r_i(\_)$ is compact, we can find for each $a \in A$ an index j_a such that $r_i(f(r_i'(a))) \leq f_{j_a}(a)$. Now, since the image of r_i' is finite, there is a fixed j so that $r_i(f(r_i'(a))) \leq f_j(a)$ holds for all a. The claim follows.

We define the following families of continuous functions $p_i : \mathbb{V} \to \mathbb{V}$ and $q_i : P\mathbb{V} \to P\mathbb{V}$:

$$p_i(n) = \begin{cases} n, & \text{if } |n| < i \\ \text{undefined}, & \text{otherwise} \end{cases} \qquad p_i(g) = q_i \circ g \circ p_i, \text{ if } g : \mathbb{V} \to T\mathbb{V}$$

$$q_0(U) = \emptyset \qquad\qquad q_{i+1}(U) = \downarrow\{p_i(v) \mid v \in U\}$$

Proposition 3. *The predomains* $\mathbb{V}$ *and* $P\mathbb{V}$ *are effectively algebraic by virtue of the abovedefined functions* p_i *and* q_i.

Proof. Most properties are by induction on i following, in the case of functions and subsets, the argument of the previous proposition. The fact that $\sup_i p_i = id_{\mathbb{V}}$ and $\sup_i q_i = id_{P\mathbb{V}}$ hinges on the fact that $\mathbb{V}$ is the *least* solution of its defining equation; for more detail see any account of the standard solution theory of recursive domain equations [12,2,1].

If $P \subseteq A$ and $Q \subseteq B$, we write $P {\rightarrow} Q$ for $\{f : A \rightarrow B \mid \forall a \in P. f(a) \in Q\}$. We also write $f : P \rightharpoonup Q$ to mean that $f(a) \in Q$ whenever $a \in P$ and $f(a){\downarrow}$.

We will make implicit use of the following proposition.

Proposition 4. *If A is effectively algebraic and $U \subseteq A$ is down-closed then $U^{\ddagger} = Adm(U)$.*

Proof. It suffices to show that $Adm(U)$ is down-closed. So suppose that $x \le \sup_i y_i$ where $y_i \in U$ so that $\sup_i y_i \in Adm(U)$. We have $x = \sup_i p_i x$ and each $p_i(x)$ is already contained in U by compactness and down-closedness of U. Therefore, $x \in Adm(U)$.

Definition 3. *Let A be an effectively algebraic predomain by $(r_i)_i$. A subset $U \subseteq A$ is effectively algebraic if $r_i : U \rightharpoonup U$.*

Strictly speaking, the family of retracts $(r_i)_i$ should be made part of the structure of an effectively algebraic predomain rather than merely be required to exist. For the sake of readability we do not do this.

Proposition 5. *Let A, B be effectively algebraic predomains and $P \subseteq A$ and $Q \subseteq B$. Furthermore, let Q be effectively algebraic. Then $Adm(P {\rightarrow} Q) = P {\rightarrow} Adm(Q) = Adm(P) {\rightarrow} Adm(Q)$.*

Proof. The second equality and the $\subseteq$-direction of the first equation are obvious. So, for "$\supseteq$" assume $f : P \rightarrow Adm(Q)$. Thus, for each $a \in P$, we can chose a chain $(b_{j,a})_j$ so that $\sup_j b_{j,a} = f(a)$ and $b_{j,a} \in Q$ for each j. Now, for each i we have $r_i'(f(a)) = \sup_j r_i'(b_{j,a})$ and, since $r_i'(f(a))$ is compact, we even have $r_i'(f(a)) = r_i'(b_{j,a})$ for some j. Note that $r_i'(f(a)) \ge r_i'(b_{j,a})$ always holds by monotonicity. Thus, since $b_{j,a} \in Q$ and $r_i' : Q \rightharpoonup Q$ we obtain $r_i'(f(a)) \in Q$ for all i. As a result, for each i we have $r_i' \circ f : P \rightharpoonup Q$ and thus, since $f = \sup_i r_i' \circ f$, we finally get $f \in Adm(P \rightarrow Q)$ as required.

The following counterexample shows that the extra assumption $r_i' : Q \rightharpoonup Q$ is indeed necessary here.

Example 1. Let $A = \mathbb{O}$ with $\mathbb{O} = \{\bot, \top\}$ denoting the Sierpinski space and let $B = \mathbb{Z} \rightarrow \mathbb{O}$ where $\mathbb{Z}$ stands for the flat predomain of integers as usual. Note that all functions from $\mathbb{Z}$ to $\mathbb{O}$ are continuous. If $u : \mathbb{Z} \rightarrow \mathbb{O}$ we write $dom(u) = \{n \mid u(n) = \top\}$. We also define u_0 and u_1 by $dom(u_0) = \mathbb{Z} \setminus \{0\}$ and $dom(u_1) = \mathbb{Z}$. Note that this uniquely defines u_0, u_1 and that $u_0 \le u_1$.

Let $P = A$ and $Q = \{u : \mathbb{Z} \rightarrow \mathbb{O} \mid u = u_0 \vee (dom(u) \text{ finite} \wedge 0 \in dom(u))\}$. Define $f : A \rightarrow B$ by $f(\bot) = u_0$ and $f(\top) = u_1$. We have $u_0 \in Q$ and $u_1 \in Adm(Q)$ since u_1

can be written as a supremum of functions with finite domain each containing 0. Thus, $f : P \rightarrow Adm(Q)$. However, $f \notin Adm(P{\rightarrow}Q)$. Namely, suppose that $f = \sup_i f_i$ with $f_i : P \rightarrow Q$. From some i onwards we must have $f_i(\bot) = u_0$ since it is not possible to approximate u_0 nontrivially while staying within Q. Then, by monotonicity, we must have $f_i(\top) = u_0$ or $f_i(\top) = u_1$ because $u_0 \leq u$ implies $u \in \{u_0, u_1\}$. But $u_1 \notin Q$, so $f_i(\top) = u_0$ and so $(\sup_i f_i)(\top) = u_0 \neq f(\top)$, a contradiction.

We are now ready to define our lifting of a logical relation to the Hoare powerdomain:

Definition 4. *Let A, B be effectively algebraic predomains and let $E \subseteq A \times B$ be admissible. We define a relation $P_0 E \subseteq PA \times PB$ by*

$$P_0 E = \{(U, V) \mid \forall a \in U. \exists b \in V. aEb\}$$

We then define an admissible relation $PE \subseteq PA \times PB$ by

$$PE = Adm(P_0)$$

Note that, in general, $P_0 E$ will not be admissible, intuitively because the existential witnesses in a chain might not form a chain themselves.

7 Typed Program Equivalence

We now define a type system in order to be able to state and prove type-dependent equivalences. We also use the type system in order to assert equivalence of the operational and the denotational semantics. In both cases, the central tool will be a logical relation built from the blocks developed in the previous section.

Types are given by the grammar

$$\tau ::= \beta \mid \tau {\rightarrow} \tau'$$

where β ranges over a set of base types including in particular bool and int. For each constant op we assume three basic types $\beta_0^{\mathrm{op}}, \beta_1^{\mathrm{op}}, \beta_2^{\mathrm{op}}$ describing the two arguments and the result of the operator. A typing context Γ is a finite map from variables to types. The typing judgement takes the form $\Gamma \vdash t : \tau$ and is given by the rules in Figure 3. We also allow typing axioms of the form (v, v', τ) where v, v' are closed values. Intuitively, such an axiom asserts that v and v' both have type τ and are equivalent at type τ. Such axioms be justified semantically. We now define for each type τ a relation $[\![\tau]\!] \subseteq \mathbb{V} \times \mathbb{V}$ by the following clauses.

$$
\begin{aligned}
[\![\texttt{int}]\!] \quad &= \{(n, n) \mid n \in \mathbb{Z}\} \\
[\![\texttt{bool}]\!] \quad &= \{(n, n') \mid n, n' \in \mathbb{Z} \land (n{=}0{\Leftrightarrow}n'{=}0)\} \\
[\![\tau \rightarrow \tau']\!] &= \{(f, f') \mid \forall v, v'. v[\![\tau]\!]v' \Rightarrow f(v)P[\![\tau']\!]f'(v')\}
\end{aligned}
$$

For each base type β other than bool, int such a relation $[\![\beta]\!]$ must be provided so as to satisfy the conditions of the following lemma.

Lemma 2. *Each relation $[\![\tau]\!]$ is admissible, effectively algebraic, transitive, and reflexive in the sense that $v[\![\tau]\!]v'$ implies $v[\![\tau]\!]v$. Moreover, if $v[\![\tau]\!]v'$ and $v_0 \leq v$ and $v' \leq v_0'$ then $v_0[\![\tau]\!]v_0'$, too.*

$$\Gamma \vdash n : \texttt{int} \quad \Gamma \vdash v : \texttt{bool} \quad \frac{\Gamma \vdash v_0 \text{ op } v_1 : \beta_2^{\text{op}}}{\Gamma \vdash v_0 : \beta_0^{\text{op}} \quad \Gamma \vdash v_1 : \beta_1^{\text{op}}} \quad \Gamma \vdash ? : \texttt{bool}$$

$$\frac{\Gamma \vdash \texttt{if } v \texttt{ then } t_1 \texttt{ else } t_2 : \tau}{\Gamma \vdash v : \texttt{bool} \quad \Gamma \vdash t_1 : \tau \quad \Gamma \vdash t_2 : \tau} \qquad \frac{\Gamma \vdash \texttt{let } x = t_1 \texttt{ in } t_2 : \tau_2}{\Gamma \vdash t_1 : \tau_1 \quad \Gamma, x{:}\tau_1 \vdash t_2 : \tau_2}$$

$$\frac{\Gamma \vdash \texttt{rec } x\, f.t : \tau_1 \rightarrow \tau_2}{\Gamma, x{:}\tau_1, f{:}\tau_1 \rightarrow \tau_2 \vdash t : \tau_1 \rightarrow \tau_2} \qquad \frac{\Gamma \vdash v : \tau}{(v, v', \tau) \text{ or } (v', v, \tau) \text{ an axiom}}$$

Fig. 3. Typing rules

Proof. By induction on types. Suppose that $f[\![\tau \rightarrow \tau']\!]f'$. We must show that $q_i \circ f \circ p_i[\![\tau \rightarrow \tau']\!](q_i \circ f' \circ p_i)$, too. Assume $v[\![\tau]\!]v'$. By induction hypothesis, we have $p_i(v)[\![\tau]\!]p_i(v')$ and thus $f(p_i(v))P[\![\tau']\!]f'(p_i(v'))$. We need to conclude that

$$q_i(f(p_i(v)))P[\![\tau']\!]q_i(f'(p_i(v')))$$

If $i = 0$ this is obvious. Otherwise, pick chains $f(p_i(v)) = \sup_j U_j$ and $f'(p_i(v')) = \sup_j U'_j$ with $U_j P_0[\![\tau']\!]U'_j$. By compactness, there exists j such that $q_i(f(p_i(v))) = q_i(U_j)$ and $q_i(f'(p_i(v'))) = q_i(U'_j)$. So, pick $a \in q_i(U_j)$. This means that $a \leq p_{i-1}(b)$ for some $b \in U_j$. By assumption, we find $b' \in U'_j$ with $b[\![\tau']\!]b'$. By induction hypothesis, we then have $p_{i-1}(b)[\![\tau']\!]p_{i-1}(b')$ and $a[\![\tau']\!]p_{i-1}(b')$. But $p_{i-1}(b') \in q_i(U')$, so we are done.

The other properties are obvious.

Theorem 1. *Suppose that* $\Gamma \vdash t : \tau$ *and* η, η' *are environments such that* $\eta(x)[\![\Gamma(x)]\!]\eta'(x)$ *for all* $x \in \text{dom}(\Gamma)$. *Suppose furthermore that whenever* (v, v', τ') *is an axiom then* $[\![v]\!][\![\tau']\!][\![v']\!]$. *Then* $[\![t]\!]\eta P[\![\tau]\!][\![t]\!]\eta'$.

This theorem is actually a special case of the following binary version that establishes soundness of the inequational theory given in Figure 4

$$\Gamma \vdash n \leq n : \texttt{int} \quad \Gamma \vdash v \leq v : \texttt{bool} \quad \frac{\Gamma \vdash v_0 \text{ op } v_1 \leq v'_0 \text{ op } v'_1 : \beta_2^{\text{op}}}{\Gamma \vdash v_0 \leq v'_0 : \beta_0^{\text{op}} \quad \Gamma \vdash v_1 \leq v'_1 : \beta_1^{\text{op}}}$$

$$\Gamma \vdash ? \leq ? : \texttt{bool} \qquad \frac{\Gamma \vdash \texttt{if } v \texttt{ then } t_1 \texttt{ else } t_2 \leq \texttt{if } v' \texttt{ then } t'_1 \texttt{ else } t'_2 : \tau}{\Gamma \vdash v \leq v' : \texttt{bool} \quad \Gamma \vdash t_1 \leq t'_1 : \tau \quad \Gamma \vdash t_2 \leq t'_2 : \tau}$$

$$\frac{\Gamma \vdash \texttt{let } x = t_1 \texttt{ in } t_2 \leq \texttt{let } x = t'_1 \texttt{ in } t'_2 : \tau_2}{\Gamma \vdash t_1 \leq t'_1 : \tau_1 \quad \Gamma, x{:}\tau_1 \vdash t_2 \leq t'_2 : \tau_2} \qquad \frac{\Gamma \vdash \texttt{rec } x\, f.t \leq \texttt{rec } x\, f.t' : \tau_1 \rightarrow \tau_2}{\Gamma, x{:}\tau_1, f{:}\tau_1 \rightarrow \tau_2 \vdash t \leq t' : \tau_1 \rightarrow \tau_2}$$

$$\frac{\Gamma \vdash v \leq v' : \tau}{(v, v', \tau) \text{ an axiom}} \qquad \frac{\Gamma \vdash t \leq t : \tau}{\Gamma \vdash t : \tau} \qquad \frac{\Gamma \vdash t \leq t' : \tau}{\Gamma \vdash t \leq t' : \tau \quad \Gamma \vdash t' \leq t'' : \tau}$$

Fig. 4. Inequational theory

Theorem 2. *Suppose that* $\Gamma \vdash t \leq t' : \tau$ *and* η, η' *are environments such that* $\eta(x)[\![\Gamma(x)]\!]$ $\eta'(x)$ *for all* $x \in \mathrm{dom}(\Gamma)$. *Suppose furthermore that whenever* (v, v', τ') *is an axiom then* $[\![v]\!][\![\tau']\!][\![v']\!]$. *Then* $[\![t]\!]\eta P[\![\tau]\!][\![t']\!]\eta'$.

Proof. By induction on derivations. Most cases are obvious from the definitions. The congruence rule for the recursion operator relies on the admissibility of all the $[\![\tau]\!]$-relations. The congruence rule for let uses Proposition 5 as follows.

We assume $\eta[\![\Gamma]\!]\eta'$ (note the shorthand) and the induction hypothesis then gives $[\![t_1]\!]\eta P[\![\tau_1]\!][\![t_1']\!]\eta'$. Let us define $f(v) = [\![t_2]\!]\eta[x \mapsto v]$ and $f'(v') = [\![t_2]\!]\eta[x \mapsto v']$. The induction hypothesis also shows $f[\![\tau_1]\!] \to P[\![\tau_2]\!]f'$ (strictly speaking: $f \times f' \in [\![\tau_1]\!] \to P[\![\tau_2]\!]$). Now, Proposition 5 shows that, in fact, $fAdm([\![\tau]\!] \to P_0[\![\tau_2]\!])f'$. In view of Prop. 1 and the fact that what we must prove is also of the form $\cdots \in Adm(\ldots)$ we can then assume without loss of generality that $[\![t_1]\!]\eta P_0[\![\tau_1]\!][\![t_1']\!]\eta'$ and $v[\![\tau_1]\!]v' \Rightarrow f(v)P_0[\![\tau_2]\!]f'(v')$. The rest is now plain sailing: Pick $a \in [\![\text{let } x = t_1 \text{ in } t_2]\!]\eta$. If a is the supremum of a chain we can use admissibility of $P[\![\tau_2]\!]$. Otherwise, we must have $a \in f(v)$ for some $v \in [\![t_1]\!]\eta$. The assumption furnishes $v' \in [\![t_1']\!]\eta'$ with $v[\![\tau_1]\!]v'$. Thus, $f(v)[\![\tau_2]\!]f'(v')$ and we get a matching $a' \in f'(v')$ such that $a[\![\tau_2]\!]a'$. We omit the other cases.

8   Observational Equivalence

We now show how the logical relation entails observational equivalence and approximation.

Definition 5. *Let* $v, v' \in \mathbb{V}$. *We say that* v *observationally approximates* v' *at type* τ, *written* $v \leq_\tau v'$, *if for each closed value* f *of type* $\tau \to$ bool, *i.e.* $\vdash f : \tau \to$ bool, *we have that* $[\![f]\!]v \subseteq [\![f]\!]v'$. *The values are observationally equivalent, written* $v =_\tau v'$ *if* $v \leq_\tau v'$ *and* $v' \leq_\tau v$.

If v, v' *are syntactic closed values we may abbreviate* $[\![v]\!] \leq_\tau [\![v']\!]$ *by* $v \leq_\tau v'$ *and likewise for* $=_\tau$.

Observational equivalence means that v and v' yield the same observable results no matter which context f they are being used in. Note that if τ is a functional type, then the context may invoke v and v' several times and on arguments that depend on earlier calls.

Theorem 3. *If* $v[\![\tau]\!]v'$ *then* $v \leq_\tau v'$.

Proof. Suppose that $\vdash f : \tau \to$ bool. By Theorem 1 we get $[\![f]\!]vP[\![\text{bool}]\!][\![f]\!]v'$. This immediately entails the desired result.

We can therefore use semantic reasoning so as to establish observational equivalences. Recall the following analogue of Shannon expansion:

$$v := \lambda f.f =_{\text{bool} \to \text{bool}} \lambda f.\lambda x.\text{if } x \text{ then } f\, 0 \text{ else } f\, 1 =: v'$$

Indeed, to show this, we merely need to show $v[\![\text{bool} \to \text{bool}]\!]v'$ and $v'[\![\text{bool} \to \text{bool}]\!]v$ which is trivial. We can now introduce the axiom $(v, v', \text{bool} \to \text{bool})$ and its converse which allows us to conclude further observational equivalences using the inequational theory in Fig. 4.

Consider, as already suggested, a base type int7 of integers modulo 7. Putting $[\![\mathtt{int7}]\!] = \{(n, n') \mid n \equiv n' \pmod{7}\}$ we then have $v[\![\mathtt{int7} \rightarrow \mathtt{int}]\!] v'$ where $v = \lambda x.x+1$ and $v' = \lambda x. \mathtt{if}\ x \geq 6\ \mathtt{then}\ x - 6\ \mathtt{else}\ x + 1$.

9   Operational Adequacy

We can also use a logical relation to establish the correspondence between the operational and the denotational semantics by generalising the classical method [10] to nondeterminism.

Proposition 6. *If* $t \longrightarrow n$ *then* $n \in [\![t]\!]$.

Proof. By induction on the derivation of $t \longrightarrow n$. As an illustrative example we show the case where $t = u\ v$ with $u = \mathtt{rec}\ x\ f.t'$. If $t \longrightarrow n$ then $t'[v/x, u/f] \longrightarrow n$ with a shorter derivation. Thus, by induction, $n \in [\![t'[v/x, u/f]]\!]$, but $[\![u\ v]\!] = [\![t'[v/x, u/f]]\!]$, so we are done.

We now prove the converse direction for typed values using a logical relation. It also holds for untyped values; for this a mixed recursive definition of an untyped logical relation. For lack of space, we must omit this generalisation.

Definition 6. *For each type* τ *we define a relation* $\triangleright\tau$ *between* $\mathbb{V}$ *and closed syntactic values.*

$$\begin{aligned}
\triangleright_{\mathtt{int}} &= \{(n, n) \mid n \in \mathbb{Z}\} \\
\triangleright_{\mathtt{bool}} &= \{(n, n') \mid n, n' \in \mathbb{Z} \wedge (n=0 \iff n'=0)\} \\
\triangleright_{\tau \rightarrow \tau'} &= \{(f, f') \mid \forall v, v'.v \triangleright_\tau v' \Rightarrow f(v) P \triangleright_{\tau'} \{a \mid f'(v') \longrightarrow a\}\}
\end{aligned}$$

In the last clause the set of closed syntactic values is understood as a flat predomain.

Theorem 4. *If* $\Gamma \vdash t : \tau$ *and* $\eta(x) \triangleright_{\Gamma(x)} \rho(x)$ *then* $[\![t]\!] P \triangleright_\tau \{a \mid t[\rho] \longrightarrow a\}$.

Proof. By induction on typing derivations. The structure of the proof follows that of Theorem 1. For the rec-case one must introduce the syntactic approximations $\mathtt{rec}_n x f.t$ by $\mathtt{rec}_0\ x\ f.t = \mathtt{rec}\ x\ f.f\ x$ and $\mathtt{rec}_{n+1}\ x\ f.t = \lambda x.t[\mathtt{rec}\ x\ f.tn/f]$. One shows that $\mathtt{rec}\ x\ f.tv \longrightarrow a$ iff $\mathtt{rec}_n\ x\ f.t\ v \longrightarrow a$ for some n.

Corollary 1. *If* $\vdash t : \mathtt{int}$ *and* $n \in [\![t]\!]$ *then* $t \longrightarrow n$.

Proof. From the Theorem we get $[\![t]\!] P \triangleright_{\mathtt{int}} \{a \mid t \longrightarrow a\}$. The claim follows directly from this.

10   Conclusion

We have demonstrated how to extend a logical relation to the Hoare powerdomain in the presence of general recursion. This yields a powerful proof principle for observational equivalence (in the may sense) and also allows one to generalise Plotkin's proof of computational adequacy for PCF to nondeterminism. The crucial technical innovation is the use of the admissible closure (*Adm*) in order to heal the lack of admissibility of the obvious ∀∃-existension of a logical relation to the power domain. In particular, we have highlighted the importance of the canonical projections ("effective algebraicity") for the well-behavedness of this closure.

There have been other proposals to lift a logical relation to arbitrary monads including, of course, the Hoare powerdomain, see e.g. [7], all of which are based on a variation of continuation passing style known as ⊤⊤-closure [8]. In general, these extensions are easier to define than ours, but are difficult to work with in concrete applications. In particular, we were unable to define parallel composition for such an extension and to prove effect-dependent equivalences using it. For the particular applications in this paper, ⊤⊤-closure might be workable, but the main purpose was to illustrate the admissible closure in a simple yet nontrivial case. In [3] we use these ideas to justify a theory of effect-dependent program equivalences including a parallelization theorem.

Since its heyday in the 80s, denotational semantics has lost quite a bit of popularity due to the fact that many difficult technical problems such as the solution of mixed-variance equations or, indeed, logical relations, simply evaporate when one moves to a syntactic setting. On the other hand, syntactic theories have also become fairly complicated (for a recent example see the definition of safety on p10 of [4]) and, arguably, less intuitive than denotational models where functions *are* functions, and once technical lemmas such as our Proposition 5 have been asserted, can be handled in much the same way as plain set-theoretic functions. We thus hope that this work will help to bring denotational semantics back to the mainstream toolbox in programming language semantics.

References

1. Abramsky, S., Jung, A.: Domain theory. Online Lecture Notes, avaliable from CiteSeerX (1994)
2. Amadio, R.M., Cardelli, L.: Subtyping recursive types, pp. 575–631 (1993)
3. Benton, N., Hofmann, M., Nigam, V.: Abstract effects and concurrency (under review 2014)
4. Birkedal, L., Sieczkowski, F., Thamsborg, J.: A concurrent logical relation. In: Cégielski, P., Durand, A. (eds.) CSL. LIPIcs, vol. 16, pp. 107–121. Schloss Dagstuhl - Leibniz-Zentrum fuer Informatik (2012)
5. Broy, M., Gnatz, R., Wirsing, M.: Semantics of nondeterministic and noncontinuous constructs. In: Gerhart, S.L., et al. (eds.) Program Construction. LNCS, vol. 69, pp. 553–592. Springer, Heidelberg (1979)
6. Broy, M., Wirsing, M.: On the algebraic specification of nondeterministic programming languages. In: Astesiano, E., Böhm, C. (eds.) CAAP 1981. LNCS, vol. 112, pp. 162–179. Springer, Heidelberg (1981)
7. Katsumata, S.-y.: Relating computational effects by ⊤⊤-lifting. In: Aceto, L., Henzinger, M., Sgall, J. (eds.) ICALP 2011, Part II. LNCS, vol. 6756, pp. 174–185. Springer, Heidelberg (2011)
8. Krivine, J.-L.: Classical logic, storage operators and second-order lambda-calculus. Ann. Pure Appl. Logic 68(1), 53–78 (1994)
9. Plotkin, G.D.: A powerdomain construction. SIAM J. Comput. 5(3), 452–487 (1976)

10. Plotkin, G.D.: "lcf" considered as a programming language. Theor. Comput. Sci. 5(3), 223–255 (1977)
11. Sieber, K.: Call-by-value and nondeterminism. In: Bezem, M., Groote, J.F. (eds.) TLCA 1993. LNCS, vol. 664, pp. 376–390. Springer, Heidelberg (1993)
12. Smyth, M.B., Plotkin, G.D.: The category-theoretic solution of recursive domain equations. SIAM J. Comput. 11(4), 761–783 (1982)

Simplified Coalgebraic Trace Equivalence

Alexander Kurz[1], Stefan Milius[3,*], Dirk Pattinson[2], and Lutz Schröder[3,**]

[1] University of Leicester, UK
[2] The Australian National University, Australia
[3] Friedrich-Alexander-Universität Erlangen-Nürnberg, Germany

Abstract. The analysis of concurrent and reactive systems is based to a large degree on various notions of process equivalence, ranging, on the so-called linear-time/branching-time spectrum, from fine-grained equivalences such as strong bisimilarity to coarse-grained ones such as trace equivalence. The theory of concurrent systems at large has benefited from developments in coalgebra, which has enabled uniform definitions and results that provide a common umbrella for seemingly disparate system types including non-deterministic, weighted, probabilistic, and game-based systems. In particular, there has been some success in identifying a generic coalgebraic theory of bisimulation that matches known definitions in many concrete cases. The situation is currently somewhat less settled regarding trace equivalence. A number of coalgebraic approaches to trace equivalence have been proposed, none of which however cover all cases of interest; notably, all these approaches depend on explicit termination, which is not always imposed in standard systems, e.g. labelled transition systems. Here, we discuss a joint generalization of these approaches based on embedding functors modelling various aspects of the system, such as transition and braching, into a global monad; this approach appears to cover all cases considered previously and some additional ones, notably standard and probabilistic labelled transition systems.

1 Introduction

It was recognized early on that the initial algebra semantics of Goguen and Thatcher [10] needs to be extended to account for notions of observational or behavioural equivalence, see Giarratana, Gimona and Montanari [9], Reichel [18], and Hennicker and Wirsing [12]. When Aczel [2] discovered that at least one important notion of behavioural equivalence—the bisimilarity of process algebra—is captured by final coalgebra semantics, the study of coalgebras fully entered computer science. Whereas early work emphasized the duality between algebra and coalgebra, it became soon clear that both areas have to be taken together. For example, in the work of Turi and Plotkin [22], monads represent the programs, comonads represent their behaviour (operational semantics), and a distributive law between them ensures that the behaviour of a composed system is given by the behaviours of the components, or, more technically, that bisimilarity is a congruence.

* Supported by the Deutsche Forschungsgemeinschaft (DFG) under project MI 717/5-1
** Supported by the Deutsche Forschungsgemeinschaft (DFG) under project SCHR 1118/11-1

R. De Nicola and R. Hennicker (Eds.): Wirsing Festschrift, LNCS 8950, pp. 75–90, 2015.

Another example of the interplay of algebraic and coalgebraic structure arises from the desire to make coalgebraic methods available for a larger range of program equivalences, e.g. the ones described in van Glabbeek [23]. To this end, Power and Turi [17] argued that trace equivalence arises from a distributive law $TF \to FT$ between a monad T describing the non-deterministic part and a functor F describing the deterministic part of a transition system $X \to TFX$. This was taken up by Hasuo et al. [11] and gave rise to a sequence of papers [16,14,20,7,8] that discuss coalgebraic aspects of trace equivalence.

We generalize this approach and call a trace semantics for coalgebras $X \to GX$ simply a natural transformation $G \to M$ for some monad M. This allows us, for example, and opposed to the work cited in the previous paragraph, to account for non-deterministic transition systems without explicit termination. Moreover, because of the flexibility afforded by choosing M, both trace semantics and bisimilarity can be accounted for in the same setting. We also show that for G being of the specific forms investigated in [11] and in [20,7,14] there is a uniform way of constructing a natural transformation of type $G \to M$ that induces the same generic trace semantics up to canonical forgetting of deadlocks.

2   Preliminaries

We assume that readers are familiar with basic notions of category theory. We work with a base category $\mathbf{C}$, which we may assume for simplicity to be locally finitely presentable, such as the category Set of sets and functions (see e.g. Adámek and Rosický [4] for basics on locally finitely presentable categories and finitary functors).

Given a functor $G : \mathbf{C} \to \mathbf{C}$, a *G-coalgebra* is an arrow $\gamma : X \to GX$. Given two coalgebras $\gamma : X \to GX$ and $\gamma' : X' \to GX'$, a *coalgebra morphism* $f : (X, \gamma) \to (X', \gamma')$ is an arrow $f : X \to X'$ in $\mathbf{C}$ such that $\gamma' \circ f = Gf \circ \gamma$.

When $\mathbf{C}$ is a concrete category, i.e. $\mathbf{C}$ comes equipped with a faithful functor $\mathbf{C} \to$ Set, we say that two states $x \in X$ and $x' \in X'$ in two coalgebras (X, γ) and (X', γ') are *behaviourally equivalent* if there are coalgebra morphisms f, f' with common codomain (Y, δ) such that $f(x) = f'(x')$.

Behavioural equivalence can be computed in a partition-refinement style using the *final coalgebra sequence* $(G^n 1)_{n < \omega}$ where 1 is a final object in $\mathbf{C}$ and G^n is n-fold application of G. The projections $p_n^{n+1} : G^{n+1}1 \to G^n 1$ are defined by induction where $p_0^1 : G \to 1$ is the unique arrow to 1 and $p_{n+1}^{n+2} = G(p_n^{n+1})$.

For any coalgebra (X, γ), there is a *canonical cone* $\gamma_n : X \to G^n 1$ defined inductively by $\gamma_0 : X \to 1$ and $\gamma_{n+1} = G(\gamma_n) \circ \gamma$. We say that two states $x, x' \in X$ in (X, γ) are *finite-depth behaviourally equivalent* if $\gamma_n(x) = \gamma_n(x')$ for all $n < \omega$. (Note that if G is a finitary set functor, then finite-depth behavioural equivalence implies behavioural equivalence; this follows from the results of Worrell [24].)

A *monad* is given by an operation M on the objects of $\mathbf{C}$ and, for each set X, a function $\eta_X : X \to MX$ and, for each $f : X \to MY$, a so-called Kleisli star $f^* : MX \to MY$ satisfying (i) $\eta_X^* = id_{MX}$, (ii) $f^* \circ \eta_X = f$, (iii) $(g^* \circ f)^* = g^* \circ f^*$ for all $g : Y \to MZ$. It follows that M is a functor, given by $Mf = (\eta \circ f)^*$, and η a natural transformation. Moreover, $\mu = id^* : MM \to M$ is a natural transformation

and satisfies $\mu \circ M\eta = \mu \circ \eta M = id$ and $\mu \circ M\mu = \mu \circ \mu M$. We obtain the Kleisli
star back from μ and M by $f^* = \mu_Y \circ Mf$.

An *Eilenberg-Moore algebra* for the monad M is an arrow $\xi : MX \to X$ such that
$\xi \circ \eta_X = id_X$ and $\xi \circ M\xi = \xi \circ \mu_X$.

Recall (e.g. from Kelly [15]) that an endofunctor G on a category $\mathbf{C}$ is said to generate an *algebraically-free* monad G^* if the category of Eilenberg-Moore algebras of
G^* is isomorphic over $\mathbf{C}$ to the category of G-algebras (i.e. morphisms $GX \to X$).
The monad G^* is then also the free monad over G; conversely, free monads are
algebraically-free if the base category $\mathbf{C}$ is complete [5,15]. For example, when $\mathbf{C}$
is locally finitely presentable, then every finitary functor on $\mathbf{C}$, representing a type of
finitely-branching systems, generates an (algebraically-)free monad (this follows from
the free algebra construction in Adámek [3]).

3   A Simple Definition of Coalgebraic Trace Equivalence

Recall the classical distinction between bisimilarity and trace equivalence, the two ends
of the *linear-time-branching time spectrum* [23]: to cite a much-belaboured standard
example, the two labelled transition systems (over the alphabet $\Sigma = \{a, b, c\}$)

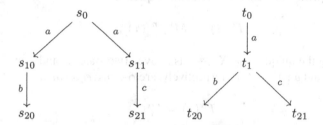

are *trace equivalent* in the usual sense [1], as they both admit exactly the traces ab
and ac (and prefixes thereof), but not bisimilar, as bisimilarity is sensitive to the fact
that the left hand side decides in the first step whether b or c will be enabled in the
second step, while the right hand side leaves the decision between b and c open in the
first step. In other words, trace equivalence collapses all future branches, retaining only
the branching at the current state. Now observe that we can nevertheless construct the
trace semantics by stepwise unfolding; to do this, we need to a) remember the last step
reached by a given trace in order to continue the trace correctly, and b) implement the
collapsing correctly in each step. E.g. for s_0 above, this takes the following form: let us
call a pair (u, x) consisting of a word over Σ and a state x a *pretrace*. Before the first
step, we assign, by default, the set $\{(\epsilon, s_0)\}$ of pretraces, where ϵ denotes the empty
word. After the first step, we reach, applying both transitions simultaneously, the set
$\{(a, s_{10}), (a, s_{11})\}$. After the second step, we reach, again applying two transitions,
$\{(ab, s_{20}), (ac, s_{21})\}$. Note that after the third step, the set of pretraces will become
empty if we proceed in the same manner, as s_{20} and s_{21} are both deadlocks. Thus,
we will in general need to remember all the finite unfoldings of the set of pretraces,
as traces ending in deadlocks will be lost on the way. Of course, for purposes of trace
equivalence we are no longer interested in the states reached by a given trace, so we

forget the state components of all pretraces that we have accumulated, obtaining the expected prefix-closed trace set $\{\epsilon, a, ab, ac\}$.

Recall that we can understand labelled transition systems as coalgebras $\gamma : X \to \mathcal{P}(\Sigma \times X)$. What is happening in the unfolding steps is easily recognized as composition with γ in the Kleisli category of a suitable monad, specifically $M = \mathcal{P}(\Sigma^* \times \_)$, a monad that contains the functor $\mathcal{P}(\Sigma \times \_)$ via an obvious natural transformation α. Defining $\gamma^{(n)}$ as the n-fold iteration of the morphism $\alpha\gamma$ in the Kleisli category of M, we have $\gamma^{(0)}(s_0) = \{(\epsilon, s_0)\}$, $\gamma^{(1)}(s_0) = \{(a, s_{10}), (a, s_{11})\}$, $\gamma^{(2)}(s_0) = \{(ab, s_{20}), (ac, s_{21})\}$, and $\gamma^{(3)}(s_0) = \emptyset$. Forgetting the state component of the pretraces in these sets amounts to postcomposing with $M!$, where ! is the unique map into $1 = \{*\}$. These considerations lead to the following definitions.

Definition 1. A *trace semantics* for a functor G is a natural transformation $\alpha : G \to M$ into a monad M, the *global monad*. Given such an α and a G-coalgebra $\gamma : X \to GX$, we define the *iterations* $\gamma^{(n)} : X \to MX$ of γ, for $n \geq 0$, inductively by

$$\gamma^{(0)} = \eta_X \qquad \gamma^{(n+1)} = (\alpha\gamma)^* \gamma^{(n)}$$

where the unit η and the Kleisli star $*$ are those of M (in particular $\gamma^{(1)} = \alpha\gamma$). Then the α-*trace sequence* of a state $x \in X$ is the sequence

$$T_\gamma^\alpha(x) = (M!\gamma^{(n)}(x))_{n<\omega},$$

with ! denoting the unique map $X \to 1$ as above. Two states x and y in G-coalgebras $\gamma : X \to GX$ and $\delta : Y \to GY$, respectively, are α-*trace equivalent* if

$$T_\gamma^\alpha(x) = T_\delta^\alpha(y).$$

(Although we use an element-based formulation for readability, this definition clearly does make sense over arbitrary complete base categories.)

Of course, one shows by induction over n that

$$\gamma^{(n+1)} = (\gamma^{(n)})^* \alpha\gamma \quad \text{for all } n < \omega. \tag{1}$$

We first note that the trace sequence factors through the initial ω-segment of the terminal sequence. Recall from Section 2 that a G-coalgebra γ induces a cone (γ_n) into the final sequence.

Lemma 2. *Let $\alpha : G \to M$ be a trace semantics for G, and define natural transformations $\alpha_n : G^n \to M$ for $n < \omega$ recursively by $\alpha_0 = \eta$ and $\alpha_{n+1} = \mu\alpha G\alpha_n$. If γ is a G-coalgebra, then*

$$M!\gamma^{(n)} = \alpha_n\gamma_n \quad \text{for all } n < \omega.$$

Proof. Induction on n.

$n = 0$: We have $M!\gamma^{(0)} = M!\eta = \eta! = \alpha_0\gamma_0$.

$n \mapsto n + 1$: We have

$$
\begin{aligned}
\alpha_{n+1}\gamma_{n+1} \\
= \mu\alpha G(\alpha_n)G\gamma_n\gamma && \text{(Definitions of } \gamma_{n+1}, \alpha_{n+1}) \\
= \mu\alpha G(M!\gamma^{(n)})\gamma && \text{(Inductive hypothesis)} \\
= \mu M(M!\gamma^{(n)})\alpha\gamma && \text{(Naturality of } \alpha) \\
= M!\mu M\gamma^{(n)}\alpha\gamma && \text{(Naturality of } \mu) \\
= M!(\gamma^{(n)})^*\alpha\gamma \\
= M!\gamma^{(n+1)} && (1).
\end{aligned}
$$

$\square$

Corollary 3. *Finite-depth behaviourally equivalent states are α-trace equivalent.*

Remark 4. In most items of related work, stronger assumptions than we make here allow for identifying an *object* of traces in a suitable category, such as the Kleisli category [11] or the Eilenberg-Moore category [14,7] of a monad that forms part of the type functor. In our setting, a similar endeavour boils down to characterizing, possibly by means of a limit of a suitable diagram, those α-trace sequences that are *G-realizable*, i.e. induced by a state in some G-coalgebra. We do not currently have a general answer for this but point out that in a variant of the special case treated in the beginning of the section where we take G to be $\mathcal{P}^*(\Sigma \times \_)$, with $\mathcal{P}^*$ denoting nonempty powerset, and $M = \mathcal{P}(\Sigma^* \times \_))$, the set of G-realizable traces is the limit of the infinite diagram

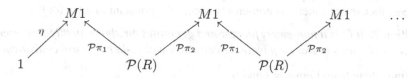

where R denotes the immediate prefix relation $R = \{(u, ua) \mid u \in \Sigma^*, a \in \Sigma\}$ with projections $\pi_1, \pi_2 : R \to \Sigma^*$. We expect that this description generalizes to cases where G and M have the form TF and TF^*, respectively, where T is a monad and F^* is the free monad over the functor F, possibly under additional assumptions. In the case at hand, the limit of the diagram is the set of all subsets A of $\Sigma^* \times 1 \cong \Sigma^*$ that are prefix-closed and *extensible* in the sense that for every $u \in A$ there exists $a \in \Sigma$ such that $ua \in A$.

4 Examples

We show that various process equivalences are subsumed under α-trace equivalence.

Finite-Depth Behavioural Equivalence. Similarly to the approach via Eilenberg-Moore liftings (explained in more detail in Section 5), α-trace equivalence spans, at least for finitely branching systems, the entire length of the linear-time-branching-time spectrum, in the sense that even (finite-depth) behavioural equivalence coincides with α-trace equivalence for a suitable α. This is conveniently formulated using the following terminology.

Definition 5. We say that an endofunctor G on a category with a terminal object 1 is *non-empty* if $G1$ has a global element, i.e. there exists a morphism $1 \to G1$.

Non-emptiness of an endofunctor entails that the component of α_n at 1 are sections where α_n is as in Lemma 2.

Lemma 6. *If G is non-empty and generates an algebraically-free monad G^* with universal arrow α, then $(\alpha_n)_1$ (the component of α_n at the terminal object) is a section for every $n < \omega$.*

Proof. For each set X, G^*X is the initial $G + X$-algebra, with structure map

$$[\mu\alpha, \eta] : GG^*X + X \to G^*X$$

where μ and η are the multiplication and unit of G^* [5]. By Lambek's lemma, it follows that $[\mu\alpha, \eta]$ is an isomorphism. Since both summands of the coproduct $GG^*1 + 1$ are nonempty (for GG^*1, this follows from non-emptiness of G: we obtain a global element of GG^*1 by postcomposing a global element of $G1$ with $G\eta_1 : G1 \to GG^*1$), the coproduct injections are sections, so we obtain that $\mu\alpha$ and η are sections, each being the composite of a section with an isomorphism. Using (1), it follows by induction that α_n is a section for each $n < \omega$. $\square$

(Notice that G is non-empty as soon as any GX has a global element; if the base category is Set, then every functor is non-empty except the constant functor for $\emptyset$.)

Proposition 7. *If G is a non-empty functor and generates an algebraically-free monad via $\alpha : G \to G^*$, then α-trace equivalence coincides with ω-behavioural equivalence.*

Proof. Immediate from Lemmas 2 and 6. $\square$

Labelled Transition Systems (LTS). We provide some additional details for our initial example: We have $GX = \mathcal{P}(\Sigma \times X)$ and $MX = \mathcal{P}(\Sigma^* \times X)$, with α the obvious inclusion. The monad M arises from G, as we will see later again in (2), from a distributive law $\delta_X : \Sigma \times \mathcal{P}(X) \to \mathcal{P}(\Sigma \times X)$ which maps a pair (a, S) to $\{a\} \times S$. Explicitly, the unit of M is given by $\eta(x) = \{(\epsilon, x)\}$, and the multiplication by $\mu(\mathfrak{A}) = \{(uv, x) \mid \exists (u, S) \in \mathfrak{A}. (v, x) \in S\}$ for $\mathfrak{A} \in \mathcal{P}(\Sigma^* \times \mathcal{P}(\Sigma^* \times X))$. For each n and each state x in an LTS $\gamma : X \to \mathcal{P}(\Sigma \times X)$, $\gamma^{(n)}(x)$ consists of the pretraces of x of length exactly n, i.e.

$$\gamma^{(n)}(x) = \{(u, y) \mid x \xrightarrow{u} y, u \in \Sigma^n\}$$

where $\xrightarrow{u}$ denotes the usual extension of the transition relation to words $u \in \Sigma^*$. Thus, $M!\gamma^{(n)}(x)$ consists of the traces of x of length n, i.e.

$$M!\gamma^{(n)}(x) = \{(u, *) \mid x \xrightarrow{u}, u \in \Sigma^n\}$$

(where, as usual, $x \xrightarrow{u}$ denotes $\exists y. x \xrightarrow{u} y$). Thus, states x and y are α-trace equivalent iff they are trace equivalent in the usual sense, i.e. iff

$$\{u \in \Sigma^* \mid x \xrightarrow{u}\} = \{u \in \Sigma^* \mid y \xrightarrow{u}\}.$$

The entire scenario transfers verbatim to the case of finitely branching LTS, with $G = \mathcal{P}_\omega(\Sigma \times \_)$ and $M = \mathcal{P}_{<\omega}(\Sigma^* \times \_)$, where $\mathcal{P}_{<\omega}$ denotes finite powerset.

LTS with Explicit Termination. The leading example treated in related work on coalgebraic trace semantics [11,14,7] is LTSs with explicit termination, described as coalgebras for the functor

$$\mathcal{P}(1 + \Sigma \times \_) \cong 2 \times \mathcal{P}^\Sigma.$$

A state in an LTS with explicit termination can be seen as a non-deterministic automaton; this suggests that one might expect the traces of such a state to be the words accepted by the corresponding automaton, and, in fact, this is the stance taken in previous work [11,14,7]; for the sake of distinction, let us call this form of trace semantics *language semantics*. Staring at the problem for a moment reveals that language semantics does not fit directly into our framework: Basically, our definition of trace sequence assembles the traces via successive iteration of the coalgebra structure, and remembers the traces reached in each iteration step. Contrastingly, language semantics will drop a word from the trace set if it turns out that upon complete execution of the word, no accepting state is reached – in α-trace semantics, on the other hand, we will have recorded prefixes of the word on the way, and our incremental approach does not foresee forgetting these prefixes. See Section 5 for a discussion of how α-trace sequences can be further quotiented to obtain language semantics.

Indeed one might contend that a more natural trace semantics of an LTS with explicit termination will distinguish two types of traces: those induced by the plain LTS structure, disregarding acceptance, and those that additionally end up in accepting states; this is related to the trace semantics of CSP [13], which distinguishes deadlock from successful termination $\checkmark$. Such a semantics is generated by our framework as follows. As the global monad, we take $MX = \mathcal{P}(\Sigma^* \times (X + 1))$ (where we regard X and $1 = \{\checkmark\}$ as subsets of $X + 1$), with $\eta(x) = \{(\epsilon, x)\}$ and

$$f^*(S) = \{(uv, b) \mid \exists (u, x) \in S \cap (\Sigma^* \times X). (v, b) \in f(x)\} \cup (S \cap (\Sigma^* \times 1))$$

for $f : X \to MY$ and $S \in MY$. This is exactly the monad induced by the distributive law $\lambda_X : 1 + \Sigma \times \mathcal{P}(X) \to \mathcal{P}(1 + \Sigma \times X)$ with $\lambda_X(\checkmark) = \{\checkmark\}$ and $\lambda_X(a, S) = a \times S$ as used by Hasuo et al. [11]. We embed $\mathcal{P}(1 + \Sigma \times \_)$ into M by the natural transformation α given by

$$\alpha_X(S) = \{(\epsilon, \checkmark) \mid \checkmark \in S\} \cup \{(a, x) \mid (a, x) \in S\}$$

(implicitly converting letters into words in the second part). Then $M1 \cong \mathcal{P}(\Sigma^*)^2$ where the first components records accepted words and the second component non-blocked words; in α-trace sequences, the first component is always contained in the second one, and increases monotonically over the sequence as the Kleisli star as defined above always keeps traces that are already accepted. Two states are α-trace equivalent iff they generate the same traces and the same accepted traces, in the sense discussed above.

Our framework also covers the language semantics of non-deterministic automata. Note that we can impose w.l.o.g. that a non-deterministic automaton never blocks an input letter – if a state fails to have an a-successor, just add an a-transition into a non-accepting state that loops on all input letters and has no transitions into other states; this clearly leaves the language of the automaton unchanged. This restriction amounts to considering coalgebras for the subfunctor

$$G = 2 \times (\mathcal{P}^*)^{\Sigma}$$

of the functor $\mathcal{P}(1 + \Sigma \times \_)$ modelling LTS with explicit termination, where $\mathcal{P}^*$ denotes non-empty powerset. We embed this functor into the same monad M as above, by restricting $\alpha : \mathcal{P}(1 + \Sigma \times \_) \to M$ to G. Calling G-coalgebras *non-blocking non-deterministic automata*, we now have that *two states in a non-blocking non-deterministic automaton are α-trace equivalent iff they accept the same language*. For a coalgebra $\gamma : X \to GX$, the maps $\gamma^{(n)} : X \to M1$, of course, still record accepted traces as well as plain traces, but the plain traces no longer carry any information: all α-trace sequences have the form $(L_n, \Sigma^n)_{n<\omega}$ (with $L_n \subseteq \Sigma^*$ recording the accepted words of length at most n).

Probabilistic Transition Systems. Recall that *generative probabilistic (transition) systems* (for simplicity without the possibility of deadlock, not to be confused with explicit termination) are modelled as coalgebras for the functor $\mathcal{D}(\Sigma \times \_)$ where $\mathcal{D}$ denotes the discrete distribution functor (i.e. $\mathcal{D}(X)$ is the set of discrete probability distributions on X, and $\mathcal{D}(f)$ takes image measures under f). That is, each state has a probability distribution over pairs of actions and successor states. We embed $\mathcal{D}(\Sigma \times \_)$ into the global monad $MX = \mathcal{D}(\Sigma^* \times \_)$ via the natural transformation α that takes a discrete distribution μ on $\Sigma \times X$ to the discrete distribution on $\Sigma^* \times X$ that behaves like μ on $\Sigma \times X$ (where we see Σ as a subset of Σ^*) and is 0 outside $\Sigma \times X$. The unit η of M maps $x \in X$ to the Dirac distribution at (ϵ, x), and for $f : X \to MY$,

$$f^*(\mu)(u, y) = \sum_{u=vw, x\in X} \mu(v, x) f(x)(w, y)$$

for all $\mu \in MX, (u, y) \in \Sigma^* \times Y$. This is the monad induced by the canonical distributive law $\lambda : \Sigma \times \mathcal{D} \to \mathcal{D}(\Sigma \times \_)$ given by $\lambda_X(a, \mu) = \delta(a) * \mu$ where δ forms Dirac measures and $*$ is product measure [11]. We identify $M1$ with $\mathcal{D}(\Sigma^*)$. Given these data, observe that for $\gamma : X \to \mathcal{D}(\Sigma \times X)$ and $x \in X$, each distribution $M!\gamma^{(n)}(x)$ is concentrated at traces of length n.

Assume from now on that Σ is finite. Recall that the usual σ-algebra on the set Σ^ω of infinite words over Σ is generated by the *cones*, i.e. the sets $v\uparrow = \{vw \mid w \in \Sigma^\omega\}$, $v \in \Sigma^*$, which (by finiteness of Σ) form a semiring of sets. We let states x in a coalgebra $\gamma : X \to \mathcal{D}(\Sigma \times X)$ *induce* distributions μ_x on Σ^ω via the Hahn-Kolmogorov theorem [21], defining a content $\mu(v\uparrow)$ inductively by

$$\mu_x(\epsilon\uparrow) = 1$$
$$\mu_x(av\uparrow) = \sum_{x'\in X} \gamma(a, x') \mu_{x'}(v\uparrow)$$

– a compactness argument, again hinging on the finiteness of Σ, shows that no cone can be written as a countably infinite disjoint union of cones, so μ is in fact a pre-measure, i.e. σ-additive.

We note explicitly

Proposition 8. *States in generative probabilistic systems over a finite alphabet Σ are α-trace equivalent iff they induce the same distribution on Σ^{ω}.*

Proof. For v a word of length n and x a state in a generative probabilistic system, we have $\mu_x(v{\uparrow}) = (M! \gamma^{(n)}(x))(v)$. $\square$

5   Relation to Other Frameworks

Kleisli Liftings. Hasuo et al. [11] treat the case where the type functor G has the form TF for a monad T and a finitary endofunctor F on sets. They require that F lifts to a functor $\bar{F}$ on the Kleisli category of T, which is equivalent to having a (functor-over-monad) distributive law

$$\lambda : FT \to TF.$$

They impose further conditions that include a cppo structure on the hom-sets[1] of the Kleisli category $\mathsf{Kl}(T)$ of T and ensure that

- $T\emptyset$ is a singleton, so that $\emptyset$ is a terminal object in $\mathsf{Kl}(T)$ (unique Kleisli morphisms into $\emptyset$ of course being $\bot$); and
- the final sequence of $\bar{F}$ coincides on objects with the initial sequence of F, and converges to the final $\bar{F}$-coalgebra in ω steps.

The trace semantics of a TF-coalgebra is then defined as the unique Kleisli morphism into the final $\bar{F}$-coalgebra; in keeping with distinguishing terminology used in Section 4, we refer to this as language semantics. Thus, two states in a TF-coalgebra are *language equivalent*, i.e. trace equivalent in the sense of Hasuo et al., iff they map to the same values in the final sequence of $\bar{F}$ under the cones induced by the respective coalgebras. Explicitly: the underlying sets of the final sequence of $\bar{F}$ have the form $TF^n\emptyset$, $n < \omega$, and given a coalgebra $\gamma : X \to TFX$, the canonical cone $(\bar{\gamma}_n : X \to TF^n\emptyset)_{n<\omega}$ is defined recursively by $\gamma_0 = \bot$ and

$$\bar{\gamma}_{n+1} = \; X \xrightarrow{\;\gamma\;} TFX \xrightarrow{\;TF\bar{\gamma}_n\;} TFTF^n\emptyset \xrightarrow{\;T\lambda\;} TTF^{n+1}\emptyset \xrightarrow{\;\mu\;} TF^{n+1}\emptyset.$$

Now the distributive law λ induces a monad structure on the functor

$$M = TF^*, \tag{2}$$

where F^* denotes the (algebraically-)free monad on F (cf. Section 4), and we have a natural transformation $\alpha : TF \to M$, so that the situation fits our current framework. The sets TF^nX embed into MX, so that the objects in the final sequence of $\bar{F}$ can be

---

[1] More precisely, hom-sets are partial orders with a least element $\bot$, joins of ω-chains and composition is continuous in both arguments and *left-strict*, i.e. $\bot \circ f = \bot$.

seen as living in $M0$. The definition of $\bar{\gamma}_{n+1}$ is then seen to be just an explicit form of Kleisli composition in M; that is, we can, for purposes of language equivalence, replace the $\bar{\gamma}_n$ with maps $\tilde{\gamma}_n : X \to M0$ defined recursively by

$$\tilde{\gamma}_0 = \perp \qquad \tilde{\gamma}_{n+1} = \tilde{\gamma}_n^* \alpha \gamma$$

where the Kleisli star is that of M. Comparing with (1), we see that the only difference with the definition of $\gamma^{(n)}$ is in the base of the recursion: $\gamma^{(0)} = \eta_X$. Noting moreover that

$$\perp^* M! \eta_X = \perp^* \eta! = \perp! = \perp,$$

we obtain

$$\tilde{\gamma}_n = \perp^* M! \gamma^{(n)}.$$

(Kissig and Kurz [16] use a very similar definition in a more general setting that in particular, for non-commutative T, does not restrict $T\emptyset$ to be a singleton, and instead assume some distinguished element $e \in T\emptyset$. They then put $\tilde{\gamma}_0 = \lambda x. \, e$; the comparison with our framework is then entirely analogous.)

Summing up, *language equivalence is induced from α-trace equivalence by post-composing α-trace sequences with* $\perp^* : M1 \to M0$. Intuitively, this means that any information tied to poststates in a pretrace is erased in language equivalence, as opposed to just forgetting the poststate itself in α-trace equivalence. An example of this phenomenon are LTS with explicit termination as discussed in Section 4. Moreover, this observation elucidates why language equivalence becomes trivial in cases without explicit termination, such as standard LTS: here, all traces are tied to poststates and hence are erased when postcomposing with $\perp^*$. (This is also easily seen directly [11]: without explicit termination, e.g. $F = \Sigma \times \_$, one typically has $F\emptyset = \emptyset$ so that the final $\bar{F}$-coalgebra is trivial in the Kleisli category of M.)

Eilenberg-Moore Liftings. An alternative route to final objects for trace semantics was first suggested by the generalized powerset construction of Silva et al. [19] and explicitly formulated in [7] (see also Jacobs et al. [14] where this is compared to the semantics given by Kleisli liftings). In this approach one considers liftings of functors to Eilenberg-Moore categories in lieu of Kleisli categories. The setup applies to functors of the form $G = FT$ where F is an endofunctor and T is a monad on a base category $\mathbf{C}$. It is based on assuming a final F-coalgebra Z and a (functor-over-monad) distributive law

$$\rho : TF \to FT.$$

Under these assumptions, F lifts to an endofunctor $\hat{F}$ on the Eilenberg-Moore category $\mathbf{C}^T$ of T, and the free-algebra functor $\mathbf{C} \to \mathbf{C}^T$ lifts to a functor D from FT-coalgebras to $\hat{F}$-coalgebras, which can be seen as a generalized powerset construction (the standard powerset construction is obtained by taking $FX = 2 \times X^\Sigma$, $T = \mathcal{P}$). Explicitly, $D(\gamma) = F\mu_X^T \rho_{TX} T\gamma$ for $\gamma : X \to FTX$, where μ^T denotes the multiplication of T. In other words, $D(\gamma) : TX \to FTX$ is the unique T-algebra morphism with $D(\gamma) \cdot \eta_X^T = \gamma$. Moreover, $\hat{F}$ has a final coalgebra with carrier Z. The *extension semantics* (i.e. trace semantics obtained via the powerset extension) of an FT-coalgebra

$\gamma : X \to FTX$ is then obtained by first applying D to γ, obtaining a $\hat{F}$-coalgebra with carrier TX and hence a $\hat{F}$-coalgebra map $TX \to Z$, and finally precomposing with $\eta^T_X : X \to TX$ where η^T denotes the unit of T. Similarly to our approach, one obtains standard bisimilarity as a special case of trace equivalence by taking $T = Id$.

In order to compare this with our framework, in which we currently consider only finite iterates of the given coalgebra, we need to assume that F-behavioural equivalence coincides with finite-depth behavioural equivalence; this is ensured e.g. by assuming that F is a finitary endofunctor on Set. In this case, two states have the same extension semantics iff they induce the same values in the first ω steps of the final sequence of $\hat{F}$, whose carriers coincide with the final sequence of F. Combining the definition of $D\gamma$ for a coalgebra $\gamma : X \to FTX$ with the usual construction of the canonical cone for $D\gamma$, which we denote by $\bar{\gamma}_n : TX \to F^n 1$ for distinction from the canonical cone of γ in the final sequence of FT, we obtain that $\bar{\gamma}_n$ is recursively defined by

$$\bar{\gamma}_0 = !_{TX} : TX \to 1$$
$$\bar{\gamma}_{n+1} = F\bar{\gamma}_n T\gamma\rho F\mu^T.$$

Now let us also assume that T is a finitary monad on Set. Then Set^T is a locally finitely presentable category, and since the forgetful functor to Set creates filtered colimits, we see that the lifting $\hat{F}$ is finitary on Set^T. Hence free $\hat{F}$-algebras exists, which implies that we have the adjunction on the right below

$$\mathsf{Set} \underset{\longleftarrow}{\overset{\perp}{\longrightarrow}} \mathsf{Set}^T \underset{\longleftarrow}{\overset{\perp}{\longrightarrow}} \mathsf{Alg}\,\hat{F},$$

and the adjunction on the left is the canonical one. We define M to be the monad of the composed adjunction; it assigns to a set X the underlying set $\hat{F}^*TX$ of a free $\hat{F}$-algebra on the free T-algebra TX; here $\hat{F}^*$ denotes the free monad on $\hat{F}$ (notice that this is not in general a lifing of the free monad on F to Set^T). Intuitively, M is defined by forming the disjoint union of the algebraic theories associated to T and F, respectively, and then imposing the distributive law between the operations of T and F embodied by ρ. In the following we shall denote the unit and multiplication of $\hat{F}^*$ by $\hat{\eta}$ and $\hat{\mu}$, respectively. We also write $\hat{\varphi}_X : \hat{F}\hat{F}^*X \to \hat{F}^*X$ for the structures of the free $\hat{F}$-algebras and note that these yield a natural transformation $\hat{\varphi}$.

Now denote by $\hat{\kappa} : \hat{F} \to \hat{F}^*$ the universal natural transformation into the free monad; it is easy to see that $\hat{\kappa} = \hat{\varphi} \cdot \hat{F}\hat{\eta}$. Then it follows that $\alpha = \hat{\kappa}T$ yields a natural transformation from FT to M (on Set). Let us further recall that there exist canonical natural transformations $\hat{\beta}^n : \hat{F}^n \to \hat{F}^*$ defined inductively by

$$\hat{\beta}^0 = (Id \overset{\hat{\eta}}{\longrightarrow} \hat{F}^*) \quad \text{and} \quad \hat{\beta}^{n+1} = (\hat{F}^{n+1} = \hat{F}\hat{F}^n \overset{\hat{F}\hat{\beta}^n}{\longrightarrow} \hat{F}\hat{F}^* \overset{\hat{\varphi}}{\longrightarrow} \hat{F}^*).$$

We can assume w.l.o.g. that F preserves monos (hence, so does $\hat{F}$ since monos in Set^T are precisely injective T-algebra homomorphisms) and that coproduct injections are monic in Set^T. Then an easy induction shows that the β^n are monic, too. (One uses that $[\hat{\eta}, \hat{\phi}] : Id + \hat{F}\hat{F}^* \cong \hat{F}^*$.) This implies that for testing equivalence in the extension semantics we can replace $\bar{\gamma}_n$ with

$$\hat{\gamma}_n = \beta^n_1 \cdot \bar{\gamma}_n : TX \to \hat{F}^*1.$$

We are now ready to state the semantic comparison result:

Theorem 9. *Let F be a finitary endofunctor, and let T be a finitary monad, both on* Set. *Further let $\rho : TF \to FT$ be a functor-over-monad distributive law. Then two states in FT-coalgebras are equivalent under the extension semantics iff for $\alpha : FT \to M$ as given above, their α-trace sequences are identified under componentwise postcomposition with $\hat{F}^* !_{T1}$. That is, in the above notation,*

$$\hat{\gamma}_n \cdot \eta_X^T = \hat{F}^* !_{T1} \cdot M!_X \cdot \gamma^{(n)}. \tag{3}$$

Proof. We first recall how the Kleisli extension $f \mapsto f^*$ for the monad M is obtained. Given $f : X \to MY$ one first extends this to the unique T-algebra morphism $f^\sharp : TX \to MY$ with $f^\sharp \cdot \eta_X^T = f$ (i.e. one applies the Kleisli extension of T). Then one obtains $f^* : MX = \hat{F}^*TX \to \hat{F}^*TY = MY$ as the unique $\hat{F}$-algebra morphism with $f^* \cdot \hat{\eta}_{TX} = f^\sharp$. Notice that in this notation we have $D(\gamma) = \gamma^\sharp$ and that the inductive step of the definition on $\bar{\gamma}_n$ can be written as $\bar{\gamma}_{n+1} = \hat{F}\bar{\gamma}_n \cdot \gamma^\sharp : TX \to \hat{F}^n 1$. Observe further that, since $\hat{\gamma}_n$, $\hat{F}^* !_{T1}$ and $M!$ are T-algebra homomorphisms, (3) is equivalent to

$$\hat{\gamma}_n = \hat{F}^* !_{T1} \cdot M!_X \cdot (\gamma^{(n)})^\sharp. \tag{4}$$

We now prove (3) by induction on n. For the base case $n = 0$ we have:

$$
\begin{aligned}
\hat{F}^* !_{T1} \cdot M!_X \cdot \gamma^{(0)} &= \hat{F}^* !_{T1} \cdot \hat{F}^*T!_X \cdot \eta_X^M && M = \hat{F}^*T \text{ and def. of } \gamma^{(0)} \\
&= \hat{F}^* !_{T1} \cdot \hat{F}^*T!_X \cdot \hat{\eta}_{TX} \cdot \eta_X^T && \text{since } \eta^M = \hat{\eta}T \cdot \eta^T \\
&= \hat{\eta}_1 \cdot !_{T1} \cdot T!_X \cdot \eta_X^T && \text{naturality of } \hat{\eta} \\
&= \hat{\eta}_1 \cdot !_{TX} \cdot \eta_X^T && \text{uniqueness of } !_{TX} \\
&= \hat{\beta}_1^0 \cdot \bar{\gamma}_0 \cdot \eta_X^T && \text{def. of } \hat{\beta}^0 \text{ and } \bar{\gamma}_0 \\
&= \hat{\gamma}_0 \cdot \eta_X^T && \text{def. of } \hat{\gamma}_0.
\end{aligned}
$$

For the induction step we compute:

$$
\begin{aligned}
\hat{F}^* &!_{T1} \cdot M!_X \cdot \gamma^{(n+1)} \\
&= \hat{F}^* !_{T1} \cdot \hat{F}^*T!_X \cdot (\gamma^{(n)})^* \cdot \alpha_X \cdot \gamma && M = \hat{F}^*T \text{ and def. of } \gamma^{(n+1)} \\
&= \hat{F}^* !_{T1} \cdot \hat{F}^*T!_X \cdot (\gamma^{(n)})^* \cdot \hat{\varphi}_X \cdot \hat{F}\hat{\eta}_{TX} \cdot \gamma && \text{def. of } \alpha \\
&= \hat{\varphi}_1 \cdot \hat{F}\hat{F}^* !_{T1} \cdot \hat{F}\hat{F}^*T!_X \cdot \hat{F}(\gamma^{(n)})^* \cdot \hat{F}\hat{\eta}_{TX} \cdot \gamma && \hat{F}\text{-algebra morphisms} \\
&= \hat{\varphi}_1 \cdot \hat{F}\hat{F}^* !_{T1} \cdot \hat{F}\hat{F}^*T!_X \cdot \hat{F}(\gamma^{(n)})^\sharp \cdot \gamma && \text{def. of } (-)^* \\
&= \hat{\varphi}_1 \cdot \hat{F}\hat{\gamma}_n \cdot \gamma && \text{induction hypothesis (4)} \\
&= \hat{\varphi}_1 \cdot \hat{F}\hat{\beta}_1^n \cdot \hat{F}\bar{\gamma}_n \cdot \gamma && \text{def. of } \hat{\gamma}^n \\
&= \hat{\beta}_1^{n+1} \cdot \hat{F}\bar{\gamma}_n \cdot \gamma && \text{def. of } \beta^{n+1} \\
&= \hat{\beta}_1^{n+1} \cdot \hat{F}\bar{\gamma}_n \cdot \gamma^\sharp \cdot \eta_X^T && (-)^\sharp \text{ Kleisli extension} \\
&= \hat{\beta}_1^{n+1} \cdot \bar{\gamma}_{n+1} \cdot \eta_X^T && \text{def. of } \bar{\gamma}_{n+1} \\
&= \hat{\gamma}_{n+1} \cdot \eta_X^T. && \text{def. of } \hat{\gamma}_{n+1}. \qquad \square
\end{aligned}
$$

In the base example in work on extension semantics [14,7], the case of non-deterministic automata understood as coalgebras of the form $\gamma : X \to 2 \times \mathcal{P}(X)^\Sigma$, the situation is as follows. The extension semantics of γ [14, Section 5.1] yields a map

$tr : X \to \mathcal{P}(\Sigma^*)$ that maps each state $x \in X$ to the language accepted by the automaton with starting state x.

To understand the above theorem in terms of this concrete example, we fix $FX = 2 \times X^\Sigma$ and $TX = \mathcal{P}_{<\omega}(X)$ (to ensure finitarity). Understood as an algebraic signature, F can be represented by two Σ-ary function symbols y and n. The monad $M = \hat{F}^*T$ has these operations and those of $\mathcal{P}_{<\omega}$, i.e. the join semilattice operations, which we write using set notation; the distributive law ρ allows us to distribute joins over y and n, favouring y over n to reflect the acceptance condition of (existential) non-deterministic automata. The trace semantics $\alpha_X : FTX \to MX$ embeds flat terms, i.e. terms of the form $y((U_a)_{a \in \Sigma})$ or $n((U_a)_{a \in \Sigma}) \in FTX$ (with $U_a \in \mathcal{P}(X)$), into general (non-flat) terms. Every step in the construction of $\gamma^n(c)$ puts a flat term on top of terms constructed in the previous step, and then distributes T-operations (joins) over their arguments as indicated. Therefore, the terms $\gamma^{(n)}(c)$ are terms of uniform depth in the F-operations over sets of variables, i.e. they are elements of F^nTC. For the alphabet $\Sigma = \{0, 1\}$, a typical component of the trace sequence $T_\gamma^\alpha(c)$, i.e. $M!_X\gamma^{(n)}(c)$ for some n can be visualised as a tree like the one on the left:

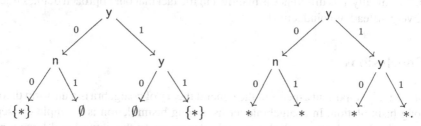

This tree conveys the information that the empty word ϵ and the word 1 lead to final states (i.e. are accepted in the sense of language semantics), and additionally that 00 and 11 are not blocked; generally, the α-trace sequence records at each stage which words are accepted and additionally which words can be executed without deadlock. The tree on the right is then obtained by applying $\hat{F}^*!_{T1}$. This erases the information on non-blocked words, so that only the information that ϵ and 1 are accepted remains; this yields the extension semantics [14,7], i.e. language semantics of the automaton, as formally stated in Theorem 9. As noted already in Section 4, if we move to non-blocking non-deterministic automata, then α-trace equivalence coincides directly with language equivalence – note that in this case, T is the non-empty powerset monad, so that $!_{T1}$ is a bijection, i.e. postcomposing the α-trace sequence with $\hat{F}^*!_{T1}$ does not lose information. Informally, this is clear as non-acceptance of words due to deadlock never happens in a non-blocking nondeterministic automaton.

Fixpoint Definitions. Trace semantics, and associated linear-time logics, are also considered by Cirstea [8]. The setup is similar to that of Hasuo et al. [11] in that it applies to systems of type $X \to TFX$ where T is a monad (that describes the branching) and F a polynomial endofunctor (modelling the traces). The monad T is required to be commutative and partially additive, thus inducing a partial additive semiring structure on $T1$. In the examples of interest, one recovers the monad T as induced by this semiring structure.

Given a system $(X, f : X \to TFX)$, trace semantics then arises as a $T1$-valued relation $R : X \times Z \to T1$ where $Z = \nu F$ is the final coalgebra of the functor F defining traces. For this to be well-defined, one additionally requires that the semiring $T1$ has suprema of chains, with order defined in the standard way.

The crucial difference to our approach is that trace semantics is defined *coinductively* on the *infinite unfolding* of the functor F defining the shape of traces, whereas our definition is *inductive* and based on *finite unfoldings*.

The difference becomes apparent when looking at examples. For labelled transition systems $X \to \mathcal{P}(A \times X)$, the trace semantics of [8] is a function $X \to \mathcal{P}(A^w)$ that maps x to the set of maximal traces, and two states are trace equivalent if they have the same set of *infinite* traces. This contrasts with our treatment where equivalent states have the same *finite* traces. Similarly, for generative probabilistic systems, i.e. systems of shape $X \to \mathcal{D}(A \times X)$ where $\mathcal{D}$ is the discrete distributions functor, the trace semantics obtained in [8] associates probabilities to maximal (infinite) traces whereas our treatment is centered around probabilities of finite prefixes. In summary, the main conceptual difference between [8] and our approach is that between infinite and finite traces. Technically, this difference is manifest in the fact that our approach defines traces inductively instead of coinductively.

6   Conclusions

One of the main important aspects of the general theory of coalgebra is a uniform theory of strong bisimulation. In coalgebraic terms, strong bisimulation is a simple concept, readily defined, supports a rich theory and instantiates to the natural and known notions for concretely given transition types. Instead of re-establishing facts about strong bisimulation on a case-by-case basis, separately for each type of transition system, the coalgebraic approach provides a general theory of which specific results for concretely given systems are mere instances: a coalgebraic success story.

The question about whether a similar success story for trace equivalence can also be told in a coalgebraic setting has been the subject of numerous papers (discussed in the previous section in detail) but has so far not received a satisfactory answer.

One of the reasons why trace semantics has so far been a more elusive concept is the fact that – even for concretely given systems such as labelled transition systems with explicit termination – there are many, equally natural, formulations of trace equivalence. This suggests that trace equivalence, by its very nature, cannot be captured by one general definition, but needs an additional parameter that defines the precise nature of traces one wants to capture.

We account for this fact by parametrising trace semantics by an embedding of a functor (that defines the coalgebraic type of system under consideration) into a monad (that allows us to sequence transitions). We have shown that our definition subsumes existing notions of generic trace semantics [11,14,7]; it is more flexible than these in that it avoids various additional technical conditions like order enrichment or partial additivity of a monad. This has allowed us to deal with new examples not covered by previous approaches, notably systems not featuring explicit termination, such as standard labelled transition systems.

Proposition 7 shows that finite-depth strong bisimilarity is a specific instance of our parametrized definition of trace equivalence, similarly as strong bisimilarity arises as a special case of Eilenberg-Moore-style extension semantics [14,7]. One important point to explore in future research is how further equivalences from the linear-time-branching time spectrum [23] fit into our framework, extending previous work on extension semantics [6]. Further open issues include a generalisation to behavioural preorders, as well as appropriate logics that characterise these preorders and ensuing equivalences.

On a more personal note, and reflecting on the last 15 years of development in universal coalgebra, we have learned that neither coalgebraic nor algebraic approaches by themselves are powerful enough to describe *all* aspects of state based systems, and that only the combination of algebraic theories (here in the form of monads) and universal coalgebra provide a satisfactory understanding.

Apart from providing a puzzle piece, we also hope to provide some physical motivation for the person honoured by this collection of papers to occasionally stand on his head, and while in this only seemingly anomalous position, to apply algebraic techniques from a coalgebraic viewpoint. We hope that this exercise will contribute to continued good health and many more insights into the algebraic foundations of our discipline. Happy Birthday, Martin!

Acknowledgements. The authors wish to thank Bartek Klin for useful discussions, and Erwin R. Catesbeiana for repeated hints regarding inconsistent monads.

References

1. Aceto, L., Ingólfsdóttir, A., Larsen, K., Srba, J.: Reactive systems: modelling, specification and verification. Cambridge University Press (2007)
2. Aczel, P.: Non-Well-Founded Sets. CSLI, Stanford (1988)
3. Adámek, J.: Free algebras and automata realizations in the language of categories. Comment. Math. Univ. Carolin. 15, 589–602 (1974)
4. Adámek, J., Rosický, J.: Locally presentable and accessible categories. Cambridge University Press (1994)
5. Barr, M.: Coequalizers and free triples. Math. Zeitschr. 116, 307–322 (1970)
6. Bonchi, F., Bonsangue, M., Caltais, G., Rutten, J., Silva, A.: Final semantics for decorated traces. In: Mathematical Foundations of Programming Semantics, MFPS 2012. ENTCS, vol. 286, pp. 73–86. Elsevier (2012)
7. Bonsangue, M.M., Milius, S., Silva, A.: Sound and complete axiomatizations of coalgebraic language equivalence. ACM Trans. Comput. Log. 14(1:7) (2013)
8. Cîrstea, C.: A coalgebraic approach to linear-time logics. In: Muscholl, A. (ed.) FOSSACS 2014 (ETAPS). LNCS, vol. 8412, pp. 426–440. Springer, Heidelberg (2014)
9. Giarratana, V., Gimona, F., Montanari, U.: Observability concepts in abstract data type specifications. In: Mazurkiewicz, A. (ed.) MFCS 1976. LNCS, vol. 45, pp. 576–587. Springer, Heidelberg (1976)
10. Goguen, J., Thatcher, J.: Initial algebra semantics. In: Switching and Automata Theory, SWAT (FOCS) 1974, pp. 63–77. IEEE Computer Society (1974)
11. Hasuo, I., Jacobs, B., Sokolova, A.: Generic trace semantics via coinduction. Log. Methods Comput. Sci. 3 (2007)

12. Hennicker, R., Wirsing, M.: Observational Specification: A Birkhoff Theorem. In: Workshop on Theory and Applications of Abstract Data Types, WADT 1985, Selected Papers, pp. 119–135. Springer (1985)
13. Hoare, A.: Communicating sequential processes. Prentice-Hall (1985)
14. Jacobs, B., Silva, A., Sokolova, A.: Trace semantics via determinization. In: Pattinson, D., Schröder, L. (eds.) CMCS 2012. LNCS, vol. 7399, pp. 109–129. Springer, Heidelberg (2012)
15. Kelly, M.: A unified treatment of transfinite constructions for free algebras, free monoids, colimits, associated sheaves, and so on. Bull. Austral. Math. Soc. 22, 1–83 (1980)
16. Kissig, C., Kurz, A.: Generic trace logics. arXiv preprint 1103.3239 (2011)
17. Power, J., Turi, D.: A coalgebraic foundation for linear time semantics. In: Coalgebraic Methods in Computer Science, CMCS 1999. ENTCS, vol. 29, pp. 259–274. Elsevier (1999)
18. Reichel, H.: Behavioural equivalence — a unifying concept for initial and final specification methods. In: Math. Models in Comp. Systems, Proc. 3rd Hungarian Comp. Sci. Conference, pp. 27–39 (1981)
19. Silva, A., Bonchi, F., Bonsangue, M., Rutten, J.: Generalizing the powerset construction, coalgebraically. In: Lodaya, K., Mahajan, M. (eds.) Proc. IARCS Annual Conference on Foundations of Software Technology and Theoretical Computer Science (FSTTCS 2010). Leibniz International Proceedings in Informatics (LIPIcs), vol. 8, pp. 272–283 (2010)
20. Silva, A., Bonchi, F., Bonsangue, M.M., Rutten, J.J.M.M.: Generalizing determinization from automata to coalgebras. Log. Methods Comput. Sci. 9(1:9) (2013)
21. Tao, T.: An Introduction to Measure Theory. AMS (2011)
22. Turi, D., Plotkin, G.: Towards a mathematical operational semantics. In: Logic in Computer Science, LICS 1997, pp. 280–291 (1997)
23. van Glabbeek, R.: The linear time-branching time spectrum (extended abstract). In: Baeten, J.C.M., Klop, J.W. (eds.) CONCUR 1990. LNCS, vol. 458, pp. 278–297. Springer, Heidelberg (1990)
24. Worrell, J.: On the final sequence of a finitary set functor. Theoret. Comput. Sci. 338, 184–199 (2005)

Localized Operational Termination
in General Logics[*]

Salvador Lucas[1,2] and José Meseguer[1]

[1] CS Dept. University of Illinois at Urbana-Champaign, IL, USA
[2] DSIC, Universitat Politècnica de València, Spain

Abstract. Termination can be thought of as the property of programs ensuring that every input is given an answer in finite time. There are, however, many different (combinations of) programming paradigms and languages for these paradigms. Is a common *formal* definition of termination of programs in any (or most) of these programming languages possible? The notion of *operational termination* provides a general definition of termination which relies on the logic-based description of (the operational semantics of) a *programming language*. The key point is capturing termination as the *absence of infinite inference*, that is: *all* proof attempts must either successfully terminate, or they must fail in finite time. This *global notion* is well-suited for most *declarative* languages, where programs are *theories* in a logic whose inference system is *specialized* to each theory to characterize its computations. Other programming languages (e.g., imperative languages) and applications (e.g., the evaluation of specific expressions and goals in functional and logic programs) require a more specialized treatment which pays attention not just to theories, but to specific *formulas* to be proved within the given theory. For instance, the execution of an imperative program can be viewed as a proof of an specific *formula* (representing the program) within the computational logic describing the operational semantics of the programming language. In such cases, an appropriate definition of termination should focus on proving the absence of infinite proofs for computations *localized* to *specific goals*. In this paper we generalize the global notion of operational termination to this new setting and adapt the recently introduced OT-framework for mechanizing proofs of operational termination to support proofs of *localized* operational termination.

Keywords: General Logics, Operational Termination, Program Termination.

1 Introduction

Martin Wirsing has made so many fundamental scientific contributions that, when trying to relate our paper for this Festschrift to them, we are forced to

[*] Partially supported by NSF grant CNS 13-19109. Salvador Lucas' research, developed during a sabbatical year at the UIUC, was also supported by the EU (FEDER), MECD grant PRX12/00214, MINECO projects TIN2010-21062-C02-02 and TIN 2013-45732-C4-1-P, and GV projects BEST/2014/026 and PROMETEO/2011/052.

R. De Nicola and R. Hennicker (Eds.): Wirsing Festschrift, LNCS 8950, pp. 91–114, 2015.
© Springer International Publishing Switzerland 2015

select only some of the important lines of research he has opened up, and, even in such lines, to mention just a few key papers.

Our present work should be viewed as closely connected with Martin's pioneering work on formal specification languages [23,24], and their use in giving a formal semantics to both programming languages [4] and sotware modeling languages [25,3]. A general idea emerging from all these papers is that formal specifications can be used either *directly* as declarative programs, or *indirectly* as providing a formal semantics for imperative languages or software modeling languages. The two main questions posed and addressed in this paper explore a practical aspect of this general idea:

1. Can we use general logics to give a language-independent notion of *termination* that applies to both declarative and imperative languages and also to modeling languages?
2. Can language-independent termination proof methods based on this general notion of termination be developed and used in practice?

Using the framework of general logics [16], we proposed, with other colleagues, the notion of *operational termination* as a first answer to question (1) focusing initially on declarative languages [15,9]. The idea is intuitively simple: a declarative program specified by a theory S in a logic $\mathcal{L}$ terminates if *no infinite proofs* are possible in S, so that an implementation trying to execute a goal will either succeed in finite time, or fail in all its proof attempts also in finite time.

More recently, we have given in [14] a first answer to question (2), also for declarative languages, by proposing a logic-independent Operational Termination Framework (OT Framework) based on the idea of *transforming* OT poblems into simpler ones by means of *processors*. This generalizes to any logic the dependency pair framework ideas of [11] used for proving termination of Term Rewriting Systems (TRS).

In this paper we answer for the first time questions (1) and (2) in their full generality; that is, for declarative languages and also for imperative languages or even for software modeling languages. The general idea is still the same: in all these cases the formal semantics will be given by an *inference system*, so that operational termination will be the absence of *infinite inference* in such a system. There is, however, a further generalization needed, namely, one allowing us to *localize* the inference to the relevant *goals*. For example, a programming language worth its salt will be Turing complete. Therefore, the operational termination of its inference system (for example, of the SOS rules defining its formal semantics) is a priori out of the question. But we are not interested in proving that *all* programs in such a language terminate: we just want to prove that *this* program P, or, more generally, *this* class $\mathcal{C}$ of programs (e.g., loop-free programs) do indeed terminate. Formally, what is needed is to *localize* the OT notion to a desired set Λ of goals (i.e., formulas) so that we can show absence of infinite inference for proof trees rooted on goals belonging to Λ. We then need to develop an OT framework parameterized by the class Λ of goals to which we are localizing our deduction.

$$\text{(Refl)} \quad \frac{}{t \to^* t} \qquad \text{(Tran)} \quad \frac{s \to u \quad u \to^* t}{s \to^* t} \qquad \text{(Cc)} \quad \frac{s \to t}{c(s) \to c(t)}$$

$$\text{(Cf)} \quad \frac{s \to t}{f(s) \to f(t)} \qquad \text{(Cg)} \quad \frac{s \to t}{g(s) \to g(t)} \qquad \text{(Repl1)} \quad \frac{}{g(a) \to c(b)}$$

$$\text{(Repl2)} \quad \frac{}{b \to f(a)} \qquad \text{(Repl3)} \quad \frac{}{f(d) \to d} \qquad \text{(Repl4)} \quad \frac{g(x) \to^* c(y)}{f(x) \to x}$$

Fig. 1. Inference rules for the CTRS in Example 1

As we show in examples, this localization idea is useful not just for imperative or modeling languages, but for declarative ones as well, because we are often interested in the termination not of all possible goals, but of a restricted class Λ. Let us consider some examples.

Example 1. The following *Conditional Term Rewriting System* (CTRS) $\mathcal{R}$:

$$\begin{aligned} g(a) &\to c(b) & f(d) &\to d \\ b &\to f(a) & f(x) &\to x \Leftarrow g(x) \to c(y) \end{aligned}$$

is *not* operationally terminating: there is an infinite proof tree for the inference system in Figure 1, which *specializes* the generic inference system of the CTRS logic (see Figure 3) to $\mathcal{R}$:

$$\frac{\dfrac{\dfrac{}{g(a) \to c(b)} \quad \dfrac{\dfrac{}{b \to f(a)}}{c(b) \to c(f(a))} \quad \dfrac{\dfrac{\vdots}{f(a) \to a}}{c(f(a)) \to c(a)} \quad c(a) \to^* c(b)}{c(f(a)) \to^* c(b)}}{\dfrac{c(b) \to^* c(b)}{\dfrac{g(a) \to^* c(b)}{f(a) \to a}}}$$

This infinite proof concerns a *single* rewriting step $f(a) \to a$.

Even though there are infinite proof trees for *goals* like $f(a) \to a$ in the example, there can be *similar* goals (e.g., $f(d) \to d$) which are *operationally terminating*, i.e., no infinite proof tree arises when a proof is attempted for such a goal. However, the current, *global* notion of operational termination of a given theory S in a logic $\mathcal{L}$ [15, Definition 4] does *not* give an account of these *local* phenomena. But such *local* phenomena are actually essential to characterize termination in other programming languages, like the imperative language **IMP** (see, e.g., [22, Chapter 2]).

Example 2. Consider the following imperative program P:

```
x:=10;
while x > 0 do x:=x-1
```

The operational semantics of imperative programming languages often describes computations as transformations from certain *configurations* involving *states* (i.e., assignments of values to the program variables) and *program expressions* and returning a final state which represents the outcome of the program (if any). The inference rules describing a big-step operational semantics for **IMP** are given in Figure 2 (see [22, Chapter 2]; for simplicity, only the inference rules that are needed for the execution of P are shown). Termination of P *cannot* be proved

(Const) $$\overline{\langle \rho \mid \mathbf{n} \rangle \Rightarrow_N n}$$ if **n** represents $n \in \mathbb{N}$ (Var) $$\overline{\langle \rho \mid \mathbf{x} \rangle \Rightarrow_N \rho(\mathbf{x})}$$

(True) $$\overline{\langle \rho \mid \mathtt{true} \rangle \Rightarrow_B \mathtt{true}}$$ (False) $$\overline{\langle \rho \mid \mathtt{false} \rangle \Rightarrow_B \mathtt{false}}$$

(GT) $$\frac{\langle \rho \mid a \rangle \Rightarrow_N n \quad \langle \rho \mid a' \rangle \Rightarrow_N n'}{\langle \rho \mid a > a' \rangle \Rightarrow_B \mathtt{true}}$$ if n is greater than n' (GF) $$\frac{\langle \rho \mid a \rangle \Rightarrow_N n \quad \langle \rho \mid a' \rangle \Rightarrow_N n'}{\langle \rho \mid a > a' \rangle \Rightarrow_B \mathtt{false}}$$ if n is not greater than n'

(Sub) $$\frac{\langle \rho \mid a \rangle \Rightarrow_N n \quad \langle \rho \mid a' \rangle \Rightarrow_N n'}{\langle \rho \mid a - a' \rangle \Rightarrow_N m}$$ where m is $n - n'$ (Assig) $$\frac{\langle \rho \mid a \rangle \Rightarrow_N n}{\langle \rho \mid x := a \rangle \Downarrow \rho[x \mapsto n]}$$

(Seq) $$\frac{\langle \rho \mid S \rangle \Downarrow \rho'' \quad \langle \rho'' \mid S' \rangle \Downarrow \rho'}{\langle \rho \mid S; S' \rangle \Downarrow \rho'}$$ (WhF) $$\frac{\langle \rho \mid b \rangle \Rightarrow_B \mathtt{false}}{\langle \rho \mid \mathtt{while}\ b\ \mathtt{do}\ S \rangle \Downarrow \rho}$$

(WhT) $$\frac{\langle \rho \mid b \rangle \Rightarrow_B \mathtt{true} \quad \langle \rho \mid S \rangle \Downarrow \rho'' \quad \langle \rho'' \mid \mathtt{while}\ b\ \mathtt{do}\ S \rangle \Downarrow \rho'}{\langle \rho \mid \mathtt{while}\ b\ \mathtt{do}\ S \rangle \Downarrow \rho'}$$

Fig. 2. Excerpt of inference rules for the programming language **IMP**

as the absence of *any* infinite proof tree for the inference system in Figure 2. In fact, since **IMP** is Turing complete, operational termination of **IMP**'s inference system would mean that all programs terminate, which is obviously false. Note also that, in sharp contrast to Figure 1 for $\mathcal{R}$ in Example 1, where each CTRS has it own, specialized inference system, the **IMP** inference system *is the same* for all (terminating or nonterminating) **IMP** programs! This problem can be solved with a *localized* notion of operational termination for *specific* goals like, e.g., the one representing the execution of P:

$$\langle \rho_0 \mid \mathtt{x:=10;\ while\ x>0\ do\ x:=x-1} \rangle \Downarrow \rho$$

where ρ_0 is an arbitrary valuation of variables.

Of course, the need for a localized notion of termination does not arise just for imperative programs, or because the logic has a single theory of interest. It is also felt for declarative programs which are understood as program-specific theories.

(Refl) $\quad \overline{t \to^* t}$	(Cong) $\dfrac{s_i \to t_i}{f(s_1, \ldots, s_i, \ldots, s_k) \to f(s_1, \ldots, t_i, \ldots, s_k)}$ for all k-ary symbols f and $1 \leq i \leq k$
(Tran) $\dfrac{s \to u \quad u \to^* t}{s \to^* t}$	(Repl) $\dfrac{s_1 \to^* t_1 \ \cdots \ s_n \to^* t_n}{\ell \to r}$ for each rule $\ell \to r \Leftarrow s_1 \to t_1 \cdots s_n \to t_n$

Fig. 3. Inference rules for the CTRS logic (all variables are universally quantified)

This is because not all formulas are equally meaningful. For example, a declarative concurrent object system can be naturally programmed with rewrite rules modulo AC [17]. But not all concurrent object configurations are meaningful: configurations where object identities are unique are essential for many purposes. See Examples 7 to 10 in Section 3 and various examples throughout the paper for other illustration of the general need for local operational termination.

In this paper we address this problem and make the following contributions: (1) we generalize the definition of operational termination to make it parametric on a set of *initial* formulas Λ which are used to restrict the number of considered proof trees; (2) we generalize the recently introduced framework for proving operational termination of theories in general logics [14] to deal with such *localized* operational termination problems; then, (3) we use the new *localized* formulation of the OT framework to illustrate how such proofs can be achieved in practice; finally, (4) we show that the notion of locality is helpful to characterize and prove termination of *imperative* programs based on their formal semantics.

2 Logics and Operational Termination

Our general notion of logic is in the spirit of both *entailment systems* in [16], and *schematic axiomatic systems* in [1], but is made more expresive by supporting inference systems (closely related to Aczels' axiomatic systems) that are *parametric* not just on signatures, but also on *theories*. This need is clearly illustrated by the CTRS inference system in Figure 3.

Example 3. When the inference system in Figure 3 is specialized to $\mathcal{R}$ in Example 1, the generic (*Cong*) rule specializes to *three* concrete rules (for c, f and g, respectively), and (*Repl*) inference rule specializes to *four* concrete inference rules, one for each rewrite rule. This specialization is shown in Figure 1.

A second feature of inference is that, even when alredy specialized to a given theory $\mathcal{S}$, the inference rules are *schematic*. That is, for $\mathcal{S}$ the CTRS in Example 1 we have a *finite* set of inference rules, but an infinite set of *instantiations* of such rules to concrete formulas in the syntax of Example 1. This is made explicit in the formulation of the (*Repl*) rule and is left implicit for the other rules, where t, r, s, u, and so on, are *meta-variables* instantiable by any term in the signature of Example 1.

Definition 1. *A logic $\mathcal{L}$ is a quadruple $\mathcal{L} = (Th(\mathcal{L}), Form, Sub, \mathcal{I})$, where: (i) $Th(\mathcal{L})$ is the class of theories of $\mathcal{L}$, (ii) Form is a mapping sending each theory $\mathcal{S} \in Th(\mathcal{L})$ to a set $Form(\mathcal{S})$ of formulas of $\mathcal{S}$, (iii) Sub is a mapping sending each $\mathcal{S} \in Th(\mathcal{L})$ to its set $Sub(\mathcal{S})$ of substitutions, with a containment $Sub(\mathcal{S}) \subseteq [Form(\mathcal{S}) \to Form(\mathcal{S})]$, and (iv) $\mathcal{I}$ is a mapping sending each $\mathcal{S} \in Th(\mathcal{L})$ to a subset $\mathcal{I}(\mathcal{S}) \subseteq Form(\mathcal{S}) \times Form(\mathcal{S})^*$, where each $(A, B_1 \ldots B_n) \in \mathcal{I}(\mathcal{S})$ is called an* inference rule *for $\mathcal{S}$ and denoted $\frac{B_1 \ldots B_n}{A}$.*

Example 4. For $\mathcal{L} = CTRS$, (i) $Th(CTRS)$ is the class of CTRSs $\mathcal{R} = (\mathcal{F}, R)$ with $\mathcal{F}$ a signature and R a set of conditional rules (with terms over the signature $\mathcal{F}$ and set of variables $\mathcal{X}$); (ii) $Form(\mathcal{R}) = \{s \to t \mid s, t \in \mathcal{T}(\mathcal{F}, \mathcal{X})\} \cup \{s \to^* t \mid s, t \in \mathcal{T}(\mathcal{F}, \mathcal{X})\}$, where $\mathcal{T}(\mathcal{F}, \mathcal{X})$ is the $\mathcal{F}$-term algebra on the variables $\mathcal{X}$; (iii) $Sub(\mathcal{R}) = \{\lambda\varphi.\sigma(\varphi) \mid \sigma \in Hom_{\mathcal{F}}[\mathcal{T}(\mathcal{F}, \mathcal{X}) \to \mathcal{T}(\mathcal{F}, \mathcal{X})]\}$, where $Hom_{\mathcal{F}}[\mathcal{T}(\mathcal{F}, \mathcal{X}) \to \mathcal{T}(\mathcal{F}, \mathcal{X})]$ denotes the set of $\mathcal{F}$-endomorphisms of $\mathcal{T}(\mathcal{F}, \mathcal{X})$, and where $\sigma(s \to t) = \sigma(s) \to \sigma(t)$, and $\sigma(s \to^* t) = \sigma(s) \to^* \sigma(t)$; and (iv) $I(\mathcal{R})$ is the instantiation of the generic inference system of Figure 3 as exemplified in Example 1.

Example 5. For $\mathcal{L} = \mathbf{IMP}$, (i) $Th(\mathbf{IMP})$ consists of a *single* theory, also denoted $\mathbf{IMP}$; (ii) $Form(\mathbf{IMP})$ consists of the following formulas:

$$Form(\mathbf{IMP}) = \{\langle \rho \mid a \rangle \Rightarrow_N n \mid \rho \in Exp_{State}, a \in ExpA, n \in \mathbb{Z}\}$$
$$\cup \{\langle \rho \mid b \rangle \Rightarrow_B t \mid \rho \in Exp_{State}, b \in ExpB, t \in Bool\}$$
$$\cup \{\langle \rho \mid S \rangle \Downarrow \rho' \mid \rho, \rho' \in Exp_{State}, S \in Stmt\}$$

where Exp_{State} consists of variables (e.g., $\rho, \rho', \ldots$) and appropriate representations of memory states (e.g., finite sequences of pairs (x, n), where $x \in Var$ is a program variable and $n \in \mathbb{Z}$); and $ExpA$, $ExpB$ and $Stmt$ are the sets of *arithmetic/boolean expressions* and *statements* which are valid in $\mathbf{IMP}$, each including variables like $a, a', \ldots, b, b', \ldots, S, S', \ldots$ which are intended to be bound to the corresponding kind of expressions. Note that *program variables* x *are treated as constant symbols* at this logical level); (iii) $Sub(\mathbf{IMP})$ are mappings from $Form(\mathbf{IMP})$ to $Form(\mathbf{IMP})$ where given $\theta \in Sub(\mathbf{IMP})$ and $\phi \in Form(\mathbf{IMP})$, $\theta(\phi)$ is obtained by simultaneously replacing all occurrences of variables ρ, a, b, S of the types indicated above by expressions of the corresponding type associated to each variable in ϕ; and (iv) $I(\mathbf{IMP})$ is the inference system of Figure 2.

Note that if $A \in Form(\mathcal{S})$ and $\sigma \in Sub(\mathcal{S})$, then its *instantiation* $\sigma(A)$, denoted by $A\sigma$, is in $Form(\mathcal{S})$. In what follows we assume some standard properties about the substitutions $\sigma \in Sub(\mathcal{S})$ by making explicit a set of terms $Term(\mathcal{S})$ and a subset of variables $Var(\mathcal{S})$ such that there is an injective mapping $Sub(\mathcal{S}) \to [Var(\mathcal{S}) \to Term(\mathcal{S})]$.

Example 6. For $\mathcal{R} \in Th(CTRS)$, $Var(\mathcal{S}) = \mathcal{X}$, $Term(\mathcal{S}) = \mathcal{T}(\mathcal{F}, \mathcal{X})$, and $\lambda\varphi.\sigma(\varphi) \in Sub(\mathcal{R})$ is identified with the substitution $\sigma : \mathcal{X} \to \mathcal{T}(\mathcal{F}, \mathcal{X})$ (with the natural extension to formulas $s \to t$ and $s \to^* t$). This is similar for $\mathbf{IMP}$.

We then define $dom(\sigma) = \{x \in Var(\mathcal{S}) \mid x\sigma \neq x\}$, and assume that there is a set $fvars(P) \subseteq Var(\mathcal{S})$ of free variables for each $P \in Form(\mathcal{S})$. We assume three standard properties: (1) *Extensibility*: if $dom(\sigma) \subseteq Z \subseteq Var(\mathcal{S})$, then there is a τ with $dom(\tau) = Z$ such that if $fvars(\varphi) \subseteq dom(\sigma)$, then $\varphi\tau = \varphi\sigma$. (2) *Renaming*: if $fvars(\varphi) \neq \emptyset$ and $Y \subseteq Var(\mathcal{S})$ is finite, there are substitutions σ, σ' with $\varphi = \varphi\sigma\sigma'$ and $fvars(\varphi\sigma) \cap (fvars(\varphi) \cup Y) = \emptyset$. (3) *Gluing*: given $\{\sigma_n\}_{n\in\mathbb{N}}$ with $dom(\sigma_i) \cap dom(\sigma_j) = \emptyset$ whenever $i \neq j$, there is a σ with $dom(\sigma) = \bigcup_{n\in\mathbb{N}} dom(\sigma_n)$, and such that whenever $fvars(\varphi) \subseteq dom(\sigma_i)$ for some $i \in \mathbb{N}$, then $\varphi\sigma = \varphi\sigma_i$. Given $\phi, \varphi \in Form(\mathcal{S})$, $mgu_{\mathcal{S}}(\phi, \varphi) \subseteq Sub(\mathcal{S})$ denotes a set such that: (i) $\forall\sigma \in mgu_{\mathcal{S}}(\phi, \varphi)$, $\varphi\sigma = \phi\sigma$; and (ii) $\forall\tau \in Sub(\mathcal{S})$ such that $\phi\tau = \varphi\tau$, there is $\sigma \in mgu_{\mathcal{S}}(\phi, \varphi), \theta \in Sub(\mathcal{S})$ such that $\tau = \sigma\theta$.

Given a logic $\mathcal{L}$ and a theory $\mathcal{S} \in Th(\mathcal{L})$ its *theorems* are the formulas of $Form(\mathcal{S})$ for which we can derive a *closed* proof tree in the following sense:

Definition 2. *Let $\mathcal{L} = (Th(\mathcal{L}), Form, Sub, \mathcal{I})$ be a logic and $\mathcal{S} \in Th(\mathcal{L})$. Then, the set of (finite) proof trees for $\mathcal{S}$ and the root of a proof tree are defined inductively as follows. A proof tree T is either*

- *an* open goal, *simply denoted as G, where $G \in Form(\mathcal{S})$. Then, we denote $root(T) = G$.*
- *a* derivation tree *with root G, denoted as*

$$\frac{T_1 \quad \cdots \quad T_n}{G}(\rho)$$

where $G \in Form(\mathcal{S})$, $T_1,\ldots,T_n$ are proof trees (for $n \geq 0$), and $\rho : \frac{B_1\ldots B_n}{A}$ is an inference rule in $\mathcal{I}(\mathcal{S})$, such that $G = A\sigma$, $root(T_1) = B_1\sigma, \ldots, root(T_n) = B_n\sigma$ for some substitution $\sigma \in Sub(\mathcal{S})$. We write $root(T) = G$.

We say that a proof tree for $\mathcal{S}$ is closed *whenever it is finite and contains no open goals. If there is a closed proof tree T for $\varphi \in Form(\mathcal{S})$ using $I(\mathcal{S})$ (i.e., such that $root(T) = \varphi$), we often denote this by writing $\mathcal{S} \vdash \varphi$. Notice the difference between G, an open goal, and $\overline{G}(\rho)$, a simple derivation tree consisting of a goal closed by a rule ρ without premises.*

Definition 3. *A proof tree T for $\mathcal{S}$ is a* proper prefix *of a proof tree T' if there are one or more open goals $G_1,\ldots,G_n$ in T such that T' is obtained from T by replacing each G_i by a derivation tree T_i with root G_i. We denote this as $T \sqsubset T'$.*

An infinite proof tree *for $\mathcal{S}$ is an infinite increasing chain of finite trees, that is, a sequence $\{T_i\}_{i\in\mathbb{N}}$ such that for all i, $T_i \sqsubset T_{i+1}$.*

Definition 4 (Well-formed proof tree). *A proof tree T for $\mathcal{S}$ is* well-formed *if it is either an open goal, or a closed proof tree, or a derivation tree*

$$\frac{T_1 \quad \cdots \quad T_n}{G}(\rho)$$

where there is i, $1 \leq i \leq n$ such that $T_1,\ldots,T_{i-1}$ are closed, T_i is well-formed but not closed, and $T_{i+1},\ldots,T_n$ are open goals. An infinite proof tree for $\mathcal{S}$ is well-formed if it is an ascending chain of well-formed finite proof trees.

Definition 5 (Operational termination). *A theory S in a logic $\mathcal{L}$ is called* operationally terminating *if no infinite well-formed proof tree for S exists.*

Remark 1. Defining operational termination as the absence of infinite *well-formed* proof trees imposes a left-to-right subgoal evaluation proof strategy[1] when evaluating subgoals (see [15] for further motivation about that). This strategy is quite natural and has important advantages: (i) is complete (will find any closed proof tree that exists), (ii) avoids building infinite proof trees with several infinite but disjoint subtrees, and (iii) pinpoints a single failure goal when a non-closed well-formed tree cannot be further extended. One can of course consider inference systems that use other proof strategies. This suggests making the proof strategy S of choice an explicit parameter, so that one could define a broader notion of S-operational termination. We leave a detailed development of such a notion as an interesting topic of future work.

3   Localized Operational Termination

As remarked in the introduction, the main purpose of this paper is extending the notion of *operational termination* to make it *localized* to specific formulas. We first define the class of *proof trees* we are interested in.

Definition 6. *Given a subset $\Lambda \subseteq Form(S)$, we say that a proof tree T for S is Λ-localized if $root(T) = \sigma(\phi)$ for some $\phi \in \Lambda$ and $\sigma \in Sub(S)$.*

Note that a proof tree is Λ-localized only if $\Lambda \neq \emptyset$.

Definition 7 (Localized operational termination). *Given $S \in Th(\mathcal{L})$ and $\Lambda \subseteq Form(S)$, we say that S is Λ-local operationally terminating if there is no infinite Λ-localized well-formed proof tree for S.*

So Λ-local operational termination means that, for all initial goals φ which are instances $\varphi = \sigma(\phi)$ of some $\phi \in \Lambda$, an $\mathcal{L}$-interpreter will either succeed in finite time in producing a closed proof tree, or will fail in finite time, not being able to close or extend further any of the possible proof trees, after exhaustively searching all such proof trees. The following fact is obvious.

Proposition 1. *Let $S \in Th(\mathcal{L})$, $\Lambda \subseteq Form(S)$, $\theta \in Sub(S)$, and $\theta(\Lambda) = \{\theta(\phi) \mid \phi \in \Lambda\}$. If S is Λ-local operationally terminating, then it is $\theta(\Lambda)$-local operationally terminating.*

Example 7. If $\Lambda = \{\langle \lambda x.0 \mid \text{x:=10; while x>0 do x:=x-1}\rangle \Downarrow \rho\}$, then termination of P in Example 2 is by definition equivalent to Λ-local operational termination of the **IMP** logic.

---

[1] In a broad sense of the word "strategy," since the choice of inference rule used to extend the proof tree is non-deterministic.

Example 8. If $\Lambda = \{s \to^* t\}$ for specific *terms* s and t, then the Λ-*local* operational termination of $\mathcal{R}$ in Example 1 implies the *decidability* of the concrete reachability problem $s \to^* t$ in $\mathcal{R}$. This implies that local operational termination is, in general, *undecidable*.

Example 9. If $\Lambda = \{f(d) \to^* x\}$ for some variable x, then the Λ-*local* operational termination of $\mathcal{R}$ in Example 1 corresponds to the operational termination of rewriting computations starting from $f(d)$. This would correspond to the notion of *local (operational) termination* (for term $f(d)$) in (conditional) term rewriting, see, e.g., [10] for a similar notion for *unconditional* term rewriting.

Example 10. If $\Lambda = \{x \to y\}$ for variables x and y, then the Λ-*local* operational termination of a CTRS corresponds to termination of proofs of *one-step* rewritings. In [13], we investigate the appropriate definition of *normal forms* in Conditional TRSs and show that, besides requiring the *irreducibility* of such terms, it is desirable to ensure that normal forms of CTRSs do not have associated infinite proof trees. CTRSs fulfilling this requirement are called *normal* [13]. The $\{x \to y\}$-local operational termination (there referred to as 1-termination) of CTRSs is a sufficient condition for CTRSs to be normal.

Every theory $\mathcal{S}$ is $\emptyset$-local operationally terminating. If a theory $\mathcal{S}$ in a logic $\mathcal{L}$ is operationally terminating, then it is Λ-local operationally terminating for all $\Lambda \subseteq Form(\mathcal{S})$. Furthermore, operational termination can be viewed as a particular case of Λ-local operational termination. Given a logic $\mathcal{L}$ and $\mathcal{S} \in Th(\mathcal{L})$, we let $\Lambda_{\mathcal{S}} = \{A \mid (A, B_1, \ldots, B_n) \in \mathcal{I}(\mathcal{S}), n > 0\}$. Then, we have the following.

Theorem 1. *A theory $\mathcal{S}$ in a logic $\mathcal{L}$ is operationally terminating if and only if it is $\Lambda_{\mathcal{S}}$-local operationally terminating.*

4   Proof Jumps and Localized Operational Termination

In [14] operational termination of a theory $\mathcal{S}$ in a logic $\mathcal{L}$ is *characterized* as the absence of chains of *proof jumps*. Proof jumps capture the use of inference rules in a particular branch of a (possibly infinite) proof tree. In the following, we often denote sequences $B_1 \cdots B_n$ of formulas by the vector $\boldsymbol{B_n}$.

Definition 8. [14, Definitions 6 and 7] *Let $\mathcal{L}$ be a logic and $\mathcal{S} \in Th(\mathcal{L})$. A proof jump for $\mathcal{S}$ is a pair $(A \Uparrow \boldsymbol{B_n})$, where $n \geq 1$ and $A, B_1, \ldots, B_n \in Form(\mathcal{S})$. Let $Jumps(\mathcal{S})$ be the set of all proof jumps for $\mathcal{S}$. The set $\mathcal{J}_{\mathcal{S}}$ of proof jumps of $\mathcal{I}(\mathcal{S})$ is:*

$$\mathcal{J}_{\mathcal{S}} = \{(A \Uparrow \boldsymbol{B_i}) \mid \frac{\boldsymbol{B_n}}{A} \in \mathcal{I}(\mathcal{S}), 1 \leq i \leq n\}.$$

Example 11. The proof jumps for the inference rules in Figure 1 are:

(Tran1) $s \to^* t \Uparrow s \to u$ (Tran2) $s \to^* t \Uparrow (s \to u, \ u \to^* t)$

(Cc) $c(s) \to c(t) \Uparrow s \to t$ (Cf) $f(s) \to f(t) \Uparrow s \to t$

(Cg) $g(s) \to g(t) \Uparrow s \to t$ (Repl3) $f(x) \to x \Uparrow g(x) \to^* c(y)$

Example 12. The proof jumps for the inference rules in Figure 2 are

(GT1) $$\langle \rho \mid a > a' \rangle \Rightarrow_B \text{true} \Uparrow \langle \rho \mid a \rangle \Rightarrow_N n$$

(GT2) $$\langle \rho \mid a > a' \rangle \Rightarrow_B \text{true} \Uparrow (\langle \rho \mid a \rangle \Rightarrow_N n, \langle \rho \mid a' \rangle \Rightarrow_N n')$$

(GF1) $$\langle \rho \mid a > a' \rangle \Rightarrow_B \text{false} \Uparrow \langle \rho \mid a \rangle \Rightarrow_N n$$

(GF2) $$\langle \rho \mid a > a' \rangle \Rightarrow_B \text{false} \Uparrow (\langle \rho \mid a \rangle \Rightarrow_N n, \langle \rho \mid a' \rangle \Rightarrow_N n')$$

(S1) $$\langle \rho \mid a - a' \rangle \Rightarrow_N m \Uparrow \langle \rho \mid a \rangle \Rightarrow_N n$$

(S2) $$\langle \rho \mid a - a' \rangle \Rightarrow_N m \Uparrow (\langle \rho \mid a \rangle \Rightarrow_N n, \langle \rho \mid a' \rangle \Rightarrow_N n')$$

(As) $$\langle \rho \mid x := a \rangle \Downarrow \rho[x \mapsto n] \Uparrow \langle \rho \mid a \rangle \Rightarrow_N n$$

(Sq1) $$\langle \rho \mid S; S' \rangle \Downarrow \rho' \Uparrow \langle \rho \mid S \rangle \Downarrow \rho''$$

(Sq2) $$\langle \rho \mid S; S' \rangle \Downarrow \rho' \Uparrow (\langle \rho \mid S \rangle \Downarrow \rho'', \langle \rho'' \mid S' \rangle \Downarrow \rho')$$

(WF) $$\langle \rho \mid \text{while } b \text{ do } S \rangle \Downarrow \rho \Uparrow \langle \rho \mid b \rangle \Rightarrow_B \text{false}$$

(WT1) $$\langle \rho \mid \text{while } b \text{ do } S \rangle \Downarrow \rho' \Uparrow \langle \rho \mid b \rangle \Rightarrow_B \text{true}$$

(WT2) $$\langle \rho \mid \text{while } b \text{ do } S \rangle \Downarrow \rho' \Uparrow (\langle \rho \mid b \rangle \Rightarrow_B \text{true}, \langle \rho \mid S \rangle \Downarrow \rho'')$$

(WT3) $\langle \rho \mid \text{while } b \text{ do } S \rangle \Downarrow \rho' \Uparrow (\langle \rho \mid b \rangle \Rightarrow_B \text{true}, \langle \rho \mid S \rangle \Downarrow \rho'', \langle \rho'' \mid \text{while } b \text{ do } S \rangle \Downarrow \rho')$

Definition 9. [14, Definition 8] *Let $\mathcal{L}$ be a logic, $\mathcal{S} \in Th(\mathcal{L})$, and $\mathcal{J} \subseteq Jumps(\mathcal{S})$. An $(\mathcal{S}, \mathcal{J})$-chain is a sequence $(\psi_i)_{i \geq 1}$ of (renamed versions of) proof jumps $\psi_i : (A^i \Uparrow B^i_{n_i}) \in \mathcal{J}$ together with a substitution σ such that for all $i \geq 1$,*

1. *$\sigma(B^i_{n_i}) = \sigma(A^{i+1})$ and,*
2. *for all j, $1 \leq j < n_i$, $\mathcal{S} \vdash \sigma(B^i_j)$ holds.*

A proof jump $\psi = A \Uparrow B_n$ is connected to the *next* one by using the *last formula* B_n in the sequence B_n, provided that (the instances of) the B_i, $1 \leq i < n$, have closed proof trees in $\mathcal{I}(\mathcal{S})$. In the following, we call A, B_{n-1} and B_n the *head*, the *conditional part* and the *hook* of ψ, respectively.

Theorem 2. [14, Theorem 1] *A theory $\mathcal{S} \in Th(\mathcal{L})$ is operationally terminating if and only if there is no infinite $(\mathcal{S}, \mathcal{J}_\mathcal{S})$-chain.*

We use previous notions to characterize localized operational termination (Theorem 3). First, we need an auxiliary definition which is essential to define the OT-framework in Section 6 and represents the idea of a *conditional* use of formulas describing local operational termination (see Definition 11).

Definition 10 (Localization). *A (possibly empty) sequence $\gamma_1, \ldots, \gamma_n$ of formulas $\gamma_i \in Form(\mathcal{S})$, $1 \leq i \leq n$ together with a formula $\phi \in Form(\mathcal{S})$ is called a localization (for $\mathcal{S}$). Let $Loc(\mathcal{S}) = Form(\mathcal{S})^* \times Form(\mathcal{S})$ be the set of all localizations (γ, ϕ) for $\mathcal{S}$. Here, ϕ is called the localizing formula and γ is the list of localized conditions (which can be empty, i.e., $\gamma = \epsilon$).*

Remark 2 (Localizations and proof jumps). A localization $(\gamma, \phi) \in Loc(\mathcal{S})$ can be written $\triangle \Uparrow \gamma, \phi$ (for $\triangle$ a *dummy* symbol which could be identified with a constant boolean value, for example) emphasizing the idea that localizations can be seen as proof jumps whose head is *never used*. This approach will be very useful in the following.

Definition 11. *Let* $L \subseteq Loc(\mathcal{S})$. *An* $(\mathcal{S}, \mathcal{J})$-*chain* $(A_i \Uparrow B^i_{n_i})_{i \geq 1}$ *with substitution* σ *is* L-*localized if there is* $(\gamma, \phi) \in L$ *such that (1) for all* $\gamma \in \gamma$, $\mathcal{S} \vdash \sigma(\gamma)$ *holds and (2)* $\sigma(A_1) = \sigma(\phi)$.

The following result, whose proof is analogous to that of Theorem 2, characterizes *localized* operational termination.

Theorem 3. *A theory* $\mathcal{S} \in Th(\mathcal{L})$ *is* Λ-*local operationally terminating for some* $\Lambda \subseteq Form(\mathcal{S})$ *if and only if there is no infinite* $(\{e\} \times \Lambda)$-*localized* $(\mathcal{S}, \mathcal{J}_{\mathcal{S}})$-*chain.*

In the following, given $\mathcal{J} \subseteq Jumps(\mathcal{S})$, we let $L_{\mathcal{J}} = \{(\epsilon, A) \mid A \Uparrow B_n \in \mathcal{J}\}$.

5   Proof Graph

We trace $(\mathcal{S}, \mathcal{J})$-chains as paths in the *proof graph* $\mathsf{PG}(\mathcal{S}, \mathcal{J})$:

Definition 12. [14, Definition 9] *The* proof graph $\mathsf{PG}(\mathcal{S}, \mathcal{J})$ *has the proof jumps in* $\mathcal{J}$ *as the set of nodes. There is an arc from* $\psi : (A \Uparrow B_m)$ *to* $\psi' : (A' \Uparrow B'_n)$ *iff there is a substitution* σ *such that* $\sigma(B_m) = \sigma(A')$ *and, for all* j, $1 \leq j < m$, $\mathcal{S} \vdash \sigma(B_j)$ *holds. Here, we assume that* $fvars(\psi) \cap fvars(\psi') = \emptyset$ *for all* $\psi, \psi' \in \mathcal{J}$, $\psi \neq \psi'$ *(renamed if necessary).*

$\mathsf{PG}(\mathcal{S}, \mathcal{J})$ is not computable due to checking for the existence of closed proof trees for the $\sigma(B_j)$. We approximate it by just omitting such a requirement.

Definition 13. [14, Definition 10] *The* estimated proof graph $\mathsf{EPG}(\mathcal{S}, \mathcal{J})$ *has the same nodes than* $\mathsf{PG}(\mathcal{S}, \mathcal{J})$. *There is an arc from* $\psi : (A \Uparrow B_m)$ *to* $\psi' : (A' \Uparrow B'_n)$ *iff there is* $\sigma \in Sub(\mathcal{S})$ *such that* $\sigma(B_m) = \sigma(A')$.

Example 13. The graph $\mathsf{EPG}(\mathcal{R}, \mathcal{J})$ for $\mathcal{J}$ in Example 11 is the following:

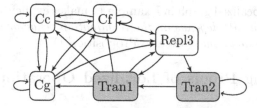

For instance, there is an arc from (Tran1) to (Cf) because $s \to u$ and $f(s') \to f(t')$ unify with substitution σ such that $\sigma(s) = f(s')$ and $\sigma(u) = f(t')$. Note that s, s', t' and u are *different variables* due to the possibility of renaming. And $\mathsf{EPG}(\mathbf{IMP}, \mathcal{J})$ for $\mathcal{J}$ in Example 12 is depicted in Figure 4.

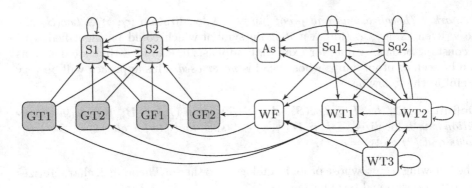

Fig. 4. Proof graph for the proof jumps in Example 12

Since L-localized chains must start at a node of the graph which unifies with some of the localizing formulas in L, we can restrict our attention to the *subgraph* of $\mathsf{PG}(\mathcal{S}, \mathcal{J})$ obtained as the *span* of such nodes. The *span* of $L \subseteq Loc(\mathcal{S})$ over $\mathsf{PG}(\mathcal{S}, \mathcal{J})$ is the subgraph of $\mathsf{PG}(\mathcal{S}, \mathcal{J})$ which is obtained from the nodes that are reachable from those nodes $A \Uparrow B$ in the graph satisfying that $\sigma(A) = \sigma(\phi)$ for some $(\gamma, \phi) \in L$ and substitution σ such that for all $\gamma \in \gamma$, $\mathcal{S} \vdash \sigma(\gamma)$ holds.

Definition 14 (Localized proof graph). *Let* $L \subseteq Loc(\mathcal{S})$. *The* L-*localized proof graph* $\mathsf{PG}_L(\mathcal{S}, \mathcal{J})$ *of* $(\mathcal{S}, \mathcal{J})$ *is the span of* L *over* $\mathsf{PG}(\mathcal{S}, \mathcal{J})$.

Again, the localized proof graph is not computable but can be approximated.

Definition 15 (Estimated localized proof graph). *Let* $L \subseteq Loc(\mathcal{S})$ *and* $L_0 = \{(\epsilon, \phi) \mid (\gamma, \phi) \in L\}$. *The* estimated L-*localized proof graph* $\mathsf{EPG}_L(\mathcal{S}, \mathcal{J})$ *of* $(\mathcal{S}, \mathcal{J})$ *is the span of* L_0 *over* $\mathsf{EPG}(\mathcal{S}, \mathcal{J})$.

Example 14. For $L = \{(\epsilon, \langle \rho \mid x := a \rangle \Downarrow \rho')\}$ (where x, a, ρ and ρ' are *variables*) and $\mathcal{J}$ in Example 12, with $\mathsf{EPG}(\mathbf{IMP}, \mathcal{J})$ in Figure 4, $\mathsf{EPG}_L(\mathbf{IMP}, \mathcal{J})$ is:

Remark 3. The L-localized graph in Example 14 makes explicit that *termination of assignment statements depends on the termination behavior of the evaluation of arithmetic expressions only* (see also Proposition 1).

6   Mechanizing Proofs of Localized Operational Termination

Let $OT(\mathcal{L})$ be the set of *Localized Operational Termination* Problems $(\mathcal{S}, \mathcal{J}, L)$, where $\mathcal{S}$ is a theory of $\mathcal{L}$, $\mathcal{J}$ is a set of proof jumps and L is a set of localizations.

$$OT(\mathcal{L}) = \{(\mathcal{S}, \mathcal{J}, L) \mid \mathcal{S} \in Th(\mathcal{L}), \mathcal{J} \subseteq Jumps(\mathcal{S}), L \subseteq Loc(\mathcal{S})\}$$

Definition 16 (Localized OT problem). *The OT problem* $\tau = (\mathcal{S}, \mathcal{J}, L)$ *is finite iff there is no infinite L-localized* $(\mathcal{S}, \mathcal{J})$-*chain;* τ *is infinite iff it is not finite, i.e., there is an infinite L-localized* $(\mathcal{S}, \mathcal{J})$-*chain.*

We can recast now Theorem 3 as follows:

Theorem 4. *A theory* $\mathcal{S}$ *in a logic* $\mathcal{L}$ *is* Λ-*local operationally terminating for some* $\Lambda \subseteq Form(\mathcal{S})$ *if and only if* $(\mathcal{S}, \mathcal{J}_\mathcal{S}, \{\epsilon\} \times \Lambda)$ *is finite.*

When proofs of Λ-local operational termination are attempted, we often refer to the OT problem $\tau_1 = (\mathcal{S}, \mathcal{J}_\mathcal{S}, \{\epsilon\} \times \Lambda)$ as the *initial* OT problem.

Example 15. With $\Lambda = \{f(d) \to t\}$ in Example 9, the *initial* OT problem for $\mathcal{R}$ in Example 1 is $\tau_1 = (\mathcal{R}, \mathcal{J}, \{(\epsilon, f(d) \to t)\})$ with $\mathcal{J}$ as in Example 11.

Example 16. With $\Lambda = \{\langle \lambda x.0 \mid \texttt{x.=10; while x>0 do x:=x-1} \rangle \Downarrow \rho\}$ for P in Example 2, the *initial* OT problem is

$$\tau_1 = (\mathbf{IMP}, \mathcal{J}, \{(\epsilon, \langle \lambda x.0 \mid \texttt{x:=10; while x>0 do x:=x-1} \rangle \Downarrow \rho\})$$

with $\mathcal{J}$ as in Example 12.

And, according to Theorem 1, we have the following.

Corollary 1. *A theory* $\mathcal{S}$ *in a logic* $\mathcal{L}$ *is operationally terminating if and only if* $(\mathcal{S}, \mathcal{J}_\mathcal{S}, \{\epsilon\} \times \Lambda_\mathcal{S})$ *is finite.*

In the OT Framework, *processors* are intended to facilitate proofs of operational termination by *simplifying* OT problems in a number of ways.

Definition 17. [14, Definition 12] *An OT processor is a function* $\mathsf{P} : OT(\mathcal{L}) \to \mathcal{P}(OT(\mathcal{L})) \cup \{\mathsf{no}\}$ *which maps an OT problem into either a set of OT problems or the answer* "no". P *is*

- *sound if for all OT problems* τ, *we have that* τ *is finite whenever* $\mathsf{P}(\tau) \neq \mathsf{no}$ *and all OT problems in* $\mathsf{P}(\tau)$ *are finite.*
- *complete if for all OT problems* τ, *we have that* τ *is infinite whenever* $\mathsf{P}(\tau) = \mathsf{no}$ *or* $\mathsf{P}(\tau)$ *contains an infinite OT problem.*

Processors transform OT problems in a *divide and conquer* scheme by decomposing OT problems into smaller ones, which are then independently treated. This yields what we call an *OTF-tree* (see Definition 18 below), which collects all successive applications until a *trivial* OT problem (which can be easily proved finite) is obtained. Trivial OT problems $(\mathcal{S}, \mathcal{J}, L)$ are those where $\mathcal{J} = \emptyset$ or $L = \emptyset$. Then, no L-localized $(\mathcal{S}, \mathcal{J})$-chain is possible.

Definition 18. [14, Definition 13] *Let* $\tau_0 \in OT(\mathcal{L})$. *We construct a tree (which we call an OTF-tree for* τ_0) *whose nodes are labeled with either OT problems or* "yes" *or* "no"; *the root is labeled with* τ_0. *For every inner node* n *with label* τ, *there is a processor* P *such that:*

1. *if* $\mathsf{P}(\tau) = \mathsf{no}$ *then* n *has a single child with label* "no".
2. *if* $\mathsf{P}(\tau) = \emptyset$ *then* n *has a single child with label* "yes".
3. *if* $\mathsf{P}(\tau) = \{\tau_1, \ldots, \tau_m\}$ *for some* $m > 0$, *then* n *has children* $\mathsf{n}_1, \ldots, \mathsf{n}_m$ *with labels* $\tau_1, \ldots, \tau_m$ *respectively*.

The following result formalizes the use of processors in our proof framework.

Theorem 5. [14, Theorem 3] *Let* $\tau \in OT(\mathcal{L})$. *If all leaves of an OTF-tree for* τ *are labeled with* "yes" *and all involved processors are sound, then* τ *is finite. If there is a leaf labeled with* "no" *and all processors used on the path from the root to this leaf are complete, then* τ *is infinite.*

Remark 4. In the following, $\mathcal{J}$ is *finite* in every OT-problem $(\mathcal{S}, \mathcal{J}, L)$.

7   Some Processors for the Localized OT Framework

This section introduces several processors to prove operational termination in the (localized) OT framework. In the following, given a set $\mathcal{J}$ of proof jumps (or localizations, viewed as proof jumps) and $\psi \in \mathcal{J}$, the (possible) *replacement* $\mathcal{J}[\mathcal{K}]_\psi$ of ψ in $\mathcal{J}$ by the (possibly empty) set of proof jumps in $\mathcal{K}$ is given by:

$$\mathcal{J}[\mathcal{K}]_\psi = \begin{cases} (\mathcal{J} - \{\psi\}) \cup \mathcal{K} & \text{if } \psi \in \mathcal{J} \\ \mathcal{J} & \text{otherwise} \end{cases}$$

Our first processor just shows that localization formulas can be handled separately in proofs of operational termination.

Theorem 6 (Decomposition of local formulas). *Let* $(\mathcal{S}, \mathcal{J}, L) \in OT(\mathcal{L})$.

$$\mathsf{P}_{DecL}(\mathcal{S}, \mathcal{J}, L) = \{(\mathcal{S}, \mathcal{J}, \{\lambda\}) \mid \lambda \in L\}$$

is a sound and complete processor.

Remark 5. If L is *infinite*, then P_{DecL} yields an OTF-tree with nodes of *infinite* degree (i.e., having infinitely many branches), which is nevertheless well defined. Although using such a tree for proving an OT problem finite is unfeasible, proofs of infiniteness of OT problems are still possible as they amount to checking that there is a branch of *finite depth* with a leaf labeled with no.

7.1   Expansion of Localizations and Proof Jumps

Recall the set $mgu_\mathcal{S}(A, B)$ of most general unifiers of formulas $A, B \in Form(\mathcal{S})$ in Section 2. If $\psi = A \Uparrow \boldsymbol{B}_n$ (where A can be $\triangle$), we let

$$\mathcal{K}_\psi(\mathcal{J}) = \{(C \Uparrow \boldsymbol{D}_m, \theta) \mid C \Uparrow \boldsymbol{D}_m \in \mathcal{J}, \theta \in mgu_\mathcal{S}(B_n, C)\}$$

representing the set of proof jumps that can *immediately follow* ψ in an $(\mathcal{S}, \mathcal{J})$-*chain*. The following processor uses proof jumps to *expand* the hook B_n of $\psi = A \Uparrow \boldsymbol{B}_n$ in such a way that all possible connections on B_n are considered.

Theorem 7 (Expansion with proof jumps). *Let* $(S, J, L) \in OT(\mathcal{L})$ *and* $\psi \in J \cup L$ *be* $\psi = A \Uparrow B_n$. *Let*

$$\mathcal{H} = \{\theta(A) \Uparrow \theta(B_1), \ldots, \theta(B_{n-1}), \theta(D_1), \ldots, \theta(D_m) \mid (C \Uparrow D_m, \theta) \in \mathcal{K}_\psi(J)\}$$

Then,

$$\mathsf{P}_{EPJ}(S, J, L) = \{(S, J[\mathcal{H}]_\psi, L[\mathcal{H}]_\psi)\}$$

is a sound and complete processor.

If $\mathcal{H}$ in Theorem 7 is *empty*, a proof jump (if $\psi \in J$) or localization (if $\psi \in L$) is *removed*.

Example 17. Consider $\tau_1 = (\mathcal{R}, J, \{(\epsilon, \mathsf{f}(\mathsf{d}) \to t)\})$ in Example 15. The expansion of $(\epsilon, \mathsf{f}(\mathsf{d}) \to t)$ (or $\triangle \Uparrow \mathsf{f}(\mathsf{d}) \to t$, in proof-jump-like notation) in Example 15 using (Cf) and (Repl3) in Example 11 yields $L' = \{(\epsilon, \mathsf{d} \to u'), (\epsilon, g(\mathsf{d}) \to^* \iota(y))\}$. Hence, $\mathsf{P}_{EPJ}(\tau_1) = \{\tau_2\}$, where $\tau_2 = (\mathcal{R}, J, L')$.

Now, $\mathsf{P}_{DecL}(\tau_2) = \{\tau_{31}, \tau_{32}\}$, where $\tau_{31} = (\mathcal{R}, J, \{(\epsilon, \mathsf{d} \to u')\})$ and $\tau_{32} = (\mathcal{R}, J, \{(\epsilon, g(\mathsf{d}) \to^* c(y))\})$. An application of P_{EPJ} to τ_{31} proves it finite, because no expansion of $\mathsf{d} \to u'$ with the proof jumps in J is possible. Therefore, $\mathsf{P}_{EPJ}(\tau_{31}) = \{(\mathcal{R}, J, \emptyset)\}$, which is a finite OT problem. On the other hand, $\mathsf{P}_{EPJ}(\tau_{32}) = \{\tau_{321}\}$, where $\tau_{321} = (\mathcal{R}, J, \{(g(\mathsf{d}) \to u, u \to^* c(y))\})$.

Example 18. For $\tau_1 = (\mathbf{IMP}, J, L)$ in Example 16, we use P_{EPJ} to transform L (using (Sq1) and (Sq2)) as follows: $\mathsf{P}_{EPJ}(\tau_1) = \{(IMP, J, L_2)\}$, where

$$L_2 = \{(\epsilon, \langle x \mapsto 0 \mid A\rangle \Downarrow \rho'), (\langle x \mapsto 0 \mid A\rangle \Downarrow \rho', \langle \rho' \mid W\rangle \Downarrow \rho)\}$$

with $A = \mathtt{x:=10}$ and $W = \mathtt{while\ x>0\ do\ x:=x-1}$. Let $\tau_2 = (IMP, J, L_2)$. Now, $\mathsf{P}_{DecL}(\tau_2) = \{\tau_{31}, \tau_{32}\}$, where $\tau_{31} = (IMP, J, L_{31})$ and $\tau_{32} = (IMP, J, L_{32})$, with $L_{31} = \{(\epsilon, \langle x \mapsto 0 \mid A\rangle \Downarrow \rho')\}$ and $L_{32} = \{(\langle x \mapsto 0 \mid A\rangle \Downarrow \rho', \langle \rho' \mid W\rangle \Downarrow \rho)\}$.

The following processor uses *inference rules* to *expand* the *internal* B_i within a given $\psi = A \Uparrow B_n$ (again, A can be $\triangle$) in such a way that all possible proof trees for any instance of the proof jump are still considered. Let $(S, J, L) \in OT(\mathcal{L})$, $\psi = A \Uparrow B_n \in J \cup L$ and i, $1 \le i < n$, we let

$$\mathcal{I}_{\psi,i}(S) = \{(\frac{D_m}{C}, \theta) \mid \frac{D_m}{C} \in \mathcal{I}(S), \theta \in mgu_S(B_n, C)\}$$

representing the set of inference rules that can be *immediately used* in a closed proof tree of $\sigma(B_i)$ for some B_i in ψ in a (S, J)-*chain*.

Theorem 8 (Expansion with inference rules). *Let* $(S, J, L) \in OT(\mathcal{L})$, $\psi \in J \cup L$ *where* $\psi = A \Uparrow B_n$, *and* i, $1 \le i < n$. *Let*

$$\mathcal{H} = \{\theta(A) \Uparrow \theta(B_{i-1}, D_m, B_{i+1}, \ldots, B_n) \mid (\frac{D_m}{C}, \theta) \in \mathcal{I}_{\psi,i}(S)\}$$

Then,

$$\mathsf{P}_{EIR}(S, J, L) = \{(S, J[\mathcal{H}]_\psi, L[\mathcal{H}]_\psi)\}$$

is a sound and complete processor.

Example 19. Consider $\tau_{321} = (\mathcal{R}, \mathcal{J}, \{(g(d) \to u, u \to^* c(y))\})$ in Example 17. Using the inference rule (Cg) in Figure 1, we have $\mathsf{P}_{EIR}(\tau_{321}) = \{\tau_{3211}\}$, where $\tau_{3211} = (\mathcal{R}, \mathcal{J}, \{(d \to t, g(t) \to^* c(y))\})$.

7.2   Removing Useless Proof Jumps and Localizations

No proof jump or localization $\psi : A \Uparrow \boldsymbol{B}_n$ with i, $1 \le i < n$ such that for all substitution σ, $\mathcal{S} \vdash \sigma(B_i)$ does *not* hold can be used in any L-localized $(\mathcal{S}, \mathcal{J})$-chain. Thus, ψ can be removed from any OT problem.

Theorem 9 (Unsatisfiable jumps). *Let* $(\mathcal{S}, \mathcal{J}, L) \in OT(\mathcal{L})$. *Let* $\psi \in \mathcal{J} \cup L$ *be such that* $\psi = (A \Uparrow \boldsymbol{B}_n)$ *and there is* i, $1 \le i < n$ *such that for all substitutions* σ, $\mathcal{S} \vdash \sigma(B_i)$ *does* not *hold. Then,*

$$\mathsf{P}_{UJ}(\mathcal{S}, \mathcal{J}, \Lambda) = \{(\mathcal{S}, \mathcal{J}[\emptyset]_\psi, L[\emptyset]_\psi)\}$$

is a sound and complete processor.

Example 20. Consider $\tau_{3211} = (\mathcal{R}, \mathcal{J}, \{(d \to t, g(t) \to^* c(y))\})$ in Example 19. Since no inference rule can be applied to $d \to t$, we have $\mathsf{P}_{UJ}(\tau_{3211}) = \{(\mathcal{R}, \mathcal{J}, \emptyset)\}$, which contains a finite problem. This finally proves the $\{f(d) \to t\}$-local operational termination of $\mathcal{R}$ in Example 1 (see Figure 5).

7.3   SCC Processor

Since we assume $\mathcal{J}$ finite (Remark 4), infinite $(\mathcal{S}, \mathcal{J})$-chains correspond to *cycles* in $\mathsf{PG}(\mathcal{S}, \mathcal{J})$. The following processor decomposes the graph associated to an OT problem into its *strongly connected components* (SCCs), i.e., maximal cycles occurring in $\mathsf{PG}(\mathcal{S}, \mathcal{J})$. In the following, given a set $\mathcal{J}$ of proof jumps, we let $\Lambda_\mathcal{J}$ be the set of *head formulas* in each proof jump in $\mathcal{J}$: $\Lambda_\mathcal{J} = \{A \mid A \Uparrow \boldsymbol{B}_n \in \mathcal{J}\}$:

Theorem 10 (SCC processor). *For each* $(\mathcal{S}, \mathcal{J}, L) \in OT(\mathcal{L})$,

$$\mathsf{P}_{SCC}(\mathcal{S}, \mathcal{J}, L) = \{(\mathcal{S}, \mathcal{J}', L_{\mathcal{J}'}) \mid \mathcal{J}' \text{ is an SCC in } \mathsf{PG}_L(\mathcal{S}, \mathcal{J})\}$$

is a sound and (if $L_{\mathcal{J}'} \subseteq L$) complete processor.

As a consequence of this theorem, we can *separately* work with the strongly connected components of $\mathsf{PG}_L(\mathcal{S}, \mathcal{J})$, disregarding other parts of the graph.

Example 21. For $\tau_{31} = (\mathbf{IMP}, \mathcal{J}, L_{31})$ in Example 18, with $\mathsf{PG}_{L_{31}}(\mathbf{IMP}, \mathcal{J})$ in Example 14, $\mathsf{P}_{SCC}(\tau_{31}) = \{\tau_{311}\}$, where $\tau_{311} = (\mathbf{IMP}, \{(S1), (S2)\}, L_{311})$, and $L_{311} = \{(\epsilon, \langle \rho \mid a - a' \rangle \Rightarrow_N m)\}$.

Note that, after using P_{SCC} most information about localization can be *lost*.

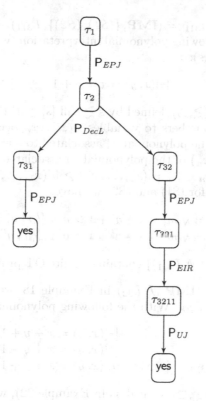

Fig. 5. OTF-tree for Λ and $\mathcal{R}$ in Example 1

7.4   Use of Well-Founded Relations

As shown in [14], well-founded relations are often useful to simplify OT problems.

Definition 19. [14, Definition 14] *A removal pair* $(\gtrsim, \sqsupset)$ *consists of a relation* $\gtrsim$, *and a well-founded relation* $\sqsupset$ *satisfying either* $\gtrsim \circ \sqsupset \, \subseteq \, \sqsupset$ *or* $\sqsupset \circ \gtrsim \, \subseteq \, \sqsupset$.

In our setting we have to be careful with localization formulas.

Theorem 11 (Removal pair processor). *Let* $(\mathcal{S}, \mathcal{J}, L) \in OT(\mathcal{L})$, *where* $\mathcal{J} = \{C \Uparrow \boldsymbol{D}_m\} \uplus \mathcal{J}_0$ *and* $L = \{\lambda\}$ *with* $\lambda = (\gamma, \phi)$. *Let* $(\gtrsim, \sqsupset)$ *be a removal pair such that, for all substitutions* σ, *(1) for all* $A \Uparrow \boldsymbol{B}_n \in \mathcal{J}_0$, *if for all* $1 \leq i < n$, $\mathcal{S} \vdash \sigma(B_i)$ *holds, then* $\sigma(A) \gtrsim \sigma(B_n)$ *holds; and (2) if for all* $1 \leq i < m$, $\mathcal{S} \vdash \sigma(B_i)$ *holds, then* $\sigma(C) \sqsupset \sigma(D_m)$. *Let* $L' = L \cup \{(\theta(\gamma \boldsymbol{D}_{m-1}), \theta(D_m)) \mid \theta \in mgu_{\mathcal{S}}(\phi, C)\}$. *Then,*

$$\mathsf{P}_{RP}(\mathcal{S}, \mathcal{J}, L) = \{(\mathcal{S}, \mathcal{J}_0, L')\}$$

is a sound and complete processor.

Example 22. We prove $\tau_{311} = (\mathbf{IMP}, \{(S1), (S2)\}, L_{311})$ in Example 21 finite using P_{RP}. With the following polynomial interpretation (with variables ranging over the natural numbers):

$$[\langle \_ \mid \_ \rangle](x, y) = y \qquad [\text{-}](x, y) = x + y + 1 \qquad [\Rightarrow_N](x, y) = x$$

we have a removal pair $(\gtrsim, \sqsupset)$ defined by $s \gtrsim t$ iff $[s] \geq [t]$ (i.e., for each possible assignment of natural numbers to variables $x_1, \ldots, x_n$ occurring in s or t the value $[s](x_1, \ldots, x_n)$ of the polynomial $[s]$ associated to s is bigger than or equal to the value $[t](x_1, \ldots, x_n)$ of the polynomial $[t]$ associated to term t, i.e., $s \gtrsim t$ if and only if $\forall x_1, \ldots, x_n \in \mathbb{N}, [s](x_1, \ldots, x_n) \geq [t](x_1, \ldots, x_n))$ and (similarly) $s \sqsupset t$ iff $[s] > [t]$. Then, for (S1) and (S2) we have:

$$[\langle \rho \mid a - a' \rangle \Rightarrow_N m] = a + a' + 1 > a = [\langle \rho \mid a \rangle \Rightarrow_N n]$$
$$[\langle \rho \mid a - a' \rangle \Rightarrow_N m] = a + a' + 1 > a' = [\langle \rho \mid a' \rangle \Rightarrow_N n']$$

and $\mathsf{P}_{RP}(\tau_{311}) = \{(\mathbf{IMP}, \emptyset, L_{311})\}$ contains a finite OT problem $(\mathbf{IMP}, \emptyset, L_{311})$.

Example 23. For $\tau_{32} = (\mathbf{IMP}, \mathcal{J}, L_{32})$ in Example 18, we remove most proof jumps from $\mathcal{J}$ by using P_{RP}. With the following polynomial interpretation:

$$\begin{aligned}
[\langle \_ \mid \_ \rangle](x, y) &= y & [\text{-}](x, y) &= x + y + 1 & [\Rightarrow_N](x, y) &= x \\
[:=](x, y) &= y + 1 & [>](x, y) &= x + y + 1 & [\Rightarrow_B](x, y) &= x \\
[;](x, y) &= x + y + 1 & [\texttt{while\_do\_}](x, y) &= x + y + 1 & [\Downarrow](x, y) &= x
\end{aligned}$$

over the naturals (and $(\gtrsim, \sqsupset)$ defined as in Example 22), we have:

$$\begin{aligned}
[\langle \rho \mid a - a' \rangle \Rightarrow_N m] &= a + a' + 1 > a = [\langle \rho \mid a \rangle \Rightarrow_N n] \\
[\langle \rho \mid a - a' \rangle \Rightarrow_N m] &= a + a' + 1 > a' = [\langle \rho \mid a' \rangle \Rightarrow_N n'] \\
[\langle \rho \mid a > a' \rangle \Rightarrow_B \texttt{false}] &= a + a' + 1 > a = [\langle \rho \mid a \rangle \Rightarrow_N n] \\
[\langle \rho \mid a > a' \rangle \Rightarrow_B \texttt{false}] &= a + a' + 1 > a' = [\langle \rho \mid a' \rangle \Rightarrow_N n'] \\
[\langle \rho \mid a > a' \rangle \Rightarrow_B \texttt{true}] &= a + a' + 1 > a = [\langle \rho \mid a \rangle \Rightarrow_N n] \\
[\langle \rho \mid a > a' \rangle \Rightarrow_B \texttt{true}] &= a + a' + 1 > a' = [\langle \rho \mid a' \rangle \Rightarrow_N n'] \\
[\langle \rho \mid x := a \rangle \Downarrow \rho[x \mapsto n]] &= a + 1 > a = [\langle \rho \mid a \rangle \Rightarrow_N n] \\
[\langle \rho \mid S; S' \rangle \Downarrow \rho'] &= S + S' + 1 > S = [\langle \rho \mid S \rangle \Downarrow \rho''] \\
[\langle \rho \mid S; S' \rangle \Downarrow \rho'] &= S + S' + 1 > S' = [\langle \rho'' \mid S' \rangle \Downarrow \rho'] \\
[\langle \rho \mid \texttt{while } b \texttt{ do } S \rangle \Downarrow \rho] &= b + S + 1 > b = [\langle \rho \mid b \rangle \Rightarrow_B \texttt{false}] \\
[\langle \rho \mid \texttt{while } b \texttt{ do } S \rangle \Downarrow \rho'] &= b + S + 1 > b = [\langle \rho \mid b \rangle \Rightarrow_B \texttt{true}] \\
[\langle \rho \mid \texttt{while } b \texttt{ do } S \rangle \Downarrow \rho'] &= b + S + 1 > S = [\langle \rho \mid S \rangle \Downarrow \rho''] \\
[\langle \rho \mid \texttt{while } b \texttt{ do } S \rangle \Downarrow \rho'] &= b + S + 1 \geq b + S + 1 = [\langle \rho'' \mid \texttt{while } b \texttt{ do } S \rangle \Downarrow \rho']
\end{aligned}$$

All proof jumps *except* (WT3) can be removed from $\mathcal{J}$ in τ_{32}: $\mathsf{P}_{RP}(\tau_{32}) = \{\tau_{321}\}$, where $\tau_{321} = (IMP, \{(WT3)\}, L_{321})$, and $L_{321} = L_{32} \cup L_{WF} \cup L_{WT1} \cup L_{WT2} \cup L_{WT3}$ with $L_{32} = \{(\langle x \mapsto 0 \mid A \rangle \Downarrow \rho', \langle \rho' \mid W \rangle \Downarrow \rho)\}$ transformed into

$$\begin{aligned}
L_{WF} &= \{(\langle x \mapsto 0 \mid A \rangle \Downarrow \rho', \langle \rho' \mid \texttt{x>0} \rangle \Rightarrow_B \texttt{false})\} \\
L_{WT1} &= \{(\langle x \mapsto 0 \mid A \rangle \Downarrow \rho', \langle \rho' \mid \texttt{x>0} \rangle \Rightarrow_B \texttt{true})\} \\
L_{WT2} &= \{(\langle x \mapsto 0 \mid A \rangle \Downarrow \rho', \langle \rho' \mid \texttt{x>0} \rangle \Rightarrow_B \texttt{true}, \langle \rho' \mid \texttt{x:=x-1} \rangle \Downarrow \rho'')\} \\
L_{WT3} &= \{(\langle x \mapsto 0 \mid A \rangle \Downarrow \rho', \langle \rho' \mid \texttt{x>0} \rangle \Rightarrow_B \texttt{true}, \langle \rho' \mid \texttt{x:=x-1} \rangle \Downarrow \rho'', \langle \rho'' \mid W \rangle \Downarrow \rho''')\}
\end{aligned}$$

Now, $\mathsf{P}_{DecL}(\tau_{321}) = \{\tau_{3211}, \tau_{3212}, \tau_{3213}, \tau_{3214}\}$, where

$$\tau_{3211} = \{(IMP, \{(WT3)\}, L_{WF})\} \qquad \tau_{3212} = \{(IMP, \{(WT3)\}, L_{WT1})\}$$
$$\tau_{3213} = \{(IMP, \{(WT3)\}, L_{WT2})\} \qquad \tau_{3214} = \{(IMP, \{(WT3)\}, L_{WT3})\}.$$

Note that P_{RP} does not take into account the information about localization to establish comparisons between the head and the hook of the proof jumps. As remarked in the introduction, taking into account the localization is essential for achieving a proof of termination for P in Example 2. The following processor uses well-founded orderings to achieve this task.

Theorem 12 (Decreasing Proof Jump). *Let* $(\mathcal{S}, \mathcal{J}, L) \in OT(\mathcal{L})$, *where* $\mathcal{J} = \{C \Uparrow \boldsymbol{D}_m\}$ *and* $L = \{\lambda\}$ *with* $\lambda = (\boldsymbol{\gamma}, \phi)$ *are such that* $mgu_\mathcal{S}(\phi, C) \neq \emptyset$. *Let* $\sqsupset$ *be a well-founded relation such that for all substitutions* σ *and* $\theta \in mgu_\mathcal{S}(\phi, C)$ *if for all* $1 \leq i < m$, $\mathcal{S} \vdash \sigma(\theta(D_i))$ *holds, then* $\sigma(\theta(C)) \sqsupset \sigma(\theta(D_m))$. *Then,*

$$\mathsf{P}_{DPJ}(\mathcal{S}, \mathcal{J}, L) = \{(\mathcal{S}, \emptyset, \emptyset)\}$$

is a sound and complete processor.

Example 24. Consider τ_{3214} in Example 23. Use P_{DPJ} to prove it finite: first note that we can really apply the processor, because the localizing formula

$$\langle \rho_\lambda'' \mid W \rangle \Downarrow \rho_\lambda''' = \langle \rho_\lambda'' \mid \texttt{while x > 0 do x:=x-1} \rangle \Downarrow \rho_\lambda'''$$

and the head $\langle \rho_\psi \mid \texttt{while } b \texttt{ do } S \rangle \Downarrow \rho_\psi'$ of (WT3) unify with (a unique, up to renaming) θ given by

$$\theta(\rho_\psi) = \rho_\lambda'' \quad \theta(b) = \texttt{x>0} \quad \theta(S) = \texttt{x:=x-1} \quad \theta(\rho_\psi') = \rho_\lambda'''$$

Now, we prove that, if **IMP** $\vdash \theta(\langle \rho_\psi \mid b \rangle \Rightarrow_B \texttt{true})$ (equivalently **IMP** $\vdash \langle \rho_\lambda'' \mid \texttt{x>0} \rangle \Rightarrow_B \texttt{true}$) and **IMP** $\vdash \theta(\langle \rho_\psi \mid S \rangle \Downarrow \rho_\psi'')$ (equivalently **IMP** $\vdash \langle \rho_\lambda'' \mid \texttt{x:=x-1} \rangle \Downarrow \rho_\psi''$) hold, then

$$\theta(\langle \rho_\psi \mid \texttt{while } b \texttt{ do } S \rangle \Downarrow \rho_\psi') = \langle \rho_\lambda'' \mid \texttt{while x>0 do x:=x-1} \rangle \Downarrow \rho_\lambda'''$$
$$\sqsupset \langle \rho_\psi'' \mid \texttt{while x>0 do x:=x-1} \rangle \Downarrow \rho_\lambda'''$$
$$= \theta(\langle \rho_\psi'' \mid \texttt{while } b \texttt{ do } S \rangle \Downarrow \rho_\psi')$$

for some well-founded relation $\sqsupset$ among **IMP** formulas. As explained in [14], we define a model of the logic **IMP** and use the provability hypothesis (together with soundness) to conclude the desired comparison between the head and the hook of the proof jump.

1. Memory states ρ are *mappings* from variables into integer numbers: $\rho \in State = Var \to \mathbb{Z}$.
2. Arithmetic expressions $a ::= \texttt{x} \mid \texttt{n} \mid a_1 - a_2$ (we do not consider addition, product, etc., which are not used here) denote mappings from states into integers: $[a] \in ExpA = State \to \mathbb{Z}$. Accordingly, we define (using the standard λ-calculus-like notation for function application):

$$[\texttt{x}]\,\rho = (\rho\;\texttt{x}) \qquad [\texttt{n}]\,\rho = n \in \mathbb{Z} \qquad (a\;[\texttt{-}]\;a')\,\rho = (a\;\rho) -_\mathbb{Z} (a'\;\rho)$$

3. Boolean expressions $b ::= \text{true} \mid \text{false} \mid a_1{>}a_2$ (again, we only consider those that are used here) denote mappings from states into booleans: $[b] \in ExpB = State \to Bool$. Accordingly, we define:

$$[\text{true}]\, \rho = \text{true} \qquad [\text{false}]\, \rho = \text{false} \qquad (a\ [{>}]\ a')\, \rho = (a\ \rho) >_{\mathbb{Z}} (a'\ \rho)$$

4. Program statements denote mappings from states into states: $[b] \in Stmt = State \to State$. Accordingly:

$$(x\ [\text{:=}]\ a)\ \rho\ y = \textit{if}\ x =_{Var} y\ \textit{then}\ (a\ \rho)\ \textit{else}\ (\rho\ y)$$
$$S\ [;]\ S'\ \rho = S'\ (S\ \rho)$$
$$[\text{while\_do\_}]\ b\ S\ \rho = \textit{if}\ (b\ \rho)\ \textit{then}\ [\text{while\_do\_}]\ b\ (S\ \rho)\ \textit{else}\ \rho$$

The last (recursive) definition could be made *explicit* by using a fixpoint operator.

5. Configurations $\langle \_ \mid \_ \rangle$ denote the *application* of the second functional component (of type $State \to \tau$ for $\tau \in \{\mathbb{Z}, Bool, State\}$) to a memory state. Rather than distinguishing three different kinds of configurations, we just assume $\langle \_ \mid \_ \rangle$ of type $State \to (State \to \tau) \to \tau$ and define $\langle \_ \mid \_ \rangle\ \rho\ f = (f\ \rho)$.

6. Predicates $\_ \Rightarrow_N \_$, $\_ \Rightarrow_B \_$, and $\_ \Downarrow \_$ just denote the *equality* between the outcome of a configuration (in the first argument) and the second argument:

$$[\_ \Rightarrow_N \_]\ n\ n' = n =_{\mathbb{Z}} n' \quad [\_ \Rightarrow_B \_]\ t\ t' = t =_{Bool} t' \quad [\_ \Downarrow \_]\ \rho\ \rho' = \rho =_{State} \rho'$$

7. It is easy to check that the previous interpretation satisfies the inference rules of **IMP**. For instance, for (Assig), we have that, whenever $[\langle \rho \mid a \rangle \Rightarrow_N n]$ holds, i.e., $(a\ \rho) =_{\mathbb{Z}} n$, then $\langle \rho \mid x := a \rangle \Downarrow \rho[x \mapsto n]$, holds as well, because $[\langle \rho \mid x := a \rangle] = \textit{if}\ x =_{Var} y\ \textit{then}\ (a\ \rho)\ \textit{else}\ (\rho\ y) = \textit{if}\ x =_{Var} y\ \textit{then}\ n\ \textit{else}\ (\rho\ y) =$ is exactly the definition of $\rho[x \mapsto n]$.

8. Now, *given variable* $x \in Var$, we define a well-founded relation $\sqsupset_x$ between formulas $\langle \rho \mid S \rangle \Downarrow \rho'$ as follows: $\langle \rho_1 \mid S \rangle \Downarrow \rho_1'\ \sqsupset_x\ \langle \rho_2 \mid S \rangle \Downarrow \rho_2'$ if and only if $(\rho_1\ x) >_{\mathbb{N}} (\rho_2\ x) \geq 0$. Note that $\sqsupset_x$ is *well-founded*.

9. Finally, we prove that, if **IMP** $\vdash \langle \rho_\lambda'' \mid x{>}0 \rangle \Rightarrow_B \text{true}$ and **IMP** $\vdash \langle \rho_\lambda'' \mid x\text{:=}x\text{-}1 \rangle \Downarrow \rho_\psi''$ hold, then

$$\langle \rho_\lambda'' \mid \text{while } x{>}0 \text{ do } x\text{:=}x\text{-}1 \rangle \Downarrow \rho_\lambda'''\ \sqsupset_x\ \langle \rho_\psi'' \mid \text{while } x{>}0 \text{ do } x\text{:=}x\text{-}1 \rangle \Downarrow \rho_\lambda'''$$

By *soundness*, we have **IMP** $\models \langle \rho_\lambda'' \mid x{>}0 \rangle \Rightarrow_B \text{true}$ and **IMP** $\models \langle \rho_\lambda'' \mid x\text{:=}x\text{-}1 \rangle \Downarrow \rho_\psi''$. Since

$$[\langle \rho_\lambda'' \mid x{>}0 \rangle \Rightarrow_B \text{true}] = ([x{>}0]\ \rho_\lambda'') =_{Bool} \text{true}$$
$$= (\rho_\lambda''\ x) >_{\mathbb{Z}} 0 =_{Bool} \text{true}$$

this means that x is bound to a *positive* number in the state ρ_λ''. And

$$[\langle \rho_\lambda'' \mid x\text{:=}x\text{-}1 \rangle \Downarrow \rho_\psi''] = ([x\text{:=}x\text{-}1]\ \rho_\lambda'') =_{State} \rho_\psi''$$
$$= \rho_\lambda''[x \mapsto ((\rho_\lambda''\ x) - 1)] =_{State} \rho_\psi''$$

means that $(\rho_\psi''\ x) =_{\mathbb{Z}} (\rho_\lambda''\ x) - 1$. Note that, since $(\rho_\lambda''\ x) > 0$, it follows $(\rho_\psi''\ x) \geq 0$. Hence, we reach the desired conclusion.

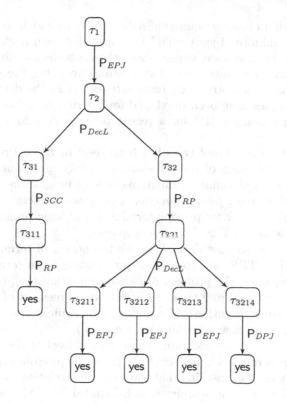

Fig. 6. OTF-tree for the program P in Example 2

Thus, $\mathsf{P}(\tau_{3214}) = \{(\mathbf{IMP}, \emptyset, L_{WT3})\}$, meaning that τ_{3214} is *finite*.

Remark 6. Example 24 shows how *semantic methods* can be successfully applied in the OT framework. Of course, the *automation* of such methods (in particular, the *automatic generation* of the *higher-order* algebraic interpretations deployed there) is not easy and deserves further investigation.

Example 25. For τ_{3211} in Example 23, the localizing formula $\langle \rho' \mid \mathtt{x>0} \rangle \Rightarrow_B$ false cannot be expanded by (WT3). Thus, $\mathsf{P}_{EPJ}(\tau_{3211}) = \{(IMP, \{(WT3)\}, \emptyset)\}$, which is *finite*. We similarly use P_{EPJ} to prove τ_{3212} and τ_{3213} finite as well. Thus, termination of P in Example 2 is finally proved (see Figure 6).

8   Related Work and Conclusions

In *lazy* functional programming and *logic* programming, the focus is naturally biased to a *localized* notion of termination due to the essential role of *initial expressions* and *goals* in computations. Lazy functional languages somehow *welcome* nontermination because of their ability to deal with *infinite data structures* (generated through an infinite number of reduction steps which steadily *approximate* the desired infinite object) would be impossible with a *global* notion of termination. Still, programmers expect that (thanks to *lazy* evaluation) *initial expressions* leading to a finite value, but possibly involving the partial development of an infinite data structure, *terminate* and yield the desired outcome. Thus, some techniques have been developed for proving such *local* termination of functional languages, see [12] for a recent paper surveying many of those developments.

The absence of infinite proof trees has been used in *Logic Programming* to provide a suitable definition of the *termination* of logic programs [5,7,20]. For instance, Dershowitz et al. define termination of a logic program as *"the finiteness of the LD-tree constructed for the program and a given query"* [7]. In [21], a *dependency pair framework* for proving termination of logic programs (inspired by the DP Framework for TRSs[2] [11]) is developed.

In Term Rewriting Systems (TRSs), where the notion of termination is traditionally *global*, i.e., TRSs are considered terminating if *no term* initiates an infinite rewrite sequence, the problem of *local* termination (i.e., termination of rewrite sequences starting from terms t taken from a *given* set of terms T) has recently deserved some attention and a number of techniques an tools for automatically proving it are now available (see, e.g., [10]).

With regard to imperative programs, the notion is *local* at the language level but *global* at the program level, meaning that: (i) not all programs terminate; and (ii) the interest focuses on ensuring that the *transition relation* (among memory states) associated to a *given program* is well-founded [6]. This includes initialization conditions (initial memory state from which the program computation starts) and user-supplied inputs, which in both cases may change the execution of the program. There have been many advances in this field as well with a host of new powerful techniques and implementations ([6] provides a good account).

Our main aim in [14] and in this paper is not *replacing* all these approaches and techniques (by somehow showing astonishing improvements in performance and efficiency, which is quite unlikely in general). It is rather to complement them by showing how *logic principles* naturally arising from the *logic description* of the operational semantics of programming languages can be used in the *definition* and *proof* of termination in a broad variety of programming languages and systems. This has two main advantages. Firstly, it makes termination proofs *semantics-based*, that is, directly based on the language's formal (*operational*) semantics, as advocated for all formal reasoning about programs in [18]. Second, it provides a variety of *language-generic* termination proof methods which can complement and enhance language-specific ones. In [14], we successfully applied the *very same* OT framework to prove and disprove termination of *Conditional Term Rewriting Systems* (CTRS), *Typed λ-calculus*, and the *Context-Sensitive Membership Equational Logic* (CS-MEL), which provides an operational princi-

---

[2] See [14] for more details about the relations between our OT framework and the DP framework for TRSs.

ple for the execution of programs in languages like CafeOBJ and Maude. In this paper, we generalize the notion of operational termination to deal with *localization*. Although the notion of localization is conceptually simple, it is powerful enough to make the OT framework applicable to imperative programming languages and other termination problems, where termination is naturally *localized*. In particular, we have exemplified its use by applying them to prove termination of *imperative programs*, and *local termination of CTRSs* in *two* different senses, regarding one-step reductions $s \rightarrow t$ starting from specific (sets of) terms s (this problem just does not exist for TRSs); and regarding many steps reductions $s \rightarrow^* t$; in both cases, this is the first time that this is investigated so far. We are able now to cover naturally *localized* notions of termination like the aforementioned ones for lazy functional programming and logic programming. We have also generalized and extended the OT framework to deal with proofs of *localized operational termination* in general logics. In particular, the processors introduced in [14] have been adapted and revised to deal with localizations.

We are working to implement the OT framework through a combined effort to improve the tools MTT [8] and MU-TERM [2]. The ability of rewriting logic and the tandem MTT/Maude to serve as a representation framework for general logics, and the implemented techniques for proving termination in MU-TERM will be essential to achieve this task. This combination of tools and methods should be very useful to further develop the theory and its applications.

Acknoledgements. We thank the anonymous referees for their useful comments.

References

1. Aczel, P.: Schematic Consequence. In: Gabbay, D. (ed.) What is a Logical System, pp. 261–272. Oxford University Press (1994)
2. Alarcón, B., Gutiérrez, R., Lucas, S., Navarro-Marset, R.: Proving Termination Properties with MU-TERM. In: Johnson, M., Pavlovic, D. (eds.) AMAST 2010. LNCS, vol. 6486, pp. 201–208. Springer, Heidelberg (2011)
3. Boronat, A., Knapp, A., Meseguer, J., Wirsing, M.: What Is a Multi-modeling Language? In: Corradini, A., Montanari, U. (eds.) WADT 2008. LNCS, vol. 5486, pp. 71–87. Springer, Heidelberg (2009)
4. Broy, M., Wirsing, M., Pepper, P.: On the Algebraic Definition of Programming Languages. ACM Transactions on Programming Languages and Systems 9(1), 54–99 (1987)
5. Codish, M., Taboch, C.: A semantic basis for the termination analysis of logic programs. Journal of Logic Programming 41, 103–123 (1999)
6. Cook, B., Rybalchenko, A., Podelski, A.: Proving Program Termination. Communications of the ACM 54(5), 88–98 (2011)
7. Dershowitz, N., Lindenstrauss, N., Sagiv, Y., Serebrenik, A.: A General Framework for Automatic Termination of Logic Programs. Applicable Algebra in Engineering, Communication and Computing 12, 117–156 (2001)
8. Durán, F., Lucas, S., Meseguer, J.: MTT: The Maude Termination Tool (System Description). In: Armando, A., Baumgartner, P., Dowek, G. (eds.) IJCAR 2008. LNCS (LNAI), vol. 5195, pp. 313–319. Springer, Heidelberg (2008)

9. Durán, F., Lucas, S., Marché, C., Meseguer, J., Urbain, X.: Proving Operational Termination of Membership Equational Programs. Higher-Order and Symbolic Computation 21(1-2), 59–88 (2008)
10. Endrullis, J., de Vrijer, R., Waldmann, J.: Local termination: theory and practice. Logical Methods in Computer Science 6(3:20), 1–37 (2010)
11. Giesl, J., Thiemann, R., Schneider-Kamp, P., Falke, S.: Mechanizing and Improving Dependency Pairs. Journal of Automatic Reasoning 37(3), 155–203 (2006)
12. Giesl, J., Swiderski, P., Schneider-Kamp, P., Thiemann, R.: Automated Termination Proofs for Haskell by Term Rewriting. ACM Transactions on Programming languages and Systems 33(2), Article 7 (2011)
13. Lucas, S., Meseguer, J.: Strong and Weak Operational Termination of Order-Sorted Rewrite Theories. In: Escobar, S. (ed.) WRLA 2014. LNCS, vol. 8663, pp. 178–194. Springer, Heidelberg (2014)
14. Lucas, S., Meseguer, J.: Proving Operational Termination Of Declarative Programs In General Logics. In: Danvy, O. (ed.) Proc. of the 16th International Symposium on Principles and Practice of Declarative Programming, PPDP 2014. ACM Press (to appear, 2014)
15. Lucas, S., Marché, C., Meseguer, J.: Operational termination of conditional term rewriting systems. Information Processing Letters 95, 446–453 (2005)
16. Meseguer, J.: General Logics. In: Ebbinghaus, H.-D., et al. (eds.) Logic Colloquium'87, pp. 275–329. North-Holland (1989)
17. Meseguer, J.: A Logical Theory of Concurrent Objects and its realization in the Maude Language. In: Agha, G., Wegner, P., Yonezawa, A. (eds.) Research Directions in Concurrent Object-Oriented Programming, pp. 314–390. The MIT Press (1993)
18. Meseguer, J., Rosu, G.: The Rewriting Logic Semantics Project: A Progress Report. Information and Computation 231, 38–69 (2013)
19. Nguyen, M.T., Giesl, J., Schneider-Kamp, P., De Schreye, D.: Termination Analysis of Logic Programs Based on Dependency Graphs. In: King, A. (ed.) LOPSTR 2007. LNCS, vol. 4915, pp. 8–22. Springer, Heidelberg (2008)
20. de Scheye, D., Decorte, S.: Termination of Logic Programs: The Never-Ending Story. Journal of Logic Programming 19, 199–260 (1994)
21. Schneider-Kamp, P., Giesl, J., Nguyen, M.T.: The Dependency Triple Framework for Termination of Logic Programs. In: De Schreye, D. (ed.) LOPSTR 2009. LNCS, vol. 6037, pp. 37–51. Springer, Heidelberg (2010)
22. Winskel, G.: The Formal Semantics of Programming Languages. The MIT Press, Cambrige Massachusetts (1993)
23. Wirsing, M.: Structured Algebraic Specifications: A Kernel Language. Theoretical Computer Science 42, 123–249 (1986)
24. Wirsing, M.: Algebraic Specification. In: Handbook of Theoretical Computer Science, Volume B: Formal Models and Sematics (B), pp. 675–788 (1990)
25. Wirsing, M., Knapp, A.: A formal approach to object-oriented software engineering. Theoretical Computer Science 285(2), 519–560 (2002)

Partial Valuation Structures
for Qualitative Soft Constraints*

Alexander Schiendorfer, Alexander Knapp, Jan-Philipp Steghöfer, Gerrit Anders,
Florian Siefert, and Wolfgang Reif

Institute for Software and Systems Engineering, University of Augsburg, Germany
{schiendorfer,knapp,steghoefer,anders,siefert,reif}@isse.de

Abstract. Soft constraints have proved to be a versatile tool for the specification and implementation of decision making in adaptive systems. A plethora of
formalisms have been devised to capture different notions of preference. Wirsing
et al. have proposed partial valuation structures as a unifying algebraic structure
for several soft constraint formalisms, including quantitative and qualitative ones,
which, in particular, supports lexicographic products in a broad range of cases.
We demonstrate the versatility of partial valuation structures by integrating the
qualitative formalism of constraint relationships as well as the hybrid concept of
constraint hierarchies. The latter inherently relies on lexicographic combinations,
but it turns out that not all can be covered directly by partial valuation structures.
We therefore investigate a notion for simulating partial valuation structures not
amenable to lexicographic combinations by better suited ones. The concepts are
illustrated by a case study in decentralized energy management.

1 Introduction

Adaptive systems consisting of a large number of interacting components as treated
in Organic Computing [26] or Ensembles [14] rely on formalisms to specify models
of their complex behavior. Equipped with adequate abstract goal models that describe a
corridor of correct behavior, these systems become amenable to formal verification [20]
as well as testing [11]. Modeling both the concrete and the abstract components' behavior in terms of relations of their system variables representing input and output naturally
leads to the framework of constraint programming. If these models are also used by
the system at runtime to actually implement the decision-making, constraint satisfaction and optimization techniques can be applied. Clearly, problems can become over-
constrained. Hence, constraint satisfaction has been extended to soft constraints [19].

In constraint hierarchies [8], users qualitatively put constraints into layers represented by a family of sets of constraints $(H_i)_{i \in I}$ where a constraint in layer H_j is
valued less important than a constraint in layer H_i if $j > i$. A lexicographic ordering
is then established by prioritizing the satisfaction degree of more important layers. This
satisfaction degree is evaluated on an assignment and may include metric real-valued

* This research is partly sponsored by the German Research Foundation (DFG) in the project
"OC-Trust" (FOR 1085).

R. De Nicola and R. Hennicker (Eds.): Wirsing Festschrift, LNCS 8950, pp. 115–133, 2015.

error functions for constraints. So-called *comparators* define the ordering over assignments. By definition, constraint hierarchies tend to ignore all constraints on higher levels which leads to a strongly hierarchical evaluation. One satisfied constraint is possibly worth more than a whole set of other, violated constraints.

More recently, constraint relationships [21] have been proposed to capture qualitative statements over soft constraints such as "Prefer a solution violating constraint a to one that violates b" without having to express this fact numerically. This allows for flexible use especially with problems changing at runtime [22,17] as faced with dynamically reconfiguring groups of power plants as described in Sect. 2. However, constraint relationships only consider predicates in lieu of using error metrics. Problems from distributed energy management [2] call for both those formalisms. If a problem admits metric real-valued error functions, one may want to use constraint hierarchies. If, on the other hand, the solution quality is measured by the number and importance of satisfied boolean properties, constraint relationships provide a less restrictive framework.

A broad variety of soft constraint approaches have been captured by the generalizing algebraic formalisms of *c-semirings* and *valued constraints*. That way, users may specify their preferences in the most suitable formalism for the task at hand and rely on a well-defined algebraic underpinning. C-semirings [5] include a set of satisfaction degrees, one operator to combine and one to compare (i.e., calculating a supremum) them as well as a minimal and maximal element to express total dissatisfaction and satisfaction. Frameworks and algorithms based on c-semirings have been devised to build a general theory of soft constraints as well as to provide common solvers [18,10]. Valued constraints [24], on the other hand, use *valuation structures*, i.e., totally ordered monoids instead of the partial order implied by the comparison operator in a c-semiring. The theoretical connection between c-semirings and valued constraints is well understood for totally ordered c-semirings [6]. Recently, the totality in valuation structures was relaxed in [12] following earlier work by Hölzl, Meier and Wirsing [13] to form *partial valuation structures* that also admit lexicographic products for many instances – as opposed to c-semirings. This combination operator offers to specify one's preferences in a more structured way to capture different criteria of descending priority. More complicated partial valuation structures can be formed from elementary ones – allowing for modular implementations and (re)combinations at runtime. These considerations pave the way for the further development of common constraint propagators [9] and search algorithms based on partial valuation structures [13].

As a unifying effort we first represent constraint relationships as partial valuation structures using an algebraically free construction in Sect. 4. For constraint hierarchies, Hosobe established that a reasonable class can be expressed as c-semirings [15]. It remained, however, unclear how to properly draw the boundary between expressible and non-expressible hierarchies. Using Wirsing's results, we can now exploit the lexicographic ordering in constraint hierarchies by mapping layers to partial valuation structures in Sect. 5. Using the insight that certain elements of monoidal soft constraints can be *collapsing* [12], i.e., making comparable elements equal when used with the combination operator, we can give necessary conditions on the partial valuation structures representing layers. In Sect. 5.2 we show that in particular idempotent comparators such as the worst-case comparator in constraint hierarchies cannot directly be represented as a collapse-free partial valuation structure and thus not used in a lexicographical product. However, in Sect. 6 we introduce a notion of *simulation* where another partial valuation structure reasonably mimics the behavior of the worst-case comparator by using a suitable p-norm to induce a collapse-free partial valuation structure.

2   Soft Constraints in Distributed Energy Management

We first give elementary definitions in the realm of classical constraint programming that are then exemplified by a real world application in distributed energy management.

A *constraint domain* (X, D) is given by a set X of *variables* and a family $D = (D_x)_{x \in X}$ of *variable domains* where each D_x is a set representing the possible values for variable x. An *assignment* for a constraint domain (X, D) is a dependent map $v \in \Pi x \in X . D_x$, i.e., $v(x) \in D_x$; we abbreviate $\Pi x \in X . D_x$ by $[X \to D]$. A *constraint* c over a constraint domain (X, D), or (X, D)-*constraint*, is given by a map $c : [X \to D] \to \mathbb{B}$. We also write $v \models c$ for $c(v) = tt$.

A *constraint satisfaction problem* (CSP) consists in finding an assignment that yields true for a set of constraints, i.e., a *solution*, and a *constraint satisfaction optimization problem* (CSOP) further seeks to optimize an objective [28] among all solutions. Classical hard constraints are generalized to soft constraints by removing the restriction of constraints to map to true or false [19] but rather an ordered domain. We call these evaluations *gradings* of assignments. In particular, we consider CSOPs that search for maximal gradings in terms of soft constraints.

Such problems occur in many adaptive systems. They are particularly interesting if individual constraint problems must be combined. Adaptive power management provides us with an illustrative example. The main task in power management systems is to maintain the balance between energy production and consumption to avoid instabilities leading to blackouts. Since the prosumers' ability to change their prosumption is subject to physical inertia (e.g., limited ramping rates), the prosumption of controllable prosumers has to be stipulated beforehand as schedules for future points in time.[1]

The concept of *Autonomous Virtual Power Plants* (AVPPs) [27] has been presented as an approach to deal with scalability issues in future smart grids. Each AVPP represents a self-organizing group of two or more prosumers of various types and has to satisfy a fraction of the overall consumption. To accomplish this task, each AVPP autonomously and periodically calculates schedules for its prosumers. Due to uncertainties such as weather conditions, AVPPs can change their composition at runtime to remain manageable. Moreover, the rising complexity with increasing numbers of controlled prosumers motivates the formation of a hierarchical structure of AVPPs following a system-of-systems approach in which hierarchy levels are dynamically created and dissolved. Hence, each AVPP controls less prosumers (including AVPPs) compared to the non-hierarchical case, resulting in shorter scheduling times for each AVPP.

When creating schedules, AVPPs not only have to respect the physical models – in terms of hard constraints – but also their prosumers' individual preferences concerning "good" schedules. For example, a baseload power plant might be reluctant to be

---

[1] We use the term "prosumer" to refer to producers and consumers, and the term "prosumption" to refer to production and consumption.

switched on and off frequently, whereas a peaking power plant is designed for exactly that purpose. Certainly, prosumers should be free to use whatever specific formalism is most adequate to model their real-life preferences. Consequently, the dynamics of this self-organizing system calls for the treatment and combination of heterogeneous preference specifications at runtime.

To illustrate these considerations, we regard a concrete example of an AVPP consisting of three prosumers: A garbage incineration plant as a thermal power plant where steam drives a generator (`thermal`), a biogas power plant using an engine to produce power (`biogas`), and an electric vehicle that can be used as a power storage when connected to the power grid (EV). Each of these prosumers is described by a relational model restricting its physically and economically feasible behavior. These individual models are combined and define the space of feasible schedules [22], ordered by the organizational goal, i.e., to keep mismatches between demand and production (violations) low and the combined preferences of the prosumers. Since blackout prevention is critical, the organizational goal is compared "pessimistically", i.e., by a schedule's worst anticipated violation over a set of future time steps. For instance, two schedules with violations $(0, 0, 3)$ and $(3, 3, 3)$, respectively, for three time steps would be esteemed equal due to the worst violation. For this process of combining shared and individual aspects [23], a common constraint domain (X, D) is used consisting of the smallest set of shared variables, e.g., those for scheduled prosumptions p_t^a for the prosumed power by prosumer a at time step t. Since we are particularly concerned with soft constraints, we deliberately omit the prosumers' hard constraints.

In addition, each prosumer defines its own set of soft constraints in a formalism of its choice over the common constraint domain and additional individual variables. As shown in Fig. 1, `biogas` and EV use constraint relationships while `thermal` uses constraint hierarchies. The overall model lexicographically arranges the organizational preference (`violation_org`) similar to constraint hierarchies where `violation_org` is put at a higher level H_1^{org} than the individual soft constraints placed on level H_2^{org} since the AVPP's primary objective is arguably to reduce the probability of blackouts. This is regulated by a limitation `maxVio` of the absolute value of the difference between demand d_t and produced power $\sum_{a \in A} p_t^a$. As indicated before, this reflects the semantics of the worst case comparator in constraint hierarchies which could not be expressed by c-semirings in [15]. We provide an explanation for this as well as a solution in Sect. 6.

The electric vehicle can also consume power to load its batteries in which case p_t^a is negative. With regard to the time horizon T schedules are created for, the error function $e_{\text{violation}_{org}}$ associated with the constraint `violation_org` maps to the maximum value by which the threshold `maxVio` is exceeded:

$$\text{violation}_{org} \equiv \forall t \in T \, . \, \left| d_t - \sum_{a \in A} p_t^a \right| \leq \text{maxVio}$$

$$e_{\text{violation}_{org}} \equiv \max_{t \in T} \max\{0, \left| d_t - \sum_{a \in A} p_t^a \right| - \text{maxVio}\}$$

The model for `biogas` specifies preferences regarding the use of its gas storage tank. It is advisable that this tank is not entirely filled and that the plant runs upon a certain filling threshold since inflow can not be regulated (`gasFull_bio`). The plant has to run if the tank is full. Furthermore, the power plant has an economic "sweet spot" which optimizes the ratio of fuel consumption to power production (`ecoSweet_bio`) and it should

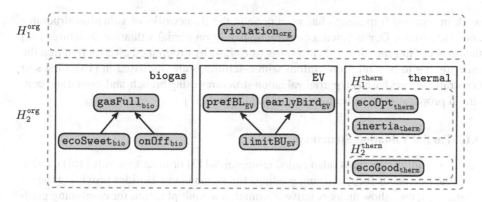

Fig. 1. Case study depicting individual and organizational preference specifications in context

not be frequently switched on and off to minimize maintenance cost ($\text{onOff}_{\text{bio}}$). Both $\text{ecoSweet}_{\text{bio}}$ and $\text{onOff}_{\text{bio}}$ are desirable but deemed less important than $\text{gasFull}_{\text{bio}}$. No statement regarding their importance is however made. It need not hold that satisfying $\text{gasFull}_{\text{bio}}$ is worth violating the two others in a strict hierarchical sense. Therefore, constraint relationships are used (see Sect. 4 for details on how an order over assignments is thereby induced).

The preferences of EV address its battery status. A preferred battery level should be maintained to allow for emergency trips ($\text{prefBL}_{\text{EV}}$). To reduce the charging cycles, a soft constraint prescribes that the amount of energy taken out of the battery should not exceed a certain threshold within a specific time frame ($\text{limitBU}_{\text{EV}}$). Finally, a higher battery charge is required in the morning to assure the trip to work ($\text{earlyBird}_{\text{EV}}$). Dually to biogas, $\text{limitBU}_{\text{EV}}$ is considered less important than the other constraints.

Finally, thermal restricts both the production ranges and the changes in power production due to inertia. The former limitation ensures economically reasonable assignments similar to biogas and the latter ensures that thermal does not have to be cooled down and heated up all the time at high costs due to energy-intensive processes. As metric error functions are easily found for these constraints, a constraint hierarchy is employed which puts constraints for economical optimality ($\text{ecoOpt}_{\text{therm}}$) and inertia-based change limits ($\text{inertia}_{\text{therm}}$) on level H_1^{therm} and constraints for economically still good ranges ($\text{ecoGood}_{\text{therm}}$) on level H_2^{therm}.

Concluding, this example presents three challenges to a soft constraint framework: Adaptive heterogeneous systems need 1) different preference formalisms, 2) combinations of such preference specifications at runtime, and 3) algorithms to solve the resulting soft constraint problems in a general manner.

3 Partial Valuation Structures as a Unifying Formalism

As presented, heterogeneous preference formalisms can show up in soft constraint based systems. Yet, algorithms to find feasible and high quality solutions need some structure to perform constraint propagation or apply branch-and-bound techniques. Seminal work in unifying formalisms has been done in the frameworks of valuation structures and c-semirings. Our following constructions rely on partial valuation structures [12] that turn out to generalize valuation structures [24] by dropping the restriction that the ordering has to be total. Connections with c-semirings are discussed in [16]. First soft constraint solvers based on partial valuation structures using branch-and-bound and constraint propagation have been presented in [13] and [17][2].

3.1 Partial Valuation Structures

Partial valuation structures (also called ic-monoids [13] or meet monoids [16]) capture essential operations for specifying gradings for assignments: Besides providing the set of gradings, they show an associative, commutative multiplication for combining gradings, a partial ordering on gradings such that the multiplication is monotone w.r.t. this ordering, and a top element w.r.t. the partial ordering capturing the best grade, i.e., total satisfaction, that simultaneously is the neutral element for the multiplication.

Definition 1. *A* partial valuation structure $M = (X, \cdot, \varepsilon, \leq)$ *is given by an* underlying set X, *an* associative *and* commutative multiplication *operation* $\cdot : X \times X \to X$, *a* neutral *element* $\varepsilon \in X$ *for* $\cdot$, *and a* partial ordering $\leq \subseteq X \times X$ *such that the multiplication* $\cdot$ *is monotone in both arguments w.r.t. to* $\leq$, *i.e.,* $m_1 \cdot m_2 \leq m_1' \cdot m_2'$ *if* $m_1 \leq m_1'$ *and* $m_2 \leq m_2'$, *and* ε *is the top element w.r.t.* $\leq$.
　We write $m_1 < m_2$ *if* $m_1 \leq m_2$ *and* $m_1 \neq m_2$, *and* $m_1 \parallel m_2$ *if neither* $m_1 \leq m_2$ *nor* $m_2 \leq m_1$. *We write* $|M|$ *for the underlying set and* $\cdot_M$, ε_M, *and* $\leq_M$ *for the other parts of* M. □

Intuitively, $m \leq n$ says that grading m is "worse than" n, so ε will be the top (and best) element of the ordering. In fact, requiring that ε is top is equivalent to requiring that $m \cdot n \leq m$. An illustrative example is the partial valuation structure $(\mathbb{N}, +, 0, \geq)$ used in weighted CSP [19]. The natural numbers represent penalties for violating constraints, with 0 representing satisfaction, and the goal is to minimize the sum of penalties. Another example (previously considered in [4] as a c-semiring) is an inclusion-based partial valuation structure $(\mathfrak{P}(A), \cup, \emptyset, \supseteq)$, where smaller sets are considered better, i.e., $\emptyset$ being best. The sets could, e.g., represent violated constraints.

3.2 Soft Constraints

Classical CSPs are turned into soft CSPs by means of soft constraints mapping assignments to arbitrary gradings instead of $\mathbb{B}$. For a partial valuation structure M, an *M-soft constraint* over a constraint domain (X, D), or (X, D)-*M-soft constraint*, is given by a map $\mu : [X \to D] \to |M|$. The *solution degree* of an assignment w.r.t. a finite set of (X, D)-M-soft constraints M is obtained by combining all gradings using $\cdot_M$, i.e., $\mathsf{M}(v) = \prod_M \{\mu(v) \mid \mu \in \mathsf{M}\}$. This gives rise to the assignment comparison $\lesssim_\mathsf{M} \subseteq [X \to D] \times [X \to D]$ with $w \lesssim_\mathsf{M} v \iff \mathsf{M}(w) \leq_M \mathsf{M}(v)$, where w is considered worse. The *maximum solution degrees* and the *maximum solutions* of M, which are the goal for solving algorithms, are given by

---

[2] See http://git.io/mH_pOg for this solver.

$$\mathsf{M}^* = \mathrm{Max}^{\leq_M}\{\mathsf{M}(v) \mid v \in [X \to D]\}\,,$$

$$\mathrm{Max}^{\leq_M}[X \to D] = \{v \in [X \to D] \mid \mathsf{M}(v) \in \mathsf{M}^*\}\,.$$

In the process of searching maximum solutions, a vital question is to ask whether the problem formulation actually admits optima. Consider, for example, the constraint domain (X, D) with $X = \{x\}$, $D_x = [0, 1]$, and the partial valuation structure $M = ([0, 1], \max, 0, \geq)$ with $\geq$ the usual ordering on real numbers. Let $\mu : [X \to D] \to |M|$ be defined by $\mu(\{x \mapsto r\}) = r$ if $r > 0$, and $\mu(\{x \mapsto 0\}) = 1$, and let $\mathsf{M} = \{\mu\}$. Then $\mathsf{M}^* = \emptyset$ since the set of solution degrees is the open interval $(0, 1]$, i.e., no maximum solution degrees and no maximum solutions exist.

Definition 2. *A set of* (X, D)-M-*soft constraints is* admissible *if* M *is finite and for each* $v \in [X \to D]$ *there is an* $m \in \mathsf{M}^*$ *such that* $\mathsf{M}(v) \leq_M m$. $\qquad\qquad\square$

Sufficient conditions for the finite set M of (X, D)-M-soft constraints to be admissible are that X and $\bigcup_{x \in X} D_x$ are finite, or that $<_M$ has no infinite ascending chains.

3.3 Product Operators for Partial Valuation Structures

For runtime combinations of different soft constraint formulations as are prevalent in adaptive systems, partial valuation structures admit finite (direct) products but also lexicographic products, as shown by Gadducci, Hölzl, Monreale, and Wirsing [12].

First, let us consider the direct product that is defined component-wise obviously yielding a partial valuation structure:

Definition 3. *Let* M *and* N *be partial valuation structures. Let*
- $P = |M| \times |N|$,
- $\cdot_P : P \times P \to P$ *given by* $(m_1, n_1) \cdot_P (m_2, n_2) = (m_1 \cdot_M m_2, n_1 \cdot_N n_2)$,
- $\varepsilon_P = (\varepsilon_M, \varepsilon_N)$,
- $\leq_P \subseteq P \times P$ *given by* $(m_1, n_1) \leq_P (m_2, n_2) \iff m_1 \leq_M m_2 \land n_1 \leq_N n_2$.
The (direct) product *of* M *and* N, *written as* $M \times N$, *is given by the partial valuation structure* $(P, \cdot_P, \varepsilon_P, \leq_P)$. $\qquad\qquad\square$

This product leaves many combinations incomparable. Let us thus turn our attention to lexicographic products introduced by [12] useful in situations where a preference is composed of multiple criteria of decreasing priority. The *lexicographic ordering* $\leq_{M \ltimes N} \subseteq |M \times N| \times |M \times N|$ on the direct product distinguishes first by $\leq_M$ and then by $\leq_N$ if the first comparison yields equality:

$$(m_1, n_1) \leq_{M \ltimes N} (m_2, n_2) \iff (m_1 <_M m_2) \lor (m_1 = m_2 \land n_1 \leq_N n_2)\,.$$

However, for $\cdot_{M \times N}$ still to be monotone now w.r.t. $\leq_{M \ltimes N}$, we would have to show that $(m_1, n_1) \cdot_{M \times N} (m, n) \leq_{M \ltimes N} (m_2, n_2) \cdot_{M \times N} (m, n)$ holds if $(m_1, n_1) \leq_{M \ltimes N} (m_2, n_2)$. But this fails, if there are $m_1, m_2, m \in |M|$ such that $m_1 <_M m_2$ and at the same time $m_1 \cdot_M m = m_2 \cdot_M m$. In this case, order-preservation w.r.t. $\leq_N$ does not hold, if $m_1 <_M m_2$ but $n_1 >_N n_2$, since we would have $(m_1, n_1) \cdot_{M \times N} (m, n) >_{M \ltimes N} (m_2, n_2) \cdot_{M \times N} (m, n)$, clearly violating monotonicity.

First, the notion of *collapsing elements* [12] captures the objectionable elements of M as the set

$$\mathfrak{C}(M) = \{m \in |M| \mid \exists m_1, m_2 \in |M| \cdot m_1 <_M m_2 \wedge m_1 \cdot_M m = m_2 \cdot_M m\}.$$

All idempotent elements w.r.t. $\cdot_M$ different from ε_M are collapsing: if $m \cdot_M m = m$, we have $m <_M \varepsilon_M$ but $m \cdot_M m = \varepsilon \cdot_M m = m$. On the other hand, $\varepsilon_M \notin \mathfrak{C}(M)$ since $m_1 <_M m_2$ implies $m_1 \cdot_M \varepsilon_M <_M m_2 \cdot_M \varepsilon_M$. Furthermore, $|M| \setminus \mathfrak{C}(M)$ is closed under $\cdot_M$, and thus $(|M| \setminus \mathfrak{C}(M), \cdot_M, \varepsilon_M, \leq_M)$ forms a partial valuation structure.

Second, the notion of *bounded partial valuation structures* [12] allows to avoid the comparison of pairs (m, n) with $m \in \mathfrak{C}(M)$ by requiring that then n must be the smallest element of N: A partial valuation structure N is *bounded* if $|N|$ has a smallest element $\perp_N$ w.r.t. $\leq_M$. Then $\perp_N$ is unique and annihilating for $\cdot_N$, i.e., $n \cdot_N \perp_N = \perp_N$ for all $n \in |N|$. We can always *lift* a partial valuation structure M into a bounded partial valuation structure $M_\perp = (|M| \cup \{\perp\}, \cdot_{M_\perp}, \varepsilon_M, \leq_{M_\perp})$ by using a fresh $\perp$ and extending $\cdot_M$ and $\leq_M$ by $m \cdot_{M_\perp} \perp = \perp$ and $\perp \leq_{M_\perp} m$ for all $m \in |M| \cup \{\perp\}$.

Equipped with these concepts, we can define the lexicographic product of partial valuation structures. The well-definedness of this construction, i.e., that it indeed yields a partial valuation structure, has been shown in [12].

Definition 4. *Let M be a partial valuation structure and let N be a bounded partial valuation structure. Let*

- $L = ((|M| \setminus \mathfrak{C}(M)) \times |N|) \cup (\mathfrak{C}(M) \times \{\perp_N\})$,
- $\cdot_L : L \times L \to L$ *given by* $(m_1, n_1) \cdot_L (m_2, n_2) = (m_1 \cdot_M m_2, n_1 \cdot_N n_2)$,
- $\varepsilon_L = (\varepsilon_M, \varepsilon_N)$,
- $\leq_L \subseteq L \times L$ *given by* $(m_1, n_1) \leq_L (m_2, n_2) \iff (m_1 <_M m_2) \vee (m_1 = m_2 \wedge n_1 \leq_N n_2)$.

The lexicographic product *of M and N, written as $M \ltimes N$, is given by the partial valuation structure* $(L, \cdot_L, \varepsilon_L, \leq_L)$.   □

Consequently, all collapsing elements have to be ignored for the lexicographic product. However, idempotent operators such as a worst case combination found in constraint hierarchies (and present in our case study in Sect. 2 when evaluating an assignment based on the worst violation over several time steps) or fuzzy and possibilistic constraints [19] necessarily lead to collapsing elements – an issue we address in Sect. 6.

However, using combinations of partial valuation structures by means of direct and lexicographic products, we are able to model the scenario depicted in Sect. 2 and also reuse them to present constraint hierarchies as partial valuation structures. But first we consider constraint relationships as a representative.

4   Constraint Relationships as Partial Valuation Structures

Partial valuation structures enable us to give an algebraic structure capable of representing preferences specified with constraint relationships. We revisit this construction first presented in [17] and [16], where we describe how to lift a quantitative preference specification over constraints to sets of violated constraints (representing assignments).

4.1 Constraint Relationships

A *directed acyclic graph*, or *DAG*, $G = (|G|, \rightarrow_G)$ is given by a set $|G|$ and a binary relation $\rightarrow_G \subseteq |G| \times |G|$ such that $\rightarrow_G^+$ is irreflexive. If $x \rightarrow_G y$, then x is a *predecessor* of y, and y is a *successor* of x. We obtain a partial order $PO\langle G \rangle = (|G|, \rightarrow_G^*)$ from G by taking the reflexive, transitive closure of $\rightarrow_G$, and write $g \leq_{PO\langle G \rangle} h$ if $g \rightarrow_G^* h$.

A *constraint relationship* over a constraint domain (X, D), or (X, D)-*constraint relationship*, is given by a DAG C with $|C|$ a finite set of (X, D)-constraints. We think of a constraint $c' \in |C|$ as *more important* than another constraint $c \in |C|$ if $c \rightarrow_C c'$.

For $V, W \subseteq |C|$, which we think of being sets of *violated* constraints by (X, D)-assignments v and w (i.e., $V = \{c \in |C| \mid v \not\models c\}$ and similarly for W), we want to express that W is *worse* than V w.r.t. C. We describe two kinds of liftings of the partial ordering induced by the DAG C to an ordering over subsets of $|C|$, using two *dominance properties* p: *single-predecessor* dominance ($p = \text{SPD}$) and *transitive-predecessors dominance* ($p = \text{TPD}$) as originally defined in [21]. Intuitively, dominance properties denote how much more important a constraint is compared to its predecessors to the quality of a solution. In SPD, a constraint can dominate only one less important one; in TPD, a single constraint is deemed more important than a whole set of predecessors.

We write $V \rightsquigarrow_C^p W$ for "V worsens to W for dominance property p over C". Both dominance properties share the following worsening rule, expressing that violating strictly more constraints is worse ($V_1 \uplus V_2$ denotes the union of V_1 and V_2 simultaneously requiring that V_1 and V_2 are disjoint):

$$V \rightsquigarrow_C^p V \uplus \{c\} \qquad\qquad \text{if } c \in |C| \qquad\qquad (\text{W})$$

The remaining rules for SPD and TPD express which constraint violations can be "traded" under the *ceteris paribus* assumption represented by $\uplus$:

$$V \uplus \{c\} \rightsquigarrow_C^{\text{SPD}} V \uplus \{c'\} \qquad\qquad \text{if } c \rightarrow_C c' \qquad\qquad (\text{SPD})$$

$$V \uplus \{c_1, \dots, c_k\} \rightsquigarrow_C^{\text{TPD}} V \uplus \{c'\} \qquad\qquad \text{if } \forall i . c_i \rightarrow_C^+ c' \qquad\qquad (\text{TPD})$$

These worsening relations induce partial orderings $\leq_C^p$ over sets of (violated) constraints for $p \in \{\text{SPD}, \text{TPD}\}$, when defining $W <_C^p V$ if, and only if, $V (\rightsquigarrow_C^p)^+ W$ (meaning repeated sequential application of the rules); this is to be read as "W is worse than V". Note that, by definition, the empty set is the *top* element w.r.t. to these orderings, meeting the intuition that "no violations" should be considered optimal since $\emptyset \rightsquigarrow_C^p V \neq \emptyset$. By abuse of notation, for assignments we also write $w <_C^p v$ if $\{c \in |C| \mid w \not\models c\} <_C^p \{c \in |C| \mid v \not\models c\}$, also read as "$w$ is worse than v".

4.2 From Constraint Relationships to Partial Valuation Structures

When abstracting from constraint relationships and casting them as a partial valuation structure, one might be tempted to start from the inclusion-based structure and extending it to accept an ordering over the constraints. The empty set, representing the fact that no constraints are violated, is the top element and simultaneously the neutral element for the union. But set union is idempotent. Consider an exemplary constraint relationship C with $|C| = \{a, b\}$ and $b \rightarrow_C a$. Then $\{a\} <_C^{\text{SPD}} \{b\}$ holds. Multiplying on both sides with $\{a\}$, i.e., taking the union, would result in $\{a\} \leq_C^{\text{SPD}} \{a, b\}$ by the required monotonicity of the multiplication. Hence, violating a only would be worse than violating both a and b, contradicting (W). However, we can patch this defect by not considering sets and their union but multisets and the multiset union as hinted by the disjointness assumptions in (SPD) and (TPD). Incidentally, when equipping multisets with an appropriate ordering induced by the partial order from the constraint relationship, the *free* partial valuation structure over the constraint relationship is obtained.

We denote the set of finite multisets over a set S by $\mathfrak{M}_{\text{fin}}(S)$, and the multiset union by $\uplus$. For a partial order $P = (|P|, \leq_P)$, we define the *upper* or *Smyth ordering*[3] on $\mathfrak{M}_{\text{fin}} |P|$ as the binary relation $\sqsubseteq^P \subseteq (\mathfrak{M}_{\text{fin}} |P|) \times (\mathfrak{M}_{\text{fin}} |P|)$ given by the transitive closure of

$$T \supseteq U \text{ implies } T \sqsubseteq^P U,$$

$$p \leq_P q \text{ implies } T \uplus \wr p \wr \sqsubseteq^P T \uplus \wr q \wr.$$

This relation is indeed a partial ordering on $\mathfrak{M}_{\text{fin}} |P|$ and $PVS\langle P \rangle = (\mathfrak{M}_{\text{fin}} |P|, \uplus, \wr \wr, \sqsubseteq^P)$ indeed a partial valuation structure. Moreover, $PVS\langle P \rangle$ is the *free* partial valuation structure over the partial order P in the sense of universal algebra. Thus, we have (for a detailed proof, see [16, §12]):

Lemma 1. *Let P be a partial order. Then $PVS\langle P \rangle = (\mathfrak{M}_{\text{fin}} |P|, \uplus, \wr \wr, \sqsubseteq^P)$ is the free partial valuation structure over P.*   □

The upper ordering, when employed for sets, exactly corresponds to $\leq_{C^{-1}}^{\text{SPD}}$ for a constraint relationship C: We need to invert C, i.e., consider $PVS\langle PO\langle C^{-1}\rangle\rangle$, as violating more important constraints has to lead to worse solutions. We get the corresponding set of (X, D)-$PVS\langle PO\langle C^{-1}\rangle\rangle$-soft constraints $\mathsf{P} = \{\varphi_c \mid c \in |C|\}$ where $\varphi_c(v) = \wr c \wr$ if $v \not\models c$ and $\wr \wr$ otherwise for $v \in [X \to D]$. However, the transitive-predecessors dominance can only be achieved by using a more specialized ordering.

This partial valuation structure can now be used to capture the preferences issued by the prosumers EV and biogas from our case study, see Fig. 1. For biogas we have the DAG $C = (\{\text{onOff}_{\text{bio}}, \text{gasFull}_{\text{bio}}, \text{ecoSweet}_{\text{bio}}\}, \{\text{onOff}_{\text{bio}} \to_C \text{gasFull}_{\text{bio}}, \text{ecoSweet}_{\text{bio}} \to_C \text{gasFull}_{\text{bio}}\})$. Assume we were to choose between the assignments v_1 and v_2 with $v_1 \not\models \{\text{gasFull}_{\text{bio}}, \text{ecoSweet}_{\text{bio}}\}$, $v_2 \not\models \{\text{onOff}_{\text{bio}}, \text{ecoSweet}_{\text{bio}}\}$. In $PVS\langle PO\langle C^{-1}\rangle\rangle$, v_1 is graded as $\mathsf{P}(v_1) = \wr \text{gasFull}_{\text{bio}}, \text{ecoSweet}_{\text{bio}} \wr$ and v_2 is graded as $\mathsf{P}(v_2) = \wr \text{onOff}_{\text{bio}}, \text{ecoSweet}_{\text{bio}} \wr$. Thus we get that $\mathsf{P}(v_1) \sqsubseteq^{PO\langle C^{-1}\rangle} \mathsf{P}(v_2)$, i.e., $\mathsf{P}(v_1)$ is worse than $\mathsf{P}(v_2)$ since $\text{gasFull}_{\text{bio}} \to_{C^{-1}} \text{onOff}_{\text{bio}}$ and therefore $\text{gasFull}_{\text{bio}} \leq_{PO\langle C^{-1}\rangle} \text{onOff}_{\text{bio}}$. This meets our intuition as $\text{gasFull}_{\text{bio}}$ is denoted more important (and thus more detrimental if violated) than $\text{onOff}_{\text{bio}}$.

5   Expressing Constraint Hierarchies as Lexicographic Products

As motivated by Sect. 2, constraint relationships provide the ability to combine unrelated preferences without introducing bias, as would occur if categorizing unrelated

---

[3] This multiset ordering mimics the eponymous ordering used in powerdomain constructions [1, Ch. 9], where partial orders are lifted to semi-lattices with an idempotent multiplication.

constraints into more or less equivalent layers in constraint hierarchies. However, constraint hierarchies are more appropriate when metric error functions are available or a clear dominance of one layer over others exists – as might be the case in relating organizational vs. individual goals. Using lexicographic combinations, both approaches can be seamlessly combined.

We first recast the original definitions of constraint hierarchies [8] to position them within the scope of partial valuation structures. In particular, we represent a constraint hierarchy as a lexicographical product of partial valuation structures in place of the layers. We discuss the existing propositions of weighting functions but increase the generality of the approach as arbitrary partial valuation structures could eventually be lexicographically combined to form hierarchies. The presence of collapsing elements gives us a criterion that algebraic structures defining a combination operation for gradings such as partial valuation structures or c-semirings representing layers in a constraint hierarchy need to show in order to be used in lexicographic combinations. Soft constraints in all but the least important layer should not map to collapsing elements to preserve all gradings. All constraint hierarchies classified as "rational" in [15] (and thus expressible as c-semirings) are void of collapsing elements.

Formally, a *constraint hierarchy* $H = (C_k)_{1 \leq k \leq n}$ over a constraint domain (X, D), or (X, D)-*constraint hierarchy*, is given by a family of sets C_k of (X, D)-constraints. The constraints in *level* $1 \leq k \leq n$ are considered as *strictly more important* than the ones in level $k + 1$. An (X, D)-constraint hierarchy is *finite* if $\bigcup_{1 \leq k \leq n} C_k$ is finite.

Let $H = (C_k)_{1 \leq k \leq n}$ be a finite (X, D)-constraint hierarchy, let $\overline{W} = (M_k)_{1 \leq k \leq n}$ be a corresponding family of partial valuation structures M_k representing the individual layers, and let for each $1 \leq k \leq n$ and for each $c \in C_k$, μ_c be the associated (X, D)-M_k-soft constraint. We call $\mathsf{H} = (\mathsf{M}_k)_{1 \leq k \leq n}$ with $\mathsf{M}_k = \{\mu_c \mid c \in C_k\}$ for $1 \leq k \leq n$ a (X, D)-$\overline{W}$-*soft constraint hierarchy*. For a $v \in [X \to D]$ the *solution degree* for $(\mathsf{M}_k)_{1 \leq k \leq n}$ of v is defined to be $(\mathsf{M}_k(v))_{1 \leq k \leq n}$. Define a binary relation $<_\mathsf{H} \subseteq [X \to D] \times [X \to D]$ by

$$w <_\mathsf{H} v \iff \exists 1 \leq k \leq n . \quad (\forall 1 \leq i \leq k - 1 . \mathsf{M}_i(w) = \mathsf{M}_i(v))$$
$$\wedge \mathsf{M}_k(w) <_{M_k} \mathsf{M}_k(v) ,$$

saying that the assignment w is *strictly worse* than the assignment v if ties up to a certain level $k - 1$ (or no ties if $k = 1$) are resolved by a strict inequality in k. This corresponds to the lexicographic order on the set $\{(\mathsf{M}_k(v))_{1 \leq k \leq n} \mid v \in [X \to D]\}$, i.e.,

$$w <_\mathsf{H} v \iff (\mathsf{M}_k(w))_{1 \leq k \leq n} <_{M_1 \ltimes \ldots \ltimes M_n} (\mathsf{M}_k(v))_{1 \leq k \leq n}$$

if, on the one hand, every M_k is a bounded partial valuation structure for all $2 \leq k \leq n$, and, on the other hand, $\mathsf{M}_k(v), \mathsf{M}_k(w) \notin \mathfrak{C}(M_k)$ for all $1 \leq k \leq n$, or, equivalently, if $\mu_c(v), \mu_c(w) \notin \mathfrak{C}(M_k)$ for each $c \in C_k$, $1 \leq k \leq n$. The first requirement, that each M_k is bounded, can be achieved by moving from M_k to its lifted variant $(M_k)_\perp$. The second hinges on the selected partial valuation structure, guaranteeing order equivalence *only if* no collapsing elements are present. In practice, this requires that no soft constraint maps to any collapsing element.

5.1   Locally Predicate Better

In the literature, many different variants are used for the comparison of solution degrees of individual layers. A straightforward approach requests that an assignment is considered worse if it is Pareto-dominated in terms of soft constraints, i.e., it violates a strict superset of constraints of another assignment's violation set. Consider a single level k of a finite (X, D)-constraint hierarchy $H = (C_k)_{1 \leq k \leq n}$, and let $C = C_k$. The so-called *locally-predicate-better* (LPB)-*comparator* [8] for C corresponds to requiring

$$w <_C^{\text{LPB}} v \iff \{c \in C \mid w \not\models c\} \supset \{c \in C \mid v \not\models c\} .$$

This is expressed by the partial valuation structure $M = (\mathfrak{P}_{\text{fin}}(C), \cup, \emptyset, \supseteq)$ where $\mathfrak{P}_{\text{fin}}(C)$ stands for finite subsets of C and the set of (X, D)-M-soft constraints $\mathsf{M} = \{\mu_c \mid c \in C\}$ with $\mu_c(v) = \{c\}$ if $v \not\models c$ and $\mu_c(v) = \emptyset$ otherwise, for each $c \in C$. However, all elements of M are idempotent, and thus the collapsing elements of M are $\mathfrak{P}_{\text{fin}}(C) \setminus \{\emptyset\}$. Hence, M is not suitable for a lexicographic product. Choosing instead the partial valuation structure $N = (\mathfrak{M}_{\text{fin}}(C), \uplus, \wr\wr, \supseteq)$, where $\mathfrak{M}_{\text{fin}}(C)$ denotes finite multisets over C, N has no collapsing elements and the set of (X, D)-N-soft constraints $\mathsf{N} = \{\nu_c \mid c \in C\}$ with $\nu_c(v) = \wr c \wr$ if $v \not\models c$ and $\nu_c(v) = \wr\wr$ otherwise, for each $c \in C$, deviates this situation, since we have for all $v, v' \in [X \to D]$ that

$$\mathsf{M}(v) \leq_M \mathsf{M}(v') \iff \mathsf{N}(v) \leq_N \mathsf{N}(v')$$

as any $\nu(c)$ adds at most one occurrence of c to the combined grading.

One may think of the ordering over $[X \to D]$ induced by M as preference *specification* that is *implemented* by N which is applicable to lexicographic products due to the absence of collapsing elements. More specifically, from a user's point of view, the used structure is not relevant as long as the intended ordering is preserved. We can generalize this idea of substituting a specifying partial valuation structure by another implementing collapse-free counterpart:

Definition 5. *A finite set of (X, D)-M-soft constraints M and a finite set of (X, D)-N-soft constraints N are* optima equivalent, *written as* $\mathsf{M} \approx \mathsf{N}$, *if* $\text{Max}^{\lesssim_M}[X \to D] = \text{Max}^{\lesssim_N}[X \to D]$. $\square$

5.2   Globally Weighted Better

The locally predicate better comparator, however, leaves us with various incomparable assignments due to the proper subset relation. Moreover, predicate evaluations may be too strict and metric error functions can take their role. Additionally, constraints may be weighted. Thus, a more general approach does not consider constraints at the individual level but maps a layer to one aggregated value (corresponding to $\mathsf{M}_k(v)$). Borning called these comparators *global* [8]. That way, we can also treat locally predicate (and metric) better as special cases.

Formally, a *weighting* for a set C of (X, D)-constraints is given by a function $g : C \times [X \to D] \to \mathbb{R}_{\geq 0}$ with $g(c, v) = 0$ iff $v \models c$ for $v \in [X \to D]$ and $c \in C$. This function subsumes both the metric aspects and weights. Traditionally, the following combinations of weights have been considered, where a valuation is deemed worse than another if its combined weight is greater than the combined weight of the other.

- *Weighted sum:* $W_1(v) = \sum_{c \in C} g(c, v)$.
- *Least squares:* $W_2(v) = \sqrt{\sum_{c \in C} g(c, v)^2}$.
- *Worst case:* $W_\infty(v) = \max\{g(c, v) \mid c \in C\}$.

These comparators can be recast as partial valuation structures based on the real numbers where the ordering is just $\geq$:

Definition 6. *A real partial valuation structure R has $0 \in |R| \subseteq \mathbb{R}_{\geq 0}$ for its underlying set, 0 as its neutral element and the (inverted) usual ordering on the real numbers $\geq$ as its ordering.* ☐

The following real partial valuation structures capture the global comparators; the notation R_∞ is justified by the well-known fact that $\lim_{p \to \infty} (r^p + s^p)^{1/p} = \max\{r, s\}$:[4]

- *Weighted sum:* $R_1 = (\mathbb{R}_{\geq 0}, \cdot_1, 0, \geq)$ with $r \cdot_1 s = r + s$;
- *Least squares:* $R_2 = (\mathbb{R}_{\geq 0}, \cdot_2, 0, \geq)$ with $r \cdot_2 s = \sqrt{r^2 + s^2}$;
- *p-norm* for $p > 0$: $R_p = (\mathbb{R}_{\geq 0}, \cdot_p, 0, \geq)$ with $r \cdot_p s = (r^p + s^p)^{1/p}$;
- *Worst case:* $R_\infty = (\mathbb{R}_{\geq 0}, \cdot_\infty, 0, \geq)$ with $r \cdot_\infty s = \max\{r, s\}$.

Given a real partial valuation structure R and a weighting $g : C \times [X \to D] \to |R| \subseteq \mathbb{R}_{\geq 0}$, the (R, g)-*weighting* of a $v \in [X \to D]$ is now given by $W_R^g(v) = \prod_R \{g(c, v) \mid c \in C\}$. Each such weighting W induces a relation $\precsim_C^W \subseteq [X \to D] \times [X \to D]$ on assignments with $w \precsim_C^W v$ denoting w is worse than v, defined by

$$w \precsim_C^W v \iff W(w) \geq W(v).$$

Let us now turn to the question how to use these real partial valuation structures in a lexicographic product. All real partial valuation structures R with $\cdot_R = \cdot_p$ for some $p > 0$ are appealing as they have no collapsing elements, since $r \cdot_p s = (r^p + s^p)^{1/p}$ is strictly monotonic in both arguments. The choices of weighted-sum-better and least-squares-better are thus readily applicable to lexicographic products. For real partial valuation structures with $\cdot_R = \cdot_\infty$, however, $\mathfrak{C}(R) = |R| \setminus \{0\}$, since $\cdot_\infty$ is idempotent. Consequently, one cannot use them to mimic the ordering of a (X, D)-W-soft constraint hierarchy using a lexicographic product since the resulting partial valuation structures would degrade to $(\{0\}, \cdot_\infty, 0, \geq)$. Assume, e.g., that C has three different constraints c_1, c_2, and c_3; that there are assignments v_1 violating only c_1, v_2 violating only c_2, v_{13} violating exactly c_1 and c_3, and v_{23} violating exactly c_2 and c_3; and that the weightings are independent of the valuation, i.e., $g(c_1, v_1) = g(c_1, v_{13})$ and $g(c_2, v_2) = g(c_2, v_{23})$ and $g(c_3, v_{13}) = g(c_3, v_{23})$. Also assume that the weightings for v_1, v_2, v_{13}, and v_{23} are related by

$$W_{R_\infty}^g(v_1) = g(c_1, v_1) > g(c_2, v_2) = W_{R_\infty}^g(v_2),$$
$$W_{R_\infty}^g(v_{13}) = \max\{g(c_1, v_{13}), g(c_3, v_{13})\} =$$
$$\max\{g(c_2, v_{23}), g(c_3, v_{23})\} = W_{R_\infty}^g(v_{23}).$$

---

[4] The choice of $\cdot_R$ for a real partial valuation structure is somewhat limited by the following theorem by Bohnenblust [7]: If $|R| = \mathbb{R}_{\geq 0}$ and $(t \cdot r) \cdot_R (t \cdot s) = t \cdot (r \cdot_R s)$ holds in the real partial valuation structure R for all $r, s, t \in \mathbb{R}_{\geq 0}$ (where $\cdot$ is the usual multiplication), then either $1 \cdot_R 1 = 1$ and $r \cdot_R s = \max\{r, s\}$ for all $r, s \in \mathbb{R}_{\geq 0}$, or $1 \cdot_R 1 > 1$ and $r \cdot_R s = (r^p + s^p)^{1/p}$ for all $r, s \in \mathbb{R}_{\geq 0}$ for some $p > 0$.

Intuitively, $g(c_3, v)$ is greater than $g(c_1, v)$ and $g(c_2, v)$ if $v \not\models c_3$, but as only the worst case is considered, all other gradings do not contribute to the distinction. Therefore, previously comparable assignments become equal when combined with $g(c_3, v)$. Any set of (X, D)-M-soft constraints $\mathsf{M} = \{\mu_c \mid c \in C\}$ reflecting the ordering induced by $W_{R_\infty}^g$ on assignments, i.e., $\mathsf{M}(v) \leq_M \mathsf{M}(v') \iff W_{R_\infty}^g(v) \geq W_{R_\infty}^g(v')$, would thus have μ_{c_3} mapping to a collapsing element in M. To still implement a partial valuation structure that meets our preference specifications originally stated in R_∞, we have to abandon the search for optima equivalence (see Def. 5) for a less restrictive property.

6 Simulating Partial Valuation Structures

A variety of application scenarios, however, motivate the evaluation of assignments based on the worst criterion including our examples in Sect. 2. To still be able to use "worst case" as a valid comparator for lexicographic products, we first relax our notion of optima equivalence to the asymmetric optima simulation. A similar effort was made by Bistarelli, Codognet, and Rossi, who discuss abstractions of c-semiring-based soft constraint problems by means of Galois connections [3]. The problem can also be seen in the context of viewpoints in model reformulation [25] in the sense that we seek an alternative partial valuation structure that reflects the same underlying user preferences.

Definition 7. *A finite set of (X, D)-N-soft constraints* N *optima simulates a finite set of (X, D)-M-soft constraints* M, *written as* $\mathsf{N} \preccurlyeq \mathsf{M}$, *if for each* $v_\mathsf{M} \in \mathrm{Max}^{\leq_M}[X \to D]$ *there is a* $v_\mathsf{N} \in \mathrm{Max}^{\leq_N}[X \to D]$ *with* $\mathsf{M}(v_\mathsf{M}) = \mathsf{M}(v_\mathsf{N})$, *and, vice versa, if for each* $v_\mathsf{N} \in \mathrm{Max}^{\leq_N}[X \to D]$ *there is a* $v_\mathsf{M} \in \mathrm{Max}^{\leq_M}[X \to D]$ *with* $\mathsf{M}(v_\mathsf{M}) = \mathsf{M}(v_\mathsf{N})$.   □

Intuitively, our definition of optima simulation allows that assignments in the same equivalence class w.r.t. M are *further* distinguished in N as long as each equivalence class in $\mathrm{Max}^{\leq_M}[X \to D]$ is represented in $\mathrm{Max}^{\leq_N}[X \to D]$ (we do not "lose" optima) and no assignment suboptimal in M is considered optimal in N. Then, N is a reasonable candidate for substituting M, constituting a kind of refinement. Obviously, $\mathsf{M} \approx \mathsf{N}$ if, and only if, $\mathsf{N} \preccurlyeq \mathsf{M}$ and $\mathsf{M} \preccurlyeq \mathsf{N}$. We can furthermore give sufficient criteria for the relations of assignments evaluated in M and N to check if $\mathsf{N} \preccurlyeq \mathsf{M}$ holds, provided that both M and N are admissible:

Lemma 2. *Let (X, D) be a constraint domain, and let M and N be admissible sets of M- and N-soft constraints over (X, D), respectively, such that for all $v, v' \in [X \to D]$*

$$\mathsf{M}(v) <_M \mathsf{M}(v') \quad \textit{implies} \quad \mathsf{N}(v) <_N \mathsf{N}(v')$$
$$\mathsf{M}(v) \parallel_M \mathsf{M}(v') \quad \textit{implies} \quad \mathsf{N}(v) \parallel_N \mathsf{N}(v')$$

Then $\mathsf{N} \preccurlyeq \mathsf{M}$.

Proof. Let first $v_1 \in \mathrm{Max}^{\leq_M}[X \to D]$. Let $v_1 \notin \mathrm{Max}^{\leq_N}[X \to D]$. Then, since N is admissible, there is a $v_2 \in \mathrm{Max}^{\leq_N}[X \to D]$ with $\mathsf{N}(v_1) <_N \mathsf{N}(v_2)$. Moreover, there is a $v_1' \in \mathrm{Max}^{\leq_M}[X \to D]$ with $\mathsf{M}(v_2) \leq_M \mathsf{M}(v_1')$, since M is admissible. But $\mathsf{M}(v_2) <_M \mathsf{M}(v_1')$ is impossible, since then also $\mathsf{N}(v_2) <_N \mathsf{N}(v_1')$ contradicting $\mathsf{N}(v_2) \in \mathsf{N}^*$.

Thus $M(v_2) = M(v_1')$. Moreover, either $M(v_1) \parallel_M M(v_1')$ or $M(v_1) = M(v_1')$ since both $M(v_1)$ and $M(v_1')$ are elements of M^*. But $M(v_1) \parallel_M M(v_1')$ is impossible, since we would have $M(v_1) \parallel_M M(v_2) = M(v_1')$ and $N(v_1) <_N N(v_2)$. Thus $M(v_2) = M(v_1') = M(v_1)$. — Now let $v_2 \in \text{Max}^{\leq_N}[X \to D]$. If $v_2 \notin \text{Max}^{\leq_M}[X \to D]$, there would be, since M is admissible, a $v_1 \in \text{Max}^{\leq_M}[X \to D]$ such that $M(v_2) <_M M(v_1)$, i.e. $N(v_2) <_N N(v_1)$, contradicting $N(v_2) \in N^*$.   □

The requirements of the lemma prove helpful in finding a collapse-free simulating partial valuation structure for a real partial valuation structure using $\cdot_\infty$. In particular, we investigate the use of $\cdot_p$ as a substitute for $\cdot_\infty$, since this directly avoids collapsing elements. For that purpose, for a $0 \in V \subseteq \mathbb{R}_{\geq 0}$, let, for each $p > 0$, V_p be the real partial valuation structure $(\langle V \rangle_p, \cdot_p, 0, \geq)$ with $\langle V \rangle_p$ the smallest subset of $\mathbb{R}_{\geq 0}$ with $r \cdot_p s \in \langle V \rangle_p$ if $r, s \in \langle V \rangle_p$; and let V_∞ denote the real partial valuation structure $(V, \cdot_\infty, 0, \geq)$. The second requirement of the lemma for moving from a V_∞ to some V_p is trivially satisfied for real partial valuation structures, since $\geq$ is total. For the first requirement we have the following characterization:

Lemma 3. *Let* $0 \in V \subseteq \mathbb{R}_{\geq 0}$, *and* $p > 0$. *Then for each* $n \geq 1$

$$\textstyle\prod_\infty \vec{r} < \prod_\infty \vec{s} \quad \text{implies} \quad \prod_p \vec{r} < \prod_p \vec{s} \quad \text{for all } \vec{r}, \vec{s} \in V^n \qquad (*_p)$$

if, and only if,

$$r < s \quad \text{implies} \quad n^{1/p} \cdot r < s \quad \text{for all } r, s \in V. \qquad (**_p)$$

Proof. Let first $(*_p)$ hold and let $r, s \in V$ with $r < s$. Choose $r_1 = \ldots = r_n = r$, $s_1 = \ldots = s_{n-1} = 0$, and $s_n = s$. Then $\prod_\infty (r_i)_{1 \leq i \leq n} = r < s = \prod_\infty (s_i)_{1 \leq i \leq n}$, and thus $n^{1/p} \cdot r = \prod_p (r_i)_{1 \leq i \leq n} < \prod_p (s_i)_{1 \leq i \leq n} = s$. — Now, let $(**_p)$ hold and let $r = \prod_\infty (r_i)_{1 \leq i \leq n} < \prod_\infty (s_i)_{1 \leq i \leq n} = s$. Define $r_1' = \ldots = r_n' = r$ and $s_1' = \ldots = s_{n-1}' = 0$, $s_n' = s$. Then $\prod_p (r_i)_{1 \leq i \leq n} \leq \prod_p (r_i')_{1 \leq i \leq n} = n^{1/p} \cdot r$, since $r_i \leq r$ for all $1 \leq i \leq n$, and $s = \prod_p (s_i')_{1 \leq i \leq n} \leq \prod_p (s_i)_{1 \leq i \leq n}$, since $0 \leq s_i$ for all $1 \leq i \leq n$. Then $\prod_p (r_i)_{1 \leq i \leq n} \leq n^{1/p} \cdot r < s \leq \prod_p (s_i)_{1 \leq i \leq n}$.   □

The lemma shows that $r < n^{1/p} \cdot r < s$ is required for all $0 \neq r < s \in V$. But this is only satisfiable if there is no $t \in V$ with $r < t \leq n^{1/p} \cdot r$, since by $(**_p)$ we would get $r < n^{1/p} \cdot r < t$. In particular, $V = \mathbb{R}_{\geq 0}$ cannot be simulated.

We call a $0 \in V \subseteq \mathbb{R}_{\geq 0}$ δ-*separated* for some $\delta > 1$ if $s/r \geq \delta$ for all $0 \neq r < s \in V$. For each δ-separated V and $n \geq 1$, $(**_p)$ holds if $p > \ln n / \ln \delta$, i.e. $n^{1/p} < \delta$: Let $r < s$ for $r, s \in V$. Then either $r = 0$, and thus $n^{1/p} \cdot r = 0 = r < s$, or $r \neq 0$, and thus $n^{1/p} \cdot r < \delta \cdot r \leq s$. Moreover, not only does δ-separation provide us with a suitable p, a set $0 \in V \subseteq \mathbb{R}_{\geq 0}$ must be δ-separated for $(**_p)$ to hold: If $0 \in V \subseteq \mathbb{R}_{\geq 0}$ for each $\delta > 1$ shows $0 \neq r < s \in V$ with $s/r < \delta$, then $(**_p)$ is violated for each $p > 0$, since we can choose $0 \neq r < s \in V$ with $s/r < n^{1/p}$, and then $n^{1/p} \cdot r > s$.

Example 1. (1) Let $0 \in V \subseteq \mathbb{R}_{\geq 0}$ be finite. Then there is a $\varepsilon > 0$ such that $|r_1 - r_2| \geq \varepsilon$ for all $r_1 \neq r_2 \in V$. Let $0 \neq r < s \in V$. Then $s/r \geq (r + \varepsilon)/r = 1 + \varepsilon/r \geq 1 + \varepsilon/\max V$. Thus V is $(1 + \varepsilon/\max V)$-separated.

(2) Let $c \in \mathbb{R}$ with $c > 1$ and let $V^c = \{c^n \mid n \in \mathbb{N}\} \cup \{0\}$. If $0 \neq r < s \in V^c$, then there are $m < n$ with $r = c^m$ and $s = c^n$. Then $c^n/c^m = c^{n-m} \geq c$ holds. Thus, V^c is c-separated and unbounded.

(3) Let $d \in \mathbb{R}$ with $d > 1$ and let $V^d = \{d^{-n} \mid n \in \mathbb{N}\} \cup \{0\}$. If $0 \neq r < s \in V^d$, then there are $m < n$ with $r = d^{-n}$ and $s = d^{-m}$. Then $d^{-m}/d^{-n} = d^{-m+n} > d$ holds. In addition, $0 < d^{-n} \leq d$ for all $n \in \mathbb{N}$. Hence, V^d is d-separated and bounded. $\qquad \square$

Wrapping up, we can define a suitable simulating partial valuation structure for V_∞ by means of a p-norm to deal with preference specifications requiring the worst case.

Proposition 1. *Let (X, D) be a constraint domain, $0 \in V \subseteq \mathbb{R}_{\geq 0}$ δ-separated, M_∞ an admissible set of (X, D)-V_∞-soft constraints, and $p > \ln |\mathsf{M}_\infty| / \ln \delta$. Define $\tau_p : |V_\infty| \to |V_p|$ by $\tau_p(r) = r$ and the finite set of (X, D)-V_p-soft constraints M_p by $\mathsf{M}_p = \{\tau_p \circ \mu \mid \mu \in \mathsf{M}_\infty\}$. If M_p is admissible, then $\mathsf{M}_p \preccurlyeq \mathsf{M}_\infty$.*

Proof. The claim that $\mathsf{M}_p \preccurlyeq \mathsf{M}_\infty$ follows from Lem. 2 by the choice of p and the totality of the order in V_∞. $\qquad \square$

This construction gives us a tool for practical scenarios requiring a worst-case comparator that are, as we showed, not directly expressible in lexicographic products of partial valuation structures or c-semirings [15] due to the presence of collapsing elements. For a finite set of (X, D)-constraints C and for a weighting $g : C \times [X \to D] \to \mathbb{R}_{\geq 0}$, let $V = \{g(c, v) \mid c \in C, v \in [X \to D]\} \cup \{0\}$. It has now to be checked that V is δ-separated for some $\delta > 1$. Classical CSPs are dealing with finite domains, and thus δ-separatedness is readily applicable in these scenarios. For real-valued possible error values, one could turn to discretizing and bounding a domain according to Ex. 1(1). We may then choose $p > \ln |C| / \ln \delta$. For each $c \in C$, we have the (X, D)-V_∞-soft constraint c_∞^g by $c_\infty^g(v) = g(c, v)$, and the (X, D)-V_p-soft constraint c_p^g by $c_p^g(v) = g(c, v)$. Then, since C is finite, we obtain $\{c_p^g \mid c \in C\} \preccurlyeq \{c_\infty^g \mid c \in C\}$, provided that both $\{c_\infty^g \mid c \in C\}$ and $\{c_p^g \mid c \in C\}$ are admissible. But if V is finite, this is guaranteed as observed in Sect. 3.2. Example 1(3), however, shows that δ-separatedness alone does not imply admissibility.

Let us apply the construction to the organizational preferences of Sect. 2. Assume that the possible error values representing violations are given by $V = \{0, 1, 2, 3\}$ and that the finite set of V_x-soft constraints $\mathsf{V}_x = \{v_t \mid t \in T\}$ represent the violations at time step $t \in T = \{1, 2, 3\}$ (with $x = \infty$ or $x = p$). Assume two assignments w_1 and w_2 such that $v_1(w_1) = 3$ and $v_t(w_1) = 0$ if $t > 1$; and further $v_t(w_2) = 2$ for all $t \in T$. Since V is finite, by Ex. 1(1) we get that it is δ-separated with $\delta = 1 + 1/3 \approx 1.3$. In fact, it is also 1.5-separated since 3 cannot take the role of r in Ex. 1(1). With $n = |V| = 3$, we get that we have to choose p greater than $\ln 3 / \ln 1.5 \approx 2.71$ for $\mathsf{V}_p \preccurlyeq \mathsf{V}_\infty$ to work. Indeed, we get that while $\mathsf{V}_\infty(w_1) = 3 > \mathsf{V}_\infty(w_2) = 2$, $p = 2$ is not high enough to preserve this ordering as $\mathsf{V}_2(w_1) = 3 < \mathsf{V}_2(w_2) \approx 3.46$, leading to an incorrect preference decision. But choosing $p = 3$ already preserves the ordering correctly as $\mathsf{V}_3(w_1) = 3 > \mathsf{V}_3(w_2) = 2.88$ and we thus have $\mathsf{V}_3 \preccurlyeq \mathsf{V}_\infty$.

This makes the construction applicable for a lexicographic product with its controlled prosumers' preferences. These are in turn also given as partial valuation structures: for biogas and EV, we use the free partial valuation structure over the partial order induced by their constraint relationships calling them P_{biogas} and P_{EV}; for thermal we use p-norms to either directly translate the desired comparators or also use simulation to get a worst-case comparator and a lexicographic product to obtain a partial valuation structure $P^1_{\text{thermal}} \ltimes P^2_{\text{thermal}}$. Since no prosumer is considered more important than the others, we combine their preferences with a direct product. In accordance with Fig. 1 we thus get the partial valuation structure

$$V_3 \ltimes (P_{\text{biogas}} \times P_{\text{EV}} \times (P^1_{\text{thermal}} \ltimes P^2_{\text{thermal}}))$$

for the overall soft constraint problem where P_{biogas} and P_{EV} are partial valuation structures originating in constraint relationships and $(P^1_{\text{thermal}} \ltimes P^2_{\text{thermal}})$ represents a constraint hierarchy.

7 Conclusions

Based on results of Wirsing et al., we showed how to express different qualitative and quantitative preference formalisms as partial valuation structures. First we expressed the representation of constraint relationships as partial valuation structures by a free construction. Second, the lexicographical product associated with partial valuation structures allowed us to reformulate constraint hierarchies to position them in a soft constraint framework. This process also led to the negative result that a direct translation of the worst-case comparator necessarily leads to partial valuation structures with collapsing elements. This fact hindered previous attempts at expressing constraint hierarchies as c-semirings. However, it is possible to look for collapsing-free partial valuation structures that fulfill several qualities regarding the assignment ordering. We therefore introduced the notion of optima simulation and provided an example of a real-valued partial valuation structure implemented with p-norms which can be used to order assignments in lieu of the original collapsing worst-case comparator. We have also demonstrated by means of a small case study that adaptive and organic computing applications can benefit from the presented ideas since reconfiguration and clustering call for compositionality which the more conventional c-semirings do not offer to the same extent.

However, our simulation result for the worst-case comparator still is burdened by some computational effort for the involved p-norms. In fact, it seems that a more general construction for optima simulation at least for totally-ordered partial valuation structures (i.e., valuation structures) is reachable, that may avoid this effort. Furthermore, based on these constructions, efficient solving and optimization algorithms and propagators need to be devised to make them available to problems of practical interest.

Dedication. The authors express their gratitude to Martin Wirsing for his encouraging style in research and teaching, displaying a kind and appreciative attitude towards the work of colleagues as well as motivating to connect rigorous methods with software engineering.

References

1. Amadio, R.M., Curien, P.L.: Domains and Lambda-Calculi. Cambridge Tracts in Theoretical Computer Science, vol. 46. Cambridge University Press (1998)
2. Anders, G., Schiendorfer, A., Steghöfer, J.P., Reif, W.: Robust Scheduling in a Self-Organizing Hierarchy of Autonomous Virtual Power Plants. In: Stechele, W., Wild, T. (eds.) Proc. 2nd Int. Wsh. Self-optimisation in Organic and Autonomic Computing Systems (SAOS 2014), pp. 1–8 (2014)
3. Bistarelli, S., Codognet, P., Rossi, F.: Abstracting Soft Constraints: Framework, Properties, Examples. Artif. Intell. 139, 175–211 (2002)
4. Bistarelli, S., Frühwirth, T., Marte, M., Rossi, F.: Soft Constraint Propagation and Solving in Constraint Handling Rules. Computational Intelligence 20(2), 287–307 (2004)
5. Bistarelli, S., Montanari, U., Rossi, F.: Semiring-based Constraint Satisfaction and Optimization. J. ACM 44(2), 201–236 (1997)
6. Bistarelli, S., Montanari, U., Rossi, F., Schiex, T., Verfaillie, G., Fargier, H.: Semiring-Based CSPs and Valued CSPs: Frameworks, Properties, and Comparison. Constraints 4(3), 199–240 (1999)
7. Bohnenblust, H.F.: An Axiomatic Characterization of L_p-spaces. Duke Math. J. 6, 627–640 (1940)
8. Borning, A., Freeman-Benson, B., Wilson, M.: Constraint Hierarchies. LISP Symb. Comp. 5, 223–270 (1992)
9. Cooper, M., Schiex, T.: Arc Consistency for Soft Constraints. Artificial Intelligence 154(1), 199–227 (2004)
10. Delgado, A., Olarte, C.A., Pérez, J.A., Rueda, C.: Implementing Semiring-Based Constraints Using Mozart. In: Van Roy, P. (ed.) MOZ 2004. LNCS, vol. 3389, pp. 224–236. Springer, Heidelberg (2005)
11. Eberhardinger, B., Seebach, H., Knapp, A., Reif, W.: Towards Testing Self-organizing, Adaptive Systems. In: Merayo, M.G., de Oca, E.M. (eds.) ICTSS 2014. LNCS, vol. 8763, pp. 180–185. Springer, Heidelberg (2014)
12. Gadducci, F., Hölzl, M., Monreale, G.V., Wirsing, M.: Soft constraints for lexicographic orders. In: Castro, F., Gelbukh, A., González, M. (eds.) MICAI 2013, Part I. LNCS, vol. 8265, pp. 68–79. Springer, Heidelberg (2013)
13. Hölzl, M., Meier, M., Wirsing, M.: Which Soft Constraints do you Prefer? In: Proc. 7th Int. Wsh. Rewriting Logic and its Applications (WRLA 2008). Electronic Notes in Theoretical Computer Science, vol. 238(3), pp. 189–205 (2009)
14. Hölzl, M., Wirsing, M.: Towards a System Model for Ensembles. In: Agha, G., Danvy, O., Meseguer, J. (eds.) Formal Modeling: Actors, Open Systems, Biological Systems. LNCS, vol. 7000, pp. 241–261. Springer, Heidelberg (2011)
15. Hosobe, H.: Constraint Hierarchies as Semiring-Based CSPs. In: Proc. 21st Int. Conf. Tools with Artificial Intelligence (ICTAI 2009), pp. 176–183 (2009)
16. Knapp, A., Schiendorfer, A.: Embedding Constraint Relationships into C-Semirings. Tech. Rep. 2014-03, Institute for Software and Systems Engineering, University of Augsburg (2014), http://opus.bibliothek.uni-augsburg.de/opus4/frontdoor/index/index/docId/2684
17. Knapp, A., Schiendorfer, A., Reif, W.: Quality over Quantity in Soft Constraints. In: Proc. 26th Int. Conf. Tools with Artificial Intelligence (ICTAI 2014), pp. 453–460 (2014)
18. Leenen, L., Anbulagan, A., Meyer, T., Ghose, A.K.: Modeling and Solving Semiring Constraint Satisfaction Problems by Transformation to Weighted Semiring Max-SAT. In: Orgun, M.A., Thornton, J. (eds.) AI 2007. LNCS (LNAI), vol. 4830, pp. 202–212. Springer, Heidelberg (2007)

19. Meseguer, P., Rossi, F., Schiex, T.: Soft Constraints. In: Rossi, F., van Beek, P., Walsh, T. (eds.) Handbook of Constraint Programming, ch. 9 (2006)
20. Nafz, F., Seebach, H., Steghöfer, J.P., Anders, G., Reif, W.: Constraining Self-organisation Through Corridors of Correct Behaviour: The Restore Invariant Approach. In: Müller-Schloer, C., Schmeck, H., Ungerer, T. (eds.) Organic Computing – A Paradigm Shift for Complex Systems. Autonomic Systems, vol. 1, pp. 79–93. Springer (2011)
21. Schiendorfer, A., Steghöfer, J.P., Knapp, A., Nafz, F., Reif, W.: Constraint Relationships for Soft Constraints. In: Bramer, M., Petridis, M. (eds.) Proc. 33rd SGAI Int. Conf. Innovative Techniques and Applications of Artificial Intelligence (AI 2013), pp. 241–255. Springer (2013)
22. Schiendorfer, A., Steghöfer, J.P., Reif, W.: Synthesis and Abstraction of Constraint Models for Hierarchical Resource Allocation Problems. In: Proc. 6th Int. Conf. Agents and Artificial Intelligence (ICAART 2014), vol. 2, pp. 15–27. SciTePress (2014)
23. Schiendorfer, A., Steghöfer, J.P., Reif, W.: Synthesised Constraint Models for Distributed Energy Management. In: Proc. 3rd Int. Wsh. Smart Energy Networks & Multi-Agent Systems (SEN-MAS 2014), pp. 1529–1538 (2014)
24. Schiex, T., Fargier, H., Verfaillie, G.: Valued Constraint Satisfaction Problems: Hard and Easy Problems. In: Proc. 14th Int. Joint Conf. Artificial Intelligence (IJCAI 1995), vol. 1, pp. 631–639. Morgan Kaufmann (1995)
25. Smith, B.M.: Modelling. In: Rossi, F., van Beek, P., Walsh, T. (eds.) Handbook of Constraint Programming, ch. 11. Elsevier (2006)
26. Steghöfer, J.-P., et al.: Trustworthy Organic Computing Systems: Challenges and Perspectives. In: Xie, B., Branke, J., Sadjadi, S.M., Zhang, D., Zhou, X. (eds.) ATC 2010. LNCS, vol. 6407, pp. 62–76. Springer, Heidelberg (2010)
27. Steghöfer, J.P., Anders, G., Siefert, F., Reif, W.: A System of Systems Approach to the Evolutionary Transformation of Power Management Systems. In: Wsh. Proc. 43th Nat. Conf. GI Jahrestagung (INFORMATIK 2013). Lect. Notes Inf., vol. P-220, Bonner Köllen Verlag (2013)
28. Tsang, E.P.K.: Foundations of Constraint Satisfaction. Computation in Cognitive Science 289. Academic Press (1993)

An Institution for Object-Z with Inheritance and Polymorphism

Hubert Baumeister[1], Mohamed Bettaz[2,3], Mourad Maouche[3],
and M'hamed Mosteghanemi[2]

[1] DTU Compute, Technical University of Denmark
huba@dtu.dk
[2] Laboratoire Méthodes de Conception de Systèmes, ESI, Algeria
{m.bettaz,m.mosteghanemi}@mesrs.dz
[3] Philadelphia University, Jordan
mmaouch@philadelphia.edu.jo

Abstract. Large software systems are best specified using a multi-paradigm approach. Depending on which aspects of a system one wants to model, some logic formalisms are better suited than others. The theory of institutions and (co)morphisms between institutions provides a general framework for describing logical systems and their connections. This is the foundation of multi-modelling languages allowing one to deal with heterogeneous specifications in a consistent way. To make Object-Z accessible as part of such a multi-modelling language, we define the institution OZS for Object-Z. We have chosen Object-Z in part because it is a prominent software modelling language and in part because it allows us to study the formalisation of object-oriented concepts, like object identity, object state, dynamic behaviour, polymorphic sorts and inheritance.

Keywords: software engineering models, Object-Z, category theory, institution, inheritance, polymorphic types.

1   Introduction

Large and complex software systems are best modelled using a multi-paradigm approach, which provides different views on the same software. The Unified Modeling Language (UML) [1] is a good example of a modelling language using different types of models to model the various aspects of a software system. Component- and class diagrams, e.g., are used to describe the structural aspects, while state-machines, activity diagrams, and interaction diagrams, e.g., focus on the behavioural aspects of the software.

In the context of formal methods, the heterogeneous tool set (Hets) [2,3] uses a similar, view based, approach to the formal specification of software systems. Hets is based on the theory of institutions developed by Goguen and Burstall in the late 1970s [4]. Originally intended to capture the basic concepts of logical systems and model theory, it was used to define the semantics of formal specification languages, like Clear [5], ASL [6], and later CASL [7], independent from

R. De Nicola and R. Hennicker (Eds.): Wirsing Festschrift, LNCS 8950, pp. 134–154, 2015.

the particular formal logic. Furthermore, institutions provide logic independent mechanisms for building larger specifications from smaller ones [6,8,9].

The concepts of (co)morphisms between institutions form the foundation for relating logical systems. They provide a mechanism to specify multifaceted software systems using appropriate languages backed by their logical systems. Such a multi-paradigm specification language has been realised with Hets.

In this paper, we present an institution for Object-Z [10], thus providing a first step to the integration of Object-Z with other specification languages in a multi-paradigm specification language.

Our interest in Object-Z is motivated by the fact that Object-Z is known as a prominent software/system modelling language based on the specification language Z [11]. It supports most of the fundamental concepts of object-orientation, such as object-identity, classes, inheritance, and polymorphism. In addition, like UML, Object-Z offers possibilities for meta-modelling. Moreover, Object-Z specifications may be enhanced by adding detailed properties required for the system under specification, that cannot be represented by using the UML alone [12].

The semantics of Object-Z in [10] is given in terms of Z, which is a first order logic framework. It has been shown in [13] that Z itself forms an institution. The contribution of this paper is, that we are addressing the issues of object identity, object state and dynamic behaviour of objects, polymorphism, and inheritance directly in the institution without resorting to the institution for Z. Using this approach, we hope to provide a better understanding of these concepts in an institution-based framework.

Other approaches for dealing with object-oriented concepts in the context of institutions is [14], where the authors define an institution for UML 2.0 static structures, starting from the abstraction of a UML class diagram example; class diagrams' methods are not given any meaning, and inheritance is interpreted as subset inclusion; in [15] and [16] the authors define a heterogeneous approach to UML semantics but are also limited to static structures, i.e., ignoring state change by methods, and thus disregarding the dynamic behaviour of objects.

The institution defined in [17] deals with the dynamic behaviour of state based systems using the concept of implicit state; however, this approach does not explicitly deal with object-oriented concepts, like object-identity and inheritance.

In this work we define an institution for Object-Z specifications that is able to deal with dynamic behaviour of the system under design by using an explicit state approach. The state of objects can be constrained by (class) invariants and changed by operations involving input/output parameters, local variables, pre/post conditions as well as operation expressions. Inheritance in Object-Z is not necessarily interpreted as subset inclusion, i.e., we are no more in the case of subsort polymorphism [18], and cannot thus treat polymorphism such as in [14]. To deal with polymorphism in our institution, we introduce the concept of polymorphic sorts. Polymorphic sorts recall type classes of Haskell or *kinds* such as defined in [19].

This contribution is in honour of Martin Wirsing who first suggested to some of the authors the use of institutions. His work entitled "What is a Multi-Modelling

Language?" [16] was the starting point of a wide research that led to this contribution. One author feels privileged to have had the chance to work closely with Martin in several EU projects.

The remainder of this paper is organised as follows: Section 1.1 recalls basic notions from institutions. In Section 1.2 we give an example aiming at introducing basic constructs from Object-Z and illustrating the concepts of our institution. Section 2 is devoted to the Object-Z institution. Section 3 discusses inheritance in an institution independent setting and its relationship to polymorphism. In Section 4 we present concluding remarks and give some directions for future work. We assume familiarity with basic notions in institutions [20] and of Object-Z [10].

1.1 Institutions

Here, we recapitulate the definition of an institution. More information can be found in [20]. An institution $\mathcal{I} = (Sig, Sen, Mod, \models)$ consists of:

- a category Sig, whose objects are called signatures and whose morphisms are called signature morphisms,
- a functor $Sen : Sig \to Set$, assigning to each signature Σ a set whose elements are called sentences over that signature, and for each signature morphism $\phi : \Sigma \to \Sigma'$ in Sig a function $Sen(\phi) : Sen(\Sigma) \to Sen(\Sigma')$, translating sentences over Σ to sentences over Σ',
- a functor $Mod : Sig \to Cat^{op}$, assigning to each Σ a category whose objects are called Σ-models and whose arrows are called Σ-homomorphisms, and for each signature morphism $\phi \in Sig$ a functor $Mod(\phi)$, most commonly written as $\_|_{\phi}$, from $Mod(\Sigma')$ to $Mod(\Sigma)$. $Mod(\phi)(M') = M'|_{\phi}$ is called the ϕ-reduct of $M' \in Mod(\Sigma')$,
- a satisfaction relation $\models_{\Sigma} \subseteq Mod(\Sigma) \times Sen(\Sigma)$ for each $\Sigma \in Sig$,

such that for each signature morphism $\phi : \Sigma \to \Sigma'$ in Sig, the satisfaction condition

$$M' \models_{\Sigma'} Sen(\phi)(\varphi) \qquad \textit{iff} \qquad M'|_{\phi} \models_{\Sigma} \varphi$$

holds for all $M' \in Mod(\Sigma')$ and $\varphi \in Sen(\Sigma)$.

1.2 An Introductory Example

In this section we give an example aiming at introducing basic constructs from Object-Z and illustrating the concepts of our institution. Inspired by [21], the example is about a liquid tank management system (LTMS) that illustrates the control and monitoring actions associated with filling and emptying of liquid containers. The operative part of the system involves two kinds of devices: liquid tanks and indicators. Each liquid tank may be equipped with an indicator which mainly serves as a display device. A (liquid tank or indicator) device is specified by a dedicated Object-Z class providing a set of elementary operations that may be invoked by an Object-Z control class.

The indicator is modelled by the class *Indicator* (Fig. 1), and its state by a state schema comprising two basic attributes, namely *light* and *danger*, where *light* is used to signal some critical situations and *danger* for storing the minimal value of the amount of liquid that has to be always available in the tank. The initial state schema *INIT* provides the two attributes *light* and *danger* with their initial values which are respectively *off* and 0. *SetLightOn*, *SetLightOff*, and *UpdateDanger* are operation schemas. *SetLightOn* and *SetLightOff* set *light* to *on*, respectively to *off*; *SetLightOn* is invoked each time a critical situation happens, and *UpdateDanger* allows to update *danger* with the value stored in the input parameter (d?).

The liquid tank is modelled by the class *Tank* (Fig. 3), where the type *Liquid-Kinds* is defined in Fig. 2; *ind* is a reference attribute, *capacity* gives the maximum liquid amount that might be contained by the tank, *level* maintains the liquid amount that is currently contained by the tank, and *liquids* identifies the various kinds of liquids that can be contained by the tank. *ind* links a liquid tank object with its equipped indicator object. The predicate ($\# ind \leq 1$) is a class invariant describing a constraint on the number of indicator devices equipping a tank device. *INIT* provides *Tank* attributes with their initial values. The operation *EmptyOut* (with input parameter q? and post-condition $level' = level - q?$) allows to withdraw an amount q? of liquid. The predicate ($level > q?$) defines a pre-condition requiring that the withdrawn amount cannot 'exceed' the amount of liquid available in the tank. *Fill* allows to add the amount q? of liquid to the tank; it is required that the new amount of liquid does not exceed the tank capacity. *SetSupportedLiquids* defines the kinds of liquids that can actually be supported by the tank. *AttachIndicator* allows to connect a liquid tank to an indicator. *AlertOn* and *AlertOff* are operation names for operation expressions. These expressions are used to send messages to objects from *Indicator* to set *light* respectively to *on* and *off*. Both operations use the scope enrichment operator (denoted by a •) to illustrate the correct use of promoted operations [10].

As an example for inheritance in Object-Z, take the specification of the *WarmingTank* (cf. Fig. 4). The *WarmingTank* class describes a special kind of liquid tank that offers the capability to warm up or cool down the liquid contained in the tank; in addition to the attributes of the liquid tank, our warming liquid tank has one more attribute: *temp* that stores the current temperature of the liquid contained in the tank. Moreover, the class invariant is constrained by an additional predicate (*flammable* $\notin$ *liquids*), and *SetSupportedLiquids* requires that flammable liquids are no more supported by the tank. *WarmingTank* provides two additional operations: *WarmUp* that allows to increase the temperature of the liquid contained by the tank, and *CoolDown* that allows to decrease the temperature of the liquid contained by the tank. Both operations have an input parameter (t?) representing respectively the amount of temperature by which the current tank temperature has to be increased or decreased from the current tank temperature.

2   The OZS Institution

In the following, we define the Object-Z institution OZS by defining signatures, models and sentences. For lack of space, we only include the definitions, facts, and proofs needed for the understanding of the construction. We refer to the technical report [22] for further details.

2.1   Signatures

Signatures declare sorts for classes and (primitive) types as well as operations for basic attributes, reference attributes and operation schemas (returning values or not returning values). We allow monomorphic sorts, like *bool*, *Nat*, *Indicator*, *Tank* and polymorphic sorts, like $[Tank] = \{Tank, WarmingTank\}$, which are sets of monomorphic class sorts.

A polymorphic sort $[c] = \{c_1, \ldots, c_n\}$ denotes a set of sorts $c_1, \ldots c_n$ instead of a single sort. That is, for an element e to be of sort $[c]$ it has to be at least an element of one of the sorts $c_1, \ldots, c_n$. As a consequence, we can access

$STATUS ::= on \mid off$

```
┌─ Indicator ──────────────────────────────────────────────
│  ┌────────────────────────────────────────────────────
│  │ light : STATUS
│  │ danger : ℕ
│  ├─ INIT ─────────────────────────────────────────────
│  │ light = off
│  │ danger = 0
│  ├─ SetLightOn ──────────────────────────────────────
│  │ Δ(light)
│  ├────────────────────────────────────────────────────
│  │ light' = on
│  ├─ SetLightOff ─────────────────────────────────────
│  │ Δ(light)
│  ├────────────────────────────────────────────────────
│  │ light' = off
│  ├─ UpdateDanger ────────────────────────────────────
│  │ Δ(danger)
│  │ d? : ℕ
│  ├────────────────────────────────────────────────────
│  │ danger' = d?
```

Fig. 1. Indicator

$LiquidKinds ::= flammable \mid ordinary \mid toxic$

Fig. 2. Liquid Kinds

an attribute or apply an operation to that element only, if this attribute or operation is common to all sorts in $[c]$. In the case, where $[c]$ is given by the set of all direct or indirect subclasses of c, then, the attributes and operations all sorts in $[c]$ have in common, are those of class c.

In the following, we often need to apply a function $g : A \to B$ to a subset $\{a_1, \ldots, a_n\}$ of A instead of just one element of A. In abuse of notation, we define $g(\{a_1, \ldots, a_n\}) = \{g(a) \mid a \in \{a_1, \ldots, a_n\}\}$. Furthermore, if g' is a function from A to $\mathbb{P}(B)$, we define $g'(\{a_1, \ldots, a_n\}) = \bigcup_{a \in \{a_1, \ldots, a_n\}} g'(a)$.

Definition 1. *A **signature** Σ in OZS is a triple $\Sigma = (S, F, \pi)$ where,*

- $S = C \cup T \cup P$ *is the disjoint union of class sorts C, primitive types T (seen as abstract data types) and polymorphic sorts P.*
- *A function $\pi : C \to 2^C$, assigning a set of class sorts for each class sort. We may write $[c]$ for $\pi(c)$.*
- *The set of **polymorphic sorts** is defined by $P = \{[c] \mid c \in C\}$.*
- $F = B \cup R \cup O$ *declares a family of operation symbols $B_{c \to t}$, $(c \in C, t \in T)$ representing basic attributes, a family of operation symbols $R_{c \to c'}$, $c \in C$, $c' \in C \cup P$, representing reference attributes, and a family of operation symbols $O_{c,w}$ and $O_{c,w,s}$, $(c \in C, w \in S^*, s \in S)$ representing operation schemas; $O_{c,w,s}$ is used for operation schemas returning values, while $O_{c,w}$ is used for operation schemas not returning values.*

*A signature **morphism** $\phi : \Sigma \to \Sigma'$, where $\Sigma = (S, F, \pi)$ and $\Sigma' = (S', F', \pi')$, is a map $\phi = (\phi_S : S \to S', \phi_F : F \to F')$ which is compatible with the sorts in S and attributes and operations in F and $\phi_S([c]) = \phi_S(\pi(c)) = \pi'(\phi_S(c)) = [\phi_S(c)]$ for all polymorphic sorts $[c] \in P$.*

In the following, we use $attr(c)$ for the set of all basic- and reference attributes of class sort $c \in C$, i.e., $attr(c) = \bigcup_{t \in T} B_{c \to t} \cup \bigcup_{c' \in C} R_{c \to c'}$.

Conceptually, $\pi(c) = [c] = \{c_1, \ldots, c_n\}$ can be thought of as the set containing c and all subclasses of c. However, this is not required by the definitions. $\pi(c)$ can be any set of class sorts and does not have to include c.

Example 1. Let's take the signature of an *Indicator* (*Ind* for short) (cf. Fig. 1) as an example. $\Sigma_{Ind} = (S_{Ind}, F_{Ind}, \pi_{Ind})$. Here $S_{Ind} = T_{Ind} \cup C_{Ind} \cup P_{Ind}$, where $T_{Ind} = \{Nat, Real, STATUS\}$, $C_{Ind} = \{Indicator\}$ and $\pi(Indicator) = \{Indicator\}$ which gives $P_{Ind} = \{[Indicator]\} = \{\{Indicator\}\}$.

Furthermore, $F_{Ind} = B_{Ind \to STATUS} \cup B_{Ind \to Nat} \cup O_{Ind,<>} \cup O_{Ind,<Nat>}$. Here, $<>$ denotes the empty sequence of sorts and $<Nat>$ a sequence of sorts consisting only of the sort Nat. Note that $R_{c \to c'}$ is empty, as *Indicator* does not have a reference to either itself, nor another class. Then we have $B_{Ind \to STATUS} = \{light\}$, $B_{Ind \to Nat} = \{danger\}$, $O_{Ind,<>} = \{SetLightOn, SetLightOff\}$, and $O_{Ind,<Nat>} = \{UpdateDanger\}$.

```
┌─ Tank ──────────────────────────────────────────────────────────────
│  ┌──────────────────────────────────────────────────────────────────
│  │ level : ℕ
│  │ capacity : ℕ
│  │ liquids : ℙ LiquidKinds
│  │ ind : ℙ Indicator
│  ├──────────────────────────────────────────────────────────────────
│  │ #ind ≤ 1
│  └──────────────────────────────────────────────────────────────────
│
│  ┌─ INIT ──────────────────────────────────────────────────────────
│  │ level = 0
│  │ capacity = 1000
│  │ ind = ∅
│  │ liquids = ∅
│  └──────────────────────────────────────────────────────────────────
│
│  ┌─ Fill ──────────────────────────────────────────────────────────
│  │ Δ(level)
│  │ q? : ℕ
│  ├──────────────────────────────────────────────────────────────────
│  │ level + q? < capacity
│  │ level' = level + q?
│  └──────────────────────────────────────────────────────────────────
│
│  ┌─ EmptyOut ──────────────────────────────────────────────────────
│  │ Δ(level)
│  │ q? : ℕ
│  ├──────────────────────────────────────────────────────────────────
│  │ level > q?
│  │ level' = level − q?
│  └──────────────────────────────────────────────────────────────────
│
│  ┌─ SetSupportedLiquids ───────────────────────────────────────────
│  │ Δ(liquids)
│  │ lk? : ℙ LiquidKinds
│  ├──────────────────────────────────────────────────────────────────
│  │ liquids' = lk?
│  └──────────────────────────────────────────────────────────────────
│
│  ┌─ AttachIndicator ───────────────────────────────────────────────
│  │ Δ(ind)
│  │ i? : Indicator
│  ├──────────────────────────────────────────────────────────────────
│  │ #ind = 0
│  │ ind' = ind ∪ {i?}
│  └──────────────────────────────────────────────────────────────────
│
│  AlertOn ≙ [i? : Indicator | i? ∈ ind ∧ i?.danger ≥ level] • i?.SetLightOn
│  AlertOff ≙ [i? : Indicator | i? ∈ ind ∧ i?.danger < level] • i?.SetLightOff
└──────────────────────────────────────────────────────────────────────
```

Fig. 3. Liquid Tank

WarmingTank

Tank

$temp : \mathbb{N}$

$flammable \notin liquids$

INIT

$temp = 0$

SetSupportedLiquids

$flammable \notin lk?$

WarmUp

$\Delta(temp)$
$t? : \mathbb{N}$

$level \neq 0$
$temp' = temp + t?$

CoolDown

$\Delta(temp)$
$t? : \mathbb{N}$

$temp' = temp - t?$

Fig. 4. Warming Tank

Example 2. To give an example of the use of polymorphic sorts, consider Fig. 5, an Object-Z specification of the system class *TankManagementSystem* (*TMS* for short) that provides references to a set of tank objects (*reference* attribute *tnks*) and a set of indicator objects (reference attribute *inds*).

Note that $\downarrow Tank$ denotes a polymorphic sort, in our case $\pi(Tank) = \{Tank, WarmingTank\}$, i.e., all subclasses of class *Tank*. Furthermore, *tnks* is a polymorphic reference to *Tank*- and *WarmingTanks* objects, that is $tnks \in R_{TMS \rightarrow [Tank]}$. This means, that *tnks* is a set that can contain at the same time, both *Tank* objects and *WarmingTank* objects. In contrast, if we had defined $tnks : \mathbb{P}(Tank)$, we could only have *Tank* objects stored in *tnks*, but not *WarmingTank* objects.

Lemma 1. *OZS signatures and OZS signature morphisms define a category denoted* Sig_{OZS}.

The identity morphism $\phi_{id} : \Sigma \rightarrow \Sigma$ is the family of identities on sorts and operations. The composition of two signature morphisms is the corresponding composition of functions on sorts and operations.

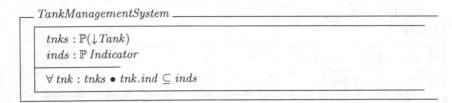

Fig. 5. Tank Management System

Proposition 1. *The category Sig_{OZS} is finitely co-complete.*

To show that Sig_{OZS} is finitely co-complete, it suffices to show that Sig_{OZS} has an initial object and pushouts [23]. Here, we only provide the construction of the initial object and the pushout without any proofs.

The initial object, $\Sigma_{init} = (\varnothing, \varnothing, \pi_\varnothing)$, in Sig_{OZS} consists of the empty set for sorts and operations, and $\pi_\varnothing$ is the empty function from $\varnothing$ to $\mathbb{P}(\varnothing)$.

Given two signature morphisms $\phi_{1/2} : \Sigma_0 \to \Sigma_{1/2}$, where $\Sigma_i = (S_i, F_i, \pi_i)$ for $i \in \{0, 1, 2\}$. The pushout of Σ_1 and Σ_2 wrt. ϕ_1 and ϕ_2, i.e., $\Sigma_{po} = (S_{po}, F_{po}, \pi_{po})$ is defined similar to the case of many-sorted signatures as the pushout of the sets of sorts S_{po} and the family of operations F_{po} [8]. In particular, since S_i is the disjoint union of C_i, T_i, and P_i, we have $S_{po} = C_{po} \cup T_{po} \cup P_{po}$, where C_{po}, T_{po}, and P_{po} are the pushouts given by the sets C_i, T_i, and P_i for $i \in \{0, 1, 2\}$, respectively.

Given the injections $(\iota_0)_S$, $(\iota_1)_S$, and $(\iota_2)_S$ from $S_{0/1/2}$ to S_{po}, restricted to class sorts from $C_{0/1/2}$ to C_{po}, given by the definition of pushouts, we can define three functions $f_i : C_i \to \mathbb{P}(C_{po})$ by $f_i(c_i) = (\iota_i)_S(\pi_i(c_i))$ for all $c_i \in C_i$ and $i \in \{0, 1, 3\}$. These three functions form a cocone from C_i to $\mathbb{P}(C_{po})$ which gives rise, by the definition of the pushout C_{po}, to a unique function $\pi_{po} : C_{po} \to \mathbb{P}(C_{po})$, the missing component of our pushout signature.

2.2   Models

Our models are based on the definition of an explicit state that associates to each object (of each class) a tuple of values of its attributes.

Definition 2. *Given a signature Σ, a Σ–model M defines:*

- *A family of pairwise disjoint sets M_s for each sort $s \in T \cup C$,*
- *A family of sets $M_{[c]} = \bigcup_{c' \in [c]} M_{c'}$ for each $[c] \in P$*
- *An (explicit) state, $state_M = \sum_{c \in C}(M_c \to \prod_{a \in attr(c)} M_{type(a)})$,*
  where $type(a) = t$ if $a \in B_{c \to t}$ for some $t \in T$ and $type(a) = pow(c')$ if $a \in R_{c \to c'}$ for some $c' \in C \cup P$ and $M_{pow(c')} = \mathbb{P}(M_{c'})$. For an element σ of $state_M$, $\sigma_c(oid)(a)$ is in M_t or in $\mathbb{P}(M_{c'})$, with $c \in C$, $oid \in M_c$, and $a \in attr(c)$,

- A function $\text{init}_M : C \to state_M$ that provides the initial state of an object of a class (assuming that the initial state is the same for all objects of the same class), and
- A function $(o_M)_c : state_M \times M_c \times M_{s_1} \times \ldots \times M_{s_n} \to \mathbb{P}(state_M)$ for each operation $o \in O_{c,w}$, and a function $(o_M)_c : state_M \times M_c \times M_{s_1} \times \ldots \times M_{s_n} \to \mathbb{P}(state_M \times M_s)$ for each operation $o \in O_{c,w,s}$, $(w = s_1 \ldots s_n)$.

Definition 3. *Given two Σ-models M_1 and M_2, then a Σ-homomorphism $h : M_1 \to M_2$ consists of a familiy of functions $h_s : (M_1)_s \to (M_2)_s$ for $s \in T \cup C$ together with a function $h_{st} : state_{M_1} \to \mathbb{P}(state_{M_2})$ such that*

- $\text{init}(c)_{M_2} \in h_{st}(\text{init}_{M_1}(c))$ for all $c \in C$
- $h_{st}((o_{M_1})_c(\sigma_1, oid, m_1, \ldots, m_n)) \subseteq$
$$(o_{M_2})_c(h_{st}(\sigma_1), h_c(oid), h_{s_1}(m_1), \ldots, h_{s_n}(m_n))$$
  for all $\sigma_1 \in state_{M_1}$, $oid \in (M_1)_c$, $m_1 \in (M_1)_{s_1}$, $\ldots m_n \in (M_n)_{s_n}$ *for* $o \in O_{c,w}$
- $(\sigma_2', h_s(v)) \in (o_{M_2})_c(h_{st}(\sigma_1), h_c(oid), h_{s_1}(m_1), \ldots, h_{s_n}(m_n))$ *for all* $(\sigma_1', v) \in (o_{M_1})_c(\sigma_1, oid, m_1, \ldots, m_n)$ *and* $\sigma_2' \in h_{st}(\sigma_1')$ *where* $\sigma_1 \in state_{M_1}$, $oid \in (M_1)_c$, $m_1 \in (M_1)_{s_1}$, $\ldots m_n \in (M_n)_{s_n}$, $v \in M_s$ *and* $o \in O_{c,w,s}$
- $h_{type(a)}(\sigma_{1\,c}(oid)(a)) \in h_{st}(\sigma_1)_c(h_c(oid))(a)$ *where* $a \in attr(c)$, $oid \in (M_1)_c$, *and* $\sigma_1 \in state_{M_1}$.

The category of Σ-models has as objects Σ-models and as morphisms Σ-homomorphisms. The identiy morphism $h : M \to M$ are the identity functions on the interpretation of sorts and $h_{st}(\sigma) = \{\sigma\}$. The composition of Σ-homomorphisms is the composition of the functions on the interpretation on sorts and $h_{1\,state}(h_{2\,state}(\sigma_1)) = \bigcup_{\sigma_2 \in h_{2\,state}(\sigma_1)} h_{1\,state}(\sigma_2)$.

Example 3. Considering again the example of the *Indicator* (Example 1), a Σ_{Ind} model M contains a set for each sort $s \in S_{Ind} = T_{Ind} \cup C_{Ind} \cup P_{Ind}$. For example, for $nat \in T_{Ind}$ we have $M_{Nat} = \mathbb{N}$, for $STATUS \in T_{Ind}$, $M_{STATUS} = \{on, off\}$ or for $Ind \in C$, we have $M_{Ind} = \{i_1, i_2, \ldots\}$.

$P_{Ind} = \{[Ind]\}$ and $M_{[Ind]} = M_{Ind}$ because Ind is the only element of $[Ind]$.

The value of attributes and object references is given by the state element $\sigma \in state_M$. For example, for $light \in B_{Ind \to STATUS}$ and $i \in M_{Ind}$, we have σ_{Ind} is of type $M_{Ind} \to \prod_{a \in B_{c \to t} \cup R_{c \to c'}} M_{type(a)}$, that is, $\sigma_{Ind}(i)(light) = off \in M_{STATUS}$.

The *SetLightOff* operation in $O_{Ind,<>}$ is the function $SetLightOff_M : state_M \times M_{Ind} \to \mathbb{P}(state_M)$, such that $\sigma' \in SetLightOff_M(\sigma, i)$ iff $\sigma_{Ind}'(i)(light) = off$ and $\sigma_{Ind}'(i')(light) = \sigma_{Ind}(i')(light)$ for $i \neq i'$ and $\sigma_{Ind}'(i'')(danger) = \sigma_{Ind}(i'')(danger)$ for all $i, i', i'' \in M_{Ind}$ and $\sigma', \sigma \in state_M$.

Example 4. Continuing the *TankManagementSystem* example (*TMS*), we have $M_{[Tank]} = M_{Tank} \cup M_{WarmingTank}$ for the polymorphic sort $[Tank]$ in a Σ_{TMS}-model M. That means, that for $\sigma \in state_M$ and reference $tnks \in B_{TMS \to [Tank]}$, we have that $\sigma_{TMS}(tms)(tnks) \in \mathbb{P}(M_{Tank} \cup M_{WarmingTank})$ for an element $tms \in M_{TMS}$. Thus the attribute $tnks$ is a reference to a set of objects, both from M_{Tank} and $M_{WarmingTank}$. If we had defined $tnks$ as $tnks : \mathbb{P}(Tank)$, $tnks$

would be in $B_{TMS \to Tank}$ and thus $\sigma_{TMS}(tms)(tnks) \in \mathbb{P}(M_{Tank})$. In this case $tnks$ could only reference sets of objects with elements of sort M_{Tank}.

Definition 4. *Given a signature morphism* $\phi : \Sigma \to \Sigma'$ *in* Sig_{OZS} *and a* Σ'-*model* M, *the* ϕ-**reduct** *of* M *is defined by:*

- $(M|_\phi)_s = M_{\phi s(s)}$ *for* $s \in T \cup C$,
- $(M|_\phi)_{[c]} = M|_{[\phi s(c)]}$ *for* $[c] \in P$,
- $(o_{M|_\phi})_c(\sigma, oid, v_1, \ldots, v_n) =$
    $\{\sigma''|_\phi \mid \exists \sigma' : \sigma'|_\phi = \sigma \text{ and } \sigma'' \in (\phi_F(o)_M)_{\phi s(c)}(\sigma', oid, v_1, \ldots, v_n)\}$
  for all $o \in O_{c,w}$, $v_i \in (M|_\phi)_{s_i}$, $oid \in (M|_\phi)_c$,
- $(o_{M|_\phi})_c(\sigma, oid, v_1, \ldots, v_n) = \{(\sigma''|_\phi, v) \mid \exists \sigma' : \sigma'|_\phi = \sigma$
    and $(\sigma'', v) \in (\phi_F(o)_M)_{\phi s(c)}(\sigma', oid, v_1, \ldots, v_n)\}$ *for all* $o \in O_{c,w,s}$, $v_i \in (M|_\phi)_{s_i}$, $v \in (M|_\phi)_s$, *and* $oid \in (M|_\phi)_c$.

If h *is a* Σ'-*homomorphism from* M_1' *to* M_2', *then* $h|_\phi$ *is given by:*

- $(h|_\phi)_s = h_{\phi(s)}$
- $(h|_\phi)_{st}(\sigma_1) = h_{st}(\phi(\sigma_1))|_\phi$ *where* $\phi(\sigma_1) = \{\sigma_1' \in state_{M_1'} \mid \sigma_1'|_\phi = \sigma_1\}$ *and* $(\sigma_1'|_\phi)_c(oid)(a) = \sigma'_{\phi s(c)}(oid)(\phi_F(a))$ *for all* $c \in C$, $oid \in (M_1'|_\phi)_c = (M_1')_{\phi s(c)}$

Note that $state_{M|_\phi}$ is completely given by the family of sets $(M|_\phi)_s$ for $s \in S$. Furthermore, any state σ in $state_M$ has a reduct $\sigma|_\phi$ in $state_{M|_\phi}$ given by $(\sigma|_\phi)_c(oid)(a) = \sigma_{\phi s(c)}(oid)(\phi_F(a))$ for $oid \in (M|_\phi)_c$, $c \in C$, $\sigma \in state_M$ and $a \in B \cup R$. However, there may be situations, where not every state σ in $state_{M|_\phi}$ can be extended to a state σ' in $state_M$ such that $\sigma = \sigma'|_\phi$. This is, for example, the case, when a signature morphism maps two different attributes of a class c in Σ to the same attribute in Σ'.

Example 5. Since *WarmingTank* inherits from *Tank* (cf. Fig. 4), there exists a signature morphism ϕ from Σ_{Tank} to $\Sigma_{WarmingTank}$. ϕ maps *Tank* to *Warming-Tank* and is the identity on all other components (sorts, attributes and operations) (cf. Sect. 3). Given a $\Sigma_{WarmingTank}$-model M, $M|_\phi$ is a Σ_{Tank}-model.

For example, $(M|_\phi)_{Ind} = M_{\phi(Ind)} = M_{Ind}$ and $(M|_\phi)_{Tank} = M_{\phi(Tank)} = M_{WarmingTank}$ for sort Ind, $Tank \in C_{Tank}$, Ind, $WarmingTank \in C_{WarmingTank}$ and $\phi(Ind) = Ind$ and $\phi(Tank) = WarmingTank$.

For $\sigma \in state_M$ and an attribute, e.g., $level \in (B_{Tank})_{Tank \to Nat}$, i.e., $level$ is a basic attribute of Σ_{Tank}, its evaluation wrt. $\sigma|_\phi$ is defined by $(\sigma|_\phi)_{Tank}(oid)(level) = \sigma_{\phi s(Tank)}(oid)(\phi_F(level)) = \sigma_{WarmingTank}(oid)(level)$ for all $oid \in (M|_\phi)_{Tank} = M_{WarmingTank}$.

For an operation, e.g., $AttachIndicator \in (O_{Tank})_{Tank, <Ind>}$, σ and σ' in $state_M$, we have $\sigma'|_\phi \in AttachIndicator_{(M|_\phi)}(\sigma|_\phi, oid, i)$ iff $\sigma' \in AttachIndicator_M(\sigma, oid, i)$ for $oid \in (M|_\phi)_{Tank} = M_{WarmingTank}$ and $i \in (M|_\phi)_{Ind} = M_{Ind}$.

The functor Mod_{OZS} from Sig_{OZS} to Cat takes each signature Σ to the category having as objects Σ-models and as morphisms Σ-homomorphisms, and each Sig_{OZS}-morphism ϕ from Σ to Σ' to a functor from the category $Mod_{OZS}(\Sigma')$ to the category $Mod_{OZS}(\Sigma)$, sending each Σ'-model M to its ϕ-reduct $M|_\phi$ and each Σ'-homomorphism h to its ϕ-reduct $h|_\phi$.

2.3 Sentences

Sentences are defined using EBNF. Here, o denotes an operation symbol, id an identifier, and λ is the empty list. inv_c, $init_c$ and the symbols $(,), ?, [,], :$, etc. are terminal symbols, while S, P, OE, $Declaration$, etc. are nonterminal symbols. Finally, $::=$ is used to define a production rule and the vertical bar separates alternatives.

- Sentences $S ::= o(id? : id, \ldots, id? : id; \; id! : id)[id, \ldots, id] : P \mid inv_c : P \mid$
  $init_c : P \mid o \cong OE$
- Operation Expressions $OE ::= E.o \mid [P] \mid [Declaration \mid P] \mid OE \wedge OE \mid$
  $OE \bullet OE$
- $Declaration ::= Delta{-}list \; Params$
- $Delta{-}list ::= \lambda \mid \Delta(id, \ldots, id)$
- $Params ::= \lambda \mid id? : id...id? : id; \; id! : id \mid id? : id...id? : id \mid id! : id$
- Predicates $P ::= E \; op \; E \mid E \in E \mid E \subseteq E \mid P \wedge P \mid P \vee P \mid P \Rightarrow P \mid \neg P \mid$
  $\forall X : E.P \mid \exists X : E.P$, where $op \in \{=, <, \leq, >, \geq\}$
- Expressions $E ::= id \mid id \; Decoration \mid E \; bop \; E \mid \#E \mid E.id$
- $Decoration ::= \; ' \mid ? \mid !$

Example 6. Examples of sentences are

- $inv_{TMS} : \forall \; tnk : tnks. \quad tnk.ind \subseteq inds$ from $TankManagementSystem$,
- $UpdateDanger(d? : \mathbb{N})[danger] : danger' = d?$ from $Tank$,
- $init_{Ind} : light = off \wedge danger = 0$ from $Indicator$, and
- $AlertOn \cong [i? : Indicator \mid i? \in ind \wedge i?.danger \geq level] \bullet i?.SetLightOn$
  from $Tank$.

The concept of well-formedness of sentences is introduced to make sure that the evaluation of sentences is always defined. Well-formedness can be seen as static type checking of sentences. To this end, we introduce the concept of a variable environment. The basic idea of a variable environment is, that it keeps track of the available identifiers for evaluating the expressions, like the class c the expression is evaluated in, together with its attributes (undecorated, e.g. $a \in attr(c)$, representing the state before an operation, and decorated with a prime, e.g. a', representing the state after an operation). In addition to the attributes of a class, the variable environment keeps track of variables V and their type (using a function τ from variables V to their type).

Given a signature Σ with class sorts C and polymorphic sorts P. For a sort $c \in C$ or a polymorphic sort $[c] \in P$, let $pow(c)$ and $pow([c])$ denote the sort representing the powerset of c and $[c]$, respectively. Given a Σ-model M, then $pow(c)$ represents the set $M_{pow(c)} = \mathbb{P}(M_c)$ and $pow([c])$ represents the set $M_{pow([c])} = \mathbb{P}(M_{c_1} \cup \cdots \cup M_{c_n})$ for $[c] = \{c_1, \ldots, c_n\}$.

Definition 5. *Let Σ be a signature, $X \subseteq V \cup \{v? \mid v \in V\} \cup \{v! \mid v \in V\}$, V a set of variables/identifiers, $\tau : X \to S \cup \{pow(c) \mid c \in C\} \cup \{pow([c]) \mid [c] \in P\}$ a mapping of undecorated, i.e., elements of V, and decorated variables/identifiers, i.e., of the form $v?$ or $v!$ where $v \in V$, in X to sorts of Σ, $c \in C$, $\varsigma \subseteq B_{c \to t} \cup R_{c \to c'}$ and $\varsigma' = \{a' \mid a \in Attr\}$ where $Attr \subseteq B_{c \to t} \cup R_{c \to c'}$, then a* **variable environment** *γ is defined as a triple $(\Sigma, (X, \tau), (c, \varsigma, \varsigma'))$.*

In the next definition, we define the well-formedness of predicates and expressions. Note that we here present only the interesting cases. The other cases can be found in the technical report [22].

Let's first look at the well-formedness of expressions $e.id$ and $e.o$, where e is of polymorphic sort $[c] = \{c_1, \ldots, c_n\}$. Basically, well-formedness of $e.id$ requires that id has to be an attribute common to all the class sorts in $[c]$. Similarly, for $e.o$, o has to be an operation defined for all class sorts $c_i \in [c]$ ($1 \leq i \leq n$).

Let o be an operation belonging to class c. Then $o(x_1? : s_1, \ldots, x_n? : s_n; x! : s)[a_1, \ldots, a_m] : P$ is an operation expression, that defines an operation o through a predicate P over the values of an object's attributes before and after the execution of o. The well-formedness of such an operation expression requires that P is well-formed in a variable environment where P has access to the attributes $a_1, \ldots, a_m$ of class c in the state before the execution of o and after the execution of o, that is, undecorated, i.e., a_i, and decorated, i.e., a_i', and where the input variables $x_i?$ are of sort s_i, the output variable $x!$ is of sort s.

Definition 6. *Given a variable environment γ, we define the* **well-formedness** *of predicates and expressions as follows.*

- *id is well-formed wrt. γ if either $id \in X$ or $id \in \varsigma$, the type of id is $\tau(id)$ if $id \in X$ or t if $id \in \varsigma$ and $id \in B_{c \to t}$ or $pow(c')$ if $id \in \varsigma$ and $id \in R_{c \to c'}$*
- *$e.id$ is well-formed wrt. γ if e is well-formed wrt. γ and has type c and c is a class sort in Σ and $id \in attr(c)$. The type of $e.id$ is either t or $pow(c')$, depending on whether id was in $B_{c \to t}$ or in $R_{c \to c'}$ for some $t \in T$ and $c' \in C \cup P$.*
- *$e.id$ is well-formed wrt. γ if e is well-formed wrt. γ and has type $[c]$ and $[c]$ is a polymorphic sort in P and $id \in \bigcap_{c'' \in [c]} (B_{c'' \to t} \cup R_{c'' \to c'})$. The type of $e.id$ is either t or $pow(c')$, depending on whether id was in $B_{c \to t}$ or in $R_{c \to c'}$*

Then, the well-formedness of operation expressions is defined as:

- *Operation expression $e.o$ is well-formed wrt. γ if e is well-formed wrt. γ and the type of e is c for $o \in O_{c,w} \cup O_{c,w,s}$*
- *Operation expression $e.o$ is well-formed wrt. γ if e is well-formed wrt. γ and the type of e is $[c]$ is a polymorphic sort for $o \in \bigcap_{c'' \in [c]} O_{c'',w} \cup O_{c'',w,s}$*
- *$[P]$ is well-formed wrt. γ if predicate P is well-formed wrt. γ*
- *$[\Delta(a_1, \ldots, a_m) \mid x_1? : s_1, \ldots, x_n? : s_n; x! : s \mid P]$ is well-formed wrt. $\gamma = (\Sigma, (X, \tau), (c, \varsigma, \varsigma'))$ if P is well-formed wrt. $\gamma' = (\Sigma, (X \cup \{x_1?, \ldots, x_n?, x!\}, \tau'), (c, \varsigma \cup \{a_1, \ldots, a_m\}, \varsigma' \cup \{a_1', \ldots, a_m'\})), \tau'(x_1?) = s_1, \ldots, \tau'(x_n?) = s_n, \tau'(x!) = s$ with $\tau'(x) = \tau(x)$ if $x \notin \{x_1?, \ldots, x_n?, x!\}$, $a_i \in attr(c)$ for $1 \leq i \leq n$.*

- $oe_1 \wedge oe_2$ is well-formed wrt. γ if oe_1 is well-formed wrt. γ and oe_2 is well-formed wrt. γ.
- $oe_1 \bullet oe_2$ is well-formed wrt. γ if oe_1 is well-formed wrt. γ_1 and oe_2 is well-formed wrt. γ_2, where $\gamma_1 = (\Sigma, (X, \tau), (\varsigma, \varsigma'))$ and $\gamma_2 = (\Sigma, (X \cup \{x_1?, \ldots, x_n?, x!\}, \tau \cup \{(x_1?, s_1), \ldots, (x_n?, s_n), (x!, s)\}), (\varsigma, \varsigma'))$, where $x_1?, \ldots, x_n?, x!$ are the input/output variables defined in oe_1 with their corresponding type s_i, where $i \in \{1, \ldots, n\}$, and s.

Based on these definitions, we define the well-formedness of sentences:

- $o(x_1? : s_1, \ldots, x_n? : s_n; \ x! : s)[a_1, \ldots, a_m] : P$ is well-formed wrt. Σ if P is well-formed wrt. $\gamma = (\Sigma, (\{x_1?, \ldots, x_n?, x!\}, \tau), (c, \{a_1, \ldots, a_m\}, \{a'_1, \ldots, a'_m\}))$, $\tau(x_1?) = s_1, \ldots, \tau(x_n?) = s_n, \tau(x!) = s$, $o \in O_{c,w} \cup O_{c,w,s}$, and $a_i \in attr(c)$.
- $inv_c : P$ is well-formed wrt. Σ if P is well-formed wrt. $\gamma = (\Sigma, (\varnothing, \varnothing), (c, attr(c), \varnothing))$.
- $init_c : P$ is well-formed wrt. Σ if P is well-formed wrt. $\gamma = (\Sigma, (\varnothing, \varnothing), (c, B_{c \rightarrow t} \cup R_{c \rightarrow c'}, \varnothing))$.
- $o(x_1? : s_1, \ldots, x_n? : s_n; \ x! : s) \mathrel{\widehat{=}} oe$ is well-formed wrt. Σ if oe is well-formed wrt. $\gamma = (\Sigma, (\{x_1?, \ldots, x_n?, x!\}, \tau), (c, attr(c), \varnothing))$ where $\tau(x_1?) = s_1, \ldots, \tau(x_n?) = s_n, \tau(x!) = s$ and $o \in O_{c,w} \cup O_{c,w,s}$.

Example 7. In the following, we look at the well-formedness of the sentences from Example 6.

- $inv_{TMS} : \forall tnk : tnks. \ \ tnk.ind \subseteq inds$ is well-formed wrt. Σ_{TMS} because $\forall tnk : tnks. \ \ tnk.ind \subseteq inds$ is well-formed wrt.
  $\gamma = (\Sigma_{TMS}, (\varnothing, \varnothing), (TMS, \{tnks, inds\}, \varnothing))$, where $tnks \in R_{TMS \rightarrow [Tank]}$ and $inds \in R_{TMS \rightarrow Ind}$. We are not looking at the well-formedness of the overall expression, but focus on $tnk.ind$. The type of tnk is $[Tank]$ because the type of $tnks$ is $pow([Tank])$ given that $tnks \in R_{TMS \rightarrow [Tank]}$. For $tnk.ind$ to be well-formed, we have to check that ind is an attribute for all sorts in $[Tank]$. Since $[Tank] = \{Tank, WarmingTank\}$ and $ind \in R_{Tank \rightarrow Indicator}$ and $ind \in R_{WarmingTank \rightarrow Indicator}$, we get that $tnk.ind$ is well-formed.
- $UpdateDanger(d? : \mathbb{N})[danger] : danger' = d?$ is well-formed wrt. Σ_{Tank} if $danger' = d?$ is well-formed wrt.
  $\gamma = (\Sigma_{Tank}, (\{d?\}, \tau), (Tank, \{danger\}, \{danger'\}))$ where $\tau(d?) = Nat$. Then $danger' = d?$ is well-formed wrt. γ, because $danger \in B_{Tank \rightarrow Nat}$ and thus $danger?$ has type Nat and $\tau(d?) = Nat$.
- $init_{Ind} : light = off \wedge danger = 0$ is well-formed wrt. Σ_{Ind} if $light = off \wedge danger = 0$ is well-formed wrt. $\gamma = (\Sigma_{Ind}, (\varnothing, \varnothing), (Ind, \{light, danger\}, \varnothing))$. This is true, because $danger$ and $light$ are in γ and $danger \in B_{Ind \rightarrow Nat}$ and $light \in B_{Ind \rightarrow STATUS}$.
- $AlertOn \mathrel{\widehat{=}} [i? : Indicator \mid i? \in ind \wedge i?.danger \geq level] \bullet i?.SetLightOn$ is well-formed wrt. Σ_{Tank} if $[i? : Indicator \mid i? \in ind \wedge i?.danger \geq level]$ is well-formed wrt. $\gamma = (\Sigma_{Tank}, (\varnothing, \varnothing), (Tank, \{level, capacity, liquids, ind\}, \varnothing))$ and $[i? : Indicator \mid i? \in ind \wedge i?.danger \geq level]$ is well-formed wrt. γ, which is the case if $i? \in ind \wedge i?.danger \geq level$ is well-formed wrt.

$$\gamma_1 = (\Sigma_{Tank}(\{i?\}, \tau(i?) = Ind), (Tank, \{level, capacity, liquids, ind\}, \varnothing))$$

which is easy to show.

Furthermore $i?.SetLightOn$ needs to be well-formed wrt.

$$\gamma_1 = (\Sigma_{Tank}, (\{i?\}, \tau(id?) = Ind), (Tank, \{levels, capacity, liquids, ind\}, \varnothing)).$$

This is true, because $\tau(i?) = Ind$ and

$SetLightOn \in O_{Ind,<>}$.

Definition 7. *The functor Sen_{OZS} maps OZS-signatures Σ to well-formed sentences over Σ and signature morphisms $\phi : \Sigma \to \Sigma'$ to a function from Σ-sentences to Σ'-sentences by replacing symbols f from Σ in a Σ-sentence with symbols $\phi(f)$ from Σ'.*

2.4 Satisfaction

The semantics is defined wrt. an evaluation environment ϵ compatible with a variable environment γ. This means, that the evaluation environment provides a concrete object, *oid*, together with a variable assignment of the variables in the variable environment and finally, two states σ and σ' representing the state before and after the execution of an operation.

Definition 8. *Let $\gamma = (\Sigma, (X, \tau), (c, \varsigma, \varsigma'))$ be a variable environment and M a Σ-model. Then $\epsilon = (oid, \{(x_1, v_1), \ldots, (x_n, v_n)\}, \sigma, \sigma')$ is an **evaluation environment compatible with** γ if $oid \in M_c$, $x_i \in X$ and $v_i \in M_{\tau(x_i)}$ and σ and σ' are in state$_M$.*

In the following definition of the semantics of expressions and predicates, we only present the interesting cases.

First, we look at the cases $e.id$ and $e.o$ where e is of polymorphic sort $[c] = \{c_1, \ldots, c_n\}$. Let M be a Σ-model. The result of evaluating e in an evaluation environment is an object identifier $oid \in M_{c_i}$, for exactly one $c_i \in [c]$, because we have required that all sets M_c for $c \in C$ are disjoint. For an identifier id, representing an attribute of c, we then look at the state σ and return $\sigma_{c_i}(oid)(id)$. Note that this is well defined regardless the choice of $c_i \in [c]$, because id is an attribute common to all sorts $c_i \in [c]$.

The evaluation of an operation expression $e.o$ is either true or false and does not return, as one might expect, a set of states. The reason is, that $e.o$ represents a relation between pre- and post states. Again, well-formedness of $e.o$ requires that o is an operation common to all sorts $c_i \in [c]$. This means, that $e.o$ evaluates to true in an evaluation environment, if the post-state σ' and the resulting value v is in the set of states and result values returned by the interpretation of the operation o of M, i.e., $(o_M)_{c_i}$, when applied to the object identifier oid, i.e., the result of evaluating e, and the values $v_1, \ldots, v_n$. That is, $e.o$ evaluates to true in an evaluation environment iff $(\sigma', v) \in (o_M)_{c_i}(\sigma, oid, v_1, \ldots, v_n)$.

Definition 9. *Given an evaluation environment ϵ compatible with a variable environment γ, then we define the **semantics** of expressions and predicates wrt. ϵ as follows.*

- $[\![id]\!]_\epsilon = v_i$ if id is well-formed wrt.
  $\gamma = (\Sigma, (X, \tau), (c, \varsigma, \varsigma'))$, $\epsilon = (oid, \{(x_1, v_1), \ldots, (x_n, v_n)\}, \sigma, \sigma')$, and id = x_i. Or $[\![id]\!]_\epsilon = \sigma_c(oid)(id)$ if id $\in \varsigma$

And for operation expressions:

- $[\![e.o]\!]_\epsilon$ *evaluates to true if* $[\![e]\!]_{\epsilon'} = oid'$ *where* $oid' \in M_{c'}$ *and* $(\sigma', v) \in (o_M)_{c'}(\sigma, oid', v_1, \ldots, v_n)$ *for* $o \in O_{c',w} \cup O_{c',w,s}$,
  $\epsilon = (oid, \{(x_1?, v_1), \ldots, (x_n?, v_n), (x!, v)\}, \sigma, \sigma')$, *and* $\epsilon' = (oid', \{\}, \sigma, \sigma')$. *If the type of e is the monomorphic type* c'' *then* $c' = c''$, *and if the type of e is the polymorphic type* $[c]$ *then* $c' \in [c]$.
- $[\![[p]]\!]_\epsilon$ *evaluates to true if* $[\![p]\!]_\epsilon$ *evaluates to true.*
- $[\![[\Delta(a_1, \ldots, a_m), x_1? : s_1, \ldots, x_n? : s_n; \ x! : s \mid p]]\!]_\epsilon$ *evaluates to true if* $[\![p]\!]_{\epsilon'}$ *evaluates to true, where* $\epsilon = (oid, \{(y_1?, v_1), \ldots, (y_n?, v_n), (y!, v)\}, \sigma, \sigma')$ *and* $\epsilon' = (oid, \{(x_1?, v_1), \ldots, (x_n?, v_n), (x!, v))\}, \sigma, \sigma')$
- $[\![oe_1 \wedge oe_2]\!]_\epsilon$ *evaluates to true if* $[\![oe_1]\!]_\epsilon$ *and* $[\![oe_2]\!]_\epsilon$ *evaluate both to true.*
- $[\![oe_1 \bullet oe_2]\!]_\epsilon$ *evaluates to true if* $[\![oe_1]\!]_{\epsilon'}$ *evaluates to true then* $[\![oe_2]\!]_{\epsilon'}$ *evaluates to true for* $\epsilon = (oid, \{(y_1?, v_1), \ldots, (y_n?, v_n), (y!, v)\}, \sigma, \sigma')$ *and* $\epsilon' = (oid, \{(x_1?, v_1), \ldots, (x_n?, v_n), (x, v)\}, \sigma, \sigma')$.

Let o be an operation defined for class sort c. Then an operation expression $o(x_1? : s_1, \ldots, x_n? : s_n; \ x! : s)[a_1, \ldots, a_m] : P$ is satisfied in a model M, if P evaluates to true for all object identifiers $oid \in M_c$, variable assignments $(x?_i, v_i)$ and $(x!, v)$ for the input and output variables, and for all states σ and σ' representing the state of the system before and after the execution of o, where (σ', v) is in $(o_M)_c(\sigma, oid, v_1, \ldots, v_n)$. In addition, it is required that σ and σ' are the same for all attributes in class c that are not in the list $[a_1, \ldots, a_m]$. That is, only the value of the attributes $[a_1, \ldots, a_m]$ of class c are allowed to change.

Definition 10. *Finally the* **satisfaction** *of* Σ-*sentences* φ *in a* Σ-*model* M, *i.e.,* $M \models_\Sigma \varphi$ *is defined by:*

- $M \models_\Sigma inv_c : P$ *iff for all* $oid \in M_c$, $\sigma \in state_M$, $\epsilon = (oid, \varnothing, \sigma, \varnothing)$ *we have* $[\![P]\!]_\epsilon$ *evaluates to true.*
- $M \models_\Sigma o(x_1? : s_1, \ldots, x_n? : s_n; \ x! : s)[a_1, \ldots, a_m] : P$ *iff*
  for all $\sigma, \sigma' \in state_M$, $oid \in M_c$, *if* $(\sigma', v) \in (o_M)_c(\sigma, oid, v_1, \ldots, v_n)$ *then* $[\![P]\!]_\epsilon$ *evaluates to true and* $\sigma_c(oid)(a_j) = \sigma'_c(oid)(a_j)$ *for* $a_j \in attr(c) \setminus \{a_1, \ldots, a_m\}$, *where* $\epsilon = (oid, \{(x_1?, v_1), \ldots, (x_n?, v_n), (x!, v)\}, \sigma, \sigma')$.
- $M \models_\Sigma init_c : P$ *iff for all* $oid \in M_c$ *we have that* $[\![P]\!]_\epsilon$ *evaluates to true for* $\epsilon = (oid, \varnothing, init_M(c), \varnothing)$.
- $M \models_\Sigma o \ \widehat{=} \ oe$ *iff for all* $(\sigma', v) \in (o_M)_c(\sigma, oid, v_1, \ldots, v_n)$ *and* $[\![oe]\!]_\epsilon$ *evaluates to true for* $\epsilon = (oid, \{(x_1?, v_1), \ldots, (x_n?, v_n), (x!, v)\}, \sigma, \sigma')$.

Example 8. Here we look at the satisfaction of the sentences defined in Example 6:

- Let M be a Σ_{TMS}-model then $M \models \text{inv}_{TMS} : \forall\, tnk : tnks.\ tnk.ind \subseteq inds$ iff $\forall\, oid \in M_{TMS}$, $\sigma \in state_M$, $\epsilon = (oid, \varnothing, \sigma, \varnothing)$ we have $[\![\forall\, tnk : tnks.\ tnk.ind \subseteq inds]\!]_{\epsilon}$ evaluates to true. We focus on $[\![tnk.ind \subseteq inds]\!]_{\epsilon'}$ where $\epsilon' = (oid, \{(tnk, tid)\}, \sigma, \varnothing)$ for all $tid \in [\![tnks]\!]_{\epsilon}$ where $[\![tnks]\!]_{\epsilon} = \sigma_{TMS}(oid)(tnks)$. Then $tid \in M_{[Tank]} = M_{Tank} \cup M_{WarmingTank}$ because the type of $tnks$ is $pow([Tank])$.

  We have $[\![tnk.ind \subseteq inds]\!]_{\epsilon'} = true$ iff $\sigma_c(tid)(ind) \subseteq \sigma_{TMS}(oid)(inds)$ where c is $Tank$ if $tid \in M_{Tank}$ or c is $WarmingTank$ if $tid \in M_{WarmingTank}$.

- Let M be a Σ_{Tank}-model, then $M \models UpdateDanger(d? : \mathbb{N})[danger] :$ $danger' = d?$ iff $\forall\, oid \in M_{Tank}$, $\sigma, \sigma' \in state_M$, if $\sigma' \in UpdateDanger_M(\sigma, n)$ then $[\![danger' = d?]\!]_{\epsilon} = true$ where $\epsilon = (oid, \{(d?, n)\}, \sigma, \sigma')$ and $\sigma_{Tank}(oid)(a) = \sigma'_{Tank}(oid)(a)$ forall $a \neq danger$. Then $[\![danger' = d?]\!]_{\epsilon} = true$ iff $\sigma'_{Tank}(oid)(danger) = n$ for all $n \in \mathbb{N}$.

- Let M be a Σ_{Ind}-model, then $M \models \text{init}_{Ind} : light = off \wedge danger = 0$ iff $\forall\, oid \in M_{Ind}$, $[\![light = 0ff \wedge danger = 0]\!]_{\epsilon} = true$ for $\epsilon = (oid, \{\}, \text{init}_M(Ind), \varnothing)$. Let $\sigma = \text{init}_M(Ind)$, then this is the case when for all $oid \in M_{Tank}$ we have $\sigma_{Ind}(oid)(light) = off$ and $\sigma_{Ind}(oid)(danger) = 0$.

- Let M be a Σ_{Tank}-model then $M \models AlertOn \,\widehat{=}\, [i? : Indicator \mid i? \in ind \wedge i?.danger \geq level] \bullet i?.SetLightOn$ iff $\forall\, oid \in M_{Tank}$, $\sigma, \sigma' \in state_M$ if $\sigma' \in AlertOn_M(\sigma)$ then $[\![[i? : Indicator \mid i? \in ind \wedge i?.danger \geq level] \bullet i?.SetLightOn]\!]_{\epsilon} = true$ for $\epsilon = (oid, \{\}, \sigma, \sigma')$.

  The latter is true if $[\![[i? : Indicator \mid i? \in ind \wedge i?.danger \geq level]]\!]_{\epsilon}$ evaluates to true then $[\![i?.SetLightOn]\!]_{\epsilon'}$ evaluates to true where $\epsilon' = (oid, \{(i?, i)\}, \sigma, \sigma')$.

  $[\![[i? : Indicator \mid i? \in ind \wedge i?.danger \geq level]]\!]_{\epsilon}$ evaluates to true if $[\![i? \in ind \wedge i?.danger \geq level]\!]_{\epsilon''}$ evaluates to true, where $\epsilon'' = (oid, \{(i?, i)\}, \sigma, \sigma')$ for all $i \in M_{Ind}$. This is true if $i \in \sigma_{Tank}(oid)(ind)$ and $\sigma_{Ind}(i)(danger) \geq \sigma_{Tank}(oid)(level)$.

  Then $[\![i?.SetLightOn]\!]_{\epsilon'} = true$ if $\sigma' \in SetLightOn_{Ind}(i)(\sigma)$.

Proposition 2. Satisfaction condition. *Given a signature morphism ϕ from Σ to Σ', a Σ'-model M and a formula $\varphi \in Sen_{OZS}(\Sigma)$, then $M|_{\phi} \models_{\Sigma} \varphi$ iff $M \models_{\Sigma'} Sen_{OZS}(\phi)(\varphi)$.*

Proposition 3. *The institution OZS has amalgamation.*

The proof sketches for the satisfaction condition and amalgamation can be found in the technical report [22].

3   Inheritance and Polymorphism

In the following, we will explain how to use inheritance in Object-Z. Inheritance is a general construction that works in any institution $\mathcal{I}$, not just in the institution OZS being defined in this paper. To do this, we first introduce the well-known concept of a specification over $\mathcal{I}$ (e.g. [17]).

A specification $Sp = (\Sigma, \Phi)$ over an institution $\mathcal{I}$ consists of a signature $\Sigma \in Sig$ and a collection of Σ-sentences $\Phi \subseteq Sen(\Sigma)$. A specification morphism

$\phi : (\Sigma, \Phi) \rightarrow (\Sigma', \Phi')$ is a signature morphism $\phi : \Sigma \rightarrow \Sigma'$ preserving the truth of sentences, i.e., for all Σ' models M' such that $M' \models_{\Sigma'} \Phi'$, we have that $M' \models_{\Sigma'} Sen(\phi)(\Phi)$. Specification and specification morphism form the category $Spec_{\mathcal{I}}$. It is a well-known fact, e.g., [17], that $Spec_{\mathcal{I}}$ is co-complete whenever the category Sig of the underlying institution $\mathcal{I}$ is co-complete. That is, if we can glue smaller signatures together to form larger signatures via colimits, then we can also glue specifications together.

Now we can define inheritance between specifications as follows:

Definition 11. *Let $Sp_1 = (\Sigma_1, \Phi_1)$ be a specification in $Spec_{\mathcal{I}}$ and ϕ a signature morphism from Σ_1 to Σ_2. Let Φ be a set of sentences over Σ_2. Then $Sp_3 = (\Sigma_2, Sen(\phi)(\Phi_1) \cup \Phi)$ is a specification created by inheriting the specification Sp_1 via ϕ.*

Lemma 2. *If Sp_3 is a specification created by inheriting from specification Sp_1 via ϕ, then ϕ is a specification morphism from Sp_1 to Sp_3.*

As an example, take the specification of the *Warming Tank* from Fig. 4. We see that *Warming Tank* is defined by inheritance from *Tank* due to the inclusion of *Tank* in *Warming Tank*. In particular, let $Sp_{Tank} = (\Sigma_{Tank}, \Phi_{Tank})$, we have that $Sp_{WarmingTank} = (\Sigma_{WarmingTank}, Sen_{OZS}(\phi)(\Phi_{Tank}) \cup \Phi_{WarmingTank})$, where $\phi : \Sigma_{Tank} \rightarrow \Sigma_{WarmingTank}$ is a signature morphism mapping *Tank* to *Warming Tank* and is the identity on attributes, operations, and the remaining sorts. According to Lemma 2 we have that ϕ is a specification morphism from Sp_{Tank} to $Sp_{WarmingTank}$. This means, in particular, that *Warming Tank* satisfies all the properties of *Tank*. Or, in other words, *Warming Tank* inherits all the attributes, operations, and properties from *Tank*.

As we have seen, inheritance allows one to define a new class sort based on an existing class sort. When a new specification is created by inheriting from another specification, e.g., $Sp_{WarmingTank} = (\Sigma_{WarmingTank}, \phi(\Phi_{Tank}) \cup \Phi_{WarmingTank})$, then $Sp_{WarmingTank}$ only contains the sort *Warming Tank* but not the sort *Tank*. To have both sorts in the specification, we have to form the union of $Sp_{WarmingTank}$ and Sp_{Tank}.

In general, an OZS specification is given as several class specifications Sp_c that are added to a global specification Sp_{all}. That is, each additional specification is added to the global specification in the following way: $Sp_{all} = Sp_{all}^{pre} \cup Sp_c$, where originally Sp_{all}^{pre} is the empty specification, i.e. $(\Sigma_0, \varnothing)$ where $\Sigma_0 = (\varnothing, \varnothing, \pi_0 : \varnothing \rightarrow 2^{\varnothing})$.

In contrast, polymorphic sorts allow one to apply operations and access to attributes of objects belonging to different classes. Given an expression e of polymorphic sort $[c] = \{c_1, \ldots, c_n\}$, then any operation or attribute that is common to all $c_i \in [c]$ can be applied to e. For example, in case of $[Tank] = \{Tank, WarmingTank\}$, all sorts have attributes *level*, *capacity*, *liquids*, and *ind* and operations *Fill*, *EmptyOut*, *SetSupportedLiquids*, *AttachIndicator*, *AlertOn*, and *AlertOff* in common.

In general, a polymorphic sort $[c] = \{c_1, \ldots, c_n\}$ describes a union of sorts, that have attributes and operations in common, but are not necessarily required to be in a subclass relationship. Evaluating an expression e, i.e. $[\![e]\!]_\epsilon = oid$, results in an $oid \in M_{c_i}$ for some $c_i \in [c]$. Since we have required that the set of M_c for $c \in C$ is pairwise disjoint (cf. Def. 2), M_{c_i} is unique. This uniqueness allows us to choose the right value when accessing an attribute a of e, e.g. by evaluating $\sigma_{c'}(oid)(a)$. Similarly, for operations, this allows us to choose the right operation $(o_M)_{c'} : state_M \times M_{c'} \to \mathbb{P}(state_M)$.

However, a motivation for the definition of polymorphic sorts is that a polymorphic sort $[c]$ contains all the subclasses of c defined by inheritance of specifications. Therefore, whenever we define a specification Sp_2 by the inheritance of Sp_1, where c_1 is the main class sort of Sp_1 and c_2 is the main class sort of Sp_2, we add $\pi_{all}^{pre}(c_2)$ to π_{all}, i.e., $\pi_{all}(c_1) = \{c_2\} \cup \pi_{all}^{pre}(c_1)$, when forming $Sp_{all} = Sp_{all}^{pre} \cup Sp_2$. Informally this means to add the subclass c_2 of c_1 and all the direct and indirect subclasses of c_2, i.e., $[c_2]$, to the polymorphic type $[c_1]$.

4   Concluding Remarks

We have shown in this work how to build an institution for Object-Z including its static and dynamic aspects. We have included polymorphic sorts into the definition and discussed inheritance and its relationship to polymorphic sorts. The category of signatures is co-complete (cf. Prop. 1) and the institution has amalgamation (cf. Prop. 3). Both properties are essential for building modular systems, i.e., larger specifications from smaller ones.

In order to permit multi-paradigm formal specification including the use of Object-Z institution, we plan, in a future work, to integrate OZS into heterogeneous tool set (Hets) [2,3]. We have defined the institution for Object-Z, but for the integration into Hets, (co)morphisms between OZS and CASL [7] (the core language of Hets) still have to be defined.

As an additional advantage, the set of proof tools, e.g. [24,25,26], that has been developed by the Object-Z community, will enrich the set of proof tools available in Hets. Moreover the Object-Z community will also take benefit from some proof tools offered, for instance, by Maude and CASL, whose institutions are already embedded into Hets.

To this end, we have to design and implement an interface allowing to provide OZS with necessary tools for parsing and (static) analysis of OZS specifications. This might be achieved using an institution independent abstract interface coded into Haskell, the implementation language of Hets. This abstract interface will be implemented by instantiating the so-called 'Logic' Haskell type class of Hets for our target language, i.e., Object-Z. This class provides a set of methods that implement a parser for basic Object-Z specifications, a static analyser transforming basic specifications into theories (signature and sentences) of the Object-Z institution, a sentence translator that gives the translation of a sentence along a signature morphism [27]. The 'Logic' type class will be supported by a set of related Haskell type classes that encode the language Object-Z itself (Object-Z abstract syntax) and the Object-Z institution (signature, sentences, morphisms).

References

1. Rumbaugh, J., Jacobson, I., Booch, G.: The Unified Modeling Language. Reference Manual, 2nd edn. Addison-Wesley Professional (2004)
2. Mossakowski, T., Maeder, C., Codescu, M.: Hets user guide - verion 0.99. DKFI GmbH, Bremen, Germany (2013)
3. Mossakowski, T.: Heterogeneous specification and the heterogeneous tool set. Habilitation thesis, University of Bremen (2005)
4. Goguen, J.A., Burstall, R.M.: Introducing institutions. In: Clarke, E., Kozen, D. (eds.) Logic of Programs 1983. LNCS, vol. 164, pp. 221–256. Springer, Heidelberg (1984)
5. Burstall, R.M., Goguen, J.A.: The semantics of Clear, a specification language. In: Bjorner, D. (ed.) Abstract Software Specifications. LNCS, vol. 86, pp. 292–332. Springer, Heidelberg (1980)
6. Sannella, D., Tarlecki, A.: Specifications in an arbitrary institution. Information and Computation (1988)
7. Mosses, P.D. (ed.): CASL Reference Manual. LNCS, vol. 2960. Springer, Heidelberg (2004)
8. Ehrig, H., Mahr, B.: Fundamentals of algebraic specification 1: Equations and initial semantics. Springer (1985)
9. Smith, D.R.: Composition by colimit and formal software development. In: Futatsugi, K., Jouannaud, J.-P., Meseguer, J. (eds.) Algebra, Meaning, and Computation. LNCS, vol. 4060, pp. 317–332. Springer, Heidelberg (2006)
10. Smith, G.: The Object-Z specification language. Kluwer Academic Publisher (2000)
11. Spivey, J.M.: The Z Notation - A Reference manual. Prentice-Hall (1989)
12. Kim, S.-K., Carrington, D.: A formal mapping between UML models and object-Z specifications. In: Bowen, J.P., Dunne, S., Galloway, A., King, S. (eds.) B 2000, ZUM 2000, and ZB 2000. LNCS, vol. 1878, pp. 2–21. Springer, Heidelberg (2000)
13. Baumeister, H.: Relating abstract datatypes and Z-schemata. In: Bert, D., Choppy, C., Mosses, P.D. (eds.) WADT 1999. LNCS, vol. 1827, pp. 366–382. Springer, Heidelberg (2000)
14. Cengarle, M.V., Knapp, A.: An institution for UML 2.0 static structures. Technical Report TUM-10807, Technische Universität München (2008)
15. Cengarle, M.V., Knapp, A., Tarlecki, A., Wirsing, M.: A heterogeneous approach to UML semantics. In: Degano, P., De Nicola, R., Meseguer, J. (eds.) Concurrency, Graphs and Models. LNCS, vol. 5065, pp. 383–402. Springer, Heidelberg (2008)
16. Boronat, A., Knapp, A., Meseguer, J., Wirsing, M.: What is a multi-modeling language? In: Corradini, A., Montanari, U. (eds.) WADT 2008. LNCS, vol. 5486, pp. 71–87. Springer, Heidelberg (2009)
17. Baumeister, H.: Relations between Abstract Datatypes modeled as Abstract Datatypes. PhD thesis, University of Saarbrücken (1999)
18. Goguen, J.A., Meseguer, J.: Order-sorted algebra I: Equational deduction for multiple inheritance, overloading, exceptions and partial operations. Theoretical Computer Science 105(2), 217–273 (1992)
19. Meseguer, J.: Membership algebra as a logical framework for equational specification. In: Parisi-Presicce, F. (ed.) WADT 1997. LNCS, vol. 1376, pp. 18–61. Springer, Heidelberg (1998)
20. Goguen, J.A., Burstall, R.M.: Institutions: Abstract model theory for specification and programming. Journal of the ACM (JACM) 39(1), 95–146 (1992)

21. Somerville, I.: Model-based specification (2000), http://www.cs.st-andrews.ac.uk/~ifs/Resources/Notes/FormalSpec/ModelSpec.pdf
22. Baumeister, H., Bettaz, M., Maouche, M., Mosteghanemi, M.: Institutions for Object-Z — technical report (2014), http://people.compute.dtu.dk/huba/publications/OZReport.pdf
23. Mac Lane, S.: Categories for the working mathematician, 2nd edn., vol. 5. Springer (1998)
24. Wen, Z., Miao, H., Zeng, H.: Generating proof obligation to verify Object-Z specification. In: IEEE International Conference on Software Engineering Advances, pp. 38–38 (2006)
25. Stevens, B.: Implementing Object-Z with Perfect Developer. Journal of Object Technology 5(2), 189–202 (2006)
26. Paige, R.F., Brooke, P.J.: Integrating BON and Object-Z. Journal of Object Technology 3(3), 121–141 (2004)
27. Codescu, M., Horozal, F., Jakubauskas, A., Mossakowski, T., Rabe, F.: Compiling logics. In: Martí-Oliet, N., Palomino, M. (eds.) WADT 2012. LNCS, vol. 7841, pp. 111–126. Springer, Heidelberg (2013)

Abstract Constraint Data Types

José Luiz Fiadeiro[1] and Fernando Orejas[2]

[1] Dep. of Computer Science, Royal Holloway University of London,
Egham TW20 0EX, UK
jose.fiadeiro@rhul.ac.uk

[2] Dep. de Llenguatges i Sistemes Informàtics, Universitat Politècnica de Catalunya,
08034 Barcelona, Spain
orejas@lsi.upc.edu

Abstract. Martin Wirsing is one of the earliest contributors to the area of Algebraic Specification (e.g., [2]), which he explored in a variety of domains over many years. Throughout his career, he has also inspired countless researchers in related areas. This paper is inspired by one of the domains that he explored thirty years or so after his first contributions when leading the FET Integrated Project SENSORIA [14]: the use of constraint systems to deal with non-functional requirements and preferences [13,8]. Following in his footsteps, we provide an extension of the traditional notion of algebraic data type specification to encompass soft-constraints as formalised in [1]. Finally, we relate this extension with institutions [6] and recent work on graded consequence in institutions [3].

1 Introduction

Service-Oriented Architecture (SOA) [10] is a paradigm for the flexible construction of systems based on the dynamic interconnection of components. This interconnection takes place when a given component (*the requester*) needs to discover another component that can provide a service that it needs, i.e., a component (*the provider*) that, through an interface, offers the properties required by the requester. In addition to the usual functional properties, components may express preferences in their interfaces, in which case the requester will choose a provider that can maximise the way those preferences are satisfied.

Interfaces are abstractions through which components can express properties that are independent of their implementations. Algebraic specification of abstract data types [12] are one of the most established formalisms in which interfaces can be defined. However, they are limited to functional properties of the input/output behaviour of the operations that components implement. In this paper, we extend algebraic specifications of component interfaces so that preferences can be expressed as *constraints* and matching can be formalised in terms of *constraint satisfaction and optimisation*.

In [1], Bistarelli, Montanari, and Rossi define a general framework for the definition of constraint systems of several kinds. More precisely, their approach allows us to describe both hard and (different types of) soft constraint systems.

R. De Nicola and R. Hennicker (Eds.): Wirsing Festschrift, LNCS 8950, pp. 155–170, 2015.

The idea is to consider that constraint values form a semiring, where 0 represents unsatisfiability, 1 represents satisfaction and the rest of the values represent the different degrees of satisfiability of the given constraint system. The approach outlined in this paper combines the ideas presented in [1] with algebraic specification to include preferences in component interfaces. Our ideas are presented using the specification of a travel request as a running example.

The paper is organized as follows. In Section 2, we recall some basic elements of algebraic specification theory (which does not dispense consulting [12]). In Section 3, we extend algebraic specifications for the specification of constraints. Then, in Section 4 we study how we can combine constraint specifications. Section 5 is dedicated to presenting our ideas in the framework of institutions. Finally, in Section 6 we draw some conclusions.

2   Basic Algebraic Concepts and Notation

We assume that the reader has some familiarity with category theory (for example, at the level of the first chapters of [5].)

A signature Σ is a pair $\langle S, \Omega \rangle$ where S is a finite set of sorts, and Ω is a finite family of sets of operation and predicate symbols typed over sorts. A Σ-algebra A consists of an S-indexed family of sets $\{A_s\}_{s \in S}$ and a function op_A (resp., a relation pr_A) for each operation symbol op (resp., predicate symbol pr) in the signature[1]. A Σ-homomorphism $h \colon A \to A'$ consists of an S-indexed family of functions $\{h_s : A_s \to A'_s\}_{s \in S}$ commuting with the functions and preserving the relations. Σ-algebras and Σ-homomorphisms form the category $\mathbf{Alg}_\Sigma$.

Given a signature Σ, we denote by T_Σ the term algebra, which consists of all the possible Σ-(ground) terms – where a ground term is either a nullary function symbol or an expression of an operation symbol being applied to ground terms of the types required by the operation. Given any Σ-algebra A there is a unique homomorphism $h_A \colon T_\Sigma \to A$ through which h_A yields the value of every term of sort $s \in S$ in A_s.

Given a set X of variables typed over S, we denote by $T_\Sigma(X)$ the algebra of all Σ-terms with variables in X, and given a variable assignment $\sigma \colon X \to A$, this assignment extends to a unique homomorphism $\sigma^\# \colon T_\Sigma(X) \to A$ yielding the value of each term after the replacement of each variable x by its value $\sigma(x)$. In particular, when an assignment is defined over the term algebra, i.e. $\sigma \colon X \to T_\Sigma$, then $\sigma^\#(t)$ denotes the term obtained by substituting each variable x in t by the term $\sigma(x)$. However, for simplicity, even if it is an abuse of notation, we will write $\sigma(t)$ instead of $\sigma^\#(t)$.

Given a signature $\Sigma = \langle S, \Omega \rangle$ and a set X of variables typed over S, we can build sentences, which are either equalities of the form $(t_1 =_s t_2)$ where t_1 and t_2 are terms of sort s, or predicates of the form $p(t_1, \cdots, t_n)$, or a result of applying the usual Boolean connectives over sentences. All sentences are implicitly

---

[1] Predicates are not part of the usual staple of algebraic data type specification but they are convenient for our purposes in this paper.

universally quantified[2], i.e., a sentence is true over a Σ-algebra A if, for each possible variable assignment $\sigma\colon X \to A$, the sentence is true, i.e., the two terms of an equality $(t_1 =_s t_2)$ have the same values — $\sigma(t_1)$ is the same as $\sigma(t_2)$, the value of the terms $t_1, \cdots, t_n$ of a predicate $p(t_1, \cdots, t_n)$ belong to the relation p_A — $(\sigma(t_1), \cdots, \sigma(t_n)) \in p_A$, or the Boolean operators return true when applied to the sentences that they connect.

In this paper, we use distinguished variables for defining constraints and use them to extend signatures and algebras. Given a set V of variables typed over S, we denote by $\Sigma \cup V$ the extension of Σ with the variables taken as unary operation symbols and, given a Σ-algebra A and an assignment $\chi\colon V \to A$, we denote by $A \cup \chi$ the extension of A to $\Sigma \cup V$ that coincides with χ on V. New 'normal' variables can be superposed using the usual construction of terms with variables as explained above.

3   Extending Algebraic Specifications with Constraints

We put forward a number of definitions that relate to the so-called c-semiring approach to constraint satisfaction and optimisation proposed in [1]. As explained therein, that approach is quite general and allows us to work with constraints of different kinds, both hard and 'soft', the latter in many grades (fuzzy, weighted, and so on). The c-semiring approach supports selection based on a characterisation of 'best solution' supported by multi-dimensional criteria, for example minimizing the cost of a resource while maximizing the work it supports.

We recall that a c-semiring is a commutative idempotent semiring where addition is extended to infinite sets. In summary, a c-semiring is a tuple $\langle R, \vee, \wedge, 0, 1 \rangle$ such that:

- R is a set and 0, 1 are elements of that set.
- $\vee$ is a commutative, associative, idempotent operation over subsets of R with unit 0; we use $\sum$ for sums over sets and reserve $\vee$ for the binary case.
- $\wedge$ is a binary, commutative, associative operation with unit 1 for which 0 is absorbing, i.e., $(a \wedge 0 = 0)$ for every a; we use $\prod$ for products over finite sets.
- $\wedge$ distributes over $\vee$.

The intuition is that R — the *domain* of the semiring — represents a space of degrees of satisfaction, for example the set $\{0, 1\}$ for 'yes'/'no' or the interval $[0, 1]$ for intermediate degrees of satisfaction (which gives us a constraint model that is richer than Boolean algebra). The operations $\wedge$ and $\vee$ are used for composition (conjunction) and choice, respectively.

A partial order $\leq_R$ (of satisfaction) is defined over R as follows: $a \leq_R b$ iff $a \vee b = b$. That is, b is better than a iff the choice between a and b is b. It follows that 0 is worse than any other degree of satisfaction — it represents dissatisfaction, and 1 is better than any other degree of satisfaction — it represents total satisfaction. This partial order defines a complete distributive lattice.

---

[2] Note that implicit quantification in many-sorted equational logic raises problems at the level of proof theory, which we do not discuss herein [7].

In order to define specifications that capture constraints interpreted over c-semirings, we extend the traditional notion of signature as follows.

Definition 1 (Constraint Signature). *A constraint signature (or c-signature for short) is a tuple* $\langle S, \Omega, V, sat, 0, 1, \leq \rangle$ *where*

- $\langle S, \Omega \rangle$ *is a signature as recalled above.*
- *V is a finite set of (constraint) variables (c-variables for short) disjoint from* Ω.
- $sat \in S$ *is a distinguished sort,* $0, 1 \in \Omega_{sat}$ *are distinguished constants, and* $\leq$ *is a distinguished predicate symbol over sat.*

For simplicity, we will often use Σ to denote both a c-signature and its underlying algebraic signature and denote by V_Σ its set of c-variables. We will denote by Σ^c the algebraic signature $\langle S, \Omega \cup V_\Sigma \rangle$.

Definition 2 (Constraint Algebra). *Let* Σ *be a c-signature. A constraint algebra (c-algebra for short) for* Σ *is a triple* $\langle A, R, \chi \rangle$ *consisting of:*

- *A c-semiring R.*
- *A* $\langle S, \Omega \rangle$-*algebra A such that* A_{sat} *is the domain of R,* 0_A *and* 1_A *are the units of R, and* $\leq_A$ *is the partial order defined by R.*
- *An assignment* $\chi \colon V \to A$ *of values to the c-variables.*

Notice that, given a term t in T_{Σ^c}, $\chi(t)$ is the value that is assigned to t in the extended algebra $A \cup \chi$.

We now adapt to our algebraic setting the concepts put forward in [1] for expressing constraints:

Definition 3 (Constraints). *Let* Σ *be a c-signature.*

- *A constraint is a term* $q \in T_{\Sigma^c sat}$, *i.e., a ground term of sort sat.*
- *A constraint problem (c-problem for short) C is a finite set of constraints.*

In our running example, we consider the case of a customer who wants to book a flight. The data signature of our example could be as depicted in Fig. 1: it sets out the domain of airports, cities, airlines and flights that are relevant for a particular customer.

The c-signature of the customer, i.e., the one in which constraint variables are introduced, could then be the extension of flightDataSign depicted in Fig. 2.

This signature includes three c-variables — flight, flightCost and payMode — meaning that the customer wants to optimise the choice of the flight and the payment mode. We use {DC, CC} as an abbreviation for a sort with two different constants DC and CC. In order to express the constraints that apply to that optimisation, three operations are declared for expressing preferences (i.e., operations of sort *sat*): airlinePref, stopsPref, distPref.

The constraints themselves are expressed as terms of type *sat*, for example:

Signature flightDataSign
    Sorts nat, bool, city, airport, airline, money, flightCode
    Opns distance : airport city $\rightarrow$ nat
          cost : airport city $\rightarrow$ money
          LHR, LGW, LTN, STN, BCN, GRO, ... : airport
          Iberia, BritishAirways, EasyJet, RyanAir, Vueling, ... : airline
          IB001, IB002, BA001, BA002, EZ001, RN001, VL001, ... : flightCode
          Egham, Barcelona, ... : city
          stops : flightCode $\rightarrow$ nat
          airline : flightCode $\rightarrow$ airline
          airDept, airDest : flightCode $\rightarrow$ airport

Fig. 1. The signature flightDataSign

Signature customerSign **extends** flightDataSign **with**
    Opns departure, destination : city
          totalCost : flightCode $\rightarrow$ money
          airlinePref : airline $\rightarrow$ sat
          payPref : {DC, CC} $\rightarrow$ sat
          stopsPref : nat money $\rightarrow$ sat
          distPref : nat $\rightarrow$ sat
    c-Vars flight : flightCode; flightCost : money; payMode : {DC, CC}

Fig. 2. The signature customerSign

airlinePref(airline(flight)) — meaning that the customer has a preference on the airline.

payPref(payMode) — meaning that the customer has a preference on the payment mode.

stopsPref(stops(flight),totalCost(flight)) — meaning that the customer wishes to optimise the number of stops relative to the total cost of the journey.

distPref(distance(airDest(flight),destination)) — meaning that the customer wishes to optimise the distance between the destination airport and city.

We discuss now how these preferences are evaluated.

Definition 4 (Constraint Evaluation).
Let Σ be a c-signature and $\langle A, R, \chi \rangle$ a c-algebra for Σ.

- *The degree of satisfaction of a constraint q is $\chi(q)$.*
- *Given a c-problem C:*
  - *The degree of satisfaction $\chi(C)$ of C is $\prod_{q \in C} \chi(q)$. That is, we take the minimum of the degrees of satisfaction that χ assigns to the constraints in C.*
  - *The best level of consistency of C over A and R is $\sum_{\chi:V \to A} \chi(C)$, which we denote by $blevel_{A,R}(C)$. That is, we take the maximum degree of satisfaction across all assignments.*

- *A c-problem C is consistent over A and R iff $blevel_{A,R}(C) > 0$, i.e., if there is an assignment for which all constraints have a non-zero degree of satisfaction.*
- *A solution to a consistent c-problem C over A and R is an assignment χ such that $\chi(C) > 0$. A best solution is an assignment χ such that $\chi(C) = blevel_{A,R}(C)$.*

We now consider specifications over a signature.

Definition 5 (Constraint Specification). *A constraint specification (c-spec for short) is a triple $\langle \Sigma, \Phi, C \rangle$ where Σ is a c-signature, Φ is a finite set of sentences over Σ^c and C is a finite set of constraints over Σ.*

A model of $\langle \Sigma, \Phi, C \rangle$ is a c-algebra $\langle A, R, \chi \rangle$ such that $(A \cup \chi) \models_{\Sigma^c} \Phi$ and $\chi(C) > 0$, i.e., the sentences in Φ are true and χ is a solution to C.

A best model of $\langle \Sigma, \Phi, C \rangle$ is a model $\langle A, R, \chi \rangle$ such that $\chi(C) = blevel_{A,R}(C)$.

Notice that, as usual in algebraic specifications, Φ may involve (data) variables, which should not be confused with the c-variables. The specification is quantified over the former but not the latter.

Consider again our running example. The specification of the underlying data type could be as depicted in Fig. 3. For simplicity, we use a tabular representation

Specification flightData
    Signature flightDataSign
        Axioms distance(X,Y)=D, cost(X,Y)=C **where:**

X	Y	D	C
BCN	Barcelona	10	5
GRO	Barcelona	60	15
LHR	Egham	10	5
LGW	Egham	35	20
LTN	Egham	40	30
STN	Egham	70	50
...	...	...	...

airDept(X)=X1, airDest(X)=X2, airline(X)=X3, stops(X)=X4 **where:**

X	X1	X2	X3	X4
IB001	LHR	BCN	Iberia	0
IB002	LGW	BCN	Iberia	1
BA001	LHR	BCN	BritishAirways	0
BA002	LGW	BCN	BritishAirways	1
EZ001	LTN	BCN	EasyJet	0
RN001	STN	GRO	RyanAir	0
VL001	LGW	BCN	Vueling	0
...	...	...	...	...

Fig. 3. The specification flightData

for groups of equations; for example, the specification would contain the equations distance(BCN,Barcelona)=10, cost(BCN,Barcelona)=5 and so on.

The specification of the customer could be as depicted in Fig. 4 (note that all sentences are universally quantified). For example, the customer is not satisfied with any flight that has two or more stops, no matter the total cost; nor is the customer satisfied with any flight whose destination airport is fifty or more miles away from the destination city, though if that distance is less than 50 miles, the closer the better. The customer is also willing to pay 20% more for a non-stop flight but prefers the cheaper between any two flights with the same number of stops.

Notice that a specification does not necessarily fix a c-semiring: a specifier is more likely to express conditions on preferences, as is the case of customer, which will determine what c-semirings can be chosen to accommodate them.

Because customer does not have information on the actual cost of flights, we cannot get a best choice for the c-constraints flight, flightCost and payMode. In the next section we show how, by connecting the customer to a supplier (with flight costs and own preferences) it is more meaningful to compute a best choice, and also how to compare between different suppliers so that the one that offers the best solution can be chosen by the customer.

> **Specification** customer **extends** flightData **with**
>   **Signature** customerSign
>   **Axioms** d, d', n, m, m' : nat
>   departure = Egham
>   destination = Barcelona
>   totalCost(F) = flightCost +
>   cost(airDest(F),destination) + cost(airDept(F),departure)
>   payPref(CC) > payPref(DC)
>   airlinePref(Iberia) > airlinePref(RyanAir)
>   airlinePref(Iberia) > airlinePref(EasyJet)
>   airlinePref(Iberia) = airlinePref(Vueling)
>   airlinePref(Iberia) = airlinePref(BritishAirways)
>   stopsPref(0,m) < stopsPref(1,m') **if** m > m'*1.2
>   stopsPref(0,m) > stopsPref(1,m') **if** m ≤ m'*1.2
>   stopsPref(n,m) > stopsPref(n,m') **if** m < m' ∧ n ≤ 1
>   stopsPref(n,m) = 0 **if** n ≥ 2
>   distPref(d) = 0 **if** d ≥ 50
>   distPref(d) > distPref(d') **if** d < d' < 50
>   **Constraints**
>   airlinePref(airline(flight))
>   payPref(payMode)
>   stopsPref(stops(flight),totalCost(flight))
>   distPref(distance(airDest(flight),destination))

Fig. 4. The specification customer

4 Composing Specifications

We start by stating some of the category-theory properties of c-specs, which are useful to bring abstract constraint data types to the more established mathematical frameworks of algebraic specification (see [4,12]).

Definition 6 (Morphisms of C-Signatures). *A morphism of c-signatures* $\sigma\colon \Sigma \to \Sigma'$ *consists of:*

- *A morphism between the algebraic signatures that preserves the distinguished elements.*
- *A total function between the sets of c-variables.*

The image of a c-problem C *by a c-signature morphism* $\sigma\colon \Sigma \to \Sigma'$ *is* $\sigma(C)$ *where* $\sigma(\langle V_k, q_k \rangle)$ *is the* Σ'*-constraint* $\langle \sigma(V_k), \sigma(q_k) \rangle$.

Proposition 7 (Category of C-Signatures). *C-signatures form a finitely co-complete category, which we denote by* c-SIG. *The c-signature* $\langle \{sat\}, 0, 1, \leq, \emptyset \rangle$, *which we denote by* $\Sigma_\emptyset$, *is an initial object and pushouts operate independently over the algebraic signature and the c-variables.*

Proposition and Definition 8 (Category of C-Specs). *A morphism of constraint specifications* $\sigma\colon \langle \Sigma, \Phi, C \rangle \to \langle \Sigma', \Phi', C' \rangle$ *is a morphism of c-signatures* $\sigma\colon \Sigma \to \Sigma'$ *such that* $\Phi' \models_{\Sigma'^c} \sigma(\Phi)$ *and* $\sigma(C) \subseteq C'$.
    Morphisms of c-specs define a category, which we denote by CCS. *This category is finitely co-complete.*

Proof. That a category is defined is trivial to prove. Finite co-completeness is proved as follows:

Existence of Initial Objects. *It is easy to prove that* $\langle \Sigma_\emptyset, \emptyset, \emptyset \rangle$, *where* $\Sigma_\emptyset = \langle \{sat\}, \{0 : sat,\ 1 : sat,\ \leq : sat\ sat\}, \emptyset, sat, 0, 1, \leq \rangle$ *is the initial c-signature, is an initial object of* CCS.

Existence of Pushouts. *Let* $\sigma_i\colon \langle \Sigma, \Phi, C \rangle \to \langle \Sigma_i, \Phi_i, C_i \rangle$ *(i = 1, 2) be two morphisms and* $\mu_i\colon \Sigma_i \to \Sigma'$ *a pushout of the corresponding c-signature morphisms. Then,* $\mu_i\colon \langle \Sigma_i, \Phi_i, p_i \rangle \to \langle \Sigma', \mu_1(\Phi_1) \cup \mu_2(\Phi_2), \mu_1(C_1) \cup \mu_2(C_2) \rangle$ *is easily proved to be a pushout of c-specs.*

Pushouts compute amalgamated unions, which provide the means for composing specifications. The amalgamation is done over what is designated to be the 'intersection' of the two signatures, i.e., the sorts, operations, predicates and c-variables that they are designated to share (composition is not based on syntactic sharing, i.e., names are not considered to be universal but local to specifications). The exceptions are the sort sat and the constants 0 and 1 of the c-semiring, which are shared by construction – i.e., the initial c-signature $\Sigma_\emptyset$ is shared by all c-specifications. An example of composition is given below.

Definition 9 (Reducts). *Let* $\sigma\colon \Sigma \to \Sigma'$ *be a morphism of c-signatures. The* σ*-reduct of a c-algebra* $\langle A', R', \chi' \rangle$ *for* Σ' *is the c-algebra* $\langle A'|_\sigma, R'|_\sigma, \chi'|_\sigma \rangle$ *for* Σ *where:*

- $A'|_\sigma$ is the σ-reduct of A' in the usual algebraic sense, i.e., $(A'|_\sigma)_s = A'_{\sigma(s)}$ for every sort s and, for every operation or predicate op, $op_{A'|_\sigma} = \sigma(op)_{A'}$.
- $R'|_\sigma = R'$.
- $\chi'|_\sigma = \sigma; \chi'$.

That is, models are translated back along a morphism by adopting the same data carriers and c-semiring, and giving symbols and variables at the source the interpretations that their translations have in the models being translated.

It is important to study how properties of models relate to those of their reducts:

Proposition and Definition 10. *Let* $\sigma\colon \langle \Sigma, \Phi, C \rangle \to \langle \Sigma', \Phi', C' \rangle$ *be a morphism of c-specs and* $\langle A', R', \chi' \rangle$ *a model of* $\langle \Sigma', \Phi', C' \rangle$. *The following properties hold:*

1. $\langle A'|_\sigma, R'|_\sigma, \chi'|_\sigma \rangle$ *is a model of* $\langle \Sigma, \Phi, C \rangle$.
2. $\chi'(\sigma(C)) = \chi'|_\sigma(C) \geq \chi'(C')$.
3. $blevel_{A'|_\sigma, R'|_\sigma}(C) \geq blevel_{A', R'}(\sigma(C)) \geq blevel_{A', R'}(C')$.
4. *If* σ *is injective on* V_Σ, *then* $blevel_{A'|_\sigma, R'|_\sigma}(C) = blevel_{A', R'}(\sigma(C))$.
5. *If* C' *is consistent over* $\langle A', R' \rangle$, *then* C *is consistent over* $\langle A'|_\sigma, R'|_\sigma \rangle$ *and, for every solution* χ' *of* C', $\chi'|_\sigma$ *is a solution of* C.

Proof. All properties are easy to prove.

Notice that the difference between 3 and 4 is that, if σ is not injective on V_Σ, the range of assignments to c-variables allowed by Σ' is more restricted than that allowed by Σ — certain c-variables are identified through σ. Property 5 is particularly important because it shows that consistency and solutions of c-problems are preserved by reducts, i.e., by extending a specification, one does not create new solutions for or make existing c-problems consistent; naturally, one may lose solutions or make c-problems inconsistent because new constraints can be introduced through the extension.

Let us analyze how we can check when a requester component and a provider component can be connected. If the constraint specification $\langle \Sigma, \Phi, C \rangle$ states the preferences and conditions defined by the requester, and $\langle \Sigma', \Phi', C' \rangle$ states the functionality offered and the conditions that the provider can accept, then what we need is that requester and the provider constraints are consistent. More precisely, that if we put together the two specifications:

$$\begin{array}{ccc} \langle \Sigma_0, \emptyset, \emptyset \rangle & \longrightarrow & \langle \Sigma, \Phi, C \rangle \\ \downarrow & {\scriptstyle po} & \downarrow \\ \langle \Sigma', \Phi', C' \rangle & \longrightarrow & \langle \Sigma'', \Phi'', C'' \rangle \end{array}$$

where Σ_0 is the common subsignature of Σ and Σ', then the resulting specification must be satisfiable, meaning that there must be a model of $\langle \Sigma'', \Phi'', C'' \rangle$.

In order to illustrate this construction, we connect customers with suppliers. Consider the following specification of a supplier given in Fig. 6 based on the

Signature supplierSign **extends** flightDataSign **with**
    Opns price : flightCode money payMode $\rightarrow$ sat
         available : flightCode $\rightarrow$ sat
   c-Vars flight : flightCode; flightCost : money; payMode : {DC, CC}

Fig. 5. The c-signature supplierSign

Specification supplier **extends** flightData **with**
   Signature supplierSign
     Axioms available(F)=1 **iff** F$\in${IB001,IB002,BA001,BA002,EZ001,RN001}
     price(F,M,C)=S **where**:

id	F	M	C	S
A1	IB001	120	DC	1
A2	IB001	120	CC	1
A3	IB002	150	DC	1
A4	IB002	150	CC	1
A5	BA001	250	DC	1
A6	BA001	250	CC	1
A7	BA002	145	DC	1
A8	BA002	145	CC	1
A9	EZ001	60	DC	1
A10	EZ001	65	CC	1
A11	RN001	40	DC	1
A12	RN001	45	CC	1
	F	M	C	0

Constraints available(flight)
             price(flight,flightCost,payMode)

Fig. 6. The specification supplier

signature given in Fig. 5. A supplier has a number of flights available for sale, for each of which it has a price depending on the payment mode. All the constraints are crisp meaning that the supplier will only accept to sell flights that it has available and for the stated prices.

As before, we have used a tabular form to simplify the specification. In addition, we have named equations (using the attribute *id*): this is just for convenience when discussing constraint optimisation and is not part of the formal specification, i.e., it has no semantics.

Consider now the amalgamated sum (pushout) of customer and supplier assuming that sorts, operations, predicates and c-variables with the same names are shared. The set of constraints is, as explained in Def. 8:

c_0 : airline(flight)
c_1 : payPref(payMode)

c_2 : stopsPref(stops(flight),totalCost(flight))
c_3 : distPref(distance(airDest(flight),destination))
c_4 : available(flight)
c_5 : price(flight,flightCost,payMode)

Again, we have named constraints to simplify the way we refer to them.

The crisp constraint c_4 reduces the space of solutions to the triples (F,M,C) — corresponding to flight code, flight cost and payment mode, respectively — on rows A1-A12. The constraint c_3 eliminates the triples (F,M,C) on rows A11-A12 from that set. For each of the remaining constraints, we can derive the following properties where we use $=$ and $>$ to compare the way those assignments order the satisfaction of the corresponding constraint:

c_0 : A1=A2=A3=A4 > A9=A10, and A5=A6=A7=A8 > A9=A10
c_1 : A2=A4=A6=A8=A10 > A1=A3=A5=A7=A9
c_2 : A9 > A10 > A1=A2 > A7=A8 > A3=A4 > A5=A6
c_3 : A1=A2=A3=A4=A5=A6=A7=A8=A9=A10
c_4 : A1=A2=A3=A4=A5=A6=A7=A8=A9=A10
c_5 : A1=A2=A3=A4=A5=A6=A7=A8=A9=A10

In order to calculate c_2, we computed the total costs as specified in the specification customer (see Fig. 4):

id	total cost	id	total cost	id	total cost	id	total cost
A1	130	A2	130	A3	175	A4	175
A5	260	A6	260	A7	160	A8	160
A9	95	A10	100	A11	105	A12	110

No best solution can be derived from these inequalities: for example, the pay-mode preference conflicts with those that relate costs. Notice that, for every algebra that satisfies the specification, a best solution can be obtained because a specific level of satisfaction is assigned to every constraint. What happens in this case is that there is no solution that is optimal for all such algebras.

In general, we can think that a customer could also wish to express an ordering of importance on constraints, for example that c_2 is the most important, followed by c_3, then c_1, and then c_0. This can be achieved by means of another preference function, this time applied to sat:

$$\text{constPref} : \text{sat sat} \rightarrow \text{sat}$$

axiomatized by

constPref(N,M) = 0 **if** N=0
constPref(N,M) < constPref(N',M) **if** N<N'
constPref(N,M) > constPref(N',M) **if** N>N'>0
constPref(N,M) > constPref(N',M') **if** N≠0 ∧ M>M'

One would then replace c_0, c_1, c_2, c_3 by

$$c : \mathsf{constPref}(c_0, \mathsf{constPref}(c_1, \mathsf{constPref}(c_3, c_2)))$$

which would again exclude the triples on rows A11-A12 from the space of solutions and return:

$c :$ A9 > A10 > A1 > A2 > A7 > A8 > A3 > A4 > A5 > A6
$c_4 :$ A1=A2=A3=A4=A5=A6=A7=A8=A9=A10
$c_5 :$ A1=A2=A3=A4=A5=A6=A7=A8=A9=A10

This time, there is a best solution for the customer: the triple (EZ001,95,DC).

Our framework can also be used for selecting a best supplier (if one exists), by analysing the composition of customer with that of every other supplier. For example. consider the following specification of a different supplier depicted in Fig. 7. The crisp constraint c_4 now reduces the space of solutions to the triples (F,M,C) on rows B1-B6. The constraint c_3 eliminates the triples (F,M,C) on rows B5-B6 from that set. The total costs are now:

id	total cost
B1	75
B2	80
B3	90
B4	95

For each of the remaining constraints, we can derive the following properties where we use the row numbers to refer to the triples:

$c_0 :$ B1=B2 > B3=B4
$c_1 :$ B2=B4 > B1=B3
$c_2 :$ B1 > B2 > B3 > B4
$c_3 :$ B1=B2=B3=B4
$c_4 :$ B1=B2=B3=B4
$c_5 :$ B1=B2=B3=B4

Applying the order on the customer's constraints we obtain:

$c :$ B1 > B2 > B3 > B4
$c_4 :$ B1=B2=B3=B4
$c_5 :$ B1=B2=B3=B4

From this set we can derive that (VL001,40,DC) is the best solution.

Consider now the combined specifications of the customer with the two suppliers, sharing the data specification but nothing else. The amalgamation will distinguish the triples that result from one pairing from those resulting from the other pairing, leading effectively to the union of the two tables. This means that

Specification otherSupplier **extends** flightData **with**
  Signature supplierSign
    Axioms available(F)=1 **iff** F∈{EZ001,RN001,VL001}
      price(F,M,C)=S **where**:

id	F	M	C	S
B1	VL001	40	DC	1
B2	VL001	45	CC	1
B3	EZ001	55	DC	1
B4	EZ001	60	CC	1
B5	RN001	40	DC	1
B6	RN001	45	CC	1
	F	M	C	0

  Constraints available(flight)
      price(flight,flightCost,payMode)

Fig. 7. The specification otherSupplier

some entries are duplicated but this is how it should be because they refer to c-variables coming from different sources:

id	F	M	C	S	id	F	M	C	S
A1	IB001	120	DC	1	A2	IB001	120	CC	1
A3	IB002	150	DC	1	A4	IB002	150	CC	1
A5	BA001	250	DC	1	A6	BA001	250	CC	1
A7	BA002	145	DC	1	A8	BA002	145	CC	1
A9	EZ001	60	DC	1	A10	EZ001	65	CC	1
B1	VL001	40	DC	1	B2	VL001	45	CC	1
B3	EZ001	55	DC	1	B4	EZ001	60	CC	1

For each of the constraints, we derive:

c_0 : B1=B2=A1=A2=A3=A4 > A9=A10=B3=B4
   and A5=A6=A7=A8 > A9=A10=B3=B4
c_1 : B2=B4=A2=A4=A6=A8=A10 > B1=B3=A1=A3=A5=A7=A9
c_2 : B1 > B2 > B3 > B4=A9 > A10 > A1=A2 > A7=A8 > A3=A4 > A5=A6
c_3 : B1=B2=B3=B4=A1=A2=A3=A4=A5=A6=A7=A8=A9=A10

If we use the ordering on the customer's constraints, then we get:

c : B1 > B2 > B3 > B4=A9 > A10 > A1=A2 > A7=A8 > A3=A4 > A5=A6

which means that, from the customer's point of view, the optimal solution is the triple (VL001,40,DC) and, therefore, the customer would prefer otherSupplier over supplier.

5   Relationship with Institutions

Algebraic specification of abstract data types has traditionally been studied in the context of institutions [6,11]:

Definition 11 (Institution). *An institution* $\langle Sig, Sen, Mod, \models \rangle$ *consists of*

- *a category Sig of* signatures *and* signature morphisms,
- *a functor Sen* : *Sig* → *Set, defining for every signature* Σ *the set Sen(Σ) of Σ-sentences, and for every signature morphism* $\sigma : \Sigma \to \Sigma'$ *a sentence translation map Sen(σ)* : *Sen(Σ)* → *Sen(Σ'),*
- *a functor Mod* : *Sig* → *Cat^{op}, defining for every signature* Σ *the category Mod(Σ) of Σ-models and Σ-model homomorphisms, and for every signature morphism* $\sigma : \Sigma \to \Sigma'$ *the* reduct functor *Mod(σ)* : *Mod(Σ')* → *Mod(Σ),*
- *a family of* satisfaction relations $\models_{\Sigma} \subseteq |Mod(\Sigma)| \times Sen(\Sigma)$, *indexed by signatures,*

such that the following satisfaction condition *holds:*

$$M' \models_{\Sigma'} Sen(\sigma)(\rho) \quad \text{if and only if} \quad Mod(\sigma)(M') \models_{\Sigma} \rho,$$

for every signature morphism $\sigma : \Sigma \to \Sigma'$, Σ'*-model M and Σ-sentence* ρ.

The algebraic specification of abstract data types as recalled in Sect. 2 is a variant of the institutions reviewed in [11].

Proposition 12. *The extension to c-specifications as defined in Sect. 3 and 4 defines an institution:*

- *The category of signatures is as defined in Prop. 7;*
- *The sentence functor is the extension of classical conditional equational logic with c-constraints as defined in Def. 3, i.e., sentences are either conditional equations or c-constraints;*
- *The model functor is as in Def. 2 and Def. 9.*
- *The satisfaction relation is as usual on conditional equations and on c-constraints is defined by*

$$\langle A, R, \chi \rangle \models c \quad \text{iff} \quad \chi(c) > 0$$

The results presented in Sect. 4 about c-specifications actually follow from the fact that c-constraints define an institution.

Another way of defining an institution of c-constraints is by framing them in the context of institutions of graded consequence recently proposed by Razvan Diaconescu [3], which differ from institutions by letting the satisfaction relations take values in a space L, i.e., for every signature Σ,

$$\models_{\Sigma} : \ |Mod(\Sigma)| \times Sen(\Sigma) \to L$$

In this case, we would just have to take the domain of the c-semiring as the space L and interpret the sentences that are not c-constraints as having the c-semiring values 1 or 0 depending on whether they are satisfied or not satisfied in a model, respectively. That is, we would treat equations as crisp constraints.

6   Conclusions and Further Work

In this paper, we outlined a way in which specifications of abstract data types can be extended to accommodate constraint specification using the c-semiring approach proposed in [1]. This brings together two areas to which Martin Wirsing has made extensive contributions: algebraic specification theory (e.g., [12]) and the use of constraint systems to deal with non-functional requirements in service-oriented systems [13,14].

This work sets the stage for a more ambitious project of revisiting the formalism of symbolic graphs, proposed in [9], to use it as the basis for describing service-oriented systems, where a symbolic graph is a typed attributed graph together with a set of constraints. In particular, we can use symbolic graphs to describe the states of systems and symbolic graph transformation rules to describe computations including the interconnection of components. In this context, constraints could be used to describe quality of service requirements, so that computing service level agreements could be part of the computation associated with component interconnection.

Acknowledgments. This work was developed while J L Fiadeiro was on study leave at Universitat Politècnica de Catalunya with the generous support of the Dep. de Llenguatges i Sistemes Informàtics.

References

1. Bistarelli, S., Montanari, U., Rossi, F.: Semiring-based constraint satisfaction and optimization. J. ACM 44(2), 201–236 (1997)
2. Broy, M., Dosch, W., Partsch, H., Pepper, P., Wirsing, M.: Existential quantifiers in abstract data types. In: Maurer, H.A. (ed.) ICALP 1979. LNCS, vol. 71, pp. 73–87. Springer, Heidelberg (1979)
3. Diaconescu, R.: Graded consequence: an institution theoretic study. Soft Comput. 18(7), 1247–1267 (2014)
4. Ehrig, H., Mahr, B.: Fundamentals of Algebraic Specification 1: Equations and Initial Semantics. Monographs in Theoretical Computer Science. An EATCS Series. Springer (1985)
5. Fiadeiro, J.L.: Categories for Software Engineering. Springer (2004)
6. Goguen, J.A., Burstall, R.M.: Institutions: Abstract model theory for specification and programming. J. ACM 39(1), 95–146 (1992)
7. Goguen, J.A., Meseguer, J.: Universal realization, persistent interconnection and implementation of abstract modules. In: Nielsen, M., Schmidt, E.M. (eds.) ICALP 1982. LNCS, vol. 140, pp. 265–281. Springer, Heidelberg (1982)
8. Hölzl, M.M., Meier, M., Wirsing, M.: Which soft constraints do you prefer? Electr. Notes Theor. Comput. Sci. 238(3), 189–205 (2009)
9. Orejas, F., Lambers, L.: Lazy graph transformation. Fundam. Inform. 118(1-2), 65–96 (2012)
10. Papazoglou, M.P., Traverso, P., Dustdar, S., Leymann, F.: Service-oriented computing: State of the art and research challenges. IEEE Computer 40(11), 38–45 (2007)

11. Sannella, D., Tarlecki, A.: Foundations of Algebraic Specification and Formal Software Development. In: Monographs in Theoretical Computer Science. An EATCS Series. Springer (2012)
12. Wirsing, M.: Algebraic specification. In: Handbook of Theoretical Computer Science, Volume B: Formal Models and Semantics (B), pp. 675–788. MIT Press, Cambridge (1990)
13. Wirsing, M., Denker, G., Talcott, C.L., Poggio, A., Briesemeister, L.: A rewriting logic framework for soft constraints. Electr. Notes Theor. Comput. Sci. 176(4), 181–197 (2007)
14. Wirsing, M., Hölzl, M. (eds.): SENSORIA. LNCS, vol. 6582. Springer, Heidelberg (2011)

Generate & Check Method
for Verifying Transition Systems in CafeOBJ

Kokichi Futatsugi

Research Center for Software Verification (RCSV)
Japan Advanced Institute of Science and Technology (JAIST)
1-1 Asahidai, Nomi, Ishikawa 923-1292, Japan

Abstract. An interactive theorem proving method for the verification
of infinite state transition systems is described.

The state space of a transition system is defined as a quotient set (i.e. a
set of equivalence classes) of terms of a topmost sort `State`, and the transitions are defined with conditional rewrite rules over the quotient set. A
property to be verified is either (1) an invariant (i.e. a state predicate that
is valid for all reachable states) or (2) a (`p leads-to q`) property for two
state predicates `p` and `q`, where (`p leads-to q`) means that from any reachable state `s` with (`p(s) = true`) the system will get into a state `t` with (`q(t)`
`= true`) no matter what transition sequence is taken.

Verification is achieved by developing proof scores in CafeOBJ. Sufficient verification conditions are formalized for verifying invariants and
(`p leads-to q`) properties. For each verification condition, a proof score
is constructed to (1) generate a finite set of state patterns that covers all
possible infinite states and (2) check validity of the verification condition
for all the covering state patterns by reductions.

The method achieves significant automation of proof score developments.

1 Introduction

Constructing specifications and verifying them in the upstream of software development are still one of the most important challenges in formal software
engineering. It is because quite a few critical bugs are caused at the level of domains, requirements, and/or designs specifications. Proof scores are intended to
meet this challenge [9,10]. In the proof score approach, an executable algebraic
specification language (i.e. CafeOBJ [3] in our case) is used to specify a system
and system properties, and the reduction (or rewriting) engine of the language is
used as a proof engine to prove that the system satisfy the properties of interest.

Proof plans for verifying the system properties are coded into proof scores, and
are also written in the algebraic specification language. Usually, a proof score
describes modules and predicates in the modules that constitute a sufficient
condition for verifying a system property. The language processor interprets the
specification and proof score and verifies the validity of the sufficient condition by
checking all the predicates with reductions. Logical soundness of the reductions

R. De Nicola and R. Hennicker (Eds.): Wirsing Festschrift, LNCS 8950, pp. 171–192, 2015.

is guaranteed by the fact that the reductions are consistent with the equational reasoning with the equations in the specification and the proof score [11].

The concept of proof supported by proof scores is similar to that of LP [14]. Proof scripts written in tactic languages provided by theorem provers (proof assistants) such as Coq [6] and Isabelle/HOL [19] have similar nature as proof scores. However, proof scores are written uniformly with specifications in an executable algebraic specification language and can enjoy a transparent, simple, executable and efficient logical foundation based on the equational and rewriting logics [11,17].

Effective coordination of inference (à la theorem proving, e.g. [6,15,19,23]) and search (à la model checking, e.g. [5,13]) is important for making proof scores more effective and powerful, and we have developed several techniques [22,10]. The generate & check method described in this paper is a recent development of this kind. The method is based on (1) a state representation as a set of observers, and (2) systematic generation of finite state patterns that cover all possible infinite cases.

The rest of the paper is organized as follows. Section 2 explains necessary mathematical concepts and notations. Section 3 presents system and property specifications of the QLOCK protocol in the CafeOBJ language. Section 4 describes the generate & check method with necessary theoretical expositions. Section 5 presents proof scores for QLOCK through the generate & check method. Section 6 explains related work and future issue.

2   Preliminaries

2.1   Equational Specifications and Quotient Term Algebras

Let $\Sigma = (S, \leq, F)$ be a regular order-sorted signature [12], where S is a set of sorts, $\leq$ is a partial order on S, and $F \overset{\text{def}}{=} \{F_{s_1 \cdots s_m s}\}_{s_1 \cdots s_m s \in S^+}$ is S^+-sorted set of function symbols. Let $X = \{X_s\}_{s \in S}$ be an S-sorted set of variables, then the S-**sorted set of** $\Sigma(X)$-**term** is defined inductively as follows. Regularity of an order-sorted signature guarantees the existence of the least sort of a term and makes the definition consistent [12].

- each constant $f \in F_s$ is a $\Sigma(X)$-term of sort s,
- each variable $x \in X_s$ is a $\Sigma(X)$-term of sort s,
- t is a $\Sigma(X)$-term of sort s' if t is a $\Sigma(X)$-term of sort s and $s < s'$, and
- $f(t_1, \ldots, t_n)$ is a $\Sigma(X)$-term of sort s for each operator $f \in F_{s_1 \ldots s_n s}$ and $\Sigma(X)$-terms t_i of sort s_i for $i \in \{1, \ldots, n\}$.

Let $T_\Sigma(X)_s$ denote a set of $\Sigma(X)$-terms of sort s, and let $T_\Sigma(X) \overset{\text{def}}{=} \{T_\Sigma(X)_s\}_{s \in S}$, and let $T_\Sigma \overset{\text{def}}{=} T_\Sigma(\{\})$. $T_\Sigma(X)$ is called an S-sorted set of $\Sigma(X)$-terms, and T_Σ is called an S-sorted set of Σ-terms. A Σ-term is also called a ground term or a term without variables. $T_\Sigma(X)$ can be organized as $(\Sigma \cup X)$-algebras in the obvious way by using the above inductive definition of $\Sigma(X)$-terms, where $\Sigma \cup X$ is a signature obtained by interpreting X as an order-sorted set of fresh constants. Similarly, T_Σ can be organized as Σ-algebras. For an S-sorted set T, let $(t \in T) \stackrel{\text{def}}{=} (\exists s \in S)(s \in T_s)$.

Let $l, r \in T_\Sigma(X)_s$ for some $s \in S$ and $c \in T_\Sigma(X)_{\texttt{Bool}}$ for a special sort $\texttt{Bool}$ with the two constructors $\texttt{true}$ and $\texttt{false}$, a Σ-equation is defined as a sentence of the form $(\forall X)\,(l = r \texttt{ if } c)$. If the condition c is the constant predicate $\texttt{true}$, the equation is called unconditional and written as $(\forall X)\,(l = r)$. An equation that is not unconditional is called conditional. Throughout this paper an equation may be conditional, and the theory and the method presented are valid even if considering conditional equations.

For a finite set of equations $E = \{e_1, \cdots, e_n\}$, (Σ, E) represents an equational specification. (Σ, E) defines an order-sorted quotient term algebra $T_\Sigma/{=_E} \stackrel{\text{def}}{=} \{(T_\Sigma)_s/(=_E)_s\}_{s \in S}$, where E defines an order-sorted congruence relation $=_E \stackrel{\text{def}}{=} \{(=_E)_s\}_{s \in S}$ on $T_\Sigma = \{T_{\Sigma s}\}_{s \in S}$. Note that if $e_i = (\forall X)(l_i = r_i \texttt{ if } c_i)$ for $i \in \{1, \cdots, n\}$ and Y is disjoint from X, then $T_\Sigma(Y)/{=_E}$ can be defined similarly by interpreting $T_\Sigma(Y)$ as $T_{\Sigma \cup Y}$, where $\Sigma \cup Y$ is a signature obtained by interpreting Y as an order-sorted set of fresh constants.

Proof scores in CafeOBJ are mainly developed for an equational specification (Σ, E) (i.e. for $T_\Sigma/{=_E}$). Note that the description of $T_\Sigma/{=_E}$ here is quite casual, and refer to [11] for more detailed and precise descriptions including constructor-based signatures, models and satisfaction, equational and specification calculi.

2.2 Rewrite Rules and Reductions

If each variable in r or c is a variable in l (i.e. $(\forall Y)(l \in T_\Sigma(Y) \texttt{ implies } r, c \in T_\Sigma(Y))$) and l is not a variable, an equation $(\forall X)(l = r \texttt{ if } c)$ can be interpreted as a rewrite rule $(\forall X)(l \rightarrow r \texttt{ if } c)$. Given a set of Σ-equations E that can be interpreted as a set of rewrite rules, the equational specification (Σ, E) defines the one step rewrite relation $\rightarrow_E$ on T_Σ. Note that the definition of $\rightarrow_E$ is not trivial because some rule in E may have a condition (see Section 2.2 of [18] or [26] for details).

The reduction (or rewriting) defined by (Σ, E) is the transitive and reflective closure $\rightarrow_E^*$ of $\rightarrow_E$. In CafeOBJ each equation is interpreted as a rewrite rule, and the reduction is used to check validity of predicates. The following is a fundamental lemma about $=_E$ and $\rightarrow_E^*$.

Lemma 1 [Reduction Lemma]. $(\forall t, t' \in T_\Sigma)((t \rightarrow_E^* t') \texttt{ implies } (t =_E t'))$ □

Note that the Reduction Lemma holds even if the rewriting relation defined by a specification (Σ, E) is not "terminating", "confluent", and "sufficiently complete". These properties of the rewriting relation are desirable but not necessary for the theory and the method presented in this paper.

Let $\theta \in T_\Sigma(Y)^X$ be a substitution (i.e. a map) from X to $T_\Sigma(Y)$ for disjoint X and Y then θ extends to a morphism from $T_\Sigma(X)$ to $T_\Sigma(Y)$, and $t\theta$ is the term obtained by substituting $x \in X$ in t with $x\,\theta$.

The following lemma about the reduction plays an important role in the generate & check method.

Lemma 2 [Substitution Lemma].

$$(\forall p \in T_\Sigma(X)_{\text{Bool}})((p \rightarrow_E^* \text{true}) \text{ implies } (\forall \theta \in T_\Sigma(Y)^X)(p\theta \rightarrow_E^* \text{true}))$$

and

$$(\forall p \in T_\Sigma(X)_{\text{Bool}})((p \rightarrow_E^* \text{false}) \text{ implies } (\forall \theta \in T_\Sigma(Y)^X)(p\theta \rightarrow_E^* \text{false}))$$

where each $x \in X$ in p and each $y \in Y$ in $p\theta$ are treated as fresh constants in the reductions $(p \rightarrow_E^* \text{true})$, $(p \rightarrow_E^* \text{false})$ and $(p\theta \rightarrow_E^* \text{true})$, $(p\theta \rightarrow_E^* \text{false})$ respectively. ☐

Lemma 1 and lemma 2 with $Y = \{\}$ imply the following lemma, where $(\forall X)(p =_E \text{true}) \overset{\text{def}}{=} (\forall \theta \in T_\Sigma^X)(p\theta =_E \text{true})$.

Lemma 3 [Lemma of Constants].

$$(\forall p \in T_\Sigma(X)_{\text{Bool}})((p \rightarrow_E^* \text{true}) \text{ implies } (\forall X)(p =_E \text{true}))$$

where each $x \in X$ in p is treated as a fresh constant in the reduction $(p \rightarrow_E^* \text{true})$. ☐

2.3 Transition Systems

It is widely recognized that the majority of systems/problems in many fields can be modeled as transition systems and their invariants.

A **transition system** is defined as a three tuple (St, Tr, In). St is a set of states, $Tr \subseteq St \times St$ is a set of transitions on the states, and $In \subseteq St$ is a set of initial states. $(s, s') \in Tr$ denotes a transition from the state s to the state s'. A sequence of states $s_1 s_2 \cdots s_n$ with $(s_i, s_{i+1}) \in Tr$ for each $i \in \{1, \cdots, n-1\}$ is defined to be a **transition sequence**. Note that any $s \in St$ is defined to be a transition sequence of length 1[1]. A state $s^r \in St$ is defined to be **reachable** if there exists a transition sequence $s_1 s_2 \cdots s_n$ with $s_n = s^r$ for $n \in \{1, 2, \cdots\}$ such that $s_1 \in In$. A state predicate p (i.e. a function from St to Bool) is defined to be an **invariant** (or an invariant property) if $(p(s^r) = \text{true})$ for any reachable state s^r.

Let (Σ, E) be an equational specification with a unique topmost sort (i.e. a sort without subsorts) State, and let $tr = (\forall X)(l \rightarrow r \text{ if } c)$ be a rewrite rule with $l, r \in T_\Sigma(X)_{\text{State}}$ and $c \in T_\Sigma(X)_{\text{Bool}}$, then tr is called a transition rule and defines the one step transition relation $\rightarrow_{tr} \in T_\Sigma(Y)_{\text{State}} \times T_\Sigma(Y)_{\text{State}}$ for Y being disjoint from X as follows.

$$(s \rightarrow_{tr} s') \overset{\text{def}}{=} (\exists \theta \in T_\Sigma(Y)^X)((s =_E l\theta) \text{ and } (s' =_E r\theta) \text{ and } (c\theta =_E \text{true}))$$

---

[1] For the case in which $n = 1$, $s_1 s_2 \cdots s_n$ is s_1 and $\{1, \cdots, 0\}$ is the empty set, and $((s_i, s_{i+1}) \in Tr$ for each $i \in \{1, \cdots, 0\})$ could be interpreted valid.

Note that the rewriting mechanism is used to define the transition relation but it is different from the rewrite relation that defines the one way (or non-commutative) equality. Note also that $=_E$ is understood to be defined with $((\Sigma \cup Y), E)$ by considering $y \in Y$ as a fresh constant if Y is not empty.

Let $TR = \{tr_1, \cdots, tr_m\}$ be a set of transition rules, let $\rightarrow_{TR} \stackrel{\text{def}}{=} \bigcup_{i=1}^{m} \rightarrow_{tr_i}$, and let $In \subseteq (T_\Sigma)_{\text{State}}/(=_E)_{\text{State}}$. Then (Σ, E, TR) defines a transition system $((T_\Sigma)_{\text{State}}/(=_E)_{\text{State}}, \rightarrow_{TR}, In)$.[2] A specification (Σ, E, TR) is called a transition specification.

The idea underlies the transition specification (Σ, E, TR) and the transition system $((T_\Sigma)_{\text{State}}/(=_E)_{\text{State}}, \rightarrow_{TR}, In)$ is same as the one for the topmost rewrite theory [24,25,17]. The generate & check method for (Σ, E, TR) is based on, however, only reductions in proof scores.

2.4 Verification of Invariant Properties

Given a transition system $TS = (St, Tr, In)$, let $init$ be a state predicate that specifies the initial states (i.e. $(\forall s \in St)(init(s) \text{ iff } (s \in In)))$, and let $p_1, p_2, \cdots, p_n$ $(n \in \{1, 2, \cdots\})$ be state predicates of TS, and $inv(s) \stackrel{\text{def}}{=} (p_1(s) \text{ and } p_2(s) \text{ and } \cdots \text{ and } p_n(s))$ for $s \in St$.

Lemma 4 [Invariant Lemma]. The following three conditions are sufficient for p^t to be an invariant.

> (1) $(\forall s \in St)(inv(s) \text{ implies } p^t(s))$
> (2) $(\forall s \in St)(init(s) \text{ implies } inv(s))$
> (3) $(\forall (s, s') \in Tr)(inv(s) \text{ implies } inv(s'))$

$\square$

A predicate that satisfies the conditions (2) and (3) like inv is called an **inductive invariant**. If p^t itself is an inductive invariant then taking $p_1 = p^t$ and $n = 1$ is enough. However, $p_1, p_2, \cdots, p_n$ $(n > 1)$ are almost always needed to be found for getting an inductive invariant, and to find them is a most difficult part of the invariant verification.

It is worthwhile to note that there are following two contrasting approaches for formalizing $p_1, p_2, \cdots, p_n$ for a transition system and its property p^t.

- Make $p_1, p_2, \cdots, p_n$ as minimal as possible to imply the target property p^t;
  - usually done by lemma finding in interactive theorem proving,
  - it is difficult to find lemmas without some comprehensive understanding of the system.
- Make $p_1, p_2, \cdots, p_n$ as comprehensive as possible to characterize the system;
  - usually done by specifying elemental properties of the system as much as possible in formal specification development,
  - it is difficult to identify the elemental properties without focusing on the property to be proved (i.e. p^t).

---

[2] Note that $(T_\Sigma)_{\text{State}}/(=_E)_{\text{State}}$ is better to be understood as $T_\Sigma/=_E$, for usually the sort State can only be understood together with other related sorts like Bool, Nat, Queue, etc.

3 Specifications of QLOCK in CafeOBJ

A simple but non-trivial example QLOCK is used to explain the generate & check method in this section and Section 5. You can find all the specifications and proof scores for verifying QLOCK with the generate & check method on the following web page.

    http://www.jaist.ac.jp/~kokichi/misc/1411gcmvtsco/

Specifications and proof scores in CafeOBJ on the web page contain quite a few comments that explain not only CafeOBJ language but also proof strategy and technique used, and interested readers are encouraged to look into the web page.

This section contains a description, and explains system and property specifications of QLOCK. Section 5 explains proof scores for verifying QLOCK with the generate & check method.

3.1 QLOCK Description

The example used is a mutual exclusion protocol QLOCK. A mutual exclusion protocol can be described as follows:

> Assume that many agents (or processes) are competing for a common equipment (e.g. a printer or a file system), but at any moment of time only one agent can use the equipment. That is, the agents are mutually excluded in using the equipment. A protocol (mechanism or algorithm) which can achieve the mutual exclusion is called "mutual exclusion protocol".

QLOCK is realized by using a global queue (first in first out storage) of agent names (or identifiers) as follows.

- Each of unbounded number of agents who participates in the protocol behaves as follows:
  - If the agent wants to use the common equipment and its name is not in the queue yet, put its name at the bottom of the queue.
  - If the agent wants to use the common equipment and its name is already in the queue, check if its name is on the top of the queue. If its name is on the top of the queue, start to use the common equipment. If its name is not on the top of the queue, wait until its name is on the top of the queue.
  - If the agent finishes to use the common equipment, remove its name from the top of the queue.
- The protocol starts from the state with the empty queue.

3.2 System Specification

The file qlock-sys.cafe on the web page contains a system specification of QLOCK in CafeOBJ.

OTS (Obervational Transition System) is a scheme for formalizing transition systems. A state is formalized as a collection of typed observed values given by

observers (or observation operations). A state transition is formalized as an **action** that defines changes of the observed values between the current state and the next state.

For the generate & check method, generations of finite state patterns (i.e. state terms composed of constructors and variables) that subsume all the possible infinite states is a key procedure, and states are assumed to be represented with an appropriate data structure (or configuration). This is different from the original OTS scheme where there is no assumption on the structure of a state [20,21].

AOB, AID-QUEUE, and STATE: A state of QLOCK is defined as a pair of a queue Qu and a set of observers Aobs by the following module STATE.

```
-- agent observer
mod! AOB {pr(LABEL) pr(AID)
[Aob] op (lb[_]:_) : Aid Label -> Aob {constr} .}
-- queue of Aid
mod! AID-QUEUE {pr(QUEUE(AID{sort Elt -> Aid}))}
-- a state is defined as a pair of a queue of Aid and a set of Aob
mod! STATE{pr(AID-QUEUE) pr(SET(AOB{sort Elt -> Aob})*{sort Set -> Aobs})
-- a state is a pair of Qu and Aobs
[State] op _$_ : Qu Aobs -> State {constr} .}
```

pr(_) indicates a **protecting** importation, and declares to import a module without changing its models. The module LABEL defines the three labels rs (remainder section), ws (waiting section), cs (critical section) for indicating the status of each agent. The module AID defines unbounded number of agent names. The parameterized modules QUEUE and SET define the data structures needed to define STATE. QUEUE(AID{sort Elt -> Aid}) defines the module obtained by instantiating the parameter X of QUEUE by AID with the interpretation of Elt as Aid. Similarly SET(AOB{sort Elt -> Aob}) defines sets of observers. *{sort Set -> State} defines the renaming of Set to State. As a result, a state is presented as a pair of a Q:Qu and a set of (lb[A:Aid]: L:Label) for all A:Aid, where the term (lb[A:Aid]: L:Label) denotes that an agent A is in the status L.

Let STATE-n denote STATE with a n agent ids (i.e. Aid = $\{a_1, \cdots, a_n\}$), and let $\Sigma_{\text{STATE}-n}$ be a signature of STATE-n, then the state space of STATE-n is defined as $St_{\text{STATE}-n} \overset{\text{def}}{=} T_{\Sigma_{\text{STATE}-n}}$.

WT, TY, EX, and QLOCKsys: The QLOCK protocol is defined by the following four modules. The transition rule of the module TY indicates that if the top element of the queue is A:Aid (i.e. Qu is (A:Aid & Q:Qu)) and the agent A is at ws (i.e. (lb[A:Aid]: ws)) then A gets into cs (i.e. (lb[A]: cs)) without changing contents of the queue (i.e. Qu is (A & Q)). The other two transition rules can be read similarly. Note that the module WT, TY, EX formulate the three actions explained in the beginning of the Section 3 precisely and succinctly. QLOCKsys is just combining the three modules.

```
-- wt: want transition
mod! WT {pr(STATE)
trans[wt]:    (Q:Qu    $ ((lb[A:Aid]: rs) AS:Aobs))
         => ((Q & A)  $ ((lb[A]:     ws) AS)) . }
-- ty: try transition
mod! TY {pr(STATE)
trans[ty]:    ((A:Aid & Q:Qu) $ ((lb[A]: ws) AS:Aobs))
          => ((A     & Q)    $ ((lb[A]: cs) AS)) . }
-- ex: exit transition
-- this transition can be defined by 'trans' rule with two
-- (A:Aid)s in the left hand side like [ty], 'ctrans' is used
-- here to show an example of conditional transition rule
mod! EX {pr(STATE)
ctrans[ex]:   ((A1:Aid & Q:Qu) $ ((lb[A2:Aid]: cs) AS:Aobs))
          =>            (Q    $ ((lb[A2]:     rs) AS))
              if (A1 = A2) . }
-- system specification of QLOCK
mod! QLOCKsys{pr(WT + TY + EX)}
```

A declaration of a transition rule starts with **trans**, contains rule's name [_]:, current state term and next state term are placed before and after => respectively, and ends with ".". Note that because a state configuration is a set (i.e. a term composed of associative, commutative, and idempotent binary constructors (_ _)) the component of the left hand side (lb[A:Aid]: rs) of the rule **wt** can match any agent in a state. This implies that the transition rule **wt** can define unbounded number of transitions depending on the number of agents a state includes. The same holds for the rules **ty** and **ex**.

For STATE-n with Aid = $\{a_1, \cdots, a_n\}$, the **trans** or **ctrans** rules **wt,ty,ex** defines the one step transition relations $\rightarrow_{wt}, \rightarrow_{ty}, \rightarrow_{ex}$ respectively on the state space $St_{STATE-n} = T_{\Sigma_{STATE-n}}$. QLOCKsys-$n$ with STATE-n defines a set of transitions $Tr_{QLOCKsys-n} \subseteq (St_{STATE-n} \times St_{STATE-n})$ as $Tr_{QLOCKsys-n} \stackrel{def}{=} (\rightarrow_{wt} \cup \rightarrow_{ty} \cup \rightarrow_{ex})$.

3.3 Property Specification

The file **qlock-prop.cafe** on the web page contains a property specification of QLOCK in CafeOBJ.

Property specification is supposed to define the initial state predicate *init* and the possible inductive invariant *inv* in lemma 4. Both of *init* and *inv* are going to be defined as conjunctions of elemental predicates. For defining the elemental predicates of QLOCK, the module **PNAT** for Peano style unary natural numbers **Nat** with addition _+_and greater than _>_operations is prepared. Using **PNAT**, fundamental functions on **State** like "the number of a label in a state", "the number of an aid in a state", "the number of an aid in a queue", "label of an agent in a State" are defined. All of these functions are naturally defined with recursive equations.

In this property specification of QLOC, we adopt a strategy to formalize necessary predicates based on the Peano style natural number **PNAT**. The strategy works well especially for verifying a (p leads-to q) property (a liveness property, see Section 5.2).

INIT: Using the fundamental functions on `State`, elemental state predicates like "at least one agent in a state" (`aoa`), "no duplication of an Aid in a state" (`1a`), "the queue is empty" (`qe`), "any Aid is in `rs` status" (`allRs`) are defined. Using the elemental state predicates, the initial state predicate `init` of QLOCK is defined as follows.

```
-- an initial state predicate
mod! INIT {pr(STATEpred-init)
op init : -> PnameSeq .   eq init = aoa 1a qe allRs .
-- initial state predicate
pred init : State . eq init(S:State) = cj(init,S) . }
```

Note that `cj` is defined recursively based on the recursive structure of `PnameSeq` as follows:

```
op cj : PnameSeq State -> Bool .
eq cj((PN:Pname PNS:PnameSeq),S:State) = cj(PN,S) and cj(PNS,S) .
```

and a conjunction of predicates is represented as a sequence of `Pname` (i.e. an element of sort `PnameSeq`). The module `PNAMEcj` in the file `qlock-prop.cafe` defines `Pname` and `PnameSeq`.

INV and QLOCKprop: The target predicate of QLOCK is a mutual exclusion predicate defined as follows.

```
-- mutual exclusion predicate; this is the target predicate
op mx : -> Pname .
eq[mx]: cj(mx,S:State) = (#ls(S,cs) = 0) or (#ls(S,cs) = (s 0)) .
pred mx : State .   eq mx(S:State) = cj(mx,S) .
```

where `(#ls(S,cs) = 0) or (#ls(S,cs) = (s 0))` means there is zero or one agent with `cs` status in a state. Elemental state predicates for the possible inductive invariant are selected to specify the statuses like "if queue is empty" (`qep`), "if agent is in `rs`" (`rs`), "if agent is in `ws`" (`ws`), "if agent is in `cs`" (`cs`), "if `cs` then it should be the top of the queue" (`cst`), and the possible inductive invariant `inv` of QLOCK is defined by the module `INV` as follows. The module `QLOCKprop` for QLOCK property specification is just combining INIT and INV.

```
-- a possible inductive invariant predicate
mod! INV {pr(STATEpred-inv)
op inv : -> PnameSeq . eq inv = aoa 1a mx qep rs ws cs cst .
pred inv : State .   eq inv(S:State) = cj(inv,S) .
}
-- property specification of QLOCK
mod! QLOCKprop{pr(INIT + INV)}
```

4   Generate & Check Method

The idea underlies the generate & check method is simple and general. Let Srt be a sort and p be a predicate on Srt, then by lemma 2 (Substitution Lemma)

$$(p(X:Srt) \to_E^* \text{true}) \text{ implies } (\forall t \in (T_\Sigma)_{Srt})(p(t) =_E \text{true})$$

holds, and $(p(X:Srt) \to_E^* \text{true})$ is sufficient to prove $(\forall t)p(t)$. However, usually p is not simple enough to obtain $(p(X:Srt) \to_E^* \text{true})$ directly, and we need to analyze the structure of terms in $(T_\Sigma)_{Srt}$ and E for (1) **generating** a set of terms $\{t_1, \cdots, t_m\} \subseteq T_\Sigma(Y)_{Srt}$ that covers all possible cases of $(T_\Sigma)_{Srt}$, and (2) **checking** $(p(t_i) \to_E^* \text{true})$ for each $i \in \{1, \cdots, m\}$.

Note that the generate & check method is general enough for applying not only to the sort State but also to any sort Srt. As a matter of fact, it can be applied in quite a few occasions in which the necessary cases to be analyzed can be covered by a finite set of term patterns of sort Srt. This paper only describes a special but most important application to the sort State.

Note also that **induction** is an already established technique for proving $(p(X:Srt) \to_E^* \text{true})$ for a constrained sort Srt with proof scores [11], and the generate & check method is another independent technique for coping with sometimes a large number of cases.

4.1   Generate & Check for $\forall st \in St$

A term $t' \in T_\Sigma(Y)$ is defined to be an **instance** of a term $t \in T_\Sigma(X)$ iff there exits a substitution $\theta \in T_\Sigma(Y)^X$ such that $t' = t\,\theta$.

A finite set of terms $C \subseteq T_\Sigma(X)$ is defined to **subsume** a (may be infinite) set of ground terms $G \subseteq T_\Sigma$ iff for any $t' \in G$ there exits $t \in C$ such that t' is an instance of t.

Lemma 5 [Subsume Lemma].

Let a finite set of state terms $C \subseteq T_\Sigma(X)_{\text{State}}$ subsume the set of all ground state terms $(T_\Sigma)_{\text{State}}$, and let p be a state predicate, then the following holds.

$$((\forall s \in C)(p(s) \to_E^* \text{true})) \text{ implies } ((\forall t \in (T_\Sigma)_{\text{State}})(p(t) \to_E^* \text{true}))$$

Proof. Let $C = \{s_1, \cdots, s_m\}$. Note that $p(s_i) \in T_\Sigma(X)_{\text{Bool}}$ for any $s_i \in \{s_1, \cdots, s_m\}$. Then, by the definition of "subsume", for any ground state term $t \in (T_\Sigma)_{\text{State}}$, there exits $s_j \in \{s_1, \cdots, s_m\}$ and a substitution $\theta \in T_\Sigma^X$ such that $t = s_j\theta$. Hence, if $(p(s_i) \to_E^* \text{true})$ for all $s_i \in \{s_1, \cdots, s_m\}$ then $(p(s_j) \to_E^*$ true), and, by lemma 2 (Substitution Lemma), $((p(s_j)\theta = p(s_j\theta) = t) \to_E^*$ true) holds. $\qquad\square$

Lemma 5 and lemma 1 imply the validity of following **Generate&Check-S**. Note that $(t_1 \to_E^* t_2)$ means that the term t_1 is reduced to the term t_2 by the CafeOBJ's reduction engine, and $(t_1 \twoheadrightarrow_E^* t_2)$ implies $(t_1 \to_E^* t_2)$ but not necessary $(t_1 \to_E^* t_2)$ implies $(t_1 \twoheadrightarrow_E^* t_2)$.

Generate&Check-S. Let $((T_\Sigma)_{\text{State}}/(=_E)_{\text{State}}, \to_{TR}, In)$ be a transition system defined by a transition specification (Σ, E, TR) (see Section 2.3). Then doing the following **Generate** and **Check** are sufficient for verifying

$$(\forall t \in (T_\Sigma)_{\text{State}})(p_{st}(t) =_E \text{true})$$

for a state predicate p_{st}.

Generate a finite set of state terms $C \subseteq T_\Sigma(X)_{\text{State}}$ that subsumes $(T_\Sigma)_{\text{State}}$.
Check $(p_{st}(s) \to_E^* \text{true})$ for each $s \in C$.

□

4.2   Built-in Search Predicate of CafeOBJ

The verification condition (3) for invariant verification in lemma 4 contains a universal quantification over the set of transitions Tr, and it is generally difficult to specify Tr as a sort. CafeOBJ's built-in search predicate makes it possible to translate a universal quantification over Tr into a universal quantification over St.

The built-in search predicate is declared as follows.

```
pred _=(*,1)=>+_if_suchThat_{_} : State State Bool Bool Info .
```

`Info` is a sort for showing necessary information. The first argument is the current state `S:State`; the second argument is the variable for binding the found next state `SS:State`; the third argument is the variable for binding the found condition `CC:Bool`; the fourth argument is a predicate `p(S,SS,CC)` whose validity is to be checked; the fifth argument is a term `i(S,SS,CC)` for showing the necessary information. Note that in the use of this predicate the second and third arguments is always variables like `SS:State` and `CC:Bool` for binding the found next state and condition respectively.

Let $((T_\Sigma)_{\text{State}}/(=_E)_{\text{State}}, \to_{TR}, In)$ be a transition system defined by a transition specification (Σ, E, TR) (see Section 2.3), and let $TR = \{tr_1, \cdots, tr_m\}$. For a state term $s \in T_\Sigma(Y)_{\text{State}}$, the reduction of a Boolean term:

```
s =(*,1)=>+ SS:State if CC:Bool suchThat p(s,SS,CC) {i(s,SS,CC)}
```

with $\to_E^* \cup \to_{TR}$ is defined to behave as follows.

1. Search for every pair (tr_j, θ) of a transition rule $tr_j = (\forall X)(l_j \to r_j \text{ if } c_j)$ in Tr and a substitution $\theta \in T_\Sigma(Y)^X$ such that $s = l_j \theta$.
2. For each found (tr_j, θ), let $(\text{SS} = r_j \theta)$ and $(\text{CC} = c_j \theta)$ and print out $i(l_j \theta, r_j \theta, c_j \theta)$ and tr_j if $(p(l_j \theta, r_j \theta, c_j \theta) \to_E^* \text{true})$ holds.
3. Returns `true` if some print out exits, and returns `false` otherwise.

Note that a user can define `p(s,SS,CC)` and `i(s,SS,CC)` freely, and it makes many kinds of checks and result displays possible. Most typical usages are (1) to check whether some predicate holds between a current state `s` and a next state `SS`, and (2) to check whether $(\text{CC}=c_j \theta \to_E^* \text{true})$ for a pair (tr_j, θ).

4.3   Generate & Check for $\forall tr \in Tr$

Let `q` be a predicate "`pred q : State State`" for stating some relation of the current state and the next state, like $(inv(s) \text{ implies } inv(s'))$ in the condition (3) for invariant verification in lemma 4. Let the predicates _then_ and valid-q be defined as follows in CafeOBJ using the built-in search predicate. Note that _then_ is different from _implies_ because (B:Bool implies true = true) for _implies_ but only (true then true = true) for _then_.

```
pred _then_ : Bool Bool .
eq (true then B:Bool) = B . eq (false then B:Bool) = true .
pred valid-q : State State Bool .
eq valid-q(S:State,SS:State,CC:Bool) =
   not(S =(*,1)=>+ SS if CC suchThat not((CC then q(s,SS))) == true)
     {i(S,SS,CC)}) .
```

For a state term $s \in T_\Sigma(Y)_{\text{State}}$, the reduction of the Boolean term:
$$\text{valid-q}(s,\text{SS:State},\text{CC:Bool})$$
with $\twoheadrightarrow^*_E \cup \rightarrow_{TR}$ behaves as follows based on the definition of the behavior of the built-in search predicate.

1. Search for evey pair (tr_j, θ) of a transition rule $tr_j = (\forall X)(l_j \to r_j \text{ if } c_j)$ in Tr and a substitution $\theta \in T_\Sigma(Y)^X$ such that $s = l_j\,\theta$.
2. For each found (tr_j, θ), let $(\text{SS} = r_j\,\theta)$ and $(\text{CC} = c_j\,\theta)$ and print out $i(l_j\,\theta, r_j\,\theta, c_j\,\theta)$ and tr_j if $(\text{not}((c_j\,\theta \text{ then } q(l_j\,\theta, r_j\,\theta)) == \text{true}) \twoheadrightarrow^*_E \text{true})$.
3. Returns false if any print out exits, and returns true otherwise.

Note that $(\text{not}((c_j\,\theta \text{ then } q(l_j\,\theta, r_j\,\theta)) == \text{true}) \twoheadrightarrow^*_E \text{true})$ means $((c_j\,\theta \text{ then } q(l_j\,\theta, r_j\,\theta)) \twoheadrightarrow^*_E \text{false})$ or $((c_j\,\theta \text{ then } q(l_j\,\theta, r_j\,\theta)) \twoheadrightarrow^*_E \text{<not-true-or-false>})$, and no print out for (tr_j, θ) means that $((c_j\,\theta \text{ then } q(l_j\,\theta, r_j\,\theta)) \twoheadrightarrow^*_E \text{true})$. It in turn means $(c_j\,\theta \twoheadrightarrow^*_E \text{false})$ or $((c_j\,\theta \twoheadrightarrow^*_E \text{true})$ and $(q(l_j\,\theta, r_j\,\theta) \twoheadrightarrow^*_E \text{true}))$. Hence, if $(\text{valid-q}(s,\text{SS:State},\text{CC:Bool}) \twoheadrightarrow^*_E \cup \rightarrow_{TR} \text{true})$ for $s \in T_\Sigma(Y)$, $((c_j\,\theta \twoheadrightarrow^*_E \text{false})$ or $((c_j\,\theta \twoheadrightarrow^*_E \text{true})$ and $(q(l_j\,\theta, r_j\,\theta) \twoheadrightarrow^*_E \text{true})))$ for any (tr_j, θ) such that $(s = l_j\,\theta)$.

We need the following definition of **cover set** for "Generate & Check for $\forall tr \in Tr$".

Definition 6 [Cover] Let $C \subseteq T_\Sigma(Y)$ and $C' \subseteq T_\Sigma(X)$ be finite sets. C is defined to **cover** C' iff for any ground instance $t'_g \in T_\Sigma$ of any $t' \in C'$, there exits $t \in C$ such that t'_g is an instance of t and t is an instance of t'. □

The following lemma holds for cover sets.

Lemma 7 [Cover Lemma 1]. Let $C' \subseteq T_\Sigma(X)_{\text{State}}$ be the set of all the left hand sides of the transition rules in TR, and let $C \subseteq T_\Sigma(Y)$ cover C', then the following holds.

$$(\forall t \in C)(\text{valid-q}(t,\text{SS:State},\text{CC:Bool}) \twoheadrightarrow^*_E \cup \rightarrow_{TR} \text{true})$$
$$\text{implies}$$
$$(\forall (s, s') \in ((T_\Sigma \times T_\Sigma) \cap \rightarrow_{TR}))(q(s, s') \twoheadrightarrow^*_E \text{true}))$$

Proof. For any $(s, s') \in T_\Sigma \times T_\Sigma$, if $(s, s') \in \rightarrow_{TR}$, there exits a transition rule $tr_i = (\forall X)(l_i \to r_i \text{ if } c_i) \in TR$ and a substitution $\theta_s \in T_\Sigma^X$ such that $(s = l_i\,\theta_s)$

and $(s' = r_i \theta_s)$ and $(c_i \theta_s =_E \textbf{true})$ by the definition of $\rightarrow_{TR}$ (see Section 2.3). Because s is a ground instance of $l_i \in C'$ and C covers C', there exits $t \in C$ such that $(t = l_i \theta_t)$ for a substitution $\theta_t \in T_\Sigma(Y)^X$ (i.e. t is an instance of l_i) and $(s = t \eta_s)$ for a substitution $\eta_s \in T_\Sigma^Y$ (i.e. s is an instance of t). If we assume (valid-q(t,SS:State,CC:Bool) $\twoheadrightarrow_E^* \cup \rightarrow_{TR} \textbf{true}$), because $(t = l_i \theta_t)$ for the substitution $\theta_t \in T_\Sigma(Y)^X$, we get $((c_i \theta_t \twoheadrightarrow_E^* \textbf{false})$ or $((c_i \theta_t \twoheadrightarrow_E^* \textbf{true})$ and (q($l_i \theta_t, r_i \theta_t$) $\twoheadrightarrow_E^* \textbf{true}$))). By using lemma 2 (Substitution Lemma) with Y for X and $\{\}$ for Y and the fact $(\twoheadrightarrow_E^*$ implies $\rightarrow_E^*)$, we get $((c_i \theta_t \eta_s \twoheadrightarrow_E^* \textbf{false})$ or $((c_i \theta_t \eta_s \twoheadrightarrow_E^* \textbf{true})$ and (q($l_i \theta_t, r_i \theta_t$)$\eta_s$ = q($l_i \theta_t \eta_s, r_i \theta_t \eta_s$) $\twoheadrightarrow_E^* \textbf{true}$))). Because $(c_i \theta_t \eta_s = c_i \theta_s)$ and $(c_i \theta_s =_E \textbf{true})$, $(c_i \theta_t \eta_s \twoheadrightarrow_E^* \textbf{false})$ can not hold, and we get (q($l_i \theta_t \eta_s, r_i \theta_t \eta_s$) $\twoheadrightarrow_E^* \textbf{true}$). Because $(l_i \theta_t \eta_s = l_i \theta_s)$ and $(r_i \theta_t \eta_s = r_i \theta_s)$, it implies (q($s, s'$) $\twoheadrightarrow_E^* \textbf{true}$).

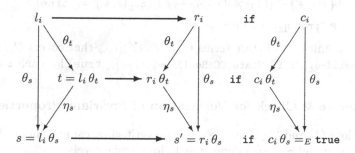

Fig. 1. Commutative Diagrams for the Cover Lemma 1

□

Lemma 7 and lemma 1 imply the validity of following **Generate&Check-T1**.

Generate&Check-T1. Let $((T_\Sigma)_{\text{State}}/(=_E)_{\text{State}}, \rightarrow_{TR}, In)$ be a transition system defined by a transition specification (Σ, E, TR) (see Section 2.3), and let $C' \subseteq T_\Sigma(X)$ be the set of all the left hand sides of the transition rules in TR. Then doing the following **Generate** and **Check** are sufficient for verifying

$$(\forall(s, s') \in ((T_\Sigma \times T_\Sigma) \cap \rightarrow_{TR}))(\textbf{q}_{\textbf{tr}}(s, s') =_E \textbf{true})$$

for a predicate "pred $\textbf{q}_{\textbf{tr}}$: State State".

Generate a finite set of state terms $C \subseteq T_\Sigma(Y)_{\text{State}}$ that covers C'.
Check (valid-$\textbf{q}_{\textbf{tr}}$(t,SS:State,CC:Bool) $\twoheadrightarrow_E^* \cup \rightarrow_{TR} \textbf{true}$) for each $\textbf{t} \in C$.

□

By investigating the proof of lemma 7, it is seen that the following lemma holds.

Lemma 8 [Cover Lemma 2]. Let $TR = \{tr_1, \cdots, tr_m\}$ be a set of transition rules. For $i \in \{1, \cdots, m\}$, let $tr_i = (\forall X)(l_i \rightarrow r_i \textbf{ if } c_i)$ and let $C_i \subseteq T_\Sigma(Y)$ cover $\{l_i\}$. Then the following holds.

$(\forall i \in \{1, \cdots, m\})(\forall t \in C_i)(\texttt{valid-q(t,SS:State,CC:Bool)} \twoheadrightarrow^*_E \cup \to_{tr_i} \texttt{true})$
implies
$(\forall (s, s') \in ((T_\Sigma \times T_\Sigma) \cap \to_{TR}))(\texttt{q}(s, s') \to^*_E \texttt{true})$

$\square$

Lemma 8 and lemma 1 imply the validity of following **Generate&Check-T2**.

Generate&Check-T2. Let $TR = \{tr_1, \cdots, tr_m\}$ be a set of transition rules, and let $tr_i = (\forall X)(l_i \to r_i \text{ if } c_i)$ for $i \in \{1, \cdots, m\}$. Then doing the following **Generate** and **Check** for all of $i \in \{1, \cdots, m\}$ is sufficient for verifying

$$(\forall (s, s') \in ((T_\Sigma \times T_\Sigma) \cap \to_{TR}))(\texttt{q}_{\texttt{tr}}(s, s') =_E \texttt{true})$$

for a predicate "$\texttt{pred q}_{\texttt{tr}} : \texttt{State State}$".

Generate a finite set of state terms $C_i \subseteq T_\Sigma(Y)_{\texttt{State}}$ that covers $\{l_i\}$.
Check ($\texttt{valid-q}_{\texttt{tr}}\texttt{(t,SS:State,CC:Bool)} \twoheadrightarrow^*_E \cup \to_{tr_i} \texttt{true}$) for each $\texttt{t} \in C$. $\square$

4.4 Generate & Check for Verification of Invariant Properties

The conditions (1) and (2) of lemma 4 can be verified by using Generate&Check-S with $\texttt{p}_{\texttt{st-1}}(s)$ and $\texttt{p}_{\texttt{st-2}}(s)$ defined as follows respectively.

(1) $\texttt{p}_{\texttt{st-1}}(s) = (inv(s) \texttt{ implies } p^t(s))$
(2) $\texttt{p}_{\texttt{st-2}}(s) = (init(s) \texttt{ implies } inv(s))$

Note that, if $inv \stackrel{\text{def}}{=} (p_1 \texttt{ and} \cdots \texttt{ and } p_n)$, usually $p^t = (p_{i_1} \texttt{ and} \cdots \texttt{ and } p_{i_m})$ for $\{i_1, \cdots, i_m\} \subseteq \{1, \cdots, n\}$, and condition (1) is directly obtained and no need to use Generate&Check-S.

The condition (3) of lemma 4 can be verified by using Generate&Check-T1 or T2 with $\texttt{q}_{\texttt{tr-3}}(s, s')$ defined as follows.

(3) $\texttt{q}_{\texttt{tr-3}}(s, s') = (inv(s) \texttt{ implies } inv(s'))$

4.5 Verification of (p leads-to q) Properties

Invariants are fundamentally important properties of transition systems. They are asserting that something bad will not happen (i.e. safety property). However, it is sometimes also important to assert that something good will surely happen (i.e. liveness property). A (p leads-to q) property is a liveness property defined as follows.

Definition 9 [p leads-to q]. Let $TS = (St, Tr, In)$ be a transition system, let Rst be the set of reachable states of TS, let $Tseq$ be the set of transition sequences of TS, and let p, q be predicates with arity $(St, Data)$ of TS, where $Data$

is a data sort needed to specify p, q^3. Then (p leads-to q) is defined to be valid for TS iff the following holds, where St^+ denotes the set of state sequences with length more than zero, and $s \in \alpha$ means that s is an element in α for $\alpha \in St^+$.

$$(\forall s\alpha \in Tseq)(\forall d \in Data)$$
$$(((s \in Rst) \text{ and } p(s,d) \text{ and } (\forall s' \in s\alpha)(\text{not } q(s',d)))$$
$$\texttt{implies}$$
$$(\exists \beta t \in St^+)(q(t,d) \text{ and } s\alpha\beta t \in Tseq))$$

It means that the system will get into a state t with $q(t,d)$ from a state s with $p(s,d)$ no matter what transition sequence is taken. □

The (p leads-to q) property is adopted from the UNITY logic [4], the above definition is, however, not the same as the original one. In the UNITY logic, the basic model is the parallel program with parallel assignments, and (p leads-to q) is defined through applications of inference rules.

It is worthwhile to note that ($s \in Rst$) is assumed in the premiss of the definition of (p leads-to q) properties.

Lemma 10 [p leads-to q]. Based on the original transition system $TS = (St, Tr, In)$, let $\widehat{St} \overset{\text{def}}{=} St \times Data$, let $(((s,d),(s',d)) \in \widehat{Tr}) \overset{\text{def}}{=} ((s,s') \in Tr)$, let $\widehat{In} \overset{\text{def}}{=} In \times Data$, and let $\widehat{TS} \overset{\text{def}}{=} (\widehat{St}, \widehat{Tr}, \widehat{In})$. Let inv be an invariant of $\widehat{TS}$ and let m be a function from $\widehat{St}$ to Nat (the set of natural numbers), then the following 4 conditions are sufficient for the property (p leads-to q) to be valid for $\widehat{TS}$. Here $\widehat{s} \overset{\text{def}}{=} (s,d)$ for any $d \in Data$, $p(\widehat{s}) \overset{\text{def}}{=} p(s,d)$ and $q(\widehat{s}) \overset{\text{def}}{=} q(s,d)$.

(1) $(\forall(\widehat{s}, \widehat{s'}) \in \widehat{Tr})$
    $((inv(\widehat{s}) \text{ and } p(\widehat{s}) \text{ and } (\text{not } q(\widehat{s}))) \text{ implies } (p(\widehat{s'}) \text{ or } q(\widehat{s'})))$
(2) $(\forall(\widehat{s}, \widehat{s'}) \in \widehat{Tr})$
    $((inv(\widehat{s}) \text{ and } p(\widehat{s}) \text{ and } (\text{not } q(\widehat{s}))) \text{ implies } (m(\widehat{s}) > m(\widehat{s'})))$
(3) $(\forall \widehat{s} \in \widehat{St})$
    $((inv(\widehat{s}) \text{ and } p(\widehat{s}) \text{ and } (\text{not } q(\widehat{s}))) \text{ implies } (\exists \widehat{s'} \in \widehat{St})((\widehat{s}, \widehat{s'}) \in \widehat{Tr}))$
(4) $(\forall \widehat{s} \in \widehat{St})$
    $((inv(\widehat{s}) \text{ and } (p(\widehat{s}) \text{ or } q(\widehat{s})) \text{ and } (m(\widehat{s}) = 0)) \text{ implies } q(\widehat{s}))$

Proof. Note that ⌢s are omitted in the following. The condition (1) asserts that if ($p(s)$ and (not $q(s)$)) for any reachable state s, and (not $q(s')$)) for any next state s' of s, then $p(s')$. This implies, by induction on the length of a transition sequence from s, that for any transition sequence $s\alpha \in Tseq$, if $(\forall s' \in s\alpha)(\text{not } q(s'))$ then $(\forall s' \in s\alpha)(p(s'))$. It means $p(s')$ keeps to hold while (not $q(s')$). (2) asserts that $m(s)$ decreases properly for any next state s' of s, if ($p(s)$ and (not $q(s)$)). (3) asserts that a next state exits while ($p(s')$ and (not $q(s')$)). Hence, (2) and (3) imply that $m(s')$ keeps to decease properly while (not $q(s')$), but $m(s')$ is a natural

---

[3] We may need some *Data* for specifying a predicate on a transition system like "the agent with the name N is working" where N is *Data*.

number and should stop to decrease in finite steps, and should get to the state t with $((p(t) \text{ or } q(t)) \text{ and } (m(t) = 0))$. (4) asserts that $((p(t) \text{ or } q(t)) \text{ and } (m(t) = 0))$ implies $q(t)$. Hence, $(\exists \beta t \in St^+)(q(t) \text{ and } s\alpha\beta t \in Tseq))$.   □

4.6   Generat & Check for Verification of (p leads-to q) Properties

The conditions (1) and (2) of lemma 10 can be verified by using Generate &Check-T1 or T2 in Section 4.3 with $q_{tr-1}(s, s')$ and $q_{tr-2}(s, s')$ defined as follows respectively[4].

(1) $q_{tr-1}(s, s') = ((inv(s) \text{ and } p(s) \text{ and } (\text{not } q(s))) \text{ implies } (p(s') \text{ or } q(s')))$
(2) $q_{tr-2}(s, s') = ((inv(s) \text{ and } p(s) \text{ and } (\text{not } q(s))) \text{ implies } (m(s) > m(s')))$

The conditions (3) and (4) of lemma 10 can be verified by using Generate &Check-S in Section 4.1 with $p_{st-3}(s)$ and $p_{st-4}(s)$ defined as follows respectively.

(3) $p_{st-3}(s) = ((inv(s) \text{ and } p(s) \text{ and } (\text{not } q(s))) \text{ implies } (s \texttt{ =(*,1)=+ SS:State}))$
(4) $p_{st-4}(s) = ((inv(s) \text{ and } (p(s) \text{ or } q(s)) \text{ and } (m(s) = 0)) \text{ implies } q(s))$

Note that $(s \texttt{ =(*,1)=+ SS:State})$ is a built-in search predicate that returns **true** if there exits $s' \in St$ such that $(s, s') \in Tr$.

5   Proof Scores for QLOCK

Interested readers are encouraged to visit the web page:
        http://www.jaist.ac.jp/~kokichi/misc/1411gcmvtsco/
for the full proof scores.

5.1   Proof Scores for Invariant Properties

The module INV of the QLOCK property specification in Section 3.3 defines a possible inductive invariant inv as the conjunction of seven state predicates as follows.

        eq inv = aoa 1a mx qep rs ws cs cst .

The target predicate for QLOCK is mx, and the condition (1) of lemma 4 is proved directly.

Proof Scores for $(\forall s \in St)(init(s) \text{ implies } inv(s))$. The condition (2) of lemma 4 for QLOCK is verified by using Generate&Check-S of Section 4.1. The file qlock-init-ps.cafe on the web page contains proof scores for verifying the condition.

Just generating a set $C \subseteq T_\Sigma(Y)_{\texttt{State}}$ that subsumes $(T_\Sigma)_{\texttt{State}}$ or covers a set $C' \subseteq T_\Sigma(X)_{\texttt{State}}$ is trivial. You can take $C = \{S\texttt{:State}\}$ for the subsuming

---

[4] ^s are omitted.

and $C = C'[X \to Y]$ for the covering. The challenging part is to guarantee that for the target predicate p the check $(p(t_i) \to_E^* \text{true})$ for each $t_i \in C$ is successful. Let a set $C \subseteq T_\Sigma(Y)_{\text{State}}$ be called p-effective iff the check $(p(t_i) \to_E^* \text{true})$ for each $t_i \in C$ is successful.

The following set of state patterns $\{s1, s2, \ldots, s7\}$ covers the singleton set of the most general state pattern $\{(\text{Q:Qu} \$ \text{ AS:Aobs})\}$ and subsumes the set of all the ground state terms $(T_\Sigma)_{\text{State}}$.

```
--> case[1]: S:State = (Q:Qu $ empty)
eq s1  = (q $ empty) .
--> case[2]: S:State = (Q:Qu $ ((lb[A:Aid]: L:Label) AS:Aobs))
eq s2  = (empQ $ ((lb[a1]: rs) as)) .        -- wt
eq s3  = (empQ $ ((lb[a1]: ws) as)) .
eq s4  = (empQ $ ((lb[a1]: cs) as)) .
--
eq s5  = ((a1 & q) $ ((lb[a2]: rs) as)) .    -- wt
eq s6  = ((a1 & q) $ ((lb[a2]: ws) as)) .    -- ty
eq s7  = ((a1 & q) $ ((lb[a2]: cs) as)) .    -- ex
}
```

Here q is a variable of sort Qu, as is a variable of sort Aobs, a1, a2 are variables of sort Aid. Note that variables q, as, a1, a2 are appearing in the terms to be reduced and are declared as fresh constants in the proof scores in CafeOBJ.

It is easy to see that there is no overlap among s1,s2,...,s7 and they list up all the state patterns with (1) the Qu part is empQ or (A1:Aid & Q:Qu), and (2) the Aobs part is empty or ((lb[A:Aid]: L:Label) as:Aobs).

Let init-c be defined as:

```
pred init-c : State .
eq init-c(S:State) = init(S) implies inv(S) .
```

then it is shown that $\{s1, s2, \ldots, s7\}$ is a (init-c)-effective set by checking $(\text{init-c}(si) \to_E^* \text{true})$ (i.e. "red init-c(si) ." returns true) for each $si \in \{s1, s2, \ldots, s7\}$.

The cover set $\{s1, s2, \ldots, s7\}$ can be generated by the following combinatorial generation script.

```
[(tg(2)[q,empty])]
     ||
[(tg(2)[(empQ),(tg(1)[(a1),(rs;ws;cs),(as)])])]
     ||
[(tg(2)[(a1 & q),(tg(1)[(a2),(rs;ws;cs),(as)])])]

-- t(1)/tg(1) and t(2)/tg(2) construct state terms
-- defined by the following two equations:
eq t(1)(A:Aid,L:Label,as:Aobs) = ((lb[A]: L) as) .
eq t(2)(Q:Qu,AS:Aobs) = (Q $ AS) .
```

Using the combinatorial generation of the cover set, Generate&Check-S for the state predicate init-c can be done automatically by one reduction command in CafeOBJ.

Proof Scores for $(\forall(s, s') \in Tr)(inv(s)$ implies $inv(s'))$. The condition
(3) of lemma 4 for QLOCK is verified by using Generate&Check-T2 of Section 4.3. The file qlock-inv-ps.cafe on the web page contains proof scores for verifying the condition.

In the QLOCK specification, the three transition rules wt, ty, ex are defined in the module WT, TY, EX in Section 3.2 and the three left hand sides of the transition rules are as follows.

```
11 =              (Q:Qu  $ ((lb[A:Aid]:   rs) as:Aobs))
12 =  ((A:Aid & Q:Qu) $ ((lb[A]:        ws) as:Aobs))
13 = ((A1:Aid & Q:Qu) $ ((lb[A2:Aid]: cs) as:Aobs))
```

Hence, a minimal set that covers {11,12,13} can be obtained as follows.

```
-- State patterns
ops t1 t2 t3 t4 t5 t6 : -> State .
-- covering 11
eq t1 = (empQ $ ((lb[b1]: rs) as)) .        -- wt
eq t2 = ((b1 & q) $ ((lb[b1]: rs) as)) .   -- wt
eq t3 = ((b1 & q) $ ((lb[b2]: rs) as)) .   -- wt
-- covering 12
eq t4 = ((b1 & q) $ ((lb[b1]: ws) as)) .   -- ty
-- covering 12
eq t5 = ((b1 & q) $ ((lb[b1]: cs) as)) .   -- ex
eq t6 = ((b1 & q) $ ((lb[b2]: cs) as)) .   -- ex
```

Here b1, b2, b3 are literal variables of sort Aid. **Literal variables** are defined to be variables which obey the rule that different literals variables denote different objects, and literal variables b1, b2, b3 denote different elements of sort Aid. Variables q, as, b1, b2, b3 are also declared as fresh constants. Let q and inv-c be defined as follows, where valid-q is defined as in Section 4.3.

```
pred q : State State .
eq q(S:State,SS:State) = (inv(S) implies inv(SS)) .
--
pred inv-c : State State Bool .
eq inv-c(S:State,SS:State,CC:Bool) = valid-q(S,SS,CC) .
```

Let a set $C \subseteq T_\Sigma(Y)_{\text{State}}$ be called p-**effective with** TR iff the check $(p(t_i) \twoheadrightarrow^*_E \cup \to_{TR}$ true) for each $t_i \in C$ is successful. Then it is shown that (1) {t1, t2, t3} is (inv-c)-effective with {wt}, (2) {t4} is (inv-c)-effective with {ty}, and (3) {t5, t6} is (inv-c)-effective with {ex}. This implies that {t1,...,t6} is (inv-c)-effective with {wt,ty,ex}.

The cover set {t1,...,t6} can be generated by the following combinatorial generation script.

```
[(tg(2)[(empQ),(tg(1)[(),(b1),rs,(as)])])]
   ||
[(tg(2)[(b1 & q),(tg(1)[(),(b1),(rs;ws;cs),(as)])])]
   ||
[(tg(2)[(b1 & q),(tg(1)[(),(b2),(rs;cs),(as)])])]
```

Using the combinatorial generation of the cover set, Generate&Check-T1 for showing that {t1,...,t6} is (inv-c)-effective with {wt,ty,ex} can be done automatically by one reduction command in CafeOBJ.

5.2   Proof Scores for a (p leads-to q) Property

The file qlock-pqp-ps.cafe on the web page contains proof scores for verifying a (p leads-to q) property of QLOCK.

QLOCK has an interesting (p leads-to q) property. Let lags be defined as follows; where aos is a destructor for getting the Aobs part from a State.

```
-- label of an agent in a Aobs
op laga : Aobs Aid -> Label .
eq laga(((lb[A1:Aid]: L:Label) AS:Aobs),A2:Aid) =
  if (A1 = A2) then L else laga((AS),A2) fi .
-- label of an agent in a State
op lags : State Aid -> Label .
eq lags(S:State,A:Aid) = laga(aos(S),A) .
```

Then QLOCK enjoys ((lags(S,A) = ws) leads-to (lags(S,A) = cs)) property. That is, if an agent gets into the queue, it will get to the top of the queue with "cs" label.

If we can identify inv and m of the lemma 10, proof scores for verifying this property can be developed by using the generate & check method as shown in Section 4.6. It turns out that it is sufficient to take $(inv(\text{S:State}) = \text{inv(S)})$ and $(m(\text{S:State,A:Aid}) = \text{\#dms(S,A)})$, where, inv is the state predicate proved to be an inductive invariant in Section 5.1, and #dms is defined as follows.

```
-- the number of a label in a Aobs
op #lss : Aobs Label -> Nat .
eq #lss(empty,L:Label) = 0 .
eq #lss(((lb[A:Aid]: L1:Label) AS:Aobs),L2:Label) =
  if (L1 = L2) then (s 0) + #lss((AS),L2)
    else #lss((AS),L2) fi .
-- the number of a label in a state
op #ls : State Label -> Nat .
eq #ls(S:State,L:Label) = #lss(aos(S),L) .
-- the depth of the first appearence of an aid in a queue
op #daq : Qu Aid -> Nat .
eq #daq(A1:Aid & Q:Qu,A2:Aid) =
  if (A1 = A2) then 0 else s(#daq(Q,A2)) fi .
-- counter count of cs
op #ccs : State -> Nat .
eq #ccs(S:State) = if (#ls(S,cs) > 0) then 0 else (s 0) fi .
-- decreasing Nat measure for the lockout freedom verification
op #dms : State Aid -> Nat .
eq #dms(S:State,A:Aid) = ((s s s 0) * #daq(qu(S),A))
                           + #ls(S,rs) + #ccs(S) .
```

The combinatorial generation scripts used are almost same as ones used in Section 5.1, except we need to generate for the pattern (`Q:Qu $ AS:Aobs, A:Aid`) instead of for the pattern (`Q:Qu $ AS:Aobs`).

6 Related Work and Conclusion

Related Work. There are a large number of researches and publications on verifications of transition systems, and it is beyond the scope of this paper to survey all the related work. We only give a brief general view and point out most related recent researches based on the Maude [16].

Verification methods for transition systems are largely classified into deductive and algorithmic ones. Majority of the deductive methods are applications of theorem proving methods/systems [6,15,19,23] to verifications of concurrent systems or distributed protocols with infinite states. Most dominant algorithmic methods are based on model checking methods/systems [2,5] and are targeting to automatic verifications of temporal properties of finite state transition systems. The generate & check method described in this paper is a deductive method with algorithmic combinatorial generations of cover sets. Moreover, reduction is only one deductive mechanism, and it makes theories and proof scores for the method simple and transparent.

Maude [16] is a sister language of CafeOBJ and both languages share many important features. Maude's basic logic is rewriting logic [17] and verification of transition systems with Maude focuses on sophisticated model checking with a powerful associative and/or commutative rewriting engine. There are recent attempts to extend the model checking with Maude for verifying infinite state transition systems [1,8]. They are based on narrowing with unification, whereas the generate & check method is based on cover sets with ordinary matching and reduction.

Searches on Time Versus Space. There are quite a few researches on search techniques in model checking [5,13]. It is interesting to observe that what we have done for the generate & check method in this paper is a search in state space with the built-in search predicate that amounts to the complete search across all one step transitions, whereas the search for model checking is along time axis (i.e. transition sequences) as shown in Figure 2.

Future Issue. This paper only describes CafeOBJ specifications and proof scores for the rather small QLOCK example. We have, however, already checked that the method proposed can be applied to larger examples like ABP (Alternating Bit Protocol [21]). In the ABP example, a state configuration is a 4 tuple of two agents and two channels, and is a little complex than that the QLOCK example. As a result, the generate & check method should be used more extensively in the ABP example. Generally speaking, the generate & check method should be more important for large problems, for it is difficult to do case analyses manually for them. Once a state configuration is properly designed, large

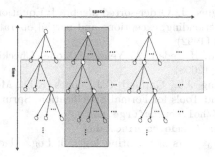

Fig. 2. Searches on Time versus Space

number of patterns (i.e. elements of a cover set) that cover all possible cases are generated and checked easily, and it is an important future issue to construct proof scores for important problems/systems of significant sizes and do experiments for developing practical methods to obtain effective cover sets.

Acknowledgments. It is a great pleasure for the author (KF) to have the chance to prepare this article for the Festschrift in honor of Professor Martin Wirsing.

The author thanks referees for their valuable comments to improve the paper.

This work was supported in part by Grant-in-Aid for Scientific Research (S) 23220002 from Japan Society for the Promotion of Science (JSPS).

References

1. Bae, K., Escobar, S., Meseguer, J.: Abstract logical model checking of infinite-state systems using narrowing. In: van Raamsdonk, F. (ed.) RTA. LIPIcs, vol. 21, pp. 81–96. Schloss Dagstuhl - Leibniz-Zentrum fuer Informatik (2013)
2. Baier, C., Katoen, J.P.: Principles of model checking, pp. 1–975. MIT Press (2008)
3. CafeOBJ (2014), http://cafeobj.org/, http://www.ldl.jaist.ac.jp/cafeobj/
4. Chandy, K.M., Misra, J.: Parallel program design - a foundation. Addison-Wesley (1989)
5. Clarke, E.M., Grumberg, O., Peled, D.: Model checking. MIT Press (2001)
6. Coq (2014), http://coq.inria.fr
7. Dong, J.S., Zhu, H. (eds.): ICFEM 2010. LNCS, vol. 6447. Springer, Heidelberg (2010)
8. Escobar, S., Meseguer, J.: Symbolic model checking of infinite-state systems using narrowing. In: Baader, F. (ed.) RTA 2007. LNCS, vol. 4533, pp. 153–168. Springer, Heidelberg (2007)
9. Futatsugi, K.: Verifying specifications with proof scores in CafeOBJ. In: Proc. of 21st IEEE/ACM International Conference on Automated Software Engineering (ASE 2006), pp. 3–10. IEEE Computer Society (2006)
10. Futatsugi, K.: Fostering proof scores in CafeOBJ. In: Dong, Zhu (eds.) [7], pp. 1–20
11. Futatsugi, K., Găină, D., Ogata, K.: Principles of proof scores in CafeOBJ. Theor. Comput. Sci. 464, 90–112 (2012)

12. Goguen, J.A., Meseguer, J.: Order-sorted algebra I: Equational deduction for multiple inheritance, overloading, exceptions and partial operations. Theor. Comput. Sci. 105(2), 217–273 (1992)
13. Grumberg, O., Veith, H. (eds.): 25 Years of Model Checking. LNCS, vol. 5000. Springer, Heidelberg (2008)
14. Guttag, J.V., Horning, J.J., Garland, S.J., Jones, K.D., Modet, A., Wing, J.M.: Larch: Languages and Tools for Formal Specification. Springer (1993)
15. HOL (2014), http://hol.sourceforge.net
16. Maude (2014), http://maude.cs.uiuc.edu/
17. Meseguer, J.: Twenty years of rewriting logic. J. Log. Algebr. Program. 81(7-8), 721–781 (2012)
18. Nakamura, M., Ogata, K., Futatsugi, K.: Incremental proofs of termination, confluence and sufficient completeness of OBJ specifications. In: Iida, S., Meseguer, J., Ogata, K. (eds.) Specification, Algebra, and Software. LNCS, vol. 8373, pp. 92–109. Springer, Heidelberg (2014)
19. Nipkow, T., Paulson, L.C., Wenzel, M.: Isabelle/HOL. LNCS, vol. 2283. Springer, Heidelberg (2002)
20. Ogata, K., Futatsugi, K.: Proof scores in the oTS/CafeOBJ method. In: Najm, E., Nestmann, U., Stevens, P. (eds.) FMOODS 2003. LNCS, vol. 2884, pp. 170–184. Springer, Heidelberg (2003)
21. Ogata, K., Futatsugi, K.: Simulation-based verification for invariant properties in the OTS/CafeOBJ method. Electr. Notes Theor. Comput. Sci. 201, 127–154 (2008)
22. Ogata, K., Futatsugi, K.: A combination of forward and backward reachability analysis methods. In: Dong, Zhu (eds.) [7], pp. 501–517 (2010)
23. PVS (2014), http://pvs.csl.sri.com
24. Rocha, C., Meseguer, J.: Proving safety properties of rewrite theories. technical report. Tech. rep., University of Illinois at Urbana-Champaign (2010)
25. Rocha, C., Meseguer, J.: Proving safety properties of rewrite theories. In: Corradini, A., Klin, B., Cîrstea, C. (eds.) CALCO 2011. LNCS, vol. 6859, pp. 314–328. Springer, Heidelberg (2011)
26. TeReSe (ed.): Term Rewriting Systems. Cambridge Tracts in Theoretical Computer Science, vol. 55. Cambridge University Press (2003)

Institutions for OCL-Like Expression Languages

Alexander Knapp[1] and María Victoria Cengarle[2]

[1] Universität Augsburg, Germany
knapp@informatik.uni-augsburg.de
[2] Technische Universität München, Germany
cengarle@in.tum.de

Abstract. In 2008, Martin Wirsing initiated the project of conceiving the "Unified Modeling Language" (UML) as a heterogeneous modelling language. He proposed to use the theory of heterogeneous institutions for providing individual semantics to each sub-language, that can then be integrated using institution (co-)morphisms. In particular, the proposal allows for seamlessly capturing the notorious semantic variation points of UML with mathematical rigour. In this line of research, we contribute an institutional framework for the "Object Constraint Language" (OCL), UML's language for expressing constraints.

1 Introduction

The "Unified Modeling Language" (UML), in its inception and according to its own definition, "is a graphical language for visualizing, specifying, constructing, and documenting the artifacts of a software-intensive system" [1, p. XV]. The UML, on the one hand, has been repeatedly criticized because of its lack of formal semantics. On the other hand, UML has been praised for being the "lingua franca" that acts as an Esperanto among stakeholders, be these application domain experts, system designers, program developers, or clients.[1] The scientific community has spent some effort in providing UML with a formal semantics that, among other things, allows for the rigorous verification of properties of interest of the software system under consideration. These efforts, however, have not been crowned with the success they might deserve, probably because they impose a "straitjacket" to UML users, what in its turn is against a stance advocated by the UML language designers that UML be somehow free in the way it should be understood. Indeed, the standard foresees so-called semantic variation points that allow language users to interpret language constructs differently.

Martin Wirsing, therefore, proposed a heterogeneous approach that allows UML users the definition of the preferred semantics to the individual UML sub-languages, and is such that the composition of those languages and their attached semantics permits compositional proofs; see [4] and also [2]. The proposed approach builds on the abstract model theory framework of institutions [8], where each sub-language is captured as an institution. Originally, institutions have been devised for formalizing logical systems with their signatures, sentences, structures, and satisfaction relation, imposing only minimal constraints, namely that satisfaction be invariable under change of syntax. Formally,

---

[1] Empirical evidence for the various, but rather limited usages of the UML in industrial practice has been gathered by Petre [18].

R. De Nicola and R. Hennicker (Eds.): Wirsing Festschrift, LNCS 8950, pp. 193–214, 2015.
© Springer International Publishing Switzerland 2015

an *institution* (Sig, *Str*, *Sen*, $\models$) is given by (i) a category Sig whose objects are called *signatures*; (ii) a contravariant functor Str : Sig^{op} $\to$ Cat, called the *structure functor*, from Sig to Cat, the category of categories; (iii) a functor Sen : Sig $\to$ Set, called the *sentence functor*, from Sig to Set, the category of sets; and (iv) a family $\models = \{\models_\Sigma\}_{\Sigma \in \text{Sig}}$ of *satisfaction relations* between Σ-structures $M \in Str(\Sigma)$ and Σ-sentences $\varphi \in Sen(\Sigma)$, such that for each $\sigma : \Sigma \to \Sigma'$ in Sig, $M' \in Str(\Sigma)$, and $\varphi \in Sen(\Sigma)$, the following *satisfaction condition* holds:

$$Str(\sigma)(M') \models_\Sigma \varphi \iff M' \models_{\Sigma'} Sen(\sigma)(\varphi) \,.$$

For the application to UML sub-languages, the syntactic elements available in each sub-language are rendered as signatures, their meaning as structures, and their possible combinations as sentences. Semantic variation points or particular domain-specific usages of a sub-language lead to different institutions. The framework of institutions provides a rich family of institution (co-)morphisms for relating institutions in terms of embeddings and projections. For UML sub-languages expressed as institutions, these (co-)morphisms can be applied to express refinements and consistency conditions between sub-languages and different resolutions of semantic variation points.

The aim of this work is to give a definition of the "Object Constraint Language" (OCL [16]) that satisfies the conditions associated with institutions. The OCL provides a textual expression language for navigating through UML models, specifying guards and pre-/post-conditions, and for defining constraints, like invariants, on model elements. In the UML specification [15] the OCL is used for specifying well-formedness rules on models. Though strictly speaking not a UML sub-language, the OCL constitutes a natural modelling ingredient complementing the visual notation of the UML.

The first difficulty, that at first sight seems an incompatibility, is that OCL focuses on terms and not on truth. This way, for instance, a three-valued logic is possible. So, the core property of institutions, namely the satisfaction condition, needs be defined for terms, in the form of an evaluation condition. In fact, this is already the case for, e.g., classical first-order predicate logic with function symbols (for term construction), predicate symbols (for atom construction), and logical connectives and quantifiers (for formula construction). This means, the property called for is satisfied in the classical setting and needs only be mimicked for a definition of OCL terms. Thus, it should be possible to use some formal OCL expression semantics, like, e.g., [3], and derive an institution directly. However, it turns out that some OCL constructs like if-then-else, iterate, or allInstances are more naturally handled as special term formers than as function symbols directly. This motivates a two-level language definition for OCL terms, namely the already mentioned function symbols and a construction functor for the term formers. Using the language of indexed categories (see Sect. 2), we define the notion of term charters for capturing such general term languages, their evaluation, and, in particular, an evaluation condition in Sect. 3. We also show how languages defined by means of term charters can be turned into an institution.[2]

A further characteristics of OCL is that it is constituted by many sub-theories: order-sortedness, non-strict evaluation, three-valued logic, non-determinism, etc. For particular

---

[2] The manuscript accompanying this article, that shows the proof of every assertion here, can be found in [11].

domains, different combinations or extensions of the sub-theories may be useful, see, e.g., [3,12]. For this reason, and in order to provide the modelling language designer with a powerful tool, means are defined that allow for a compositional definition of a term-based constraint language. Each sub-language can be defined separately, and it is possible to build different constraint languages, that contain the needed theories for the situation at hand, by putting up different sub-theories. Therefore, a further goal of this work is the elucidation of a (meta-)theory for the compositional integration of those sub-theories. This is akin to the specification-building operators defined by Martin Wirsing in [21], only on a meta-level. Examples of OCL theories are shown in Sect. 4, means for their composition are presented in Sect. 5.

2 Indexed Categories

We briefly recall the basic notions of indexed categories (see, e.g., [20]) mainly for fixing the notation.

An *indexed category* N over an index category I is a functor $N : I^{op} \to$ Cat. Given an I-indexed category $N : I^{op} \to$ Cat, the *Grothendieck category* $\mathcal{G}(N)$ over N has as objects the pairs $\langle i, O \rangle$ with $i \in |I|$ and $O \in |N(i)|$, and as morphisms from $\langle i, O \rangle$ to $\langle i', O' \rangle$ the pairs $\langle u, o \rangle$ with $u \in I(i, i')$ and $o \in N(i)(O, N(u)(O'))$; the identity morphism on $\langle i, O \rangle$ is $\langle 1_i, 1_O \rangle$, the composition of morphisms $\langle u, o \rangle : \langle i, O \rangle \to \langle i', O' \rangle$ and $\langle u', o' \rangle : \langle i', O' \rangle \to \langle i'', O'' \rangle$ is $\langle u, o \rangle; \langle u', o' \rangle = \langle u; u', o; N(u)(o') \rangle$.

The *projection functor* π_N from $\mathcal{G}(N)$ to I is defined by $\pi_N(\langle i, O \rangle) = i$ and $\pi_N(\langle u, o \rangle) = u$. For an $i \in |I|$, $\mathcal{G}(N)(i)$ denotes the sub-category of $\mathcal{G}(N)$ with objects $\langle i, O \rangle$ and morphisms $\langle 1_i, o \rangle$.

A morphism $u : i \to i'$ in I induces the *reduct functor* $-|_N u : \mathcal{G}(N)(i') \to \mathcal{G}(N)(i)$ with $\langle i', O' \rangle|_N u = \langle i, N(u)(O') \rangle$ and $\langle 1_{i'}, o' \rangle|_N u = \langle 1_i, N(u)(o') \rangle$. For $\langle i', O' \rangle \in |\mathcal{G}(N)|$, $u : i \to i'$ also induces the *forward morphism* $u|^{N\langle i', O' \rangle} = \langle u, 1_{N(u)(O')} \rangle : \langle i, N(u)(O') \rangle \to \langle i', O' \rangle$; in particular, $u|^{N^-} : -|_N u \to 1_{\mathcal{G}(N)(i')}$ is a natural transformation. Each morphism $\langle u, o \rangle : \langle i, O \rangle \to \langle i', O' \rangle$ can be uniquely factorized as $\langle u, o \rangle = \langle 1_i, o \rangle; u|^{N\langle i', O' \rangle}$ with $\langle 1_i, o \rangle : \langle i, O \rangle \to \langle i', O' \rangle|_N u$; we denote $\langle 1_i, o \rangle$ by $\langle u, o \rangle|_N$.

An *indexed functor* F from an I-indexed category M to an I-indexed category N is a natural transformation $F : M \overset{\cdot}{\to} N$. The *Grothendieck functor* $\mathcal{G}(F) : \mathcal{G}(M) \to \mathcal{G}(N)$ over F is defined by $\mathcal{G}(F)(\langle i, O \rangle) = \langle i, F_i(O) \rangle$ and $\mathcal{G}(F)(\langle u, o \rangle : \langle i, O \rangle \to \langle i', O' \rangle) = \langle u, F_i(o) \rangle : \langle i, F_i(O) \rangle \to \langle i', F_{i'}(O') \rangle$.

Lemma 1. *Let* $M, N : I^{op} \to$ Cat *be indexed categories and* $F : M \overset{\cdot}{\to} N$ *an indexed functor. Let* $u : i \to i'$ *in* I *and* $\langle i', O' \rangle \in |\mathcal{G}(M)|$. *Then*

(1) $\mathcal{G}(F); (-|_N u) = (-|_M u); \mathcal{G}(F)$;
(2) $u|^{N\mathcal{G}(F)(\langle i', O' \rangle)} = \mathcal{G}(F)(u|^{M\langle i', O' \rangle})$;
(3) $\pi_M = \mathcal{G}(F); \pi_N$.

3 Term Charters

The core part of the OCL is an expression or term language, where formulae are captured as Boolean expressions that can then be used as guards, invariants, or pre-/post-conditions. When institutionalizing OCL we thus want to focus on its expressions in their own right and extend the satisfaction condition for formulae to an "evaluation condition" for terms. We therefore employ a framework that mimics and generalizes classical term evaluation with valuations for variables [21]: Terms over a signature are built by a construction functor $\mathscr{C}$ that takes values as variables X from a signature-indexed category Val and yields the term language, again in Val. Evaluation of a term over a given valuation β is described by a lifting $(\beta)^{\natural}{}_M$ from $\mathscr{C}(X)$ to the values in a structure M from a signature-indexed category Str. The evaluation condition requires that evaluation is invariant w.r.t. signature changes.

We call our evaluation framework "term charters", as it is inspired by the notion of charters [7] for constructing institutions. A charter is given by an adjunction $(U, F, \eta, (-)^{\sharp})$ between a category of signatures Sign and a category of syntactic systems Syn, a ground object $G \in |\text{Syn}|$ and a base functor $B : \text{Syn} \to \text{Set}$ with $B(G) = \{f\!f, tt\}$. An institution is obtained from a charter by using Sign as the signatures, and defining, for each $\Sigma \in |\text{Sign}|$, the Σ-structures as the Sign-morphisms $m : \Sigma \to U(G)$, the Σ-sentences as $B(F(\Sigma))$, and the satisfaction relation by $m \models_{\Sigma} e$ if, and only if $B(m^{\sharp})(e) = tt$.[3] Term charters mainly deviate from charters in making the variables of terms explicit in the indexed category Val such that evaluation by means of $(-)^{\sharp}$ is shifted to taking into account valuations. In charters, these valuations are contained in the single semantic ground object that also comprises all possible interpretations of the signatures, necessitating a "Procrustean ground signature" [7, p. 324] of this ground object which sometimes may not seem the most natural choice; in term charters the ground object is split into several semantic structure objects from the indexed category Str representing different interpretations. Finally, term charters do not insist on an adjunction between the syntactic domain $\mathcal{G}(Val)$ and the semantic domain $\mathcal{G}(Str)$ which makes them applicable in situations where the evaluation structures should only consist in standard interpretations but the syntactic domain may lead to non-standard interpretations, as, e.g., for pre-defined data types or higher-order functions. However, we show below that such an adjunction indeed induces a term charter.

3.1 Term Charter Domains and Term Charters

A term charter is defined over a term charter domain that fixes the signatures, the values and variables, the semantic structures, and how the values are extracted from a structure. A term charter then adds how terms or expressions over variables are constructed and how they are evaluated over the values of a structure. We first give the formal definition and then illustrate the notion of term charters by means of order-sorted algebras [21].

A *term charter domain* $D = (\mathbb{S}, Val, Str, U)$ is given by a category $\mathbb{S}$ of *signatures*, an indexed category $Val : \mathbb{S}^{\text{op}} \to \text{Cat}$ of *values*, an indexed category $Str : \mathbb{S}^{\text{op}} \to \text{Cat}$ of *structures*, and an *underlying* indexed functor $U : Str \overset{.}{\to} Val$.

A *term charter* $\mathfrak{T} = (\mathscr{C}, \nu, (-)^{\natural})$ over a term charter domain $(\mathbb{S}, Val, Str, U)$ is given by a *construction* functor $\mathscr{C} : \mathcal{G}(Val) \to \mathcal{G}(Val)$ with $\pi_{Val} = \mathscr{C}; \pi_{Val}$; an *embedding*

---

[3] In fact, an adjunction for a charter can be obtained systematically when using the notion of parchments [7,17] that induce a suitable category of syntactic systems as the Grothendieck category $\mathcal{G}(Syn)$ with $Syn(\Sigma) = Alg(Lang(\Sigma))$ where $Lang$ is a functor from the signatures to (many-sorted) algebraic signatures and the functor Alg yields the (many-sorted) algebras over an algebraic signature.

natural transformation $\nu : 1_{\mathcal{G}(Val)} \dot{\to} \mathscr{C}$ with $\nu_X : X \to \mathscr{C}(X)$ in $\mathcal{G}(Val)(\pi_{Val}(X))$; and a $|\mathcal{G}(Str)|$-family $(-)^{\natural} = ((-)^{\natural}_M)_{M \in |\mathcal{G}(Str)|}$ associating for each $\Sigma \in |\mathbb{S}|$ and $M \in |\mathcal{G}(Str)(\Sigma)|$ to each morphism $\beta : X \to \mathcal{G}(U)(M)$ in $\mathcal{G}(Val)(\Sigma)$ a morphism $(\beta)^{\natural}_M : \mathscr{C}(X) \to \mathcal{G}(U)(M)$ in $\mathcal{G}(Val)(\Sigma)$ such that

– for all $\Sigma \in \mathbb{S}$, $M \in |\mathcal{G}(Str)(\Sigma)|$, $\beta : X \to \mathcal{G}(U)(M)$ in $\mathcal{G}(Val)(\Sigma)$, and $\xi : Y \to X$ in $\mathcal{G}(Val)(\Sigma)$ the following diagrams commute:

$$
(C) \quad
\begin{array}{ccc}
X & \xrightarrow{\nu_X} & \mathscr{C}(X) \\
 & \searrow{\scriptstyle \beta} & \downarrow{\scriptstyle (\beta)^{\natural}_M} \\
 & & \mathcal{G}(U)(M)
\end{array}
\qquad
(K) \quad
\begin{array}{ccc}
\mathscr{C}(Y) & \xrightarrow{\mathscr{C}(\xi)} & \mathscr{C}(X) \\
 & \searrow{\scriptstyle (\xi; \beta)^{\natural}_M} & \downarrow{\scriptstyle (\beta)^{\natural}_M} \\
 & & \mathcal{G}(U)(M)
\end{array}
$$

– for all $\sigma : \Sigma \to \Sigma'$ in $\mathbb{S}$, $M' \in |\mathcal{G}(Str)(\Sigma')|$, and $\beta' : X' \to \mathcal{G}(U)(M')$ in $\mathcal{G}(Val)(\Sigma')$ the following diagram commutes:

$$
(E) \quad
\begin{array}{ccc}
\mathscr{C}(X'|_{Val}\sigma) & \xrightarrow{\mathscr{C}(\sigma|_{Val}X')} & \mathscr{C}(X') \\
{\scriptstyle (\beta'|_{Val}\sigma)^{\natural}_{M'|_{Str}\sigma}} \downarrow & & \downarrow {\scriptstyle (\beta')^{\natural}_{M'}} \\
\mathcal{G}(U)(M'|_{Str}\sigma) & \xrightarrow{\mathcal{G}(U)(\sigma|_{Str}M')} & \mathcal{G}(U)(M')
\end{array}
$$

Requirement (E) is called the *evaluation condition* expressing that evaluation is invariant w.r.t. signature changes. Condition (C) and (K) ensure that valuations are respected by evaluation and that evaluation is compatible with variable renaming.

Example 1. In order to illustrate term charters, we reformulate order-sorted algebras and their terms. For establishing a suitable term charter domain, we first have to fix order-sorted signatures, value domains, and structures.

The category $\mathbb{S}^{\leq}$ of *order-sorted signatures* has as objects the pairs (S, D) with $S = (|S|, \leq_S)$ a partial order for the *sorts* and $D = (|D|, \delta_D)$ *function declarations* with $\delta_D : |S|^* \times |S| \to \mathcal{P}(|D|)$; and as morphisms pairs $(\gamma, \rho) : (S, D) \to (S', D')$ of a monotone function on the sorts and a sort-compatible function renaming.

For a $\Sigma = (S, D)$, a Σ-*value domain* V consists of a family $(V_s)_{s \in |S|}$ of *values* respecting sub-sorting, i.e., $V_s \subseteq V_{s'}$ if $s \leq_S s'$; and a Σ-*value domain morphism* $\omega : V \to V'$ is given by a family of mappings $\omega = (\omega_s : V_s \to V'_s)_{s \in |S|}$. Similarly, a Σ-*structure* (V, E) consists of a Σ-value domain V and a family E of *evaluation functions* $E = (E_{\overline{s}, s})_{\overline{s} \in |S|^*, s \in |S|}$, where $E_{\overline{s}, s} : \delta_D(\overline{s}, s) \to (V_{\overline{s}} \to V_s)$, that is, E assigns to each function type in $|D|$ a set of functions on the corresponding values; and a Σ-*structure morphism* $\omega : (V, E) \to (V', E')$ is given by a Σ-value domain morphism $\omega : V \to V'$ satisfying the *homomorphism condition* $\omega_s(E_{\overline{s}, s}(d)(\overline{v})) = E'_{\overline{s}, s}(d)(\omega_{\overline{s}}(\overline{v}))$. The indexed categories $Val^{\leq}, Str^{\leq} : (\mathbb{S}^{\leq})^{op} \to \mathbf{Cat}$ map each Σ to $Val^{\leq}(\Sigma)$ and $Str^{\leq}(\Sigma)$, respectively, and each order-sorted signature morphism to the usual renaming reduct functors. The indexed functor $U^{\leq} : Str^{\leq} \to Val^{\leq}$ "forgets" the evaluation functions of a structure.

We thus obtain the term charter domain $(\mathbb{S}^{\leq}, Val^{\leq}, Str^{\leq}, U^{\leq})$. For a term charter for order-sorted terms, we now address term construction and evaluation.

The construction functor $\mathscr{C}^{\leq} : \mathcal{G}(Val^{\leq}) \to \mathcal{G}(Val^{\leq})$ assigns to $\langle \Sigma, X \rangle \in |\mathcal{G}(Val^{\leq})|$ with $\Sigma = (S, D)$ the value domain $\mathscr{C}^{\leq}(\langle \Sigma, X \rangle) = \langle \Sigma, V_X^{\leq} \rangle$ such that for each $s \in |S|$ the values in $V_{X,s}^{\leq}$ are given inductively by

- $x \in V_{X,s}^{\leq}$ for $x \in X_s$;
- $d(\vec{v}) \in V_{X,s'}^{\leq}$ for all $s' \geq_S s$ if $d \in \delta_D(\bar{s}, s)$ and $\vec{v} \in V_{X,\bar{s}}^{\leq}$.

For the morphisms in $\mathcal{G}(Val^{\leq})$, $\mathscr{C}^{\leq}$ yields the corresponding renaming morphism in $\mathcal{G}(Val^{\leq})$. As natural transformation $\nu^{\leq} : 1_{\mathcal{G}(Val^{\leq})} \dot{\to} \mathscr{C}^{\leq}$ for *embedding* values or variables into the order-sorted terms we may simply choose the inclusions.

For *evaluating* order-sorted terms over a structure $M = \langle \Sigma, (V, E) \rangle$ in $|\mathcal{G}(Str^{\leq})|$ given a *valuation* $\beta = \langle 1_\Sigma, \beta^{\leq} \rangle : \langle \Sigma, X \rangle \to \mathcal{G}(U^{\leq})(\langle \Sigma, (V, E) \rangle)$ define $(\beta)^{\natural_M^{\leq}} = \langle 1_\Sigma, (\beta^{\leq})^{\natural_M^{\leq}} \rangle : \mathscr{C}^{\leq}(\langle \Sigma, X \rangle) \to \langle \Sigma, (V, E) \rangle$ inductively by

- $(\beta^{\leq})_s^{\natural_M^{\leq}}(x) = \beta_s^{\leq}(x)$ for $x \in X_s$;
- $(\beta^{\leq})_s^{\natural_M^{\leq}}(d(\vec{v})) = E_{\bar{s},s}(d)((\beta^{\leq})_{\bar{s}}^{\natural_M^{\leq}})(\vec{v}))$.

With these definitions, the term charter conditions (C), (K) and, (E) can be checked straightforwardly by induction. Thus we obtain the *order-sorted term charter* $(\mathscr{C}^{\leq}, \nu^{\leq}, (-)^{\natural^{\leq}})$ over the term charter domain $(\mathbb{S}^{\leq}, Val^{\leq}, Str^{\leq}, U^{\leq})$.   □

3.2   Term Charters from Adjunctions

The concrete construction of a term charter often involves quite many routine checks, as already illustrated by the previous example of the order-sorted term charter. In the special situation of an adjunction between the syntactic side of *Val* and the semantic side of *Str* this effort can be avoided completely.

In fact, let $D = (\mathbb{S}, Val, Str, U)$ be a term charter domain and assume that $(\mathcal{G}(U), \mathscr{T}, \eta, (-)^{\natural})$ forms an adjunction (expressed as a free construction [19]) with the functor $\mathscr{T} : \mathcal{G}(Val) \to \mathcal{G}(Str)$ satisfying $\pi_{Val} = \mathscr{T}; \pi_{Str}$ the left-adjoint to $\mathcal{G}(U)$, the natural transformation $\eta : 1_{\mathcal{G}(Val)} \dot{\to} \mathscr{T}; \mathcal{G}(U)$ with $\eta_X : X \to \mathcal{G}(U)(\mathscr{T}(X))$ in $\mathcal{G}(Val)(\pi_{Val}(X))$ the unit, and the $\mathbb{S}$-family $(-)^{\natural} = ((-)^{\natural_\Sigma})_{\Sigma \in |\mathbb{S}|}$ associating for each $\sigma \in |\mathbb{S}|$ and $M \in |\mathcal{G}(Str)(\Sigma)|$ to each morphism $\beta : X \to \mathcal{G}(U)(M)$ in $\mathcal{G}(Val)(\Sigma)$ a morphism $\beta^{\natural_\Sigma} : \mathscr{T}(X) \to M$ in $\mathcal{G}(Str)(\Sigma)$ the lifting. Then it can be shown that for each $\sigma : \Sigma \to \Sigma'$ in $\mathbb{S}$, $M' \in |\mathcal{G}(Str)(\Sigma')|$, and $\beta' : X' \to \mathcal{G}(U)(M')$ in $\mathcal{G}(Val)(\Sigma')$ the following diagram expressing the evaluation condition commutes:

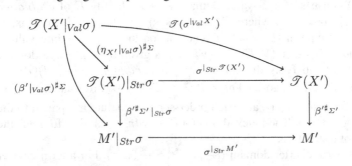

Using this form of the evaluation condition we obtain

Proposition 1. *Let* $(\mathcal{G}(U), \mathcal{T}, \eta, (-)^\natural)$ *form an adjunction. Then* $(\mathcal{T}; \mathcal{G}(U), \eta, (-)^\natural)$ *with* $(\beta)^\natural_M = \mathcal{G}(U)(\beta^{\natural_\Sigma})$ *for each* $\Sigma \in |\mathbb{S}|, X \in |\mathcal{G}(Val)(\Sigma)|, M \in |\mathcal{G}(Str)(\Sigma)|,$ *and* $\beta : X \to \mathcal{G}(U)(M)$ *is a term charter.*   □

3.3 Constructing an Institution from a Term Charter

Let $\mathfrak{T} = (\mathcal{C}, \eta, (-)^\natural)$ be a term charter over the term charter domain $(\mathbb{S}, Val, Str, U)$. Let $\mathcal{U}_{Val} : \mathcal{G}(Val) \to Set$ be a functor such that $\mathcal{U}_{Val}(\sigma^{|_{Val}X'})$ is the inclusion map from $\mathcal{U}_{Val}(X'|_{Val}\sigma)$ to $\mathcal{U}_{Val}(X')$ for $\sigma : \Sigma \to \Sigma'$ in $\mathbb{S}$ and $X' \in |\mathcal{G}(Val)(\Sigma')|$, and the *semantic truth value* $* \in \mathcal{U}_{Val}(X)$ for all $X \in |\mathcal{G}(Str); \mathcal{G}(U)| \subseteq |\mathcal{G}(Val)|$.

- Define the category $Sig^{\mathcal{U}_{Val}}_{\mathfrak{T}}$ as $\mathcal{G}(Val)$.
- Define the functor $Sen^{\mathcal{U}_{Val}}_{\mathfrak{T}} : Sig^{\mathcal{U}_{Val}}_{\mathfrak{T}} \to Set$ as $\mathcal{C}; \mathcal{U}_{Val}$.
- Define the functor $Str^{\mathcal{U}_{Val}}_{\mathfrak{T}} : \mathcal{G}(Val)^{op} \to Cat$ as

  - the category $Str^{\mathcal{U}_{Val}}_{\mathfrak{T}}(X)$, where $\Sigma = \pi_{Val}(X)$, with the class of objects the pairs (M, β) with $M \in |\mathcal{G}(Str)(\Sigma)|$ and $\beta : X \to \mathcal{G}(U)(M)$ in $\mathcal{G}(Val)(\Sigma)$, and the morphisms $\mu : (M_1, \beta_1) \to (M_2, \beta_2)$ where $\mu \in \mathcal{G}(Str)(\Sigma)(M_1, M_2)$ and $\beta_i : X \to \mathcal{G}(U)(M_i)$ for $1 \leq i \leq 2$ such that $\beta_1; \mathcal{G}(U)(\mu) = \beta_2$;
  - the functor $Str^{\mathcal{U}_{Val}}_{\mathfrak{T}}(\xi : X \to X') : Str^{\mathcal{U}_{Val}}_{\mathfrak{T}}(X') \to Str^{\mathcal{U}_{Val}}_{\mathfrak{T}}(X)$, where $\sigma = \pi_{Val}(\xi)$, with

$$Str^{\mathcal{U}_{Val}}_{\mathfrak{T}}(\xi)(M', \beta') = (M'|_{Str}\sigma, \xi|_{Val}; \beta'|_{Val}\sigma)$$
$$Str^{\mathcal{U}_{Val}}_{\mathfrak{T}}(\xi)(\mu' : (M_1', \beta_1') \to (M_2', \beta_2')) = \mu'|_{Str}\sigma \,.$$

  This is well-defined, since $\beta_1'; \mathcal{G}(U)(\mu') = \beta_2'$ and hence also $\xi|_{Val}; \beta_1'|_{Val}\sigma;$ $\mathcal{G}(U)(\mu')|_{Val}\sigma = \xi|_{Val}; \beta_1'|_{Val}\sigma; \mathcal{G}(U)(\mu'|_{Str}\sigma) = \xi|_{Val}; \beta_2'|_{Val}\sigma.$

- Define the family of relations $(\models^{\mathcal{U}_{Val}}_{\mathfrak{T},X})_{X \in |Sig^{\mathcal{U}_{Val}}_{\mathfrak{T}}|}$ with $\models^{\mathcal{U}_{Val}}_{\mathfrak{T},X} \subseteq |Str^{\mathcal{U}_{Val}}_{\mathfrak{T}}(X)| \times |Sen^{\mathcal{U}_{Val}}_{\mathfrak{T}}(X)|$ by

$$(M, \beta) \models^{\mathcal{U}_{Val}}_{\mathfrak{T},X} \varphi \quad \text{iff} \quad \mathcal{U}_{Val}((\beta)^\natural_M)(\varphi) = * \,.$$

Proposition 2. $(Sig^{\mathcal{U}_{Val}}_{\mathfrak{T}}, Str^{\mathcal{U}_{Val}}_{\mathfrak{T}}, Sen^{\mathcal{U}_{Val}}_{\mathfrak{T}}, \models^{\mathcal{U}_{Val}}_{\mathfrak{T}})$ *is an institution.*

Proof. We have to show the satisfaction condition

$$Str^{\mathcal{U}_{Val}}_{\mathfrak{T}}(\xi)(M', \beta') \models^{\mathcal{U}_{Val}}_{\mathfrak{T},X} \varphi \quad \text{iff} \quad (M', \beta') \models^{\mathcal{U}_{Val}}_{\mathfrak{T},X'} Sen^{\mathcal{U}_{Val}}_{\mathfrak{T}}(\xi)(\varphi)$$

with $\varphi \in Sen^{\mathcal{U}_{Val}}_{\mathfrak{T}}(X), \xi : X \to X'$ and $\beta' : X' \to \mathcal{G}(U)(M')$. It suffices to prove

$$\mathcal{U}_{Val}((\xi|_{Val}; \beta'|_{Val}\sigma)^\natural_{M'|_{Str}\sigma})(\varphi) = \mathcal{U}_{Val}(\mathcal{C}(\xi; (\beta')^\natural_{M'}))(\varphi)$$

with $\sigma = \pi_{Val}(\xi)$. We have

$$(\xi|_{Val};\beta'|_{Val}\sigma)^{\natural M'|_{Str}\sigma};\sigma|_{Val}\mathcal{G}(U)(M')\overset{(\mathbf{K})}{=}$$

$$\mathscr{C}(\xi|_{Val});(\beta'|_{Val}\sigma)^{\natural M'|_{Str}\sigma};\sigma|_{Val}\mathcal{G}(U)(M')\overset{(\mathbf{E})}{=}\mathscr{C}(\xi|_{Val});\mathscr{C}(\sigma|_{Val}X');(\beta')^{\natural M'}=$$

$$\mathscr{C}(\xi|_{Val};\sigma|_{Val}X');(\beta')^{\natural M'}=\mathscr{C}(\xi);(\beta')^{\natural M'}.$$

The image $\mathcal{U}_{Val}(\sigma|_{Val}\mathcal{G}(U)(M'))$ of the forward morphism is an inclusion map. Therefore,

$$\mathcal{U}_{Val}((\xi|_{Val};\beta'|_{Val}\sigma)^{\natural M'|_{Str}\sigma};\sigma|_{Val}\mathcal{G}(U)(M'))(\varphi)=$$

$$\mathcal{U}_{Val}((\xi|_{Val};\beta'|_{Val}\sigma)^{\natural M'|_{Str}\sigma})(\varphi).$$

$\square$

Now additionally assume that for each $\Sigma\in|\mathbb{S}|$ there is an object X^{Σ} that is initial in $\mathcal{G}(Val)(\Sigma)$. Then, for each each $X\in|\mathcal{G}(Val)|$, there is a unique morphism $\xi^X:X^{\Sigma}\to X$ in $\mathcal{G}(Val)(\Sigma)$. In particular, for each $M\in|\mathcal{G}(Str)(\Sigma)|$, there is a unique morphism $\beta^{\Sigma}:X^{\Sigma}\to\mathcal{G}(U)(M)$ in $\mathcal{G}(Val)(\Sigma)$. In this case, we can define a more "classical" institution from the term charter $\mathfrak{T}=(\mathscr{C},\nu,(-)^{\natural})$ as follows:

– Define the category $\mathrm{CSig}_{\mathfrak{T}}^{\mathcal{U}_{Val}}$ as $\mathbb{S}$.
– Define the functor $\mathit{CSen}_{\mathfrak{T}}^{\mathcal{U}_{Val}}:\mathrm{CSig}_{\mathfrak{T}}^{\mathcal{U}_{Val}}\to\mathrm{Set}$ as

$$\mathit{CSen}_{\mathfrak{T}}^{\mathcal{U}_{Val}}(\Sigma)=\mathcal{U}_{Val}(\mathscr{C}(X^{\Sigma}))\quad\text{and}$$

$$\mathit{CSen}_{\mathfrak{T}}^{\mathcal{U}_{Val}}(\sigma:\Sigma\to\Sigma')=\mathcal{U}_{Val}(\mathscr{C}(\xi^{X^{\Sigma'}}|_{Val}\sigma;\sigma|_{Val}X^{\Sigma'})).$$

– Define the functor $\mathit{CStr}_{\mathfrak{T}}^{\mathcal{U}_{Val}}:(\mathrm{CSig}_{\mathfrak{T}}^{\mathcal{U}_{Val}})^{\mathrm{op}}\to\mathrm{Cat}$ as $\mathit{Str}:\mathbb{S}^{\mathrm{op}}\to\mathrm{Cat}$.
– Define the family of relations $(\models_{\mathfrak{T},\Sigma}^{\mathcal{U}_{Val}})_{\Sigma\in|\mathrm{CSig}_{\mathfrak{T}}^{\mathcal{U}_{Val}}|}$ with $\models_{\mathfrak{T},\Sigma}^{\mathcal{U}_{Val}}\subseteq|\mathit{CStr}_{\mathfrak{T}}^{\mathcal{U}_{Val}}(\Sigma)|\times|\mathit{CSen}_{\mathfrak{T}}^{\mathcal{U}_{Val}}(\Sigma)|$ by

$$M\models_{\mathfrak{T},\Sigma}^{\mathcal{U}_{Val}}\varphi\quad\text{iff}\quad\mathcal{U}_{Val}((\beta^{\Sigma})^{\natural M})(\varphi)=*.$$

Corollary 1. $(\mathrm{CSig}_{\mathfrak{T}}^{\mathcal{U}_{Val}},\mathit{CStr}_{\mathfrak{T}}^{\mathcal{U}_{Val}},\mathit{CSen}_{\mathfrak{T}}^{\mathcal{U}_{Val}},\models_{\mathfrak{T}}^{\mathcal{U}_{Val}})$ *is an institution.* $\square$

4 OCL Terms and Evaluation

The main use of OCL for UML models is navigation through a system's maze of objects and links. A domain for this task is quite naturally captured by the notion of order-sorted algebras [9], where the sort hierarchy of an order-sorted signature is induced by the inheritance relation of a given model and its function symbols represent the properties and queries specified in the model [10]. Following, the "states-as-algebras" paradigm [6], each order-sorted algebra represents a particular configuration of objects and links. In fact, we use order-sorted signatures, structures, and terms as substitutes for the precise OCL declarations in order to avoid some of its idiosyncrasies [3].

For expressiveness and ease of use, the OCL provides a set of built-in types, like `Boolean` or `Integer`, and collection constructors, like `Sequence` or `Set`, as well as a rich standard library. On the one hand, this library features primitive functions for computations on values like `c->including(e)` for adding e to the sequence or set c. On the other hand, the construct `c->iterate(i; a = e_0 | e)` is available on collections which after initializing the accumulator variable a by e_0 successively binds the iteration variable i to the values in the collection c updating the accumulator with the result of evaluating e for the current values of i and a, and finally returns the value stored in a. Numerous operations on collections, like `select`, `reject`, or `collect`, but also `forAll` and `exists`, are built on top of this general iteration construct [5]. For accessing the currently available objects of a class `allInstances()` can be called on a type identifier; this call only succeeds when a type with finitely many inhabitants is used, such that `Integer.allInstances()` will not work.

In fact, OCL introduces a special value `undefined` for expressions like `Integer.allInstances()` or division by zero that do not yield a proper value. Instead of exception handling, the particular function `isUndefined()` can be used to check whether an expression results in `undefined`. The built-in Boolean functions `and` and `or` show a "parallel" (non-strict) behaviour for `undefined`, mandating that `true or e` and `e or true` always result in `true`, regardless of whether e yields `undefined` or not, and similarly for `false and e` and `e and false`.

We now consider these OCL features w.r.t. terms and evaluation one by one, but separately, starting with the order-sorted framework as a term charter and then accordingly adapting this framework. We restrict ourselves to an informal account of the notions mentioned above, that constitute the interesting cases within OCL. Formal, rigorous definitions can be found in the Appendix A.

4.1 Built-ins

The built-in types of OCL can be viewed as a particular case of the order-sorted framework in Ex. 1, namely the one that contains certain sorts and declarations and interprets them in the "standard" way. If we want, for instance, sequences and sets with membership test, then we require $\mathsf{Bool} \in |S|$ with $\{\mathsf{true}, \mathsf{false}\} \subseteq \delta_D(\mathsf{Bool})$, and $\{\mathsf{Seq}(s), \mathsf{Set}(s)\} \subseteq |S|$ with $- - \!\!\rightarrow\!\mathrm{including}(-) \in \delta_D(\mathsf{Seq}(s)\ s, \mathsf{Seq}(s)) \cap \delta_D(\mathsf{Set}(s)\ s, \mathsf{Set}(s))$ (together with some sanity conditions). The morphisms are required to be the identity on these built-in types and function names. The signatures and morphisms fulfilling these requirements are called *primitives closed*, the sub-category they define is denoted by $\mathbb{S}^\circ$. Primitives-closed structures interpret built-in sorts and declarations in the standard way; this contravariant structure functor is denoted by Str°. Value domains, however, are not restricted: this means, in particular, that the value domain for $\mathsf{Set}(s)$ not necessarily consists of the (finite) sets of values in the value domain for s. The indexed category of values is thus the same as for order-sorted term charter, namely $Val^\leq$. The underlying indexed functor relating structures and values is denoted by U°. The terms are constructed in the same manner as those of the order-sorted case. This way, we obtain the *primitives-closed order-sorted term charter* $(\mathscr{C}^\leq, \nu^\leq, (-)^{\natural\leq})$ over the term charter domain $(\mathbb{S}^\circ, Val^\leq, Str^\circ, U^\circ)$.

4.2 Iteration, All Instances, Undefinedness

The iteration construct of OCL is, in fact, a higher-order instrument since it binds both an iteration variable and an accumulator variable. Therefore, it cannot be treated as the built-ins of above. It can however be added to primitive-closed term charters by including a further inductive case to the definition of the term language. Besides the base case of variables being a term and the inductive case of function symbols applied to previously defined terms, we have a second inductive case constructing an OCL iteration term: $t' \rightarrow \text{iterate}(x'; x = t_0 \,|\, t)$ where t' is a term of collection type (with elements of type s'), t_0 is a term of arbitrary type s, x and x' are "new" variables of type s' and s, respectively, and t is a term of type s possibly containing x and x'. (For the sake of simplicity, we disregard here sub-sorting.) The extension of order-sorted signature morphisms to iteration terms is straightforward. The evaluation $(\beta)^{\natural^{it}}$ along a valuation β is defined on iteration terms, if not in a straightforward, nevertheless in relatively simple manner by

$$(\beta^{it})^{\natural^{it}}_{s'M}(t' \rightarrow \text{iterate}(x'; x = t_0 \,|\, t)) =$$
$$it((\beta^{it})^{\natural^{it}}_{s'M}(t'), (\beta^{it})^{\natural^{it}}_{sM}(t_0),$$
$$\{(t_1, t_2) \mapsto ((\beta^{it}\{x : s \mapsto t_2, x' : s' \mapsto t_1\})^{\natural^{it}}_{sM}(t))\})$$

where $it(\varepsilon, t_a, f) = t_a$ and $it(t_i :: \ell, t_a, f) = it(\ell, f(t_i, t_a), f)$

The charter domain used here is the one of order-sorted signatures, that is, the obtained *iteration term charter* $(\mathscr{C}^{it}, \nu^{it}, (-)^{\natural^{it}})$ is defined over the term charter domain $(\mathbb{S}^\circ, Val^\leq, Str^\circ, U^\circ)$.

Now, the introduction of the OCL query that returns all the instances of a given type, namely allInstances, conveys the introduction of an undefined return value if the type is infinite. Thus we consider a further special case of order-sorted value domains: those that contain the undefined constant $\dagger$. More formally, the value domains remain unchanged, only the morphisms are "undef-lifted" and, in particular, the structures do not change, i.e., they do not contain $\dagger$. This yields an indexed category $Val^\dagger : (\mathbb{S}^\leq)^{op} \rightarrow \text{Cat}$ and thus an indexed functor $U^\dagger : Str^\circ \dashrightarrow Val^\dagger$. Similarly as for iteration, a further inductive case is added to the definition of term language, namely $s.\text{allInstances}()$ with s a sort. The extension of order-sorted signature morphisms as well as the (strict) extension of valuations to allInstances is straightforward:

$$(\beta^a)^{\natural^a}_{s'M}(s.\text{allInstances}()) = \begin{cases} V_s & \text{if } |V_s| < \infty \\ \dagger & \text{otherwise} \end{cases}$$

and in any other case the extension of the valuation β is strict. An *all-instances term charter* $(\mathscr{C}^a, \nu^a, (-)^{\natural^a})$ over the term charter domain $(\mathbb{S}^\circ, Val^\dagger, Str^\circ, U^\dagger)$ is obtained.

Having a way to treat undefinedness of allInstances, the possibility of treating undefinedness in general opens up. So, for instance, non-strict functions as, e.g., if-then-else can be terms of the language. Three-valued Boolean connectives, moreover, need be defined. Again, not function symbols are assumed but further cases to the inductive definition of terms are added; in particular, the constant undef, the term construction $t.\text{isUndef}()$ for t a term, t_1 and t_2 and t_1 or t_2 are terms if t_1 and t_2 are terms of sort Bool, and if t then t_1 else t_2 endif is a term if t is a term of sort Bool and t_1 and t_2 are of the same sort (disregarding sub-sorting here for the sake of simplicity). Both undef-lifted order-sorted signature morphisms and valuations are customarily defined on these new terms, with valuations strict but for if-then-else:

$$(\beta^u)_s^{\natural_M^u}(v_1 \text{ and } v_2) = \begin{cases} tt & \text{if } (\beta^u)_{\text{Bool}}^{\natural_M^u}(v_1) = tt \text{ and } (\beta^u)_{\text{Bool}}^{\natural_M^u}(v_2) = tt \\ ff & \text{if } (\beta^u)_{\text{Bool}}^{\natural_M^u}(v_1) = ff \text{ or } (\beta^u)_{\text{Bool}}^{\natural_M^u}(v_2) = ff \\ \dagger & \text{otherwise} \end{cases}$$

$$(\beta^u)_s^{\natural_M^u}(\text{if } v \text{ then } v_1 \text{ else } v_2 \text{ endif}) = \begin{cases} (\beta^u)_s^{\natural_M^u}(v_1) & \text{if } (\beta^u)_s^{\natural_M^u}(v) = tt \\ (\beta^u)_s^{\natural_M^u}(v_2) & \text{if } (\beta^u)_s^{\natural_M^u}(v) = ff \\ \dagger & \text{otherwise} \end{cases}$$

The *undefinedness term charter* $(\mathscr{C}^u, \nu^u, (-)^{\natural^u})$ is thus defined over the term charter domain $(\mathbb{S}^\circ, Val^\dagger, Str^\circ, U^\dagger)$, i.e., over the same term charter domain as "all instances".

4.3 Institutions for OCL Sub-languages

The term charters of the preceding sections use primitives-closed signatures and structures. From each of them, by Prop. 2, corresponding institutions can be constructed by instantiating $\mathcal{U}_{Val^\dagger}$ and $*$. One possible choice is $\mathcal{U}_{Val^\dagger}(\langle \Sigma, V \rangle) = V_{\text{Bool}}$ and taking the semantic truth value $*$ to be tt. With this choice a term of type Bool evaluating to $\dagger$ is per se not "true". Due to the satisfaction condition, this evaluation is invariant under change of notation.

Example 2. Assume that equality is one of the built-ins considered in Sect. 4.1 and let us write $t_1 = t_2$ instead of $=(t_1, t_2)$. In the undefinedness term charter $\mathfrak{T}^u$ with $\Sigma \in |\mathbb{S}^\circ|$, $X \in |\mathcal{G}(Val^\dagger)(\Sigma)|$, $M \in |\mathcal{G}(Str^\circ)(\Sigma)|$, and $\beta : X \to \mathcal{G}(U^\dagger)(M)$, we have $(\beta)_M^{\natural^u}(\text{undef} = \text{true}) = \dagger$ and therefore $(M, \beta) \not\models_{\mathfrak{T}^u, X}^{\mathcal{U}_{Val^\dagger}} \text{undef} = \text{true}$. Similarly, $(\beta)_M^{\natural^u}(\text{false} = \text{true}) = ff$, and again $(M, \beta) \not\models_{\mathfrak{T}^u, X}^{\mathcal{U}_{Val^\dagger}} \text{false} = \text{true}$. □

5 Operators on Term Charters

Having provided a series of examples for term charters for various OCL features in isolation, we now want to combine these term charters and thus the OCL features to obtain a coherent OCL semantics out of which we can also form an institution. We provide two first operators, which, however, both currently assume that all the involved term charters are given over the same term charter domain.

By sequencing term charters we can stack construction functors and thus get a levelled combination of their terms. Consider for example the all-instances term charter $\mathfrak{T}^a = (\mathscr{C}^a, \nu^a, (-)^{\natural^a})$ and the undefinedness term charter $\mathfrak{T}^u = (\mathscr{C}^u, \nu^u, (-)^{\natural^u})$ of Sect. 4.2 which are both defined over $(\mathbb{S}^\circ, Val^\dagger, Str^\circ, U^\dagger)$. In the term charter $\mathfrak{T}^a \triangleright \mathfrak{T}^u = (\mathscr{C}, \nu, (-)^\natural)$ resulting from sequencing these two term charters we obtain the "heterogeneous" term $(s.\text{allInstances}()).\text{isUndef}()$. This sequencing can be iterated thus adding more levels; a full combination, that allows the occurrence of terms from both term charters on all levels, is in a co-limit construction provided below of the chain $\nu_{\mathscr{C}(n)} : \mathscr{C}^{(n)} \to \mathscr{C}^{(n+1)}$ where $\mathscr{C}^{(n)}$ is the construction functor of the n-th level.

Both operators, sequencing and co-limit, work in the category $\mathrm{TmCh}(\mathsf{D})$ of term charters over a given term charter domain D, where a *term charter morphism* $\mu :$ $\mathfrak{T}_1 \to \mathfrak{T}_2$ with term charters $\mathfrak{T}_1 = (\mathscr{C}_1, \nu_1, (-)^{\natural_1})$ and $\mathfrak{T}_2 = (\mathscr{C}_2, \nu_2, (-)^{\natural_2})$ over $\mathsf{D} = (\mathbb{S}, Val, Str, U)$ is given by a natural transformation $\mu : \mathscr{C}_1 \to \mathscr{C}_2$ such that for all $\Sigma \in |\mathbb{S}|$, $X \in |\mathcal{G}(Val)(\Sigma)|$, $M \in |\mathcal{G}(Str)(\Sigma)|$ and $\beta : X \to \mathcal{G}(U)(M)$ in $\mathcal{G}(Val)(\Sigma)$ the conditions $\nu_{1,X}; \mu_X = \nu_{2,X}$ and $\mu_X; (\beta)^{\natural_{2,M}} = (\beta)^{\natural_{1,M}}$ hold.

5.1 Sequencing of Term Charters

Let $\mathfrak{T}_1 = (\mathscr{C}_1, \nu_1, (-)^{\natural_1})$ and $\mathfrak{T}_2 = (\mathscr{C}_2, \nu_2, (-)^{\natural_2})$ be term charters over the term charter domain $(\mathbb{S}, Val, Str, U)$. Then the *sequencing* $\mathfrak{T}_1 \rhd \mathfrak{T}_2 = (\mathscr{C}, \nu, (-)^{\natural})$ of first $\mathfrak{T}_1$ and then $\mathfrak{T}_2$ is defined by

$$\mathscr{C} = \mathscr{C}_1; \mathscr{C}_2 : \mathcal{G}(Val) \to \mathcal{G}(Val)$$
$$\nu_X = \nu_{1,X}; \nu_{2,\mathscr{C}_1(X)} = \nu_{2,X}; \mathscr{C}_2(\nu_{1,X}) : X \to \mathscr{C}_2(\mathscr{C}_1(X))$$
$$\beta^{\natural_M} = (\beta^{\natural_{1,M}})^{\natural_{2,M}}$$

for all $X \in |\mathcal{G}(Val)(\Sigma)|$, $M \in |\mathcal{G}(Str)(\Sigma)|$, and $\beta : X \to \mathcal{G}(U)(M)$ in $\mathcal{G}(Val)(\Sigma)$.

Proposition 3. *Let* $\mathsf{D} = (\mathbb{S}, Val, Str, U)$ *be a term charter domain. Let* $\mathfrak{T}_1 = (\mathscr{C}_1, \nu_1, (-)^{\natural_1})$ *and* $\mathfrak{T}_2 = (\mathscr{C}_2, \nu_2, (-)^{\natural_2})$ *be term charters over* D. *Then* $\mathfrak{T}_1 \rhd \mathfrak{T}_2$ *is a term charter over* D. $\qquad\square$

Example 3. Consider the "heterogeneous" term (Integer.allInstances()).isUndef() of $\mathfrak{T}^a \rhd \mathfrak{T}^u$ where we assume that Integer is a built-in sort standardly interpreted by $\mathbb{Z}$. This term is built by first constructing Integer.allInstances() in $\mathfrak{T}^a$, then taking this term as a variable, which we may abbreviate by x, and constructing x.isUndef() in $\mathfrak{T}^u$. Consequently, the evaluation of

$$((\beta)^{\natural^a}_M)^{\natural^u}_M((\text{Integer.allInstances()}).\text{isUndef}()) = ((\beta)^{\natural^a}_M)^{\natural^u}_M(x.\text{isUndef}())$$

for an arbitrary $\beta : X \to \mathcal{G}(U^\dagger)(M)$ with $X \in |\mathcal{G}(Val^\dagger)(\Sigma)|$, $M \in |\mathcal{G}(Str^\circ)(\Sigma)|$, and $\Sigma \in |\mathbb{S}^\circ|$ first evaluates $((\beta)^{\natural^a}_M)^{\natural^u}_M(x)$, amounting to $(\beta)^{\natural^a}_M(x)$, since x is a variable, which yields $\dagger$. Thus the overall result is tt. $\qquad\square$

Also the natural transformation $\nu_{2,\mathscr{C}_1(-)} : \mathscr{C}_1 \to \mathscr{C}_1; \mathscr{C}_2$ induces a term charter morphism from $\mathfrak{T}_1$ to $\mathfrak{T}_1 \rhd \mathfrak{T}_2$, and, likewise, the natural transformation $\mathscr{C}_2(\nu_1) : \mathscr{C}_2 \to \mathscr{C}_1; \mathscr{C}_2$ induces a term charter morphism from $\mathfrak{T}_2$ to $\mathfrak{T}_1 \rhd \mathfrak{T}_2$. The *n-th iteration* $\mathfrak{T}^{(n)}$ of a term charter $\mathfrak{T}$ for $n \geq 1$ is inductively defined by $\mathfrak{T}^{(1)} = \mathfrak{T}$ and $\mathfrak{T}^{(n+1)} = \mathfrak{T}^{(n)} \rhd \mathfrak{T}$.

5.2 Co-limits of Term Charters

Let $\mathsf{D} = (\Sigma, Val, Str, U)$ be a term charter domain. For a term charter $\mathfrak{T} = (\mathscr{C}, \nu, (-)^{\natural}) \in |\mathrm{TmCh}(\mathsf{D})|$ let us write $\mathfrak{T}_{\mathscr{C}}$, $\mathfrak{T}_\nu$, and $\mathfrak{T}_\natural$ for the components of $\mathfrak{T}$. Consider a diagram $F : J \to \mathrm{TmCh}(\mathsf{D})$ where J is a small connected category. Assume that for every $X \in |\mathcal{G}(Val)(\Sigma)|$ with $\Sigma \in |\mathbb{S}|$, the diagram $F_{\mathscr{C},X} : J \to \mathcal{G}(Val)(\Sigma)$

with $F_{\mathscr{C},X}(j) = F(j)_{\mathscr{C}}(X)$ and $F_{\mathscr{C},X}(f : j \to j') = F(f)_X$ has co-limit ($C_{F,X} \in \mathcal{G}(Val)(\Sigma), \gamma_{F,X} : F_{\mathscr{C},X} \dashrightarrow \Delta(C_{F,X})$) (where, for a category $\mathbb{C}$, $\Delta : \mathbb{C} \to \mathbb{C}^J$ denotes the diagonal functor mapping a $C \in |\mathbb{C}|$ to the functor $\Delta(C) : J \to \mathbb{C}$ with $\Delta(C)(j) = C$ and $\Delta(C)(f : j \to j') = 1_C$). Then, by universality, for each $\xi : X \to Y$ in $\mathcal{G}(Val)(\Sigma)$ there is a unique arrow $c_{F,\xi} : C_{F,X} \to C_{F,Y}$ such that

$$F(j)_{\mathscr{C}}(\xi); \gamma_{F,Y,j} = \gamma_{F,X,j}; c_{F,\xi} \quad \text{for all } j \in |J|.$$

Define $\mathscr{C}^F(X) = C_{F,X}$ and $\mathscr{C}^F(\xi) = c_{F,\xi}$. Furthermore, for all $f : j \to j'$ in J,

$$(F(j)_\nu)_X; F(f)_X = (F(j')_\nu)_X \quad \text{and} \quad \gamma_{F,X,j} = F(f)_X; \gamma_{F,X,j'}$$

Define $\nu_X^F = (F(j)_\nu)_X; \zeta_{F,X,j}$ for some $j \in |J|$. For a morphism $\beta : X \to \mathcal{G}(U)(M)$ in $\mathcal{G}(Val)(\Sigma)$ with $M \in |\mathcal{G}(Str)(\Sigma)|$ let $(\beta)_M^{\natural^F} : \mathscr{C}^F(X) \to \mathcal{G}(U)(M)$ be the unique morphism with $\zeta_{F,X,j}; (\beta)_M^{\natural^F} = F(j)_\natural(\beta)$ for all $j \in |J|$ which exists since

$$F(f)_X; F(j)_{\natural M}(\beta) = F(j')_{\natural M}(\beta) \quad \text{for all } f : j \to j' \text{ in } J.$$

Then $\mathfrak{T}^F = (\mathscr{C}^F, \nu^F, (-)^{\natural^F})$ is a term charter and all $\gamma_{F,-,j}$ are term charter morphisms. In fact, $(\mathfrak{T}^F, \gamma^F)$ with $(\gamma_j^F)_X = \gamma_{F,X,j}$ is the co-limit of F.

Proposition 4. $(-)_{\mathscr{C}} : \mathrm{TmCh}(\mathbb{S}, Val, Str, U) \to \mathrm{Fun}(\mathcal{G}(Val), \mathcal{G}(Val))$ *creates parameterized small connected co-limits.* □

Example 4. Continuing the previous example, we now want to consider arbitrarily nested terms from the all-instances term charter $\mathfrak{T}^a$ and the undefinedness term charter $\mathfrak{T}^u$. We thus consider the chain $\mathfrak{T} \xrightarrow{\nu_1} \mathfrak{T}^{(2)} \xrightarrow{\nu_2} \mathfrak{T}^{(3)} \xrightarrow{\nu_3} \cdots$ for $\mathfrak{T} = \mathfrak{T}^a \triangleright \mathfrak{T}^u$. Writing $\mathscr{C}$ for the construction functor $\mathscr{C}^a; \mathscr{C}^u$, we have to check that the chain $\mathscr{C}(X) \xrightarrow{\nu_{1,X}} \mathscr{C}^{(2)}(X) \xrightarrow{\nu_{2,X}} \mathscr{C}^{(3)}(X) \xrightarrow{\nu_{3,X}} \cdots$ has a co-limit in $\mathcal{G}(Val^\dagger)(\Sigma)$ for $X \in |\mathcal{G}(Val^\dagger)(\Sigma)|$. Indeed, the co-limit object of this chain is simply given by the component-wise union of the value domains and thus we obtain a co-limit term charter by Prop. 4. The evaluation of a term at a nesting level n of $\mathfrak{T}^a$ and $\mathfrak{T}^u$ then proceeds like in $\mathfrak{T}^{(n)}$. □

6   Conclusions and Future Work

Along the lines of Martin Wirsing's proposal for the definition of an heterogeneous semantics of UML in [4], we have presented above a semantics for the constraints language OCL. The distinct characteristic of this approach is the compositional construction of theories out of basic ones. Indeed, OCL can be obtained by sequencing term charters and building the co-limit of the result. This way only the theories, presented as term charters and needed for the situation at hand, are combined into an OCL sub-language (and therefore the theories that are dispensable need not be included).

Let us emphasize that OCL is not a logic but a term language. It it is imperative to deal with its particularities, too, especially undefinedness and non-termination. The OCL setting defines a logic that is not binary. That is, we have to deal with formulase that, instead of being either true or not, may be true, false, undefined or even non-terminating. In order to mimic the implied three- or four-valued OCL logic (see [3] and also [12]), the most natural to do is, on the one hand, to follow the definition of OCL as closely as possible and construct a term language whose equality, on the other hand, is invariant under change of notation. As pointed out above, we moreover addressed the OCL sub-languages one by one, thus supporting compositional construction of term languages that comply the satisfaction condition and can consequently be presented as institutions.

Indeed, term charters for the OCL sub-languages can be composed by means of the sequencing operator and the co-limit construction of Sect. 5, provided they are defined over the same term charter domain. In particular, an OCL term charter can be obtained by composing the term charters sketched in Sect. 4, that is, the primitives-closed order-sorted term charter (see Sect. A.2), the iteration term charter (see Sect. A.3), the all-instances term charter (see Sect. A.4), and the undefinedness term charter (see Sect. A.5), only after their reformulation as term charters over a single term charter domain. By Prop. 2, the resulting OCL term charter defines an institution for OCL.

Useful would be the possibility of combining term charters defined over different term charter domains. The use of heterogeneous term charter domains could support the construction of the four-valued logic with undef and non-termination by means of operators on the corresponding three-valued term charters, i.e., by composing them directly, instead of resorting to their redefinition for a four-valued term charter domain. A property not demonstrated yet is the associativity of sequencing. A further issue, to be included in the framework presented in this work, is the treatment of pre-/post-conditions. The present idea consists in testing them on pairs of "states", one that represents the state at the time before the execution of a method and one that represents the state afterwards. In the long term, we aim to define an entailment system for OCL which, combined with the institution above, would yield an general logic; see [13]. Finally, an integration into the institution-based Heterogeneous Tool Set [14] for analysis and proof support in multi-logic specifications is planned.

Acknowledgements. We thank Till Mossakowski and Hubert Baumeister for fruitful discussions and comments on previous drafts of this work. We especially want to express our deep gratitude to Martin Wirsing for initiating this work, accompanying our scientific lives, and particularly for being, both from the academic and personal point of view, precisely Martin Wirsing.

References

1. Booch, G., Rumbaugh, J., Jacobson, I.: The Unified Modeling Language User Guide. Addison-Wesley (1999)
2. Boronat, A., Knapp, A., Meseguer, J., Wirsing, M.: What Is a Multi-modeling Language? In: Corradini, A., Montanari, U. (eds.) WADT 2008. LNCS, vol. 5486, pp. 71–87. Springer, Heidelberg (2009)
3. Cengarle, M.V., Knapp, A.: OCL 1.4/1.5 vs. OCL 2.0 Expressions: Formal Semantics and Expressiveness. Softw. Syst. Model. 3(1), 9–30 (2004)

4. Cengarle, M.V., Knapp, A., Tarlecki, A., Wirsing, M.: A Heterogeneous Approach to UML Semantics. In: Degano, P., De Nicola, R., Meseguer, J. (eds.) Concurrency, Graphs and Models. LNCS, vol. 5065, pp. 383–402. Springer, Heidelberg (2008)

5. Clark, T.: Typechecking UML Static Models. In: France, R.B. (ed.) UML 1999. LNCS, vol. 1723, pp. 503–517. Springer, Heidelberg (1999)

6. Ganzinger, H.: Programs as Transformations of Algebraic Theories (Extended Abstract). Informatik Fachberichte 50, 22–41 (1981)

7. Goguen, J.A., Burstall, R.M.: A Study in the Foundation of Programming Methodology: Specifications, Institutions, Charters, and Parchments. In: Poigné, A., Pitt, D.H., Rydeheard, D.E., Abramsky, S. (eds.) Category Theory and Computer Programming. LNCS, vol. 240, pp. 313–333. Springer, Heidelberg (1986)

8. Goguen, J.A., Burstall, R.M.: Institutions: Abstract Model Theory for Specification and Programming. J. ACM 39(1), 95–146 (1992)

9. Goguen, J.A., Meseguer, J.: Order-sorted Algebra I: Equational Deduction for Multiple Inheritance, Overloading, Exceptions and Partial Operations. Theo. Comp. Sci. 105(2), 217–273 (1992)

10. Hennicker, R., Knapp, A., Baumeister, H.: Semantics of OCL Operation Specifications. In: Schmitt, P.H. (ed.) Proc. Wsh. OCL 2.0 — Industry Standard or Scientific Playground? (WOCL 2003). Electr. Notes Theo. Comp. Sci., vol. 120, pp. 111–132. Elsevier (2004)

11. Knapp, A., Cengarle, M.V.: Institutions for OCL-like Expression Languages. Manuscript, Universitt Augsburg (2014),
    http://www.informatik.uni-augsburg.de/lehrstuehle/swt/sse/veroeffentlichungen/uau-2014/ocl-institutions.pdf

12. Lano, K.: Null Considered Harmful (for Transformation Verification). In: Proc. 3rd Int. Wsh. Verification of Model Transformations, VOLT 2014 (2014), http://volt2014.big.tuwien.ac.at/papers/volt2014_paper_3.pdf

13. Meseguer, J.: General Logics. In: Ebbinghaus, H.D., Fernández-Prida, J., Garrido, M., Lascar, D., Rodríguez Artalejo, M. (eds.) Proc. Logic Colloquium 1987, pp. 275–329. North-Holland (1989)

14. Mossakowski, T., Maeder, C., Lüttich, K.: The Heterogeneous Tool Set, HETS. In: Grumberg, O., Huth, M. (eds.) TACAS 2007. LNCS, vol. 4424, pp. 519–522. Springer, Heidelberg (2007)

15. Object Management Group: Unified Modeling Language, Superstructure. Version 2.4.1. Specification formal/2011-08-06, OMG (2011)

16. Object Management Group: Object Constraint Language. Version 2.3.1. Specification formal/2012-01-01, OMG (2012)

17. Pawłowski, W.: Context Parchments. In: Parisi-Presicce, F. (ed.) WADT 1997. LNCS, vol. 1376, pp. 381–401. Springer, Heidelberg (1998)

18. Petre, M.: UML in Practice. In: Proc. 35th Int. Conf. Software Engineering (ICSE 2013), pp. 722–731. IEEE (2013)

19. Sannella, D., Tarlecki, A.: Foundations of Algebraic Specification and Formal Software Development. EATCS Monographs in Theoretical Computer Science. Springer (2012)

20. Tarlecki, A., Burstall, R.M., Goguen, J.A.: Some Fundamental Algebraic Tools for the Semantics of Computation, Part 3: Indexed Categories. Theo. Comp. Sci. 91, 239–264 (1991)

21. Wirsing, M.: Algebraic Specification. In: van Leeuwen, J. (ed.) Handbook of Theoretical Computer Science, Volume B: Formal Models and Semantics, pp. 675–788. Elsevier and MIT Press (1990)

A OCL Terms and Evaluation

We formally define the OCL features discussed in Sect. 4 following the same strategy, i.e., one by one and each time adapting the framework.

A.1 Order-Sorted Terms and Evaluation

For the first basic step, we recapitulate the notions of order-sorted signatures, structures, terms, and evaluation in terms of indexed categories.

Signatures, Values, and Structures. An *order-sorted signature* (S, D) consists of a *sort hierarchy* S and a *function declaration* pair over S; where $S = (|S|, \leq_S)$ is a partial order with a set of sort names $|S|$ and a sub-sorting relation $\leq_S$; and $D = (|D|, \delta_D)$ is a pair with $|D|$ a set of function names and $\delta_D : |S|^* \times |S| \to \mathcal{P}(|D|)$ a function such that $|D| = \bigcup\{\delta_D(\overline{s}, s) \mid \overline{s} \in |S|^*, s \in |S|\}$. An *order-sorted signature morphism* $(\gamma, \rho) : (S, D) \to (S', D')$ is given by a monotone function $\gamma : S \to S'$ and a function $\rho : |D| \to |D'|$ such that $\rho(d) \in \delta_{D'}(\gamma(\overline{s}), \gamma(s))$ for each $d \in \delta_D(\overline{s}, s)$. Order-sorted signatures and morphisms between them define a category which we denote by $\mathbb{S}^{\leq}$.

An (S, D)-*value domain* V consists of a family $V = (V_s)_{s \in |S|}$ of sets of *values* with $V_s \subseteq V_{s'}$ if $s \leq_S s'$. An (S, D)-*value domain morphism* $\omega : V \to V'$ is given by a family of mappings $\omega = (\omega_s : V_s \to V'_s)_{s \in |S|}$. (S, D)-value domains and morphisms define a category $Val^{\leq}(S, D)$. The indexed category $Val^{\leq} : (\mathbb{S}^{\leq})^{\mathrm{op}} \to \mathbf{Cat}$ maps each $\Sigma = (S, D)$ to $Val^{\leq}(\Sigma)$ and each $(\gamma, \rho) : \Sigma \to \Sigma' = (S', D')$ to the functor $Val^{\leq}(\gamma, \rho) : Val^{\leq}(\Sigma') \to Val^{\leq}(\Sigma)$ with $Val^{\leq}(\gamma, \rho)((V'_{s'})_{s' \in |S'|}) = (V'_{\gamma(s)})_{s \in |S|}$ and $Val^{\leq}(\gamma, \rho)((\omega'_{s'} : V'_{1,s'} \to V'_{2,s'})_{s' \in |S'|}) = (\omega'_{\gamma(s)} : V'_{1,\gamma(s)} \to V'_{2,\gamma(s)})_{s \in |S|}$.

An (S, D)-*structure* (V, E) consists of an (S, D)-value domain and a family of *evaluation* functions $E = (E_{\overline{s},s})_{\overline{s} \in |S|^*, s \in |S|}$ with $E_{\overline{s},s} : \delta_D(\overline{s}, s) \to (V_{\overline{s}} \to V_s)$. An (S, D)-*structure morphism* $\omega : (V, E) \to (V', E')$ is given by an (S, D)-value domain morphism $\omega : V \to V'$ such that the *homomorphism condition* $\omega_s(E_{\overline{s},s}(d)(\overline{v})) = E'_{\overline{s},s}(d)(\omega_{\overline{s}}(\overline{v}))$ is satisfied. (S, D)-structures and morphisms define a category $Str^{\leq}(S, D)$. The indexed category $Str^{\leq} : (\mathbb{S}^{\leq})^{\mathrm{op}} \to \mathbf{Cat}$ maps each Σ to $Str^{\leq}(\Sigma)$ and each $(\gamma, \rho) : \Sigma \to \Sigma' = (S', D')$ to the functor $Str^{\leq}(\gamma, \rho) : Str^{\leq}(\Sigma') \to Str^{\leq}(\Sigma)$ with $Str^{\leq}(\gamma, \rho)((V'_{s'})_{s' \in |S'|}, (E'_{\overline{s}',s'})_{\overline{s}' \in |S'|^*, s' \in |S'|}) = ((V'_{\gamma(s)})_{s \in |S|}, ((E' \circ \rho)_{\gamma(\overline{s}),\gamma(s)})_{\overline{s} \in |S|^*, s \in |S|})$ and $Str^{\leq}(\gamma, \rho)(\omega') = Val^{\leq}(\gamma, \rho)(\omega')$.

The indexed functor $U^{\leq} : Str^{\leq} \dashrightarrow Val^{\leq}$ "forgets" the evaluation functions of a structure.

Terms and Evaluation. For constructing *order-sorted terms* over an order-sorted value domain we define a functor $\mathscr{C}^{\leq} : \mathcal{G}(Val^{\leq}) \to \mathcal{G}(Val^{\leq})$ as follows: For an object $\langle \Sigma, X \rangle \in |\mathcal{G}(Val^{\leq})|$ with $\Sigma = (S, D)$ set $\mathscr{C}^{\leq}(\langle \Sigma, X \rangle) = \langle \Sigma, V_X^{\leq} \rangle$ such that for each $s \in |S|$ the values in $V_s^{\leq}$ are given inductively by

- $x \in V_{\overline{X},s}^{\leq}$ for $x \in X_s$;
- $d(\overline{v}) \in V_{\overline{X},s'}^{\leq}$ for all $s' \geq_S s$ if $d \in \delta_D(\overline{s}, s)$ and $\overline{v} \in V_{\overline{X},\overline{s}}^{\leq}$;

For a morphism $\langle \sigma, \omega \rangle : \langle \Sigma, X \rangle \to \langle \Sigma', X' \rangle$ in $\mathcal{G}(Val^{\leq})$ with $\sigma = (\gamma, \rho)$ and $\Sigma = (S, D)$ set $\mathscr{C}^{\leq}(\langle \sigma, \omega \rangle) = \langle \sigma, \omega^{\leq} \rangle : \mathscr{C}^{\leq}(\langle \Sigma, X \rangle) \to \mathscr{C}^{\leq}(\langle \Sigma', X' \rangle)$ such that inductively $\omega_{\bar{s}}^{\leq}(x) = \omega_s(x)$ for $x \in X_s$ and $\omega_{\bar{s}}^{\leq}(d(\vec{v})) = \rho(d)(\omega_{\bar{\bar{s}}}^{\leq}(\vec{v}))$.

For *evaluating* order-sorted terms over a Σ-structure $M = \langle \Sigma, (V, E) \rangle$ in $|\mathcal{G}(Str^{\leq})|$ given a *valuation* $\beta = \langle 1_{\Sigma}, \beta^{\leq} \rangle : \langle \Sigma, X \rangle \to \mathcal{G}(U^{\leq})(\langle \Sigma, (V, E) \rangle)$ define $(\beta)^{\flat_M^{\leq}} = \langle 1_{\Sigma}, ((\beta^{\leq}))^{\flat_M^{\leq}} \rangle : \mathscr{C}^{\leq}(\langle \Sigma, X \rangle) \to \langle \Sigma, (V, E) \rangle$ inductively by

- $(\beta^{\leq})_{\bar{s}}^{\flat_M^{\leq}}(x) = \beta_{\bar{s}}^{\leq}(x)$ for $x \in X_s$;
- $(\beta^{\leq})_{\bar{s}}^{\flat_M^{\leq}}(d(\vec{v})) = E_{\bar{\bar{s}}, s}(d)((\beta^{\leq})_{\bar{\bar{s}}}^{\flat_M^{\leq}})(\vec{v}))$.

Term Charter. Given an order-sorted signature morphism $\sigma : \Sigma \to \Sigma'$ in $\mathbb{S}^{\leq}$, a Σ'-structure $\langle \Sigma', (V', E') \rangle \in |\mathcal{G}(Str^{\leq})(\Sigma')|$, and a valuation $\beta' : \langle \Sigma', X' \rangle \to \mathcal{G}(U^{\leq})(\langle \Sigma', (V', E') \rangle)$ in $\mathcal{G}(Val^{\leq})(\Sigma')$ it is straightforwardly checked that the evaluation condition (E) for term charters

$$
\begin{array}{ccc}
\mathscr{C}^{\leq}(\langle \Sigma', X' \rangle|_{Val^{\leq}\sigma}) & \xrightarrow{\mathscr{C}^{\leq}(\sigma|_{Val^{\leq}}\langle \Sigma', X' \rangle)} & \mathscr{C}^{\leq}(\langle \Sigma', X' \rangle) \\
{\scriptstyle (\beta'|_{Val^{\leq}\sigma})^{\flat_{\langle \Sigma', (V', E') \rangle}^{\leq}}|_{Str^{\leq}\sigma}} \downarrow & & \downarrow {\scriptstyle (\beta')^{\flat_{\langle \Sigma', (V', E') \rangle}^{\leq}}} \\
\mathcal{G}(U^{\leq})(\langle \Sigma', (V', E') \rangle|_{Str^{\leq}\sigma}) & \xrightarrow{\mathcal{G}(U^{\leq})(\sigma|_{Str^{\leq}}\langle \Sigma', (V', E') \rangle)} & \mathcal{G}(U^{\leq})(\langle \Sigma', (V', E') \rangle)
\end{array}
$$

indeed is satisfied. Also condition (K) is easily shown. As natural transformation $\nu^{\leq} : 1_{\mathcal{G}(Val^{\leq})} \dot{\to} \mathscr{C}^{\leq}$ for embedding values or variables into the order-sorted terms we may simply choose the inclusions, i.e., $\nu_{\langle (S, D), X \rangle}^{\leq} = \langle 1_{(S, D)}, (\iota_{\langle (S, D), X \rangle, s} : X_s \to V_{X, s}^{\leq})_{s \in |S|} \rangle$ which also satisfies (C).

Thus we obtain the *order-sorted term charter* $(\mathscr{C}^{\leq}, \nu^{\leq}, (-)^{\flat^{\leq}})$ over the term charter domain $(\mathbb{S}^{\leq}, Val^{\leq}, Str^{\leq}, U^{\leq})$.

A.2   Adding Built-ins

The addition of OCL's built-in types can be handled by a specialization of order-sorted signatures and structures, requiring them to contain and interpret particular sorts and declarations in a standard way. We demonstrate this by adding Booleans, sequences, and sets as well as a few functions; these additions are by far not exhaustive, but meant to be exemplarily. Nevertheless, we call the resulting order-sorted signatures and structures "primitives closed".

Signatures and Structures. An order-sorted signature (S, D) with $S = (|S|, \leq_S)$ and $D = (|D|, \delta_D)$ is *primitives-closed* whenever $\mathsf{Bool} \in |S|$, and $\mathsf{true} \in \delta_D(\mathsf{Bool})$ and $\mathsf{false} \in \delta_D(\mathsf{Bool})$; and the following conditions hold for all $\tau \in \{\mathsf{Seq}, \mathsf{Set}\}$ and all $s, s' \in |S|$:

- $\tau(s) \in |S|$ if, and only if, $s \in |S|$;
- $\tau(s) \leq_S \tau(s')$ if, and only if, $s \leq_S s'$;
- $\tau\{\} \in \delta_D(\tau(s))$ and $-\!-\!\to\mathsf{including}(-) \in \delta_D(\tau(s)\ s, \tau(s))$.

A morphism $(\gamma, \rho) : (S, D) \to (S', D')$ between primitives-closed order-sorted signatures is *primitives-closed* if $\gamma(\mathsf{Bool}) = \mathsf{Bool}$, and $\rho(\mathsf{true}) = \mathsf{true}$ and $\rho(\mathsf{false}) = \mathsf{false}$; and the following conditions hold for all $\tau \in \{\mathsf{Seq}, \mathsf{Set}\}$ and all $s \in |S|$:

- $\gamma(\tau(s)) = \tau(\gamma(s))$;
- $\rho(\tau\{\}) = \tau\{\}$ and $\rho(-\!-\!\to\!\mathsf{including}(-)) = -\!-\!\to\!\mathsf{including}(-)$.

Let $\mathbb{S}^\circ$ be the sub-category of order-sorted signatures consisting of all the primitives-closed order-sorted signatures and all the primitives-closed morphisms between them.

An (S, D)-structure (V, E) over a primitives-closed order-sorted signature (S, D) is *primitives-closed* if $V_{\mathsf{Bool}} = \{tt, f\!f\}$, and $E_{\mathsf{Bool}}(\mathsf{true}) = tt$ and $E_{\mathsf{Bool}}(\mathsf{false}) = f\!f$; and for all $s \in |S|$:

- $V_{\mathsf{Seq}(s)} = (V_s)^*$ and $V_{\mathsf{Set}(s)} = \mathcal{P}_{\mathrm{fin}}(V_s)$ (i.e., all finite lists and sets over V_s);
- $E_{\mathsf{Seq}(s)}(\mathsf{Seq}\{\}) = \varepsilon$ and $E_{\mathsf{Set}(s)}(\mathsf{Set}\{\}) = \emptyset$ (i.e., the empty list and set);
- $E_{\mathsf{Seq}(s)\,s,\mathsf{Seq}(s)}(-\!-\!\to\!\mathsf{including}(-)) = \{(l, v) \mapsto v :: l\}$ (i.e., prepending an element to a list) and $E_{\mathsf{Set}(s)\,s,\mathsf{Set}(s)}(-\!-\!\to\!\mathsf{including}(-)) = \{(m, v) \mapsto \{v\} \cup m\}$ (i.e., adding an element to a set);

An (S, D)-structure morphism $\omega : (V, E) \to (V', E')$ over a primitives-closed order-sorted signature (S, D) is *primitives-closed* if $\omega_{\mathsf{Bool}}(tt) = tt$ and $\omega_{\mathsf{Bool}}(f\!f) = f\!f$; and for all $s \in |S|$:

- $\omega_{\mathsf{Seq}(s)}(\varepsilon) = \varepsilon$ and $\omega_{\mathsf{Set}(s)}(\emptyset) = \emptyset$;
- $\omega_{\mathsf{Seq}(s)}(v :: l) = \omega_s(v) :: \omega_{\mathsf{Seq}(s)}(l)$ and $\omega_{\mathsf{Set}(s)}(\{v\} \cup m) = \{\omega_s(v)\} \cup \omega_{\mathsf{Set}(s)}(m)$.

The indexed category $Str^\circ : (\mathbb{S}^\circ)^{\mathrm{op}} \to \mathbf{Cat}$ is defined like $Str^{\leq}$ but only involves primitives-closed order-sorted signatures, structures, and morphisms.

The indexed functor $U^\circ : Str^\circ \overset{\cdot}{\to} Val^{\leq}$ is defined by $U^{\leq}$ restricted to Str°.

Terms and Evaluation. As construction functor for *primitives-closed* order-sorted terms we can still use $\mathscr{C}^{\leq} : \mathcal{G}(Val^{\leq}) \to \mathcal{G}(Val^{\leq})$ as defined in Sect. A.1. Also the definition of the evaluation of primitives-closed order-sorted terms, though now involving primitives-closed signatures and structures, stays the same, such that the corresponding evaluation condition (E) again is satisfied. However, the primitives-closed order-sorted terms do not directly give rise to primitives-closed structures (in the sense of term algebras) due to the "standard interpretation" requirements on sequences and sets.

Term Charter. In particular, we obtain the *primitives-closed order-sorted term charter* $(\mathscr{C}^{\leq}, \nu^{\leq}, (-)^{\natural\leq})$ over the term charter domain $(\mathbb{S}^\circ, Val^{\leq}, Str^\circ, U^\circ)$. Furthermore, setting $\mathcal{U}_{Val^{\leq}}(\langle \Sigma, V \rangle) = V_{\mathsf{Bool}}$ and $* = tt$ we obtain, by applying Prop. 2, an institution for the primitives-closed order-sorted term charter. Since $Val^{\leq}(\Sigma)$ has initial value domains for each $\Sigma \in |\mathbb{S}^\circ|$, we can also apply Cor. 1 and obtain a "classical" institution.

A.3　Iteration

For handling OCL's iteration construct, we only extend the term language, but keep working over primitives-closed order-sorted signatures and structures. In fact, iteration is not straightforwardly integrable into order-sorted signatures and structures themselves, since it binds the iteration and the accumulator variable and thus involves higher-order terms.

Terms and Evaluation. The construction functor for *iteration terms* $\mathscr{C}^{\text{it}} : \mathcal{G}(Val^{\leq}) \to \mathcal{G}(Val^{\leq})$ is defined as follows: For the objects, set $\mathscr{C}^{\text{it}}(\langle\langle(S,D),X\rangle\rangle) = \langle(S,D),V_X^{\text{it}}\rangle$ such that inductively

- $x \in V_{X,s}^{\text{it}}$ if $x \in X_s$;
- $d(\vec{v}) \in V_{X,s'}^{\text{it}}$ for all $s' \geq_S s$ if $d \in \delta_D(\overline{s}, s)$ and $\vec{v} \in V_{X,\overline{s}}^{\text{it}}$;
- $v' \to \text{iterate}(y'; y = v_0 \,|\, v) \in V_{X,s}^{\text{it}}$ if $v' \in V_{X,\text{Seq}(s')}^{\text{it}}$ with $s' \in |S|$, $v_0 \in V_{X,s}^{\text{it}}$, and $v \in V_{X \uplus \{y:s,y':s'\},s}^{\text{it}}$ (where, for $s_0, s_1 \in |S|$, $y_0 \notin X_{s_0'}$ for any $s_0' \geq_S s_0$, $(X \uplus \{y_0 : s_0\})_{s_1}$ is defined by X_{s_1} if $s_0 \not\leq_S s_1$ and by $X_{s_1} \cup \{y_0\}$ if $s_0 \leq_S s_1$).

For the morphisms, define the morphism $\mathscr{C}^{\text{it}}(\langle\langle(\gamma,\rho),\omega\rangle) = \langle\langle(\gamma,\rho),\omega^{\text{it}}\rangle : \mathscr{C}^{\text{it}}(\langle\langle(S,D), X\rangle\rangle) \to \mathscr{C}^{\text{it}}(\langle\langle(S',D'),X'\rangle\rangle)$ such that, by simultaneous induction, $\omega_s^{\text{it}}(x) = \omega_s(x)$ for $x \in X_s$; $\omega_s^{\text{it}}(d(\vec{v})) = \rho(d)(\omega_{\overline{s}}^{\text{it}}(\vec{v}))$; and $\omega_s^{\text{it}}(v' \to \text{iterate}(y'; y = v_0 \,|\, v)) = \omega_{s'}^{\text{it}}(v') \to \text{iterate}(y'; y = \omega_s^{\text{it}}(v_0) \,|\, (\omega\{y : s \mapsto y : \gamma(s), y' : s' \mapsto y' : \gamma(s')\})_s^{\text{it}}(v))$.

For each $M = \langle \Sigma, (V,E)\rangle \in |\mathcal{G}(Str^\circ)|$ with $\Sigma = (S,D)$ and each morphism $\beta = \langle 1_\Sigma, \beta^{\text{it}}\rangle : \langle\Sigma, X\rangle \to \mathcal{G}(U^\circ)(M)$ define $(\beta)_\Sigma^{\natural^{\text{it}}} = \langle 1_\Sigma, (\beta^{\text{it}})_\Sigma^{\natural^{\text{it}}}\rangle : \mathscr{C}^{\text{it}}(\langle\Sigma, X\rangle) \to \mathcal{G}(U^\circ)(M)$ inductively by

- $(\beta^{\text{it}})_s^{\natural_M^{\text{it}}}(x) = \beta_s(x)$ for $x \in X_s$;
- $(\beta^{\text{it}})_s^{\natural_M^{\text{it}}}(d(\vec{v})) = E_{\overline{s},s}(d)((\beta^{\text{it}})_{\overline{s}}^{\natural_M^{\text{it}}}(\vec{v}))$;
- $(\beta^{\text{it}})_s^{\natural_M^{\text{it}}}(v' \to \text{iterate}(y'; y = v_0 \,|\, v)) = it((\beta^{\text{it}})_{s'}^{\natural_M^{\text{it}}}(v'), (\beta^{\text{it}})_s^{\natural_M^{\text{it}}}(v_0),$

$$\{(v_1,v_2) \mapsto ((\beta^{\text{it}}\{y : s \mapsto v_2, y' : s' \mapsto v_1\})_s^{\natural_M^{\text{it}}}(v)\})\}),$$

where $it(\varepsilon, v_a, f) = v_a$ and $it(v_i :: \ell, v_a, f) = it(\ell, f(v_i, v_a), f)$.

Term Charter. We obtain the *iteration term charter* $(\mathscr{C}^{\text{it}}, \nu^{\text{it}}, (-)^{\natural^{\text{it}}})$ over the term charter domain $(S^\circ, Val^{\leq}, Str^\circ, U^\circ)$ when choosing the embedding natural transformation ν^{it} to consist out of inclusions. The evaluation of the iteration construct is completely handled by the structure over which a term is evaluated. As for primitives-closed order-sorted term charters we can construct the respective institutions.

A.4   All Instances

When accessing all instances of a type with an infinite number of inhabitants, an undefined value, which we denote by †, shall be the result. We cover this addition by lifting the order-sorted value domain morphisms to include also † in their co-domains.

Values. An *undef-lifting value domain morphism* $\omega^\dagger : V \to V'$ from an (S,D)-value domain V to an (S,D)-value domain V' over the order-sorted signature (S,D) is given by a family of mappings $\omega^\dagger = (\omega_s^\dagger : V_s \to (V_s')_\dagger)_{s \in |S|}$ where $(M)_\dagger = M \uplus \{\dagger\}$ is the *undef-lifting* of the set M extending M by the special *undefinedness symbol* †. The *composition* $\omega'^\dagger \circ \omega^\dagger : V \to V''$ of two undef-lifting value domain morphisms $\omega^\dagger : V \to V'$ and $\omega'^\dagger : V' \to V''$ between (S,D)-value domains is given by $\omega'^\dagger \circ \omega^\dagger = (\omega_s'^\dagger \circ \omega_s^\dagger : V_s \to (V_s'')_\dagger)_{s \in |S|}$ with $(\omega_s'^\dagger \circ \omega_s^\dagger)(v) = \dagger$ if $\omega_s^\dagger(v) = \dagger$ and $(\omega_s'^\dagger \circ \omega_s^\dagger)(v) = \omega_s'^\dagger(\omega_s^\dagger(v))$ otherwise; i.e., composition is strict w.r.t. undefinedness. The *identity* undef-lifting value domain morphism $1_V^\dagger : V \to V$ between an (S,D)-value domain V is given by $1_V^\dagger = (1_{V,s}^\dagger : V_s \to (V_s)_\dagger)_{s \in |S|}$ with $1_{V,s}^\dagger(v) = v$.

(S, D)-value domains and undef-lifting morphisms between (S, D)-value domains define a category which we denote by $Val^\dagger(S, D)$. The indexed category $Val^\dagger : (\mathbb{S}^{\leq})^{\mathrm{op}} \to \mathbf{Cat}$ maps each order-sorted signature (S, D) to $Val^\dagger(S, D)$ and each order-sorted signature morphism $(\gamma, \rho) : (S, D) \to (S', D')$ to the functor $Val^\dagger(\gamma, \rho) : Val^\dagger(S', D') \to Val^\dagger(S, D)$ with $Val^\dagger(\gamma, \rho)((V'_{s'})_{s' \in |S'|}) = (V'_{\gamma(s)})_{s \in |S|}$ and $Val^\dagger(\gamma, \rho)((\omega'^\dagger_{s'} : V'_{1,s'} \to (V'_{2,s'})_\dagger)_{s' \in |S|}) = (\omega'^\dagger_{\gamma(s)} : V'_{1,\gamma(s)} \to (V'_{2,\gamma(s)})_\dagger)_{s \in |S|}$.

For a primitives-closed $\Sigma = (S, D)$-structure (V, E) define $U^\dagger_\Sigma(V, E) = V$. For a structure morphism $\omega : (V, E) \to (V', E')$ between primitives-closed Σ-structures define $U^\dagger_\Sigma(\omega) = (\omega^\dagger_s : V_s \to (V'_s)_\dagger)_{s \in |S|}$ with $\omega^\dagger_s(v) = \omega(v)$ which is an undef-lifting value domain morphism from $U^\dagger_\Sigma(V, E)$ to $U^\dagger_\Sigma(V', E')$. This yields the indexed functor $U^\dagger : Str^\circ \dot\to Val^\dagger$.

Terms and Evaluation. The construction functor for *all-instances terms* $\mathscr{C}^{\mathrm{a}} : \mathcal{G}(Val^\dagger) \to \mathcal{G}(Val^\dagger)$ is defined as follows: For the objects, let $\mathscr{C}^{\mathrm{a}}(\langle(S, D), X\rangle) = \langle(S, D), V^{\mathrm{a}}_X\rangle$ such that inductively

- $x \in V^{\mathrm{a}}_{X,s}$ if $x \in X_s$;
- $d(\vec{v}) \in V^{\mathrm{a}}_{X,s'}$ for all $s' \geq_S s$ if $d \in \delta_D(\bar{s}, s)$ and $\vec{v} \in V^{\mathrm{a}}_{X,\bar{s}}$;
- $s.\mathsf{allInstances}() \in V^{\mathrm{a}}_{X,s'}$ for all $s \in |S|$ and $s' \geq_S \mathsf{Set}(s)$;

For the morphisms, define $\mathscr{C}^{\mathrm{a}}(\langle(\gamma, \rho), \omega^\dagger\rangle) = \langle(\gamma, \rho), (\omega^\dagger)^{\mathrm{a}}\rangle : \mathscr{C}^{\mathrm{a}}(\langle(S, D), X\rangle) \to \mathscr{C}^{\mathrm{a}}(\langle(S', D'), X'\rangle)$ such that, by simultaneous induction,

- $(\omega^\dagger)^{\mathrm{a}}_s(x) = \omega^\dagger_s(x)$ for $x \in X_s$;
- $(\omega^\dagger)^{\mathrm{a}}_{s'}(d(\vec{v})) = \begin{cases} \rho(d)((\omega^\dagger)^{\mathrm{a}}_{\bar{s}}(\vec{v})) & \text{if } \omega^\dagger_{\bar{s}_i}(\vec{v}_i) \neq \dagger \text{ for all } 1 \leq i \leq |\vec{v}| \\ \dagger & \text{otherwise} \end{cases}$;
- $(\omega^\dagger)^{\mathrm{a}}_{s'}(s.\mathsf{allInstances}()) = \gamma(s).\mathsf{allInstances}()$.

For each $M = \langle\Sigma, (V, E)\rangle$ in $|\mathcal{G}(Str^\circ)|$ with $\Sigma = (S, D)$ and each $\beta = \langle 1_\Sigma, \beta^{\mathrm{a}}\rangle : \langle\Sigma, X\rangle \to \mathcal{G}(U^\dagger)(M)$ define $(\beta)^{\natural^{\mathrm{a}}}_M = \langle 1_\Sigma, (\beta^{\mathrm{a}})^{\natural^{\mathrm{a}}}_M\rangle : \mathscr{C}^{\mathrm{a}}(\langle\Sigma, X\rangle) \to \mathcal{G}(U^\dagger)(M)$ inductively by

- $(\beta^{\mathrm{a}})^{\natural^{\mathrm{a}}}_{M\,s}(x) = \beta^{\mathrm{a}}_s(x)$ for $x \in X_s$;
- $(\beta^{\mathrm{a}})^{\natural^{\mathrm{a}}}_{M\,s'}(d(\vec{v})) = \begin{cases} E_{\bar{s},s}(d)((\beta^{\mathrm{a}})^{\natural^{\mathrm{a}}}_{M\,\bar{s}}(\vec{v})) & \text{if } (\beta^{\mathrm{a}})^{\natural^{\mathrm{a}}}_{M\,\bar{s}_i}(\vec{v}_i) \neq \dagger \text{ for all } 1 \leq i \leq |\vec{v}| \\ \dagger & \text{otherwise} \end{cases}$;
- $(\beta^{\mathrm{a}})^{\natural^{\mathrm{a}}}_{M\,s'}(s.\mathsf{allInstances}()) = \begin{cases} V_s & \text{if } |V_s| < \infty \\ \dagger & \text{otherwise} \end{cases}$.

Term Charter. Define the embedding natural transformation $\nu^{\mathrm{a}} : 1_{\mathcal{G}(Val^\dagger)} \dot\to \mathscr{C}^{\mathrm{a}}$ again as inclusions, though now as undef-lifting value domain morphisms, i.e., $\nu^{\mathrm{a}}_{\langle(S,D),X\rangle} = \langle 1_{(S,D)}, (\iota^{\mathrm{a}}_{\langle(S,D),X\rangle,s} : X_s \to (V^{\mathrm{a}}_{X,s})_\dagger)_{s \in |S|}\rangle$. This yields the *all-instances term charter* $(\mathscr{C}^{\mathrm{a}}, \nu^{\mathrm{a}}, (-)^{\natural^{\mathrm{a}}})$ over the term charter domain $(\mathbb{S}^\circ, Val^\dagger, Str^\circ, U^\dagger)$, though checking the term charter conditions (C), (K), and (E) becomes a little bit more tedious because of case distinctions.

A.5 Undefinedness

Finally, let us consider OCL's handling of undefinedness. We also add an if-then-else clause as another non-strict function besides the test on undefinedness and the three-valued Boolean connectives.

Terms and Evaluation. The construction functor for *undefinedness terms* $\mathscr{C}^u$: $\mathcal{G}(Val^\dagger) \to \mathcal{G}(Val^\dagger)$ is defined as follows: For the objects, set $\mathscr{C}^u(\langle\langle(S, D), X\rangle\rangle) = \langle(S, D), V^u_X\rangle$ such that inductively

- $x \in V^u_{X,s}$ if $x \in X_s$;
- $d(\vec{v}) \in V^u_{X,s'}$ for all $s' \geq_S s$ if $d \in \delta_D(\bar{s}, s)$ and $\vec{v} \in V^u_{X,\bar{s}}$;
- $\mathsf{undef} \in V^u_{X,s}$ for all $s \in |S|$;
- $v.\mathsf{isUndef}() \in V^u_{X,s'}$ for all $s' \geq_S$ Bool if $v \in V^u_{X,s}$ for $s \in |S|$;
- v_1 and $v_2 \in V^u_{X,s}$ and v_1 or $v_2 \in V^u_{X,s}$ for all $v_1, v_2 \in V^u_{X,\mathsf{Bool}}$ and $s \geq_S$ Bool;
- if v then v_1 else v_2 endif $\in V^u_{X,s'}$ for all $v \in V^u_{X,\mathsf{Bool}}$ and $v_1, v_2 \in V^u_{X,s}$ with $s' \geq_S s$.

For the morphisms, define $\mathscr{C}^u(\langle\langle(\gamma, \rho), \omega^\dagger\rangle\rangle) = \langle(\gamma, \rho), (\omega^\dagger)^u\rangle : \mathscr{C}^u(\langle\langle(S, D), X\rangle\rangle) \to \mathscr{C}^u(\langle\langle(S', D'), X'\rangle\rangle)$ such that, by simultaneous induction,

- $(\omega^\dagger)^u_s(x) = \begin{cases} \mathsf{undef} & \text{if } \omega^\dagger_s(x) = \dagger \\ \omega^\dagger_s(x) & \text{otherwise} \end{cases}$ for $x \in X_s$;
- $(\omega^\dagger)^u_{s'}(d(\vec{v})) = \rho(d)((\omega^\dagger)^u_{\bar{s}}(\vec{v}))$ for $d \in \delta_D(\bar{s}, s)$;
- $(\omega^\dagger)^u_s(\mathsf{undef}) = \mathsf{undef}$;
- $(\omega^\dagger)^u_{s'}(v.\mathsf{isUndef}()) = (\omega^\dagger)^u_s(v).\mathsf{isUndef}()$;
- $(\omega^\dagger)^u_s(v_1 \ bop \ v_2) = (\omega^\dagger)^u_{\mathsf{Bool}}(v_1) \ bop \ (\omega^\dagger)^u_{\mathsf{Bool}}(v_2)$ for $bop \in \{\mathsf{and}, \mathsf{or}\}$;
- $(\omega^\dagger)^u_{s'}(\text{if } v \text{ then } v_1 \text{ else } v_2 \text{ endif}) = \text{if } (\omega^\dagger)^u_{\mathsf{Bool}}(v) \text{ then } (\omega^\dagger)^u_s(v_1) \text{ else } (\omega^\dagger)^u_s(v_2) \text{ endif}$.

(Although $(\omega^\dagger)^u_s(x) = \omega^\dagger_s(x)$ together with a strict extension for $d(\vec{v})$ could have been defined, special measures for if v then v_1 else v_2 endif would have to be taken.)

For each $M = \langle\Sigma, (V, E)\rangle$ in $|\mathcal{G}(Str^\circ)|$ with $\Sigma = (S, D)$ and each $\beta = \langle1_\Sigma, \beta^u\rangle : \langle\Sigma, X\rangle \to \mathcal{G}(U^\dagger)(M)$ define $(\beta)^{\natural^u_M} = \langle1_\Sigma, (\beta^u)^{\natural^u_M}\rangle : \mathscr{C}^u(\langle\Sigma, X\rangle) \to \mathcal{G}(U^\dagger)(M)$ inductively by

- $(\beta^u)^{\natural^u_M}_s(x) = \beta^u_s(x)$ for $x \in X_s$;
- $(\beta^u)^{\natural^u_M}_{s'}(d(\vec{v})) = \begin{cases} E_{\bar{s},s}(d)((\beta^u)^{\natural^u_M}_{\bar{s}}(\vec{v})) & \text{if } (\beta^u)^{\natural^u_M}_{\bar{s}_i}(\vec{v}_i) \neq \dagger \text{ for all } 1 \leq i \leq |\vec{v}| \\ \dagger & \text{otherwise} \end{cases}$;
- $(\beta^u)^{\natural^u_M}_s(\mathsf{undef}) = \dagger$;
- $(\beta^u)^{\natural^u_M}_{s'}(v.\mathsf{isUndef}()) = \begin{cases} tt & \text{if } (\beta^u)^{\natural^u_M}_s(v) = \dagger \\ f\!f & \text{otherwise} \end{cases}$;
- $(\beta^u)^{\natural^u_M}_s(v_1 \text{ and } v_2) = \begin{cases} tt & \text{if } (\beta^u)^{\natural^u_M}_{\mathsf{Bool}}(v_1) = tt \text{ and } (\beta^u)^{\natural^u_M}_{\mathsf{Bool}}(v_2) = tt \\ f\!f & \text{if } (\beta^u)^{\natural^u_M}_{\mathsf{Bool}}(v_1) = f\!f \text{ or } (\beta^u)^{\natural^u_M}_{\mathsf{Bool}}(v_2) = f\!f \\ \dagger & \text{otherwise} \end{cases}$;
- $(\beta^u)^{\natural^u_M}_s(v_1 \text{ or } v_2) = \begin{cases} tt & \text{if } (\beta^u)^{\natural^u_M}_{\mathsf{Bool}}(v_1) = tt \text{ or } (\beta^u)^{\natural^u_M}_{\mathsf{Bool}}(v_2) = tt \\ f\!f & \text{if } (\beta^u)^{\natural^u_M}_{\mathsf{Bool}}(v_1) = f\!f \text{ and } (\beta^u)^{\natural^u_M}_{\mathsf{Bool}}(v_2) = f\!f \\ \dagger & \text{otherwise} \end{cases}$

$$- (\beta^{\mathrm{u}})_s^{\natural_M^{\mathrm{u}}} (\text{if } v \text{ then } v_1 \text{ else } v_2 \text{ endif}) = \begin{cases} (\beta^{\mathrm{u}})_s^{\natural_M^{\mathrm{u}}} (v_1) & \text{if } (\beta^{\mathrm{u}})_s^{\natural_M^{\mathrm{u}}} (v) = tt \\ (\beta^{\mathrm{u}})_s^{\natural_M^{\mathrm{u}}} (v_2) & \text{if } (\beta^{\mathrm{u}})_s^{\natural_M^{\mathrm{u}}} (v) = f\!f \\ \dagger & \text{otherwise} \end{cases}.$$

Term Charter. The *undefinedness term charter* $(\mathscr{C}^{\mathrm{u}}, \nu^{\mathrm{u}}, (-)^{\natural^{\mathrm{u}}})$ over the term charter domain $(\mathbb{S}^\circ, Val^\dagger, Str^\circ, U^\dagger)$ uses the analogous embedding natural transformation $\nu^{\mathrm{u}} : 1_{\mathcal{G}(Val^\dagger)} \overset{\cdot}{\to} \mathscr{C}^{\mathrm{u}}$ as the all-instances term charter. Checking the term charter conditions (C), (K), and (E) now involves even more case distinctions. In contrast to the all-instances case, the undef-lifting value domain morphism constructed by $\mathscr{C}^{\mathrm{u}}$ not simply is a strict extension to terms, but treats $\dagger$ specially in order to avoid problems with the if-then-else clause.

Towards an Institutional Framework
for Heterogeneous Formal Development in UML
— A Position Paper —

Alexander Knapp[1], Till Mossakowski[2], and Markus Roggenbach[3]

[1] Universität Augsburg, Germany
[2] Otto-von-Guericke Universität Magdeburg, Germany
[3] Swansea University, UK

Abstract. We present a framework for formal software development with UML. In contrast to previous approaches to equipping UML with a formal semantics, we propose an institution-based heterogeneous approach. This can express suitable formal semantics of the different UML diagram types directly, without the need to map everything to one specific formalism (let it be first-order logic or graph grammars). We provide ideas how different aspects of the formal development process can be coherently formalised, ranging from requirements over design and Hoare-style conditions on code to the implementation itself. The framework can be used to verify consistency of different UML diagrams both horizontally (e.g., consistency among various requirements) as well as vertically (e.g., correctness of design or implementation w.r.t. the requirements).

Keywords: UML, heterogeneous formal methods, institutions.

1 Introduction

In Martin Wirsing's research, the development of applicable formal methods plays an important role. Martin has examined real-world modeling and programming languages like UML and Java, and has studied suitable formal theories that can lead to increased trustworthiness due to the possibility of formal verification. In this work, we build on and extend the first author's joint work with Martin Wirsing about views in software development, heterogeneous semantics of UML, and multi-modeling languages [24,34,3,7]. In fact, the integration of different, heterogeneous views on and in a software system is a continual theme in Martin's research, be it for data bases [10], multimedia systems [20], or mobile systems [22]. We also build on joint work of Martin Wirsing with the second and third author on the design of CASL [31]; indeed, in the 1990s, Martin hosted some of the CASL/CoFI meetings and provided valuable input for the CASL design. For the present paper, CASL forms a building block for the distributed ontology, modeling and specification language (DOL), which has evolved from a generalisation of CASL to heterogeneous specifications.

In the industrial design of software for critical systems, the Unified Modeling Language (UML) is an often used development mechanism. In aerospace industry, e.g., the company Aero Engine Controls (AEC)[1] uses the UML to define the software architecture

---

[1] AEC is the former name of Rolls-Royce Control and Data Services,
http://www.controlsdata.com

R. De Nicola and R. Hennicker (Eds.): Wirsing Festschrift, LNCS 8950, pp. 215–230, 2015.

of aeroplane engine controllers through various levels of abstraction from a layered architecture overview to a detailed class, operation and attribute definition of the software components. This model is then used for code generation. Typically, the software components developed are either reactive or logic-based and/or stateful in nature, where notations such as UML state diagrams are used to define the required behaviour [17]. Micro-controllers in the automotive sector or, in the medical sector, ventricular assistance devices exemplify further uses of UML in the development of critical systems.

The UML is an OMG standard [32], which describes a language family of 14 types of diagrams, of structural and behavioural nature. A typical development by AEC involves about eight different UML diagrams [18]. The OMG specification provides an informal semantics of nine sub-languages in isolation. The languages are mostly linked through a common meta-model, i.e., through abstract syntax only. This situation leads to a gap between standards' recommendation to apply formal methods, and current industrial practice, which by using the UML lacks the semantic foundations to apply such methods. One common approach to deal with this gap is to define a comprehensive semantics for the UML using a system model, e.g., [4,5]. However, this is a thorny business, as every detail has to be encoded into one, necessarily quite complex semantics. Furthermore, such an approach has difficulties to cater for UML's variations of usage, leading to company or domain-specific variations. On the other hand, there are many approaches like component models (e.g. [16,2]) which are based on sound theory, but do not meet the main goal of the present work: to set up a framework in which one can eventually capture precisely the semantics and semantic variation points of the UML standard (including all its idiosyncrasies), such that a holistic model-driven development in UML can be complemented with rigorous consistency and verification conditions.

In this position paper, we outline a competing approach by providing a heterogeneous semantics, where we extend [7] by considering a subset of diagrams rich enough for industrial use, adding components and composite structures as well as behavioural and protocol state machines. We substantiate this claim by a small case study that is modelled holistically, using a variety of different diagram types. We distinguish between diagrams for properties, types and instances, where we express the meaning of a model in a sub-language/diagram directly in an appropriate semantic domain. We also distinguish diagrams for requirements, design, deployment and implementation. This degree of completeness in the coverage of the development process has not been achieved so far.

We further systematically identify meaningful connections given by the abstract syntax of the UML specification or which can be gleaned from its semantic description. The separation between the meaning of the individual diagrams and their relation allows our approach to be adopted by different methodologies, for instance an object-oriented approach or a component-based one.

2   Methodology

Our overall aim is to provide qualified formal methods for dependable software design for critical systems, especially embedded, reactive systems based on UML. We illustrate this aim by first giving a case study in UML and then discussing desirable checks for consistency between the various artefacts. We then explain how languages and UML diagram types involved in a software design can be viewed as types, instances, and properties, either on the modelling level or on the implementation level. Finally, we address the topic of semantic variation points.

2.1 ATM Case Study

In order to illustrate our heterogeneous semantics and method, we present as a running example the design of a traditional automatic teller machine (ATM) connected to a bank. For simplicity, we only describe the handling of entering a card and a PIN with the ATM. After entering the card, one has three trials for entering the correct PIN (which is checked by the bank). After three unsuccessful trials the card is kept.

Requirements. Figure 1(a) shows a possible *interaction* between an atm and a bank, which consists out of four messages: the atm requests the bank to verify if a card and PIN number combination is valid, in the first case the bank requests to reenter the PIN, in the second case the verification is successful.

The composite structure of the ATM-bank system is specified in the *component diagram* in Fig. 1(b). In order to communicate with a bank component, the atm component has a *behaviour port* called bankCom and the bank component has a behaviour port atmCom. Furthermore, atm has a port userCom to a user. Figure 1(c) provides structural information in the form of the interfaces specifying what is provided at the userCom port of the atm instance (UserIn) and what is required (UserOut). An interface is a set of operations that other model elements have to implement. In our case, the interface is described in a *class diagram*. Here, the operation keepCard is enriched with the OCL constraint trialsNum >= 3, which refines its semantics: keepCard can only be invoked if the OCL constraints hold.

The communication protocol required between the atm's port bankCom and the bank's port atmCom is captured with a protocol state machine, see Fig. 1(d): After a verify message from atm, either verified or reenterPIN can be sent as a reply from bank; atm can request a card to be rendered invalid whenever it has not just asked to verify a card and a PIN.

Design. The dynamic behaviour of the atm component is specified by the *state machine* shown in Fig. 1(e). The machine consists of five states including Idle, CardEntered, etc. Beginning in the initial Idle state, the user can *trigger* a state change by entering the card, where we indicate that the event card has to occur at port userCom. This has the *effect* that the parameter c from the card event (declared for operation card in Fig. 1(c)) is assigned to the cardId in the atm component. Entering a PIN triggers another transition to PINEntered. Then the ATM requests verification from the bank using its bankCom port. The transition to Verifying uses a *completion event*: No explicit trigger is declared and the machine autonomously creates such an event whenever a state is completed, i.e., all internal activities of the state are finished (in our example there are no such activities). In case the interaction with the bank results in reenterPIN, and the *guard* trialsNum < 3 is true, the user can again enter a PIN. If, on the other hand, trialsNum >= 3, the user

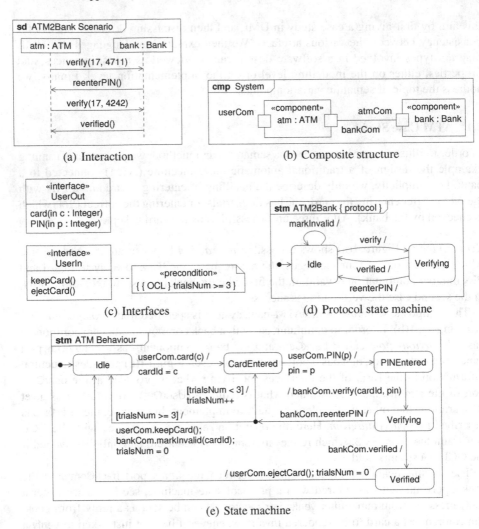

Fig. 1. ATM example

is informed that the card is kept by userCom.keepCard(), and the bank is informed to render the card invalid by bankCom.markInvalid(cardId).

Deployment. Although the UML allows to specify which component instances should run on which computational resources and which physical connectors transport their communication, we currently restrict ourselves to specifying which component and connector instances have to be present at system start. This initial configuration is described in a *composite structure diagram*, see Fig. 1(b) now interpreted at the component instance level. In particular, instances of the behaviour specifications for the components have to be deployed accordingly. The starting configuration could change over time by changing the wiring of the connectors to ports as well as creating or deleting component instances.

Code. The state machine shown in Fig. 1(e) can be implemented in the programming language C, enriched with pre-/post-conditions written in the ANSI/ISO C Specification Language (ACSL). The code example below shows how the event card is encoded as a C function, where the ACSL annotations ensure that the system is in some defined state and that the number of trials to re-enter the PIN is smaller than three.

```
typedef enum states {
  EMPTY = 0, IDLE = 1, CARDENTERED = 2,
  PINENTERED = 3, VERIFYING = 4, PINVERIFIED = 5
} states_t;
int cardId = 0; int pin = 0; int trialsNum = 0;
states_t state = EMPTY;

/*@
requires state != EMPTY; requires trialsNum <= 3;
ensures state != EMPTY;  ensures trialsNum <= 3;
@*/
void card(int c) {
  switch (state) {
    case IDLE:
      cardId = c;
      state = CARDENTERED;
      break;
    default:
  }
}
```

2.2   Consistency and Satisfaction

A typical software devolopment for a critical system will cover requirements, design, deployment, and code using several sub-languages and diagram types summarised in Fig. 2 and classified towards a software design process. In fact, class and component diagrams also will be used for expressing requirement, as already illustrated by our small case study.

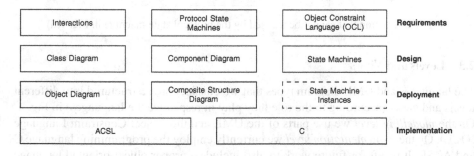

Fig. 2. Methodological use of languages and diagrams considered

It is desirable to detect inconsistencies at an early stage of the development in order to ease corrections and avoid costly re-engineering at a late stage (e.g. during the implementation phase). While there are some tools providing static inconsistency checks based on UML's meta-model, only few works consider dynamic checks, and generally only for specific UML diagram types, e.g. [25].

The analysis of UML models can proceed either horizontally within the requirements or within the design level checking for consistency within the level, or vertically checking for satisfaction between these two levels, see Fig. 4. A typical horizontal consistency check on the requirements level would ask if the sequential composition of actions in an interaction diagram is justified by an accompanying OCL specification. A typical vertical satisfaction check between the requirements and the design level would ask if the behaviour prescribed in an interaction diagram is realisable by several state machine (instance)s cooperating according to a composite structure diagram. The notion of a state machine instance will be explained in the next section. Code generation transforms a UML logical design to code templates with semantic annotations in the form of pre-/post-conditions and invariants. If the templates are completed satisfying the semantic annotations, it is guaranteed that the resulting code is a correct model of the logical design and therefore, by the vertical checks, also for the requirements.

Concerning Fig. 1, there are the following (succeeding) consistency and satisfiability checks: speaking horizontally, the interaction in Fig. 1(a) can be realised by the protocol state machine in Fig. 1(d), which in turn (vertically) refines to the behavioural state machine in Fig. 1(e), which in turn (vertically) refines to the C code shown at the end of Section 2.1.

A simple example for a failing horizontal check among several requirements is the interaction in Fig. 3, which cannot be realised by the protocol state machine in Fig. 1(d).

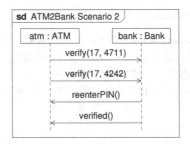

Fig. 3. Interaction that cannot be realised by the protocol state machine in Fig. 1(d)

2.3 Levels and Views

The languages and UML diagram types that we consider are restructured into different levels and views (according to the role they play in respective the languages) in Fig. 4. On the *modelling level* we use parts of the UML and the Object Constraint Language (OCL). On the *implementation level* we currently employ the programming language C and ACSL. It is left for future work to also include a proper object-oriented language such as Java together with some specification formalism.

In the *types view* of the modelling level we look at class diagrams for modelling data; component diagrams for modelling components; and state machines for specifying dynamic behaviour. These diagrams can be instantiated in the *instance view* using composite structure diagrams for showing component configurations; and object diagrams for showing concrete data. Although they are not present in UML, we also have added state machine instances (in a dashed box). Constraints on the models can be specified in the *properties view* using interactions, i.e., sequence diagrams or communication diagrams, for prescribing message exchanges between components and objects; protocol state machines for specifying port behaviour; and the OCL for detailing the behaviour of components and objects in terms of invariants and method pre-/post-conditions.

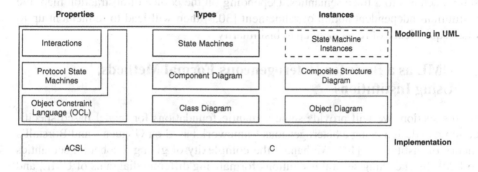

Fig. 4. Languages and diagrams considered

2.4   Semantic Variation Points

The UML specification uses the notion of "semantic variation point" whenever she does not want to fix or enforce a particular meaning for a construct, but sees room for variable but valid interpretations useful in different contexts. Examples of such semantic variation points include the behaviour of an operation invocation when a pre-condition is not satisfied; the compatibility of connectable elements, like components; the forwarding of requests at a port with several outgoing connectors; the ordering of events in event pools; the time intervals between event occurrence, event dispatching, and consumption; or the reception of an event in an unexpected situation for a protocol state machine. Different domains or implementation technologies will require different resolutions, like whether message overtaking is possible in a middle-ware. Additionally, some resolutions may enable particular validation or verification techniques, e.g., when using multi-sets or bounded queues for event pools.

However, the specification does not show clear-cut means to resolve these variation points: Not surprisingly, no parameterised semantics is explained where the resolution of a semantic variation point would simply amount to setting a particular value — which, in fact, would be quite hard more often than not. More embarrassingly, also no dedicated syntactic means are provided for at least specifying that a particular meaning is intended by the use of a feature subject to semantic variation. For the syntactical side, the most common, though rather *ad hoc*, resort is to employ stereotypes to express that, say, the event pool for a state machine is to be realised as a queue, or that the violation of an operation's precondition will result in an error. For the semantical issues, the use of a comprehensive system model approach would require to corral all possible inter-pretations of a semantic variation point into a single common ground using, e.g., loose specifications.

By contrast, heterogeneous institutional semantics offer the additional possibility to provide particular stand-alone semantics for different resolutions of semantic vari-ation points. The mutual effects of combining different resolutions can be identified and consistent resolutions can be plugged together. Also, different choices for semantic variation points can be related via abstraction maps. For example, it is easy to design an institution comorphism that abstracts the labelled transition system semantics of state machines to a trace semantics. Depending on the choice of abstraction map, the institution-independent notion of refinement [30,8] then will lead to refinement up to trace equivalence of refinement up to bisimilarity.

3   UML as a Basis for Heterogeneous Formal Methods, Using Institutions

In this section, we will provide some semantic foundations for model based specifi-cation and design using a heterogeneous framework based on Goguen's and Burstall's theory of institutions [14]. We handle the complexity of giving a coherent semantics to UML by sketching several institutions formalising different diagrams of UML, and several institution translations (formalised as so-called institution morphisms and co-morphisms) describing their interaction and information flow. The central advantage of this approach over previous approaches to formal semantics for UML (e.g. [25]) is that each UML diagram type can stay "as-is", without the need of a coding using graph grammars (as in [12]) or some logic (as in [25]). This also keeps full flexibility in the choice of both the development method and the verification mechanisms. The for-malisation of UML diagrams as institutions has the additional benefit that a notion of refinement comes for free, see [30,8]. The exact nature of the thus obtained refinement relation depends on the semantic choices that have been made.

This systematic coverage in a single semantic based meta-formalism is unique. We discuss semantic links in the form of institution (co-)morphisms, that, on the one hand, provide the basis for correct model transformations and validations, and on the other hand give rise to an integrated semantic view (via the so-called Grothendieck institution [9,26]) on the identified UML subset as well as the target implementation languages. Institution theory provides an adequate abstraction level for such a semantic integration. The framework is flexible enough to support various development paradigms as well as different resolutions of UML's semantic variation points. This is the crucial advantage of the proposed approach to the semantics of UML, compared to existing approaches in the literature which map UML to a specific global semantic domain in a fixed way.

3.1   Institutions and Their (Co)Morphisms

Institutions [14] are an abstract formalisation of the notion of logical system. Informally, institutions provide four different logical notions: signatures, sentences, models and satisfaction. Signatures provide the vocabulary that may appear in sentences and that is interpreted in models. The satisfaction relation determines whether a given sentence is satisfied in a given model. The exact nature of signatures, sentences and models is left unspecified, which leads to a great flexibility. This is crucial for the possibility to model UML diagrams types (which do not at first sight look like logics) as institutions.

An important feature of institutions is the presence of signature morphisms, which can be seen as mappings between signatures. Sentences can be translated along signature morphisms, and models reduced *against* signature morphisms. The satisfaction condition states that satisfaction is invariant under change of notation and enlargement of context (along a signature morphism). For details, we refer to [14,33].

It is possible to define standard logical notions like logical consequence, logical theory, satisfiabilty etc. as well as languages for structured specification and refinement in an institution-independent way [33].

For relating institutions in a semantics preserving way, we consider institution morphisms [14]. Given institutions I and J, an *institution morphism* consists of (i) a mapping from I-signatures to J-signatures (also for signature morphisms); (ii) a mapping from J-sentences to I-sentences; and (iii) a mapping from I-models to J-models. Again, there is a satisfaction condition governing these mappings. Dually, we consider institution comorphisms [15]. They are like institution morphisms, except that the direction of sentence and model translations are reversed.

The methodological need for these two kinds of mappings between institutions will be explained in Sect. 3.4 below. Both morphisms and comorphisms also come in a "semi" variant (i.e. semi-morphisms and semi-comorphisms) [15]. These omit both the sentence translation and the satisfaction condition. Semi-(co-)morphisms can provide a model-theoretic link between institutions that are too different to permit a sentence translation, e.g. OCL and state machines.

3.2   Heterogeneous Formal Semantics of Languages and Diagrams

Carrying out our program of institutionalising UML is ongoing work. In this position paper, we review this work and sketch how it can be extended to all diagrams in Fig. 2.

Building on existing UML semantics, see [25] for an overview, we want to turn UML's sub-languages and diagram types into separate institutions[2]. For substantial fragments of several UML diagram types, we have already provided a formalisation as institutions:

Class diagrams In [7], we have sketched an institution for class diagrams, which has
  been detailed in [19]. It includes a construction for stereotypes.
Component diagrams form an institution similar to that for class diagrams. The main
  difference are the connector and port types, which however are quite similar to
  associations.
Object diagrams are essentially reifications of models of class diagrams.
Composite structure diagrams are similar to object diagrams. The main difference
  are the connectors, which however are quite similar to the links of object diagrams.

---

[2] Alternative or complementing approaches like statecharts instead of UML state machines or SysML/MARTE components could be added to this family of institutions.

Interactions In [7], we have sketched an institution for interactions, as well as their interconnection (also with class diagrams) via institution comorphisms.

OCL In [7], we have sketched institutions for OCL. In [6], the OCL semantics is presented in more detail. An institution based on this is in preparation.

State machines In [23], we have provided in full detail institutions for UML state machines and protocol state machines (so far only for non-hierarchical states, a generalization to hierarchical states is in preparation). Both institutions are very similar; only their sentences differ in that UML protocol state machines have a post condition instead of an action. Post conditions can also speak about messages being sent (using OCL).

Formalising both C and ACSL as institutions is future work.

3.3 Institutional Interaction of Heterogeneous UML Diagrams

We now will discuss how different diagram types can be linked using the institutional approach. A characteristic example is the interplay between class diagrams, component diagrams and state machines. Here, an *environment* institution [23] provides the interface necessary to define state machines. Signatures in this environment institution fix the conditions which can be used in guards of transitions, the actions for the effects of transitions, and also the messages that can be sent from a state machine. The source of this information are the class and component diagrams: The conditions and actions involve the properties available in the classes or components, the messages are derived from the available signals and operations. The sentences of this environment institution form a simple dynamic logic (inspired by OCL). This logic can express that if a guard holds as pre-condition when executing an action, then a certain set of messages has been sent out and another guard holds as post-condition. In particular, this environment institution forms the interface to the outside; different institutions for classes and components can be linked to it via (co-)morphisms.

A family of institutions for *state machines* (and similarly for protocol state machines) is then parameterized over such environment institutions. Using a product construction on the state machine institution, *communicating state machines*, with their linkage described in a composite structure, can be captured. The essential idea behind the product construction is to control the flow of messages in such a way that each message is sent to the correct event pool.

Example 1. Consider the composite structure diagram in Fig. 1(b), showing instances atm and bank of the ATM and Bank components, respectively, that are connected through their bankCom and atmCom ports. In execution, atm and bank will exchange messages, as prescribed by their state machines, and this exchange is reflected by the product which internalises those events that are part of the common signature. On the other hand, messages to the outside, i.e., through the userCom port are still visible.

3.4 Transformations Among UML institutions

Figure 5 gives an overview of the transformations to be developed between the modeling languages, diagram types, and additional languages. We claim that the transformations in this Figure can be formalised as institution morphisms and comorphisms. An institution morphism (represented by a solid line in the figure) roughly corresponds to a projection from a "richer" to a "poorer" logic, expressing that the "richer" logic has some more features, which are forgotten by the morphism. The main purpose of the institution morphisms is the ability to express, e.g., that an interaction diagram and a state machine are compatible because they are expressed over the same class diagram. Institution morphisms thus enable the formalisation of heterogeneous UML specifications as structured specifications over the Grothendieck institution, a flattening of the diagram of institutions and morphisms [9]. Practically, these structured Grothendieck specifications can be formulated in the distributed ontology, modeling and specification language (DOL), which currently is being standardized in the OMG (see `ontoiop.org` and [28]).

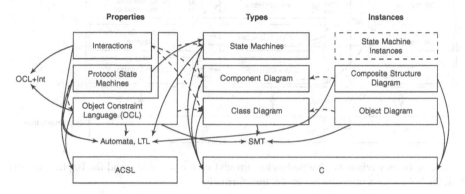

Fig. 5. Institution morphisms (dashed arrows) and institution co-morphisms (solid arrows) between the languages and diagrams

By contrast, institution comorphisms (represented by dashed lines in Fig. 5) are often more complex. Roughly, a comorphism corresponds to an encoding of one logic into another one. The purpose of institution comorphisms is threefold: **(1)** to provide a means for expressing the dynamic checks (see below) in the institutional framework, **(2)** to obtain tool support for the various UML diagrams by using comorphisms into tool-supported institutions, and **(3)** to transform UML diagrams into ACSL specifications and C programs.

Dynamic checks and tool support involve additional institutions (also depicted in Fig. 5, but not formalised in detail here) for certain automata, like those used in the model checker SPIN, and satisfiability modulo theories (SMT) provers, as well as linear temporal logic. The modeling language institutions can be embedded into these, paving the way for tool and prover support.

3.5 Consistency and Satisfaction, Revisited

The horizontal dimension of the relationship between the different models has to ensure *consistency* of the models, i.e., that the models fit together and describe a coherent

system. The same has to be checked on the implementation level for the consistency between the C program and the ACSL specification; however, here we can reuse existing
theory and tools.

There are different kinds of consistency checks on the modelling level: Static checks
ensuring type consistency and type correctness between types and instances. Dynamic
checks include the properties and one or several cooperating instances or types. Most of
the dynamic checks are theoretically undecidable, thus fully automatic tools will not be
able to answer all instances. However, in many cases, useful automatic approximations
are possible, while in other cases, manual effort may be involved.

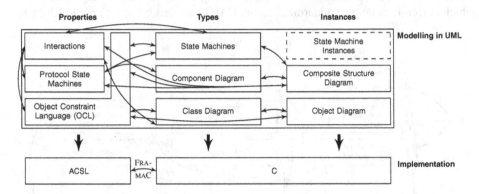

Fig. 6. Consistency relations (double-headed arrows) on the modelling and the implementation
level; the bold arrows represent the model transformations

Figure 6 gives an overview of useful relations between different kinds of diagrams,
along which consistency checks are possible. Here, we list only a few of these. Some
useful static checks are:

S1. Does an OCL specification or a composite structure diagram only use the methods
    of a class diagram?
S2. Does a state machine or an interaction comply with the interfaces referred to in a
    composite structure diagram?
S3. Does an instance diagram (an object or a composite structure diagram) comply to
    its corresponding type diagram (a class or a component diagram)?
S4. Do the objects used in an interaction diagram form an object diagram complying
    to a class diagram?

Here are some useful dynamic checks:

D1. Does an object or composite structure diagram satisfy an OCL invariant? Here
    we use institution semi-comorphisms from the OCL institution to the object and
    composite structure diagram institution that turn a model of the object or composite
    structure diagram into a model of the OCL invariant.
D2. Does a state machine satisfy an OCL invariant or an OCL pre-/post-condition?
    Here we use a semi-comorphism from the OCL institution to the state machines
    institution that takes the runs of the state machine and selects those states and tran-
    sitions that are relevant for the invariant or the method with pre-/post-conditions.

However, the UML does not specify the time point when the OCL post-condition should be evaluated; one possibility is to choose the finishing of the fired transition.

D3. Do the protocol state machines at the ends of a connector of a composite structure diagram fit together? Here we use a comorphism from the protocol state machine institution into a temporal logic institution [13], where we can form the product of the protocol state machines along the connector. However, the precise nature of compatibility may be seen as a "semantic variation point". An important question is the absence of deadlocks and buffer overruns.

D4. Is the sequential composition of methods in an interaction diagram justified by the state machines and/or the OCL specification? For the relation to an OCL specification we use a co-span of institution comorphisms between the interactions institution and the OCL institution [7]. At least two links are possible: In a strict interpretation, for each pair of successive methods in the interaction there must be a state meeting the post-condition of the first method and the pre-condition of the second method. In a more loose interpretation, a sequence of additional method calls, not prescribed but also not excluded by the interaction, must be possible to reach the pre-condition of the second method from the post-condition of the first method. For also considering state machines, the co-span approach is extended by also involving the state machines institution.

D5. Does an interaction comply with the protocol state machines? Here we proceed similarly to the case where an interaction is checked against a state machine and an OCL specification using a comorphism turning the protocol state machine into an OCL specification.

D6. Does a state machine refine the protocol state machines in a component diagram? This is expressible as a heterogeneous refinement from the protocol state machines to the state machine using a semi-comorphism which keeps signatures and models as they are (protocol state machines and state machines only differ in their sentences).

Example 2. Though our running example of an ATM machine is quite simple, it is rich enough to illustrate some dynamic checks. The interface UserIn in Fig. 1(c) requires the operation keepCard only to be invoked when the precondition trialsNum >= 3 holds. This property holds for the state machine in Fig. 1(e) thanks to the guard trialsNum < 3 – an illustration of check D1. This property trivially holds for the interaction shown in Figure 1(a) as keepCard is not invoked – an illustration of check D3.

4   Tools

The Heterogeneous Tool Set (Hets) [27,29] provides analysis and proof support for multi-logic specifications. The central idea of Hets is to provide a general framework for formal methods integration and proof management that is equipped with a strong semantic (institution-based) backbone. One can think of Hets acting like a motherboard where different expansion cards can be plugged in, the expansion cards here being individual institutions (with their analysis and proof tools) as well as institution (co)morphisms. The Hets motherboard already has plugged in a number of expansion cards (e.g., SAT solvers, automated and interactive theorem provers, model finders, model checkers, and more). Hence, a variety of tools is available, without the need to hard-wire each tool to the logic at hand. Via suitable translations, new formalisms can be connected to existing tools.

We have just started to integrate first institutions for UML, such as class diagrams, into Hets. In order to obtain proof support for the methodology presented in this paper, beyond the individual institutions, also the morphisms and comorphisms need to be implemented in Hets. Moreover, we plan to connect Hets to the tool HugoRT [21]. HugoRT can, on the one hand, perform certain static checks on UML diagrams. Moreover, it provides transformations of UML diagrams to automata and linear temporal logic formulas, which can then be fed into model checkers like SPIN in order to check certain properties. The crucial benefit of our approach is a clear separation of concerns: verification conditions for consistency and satisfaction checks can be formulated abstractly in terms of the UML institutions and (co)morphisms described above. In a second step, these checks can then be reformulated in terms of specific logics and tools that have been connected to Hets.

5 Conclusion

We have outlined an institution-based semantics for the main UML diagrams. Moreover, we have sketched a methodology how consistency among UML diagrams and with implementation languages can be modeled at the institutional level and supported with tools.

Much remains to be done to fill in the details. Semantically, the greatest missing bit is certainly the institutional formalisation of programming languages and their Hoare logics, like C and ACSL, or Java and JML. Here, we want to follow the ideas sketched by A. Tarlecki and D. Sannella [33, Ex. 4.1.32, Ex. 10.1.17] for rendering an imperative programming language as an institution. The semantic basis could be a simplified version of the operational semantics of C. Ellison and G. Rosu [11]. The concepts for institutionalising a Hoare logic like ACSL on the basis of its specification [1] can be similar as for OCL. On the tools side, it is future work to make UML institutions, checks and code generation part of the tool Hets. This will allow also non-experts in institution theory to apply the suggested framework.

Acknowledgements. The authors would like to thank the reviewers of their valuable feedback, the editors for their considered handling of this paper, and Erwin R. Catesbeiana for pointing out the many sources of inconsistency.

References

1. Baudin, P., Cuoq, P., Filliâtre, J.-C., Marché, C., Monate, B., Moy, Y., Prevosto, V.: ACSL: ANSI/ISO C Specification Language. Report. In: CEA 2012 (2012)
2. Bauer, S.S., Hennicker, R.: Views on Behaviour Protocols and Their Semantic Foundation. In: Kurz, A., Lenisa, M., Tarlecki, A. (eds.) CALCO 2009. LNCS, vol. 5728, pp. 367–382. Springer, Heidelbrg (2009)

3. Boronat, A., Knapp, A., Meseguer, J., Wirsing, M.: What Is a Multi-modeling Language? In: Corradini, A., Montanari, U. (eds.) WADT 2008. LNCS, vol. 5486, pp. 71–87. Springer, Heidelberg (2009)
4. Broy, M., Cengarle, M.V., Grönniger, H., Rumpe, B.: Considerations and Rationale for a UML System Model. In: Lano (ed.) [25], ch. 3, pp. 43–60
5. Broy, M., Cengarle, M.V., Grönniger, H., Rumpe, B.: Definition of the System Model. In: Lano (ed.) [25], ch. 4, pp. 61–93
6. Cengarle, M.V., Knapp, A.: OCL 1.4/5 vs. 2.0 Expressions — Formal Semantics and Expressiveness. Softw. Syst. Model. 3(1), 9–30 (2004)
7. Cengarle, M.V., Knapp, A., Tarlecki, A., Wirsing, M.: A Heterogeneous Approach to UML Semantics. In: Degano, P., De Nicola, R., Meseguer, J. (eds.) Concurrency, Graphs and Models. LNCS, vol. 5065, pp. 383–402. Springer, Heidelberg (2008)
8. Codescu, M., Mossakowski, T., Sannella, D., Tarlecki, A.: Specification Refinements: Calculi, Tools, and Applications (Submitted, 2014)
9. Diaconescu, R.: Grothendieck Institutions. Applied Cat. Struct. 10, 383–402 (2002)
10. Dosch, W., Mascari, G., Wirsing, M.: On the Algebraic Specification of Databases. In: Proc. 8th Int. Conf. Very Large Data Bases (VLDB 1982), pp. 370–385. Morgan Kaufmann (1982)
11. Ellison, C., Rosu, G.: An Executable Formal Semantics of C With Applications. In: Field, J., Hicks, M. (eds.) Proc. 39th ACM SIGPLAN-SIGACT Symp. Principles of Programming Languages (POPL 2012), pp. 533–544. ACM (2012)
12. Engels, G., Heckel, R., Küster, J.M.: The Consistency Workbench: A Tool for Consistency Management in UML-Based Development. In: Stevens, P., Whittle, J., Booch, G. (eds.) UML 2003. LNCS, vol. 2863, pp. 356–359. Springer, Heidelberg (2003)
13. Fiadeiro, J.L.: Categories for Software Engineering. Springer (2005)
14. Goguen, J.A., Burstall, R.M.: Institutions: Abstract Model Theory for Specification and Programming. J. ACM 39, 95–146 (1992)
15. Goguen, J.A., Rosu, G.: Institution Morphisms. Formal Asp. Comp. 13, 274–307 (2002)
16. Hennicker, R., Janisch, S., Knapp, A.: On the Observable Behaviour of Composite Components. In: Proc. 5th Int. Wsh. Formal Aspects of Component Software (FACS 2008). ENTCS 260, pp. 125–153 (2010)
17. Hutchesson, S.: Chief software architect at AEC. Industrial case study outline (2012)
18. Hutchesson, S.: Chief software architect at AEC. Personal communication (2012)
19. James, P., Knapp, A., Mossakowski, T., Roggenbach, M.: Designing Domain Specific Languages – A Craftsman's Approach for the Railway Domain Using CASL. In: Martí-Oliet, N., Palomino, M. (eds.) WADT 2012. LNCS, vol. 7841, pp. 178–194. Springer, Heidelberg (2013)
20. Knapp, A., et al.: Epk-fix: Methods and tools for engineering electronic product catalogues. In: Steinmetz, R. (ed.) IDMS 1997. LNCS, vol. 1309, pp. 199–209. Springer, Heidelberg (1997)
21. Knapp, A., Merz, S., Rauh, C.: Model checking - timed UML state machines and collaborations. In: Damm, W., Olderog, E.-R. (eds.) FTRTFT 2002. LNCS, vol. 2469, pp. 395–416. Springer, Heidelberg (2002)
22. Knapp, A., Merz, S., Wirsing, M., Zappe, J.: Specification and Refinement of Mobile Systems in MTLA and Mobile UML. Theo. Comp. Sci. 351(2), 184–202 (2006)
23. Knapp, A., Mossakowski, T., Roggenbach, M., Glauer, M.: An Institution for Simple UML State Machines. In: Egyed, A., Schaefer, I. (eds.) FASE 2015. LNCS. Springer (to appear, 2015)
24. Knapp, A., Wirsing, M.: A Formal Approach to Object-Oriented Software Engineering. Theo. Comp. Sci. 285, 519–560 (2002)
25. Lano, K.: UML 2 — Semantics and Applications. Wiley, Chichester (2009)

26. Mossakowski, T.: Comorphism-Based Grothendieck Logics. In: Diks, K., Rytter, W. (eds.) MFCS 2002. LNCS, vol. 2420, pp. 593–604. Springer, Heidelberg (2002)
27. Mossakowski, T., Autexier, S., Hutter, D.: Development Graphs — Proof Management for Structured Specifications. J. Log. Alg. Program. 67(1–2), 114–145 (2006)
28. Mossakowski, T., Kutz, O., Codescu, M., Lange, C.: The Distributed Ontology, Modeling and Specification Language. In: Proc. 7th Int. Wsh. Modular Ontologies (WoMO 2013). CEUR-WS 1081, CEUR (2013)
29. Mossakowski, T., Maeder, C., Lüttich, K.: The Heterogeneous Tool Set, HETS. In: Grumberg, O., Huth, M. (eds.) TACAS 2007. LNCS, vol. 4424, pp. 519–522. Springer, Heidelberg (2007)
30. Mossakowski, T., Sannella, D., Tarlecki, A.: A Simple Refinement Language for CASL. In: Fiadeiro, J.L., Mosses, P.D., Orejas, F. (eds.) WADT 2004. LNCS, vol. 3423, pp. 162–185. Springer, Heidelberg (2005)
31. Mosses, P.D. (ed.): CASL Reference Manual. LNCS, vol. 2960. Springer, Heidelberg (2004), Free online version available at http://www.cofi.info
32. Object Management Group. Unified Modeling Language. Standard, OMG (2011)
33. Sannella, D., Tarlecki, A.: Foundations of Algebraic Specification and Formal Software Development. EATCS Monographs in Theoretical Computer Science. Springer, Heidelberg (2012)
34. Wirsing, M., Knapp, A.: View Consistency in Software Development. In: Wirsing, M., Knapp, A., Balsamo, S. (eds.) RISSEF 2002. LNCS, vol. 2941, pp. 341–357. Springer, Heidelberg (2004)

Formal Analysis of Leader Election in MANETs Using Real-Time Maude[*]

Si Liu[1], Peter Csaba Ölveczky[2], and José Meseguer[1]

[1] University of Illinois at Urbana-Champaign, USA
[2] University of Oslo, Norway

Abstract. The modeling and analysis of mobile ad hoc networks (MANETs) pose non-trivial challenges to formal methods. Time, geometry, communication delays and failures, mobility, and uni- and bidirectionality can interact in unforeseen ways that are hard to model and analyze by automatic formal methods. In this work we use rewriting logic and Real-Time Maude to address this challenge. We propose a composable formal framework for MANET protocols and their mobility models that can take into account such complex interactions. We illustrate our framework by analyzing a well-studied leader election protocol for MANETs in the presence of both mobility and uni- and bidirectional links.

1   Introduction

The human factor is *everything*, particularly in scientific research. Thanks to the friendship, the creativity, the intellectual generosity, and the inspiration of Martin Wirsing and his pioneering work (with Kosiuczenko) on *timed rewriting logic* [20,11], two of us (Ölveczky and Meseguer) started working together on a line of research that has kept us busy for almost twenty years and is at the core of the present work. In 1995 Ölveczky visited Martin at LMU and was fired up by Martin's new ideas on formally modeling real-time systems with rewrite rules. By various circumstances he made his way to Menlo Park, fell in love with the place, and was allowed to work for his Bergen Ph.D. under Meseguer at SRI. At the time it was not clear how timed rewriting logic and standard rewriting logic, though by design very close to each other, were precisely related. This was clarified in [21] and in Ölveczky's dissertation [19], which proposed the alternative model of *real-time rewrite theories* as a *special class* of ordinary rewrite theories to specify real-time and hybrid systems. The associated Real-Time Maude tool [18] also started in [19], and has since then been applied to a wide range of real-time systems (see [17] for an overview).

It therefore seems fitting to honor Martin Wirsing on this festive occasion with a work in an area that he initiated and to which he has continued making important contributions up to this date. One of the key strengths of the

[*] Partially supported by NSF Grant CNS 13-19109 and AFOSR Grant FA8750-11-2-0084.

R. De Nicola and R. Hennicker (Eds.): Wirsing Festschrift, LNCS 8950, pp. 231–252, 2015.

rewriting logic approach to the modeling and formal analysis of real-time systems is the flexibility and naturalness with which it can specify and analyze many distributed object-based real-time systems whose discrete states may have unbounded data structures and are therefore beyond the pale of timed automata models [2]. Furthermore, this is accomplished without losing completeness of the analysis and useful decidability properties [22].

The present work illustrates the use of the expressive power of real-time rewrite theories to model not only time and distributed objects, but also *geometry, mobility,* and *wireless communication,* which are needed for wireless applications such as wireless sensor networks and mobile ad hoc networks (MANETs). Real-Time Maude was first used on sensor network protocols in [24], and for MANETs in the work started in [13] and continued here. The work in [13], which is further developed in this paper, provides a general framework for modeling and analyzing MANETs in which a protocol can be seamlessly *composed* with various mobility models by exploiting the class inheritance features of Real-Time Maude in the style of [23]. In particular, our framework allows us to formally model different kinds of MANET protocols, and then formally analyze them together with reasonably precise models of both

- any of several commonly used models for node mobility, and
- spatially bounded wireless communication, which takes into account both link directionality (uni- or bidirectional) and the interplay between communication delay and mobility.

Simulation tools typically represent node locations explicitly and analyze MANETs using common node mobility models [25,6], whereas formal approaches to MANETs usually abstract from node locations and consider arbitrary topology changes (if any), as explained in Section 7. Our framework allows us to see Real-Time Maude as *both* a simulation tool and a formal analysis tool for MANETs.

In [13] we showed the power and flexibility of our framework by analyzing the Ad hoc On-Demand Distance Vector (AODV) routing protocol under various mobility models. In this paper we apply our framework on the well known leader election (LE) protocol for MANETS by Vasudevan, Kurose, and Towsley [32]. Modeling and analyzing the LE protocol pose a number of challenges not encountered in the analysis of AODV, including:

- LE assumes that the underlying framework detects new and lost links that appear/disappear due to nodes moving into, or out of, the transmission ranges of other nodes; however, no neighborhood discovery process is given.
- LE features both *one-hop* and *multi-hop* communication; however, LE does not present any transport protocol, but just assumes that the underlying communication framework provides certain guarantees, such as "a message must eventually be received if the receiver is connected to the sender forever."

LE is defined and verified only for bidirectional links [31], but its developers conjecture that LE also works correctly in the presence of unidirectional links.

Apart from providing a formal model of LE, our novel contributions in the LE case study include:

- Defining fairly abstract executable models of both multi-hop communication and of neighbor discovery in MANETs.
- Defining LE also for unidirectional links.
- Model checking LE in a number of different settings, including with unidirectional links, without finding flaws significant in LE, thereby strengthening the confidence that LE also works correctly with unidirectional links.

This paper is organized as follows: Section 2 gives a background to Real-Time Maude. Section 3 recapitulates our framework for modeling MANETs in Real-Time Maude. Section 4 gives an overview of the LE protocol. Section 5 presents our Real-Time Maude model of LE, and Section 6 describes its formal analysis. Finally, Section 7 discusses related work and gives some concluding remarks.

2   Real-Time Maude

Real-Time Maude [18] extends Maude [5] to support the formal specification and analysis of real-time systems. The specification formalism emphasizes *ease* and *generality* of specification, and is particularly suitable for modeling distributed real-time systems in an object-oriented style. Real-Time Maude specifications are executable, and the tool provides a variety of formal analysis methods, including simulation, reachability analysis, and LTL and timed CTL model checking.

Specification. A Real-Time Maude module specifies a *real-time rewrite theory* [18] $(\Sigma, E \cup A, IR, TR)$, where:

- Σ is an algebraic *signature*; that is, declarations of *sorts*, *subsorts*, and *function symbols*, including a data type for time, which can be discrete or dense.
- $(\Sigma, E \cup A)$ is a *membership equational logic theory* [3], with E a set of (possibly conditional) equations, and A a set of equational axioms such as associativity, commutativity, and identity. $(\Sigma, E \cup A)$ specifies the system's state space as an algebraic data type.
- IR is a set of *labeled conditional rewrite rules* specifying the system's local transitions, each of which has the form[1] $[l] : t \longrightarrow t'$ **if** $\bigwedge_{j=1}^{m} cond_j$, where each $cond_j$ is either an equality $u_j = v_j$ (u_j and v_j have the same normal form) or a rewrite $t_j \longrightarrow t'_j$ (t_j rewrites to t'_j in zero or more steps), and l is a *label*. Such a rule specifies an *instantaneous transition* from an instance of t to the corresponding instance of t', *provided* the condition holds.
- TR is a set of *tick rules* $l : \{t\} \longrightarrow \{t'\}$ **in time** τ **if** $cond$ that advance time in the *entire* state t by τ time units.

We briefly summarize the syntax of Real-Time Maude and refer to [5] for more details. Operators are declared op $f : s_1 \ldots s_n$ -> s, and can have user-definable syntax, with underbars '_' marking the argument positions. Some operators can have equational *attributes*, such as assoc, comm, and id, stating, respectively,

---

[1] An equational condition $u_i = v_i$ can also be a *matching equation*, written $u_i := v_i$, which instantiates the variables in u_i to the values that make $u_i = v_i$ hold, if any.

that the operator is associative and commutative and has a certain identity element, so that rewriting is performed *modulo* the declared axioms. Equations and rewrite rules are introduced with, respectively, keywords eq, or ceq for conditional equations, and rl and crl. The mathematical variables in such statements are declared with the keywords var and vars. An equation $f(t_1, \ldots, t_n) = t$ with the owise (for "otherwise") attribute can be applied to a term $f(\ldots)$ only if no other equation with left-hand side $f(u_1, \ldots, u_n)$ can be applied.

A class declaration   class $C \mid att_1 : s_1, \ldots, att_n : s_n$ declares a class C with attributes att_1 to att_n of sorts s_1 to s_n. An *object* of class C in a given state is represented as a term $<O : C \mid att_1 : val_1, \ldots, att_n : val_n>$ of sort Object, where O, of sort Oid, is the object's *identifier*, and where val_1 to val_n are the current values of the attributes att_1 to att_n. A *message* is a term of sort Msg.

The state of an object-oriented specification is a term of sort Configuration, and is a *multiset* of objects and messages. Multiset union is denoted by an associative and commutative juxtaposition operator, so that rewriting is *multiset rewriting*. For example, the rewrite rule

```
rl [l] :  m(0,w)
          < 0 : C | a1 : x, a2 : 0', a3 : z, a4 : y >
          =>
          < 0 : C | a1 : x + w, a2 : 0', a3 : z, a4 : y >
          dly(m'(0',x), y) .
```

defines a family of transitions in which a message m, with parameters 0 and w, is read and consumed by an object 0 of class C, the attribute a1 of object 0 is changed to x + w, and a new message m'(0',x) is generated; this message has a *message delay* y, and will become the "ripe" message m'(0',x) in y time units. Attributes whose values do not change and do not affect the next state of other attributes or messages, such as a3, need not be mentioned in a rule. Attributes that are unchanged, such as a2, can be omitted from right-hand sides of rules.

A *subclass* inherits all the attributes and rules of its superclasses.

Formal Analysis. Real-Time Maude's *timed rewrite* command simulates *one* of the many possible system behaviors from the initial state by rewriting the initial state up to a certain duration. The timed *search* command uses a breadth-first strategy to search for states matching a search pattern that are reachable from the initial state t within a certain time interval.

Real-Time Maude's *linear temporal logic model checker* analyzes whether *each* behavior satisfies a temporal logic formula. *State propositions* are operators of sort Prop, and their semantics is defined by equations of the form

```
ceq statePattern |= prop = b if cond
```

for b a term of sort Bool, which defines *prop* to hold in all states t where t |= *prop* evaluates to true. A temporal logic *formula* is constructed by state propositions and temporal logic operators such as True, False, ~ (negation), /\, \/, -> (implication), [] ("always"), <> ("eventually"), and U ("until"). Real-Time Maude provides both *unbounded* and *time-bounded* LTL model checking.

If the reachable state space is finite, the unbounded model checking command (mc t |=u *formula* .)   checks whether the temporal logic formula *formula* holds in all behaviors starting from the initial state t. If the reachable state space is infinite, the *time-bounded* model checking command

(mc t |=t *formula* in time <= *timeLimit* .)

in which each behavior is only analyzed up to time *timeLimit*, can be used to ensure termination of the analysis.

3   Modeling MANETs in Real-Time Maude

Analyzing MANET protocols under reasonably realistic conditions is challenging. Models of node movement are needed, and must be combined with wireless communication, where typically only nodes within a certain distance of the sender receive a message with sufficient signal strength. Since *both* the sender *and* a potential receiver may move during the "messaging delay," the potential receiver could move *into*, or *out of*, the transmission range of the sender *during* the messaging delay.

Combining node mobility with reasonably precise models of wireless communication is therefore nontrivial and is currently barely addressed by formal methods. In [13] we propose a framework for specifying and analyzing MANET protocols under different mobility models in Real-Time Maude by: (i) formally specifying several popular *mobility models*; (ii) studying the different constituents of wireless "messaging delay"; (iii) defining a model of wireless communication in the presence of node movement; and (iv) explaining how our model of mobility and communication is easily composable with a Real-Time Maude specification of a MANET protocol. This section briefly recapitulates our framework.

Mobility Models. A number of different *entity mobility patterns*, where a node's movement is independent of the movements of the other nodes, have been proposed to model node mobility in realistic scenarios. The following main entity mobility models [4] are illustrated in Fig. 1:

- *Random Walk:* The node moves in "rounds" of fixed durations. At the beginning of each round, the *new speed* and the *new direction* of a node are randomly chosen, and the node moves accordingly.
- *Random Waypoint:* In each round, the node first pauses for some time, and then randomly chooses a *new destination* and a *new speed*, and travels to that destination at the chosen speed.
- *Random Direction:* The node chooses a *random direction and speed*, and travels until it reaches the boundary of the area. The node then pauses for some time, before randomly selecting a new direction and speed, and so on.

Fig. 1. Motion paths of a mobile node in three mobility models, where a bullet • depicts a pause in the movement

Communication Delay. The per-hop communication delay can be seen as consisting of three parts [30]. The *sending delay* is the time from the moment a sender wants to send a message until the moment it is sent. This includes the time that the sender needs to buffer the message in its radio output buffer, the *media access delay* waiting for a clear channel to transmit, and the time needed to transmit the message. The *radio propagation delay* is the time it takes for a message to travel through the air from sender to receiver. The *receiving delay* denotes the time spent on the receiver side to pass the received message from device to application. Since the transmission range in MANETs usually ranges from 10 to 100 meters, while the radio propagation speed is approximately 3×10^8 meters per second, we abstract from the radio propagation delay.

Formal Model of Mobility and Wireless Communication. We summarize the Real-Time Maude model of mobility and wireless communication first presented in [13] and improved in our current work (see [15] for more details).

Mobility Models. We assume that nodes move in a two-dimensional square with length `areaSize`. A *location* is then represented as a pair x . y of rational numbers. We model a MANET node as an object of (a subclass of) the class `Node`, whose attributes denote the node's current location and its transmission range:

```
class Node | currentLocation : Location, transRange : Nat .
```

Since different nodes can have different transmission ranges, we may have *unidirectional* connections.

A *stationary* node is an object instance of the subclass `StationaryNode`:

```
class StationaryNode .          subclass StationaryNode < Node .
```

A mobile node is modeled as an object of a subclass of the class `MobileNode`:

```
class MobileNode | speedVector : SpeedVector,    timer : TimeInf .
subclass MobileNode < Node .
```

`speedVector` is a term < *xSpeed* , *ySpeed* > denoting the node's speed *and* direction, with *xSpeed* (resp., *ySpeed*) denoting the distance traveled along the *x*-axis (resp., *y*-axis) during one time unit. The `timer` attribute is used to ensure that a node changes its movement (or lack thereof) in a timely manner.

A node moving according to the *random walk* (resp., *random waypoint*) model is modeled by an object of the subclass `RWNode` or `RWPNode`, respectively:

```
class RWNode  | speedVectorRange : SpeedVectorRange,
                boundaryTimer : TimeInf .
class RWPNode | speedRange : SpeedRange,  destRange : DestRange,
                status : Status .
subclass RWNode  RWPNode < MobileNode .
```

`speedVectorRange`, `speedRange`, and `destRange` denote the set of possible speed vectors, speeds, and destinations, respectively. The `status` attribute is either `pausing` or `moving`, and `boundaryTimer` denotes the time until the node hits the area boundary. The rewrite rules modeling node movement are given in [15].

Modeling Wireless Communication in Mobile Systems. As mentioned above, if we abstract from the radio propagation delay, the per-hop delay can be seen to consist of two parts: the delay at the sender side and the delay at the receiver side. The point is that exactly those nodes that are within the transmission range of the sender *when the sending delay ends* should receive a message. Our communication model assumes that the one-hop sending delay is a *constant* `sendDly`; it therefore abstracts from issues such as buffering of multiple messages at the sender or dynamic delays caused by network congestion, etc.

One-hop broadcast, one-hop unicast, and *one-hop multicast* are modeled using the following "message wrappers:"

```
msg broadcast_from_ : MsgContent Oid -> Msg .
msg unicast_from_to_ : MsgContent Oid Oid -> Msg .
msg multicast_from_to_ : MsgContent Oid OidSet -> Msg .
```

where `Oid` is the identifier of a node; `OidSet` denotes sets of node identifiers; and `MsgContent` is the sort for message contents. For example, when a node *sender* wants to broadcast some message content *mc* in one hop, it sends a "message" `broadcast` *mc* `from` *sender*.

Each node (in the set of intended receivers) that is within the transmission range of the sender exactly when the sending delay expires should receive the message, as a *single* message of the form *mc* `from` *sender* `to` *receiver*.[2]

Compositionality. A MANET protocol *P* can be specified, without having to take mobility and communication into account, by letting a node in the protocol description be specified as a subclass of `Node`:

---

[2] Since there is also a delay on the receiver side, this message can only be read/consumed when also the receiving delay has elapsed.

```
class PNode | protocol-specific attributes .
subclass PNode < Node .
```

A specification involving nodes of class PNode can then be analyzed under
different mobility models by defining the nodes in the initial state to be object
instances of a subclass of *both* PNode and a mobility class, such as RWPNode:

```
class RWPPNode .
subclass RWPPNode < RWPNode PNode .
```

4   The LE Leader Election Algorithm for MANETs

Leader election is a fundamental problem in distributed systems, and has a
variety of applications in wireless networks, such as key distribution, routing
coordination, and general control. One of the most well known leader election
algorithms targeting MANETs is the algorithm, which we call LE, of Vasudevan,
Kurose, and Towsley in [32]. The LE algorithm aims at electing the *best-valued*
node (according to some measure, such as the amount of remaining battery life)
in each connected component as the leader of that connected component.

In a *static* topology, LE works as follows. When an election is triggered at
a node, the node broadcasts an *election* message to its immediate neighbors. A
node that receives an *election* message for the *first* time, records the sender of
the message as its *parent* in the spanning tree under construction, and multicasts
an *election* message to its other immediate neighbors. When a node receives an
election message from a node that is not its parent, it immediately responds
with an *ack* message. When a node has received *ack* messages from all of its
children, it sends an *ack* message to its parent. Each such *ack* message to a
parent includes the identity and value of the best-valued node in the subtree
(of the spanning tree defined by the "parent" relation) rooted at the sender.
Therefore, when the source node has received an *ack* message from all of its
children, it can determine the best-valued node in the entire spanning tree. The
source node then broadcasts a *leader* message announcing the identity of this
new leader. Figure 2 shows a run of LE under a static topology of five nodes,
with node 1 being the source and node 5 the best-valued node (the higher the
node number, the better value it has).

Multiple nodes can concurrently initiate *multiple* elections; in this case, only
one election should "survive." This is done by associating to each election a
priority, so that a node already in an election ignores incoming elections with
lower priority, but participates in an election with *higher* priority.

To deal with *dynamic* settings, with node mobility and the resulting new and
lost links, the algorithm is extended as follows:

1. When a parent-child pair becomes disconnected during the election process,
   the parent removes the child from its waiting list of acknowledgments and
   continues its election. The child terminates the current election by announcing as the leader its maximal downstream node.

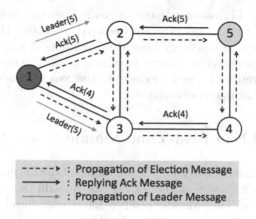

----→ : Propagation of Election Message
——→ : Replying Ack Message
——→ : Propagation of Leader Message

Fig. 2. An LE run in a static topology

2. When a new link forms between two nodes that have already finished their elections, the new neighbors exchange leader information. The node with the lower-valued leader adopts the higher-valued leader as its new leader, and propagates this new leader to the other nodes in its connected component. If one or both of the nodes in the new link are still in the process of electing a leader, they continue their separate election processes. When they have both terminated their local leader elections, they exchange leader information with each other and proceed as in the above case.

The report [31] gives a detailed pseudo-code specification of LE.

In [32,31] the authors prove the following main correctness theorem: The system will reach the following situation: Each node i has a leader, which, furthermore, is the best-valued node reachable from i. The authors of [32] state that they assume that the links are bidirectional, but add that "the algorithm should work correctly even in the case of unidirectional links, provided that there is symmetric connectivity between nodes."

Communication. In LE, *election* messages are sent to "immediate neighbors," which should amount to one-hop broadcast/multicast. On the other hand, *ack* messages use source-to-destination (i.e., "multi-hop") unicast, and therefore rely on the network infrastructure being able to transport messages to a given node. This can be achieved by composing LE with some routing protocol, such as AODV, and some transport protocol, such as UDP or TCP, that uses the obtained routing information to transport messages from source to destination. However, the description of LE does not specify any routing or message transport. Instead, [31] assumes that (i) links between two neighbors are bidirectional and FIFO, and (ii) that "a message sent by a node is eventually received by the intended receiver, provided that the two nodes remain connected forever starting from the instant the message is sent."

Neighbor Discovery. LE assumes that each node knows its neighbors, and that new links formed by node mobility are detected somehow. However, LE does not specify any neighbor discovery algorithm, nor does it make explicit the assumptions/requirements on the discovery of new links. The exception is that an explicit "probe" protocol is used to discover the loss of connection to a node from which a node awaits an *ack* message.

5   Modeling LE in Real-Time Maude

This section presents our Real-Time Maude model of the LE protocol as specified in detail in [31]. We show 8 of the 23 rewrite rules in our specification. The entire executable Real-Time Maude specification is available at https://sites.google.com/site/siliunobi/leader-election.

5.1   Nodes and Messages

We model an LE node as an object of a subclass `LENode` of the class `Node`. The new attributes are the identifier of the leader (`leader`), the parent (`parent`), the current best-valued node (`max`), the node's computation number (`number`), its computation index (`src`), the set of neighbors from which the node has yet to receive an *ack* message (`acks`), a flag indicating whether the node is currently in an election (`eflag`), a flag indicating whether the node has sent an acknowledgement to its parent (`pflag`), the node's (immediate) neighbors (`neighbors`), the new neighbors found by the neighbor discovery process (`newNbs`), and the relevant nodes which can no longer reach the node (`lostConxs`):

```
class LENode | leader : Oid,        parent : Oid,      max : Oid,
               number : Nat,        src : CompIndex,   acks : OidSet,
               eflag : Bool,        pflag : Bool,      neighbors : OidSet,
               newNbs : OidSet,     lostConxs : OidSet .
subclass LENode < Node .
```

A computation index is a pair $o \sim k$, with o a node identifier and k a computation number. As in [32], we assume that a node's identifier determines its value.

The three message types in LE are represented as message contents of the forms `election(...)`, `ack(...)`, and `leader(...)`.

5.2   Modeling Communication

In LE, nodes broadcast/multicast *election* messages to *immediate neighbors*, and unicast *ack* messages to their parent (and other) nodes. Sending to immediate neighbors may be seen as *one-hop* broadcast/multicast, which we model as explained in Section 3: the sender sends a "broadcast message;" after time `sendDly` this broadcast message is distributed to all nodes within transmission range of the sender *at that moment*, and will arrive `rcvDly` time units later.

Unicasting *ack* messages, however, may involve multiple hops, since a node may have moved away from its parent by the time the *ack* message should be sent. As mentioned in Section 4, LE does not specify a transport protocol to transmit such messages, but only requires (i) that communication between neighbors is FIFO and (ii) that the destination node must get the message if it is connected to the sender forever from the time when the message is sent.

In this paper, we abstract from details about how messages are routed, and model multi-hop message transmission as follows:

- the sender sends a `multiHopUnicast` message to the destination node;
- if there *exists* a communication path from source to destination exactly `multiHopSendDelay` time units later, the message will be received by the destination node `multiHopSendDly` + `rcvDly` time units after it was sent.

We model such communication as follows:[3]

```
op multiHopUnicast_from_to_ : MsgContent Oid Oid -> Msg .
op mhTransfer : MsgContent Oid Oid -> Configuration .

eq multiHopUnicast MC from O1 to O2 = dly(mhTransfer(MC, O1, O2), multiHopSendDly).
eq {mhTransfer(MC, O1, O2) CONF}
= if O2 in reachable(O1, CONF) then {dly(MC from O1 to O2, rcvDly) CONF}
   else {CONF} fi .

op reachable : OidSet Configuration -> OidSet .

ceq reachable(O1 ; OS,              --- add O2 to nodes reachable from (O1 ; OS)
              < O1 : Node | currentLocation : L1, transRange : R >
              < O2 : Node | currentLocation : L2 >  CONF)
= reachable(O1 ; O2 ; OS,  < O1 : Node | >  < O2 : Node | >  CONF)
  if not (O2 in (O1 ; OS)) /\ L2 withinTransRange R of L1 .

eq reachable(OS, CONF) = OS [owise] .    --- fixed point reached
```

Since this model abstracts from the actual route by which a message is transported, a message that happens to be transferred in one hop has the same delay as one that uses 10 hops. Our model satisfies the requirement that messages are delivered if there is a path from source to destination forever. However, our model does not guarantee FIFO transmission between neighbors for two reasons:

1. Two one-hop messages sent "at the same time" results in two messages with the same delay, since our model abstracts from details about the buffering of outgoing messages.
2. Since we abstract from routing details, a "multi-hop" message has sending delay `multiHopSendDly` even if it happens to need only one hop, and could be overtaken by a one-hop broadcast message sent later along the same link.

---

[3] We do not show the declarations of mathematical variables; they follow the Maude convention that such variables are written with capital letters.

5.3   Neighbor and Connectivity Discovery

LE assumes that new (one-hop) links caused by node movement are detected. We model such neighbor discovery abstractly by periodically updating the `newNbs` attribute of each node with those nodes that are within transmission range but are not included in the node's `neighbors` attribute, and by removing from `neighbors` those nodes that are no longer within transmission range.

In LE, the leader of a component "periodically sends out a heartbeat message to other nodes," which can then discover whether they are disconnected from the leader. Each node n also periodically sends a *probe* message to each node n' from which it awaits an *ack* message. If n does not receive a *reply* message from n' within certain time, it assumes that the connection to n' is lost. Finally, LE assumes that a node knows when it becomes disconnected from its parent. We abstract from heartbeat and probe/reply protocols, and instead periodically check whether a connection is lost to nodes in `acks`, the leader, or the parent.

We include in the state a timer object `< 100 : GlobalND | timer : t >` that triggers both the neighbor discovery process and the lost connectivity process, periodically, each time the timer expires:

```
rl [computeNewNbsAndLostConnections] :
   {< O : GlobalND | timer : O >   CONF} =>
   {< O : GlobalND | timer : period >  updateNbsAndAck(CONF)} .
```

where, for each node object o in CONF, `updateNbsAndAck`:

1. sets o's `newNbs` attribute to o's current immediate neighbors minus the nodes already in o's `neighbors` attribute;
2. removes all nodes which are no longer o's neighbors from o's `neighbors` attribute;
3. sets o's `lostConxs` attributes to those relevant nodes that cannot reach o (in multiple hops).

We refer to the online specification for the definition of this function.

5.4   Modeling the Behavior of LE

LE consists of five parts: initiating leader election, handling an *election* message, handling an *ack* message, handling a *leader* message, and dealing with new neighbors and lost connections.

Starting Leader Election. A "message" `electLeader(o)` kicks off a run of LE with node o as initiator. Node o multicasts a message `election(o~n)` to all its immediate neighbors, where n is the latest computation number.[4] The source will then wait for the *ack* messages from those neighbors by setting `acks` to OS. Moreover, it sets `eflag` to `true`, indicating that it is currently in an election:

---

[4] In case there are multiple concurrent runs of the protocol, this index helps deciding which run should continue.

```
rl [init-leader-election] :
   electLeader(O)
   < O : LENode | eflag : false,  neighbors : OS,  number : N,  leader : O2 >
 =>
   < O : LENode | acks : OS,       src : O ~ N,     number : N + 1,
                       eflag : true, pflag : false, parent : O,  max : O >
   (multicast election(O ~ N, O2) from O to OS) .
```

Receiving an Election Message. When a node that is not involved in an election
(eflag is false) receives an election message from SND, the node sets SND as
its parent, and sets its src, eflag, and pflag attributes accordingly. The node
multicasts an election message to all its neighbors except the parent:[5]

```
crl [join-1] :
   (election(I, LID) from SND to O)
   < O : LENode | eflag : false, leader : LID, neighbors : OS1 >
 =>
   < O : LENode | src : I, acks : OS2, eflag : true, pflag : false,
                    parent : SND, max : O >
   (multicast election(I, LID) from O to OS2)
 if OS2 := delete(SND, OS1) .
```

There are five more rules for handling election messages; see [14] for details.

Receiving Ack Messages. When a node receives an ack message, for the current
computation I, from a node SND, it deletes SND from the set acks. If the reported
best node M' is better than the node's current best-valued node M, then the max
attribute is also updated accordingly:

```
rl [update-acks] :
   (ack(I, FL, M') from SND to O)
   < O : LENode | pflag : false, src : I, acks : OS, max : M >
 =>
   < O : LENode | acks : delete(SND, OS),
                    max : (if FL and M' > M then M' else M fi) > .
```

All acks Received. When a node is no longer waiting for any ack message (acks
is empty), and it has not yet sent an ack to its parent (pflag is false), it sends
an ack message to its parent, with its best-valued node M. However, if the node
initiated this round of the protocol (and therefore is the root node) it starts
propagating the leader M to its immediate neighbors:

```
rl [all-acks-received-1] :
   < O : LENode | acks : empty, src : (O' ~ N), pflag : false,
                 parent : P,   max : M,       neighbors : OS >
 =>
   if O =/= O'   --- not root node
```

---

[5] Multicast to the empty set generates no messages in our communication model [15].

```
then < O : LENode | pflag : true >
     (multiHopUnicast ack(O' ~ N, true, M) from O to P)
else < O : LENode | eflag : false, leader : M >
     (multicast leader(O' ~ N, M) from O to OS)   fi .
```

Leader Message Handling. If a node already in an election receives a `leader` message for the first time, it just updates the local `leader`, clears the `eflag` (its election is over), and propagates the received message:

```
crl [adopt-new-leader-1] :
   (leader(I, LID) from SND to O)
   < O : LENode | pflag : true, eflag : true, max : M, neighbors : OS >
 =>
   < O : LENode | leader : LID, eflag : false, src : I >
   (multicast leader(I, LID) from O to OS)   if M <= LID .
```

New Links. If one or more new neighbors have been found from a node O that has already finished its election, then the node multicasts the leader message to the new immediate neighbors:

```
rl [new-links-found] :
   < O : LENode | newNbs : O' ; OS, eflag : B, src : I, leader : LID >
 =>
   < O : LENode | newNbs : empty >
   (if not B and LID =/= O then
       (multicast leader(I, LID) from O to (O' ; OS))   else none fi) .
```

Lost Connections. If a node gets disconnected from its parent while still in an election, it terminates the diffusing computation by announcing its maximal downstream node as the leader:

```
rl [disconnected-from-parent] :
   < O : LENode | lostConxs : OS ; P, pflag : true, eflag : true,
                  parent : P, max : M, src : I, neighbors : OS2 >
 =>
   < O : LENode | lostConxs : OS, eflag : false, leader : M >
   (multicast leader(I, M) from O to OS2) .
```

Timed Behavior. Due to lack of space, we refer to [15,14] for the definition of the timed behaviors. The main point is that time cannot advance when an instantaneous rule is enabled, so that all actions are performed in a timely manner.

6   Formal Analysis of the LE Protocol

This section shows how our modeling framework for MANETs can be composed with our model of the LE protocol to analyze LE under realistic mobility and communication models. As already mentioned, the LE developers prove the correctness of LE only for bidirectional links, although they "strongly believe that

[LE] would still work correctly if links were unidirectional, as long as all nodes have a path to each other." We analyze LE with both bidirectional links and unidirectional links; the latter are a consequence, e.g., of nodes sending with different signaling power. We consider both static and dynamic topologies, and also analyze a system with two connected components that repeatedly merge and partition because of node movement.

Although many papers (e.g., [32,7,27,9,26,12,28,29,16,8]) have studied LE, little is known by way of formal analysis about how it behaves with unidirectional connections or under realistic mobility scenarios. We are also not aware of any study taking into account the joint effects of communication delay and mobility.

6.1 Nodes

As mentioned in Section 3, we can combine our protocol specification with a node mobility model by having nodes as object instances of a subclass of both LENode and a mobility class, such as RWPNode for random waypoint mobility and StationaryNode for stationary nodes:

```
class RWPLENode .          subclass RWPLENode < RWPNode LENode .
class SLENode .            subclass SLENode < StationaryNode LENode .
```

6.2 Modeling Checking the Correctness Property

We use model checking to analyze the main correctness property of LE, as described in [32]:

> "[E]very connected component will eventually select a unique leader, which is the most-valued-node from among the nodes in that component."

The following atomic proposition unique-leaders holds if and only if all nodes in a connected component have the same leader, which is, furthermore, the highest-valued node in that connected component:[6]

```
op unique-leaders : -> Prop [ctor] .

eq {< O : LENode | leader : O > REST} |= unique-leaders = false .
--- no leader ('O') selected by some node

ceq {< O : LENode | leader : O' > REST}
    |= unique-leaders = false if O' < O .   --- O better than its leader

ceq {< O1 : LENode | leader : O' > < O2 : LENode | > REST}
    |= unique-leaders = false
   if O' < O2     --- wrong leader selected by O1
      /\ O2 in reachable(O1, < O1 : LENode | > < O2 : LENode | > REST) .

eq {SYSTEM} |= unique-leaders = true [owise] .
```

---

[6] Remember that the value of a node is given by its identifier.

The main correctness property can then be formalized as the LTL formula
`<> unique-leaders`. Given an initial state `initConf`, the following commands
return `true` if the property holds (possibly up to the duration of the test round,
`roundTime`); otherwise, a trace illustrating the counterexample is shown.

```
(mc {initConf} |=u <> unique-leaders .)
(mc {initConf} |=t <> unique-leaders in time <= roundTime .)
```

We can use unbounded model checking for static topologies. In dynamic topologies, the locations of the moving nodes contribute to an infinite reachable state space, and model checking must be time-bounded in order to terminate.

6.3   Scenarios and Analysis

Our model enables us to experiment with LE under many different scenarios by changing the values of system parameters such as node locations and movement patterns, transmission ranges, one-hop and multi-hop send delays, node velocities, the frequency of the neighbor/connectivity detection process, the number of concurrent runs of the protocol, and so on.

We use the following setting for our experiments, with additional scenario-specific settings presented separately:

- The transmission range of a node is $10\,m$, and the test area is $100\,m \times 100\,m$.
- The one-hop delays at the sender side and the receiver side are 1 time unit and 0, respectively. The multi-hop "send" delay is 2 time units.
- `roundTime` (i.e., the time bound in the model checking) is 20.

Scenario I. Scenario I corresponds to the topology in Fig. 2, and consists of five stationary nodes with bidirectional connections. The nodes 1, 2, 3, 4, and 5 are located at (45 . 45), (50 . 50), (50 . 40), (60 . 40), and (60 . 50), respectively. We consider two sub-scenarios: (a) only node 1 initiates a round of the leader election protocol; and (b) all five nodes initiate a run of the protocol. Time-bounded model checking shows that the property holds: all five nodes elect the best-valued node 5 as their leader within 20 time units; the execution times of the analyses are 150 milliseconds (ms) and 4500 ms, respectively.

Scenario II. This scenario, shown in Fig. 3 (where a solid line denotes a bidirectional link, an arrow denotes a unidirectional link, and a dashed circle shows a node's transmission area), considers a topology with three stationary nodes, where the links between nodes 2 and 3 and between 3 and 1 are unidirectional. This scenario defines a single connected component in the sense that there is a directed path from each node to any other node. To form such a *unidirectional* but *connected* component, we set the transmission ranges of the source 1 and other two nodes 2 and 3 to $10\,m$, $30\,m$, and $20\,m$, respectively.

Real-Time Maude model checking shows (in 100 ms CPU time) that the desired property is satisfied in this topology with the above system parameters.

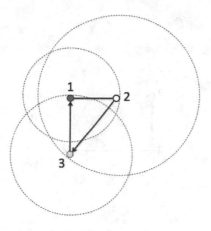

Fig. 3. Topology in Scenario II

Scenario III. Scenario III, shown in Fig. 4 (where a dashed arrow denotes a node's motion path), considers a bidirectional *dynamic* topology with three nodes, where the source node 1 is located at (50 . 50), and nodes 2 and 3 are initially at (60 . 50) and (50 . 55), respectively. Node 3 is a *random waypoint* node that moves back and forth along the dashed arrow with end points (50 . 55) and (60 . 55) (denoted by 3'). Note that the topology remains a connected component despite node 3's movement. We set the pause time of the moving node to 0 and the period of the neighbor/connectivity discovery process to 2.

We experiment with three sub-scenarios: (a) the speed of the moving node is 10; i.e., the speedRange attribute is the singleton 10; (b) the speed is 5; and (c) the speed is again 10, but now the pause time is 1 time unit. The initial state of Scenario III-a is given by the term (with parts of the term replaced by '...'):

```
eq period = 2 .     eq pauseTime = 0 .
eq initConfig
= electLeader(1)
  < 100 : GlobalND | timer : period >
  < 1 : SLENode | currentLocation : 50.50, transRange : 10, leader : 0, max : 0,
                  neighbors : (2 ; 3), parent : 0, number : 100, src : 0 ~ 0,
                  acks : empty, eflag : false, pflag : false, newNbs : empty,
                  lostConxs : empty >
  < 2 : SLENode | currentLocation : 60.50, transRange : 10, leader : 0, max : 0,
                  neighbors : 1, parent : 0, ... >
  < 3 : RWPLENode | currentLocation : 50.55, transRange : 10, speed : 0,
                  speedVector : <0,0>, speedRange : 10,
                  destRange : (60 . 55) ; (50 . 55), timer : pauseTime,
                  status : pausing, leader : 0, neighbors : 1, ... > .
```

Real-Time Maude model checking of Scenario III-a shows (in 240 ms CPU time) that the desired property is *not* satisfied: Node 3 moves away from Node 1 *during* Node 1's multicast to "immediate neighbors," and is not within Node 1's

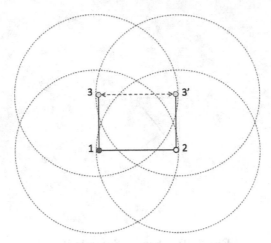

Fig. 4. Topology in Scenario III

transmission range when the sending delay of the one-hop multicast of `election` messages to "immediate neighbors" *expires*. Therefore, Node 3 does not get this message. Furthermore, the neighbor discovery process takes place every 2 time units, which exactly coincides with the moments when Node 3 is close to Node 1! The neighbor discovery process therefore never discovers that Node 3 is *not* an immediate neighbor of Node 1, and will hence never discover that Node 3 is a *new* neighbor. Node 3 will therefore be left out of the election process forever.

We cannot claim that this behavior *invalidates* the LE protocol, since LE may be based on other assumptions, such as "continuous neighbor discovery" and/or multi-hop communication even to nodes that are immediate neighbors when a sending event begins. However, our "counterexample" shows the need to make explicit subtle requirements of the underlying neighbor discovery process, and to make more precise the meaning of sending to "immediate neighbors" when an immediate neighbor may cease to be one *during* the sending process.

Real-Time Maude model checking of Scenarios III-b and III-c show that the desired property holds in these scenarios. The only difference between Scenarios III-a and III-c is that `pauseTime` is 1 in Scenario III-c. This implies that Node 3 takes three time units to move from location 3 to location 3', and back. Since the neighbor discovery process takes place every two time units, it will sooner or later take place when Node 3 is in location 3' in Fig 4, and hence no longer is an immediate neighbor of Node 1. Some time later, the neighbor discovery will take place when Node 3 is again close to Node 1, and will discover the "new" link between Nodes 1 and 3, and will then involve Node 3 in the election.

In Scenario III-b, it takes Node 3 two time units to move between the locations 3 and 3' in Fig. 4, and the neighbor discovery process will therefore update the neighbor information every time Node 3 reaches one of these end-points.

Scenario IV. Finally, to analyze merge and partition of connected components we consider the system with two connected components (consisting of Nodes 1

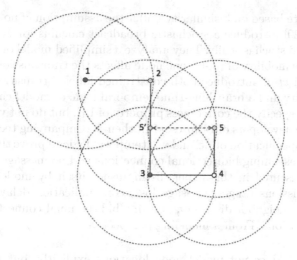

Fig. 5. Topology in Scenario IV

and 2, and of Nodes 3, 4, and 5, respectively) in Fig. 5. Since Node 5 moves back and forth between position 5 and position 5' in Fig. 5, the two connected components will repeatedly merge (when Node 5 is close to position 5') and partition (when Node 5 is close to position 5).

Our model checking analysis shows that the property holds when both Node 1 and Node 3 initiate elections at the same time and when `pauseTime` is 8.

7   Related Work and Conclusions

LE has been subjected to a number of formal analysis efforts in recent years. Gelastou et al. [7] specify and verify LE using both I/O automata and process algebra. They only consider static bidirectional topologies with non-lossy channels, and communication delay is not taken into consideration. Singh et al. [27] present the ω-calculus for formally modeling and reasoning about MANETs, and illustrate their techniques by developing and analyzing a formal model of LE. They only consider dynamic bidirectional topologies where a node is free to move as long as the network remains connected, without taking into account unidirectional scenarios, communication delay, and message loss. Ghassemi et al. [9] provide a framework for modeling and analyzing both qualitative and quantitative aspects of MANET protocols, where communication delay and dynamic topologies (modeled by probabilistic message loss) are considered. They focus on the performance of LE under various parameters without giving any qualitative results. Sibilio et al. [26,16] propose a calculus for trustworthy MANETs with which they analyze a secure version of LE (neighbors trust each other at some security level) with three stationary nodes connected by bidirectional links. Kouzapas et al. [12] propose a calculus of dynamic networks whose semantics contain rules mimicking the behavior of a neighbor discovery protocol. They analyze LE with an arbitrary derivative of the initial state based on bisimilarity under the assumption of no message loss. Song *et al.* [28,29] introduce a stochastic broadcast calculus for MANETs with mobility modeled stochastically. They analyze a simplified model of LE with four nodes, where the mobility of (only) one node affects the transmission probability. In [8], Ghassemi *et al.* introduce both constrained labeled transition systems to represent mobility and a branching-time temporal logic to model check MANET protocols. They specify the correctness property of LE, but do not verify it in detail. Finally, the developers of LE present in their accompanying technical report [31] a "formal" specification of LE and use temporal logic to prove the correctness of the protocol, assuming bidirectional connections and no message loss.

The work presented in this paper distinguishes itself by modeling node locations, transmissions ranges, message loss, communication delay, well known mobility models, neighbor discovery, and uni/bidirectional connectivity, as well as their interrelations. From a modeling perspective:

- Related work does not model node locations explicitly, but represent the topologies abstractly as "neighborhood graphs."
- Related work therefore does not consider *realistic mobility models*, but only static topologies or simple dynamic topologies with arbitrary link breaks.
- Related work does not consider *unidirectional connectivity*.
- Our work is the only one that models a *neighbor discovery* process.
- Only [9,28,29] consider *communication delay*.
- No related work considers the the *interplay of all the above ingredients*.

Maude and Real-Time Maude have been applied to analyze wireless systems. Our previous work [13] builds the modeling framework that serves as the basis for this paper, and analyzes the Ad hoc On-Demand Distance Vector (AODV) routing protocol under different mobility models. The papers [10,24] model wireless sensor networks in (Real-Time) Maude, but do not consider node mobility.

In this work we have used rewriting logic and Real-Time Maude to address what we see as a real gap between the current application of formal methods to MANETs and actual practice. Specifically, there is a need to formally analyze MANET protocols with realistic models of node mobility and wireless communication. Our solution has taken the form of a composable formal framework in rewriting logic for MANET protocols and mobility models that can take into account time, space, directionality, and transmission failures and delays. We have illustrated the usefulness of this approach by showing how it can discover a potential problem with LE that is caused by the subtle interplay of neighbor discovery, communication with "immediate neighbors," and node movement *during* a communication event.

Much work remains ahead. We should apply our framework to the analysis of other MANET protocols and composition of protocols under various modes of use. Finally, by using probabilistic rewrite theories and statistical model checking in the style of [1], our framework could also be used for formal quantitative analysis of MANET protocols to evaluate their performance and reliability.

References

1. Agha, G., Meseguer, J., Sen, K.: PMaude: Rewrite-based specification language for probabilistic object systems. Electronic Notes in Theoretical Computer Science 153(2), 213–239 (2006)
2. Alur, R., Dill, D.L.: A theory of timed automata. Theoretical Computer Science 126(2), 183–235 (1994)
3. Bouhoula, A., Jouannaud, J.P., Meseguer, J.: Specification and proof in membership equational logic. Theoretical Computer Science 236(1-2), 35–132 (2000)
4. Camp, T., Boleng, J., Davies, V.: A survey of mobility models for ad hoc network research. Wireless Communications and Mobile Computing 2(5), 483–502 (2002)
5. Clavel, M., Durán, F., Eker, S., Lincoln, P., Martí-Oliet, N., Meseguer, J., Talcott, C.: All About Maude - A High-Performance Logical Framework. LNCS, vol. 4350. Springer, Heidelberg (2007)
6. Fall, K., Varadhan, K.: The *ns* Manual (2011), http://www.isi.edu/nsnam/ns/doc/ns_doc.pdf
7. Gelastou, M., Georgiou, C., Philippou, A.: On the application of formal methods for specifying and verifying distributed protocols. In: Proc. NCA 2008. IEEE (2008)
8. Ghassemi, F., Ahmadi, S., Fokkink, W., Movaghar, A.: Model checking MANETs with arbitrary mobility. In: Arbab, F., Sirjani, M. (eds.) FSEN 2013. LNCS, vol. 8161, pp. 217–232. Springer, Heidelberg (2013)
9. Ghassemi, F., Talebi, M., Movaghar, A., Fokkink, W.: Stochastic restricted broadcast process theory. In: Thomas, N. (ed.) EPEW 2011. LNCS, vol. 6977, pp. 72–86. Springer, Heidelberg (2011)
10. Katelman, M., Meseguer, J., Hou, J.: Redesign of the LMST wireless sensor protocol through formal modeling and statistical model checking. In: Barthe, G., de Boer, F.S. (eds.) FMOODS 2008. LNCS, vol. 5051, pp. 150–169. Springer, Heidelberg (2008)
11. Kosiuczenko, P., Wirsing, M.: Timed rewriting logic with an application to object-based specification. Science of Computer Programming 28(2-3), 225–246 (1997)
12. Kouzapas, D., Philippou, A.: A process calculus for dynamic networks. In: Bruni, R., Dingel, J. (eds.) FORTE 2011 and FMOODS 2011. LNCS, vol. 6722, pp. 213–227. Springer, Heidelberg (2011)
13. Liu, S., Ölveczky, P.C., Meseguer, J.: A framework for mobile ad hoc networks in real-time maude. In: Escobar, S. (ed.) WRLA 2014. LNCS, vol. 8663, pp. 162–177. Springer, Heidelberg (2014)
14. Liu, S., Ölveczky, P.C., Meseguer, J.: Formal analysis of leader election in MANETs using Real-Time Maude (2014), http://www.ifi.uio.no/RealTimeMaude/leader-election-report.pdf
15. Liu, S., Ölveczky, P.C., Meseguer, J.: Modeling and analyzing mobile ad hoc networks in Real-Time Maude (submitted for publication, 2014), http://www.ifi.uio.no/RealTimeMaude/manets-report.pdf
16. Merro, M., Sibilio, E.: A calculus of trustworthy ad hoc networks. Formal Aspects of Computing 25(5), 801–832 (2013)
17. Ölveczky, P.C.: Real-Time Maude and its applications. In: Escobar, S. (ed.) WRLA 2014. LNCS, vol. 8663, pp. 42–79. Springer, Heidelberg (2014)
18. Ölveczky, P.C., Meseguer, J.: Semantics and pragmatics of Real-Time Maude. Higher-order and Symbolic Computation 20(1-2), 161–196 (2007)
19. Ölveczky, P.C.: Specification and Analysis of Real-Time and Hybrid Systems in Rewriting Logic. Ph.D. thesis, University of Bergen, Norway (2000), http://maude.csl.sri.com/papers

20. Ölveczky, P.C., Kosiuczenko, P., Wirsing, M.: An object-oriented algebraic steam-boiler control specification. In: Abrial, J.-R., Börger, E., Langmaack, H. (eds.) Formal Methods for Industrial Applications. LNCS, vol. 1165, pp. 379–402. Springer, Heidelberg (1996)
21. Ölveczky, P.C., Meseguer, J.: Specification of real-time and hybrid systems in rewriting logic. Theoretical Computer Science 285, 359–405 (2002)
22. Ölveczky, P.C., Meseguer, J.: Abstraction and completeness for Real-Time Maude. Electronic Notes in Theoretical Computer Science 176(4), 5–27 (2007)
23. Ölveczky, P.C., Meseguer, J., Talcott, C.L.: Specification and analysis of the AER/NCA active network protocol suite in Real-Time Maude. Formal Methods in System Design 29(3), 253–293 (2006)
24. Ölveczky, P.C., Thorvaldsen, S.: Formal modeling, performance estimation, and model checking of wireless sensor network algorithms in Real-Time Maude. Theoretical Computer Science 410(2-3), 254–280 (2009)
25. OMNeT++., http://www.omnetpp.org/ (accessed November 24, 2014)
26. Sibilio, E.: Formal methods for wireless systems. Ph.D. Thesis, University of Verona (2011)
27. Singh, A., Ramakrishnan, C.R., Smolka, S.A.: A process calculus for mobile ad hoc networks. Science of Computer Programming 75(6), 440–469 (2010)
28. Song, L.: Probabilistic models and process calculi for mobile ad hoc networks. Ph.D. Thesis, IT University of Copenhagen (2012)
29. Song, L., Godskesen, J.C.: Broadcast abstraction in a stochastic calculus for mobile networks. In: Baeten, J.C.M., Ball, T., de Boer, F.S. (eds.) TCS 2012. LNCS, vol. 7604, pp. 342–356. Springer, Heidelberg (2012)
30. Su, P.: Delay measurement time synchronization for wireless sensor networks. Tech. Rep. IRB-TR-03-013, Intel Research Berkeley Lab (2003)
31. Vasudevan, S., Kurose, J.F., Towsley, D.F.: Design and analysis of a leader election algorithm for mobile ad hoc networks. Tech. Rep. UMass CMPSCI 03-20, University of Massachusetts (2003)
32. Vasudevan, S., Kurose, J.F., Towsley, D.F.: Design and analysis of a leader election algorithm for mobile ad hoc networks. In: Proc. ICNP 2004. IEEE (2004)

The Foundational Legacy of ASL*

Donald Sannella[1] and Andrzej Tarlecki[2]

[1] Laboratory for Foundations of Computer Science, University of Edinburgh, UK
[2] Institute of Informatics, University of Warsaw, Poland

Abstract. We recall the kernel algebraic specification language ASL and outline its main features in the context of the state of research on algebraic specification at the time it was conceived in the early 1980s. We discuss the most significant new ideas in ASL and the influence they had on subsequent developments in the field and on our own work in particular.

1 Introduction

One of Martin Wirsing's most important contributions to the field of algebraic specification was his work on the ASL specification language. ASL is one of the milestones of the field and is one of Martin's most influential lines of work. It was also the highlight of our long-term collaboration and friendship with him — **many thanks, Martin!!!**

ASL is a simple algebraic specification language containing a small set of orthogonal constructs. Preliminary ideas were sketched in [Wir82], then modified and further developed in [SW83], with [Wir86] offering a complete, extended presentation. At the time, the first fully-fledged algebraic specification languages had recently been defined (Clear [BG80], CIP-L [BBB⁺85] etc.). In contrast, ASL was conceived as a *kernel language*, with stress on expressive power, conceptual clarity, and simplicity, rather than on convenience of use. The idea was to penetrate to the essential concepts, suitable for foundational studies and supplying a basis that could be used to define other specification languages.

Among the key characteristics of ASL, as listed in [Wir86], are the following:

- "ASL is a language for describing *classes of algebras* rather than for building sets of axioms (theories)"; in particular, "an ASL specification may be *loose* (meaning that it may possess nonisomorphic models)": We will discuss the semantics of specifications in Sect. 3, including the relationship between model-class semantics and theory-level semantics.
- "The expressive power of ASL allows the choice of a *simple notion of implementation*" and "parameterization in ASL is *λ-abstraction*": We will discuss aspects of the software development process, as influenced by these two ideas, in Sect. 4.
- "ASL is oriented towards a *'behavioural' approach* ... ASL includes a very general *observability* operation which can be used to behaviourally abstract from a specification": We will discuss the technicalities of behavioural abstraction and its role in the software development process in Sect. 5.

---

* This work has been partially supported by the National Science Centre, grant UMO-2013/11/B/ST6/01381 (AT).

R. De Nicola and R. Hennicker (Eds.): Wirsing Festschrift, LNCS 8950, pp. 253–272, 2015.

Further characteristics, also listed in [Wir86], are:

- *"Infinite signatures* and *infinite sets of axioms* can be described by finite ASL expressions" and "Algebras in ASL are *generalized algebras* ... suitable for the description of strict and nonstrict operations": We are not going to dwell on these
  points as they are subsumed by the more general setup of [ST88a], where the semantics of ASL is given for an arbitrary logical system (institution); we will follow
  this approach in Sects. 2–4. The particular choices made in [Wir82], [SW83] and
  [Wir86] arise from particular institutions.
- "ASL can be seen as an applicative (programming) language where the basic modes
  are not only natural numbers, integers, or strings, but sorts, operation symbols,
  terms, formulas, signatures, and specifications": The novel feature here is that each
  of these modes was treated as a first-class citizen in ASL. As far as we know, this
  aspect of ASL has not been explicitly taken up in later work, at least not to the same
  extent.
- "ASL is a *universal specification language* allowing to write every computable
  transformation of specifications": The power of parameterization in ASL comes
  partly from the previous point. This universality property was an interesting technical point but in our view it evades the real question, concerning which *semantic*
  entities (model classes and transformations between them) can be captured.

As indicated above, this paper discusses some of the ideas and themes that were
prominent in ASL and influenced further work. We comment on these from today's
perspective, supported by pointers to the subsequent literature.

2 Preliminaries

We will rely here on the usual notions of many-sorted algebraic signatures $\Sigma = \langle S, \Omega \rangle$
and signature morphisms $\sigma: \Sigma \to \Sigma'$ mapping sorts in Σ to sorts in Σ' and operation names in Σ to operation names with corresponding arity and result sorts in
Σ'. This yields the category **AlgSig**. For each algebraic signature Σ, $\mathbf{Alg}(\Sigma)$ stands
for the usual category of Σ-algebras and their homomorphisms. We restrict attention
to algebras with non-empty carriers to avoid minor technical problems in the sequel,
which are by now well-understood, see [Tar11]. As usual, each signature morphism
$\sigma: \Sigma \to \Sigma'$ determines a *reduct* functor $\_|_\sigma: \mathbf{Alg}(\Sigma') \to \mathbf{Alg}(\Sigma)$. This yields a
functor $\mathbf{Alg}: \mathbf{AlgSig}^{op} \to \mathbf{Cat}$. See [ST12] for a more detailed presentation.

Given a signature Σ, Σ-terms, Σ-equations, and first-order Σ-formulae with equality are defined as usual. The set of all Σ-terms with variables from X is denoted by
$T_\Sigma(X)$, and for sets IN, OUT of sorts in Σ, $T_\Sigma(X_{IN})_{OUT}$ denotes the set of Σ-terms
of sorts in OUT with variables of sorts in IN. Given a Σ-algebra A, a set of variables
X and a valuation $v: X \to |A|$, the *value* $t_{A[v]}$ of a Σ-term t with variables X in A
under v and the *satisfaction* $A[v] \models \varphi$ of a formula φ with variables X in A under v
are defined as usual. The parameter v is omitted when X is empty.

A *derived signature morphism* $\delta: \Sigma \to \Sigma'$ maps sorts in Σ to sorts in Σ' and
function symbols $f: s_1 \times \ldots \times s_n \to s$ in Σ to Σ'-terms of sort $\delta(s)$ with variables
$\{x_1{:}\delta(s_1), \ldots, x_n{:}\delta(s_n)\}$. This generalises "ordinary" algebraic signature morphisms

as recalled above. A derived signature morphism $\delta\colon \Sigma \to \Sigma'$ still determines a reduct functor $_-|_\delta\colon \mathbf{Alg}(\Sigma') \to \mathbf{Alg}(\Sigma)$.

Given a (derived) signature morphism $\delta\colon \Sigma \to \Sigma'$, the δ-translation of Σ-terms, Σ-equations, and first-order Σ-formulae to Σ'-terms, Σ'-equations, and first-order Σ'-formulae are as usual: we write $\delta(t)$ etc. For any term $t \in T_\Sigma(X)$, Σ'-algebra A', and valuation $v'\colon \delta(X) \to |A'|$, where $\delta(X)_{s'} = \biguplus_{\delta(s)=s'} X_s$, we have $t_{(A'|_\delta)[v]} = \delta(t)_{A'[v']}$, where $v\colon X \to |A'|_\delta|$ is the valuation of variables in X that corresponds to v' in the obvious way. Similarly for Σ-equations and Σ-formulae φ with free variables $X\colon (A'|_\delta)[v] \models \varphi$ iff $A'[v'] \models \delta(\varphi)$.

An *institution* [GB92] **INS** consists of:

- a category $\mathbf{Sign}_{\mathbf{INS}}$ of *signatures*;
- a functor $\mathbf{Sen}_{\mathbf{INS}}\colon \mathbf{Sign}_{\mathbf{INS}} \to \mathbf{Set}$, giving a set $\mathbf{Sen}_{\mathbf{INS}}(\Sigma)$ of Σ-*sentences* for each signature $\Sigma \in |\mathbf{Sign}_{\mathbf{INS}}|$;
- a functor $\mathbf{Mod}_{\mathbf{INS}}\colon \mathbf{Sign}_{\mathbf{INS}}^{op} \to \mathbf{Cat}$, giving a category $\mathbf{Mod}_{\mathbf{INS}}(\Sigma)$ of Σ-*models* for each signature $\Sigma \in |\mathbf{Sign}_{\mathbf{INS}}|$; and
- a family $\langle \models_{\mathbf{INS},\Sigma} \subseteq |\mathbf{Mod}_{\mathbf{INS}}(\Sigma)| \times \mathbf{Sen}_{\mathbf{INS}}(\Sigma)\rangle_{\Sigma \in |\mathbf{Sign}_{\mathbf{INS}}|}$ of *satisfaction relations*

such that for any signature morphism $\sigma\colon \Sigma \to \Sigma'$ the translations $\mathbf{Mod}_{\mathbf{INS}}(\sigma)$ of models and $\mathbf{Sen}_{\mathbf{INS}}(\sigma)$ of sentences preserve the satisfaction relation, that is, for any $\varphi \in \mathbf{Sen}_{\mathbf{INS}}(\Sigma)$ and $M' \in |\mathbf{Mod}_{\mathbf{INS}}(\Sigma')|$ the following *satisfaction condition* holds:

$$M' \models_{\mathbf{INS},\Sigma'} \mathbf{Sen}_{\mathbf{INS}}(\sigma)(\varphi) \quad \text{iff} \quad \mathbf{Mod}_{\mathbf{INS}}(\sigma)(M') \models_{\mathbf{INS},\Sigma} \varphi$$

We will omit the subscripts **INS** and Σ whenever they are obvious from the context. For any signature morphism $\sigma\colon \Sigma \to \Sigma'$, the translation $\mathbf{Sen}(\sigma)\colon \mathbf{Sen}(\Sigma) \to \mathbf{Sen}(\Sigma')$ will be denoted by $\sigma\colon \mathbf{Sen}(\Sigma) \to \mathbf{Sen}(\Sigma')$, and the reduct $\mathbf{Mod}(\sigma)\colon \mathbf{Mod}(\Sigma') \to \mathbf{Mod}(\Sigma)$ by $_-|_\sigma\colon \mathbf{Mod}(\Sigma') \to \mathbf{Mod}(\Sigma)$. Thus, the satisfaction condition may be re-stated as: $M' \models \sigma(\varphi)$ iff $M'|_\sigma \models \varphi$. For any signature Σ, the satisfaction relation extends naturally to sets of Σ-sentences and classes of Σ-models.

Examples of institutions abound. The institution **EQ** of equational logic has the category $\mathbf{Sign}_{\mathbf{EQ}} = \mathbf{AlgSig}$ of many-sorted algebraic signatures as its category of signatures; its models are algebras, so $\mathbf{Mod}_{\mathbf{EQ}}$ is $\mathbf{Alg}\colon \mathbf{AlgSig}^{op} \to \mathbf{Cat}$; for any signature $\Sigma \in |\mathbf{AlgSig}|$, $\mathbf{Sen}_{\mathbf{EQ}}(\Sigma)$ is the set of all (universally quantified) Σ-equations, with $\mathbf{Sen}_{\mathbf{EQ}}(\sigma)\colon \mathbf{Sen}_{\mathbf{EQ}}(\Sigma) \to \mathbf{Sen}_{\mathbf{EQ}}(\Sigma')$ being the translation of Σ-equations to Σ'-equations for any signature morphism $\sigma\colon \Sigma \to \Sigma'$ in $\mathbf{AlgSig}$. Finally, the satisfaction relations $\models_{\mathbf{EQ},\Sigma} \subseteq |\mathbf{Alg}(\Sigma)| \times \mathbf{Sen}_{\mathbf{EQ}}(\Sigma)$ are defined as usual: $A \models_{\mathbf{EQ},\Sigma} \forall X.t = t'$ iff $t_{A[v]} = t'_{A[v]}$ for all valuations $v\colon X \to |A|$. The institution **FOEQ** of first-order equational logic shares with **EQ** its category of signatures and its model functor, with its sets of sentences extended to include all closed formulae of first-order logic with equality, together with the standard satisfaction relations. Any institution having the same category of signatures and the same model functor as **EQ** (and **FOEQ**) will be called *standard algebraic*. See [ST12] for detailed definitions of many other institutions.

For any signature Σ, a Σ-sentence $\varphi \in \mathbf{Sen}(\Sigma)$ is a *semantic consequence* of a set of Σ-sentences $\Phi \subseteq \mathbf{Sen}(\Sigma)$, written $\Phi \models_\Sigma \varphi$ or simply $\Phi \models \varphi$, if for all Σ-models

$M \in |\mathbf{Mod}(\Sigma)|$, $M \models \varphi$ whenever $M \models \Phi$. A Σ-*theory* is a set of Σ-sentences that is closed under semantic consequence.

Semantic consequence is often approximated by an *entailment system*, that is, a family of relations $\langle \vdash_\Sigma \rangle_{\Sigma \in |\mathbf{Sign}|}$ where, for $\Sigma \in |\mathbf{Sign}|$, $\vdash_\Sigma$ is a relation between sets of Σ-sentences and individual Σ-sentences, subject to the usual requirements (reflexivity, transitivity, weakening). An entailment system (and its presentation via a system of proof rules) is sound for **INS** if for $\Sigma \in |\mathbf{Sign}|$, $\Phi \subseteq \mathbf{Sen}(\Sigma)$ and $\varphi \in \mathbf{Sen}(\Sigma)$, $\Phi \vdash_\Sigma \varphi$ implies $\Phi \models_\Sigma \varphi$, and it is complete if the opposite implication holds. Sound and complete proof systems for **EQ** and **FOEQ** are well known.

Institutional structure is rich enough to enable a number of key features of logical systems to be expressed. For instance, amalgamation and interpolation properties may be captured as follows.

Consider the following commuting diagram in **Sign**:

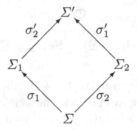

This diagram *admits amalgamation* if for any two models $M_1 \in |\mathbf{Mod}(\Sigma_1)|$ and $M_2 \in |\mathbf{Mod}(\Sigma_2)|$ such that $M_1|_{\sigma_1} = M_2|_{\sigma_2}$, there exists a unique model $M' \in |\mathbf{Mod}(\Sigma')|$ such that $M'|_{\sigma_2'} = M_1$ and $M'|_{\sigma_1'} = M_2$ and similarly for model morphisms. An institution is *semi-exact* if pushouts of signature morphisms always exist and admit amalgamation. It is well-known that any standard algebraic institution (in particular, **EQ** and **FOEQ**) is semi-exact.

The above diagram *admits parameterized interpolation* if for any $\Phi_1 \subseteq \mathbf{Sen}(\Sigma_1)$, $\Phi_2 \subseteq \mathbf{Sen}(\Sigma_2)$ and $\varphi_2 \in \mathbf{Sen}(\Sigma_2)$, whenever $\sigma_2'(\Phi_1) \cup \sigma_1'(\Phi_2) \models \sigma_1'(\varphi_2)$ then for some $\Phi \subseteq \mathbf{Sen}(\Sigma)$ such that $\Phi_1 \models \sigma_1(\Phi)$ we have $\Phi_2 \cup \sigma_2(\Phi) \models \varphi_2$. The diagram *admits Craig interpolation* if it admits parameterized interpolation with "parameter set" $\Phi_2 = \emptyset$. **INS** *admits parameterized* (resp. *Craig*) *interpolation* if all pushouts in the category of signatures admit parameterized (resp. Craig) interpolation.

The above reformulation of classical (first-order) Craig interpolation [CK90] has its source in [Tar86]. It is well-known that single-sorted first-order equational logic admits Craig as well as parameterized interpolation. But in the many-sorted case, interpolation requires additional assumptions on the signature morphisms involved: a pushout in **FOEQ** admits Craig and parameterized interpolation when at least one source morphism involved is injective on sorts, see [Bor05]. Interpolation properties for equational logic are even more delicate. **EQ** admits Craig interpolation for pushouts in which all morphisms are injective, but the restriction to non-empty carriers cannot be dropped [RG00], [Tar11]. Parameterized interpolation for **EQ** fails, unless injectivity and strong "encapsulation" properties are imposed on the morphisms in the pushouts considered, see [Dia08].

The interpolation requirement for an institution may be parameterized by classes of morphisms used in the pushouts considered. For simplicity of exposition we avoid this complication here; see [Bor05], [Dia08] for details.

3 Specifications and Their Semantics

Taking an institution as a starting point for talking about specifications and software development, each signature Σ captures static information about the interface of a software system with each Σ-model representing a possible realisation of such a system, and with Σ-sentences used to describe properties (axioms) that a realisation is required to satisfy. As a consequence, it is natural to regard the meaning of any specification SP built in an institution $\mathbf{INS} = \langle \mathbf{Sign}, \mathbf{Sen}, \mathbf{Mod}, \langle \models_\Sigma \rangle_{\Sigma \in |\mathbf{Sign}|} \rangle$ as given by its signature $Sig[SP] \in |\mathbf{Sign}|$ together with a class $Mod[SP]$ of $Sig[SP]$-models. Specifications SP with $Sig[SP] = \Sigma$ are referred to as Σ-specifications.

The stress here is not only on the use of model classes to capture the semantics of specifications, but also on the lack of restriction on the models in the class and on the class itself — so-called "loose semantics". This is in contrast to the approach of ADJ [GTW76] and its followers, see e.g. [EM85], in which the meaning of an (equational) specification SP was taken to be the isomorphism class of the *initial* models of SP. Similar restrictions appear in other early approaches: final models [Wan79], generated models [BBB+85], etc. The clear benefit of the loose approach is that it avoids placing premature constraints on the semantics of specifications, leaving choices of implementation details open for later stages of the development process. Although based in earlier work — the notion of the class of models of a set of axioms is a backbone of mathematical logic — in the context of algebraic specification this loose view was first consequently adopted in the work on ASL.

Different formulations of ASL share a kernel where specifications are built from *basic specifications* using *union*, *translation* and *hiding*. We use a syntax that is close to that of CASL [BM04], rather than choosing one of the variants in the ASL literature.

basic specifications: For any signature $\Sigma \in |\mathbf{Sign}|$ and set $\Phi \subseteq \mathbf{Sen}(\Sigma)$ of Σ-sentences, the *basic specification* $\langle \Sigma, \Phi \rangle$ is a specification with:

$$Sig[\langle \Sigma, \Phi \rangle] = \Sigma$$
$$Mod[\langle \Sigma, \Phi \rangle] = \{M \in \mathbf{Mod}(\Sigma) \mid M \models \Phi\}$$

union: For any signature $\Sigma \in |\mathbf{Sign}|$, given Σ-specifications SP_1 and SP_2, their *union* $SP_1 \cup SP_2$ is a specification with:

$$Sig[SP_1 \cup SP_2] = \Sigma$$
$$Mod[SP_1 \cup SP_2] = Mod[SP_1] \cap Mod[SP_2]$$

translation: For any signature morphism $\sigma \colon \Sigma \to \Sigma'$ and Σ-specification SP, SP **with** σ is a specification with:

$$Sig[SP \text{ with } \sigma] = \Sigma'$$
$$Mod[SP \text{ with } \sigma] = \{M' \in \mathbf{Mod}(\Sigma') \mid M'|_\sigma \in Mod[SP]\}$$

hiding: For any signature morphism $\sigma \colon \Sigma \to \Sigma'$ and Σ'-specification SP', SP' **hide via** σ is a specification with:

$$Sig[SP' \text{ hide via } \sigma] = \Sigma$$
$$Mod[SP' \text{ hide via } \sigma] = \{M'|_\sigma \mid M' \in Mod[SP']\}$$

Using this semantics as a basis, we can now study the expressible properties that a specification ensures.

A Σ-sentence $\varphi \in \mathbf{Sen}(\Sigma)$ is a *semantic consequence* of a specification SP with $Sig[SP] = \Sigma$ if $Mod[SP] \models \varphi$; we write this $SP \models \varphi$. The set of all semantic consequences of SP is called the *theory* of SP.

An alternative to the ASL model-class semantics for specifications is to assign a theory to a specification as its meaning. This goes back to Clear [BG80], and is the stance taken for instance in [DGS93] and [GR04]. See [ST14] for a careful analysis of this alternative.

One standard way of presenting such a semantics is by giving a proof system for deriving consequences of specifications. For the class of specifications described above, the following proof rules are standard [ST88a]:

$$\frac{SP \vdash \varphi \text{ for each } \varphi \in \Phi \quad \Phi \vdash \psi}{SP \vdash \psi} \qquad \frac{}{\langle \Sigma, \Phi \rangle \vdash \varphi} \; \varphi \in \Phi$$

$$\frac{SP_1 \vdash \varphi}{SP_1 \cup SP_2 \vdash \varphi} \qquad \frac{SP_2 \vdash \varphi}{SP_1 \cup SP_2 \vdash \varphi}$$

$$\frac{SP \vdash \varphi}{SP \text{ with } \sigma \vdash \sigma(\varphi)} \qquad \frac{SP \vdash \sigma(\varphi)}{SP \text{ hide via } \sigma \vdash \varphi}$$

where $\Phi \vdash \psi$ calls upon a sound entailment system for the underlying institution **INS**. This proof system is sound: $SP \vdash \varphi$ implies $SP \models \varphi$. Completeness ($SP \models \varphi$ implies $SP \vdash \varphi$) is more difficult.

Theorem 3.1 ([ST14]). *Given an institution* **INS** *that admits amalgamation, and an entailment system* $\langle \vdash_\Sigma \rangle_{\Sigma \in |\mathbf{Sign}|}$ *for* **INS** *that is sound and complete, the above proof system is sound and complete for consequences of specifications built from basic specifications using union, translation and hiding if and only if* **INS** *admits parameterized interpolation.*

The assumption that **INS** admits parameterized interpolation is a rather strong one, excluding important examples like **EQ** except under restrictive conditions (Sect. 2). But strengthening the proof system above in an attempt to make it complete even in the absence of this assumption has a high price. As explained in full technical detail in [ST14], the above proof system cannot be improved without breaking the well-known compositionality principle, whereby consequences of a specification are inferred from consequences of its immediate component subspecifications.

It follows that a compositional theory-level semantics for the above class of structured specifications — or any larger class — that would assign to any specification the theory of its model class can be given only under a rather strong assumption about the underlying logical system.

This negative conclusion shows that there is an unavoidable discrepancy between compositional theory-level and model-class semantics for specifications. As usual, proof theory gives an approximation to semantic truth, and where there is a difference the latter provides the definitive reference point.

That said, non-compositional sound and complete proof systems for consequences of specifications can be given by collapsing the structure of specifications via normalisation [Bor05], even if **INS** does not admit interpolation. Various ways of avoiding complete collapse of specification structure are possible, see [MAH06] and [MT14].

We may take the theory-level view a bit further and study consequence relative to a specification. Any Σ-specification SP determines a consequence relation $\models_{SP}$ where for any set Φ of Σ-sentences and any Σ-sentence φ, $\Phi \models_{SP} \varphi$ if φ holds in all models of SP that satisfy Φ. The corresponding semantics assigns to each specification an entailment relation, possibly given by a proof system as in [HWB97]. The standard proof rules for the above specifications are the following:

$$\frac{\Phi \vdash \psi}{\Phi \vdash_{SP} \psi} \qquad \frac{}{\vdash_{\langle \Sigma, \Phi \rangle} \varphi} \; \varphi \in \Phi$$

$$\frac{\Phi \vdash_{SP_1} \varphi}{\Phi \vdash_{SP_1 \cup SP_2} \varphi} \qquad \frac{\Phi \vdash_{SP_2} \varphi}{\Phi \vdash_{SP_1 \cup SP_2} \varphi}$$

$$\frac{\Phi \vdash_{SP} \varphi}{\sigma(\Phi) \vdash_{SP \; \mathbf{with} \; \sigma} \sigma(\varphi)} \qquad \frac{\sigma(\Phi) \vdash_{SP} \sigma(\varphi)}{\Phi \vdash_{SP \; \mathbf{hide} \; \mathbf{via} \; \sigma} \varphi}$$

These rules are sound: $\Phi \vdash_{SP} \varphi$ implies $\Phi \models_{SP} \varphi$. Again, completeness ($\Phi \models_{SP} \varphi$ implies $\Phi \vdash_{SP} \varphi$) holds only under strong assumptions.

Theorem 3.2 ([Dia08]). *Given an institution* **INS** *that admits amalgamation, and an entailment system* $\langle \vdash_\Sigma \rangle_{\Sigma \in |\mathbf{Sign}|}$ *for* **INS** *that is sound and complete, the above proof system is sound and complete for consequence relative to specifications built from basic specifications using union, translation and hiding if and only if* **INS** *admits parameterized interpolation.*

The negative remarks above concerning compositional theory-level semantics carry over here as well.

3.1 An Example

Without complicating the semantic foundations, we may add specification-building operations that are defined in terms of the ones above. For instance, in any algebraic institution, we may use the following operations:

sum: For any Σ-specification SP and Σ'-specification SP', their *sum* is:

SP **and** $SP' = (SP \; \mathbf{with} \; \iota) \cup (SP' \; \mathbf{with} \; \iota')$

where $\iota \colon \Sigma \hookrightarrow \Sigma \cup \Sigma'$ and $\iota' \colon \Sigma' \hookrightarrow \Sigma \cup \Sigma'$ are the signature inclusions.

enrichment: For any Σ-specification SP with $\Sigma = \langle S, \Omega \rangle$, set S' of sort names, set Ω' of operation names with arities and result sorts over $S \cup S'$, and set Φ' of sentences over the signature $\Sigma' = \langle S \cup S', \Omega \cup \Omega' \rangle$, we define:

SP **then sorts** S' **ops** Ω' • $\Phi' = (SP \; \mathbf{with} \; \iota) \cup \langle \Sigma', \Phi' \rangle$

where $\iota \colon \Sigma \hookrightarrow \Sigma'$ is the signature inclusion. Obvious notational variants (e.g. omitting "**sorts**" when $S' = \emptyset$) are used to enhance convenience.

***hiding*:** Hiding with respect to signature inclusion may be written by listing the hidden symbols. So, for any Σ-specification SP with $\Sigma = \langle S, \Omega \rangle$ and signature inclusion $\iota\colon \langle S', \Omega' \rangle \hookrightarrow \Sigma$, we define:

$$SP \text{ hide sorts } S \setminus S' \text{ ops } \Omega \setminus \Omega' = SP \text{ hide via } \iota$$

Assume given specifications BOOL of Booleans and NAT of natural numbers. Then, working in **FOEQ**, we can build the following specifications:

spec NATBOOL =
  NAT **and** BOOL **then**
    ops $\_ > \_ \colon nat \times nat \to bool$
    $\forall n, m \colon nat$
       • $0 > n = false$
       • $succ(n) > 0 = true$
       • $succ(n) > succ(m) = n > m$

spec BAG =
  NATBOOL **then**
    sorts bag
    ops $empty \colon bag$
          $add \colon nat \times bag \to bag$
          $count \colon nat \times bag \to nat$
    $\forall x, y \colon nat, B \colon bag$
       • $count(x, empty) = 0$
       • $count(x, add(x, B)) = succ(count(x, B))$
       • $x \neq y \Rightarrow count(x, add(y, B)) = count(x, B)$

spec CONTAINER =
  (BAG **then**
      ops $isin \colon nat \times bag \to bool$
      $\forall x \colon nat, B \colon bag$
        • $isin(x, B) = count(x, B) > 0$)
  hide ops $count$

It is now easy to check that, for instance,

    CONTAINER $\models \forall x{:}nat, B{:}bag.\ isin(x, add(x, B)) = true$
    CONTAINER $\models \forall x, y{:}nat, B{:}bag.\ isin(x, add(y, add(x, B))) = true$
    CONTAINER $\models \forall x{:}nat.\ isin(x, empty) = false$.

Since we are working in **FOEQ**, which admits parameterized interpolation, by Theorem 3.1 these can be proved using the proof system given above. We encourage the reader to write out the details.

One may now attempt to upgrade CONTAINER to give a specification of sets, for example:

spec EXTCONTAINER =
  CONTAINER **then**
    $\forall B, B' \colon bag$
      • $(\forall x{:}nat.\ isin(x, B) = isin(x, B')) \Rightarrow B = B'$

However, this specification has no models. To see this, note that[1]

$$\text{BAG} \models \forall x{:}nat.\ add(x, add(x, empty)) \neq add(x, empty)$$

from which we encourage the reader to derive $\text{EXTCONTAINER} \models \phi$ for all first-order formulae ϕ.

Instead, we may define

> **spec** SET =
>   NATBOOL **then**
>   **sorts** *bag*
>   **ops** *empty* : *bag*
>   *add* : *nat* × *bag* → *bag*
>   *isin* : *nat* × *bag* → *bool*
> $\forall x, y : nat, B : bag$
>   • $isin(x, empty) = false$
>   • $isin(x, add(x, B)) = true$
>   • $x \neq y \Rightarrow isin(x, add(y, B)) = isin(x, B)$

and then

> **spec** EXTSET =
>   SET **then**
> $\forall B, B' : bag$
>   • $(\forall x{:}nat.\ isin(x, B) = isin(x, B')) \Rightarrow B = B'$

We may now prove

$$\text{EXTSET} \models \forall x, y{:}nat, B{:}bag.\ add(x, add(y, B)) = add(y, add(x, B))$$
$$\text{EXTSET} \models \forall x{:}nat, B{:}bag.\ isin(x, B) = true \Rightarrow add(x, B) = B$$

as well as

$$\text{EXTSET} \models \forall x{:}nat, B{:}bag.\ isin(x, add(x, B)) = true$$
$$\text{EXTSET} \models \forall x, y{:}nat, B{:}bag.\ isin(x, add(y, add(x, B))) = true$$
$$\text{EXTSET} \models \forall x{:}nat.\ isin(x, empty) = false.$$

We will refer to these specifications throughout the rest of the paper.

4 Implementations and Parameterization

At the time when work on ASL began, one of the hottest research topics in algebraic specification was the search for the "right" definition of implementation of one specification by another. The goal was to achieve the expected composability properties [GB80] while capturing practical data representation and refinement techniques. Various approaches were proposed, of which the concept of implementation given in [EKMP82] was probably the most influential and well developed; see [SW82] for a

---

[1] This follows from NAT $\models \forall n{:}nat.\ succ(n) \neq n$.

contribution from Martin. "Vertical composition" (transitivity) of two such implementations was the crucial goal, but this was not always possible except under additional assumptions about the specifications involved. In retrospect, this is no surprise, since the definitions proposed were all based on syntactic concepts and composition required some form of normalisation of the transition from implemented to implementing specifications. This corresponds to requiring programs to be written in a rather restricted programming language that provides no means of composing modules without syntactically merging their actual code. In addition to problems with vertical composition, these early definitions failed to cover certain naturally arising examples, and most disregarded loose specifications.

The breakthrough of ASL for implementations was to take seriously the idea that a loose specification has all of its legal realisations as models. Proceeding from an abstract specification of requirements to a more refined specification is then a matter of making a series of design decisions, each of which narrows the class of models under consideration. Thus, implementation corresponds simply to the inclusion of model classes of the specifications involved.

Given specifications SP and SP' with $Sig[SP] = Sig[SP']$, we say that SP' is a *simple implementation* of SP, written $SP \rightsquigarrow SP'$, if $Mod[SP] \supseteq Mod[SP']$. For instance, referring to Sect. 3.1, SET $\rightsquigarrow$ CONTAINER. (But CONTAINER $\not\rightsquigarrow$ SET.)

Vertical composition is now immediate: if $SP \rightsquigarrow SP'$ and $SP' \rightsquigarrow SP''$ then $SP \rightsquigarrow SP''$. Thus, given a chain $SP_0 \rightsquigarrow SP_1 \rightsquigarrow \cdots \rightsquigarrow SP_n$ of simple implementation steps and a model $M \in Mod[SP_n]$, we have $M \in Mod[SP_0]$. This ensures that the correctness of the final outcome of stepwise development may be inferred from the correctness of the individual implementation steps.

The definition of simple implementation requires the signatures of both specifications to be the same. Hiding may be used to adjust the signatures (for example, by hiding auxiliary functions in the implementing specification) if this is not the case. This is just one example of "wrapping" around specifications that may be needed to capture the relationship between implemented and implementing specifications when using simple implementations. In general, such wrapping may incorporate design decisions like definitions of types and operations in terms of other components that are yet to be implemented. These are expressible using the simple specification constructs defined in the last section, where definitions can be expressed using hiding via a derived signature morphism. Proceeding this way, successive specifications in the chain will incorporate more and more details arising from successive design decisions. Thereby, some parts become fully determined, and remain unchanged as a part of the specification until the final program is obtained. The following diagram is a visual representation of this situation, where $\kappa_1, \ldots, \kappa_n$ label the parts that become determined at consecutive steps:

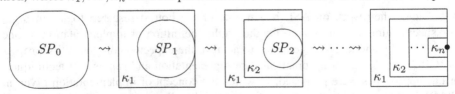

It is more convenient to separate the finished parts from the specification, putting them aside, and proceeding with the development of the unresolved parts only:

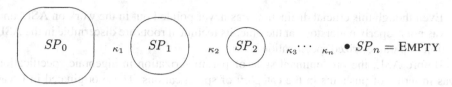

where EMPTY is a specification for which a standard model empty $\in Mod[\text{EMPTY}]$ is available.

Semantically, the finished parts $\kappa_1, \ldots, \kappa_n$ are functions that map any realisation of the unresolved part to a realisation of what is being implemented. We call such functions *constructors* and capture the corresponding concept of implementation as follows [ST88b]: given specifications SP and SP', we say that SP' is a *constructor implementation of SP via κ*, written $SP \underset{\kappa}{\;} SP'$, if κ is a constructor from SP' to SP, that is, a function $\kappa \colon |\mathbf{Mod}(Sig[SP'])| \to |\mathbf{Mod}(Sig[SP])|$ such that $\kappa(M') \in Mod[SP]$ for all $M' \in Mod[SP']$. Again, vertical composition follows immediately: if $SP \underset{\kappa}{\;} SP'$ and $SP' \underset{\kappa'}{\;} SP''$ then $SP \underset{\kappa';\kappa}{\;} SP''$. Furthermore, given a chain of constructor implementation steps $SP_0 \underset{\kappa_1}{\;} SP_1 \underset{\kappa_2}{\;} \cdots \underset{\kappa_n}{\;} SP_n = \text{EMPTY}$ we have $\kappa_1(\kappa_2(\ldots \kappa_n(\text{empty})\ldots)) \in Mod[SP_0]$.

The general notion of a constructor above covers various constructs used in early notions of implementation. An important class of examples is reducts with respect to derived signature morphisms $\delta \colon Sig[SP] \to Sig[SP']$ which capture definitions of types and operations in SP terms of components in SP'.[2] By definition, this yields $SP \underset{-|\delta}{\;} SP'$ if $M'|_\delta \in Mod[SP]$ for all models $M' \in Mod[SP']$, which is a semantic statement of the correctness condition that needs to be verified.

For example, CONTAINER $\underset{-|\delta}{\;}$ BAG where $\delta \colon Sig[\text{CONTAINER}] \to Sig[\text{BAG}]$ maps *isin* to the term $count(x_1, x_2) > 0$.

This successfully deals with the definition of implementation and the issue of vertical composition. The other dimension, "horizontal composition" [GB80], captures the idea that combining implementations of components of a structured specification should yield an implementation of the whole original specification. This supposedly provides for modular decomposition of development tasks during the stepwise development process. Unfortunately, this does not allow for the very real possibility that there may be a mismatch between the structure of the original requirements specification and its realisation, see [FJ90]. For example, an implementation of CONTAINER would not need to be built on top of an implementation of BAG. The requirement of horizontal composition is missing a way of distinguishing between, on the one hand, the structure of the requirements specification used to facilitate its construction and understanding, and on the other hand, binding decisions made during the development process concerning the structure of the realisation. The latter fixes the design of the system architecture, and horizontal composition with respect to this structure is what really matters, see [ST06]. CASL [BM04] provides a way to capture designs of system architecture in the form of *architectural specifications* [BST02].

---

[2] This essentially gives a simple functional programming language if one generalises the notion of derived signature morphisms by allowing terms that involve constructs like conditionals, local (recursive) definitions, etc., see e.g. Example 4.1.25 of [ST12].

Even though this crucial distinction was never pointed out in the work on ASL, and it was not properly understood at the time, its technical roots are discernible in the ASL notion of parameterized specification.

Before ASL, the predominant style of parameterization in algebraic specification was in terms of pushouts in the category of specifications. These originated in Clear [BG80] and were then taken further in [TWW82], [EM85]. There, parameterized specifications were viewed both as specification-building operations and as specifications for the (free) functor mapping models of the parameter specification to models of the result specification, with compatibility between the two views being a cornerstone of this approach. This two-level view is another manifestation of the confusion between the structure of requirement specifications and the structure of realisations.

Parameterized specifications in ASL were quite different, formed by λ-abstracting specification expressions with respect to a specification variable. This obviously yields a function from specifications to specifications, but in general such a function will not correspond in any natural way to a function on the level of models, and in ASL there was never any intention that it would.

For instance, define

spec EXT =
  $\lambda\mathcal{X}:Sig[\text{SET}] \bullet$
  $\mathcal{X}$ **then**
    $\forall B, B': bag$
    $\bullet\ (\forall x:nat.\ isin(x, B) = isin(x, B')) \Rightarrow B = B'$

Then EXTCONTAINER = EXT(CONTAINER) and EXTSET = EXT(SET). Clearly, EXT does not correspond to a function on the level of individual models: CONTAINER has models but EXT(CONTAINER) does not.

An analysis of this situation suggests that what is missing is a distinction between parameterized specifications and specifications of parameterized models (*viz.* generic modules, constructors, ML-style functors). We studied this distinction in [SST92]: parameterized specifications denote functions that map model classes to model classes, while parameterized programs denote functions that map models to models and specifications of parameterized programs denote classes of such functions. The slogan is

parameterized (program specification) $\neq$ *(parameterized program) specification.*

Given this distinction, different specification constructs are appropriate for the two kinds of specifications. We used the notation $\Pi X:SP \bullet SP'[X]$ for the latter, following dependent type theory, and ASL-style λ-abstraction as above for the former. There is a Galois connection which links the two semantic domains, with closed elements corresponding to functions mapping models to non-empty classes of models [SST92]. A natural example is to generalise from SET by taking the sort of elements as a parameter, in place of nat.

This can be taken further, to higher-order parameterization mechanisms in which objects of all kinds (parameterized specifications, parameterized programs, their specifications, etc.) are permitted as arguments and as results. This results in a complex hierarchy with some "types" of objects in this hierarchy being more useful than others

[Asp97] and is closely related to issues involved in the design of module systems, see e.g. [LB88] and [KBS91]. CASL architectural specifications, which feature parameterized units and their specifications, may be viewed as providing a simple module system, raising familiar issues of shared substructure [BST02].

5 Behavioural Specifications

Probably the most novel feature of ASL, which first appeared in [SW83], was *behavioural abstraction*. If two algebras "behave the same", and one is a model of a specification, then it is natural to consider the specification in which the other is a model as well. Behavioural abstraction performs such a closure, with respect to an equivalence which is chosen to reflect the desired meaning of "behaves the same".

There had been some work on behavioural interpretation of specifications before ASL, notably [GGM76], [Rei81], [GM82] and [Gan83]. ASL introduced behavioural abstraction as an explicit construct, which facilitated understanding of the relationship between behaviourally abstracted specifications and "normal" specifications in a single language. It also proposed a general notion of behavioural equivalence, parameterized by an arbitrary set of terms W to be regarded as observable, which covered various notions of behavioural equivalence proposed in the literature and more.

In the previous sections, we have been working in the context of an arbitrary institution, but discussion of behavioural equivalence and behavioural abstraction is simplest in the context of ordinary algebraic signatures and algebras. Therefore, in this section we will restrict attention to algebraic institutions, which share signatures and models with **EQ** and **FOEQ**. See [ST87] for a possible generalisation to the framework of an arbitrary institution, and Sect. 8.5.3 of [ST12] for some further remarks in this direction.

Given an algebraic signature $\Sigma = \langle S, \Omega \rangle$, an S-sorted set of variables X, and a set $W \subseteq T_\Sigma(X)$ of Σ-terms, two Σ-algebras A, B are W-*equivalent via* X, written $A \equiv^{ASL}_{W(X)} B$, if there are surjective valuations $v_A \colon X \to |A|$, $v_B \colon X \to |B|$ such that for all terms $t, t' \in W$ of the same sort, $t_{A[v_A]} = t'_{A[v_A]}$ iff $t_{B[v_B]} = t'_{B[v_B]}$.

The relation $\equiv^{ASL}_{W(X)}$ is clearly not reflexive on $\mathbf{Alg}(\Sigma)$: for algebras A with carrier of cardinality larger than that of X, $A \not\equiv^{ASL}_{W(X)} A$. This was not a problem for ASL, where only countable algebras were considered. However, a problem that has been overlooked so far is that, in general, $\equiv^{ASL}_{W(X)}$ is not transitive either.

Counterexample 5.1. Consider a signature Σ with sorts s, $bool$ and operations $g \colon s \to bool$ and $true, false \colon bool$, with $X = \{x, y{:}s, t, f{:}bool\}$ and $W = \{g(x), true, false\}$; crucially, $g(y) \notin W$. Consider Σ-algebras A, B, C such that $A_s = B_s = C_s = \{a, b\}$ and $A_{bool} = B_{bool} = C_{bool} = \{tt, ff\}$, with $true_A = true_B = true_C = tt$, $false_A = false_B = false_C = ff$, and $g_A(a) = g_A(b) = tt$, $g_B(a) = tt$ but $g_B(b) = ff$, and $g_C(a) = g_C(b) = ff$. Then $A \equiv^{ASL}_{W(X)} B$ via valuations v_A, v_B with $v_A(x) = v_B(x) = a$, $v_A(y) = v_B(y) = b$, and $B \equiv^{ASL}_{W(X)} C$ via valuations w_B, w_C with $w_B(x) = w_C(x) = b$, $w_B(y) = w_C(y) = a$ (extended surjectively to $bool$). But $A \not\equiv^{ASL}_{W(X)} C$.

A consequence of this is that ASL's behavioural abstraction as a function on model classes is not a closure operation, contrary to some of the laws in [SW83], [Wir86].

The source of the problem indicated by the above counterexample is that when the set of terms considered is not closed under renaming of variables, two algebras A, B remain in the relation defined above if for each set of terms in W that share common variables we can identify subalgebras of A and B in which these terms have the same behaviour. Clearly, this is quite different from requiring these terms (and all terms in W) to have the same behaviour throughout A and B, and leads to the failure of transitivity.

To alleviate the above problems, we therefore need to allow the set of variables to be arbitrarily enlarged and the set of terms to be closed under renaming of variables.

Given a set $W \subseteq T_\Sigma(X)$ of Σ-terms and another set Y of variables, the *closure of W from X to Y* is $W[X \mapsto Y] = \{\theta(t) \mid \theta : X \to Y, t \in W\}$. W is *closed under renaming of variables* if $W = W[X \mapsto X]$.

Now, we define two Σ-algebras A, B to be *W-equivalent*, written $A \equiv_W B$, if there is a set Y of variables such that $A \equiv^{ASL}_{W[X \mapsto Y]} B$. Then we define

abstraction: For any Σ-specification SP and set $W \subseteq T_\Sigma(X)$ of Σ-terms with variables in X, **abstract SP wrt W** is a specification with:

$Sig[\textbf{abstract } SP \textbf{ wrt } W] = \Sigma$
$Mod[\textbf{abstract } SP \textbf{ wrt } W] =$
$\quad \{A \in \textbf{Mod}(\Sigma) \mid A \equiv_W B \text{ for some } B \in Mod[SP]\}$

Proposition 5.2. *For any signature Σ and set $W \subseteq T_\Sigma(X)$ of Σ-terms with variables in X, W-equivalence is indeed an equivalence on $\textbf{Alg}(\Sigma)$.*

Proof. Reflexivity and symmetry are obvious. For transitivity, suppose $A \equiv_W B$ as witnessed by a set Y of variables with valuations $v_A : Y \to |A|$ and $v_B : Y \to |B|$, and $B \equiv_W C$ as witnessed by a set Z of variables with valuations $w_B : Z \to |B|$ and $w_C : Z \to |C|$. Take YZ to be the set of variables given by a pullback $v' : YZ \to Y$, $w' : YZ \to Z$ of v_B and w_B. Then the equivalence $A \equiv_W C$ is witnessed by YZ with valuations $v';v_A : YZ \to |A|$ and $w';w_C : YZ \to |C|$. First, since v_B and w_B are surjective, so are v' and w', and hence also $v';v_A$ and $w';w_C$. Then, for any terms $t, t' \in W$ of the same sort, and $\theta : X \to YZ$, we have: $\theta(t)_{A[v';v_A]} = \theta(t')_{A[v';v_A]}$ iff $(\theta;v')(t)_{A[v_A]} = (\theta;v')(t')_{A[v_A]}$ iff (since Y, v_A, v_B witness $A \equiv_W B$) $(\theta;v')(t)_{B[v_B]} = (\theta;v')(t')_{B[v_B]}$ iff $\theta(t)_{B[v';v_B]} = \theta(t')_{B[v';v_B]}$ iff (since $v';v_B = w';w_B$) $\theta(t)_{B[w';w_B]} = \theta(t')_{B[w';w_B]}$ iff $(\theta;w')(t)_{B[w_B]} = (\theta;w')(t')_{B[w_B]}$ iff (since Z, w_B, w_C witness $B \equiv_W C$) $(\theta;w')(t)_{C[w_C]} = (\theta;w')(t')_{C[w_C]}$ iff $\theta(t)_{C[w';w_C]} = \theta(t')_{C[w';w_C]}$.

We do not need to assume here that the set W is closed under renaming of variables — the definition of W-equivalence invokes the closure now.

Furthermore, W-equivalence properly generalises the equivalence used in ASL:

Proposition 5.3. *$A \equiv_W B$ iff $A \equiv^{ASL}_{W(X)} B$ provided that W is closed under renaming of variables and $card(X) \geq card(|A|) + card(|B|)$.*

Proof. We take the easy direction first: if $A \equiv^{ASL}_{W(X)} B$ is witnessed by $v_A : X \to |A|$, $v_B : X \to |B|$ then, since W is closed under renaming of variables, $A \equiv_W B$ is witnessed by X with the same valuations.

For the opposite implication: suppose $A \equiv_W B$ is witnessed by Y with valuations $v_A\colon Y \to |A|$, $v_B\colon Y \to |B|$. Then, given the cardinality assumption to ensure that X is sufficiently large, there exists $\theta\colon X \to Y$ such that $\theta;v_A\colon X \to |A|$ and $\theta;v_B\colon X \to |B|$ are surjective. $A \equiv_{W(X)}^{ASL} B$ is witnessed by $\theta;v_A$ and $\theta;v_B$.

Completely arbitrary choices of W, as permitted in ASL, may yield odd equivalences. Even closing the sets of terms under variable renaming leaves an enormous wealth of possibilities. Only a few of these have ever been used, capturing different notions of behavioural equivalence. The most typical situation is where we want to indicate a set IN of sorts to be viewed as input data, and a set OUT of sorts to be viewed as observable outputs. Then $\equiv_{T_\Sigma(X_{IN})_{OUT}}$ identifies algebras that display the same input/output behaviour for observable computations (presented as Σ-terms) taking inputs from IN and yielding results in OUT. Often, one identifies a single set OBS of *observable sorts* and takes $IN = OUT = OBS$. An important twist is to select a subset of operations that are used to build observable terms, by considering $\equiv_{T_{\Sigma'}(X_{IN})_{OUT}}$ for a subsignature Σ' of Σ, see for instance [BH06].

The natural choice of observable sorts for the specifications SET, EXTSET and CONTAINER in Sect. 3.1 is $OBS = \{bool, nat\}$; in particular, $bag \notin OBS$. One may now check that, in this context, it is sufficient to consider as observable terms W^{SET} all variables of sorts nat and $bool$ as well as all terms of the form $isin(x, t_{bag})$ where x is a variable of sort nat and t_{bag} is a term of sort bag built using $empty$, add, and variables of sort nat.

A more general interesting case arises in the following situation. We consider an additional signature $\widehat{\Sigma}$ with sets IN and OUT of input and output sorts, together with a derived signature morphism $\delta\colon \widehat{\Sigma} \to \Sigma$. We may think of δ as defining $\widehat{\Sigma}$-operations in terms of Σ-operations. Suppose that we want to observe $\widehat{\Sigma}$-computations carried out in Σ-algebras according to the definitions given by δ. Then the relevant equivalence on Σ-algebras is given by the following set of terms: $W_{\delta(IN,OUT)} = \delta(T_{\widehat{\Sigma}}(\widehat{X}_{IN})_{OUT})$, where $X = \delta(\widehat{X}_{IN})$.

In ASL, the abstraction construct defined above was available for arbitrary use, freely intermixed with other specification constructs. This is in line with the idea that ASL is a kernel language which provides raw specification power, free from pragmatic or methodologically-motivated constraints.

In specification practice, the use of abstraction can be limited to specific contexts where it fits a methodological need. In particular, if SP is a requirements specification and W captures all of the computations that the user wishes to carry out in its realisation, then any implementation of **abstract** SP **wrt** W will be satisfactory. So this is the specification that should be used as the starting point in the development. That is, we want to have the liberty to implement SP up to $\equiv_W$. However, when using a realisation of another specification SP' to implement SP, we still want to be allowed to assume that it satisfies SP' "literally". This is captured by the following definition.[3]

We say that SP' is a *behavioural implementation of SP via κ wrt W*, written $SP \sqsupseteq_\kappa^W SP'$, if **abstract** SP **wrt** $W \sqsupseteq_\kappa SP'$. Obviously, whenever $SP \sqsupseteq_\kappa SP'$ then also $SP \sqsupseteq_\kappa^W$

---

[3] This is a special case of *abstractor implementations* as introduced in [ST88b]. We follow the terminology of Sect. 8.4 in [ST12] but generalise the concept from equivalence with respect to observable sorts to equivalence with respect to observable terms.

SP'. Hence, for instance, we have CONTAINER $W^{\text{SET}}_{-|_\delta}$ BAG where δ: $Sig[\text{CONTAINER}] \rightarrow$ $Sig[\text{BAG}]$ maps $isin$ to the term $count(x_1, x_2) > 0$ and W^{SET} is as described above. However, we also have EXTSET $W^{\text{SET}}_{-|_\delta}$ BAG even though EXTSET $\not\sim_{-|_\delta}$ BAG.

The alert reader will have sensed that we are about to run into a problem: vertical composability does not hold in general. $SP \; {}^W_{\kappa} \; SP'$ and $SP' \; {}^{W'}_{\kappa'} \; SP''$ does not imply $SP \; {}^W_{\kappa';\kappa} \; SP''$. However, these behavioural implementations compose if the constructor κ is *stable* with respect to W' and W, that is, $\equiv_{W'} \subseteq \kappa^{-1}(\equiv_W)$. Or, spelling this out, we require that for any $A', B' \in \mathbf{Alg}(Sig[SP'])$, whenever $A' \equiv_{W'} B'$ then $\kappa(A') \equiv_W \kappa(B')$ [Sch90], [ST88b]. This technical notion captures a methodological point: κ must not differentiate between behaviourally equivalent realisations of SP'. This is exactly the encapsulation principle of data abstraction and hierarchical decomposition.

Now, given a chain of behavioural implementation steps using stable constructors

$$SP_0 \; {}^{W_0}_{\kappa_1} SP_1 \; {}^{W_1}_{\kappa_2} \cdots {}^{W_{n-1}}_{\kappa_n} SP_n = \text{EMPTY}$$

we have $\kappa_1(\kappa_2(\ldots \kappa_n(\text{empty}) \ldots)) \equiv_{W_0} A_0$, for some $A_0 \in Mod[SP_0]$.

The crucial stability requirement on constructors may be approached in two different ways. On the one hand, following the ideas in [Sch90] and [BST08], we can fix the family of behavioural equivalences considered, referring to a fixed set of observable built-in sorts (booleans, etc.), and then limit constructors to those that preserve that equivalence. This is guaranteed by use of a programming language that appropriately enforces abstraction barriers. The other option is, at each development step, to determine the behavioural equivalence that is appropriate to the context of use. Technically, this means that given a behavioural implementation step $SP \; {}^W_{\kappa} \; SP'$, we need a set W' of $Sig[SP']$-terms such that κ is stable with respect to W' and W. Picking W' to achieve $\equiv_{W'} = \kappa^{-1}(\equiv_W)$ gives maximal flexibility for further implementations of SP', since only the precise context of use in the implementation of SP by SP' via κ matters.

The latter option was proposed in [ST88b] but it does not seem to have been properly explored. The following simple fact shows how this might go.

Proposition 5.4. *Given a derived signature morphism $\delta \colon \Sigma \rightarrow \Sigma'$ and set $W \subseteq T_\Sigma(X)$ of Σ-terms closed under renaming of variables, let $W' = \delta(W) \subseteq T_{\Sigma'}(X')$ where $X' = \delta(X)$. Then for any Σ'-algebras A', B', $A' \equiv_{W'} B'$ iff $A'|_\delta \equiv_W B'|_\delta$. In particular the δ-reduct constructor is stable with respect to W' and W.*

Proof. *Suppose in Σ', $A' \equiv_{W'} B'$ is witnessed by Y' with valuations $v'_{A'} \colon Y' \rightarrow |A'|$ and $v'_{B'} \colon Y' \rightarrow |B'|$. Then in Σ, $A'|_\delta \equiv_W B'|_\delta$ is witnessed by $Y = Y'|_\delta$ (only the mapping on sorts matters here) with valuations $v'_{A'}|_\delta \colon Y \rightarrow |A'|_\delta|$ and $v'_{B'}|_\delta \colon Y \rightarrow |B'|_\delta|$.*

Let then in Σ, $A'|_\delta \equiv_W B'|_\delta$ be witnessed by Y with valuations $v_1 \colon Y \rightarrow |A'|_\delta|$ and $v_2 \colon Y \rightarrow |B'|_\delta|$. Let Y' be $\delta(Y)$ on sorts in the image of δ and $Y'_{s'} = |A'|_{s'} \uplus |B'|_{s'}$ for all sorts s' not in the image of δ. Let $v'_{A'} \colon Y' \rightarrow |A'|$ be given by v_1 on variables in $\delta(Y)$, and be any surjective function on the sorts not in the image of δ; similarly, let $v'_{B'} \colon Y' \rightarrow |B'|$ be given by v_2 on variables in $\delta(Y)$, and be any surjective function on *the sorts not in the image of δ. Then $A' \equiv_{W'} B'$ is witnessed by Y' with valuations $v'_{A'}$ and $v'_{B'}$.*

Stability of the reduct is just the former implication.

For instance, in the context of use of BAG taken as an implementation of EXTSET as indicated above, EXTSET $\overset{W^{\text{SET}}}{\underset{\text{-}|\delta}{}}$ BAG, the relevant set of observable terms to determine equivalence up to which BAG is to be implemented is $\delta(W^{\text{SET}})$ which consists of all variables of sorts nat and $bool$ as well as all terms of the form $count(x, t_{bag}) > 0$ where x is a variable of sort nat and t_{bag} is a term of sort bag built using $empty$, add, and variables of sort nat. In particular, we do not care about keeping the exact count of the number of occurrences in a bag, as long as we can distinguish between the cases where it is 0 versus strictly positive.

6 Final Remarks

In this essay we have presented what we see as the key characteristics of ASL and have outlined some of the developments that later emerged from this basis. We have focused on tracing the flow of ideas rather than on technical details or new results, although the technicalities in Sect. 5 regarding W-equivalence seem new.

Even though there has been a lot of work on these topics, some corners are worth further exploration.

Semantics: It seems to us that the relationship between model-class and theory-level semantics is completely resolved by Theorem 3.1 and its consequences, as discussed in Sect. 3, even if the choice between the two may remain controversial in some quarters. The class of specifications we consider is particularly well-understood with clear proof techniques etc. For some other specification constructs, including for instance behavioural abstraction, this is much less true.

Implementation: The semantic concept of implementation in Sect. 4 together with its refinement in Sect. 5 capture what is needed. We have not discussed issues arising from the need for proof techniques to establish the correctness of implementation steps — see Chap. 9 of [ST12] for our summary of the state of the art.

Parameterization: All of the syntactic and semantic concepts are established but in a raw form that is a little hard to use. We feel that this is still a somewhat open area where more ideas are needed to limit the scope of possibilities to what is really required and useful in practice.

Behavioural specifications: Following ASL, in Sect. 5 we sketched the "external" approach to behavioural interpretation of specifications, based on behavioural equivalence between algebras. A widely-studied alternative is to re-interpret the meaning of axioms, and hence of specifications, using the "internal" indistinguishability between values. The relationship between the two approaches is now well-understood, see [BHW95], but only for behavioural equivalence with respect to a set of observable sorts. It would be interesting to investigate the same relationship for W-equivalence. We also think that the methodological ideas on the use of context-tailored behavioural equivalence at the end of Sect. 5 are worth further exploration.

References

[Asp97]   Aspinall, D.: Type Systems for Modular Programming and Specification. Ph.D. thesis, University of Edinburgh, Department of Computer Science (1997)

[BBB⁺85]   Bauer, F.L., Berghammer, R., Broy, M., Dosch, W., Geiselbrechtinger, F., Gnatz, R., Hangel, E., Hesse, W., Krieg-Brückner, B., Laut, A., Matzner, T., Möller, B., Nickl, F., Partsch, H., Pepper, P.A., Samelson, K., Wirsing, M., Wössner, H.: The Munich Project CIP. LNCS, vol. 183. Springer, Heidelberg (1985)

[BG80]   Burstall, R.M., Goguen, J.A.: The semantics of Clear, a specification language. In: Bjorner, D. (ed.) Abstract Software Specifications. LNCS, vol. 86, pp. 292–332. Springer, Heidelberg (1980)

[BH06]   Bidoit, M., Hennicker, R.: Constructor-based observational logic. Journal of Logic and Algebraic Programming 67(1-2), 3–51 (2006)

[BHW95]   Bidoit, M., Hennicker, R., Wirsing, M.: Behavioural and abstractor specifications. Science of Computer Programming 25(2-3), 149–186 (1995)

[BM04]   Bidoit, M., Mosses, P.D. (eds.): CASL User Manual. LNCS, vol. 2900. Springer, Heidelberg (2004), http://www.informatik.uni-bremen.de/cofi/index.php/CASL

[Bor05]   Borzyszkowski, T.: Generalized interpolation in first order logic. Fundamenta Informaticae 66(3), 199–219 (2005)

[BST02]   Bidoit, M., Sannella, D., Tarlecki, A.: Architectural specifications in CASL. Formal Aspects of Computing 13, 252–273 (2002)

[BST08]   Bidoit, M., Sannella, D., Tarlecki, A.: Observational interpretation of CASL specifications. Mathematical Structures in Computer Science 18, 325–371 (2008)

[CK90]   Chang, C.-C., Keisler, H.J.: Model Theory, 3rd edn. North-Holland (1990)

[DGS93]   Diaconescu, R., Goguen, J.A., Stefaneas, P.: Logical support for modularisation. In: Huet, G., Plotkin, G. (eds.) Logical Environments, pp. 83–130. Cambridge University Press (1993)

[Dia08]   Diaconescu, R.: Institution-Independent Model Theory. Birkhäuser (2008)

[EKMP82]   Ehrig, H., Kreowski, H.-J., Mahr, B., Padawitz, P.: Algebraic implementation of abstract data types. Theoretical Computer Science 20, 209–263 (1982)

[EM85]   Ehrig, H., Mahr, B.: Fundamentals of Algebraic Specification 1. In: EATCS Monographs on Theoretical Computer Science, vol. 6. Springer (1985)

[FJ90]   Fitzgerald, J.S., Jones, C.B.: Modularizing the formal description of a database system. In: Langmaack, H., Hoare, C.A.R., Bjorner, D. (eds.) VDM 1990. LNCS, vol. 428, pp. 189–210. Springer, Heidelberg (1990)

[Gan83]   Ganzinger, H.: Parameterized specifications: Parameter passing and implementation with respect to observability. ACM Transactions on Programming Languages and Systems 5(3), 318–354 (1983)

[GB80]   Goguen, J.A., Burstall, R.M.: CAT, a system for the structured elaboration of correct programs from structured specifications. Technical Report CSL-118, Computer Science Laboratory, SRI International (1980)

[GB92]   Goguen, J.A., Burstall, R.M.: Institutions: Abstract model theory for specification and programming. Journal of the Association for Computing Machinery 39(1), 95–146 (1992)

[GGM76]   Giarratana, V., Gimona, F., Montanari, U.: Observability concepts in abstract data type specifications. In: Mazurkiewicz, A. (ed.) MFCS 1976. LNCS, vol. 45, pp. 567–578. Springer, Heidelberg (1976)

[GM82]   Goguen, J.A., Meseguer, J.: Universal realization, persistent interconnection and implementation of abstract modules. In: Nielsen, M., Schmidt, E.M. (eds.) ICALP 1982. LNCS, vol. 140, pp. 265–281. Springer, Heidelberg (1982)

[GR04]   Goguen, J.A., Roșu, G.: Composing hidden information modules over inclusive institutions. In: Owe, O., Krogdahl, S., Lyche, T. (eds.) From Object-Orientation to Formal Methods. LNCS, vol. 2635, pp. 96–123. Springer, Heidelberg (2004)

[GTW76]   Goguen, J.A., Thatcher, J.W., Wagner, E.G.: An initial algebra approach to the specification, correctness and implementation of abstract data types. Technical Report RC 6487, IBM Watson Research Center, Yorktown Heights NY (1976), Also in: Yeh, R.T. (ed.): Current Trends in Programming Methodology. Data Structuring, vol. IV, pp. 80–149. Prentice-Hall (1978)

[HWB97]   Hennicker, R., Wirsing, M., Bidoit, M.: Proof systems for structured specifications with observability operators. Theoretical Computer Science 173(2), 393–443 (1997)

[KBS91]   Krieg-Brückner, B., Sannella, D.: Structuring specifications in-the-large and in-the-small: Higher-order functions, dependent types and inheritance in SPECTRAL. In: Abramsky, S. (ed.) TAPSOFT 1991, CCPSD 1991, and ADC-Talks 1991. LNCS, vol. 494, pp. 103–120. Springer, Heidelberg (1991)

[LB88]   Lampson, B., Burstall, R.M.: Pebble, a kernel language for modules and abstract data types. Information and Computation 76(2-3), 278–346 (1988)

[MAH06]   Mossakowski, T., Autexier, S., Hutter, D.: Development graphs — proof management for structured specifications. Journal of Logic and Algebraic Programming 67(1-2), 114–145 (2006)

[MT14]   Mossakowski, T., Tarlecki, A.: A relatively complete calculus for structured heterogeneous specifications. In: Muscholl, A. (ed.) FOSSACS 2014 (ETAPS). LNCS, vol. 8412, pp. 441–456. Springer, Heidelberg (2014)

[Rei81]   Reichel, H.: Behavioural equivalence — a unifying concept for initial and final specification methods. In: Proceedings of the 3rd Hungarian Computer Science Conference, pp. 27–39 (1981)

[RG00]   Roșu, G., Goguen, J.A.: On equational Craig interpolation. Journal of Universal Computer Science 6(1), 194–200 (2000)

[Sch90]   Schoett, O.: Behavioural correctness of data representations. Science of Computer Programming 14(1), 43–57 (1990)

[SST92]   Sannella, D., Sokołowski, S., Tarlecki, A.: Toward formal development of programs from algebraic specifications: Parameterisation revisited. Acta Informatica 29(8), 689–736 (1992)

[ST87]   Sannella, D., Tarlecki, A.: On observational equivalence and algebraic specification. Journal of Computer and System Sciences 34, 150–178 (1987)

[ST88a]   Sannella, D., Tarlecki, A.: Specifications in an arbitrary institution. Information and Computation 76(2-3), 165–210 (1988)

[ST88b]   Sannella, D., Tarlecki, A.: Toward formal development of programs from algebraic specifications: Implementations revisited. Acta Informatica 25, 233–281 (1988)

[ST06]   Sannella, D., Tarlecki, A.: Horizontal composability revisited. In: Futatsugi, K., Jouannaud, J.-P., Meseguer, J. (eds.) Algebra, Meaning, and Computation. LNCS, vol. 4060, pp. 296–316. Springer, Heidelberg (2006)

[ST12]   Sannella, D., Tarlecki, A.: Foundations of Algebraic Specification and Formal Software Development. In: Monographs in Theoretical Computer Science. An EATCS Series. Springer (2012)

[ST14]   Sannella, D., Tarlecki, A.: Property-oriented semantics of structured specifications. Mathematical Structures in Computer Science 24(2), e240205 (2014)

[SW82]   Sannella, D., Wirsing, M.: Implementation of parameterised specifications. In: Nielsen, M., Schmidt, E.M. (eds.) ICALP 1982. LNCS, vol. 140, pp. 473–488. Springer, Heidelberg (1982)

[SW83]   Sannella, D., Wirsing, M.: A kernel language for algebraic specification and implementation. In: Karpinski, M. (ed.) FCT 1983. LNCS, vol. 158, pp. 413–427. Springer, Heidelberg (1983)

[Tar86]   Tarlecki, A.: Bits and pieces of the theory of institutions. In: Poigné, A., Pitt, D.H., Rydeheard, D.E., Abramsky, S. (eds.) Category Theory and Computer Programming. LNCS, vol. 240, pp. 334–360. Springer, Heidelberg (1986)

[Tar11]   Tarlecki, A.: Some nuances of many-sorted universal algebra: A review. Bulletin of the European Association for Theoretical Computer Science 104, 89–111 (2011)

[TWW82]   Thatcher, J.W., Wagner, E.G., Wright, J.B.: Data type specification: Parameterization and the power of specification techniques. ACM Transactions on Programming Languages and Systems 4(4), 711–732 (1982)

[Wan79]   Wand, M.: Final algebra semantics and data type extensions. Journal of Computer and System Sciences 19, 27–44 (1979)

[Wir82]   Wirsing, M.: Structured algebraic specifications. In: Proceedings of the AFCET Symposium on Mathematics for Computer Science, Paris, pp. 93–107 (1982)

[Wir86]   Wirsing, M.: Structured algebraic specifications: A kernel language. Theoretical Computer Science 42(2), 123–249 (1986)

Soft Agents: Exploring Soft Constraints to Model Robust Adaptive Distributed Cyber-Physical Agent Systems

Carolyn Talcott[1], Farhad Arbab[2], and Maneesh Yadav[1]

[1] SRI International, Menlo Park, CA 94025, USA
{carolyn.talcott,maneesh.yadav}@sri.com
[2] CWI Amsterdam, The Netherlands
Farhad.Arbab@cwi.nl

Abstract. We are interested in principles for designing and building open distributed systems consisting of multiple cyber-physical agents, specifically, where a coherent global view is unattainable and timely consensus is impossible. Such agents attempt to contribute to a system goal by making local decisions to sense and effect their environment based on local information. In this paper we propose a model, formalized in the Maude rewriting logic system, that allows experimenting with and reasoning about designs of such systems. Features of the model include communication via sharing of partially ordered knowledge, making explicit the physical state as well as the cyber perception of this state, and the use of a notion of soft constraints developed by Martin Wirsing and his team to specify agent behavior. The paper begins with a discussion of desiderata for such models and concludes with a small case study to illustrate the use of the modeling framework.

With Best Wishes to Martin Wirsing

This work has roots in the joint work with Martin on the PAGODA project and soft constraint solving[1], carried out when Martin spent a sabbatical at SRI in 2005. This work was continued by Martin, Max Meier and Matthias Hölzl [2,3], leading to a new notion of soft constraints that seems very well suited to the world of cyber-physical agents. The present work also builds on many discussions over the last few years on the challenges of cyber-physical systems, including several Interlink workshops [4] lead by Martin.

It has been a great privilege and pleasure to know Martin, to have the opportunity to work together from time to time, and to exchange ideas as our paths have crossed over the years. I look forward to many more years of exchanging ideas and tackling challenging problems.

1 Introduction

Consider a future in which an explosion of small applications running on mobile devices combine and collaborate to provide powerful new functionality not only in the realms

R. De Nicola and R. Hennicker (Eds.): Wirsing Festschrift, LNCS 8950, pp. 273–290, 2015.

such as large collections of automated vehicles, but also harnessing the underlying communication and robust people power for new kinds of cyber crowd sourcing tasks.

Complex cyber-physical agents are becoming increasingly ubiquitous, in part, due to increased computational performance of commodity hardware and the widespread adoption of standard mobile computing environments (e.g. Android). At the time of writing, one can purchase (for a few hundred US dollars in the retail market) a four rotor "drone" capable of precise, controlled hovering that can be equipped with a portable Android phone that provides integrated communication (e.g. wifi ad hoc) and sensing (e.g. high resolution camera) capability as well as considerable processing power (e.g. multiple GPU cores) and memory. The increasingly impressive capabilities of such platforms have led to autonomous cyber-physical systems that implement realtime methods for computer vision[5], machine learning[6] and computational aerodynamics[7]. Technology has progressed to the point that many of these capabilities can be easily applied by non-specialists.

The disparity between the growing sophistication of cyber-physical agents and practical, scalable methods that autonomously coordinate agent collectives (without central control) is clear from the lack of widely available frameworks. There are very few practical tools available to non-specialists that would enable them to specify joint goals across a cyber-physical agent collectives in a way that is robust to a dynamic environment.

The specification of goals and constraints for agent collectives broadly falls under a number of problem representations that have been long explored, these include Distributed Constraint Satisfaction Problems [8], Distributed Control Optimization Problems [9], Distributed Continual Planning [10], Multi-Agent Planning [11] and multi-agent coordination[12]. Not all methods that we have surveyed in the literature have proven correctness or bounds, but amongst those that have, coordination is clearly difficult since all methods that we are aware of are exponential in the number of messages sent (with the exception of DPOP[13], where the number of messages is kept linear at the cost of exponential memory usage).

Most methods focus on *distributed* systems, but practical distributed systems are often further complicated from unexpected changes in goals, (partial) agent failure and delays in agent communication. In the context of such complicating factors, some coordination methods will suffer (unbounded) delays in performing actions towards a specified goal (e.g., halt during consensus formation), when it would make eminent sense for the agents to begin *doing something* towards achieving their goal. While many of the problem representations that have explored distributed systems have carefully considered dynamic environments and failure, we use the term *fractionated* to emphasize these aspects.

Our intent is to address the design, prototyping and eventually implementation of systems which we call *Fractionated Cyber-Physical Systems* (FCPS) [14,15]. FCPS are distributed systems composed of many small cyber-physical agents that must act using only local knowledge in the context of an uncertain environment, communication delays as well as agent failure/replacement/addition. Agents in FCPS interact by sharing knowledge that is gained by sensing and by reasoning. We are particularly interested in principles for designing FCPS in which desired cooperation/coordination emerges from local behaviors, under practical conditions.

FCPS promise robustness and fault tolerance using many small entities such that no specific individual is critical. Entities can come and go without disrupting the system, as long as the needed functionality is sufficiently represented. Defective, worn out, or out-of-date entities can be easily replaced by fresh, improved versions. The term "fractionated" was originally coined to describe replacing small sets of multifunctional space satellites with an collective of smaller more specialized "nanosats" that could be launched cheaply and easily replaced, providing a resilient system capable of complex functionality at a lower overall cost[16]. We suggest that this notion has become much more relevant with the advent of ubiquitous mobile computing and applicable to "down to earth" problems such as package delivery.

Towards these goals, we propose a framework we call *Soft Agents* and describe a prototype implementation in the Maude rewriting logic system [17] along with a small package delivery case-study to illustrate the ideas.

The notion of fractionated cyber-physical systems is very similar to the notion of *ensemble* that emerged from the Interlink project [4,18] and that has been a central theme of the ASCENS (Autonomic Service-Component Ensembles) project [19]. In [20] a mathematical system model for ensembles is presented. Similar to FCPS and soft agents, the mathematical model treats both cyber and physical aspects of a system. A notion of fitness is defined that supports reasoning about level of satisfaction. Adaptability is also treated. In contrast to the soft-agent framework which provides an executable model, the system model for ensembles is denotational. The two approached are both compatible and complementary and joining them could lead to a very expressive framework supporting both high-level specification and concrete design methodologies.

The soft agents framework combines ideas from several previous works: the use of soft constraints [1,2,3] and soft constraint automata [21] for specifying robust and adaptive behavior; partially ordered knowledge sharing for communication in disrupted environments [14,22,23,15], and the Real-time Maude approach to modeling timed systems [24].

Soft constraints allow composition in multiple dimensions, including different concerns for a given agent, and composition of constraints for multiple agents. In [2] a new system for expressing soft constraints called Monoidal Soft Constraints is proposed. This generalizes the Semi-ring approach to support more complex preference relations. In [3] partially ordered valuation structures are explored to provide operators for combination of constraints for different features that respects the relative importance of the features.

Given local constraints, a global theoretical model can be formed as a cross product, that considers all inter-leavings of actions of individual agents. This is generally an infeasibly complex problem to solve. We propose solving the complex problem by concurrent distributed solution of simpler local problems. This leads us to study questions such as

- Under what conditions are the local solutions good enough?
- Under what conditions would it not be possible?
- How much knowledge is needed for satisfactory solution/behavior?
- What frequency of decision making is needed so that local solutions are safe and effective?

Plan. Section 2 discusses desiderata for a framework for FCPS. Section 3 presents the proposed framework and its formalization in Maude. Section 4 illustrates the application of soft-agents to a simple autonomous drone packet deliver system. Section 5 summarizes and discusses future directions.

2   Desiderata for Soft Agents

CPS agents must maintain an overall situation, location, and time awareness and make safe decisions that progress towards an objective in spite of uncertainty, partial knowledge and intermittent connectivity. The big question is: how do we design, build, and understand such systems? We want principles/tools for system designs that achieve adaptive, robust functionality using diversity, redundancy and probabilistic behavior.

The primary desiderata for our FCPS are *localness*, *liveness* and *softness*. We explicitly exclude considering insincere or malicious agents in our current formulation.[1]

Localness. Cooperation and coordination should emerge from local behavior based on local knowledge. This is traditionally done by consensus formation algorithms. Consensus involves agreeing on what actions to take, which usually requires a shared view of the system state. In a distributed system spread over a large geographic area beyond the communication reach of individual agents, consensus can take considerable time and resources, but an FCPS agent must keep going. Thus consensus may emerge but can't be relied on, nor can it be be forced.

In less than ideal conditions what is needed is a notion of *satisficing consensus*: for any agent, consensus is satisficed when enough of a consensus is present so that agents can begin executing actions that are likely to be a part of a successful plan, given that there is some expectation for the environment to change.

Our POKS knowledge dissemination framework underlying an FCPS takes care of agreeing on state to the degree possible. In a quiescent connected situation all agents will eventually have the same knowledge base. As communication improves, an FCPS approaches a typical distributed system without complicating factors. This should increase the likelihood of reaching actual consensus, and achieving ideal behaviors.

A key question here is how a system determines the minimal required level of consensus? In particular what quality of connection/communication is required to support formation of this minimum level of consensus?

Safety and Liveness. Another formal property of an FCPS to consider concerns safety and liveness: something bad does not happen and something good will eventually happen. From a local perspective this could mean avoiding preventable disaster/failure as well as making progress and eventually sufficiently satisfying a given goal.

- An agent will never wait for an unbounded time to act.
- An agent can always act if local environment/knowledge/situation demands.

---

[1] This is a strong assumption, although not unusual. The soft agents framework supports modeling of an unpredictable or even "malicious" environment. We discus the issue of trust or confidence in knowledge received as part of future work.

- An agent will react in a timely manner based on local information.
- An agent should keep itself "safe".

We note that the quality calculus [25,26] provides language primitives to support programming to meet such liveness requirements and robustness analysis methods for verification. One of the motivations of the Quality Calculus was to deal with unrealiable communication. It will be interesting to investigate how soft constraints and the quality calculus approach might be combined to provide higher level specification and programming paradigms.

Softness. We want to reason about systems at both the system and cyber-physical entity/agent level and systematically connect the two levels. Agent behavior must allow for uncertainty and partial information, as well as preferences when multiple actions are possible to accomplish a task, as often is the case.

Specification in terms of constraints is a natural way to allow for partiality. *Soft constraints* provide a mechanism to rank different solutions and compose constraints concerning different aspects. We refer to [2] for an excellent review of different soft constraint systems. Given a problem there will be system wide constraints characterizing acceptable solutions, and perhaps giving measures to rank possible behaviors/solutions. Rather than looking for distributed solution of global constraints, each agent will be driven by a local constraint system. Multiple soft constraint systems maybe be involved (multiple agent classes) and multiple agents may be driven by the same soft constraint system.

3   Soft Agent Model Formalized in Maude

3.1   Networked Cyber-Physical Systems and Partially-Ordered Knowledge Sharing

To motivate the formal model we give a brief overview of our Networked cyber-physical systems (NCPS) framework. The theoretical foundation is a distributed computing model based on sharing knowledge that is partially ordered (POKS) [22,14,15]. An NCPS is a collection of cyber-physical agents (CPAs or simply agents) with diverse capabilities and resource limitations. They may cooperate and/or compete to achieve some global or local goal. An agent can communicate directly with connected peers to share knowledge. Information propagates opportunistically when connections arise. Communication, as well as an agent's own sensors, may update the agent's local knowledge base. A CPA must function somewhat autonomously, making decisions based on local information. It should function safely even in absence of communication and should be capable of a wide spectrum of operation between autonomy and consensus/cooperation to adapt to resource constraints and disruptions in communication. Interpreting knowledge items as facts or goals enables declarative specification of sensing and control. Conflicts between information received from various peers, through various channels, and/or local sensors, acquired/received at different times, need to be resolved. The partial order on knowledge provides a mechanism for revision, control, conflict resolution and consensus under suitable conditions.

Soft agents are based on the NCPS framework with two additional features: formulation of an agent's goals as soft constraint problems and representation of an agent's physical state separated from its knowledge. Actions are carried out based on the physical state, and an agent makes decisions based on its local knowledge. In the following we describe the formalization of Soft Agents in the Maude rewriting logic language [17].

3.2   Soft Agents in Maude

A Maude cyber-physical soft-constraint system is an executable model with two parts: (1) the application independent modules (SOFT-AGENTS, SOFT-AGENT-RULES) and (2) modules specifying capabilities and behavior of the agents by defining the abstract functions used in the rewrite rules.

The following is a brief summary of the data structures and behavior rules used to specify the framework, including the functions that must be defined for each application. We present fragments of Maude code followed by informal discussion to clarify and augment the fragments. [2]

Knowledge. We use knowledge to represent properties of the world (the environment perspective) as well as an agents local view. An agent can receive or post knowledge. The environment, represented by rewrite rules, provides sensor information to agents.

```
sorts PKItem TKItem KItem  Info .
subsort PKItem TKItem < KItem .
op _@_ : Info Nat -> TKItem .
```

Knowledge is represented as a set of knowledge items (sort KItem), and comes in two flavors: persistent (sort PKItem) and ephemeral/temporary (sort TKItem). Persistent knowledge is knowledge that doesn't change over time, such as the class of an agent, size of a packet or capacity of a drone. Ephemeral knowledge concerns things that are expected to change over time such as sensor information, delivered by the environment, (received) logical and shared state knowledge (received and/or posted). Ephemeral knowledge is constructed from the underlying information (sort Info) and a timestamp (info @ t).

```
op _<<_ : KItem KItem -> Bool .   *** knowledge partial order
eq kitem << kitem' = false [owise] . *** not ordered default
```

Knowledge is partially ordered (<<) providing a mechanism to discard knowledge that is no longer valid/relevant. This allows an agent to deal with situations where, for example, newer state knowledge is available, or knowledge representing a goal is no longer valid because the goal has been satisfied or timed out. The equation with the [owise]

---

[2] Maude specifications consist of sort and subsort declarations, specifying the data type hierarchy, function and constant declarations (keyword op) giving argument and result sorts, equations (keyword eq) used to define functions, and rewrite rules rl[rulename]: lhs => rhs. --- and *** precede comments.

label says that the default is that two items are not ordered. It will be used if no other equation for the relation << matches.

An agent is modeled by a structure of the form

```
[id : class | envkb | localkb | cachedkb | events ]
```

where id is the agent's identity and class is the agent's class. The terms envkb, localkb, and cachekb denote knowledge bases—sets of knowledge items, where envkb contains facts representing an agent's physical state. In mobile settings it will include location and may include energy or fuel level, load, weight, etc.. The agent doesn't see envkb directly, only via sensor readings which maybe posted automatically or upon request. The knowledge items in localkb contain the agent's perception of its state and other knowledge which could include mode, plans, and knowledge posted by other agents. The knowledge items in cachedkb form the local cache of knowledge, used by the environment to implement knowledge sharing. It is not directly visible by the agent, although the agent has had the opportunity to process the knowledge in the cache. An agent system evolves by application of event handling rules. Rules for different types of event use information from different knowledge bases as appropriate.

Events, actions and tasks. Events include those that an agent handles and those handled by the environment. There are four classes of event:

- received knowledge such as local sensor information or shared knowledge, handled by the agent
- tasks scheduled by the agent, possibly with delay, to be handled by the agent
- actions to execute posted by agents, possibly with delay, handled by the environment (using rewrite rules that reflect the model physics)
- knowledge posted by an agent, handled by the communication system rewrite rules

```
sorts IEvent DEvent Event .
subsort  IEvent DEvent < Event .   --- immediate/delayed events
sorts Action Task ActTask .        --- delayed event body
subsort Action Task < ActTask .
```

Events are classified as immediate (sort IEvent) or delayed (sort DEvent). Delayed events are actions or tasks with a timestamp. The following are the event constructors.

```
op _@_ : ActTask Nat -> DEvent .
op rcv : KB -> IEvent [ctor] .         *** receive event
op post : InfoSet -> IEvent  [ctor] . *** posting information
op done : Action Bool -> Info  [ctor] . *** action status
op tick : -> Task .                    *** built in task
```

Time For initial studies we assume a global clock. Agents can run at different speeds by scheduling actions with different delays. In the current simple model only tasks and actions cause time to pass. Other events are handled instantaneously. An agent's behavior rules can cause delay in handling received knowledge by posting tasks.

3.3 Rules

An agent system has the form

```
{ aconf clock(t) }
```

where aconf is a multiset of agents, assumed to have distinct identifiers, and clock(t) is the global clock. There are five rewrite rules for describing how an agent system evolves over time. An agent may be reactive, and only respond when new knowledge is received, or agents may be proactive, scheduling tasks rather than waiting for input.

Rules for communication, posting and receiving knowledge, and handling scheduled tasks operate on a local part of the agent configuration. The rule for executing actions and the rule for passing time must capture the whole system.

Knowledge sharing. Notation convention: In the following we use id (and decorated variants) to range over agent identifiers, cl to range over agent classes, ekb for environment knowledge bases, lkb for local knowledge bases, ckb for cache knowledge bases, evs for event sets, and rcvk for received knowledge bases. For example, in the following code ekb1 is the environment knowledge base of the agent with identity id1, and evs1 is the set of pending events for this agent.

```
crl[KnowledgeSharing]:
[id1 : cl1 | ekb1 | lkb1 | ckb1 | evs1 ]
[id2 : cl2 | ekb2 | lkb2 | ckb2 | evs2]
=>
[id1 : cl1 | ekb1 | lkb1 | ckb11 |
        evs1 (if rcvk1 == none then none else rcv(rcvk1) fi)]
[id2 : cl2 | ekb2 | lkb2 | ckb21 |
        evs2 (if rcvk2 == none then none else rcv(rcvk2) fi)]
if inContact(id1,ekb1,id2,ekb2)
/\ {ckb11, rcvk1} := share(ckb2,ckb1,none) --- ckb2 to ckb1
/\ {ckb21, rcvk2} := share(ckb1,ckb2,none) --- ckb1 to ckb2
/\ rcvk2 rcvk1 =/= none .
```

Knowledge is propagated to neighbors upon contact. The definition of contact is part of each specific model and a model could have several different forms of contact. This is formalized by declaring a function inContact(id1,ekb1,id2,ekb2) that takes two agent identifiers and their corresponding environment knowledge bases and returns a boolean. A simple notion of contact is for two agents to be within a given distance of each other. Upon contact two agents fully exchange knowledge in their cache knowledge base and each agent is notified (via a receive event) of any new knowledge obtained. The function share(ckb2,ckb1,none) returns ckb11,rcvk1, where ckb11 is ckb1 updated with knowledge from ckb2 that is not present or subsumed/replaced by knowledge already in ckb1, and rcvk1 is the set of knowledge items newly added, used to notify the agent via the rcv(rcvk1) event.

Future work could limit the number of knowledge items that can be exchanged upon each contact, controlled by a policy or by the physics. Other properties of channels could be modeled as well, such as one way channels.

Posted Knowledge.

```
crl[post]:
[a : cl | ekb | lkb | ckb | post(iset) evs ] clock(t)
=>
[a : cl | ekb | lkb' | ckb' | evs ]    clock(t)
if kb := tstamp(iset,t)
/\ ckb' := addK(ckb,kb)
/\ lkb' := addK(lkb,kb) .
```

Posted knowledge is time stamped (`tstamp(iset,t)`) with the current time and added to the cached knowledge base and the local knowledge base. The function `addK` adds knowledge items from its second argument, `kb1`, to its first argument, `kb0`, that are not less than in the partial order to knowledge already present in `kb0`. It also removes elements of `kb0` that are less in the partial order than a newly added item.

Receiving Knowledge.

```
crl[rcv]:
[id : cl | ekb | lkb | ckb | rcv(rcvk) evs ] clock(t)
=>
[id : cl | ekb | lkb' | ckb | evs fixTime(evs',t) ]    clock(t)
if {lkb', evs'} := handle(cl,id, lkb,rcvk) .
```

Agents have class specific procedures for handling new knowledge. These procedures specify how the local knowledge base is updated, possibly raising new events to schedule. This is formalized by the function

```
    handle(class,id,lkb,rcvkb) = {lkb1,evs1}
```

where `lkb` is the current local knowledge base, `lkb1` is the updated local knowledge base, and `evs1` is the possibly empty set of events to schedule.

Tasks. Tasks provide a mechanism for an agent to control scheduling its activity.

```
crl[doTask]:
[id : cl | ekb | lkb | ckb | (task @ t) evs ] clock(t')
=>
[id : cl | ekb | lkb | ckb | evs fixTime(ev,t')] clock(t')
if t <= t'
/\ ev evs' := doTask(cl, id, task,lkb) .
```

The event `task @ t` expresses that the agent plans to carry out `task` at time `t`. The task can be carried out if its time stamp is not greater than the current time. The task handling function, `doTask(class,id,lkb,task)`, returns a set of alternative actions. `task` is the task to be carried out, `lkb` is the agents local knowledge base. One of the alternative actions is chosen non deterministically and added to the agents event set. The pattern `ev evs'` models the selection of an event from a non-empty set of events.

The framework provides a generic task `tick` which an agent can use as a mechanism to periodically check the local state and decide on possible actions, if any. In our applications the agent solves a soft constraint problem for this purpose, but the framework allows other methods of deciding on actions.

Actions. For each agent class there is a (possibly empty) set of actions that its instances can perform. The event `act @ t` expresses that the agent intends to execute the action `act` at time `t`. For example the agent could move to a new location, press a button, pickup or drop an object.

```
crl[doAct]:
{[id : cl | ekb | lkb | ckb | (act @ t') evs ] clock(t) aconf}
=>
{ updateAConf([id : cl | ekb | lkb | ckb | evs ],{id,ekb',evs'})
  updateAConf( aconf,idkbevset)  clock(t) }
if t' <= t
/\ {id,ekb',evs'} idkbevset := doAction(cl,id,act,t,ekb,aconf) .
```

The environment has an action execution function, `doAction`, parameterized by agent class, formalizing the physics of the model. The physics may involve the state of the local environment, which is represented in the environment knowledge base of nearby agents. This is formalized by the abstract equation

$$doAction(class,id,act,t,ekb,aconf) = idekbevents$$

where `act` is the action to be executed, `ekb` is the agent's local environment knowledge base, and `aconf` contains the nearby agents. The variable `idekbevents` stands for a set of updates of the form `id,ekb',evs'`, one for the agent doing the action and one for any nearby agent affected by the action. `ekb'` is the new environment knowledge base and `evs'` is added to the existing event set.

Advancing time.

```
crl[timeStep]:
{ aconf clock(t) } => { aconf clock(ni) }
if ni := minTime(aconf,t)
/\ ni :: Nat .
```

Following the real-time Maude approach [24], time passes if there is nothing else to do at the current time. The function `minTime` returns infinity (which will not satisfy the membership `ni :: Nat`) if there are any immediate events or any knowledge sharing enabled. Otherwise, it returns the smallest timestamp of a delayed action or task.

4   A Simple Packet Delivery System

The drones and packets simple package delivery problem was inspired by a small startup in San Francisco developing an instant package delivery/courier service. There is a service area; packets at various locations in the service area, that want to be at another location (called the destination); and drones (mobile agents capable of moving around) that can transport packets. Drones use energy when moving and there are charging stations where a drone can recharge. We start with a simple case where there is one kind of packet and one kind of drone. The service area is a grid, locations are points on the grid, some of these locations are charging stations.

Knowledge partial order. The partially ordered knowledge for drones and packets adds three kinds of knowledge items for packet state

```
dest(idp,loc)              *** the destination of packet pid
pickupOk(pid,id,b) @ t *** models a pickup light indicating
                           *** permission for drone id to pickup pid
delivered(pid) @ t         *** packet pid has been delivered
```

and one item for drone state

```
energy(id,e) @ t     *** drone id has energy reserve e
```

where we use `idp` and `id` as variables for packet and drone identifiers; `t`, `t0`, `t1` range over natural numbers representing discrete time; and `loc`, `l0`, `l1` range over locations. The partial order is given by the following equations.

```
ceq (atloc(id,l0) @ t0) << (atloc(id,l1) @ t1)
      = true if t0 < t1 .
ceq (energy(id,n0) @ t0) << (energy(id,n1) @ t1)
      = true if t0 < t1 .

*** once delivered, packet info disappears.
eq (atloc(idp,l0) @ t0) << (delivered(idp) @ t1) = true .
eq dest(idp,l0) << (delivered(idp) @ t1) = true .
eq (pickupOk(idp,id,b0) @ t0) << (delivered(idp) @ t1) = true .
eq class(idp,packet) << (delivered(idp) @ t1) = true .
```

The first two equations say that new information about energy or location of an agent replaces older information. The last four formalize the policy that once a packet is delivered, it is no longer part of the system.

Actions. Drones are proactive, periodically choosing an action and executing it. The possible drone actions are

- `mv(dir)`: moving in direction `dir` to an adjacent grid point, where `dir` is one of `N,S,E,W`.
- `charge`: charge one charge unit, if located at a charging station
- `pickup(idp)`: picking up packet `idp`, if permitted
- `drop(idp)`: dropping packet `idp`, if carrying `idp`

It is permitted for a drone to pickup a packet if they are co-located and the packet agrees to ride (it may prefer another drone). Packets are largely passive, they react to sensing the presence of a drone by indicating whether they will accept a ride from that drone. This is done by action `setPickUpOk(id,b)`, where b is a boolean. If b is *true* the pickup light should turn on, otherwise it turn off.

The system objective is that packets get delivered with minimal delay and minimal cost (drone energy). Less delay gives more satisfaction as does less energy consumption.

Choosing actions. As a first step, drones operate independently. A drone repeatedly chooses an allowed action to execute. The choice is formulated as a family of soft-constraint problems parameterized by the drone's local knowledge. This pro-activity of individual drones is insufficient by itself to ensure liveness of the system, there are two local criteria to consider, in designing the soft constraints.

(Safety) The drone should not run out of energy.

(Benefit) If there are packets needing transport, the drone should pick a packet according to some notion of benefit gained for work done and transport that packet.

We start with a simple drone behavior in which the drone will try to pick a packet that requires the least work to deliver, where work to deliver is a function of the distance to the packets destination, going via the packet's current location.

We use the definition of Soft Constraint Problem (SCP) presented in [2]. An SCP over a set of variables V with values in domain D consists of a tuple of grading functions

$$[(G_i, c_i) | 1 \leq i \leq k]$$

together with a ranking structure

$$(R, [p_i | 1 \leq i \leq k], I)$$

where each G_i is a monoid, c_i maps variable value tuples $\bar{d}$ to the domain of G_i, and p_i is an action of G_i on R ($p_i(g_i) : R \to R$). The solution is the set of variable value tuples with maximal rank.

$$maxS(SCP) = \{(\bar{d}, S(\bar{d}) | S(\bar{d}) \text{ is maximal over } D^V\}$$

where $S(\bar{d}) = \bigcirc_{1 \leq i \leq k}(p_i(c_i((\bar{d}))(I)))$. Here $\bigcirc$ is the binary operation in the ranking structure, $*$ in our case.

In the independent drone problem there is one variable, the action, and actions are graded based on the state predicted to result from executing the action. Thus the drone soft constraint problem $DSCP$ is a family of SCPs parameterized by the drone identifier and local knowledge base (the drones view of the system state). We use two grading functions one for the Benefit criteria, one for the Safety constraint. Safety is a crisp constraint – the value of an action is 0 if it leads to an unsafe situation and 1 otherwise. An action is deemed safe if in the resulting state the drone has sufficient energy to reach a charging station. Thus it should be provable that if a drone is initially in a safe condition, it will remain safe. (Although it may not be able to move.)

Benefit ranges from 0 to `maxBenefit`. The ranking function combines Safety and Benefit by multiplication, thus ensuring an unsafe action has rank 0.

$DCP(id, lkb) =$

    $[(NatMax, Benefit(id, lkb)),$

    $(ZeroOne, Safety(id, lkb)),$

    $(NatMult, *, 1)]$

where $NatMax$ is the natural numbers ordered as usual taking max as the binary operator, and `maxBenefit` as the identity. $NatMult$ is the natural numbers with multiplication as the binary operator and 1 as the identity. $ZeroOne$ is like the boolean ordered monoid using $0, 1$ rather than booleans to support the multiplicative action.

Only moves perceived to be possible are considered. Thus `drop` won't be considered if the drone is not carrying a packet, and moves off the grid or to a point thought to be occupied by another drone will not be considered. This is done just to simplify the grading functions, as such moves will be given a 0 grade.

The *Benefit* function is the key. It depends on the drone's mode: searching (for a packet) or carrying (a packet). In searching mode, if the drone is co-located with a packet the only action with a non-zero grade is to pickup the packet. Otherwise the grade is the max of 1 and the gain for delivering known packets, where the gain is the max possible cost minus the actual cost. The actual cost for delivering a given packet is the distance to the packets destination going via the packet's current location.

In carrying mode if the drone's location is the packet's destination then the only action with a non-zero grade is dropping the packet. Otherwise moves that decrease distance to destination are preferred. Charging gets a maximal grade if the drone is at a charging station and its energy is below the upper bound.

The doTask function for drones formalizes the above.

```
ceq doTask(drone,id,tick,lkb) = tstampA(bestActs,0)
if acts := droneActs(id,lkb)
/\ bestActs := selectMax(rankDroneActs(id,lkb,acts),1,none) .
```

The function droneActs(id,lkb) enumerates the allowed actions, and the function tstampA(acts,n) stamps each action in acts with delay n (0 in the above equation). The function selectMax(rankDroneActs(...)...) selects the maximal solutions.

4.1   The doAction and Handle Functions

The doAction function specifies the physical effects of an action as updates on local environment knowledge bases and the perceived/sensed effects of the action by information in a rcv event. Part of the sensed effects of the agent executing an action act is the information item done(act,b) @ t where b is a boolean indicating success or failure, and t is the time at which the action was executed.

Drone actions. The drone move and charge actions effect only the drone state. For example the equation defining a move is

```
ceq doAction(drone,id,mv(dir),t,ekb,aconf) =
  {id, addK(ekb,mvkb), rcv((done(mv(dir),b) @ t) mvkb)}
if 10 := getLoc(id,ekb)
/\ 11 := doMv(10,dir)
/\  e := getEnergy(id,ekb)
/\  b := not(occupied(11,aconf)) and e > 1
/\ mvkb := (if b
            then mvInfo(id,11,sd(e,1),t)
            else mvInfo(id,10,e,t) fi) .
```

where mvInfo computes the new location and energy information items for the drone. The charging action succeeds if the drone is located at a charging station and the new information is the new energy level.

The `handle` function for drones for response to receiving action information adds the new information to the local knowledge base of the drone, schedules a `tick` at delay `droneDelay` and posts new location information if any.

The drone `pickup(idp)`/`drop(idp)` actions, if successful also affect the packet `idp`. In the case of a successful `pickup(idp)`/`drop(idp)` action the packet is added/removed from the drone's environment knowledge base. The packet environment knowledge base is updated with new packet location and the packet is notified of its new location. When the packet handles the new location information it will post this information, thus the drone local knowledge base will be updated as well. A `pickup(idp)` by a drone will fail if not co-located or if the packet environment knowledge base has the pickupOk light off (explicitly or by default). A `drop(idp)` fails if the packet is not carried by the drone (which should not happen in our simple setting). If `pickup` or `drop` fails then nothing changes (except that the time stamp on packet location may be updated).

Drones respond to received information that is not an action report by adding the new information to their local knowledge bases.

Packet actions. The only packet action is `setPickupOk(id,b)`. If the boolean `b` is `true`, the action turns on the pickupOk light for `id` in the packet's environment knowledge base. This is represented by the knowledge item `pickupOk(id,true)` @ `t` in the environment and local knowledge bases. When the boolean is `false`, the pickupOk light is turned off. This is represented by `pickupOk(id,false)` in the knowledge base, or by absence of a `pickupOk` fact. The packet is also notified of the `pickupOk` information. This action should succeed (unless the light is broken).

A packet that is delivered, `delivered(idp)` @ `t` in the local knowledge base, handles new information by ignoring it. A packet that is still active handles new self location information `atloc(idp,loc)` @ `t` according to whether `loc` is its destination or not. In the first case, the packet posts `delivered(idp)` which will remove other information about the packet as it propagates using the partial ordering. Otherwise the packet remembers the new location (adds it to the local knowledge bases) and also posts it.

A packet responds to new location for drone `id` by scheduling a `setPickupOk` action for `id` with boolean `true` if the drone becomes co-located. In either case it also remembers the new location. In other cases a packet simply remembers the new information.

4.2 Experiments

We now describe the results of a few simple experiments in the setting of the drones and packets model. The are number of parameters to be set. For this set of experiments, these are fixed as follows.

```
eq commDistance = 2 .       *** upper bound on contact distance
eq gridX = 10 .             *** grid dimensions
eq gridY = 10 .
eq chargeLocs = pt(5,5) .   *** one charging station at 5,5
eq maxBenefit = 20 .
```

```
eq maxCharge = 25 .        *** stop charging when full
eq costMv = 1 .            *** energy used in a move
eq chargeUnit = 5 .        *** energy gained per charge action
eq droneDelay = 2 .        *** delay on tick action
```

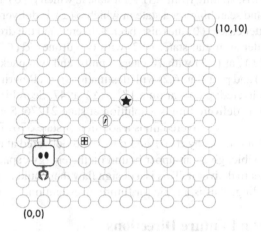

Fig. 1. A depiction of the location grid with the drone at (2,2). packet at (4,4), charging station at (5,5) and destination at (6,6).

Here is a simple ASystem, AS0, with one drone, d(0), at (2,2) with 10 energy units, and one packet p(0) at (4,4) with destination (6,6).

```
AS0 =
{clock(1)
[d(0) : drone
   | (atloc(d(0),pt(2,2)) @ 0)(energy(d(0),10) @ 0)class(d(0),drone)
   | (atloc(d(0), pt(2, 2)) @ 0) (atloc(p(0), pt(4, 4)) @ 0)
     (energy(d(0),10) @ 0) class(d(0),drone) class(p(0), packet)
     dest(p(0), pt(6, 6))
   | none
   | tick @ 1]
[p(0) : packet
   | (atloc(p(0),pt(4,4)) @ 0) class(p(0),packet)
   | (atloc(p(0),pt(4,4)) @ 0) class(d(0),drone) class(p(0),packet)
     dest(p(0),pt(6,6))
   | none
   | none]}
```

Rewriting this configuration with a limit of 100 results in a system state in which p(0) was delivered at time 25, (delivered(p(0)) @ 25) is in the local KB of p(0). Searching starting with AS0 for a state with p(0) delivered at some time using the search pattern

```
{[ p(0) : packet | ekb:KB | lkb:KB (delivered(p(0)) @ t:Nat)
                 | ckb:KB | evs:EventSet] ac:Conf }
```

finds a solution at state 201. If the drones initial energy is only 5, it will not move, as it is in an unsafe situation. If the initial energy is 8, the drone will recharge before it drops the packet.

As a next example we use an initial state, AS1, with one drone, d(0), at (2,2) with 10 energy units, and two packets p(0) at (2,6) with destination (4,6) and p(1) at (6,2) with destination (6,6). Searching from AS1 for a state in which p(0) is delivered finds a solution at state 66, and searching for a state in which p(1) is delivered finds a solution at state 459. It the latter case p(0) has also been delivered and the drone has recharged.

Finally, we consider an initial state, AS2, with two drones, d(0), at (2,2) with 10 energy units and d(1), at (7,7) with 10 energy units, and two packets p(0) at (2,6) with destination (4,6) and p(1) at (6,2) with destination (6,6). Rewriting leads to a state with both packets delivered: p(0) at time 17, p(1) at 47. Searching from AS2 for a state in which p(0) is delivered finds a solution at state 21276. Searching from AS2 for a state in which p(1) is delivered finds a solution at state 576171. In this solution p(0) was delivered at time 15 by d(0) and p(1) was delivered at time 41 by d(1).

Note that it is possible, given an upper bound on the energy capacity that the drone can not reach a packet to deliver it. This is a design flaw that could hopefully be discovered by formal modeling. This is a topic for future investigation.

5   Conclusions and Future Directions

We have presented a framework for modeling fractionated cyber-physical systems called Soft Agents, and a prototype using the Maude rewriting logic system. Three key features of the framework are the partially ordered knowledge model of communication; soft constraint problems for specifying robust, adaptive agent behavior; and explicit representation of the physical state of an agent as well as its knowledge state. Use of the framework was illustrated with a simple drones and packets case study, showing how soft constraints can be used, and the use of partial ordering on knowledge to keep the knowledge state relevant and simple.

The soft agents framework supports, but does not enforce, liveness as discussed in section 2. Agents can control how often to check whether some action is needed, and agents can be notified about change in their local state. It is up to the system designer to use these capabilities to achieve the desired/necessary liveness.

The present work is just a first step. It lays a foundation for further exploration and experimentation to understand the tradeoffs and the nature of emerging behavior. One point of being able to experiment is to guide attempts to prove general properties.

The drones and packets case study can be complicated in many ways to explore principles for defining soft constraints. For example, packets can have different weights, require special accommodation such as refrigeration, and drones can have different load capacity (with/without refrigeration), speed, energy consumption, etc. New packets can appear as the system evolves. Packets can post ratings of their ride — giving other packets a reason to refuse a ride from a low rated drone, and giving drones motivation to provide better service. In addition, one can also consider local clocks, rather than a global clock, to study different forms of synchronization.

In the presented case study, drones just planned one step ahead and didn't try to account for actions of other drones. A next challenge is to consider multistep planning both independently and with knowledge of what other agents are planning. An agent would make a plan (a set of reasonable plans) to achieve some objective, and start executing a plan that it (locally) deems best. It would re-evaluate under certain conditions, for example at every step, or when the next step is not possible. One possible approach would be the reflecting planning approach that was used in a disruption tolerant networking project [27]. The idea is to reflect a model of the system based on the local knowledge base to the meta-level, search for paths to a goal or subgoal, and use results as the space of solutions for soft constraint solving. This would not generally be efficient but might lead to useful insights.

In our simple example with one variable, finding the maximal solutions to a constraint problem is simple. With multi-step plans and consideration of multiple agents methods for efficient solution will be needed. There are some suggestions in [2]. Methods to reuse partial plans could also be useful.

As indicated by the number of states to be searched to find a solution for both packets being delivered starting from the initial state, AS2, with 2 drones and 2 packets, work is needed to scale the analysis. Interestingly, simple rewriting finds a solution, although it may not be the best one, and it is very fast even for AS2. Methods to reduce the interleaving need to be investigated. Another direction is to move to a probabilistic model and use Monte-Carlo like simulation and statistical model checking.

The Fractionated CPS model assumes honest, non-malicious agents and provides only weak guarantees about knowledge dissemination. The latter is to provide a general and realistic model. Furthermore agents are anonymous, identities are not revealed by by the system. A challenging problem is to identify primitives that, under suitable conditions, support stronger communication guarantees, and primitives that support building of trust both in the knowledge posted by other agents and in the capabilities and stated intents of other agents. It is important to have a balance between strong guarantees and the robustness enabled by weaker guarantees.

References

1. Wirsing, M., Denker, G., Talcott, C., Poggio, A., Briesemeister, L.: A rewriting logic framework for soft constraints. In: Sixth International Workshop on Rewriting Logic and Its Applications (WRLA 2006). Electronic Notes in Theoretical Computer Science. Elsevier (2006)
2. Hölzl, M., Meier, M., Wirsing, M.: Which soft constraints do you prefer? In: Seventh International Workshop on Rewriting Logic and Its Applications (WRLA 2008). Electronic Notes in Theoretical Computer Science, Elsevier (2008)
3. Gadducci, F., Hölzl, M., Monreale, G.V., Wirsing, M.: Soft constraints for lexicographic orders. In: Castro, F., Gelbukh, A., González, M. (eds.) MICAI 2013, Part I. LNCS, vol. 8265, pp. 68–79. Springer, Heidelberg (2013)
4. Interlink project (last accessed November 15, 2014)
5. Bristeau, P.J., Callou, F., Vissiére, D., Petit, N., et al.: The navigation and control technology inside the ar. drone micro uav. In: 18th IFAC world congress, vol. 18, pp. 1477–1484 (2011)
6. Krajník, T., Vonásek, V., Fišer, D., Faigl, J.: AR-Drone as a Platform for Robotic Research and Education. In: Obdržálek, D., Gottscheber, A. (eds.) EUROBOT 2011. CCIS, vol. 161, pp. 172–186. Springer, Heidelberg (2011)
7. Meng, L., Li, L., Veres, S.: Aerodynamic parameter estimation of an unmanned aerial vehicle based on extended kalman filter and its higher order approach. In: 2010 2nd International Conference on Advanced Computer Control (ICACC), vol. 5, pp. 526–531. IEEE (2010)

 8. Yokoo, M., Durfee, E.H., Ishida, T., Kuwabara, K.: The distributed constraint satisfaction problem: Formalization and algorithms. IEEE Transactions on Formalization and algorithms. Knowledge and Data Engineering 10(5), 673–685 (1998)
 9. Modi, P.J., Shen, W.M., Tambe, M., Yokoo, M.: ADOPT: Asynchronous distributed constraint optimization with quality guarantees. Artificial Intelligence 161(1), 149–180 (2005)
10. des Jardins, M.E., Durfee, E.H., Charles, L., Ortiz, J., Wolverton, M.J.: A survey of research in distributed, continual planning. AI Magazine 20(4), 13 (1999)
11. de Weerdt, M., Clement, B.: Introduction to planning in multiagent systems. Multiagent Grid Syst. 5(4), 345–355 (2009)
12. Bullo, F., Cortés, J., Martínez, S.: Distributed Control of Robotic Networks. Applied Mathematics Series. Princeton University Press (2009), Electronically available at http://coordinationbook.info
13. Petcu, A., Faltings, B.: A scalable method for multiagent constraint optimization. In: Proceedings of the 19th International Joint Conference on Artificial Intelligence, IJCAI 2005, pp. 266–271. Morgan Kaufmann Publishers Inc, San Francisco (2005)
14. Stehr, M.-O., Talcott, C., Rushby, J., Lincoln, P., Kim, M., Cheung, S., Poggio, A.: Fractionated software for networked cyber-physical systems: Research directions and long-term vision. In: Agha, G., Danvy, O., Meseguer, J. (eds.) Formal Modeling: Actors, Open Systems, Biological Systems. LNCS, vol. 7000, pp. 110–143. Springer, Heidelberg (2011)
15. Stehr, M.-O., Kim, M., Talcott, C.: Partially ordered knowledge sharing and fractionated systems in the context of other models for distributed computing. In: Iida, S., Meseguer, J., Ogata, K. (eds.) Specification, Algebra, and Software. LNCS, vol. 8373, pp. 402–433. Springer, Heidelberg (2014)
16. Brown, O., Eremenko, P.: The value proposition for fractionated space architectures. In: Proc. of AIAA, San Jose, CA (September 2006)
17. Clavel, M., Durán, F., Eker, S., Lincoln, P., Martí-Oliet, N., Meseguer, J., Talcott, C.: All About Maude - A High-Performance Logical Framework. LNCS, vol. 4350. Springer, Heidelberg (2007)
18. Hölzl, M., Rauschmayer, A., Wirsing, M.: Engineering of software-intensive systems: State of the art and research challenges. In: Wirsing, M., Banâtre, J.-P., Hölzl, M., Rauschmayer, A. (eds.) Soft-Ware Intensive Systems. LNCS, vol. 5380, pp. 1–44. Springer, Heidelberg (2008)
19. Ascens: Autonomic service-component ensembles (last accessed: November 15, 2014)
20. Hölzl, M., Wirsing, M.: Towards a system model for ensembles. In: Agha, G., Danvy, O., Meseguer, J. (eds.) Formal Modeling: Actors, Open Systems, Biological Systems. LNCS, vol. 7000, pp. 241–261. Springer, Heidelberg (2011)
21. Arbab, F., Santini, F.: Preference and similarity-based behavioral discovery of services. In: Formal Methods (2012)
22. Kim, M., Stehr, M.O., Talcott, C.: A distributed logic for networked cyber-physical systems. Science of Computer Programming (2012)
23. Choi, J.S., McCarthy, T., Yadav, M., Kim, M., Talcott, C., Gressier-Soudan, E.: Application patterns for cyber-physical systems. In: Cyber-physical Systems Networks and Applications (2013)
24. Ölveczky, P.C., Meseguer, J.: Semantics and pragmatics of real-time maude. Higher-Order and Symbolic Computation 20(1-2), 161–196 (2007)
25. Nielson, H.R., Nielson, F., Vigo, R.: A calculus for quality. In: Păsăreanu, C.S., Salaün, G. (eds.) FACS 2012. LNCS, vol. 7684, pp. 188–204. Springer, Heidelberg (2013)
26. Nielson, H.R., Nielson, F.: Safety versus security in the quality calculus. In: Liu, Z., Woodcock, J., Zhu, H. (eds.) Theories of Programming and Formal Methods. LNCS, vol. 8051, pp. 285–303. Springer, Heidelberg (2013)
27. Stehr, M.O., Talcott, C.: Planning and learning algorithms for routing in disruption-tolerant networks. In: MILCOM 2008. IEEE (2008)

Structured Document Algebra in Action

Don Batory[1], Peter Höfner[2], Dominik Köppl[3],
Bernhard Möller[4], and Andreas Zelend[4]

[1] Dept. of Computer Science, University of Texas at Austin, USA
[2] NICTA and UNSW, Australia
[3] Department of Computer Science, TU Dortmund, Germany
[4] Institut für Informatik, Universität Augsburg, Germany

Abstract. A *Structured Document Algebra (SDA)* defines modules with variation points and how such modules compose. The basic operations are module addition and replacement. Repeated addition can create nested module structures. SDA also allows the decomposition of modules into smaller parts. In this paper we show how SDA modules can be used to deal algebraically with *Software Product Lines (SPLs)*. In particular, we treat some fundamental concepts of SPLs, such as refinement and refactoring. This leads to mathematically precise formalization of fundamental concepts used in SPLs, which can be used for improved *Feature-Oriented Software Development* (FOSD) tooling.

Keywords: software product lines, feature-oriented design, algebraic reasoning.

It is our pleasure to dedicate this paper to Martin Wirsing on the occasion of his Formal Retirement. We contribute a study on a recently developed algebra for all kinds of structured and interconnected documents, but particularly the ones that describe product families or product lines in Feature Oriented Software Design — a topic on which Martin has been quite active for a while now. The frame of this are general formal methods and semantics. We pick up this latter theme to endow the algebra, which previously had a more syntactic flavor, with a semantic component, too. The particular approach we take uses the terminology of algebraic specification; this gives the fourth author the opportunity to fondly remember the days of the CIP project at TU Munich, in which Martin and he cooperated quite a lot on that topic. We hope that Martin will enjoy that bit of scientific nostalgia, too! Best wishes, Martin, for your Formal Retirement — enjoy! — but also for many further successful years, since we do hope that your Retirement is only Formal!

1 Introduction

A *Software Product Line (SPL)* is a family of related programs constructed from a common set of assets. Variations in programs are explained by *features*—increments in program functionality. The assets of an SPL are modules that implement features. These modules are the building blocks of SPL programs [2].

R. De Nicola and R. Hennicker (Eds.): Wirsing Festschrift, LNCS 8950, pp. 291–311, 2015.

Today's SPL researchers are exploring two rather different forms of feature-based modularity: alternative-based variation (a.k.a. *classical modularity*) and projectional variation (a.k.a. *SYSGEN* or *virtual modularity*). Classical modularity is what you would expect: there are physical files that define a feature module and tools that compose modules to produce a desired program. Here, files refer to arbitrary documents, such as specifications, code composed of elementary program features, text fragments or manuals. In contrast, virtual feature modularity is a preprocessor technology called *coloring*. The idea is simple: the code of the `Blue` feature is painted blue; code of the `Green` feature is painted green. Whenever `Blue` is not needed in a product, all blue-colored code is removed or is said to be *projected out*. The tools for virtual modularity are historically based on text preprocessors; more advanced tools color *abstract syntax trees (ASTs)* [5,15,18]. The current debate is which implementation technique is most appropriate for an SPL. Our position is that both implement the same abstractions—feature modules—in very different ways. *What is important is to understand the algebraic nature of these abstractions.*

The *Structured Document Algebra (SDA)*, partially first presented in [6], aims at providing a simple, yet effective, algebra of feature modularity (e.g., the modularization of text files, text fragments, ASTs, etc.).

It is completely independent of the underlying programming paradigm, such as Object-Oriented Programming or Functional Programming. In fact, it is even independent of programming, since it is abstract enough to cover also general structured documents, such as manuals or collections of web pages. It is meant as an aid for formal reasoning about the process of decomposing larger document pieces into smaller ones (and vice versa). It can be implemented on top of or inside any text editor, IDE or web page editor. Depending on the desired level of reasoning, it can be used purely syntactically or at a semantic level, as demonstrated in the Appendix. Phenomena modelled by the algebra include coherence, uniform transformations, deletion, overriding. In the special case of SPL documents, SDA additionally allows a description of their fine structure. This is in contrast to other algebraic approaches in this area (e.g., [1,24,25]), where modules are often treated as atomic units.

In the present paper we extend the basic repertoire of the version of SDA from [6] and show how it can be used to formally describe some standard techniques used in feature oriented software construction and SPLs.

The basis of SDA are structured, inter-linked documents or document *fragments*. A link is represented as a *Variation Point (VP)*, i.e., a labeled position in a fragment where contents can be inserted to yield a larger fragment. The association between VPs and their assigned fragments, if any, is provided by *modules*, i.e., partial functions from VPs to fragments.

SDA allows multiple "applied occurrences", i.e., replication of one and the same VP v; they all stand for (or share) the fragment assigned to v by some module. Conversely, different VPs may be associated with the same fragment (a module need not be an injective partial function).

In this paper we show how modules and fragments can be treated algebraically and discuss algebraic operations for module (de)composition and present an operation for overriding.

2   Structured Document Algebra

This section recapitulates a formal model of VPs, modules containing VPs, and compositions of such modules first presented in [6]. To keep SDA language-independent, we leave the exact nature of fragments (e.g., text or abstract syntax trees) unspecified and view it as a parameter of the algebra. For our examples we will use Java code fragments.

2.1   SDA Basics

Variation Points and Fragments. We now formalize the notions mentioned above. Let V be a set of VPs, denoted by $v_1, v_2, \ldots$ at which fragments may be inserted and $F(V)$ be a set of *fragments*, denoted by $f_1, f_2, \ldots$. Fragments may contain VPs from V.

In incremental software design it is often advantageous to leave certain parts unspecified and to insert placeholders where (optionally) further features may be added. As an abstraction of such placeholders we use *default fragments*. In addition, it is convenient to introduce a special pseudo-fragment that represents an error, namely that there has been an attempt to assign two or more non-default and different fragments to the same VP. To this end we assume that the set $F(V)$ includes two special elements, a default fragment 0 and an error $\frac{1}{2}$.

The addition, or supremum, operator $+$ on fragments has the axioms

$$0 + x = x , \quad \frac{1}{2} + x = \frac{1}{2} , \quad f_i + f_j = \frac{1}{2} \; (i \neq j) ,$$

where $x, f_i, f_j \in F(V)$ with $f_i, f_j \neq 0$. If we assume associativity, idempotence and commutativity of addition, this structure forms a flat lattice with least element 0 and greatest element $\frac{1}{2}$.

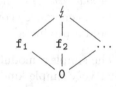

Modules. A *module* is a partial function $m : V \rightsquigarrow F(V)$. A VP v is *assigned* by m if $v \in \mathrm{dom}(m)$, otherwise *unassigned* or *external*. Thus the domain $\mathrm{dom}(m)$ of a module is the set of VPs it "knows about" or administers. By using partial functions rather than relations, a VP can be filled with at most one fragment (*uniqueness*).

Example 2.1. Figure 1(a) is a sample file/module, structured by the assignment of fragments to its VPs. Its partial function is given in Figure 1(b).   □

Ducasse et al. [12] also use a flat lattice of composable units, called *traits*. Our modules correspond to the *method dictionaries* there. However, these have to be total rather than partial maps, which makes distinguishing assigned and external VPs difficult. Had we taken the same decision, our algebraic laws would have become much more cumbersome.

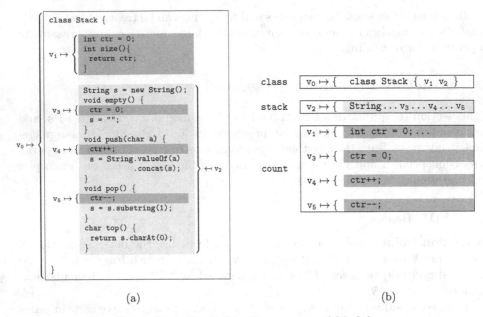

Fig. 1. Variation Points, Fragments and Modules

A module m can be viewed in different ways:

- as a collection of fragments that instantiate the VPs of dom(m), i.e., a structured document;
- as filling certain VPs with contents (in term rewriting etc., it would be called a *substitution*); and
- as a generalized context-free grammar with dom(m) as the set of nonterminals and a production v ↦ m(v) for each v ∈ dom(m).

The simplest module is the *empty module* **0**, i.e., the empty partial map. Another very simple kind of module is provided by *constant modules*, i.e., modules which assign one and the same fragment—for instance 0—to a number of VPs. Let W ⊆ V be a set of VPs and f a fragment. We set

$$[W \mapsto f](v) =_{df} \begin{cases} f & \text{if } v \in W, \\ \text{undefined} & \text{otherwise.} \end{cases}$$

If W = {w} is a singleton set, we abbreviate [{w} ↦ f] to [w ↦ f]. Such *singleton modules* are the atomic building blocks from which all other modules can be constructed by the addition operation introduced next.

Module Addition. We want to construct larger modules step by step by assigning more and more fragments to VPs. The central operation for this is module addition (+), which fuses two modules while maintaining uniqueness (and signaling an error upon a conflict). Basically, module addition can be viewed as union with flagged inconsistent VP/fragment associations. Desirable properties for + are commutativity and associativity. If two modules have no VPs in common, the partial functions characterizing them can easily be combined. For example, class + stack (Figure 1(b)) is the partial function

$$\text{class} + \text{stack} = \begin{cases} v_0 \mapsto \text{class Stack } \{v_1 \ v_2\} \\ v_2 \mapsto \text{String} \ ... \ v_3 \ ... \ v_4 \ ... \ v_5 \end{cases}$$

Module addition can be defined as the lifting of + on fragments

$$(m + n)(v) =_{df} \begin{cases} m(v) & \text{if } v \in \text{dom}(m) - \text{dom}(n) \\ n(v) & \text{if } v \in \text{dom}(n) - \text{dom}(m) \\ m(v) + n(v) & \text{if } v \in \text{dom}(m) \cap \text{dom}(n) \\ \text{undefined} & \text{if } v \notin \text{dom}(m) \cup \text{dom}(n) \end{cases}$$

If in the third case $m(v) \neq n(v)$ and $m(v), n(v) \neq 0$ then $(m + n)(v) = \lightning$, thus signaling an error. By the above laws for fragment addition, the set of modules forms a commutative and idempotent monoid under $+$.[1] Therefore we can define a *submodule relation* as the natural order

$$m \leq n \Leftrightarrow_{df} m + n = n. \tag{1}$$

Example 2.2. Figure 1(b) shows three modules: class and stack contain single fragments, assigned to v_0 and v_2 respectively; count contains fragments assigned to v_1, v_3, v_4, and v_5. The module addition class + stack + count corresponds to the code in Figure 1(a). □

Implementation. A simple example suggests several ways in which SDA modules can be implemented. Figure 2(a) shows how preprocessor macros might define three non-default fragments (labeled BLUE, GREEN, RED) and a default for an implicit variation point. Figure 2(b) shows how this might be rendered in a "coloring" tool (e.g., the one contained in the integrated development environment CIDE [18,19,2]) where the fragments assigned to the VPs are explicitly shown. (There is no need to actually "see" the names of VPs). However, Figure 2(b) would require significant engineering: a Java compiler would have to understand the preprocessor semantics of coloring (Figure 2(a)) so as not to alert programmers that the GREEN fragments and beyond are unreachable if BLUE is true. In a Java-like language this can be accomplished by defining feature variables as static Booleans and put a wrapper if (feature){ fragment } around each fragment. So if the feature variable is false, the compiler will effectively ignore the fragment as dead code. This is, for instance, offered by the CIDE compiler.

A more likely possibility—which is consistent with current text coloring tools—would be to "fool" the compiler by pretending that the code of Figure 2(c) is the definition of the add method, where a projection would produce a simpler method with only one assignment to the variable result.

---

[1] Modules and module addition can be recoded in terms of total functions, which makes it easier to see that the + operation indeed is commutative, associative and idempotent, hence induces a lattice, too. Moreover, it has the empty module 0 as its neutral element and satisfies $\text{dom}(m + n) = \text{dom}(m) \cup \text{dom}(n)$.

```
int add(int x) {
#if BLUE
    return x+3;
#elif GREEN
    return x+5;
#elif RED
    return x+11;
#else
    return x+1
#endif
}
```

```
int add(int x) {

v₁ ↦ { return x+3;
v₁ ↦ { return x+5;
v₁ ↦ { return x+11;
v₁ ↦ { return x+1;

}
```

```
int add(int x) {

v₁ ↦ { result = x+3;
v₁ ↦ { result = x+5;
v₁ ↦ { result = x+11;
v₁ ↦ { result = x+1;
        return result;

}
```

(a)   (b)   (c)

Fig. 2. Module Implementations

These ideas are, in effect, standard fare for SPL development, except that the tool support needs to be beautified by coloring and VP recognition. Code fragments or *mini-modules* can indeed be expressed in terms of classical module systems; see [10] for examples. Coloring also presents the connection between modules and virtual modularity (cf. Sect. 1).

2.2 Structural Properties of Modules

Since fragments may contain VPs, cycles could occur when composing modules. A module, however, should be cycle-free. To handle this we use a dependence relation.

Cycle-Freeness. For a fragment $f \in F(V)$ let $VP(f)$ be the set of VPs that occur in f. We define a *direct dependence relation* $\mathrm{dep_m} \subseteq V \times V$ within a module m by

$$v \; \mathrm{dep_m} \; w \quad \Leftrightarrow_{df} \quad v \in \mathrm{dom}(m) \wedge w \in VP(m(v)) \; .$$

This means that VP w occurs in the fragment assigned to VP v by m, so that v depends on w. For example, in Figure 1(b), $v_2 \; \mathrm{dep_{stack}} \; v_3$. A module m is *acyclic* if no VP depends directly or indirectly on itself, i.e., no VP v satisfies $v \; \mathrm{dep_m^+} \; v$, where $\mathrm{dep_m^+}$ is the transitive closure of $\mathrm{dep_m}$. Henceforth we only consider cycle-free modules.

The concepts of dependence and module addition do not interfere. Since the latter is just the "union" of VP/fragment associations, for acyclicity it does not matter whether dependences occur inside one module or between different modules.

Assembling Fragments. We now describe how to assemble a structured document into a single fragment (while "forgetting" the structure). To define this formally we use an auxiliary function $\mathrm{single\_fill}(f,m)$. It takes a fragment f and a module m and yields the fragment that results from f by replacing, in parallel, all occurrences of every $v \in VP(f)$ by the corresponding fragment $m(v)$

(if any). The precise definition of `single_fill` depends on the special type of fragments considered; as stated in the introduction we want to keep that parametric. For an acyclic module m and $v \in \text{dom}(m)$, the fragment $\text{frag}(v, m)$ can be computed by iterating the `single_fill` function. By the assumed acyclicity of m this always terminates. To cope with unassigned (= external) VPs we assume that every VP is also a fragment, i.e., that $V \subseteq F(V)$. Then the external VPs can simply be left unchanged by the assembly function. A corresponding program looks as follows:

```
fragment frag (vp v, module m){
  fragment f = v;
  while (VP(f) ∩ dom(m) ≠ ∅)
    f = single_fill(f, m);
  return f; }
```

Note that $\text{frag}(v, m) = v$ if $v \notin \text{dom}(m)$.

Module Equivalence. Two modules m, n are *equivalent* if they generate the same fragments for all VPs:

$$m \equiv n \iff_{df} \forall v \in VP : \text{frag}(v, m) = \text{frag}(v, n) .$$

Lemma 2.3. *For modules* m, n *we have* $m \equiv n \implies \text{dom}(m) = \text{dom}(n)$.

Restructuring. Module m *restructures into* module n, in symbols $m \sqsubseteq n$, if
$$m \sqsubseteq n \iff_{df} \text{dom}(m) \subseteq \text{dom}(n) \wedge \forall v \in \text{dom}(m) : \text{frag}(v, m) = \text{frag}(v, n) .$$

This means that n offers a possibly more detailed representation of the fragments of m using auxiliary VPs in $\text{dom}(n) - \text{dom}(m)$. The empty module is the smallest one w.r.t. $\sqsubseteq$, since it does not offer any choice—in particular since $\text{dom}(0) = \emptyset$.

It is easy to check that the relation $\sqsubseteq$ is reflexive and transitive, i.e., a preorder. It is, however, not antisymmetric as the following example shows.

Example 2.4. Consider the modules m and n defined as follows:

$$
\begin{array}{llll}
m : & v \mapsto i\text{++; } w; & \text{and} & w \mapsto j\text{++;} \\
n : & v \mapsto i\text{++; } j\text{++;} & \text{and} & w \mapsto j\text{++;}
\end{array}
$$

These are equivalent, i.e., $m \equiv n$, in that they produce the same text. Hence, $m \sqsubseteq n$ and $n \sqsubseteq m$. If $\sqsubseteq$ were antisymmetric, this should imply $m = n$, but m and n are different as modules.   □

However, we always have $m \sqsubseteq n \wedge n \sqsubseteq m \iff m \equiv n$.

We provide some basic properties of $\sqsubseteq$ that can be used to restructure larger modules in a modular fashion. To state them we define the set of all VPs occurring in a module m by $VP(m) =_{df} \text{dom}(m) \cup \bigcup_{v \in \text{dom}(m)} VP(m(v))$. First we treat the case of decomposing the fragment belonging to a single VP.

Lemma 2.5. *Assume fragments* f, g *and a module* m *with* $\text{dom}(m) = VP(g)$ *and* $f = \text{single\_fill}(g, m)$. *This means that the VPs in* g *are filled by* m *yielding* f. *Moreover let* v *be a fresh VP, i.e.,* $v \notin \text{dom}(m) \cup VP(m)$. *Then*

$$[v \mapsto f] \sqsubseteq ([v \mapsto g] + m) .$$

The proof is immediate from the definitions and assumptions.

Lemma 2.6. *For modules* $m_i \sqsubseteq n_i (i = 1, 2)$ *with* $VP(n_1) \cap VP(n_2) = \emptyset$ *we have*

$$m_1 + m_2 \sqsubseteq n_1 + n_2 .$$

Proof. (Sketch) We first state an auxiliary property. Assume modules m, n such that $m + n$ is acyclic and $VP(m) \cap VP(n) = \emptyset$. Then $\forall v \in \mathrm{dom}(m) : \mathrm{frag}(v, m + n) = \mathrm{frag}(v, m)$. In words, if n does not mention the VPs of m then it cannot influence the fragment represented by m. This is shown by induction on the length of the longest dep_m-path (or equivalently the smallest natural number i such that $\mathrm{dep}_m^i = \emptyset$), which exists by the assumed acyclicity of $m + n$ and hence also of m.

With that, the main claim follows easily from the definition of $\sqsubseteq$, because $VP(n_1) \cap VP(n_2) = \emptyset$ implies $VP(m_i) \cap VP(n_j) = \emptyset$ $(i \neq j)$.   □

3   Additional SDA Operators

3.1   Subtraction

In this section we present a way of defining an "inverse" to addition. The usefulness of this operation might not be straightforward. However, as we will show, it lays the foundation for more sophisticated operations such as overriding, which is a common technique in feature-oriented software development.

For modules m and n we define the *subtraction* $m - n$ via restriction $|$ as

$$m - n =_{df} m \mid_{\mathrm{dom}(m) - \mathrm{dom}(n)} .^2$$

This spells out to

$$(m - n)(v) =_{df} \begin{cases} m(v) & \text{if } v \in (\mathrm{dom}(m) - \mathrm{dom}(n)) \\ \text{undefined} & \text{otherwise} . \end{cases}$$

Among others, subtraction satisfies, for arbitrary modules m, n and p, the following laws. (Proofs are straightforward.)

$$
\begin{array}{ll}
\mathrm{dom}(m - n) = \mathrm{dom}(m) - \mathrm{dom}(n) & \quad m - n \leq m \\
(m + n) - p = (m - p) + (n - p) & \quad m - 0 = m \\
m - (n + p) = (m - n) - p & \quad m - m = 0 \\
m \leq n \Rightarrow m - n = 0 & \quad 0 - n = 0 .
\end{array}
$$

Note that the left law in the last line is only an implication, while the corresponding one for set theoretic difference is an equivalence. For the reverse direction we only have $m - n = 0 \Rightarrow \mathrm{dom}(m) \subseteq \mathrm{dom}(n)$. Moreover, $m - n \sqsubseteq m$ need not hold. Subtraction is isotone in its right argument and antitone in its left, i.e.,

$$m \leq n \Rightarrow m - o \leq n - o , \quad \text{and} \quad n \leq o \Rightarrow m - o \leq m - n .$$

---

[2] Instead, one could define another subtraction operator $\ominus$ of type $(V \rightsquigarrow F(V)) \times \mathcal{P}(V) \to (V \rightsquigarrow F(V))$ by $m \ominus U =_{df} m \mid_{\mathrm{dom}(m) - U}$ and then set $m - n =_{df} m \ominus \mathrm{dom}(n)$.

3.2   Overriding

Ideally, modules that are composed have disjoint domains. And by using subtraction or deletion, modules can be customized. Still, object-oriented programmers are used to the notion of *overriding* or *replacing* definitions, an operation that can be defined in terms of subtraction and addition. The module $m \dashrightarrow n$ which results from overriding n by m is defined as

$$m \dashrightarrow n =_{df} m + (n - m) .$$

This replaces all assignments in n for which m also provides a value. It may destroy acyclicity. $\dashrightarrow$ is associative and idempotent with neutral element 0, but not commutative.

Example 3.1. A classic example of feature interaction and product lines is the fire-and-flood control [17]. Assume a building is equipped with two systems: a fire control and a flood control. The flood control turns off the water supply as soon as sensors in the building indicate a water level is too high. It is specified by the following module.

$$\text{Flood}: \begin{cases} \text{pv} \mapsto \text{void flood()\{ pt \}} \\ \text{pt} \mapsto \text{if(isWaterHigh()) waterOff(); else waterOn();} \end{cases}$$

Fire control works in an opposite manner: as soon as sensors detect a too high temperature, sprinklers are turned on.

$$\text{Fire}: \begin{cases} \text{pw} \mapsto \text{void fire()\{ i1 \}} \\ \text{i1} \mapsto \text{if(isTemperatureHigh()) spriOn(); else spriOff();} \end{cases}$$

Note that the sprinklers' functionality depends on a working water supply. Their composition/sum is FplusF = Fire + Flood:

$$\text{FplusF}: \begin{cases} \text{pv} \mapsto \text{void flood()\{ pt \}} \\ \text{pt} \mapsto \text{if(isWaterHigh()) waterOff(); else waterOn();} \\ \text{pw} \mapsto \text{void fire()\{ i1 \}} \\ \text{i1} \mapsto \text{if(isTemperatureHigh()) spriOn(); else spriOff();} \end{cases}$$

After a fire has been detected, it must be guaranteed that the water supply is not turned off; otherwise the building would burn down. This is not guaranteed with Fire + Flood; it depends on a race condition determined by the order of fire() and flood() execution.

The solution is to impose one more module, representing a feature interaction FI, denoted Fire#Flood in [5], whose alterations make Flood and Fire work correctly together. This is achieved by a shared VP pv and the use of overriding. FI replaces Flood's fragment at pv with FI's fragment:

$$\text{FI}: \begin{cases} \texttt{pv} \mapsto \texttt{void flood()\{ i2 \}} \\ \texttt{i2} \mapsto \texttt{if(isTemperatureHigh()) waterOn(); else \{ pt \}} \end{cases}$$

The occurrence of $\texttt{pt}$ in the fragment of $\texttt{i2}$ may be viewed as an $\texttt{original}$ call to the respective method (e.g., [8]).

The composition of all three modules, $\texttt{FandF} = \texttt{FI} \dashrightarrow (\texttt{Fire} + \texttt{Flood})$, yields a correct implementation:

$$\text{FandF}: \begin{cases} \texttt{pw} \mapsto \texttt{void fire()\{ i1 \}} \\ \texttt{i1} \mapsto \texttt{if(isTemperatureHigh()) spriOn(); else spriOff();} \\ \texttt{pv} \mapsto \texttt{void flood()\{ i2 \}} \\ \texttt{i2} \mapsto \texttt{if(isTemperatureHigh()) waterOn(); else \{ pt \}} \\ \texttt{pt} \mapsto \texttt{if(isWaterHigh()) waterOff(); else waterOn();} \end{cases}$$

$\square$

To state further laws, we call modules $\texttt{m}$ and $\texttt{n}$ *compatible*, in signs $\texttt{m} \downarrow \texttt{n}$, if their fragments coincide on their shared domains. Formally,

$$\texttt{m} \downarrow \texttt{n} \Leftrightarrow_{df} \forall \texttt{v} \in \text{dom}(\texttt{m}) \cap \text{dom}(\texttt{n}) : \texttt{m}(\texttt{v}) = \texttt{n}(\texttt{v}) .$$

All submodules of a module are pairwise compatible with each other. It follows that the properties below are equivalent:

$$\texttt{m} \downarrow \texttt{n} \ \Leftrightarrow \ \texttt{m} \dashrightarrow \texttt{n} = \texttt{m} + \texttt{n} \ \Leftrightarrow \ \texttt{m} \dashrightarrow \texttt{n} = \texttt{n} \dashrightarrow \texttt{m}$$

Module addition and overriding interact by the following laws, where the left implication $\Leftarrow$ means "provided".

$$
\begin{array}{lll}
\texttt{m} \dashrightarrow (\texttt{n} + \texttt{p}) = (\texttt{m} \dashrightarrow \texttt{n}) + (\texttt{m} \dashrightarrow \texttt{p}) & & \text{(left distributivity)} \\
(\texttt{m} + \texttt{n}) \dashrightarrow \texttt{p} = \texttt{m} \dashrightarrow (\texttt{n} \dashrightarrow \texttt{p}) & \Leftarrow \ \texttt{m} \downarrow \texttt{n} & \text{(sequentialisation)} \\
(\texttt{m} + \texttt{n}) \dashrightarrow \texttt{p} = \texttt{n} \dashrightarrow \texttt{p} & \Leftarrow \ \texttt{m} \downarrow \texttt{n} \wedge \texttt{m} \dashrightarrow \texttt{n} = \texttt{n} & \text{(absorption I)} \\
(\texttt{m} + \texttt{n}) \dashrightarrow \texttt{p} = \texttt{m} \dashrightarrow \texttt{p} & \Leftarrow \ \texttt{m} \downarrow \texttt{n} \wedge \texttt{n} \dashrightarrow \texttt{p} = \texttt{p} & \text{(absorption II)} \\
\texttt{m} \dashrightarrow (\texttt{n} + \texttt{p}) = \texttt{n} + (\texttt{m} \dashrightarrow \texttt{p}) & \Leftarrow \ \text{dom}(\texttt{m}) \cap \text{dom}(\texttt{n}) = \emptyset & \text{(localisation)}
\end{array}
$$

The sequentialisation law means that a complex overriding may also be done by two successive simpler overridings. Absorption II, which is an immediate consequence of sequentialisation, allows simplifying a complex overriding by omitting the part that is "already there". Finally, localisation allows propagating an overriding to the submodule it really affects.

The previous laws for overriding dealt with immediate links from VPs to fragments. We now deal with preservation of transitive links under overriding. Let $\text{dep}_\texttt{m}^*$ be the reflexive, transitive closure of $\text{dep}_\texttt{m}$. For a module $\texttt{m}$ and a VP $\texttt{v} \in \text{dom}(\texttt{m})$ we define $\text{deps}(\texttt{v}, \texttt{m}) =_{df} \{\texttt{w} \mid \texttt{v} \ \text{dep}_\texttt{m}^* \ \texttt{w}\}$, i.e., the set of VPs on which $\texttt{v}$ depends transitively, plus $\texttt{v}$ itself. We now want to override or extend a module $\texttt{n}$ with a module $\texttt{m}$. If $\texttt{n}$ does not alter the assignments of the VPs on which $\texttt{v}$ transitively depends in $\texttt{m}$ then the overriding/extension does not change the transitive dependence of $\texttt{v}$ (cf. [23,13]):

$$\left. \begin{array}{l} \text{deps}(\texttt{v}, \texttt{m} + \texttt{n}) = \text{deps}(\texttt{v}, \texttt{m}) \\ \text{deps}(\texttt{v}, \texttt{m} \dashrightarrow \texttt{n}) = \text{deps}(\texttt{v}, \texttt{m}) \end{array} \right\} \ \Leftarrow \ \text{deps}(\texttt{v}, \texttt{m}) \cap \text{dom}(\texttt{n}) = \emptyset .$$

3.3   Solving Module Equations

As discussed in [5], it is useful to be able to solve module equations. Subtraction and its relatives enable us to do so. Suppose that m is a submodule of n, i.e., $m \leq n$ (see Equation (1)). Then the equation $m + x = n$ has $x = n - m$ as a solution. Moreover, this is the unique solution that is domain-disjoint from m.[3]

Example 3.2. Consider a composition $comp = a + b + c + d$ with pairwise domain-disjoint modules a, b, c, d. Then the equation $a + x + b + d = comp$ has the unique solution $x = c$ domain-disjoint from $a + b + d$. $\qquad\square$

Note that the condition $dom(m) \subseteq dom(n)$ is necessary for $m + x = n$ to be solvable, because we need to have $dom(m + x) = dom(m) \cup dom(x) = dom(n)$, which implies $dom(m) \subseteq dom(n)$. The above assumption $m \leq n$ implies that necessary condition. In fact, solvability of $m + x = n$ conversely implies $m \leq n$, since

$$m + n = m + (m + x) = (m + m) + x = m + x = n \, .$$

In short: $m + x = n$ is solvable iff $m \leq n$.

Next, we have a brief look at equations involving overriding. Since

$$dom(m \dashrightarrow n) = dom(n \dashrightarrow m) = dom(m) \cup dom(n) \, ,$$

again $dom(m) \subseteq dom(n)$ is necessary for $m \dashrightarrow x = n$ and $x \dashrightarrow m = n$ to be solvable. But by the definition of $\dashrightarrow$, solvability of $m \dashrightarrow x = n$ even implies the stronger necessary condition $m \leq n$. In this case again $x = n - m$ is the unique solution domain-disjoint from m. A closer inspection shows that the same is the case for the equation $x \dashrightarrow m = n$. This means that it is sufficient to restrict interest to the solution of equations involving $+$.

3.4   Transformations

In this section we sketch another extension of SDA, intended to cope with some standard techniques in software refactoring (e.g., [4,20]). Examples of such techniques are consistent renaming of methods or classes in a large software system. To stay at the same level of abstraction as before, we realize this by a mechanism for generally modifying the fragments in SDA modules.

By a *transformation* or *modification* or *refactoring* we mean a total function $T : F(V) \to F(V)$. By $T \cdot m$ we denote the *application* of T to a module m. It yields a new module defined by

$$(T \cdot m)(v) =_{df} \begin{cases} T(m(v)) & \text{if } v \in dom(m) \\ \text{undefined otherwise} \, . \end{cases}$$

We use the convention that $\cdot$ binds stronger than all other operators. The following properties hold:

(1) $dom(T \cdot m) = dom(m)$,   (2) $T \cdot (m + n) = T \cdot m + T \cdot n \quad \Leftarrow \quad m \downarrow n$,
(3) $T \cdot (m - n) = T \cdot m - T \cdot n$,   (4) $T \cdot (m \dashrightarrow n) = T \cdot m \dashrightarrow T \cdot n$.

---

[3] Another solution is $x = n$, since $m \leq n$ means $m + n = n$. Such solutions are uninteresting.

The proofs are straightforward calculations.

The analogue of Equation (2) is also used in the feature algebra of [1]; it entails that a transformation T is propagated and applied to all components of a composed module.

This applies, in particular, to transformations like method renaming; there T would be implemented using a global table with all the old-name/new-name associations which would be consistently applied in all submodules of the overall module under consideration. Note that, although T is supposed to be a total function on all fragments, it might well leave many of those unchanged, i.e., act as the identity on them.

Future work in this area will deal with further operators that reflect extended transformations concerning several modules, like moving methods from one module to another.

4 Using the Algebra

4.1 Projecting Out

Next, we deal with some aspects of modularity. In *classical modularity* there are physical files that define the feature modules and tools that compose them to produce a desired program. This is also known as *alternative-based variation*. Contrarily, *virtual modularity,* also known as *SYSGEN* (e.g. [14]) or *projectional variation* is a preprocessor technology. A prominent representative of this technique is the *coloring* approach of [5,15,18]. The idea is simple: every document is painted in different colors, one color per feature. A color C that appears "inside" another color D indicates a feature interaction—C changes the source of D (denoted C#D in [5]). VPs are implicit in coloring. At every point in a document where coloring changes, an implicit VP is created. Figure 1 is not only an example for variation points, fragments and modules, but also for coloring: the code is colored white, light gray and dark gray. If a feature is not needed in a product, all code colored in the corresponding color (e.g., dark gray) is *projected out*, i.e., does not show up in the final product. Since one colors the entire code base of a product line, it is possible to compute the contents of SDA modules and their VPs.

We now show how this operation can be expressed in our algebra. Assume a module m and a subset $U \subseteq \mathtt{dom}(m)$. Projection to U is supposed to hide everything that does not correspond to a VP in U. This needs to be done in such a way that later the hidden parts can be uncovered again. Therefore, a corresponding operation should not remove the VPs outside U from m. We preserve the hidden part $n =_{df} m|_{\mathtt{dom}(m)-U}$ and temporarily work with the module $p =_{df} [(\mathtt{dom}(m) - U) \mapsto 0] \rightarrow m$ which masks all VPs outside U with the default fragment. To restore the original module, i.e., to switch the masked parts back on again we use that $n \rightarrow p = m$.

The difference between restriction and projecting out is that in the former case all VPs outside U are removed and hence become external to the resulting module so that they would be considered as "fresh" there, whereas after projection they are still "known" and hence "protected" against unintentional change, so that they can be refilled later.

4.2   Introducing Wrappers

We can use overriding for adding a wrapper to a module. Let m be a module and $v \in dom(m)$ be the VP where we want to insert the wrapper. Choose a "fresh" VP $w \notin dom(m)$ and a non-trivial wrapper fragment f such that $VP(f) = \{w\}$ and w occurs only once in f. Then w marks the place in f where the original "contents" of v is to be put and thereby wrapped. The old contents m(v) of v is remembered by a link from w to it, so that it can be overridden by a link from v to the wrapper f. Algebraically, the module with the wrapper is expressed by

$$m' =_{df} ([v \mapsto f] \twoheadrightarrow m) + [w \mapsto m(v)] .$$

An illustration is given in Figure 3.

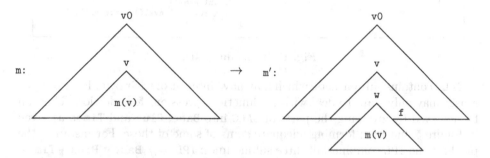

Fig. 3. Introducing a Wrapper (Splicing)

5   Small Case Study: Constructing Product Lines

There are often multiple ways how a finished product (i.e., a single fragment without further VPs) can result within a product line. This is, for example, the case when modules can be grouped into sets of features that are orthogonal to each other. Conversely, one may wish to refactor an existing monolithic system by decomposing it into directly re-usable or at least easily adaptable parts.

We illustrate this by taking up an example from [7]. Notationally we deviate a bit from that paper by not distinguishing "defining" and "applied" occurrences of VPs. All VP names start with @ (for text processing reasons); in a module every VP is assigned the text indented to the position after the VP name. If no text appears to the right of a VP this means that the default is assigned to it.

We look at software for a basic calculator. It deals with arithmetic expressions composed by the operations addition and multiplication; expressions can be displayed and evaluated. First we present a program (or single module) CALC, given in [7] (see Figure 4). Formally, this is a module that has only one single root VP @0 to which the complete program is assigned, without any VPs in its text. However, to prepare the restructuring to come, we already indicate a number of further VPs, to be read as comments at this level. For operator signs op, such as + or *, the abbreviation ?op? stands for the string concatenation + "op" +.

```
CALC
┌─────────────────────────────────────────────────────────────────────────┐
│ @0 abstract class Exp {              class Plus extends Exp {             │
│     @1 String print();                   Exp l,r;                        │
│     @2 int eval();                       Plus(Exp L, Exp R) {l=L; r=R;}   │
│     }                                    @5 String print()               │
│                                             { return l.print() ?+? r.print(); } │
│                                          @6 int eval()                    │
│                                             { return l.eval() + r.eval(); } │
│                                          }                                │
│                                                                          │
│     class Int extends Exp {          class Times extends Exp {            │
│         int v;                           Exp l,r;                        │
│         Int(int a) { v=a; }              Times(Exp L, Exp R) {l=L; r=R;}  │
│         @3 String print() { return v; }  @7 String print()               │
│         @4 int eval() { return v; }         { return l.print() ?*? r.print();} │
│         }                                @8 int eval()                    │
│                                             { return l.eval() * r.eval(); } │
│                                          }                                │
└─────────────────────────────────────────────────────────────────────────┘
```

Fig. 4. The module CALC

CALC contains sub-packets, which may have interest of their own. For example, a user may only want to deal with arithmetic expressions for addition. This can be achieved by grouping the parts of CALC into Base, Plus and Times as given in Figure 5 and then forming adequate sums of some of these. For instance, the product line TPL combines all three submodules: TPL $=_{df}$ Base + Plus + Times. Using the restructuring preorder from Sect. 2.2, we have the relation CALC $\sqsubseteq$ TPL between the original code base CALC and TPL.

A second restructuring reflects that some users may only wish to evaluate expressions but not to print them. This can be accommodated by decomposing the original code base CALC into a Core module and two optional modules Print and Eval, whose definitions are given in Figure 6. A new product line CPE $=_{df}$ Core + Print + Eval combines these three submodules.

The original product line CALC relates to the new one by CALC $\sqsubseteq$ CPE.

Finally we can form a common restructuring of CPE and TPL. This SPL is presented in Figure 7 and corresponds to the EPL matrix of [7]. We use two sets of feature names, F $=_{df}$ {core, print, eval} and G $=_{df}$ {base, plus, times}. We use lower-case names here, since these are not module names but will serve as indices for a matrix EPLmat, where every entry EPLmat$_{ij}$ (i $\in$ F, j $\in$ G) is a submodule. Then setting EPL $=_{df} \sum_{i \in F} \sum_{j \in G}$ EPLmat$_{ij}$ we obtain our finest restructuring of the original program CALC. As a consequence we have

$$CPE \sqsubseteq EPL \wedge TPL \sqsubseteq EPL \,.$$

```
TPL:
Base:                        Plus:                        Times:
@0 abstract class Exp {      @+ class Plus extends Exp {  @* class Times extends Exp {
     String print();              Exp l,r;                     Exp l,r;
     int eval();                  Plus(Exp L, Exp R)           Times(Exp L, Exp R)
   }                                {l=L; r=R;}                  {l=L; r=R;}
                                  String print()               String print()
   class Int extends Exp {          { return l.print() ?+?       { return l.print() ?*?
     int v;                                    r.print(); }                r.print();}
     Int(int a) { v=a; }                                     int eval()
     String print()               int eval()                   { return l.eval() *
       { return v; }                { return l.eval() +                   r.eval(); }
     int eval()                                r.eval(); }    }
       { return v; }            }
   }

   @+
   @*
```

Fig. 5. The module TPL

```
CPE:
Core:                        Print:                       Eval:
@0 abstract class Exp {
     @1                       @1 String print();           @2 int eval();
     @2
   }

   class Int extends Exp {
     int v;
     Int(int a) { v=a; }
     @3                       @3 String print()            @4 int eval()
     @4                          { return v; }                { return v; }
   }

   class Plus extends Exp {
     Exp l,r;
     Plus(Exp L, Exp R)
       {l=L; r=R;}
     @5                       @5 String print()            @6 int eval()
     @6                          { return l.print()           { return l.eval()
   }                              ?+? r.print(); }             + r.eval(); }

   class Times extends Exp {
     Exp l,r;
     Times(Exp L, Exp R)
       {l=L; r=R;}
     @7                       @7 String print()            @8 int eval()
     @8                          { return l.print()           { return l.eval()
   }                              ?*? r.print(); }             * r.eval(); }
```

Fig. 6. The module CPE

If we sum the columns of EPLmat we obtain the constituent modules of CPE, while the row sums give the constituent modules of TPL. Hence the small modules in EPLmat can be considered as the elementary features in this product line. Of course, by transitivity of $\sqsubseteq$, the original code base is an element of this product line too, i.e., CALC $\sqsubseteq$ EPL; but EPL offers many more products.

EPLmat		
	core	print	eval

	core	print	eval

base	`@0 abstract class Exp {`
	`    @1`
	`    @2`
	`}`
	
	`class Int extends Exp {`
	`    int v;`
	`    Int(int a) { v=a; }`
	`    @3`
	`    @4`
	`}`
	`@*`
	`@+`
		`@1 String print();`
		`        eval print core`
		
		`@3 String print()`
		`        { return v; }`
			`@2 int eval();`
			
			`@4 int eval()`
			`        { return v; }`

plus	`@+ class Plus extends Exp {`
	`    Exp l,r;`
	`    Plus(Exp L, Exp R)`
	`        {l=L; r=R;}`
	`    @5`
	`    @6`
	`}`
		`@5 String print()`
		`        { return l.print()`
		`          ?+? r.print(); }`
			`@6 int eval()`
			`        { return l.eval()`
			`          + r.eval(); }`

times	`@* class Times extends Exp {`
	`    Exp l,r;`
	`    Times(Exp L, Exp R)`
	`        {l=L; r=R;}`
	`    @7`
	`    @8`
	`}`
		`@7 String print()`
		`        { return l.print()`
		`          ?*? r.print(); }`
			`@8 int eval()`
			`        { return l.eval()`
			`          * r.eval(); }`

Fig. 7. The matrix `EPLmat`

6   Related Work

Ideas similar to those of SDA can be found in [9], where elements of UML models could be tagged with feature predicates. Given a set of selected features, an element is removed from a model if its predicate is false.

Derivatives [21] were the first identified building blocks of feature modules. Unfortunately, the mathematics of derivatives was incomplete, as composition of derivatives was not associative. This made it impossible to algebraically calculate the results of feature splitting (replacing T with R × S if T is split into features R and S) and feature merging (replacing R × S with T). CIDE [18] showed a simple and elegant way to visualize features and their interactions, resulting in the coloring algebra, which does support splitting and merging.

Other algebras for feature-based composition, such as [1,22], focus on the internal structure of modules. The algebra presented in [1] is (to our knowledge) the first that dealt with feature replication. It uses the algebraic law of *distant idempotence* (a form of idempotence where adjacency of identical features is not required). Feature composition is not commutative and there is no operation of subtraction on feature modules (called feature structure trees there). An algebra that also captures replicas is presented in [16]. However, this algebra only works at a semantic level and cannot cope with real source code, as SDA does.

The *Choice Calculus (CC)* [25] offers an interesting and alternative approach to our work. Among the goals of CC are to integrate classical and virtual modularity, but to do so in the context of a formal programming language. Large-scale fragments can be placed in modules of their own, while small-scale fragments (suitable for annotations) can be embedded into other modules. As in coloring and `ifdef` preprocessing, variation points are implicit. The key difference between our work and CC is that the issues of classical and virtual modularity are not limited to a fixed set of programming languages.

Delta Oriented Programming (DOP) [24] is another interesting language-based approach within our field. Delta modules are qualified to be composed into a product when the corresponding `where` clause is satisfied. Such a clause is a propositional formula over features, namely the conjunction of the feature formulas that arise in coloring. Disjunction allows a single module to be reused in different contexts (rather than requiring a module to be replicated for each context). Negation seems to offer a more general way for defining alternatives. Understanding this connection will be the subject of future work. Delta modules also have `after` clauses, which specify a partial order in which to compose them. We express the composition order of modules explicitly with our overriding operator $\rightarrow$.

A project close in spirit and ideas is Kästner's *CIDE* [18,19,2]. It started out with a tool for software product line development (esp. analyzing and decomposing legacy code), following the paradigm of virtual separation of concerns. For this it offers the possibility of distinguishing fragments within the original code by different background colors. CIDE is also a compiler (and an IDE), closely related to conditional compilation with preprocessors. Additionally it analyzes the deep structure of the code and hence guarantees syntactic correctness as well as type correctness of all generated products. Hence CIDE already provides, at the tool level, some of the functionality that our algebra treats at the abstract level.

7   Conclusions and Outlook

We have presented a structured document algebra not only in concept, but also at work on some essential phenomena of large-scale software construction. We hope to have convinced the reader that SDA is both concise and precise, and comes with a number of useful laws. These can be used to construct and reason about structured modules in an algebraic fashion.

The main aim is to provide a formal basis for governing variability in large interconnected collections of documents, in particular ones that define SPLs. SDA can be used to implement tools which relieve developers from managing variability manually. In particular, it provides a basis for precise reasoning about complex and error-prone operations such as subtraction, overriding, and various refactorings. Currently, work on a pilot implementation is under way.

The algebra has interesting connections to other structures, such as the pointer algebras presented in [13,23] and to the concept of the demonic join or compatible union [3,11].

While so far SDA is presented along a concrete mathematical model, an abstraction to more general concepts like monoids, semirings and modules in the linear algebra sense is under way.

Finally, so far SDA has a very syntactic flavor, since the nature of fragments is left open. However, it is possible to work with fragments that have a semantic character, such as functions from valuations of VPs in some semantic model to a semantic value. We have sketched this in an Appendix; the elaboration of these ideas will be the subject of future investigations.

Acknowledgments. We are grateful to the anonymous referees for helpful comments and suggestions. We gratefully acknowledge support for this work by NSF grants CCF 0724979 and OCI-1148125, as well as by DFG grant MO 690/7-2. NICTA is funded by the Australian Government through the Department of Communications and the Australian Research Council through the ICT Centre of Excellence Program.

References

1. Apel, S., Lengauer, C., Möller, B., Kästner, C.: An algebraic foundation for automatic feature-based program synthesis. SCP 75(11), 1022–1047 (2010)
2. Apel, S., Batory, D., Kästner, C., Saake, G.: Feature-Oriented Software Product Lines. Springer (2013)
3. Backhouse, R., van der Woude, J.: Demonic operators and monotype factors. Mathematical Structures in Computer Science 3(4), 417–433 (1993)
4. Batory, D.: Program refactoring, program synthesis, and model-driven development. In: Adsul, B., Odersky, M. (eds.) CC 2007. LNCS, vol. 4420, pp. 156–171. Springer, Heidelberg (2007)
5. Batory, D., Höfner, P., Kim, J.: Feature interactions, products, and composition. In: Generative Programming and Component Engineering (GPCE 2011), pp. 13–22. ACM (2011)
6. Batory, D., Höfner, P., Möller, B., Zelend, A.: Features, modularity, and variation points. In: Feature-Oriented Software Development, pp. 9–16. ACM (2013)
7. Batory, D., Shepherd, C.: Product lines of product lines, Department of Computer Science, University of Texas at Austin (submitted, 2013)
8. Bergel, A., Ducasse, S., Nierstrasz, O.: Classbox/J: Controlling the scope of change in Java. SIGPLAN Not. 40(10), 177–189 (2005)
9. Czarnecki, K., Antkiewicz, M.: Mapping features to models: A template approach based on superimposed variants. In: Glück, R., Lowry, M. (eds.) GPCE 2005. LNCS, vol. 3676, pp. 422–437. Springer, Heidelberg (2005)
10. Delaware, B., Cook, W.R., Batory, D.S.: Product lines of theorems. In: Lopes, C.V., Fisher, K. (eds.) Proceedings of the 26th Annual ACM SIGPLAN Conference on Object-Oriented Programming, Systems, Languages, and Applications, OOPSLA 2011, part of SPLASH 2011, Portland, OR, USA, October 22-27, vol. 10, pp. 595–608. ACM (2011)

11. Desharnais, J., Belkhiter, N., Sghaier, S.B.M., Tchier, F., Jaoua, A., Mili, A., Zaguia, N.: Embedding a demonic semilattice in a relational algebra. Theor. Comput. Sci. 149(2), 333–360 (1995)
12. Ducasse, S., Nierstrasz, O., Schärli, N., Wuyts, R., Black, P.: Traits: A mechanism for fine-grained reuse. ACM Trans. Program. Lang. Syst. 28(2), 331–388 (2006)
13. Ehm, T.: The Kleene Algebra of Nested Pointer Structures: Theory and Applications. Ph.D. thesis, Fakultät für Angewandte Informatik, Universität Augsburg (2003)
14. Gomaa, H.: Designing Software Product Lines with UML: From Use Cases to Pattern-Based Software Architectures. Addison-Wesley (2004)
15. Heidenreich, F.: Towards systematic ensuring well-formedness of software product lines. In: Feature-Oriented Software Development, ACM (2009)
16. Höfner, P., Khedri, R., Möller, B.: Feature algebra. In: Misra, J., Nipkow, T., Sekerinski, E. (eds.) FM 2006. LNCS, vol. 4085, pp. 300–315. Springer, Heidelberg (2006)
17. Kang, K., Cohen, S., Hess, J., Novak, W., Peterson, A.: Feature-oriented domain analysis (foda) feasibility study. Tech. Rep. CMU/SEI-90-TR-021, Carnegie Mellon Software Engineering Institute, Carnegie Mellon University (1990)
18. Kästner, C., Apel, S., Kuhlemann, M.: Granularity in software product lines. In: Schäfer, W., Dwyer, M., Gruhn, V. (eds.) Conference on Software Engineering (ICSE 2008). ACM (2008)
19. Kästner, C.: Virtual separation of concerns: toward preprocessors 2.0. Ph.D. thesis, Otto von Guericke University Magdeburg (2010)
20. Kuhlemann, M., Batory, D., Apel, S.: Refactoring feature modules. In: Edwards, S.H., Kulczycki, G. (eds.) ICSR 2009. LNCS, vol. 5791, pp. 106–115. Springer, Heidelberg (2009)
21. Liu, J., Batory, D.S., Lengauer, C.: Feature oriented refactoring of legacy applications. In: Osterweil, L.J., Rombach, H.D., Soffa, M.L. (eds.) 28th International Conference on Software Engineering (ICSE 2006), Shanghai, China, May 20-28, pp. 112–121. ACM (2006)
22. Lopez-Herrejon, R., Batory, D., Lengauer, C.: A disciplined approach to aspect composition. In: Partial Evaluation and Semantics-based Program Manipulation (PEPM 2006). ACM (2006)
23. Möller, B.: Towards pointer algebra. SCP 21(1), 57–90 (1993)
24. Schaefer, I., Bettini, L., Bono, V., Damiani, F., Tanzarella, N.: Delta-oriented programming of software product lines. In: Bosch, J., Lee, J. (eds.) SPLC 2010. LNCS, vol. 6287, pp. 77–91. Springer, Heidelberg (2010)
25. Walkingshaw, E., Erwig, M.: A calculus for modeling and implementing variation. In: Generative Programming and Component Engineering, pp. 132–140. ACM (2012)
26. Wirsing, M.: Algebraic specification. In: Handbook of Theoretical Computer Science, Volume B: Formal Models and Semantics (B), pp. 675–788 (1990)

Appendix: Sketch of a Semantic Model of SDA

For historical reasons, in particular in honour of Martin Wirsing, we have chosen an approach based on the notions of algebraic specification [26]. Other variants are conceivable, too.

Basic Definitions. Assume a signature $\Sigma = (s, F)$ with a sort s and a set F of operators $f : s^n \to s$. (For simplicity we restrict ourselves to the one-sorted case; the generalisation to many sorts is straightforward.) The number n is called the *arity* of f. An operator of arity 0 is called a *constant operator*. We also assume a set V of *variation points* such that V is disjoint from the set of constant operators of Σ (in logic the elements of V would be called *variables*). The set $T(\Sigma, V)$ of *terms* over Σ and V is defined as usual. If $VP(t) = \emptyset$ then t is called *closed* or a *ground term*. For describing SDA modules we assume a signature with two special constant symbols $0, \frac{t}{t}$.

A Σ-*algebra* is a pair $A = (s^A, F^A)$ where s^A is a nonempty *carrier set* and $F^A = \{f^A \mid f \in F\}$ is a set of *operations* $f^A : (s^A)^n \to s^A$ associated with the $f : s^n \to s \in F$. The set $T(\Sigma, V)$ can be made into a Σ-algebra in the usual way. A *valuation* of V in a Σ-algebra A (also called an *environment*) is a partial function $e : V \rightsquigarrow s^A$. The set of all environments is denoted by $\mathcal{E}^A$.

Syntactic Modules. A *syntactic fragment* simply is an element of $T(\Sigma, V)$. By this, all VPs are fragments, too. A *syntactic module* is an environment $m : V \rightsquigarrow T(\Sigma, V)$ from $\mathcal{E}^{T(\Sigma, V)}$. The function $\mathtt{single\_fill(t, m)}$ is defined inductively as syntactic substitution:

1. If $t = v \in V$ is a VP then

$$\mathtt{single\_fill(t, m)} =_{df} \begin{cases} e(v) & \text{if } v \in \mathrm{dom}(e) , \\ v & \text{otherwise} . \end{cases}$$

2. If $t = f(t_1, \ldots, t_n)$ then

$$\mathtt{single\_fill(t, m)} =_{df} f(\mathtt{single\_fill(t_1, m)}, \ldots, \mathtt{single\_fill(t_n, m)}) .$$

For a constant operator f hence $\mathtt{single\_fill(t, m)} = f$.

Term Evaluation. For a Σ-algebra A we define inductively the *evaluation* $[\![\_]\!] : T(\Sigma, V) \to (\mathcal{E}^A \rightsquigarrow s^A)$ that assigns to every term a value using an environment, if possible.

– For VP v we set

$$[\![v]\!](e) =_{df} \begin{cases} e(v) & \text{if } v \in \mathrm{dom}(e) , \\ \text{undefined} & \text{otherwise} . \end{cases}$$

– For other terms we set

$$[\![f(t_1, \ldots, t_n)]\!](e) =_{df}$$
$$\begin{cases} f^A(u_1, \ldots, u_n) & \text{if all } [\![t_i]\!](e) \text{ are defined and } u_i = [\![t_i]\!](e) , \\ \text{undefined} & \text{otherwise} . \end{cases}$$

Hence for a constant symbol f we have $[\![f]\!](e) = f^A$ for all e.

This definition entails what is called the *Coincidence Lemma* in logic; the proof is a straightforward induction.

Lemma 7.1. *If two environments* e, e' *agree on the VPs of a term* t, *i.e., if* $e|_{VP(t)} = e'|_{VP(t)}$, *then* $[\![t]\!](e) = [\![t]\!](e')$.

Semantic Modules. The idea is now to make the mapping $[\![t]\!] : \mathcal{E}^A \rightsquigarrow s^A$ somehow into a *semantic fragment* corresponding to the syntactic object t and to define a semantic module as a partial function from VPs to semantic fragments. However, this is not entirely straightforward, since we need to have VP information in some way to still be able to talk about cycle-freeness of modules. The solution proposed here is to enrich a semantic fragment by a set of VPs it "administers". A *semantic fragment* over a set V of VPs and a Σ-algebra A is a pair (W, g) where $W \subseteq V$ and $g : \mathcal{E}^A \rightsquigarrow s^A$ satisfies the *coincidence property* on W:

$$\forall e, e' : e|_W = e'|_W \Rightarrow g(e) = g(e') .$$

We set $VP(W, g) =_{df} W$ and $ev(W, g) =_{df} g$. The dependence relation for semantic modules uses this definition of VP.

Every VP v can be made into the fragment $(\{v\}, \lambda e . 0^A)$.

A *semantic module* is a partial function from V to the set of semantic fragments. We can translate every syntactic module m into a semantic one called $\hat{m}$ by setting $\hat{m}(v) =_{df} (VP(m(v)), [\![m(v)]\!])$. If m is cycle-free then so is $\hat{m}$.

The Single Fill Function for Semantic Modules. To make SDA work for semantic modules we have to define the `single_fill` function suitably:

$$\texttt{single\_fill}((W, g), m) =_{df} ((W - \text{dom}(m)) \cup Z, \lambda e . g(e')) ,$$

where $Z =_{df} \bigcup_{v \in \text{dom}(m)} VP(m(v))$ and

$$e'(v) =_{df} \begin{cases} m(v)(e) & \text{if } v \in \text{dom}(m) , \\ e(v) & \text{otherwise} . \end{cases}$$

From EU Projects to a Family of Model Checkers

From Kandinsky to KandISTI

Maurice H. ter Beek, Stefania Gnesi, and Franco Mazzanti

Formal Methods && Tools lab (FM&&T)
Istituto di Scienza e Tecnologie dell'Informazione "A. Faedo" (ISTI)
Consiglio Nazionale delle Ricerche (CNR)
Via G. Moruzzi 1, 56124 Pisa, Italy
{terbeek,gnesi,mazzanti}@isti.cnr.it

Abstract. We describe the development of the KandISTI family of model checkers from its origins nearly two decades ago until its very recent latest addition. Most progress was made, however, during two integrated European projects, AGILE and SENSORIA, in which our FM&&T lab participated under the scientific coordination of Martin Wirsing. Moreover, the very name of the family of model checkers is partly due to Martin Wirsing's passion for art and science.

1 Introduction

We have had the pleasure to work with Martin in two European projects, namely FP5-IP-IST-2001-32747 AGILE [2] and the FP6-IP-IST-016004 SENSORIA [57]. He coordinated both in an excellent manner.

AGILE created primitives for explicitly addressing mobility in architectural models. Therefore algebraic models based on graph transformation techniques were defined for the underlying processes to relate the reconfiguration of the coordination structure and the mobility of components across the distribution topology. Moreover, an extension of UML for mobility was developed to make the architectural primitives available to practitioners, together with tool support.

SENSORIA resolved problems from Service-Oriented Computing (SOC) by building novel theories, methods, and tools supporting the engineering of software systems for service-oriented overlay computers. The results include a comprehensive service ontology, new semantically well-defined modeling and programming primitives for services, new powerful mathematical analysis and verification techniques, tools for system behavior and quality of service properties, and novel model-based transformation and development techniques [57].

Based on our expertise, our involvement in AGILE was mainly to develop analysis techniques to support compositional verification of properties addressing the evolution of computation, coordination and distribution. In SENSORIA, instead, we developed a logical verification framework for the analysis of functional properties in SOC. In both projects, our work was strongly focused on the realization of a model-checking framework, as a result of which we now have a family of model checkers that we will describe in this paper.

R. De Nicola and R. Hennicker (Eds.): Wirsing Festschrift, LNCS 8950, pp. 312–328, 2015.

This paper is organized as follows. In Sect. 2 we explain the name we gave to our family of model checkers, after which we briefly describe each family member in Sect. 3–6. We then sketch their overall structure in Sect. 7, after which we conclude the paper in Sect. 8.

2 From Kandinsky to KandISTI

In the beginning of 2008, one of the SENSORIA meetings included as social event a visit to the Lenbachhaus, a museum which preserves one of the richest collections of Wassily Kandinsky. At that time we were in the middle of the process of reshaping our family of model checkers by separating the specification language dependent details of the underlying *ground* computational model from its abstract representation in terms of a so-called Doubly-Labeled Transition System (L^2TS) [33], on which to carry out the analysis. While our ground computational models (state machines, process algebras) are already a simplified model of a real system, their correspondence with reality is still very immediate as they directly reflect the real system structure and behavior. Observing a model at this level, as explicitly allowed by our model-checking framework, is like exploring the real system which is being modeled. In some sense, our ground models are similar to the early paintings of Kandinsky (*e.g.* Fig. 1(a)) in which the correspondence of the painting to the reality is immediate.[1]

(a) Kallmünz - Gabriele Münter Painting II, 1903   (b) St. George III, 1911   (c) Red Spot II, 1921

Fig. 1. By Wassily Kandinsky (Städtische Galerie im Lenbachhaus, Munich, Germany)

In a very short time, however, Kandinsky's style of painting started to evolve into a more abstract style and his paintings started to no longer directly reflect reality in all its details. Instead, the painter chose to communicate just what he felt was relevant to him (*e.g.* Fig. 1(b)). Again, this is precisely what we intend

---

[1] The depicted thumbnails of Kandinsky paintings are among those observable on the official website of the Städtische Galerie im Lenbachhaus in Munich, Germany (*cf.* http://www.lenbachhaus.de/collection/the-blue-rider/), and are used here for non-commercial and strictly illustrative purposes.

to achieve in our family of model checkers, when we define *abstraction rules* which allow to represent the system as an L^2TS in which the labels on the states and edges directly represent just the abstract pieces of information we want to observe, to be able to express the properties we want to verify. A specific feature of our framework displays the model precisely at this abstraction level, even if at this level we are still able to find a correspondence between the abstract L^2TS and the underlying computational model, since each state and each edge can still be mapped back to a precise system state and system evolution.

In the last series of Kandinsky paintings, the disconnection between the observed reality and the represented images is almost complete (*e.g.* Fig. 1(c)). His paintings directly express just the author's feelings that the observation of reality stimulates. In our framework we have the possibility to apply to our abstract L^2TS a powerful minimization technique, which allows to observe in a graphical and very concise way the system behavior with respect to the abstract pieces of information we have selected to observe. In this way the resulting picture loses its direct connection with the underlying model (it is no longer possible to map a node to a single system state) and directly communicates most of the system properties regarding the observed aspects of the system. The intuition on the correctness of a system can be gained by just observing the representation of its abstract minimized behavior.

During the aforementioned visit to the Lenbachhaus, Martin Wirsing did not fail to notice the reminiscence of the various abstraction levels of our verification framework to the various approaches to painting through which Kandinsky's style has evolved, and we enjoyed together this wonderful matching. This visit inspired us to name our ISTI verification framework in a way that somehow reflects and honors Kandinsky's contribution to the art of painting, and this is why we have decided to name it KandISTI.

The development of the KandISTI family of model checkers is an ongoing effort [24,40,17]. The current versions of its family members are freely usable online via:

http://fmt.isti.cnr.it/kandisti/

On that page you will see the front-end of the family depicted in Fig. 2 and by clicking on one of its family members the specific tool will open.

In the next four sections, we briefly describe the different computational models underlying the model-checking tools of KandISTI, after which we will describe the unique logical verification environment in more detail in Sect. 7.

3   FMC: The Origin of Our On-the-Fly Model-Checking Approach

Experiments at ISTI with on-the-fly model checking began with the FMC model checker [39] for action-based CTL (ACTL) [32] extended with fixed-point operators. In FMC, a system is a hierarchical composition (net) of sequential automata (terms). Terms can be recursively defined using a simple process algebra which supports features coming from CCS, CSP and LOTOS [36]. Communication and synchronization among terms is achieved through synchronous operations over

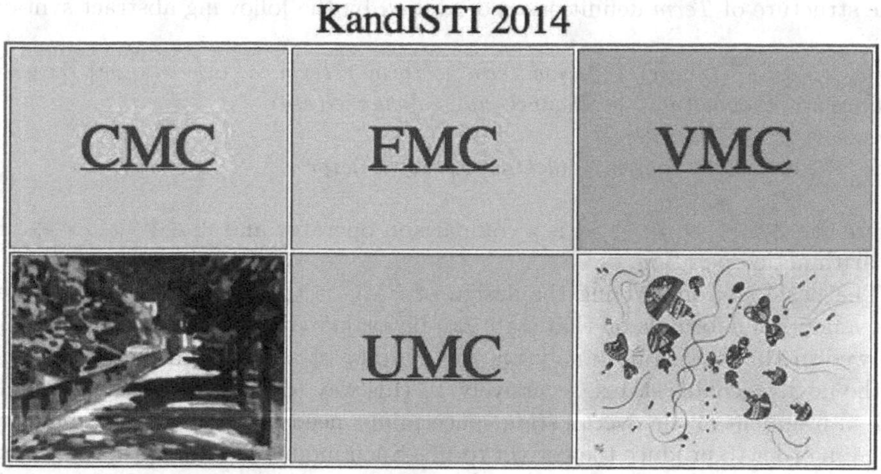

KandISTI 2014

CMC	FMC	VMC
	UMC	

Fig. 2. The front-end of the KandISTI family of model checkers

channels. The parallel operator / *Channels* / defined in the syntax below allows the CCS synchronization between two participating networks, requires the CSP-like synchronization when the participating networks evolve with a communication action controlled by the specified list of Channels, and lets the participants proceed in interleaving when executing CSP actions not explicitly controlled. Moreover, all participants of a communication/synchronization must agree on the set of values exchanged during the operation.

All this allows to naturally model both binary client-server interactions and n-ary barrier-like synchronizations. Term definitions can be parametrized, and communication operations allow value passing. The only supported form of values are integer numbers, stand-alone identifiers can also be used as values and behave like special implementation defined integer constants.

Summarizing, the structure of the process algebra accepted by FMC is described by the following abstract syntax (where only the case in which term definitions and communication actions have precisely one parameter is depicted, but obviously their number can be arbitrary):

$System$ ::= [Net]
Net ::= $T(expr)$ | Net / *Channels* / Net | $Net \setminus channel$ | Net [$channel/channel$]

where [Net] denotes a *closed* system, *i.e.* a process that cannot evolve on actions that rely on input parameters ($channel(?variable)$ as defined below); $T(expr)$ is a process instantiation from the set of process declarations of the form $T(variable) \stackrel{\text{def}}{=} Term$; and *Channels* is a list of channel names. Next to the *parallel* operator / *Channels* / mentioned before, $\setminus channel$ and [$channel/channel$] denote the classical operators of channel *restriction* and *renaming*, respectively.

The structure of *Term* definitions is described by the following abstract syntax:

$$Term ::= nil \mid T(expr) \mid Action.Term \mid Term + Term \mid [\, expr \bowtie expr \,]\, Term$$
$$Action ::= channel(arg) \mid ?channel(arg) \mid !channel(arg)$$
$$arg ::= expr \mid ?variable$$
$$expr ::= variable \mid integer \mid identifier \mid expr \pm expr$$

where $\bowtie \in \{<, \leq, =, \neq, \geq, >\}$ is a comparison operator and $\pm \in \{+, -, \times, \div\}$ is an arithmetic operation.

The basic idea underlying the design of FMC is that, given a system state, the validity of a formula on that state can be evaluated analyzing the transitions allowed in that state, and analyzing the validity of a subformula in only some of the next reachable states, recursively. In this way (depending on the formula) only a fragment of the overall state space might need to be generated and analyzed in order to produce the correct result. Such model-checking procedures are also called *local*, in order to distinguish them from those called *global*, in which the whole state space is explored to check the validity of a formula (*cf.* [27,7]).

For the evaluation of a formula, in order to be able to partially deal also with infinite-state systems (potentially introduced by the presence of integer values), a so-called *bounded* model-checking approach is adopted (*cf.* [27,7]). The evaluation is started by assuming a certain value as a maximum depth of the evaluation. If the evaluation of the formula reaches a result within the requested depth, then the result holds for the whole system; otherwise the maximum depth is increased and the evaluation is retried (preserving all useful partial results already found). This approach, initially introduced to address infinite state spaces, can turn out to be useful also for another reason: by setting a small initial maximum depth and a small automatic increment of this bound at each re-evaluation failure, once a result is finally found then we might also have a usable explanation for it. Note, however, that depending on the structure of the formula (*e.g.* requesting a check on all reachable states) and on the structure of the model (*e.g.* of a too big size[2]) no result might be returned by the tool when all the available resources (*e.g.* memory) are consumed.

The logic initially supported by FMC is an action-based branching-time logic inspired by ACTL and enriched with weak until operators, box and diamond operators and fixed-point operators. The fragment of this logic without fixed-point operators allows verifications with a complexity which is linear with respect to the size of the model and the size of the formula. With the integrations of the other tools of the family this logic has been over the time extended with the new features introduced for the support of state properties and data correlations among actions.

So far, FMC has been used mainly in didactic contexts for the experimentation of various modeling and verification techniques. Its main limit for heavier industrial use is the lack of support for more structured data types (*e.g.* lists, sets, maps, vectors).

---

[2] The current limit for an exhaustive verification is a statespace of millions of states.

4   UMC: Support for State/Event-Based Models and Logics

As an attempt to reduce the gap between software engineers and theoreticians, the very same model-checking approach that was adopted for FMC has subsequently been applied to a computational model directly inspired by UML statecharts (*cf.* http://www.uml.org). This prompted the switching to an action- *and* state-based logic, that would allow to express in a natural way not only properties of evolution steps (*i.e.* related to the executed actions) but also internal properties of states (*e.g.* related to the values of object attributes). The result of this process has been the UMC model checker and its associated UCTL logic [14].

The initial part of the design, development, and experimentation of the approach has been carried out in the context of the AGILE project. The purpose of the project was the development of an architectural approach in which mobility aspects could be modeled explicitly. The project proposed extensions of UML to support mobile and distributed system design, including linguistic extensions of the UML diagrammatic notations, extensions of the Unified Process and a prototype for simulating and analyzing the dynamic behavior of designs of mobile and distributed systems.

According to the UML paradigm, a dynamic system is seen as a set of evolving and communicating objects, where objects are class instances. The set of objects and classes which constitute a system can be described in UML by a structure diagram, while the dynamic behavior of the objects can be described by associating a statechart diagram to their classes. Each object of the system will therefore behave like a state machine; it will have a set of local attributes, an event pool collecting the events that need to be processed, and a current progress status. The progress status of a state machine is given by the set of currently active states of the statechart diagram.

In UMC a system is described as a set of communicating UML-like state machines. The structure of a state machine in UMC is defined by a Class declaration, which has the following general structure:

```
class <name> is
  Signals:
  <list of asynchronous signals managed by the class' objects>
  Operations:
  <list of synchronous call ops managed by the class' objects>
  Vars:
  <list of local vars belonging to the class' objects state>
  Behavior:
  <list of rules defining state evolutions of the class' objects>
end <name>
```

The **Behavior** part of a class definition describes the possible evolutions of the system. This part contains a list of transition rules which have the following generic form:

```
<Source> --> <Target> {<EventTrigger>[<Guard> ] /<Actions> }
```

Each rule intuitively states that when the system is in state *Source*, the specified *EventTrigger* is available and the *Guard* is satisfied, then all *Actions* of the transition are executed and the system state passes from *Source* to *Target*.

In UMC, the actual structure of the system is defined by a set of active object instantiations. A full UMC model is defined by a sequence of Class and Object declarations and by a final definition of a set of Abstraction rules. The overall behavior of a system is in fact formalized as an abstract L^2TS and the Abstraction rules allow to define what we want to see as labels of the states and edges of the L^2TS.

This approach to model the abstract system behavior as an L^2TS, showing only the essential information for the verification of system properties, proved to be a winning idea. Hence it was applied also to the other tools of the family, thus allowing the development of a common logical verification layer for our family of model checkers, which consequently became independent from the details of the particular specification language and computational model of the various tools.

The logic initially supported by UMC was just an extension of the logic supported by FMC with the possibility of using state predicates and pure CTL-like operators. As we will see in the next section over time this logic has been extended with the new features introduced for the support of parametric formulas allowing to express data correlations among actions.

The development and the experience gained with UMC has also helped in clarifying the overall purpose for the development of our verification framework. The main purpose of our tools is not just the final validation step of a completed architectural design, but rather a formal support during all steps of the incremental design phase (*i.e.* when ongoing designs are still likely to be incomplete and, with a high probability, contain mistakes). Indeed, the UMC framework has evolved having in mind the requirements of a system designer as end user: (s)he intends to take advantage of formal approaches to achieve an early validation of the system requirements and an early detection of design errors. Therefore, the main goals of the development of UMC have been:

1. The possibility to manually explore a system's evolutions and to generate a summary of its behavior in terms of minimal abstract traces.
2. The possibility to investigate abstract system properties by using a branching-time temporal logic supported by an on-the-fly model checker.
3. The possibility to obtain a clear explanation of the model-checking results in terms of possible evolutions of the selected computational model.

In AGILE, planes landing and taking off from airports and transporting other mobile objects, namely passengers, were considered as an example of mobile objects. In a simplified scenario, departing passengers check in and board the plane, during the flight they might consume a meal, and after the plane has arrived at the destination airport, they deplane and claim their luggage. The complete dynamic behavior of the objects of classes Passenger, Airport and Plane was modeled in UMC in the form of statechart diagrams and subsequently a number of logical properties were verified [2].

The experimentation with UMC has continued also in the context of the SENSORIA project, where it was used to model and verify an asynchronous version of the SOAP communication protocol. In the same project, UMC has been used for the modeling of an automotive scenario, for the support of the SRML modeling language, and for the conflict detection of policies in a scenario from SENSORIA's Finance case study [15,1,20,8].

More recently, UMC was successfully applied, in the context of the regional project PAR-FAS-2007-2013 TRACE-IT (Train Control Enhancement via Information Technology), to the development of a model-checking-based design methodology for deadlock-free train scheduling [52,51].

5 CMC: Parametrized Logic Formulas for Expressing Data Correlations Among Actions

A third application of our on-the-fly model-checking approach has been to the process algebra COWS [44,56], developed in the context of the SENSORIA project. This project developed a novel comprehensive approach to the engineering of software systems for SOC. Foundational theories, techniques and methods were fully integrated in a pragmatic software engineering approach that focused on global services that are context-adaptive, personalizable, and which may require hard and soft constraints on resources and performance. Moreover, the fact that services have to be deployed on different, possibly interoperating global computers to provide novel and reusable service-oriented overlay computers was taken into account.

The Calculus for Orchestration of Web Services (COWS) is a modeling notation for all relevant phases of the life cycle of service-oriented applications, among which service publication, discovery, and orchestration, as well as Service-Level Agreement (SLA) negotiation. Besides service interactions and compositions, important aspects like fault and compensation handling can be modeled in COWS. Extensions moreover allow timed activities, constraints and stochastic reasoning. Application to the SENSORIA case studies [8] has demonstrated the feasibility of modeling service-oriented applications with the specific mechanisms and primitives of COWS [35].

Experimentation in this direction led to the development of the CMC model checker for COWS terms and the definition of the SocL logic [24,35]. It is too complex to explain in detail all the features and characteristics of the COWS specification language. Here we only mention that COWS is a process-algebraic language that allows recursive processes which can also be parallel process (unlike FMC, which does not not allow parallelism inside recursion). Process synchronization and communication occurs through input/output actions which have the form $p.o! < args >$ and $p.o? < params >$ where p denotes a communication partner and o an operation request. Recursion is achieved through a 'bang' operator ($*P$) meaning $P|P|P|\cdots$. The language supports also the definition of protected contexts ($\{P\}$), delimited contexts ($[k]\,P$) and kill operations ($kill(k)$).

This kind of systems require a logic that allows to express the *correlation* between dynamically generated values appearing inside actions at different times. The reason for this is that such correlation values then allow, *e.g.*, to relate the responses of a service to their specific request, or to handle the concept of a session involving a long sequence of interactions among the interacting partners. A typical example property that one would like to express in this context is that whenever a process performs a *request* operation to a partner p, providing some identification data *id*, in all cases the partner will reply with a *response* operation with the same identification data. In CMC that property can be expressed by the parametric formula:

$$AG\ [request(p, \$id)]\ AF\ response(p, \%id)\ true$$

CMC has been successfully used to model and analyze service-oriented scenarios from the SENSORIA project's Automotive and Finance case studies and to its Bowling Robot case study [19,15,20,14,21,8,35].

6 VMC: Behavioral Variability Analysis for Product Families

The final and most recent extension of the modeling and verification framework that we will describe in this paper is a tool, called the Variability Model Checker (VMC [25,16,23]), which was specifically developed for the specification and verification of so-called *product families* or *product lines*.

Software Product Line Engineering (SPLE) [30,55] is by now an established field of software-intensive system development which propagates the systematic reuse of assets or features in an attempt to lower production costs and time-to-market and to increase overall efficiency. SPLE thus aims to develop, in a cost effective way, a variety of software-intensive products that share an overall reference model, *i.e.* that together form a product family. Usually, *commonality* and *variability* are defined in terms of so-called *features*, and managing variability is about identifying variation points in a common family design and deciding which combinations of features are to be considered valid products. There is by now a large body of literature on the computer-aided analysis of feature models to extract valid products and to detect anomalies, *i.e.* undesirable properties such as superfluous or—worse—contradictory variability information (*e.g.* so-called false optional or dead features) [26].

Until a few years ago, these analyses however did not take any behavior into account, even though software products are often large and complex, and many are used in safety-critical applications in the avionics, railways, or automotive industries. The importance of specifying and verifying also *behavioral variability* was first recognized in the context of UML [43,58]. Shortly after, in [37], Modal Transition Systems (MTSs) were recognized as a promising formal method for describing in a compact way the possible operational behavior of the products in a product family. An MTS [3] is a Labeled Transition System (LTS) distinguishing between 'admissible' *may* and 'necessary' *must* transitions. By definition, every must transition is also a may transition.

In recent years, many variants and extensions of MTSs have been studied in order to elaborate a suitable formal modeling structure to describe (behavioral) variability [34,45,46,4,5,6]. This has resulted in a growing interest in modeling behavioral variability in general, which has led to the application of a number of formal methods different from MTSs but still with a transition system semantics [42,54,41,47,53,22,29,10,11,12,48,28]. As a consequence, behavioral analysis techniques like model checking have become available for the verification of (temporal) logic properties of product families.

VMC accepts the specification of an MTS in process-algebraic terms, together with an optional set of additional variability constraints. VMC then allows to perform the following two kinds of behavioral variability analyses on a given family of products:

1. A logic property expressed in a *variability-aware* version of ACTL (v-ACTL) can directly be verified against the MTS modeling the product family behavior, relying on the fact that under certain syntactic conditions the validity of the property over the MTS guarantees the validity of the same property for all products of the family.
2. The actual set of valid product behavior can explicitly be *generated* and the resulting LTSs can be verified against the same logic property (expressed in ACTL). This is surely less efficient than direct MTS verification but allows to precisely identify the set of features whose interactions may cause the original property to fail over the whole family.

The process algebra used by VMC to specify the MTS modeling of the behavior of a product family is derived from the one of FMC by removing CCS-like synchronizations and adding to the actions the notion of variability. In fact, in VMC, communication/synchronization actions can accept an additional parameter (*may*) which expresses the property that the action is not necessarily present in all derivable products of the family. The synchronization semantics is also updated by taking this parameter into consideration, in the sense that the result of the synchronization of an optional action with a mandatory action results in an optional action [3].

In more detail, the structure of the process algebra accepted by VMC is described by the following abstract syntax:

System ::= [*Net*]
Net ::= T(*expr*) | *Net* / *Labels* / *Net*

where [*Net*] denotes again a closed system, T(*expr*) is a process instantiation from the set of process declarations of the form T(*variable*) $\stackrel{\text{def}}{=}$ *Term*, and *Labels* is a list of action names.

The structure of *Term* definitions is described by the following abstract syntax:

$$Term ::= nil \mid T(expr) \mid Action.Term \mid Term + Term \mid [\,expr \bowtie expr\,]\,Term$$
$$Action ::= a(arg) \mid a(may, arg)$$
$$arg ::= expr \mid ?variable$$
$$expr ::= variable \mid integer \mid expr \pm expr$$

where $\bowtie$ is a comparison operator and $\pm$ is an arithmetic operation.

In VMC, the abstract model associated to this variability-oriented process algebra is an LTS in which edges are labeled with sets of labels, and where the additional *may* label is added to the optional edges to specify their possible absence in some of the family's products.

The logic v-ACTL is built over a subset of ACTL, but enriched with the *deontic* operators $AF\#$, $EF\#$, $\langle\rangle\#$, and $[]\#$ (*cf.* [18,23] for details). These operators are actually implemented in VMC by a translation into plain ACTL. For example, the formula $\langle a\rangle\#$ *true*, which means that there exists a mandatory evolution from the current state which satisfies action a, can be encoded in plain ACTL as $\langle a$ *and not may*$\rangle$ *true*. Similarly, $EF\#$ ϕ can be encoded in plain ACTL as $E\,[\,true\,\{not\,may\}\,U\,\phi\,]$ (where ϕ is a subformula).

We are currently experimenting with VMC in the context of the European FP7-ICT-600708 project QUANTICOL [9] (*cf.* http://www.quanticol.eu). So far the case studies taken into consideration (a bike-sharing system and a coffee machine [13,18]) are relatively small and more effort is needed to evaluate the approach on problems of a more realistic size.

7   The Overall Structure of the Model Checkers

In the previous sections, we have seen four different specification languages for the four model checkers that are part of KandISTI. While their computational models are rather different, ranging from statecharts to various kind of process algebras, the evolution of the framework over time has led to the development of a *unique* common temporal logic and verification engine, which encompasses and integrates the various specific logics initially associated to the specific tools: ACTL for FMC, UCTL for UMC, SocL for CMC and v-ACTL for VMC.

This had become feasible by splitting the statespace generation problem (which depends on the underlying computational model), from the L^2TS analysis problem, and by the introduction of an explicit abstraction mechanism which allows to specify which details of the model should be observable as labels on the states and transitions of the L^2TS.

Another essential characteristic of our family of tools, which has been preserved since its origins, is the so-called *on-the-fly* structure of the model-checking algorithm: the L^2TS corresponding to the model is generated *on-demand*, following the incremental needs of the logical verification engine. Given a state of an L^2TS, the validity of a logic formula on that state is evaluated by analyzing the transitions allowed in that state, and by analyzing the validity of the necessary subformulae possibly in some of the necessary next reachable states, all this recursively.

Indeed, each tool consists of two separate, but interacting, components: a tool-specific L^2TS generator engine and a common logical verification engine. The L^2TS generator engine is again structured in two logical components: a ground evolutions generator, strictly based on the operational semantics of the language, and an abstraction mechanism which allows to associate abstract observable events to system evolutions and abstract atomic propositions to the system states. The verification engine is the component which actually tries to evaluate a logic formula following the on-the-fly approach, and is described in more detail in [14,35].

The L^2TS generator engine maintains an archive of already generated system states in order to avoid unnecesary duplications in the computation of the possibile evolutions of states. The logical verification engine maintains an archive of logical computation fragments; this is not only useful to avoid unnecessary duplications in the evaluation of subformulae, but also necessary to deal with the recursion in the evaluation of a formula arising from the presence of loops in the models. The overall structure of the framework is shown in Fig. 3.

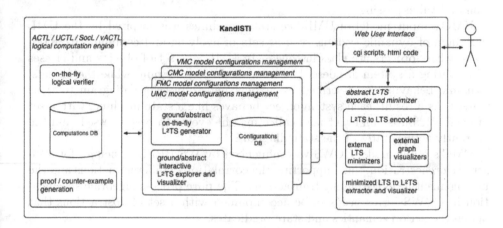

Fig. 3. The architecture of the KandISTI framework

All the model checkers of our family are constituted by a command-line version of the tool written in Ada, which can be easily compiled for the Windows, Linux, Solaris and Mac OS X platforms. These core executables are wrapped with CGI scripts handled by a web server, facilitating an html-oriented GUI and integration with graph drawing tools. It is beyond the scope of this paper to give detailed descriptions of the model-checking algorithms and architecture that underly our family of model checkers. Instead, we refer the interested reader to [24,40,14,35] for more details.

8 Discussion and Conclusions

In this paper, we have provided an overview of the KandISTI family of model-checking tools, currently consisting of FMC, UMC, CMC and VMC. We have briefly presented their different kind of underlying computational models and their different contributions to the development of a general purpose action- and state-based branching-time temporal modal logic (with special purpose dialects for each of the KandISTI variants).

The differences between the described input models stem from the specific field of application for which they were developed. In the end, however, each of them is interpreted over an L²TS, which permits to use the same logical verification engine for all, even though the specific logic associated to each of the input models again has certain features that are specifically tailored towards the application field for which they were developed.

FMC's input model of automata networks was defined as an attempt to integrate the communication and synchronization mechanisms from CCS, CSP and LOTOS in a single process-algebra, thus allowing both multi-way synchronization and value-passing.

UMC's input model of UML-like state machines was inspired by the UML paradigm of dynamic systems seen as sets of evolving and communicating objects, where objects are class instances. In UML, the set of objects and classes constituting a system are described by a structure diagram, while the objects' dynamic behaviour is described by associating a statechart diagram to their classes. As a result, each system object behaves like a state machine, with a set of local attributes, an event pool collecting the events to be processed, and the currently active states of the state diagram.

CMC's input model COWS was influenced by WS-BPEL principles for Web service orchestration, thus supporting the correlation of different actions and the management of long-running transactions. The pure process-algebraic specification in COWS terms needs to be accompanied with a set of abstractions that define the action semantics and state predicates.

VMC's input model of process-algebraic interpretations of MTSs, possibly enriched with variability constraints known from SPLE, was developed to study the feasibility of using MTSs to describe (and consequently analyze) in a compact way the possible operational behaviour of products from a product family.

The KandISTI model checkers are continuously being improved. This ranges from more efficient generation of the computational models to a more user-friendly web interface. An overall goal for the future is to experiment with industrial case studies of increasing size. In order to fulfill this aim, richer input models are needed, in particular allowing more advanced data types (e.g. tuples, sets, lists, etc., currently only supported by UMC), thus requiring more complex computational models. The addition of some kind of global data space shared among the concurrent objects/agents might moreover be a useful extension to more easily support also the underlying models of other verification frameworks, like Spin or SMV.

Future work that is specifically related to VMC concerns studying the specific fragment of v-ACTL that is guaranteed to be preserved by product refinement. This would allow built-in user notification in all cases in which a model-checking result is guaranteed to be preserved from family to product level.

As already hinted at in Section 4, the main lesson learned by the use of our framework is the usefulness of an easy-to-use formal framework for the early analysis of initial system designs, i.e. the usefulness of formal methods in the earliest stages of system design, when the first architectural/algorithmic ideas are being prototyped and debugged. This is a very different application of formal methods with respect to their classical use in the final validation/verification steps, when the system is already supposed to be (hopefully) free of errors. In the former case, it is important to be able to rely on formal frameworks which simplify and make the task of modeling and debugging a system (which with a high probability is expected to contain errors) easy, while in the latter case the emphasis can be put on the power to deal with extremely large state spaces in a very efficient way.

We believe that KandISTI can successfully match the needs of agile formal designers (which constitute its natural set of target users) while still not disregarding the issues introduced by the problems of the possible state space explosions.

Acknowledgements. Major progress on KandISTI was made during almost a decade of EU projects under the inspiring coordination of Martin Wirsing. We would like to take this opportunity to thank him for the work we did together.

The three paintings by Wassily Kandinsky that are part of the collection of the Städtische Galerie im Lenbachhaus in Munich, Germany, and whose images are used here for non-commercial strictly illustrative purposes, have entered the public domain in the EU on January 1st, 2015 (70 years *post mortem auctoris*, imposed by Article 1 of EU Directive 93/98/EEC as repealed and replaced by EU Directive 2006/116/EC).

References

1. Abreu, J., Mazzanti, F., Fiadeiro, J.L., Gnesi, S.: A Model-Checking Approach for Service Component Architectures. In: Lee, D., Lopes, A., Poetzsch-Heffter, A. (eds.) FMOODS 2009. LNCS, vol. 5522, pp. 219–224. Springer, Heidelberg (2009)
2. Andrade, L., et al.: AGILE: Software Architecture for Mobility. In: Wirsing, M., Pattinson, D., Hennicker, R. (eds.) WADT 2003. LNCS, vol. 2755, pp. 1–33. Springer, Heidelberg (2003)
3. Antonik, A., Huth, M., Larsen, K.G., Nyman, U., Wąsowski, A.: 20 Years of Modal and Mixed Specifications. Bulletin of the EATCS 95, 94–129 (2008)
4. Asirelli, P., ter Beek, M.H., Fantechi, A., Gnesi, S.: A Model-Checking Tool for Families of Services. In: Bruni, R., Dingel, J. (eds.) FORTE 2011 and FMOODS 2011. LNCS, vol. 6722, pp. 44–58. Springer, Heidelberg (2011)
5. Asirelli, P., ter Beek, M.H., Fantechi, A., Gnesi, S.: Formal Description of Variability in Product Families. In: SPLC, pp. 130–139. IEEE (2011)

6. Asirelli, P., ter Beek, M.H., Fantechi, A., Gnesi, S.: A Compositional Framework to Derive Product Line Behavioural Descriptions. In: [49], pp. 146–161
7. Baier, C., Katoen, J.-P.: Principles of Model Checking. MIT Press (2008)
8. ter Beek, M.H.: Sensoria Results Applied to the Case Studies. In: [57], pp. 655–677
9. ter Beek, M.H., Bortolussi, L., Ciancia, V., Gnesi, S., Hillston, J., Latella, D., Massink, M.: A Quantitative Approach to the Design and Analysis of Collective Adaptive Systems for Smart Cities. ERCIM News: Smart Cities 98, 32 (2014)
10. ter Beek, M.H., de Vink, E.P.: Software Product Line Analysis with mCRL2. In: [38], pp. 78–85
11. ter Beek, M.H., de Vink, E.P.: Towards Modular Verification of Software Product Lines with mCRL2. In: [50], pp. 368–385
12. ter Beek, M.H., de Vink, E.P.: Using mCRL2 for the analysis of software product lines. In: FormaliSE, pp. 31–37. IEEE (2014)
13. ter Beek, M.H., Fantechi, A., Gnesi, S.: Challenges in Modelling and Analyzing Quantitative Aspects of Bike-Sharing Systems. In: [50], pp. 351–367
14. ter Beek, M.H., Fantechi, A., Gnesi, S., Mazzanti, F.: A state/event-based model-checking approach for the analysis of abstract system properties. Science of Computer Programming 76(2), 119–135 (2011)
15. ter Beek, M.H., Gnesi, S., Koch, N., Mazzanti, F.: Formal verification of an automotive scenario in service-oriented computing. In: ICSE, pp. 613–622. ACM (2008)
16. ter Beek, M.H., Gnesi, S., Mazzanti, F.: VMC: A Tool for the Analysis of Variability in Software Product Lines. ERCIM News: Mobile Computing 93, 50–51 (2013)
17. ter Beek, M.H., Gnesi, S., Mazzanti, F.: KandISTI: A Family of Model Checkers for the Analysis of Software Designs. ERCIM News: Software Quality 99, 31–32 (2014)
18. ter Beek, M.H., Gnesi, S., Mazzanti, F.: Model Checking Value-Passing Modal Specifications. In: PSI. LNCS, Springer (to appear, 2014)
19. ter Beek, M.H., Gnesi, S., Mazzanti, F., Moiso, C.: Formal Modelling and Verification of an Asynchronous Extension of SOAP. In: ECOWS, pp. 287–296. IEEE (2006)
20. ter Beek, M.H., Gnesi, S., Montangero, C., Semini, L.: Detecting policy conflicts by model checking UML state machines. In: ICFI, pp. 59–74. IOS Press (2009)
21. ter Beek, M.H., Lapadula, A., Loreti, M., Palasciano, C.: Analysing Robot Movement Using the Sensoria Methods. In: [57], pp. 678–697
22. ter Beek, M.H., Lluch-Lafuente, A., Petrocchi, M.: Combining declarative and procedural views in the specification and analysis of product families. In: SPLC, vol. 2, pp. 10–17. ACM (2013)
23. ter Beek, M.H., Mazzanti, F.: VMC: Recent Advances and Challenges Ahead. In: [38], pp. 70–77
24. ter Beek, M.H., Mazzanti, F., Gnesi, S.: CMC–UMC: a framework for the verification of abstract service-oriented properties. In: SAC, pp. 2111–2117. ACM (2009)
25. ter Beek, M.H., Mazzanti, F., Sulova, A.: VMC: A Tool for Product Variability Analysis. In: Giannakopoulou, D., Méry, D. (eds.) FM 2012. LNCS, vol. 7436, pp. 450–454. Springer, Heidelberg (2012)
26. Benavides, D., Segura, S., Ruiz-Cortés, A.: Automated Analysis of Feature Models 20 Years Later: a Literature Review. Information Systems 35(6) (2010)
27. Clarke, E.M., Grumberg, O., Peled, D.A.: Model Checking. MIT Press (1999)
28. Classen, A., Cordy, M., Heymans, P., Legay, A., Schobbens, P.-Y.: Formal semantics, modular specification, and symbolic verification of product-line behaviour. Science of Computer Programming 80(B), 416–439 (2014)

29. Classen, A., Cordy, M., Schobbens, P.-Y., Heymans, P., Legay, A., Raskin, J.-F.: Featured Transition Systems: Foundations for Verifying Variability-Intensive Systems and Their Application to LTL Model Checking. IEEE Transactions on Software Engineering 39(8), 1069–1089 (2013)
30. Clements, P.C., Northrop, L.M.: Software Product Lines: Practices and Patterns. Addison-Wesley (2002)
31. De Nicola, R. (ed.): ESOP 2007. LNCS, vol. 4421. Springer, Heidelberg (2007)
32. De Nicola, R., Vaandrager, F.W.: Action versus State based Logics for Transition Systems. In: Guessarian, I. (ed.) LITP 1990. LNCS, vol. 469, pp. 407–419. Springer, Heidelberg (1990)
33. De Nicola, R., Vaandrager, F.W.: Three logics for branching bisimulation. Journal of the ACM 42(2), 458–487 (1995)
34. Fantechi, A., Gnesi, S.: A behavioural model for product families. In: ESEC/FSE, pp. 521–524. ACM (2007)
35. Fantechi, A., Gnesi, S., Lapadula, A., Mazzanti, F., Pugliese, R., Tiezzi, F.: A logical verification methodology for service-oriented computing. ACM Transactions on Software Engineering and Methodology 21(3), 16 (2012)
36. Fidge, C.: A Comparative Introduction to CSP, CCS and LOTOS. Technical Report 93-24, Software Verification Research Centre, University of Queensland (January 1994)
37. Fischbein, D., Uchitel, S., Braberman, V.A.: A foundation for behavioural conformance in software product line architectures. In: ROSATEA, pp. 39–48. ACM (2006)
38. Gnesi, S., Fantechi, A., ter Beek, M.H., Botterweck, G., Becker, M.: Proceedings of the 18th International Software Product Line Conference (SPLC 2014), vol. 2. ACM (2014)
39. Gnesi, S., Mazzanti, F.: On the Fly Verification of Networks of Automata. In: PDPTA, pp. 1040–1046. CSREA Press (1999)
40. Gnesi, S., Mazzanti, F.: An Abstract, on the Fly Framework for the Verification of Service-Oriented Systems. In: [57], pp. 390–407
41. Gnesi, S., Petrocchi, M.: Towards an executable algebra for product lines. In: SPLC, vol. 2, pp. 66–73. ACM (2012)
42. Gruler, A., Leucker, M., Scheidemann, K.: Modeling and Model Checking Software Product Lines. In: Barthe, G., de Boer, F.S. (eds.) FMOODS 2008. LNCS, vol. 5051, pp. 113–131. Springer, Heidelberg (2008)
43. Haugen, Ø., Stølen, K.: STAIRS – Steps To Analyze Interactions with Refinement Semantics. In: Stevens, P., Whittle, J., Booch, G. (eds.) UML 2003. LNCS, vol. 2863, pp. 388–402. Springer, Heidelberg (2003)
44. Lapadula, A., Pugliese, R., Tiezzi, F.: A Calculus for Orchestration of Web Services. In: [31], pp. 33–47
45. Larsen, K.G., Nyman, U., Wąsowski, A.: Modal I/O Automata for Interface and Product Line Theories. In: [31], pp. 64–79
46. Lauenroth, K., Pohl, K., Töhning, S.: Model Checking of Domain Artifacts in Product Line Engineering. In: ASE, pp. 269–280. IEEE (2009)
47. Leucker, M., Thoma, D.: A Formal Approach to Software Product Families. In: [49], pp. 131–145
48. Lochau, M., Mennicke, S., Baller, H., Ribbeck, L.: DeltaCCS: A Core Calculus for Behavioral Change. In: [50], pp. 320–335
49. Margaria, T., Steffen, B. (eds.): ISoLA 2012, Part I. LNCS, vol. 7609. Springer, Heidelberg (2012)

50. Margaria, T., Steffen, B. (eds.): ISoLA 2014, Part I. LNCS, vol. 8802. Springer, Heidelberg (2014)
51. Mazzanti, F., Spagnolo, G.O., Della Longa, S., Ferrari, A.: Deadlock Avoidance in Train Scheduling: A Model Checking Approach. In: Lang, F., Flammini, F. (eds.) FMICS 2014. LNCS, vol. 8718, pp. 109–123. Springer, Heidelberg (2014)
52. Mazzanti, F., Spagnolo, G.O., Ferrari, A.: Designing a Deadlock-Free Train Scheduler: A Model Checking Approach. In: Badger, J.M., Rozier, K.Y. (eds.) NFM 2014. LNCS, vol. 8430, pp. 264–269. Springer, Heidelberg (2014)
53. Millo, J.-V., Ramesh, S., Krishna, S.N., Narwane, G.K.: Compositional Verification of Software Product Lines. In: Johnsen, E.B., Petre, L. (eds.) IFM 2013. LNCS, vol. 7940, pp. 109–123. Springer, Heidelberg (2013)
54. Muschevici, R., Proença, J., Clarke, D.: Modular Modelling of Software Product Lines with Feature Nets. In: Barthe, G., Pardo, A., Schneider, G. (eds.) SEFM 2011. LNCS, vol. 7041, pp. 318–333. Springer, Heidelberg (2011)
55. Pohl, K., Böckle, G., van der Linden, F.J.: Software Product Line Engineering: Foundations, Principles, and Techniques. Springer (2005)
56. Pugliese, R., Tiezzi, F.: A Calculus for Orchestration of Web Services. Journal of Applied Logic 10(1), 2–31 (2012)
57. Wirsing, M., Hölzl, M. (eds.): SENSORIA. LNCS, vol. 6582. Springer, Heidelberg (2011)
58. Ziadi, T., Jézéquel, J.-M.: Software Product Line Engineering with the UML: Deriving Products. In: Software Product Lines: Research Issues in Engineering and Management, pp. 557–588. Springer (2006)

Pragmatic Formal Specification
of System Properties by Tables

Dedicated to Martin Wirsing on the Occasion of his Emeritation

Manfred Broy

Institut für Informatik, Technische Universität München
80290 München Germany
broy@in.tum.de
http://wwwbroy.informatik.tu-muenchen.de

A picture is worth a 1000 words

Folklore

It takes a long time to understand a 1000 words

Engineering experience

A formula may make a 1000 words superfluous

Abstract. We suggest tables as pragmatic tractable specification formalism for a precise as well as readable specification of systems, their interfaces, as well as their functional properties. Translating tables into logical formulae defines a precise semantics for them. Writing logical formulae in a structured way by tables makes them better usable for engineering purposes. Tables are considered better structured, easier to read, to comprehend, to analyze, or at least easier to communicate than large logical formulae. On the other hand logical formulae are better suited to derive properties by deduction steps applying logical calculi. By translating tables into formulae of predicate logic and vice versa, we provide a bridge between the conciseness of readable suggestive specifications and the preciseness of mathematical methods in software and systems engineering.

Keywords: Dynamic Systems, Mobility, Instantiation.

1   Introduction

Studies in the development of embedded software systems[1] show that requirements capture and system specification is one of the most decisive and critical tasks in system development. There are at least three sources of difficulties in the task of requirements engineering:

---

[1] Embedded software systems are dedicated computing and control systems that are embedded into a technical environment.

R. De Nicola and R. Hennicker (Eds.): Wirsing Festschrift, LNCS 8950, pp. 329–354, 2015.

- Requirements are not completely and not accurately identified and understood by the domain experts and system engineers and/or not properly communicated to the requirements engineers.
- Requirements are not correctly documented, even when completely and accurately identified and understood.
- Requirements are documented, using informal techniques, but not properly interpreted and conceived by the system designers and programmers due to lack of preciseness.

All three problems lead to serious errors and costly changes in the software development process. As it is well known, misinterpretations and bugs in the requirements tend to be very expensive, especially if they are captured only very late in the development so that crucial redevelopment is needed.

Of course, errors cannot be fully avoided when developing complex information processing systems. However, well worked out specification methods with adequate methods and techniques for analyzing requirements can help to avoid some pitfalls. By guaranteeing the quality and correctness of the specified requirements we obtain a better control over the development process and the functional quality of the produced documents.

There are a number of quality attributes for a tractable result of requirements engineering and documentation. These are, among others:
- validity,
- consistency,
- preciseness,
- completeness,
- conciseness,
- understandability,
- expressiveness,
- generality,
- changeability,
- tractability with respect to the development method and process.
- traceability within requirements artifacts and between requirement artifacts and for the development artifacts,
- modularity.

Obviously, several of these properties are in mutual conflicts. Therefore we have to find acceptable compromises when designing or choosing specification methods to be used in requirements engineering.

In this paper we concentrate mainly on the issues of consistency, understandability, readability, conciseness, and preciseness. The other goals might be taken care of by the development methods and the mathematical system models on which our description techniques are based.

It is well recognized that one of the most significant effects of applying formal techniques to software development consists in their potential to improve the quality and precision of specifications. A further goal is rigorous verification and the potential for tool support. Complex systems specifications tend to get fairly large and therefore have to be well structured and modular. They have to be abstract, leaving out all unnecessary detail, concentrating on the interface description - also called the *functional behavior* of systems – not taking into account implementation details or low level considerations. They have to be precise in the sense that they specify system properties unambiguously.

The main purposes and advantages of using advanced modeling and specification techniques in the system development process are fivefold:

- *Requirements engineering:* specification techniques help the requirements engineer in the process of clarifying and documenting the required system properties.
- *Communication medium:* specifications are a basis for the communication between domain experts, requirements engineers, system designers and implementers.
- *Implementation:* abstract descriptions of particular design and implementation ideas provide guidelines in system realization.
- *Documentation:* specifications document the system properties for the use and reuse of a system and its components.
- *Verification*: precisely specified requirements are the basis for verification of correctness.

Adequate specification techniques provide helpful mental models (semantic models) of systems, notations (syntactic formalism) for the concrete representation of specifications, and methods to reason about and to refine specifications (deduction and verification theory).

One of the striking arguments against mathematical and logical formalisms for the specification of software requirements are difficulties with their scalability and comprehensibility due to their technical complexity and sophistication. However, these arguments are often based on unjustified common sense and lack proper support by experimental data. On the contrary, experiments have shown that graphical formalisms are not necessarily easier to understand than textual or mathematical ones (see [14]). It is telling to observe that the problems that readers have with large diagrams are similar to those they have with large logical formulae. If diagrams get very large, they no longer provide helpful graphical patterns for intuitive understanding but rather provide a large amount of information in a fairly unstructured way. It is not clear for a reader which parts of a diagram to begin with when studying or producing a diagram and in which order to work through it systematically.

This indicates that graphical documentation techniques do not help, per se, to make specifications more readable and understandable, but need a careful choice of their content and the design of their layout. Large formulae as well as large diagrams are difficult to deal with. If the information contained in the formulae and diagrams exhibits a particular structure it might be more appropriate to gather such information outside the formulae or the diagrams and to present it in tables. Tables can be well combined with diagrams. They help to avoid an overloading of the diagrams by formulae and text. Moreover, tables support a very regular structure to present a large amount of information, in particular, when – as typical for systems – a number of case distinctions are to be considered. Then information look up is more efficient since one knows where to look for it. Moreover, the systematics of tables makes it easier to check, whether certain cases have been overlooked (completeness).

Tables are a well-known and well-accepted concept in many disciplines including mathematics and engineering. They are and have been used for a long time to provide well-structured descriptions of large amounts of information. For instance, engineers often use tables and diagrams for specifying behavior and properties of mechanical or electrical devices.

Of course, specifications are mainly thought to be helpful for documentation and communication. Therefore comprehensibility, readability, and understandability are first class goals of specification methods. Formal specifications are often considered to be hard to understand and difficult to deal with. This applies, in particular, as long as engineers are not trained and not familiar with the underlying formalisms such as predicate logic.

Formulae of predicate logic can get rather big when complex large systems are to be described. Therefore the appropriate structuring of such formulae is crucial for their practical use. However, even with a perfect structuring and a well designed layout, logical formulae may be hard to read and to comprehend, especially when dealing with long lists of case distinctions. In such situations, tables are especially helpful. We concentrate in the following, in particular, on tables for specifying interface behavior of systems. For this purpose, we introduce tables as a systematic, more readable representation of large logical formulae that provide some regular structure.

Diagrams complement tables in helping to illustrate behaviors, but often do not describe behavior precisely enough. Nevertheless, diagrams are successfully used in many fields to software engineering. However, preciseness and understandability need not be contradictory. Our goal is to address both of them. Therefore we also show how tables can be represented by diagrams and be used in connection with diagrams.

Tables and table-directed notations have been advocated many times in computing science. Prominent examples are decision tables as suggested in the 70's. Less successful were perhaps Nassi-Schneidermann style tables, an attempt to organize program text in a table-oriented style. Significant work on tables has been done by the group of David Parnas, beginning with the remarkable work on the A-7E aircraft (see [8], [9]). This work has been continued in several directions exploring many ways of working with tables in software development. What we present in the following does not actually go beyond that work. Our goal is to provide ideas for the use of tables for particular formal techniques including algebraic specifications and stream-based models for the interface behavior of systems.

The main goal of this paper is to provide simple table and diagram techniques for better structuring and readability of mathematical specification techniques. These techniques are especially helpful when used to support axiomatic specifications. Our concrete goal is the support of the algebraic specification language SPECTRUM and of the functional system specification and development technique FOCUS, for which a rich mathematical theory and powerful methods for specification, refinement, and verification are available (see [5] and [15]). Techniques to support logical formalisms by tables carry over, of course, to most of the other formal methods that work with logical formulae.

We do not advocate to use only tables or diagrams in specifications. We rather suggest to use a fine mixture of textual explanations, mathematical formulae, tables, and diagrams in well-chosen combinations side by side. We regard formulae as syntactic entities that can be represented by the tables and diagrams if they have a regular structure.

The paper is organized as follows: in Section 2 we introduce and recapitulate some basic notions from algebraic specifications that are helpful when writing formulae in multi-sorted predicate logics. Then, we take a brief look at value tables in Section 3. Section 4 introduces some instances of term tables and discusses their semantics. In Section 5 this concept is generalized to tables that carry predicates and entries. Section 6 introduces a general concept for representing formulae by tables. Section 7 discusses quantifiers and abbreviations in tables. Section 8 treats specific tables for the specification of interactive systems. Section 9 contains concluding remarks with a short discussion of the relationship of tables to diagrams.

2   Many Sorted Algebra and Predicate Logic

We are convinced that mathematical logic is a good choice for providing a firm basis for system specification. Whatever we write down in a table in the following can also be expressed by a logical formula. Typically, logical formulae are less structured, less readable and more difficult to understand for untrained persons. However, logic provides all the advantages of formal theories, such as a precise syntax and semantics as well as a logical calculus for formal manipulation, analysis, transformation, and deduction[2]. This also allows us to give precise definitions when different description methods are combined and related to form a comprehensive integrated system description. In this section, we introduce the basic concepts for our logical formulae that are rather general and common.

Since we are convinced that type information[3] is helpful for structuring and easier comprehension of system descriptions, we work with a sorted (typed) higher-order predicate logic as a mathematical basis to formulate specifications. In fact, throughout this paper we mainly use classical first order predicate logic. In particular, we use the following primitives for writing terms and formulae:

- *sorts* from a set S of sorts (including functional sorts),
- *constants* from a set F of function symbols and identifiers for data element,
- *a sort assignment* for the constants by a mapping srt: $F \rightarrow S$,
- a set X of *identifiers* used as logical variables with given sorts.

---

[2] We are aware of work that attempts to apply transformations and deductions directly to table representations and diagrams. However, even in this case it may be useful to relate these manipulations to the manipulation of logical formulas, for instance, to show the correctness of the transformation rules.

[3] We follow the tradition of algebraic specifications and speak of sorts instead of types.

The sorts in S and the function symbols in F with their associated sorts together form what is commonly called a *signature* $\Sigma = (S, F)$. Given a signature, we can form ground terms and formulae of propositional logic. Given identifiers, we can construct terms with free variables and formulae of predicate logic. Assigning carrier sets to sorts as well as elements and functions to the symbols in F, we get algebras of a particular signature and use them to interpret terms. We assume that these concepts are familiar to the reader (see [17] for an extensive introduction).

Whenever we use an identifier in a formula in the following, we fix its sort before. Hence we can always assume that the function srt assigning sorts to constants can be extended to a function

srt: $X \cup F \rightarrow S$

assigning sorts also to variables. We assume that the set of sorts S contains functional sorts as well as polymorphic sorts (like in [15]).

3   Value Tables

Tables have a long tradition in mathematics and engineering. By tables, relations between elements of given sets are represented. Therefore, tables can be used to describe relations and - as a special case - to describe functions. In their simplest form tables contain only ground terms as denotations of values as entries. Such tables are called *value tables*.

In a value table all entries are constants denoting elements. We show two simple examples of value tables in Table 3.1 and Table 3.2, namely Boolean tables defining the connective logical "or" of propositional logic.

Value tables seem to have an obvious meaning. But even for value tables different semantic interpretations might exist, in particular, when specifying relations. Since value tables are a special case of term tables as we treat them in the following section we do not give any semantics or formal translation for value tables, here.

Nota bene, value tables help only when the domain of the functions that are specified is finite and, in particular, rather small. Nevertheless, also for functions on infinite domains value tables can be used. Then, of course, only a finite set of argument/result pairs can be covered. Traditionally, in mathematics value tables have been used to provide the values of arithmetic and trigonometric functions such as logarithm, sine, cosine etc. Today, algorithms on computers have replaced them. Nevertheless, still a lot of value tables are in use in everyday life such as tax tables or timetables, etc.

Table 3.1. Value Table of the Logical Connective "or"

x	y	$x \vee y$
0	0	0
0	1	1
1	0	1
1	1	1

Table 3.2. Value Table of the Logical Connective "or" in Matrix Form

$x \vee y$	0	1
0	0	1
1	1	1

4   Term Tables

An obvious step to generalize value tables are term tables. In term tables, we permit terms with free variables as entries, in addition to ground terms and constants denoting values. A nice example of a term table is the table specifying conditional expression. The conditional expression can of course be represented by a value table (provided the domain of values is finite), in a case distinction, or by logical formulae. However, a term table as given in Table 4.1 is perhaps even more suggestive.

Table 4.1. Term Table for the Conditional **if_then_else_fi**

b	**if b then** x **else** y **fi**
1	x
0	y
$\perp$	$\perp$

Simple value tables for functions have a more or less obvious semantics. This also holds for simple term tables as given in Table 4.1. For more sophisticated term tables this no longer holds. Often, sophisticated term tables do not have an obvious interpretation, since several possible interpretations may exist. Therefore we suggest a translation of term tables into logical formulae.

Both value tables and term tables can be understood as representations of possibly large logical formulae in a canonical disjunctive normal form.

Table 4.2. A Scheme for a Term Table with m Rows and n Columns

x_1	...	x_n
...		...
t_1^i		t_n^i
...		...

Let x_1, ..., x_n be variables and t_1^i, ..., t_n^i be terms such that the sorts of the terms t_j^i and the identifiers x_j coincide. Table 4.2 represents a large formula of predicate logic. We associate with it the formal meaning as given by the following logical formula:

$$\bigvee_{i=1}^{m} \bigwedge_{j=1}^{n} x_j = t_j^i$$

Given this logical interpretation we speak of a *disjunctive table*.

Consider the example of the if-then-else-table as given in Table 4.1. Its interpretation as a disjunctive table yields the following logical formula

(b = 1   ∧ **if** b **then** x **else** y **fi** = x)

∨   (b = 0   ∧ **if** b **then** x **else** y **fi** = y)

∨   (b = ⊥   ∧ **if** b **then** x **else** y **fi** = ⊥)

This example shows already that tables can be more concise (shorter and clearer structured) than logical formulae if in the formulae certain large terms have to be repeated several times.

Disjunctive tables allow us to write only formulae with a simple logical structure as tables. More common than formulae in disjunctive form are logical implications as used in conditional equations for writing algebraic specifications. Implicative tables can capture such conditional equations. Let us consider a simple example.

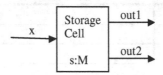

Fig. 4.1. Component with Input Channel x, Output Channels out1 and out2, and State s

Example: Specification of a storage cell

We give a specification of an interactive storage cell that stores a data message from a set of messages M = Data ∪ {®} and returns it upon request. A request is indicated by the signal ®. The syntactic interface is illustrated by a data flow node in Fig. 4.1 showing the communication channels. The state transition table given in Table 4.3 (let d, e ∈ Data) specifies the interface behavior.

Table 4.3 describes a state automaton. By i ∈ M we denote the input message on channel x, by s ∈ Data the current state of the automaton. The input i stimulates a state transition and some output. By state(s, i) we describe the successor state, by $out_1(s, i)$ the output message on the first output channel, by $out_2(s, i)$ the output message on the second output channel.

Table 4.3. Implicative Table of a State Transition System with Input i on Channel x and State s (for all elements d, e ∈ Data)

i	s	state(s, i)	$out_1(s, i)$	$out_2(s, i)$
e	d	e	®	d
®	d	d	d	®

The functions out_1 and out_2 are output functions for the cell in state s obtaining input i. The function state yields the new state after the input i has been received in state s. The vertical double line separates the input for state transitions from output. ❑

As explained, the interpretation of a table by a disjunctive formula is rather inflexible, since disjunctive tables require that all cases are covered. This is sometimes too rigid. A more flexible concept of a table is obtained by an implicative table with the general form as given in Table 4.4. Implicative tables are useful to describe weaker properties.

Table 4.4. Schematic Form of an Implicative Table

x_1	...	x_c	x_{c+1}	...	x_n
...		...	...		...
t_1^i	...	t_c^i	t_{c+1}^i	...	t_n^i
...		...	...		...

Table 4.4 has two blocks of columns separated by a vertical double line separating premises from conclusions. The first block denotes premises, the second one conclusions. The table has the semantic interpretation given by the following logical formula (again x_1, ..., x_n are identifiers (or terms) and t_1^i, ..., t_n^i are terms and the respective sorts are consistent, m denotes the number of rows):

$$\bigwedge_{i=1}^{m}\left(\left(\bigwedge_{j=1}^{c}x_j=t_j^i\right)\Rightarrow\left(\bigwedge_{j=c+1}^{n}x_j=t_j^i\right)\right)$$

If a table provides a complete and disjunctive case distinction, the implicative and the disjunctive interpretations of the table are logically equivalent (for a proof see appendix). Note that the implicative interpretation requires that the table is divided into two blocks, conditions and conclusions, that are - according to our convention - separated by the vertical double line.

According to the translation scheme for implicative tables given above for our example represented in Table 4.3 we obtain the following formulae as indicated by the vertical double line between the second and the third column (let e, d ∈ Data):

$$i = e \wedge s = d \Rightarrow \text{state}(s, i) = e \wedge \text{out}_1(s, i) = ® \wedge \text{out}_2(s, i) = d$$
$$i = ® \wedge s = d \Rightarrow \text{state}(s, i) = d \wedge \text{out}_1(s, i) = d \wedge \text{out}_2(s, i) = ®$$

These formulae show very clearly that the table exactly captures the relevant entries taken from the two conditional equations.

The vertical double line does not only show where the implication sign is to be placed. In our example it also separates input from output. This is very helpful for the intuitive understanding of implicative specifications from a conceptual and from a methodological point of view.

The well-known definition of functions by cases is written in mathematics generally as follows

$$f(x) = \begin{cases} t_1 & \text{if } c_1 \\ t_2 & \text{if } c_2 \end{cases}$$

It can be written in the form of a disjunctive table as shown in Table 4.5a or by a implicative table as given by Table 4.5b.

Table 4.5a. Disjunctive Table Describing a Complete Case Distinction

true	f(x)
c_1	t_1
c_2	t_2

Table 4.5b. Implicative Table for the Case Distinction

true	f(x)
c_1	t_1
c_2	t_2

An implicative table can also represent a case distinction. We just have to replace the vertical line in the middle of Table 4.5a by a double line as shown in Table 4.5b separating conditions from conclusions. In the case of a complete, disjoint case distinction there is no semantic difference whether we write a disjunctive or an implicative table. Replacing the single vertical line separating the two columns by a double line to separate the columns into premises and conclusions leads to a logically equivalent table as long as $c_1 \vee c_2$ and $\neg c_1 \Leftrightarrow c_2$ hold, in other words, as long as the case distinction is disjoint and complete.

In spite of the semantic equality between disjunctive and implicative tables for complete, disjunctive case distinctions, we advocate to use implicative tables rather than disjunctive ones. They provide more structure since they separate premises (conditions) from conclusions.

The tables of Parnas (see [Parnas 92]) in their most basic form can be represented in our approach, too. Parnas suggests using tables to represent formulae of the form

$$\bigwedge_{i=1}^{n} (C_i \Rightarrow \bigwedge_{j=1}^{m} v_j' = E_j^i)$$

by tables of the form shown in Table 4.6.

Table 4.6. Parnas Table

	C_1	...	C_n
...	...	...	...
v'_j	E^1_j	...	E^n_j
...	...	...	...

By such a table Parnas represents specifications of programs (statements) that work with the program variables $v_1, ..., v_n$. Primed variables $v'_1, ..., v'_n$ denote the values of the variables after the execution of the specified statements.

In our approach we may represent Table 4.6 in a straightforward way by the transposed implicative table as shown in Table 4.7.

Table 4.7. Parnas Table as an Implicative Table

true	v'_1	...	v'_m
C_1	E^1_1	...	E^1_m
...	...		...
C_n	E^n_1	...	E^n_m

This demonstrates that in its simplest form Parnas tables are a special case of implicative tables. This gives a first hint on the generality and expressiveness of our table concept.

5   Syntax and Semantics of Formula Tables

In this section we deal with a more general syntactic form of term tables and their semantics. A table is structured by a head row (called its agenda), a number of rows, and a number of columns. Also for the rows, a column with headings may be provided that may serve as comments. Every row and every column share an entry that is a term or a formula.

Often we want to talk about conditions in a table. They can be included into tables by allowing the head rows and the entries of a table to be arbitrary terms. If the head row of the column j is the term h_j of sort $s \in S$ and the entry (in a row) for this column is a predicate P for elements of sort s then $P(h_j)$ is the proposition associated with that entry in place of the equation we usually deal with. If the entry is a Boolean formula, called an assertion, that may contain h as a free variable, then it is the proposition associated with this entry.

A disjunctive table with m rows n columns represents the following logical formula (where entries E_{ij} denote logical formulae that are shown in the table entries)

$$\bigvee_{i=1}^{m} \bigwedge_{j=1}^{n} E_{ij}$$

An implicative table with c preconditions represents the following logical formula

$$\bigwedge_{i=1}^{m} ((\bigwedge_{j=1}^{c} E_{ij}) \Rightarrow (\bigwedge_{j=c+1}^{n} E_{ij}))$$

The formula E_{ij} is called the basic proposition of the entry in row i and column j. The meaning of the table is defined as follows: We distinguish three cases of entries:

(1) The head row entry hj of the jth column is of the same sort as the term t_{ij} that is the table entry in column j and row i. Then entry E_{ij} stands for the equation

$$h_j = t_{ij}$$

(2) The heading entry hj of column j is a term of sort s and the table entry P_{ij} in column j and row i is a predicate for elements of sort s. Then entry E_{ij} stands for the proposition
$$P_{ij}(h_j)$$

(3) In case the entry is a logical formula e, then e is the basic proposition. We also permit formulae as entries in which hj occurs freely in the case hj is a variable.

In the example of the storage cell above a table with predicates reads as shown in Table 5.1. Here isData is a predicate

isData: $M \rightarrow Bool$

that is specified by the following equation

isData(z) = (z $\in$ Data)

Often for this kind of tables, predicates have to be introduced. This yields some overhead, however, it may help structuring a specification and thus support its understanding provided the predicates and their names are well-chosen.

Table 5.1. Transition Systems with Predicates as Entries

i	s	state(s, i)	$out_1(s, i)$	$out_2(s, i)$
isData	isData	i	®	s
®	isData	s	s	®

6   Schematic Formulae and Their Representation by Tables

To provide sophisticated techniques for translating arbitrary formulae of predicate logic into tables is perhaps an overkill. Tables are only helpful as means of abbreviation and structuring, if they are easy to comprehend.

Example: Specification of a sender in the alternating bit protocol

As an example we specify a component that serves as the sender in the alternating bit protocol example following the FOCUS approach (see [5]). The component can be graphically illustrated by a data flow node (see [1]) as given in Fig 6.1.

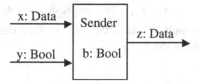

Fig. 6.1. Sender as a Data Flow Node

We are particularly interested in syntactic representations of formulae by tables. Therefore we do not give extensive explanations of the meaning of the example formulae represented by the tables. However, it is helpful to give some brief hints. In the following x, y, z are identifiers of the sort Stream of Data or Stream of Bool, as indicated in Fig 6.1. A stream is a finite or infinite sequence of elements. The identifier b is an attribute of the sort Data. The functions ft and rt operate on streams and deliver the first element of a stream and the rest of a stream without the first element respectively.

The behavior of the sender is captured by the stream function Send(b) and by instances of the logical formula of the form

$$Send(b)(x, y) = (ft.x', b')^\wedge Send(b')(x', rt.y)$$

with particular choices for the values b' and x' that depend on the actual message ft.y. These choices are instantiated as specified in Table 6.1. The table shows two instantiations of the formula above for the cases "matching acknowledgement" (Positive Ack) and "not matching acknowledgement" (Negative Ack).   ❏

Table 6.1. Table of the Instances for the Sender of the Alternating Bit Protocol

Send(b)(x, y) = (ft.x', b')^Send(b')(x', rt.y)			
case	ft.y	b'	x'
Positive Ack	b	¬b	rt.x
Negative Ack	¬b	b	x

In the example above we only work with two instantiations of the schematic formula and therefore with a table that has only two rows. More realistic protocol examples have to be represented by tables that contain many more rows and columns. This usage of a table supports separating the schematic form of a set of formulae from their often high number of instantiations.

As shown by our simple example, in specifications there often exists a set of formulae having the same structure that differ only for certain significant subexpressions. We speak of *instances* of a formula or more precisely of a formula scheme. Assume we work with a formula of the form

$$\bigwedge_{i=1}^{m} E(t_1^i, ..., t_n^i)$$

where $E(t_1^i, ..., t_n^i)$ is an arbitrary, maybe large, logical formula and where t_1^i, ..., t_n^i are terms of sort s_1, ..., s_n. Let x_1, ..., x_n be fresh variables (variables that do not occur in the considered formulae). Then, we may replace the original formula by a logically equivalent formula of the form

$$\bigwedge_{i=1}^{m} (\bigwedge_{j=1}^{n} x_j = t_j^i) \Rightarrow E(x_1, ..., x_n)$$

We represent this formula by a table as schematically shown by Table 6.2.

Table 6.2. Table for Representing a Schematic Formula and its Instances

$E(x_1, ..., x_n)$		
x_1	...	x_n
...		...
t_1^i	...	t_n^i
...		...

This form of tables for representing arbitrary schematic formulae gives us flexibility in specifications. We can choose the schematic form of the formulae freely and describe its instantiations by the entries of the table.

The simple representation of the formula above may not work properly if $E(x_1, ..., x_n)$ is a formula that contains quantifiers and some of the x_j occur in the range of the quantifiers and the terms t_j^i contain occurrences of identifiers that are bound by these quantifiers. Then we specify the meaning of the table by replacing the identifiers x_j textually by the terms t_j^i.

$$\bigwedge_{i=1}^{m} E(t_1^i, ..., t_n^i)$$

Here terms t_j^i replace the identifiers in $E(x_1, ..., x_n)$ by straightforward substitutions without renaming bound identifiers. This purely syntactic substitution is in contrast with logical substitution or with function application in λ-notation where locally bound identifiers are renamed by α-conversion to avoid name-clashes. However, we should keep in mind that the identifiers x_1, ..., x_n are not introduced for reasons of logical deduction as it is the case in predicate logic but as simple textual abbreviations and placeholders ("macros") in schematic formulae.

A note on abbreviations:
Carefully chosen abbreviations help substantially to improve the readability of formulae. For abbreviations, we distinguish between textual abbreviations, the semantics of which is explained by simple textual substitutions called "macros", and parameterized abbreviations, which introduce functions that can be applied to a range of arguments. The difference between these two paradigms becomes crucial when working with bindings of identifiers by quantifiers. Consider the following formula that is again taken from a FOCUS specification (we come back to this formula in Section 7):

$$\forall\ d \in D: f(\langle d \rangle) = \diamond \wedge \forall\ x \in M^{\omega}: \exists\ f: B(f) \wedge f(d\hat{\ }\circledR\hat{\ }x) = \langle d \rangle\hat{\ }f(x)$$

Using *textual abbreviations* we may write for this formula

$$\forall\ d \in D: Case1 \wedge Case2$$

Where Case1 and Case2 are textual abbreviations standing for the following formulae as shown below:

$$Case1 \equiv (f(\langle d \rangle) = \diamond)$$

$$Case2 \equiv (\forall\ x \in M^{\omega}: \exists\ f: B(f) \wedge f(d\hat{\ }\circledR\hat{\ }x) = d\hat{\ }f(x))$$

Using *parameterized specifications* of Case1 and Case2 we would write

$$\forall\ d \in D: Case1(d) \wedge Case2(d)$$

where Case1 and Case2 are predicates specified as follows:

$$Case1(d) \equiv (f(\langle d \rangle) = \diamond)$$

$$Case2(d) \equiv (\forall\ x \in M^{\omega}: \exists\ f: B.(f) \wedge f(d\hat{\ }\circledR\hat{\ }x) = d\hat{\ }f.(x))$$

Both concepts of dealing with abbreviations have advantages and disadvantages. Both seem helpful in their own way. Therefore in a flexible specification formalism it seems reasonable to have both concepts available.   *End_of_Note*

Of course, all the tables introduced so far are cases of the technique of representing a number of instances of a schematic formula.

Example: Specification of a Routing Cell
A routing cell has two input and two output channels. On one channel called x it receives messages and forwards them on one of its output channels, depending on the value on its second Boolean input channel called y. The routing cell acts as a switch. It can also be specified by the table technique for schematic formulae. The syntactic interface of the cell is shown as a data flow node in Fig. 6.2.

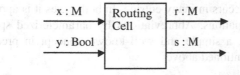

Fig. 6.2. Routing Cell as a Data Flow Node

Again we specify the set M of messages by the equation

M = Data

The formula s:d ‹ F denotes a behavior which outputs d on channel s and then behaves like F. The formula F ‹ x:d denotes a behavior which receives d on channel x and then behaves like F.

Table 6.3. Table of the Formula Specifying a Routing Cell

Cell ‹ x:m ‹ y:b = r:c ‹ s:e ‹ Cell		
b	c	e
true	m	–
false	–	m

In the sample formula of Table 6.3 we use a notation for the algebraic specification of interactive systems as introduced and explained in detail in [3].   ❑

Through the technique of schematic tables we achieve a valuable flexibility for writing conjunctions of instances of arbitrary logical formulae as tables. We can always provide a schematic formula that is instantiated by the rows listed in the table.

7   Readability of Formulae and Structuring of Tables

In our approach each table represents a formula in predicate logic. Formulae containing quantifiers can be written as tables by using the techniques of Section 6 for representing schematic formulae, which of course may contain quantifiers.

Since each table can be seen as a specific representation of a logical formula, we may combine tables like logical formulae. Of course, to form formulae with tables as sub-expressions seems to be difficult, especially when tables get large. However, we have the possibility to introduce names for tables. Then it is easy to build formulae with tables by referring to their names.

Another option of representing nested formulae by tables is the nesting of tables exactly as the logical formulae are nested. In this section we follow the second line of thought. Our goal is a general method for the representation of large complex logical formulae by hierarchically nested structured tables.

Often the terms or formulae we want to use as entries in tables get very large so that they hardly fit into the columns of tables. Then tables get unreadable. Sometimes the same large formula occurs in many entries. In both cases it is appropriate to work with well-chosen abbreviations. Abbreviations by parameterized specifications and textual abbreviations are a simple and well-known concept in predicate logic and computing science as mentioned above.

The readability of a logical formula is often difficult according to the use of local variables bound by quantifiers, especially when a number of nested quantifiers occur. For a given signature $\Sigma = (S, F)$ that defines a set of sorted names we may write a logical formula E. For such a formula we may require, in principle, that at most the symbols in F occur as free identifiers. This forces us to introduce quantifiers for all other identifiers that are used as bound local variables.

A convention that allows us to leave out and therefore to save the explicit writing of some universal quantifiers is the universal closure. If identifiers occur in a formula E that are not contained in the signature Σ, then they are assumed as (implicitly) universally quantified. Its sort then has to be deduced from the context. However, often it improves the readability to write quantifiers explicitly.

The general scheme of representing quantifiers in tables is given in the following. For the formula

$$\forall\, x \in M: P(x)$$

we write a table as shown in Table 7.1. Then we can apply a table along the lines of using tables for schematic formulae to represent the formula P(x).

Table 7.1. Universal Quantification in a Table

$\forall$ x: M:
P(x)

For the formula

$$\exists\, x \in M: P(x)$$

we write the table of the form given in Table 7.2.

Table 7.2. Existential Quantification in a Table

$\exists$ x: M:
P(x)

In spite of all the possibilities of writing formulae in a more structured style, nested quantification remains a concept that makes formulae more difficult to write, read, understand, and manipulate. Sometimes, it is possible to replace existential quantification by declarations. Existential quantification is closely related to the declaration of identifiers and their binding and vice versa. Whenever we write a declaration

Let x = t **in** e

or equivalently

e **where** x = t

its meaning can be expressed logically (provided e is a Boolean expression) by the formula:

$$\exists\, x: e \wedge x = t$$

Note that this formula is equivalent to the implicative formula

$$\forall x: x = t \Rightarrow e$$

provided the formula $\exists x: x = t$ is valid. The proposition $\exists x: x = t$ is trivially true, if every term t denotes a value[4]. So it is true in classical equational logic.

In fact, non-recursive declarations may always be understood as abbreviations for certain formulae in predicate logic. Clearly, in a declaration $x = t$ we generally assume that the formula

$$\exists x : x = t$$

is valid. This shows a remarkable difference between the roles of the sub-formula e and that of sub-formula $x = t$ in the formula

$$\exists x : e \wedge x = t.$$

The sub-formula $x = t$ can be seen as just an auxiliary construction that can be always satisfied (assuming that the term t always denotes a value) and serves as an auxiliary construct for the formulation of formula e. If the declaration "Let $x = t$" is not recursive which means that x does not occur in term t then the formula

$$\exists x : e \wedge x = t$$

expresses the same as the formula

$$e[t/x].$$

In these cases we may decompose a formula into pieces by structuring quantifiers into declarations. This idea of a structured specification of existential quantification can be generalized to formulae of the form

$$\exists x : e \wedge B(x)$$

provided the proposition

$$\exists x : B(x) \qquad\qquad (*)$$

holds. In contrast to the equation $x = t$ that we used in place of the sub-formula $B(x)$ above, the sub-formula $B(x)$ does not necessarily identify the element x uniquely. Then we may read the formula as the proposition

e   where x is arbitrary such that $B(x)$ holds

provided, the logical value of e does not depend on the choice of x as long as proposition $B(x)$ holds. Expressed in logical terms we require

$$B(x) \wedge B(x') \Rightarrow (e \equiv e[x'/x]) \qquad\qquad (**)$$

---

[4] Of course the situation gets more complicated if there are expressions t without a value (such as in the presence of partial functions) or if $x = t$ may have several solutions for x (such as in the case of recursive declarations).

Given the conditions (*) and (**) the formula $\exists\, x : e \wedge B(x)$ is equivalent to the formula[5]

$$\forall\, x: B(x) \Rightarrow e.$$

If the requirements described above are valid, we rather write the proposition $\exists\, x: t \wedge B(x)$ in the tabular form as given in Table 7.3.

Table 7.3. Representation of the Formula $\exists\, x : e \wedge B(x)$

e
where $x : B(x)$.

Here we require as a healthiness condition that propositions (*) and (**) hold.

We know how to specify the behavior of interactive systems, in principle, by logical formulae in FOCUS (see [FOCUS 92]). For complex components, these formulae can get fairly large and unreadable. Therefore a better way of structuring can make them easier to read and understand. In addition of using tables, one possibility is to use appropriate formatting concepts and conventions for formulae (see [11] for an example). In addition, the introduction of well-chosen auxiliary declarations may help to shorten the formulae occurring in tables and to provide additional structure (see [16] for an extended example).

A schematic table is used to abbreviate a sequence of implications connected by logical conjunction. Sometimes, in the premise or in the conclusion local quantifiers are used.

Example: Quantification in FOCUS
Using the description techniques of FOCUS (cf. [2]) we work with specifications defining sets of functions via equations for predicates like in the following case. Here a predicate B is specified that characterizes functions on streams:

$$B(f) \equiv \forall\, d \in D: f(\langle d \rangle) = \langle \rangle \wedge \forall\, x \in M^{\omega}: \exists\, f': B(f') \wedge f(\langle d \rangle\hat{\ }\langle \circledR \rangle\hat{\ }x) = \langle d \rangle\hat{\ }f'(x)$$

This specification of the predicate B essentially expresses that a function f mapping streams of messages to streams of messages characterizes a one element buffer. The formula indicates that f produces the empty output stream on the input stream that carries exactly one data element, and that it produces the data element d as output on the input stream that starts with the data message d followed by the request signal ® followed by the stream x. Then the output d is followed by the stream that f produces for the input stream x. The nested quantification is rather complicated here and difficult to read and to understand. A table specification as shown in Table 7.4 could provide more structure. This is a first example of a hierarchically structured table.

---

[5] As Wolfgang Naraschewski pointed out to me there is a relationship to dependent types in type theory; there we express $\exists\, x: e \wedge B(x)$ as $\Sigma\, x{:}e.B(x)$.

Table 7.4. Table of a Formula Specifying a Queue

$B \equiv (f: M^\omega \to M^\omega): \exists\, f: B(f') \land$	
$\forall\, d \in D,\ x \in M^\omega: f(i) = o$	
i	o
⟨d⟩	⟨⟩
$d\,\hat{}\,®\,\hat{}\,x$	$d\,\hat{}\,f(x)$

Here existential and universal quantifiers are written in a more structured style, which makes the formula hopefully easier to read.   ❑

We may include quantification into the heading of tables describing formulae. This allows us also to work with tables for formulae with quantifiers as shown in Table 7.4.

The readability of a formula critically depends on its layout. Especially, if a formula is large the layout should be carefully chosen. Then the difference between a table and a diagram may become more or less unimportant.

Often for large, uniformly structured formulae it may be better to choose the following layout (advocated by [11])

$\land$	t_1
$\land$	t_2
$\land$	t_3

instead of the conventional layout

$$t_1 \land t_2 \land t_3$$

This way the structure of the formulae gets clearer and more uniform making formulae get even more readable.

In a similar style it is preferable to write

	t_1
$\Rightarrow$	t_2

for large formulae t_1 and t_2 instead of the logical formula

$$t_1 \Rightarrow t_2$$

to make the formula more structured and better readable.

8   Interaction Tables

The description of the interactive behavior of reactive systems is an important but difficult task. As we have shown in earlier examples, tables are useful also for this task. In this section, we consider a specific situation, which is typical for protocols in telecommunication systems. To illustrate this issue we use again a one element buffer as a simple example, which in this case is lossy, however.

Example: Unreliable Buffer
We work with the following sets of input and output messages (let D be a set of data elements):

$$M = D \cup \{\circledR\}$$

$$N = D \cup \{\circledR, @\}$$

The behavior of the unreliable buffer is described by a nondeterministic state machine with input and output:

$$\Delta: \Sigma \times M \rightarrow \wp(\Sigma \times N)$$

where state space Σ is equal to M. The basic properties of the buffer can be described by schematic formula table (let d1, d2 $\in$ D), as it is shown in Table 8.1a.

Table 8.1a. State Transition System Described by a Table

$(\sigma', r) \in \Delta(\sigma, a)$			
σ	a	σ'	r
d1	d2	$\circledR$	$\circledR$
d1	$\circledR$	$\circledR$	$\circledR$
d1	$\circledR$	$\circledR$	d1
$\circledR$	d2	$\circledR$	$\circledR$
$\circledR$	d2	d2	@
$\circledR$	$\circledR$	$\circledR$	$\circledR$

Here σ denotes the current state, σ' the successor state, a the input message and r the output message.

The meaning of Table 8.1a is simply

$$\bigwedge_{j=1}^{6} \sigma = s_j^1 \wedge a = s_j^2 \wedge \sigma' = s_j^3 \wedge r = s_j^4 \Rightarrow (\sigma', r) \in \Delta(\sigma, a)$$

which is equal to

$$\bigwedge_{j=1}^{6} (s_j^3, s_j^4) \in \Delta(s_j^1, s_j^2)$$

Table 8.1b represents the same formula in a slightly different style. However, both formulas are weak. We get $(\circledR, d1) \in \Delta(d1, \circledR) \wedge (\circledR, \circledR) \in \Delta(d1, \circledR)$ but we do not and cannot express this way

$$\Delta(d1, \circledR) = \{(\circledR, d1), (\circledR, \circledR)\}$$

Table 8.1b. State Transition System Described by an Implicative Table

$P(\sigma) \wedge Q(a) \Rightarrow (\sigma', r) \in \Delta(\sigma, a)$			
$P\sigma$	$Q(a)$	σ'	r
$\sigma = d1$	$a = d2$	®	®
$\sigma = d1$	$a = ®$	®	®
$\sigma = d1$	$a = ®$	®	$d1$
$\sigma = ®$	$a = d2$	®	®
$\sigma = ®$	$a = d2$	$d2$	@
$\sigma = ®$	$a = ®$	®	®

The specifications by Table 8.1a und 8.b are loose; they specify what are possible reactions of the system but they do not express that these are the only possible reactions.

Now consider the conjunctive Table 8.1c. Below the heading it has 4 rows. For instance row 2 expresses

$$(\sigma = d1 \wedge a = ® \wedge (\sigma', r) \in \Delta(\sigma, a) \Rightarrow (\sigma' = ® \wedge r = ®) \vee (\sigma' = ® \wedge r = d1)$$

Since Table 8.1c is a conjunctive table we get

$$(\sigma = d1 \wedge a = d2 \wedge (\sigma', r) \in \Delta(\sigma, a) \Rightarrow \sigma' = ® \wedge r = ®)$$

$$\wedge \quad (\sigma = d1 \wedge a = ® \wedge (\sigma', r) \in \Delta(\sigma, a) \Rightarrow (\sigma' = ® \wedge r = ®) \vee (\sigma' = ® \wedge r = d1)$$

$$\wedge \quad (\sigma = ® \wedge a = d2 \wedge \wedge (\sigma', r) \in \Delta(\sigma, a) \Rightarrow (\sigma' = ® \wedge r = ®) \vee (\sigma' = d2 \wedge r = @)$$

$$\wedge \quad (\sigma = ® \wedge a = ® \wedge (\sigma', r) \in \Delta(\sigma, a) \Rightarrow \sigma' = ® \wedge r = ®)$$

Table 8.1c. State Transition System Described by a Conjunctive Table

$P(\sigma) \wedge Q(a) \wedge \wedge (\sigma', r) \in \Delta(\sigma, a) \Rightarrow \bigvee_{j=1}^{n} (\sigma', r) \in \Delta(\sigma, a)$			
$P\sigma$	$Q(a)$	σ'	r
$\sigma = d1$	$a = d2$	®	®
$\sigma = d1$	$a = ®$	®	®
		®	$d1$
$\sigma = ®$	$a = d2$	®	®
		$d2$	@
$\sigma = ®$	$a = ®$	®	®

❑

Note that, since tables are only syntactic sugar for formulae, we can freely combine tables and formulae. One additional advantage of our technique is that it allows us to translate the information given by tables into formulae of predicate logic, so that we can use tables and formulae side by side with a definition of how they correspond to each other.

9   Combining Tables with Diagrams

There are many possibilities to combine tables with diagrams. Diagrams may, like tables, be helpful to support a quick understanding of large specifications. Each table represents a finite relation between terms. It can be rewritten into a diagram. Vice versa, each diagram that is a directed labeled graph can be represented by a table.

A diagram is a labeled graph consisting of nodes and arcs. In computer science many variations of diagrams are used. Often they differ only in the form of the symbols used to represent their nodes. Of course, we cannot and do not want to treat all kinds of diagrams found in computer science in this section in a systematic way. Therefore, we demonstrate the combination of tables with diagrams only for simple state transition diagrams. For them the nodes represent states and the arcs represent transitions.

A diagram is a labeled graph with labels for its nodes and for its arcs. Every node and arc may carry several labels such as names and values. The translation of a diagram into a table and vice versa can be described by fixing the way an arc is represented by a table.

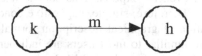

Fig. 9.1. An Arc Connecting Two Nodes

We can then associate an entry in the table with each arc as shown in Fig. 9.1 in the form of a row in the table with the following entries:

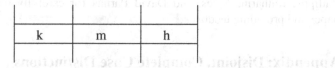

After this translation scheme has been fixed, each diagram can be translated into a table and vice versa. Note, however, that we can freely choose which columns are used to represent arcs and which represent nodes. This may lead to quite different options for diagrams to be represented by tables.

A general way to translate graphs into diagrams is sketched as follows. Assume a directed graph with labeled arcs and labeled nodes. We may easily translate the graph into a table with three columns. Then each arc corresponds to a row with the entry in the first column being the source node label, entry in the second column being the arc label and the entry in the third column being the target node label. State transition diagrams are discussed in detail in [4].

10   Concluding Remarks

Specifications that are readable but nevertheless precise constitute a valuable concept in system development. The goals of readability and preciseness are not in contradiction.

On the contrary, a vague, imprecise specification is hardly actually understandable. Of course, often complicated constructs in formulae make the understanding too difficult, however. Improvements should correspond to abstraction and not to vagueness. A well-chosen structure and layout may help a lot to keep formulae readable.

A well-chosen balance between explanatory text, formulae, tables, and diagrams is a must for useful and tractable specification methods. Such a structuring of specifications requires insights into the application area and an understanding for the specification methods and goals. Looking for methods along these lines, we are only at the beginning in software engineering. Much more experience is needed on how to apply specification techniques in practical projects. Furthermore, a scientific basis is necessary that allows us to integrate the various description formalisms. This paper is intended as an attempt to contribute to developing this basis.

The specification techniques used in practical applications in systems engineering are often not precisely defined. Typical examples are statecharts or SDL (see [10]). In both cases many proposal for semantics exist, while formal reference semantics is missing. Obviously the concepts of such languages allow for a wide variety of semantic interpretations. Experiments show that such languages lead to quite different interpretations of descriptions, even by experts. This shows that the chosen description concepts are too complex. Therefore, simple, suggestive concepts with a straightforward semantic interpretation of graphical description formalism and tables that are suggestive and often more familiar to most users are indispensable. However, if one hardly understands logical connectives, it is unlikely that one understands the meaning of the diagrams and tables.

Acknowledgement. This paper has been influenced by discussions we had during the design of [7]. I am grateful to Diego Marmsoler, Wolfgang Naraschewski, Jan Philipps, Katharina Spies, and David Parnas for carefully reading versions of this paper and providing feedback.

Appendix: Disjoint, Complete Case Distinctions

We consider a finite set of cases p_i and a finite set of consequences c_i, $1 \leq i \leq n$. We speak of a complete, disjoint case distinction if both the following two propositions hold

$$\bigvee_{i=1}^{n} p_i \qquad \{\text{completeness}\}$$

$$\bigwedge_{i=1}^{n} \bigwedge_{\substack{j=1 \\ j \neq i}}^{n} (p_i \Rightarrow \neg p_j) \qquad \{\text{disjointness}\}$$

Under these conditions we can show that the following two propositions are equivalent

$$\bigvee_{i=1}^{n} (p_i \wedge c_i) \qquad \{\text{disjunctive normal form}\}$$

$$\bigwedge_{i=1}^{n} (p_i \Rightarrow c_i) \qquad \{\text{implicative form}\}$$

We first prove the equivalence for $n = 2$. We start the deduction processes with the implicative version:

$$(p_1 \Rightarrow c_1) \wedge (p_2 \Rightarrow c_2)$$

$\equiv$ {definition of implication}

$$(\neg p_1 \vee c_1) \wedge (\neg p_2 \vee c_2)$$

$\equiv$ {distributive law}

$$(\neg p_1 \wedge \neg p_2) \vee (\neg p_1 \wedge c_2) \vee (\neg p_2 \wedge c_1) \wedge (c_1 \wedge c_2)$$

$\equiv$ {disjointness, completeness implies $\neg p_1 \equiv p_2$}

$$(p_2 \wedge c_2) \vee (p_1 \wedge c_2) \vee (c_1 \wedge c_2)$$

$\equiv$ {disjointness, completeness implies $(c_1 \wedge c_2) \Rightarrow (p_1 \wedge c_1) \vee (p_2 \wedge c_2)$}

$$(p_1 \wedge c_1) \vee (p_2 \wedge c_2)$$

We prove the equivalence for $n > 2$ by induction as follows:

$$\bigwedge_i (p_i \Rightarrow c_i)$$

$\equiv$ {definition of iterated conjunction and completeness of case distinction}

$$\left(\left(\bigvee_i p_i\right) \Rightarrow \bigwedge_i (p_i \Rightarrow c_i)\right) \wedge (p_{n+1} \Rightarrow c_{n+1})$$

$\equiv$ {by the equivalence for $n = 2$ and induction}

$$\left(\bigvee_{i=1}^{n} p_i \wedge \bigvee_{i=1}^{n} (p_i \wedge c_i)\right) \vee (p_{n+1} \wedge c_{n+1})$$

$\equiv$ {since $\bigvee_{i=1}^{n} (p_i \wedge c_i) \Rightarrow \bigvee_{i=1}^{n} p_i$ by absorption}

$$\bigwedge_{i=1}^{n+1} (p_i \wedge c_i)$$

The proved equivalence justifies the equivalence of disjunctive and implicative tables in the case of complete, disjoint case distinctions.   ❑

References

1. Broy, M.: (Inter-)Action Refinement: The Easy Way. In: Broy, M. (ed.) Program Design Calculi. Springer NATO ASI Series, Series F: Computer and System Sciences, vol. 118, pp. 121–158. Springer, Heidelberg (1993)
2. Broy, M.: Specification and Refinement of a Buffer of Length One. Marktoberdorf Summer School 1994 (1994)

3. Broy, M.: Algebraic Specification of Reactive Systems. In: Nivat, M., Wirsing, M. (eds.) AMAST 1996. LNCS, vol. 1101, pp. 487–503. Springer, Heidelberg (1996)

4. Broy, M.: The specification of System Components by State Transition Diagrams (unpublished Manuscript 1996)

5. Broy, M., Dederichs, F., Dendorfer, C., Fuchs, M., Gritzner, T.F., Weber, R.: The Design of Distributed Systems - an Introduction to Focus. Technische Universität München, Institut für Informatik, TUM-I9203 (January 1992)

6. Fuchs, M.: Funktionale Spezifikation einer Geschwindigkeitsregelung; Technische Universität München, Institut für Informatik, TUM-INFO, SFB-Bericht 342/1/93 (January 1993)

7. GRAPES-Referenzmanual, DOMINO, Integrierte Verfahrenstechnik. Siemens AG, Bereich Daten-und Informationstechnik (1990)

8. Heninger, K., Kallander, J., Parnas, D.L., Shore, J.: Software Requirementsforthe A-7E Aircraft. NRL Report 3876 (November 1978)

9. Heninger, K.L.: Specifying Software Requirements for Complex Systems: New Techniques and Their Application. IEEE Transactions Software Engineering SE-6(1) (January 1980)

10. CCITT, Recommendation Z.100, Specification and Description Language (SDL), ITU-T (1993)

11. L. Lamport: How to Write a Long Formula. DIGITAL Systems Research Center, SRC 119 (December 1993)

12. Parnas, D.L.: Tabular Representation of Relations. CRL Report #260, McMaster University (September 1992)

13. Parnas, D.L.: Predicate Logic for Software Engineering. IEEE Transactions on Software Engineering 19(9) (September 1993)

14. Petre, M.: Why Looking Isn't Always Seeing. Comm. ACM 38(6), 33–44 (1995)

15. Broy, M., Facchi, Ch., Grosu, R., Hettler, R., Hußmann, H., Nazareth, D., Regensburger, F., Stolen, K.: The Requirement and Design Specification Language SPECTRUM. Technische Universität München, Institut für Informatik, TUM-I9140 (October 1991)

16. Spies, K.: Funktionale Spezifikation eines Kommunikationsprotokolls, Technische Universität München, Institut für Informatik, TUM-I9414 (May 1994)

17. Wirsing, M.: Algebraic Specification. Handbook of Theoretical Computer Science, vol. B, pp. 675–788. North Holland, Amsterdam (1990)

Formal Modelling for Cooking Assistance

Bernd Krieg-Brückner, Serge Autexier, Martin Rink,
and Sidoine Ghomsi Nokam

German Research Center for Artificial Intelligence, DFKI, and
Universität Bremen, Germany
{Bernd.Krieg-Brueckner,Serge.Autexier}@dfki.de,
{mrink,sidoine}@informatik.uni-bremen.de

Abstract. Structured ontologies, with various facets of abstraction, are
used to model food, ingredients, recipes, cookware and workflows. They
form the uniform knowledge base for modular software assistants. Processes and monitors supervise the cooking process and advise the user.

1 Introduction

The Objective of this Paper is to show the complexity of Formal Modelling
for an application domain such as *cooking*, but at the same time to introduce
"Formal Methods Light" step by step and to illustrate their added value:

modelling data	in ontologies, analogous to data types, with more semantic rigor than in relational data bases;
flexibility, extendability	of ontologies, easier to maintain than data types;
separation of concerns	by structuring into domain ontologies;
abstraction	in several ways to conquer complexity;
modelling processes	at a high level, in particular for monitoring.

On the side of the application domain, the objective is to propose a *uniform
approach* for the *integration* of the many aspects of *cooking*, as a basis for software
"assistants", which access the knowledge base and present it appropriately for
user interaction, see Sec. 5.1.

How is our protagonist, Ms. W., going to cook when several guests with all
sorts of health and other constraints are being invited together (cf. Sec. 7)? To
try to solve this and related problems, we shall accompany Ms. W. while she
plans a meal, develops recipes, manages ingredients, goes shopping, prepares for
cooking, and finally gets the cooking done — supported by DFKI's emerging
technology, explained as we go along.

2 Food, Drink and Health

Food and drink are most likely the most important source of a persons well-being.
Chinese grandfathers and -mothers, when still living at home in the traditional
multi-generation family, supposedly live longer [26], for physical reasons, since

R. De Nicola and R. Hennicker (Eds.): Wirsing Festschrift, LNCS 8950, pp. 355–376, 2015.

they can expect a very diverse diet, but also for psychological reasons, since they are pampered with a varying and attractive meal three times a day, and live by looking forward to the next. Other great cuisines (such as the Italian or French Cuisine) also thrive on variety, locally grown ingredients — and eating (slowly!) with the family, friends, or at least colleagues, around a big table.

In modern Western (and increasingly other) societies, people suffer from health problems due to stress and hectic eating without the soothing effects of friendly society, but also unhealthy food products provided by an inconsiderate and greedy food industry, marketing dietary dreams that turn out to deteriorate health even further (e.g. "low fat", where fat is substituted by sugar to provide "taste"). One of the most important (health care political) issues is that food producers are still not obliged to (and therefore do not) provide complete details about the composition of their products, and consumers are not sufficiently informed about the effect of these products on their individual health.

Luckily, there are some (government, non-profit, and commercial) organisations, which try to provide the missing information about existing products, and software (apps) to access it [29,21,22,27,32,8]. However, information about various aspects and their interrelation is still widely dispersed, often not directly accessible to the layman, and not integrated.

We shall try to delineate an approach in the sequel to unify, integrate and standardise such information to achieve a *personalized* added value for the user.

2.1   Food Classification and Properties

Ontologies. Let us start by classifying food and drink products such that we can then add meaningful properties and relationships to other concepts. A hierarchy of concepts, a taxonomy, becomes an *ontology* when relations or more semantics are added. Every concept X at a lower level is subsumed by the parent *class* C, the concept at the next higher level; we say X *is-a* C (a directed acyclic graph). In Fig. 1, CourgetteVegetable *is-a* ... *is-a* SquashVegetable *is-a* GourdFruitVegetable and eventually ... *is-a* Vegetable, and so on upwards in the hierarchy.

Abstraction of Properties is a central strength of modelling with ontologies. In the hierarchy of concepts, each intermittent *class* concept *abstracts away* from more particular, specialised properties of descendants at lower levels, retaining the properties that hold for all descendants, while some may not hold any more for ancestors or siblings. Indeed, *class*es may be declared to be *disjoint*, such that (sub)*class*es (and associated specialised properties) cannot be shared. Unless stated, hierarchies will be disjoint in the sequel.

Relations. The *relation is-a* is the standard *relation* between (sub)*class*es. The interrelation between concepts is the core of semantics. As an example, take *fromPlant* that relates a sub*class* of PlantProduct to the biological sub*class* of Plant of which it is a part, see Sec. 2.2; *isSourceOfPlantProduct* is its *inverse*.

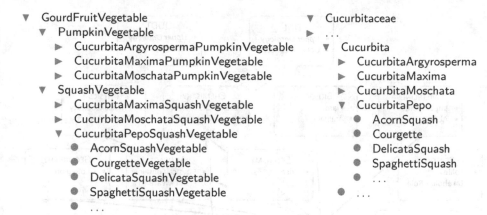

Fig. 1. PlantProduct and Plant Ontologies (Excerpts)

Multi-Lingual Ontologies. Ontologies can be made multi-lingual by attaching names or language terms as *labels* to a *class* name, one term for each desired language (or more if there are synonyms). This helps in a search, but also for automatic translation, for example of recipes. While there may be many *labels*, denoting synonyms in the same language, a *class* name is always unique.

When we want to look up *Zucchini* in German, for example, we find the class CourgetteVegetable, since *Zucchini* in German, Italian, and American English, is called *Courgette* in French, and British English — and we use primarily European terms for *class* names, i.e. British over American English.

We also take care of different traditions, e.g. by modelling German, French and English/American butcher's cuts of meat, relating them appropriately.

2.2 Where the Food Comes From

Biological Source. In fact, resolving such equivalencies between terms in several languages, even synonyms within the same language family such as English, with dictionaries alone may lead to inaccurate results, since "common names" for plants or animals are often overlapping, ambiguous, or misleading.[1]

To be safe, we should resort to relating each *food class* (and the associated linguistic labels) with the proper *biological class* with the relation *fromPlant* or *fromAnimal*, respectively. Biologists have been using taxonomic hierarchies for centuries (since Linné) to uniquely identify animals and plants (in Latin, the common language of scientists of the time), and to group them according to hereditary variations of properties. This way, we also relate breeds of cultivated plants or domestic animals to the respective "wild forms" of their ancestors.

Squash and *pumpkin* are examples of "common names"[2] *distinguishing* and classifying groups of vegetables with certain *culinary* properties, cf. Sec. 2.1. In Fig. 1,

---

[1] *Savoy cabbage* is confusingly called *chou de Milan* in French (*Wirsing* in German); *red cabbage* is regionally called *Rotkohl* or *Blaukraut*, as cooking changes its colour.

[2] Europeans need help with primarily American breeds of *squashes* and *pumpkins*.

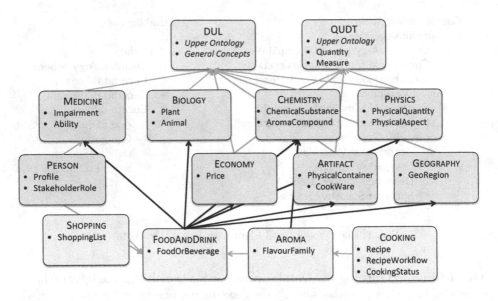

Fig. 2. Domain Ontologies and Import Structure

SquashVegetable and PumpkinVegetable are *separate class*es from a "vegetable/-culinary point of view": SquashVegetables can be cooked and eaten whole, whereas PumpkinVegetables have a hard shell, only the inside of the pumpkin shell is edible. However, they are closely *related as plants*: both are *fromPlant* Cucurbita. For example, some kinds of SquashVegetable and some kinds of PumpkinVegetable *both* are *fromPlant* CucurbitaMoschata, i.e. the *same biological class*.

Constraints on Relations in OWL. The Ontology Web Language, OWL [6], is the standard for the formulation of ontologies. Intricate relationships such as
    "all SquashVegetables are related with *fromPlant* to *only* Cucurbita"
may be axiomatised as a *subclass constraint* on the relation *fromPlant*:
    SquashVegetable ⊑ *fromPlant* **only** Cucurbita.

Structuring Ontologies. It is a good idea to structure the multitude of ontologies into separate *domain ontologies*, where one ontology *imports* (*classes, relations*, etc.) from other ontologies, cf. Fig. 2, sometimes called "hyper-ontology" [16,25]. A language for structuring ontologies by imports and morphisms is now proposed as a standard for extending OWL [25,28]. Ontologies defining very general concepts are called *upper ontologies*; we use DUL [3] (derived from DOLCE [2]) and QUDT [7] (for standardised quantities and measures).

Data Abstraction, Instances. An actual data object, e.g. a particular food product, is modelled as an *instance* of a *class* (i.e. a member of the *class* regarded as a set), and serves as source or target for the relations contained in the data. Thus the modelling by a ontology abstracts from the particular properties of tens or hundreds of thousands of products contained in data bases, and provides additional information by deductions as an "added value". In fact, with today's technology, these data cannot all be held as *instances*; instead, data base access from the ontology to several external *data bases* is provided in a hybrid approach, such that only some *instances* are held as local (copies of) objects.

Integration of Sources for Domain Modelling. Notice the large variety of aspects related to food or beverage products. It is the benefit of our modelling that we integrate and structure this variety inspired by several sources.

The internet portals WikiFood [8], or Barcoo [1] provide a (rather coarse) taxonomy and description of food and beverage products likely to be found in (European, German) food stores. WikiFood is a non-commercial portal focussing on the composition of food regarding nutrition or substances that might lead to incompatibilities; a distinctive feature is the personalized filter for food additives or content substances. WikiFood provides translation into English, German and French. Barcoo maps directly from the barcode to a variety of product information. The up-to-date management of their data bases relies on information from manufacturers, but also strongly on the community of users providing content. Challenging problems are the medical relevance and the quality (in particular the "half-life") of data regarding content substances (cf. Sec. 3.1, [11,10]). Compare also the overview of food standards in [22,17], in particular the CEN standard.

While we want to access such portals as data bases for actual food products on the market, we have to do the (integration of the) modelling, and mapping between possibly different models ourselves. The upper part of the FoodOrBeverage taxonomy (not shown here, including PlantProduct in Fig. 1) follows the hierarchy of the European Food Information Resource, EuroFIR [4,27,18], which is intended as a standard for organisations, industry, and researchers in Europe.

To enable exchange and comparison of data, an approach to indexing of data bases was established: the multi-lingual Langua aLimentaria Thesaurus, LanguaL [5,29,21]. Langual defines some relations to target domains we are modelling, but lacks e.g. information about nutrition impairments (cf. Sec. 3.1).

3   Planning a Meal

3.1   Guests and Their Peculiarities

Restricted Diets, Nutrition Impairments. When Ms. W. invites guests for dinner, she may be faced with all sorts of peculiarities: a guest may have a mere preference for a particular diet, such as a NoFlavorEnhancerDiet, or may insist on a meatless diet, such as an OvoLactoPescetarianDiet, a religiously restricted diet, such as a HalalDiet, a culturally restricted diet, such as a NoInnardsDiet, or have a more or less severe NutritionImpairment requiring a medically restricted diet, e.g. a PregnancyDietRestriction with specific *requiresDiet* constraints, cf. the list

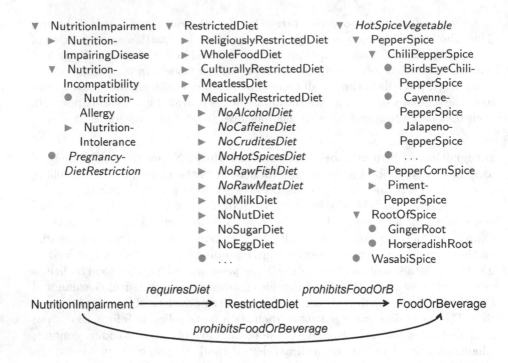

Fig. 3. PregnancyDietRestriction, RestrictedDiets, and Prohibited HotSpiceVegetables

of MedicallyRestrictedDiets marked in italics in Fig. 3. Note that diet restrictions might be elicited anonymously over a form on the Internet; anyway, a guest may state a list of RestrictedDiets individually and need not reveal her pregnancy.

Several Guests, Joining Impairments. When Ms. W. plans a meal for several such guests, she has to join impairments and associated dietary restrictions, thus the allowed foods. Similar considerations apply to a group in a restaurant.

3.2 Relating Impairments to Allowed Foods

Intermediate Abstraction. When relating PregnancyDietRestriction to allowed foods, cf. Fig. 3, it has been convenient to introduce the extra class hierarchy RestrictedDiet as an *intermediate abstraction*. It allows us to relate NutritionImpairment via *requiresDiet* to RestrictedDiet on the left, and RestrictedDiet via *prohibitsFoodOrB* to FoodOrBeverage on the right; otherwise each relationship between PregnancyDietRestriction and prohibited FoodOrBeverages would have to be defined individually for an overall *relation prohibitsFoodOrBeverage*.

On the left, we can focus on all those subclasses of RestrictedDiet that should be related to PregnancyDietRestriction, and define *subclass constraints*, e.g.

PregnancyDietRestriction ⊑ requiresDiet **only** NoHotSpicesDiet

(cf. Sec. 2.2) and analogously for NoAlcoholDiet, NoCaffeineDiet, NoRawMeatDiet, NoRawFishDiet, NoCruditesDiet. Other NutritionImpairments are similarly related to *particular* sub*classes* of MedicallyRestrictedDiet.

On the right, we can limit our attention to each sub*class* of RestrictedDiet and its relation to FoodOrBeverage, e.g. for NoHotSpicesDiet to all spicy-hot food

NoHotSpicesDiet ⊑ prohibitsFoodOrB **only** HotSpiceVegetable

and similarly for other hot food. Note that it helps considerably to cluster food into *classes* with culinary aspects, but also to define extra (super)*classes* with other properties, such as the spicy-hot aspect; then we need to define *subclass constraints* only for the clustering super*classes*, and they are inherited. In the case of HotSpiceVegetable, the culinary and the special spicy-hot aspects coincide: we distinguish the CayennePepperSpice as a HotSpiceVegetable from the BellPepperVegetable as a bland PepperFruitVegetable (although CayennePepperSpice and BellPepperVegetable are both *fromPlant* CapsicumAnnuum, cf. Sec. 2.2). The *relation prohibitsFoodOrBeverage* is defined as a *composite relation*

prohibitsFoodOrBeverage ⊑ requiresDiet ∘ prohibitsFoodOrB;

any HotSpiceVegetable is *deduced* to be prohibited for a PregnancyDietRestriction.

Separation of Concerns. The clou of *intermediate abstraction* is that *requiresDiet* and *prohibitsFoodOrB* can be described *independently*. Perhaps even more importantly, it allows us to define *subclass constraints* (cf. Sec. 2.2) for both relations *separately* at a high level of property abstraction, cf. Sec. 2.1.

Relationships established by *prohibitsFoodOrB* can be *reused* for other diet restrictions, e.g. NoHotSpicesDiet for the NutritionImpairment Gastritis.

3.3   Meals, Courses, Dishes

For the planning of a meal, potentially with a number of courses, dishes, side-dishes, etc. (cf. Sec. 5.3), we have to consider the number of guests and their joint restrictions, choose from a variety of cuisines, and select among the multitude of recipes (or invent a new one). What is the culinary secret for the combination of dishes? for a dish with an accompanying wine? or for the ingredients in a dish?

The secret is the interaction or "interplay" of aromas, their harmony, but also the contrast, coverage and variety of different *flavours* in a dish (or a combination of dishes); moreover, a similar harmony and variety of textures, colours and shapes matters, which we will disregard here.

Flavour Affinities. Why does caviar taste good with white chocolate? or Ms. W.'s heavenly Bavarian cream with raspberry sauce?

There has been considerable research in the analysis of aromas and their chemical composition. *"Food pairing"* relates two ingredients that have one (or more) flavour(s) in common: e.g. for caviar and white chocolate the flavour determining substance trimethylamine. It has become quite popular among food researchers and technologists, star chefs, sommeliers, even perfumers.

"Pairing" refers to a *semantic neighborhood* of a flavour (or aroma) that is shared by two ingredients in harmony.

Caviezel, in a commendably scientific approach, introduces a hierarchy of *flavour levels* in [19], starting with the *taste* level (sweet, sour, salty, bitter, umami, fat), the flavour created in the mouth by taste buds on the tongue, continuing with *aromas* sensed by the nose, ordered in 8 levels according to the volatility of the corresponding molecules. Thus a flavour at a low level is usually more prominent and persistent; some herbs or spices may overpower others (e.g. "spicy hot" from chili). Note that (the stage of) the cooking may significantly influence or even create a flavour, e.g. when roasting meat. In general, an ingredient contains several flavours that are more or less salient, and is thus related "in several directions" to other ingredients. Thus complex and elaborate recipes can be analysed w.r.t. the harmony and intentional contrast in their composition.

The net of [9] shows 381 regularly used ingredients and 1021 aroma substances. To conquer such complexity, we hope to achieve a manageable set of *intermediate flavour abstractions* (perhaps Caviezel's flavour level sets), which allow us to constructively *propose compositions* of ingredients, or *substitutions* of alternative ingredients in existing recipes, for creative cooking.

4   Recipes

4.1   Recipe Structure

Cooking might be defined as the process of performing certain cooking steps on a defined amount of ingredients in a specific order, utilizing cooking utensils, tools, etc. A recipe is then a structured workflow for processing such cooking steps, prescribed by recipe instructions, with corresponding ingredients (cf. Sec. 5.3).

We shall propose a structure for modelling recipes below, which takes care of a variety of "culinary" semantic relationships; for a running example, see Fig. 4 for an Italian *zucchini frittata*, a courgette omelette. The rendering in Fig. 4, ignoring the nested boxes, is similar to what you might expect in a cookbook.

Primary Ingredient(s), Culinary Options. The composition of ingredients is, quite likely, the most characteristic feature of a recipe. Often, a user will search for a recipe with one *primary ingredient*, and choose the others accordingly (cf. pairing in Sect. 3.3). The recipe author should flag, whether an ingredient is optional — an important semantic indication providing freedom for the user:

essential: not to be omitted
primary: essential reference ingredient, giving the recipe its name
optional: dispensable for a restricted diet or by personal preference
culinary: optional, intended as a special "culinary kick" by the author that would be lost if omitted (or dispensable as a fad of that author)?

In a vegetable omelette, eggs are essential; adding anchovies and capers to bland cauliflowers adds a Mediterranean culinary touch (cf. Sec. 4.2). Deleting an optional Ingredient, e.g. pepper, also deletes the dependent RecipeInstruction(s).

Balancing Amounts, Intervals. Amounts, for example, are likely to be defined in terms of the amount for a *primary ingredient*, in particular, if its quantity cannot be influenced; for example a large rather than a small turkey; for a jam, fruit (as much as could be collected) matched on-to-one by sugar; in baking, just so much yeast per flour quantity. This important dependency should be reflected in the recipe, and tools should calculate dependent measures automatically.

While it is important in such cases to keep amounts and balancing strictly controlled, the precise definition of amounts is often over-specified. The author of a recipe should recommend the interval over which the amount of an ingredient may range based on her/his expertise (and maybe indicate a preference), such that the user may vary according to her/his personal taste or other constraints.

A recommended interval should also make it easier to achieve proper rounding of measures when recomputing for a different number of portions. If, for example, for 4 portions of an omelette, 5-7 (instead of 6) eggs are prescribed, then an omelette for 3 should have 4-5 (and not 4.5) eggs in it.

Measures. There are various different approaches to measure ingredients, depending on the cultural background in different geographic regions. While flour is measured in weight (i.e. mass) in Germany, it is measured in volume in the UK, the US, or Sweden; moreover, measurement units differ. We use the QUDT ontology [7], providing quantities and measurement units, and their relation to each other; so standards can be converted to a style preferred by the user, e.g. 0.23 Liters to a LiquidCupUS; the intervals above help rounding off.

Individual Adaptation of ingredients (adjusting amounts, omission, or substitution) now becomes possible, regarding the variety of dietary constraints, see Sec. 3.1 — and flavour affinities should help find tasty substitutions, see Sec. 3.3.

In view of the abundant minced fish in Denmark, BKB substituted bacon by fish in an *Ærø zucchini frittata*, suitable for an OvoLactoPescetarianDiet.

Recipe Instructions. RecipeInstructions (see Fig. 5) have been modelled to

set up an environment	for cooking, i.e. get the requisite CookWare (see below), add Ingredients, heat the Burner, serve or store away result Ingredients (temporarily or for preservation), clean and restore CookWare for further use;
prepare Ingredients	e.g. cut in a particular way, mix, or whisk;
cook Ingredients	in the present environment, e.g. braise, or fry.

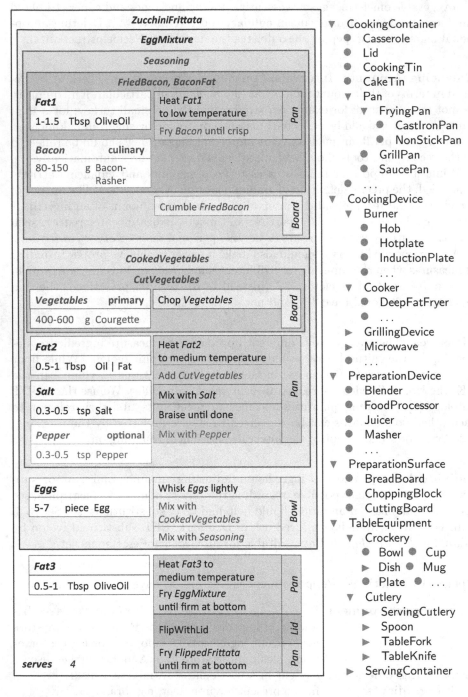

Fig. 4. *Zucchini Frittata* Recipe and CookWare Ontology (Excerpt)

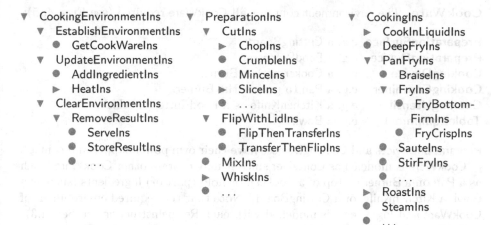

▼ CookingEnvironmentIns
  ▼ EstablishEnvironmentIns
    ● GetCookWareIns
  ▼ UpdateEnvironmentIns
    ● AddIngredientIns
    ▶ HeatIns
  ▼ ClearEnvironmentIns
    ▼ RemoveResultIns
      ● ServeIns
      ● StoreResultIns
      ● ...

▼ PreparationIns
  ▼ CutIns
    ▶ ChopIns
    ● CrumbleIns
    ● MinceIns
    ▶ SliceIns
    ● ...
  ▼ FlipWithLidIns
    ● FlipThenTransferIns
    ● TransferThenFlipIns
    ● MixIns
    ▶ WhiskIns
    ● ...

▼ CookingIns
  ▶ CookInLiquidIns
  ● DeepFryIns
  ▼ PanFryIns
    ● BraiseIns
    ▼ FryIns
      ● FryBottom-
        FirmIns
      ● FryCrispIns
    ● SauteIns
    ● StirFryIns
    ● ...
  ▶ RoastIns
  ● SteamIns
  ● ...

Fig. 5. RecipeInstruction Ontology (Excerpt; "Instruction" abbreviated as "Ins")

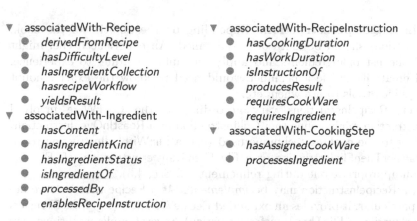

▼ associatedWith-Recipe
  ● *derivedFromRecipe*
  ● *hasDifficultyLevel*
  ● *hasIngredientCollection*
  ● *hasrecipeWorkflow*
  ● *yieldsResult*
▼ associatedWith-Ingredient
  ● *hasContent*
  ● *hasIngredientKind*
  ● *hasIngredientStatus*
  ● *isIngredientOf*
  ● *processedBy*
  ● *enablesRecipeInstruction*

▼ associatedWith-RecipeInstruction
  ● *hasCookingDuration*
  ● *hasWorkDuration*
  ● *isInstructionOf*
  ● *producesResult*
  ● *requiresCookWare*
  ● *requiresIngredient*
▼ associatedWith-CookingStep
  ● *hasAssignedCookWare*
  ● *processesIngredient*

Fig. 6. Recipe Relations in the Ontology (Excerpt)

▼ PhysicalAspect
  ▼ SizeAspect
    ● LargeSizeAspect
    ● MediumSizeAspect
    ● SmallSizeAspect
    ● TinySizeAspect
  ▼ TemperatureAspect
    ▼ BurnerTemperature
      ● HighBurnerTemperature
      ● LowBurnerTemperature
      ● MediumBurnerTemperature
    ▶ OvenTemperature

▼ TextureAspect
  ▶ CookingTextureAspect
  ● GaseousTexture
  ▶ LiquidTexture
  ▼ SolidTexture
    ● FirmTexture
    ▼ HardTexture
      ● CrispTexture
      ● PowderedTexture
      ● ...
    ● SoftTexture
  ● ...

Fig. 7. PhysicalAspect Ontology (Excerpt)

CookWare. The environment contains all CookWare required (see Figs. 4, 5):

PreparationSurface e.g. a CuttingBoard;
PreparationDevice e.g. a FoodProcessor;
CookingDevice e.g. a Cooker with a Burner;
CookingContainer e.g. a Pan to put on the Burner;
CookingUtensil e.g. a KitchenKnife as a FoodCutter, a Whisk;
TableEquipment e.g. a Bowl;

PreparationDevices and CookingDevices have their own power supply and control.

CookWare is modeled as Container since it may contain other CookWare (such as a Pan on a Burner on top of a Cooker), or hold (part of) Ingredients (such as a Bowl, a KitchenKnife, or a CuttingBoard). Note that the required environment of CookWare and Ingredients is modelled with each RecipeInstruction (cf. Sec. 4.3).

BKB hardly uses a FoodProcessor, but cannot do without his ChineseChoppingKnife that doubles as a little plate for small pieces.

Details in a RecipeInstruction. Depending on the abilities of the cook, RecipeInstructions should be more or less detailed. An experienced chef might only need the list of ingredients and apply amounts according to experience, taste and creativity, while a beginner would need to know the exact amount (interval), which tools to use when, etc.

Moreover, RecipeInstructions vary according to the CookWare involved (a RoastInstruction might refine to a GrillInstruction or a RoastInOvenInstruction) or according to the cooking technique used (e.g. a FlipWithLidInstruction to either a TransferThenFlipInstruction or a FlipThenTransferInstruction, cf. Fig. 5), choosing an appropriate one during refinement (cf. Sec. 4.3).

In fact, a RecipeInstruction may be *implementedAs* a Recipe that is more detailed; in particular, it provides an expanded RecipeWorkflow (e.g. for a TransferThenFlipInstruction or FlipThenTransferInstruction). Several implementations may be provided when defining a new RecipeInstruction, giving different amounts of detail for different user profiles (e.g. for a beginner, cf. Sec. 4.3), which may then be used for adapting the interface displayed to the user (cf. Sec. 5.2).

We also expect that modelling a RecipeInstruction explicitly, instead of just having a piece of text, will ease automatic translation of recipes.

Recipe Workflow, Nested Sub-Recipes. A RecipeWorkflow is a sequence of RecipeInstructions, which relate to Ingredients and CookWare, and finally deliver a result that is potentially used as an Ingredient later on. Since a Recipe depends on its Ingredients, and an Ingredient may be the result of another Recipe (e.g. for a seasoning), we are in fact dealing with sub-Recipes inside a Recipe, see Fig. 4. Every sub-Recipe has a name on top referring to its result Ingredient(s), e.g. *FriedBacon, BaconFat*.

A sub-Recipe may be cut out of a Recipe to become an independent, self-contained Recipe, e.g. a Recipe for a seasoning such as *CrumbledBacon*. In the example recipe, it is purposely left unspecified whether Fat2, i.e. OilOrFat, should contain leftover (flavoring) *BaconFat*; this will only be possible, if it is scheduled to be prepared before CookedVegetables, and is anyway a choice of the cook.

The *relation* Recipe *contains* Recipe is a *partial order*, denoting the dependency of a recipe on another, whose result must be available as an ingredient (cf. also dependent cooking processes in Sec. 5.3). For the *ZucchiniFrittata* to be fried, the *EggMixture* must be ready; for the *EggMixture*, the *CookedVegetables* and the *Seasoning*. The order, in which the *CookedVegetables* and the *Seasoning* have to be prepared, is unspecified (and Mix is commutative); this leaves room for choice in the scheduling of CookingSteps later on.

The overall environment of CookWare involved in a RecipeWorkflow can be deduced from the RecipeInstructions used (cf. Sec. 4.3).

4.2   Generic Recipes, Recipe Development

When trying to find a suitable recipe, the user is faced with an overwhelming number, distributed over many portals, blogs, or web-pages on the internet. Being faced with restricted diets (cf. Sec. 3.1) aggravates the issue.

We hope to eventually provide a uniform (and standardised?) modelling and data base access, not only for information about food (cf. Sec. 2.2), but also recipes. This requires a standard recipe structure and representation (cf. Sec. 4.1) to allow an intelligent search and adaptation in the presence of diet constraints.

We are looking for a way to cluster recipe *variants* together, encouraging *creativity*. Ms. W. is famous for Apfel-, Topfen- *and* Gemüse-Strudel, cf. Sec. 7.

Variables, Parameter Abstraction. One way to make recipes *generic* (generalised, schematic) is to introduce a kind of *parameter abstraction* (compare CASL generics [12]; not yet available for OWL, cf. Sec. 2.2).

The *primary ingredient* in the *zucchini frittata* (cf. Sec. 4.1), courgette/zucchini, is more generally a vegetable, as seasonally available; but is it really? Can we generalise from CourgetteVegetable to Vegetable, i.e. just navigate upwards in the class hierarchy? No, not just any vegetable, e.g. no cabbage, but perhaps Cauliflower[3]. One proper *culinary* abstraction would be SquashVegetable, serving like a *variable* that can later be substituted by any product in a sub*class*.

To further generalize, an ingredient can be defined as a set of *alternatives* as if an implicit super-*class* was created (cf. Oil | Fat for OilOrFat), e.g.
CourgetteVegetable | FennelVegetable | SpinachVegetable | RadicchioVegetable
for the classic *frittata alla verdura*; even more generally,
SquashVegetable | FlowerVegetable | StalkVegetable | PotatoVegetable |
SpinachVegetable | RadicchioVegetable
and so on. StalkVegetable includes fennel; the latter two are special sub*classes* of LeafVegetable, which we want to avoid as it includes CabbageVegetable as well.

This abstraction, allowing seasonal variants and substitutions (cf. Sec. 4.1), and ample room for creativity (cf. Sec. 3.3) with a corresponding abstraction of

---

[3] *cauliflower*, the German *Blumenkohl*, is actually not a cabbage, but a FlowerVegetable.

culinary seasoning, includes some of Ms. W.'s favourites: the Sicilian *frittata di cavolfiore* (CauliflowerVegetable, anchovies and capers) and Umbrian *frittata ai tartufi neri* (PotatoVegetable, black truffles), a sister of the *Spanish omelette*.

4.3 Refinement

Stakeholders, Refinement Stages. When the user of a generic recipe deletes options or provides substitutions for individual adaptation (cf. Sec. 4.1), chooses among alternatives, or navigates down to a particular sub*class*, in fact when being *creative*, s/he becomes an editor of a derived recipe *variant* that is a *refinement* of the original one. Refinement for adaptation will happen in *stages* at various occasions, and the editors will be different *stakeholders* (or assume such roles) with different interests and, more importantly, different *profiles*:

basic author   providing general generic recipes
culinary author   creating recipes with individual culinary kicks
host   gathering and joining the guests' requirements
meal planner   planning recipes for courses and beverages
recipe planner   adapting recipes to the joint guests' requirements
shopper   adapting recipes to (seasonally) available ingredients
kitchen planner adapting recipes to CookWare available in the kitchen
scheduler   scheduling cooks and RecipeWorkflows
cook   adapting recipes to personal cooking abilities and preferences

Ms. W., as all experienced cooks, will assume all these roles at some time, and change between them. In particular, she prefers to do the shopping herself; she might want to change her mind about a recipe, since today's offer of a fresh seasonal vegetable is so attractive. However, when planning recipes with a derived shopping list for another person as shopper, she will have to be careful to be precise about generalizations and appropriate alternatives for ingredients, keeping the personal shopping profile of the shopper in mind (who might be inclined to choose what he likes, not necessarily in line with her wishes).

Recipe Design. The author of a recipe will be assisted by a special version of a recipe editor (cf. Sec. 5.1), allowing navigation in the *class* hierarchy.

Ms. W. will start with the RecipeInstruction for the Ingredient in focus (cf. Fig. 4). When choosing Bacon as an ingredient, a FryInstruction will be suggested (modelled via *enablesRecipeInstruction*), and Ms. W. will choose the FryCrispInstruction as a refinement. The FryCrispInstruction will be related to the CrispTextureAspect, and, as a FryInstruction, require medium hot OilOrFat in a Pan; this, in turn, will suggest a Burner with a MediumBurnerTemperature, and so on. RecipeInstructions and Ingredients are modelled with corresponding specialised attributes, enabling the RECIPE ASSISTANT to suggest appropriate choices.

Similarly, the other stakeholders will be able to navigate in the (generalised) hierarchy of attributes in their refinement process; not only Ingredients, but also RecipeInstructions and CookWare are generalised.

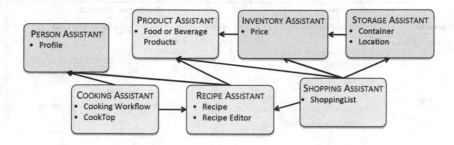

Fig. 8. Software Assistants and Use Relationship

The RECIPE ASSISTANT, as a "kitchen planner" prior to the actual cooking, will advise Ms. W. to use a NonStickPan for a Pan, since it knows, which Cook-Ware is preferred and available from her profile as a cook and the profile of the kitchen environment. BKB will get his beloved ChineseChoppingKnife.

Version and Change Management. It is important to record the whole development, a sequence of *refinements*, for future reference. Thus a new version is placed among a cluster of *variants*, sharing similar culinary properties.

Ms. W. may wish to revise previous decisions when re-using a recipe next time, omitting a particular dietary constraint, or cooking in a different kitchen. Her recipe variants are kept in a local, private repository.

5   Cooking Assistance

5.1   Software Assistants

Based on the modelling, several modular software assistants are presently under development to help Ms. W. in her tasks, cf. Fig. 8. The PERSON ASSISTANT manages profiles of stakeholders (cf. Sec. 4.3); the RECIPE ASSISTANT helps in the development of recipes, using the PRODUCT ASSISTANT and PERSON ASSISTANT; it generates a shopping list for the SHOPPING ASSISTANT, which, in turn, uses the PRODUCT ASSISTANT for information about food products, the INVENTORY ASSISTANT about their availability at home or in a shop, and the STORAGE ASSISTANT about their location.

When Ms. W. goes shopping and changes her mind about a recipe, the SHOPPING ASSISTANT will be able to trace back to the recipe, Ms. W. can adapt or change it, the shopping list is adjusted accordingly, and the INVENTORY ASSISTANT bears the availability of food products at home in mind; the PRODUCT ASSISTANT will help her choose alternatives or substitutions.

Consistency of Data Updates. The assistants (cf. Fig. 8) correspond to software modules linked to a central controller, which takes care of communication,

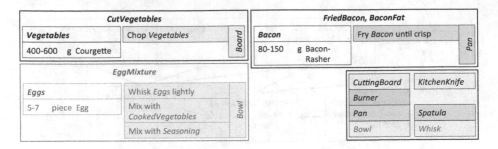

Fig. 9. CookTop View

e.g. interface modules responsible for user interaction, or utility modules for data base access. Assistant modules access data in the ontology (or associated data bases) via the controller; the controller, triggered by an interface module request, distributes the request to appropriate assistants, and forwards answers back to the interface module. The ontology is managed by the SHIP-Tool [13,15], which, apart from deductions with a standard reasoner, guarantees *consistency of data updates* generated by the processing, a unique feature. The ontology hides and abstracts from associated data bases. Since all the knowledge is represented in the ontology, the assistants only need a minimal data representation internally.

5.2   The CookTop, the Cooking Desktop

The CookTop is the touch-screen via which the cooking assistance processes communicate with the user, see Fig. 9. "Active" (sub)Recipes and CookingSteps, currently being processed, are displayed together with the required Ingredients and CookWare; already completed ones are not displayed any more, neither are those that are not enabled yet, for instance, because the required Ingredients are not yet ready as the result of other processes, or the CookWare is still in use. Once a CookingStep has been completed, the user touches the CookingStep box (or by clicking, voice interaction, etc.). This acknowledgement is recorded by the assistance processes and other possible CookingSteps become enabled. Enabled Recipes (and subsequent CookingSteps in a list) are displayed as gray; they are activated by a user's touch. Depending on the user's abilities and preferences, more or less information (e.g. associated CookWare or durations) is displayed.

5.3   Cooking Workflows, Processes

The RecipeWorkflow of a structured Recipe corresponds to a (partially ordered) tree of sequences of RecipeInstructions for the (sub)Recipes, cf. Sec. 4.1 and Fig. 4. The resulting CookingWorkflows prescribing the order of processing the RecipeInstructions, may be completely sequential, e.g. for an inexperienced cook, to do all preparation work first, and then cook strictly sequentially. However, there is a potential for parallel work by one cook (or more than one); the scheduling has to take different abilities and resulting prospective durations of workloads, preliminary preparation, actual cooking, settling and cooling phases, into account.

Process Abstractions. The assistance processes control the execution of the CookingWorkflow and can be described as *processes* in the SHIP-Tool at a high level of abstraction. The SHIP-Tool is based on a logical state representation modelling data as well as the state of the real world. States are modelled in Description Logics, which provides the semantic foundation for OWL used to model the recipes. A state consists of the defined *classes* and *relations*, and *instances* (individuals) modelling the state. Considering our running example (cf. Fig. 4): each Ingredient, CookWare, etc. is modelled as an *instance* of the respective *class* with relations to other *instances* as imposed by the class declarations and (constraint) definitions. In SHIP notation, this is expressed as follows

courgette: CourgetteVegetable, (courgette, cquant): hasIngredientQuantity

which represents that the *instance* courgette belongs to the class CourgetteVegetable, and courgette *hasIngredientQuantity* cquant. If relations are *functional* relations, then courgette.*hasIngredientQuantity* denotes the associated *instance*.

As modelling discipline we impose that all existential quantifiers have a witnessing *instance* in the ontology. For instance, CookingSteps always have at least one assigned CookWare, which is expressed by the subclass declaration CookingStep $\sqsubseteq$ $\exists$hasAssignedCookware . CookWare; if fry1 is a CookingStep, this imposes that there exists an *instance* in the ontology which is the assigned CookWare (cf. [13]). Available CookWare, the Recipe and instances of the specific Ingredients and quantities (fitting a specific number of persons) are modelled this way.

The assistance processes need to track the status of CookingSteps. To this end, we model the CookingStepStatus as StartedStatus or CompletedStatus. Ingredients necessary for the different CookingSteps and resulting from other CookingSteps create the dependencies between the CookingSteps, cf. Sec. 4.1; active CookingSteps depend on the availability of CookWare; all this information is encoded in an active CookingStep.

Based on the ontological state model, basic computation steps in SHIP are ontology updates which result in a new ontological state. The updates are restricted to *instances*, the definitions of *classes* and *relations* cannot be changed. Updates may result from the real world, such as, for instance, the user acknowledging that a specific CookingStep is completed. But updates can also be computing actions of the assistance processes, for instance to enable or initialise a new CookingStep, or to delete a completed cooking step. In SHIP, *actions* can be defined, which have ontological *preconditions*, checked on the current ontological state, and *effects* describing the update. Based on the actions as basic steps, named, recursive, parallel processes can be defined, used to describe the cooking assistance processes.

Consider the FryBacon step in Fig. 4. The corresponding cooking step assistance process is described in Fig. 10. While the process is presently written manually, we aim at automatic generation from the RecipeWorkflow, cf. Sect. 5.3.

```
1    process fryBacon (fat,bacon) = {
2      init F(fat.currentIngredientStatus:PreparedStatus and
                                        bacon.currentIngredientStatus:PreparedStatus);
3      fix pan:CookingContainer and pan:UnassignedCookWare and burner:Burner and
              burner:UnassignedCookWare;
4      createHeatupActivity(fat,pan,burner,:lowBurnerTemperature);
5      let d = fat.inv(rawIngredient)
6          prod = d.producedIngredient in
7      init F((fat,pan):at and (fat,:lowBurnerTemperature):hasTemperature and
8        (pan,:lowBurnerTemperature):hasTemperature and
9        prod.currentIngredientStatus:PreparedStatus);
10     closeActivity(d);
11     createFryActivity(bacon,pan,burner,:lowBurnerTemperature,:crisp);
12     let f = bacon.inv(rawIngredient)
13         crispbacon = f.producedIngredient in
14     init F((crispbacon,pan):containedIn and crispbacon.currentIngredientStatus:
              PreparedStatus);
15     closeActivity(f);
16     createRemovalActivity(crispbacon,pan);
17     let doRemove = crispbacon.inv(rawIngredient)
18         storage = doRemove.requiredCookWare in
19     init F((crispbacon,storage):containedIn);
20     closeActivity(doremove) }
```

Fig. 10. Assistance Process for FryBacon

The assistance process is parameterized over the specific ingredients `fat` and `bacon` of the cooking step. It then first waits until these are available, i.e. have PreparedStatus. To this end the SHIP language allows to specify linear temporal logic formulas over ontology expressions, which are monitored over the evolution of the ontological state. We use the standard temporal connectives[4] that allow to start a monitor (line 2) waiting for an ontological state, where both ingredients have PreparedStatus. Once this holds, the process execution continues and we query the current ontological state for unassigned `pan` and `burner` (line 3) and execute the action initialising the first subactivity, i.e. heating up the `fat` in the `pan` on the `burner` (line 4).

Now the information is in the ontology and can be presented to the user on the CookTop interface. We collect the *instance* d encoding the activity, but querying the ontological state for the *instance*, of which `fat` is the `rawIngredient` (line 5), as well as the *instance* `prod` introduced to denote the product of the heatup step. Next we wait until the `fat` is in the `pan` and has the right temperature, which the user or some sensing device has indicated, and the product is prepared. The activity is now closed by the action `closeActivity`, which removes the *instance* d from the ontological state. Subsequently the next subactivity is started, which

---

[4] F = Eventually (Future), G = Globally, U = Until.

```
1    monitor controlCooking () =
2      G(all s:CookingStep . ((s,r):fromRecipeInstruction and r:CookingInstruction and
3        (s,p):requiresCookWare and p:CookingDevice and
4        (p,ct):currentCookingTemperature and (p,rt):hasCookingTemperature)
5        => (ct =rt U s.yieldsResult.currentIngredientStatus:PreparedStatus))
6
7    process monitorCooking () = {
8      try { init controlCooking }
9      catch {
10       forall s:CookingStep and (s,r):fromRecipeInstruction and r:CookingInstruction and
11         (r,p):requiresCookWare and p:CookingDevice and
12         (p,ct):currentCookingTemperature and (p,rt):hasCookingTemperature and
13         r.yieldsResult.currentIngredientStatus:UnpreparedStatus and
14         ct != rt => if (ct < rt) signalHeatUp(s,p)
15                            else signalCoolDown(s,p);
16                            init F(ct =rt ⟨|⟩ not(!s))
17       }; monitorCooking}
```

Fig. 11. Monitor and Monitor Process

consists of actually frying the `bacon` until it is `crisp` and finally the subactivity
to remove it from the `pan`. Again, these subactivities follow the same patterns
of (i) initializing the sub-activity possibly preceding a monitor waiting for the
availability of Ingredients and CookWare, (ii) a monitor waiting for the user or
a sensor in the real world to acknowledge completion of the subactivity, and
(iii) closing the subactivity.

For each CookingStep of the Recipe we have respective actions and assistance
processes, i.e., `cutVegetables`, `fryBacon` and `eggMixture`. The dependencies
between these are managed by the Ingredients and CookWare when they have
been produced or become available. Hence the overall assistance process is the
parallel composition of these three processes

cutVegetables(courgettes) ⟨|⟩ fryBacon(fat,bacon) ⟨|⟩ eggMixture(eggs)

The parallel composition is an interleaving of the basic actions of the different
processes, as they all operate over the same ontological state.

Monitoring Processes. The SHIP-Tool provides the possibility to define monitors tracking ontological state evolutions, to be used alongside processes to observe the environment and react accordingly. An update violating a running
monitor causes a failure in the process semantics, which can be caught like an
exception, and processes can be defined to react. Furthermore, it is possible
to specify general properties not tied to a specific process, but rather global
invariants (in fact, the "common sense of cooking").

As an example consider the monitor controlCooking in Fig. 11. It specifies that in each state, whenever there is an active CookingStep s derived from a RecipeInstruction r that is a CookingInstruction (in particular, a FryInstruction), then the required CookingDevice p keeps the required temperature (its current temperature ct is equal to the required temperature rt associated with the CookingDevice in the CookingInstruction) until the resulting Ingredient is prepared.

This monitor can be used in a monitorCooking process, running in parallel to all other assistance processes, that monitors the invariant, signals the respective action to take in case of a violation (heatUp or coolDown) to the user, and, once the invariant is restored, recurses and resumes monitoring.

6 Conclusion

Status of the Modelling and Implementation. Structuring and modelling an intricately interwoven domain such as *Cooking* is indeed a formidable task. Presently, we do not aim for completeness, but for a very substantial coverage that allows the demonstration of nontrivial examples. As the ontology is going to be published in the public domain, we hope for community contributions.

At the same time, we plan to cooperate with other groups. The proper modelling of nutrition impairing diseases or nutrition intolerances (allergies, incompatibilities), cf. Sec. 3.1, requires medical expertise and will be a challenge in itself (see also [31,10,11]); we have only made a first attempt so far.

Supporting the CookTop and the actual cooking process by intelligent tools and an intelligent monitoring environment is another direction, where we want to bring in our expertise connected with DFKI's Bremen Ambient Assisted Living Lab, BAALL, and SHIP [14], and combine it with that of the sister Lab at DFKI Saarbrücken, focussed on smart kitchen objects and appliances.

Several Master's and Diploma's theses [20,23,24,30] are under way to complete the modelling, the deduction apparatus, and to develop prototype implementations for the corresponding assistants, to be available as web-apps online.

Cooking with Robots. While the instruction of an experienced cook should be quite terse, a beginner, or an elderly person with slight dementia, needs detailed instruction and detailed sequencing, see Sec. 4.1. It is interesting to note that a cooking robot needs a very similar, if not the same, level of detail to model cooking. We expect to share and combine our modelling with that for robots, e.g. those at Michael Beetz's lab at Universität Bremen.

7 Dedication to Martin Wirsing's Health and Well-Being

How can *Formal Modelling for Cooking Assistance* contribute to Martin Wirsing's health and well-being?

The modelling and methodology described above cite many notions and concepts that have been in the focus of Martin's research on *Formal Methods*: loose (under)specification, abstraction and refinement, processes, temporal logic, etc. He has also always appreciated interesting application domains; now Formal Methods and Cooking come together!

It is, no doubt, primarily his wife Sabine's, i.e. *Ms. W.*'s, *excellent cooking* that is responsible for Martin's good health and well-being. We, as friends, have had the pleasure of sampling it in jolly company; definitely a source of well-being for us, presumably also for Martin, and hopefully for Sabine as well.[5] However, we are getting older and have all sorts of health and other constraints[6] of what we can or wish to eat — so how is Sabine going to cook when a group of us is being invited together?[7]

We hope that Sabine, and others, will eventually get some assistance from the CookTop based on the modelling — and that Martin's good health and well-being will last for many more years to come!

References

1. Barcoo, www.barcoo.com
2. DOLCE - Descriptive Ontology for Linguistic and Cognitive Engineering, www.loa.istc.cnr.it/old/DOLCE.html
3. DUL - DOLCE+DnS Ultralite ontology - Ontology Design Patterns (ODP), www.ontologydesignpatterns.org/ont/dul/
4. EuroFIR AISBL, www.eurofir.org
5. LanguaL — the International Framework for Food Description, www.langual.org
6. OWL Web Ontology Language - Use Cases and Requirements - W3C Recommendation 10 February 2004, www.w3.org/TR/2004/REC-webont-req-20040210/
7. QUDT - Quantities, Units, Dimensions and Data Types Ontologies, www.qudt.org/
8. WikiFood – Knowing what's inside, www.wikifood.eu/wikifood/struts/welcome.do
9. Ahn, Y.-Y., Ahnert, S.E., Bagrow, J.P., Barabási, A.-L.: Flavor network and the principles of food pairing. Scientific Reports 1, 196 (January 2011)
10. Arens, A., Schnadt, S., Feidert, F., Mösges, R., Roesch, N., Herbst, R.: Preferences and satisfaction of food allergy sufferers using internet resources. Clinical and Translational Allergy 3(3), 126 (2013)
11. Arens-Volland, A., Roesch, N., Feidert, F., Harpes, P., Mösges, R.: Change frequency of ingredient descriptions and free-of labels of food items concern food allergy sufferers. Allergy (European Journal of Allergy and Clinical Immunology) 65, 92 (2010)
12. Astesiano, E., Bidoit, M., Krieg-Brückner, B., Kirchner, H., Mosses, P.D., Sannella, D., Tarlecki, A.: CASL - the Common Algebraic Specification Language. Theoretical Computer Science 286, 153–196 (2002)
13. Autexier, S., Hutter, D.: Constructive DL update and reasoning for modeling and executing the orchestration of heterogenous processes. In: Eiter, T., Glimm, B., Kazakov, Y., Krötzsch, M. (eds.) Informal Proceedings of the 26th International Workshop on Description Logics, Ulm, Germany, vol. 1014, pp. 501–512. Technical University of Aachen (RWTH) (July 2013)

---

[5] With the generic vegetable omelette abstraction of Sec. 4.2, will Sabine get new ideas for her famous vegetable strudel, so much appreciated by their friends?

[6] Martin, Sabine and family of course excluded.

[7] Many of us friends can appreciate such problems as enthusiastic amateur cooks.

14. Autexier, S., Hutter, D., Mandel, C., Stahl, C.: SHIP-Tool Live: Orchestrating the Activities in the Bremen Ambient Assisted Living Lab. In: Augusto, J.C., Wichert, R., Collier, R., Keyson, D., Salah, A.A., Tan, A.-H. (eds.) AmI 2013. LNCS, vol. 8309, pp. 269–274. Springer, Heidelberg (2013)

15. Autexier, S., Hutter, D., Stahl, C.: An Implementation, Execution and Simulation Platform for Processes in Heterogeneous Smart Environments. In: Augusto, J.C., Wichert, R., Collier, R., Keyson, D., Salah, A.A., Tan, A.-H. (eds.) AmI 2013. LNCS, vol. 8309, pp. 3–18. Springer, Heidelberg (2013)

16. Bateman, J.A., Castro, A., Normann, I., Pera, O., Garcia, L., Villaveces, J.-M.: OASIS Common hyper-ontological framework (COF). EU FP7 Project OASIS – Open architecture for Accessible Services Integration and Standardization Deliverable D1.2.1. Bremen University, Bremen (January 2010)

17. Becker, W.: Towards a CEN Standard on Food Data. European Journal of Clinical Nutrition 64, S49–S52 (2010)

18. Burgos, M., Martínez-Victoria, I., Milá, R., Farrán, A., Farré, R., Ros, G., Yago, M., Audi, N., Santana, C., Millán, L., et al.: Building a unified Spanish food database according to EuroFIR specifications. Food Chemistry 113(3), 784–788 (2009)

19. Caviezel, R., Vilgis, T.A.: Foodpairing — Harmonie und Kontrast. FONA (2012)

20. Ghomsi Nokam, S.: A Food Ontology for the Assistance of Shopping and Cooking. Master's thesis, Universität Bremen (in preparation) (in German)

21. Ireland, J., Møller, A.: What's new in LanguaL? Procedia Food Science 2, 117–121 (2013)

22. Ireland, J.D., Møller, A.: Review of international food classification and description. Journal of Food Composition and Analysis 13(4), 529–538 (2000)

23. Kolloge, P.: Modelling Dietary Restrictions. Master's thesis, Universität Bremen (in preparation) (in German)

24. Kozha, D.: Shopping Assistance from the Kitchen Cabinet to the Supermarket Shelf. Master's thesis, Universität Bremen (in preparation) (in German)

25. Kutz, O., Mossakowski, T., Lücke, D.: Carnap, Goguen, and the Hyperontologies: Logical Pluralism and Heterogeneous Structuring in Ontology Design. Logica Universalis 4(2), 255–333 (2010), Special Issue on 'Is Logic Universal?'

26. Lo, K.: Chinese Cooking and Eating for Health. Mayflower Granada Publ. (1979)

27. Møller, A., Unwin, I.D., Becker, W., Ireland, J.: EuroFIR's food databank systems for nutrients and bioactives. Trends in Food Science & Technology 18(8), 428–433 (2007)

28. Mossakowski, T., Kutz, O., Codescu, M., Lange, C.: The distributed ontology, modeling and specification language. In: Vescovo, C.D., Hahmann, T., Pearce, D., Walther, D. (eds.) WoMo 2013. CEUR-WS online proceedings, vol. 1081 (2013)

29. Pennington, J.A., Butrum, R.R.: Food descriptions using taxonomy and the LanguaL system. Trends in Food Science & Technology 2, 285–288 (1991)

30. Rink, M.: Ontology Based Product Configuration Based on User Requirements. Master's thesis, Universität Bremen (in preparation)

31. Roesch, N., Arens, A., Feidert, F., Herbst, R., Mösges, R.: Computerised identification of allergens in food ingredient descriptions. Allergy: European Journal of Allergy and Clinical Immunology 64, 363–364 (2009)

32. Snae, C., Bruckner, M.: Foods: a food-oriented ontology-driven system. In: 2nd IEEE International Conference on Digital Ecosystems and Technologies, DEST 2008, pp. 168–176. IEEE (2008)

A Framework for Defining and Comparing Modelling Methods

Gianna Reggio[1], Egidio Astesiano[1], and Christine Choppy[2]

[1] DIBRIS – Università di Genova, Italy
[2] Université Paris 13, Sorbonne Paris Cité, LIPN, CNRS UMR 7030, France

Abstract. There are a huge number of scientific papers and reports intended for practitioners, not forgetting whole books and websites, presenting modelling methods in the field of software development. Thus, many questions naturally arise concerning both the nature of method itself (say, e.g. its scope and intended use) and the relationships between different methods, to compare them and choosing the most appropriate for a specific application. Here we present a preliminary attempt at proposing a "modelling method framework" suitable for presenting the constituents, both technical and methodological, of a method in an organized and possibly precise way. The purpose of our framework is to provide a setting for answering the above mentioned questions in a systematic and well-founded way. We will illustrate our proposed framework using some existing methods for modelling service-based systems.

At the end of the paper we offer a short tribute to a long standing friendship with Martin.

1   Introduction

Nowadays, in the field of software development, the issue of modelling is well developed and a number of modelling notations/languages have been designed together with methods for their use. Having contributed to the work in the area for a while, we quite often have experienced an uneasy feeling when trying to identify our own methods in comparison with some existent ones. Indeed, we could not find a clearly defined, less to say commonly agreed, framework for defining and compare modelling methods. Thus, we have taken the occasion provided by this celebration of an outstanding contributor to the field for raising that issue and offer a preliminary proposal for addressing it.

Let us start by clarifying the term denoting the topic of this article: *modelling method*. First we recall a reasonable definition of *model*: "*A model is a representation of some aspects of an entity (either as-it-is or to-be) to be built for a specific aim*" then, the definition of a *method*: "*a way of doing something, a careful or organized plan that controls the way something is done*." So, *modelling method* means "a way to represent some aspects of an entity (either as-it-is or to-be) to be built for a specific aim".

There are a huge number of technical scientific papers and reports intended for practitioners, not forgetting whole books and websites, presenting modelling

R. De Nicola and R. Hennicker (Eds.): Wirsing Festschrift, LNCS 8950, pp. 377–408, 2015.

methods in the field of software development. Thus many questions concerning modelling methods naturally arise which are important to answer in a systematic and well-founded way, obviously after having decided whether the questions are sensible (i.e. they admit an answer or better a factual answer not just based on an opinion or a feeling). We list below some typical questions, all found either in scientific papers or in technical documentation, forums or mailing lists.

- Questions about *choosing a method*
  - Is modelling method A more appropriate than method B in a given context?
  - Which are the relationships between modelling methods A and B?
  - Does the modelling method A have any novelty with respect to method B?
  - Does the model of X produced following modelling method A contain more than/less than/the same information as the model of X produced following method B?
  - Is there a real difference between two modelling methods, i.e. can one model something in a way that cannot be done in the other, or instead might they be slightly modified to eliminate such a difference?
  - Could the models produced following modelling method A be converted into models produced following method B?

- Questions about the *key features of a modelling method*
  - Is modelling method A adequate for a specific case?
  - Is modelling method A mature?
  - Is modelling method A operative?
  - What do I have to do to learn modelling method A?
  - What do I have to do to apply modelling method A to a specific case?
  - Is there any tool support for modelling method A?

- Questions about *presenting a modelling method*
  - I have designed a new modelling method, now which is the best way to present it?
  - Is there any motivation for designing modelling method A?
  - Is there any difference between a modelling method and a modelling notation, or indicating a notation is enough to propose a modelling method?
  - How can I model X using notation N? Is this model of X prepared using notation N correct? (these kinds of questions appear very frequently in forums on the web and in mailing lists, and most frequently concern the UML).

As a contrasting remark, we note that questions of the form:

"Is notation N better than/can be easily replaced by notation M?"

"Should I use notation N or notation M in the case . . . ?"

are in our opinion ill-formed in the context of modelling methods, since only methods should be compared/related, not the notations only; indeed a smart method based on a simple notation may be more appropriate than a poor method based on a powerful notation.

To provide a setting for answering some of the previous questions, our starting consideration is that every modelling method, used as a tool for building (a model in this case), should be qualified, as any other similar tool, by a "fact sheet", so to speak, following of course a peculiar pattern expressing in its structure the essential ingredients of a modelling method. Such fact sheet will be suitable to evaluate/compare/... modelling methods in the same way we look at the fact sheet about different versions of a product/of a software to decide which is the best choice for our specific needs.

Our aim is a preliminary attempt at proposing a "framework" for presenting a modelling method in an organized and possibly precise way considering all its main constituents, both technical and methodological and their mutual relationships. In our view presenting a method following our framework should result in a fact sheet about the method covering all its main aspects. We say "main" aspects purposely, since our framework does not pretend to be complete for a number of reasons, first of all being a preliminary proposal, but also because we believe that ideally there should be a framework agreed upon by the community of the researchers in the field. For example, our current framework does not address the issue of "maturity" nor the one of "model quality". It is easy to imagine a number of extensions/enrichments, as well as refinements related either to a specific modelling subject or for capturing specific aspects, and thus making finer comparisons.

The core of the paper consists in providing our framework, with its components and their relationships. Then, to make more understandable that idea and, to some extent, to exemplify its use, we have put at work our framework considering the specific field of service-based system modelling. We could have chosen a different topic, e.g. business processes, but we have selected this specific context first of all because we are familiar with it to some extent, since we have developed some modelling methods for service-based systems, and also because many proposals are available in the literature with either similar aspects (e.g. they use the UML) or very different ones (e.g. the models are intended for formal analysis of some specific aspects or to be automatically transformed into code). We have selected several proposals in the literature, and then we have tried to present the chosen modelling techniques following our framework. We have restricted ourselves to consider approaches that are called formal at least in the sense of the syntactical level, i.e. where a notation or a specification language is used.

The roots of this work are to be found in "Formalism and Method" [2], a paper by two of the authors (originally an invited talk at TAPSOFT '97). There we were trying to distinguish and, to some extent, deemphasize the formal from other relevant aspects within a method for software development. In particular we have introduced the concept of "modelling" in its restricted meaning of connecting the target item to its formal representation. A natural evolution of those ideas was the introduction of what we have baptized well-founded methods [3], namely those methods which hide the difficulties of the formal aspects from the developers, while being grounded in solid formal foundations. And we find very appropriate to conclude this introduction acknowledging a realization at a large scale of these and similar ideas in the SENSORIA project[1], both in its overall structure and in many presentations by its leader Martin Wirsing.

---

[1] www.sensoria-ist.eu/

The paper is structured as follows. Sect. 2 introduces the modelling method framework, then its constituents are presented in Sect. 3 (Method Definition part) and 4 (Operational aspects), followed by some considerations on relating methods in Sect. 5. Related work is in Sect. 6, whereas conclusions and future developments are in Sect. 7.

2   A Modelling Method Framework

The proposed framework consists of a conceptual model of the modelling methods, exploiting their main constituents and their mutual relationships; from it we can then derive a way to collect all relevant information about a method, and to present it in a structured/organized way allowing to grasp all its aspects, facilitating the understanding of its features and the comparison with other methods.

The conceptual model of the modelling methods is described by means of a UML class diagram[2], shown in Fig. 1, and commented below. Note that an instance of Models is a set of models, and similarly, an instance of Items is a set of items.

- Items, the set of items to be modelled.
- Notation, the language used to represent the models (e.g. UML, BPMN, basic place-transition Petri nets, linear temporal logic, and description logic).
- Models, the set of models that can be produced using Notation.
- Eligible Models, the subset of Models used by the method (a constraint in Fig. 1 expresses that eligible models are included in models).
- Modelling, a binary *relationship* between the modelled items and the eligible models, linking the items with the (eligible) models "modelling" them.
- Intended Use of Models, the reason for doing the modelling and in which context (e.g. automatic generation of code for mobile applications, simulation of business processes, automatic verification of properties of protocols, documentation of object-oriented programs
- Tool Support, the available software tools to support the production and the use of the models (e.g. only editing tools, no tool at all).
- User Guidance, the *guidelines* driving the modeller in the model production.

The constituents of a method are categorized in two groups (cf. Fig. 1):

- *Method definition*: they are the essential ingredients to define the modelling, what is modelled (Items), by means of what (Notation, Models, Eligible Models), and how (Modelling).
- *Operational aspects*: they concern the support to the task of performing the modelling: why (Intended Use of Models), in which way (User Guidance), and whether can be supported by software tools (Tool Support). These constituents are optional (see the multiplicities [0..1] and * in Fig. 1 on the associations connecting them with the modelling methods), whenever they are all present we can say that the method has been made operative.

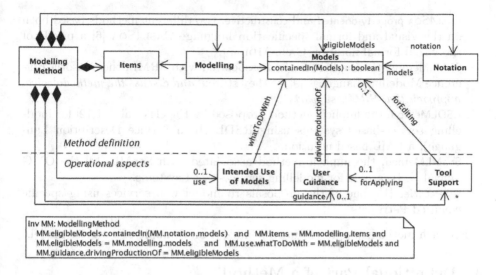

Fig. 1. Modelling Method Conceptual Model

Using our *modelling method framework* to present a method simply requires to explicitly provide all its constituents as presented before, and summarized in Table 1.

Table 1. How present a Modelling Method (* denotes that the part is mandatory)

Items *	
Notation *	
Models *	
Eligible Models *	
Modelling *	
Intended Use of Models	
Tool Support	
User Guidance	

We illustrate in the next two sections the various constituents of a method appearing in Fig. 1 by exemplifying them on the following modelling methods for service-based systems. Some of them are explicitly presented as methods, while for the others we consider the implicit method subsumed by the documents presenting a notation.

- PreciseSoa [5], a method to model service-based systems based on a very controlled and guided use of a UML profile, to overcome the fact that the UML offers a huge number of diagrams and constructs, and many have no well-defined semantics.

---

[2] We omit the multiplicity of an association whenever it is equal to 1.

- CASL4SOA property-oriented and constructive, two different methods based both on the visual and formal specification language CASL4SOA [6] a profile of the visual formal notation CASL-MDL [5].
- SRMLMethod, the implicit method associated with SRML, the Sensoria Reference Modelling Language [9], as they state: *"and discuss the methodological approach that SRML supports"*.
- RSDLMethod, the implicit method proposed by Engels et al. [11,12] for modelling service-based systems using RSDL (Rich Service Description Language), a UML based notation.
- SoaMLMethod, the implicit method associated with SoaML [14] the OMG official UML profile for modelling service-based systems.
- WSPetriNet [13] one of the proposals to model web services using specific coloured Petri nets.

For each method, we present in Appendix A an example of a service model.

3   Definitional Part of a Method

Here we introduce the constituents contributing to the method definition, precisely Items, Notation, Models, Eligible Models and Modelling.

3.1   The Items

The *items* to be modelled are one of the key ingredients of a modelling method, and to have clearly in mind what they are is fundamental to define an effective method. It is not sufficient to speak generically of service-based systems, SOA systems, business processes, businesses, cyber-physical systems, cloud, ...; first of all because there is no unique standard way to intend consider such things, second because those things may have different aspects and features, and it is not mandatory for a modelling method to consider all of them (e.g. in some cases the performance is of paramount importance for a business process whereas in other cases is completely irrelevant). So the method developers should determine which are the items that they want to model and which are their relevant features.

A clearly written and well-structured natural language text may be a sensible way to present the items, and indeed in [2] we followed this idea. Now, we propose instead to present the items in a more precise way by means of a *conceptual model*, which may be visually presented by means of a UML class diagram.

Notice however that the conceptual model of the items, that it is also the perceived/assumed/supported view of them, may be biased by the design of the modelling method; e.g. there is not "The Conceptual Model" of enterprise applications as well as there is not "The Definition" of such kind of software systems[3].

---

[3] See here, for example, some existing definitions of enterprise application: www.webopedia.com/TERM/E/enterprise_application.html, en.wikipedia.org/wiki/Enterprise_software, and msdn.microsoft.com/en-us/library/aa267045%28v=vs.60%29.aspx.

Let us now see how the selected sample modelling methods consider the items.

PreciseSoa, CASL4SOA property-oriented and constructive: Items. The items in the case of these three methods are service-based systems, and we report here the part of their description concerning the services.

A *service* is characterized by an interface, a contract, and a semantics.

The *interface* provides the static information needed to interact with the service. A service interface is conceptually seen as a set of "in" and "out" messages, where each message is characterized by a name and a list of typed parameters; the in-messages are used to require the service functionalities from the service provider and the out-messages to answer such requests.

The *service contract* defines which are the allowed interactions between who uses the service and who provides it.

The *service semantics* defines which are the functionalities offered by the service. We assume that a service is able to act over a portion of the real world (that we call the *realm* of the service); it may modify such realm as the result of receiving an in-message from a service user, and it may send out-messages to the user of the service depending on the current status of the realm. Thus, the semantics of a service consists of a description of the realm, of how the in-messages may modify it, and how the out-messages may depend on it.

Fig. 2 summarizes this conception of services by means of a conceptual model.

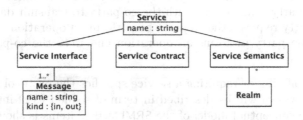

Fig. 2. PreciseSoa, CASL4SOA property-oriented and constructive: Items (conceptual model fragment)

SRMLMethod: Items. The items are service-based systems as intended in the context of *Service-Oriented Computing (SOC)*[4]. Differently from the component based paradigm, a system in SOC is considered as *"an evolving universe of software applications that service providers publish so that they can be discovered*

---

[4] *"A new computational paradigm in which interactions are no longer based on fixed or programmed exchanges between specific parties – what is known as clientship in object-oriented programming – but on the provisioning of services by external providers that are procured on the fly subject to a negotiation of service level agreements (SLAs). In SOC, the processes of discovery and selection of services are not coded (at design time) as part of the applications that implement business activities, but performed by the middleware according to functional and non-functional requirements (SLAs)."* [9].

by (and bound to) business activities as they execute. For instance, if documents need to be exchanged as part of a loan application, the bank may rely on an external courier service instead of imposing a fixed one. In this case, a courier service would be discovered for each loan application that is processed, possibly taking into account the address to which the documents need to be sent, speed of delivery, reliability, and so on. However, the added flexibility provided through SOC comes at a price – dynamic interactions impose the overhead of selecting the co-party at each invocation – which means that the choice between invoking a service and calling a component is a decision that needs to be taken according to given business goals", again from [9].

From this excerpt we can see how in this case there is a strong emphasis on the fact that services must be published and discovered dynamically. Another relevant feature of the services supported by SRMLMethod concerns the interactions between who provides and who uses a service, that may be of different kinds, precisely:

- Receive&Send, the interaction is initiated by the co-party, which expects a reply. The co-party does not block while waiting for the reply.
- Send & Receive, the interaction is initiated by the party and expects a reply from its co-party. While waiting for the reply, the party does not block.
- Receive, the co-party initiates the interaction and does not expect a reply.
- Send, the party initiates the interaction and does not expect a reply.
- Ask, the party synchronizes with the co-party to obtain data.
- Reply, the party synchronizes with the co-party to transmit data.
- Tell, the party requests the co-party to perform an operation and blocks.
- Perform, the party performs an operation and frees the co-party that requested it.

A party either offering or requiring a service specifies the protocol for accessing to that service, which will be described in term of sequences of interactions. A fragment of the conceptual model of the SRMLMethod items is shown in Fig. 3.

RSDLMethod: Items. A service-based system in the context of RSDLMethod is intended as a set of partners that offer and require services in a common "service

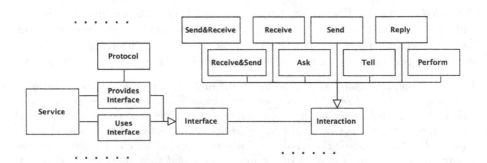

Fig. 3. SRMLMethod: Items (conceptual model fragment)

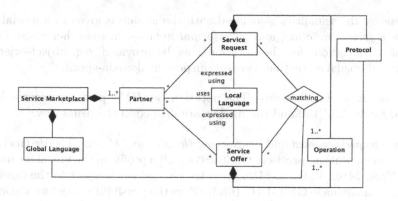

Fig. 4. RSDLMethod Items: conceptual model

marketplace", where requests will be matched by suitable offers (a specific matching mechanism based on ontologies is described in detail in [11]). The service offers and requests are described using some "local language", and each local language should be mapped to a global language specific of each marketplace; Fig. 4 shows a conceptual models of such systems (the diamond represent a UML ternary relationships).

SoaMLMethod: Items. The SoaML specification [14] (in section 3.1 "Introduction to SoaML") also introduces the underlying view of service-based systems by means of textual description (the items are quite similar to those of PreciseSoa, indeed we took inspiration from them).

WSPetriNet: Items. The items in this case are the web services as intended in the WSDL (Web Services Description Language) specification by W3C[5].

3.2   The Notation and the Models

We have decided to use here the term *notation* but, in different communities, various synonyms may be used, such as *modelling language, specification language* and *description language*. To propose a method, some appropriate documentation on the selected notation should be provided, for example user manuals.

As usual a notation should be defined by giving the set of artifacts – that we call *models* – that can be produced using it, and a description of their intended meaning (*semantics*); for example, for the UML or a UML profile, the models are defined by a metamodel accompanied by well-formedness constraints, and the semantics amounts to a natural language description of their meaning; whereas for a formal textual specification language, the models (i.e. specifications) may defined using a BNF grammar plus a type checking mechanism, and a denotational semantics may be available.

---

[5] http://www.w3schools.com/Webservices/ws_wsdl_intro.asp

Whenever the semantics associated with the models is given in a formal way we have a *formal notation*, and an *informal notation* in the other cases. Other relevant qualifications for the notation may be provided, e.g. object-oriented, agent-based, visual or textual, general purpose or domain-specific.

PreciseSoa: Notation and Models. The notation is a UML profile presented in [6] inspired by SoaML [14], and the models are defined in the usual way.

CASL4SOA property-oriented and constructive: Notation and Models. The two methods use the same notation, precisely CASL4SOA [6,4] a profile of the visual formal notation CASL-MDL [5]. CASL-MDL provides a visual counterpart to the algebraic specification language CASL-LTL [16]. It offers the possibility to define static and dynamic datatypes (where the behavior of the latter is represented by a labelled transition tree) introduced by means of type diagrams (visually presenting the various types and their mutual relationships, such as refinement); the semantics of the static and of the dynamic types may defined axiomatically by constraints (first-order many sorted branching-time with edge temporal formulas) or constructively by conditional rules and by interaction machines (a specific form of state-labelled transitions diagrams), respectively. The models are a collection of type definitions.

SRMLMethod: Notation and Models. The notation is the formal visual-textual specification language SRML [9], and the models are all possible specifications written using SRML.

RSDLMethod: Notation and Models. The RSDLMethod notation is obviously RSDL [11], and the form of the models of the services is given in Fig. 5.

A service model contains an ontology (represented by means of a UML class diagram) defining the local language, a description of the service operations,

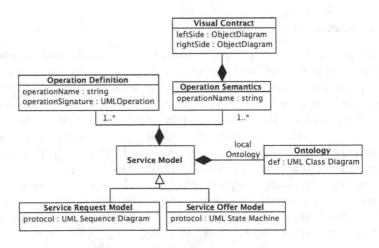

Fig. 5. RSDLMethod: Models (metamodel fragment)

where each operation is described by a signature following the WSDL standard (but represented by means of a UML operation signature), and by a visual contract specifying its semantics (expressed by a pair of object diagrams showing the situation before and after the operation call). Then, the service offer and request models differ in the way the protocol for accessing the service is described: by means of a UML sequence diagram in the case of a request and by means of UML state machine in the case of an offer.

SoaMLMethod: Notation and Models. The notation is SoaML which is a UML profile defined in [14]. The models are all the models built using such profile.

WSPetriNet: Notation and Models. The notation, SWN, is defined as an extension of coloured Petri nets with labels (that are operation names) on transitions. SWN is also a restriction of coloured Petri nets since it requires to distinguish three set of places, two special control places (initial and final), together with restrictions on the marking that makes it straightforward to associate a workflow net with an SWN. While it is not in the definition of SWN, they associate a polarity function to transitions to reflect the fact that they represent an action sending/receiving messages or not. Then, a notion of well-structuredness is defined, in relationship with the well structuredness of the associated workflow net - some constraints on how should be merged parallel branches initiated by an AND (resp. OR).

The models are coloured Petri nets of this notation SWN.

3.3 The Eligible Models and the Modelling

These two method constituents are strictly related and we present them together in this subsection.

In general not all the models provided by a notation are eligible[6] to be used by a method. For instance, the UML class, object and sequence diagrams are enough to model sequential Java programs, while the *until* and *next* temporal logic combinators are adequate to specify simple protocols, and algebraic specification whose axioms are positive conditional formula are sufficient to specify in a constructive way data structures. Our framework requires to explicitly define which are the models of the chosen notation that, following the method indication, will be the result of the chosen items modelling. Thus, the Eligible Models (technically a subset of the notation models) are another constituent of a modelling method.

Here a natural objection arises: "trying to determine which are the eligible models is losing time, just use what you need and forget the fact that there are other models around". We think that trying to determine the eligible models may be useful for the following reasons:

- the eligible models may have a well-defined semantics whereas it may be problematic to define it for other models;

---

[6] From Merriam-Webster: able to be chosen for something.

- a convenient tool support may be available only for the eligible models (e.g. a theorem prover working only for algebraic specifications built using positive conditional axioms);
- the modeller may save time by learning only the subset of the notation needed for the eligible models;
- the quality of the produced models may improve, because "bad" models are not eligible (e.g. if only UML classes with private attributes are eligible, then there is no way to violate the encapsulation principle);
- the time needed to produce a model is reduced, since the modeller has to look for the model to be produced in a restricted universe (e.g. all the 14 UML diagram types may be used versus only class, object and sequence diagrams may be used, and the latter have to be built using only the cycle and alternative combinators);
- the method designer is obliged to consider explicitly if and how to use the various constructs of the selected notation.

Clearly, there are cases where the models provided by a notation coincide with those used by a specific modelling method, especially when the notation is a Domain Specific Language, that has been designed just for being used in exactly a unique modelling method.

The *modelling* is the key ingredient of a modelling method, indeed it defines how the modelling is performed. It consists in a description (that may be just a natural language text) of a binary relationship between the items and the eligible models, usually given by stating how the features of the items are represented by the eligible models parts and, vice versa, i.e. how the parts of the eligible models represent the features of the items.

There are no specific constraints on the form of the modelling. In general it is not mandatory that the modelling is total, i.e. that it provides a means to represent all the items and all their aspects. A modelling method will be more or less *powerful* depending on how many items/aspects are considered by the modelling. Similarly, it is not mandatory that the modelling is surjective, i.e. that it hows a possible use for all the eligible models (this for example happens whenever the eligible model set coincides with all the models provided by the notation), in such case we may just state that the eligible models are not minimal. Furthermore, the modelling may also lead to have different models representing a given item also non semantically equivalent (i.e. it is not a function) or, conversely, to have that many different items are represented by the same model (it is not injective).

The modelling may be quite easy to understand and almost obvious whenever the structure of the items and of the eligible models are quite similar[7], otherwise a clever (also if perhaps not trivial) modelling may allow to use with a satisfactory result a simple or general purpose notation for modelling specific items.

In many case the "distance" (i.e. the difference) between the items and the models of the selected notation, say N, may render the definition of the modelling (and of the eligible models) very hard if not impossible to use, or resulting in

---

[7] Using a mathematical terminology we may say they are isomorphic.

a really complicate and difficult to understand modelling. In such cases, many well-established techniques may be used, for example:

- build a chain of notations $N_1, \ldots, N_k = N$, where for $i = 1, k - 1$ N_i may be translated into N_{i+1}, where N_1 is not very far from the items (e.g. build a visual notation on the top of textual one), and then use N_1 as method notation;
- extend N by means of derived constructs (i.e. new constructs that correspond however to a combination of already existing ones);
- profile N by marking in some way existing constructs to help to match them with the various aspects of the items, and possibly by modifying their meaning or by restricting their possible use; this technique has been introduced by the UML but it may be used for other notations.

The above techniques have been used for example in the case of CASL4SOA property-oriented and constructive, the used notation CASL4SOA is a profile of CASL-MDL, that it is in turn a visual counterpart to CASL-LTL textual specifications (i.e. CASL-MDL models can be translated into CASL-LTL specifications).

PreciseSoa: Eligible Models and Modelling. In the PreciseSoa case the form of the eligible models is quite precisely defined by a metamodel, and we show in Fig. 6 the fragment of such metamodel corresponding to services. The form of model service strictly matches the view of the services by PreciseSoa (see Fig. 2), indeed we can see that there are parts corresponding to the service interfaces, contracts and semantics.

The *service interface* is defined by a class stereotyped ≪service interface≫ and named as the service itself. It should realize and use two UML interfaces, defining the in and the out-messages by means of operations, respectively. The operations of the interfaces correspond to the messages exchanged between the service and the participants using and providing it. The operations may have parameters that must be typed by datatypes (either predefined or user defined), and cannot have a return type. The definition of the needed datatypes should be given together with the two interfaces, thus a service interface consists of a class diagram, that will include a class stereotyped by ≪service interface≫, the two interfaces and all needed datatypes.

The *service contract* consists of a UML collaboration stereotyped by ≪service contract≫ and named as the service itself, and by a behaviour represented by a set of UML sequence diagrams. The collaboration has exactly two parts corresponding to the roles the service provider and consumer, typed by interfaces,

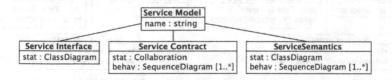

Fig. 6. PreciseSoa: Eligible Models (metamodel fragment)

and the sequence diagrams have exactly two lifelines (one for the service provider role and one for the service user role). The sequence diagrams present all possible scenarios of the provider using the service showing which messages and in which order the provider and the consumer exchange.

The *service semantics* consists of a class named service realm realizing the provided interface of the service itself, in such a way that its attributes define the current status of the realm (obviously together with the needed datatypes, and thus it will be represented by a class diagram). The behaviour part is a "refinement" of the sequence diagrams part of the service contract, depicting how the reception of the various in-messages modifies the realm status and how the out-messages are influenced by the same status (technically they are obtained by typing the provider lifeline with the realm class and adding action specifications to represent the modifications of the realm status and further guards to influence the choice of which messages to send out and which values they are carrying depending on the status of the realm).

The Modelling is in this case quite obvious, since the form of the eligible models is rather similar to that of the items.

CASL4SOA *property-oriented and constructive: Eligible Models and Modelling.* Also in this case we present only the details relative to the modelling of the services, and in Fig. 7 we present the form of the corresponding models following CASL4SOA property-oriented and constructive.

A service interface is modelled by a dynamic type whose possible transitions correspond to receive the in-messages and to send the out-messages; in more detail the service interface lists the possible labels of its transitions (in and out-messages of the service) and the contract its behavior in terms of possible sequence of in/out-messages, whereas the semantics gives another dynamic type refining the one describing the service contract by adding the information relative to its realm.

CASL4SOA property-oriented and constructive methods use the same notation but differ for the modelling and the form of the eligible models. In the first case the service contract is specified by means of a set of temporal formulas stating which transitions corresponding to out-messages must be performed by who provides the service after having received the in-messages, and which out-messages may be

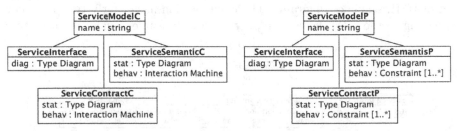

Fig. 7. CASL4SOA property-oriented and constructive: Eligible Models (metamodel fragments)

sent only after having received specific in-messages. The semantics of a service is specified in a similar way, but the formulas may related the sent messages with the current state of the realm. In the other case the contract is represented by means of an interaction machine associated with the dynamic type modelling the service provider defining all possible behaviours of the service provider for any possible in-message, the semantic is represented similarly with an interaction machine associated with the dynamic type modelling the real of the service (thus the machine transitions may be conditionated by the realm state and may affect it).

SRMLMethod: Eligible Models and Modelling. The eligible models of SRMLMethod are all possible specifications written using SRML (this is not surprising since SRML is a domain-specific notation built to be used just for this method). The modelling is quite simple since there are specific constructs for each component of the items. For example, there is a specific textual construct to define each transition type.

RSDLMethod: Eligible Models and Modelling. The eligible models coincide with the models of the RSDL notation, see Fig. 5, and the modelling is obvious since the form of the eligible models is rather similar to that of the items.

SoaMLMethod: Eligible Models and Modelling. The models are obviously all the models built using the SoaML profile, and no explicit definition of the eligible models is given, only various examples are provided in [14]. Also the modelling is presented by means of various examples.

WSPetriNet: Eligible Models and Modelling. The models are the one that follow the restrictions and extension on the coloured Petri nets as defined by the language WSN, and no explicit definition of the eligible models is given. The modelling as such is not addressed.

4   Operational Part of a Method

In this section we present the constituents of the operational part of a method, precisely Intended Use of Models, User Guidance, and Tool Support; again they will be illustrated with the considered modelling methods for service-based systems.

4.1   The Intended Use of Models

Any model should be produced having in mind some use, at least a specific use is needed to validate a modelling method, but obviously some models may be aimed at several uses.

Here there is a list of common model uses:

– documentation, and in this case it may be useful to explicitly indicate who are the expected readers of this documentation (e.g. experts of the domain, requirement engineerings, designers, implementers);

- verification, and in this case it should make explicit what it is the intended idea of verification, and which means are planned to be used to perform it (e.g. use of model checker MC that it is able to check formulas expressed using notation N);
- to support some software engineering task, e.g. requirement specification, testing;
- to (automatically/semi-automatically/by hand) generate some code, in this case which kind of code has be produced should be made explicit together with the means to use for the generation.

PreciseSoa, CASL4SOA property-oriented and constructive: Intended Use of Models. In these methods the models of service-based systems are intended for documenting the design of such systems, to help to build such systems; furthermore it is planned to use them also to generate automatically the WSDL (Web Services Description Language) description of the used services and part of the code supporting the participants to use and provide the services.

SRMLMethod: Intended Use of Models. The SRML models are intended to:
- represent the design of a service-oriented system obtained by a business model, see [9];
- perform some verifications on the modelled service-oriented systems;
- generate portions of the code of the resulting implementation.

RSDLMethod: Intended Use of Models. The RSDL models should be used to describe the services requested and offered in a service marketplace in such a way to allow the automatic matching between offers and requests.

SoaMLMethod: Intended Use of Models. The SoaMLMethod models are intended *"for the specification and design of services within a service-oriented architecture"* from [14].

WSPetriNet: Intended Use of Models. The purpose of this work is to provide a framework where service compatibility can be checked, and obviously the notation developed and the well formedness property were defined in such a way that service compatibility can be verified.

4.2 User Guidance

Once a modeller knows very well the form of the eligible models, which items s(he) may model, and how the models should be linked with the items (the modelling component of a method), s(he) still needs some help to start to produce the models to overcome the blocking effect of an empty page/screen.

The user guidance should be presented either informally using the natural language or using some visual notation for workflow (e.g. UML activity diagrams), explaining which tasks to perform and which artifacts should be produced to reach an eligible complete model.

In many cases the user guidance is introduced together with the modelling and the eligible models by just giving one or more complete examples; clearly examples are useful, but they may convey only a part of the relevant informations, and may be also convey unwanted impressions to the method users, for example by seeing a particular example s(he) may deduce that the methods can be applied only to similar cases, on the other side giving a very complex example including all the relevant features may require too much time to be prepared and space to be presented, and may yield confusion for the user to be.

PreciseSoa, CASL4SOA property-oriented and constructive: User Guidance. In these three cases the user guidance to build a model is presented using some UML activity diagrams see [6]; in Fig. 8 we show the part relative to build a model of a service following PreciseSoa[8].

SRMLMethod: User Guidance. How to build a SRML model is described together with how to use other notations developed in the Sensoria project by means of some throughly commented examples that can be found on the project web site[9]. In general, the important role of User Guidance in the Sensoria project has been recognized, as it is witnessed by the definition of the Sensoria patterns [19], presenting the user guidance to solve various development problems in the field of the service oriented systems using various notations and techniques developed in the project in form of patterns. Among them there is a pattern named "Service Modelling" that however proposes to use some Sensoria UML profiles instead of SRML.

RSDLMethod, SoaMLMethod and WSPetriNet: User Guidance. This constituent is not available at least to the best of our knowledge.

4.3   Tool Support

It is important to know whether there are software tools supporting the various activities related to applying the considered method. Many different kinds of tools may be developed, supporting for example:

- model production: indeed an editor is the most common software tool supporting the modelling, we can then distinguish if it is either a general editor for the selected notation or if it helps to produce the eligible models, e.g. by checking if they have all the required characteristics to be eligible;
- following the user guidance during the production of the models, for example a wizard;
- helping to ensure the quality of the produced models, for example a tools computing some metrics.

---

[8] The rake construct, shown by a small rake-like icon at the bottom on the right of some action rounded box, means that such action is defined by an activity with the same name defined elsewhere, e.g. **Model Service Interface**.

[9] www.sensoria-ist.eu

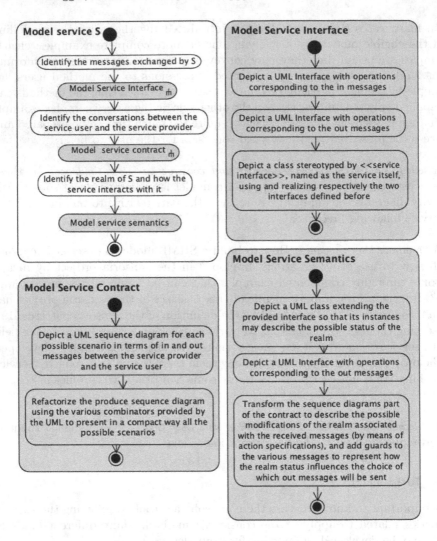

Fig. 8. PreciseSoa: User Guidance (fragment)

When listing the tools supporting a method it is of paramount importance to explicitly provide for each tool the following information:

– how to get a working copy of the tool (only tools publicly available may be considered),

– the system requirements,

– and the tool status (academic, student project, free, community edition, commercial and in this case the cost should be stated).

Concerning the tools supporting a modelling method it may be also interesting to discuss which tools are potentially "feasible", meaning that they may be built using the current knowledge and technology by a professional software developer.

PreciseSoa: Tool Support. General purpose UML editors supporting the profile mechanism are currently the only available tool support for the PreciseSoa method; among them we are now using VisualParadigm community edition, and all the UML models appearing in this paper have been produced using it. To check if a model is eligible, it is possible to implement a particular model to model transformation using ATL, where the target model is a description of the possible reasons for a model not being eligible.

CASL4SOA *property-oriented and constructive: Tool Support.* The visual syntax of CASL4SOA (as well as the one of CASL-MDL) has been defined by reusing the visual elements of the UML, thus any UML editor tool may be used to produce CASL4SOA models.

SRMLMethod: Tool Support. A model checker UMC[10] acting over communicating UML state machines able to check the validity of temporal logic formulas may be used to do some checks over the service modules, after having transformed them into state machines.

RSDLMethod: Tool Support. Not available at the best of our knowledge.

SoaMLMethod: Tool Support. General purpose UML editors supporting the profile mechanism may be used to produce SoaML models (also if specific tools are available see e.g. the one of the Visual Paradigm family[11]).

WSPetriNet: Tool Support. A tool for checking web services compatibility (similarity and equivalence verification) is built on top of PIPE[12] (Platform Independent Petri net Editor) [8] that provides editing facilities for coloured Petri nets.

5 Relating Modelling Methods

In this paper we have only the room to just give an idea of how the proposed framework may be useful to relate different modelling methods allowing to grasp the true differences among them and perhaps to discover hidden similarities, or to find suggestions for moving features from one method to another.

By looking at the considered items we can already decide whether two methods may be compared or related in some way. Just considering the definition of the items we can see that the methods for service-based systems considered in this paper were designed with quite different ideas about the services. For example in the case of PreciseSoa (and of CASL4SOA property-oriented and constructive) there is no idea of dynamic service discovery, whereas that is an important feature in the case of SRMLMethod and of RSDLMethod; instead in WSPetriNet the services are intended as software artifacts presented by means of a kind of

---

[10] fmt.isti.cnr.it/umc/V4.1/umc.html

[11] http://www.visual-paradigm.com/features/soaml-modeling/

[12] http://pipe2.sourceforge.net/

programming language. Thus, the first three methods, which consider exactly the same items, may be surely compared, whereas a detailed analysis is needed to decide whether SRMLMethod, RSDLMethod and WSPetriNet may be related, for example SRMLMethod assumes that the interactions between who provides and who consumes the services are of seven different kinds (see Fig. 3) while no classification is made by RSDLMethod and WSPetriNet.

Methods may be also related by looking at the intended use of the models; for example some kind of formal verification is considered by SRMLMethod and WSPetriNet, whereas PreciseSoa and SoaMLMethod should allow automatic generation of code from the models.

The relationships among PreciseSoa and CASL4SOA property-oriented and constructive are very strong, we can say that they are almost isomorphic methods; indeed not only they consider the same items but the form of their models is isomorphic (see Fig. 6 and 7, as well as Fig. 9, 10, and 11 where the Place Order service is modelled using the three methods), even if they use quite different notations (the informal object-oriented UML for PreciseSoa and the formal visual CASL4SOA property-oriented and constructive).

Notice that, however, initial versions of such methods have some different features [7], for example no semantics of the services was considered by the method based on the UML, and no strict guidelines on how to represent the service contract were given for CASL4SOA property-oriented (it was just required to express any relevant property on the interaction between the service provider and the service user using the temporal logic). Then, by looking at the presentations of such different methods using our framework, it was simple to see that a semantic part may be added to the method based on the UML, and that an interaction machine modelling the service contract in CASL4SOA constructive presenting all possible sequences of messages exchanged between service provider and user could be moved to CASL4SOA property-oriented as a restriction on the form of the temporal formulas specifying the contract (e.g. receiving and in-message implies that eventually some out-messages will be sent, and then ...).

Thus, the systematic presentation of modelling methods using our framework may allow also some cross-fertilization among them, suggesting how some features may be moved from one method to another one.

6   Related Work

To the best of our knowledge there are no other papers proposing a structured and organized way to present a modelling method, except our old work on formal specification methods [2]. Instead, there are many contributions considering modelling methods for particular categories of items, for example business processes and web applications, where aspects and properties specific to that items are considered.

[1] proposes a framework for comparing different business process modelling techniques along two criteria: *purpose of the model* and *model change permissiveness*. The first one corresponds to one of our method constituents (Intended Use of

Models), whereas the latter requires also to express "Strengths and Weaknesses" of a method from the point of view of the model users and of the modellers. Our proposal, instead, does not lead explicitly to make any judgement, and so in our framework there are no places where to insert the good and the bad points of a method; we are only interested to present the methods thoroughly covering any possible aspect, allowing to the modellers to decide which is the best method for their jobs. In [1], moreover, the author equates notation to method, and indeed they assume that the UML may correspond to just a unique way to model a business process, whereas we proposed at least five different methods based on the UML, see [17].

[15] proposes a procedure for selecting the most appropriate modelling method for a given specific business process, considering many aspects of these kinds of the methods (e.g. completeness, readability, etc.); then, by a decision procedure (based on the AHP Analytic Hierarchical Process) considering all the relevant aspects, the procedure ranks several methods with respect to the given business processes. However, the presented approach is difficult to evaluate, since the various methods are very vaguely presented and among them there is "π-calculus by Milner", a very abstract and scarcely readable formal notation, and "Petri nets" without any other qualifications (not considering that Petri nets is a wide range family, from very elementary to quite rich and expressive, as the coloured nets). Thus, it is difficult to evaluate the value of the proposed approach.

[10] is about a taxonomy of modelling techniques for business processes and information systems. The author understanding of the word *technique* also with respect to method is suggested by this excerpt *"Methodologies are taken to refer to modeling paradigms (for example, data focused, object oriented, and so on) and are outside the scope of this paper. Modeling methodologies are supported by a number of techniques that provide the main analytical focus of our research. Techniques are taken to refer to diagrammatic or other notations for studying and analyzing modeled systems."* [10]. By looking at the techniques considered in the paper (Data flow diagramming, Entity-relationship diagramming, State-transition diagramming, IDEF techniques, UML, Flowcharting, Petri nets, Simulation, Knowledge-based techniques and Role activity diagramming) it is not clear if this "technique" corresponds to our notation or to a typology of notations. In this paper, it is stressed that different techniques may consider different aspects of business processes and information systems (e.g. the functional, behavioral, organizational and informational perspectives) that should considered for classifying the modelling methods. However, this paper seems to suggest that the notation (also if called technique) is different from the modelling method, and that the tools have a relevant role.

[18] presents a framework to evaluate various modelling methods for web applications, again considering specific aspects of this activity (e.g. "Evolving Requirements Modelings", "Content Modeling", "Hypertext Modeling", "Presentation Modeling", "Customization Modeling", and "Structure and Behavior"), whereas other aspects correspond to constituents of our framework (e.g. "Notation", "Tool Support", "Code Generation available", and "Process / Approach", i.e. in which

process development the method will be used, in our framework this will be part of the intended use of the models). Finally, an aspect "Strength" requires a form of judgement of the methods, whereas our framework is absolutely objective.

7   Conclusions and Future Work

As announced in the introduction, we wanted to address questions about choosing a method, the key features of a modelling method, and presenting a modelling method. We have introduced a framework for presenting in a structured way the modelling methods considering all their main constituents, and we have then applied it to several modelling methods for service-based systems found in the current literature.

Using our framework a modeller may decide whether a method may be used for some specific modelling tasks, grasp the differences among several methods, and distinguish a method based on a notation from a mere notation. Whereas a method developer may be guided in presenting at the best a modelling method, and s(he) may get hints on what to add to a notation to transform it in a fully operative method. Moreover, we can now answer to the majority of the questions we have listed in the Introduction, see Appendix B.

We put our framework at work on seven different approaches to model service-based systems. In some cases the various constituents of a given method are explicitly defined or can be more or less easily recovered; in other cases there are no clues on which they may be, so this means that they may be defined in several ways thus deriving different modelling methods. Thus, as expected, in various cases several constituents of a given method cannot be given, nevertheless our effort is in our opinion valuable, indeed:

- making explicit the considered items helps to preliminary decide whether an approach is suitable for a specific case (in a local project concerning logistic systems for maintenance of ships we have to model service-based systems where each participant has to preliminary declare which services it will provide, thus the considered services are not dynamically discovered, and so the methods sharing the same view of services may be selected);
- it may be the starting point in the case the proposed approach should be transformed in a fully operative modelling method, for example the method developer may try to fill the lacking part of the framework;
- it may be of help to produce a better more structured and easy to grasp method documentation; for example, in some cases, the modelled items are not explicitly described and the form of the eligible models is mainly presented by means of examples, whereas in the case of SoaML [14] there is a nice preliminary section in the specification document clearly presenting the modelled items, but the form of the eligible models, as in many other case when a UML profile is provided, is not defined at all.

In this initial version of the modelling method framework we have tried to consider only the fundamental constituents, for what concerns the "Method Definition" part we are quite confident to have considered all of them, but other constituents may be added to the "Operational Aspects". We can think for example, of Quality Assessment concerning the means provided by the method to assess the level of quality of the produced models, obviously after having defined what it means to be of good quality.

The proposed framework is general purpose, i.e. it may be used for presenting any kind of modelling methods, but as future work we would like to investigate if it is possible to derive from it some specializations for specific tasks or specific items by adding new constituents or by specializing the form of those already present. For example, we may try to provide a general reference model of the business processes or of the service-based systems and to require that the item model should be a restriction/specialization of this one, whereas for methods intended for the automatic verification a new constituent may be "Verifiable Properties" to be defined with respect to the models.

The current version of the framework presented in this paper tries to be as much as possible agnostic and objective, avoiding to encompass personal ideas and best practice concerning the modelling activities (for example the framework does not support either "model as sketch" or "model as program" point of view, not even "the cost of producing a model is only justified if the model is used for formal verification" and "useful models are only visual"[13]. However, specific ideas concerning what should be a good modelling method may be presented using our framework, indeed it is sufficient to propose a refinement of it, either adding new constituents or specializing the form of those already present. To overcome some drawbacks of using the UML we have developed what we call *Precise UML modelling methods,* by imposing that the form of the eligible models must be given by a metamodel and by a large set of well-formedness constraints (to mitigate the excessive freedom of the UML, and to reduce the effort of the modeller to decide which among the 14 diagrams and the large number of constructs to use), and that the User Guidance must be defined by means of detailed UML activity diagrams; PreciseSoa is an example of a precise UML modelling method. These personal ideas on UML modelling could be very easily encompassed in a "precise-modelling framework", where for example the eligible models must be defined by a metamodel and by a set of constraints.

Finally, we want to acknowledge the real help provided by the referees with their careful reading and wise remarks.

References

1. Aguilar-Saén, R.S.: Business process modelling: Review and framework. International Journal of Production Economics 90(2), 129 (2004)
2. Astesiano, E., Reggio, G.: Formalism and method. Theor. Comput. Sci. 236(1-2), 3–34 (2000)

---

[13] These statements have been heard in some public events in the software engineering community in the last years.

3. Astesiano, E., Reggio, G., Cerioli, M.: From formal techniques to well-founded software development methods. In: Aichernig, B.K. (ed.) Formal Methods at the Crossroads. From Panacea to Foundational Support. LNCS, vol. 2757, pp. 132–150. Springer, Heidelberg (2003)

4. Choppy, C., Reggio, G.: A well-founded approach to service modelling with Casl4Soa: part 1 (service in isolation). In: Shin, S.Y., Ossowski, S., Schumacher, M., Palakal, M.J., Hung, C. (eds.) Proceedings of the 2010 ACM Symposium on Applied Computing (SAC), Sierre, Switzerland, March 22-26, pp. 2451–2458. ACM (2010)

5. Choppy, C., Reggio, G.: CASL-MDL, modelling dynamic systems with a formal foundation and a UML-like notation. In: Mossakowski, T., Kreowski, H.-J. (eds.) WADT 2010. LNCS, vol. 7137, pp. 76–97. Springer, Heidelberg (2012), http://www-lipn.univ-paris13.fr/~choppy/REPORTS/casl-mdl-report.pdf

6. Choppy, C., Reggio, G.: Precise and formal modelling methods for service systems. Technical Report TR-14-03, DIBRIS, Università di Genova (2014)

7. Choppy, C., Reggio, G., Tran, K.-D.: Formal or not, but precise modelling of services with CASL4SOA and SoaML. In: Hung, D.V., Vo, H.T., Sanders, J., Bui, L.T., Pham, S.B. (eds.) Fourth International Conference on Knowledge and Systems Engineering (KSE 2012), pp. 187–194. IEEE Computer Society (2012)

8. Dingle, N.J., Knottenbelt, W.J., Suto, T.: PIPE2: A tool for the performance evaluation of generalised stochastic Petri nets. SIGMETRICS Perform. Eval. Rev. 36(4), 34–39 (2009)

9. Fiadeiro, J., Lopes, A., Bocchi, L., Abreu, J.: The SENSORIA reference modelling language. In: Wirsing, M., Hölzl, M. (eds.) SENSORIA. LNCS, vol. 6582, pp. 61–114. Springer, Heidelberg (2011)

10. Giaglis, G.M.: A taxonomy of business process modeling and information systems modeling techniques. International Journal of Flexible Manufacturing Systems, 13(2), 209 (2001)

11. Huma, Z., Gerth, C., Engels, G., Juwig, O.: Towards an automatic service discovery for UML-based rich service descriptions. In: France, R.B., Kazmeier, J., Breu, R., Atkinson, C. (eds.) MODELS 2012. LNCS, vol. 7590, pp. 709–725. Springer, Heidelberg (2012)

12. Huma, Z., Gerth, C., Engels, G., Juwig, O.: A UML-based rich service description language for automatic service discovery of heterogeneous service partners. In: Proceedings of the CAiSE 2012 Forum at the 24th International Conference on Advanced Information Systems Engineering (CAiSE). CEUR Workshop Proceedings, vol. 855, pp. 90–97 (2012)

13. Li, X., Fan, Y., Sheng, Q.Z., Maamar, Z., Zhu, H.: A Petri net approach to analyzing behavioral compatibility and similarity of web services. Trans. Sys. Man Cyber. Part A 41(3), 510–521 (2011)

14. OMG. Service oriented architecture Modeling Language (SoaML) Specification, Version 1.0.1 (2012)

15. Pavlov, R., Shekhovtsov, V.A., Zlatkin, S.: Towards selecting among business process modeling methodologies. In: Proceedings of 9th International Conference on Business Information Systems, BIS 2006 (2006)

16. Reggio, G., Astesiano, E., Choppy, C.: CASL-LTL: A CASL Extension for Dynamic Reactive Systems Version 1.0–Summary. Technical Report DISI-TR-03-36, DISI – Università di Genova, Italy (2003), ftp://ftp.disi.unige.it/person/ReggioG/ReggioEtAll03b.pdf

17. Reggio, G., Leotta, M., Ricca, F., Astesiano, E.: Business process modelling: Five styles and a method to choose the most suitable one. In: Proceedings of 2nd International Workshop on Experiences and Empirical Studies in Software Modelling, EESSMod 2012, pp. 8:1–8:6. ACM (2012)
18. Schwinger, W., Koch, N.: Modeling web applications. In: Gerti, K., Birgit, P., Siegfried, R., Werner, R. (eds.) Web Engineering - The Discipline of Systematic Development of Web Applications, pp. 39–64. John Wiley (2006)
19. Wirsing, M., et al.: Sensoria patterns: Augmenting service engineering with formal analysis, transformation and dynamicity. In: Margaria, T., Steffen, B. (eds.) Leveraging Applications of Formal Methods, Verification and Validation. CCIS, vol. 17, pp. 170–190. Springer, Heidelberg (2008)

A Tribute to a Long Lasting Friendship

It has been a very wet summer here in Genoa this year, followed by an even worse autumn with some devastating floods, a pattern unfortunately not infrequent in the last two decades. But in the late seventies and the eighties we had some long periods of extremely serious drought and we still vividly remember that in one of these occasions, late eighties, a member of our group (Gianna) came up with the brilliant idea of proposing to the town Mayor inviting Martin to come to Genoa as a special guest – a remedy to the drought. There was a clear reason for that: Martin's frequent visits since 1982 were almost invariably marked by some heavy showers, "tropical" in his words; and indeed I personally remember once being trapped in my car for about twenty minutes under a so heavy rain to make impossible to pick up Martin and Sabine waiting under the arcade in the central Piazza De Ferrari.

Nevertheless the lasting feeling of those visits, and of the overall long and intense period of collaboration, does not suffer at all of the unpleasantness of some bad weather; it is instead the feeling of a warm and emotionally sunny atmosphere, the encounter with a young brilliant researcher who was also a good friend, constantly received at our department as "the most latin of the Germans we know" (copyrighted nickname of our staff at that time).

Of course there were also some really sunny days when we could work hard in the relaxing beauty of the gardens of Villa Imperiale and Villa Cambiaso, or taste some delicious fishes on the tiny beach of San Fruttuoso after a relaxing walk in the wood of the Portofino Mount. And, outside Genoa, how to forget his hospitality beginning in the Munich house in 1981 (a rose in every room), and then in Passau and again in Munich; and . . . marching together, with Fulvia and Sabine, in the middle of an exulting crowd along Rue de la République up to Place de la Bastille, the evening of the 1988 second victory of Mitterrand?

I know, I have to stop the flow of the leisure memories and speak of work and science. I will be short, since so many will have much more to say about that, and though we have coauthored a number of papers, I will concentrate on two lines of research.

Martin's work on ASL, and algebraic specifications in general, has marked a turning point in our approach to the specifications of concurrent systems.

Putting together our experience of some work about CCS and variations (Egidio and Elena) with Martin's algebraic declination of labelled transition systems has led to a joint paper presented at TAPSOFT '85. Days ago Gianna was recalling those days of hard work in Passau with Martin already involved in an amazing amount of scientific and organizational duties, and I personally cannot forget stopping a summer '84 holiday with some friends in Corsica, to feverishly improve an almost final version, then posted to Martin who was on holiday on the island of Pantelleria. That paper has been a cornerstone of our future developments on the algebraic specification of concurrent systems, that has also seen the participation of Martin as an advisor in some significant applications of that framework; to mention just two: the Cnet Italian National Project and the EEC project on the Ada Formal Definition.

Then, it was a problem left open by Martin (as a fall-out of some work with Manfred) on algebraic specifications with partial algebras the starting point of a stream of work for the Ph.D. thesis of Maura and its following. That work has meant for our group building up the knowledge that was later crucial for our contribution to the CoFI/CASL project. Though Martin was not involved himself in that project, during a three month stay in Santa Margherita and Genoa, he had a number of nice discussions with us on many technically delicate points.

Dear Martin, our best memories happily survive for us and we hope for you too.

A   Service Model Examples

In Fig. 9 to 15 we present an example of service model (or of a model fragment) for each of the methods considered in this paper.

B   Answers to Some Questions Listed in the Introduction

- Is modelling method A more appropriate than method B in a given context?
  Assuming that the context is given by one or more tasks to be done with models of specific items, in a specific application field or in a specific domain, the answer is yes.
  Indeed, we need to examine
  - the Items component of methods A and B to see to which extent they match the things to model in that context, and
  - the Intended Use of Models component of methods A and B to see to which extent they include the task required in that context.
- Which are the relationships between modelling methods A and B?
  We can state quite precisely whether the two methods concern more or less similar modelling tasks, i.e. they are about modelling more or less similar items, whether the produced models may be used for similar tasks, and whether the used notation are the same or have similar aspects.
- Does the modelling method A have any novelty with respect to method B?
  A novelty may be to be able to model a larger class of items (this may be deduced by looking at the Items components of the two methods), or to be able to model more aspects of the same class of items (either the items of A have more features than those of B, or the modelling of A provides a way to model such aspects while they were not considered by the modelling of B.
  In the case that both methods share the same items and the same notation say N, it may be that the modelling of A shows how to represent some features of the items using N in a more clever or simpler way than B.
  Another kind of novelties may be given by the fact that A has a larger set of tools supporting a larger set of tasks (e.g. a method for modelling business processes using BPMN offering a model editor and a simulator versus a method offering only an editor).
- Is modelling method A adequate for a specific case?
  First of all check whether the "thing" that you have to model in that specific case matches the items of method A, then whether the available tools and intended uses cover what you have to do in this specific case.
- Is modelling method A mature?
  A mature method should have been around for some time and should have been used extensively. The main constituents of a method considered by our framework (those defined in this paper) do not allow to answer to this question. But, as mentioned here we have given only the "main" constituents of a method, other ones may be added to capture further aspects.

Interface

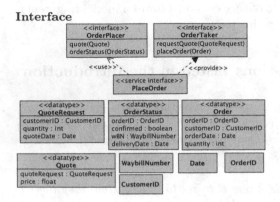

Contract

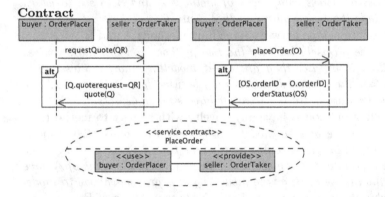

Semantics

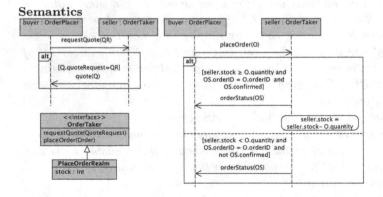

Fig. 9. PreciseSoa: service model example from [6]

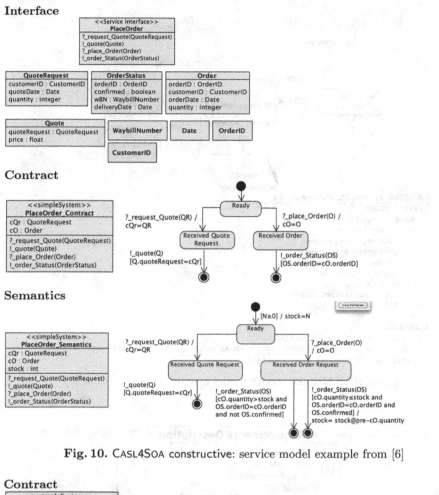

Fig. 10. CASL4SOA constructive: service model example from [6]

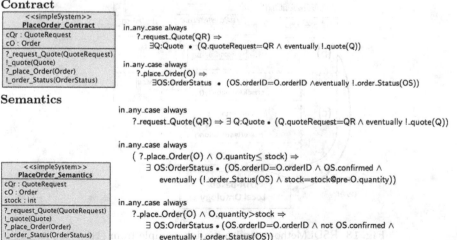

Fig. 11. CASL4SOA property-oriented: service model from [6] (interface as in Fig. 10)

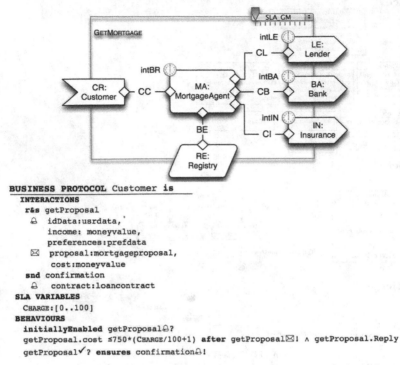

BUSINESS PROTOCOL Customer **is**
    INTERACTIONS
    r&s getProposal
       ⌂ idData:usrdata,
          income: moneyvalue,
          preferences:prefdata
       ⊠ proposal:mortgageproposal,
          cost:moneyvalue
    snd confirmation
       ⌂   contract:loancontract
  SLA VARIABLES
    CHARGE:[0..100]
  BEHAVIOURS
   initiallyEnabled getProposal⌂?
   getProposal.cost ≤750*(CHARGE/100+1) **after** getProposal⊠! ∧ getProposal.Reply
   getProposal✓? **ensures** confirmation⌂!

Fig. 12. SRMLMethod: service model example fragment from [9]

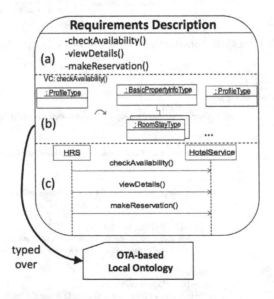

Fig. 13. RSDLMethod: service model example from [11]

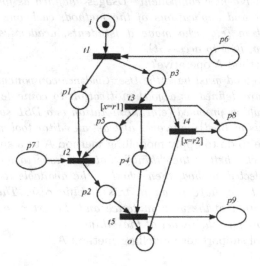

Fig. 14. WSPetriNet: service model example fragment from [13]

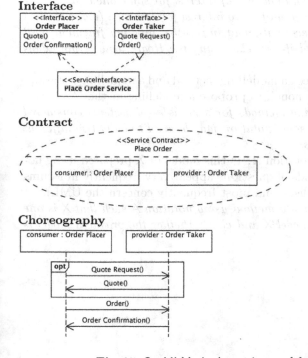

Fig. 15. SoaMLMethod: service model example from [14]

We may consider a new component "Usages" defined as follows: it is a list of cases studies and applications of the method, each one accompanied by useful information (e.g. who made it [students, academics, professionals], time, dimension, how to access it).

– Is modelling method A operative?

An operative method must have the User Guidance component, and either the Eligible Models are defined or a good motivation to coincide with the Models component should be provided (e.g. the notation is a DSL specifically defined to be used in this method); moreover at least an editor tool must be available.

– What do I have to do to apply modelling method A to a specific case?

First of all check whether the "thing" that you have to model matches the items of the selected method, then whether the available tools and intended uses cover what you have to do in this specific case. Then following the operative indication of the user guidance and the extensional indication of the modelling produce the model of the "thing".

– Is there any tool support for modelling method A?

Trivial

– I have designed a new modelling method, now which is the best way to present it?

Provide all the constituents required by the proposed framework.

– Is there any motivation for designing modelling method A?

Decide whether the considered items are of interest for some one and whether the intended use of them is again of some interest for someone (e.g. a method for verifying by hand the termination of imperative program fragment built using assignment, loop, and if-then-else using the Hoare logic is nowadays scarcely motivated).

– Is there any difference between a modelling method and a modelling notation, or indicating a notation is enough to propose a modelling method?

Trivial, the various modelling methods for service-based systems considered in this paper show how the same notation may be used to build two different methods for the same items.

– How can I model X using notation N? Is this model of X prepared using notation N correct? (these kinds of questions appear very frequently in forums on the web and in mailing lists, and most frequently concern the UML).

First of all you have to design a method using notation A such that X is one of its items, then you can model X and check whether the produced model is correct.

A Theory Agenda for Component-Based Design

Joseph Sifakis[1], Saddek Bensalem[2], Simon Bliudze[1], and Marius Bozga[2]

[1] EPFL, Rigorous System Design Laboratory, Station 14, 1015 Lausanne, Switzerland
[2] Université Grenoble Alpes, VERIMAG, 38000 Grenoble, France
CNRS, VERIMAG, 38000 Grenoble, France

Dedicated to Martin Wirsing.

Abstract. The aim of the paper is to present a theory agenda for component-based design based on results that motivated the development of the BIP component framework, to identify open problems and discuss further research directions. The focus is on proposing a semantically sound theoretical and general framework for modelling component-based systems and their properties both behavioural and architectural as well for achieving correctness by using scalable specific techniques.

We discuss the problem of composing components by proposing the concept of glue as a set of stateless composition operators defined by a certain type of operational semantics rules. We provide an overview of results about glue expressiveness and minimality. We show how interactions and associated transfer of data can be described by using connectors and in particular, how dynamic connectors can be defined as an extension of static connectors. We present two approaches for achieving correctness for component-based systems. One is by compositional inference of global properties of a composite component from properties of its constituents and interaction constraints implied by composition operators. The other is by using and composing architectures that enforce specific coordination properties. Finally, we discuss recent results on architecture specification by studying two types of logics: 1) interaction logics for the specification of sets of allowed interactions; 2) configuration logics for the characterisation of architecture styles.

1 Introduction

Component-based design is the process leading from given requirements and a set of predefined components to a system meeting the requirements.

Building systems from components is essential in any engineering discipline. Components are abstract building blocks encapsulating behaviour. They can be composed in order to build composite components. Their composition should be rigorously defined so that it is possible to infer the behaviour of composite components from the behaviour of their constituents as well as global properties from the properties of individual components.

The problem of building systems from components can be defined as follows. Given a set of components $\{C_1, \ldots, C_n\}$ and a property of their product state

R. De Nicola and R. Hennicker (Eds.): Wirsing Festschrift, LNCS 8950, pp. 409–439, 2015.
© Springer International Publishing Switzerland 2015

space Φ find a coordinator Co such that the coordinated behaviour $Co(C_1, \dots, C_n)$ meets the property Φ.

This problem can be studied as a synthesis problem [31]. The coordinator can be considered as a component that adequately restricts the behaviour of the components so that the resulting behaviour meets Φ. Synthesis techniques suffer from well-known complexity limitations. The coordinator is computed by (semi)-algorithms on the product space of the coordinated components.

System design pursues similar and even broader objectives than synthesis: incremental construction of systems meeting given requirements from a set of components. In contrast to synthesis, design lacks rigorous theoretical foundations. Existing frameworks are mostly informal. Designers use "ready-made" solutions to coordination problems, e.g. architectures, protocols, that have been proven correct practically or theoretically. In contrast to synthesis, design requires a variety of composition operators. It is based on the concept of architecture as a means to enforce specific characteristic properties by application of generic coordination principles. A key idea is to ensure correctness by construction by avoiding computationally expensive techniques implying state explosion.

Endowing component-based design with scientific foundations is a major scientific challenge. This requires:

1. *A general concept of component.* Currently there is no agreement on a single component model. System designers deal with heterogeneous components with different characteristics. One source of heterogeneity is the distinction between synchronous and asynchronous components. Hardware components as well as components in some data flow applications are synchronous. Another source of heterogeneity reflects the difference in programming styles. Thread-based programming allows for components to be accessed by an arbitrary number of threads sharing common data. It does not allow a strict separation between behaviour and coordination mechanisms as the programmer explicitly handles synchronisation primitives to ensure coherency of shared data, e.g. to avoid races. This style is hardly amenable to formalisation and analysis. On the contrary, actor-based programming assumes that each component has its own data transformed by a single local thread. Coordination is external to the atomic components of the application and can be ensured using general mechanisms such as protocols.

2. *Theory for composing components.* We need theory for describing and analysing the coordination between components in terms of tangible, well-founded and organised concepts. The theory should propose a set of composition operators meeting the following requirements:
   - Orthogonality, meaning that composition operators are stateless to respect a clear separation between behaviour and coordination. Many component-based frameworks do not meet this requirement. Some allow arbitrary behaviour in coordination mechanisms. This which precludes rigorous mathematical treatment focusing on coordination. Others allow a limited number of types of behaviour such as buffers or queues to the detriment of mathematical elegance.

- Minimality, meaning that none of the coordination primitives can be expressed as the combination of others without using behaviour.
- Expressiveness, meaning that the considered set of composition operators can be used to express any coordination problem. This requirement is further explained and formalised in the paper.

Notice that most of the existing component composition frameworks fail to satisfy these requirements. Some are formal such as process algebras, e.g. CCS, CSP, π-calculus, and use single composition operators that are not expressive enough. Others are ad hoc such as most frameworks used in software engineering, e.g. architecture description languages [28] which are not rooted in rigorous semantics and are hardly amenable to formalisation.

3. *Theory for ensuring correctness of components.* Being able to check or assert correctness of the built components using scalable techniques is an essential requirement. The idea is to avoid a posteriori verification and establish correctness incrementally by applying easy-to-check rules that follow the system construction.

   A key concept in this approach is that of architectures as well-established coordination schemes enforcing given properties. The problem is then to decompose any component coordination property as the conjunction of pre-defined characteristic properties enforced by predefined architectures.

The aim of the paper is to propose a theory agenda for rigorous component-based design. The agenda is built on existing results developed for the BIP framework [6]. It identifies work directions addressing open problems and covering a good deal of the needs. The exposition of the results is mainly informal. We provide references to technical papers for the interested reader. One of the objectives is to show mathematical relations between three hierarchically structured domains encompassing the basic concepts:

- The domain of *components* offering the possibility of interaction through their ports p and associated variables X_p through which they make available the data transferred when interactions occur.
- The domain of *connectors*, used to model coordination between components. Each connector is characterised by an interaction between ports and associated computation on the exported data. Interactions are arbitrary sets of ports. Their execution implies the atomic synchronisation of the involved components. Clearly if P is the set of the ports then the set of interactions I is a subset of 2^P.
- The domain of configurations which are sets of connectors characterising architectures. Clearly if I is the set of interactions of an architecture then the set of configurations Γ is a subset of 2^I.

The paper is structured as follows. In Section 2, we discuss the problem of composing components by proposing the concept of glue. Glue is a set of stateless composition operators defined by a certain type of operational semantics rules. We provide an overview of results about expressiveness and minimality that led to the definition of the BIP component framework. In Section 3, we show how interactions and associated data transfer can be described by using connectors. We show in particular, how dynamic connectors can be defined as an extension of static connectors. Two approaches for achieving correctness for component-based systems are presented in Section 4. One is by compositional inference of global properties of a composite component from properties of its constituents and synchronisation constraints implied by composition operators. The other is by using and composing architectures that enforce specific coordination properties. Section 5 discusses recent results on architecture specification by studying two types of logics: 1) interaction logics for the specification of sets of allowed interactions; 2) configuration logics for the characterisation of architectural styles. The last section concludes and discusses further research directions.

2   Composing Components

2.1   The Concept of Component

A component is a tuple $C = (\Sigma, P, X, \rightarrow)$, where

- Σ is a set of *control locations*;
- P is a set of *ports*;
- X is a set of variables partitioned in two disjoint sets X_L and X_P of, respectively, *local* and *port variables*; the variables in X_P are indexed by ports, that is $X_P = \{X_p\}_{p \in P}$;
- $\rightarrow \subseteq \Sigma \times P \times G(X) \times F(X) \times \Sigma$ is a *transition relation*; transitions between control locations are labeled by triplets (p, g, f) where p is a port, g and f are, respectively, a guard Boolean expression and an update function on the variables in X.

A shorthand notation $\sigma \xrightarrow{p,g,f} \sigma'$ is commonly used to denote $(\sigma, p, g, f, \sigma') \in \rightarrow$.

Intuitively, a component can be considered as an open transition system, that is a system that performs coordination-driven computation. Coordination is defined by the environment of the component and involves two aspects: *interaction* (synchronisation) and *data transfer*. Denoting by $\mathbf{X}$ the set of all valuations of the variables in X, a state of the transition system is a pair $s = (\sigma, v)$ where $\sigma \in \Sigma$ is a control location and $v \in \mathbf{X}$ is a valuation of the component variables. Thus the state space of the transition system is $S = \Sigma \times \mathbf{X}$.

If $\sigma \xrightarrow{p,g,f} \sigma'$ then the transition system has a transition from state $s = (\sigma, v)$ to state $s' = (\sigma', v')$ if $g(v) = \text{true}$ and the external environment offers an interaction involving p. The execution of a transition consists in exporting the value $v(X_p)$ of the variable X_p [1] associated with port p and receiving back a new value u_p. The resulting valuation is $v' = f\big(v[u_p/X_p]\big)$ where $v[u_p/X_p]$ is the valuation obtained by replacing, in v, the value of X_p by u_p.

---

[1] For the sake of simplicity of notations, we consider that ports p have associated exactly one variable X_p. This restriction is, however, irrelevant and we'll consider later examples where any number of variables are associated to ports.

Sometimes, for the sake of simplicity and when data treatment is irrelevant, we will use components without data, i.e. $C = (\Sigma, P, \rightarrow)$ with $\rightarrow \subseteq \Sigma \times P \times \Sigma$. Notice that, since there are no data variables, $X = \mathbf{X} = \emptyset$ and $S = \Sigma$, i.e. the notions of state and control location coincide. Therefore, in the rest of this section, we will use 's' to denote both.

The proposed concept of component does not distinguish between input and output ports. We consider that such a distinction is not specific to ports. It can be inferred from the data-flow relation between ports specified in the coordination mechanisms. Similarly, we do not distinguish between synchronous and asynchronous components. This distinction is also inferred from the context of use.

2.2   Glue Operators

The problem of component-based design can be understood as follows. Given a component framework and a property Φ, build a composite component C which satisfies Φ. A component framework comprises a set of components $\mathcal{C}$, an equivalence relation $\cong$ and a set $\mathcal{G}$ of glue operators on these components. The glue $\mathcal{G}$ includes general composition operators, i.e. behaviour transformers, such as parallel composition.

A general formalisation of the notions of component framework and glue is provided in [13]. Below, for the sake of simplicity, we assume that components are characterised by their behaviours specified directly as Labeled Transition Systems (LTS). In this context, a component framework can be considered as a term algebra equipped with an equivalence relation $\cong$ compatible with strong bisimulation on transition systems. A composite component is any (well-formed) expression built from atomic components.

The meaning of a glue operator $gl : \mathcal{C}^n \rightarrow \mathcal{C}$ can be specified by using a set of *Structural Operational Semantics* (SOS) rules [38], defining the transition relation of the composite component $gl(C_1, \ldots, C_n)$ as a partial function of transition relations of the composed components $C_1, \ldots, C_n$. A formal and general definition of glue operators on LTS components is provided in [15]. Equation (1) shows a typical—although not general—form taken by SOS rules defining glue operators.

$$\frac{\{s_i \xrightarrow{p_i} s_i'\}_{i \in I} \quad \{s_j \xrightarrow{p_j} \!\!\!\!\!\!/\,\}_{j \in J} \quad \{s_i = s_i'\}_{i \notin I}}{s_1 \ldots s_n \xrightarrow{a} s_1' \ldots s_n'}. \tag{1}$$

Note 1. In the general case, as opposed to (1), several negative premises can apply to a single component. In any case, at most one positive premise can apply to a component.

The rule (1) has two parts: *premises* (above the line) and *conclusion* (below the line). Sets $I, J \subseteq [1, n]$ (with $I \neq \emptyset$) index two subsets of components, which need *not* be disjoint: components $\{C_i\}_{i \in I}$ contribute *positive* premises $s_i \xrightarrow{p_i} s_i'$, whereas components $\{C_j\}_{j \in J}$ contribute *negative* premises $s_j \xrightarrow{p_j} \!\!\!\!\!\!/\,$.

The rule (1) is interpreted as follows. The state space Σ of the composite component is the Cartesian product of the state spaces of composed components: $\Sigma = \prod_{i=1}^{n} \Sigma_i$. If 1) for each $i \in I$, component C_i can execute a transition from the state s_i to s_i' (with $s_i, s_i' \in \Sigma_i$) labeled by the port $p_i \in P_i$ and 2) for each $j \in J$, component C_j *cannot* execute *any* transition from the state $s_j \in \Sigma_j$ labeled by the port $p_j \in P_j$, then the composite component $gl(C_1, \ldots, C_n)$ can execute a transition from the state $s = s_1 \ldots s_n$ to $s' = s_1' \ldots s_n'$ (with $s, s' \in \Sigma$) labeled by an *interaction* a, where $s_i' = s_i$, for all components that do not participate, i.e. C_i with $i \notin I$.

Notice that the negative premises play the role of priorities. A transition of the composite component can be executed only if a set of transitions of the constituent components are disabled.

An interaction a, in the conclusion of (1), corresponds to the atomic synchronous execution of transitions in the composed components. Depending on the component framework, the interaction label a is obtained by combining the ports $\{p_i\}_{i \in I}$ in different manners.

Example 1. In CCS [34], ports are actions belonging to a given set $L = A \cup \overline{A} \cup \{\tau\}$, where actions in $\overline{A} = \{\overline{a} \mid a \in A\}$ are complementary to those in A and $\tau \notin A \cup \overline{A}$ is a special "silent" action. The binary parallel composition operator is defined by the following three rules:

$$\frac{s_1 \xrightarrow{p} s_1'}{s_1 s_2 \xrightarrow{p} s_1' s_2}, \qquad \frac{s_2 \xrightarrow{p} s_2'}{s_1 s_2 \xrightarrow{p} s_1 s_2'}, \qquad \text{for all } p \in L, \tag{2}$$

$$\frac{s_1 \xrightarrow{p} s_1' \quad s_2 \xrightarrow{\overline{p}} s_2'}{s_1 s_2 \xrightarrow{\tau} s_1' s_2'}, \qquad \text{for all } p \in A \cup \overline{A} \text{ (with } \overline{\overline{p}} \stackrel{def}{=} p). \tag{3}$$

In the conclusion of the rule (3), the resulting interaction is the silent action τ, replacing the combination of two complementary actions p and $\overline{p}$. □

In [25], the authors propose a notion of *label structures*, providing a generic mechanism for defining interaction labels of the composite components. Below, for the sake of simplicity, we consider a in the conclusion of (1) to be the set of ports $\{p_i\}_{i \in I}$ in the positive premises of the rule.

As shown above, positive premises in a rule of form (1) define interactions synchronising transitions of the constituent components. In a given global state of the system, several such interactions could be possible introducing non-determinism in the composed behaviour. Negative premises define *priority rules*, which allow reducing this non-determinism.

Example 2. Consider the two components C_1 and C_2 shown in Figures 1a and 1b. Let gl be a glue operator defined by the following three rules:

$$\frac{s_1 \xrightarrow{p} s_1'}{s_1 s_2 \xrightarrow{p} s_1' s_2}, \qquad \frac{s_1 \xrightarrow{q} s_1' \quad s_2 \xrightarrow{r} s_2'}{s_1 s_2 \xrightarrow{qr} s_1' s_2'}, \qquad \frac{s_1 \xrightarrow{q} s_1' \quad s_2 \not\xrightarrow{r}}{s_1 s_2 \xrightarrow{q} s_1' s_2}. \tag{4}$$

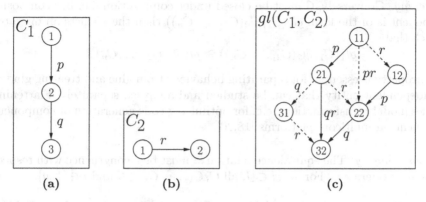

Fig. 1. Component behaviours for Example 2

The composed component $gl(C_1, C_2)$ is shown in Figure 1c. The dashed arrows show the transitions of the component obtained by composing C_1 and C_2 with the most liberal parallel composition operator, allowing any combination of transitions of the two components. Solid arrows show the transitions of $gl(C_1, C_2)$.

Among the transitions labeled by q, only the transition $22 \xrightarrow{q} 32$ is enabled and not $21 \xrightarrow{q} 31$ (Figure 1c). Indeed, the negative premise in the third rule of (4) suppresses the interaction when a transition labeled r is possible in the second component. Here, this results in giving $21 \xrightarrow{qr} 32$ "higher priority" over $21 \xrightarrow{q} 31$. Notice that, in the state 22 of $gl(C_1, C_2)$, r is no longer possible, i.e. $2 \xrightarrow{r}\!\!\!\!\!/\; $ in C_2. Hence, the third rule of (4) applies and we have $22 \xrightarrow{q} 32$.   □

Priorities are presented in more detail in Section 2.5, below.

2.3   Properties of Glue

Glue operators must meet the following requirements.

Incrementality. If a composite component is of the form $gl(C_1, C_2, \ldots, C_n)$ for $n \geq 2$, then there exist glue operators gl_1 and gl_2 such that

$$gl(C_1, C_2, \ldots, C_n) \cong gl_1(C_1, gl_2(C_2, \ldots, C_n)).$$

Incrementality is a kind of generalised associativity[2]. It requires that coordination between n components can be expressed by first coordinating $n-1$ components and then by coordinating the resulting component with the remaining argument.

---

[2] Notice that, for any permutation $\sigma : [1,n] \to [1,n]$, one can define a glue operator $gl_\sigma(C_1, \ldots, C_2) \overset{def}{=} gl(C_{\sigma(1)}, \ldots, C_{\sigma(n)})$. Applying incrementality to gl_σ with the permutation $\sigma = (2, 3, \ldots, i, 1, i+1, \ldots, n)$, we conclude that there must exist glue operators gl_1 and gl_2 such that $gl(C_1, \ldots, C_i, \ldots C_n) = gl_\sigma(C_i, C_1, \ldots, C_{i-1}, C_{i+1}, \ldots, C_n) = gl_1(C_i, gl_2(C_1, \ldots, C_{i-1}, C_{i+1}, \ldots, C_n))$, for any $i \in [1, n]$.

Flattening. Conversely, $\mathcal{G}$ must be closed under composition, i.e. if a composite component is of the form $gl_1(C_1, gl_2(C_2, \ldots, C_n))$ then there exists an operator gl such that

$$gl_1(C_1, gl_2(C_2, \ldots, C_n)) \cong gl(C_1, C_2, \ldots, C_n).$$

This property is essential for separating behaviour from glue and treating glue as an independent entity that can be studied and analysed separately. Flattening enables model transformations, e.g. for optimising code generation or component placement on multicore platforms [18,20].

Compositionality. The equivalence relation $\cong$ must be a congruence with respect to the glue operators. For all $gl \in \mathcal{G}$, all $C, C_1, \ldots, C_n \in \mathcal{C}$ and $i \in [1, n]$,

$$C_i \cong C \qquad \text{must imply} \qquad gl(C_1, \ldots, C_i, \ldots, C_n) \cong gl(C_1, \ldots C, \ldots, C_n).$$

Compositionality is fundamental for reasoning about systems. It allows considering properties of components in isolation and separately from the properties of glue operators to infer global properties of the system by construction. Furthermore, compositionality allows component providers to protect their intellectual assets by providing only an abstract specification of a component—any observationally equivalent implementation can then be substituted without affecting the semantics of the system.

It can be shown that glue operators defined by SOS rules, as in (1), are always compositional if the equivalence relation $\cong$ is compatible with strong bisimulation (recall the assumption of Section 2.2).

It should be noted that almost all existing frameworks fail to meet all three requirements. Process algebras are based on two composition operators (some form of parallel composition and hiding) which are orthogonal to behaviour, but fail to meet the flattening requirement as formulated above: in order to flatten a composite component, the operand components might have to be modified or additional components (e.g. context) might need to be introduced. General component frameworks, such as [2,24], adopt more expressive notions of composition by allowing the use of behaviour for coordination between components and thus do not separate behaviour from interaction. Furthermore, most of these frameworks are hardly amenable to formalisation through operational semantics.

2.4   Expressiveness of Glue

Comparison between different formalisms and models is often made disregarding their structure and reducing them to behaviourally equivalent formalisms, such as Turing machine. This leads to a notion of expressiveness which is not adequate for the comparison of high-level languages. All programming languages are deemed equivalent (Turing-complete) disregarding their adequacy for solving problems. For component frameworks separation between behaviour and coordination mechanisms is essential.

A notion of expressiveness for component frameworks characterising their ability to coordinate components is proposed in [15]. It allows the comparison of two component frameworks with glues $\mathcal{G}$ and $\mathcal{G}'$ respectively, the same set of components and equipped with the same congruence relation $\cong$.

We say that $\mathcal{G}'$ is *more expressive* than $\mathcal{G}$—denoted $\mathcal{G} \preccurlyeq \mathcal{G}'$—if, for any composite component $gl(C_1, \ldots, C_n)$ obtained by using $gl \in \mathcal{G}$, there exists $gl' \in \mathcal{G}'$, such that $gl(C_1, \ldots, C_n) \cong gl'(C_1, \ldots, C_n)$. That is, any coordination expressed by using $\mathcal{G}$ can be expressed by using $\mathcal{G}'$.

Example 3. Let P be a set of ports and consider two glues Bin and Ter generated respectively by families of binary and ternary rendezvous operators: $rdv_{a,b}^{(2)}$ and $rdv_{a,b,c}^{(3)}$, defined by the following rules (for all interactions $a, b, c \in 2^P$):

$$rdv_{a,b}^{(2)} : \frac{s_1 \xrightarrow{a} s_1' \quad s_2 \xrightarrow{b} s_2'}{s_1 s_2 \xrightarrow{ab} s_1' s_2'}, \quad rdv_{a,b,c}^{(3)} : \frac{s_1 \xrightarrow{a} s_1' \quad s_2 \xrightarrow{b} s_2' \quad s_3 \xrightarrow{c} s_3'}{s_1 s_2 s_3 \xrightarrow{abc} s_1' s_2' s_3'}.$$
$$(5)$$

Clearly, $Ter \preccurlyeq Bin$. Indeed, for any $a, b, c \in 2^P$, and any $C_1, C_2, C_3 \in \mathcal{C}$, we have $rdv_{a,b,c}^{(3)}(C_1, C_2, C_3) \cong rdv_{a,bc}^{(2)}(C_1, rdv_{b,c}^{(2)}(C_2, C_3))$. On the contrary, $Bin \npreccurlyeq Ter$, since any two components at any given state can only perform two actions (one action each), whereas three are needed for a ternary synchronisation. $\square$

We call *universal glue* the set $\mathcal{G}_{univ}$, which contains all glue operators that can be defined by the rules similar to (1) in the general form defined in [15] (see also Note 1). An interesting question is whether the expressiveness of $\mathcal{G}_{univ}$ can be achieved with a minimal set of operators. Results in [15] bring a positive answer to this question. It is shown that the glue of the BIP framework [6] combining two classes of operators, interactions and priorities, is as expressive as $\mathcal{G}_{univ}$. Furthermore, this glue is minimal in the sense that it loses universal expressiveness if either interactions or priorities are removed.

A consequence of these results is that most existing formal frameworks using only interaction such as process algebras are less expressive. This comparison can be strengthened by using the following weaker notion of expressiveness.

Often component frameworks consider certain behaviours, such as, for instance, FIFO buffers, to be part of the coordination primitives. To address such cases, we introduce a weaker form of expressiveness comparison. We say that $\mathcal{G}'$ is *weakly more expressive* than $\mathcal{G}$—denoted $\mathcal{G} \preccurlyeq_W \mathcal{G}'$—if there exists a *finite* set of *coordinating components* $\mathcal{D} \subseteq \mathcal{C}$, such that, for any component $gl(C_1, \ldots, C_n)$ with $gl \in \mathcal{G}$ there exist $gl' \in \mathcal{G}'$ and $D_1, \ldots, D_k \in \mathcal{D}$, such that $gl(C_1, \ldots, C_n) \cong gl'(C_1, \ldots, C_n, D_1, \ldots, D_k)$. That is, to realise the same coordination as gl, additional behaviour is needed. The term "weakly more expressive" is justified by the observation that, taking $\mathcal{D} = \emptyset$, $\mathcal{G} \preccurlyeq \mathcal{G}'$ clearly implies $\mathcal{G} \preccurlyeq_W \mathcal{G}'$.

Example 4. Taking on Example 3, it is clear that $Bin \preccurlyeq_W Ter$. Indeed, let $D = (\{*\}, \{\tau\}, \{* \xrightarrow{\tau} *\})$ (with $\tau \notin P$) be the only coordinating component. Considering τ as the "silent" action, it is easy to see that, for all $a, b \in 2^P$ and

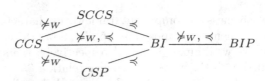

Fig. 2. Summary of relations between glues

$C_1, C_2 \in \mathcal{C}$, we have $rdv_{a,b}^{(2)}(C_1, C_2) \cong rdv_{\tau,a,b}^{(3)}(D, C_1, C_2)$. Therefore, we say that *Bin* and *Ter* are *weakly equivalent*.   □

It can be shown that glues including only interactions fail to match universal expressiveness even under this definition. Adding new atomic components does not suffice if the behaviour of the composed components is not modified.

Relations between the glues of BIP (see Section 2.5 below) and classical process algebras, namely CCS [34], SCCS [33] and CSP [26], which were obtained in [15], are summarised in Figure 2. BI denotes the BIP glue without priorities.

2.5 The BIP Component Model

In the light of the above results the BIP component model has been defined in [6,14]. BIP uses two types of glue. Given a set of atomic components $C_1, \ldots, C_n$ a composite component is modelled by an expression of the form $\pi\gamma(C_1, \ldots, C_n)$ where γ is a set of interactions and π a priority relation.

Let $C_i = (\Sigma_i, P_i, \rightarrow)$, for $i \in [1, n]$, with disjoint sets of ports, i.e. $P_i \cap P_j = \emptyset$, for $i \neq j$ and denote $P = \bigcup_{i=1}^{n} P_i$. The glue operator corresponding to a set of interactions $\gamma \subseteq 2^P$ is defined by the following set of rules in the format generalising (1) (see Note 1):

$$\frac{\left\{ s_i \xrightarrow{a \cap P_i} s_i' \right\}_{i \in I} \quad \left\{ s_i = s_i' \right\}_{i \notin I}}{s_1 \ldots s_n \xrightarrow{a} s_1' \ldots s_n'}, \qquad \text{for all } a \in \gamma, \qquad (6)$$

where $I = \{ i \in [1, n] \mid a \cap P_i \neq \emptyset \}$ is the set indexing the components that participate in the interaction. Notice that (6) has only positive premises.

Priority is a strict partial order relation $\pi \subseteq 2^P \times 2^P$. For two interactions $a, b \in 2^P$, we write $a \prec b$ as a shorthand for $(a, b) \in \pi$. As described in Section 2.2, priority introduces negative premises in the derivation rules. Intuitively, for an interaction a to be executed, it has to be enabled (cf. (6)) and all interactions with higher priority than a must be disabled.

For an interaction $a \in 2^P$, denote by $\pi(a) = \{ b \in 2^P \mid a \prec b \}$ the set of interactions having higher priority than a. For an interaction $b \in \pi(a)$ to be disabled, a corresponding transition must be disabled in at least one of the contributing components. To assign such a component to each $b \in \pi(a)$ we use, in the derivation rules (7) below, indexing functions $j : \pi(a) \rightarrow [1, n]$, such that, for all $b \in \pi(a)$, we have $b \cap P_{j(b)} \neq \emptyset$. Thus the glue operator $\pi\gamma$ is defined by the following set of rules:

$$\frac{\left\{s_i \xrightarrow{a \cap P_i} s_i'\right\}_{i \in I} \quad \left\{s_{j(b)} \xcancel{\xrightarrow{b \cap P_{j(b)}}}\right\}_{b \in \pi(a)} \quad \left\{s_i = s_i'\right\}_{i \notin I}}{s_1 \dots s_n \xrightarrow{a} s_1' \dots s_n'},$$

for all $a \in \gamma$ and $j : \pi(a) \to [1, n]$ such that $\forall b \in \pi(a), \big(b \cap P_{j(b)} \neq \emptyset\big)$,   (7)

where $I = \{i \in [1, n] \mid a \cap P_i \neq \emptyset\}$ is the set indexing the components that participate in the interaction a. In [15], we have shown that any operator of the universal glue $\mathcal{G}_{univ}$ can be obtained in such manner by combining a priority π and a set of interactions γ.

Besides meeting the universal expressiveness property, BIP meets the incrementality, flattening and compositionality requirements discussed in Section 2.3 (see the detailed discussion in [5]). Glue is a first class entity that can be analysed and composed.

The BIP model is implemented by the BIP language and an extensible toolbox. The BIP language can be considered as a general component coordination language. It leverages on C++ style variables and data type declarations, expressions and statements, and provides additional structural syntactic constructs for defining component behaviour, describing connectors and priorities. Moreover, it provides constructs for dealing with parametric and hierarchical descriptions as well as for expressing timing constraints associated with behaviour. The BIP toolbox includes tools for checking correctness, for source-to-source transformations and for code generation. Correctness can be either formally proven using invariants and abstractions, or tested by using simulation. For the latter case, simulation is driven by a specific middleware, the BIP engine, which allows exploration and inspection of traces corresponding to BIP models. Source-to-source transformations allow static optimizations as well as specific transformations towards implementation, i.e. distribution. Finally, code generation targets different platforms and operating systems support (e.g. distributed, multi-threaded, real-time, for single/multi-core platforms).

In the rest of the paper, we focus on modelling interactions by using connectors as well as the formalisation of architectures and their use for achieving correctness by construction.

3 Connectors and Their Properties

In this section we study connectors as a means for expressing coordination constraints between components. Connector descriptions involve a control part describing interactions and a data transfer part describing data transformations of the interacting components. We provide a principle for the hierarchical structuring of connectors and show how hierarchical connectors can be flattened into equivalent simple connectors. Finally, we propose a formalism for describing dynamic connectors that is currently under study.

3.1 Simple Connectors

We consider a set of components $\{C_i\}_{i \in I}$ with disjoint sets of ports $\{P_i\}_{i \in I}$. We denote for a set of ports P by X_P the associated set of variables. A connector γ is an expression of the form

$$\gamma = (a).[g(X_a) : X_a := f(X_a)],$$

where a is an interaction, that is a set of ports such that $|a \cap P_i| \le 1$ for all $i \in I$.

The interaction describes the control part of the connector. It is an n-ary atomic strong synchronisation between ports specified by the set of the synchronised ports. The term in brackets consists of a guard on the exported variables followed by an assignment. It describes the data transfer part of the connector. The execution of a connector is possible only if ports involved in the interaction a are enabled in the components and the guard g evaluates to true for the exported values. It consists in modifying the exported variables as specified by the assignment and letting the involved components complete the synchronised transitions.

The figure below depicts a connector between ports p, q and r with associated exported variables X_p, X_q and X_r. An interaction can occur only when at least two of the exported values differ (the guard is true). It is completed by assigning the maximum of their values to the port variables.

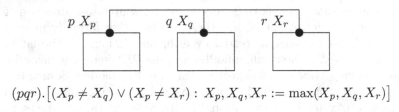

$$(pqr).[(X_p \ne X_q) \vee (X_p \ne X_r) : X_p, X_q, X_r := \max(X_p, X_q, X_r)]$$

Fig. 3. Simple connector

The effect of the application of connectors on a set of components is formally defined in [17].

3.2 Hierarchical Connectors

Hierarchical connectors are useful when we want to build systems incrementally. The idea is to equip each connector with a port and an associated variable. The port can be then used further in other connectors, and hence lead to a hierarchical structuring of connectors. Syntactically, a hierarchical connector γ is an expression of the form

$$\gamma = (w \leftarrow a).[g(X_a) : (X_w, X_L) := f_{up}(X_a) \mathbin{/\!/} X_a := f_{down}(X_w, X_L)].$$

As for simple connectors, the coordination in hierarchical connectors involves two parts. The control part $w \leftarrow a$ defines a dependency relation between the connector port w and its interaction a. That is, w is enabled if and only if the interaction a is enabled. The data part $[g(X_a) : (X_w, X_L) := f_{up}(X_a) \mathbin{/\!/} X_a := f_{down}(X_w, X_L)]$ defines the computation realised on local variables X_L and data associated to ports. The interaction is enabled and the computation is performed only if the guard $g(X_a)$ evaluates to true. In this case, computation involves two steps. First, an *up* function f_{up} is used to compute X_w and X_L depending on interaction variables X_a. Second, if an (upper) interaction involving w takes place, the *down* function f_{down} is used to update X_a based on X_w and X_L. Moreover, in an hierarchical connector, execution of up and down steps is coordinated: first, all up steps are performed bottom-up (as long as guards are satisfied), then, if a top-level interaction is executed, all down steps are performed top-down.

As an example, the coordination enforced by the simple connector presented in Figure 3 can be equally obtained by using the hierarchical connector depicted in Figure 4. The ternary connector and its associated data transfer is split in two binary connectors, glued together by the port w.

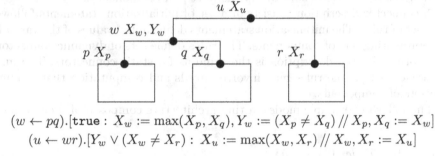

$$(w \leftarrow pq).[\mathtt{true} : X_w := \max(X_p, X_q), Y_w := (X_p \neq X_q) \mathbin{/\!/} X_p, X_q := X_w]$$
$$(u \leftarrow wr).[Y_w \vee (X_w \neq X_r) : X_u := \max(X_w, X_r) \mathbin{/\!/} X_w, X_r := X_u]$$

Fig. 4. Hierarchical connector

Hierarchical connectors can be statically flattened, that is, transformed into functionally equivalent simple connectors. For the control part, flattening amounts to substituting the inner connector ports by the associated interactions. For the data part, it reduces to static composition of up and down functions together with propagation of the guards. Flattening has been formally defined as a rewriting system on hierarchical connectors and proven confluent and terminating [17]. As an example, flattening of the connector from Figure 4 transforms it back into the simple connector from Figure 3.

3.3 Dynamic Connectors

How can we reason about architectures whose structure changes dynamically? There exists a variety of paradigms dealing with dynamic change in coordination. One is based on the use of process algebras such as the π-calculus [35]. Nonetheless, there is no clear distinction between behaviour and coordination and thus it is hard to come up with a concept of architecture in this context.

Another considers architectures as graphs and studies their possible configurations by using graph grammars. Technically architecture styles and possible configurations are described by context-free graph grammars [32,36]. This approach implicitly assumes the existence of a global coordinator. Furthermore, the focus is on changing structure and it is not easy to account for data transfer. Other more ad hoc techniques consider that dynamic architectures are just coordinators between components that can modify the architecture connectivity [1]. The approach closest to the one presented below is explored in [21], where *dynamic BI(P)* (BIP without priorities) allows spawning new components and interactions during execution.

We show below how dynamic connectors can be defined as a direct extension of connectors in BIP. We assume that system models are built using arbitrary numbers of typed components. The type T of a component defines its set of ports and associated exported variables. Two kinds of variables can be used in descriptions: 1) component variables c_i with an associated component type T, denoted $c_i : T$; 2) variables U_i representing sets of components of the same type T, denoted $U_i : T$. We denote by $c.p$ the port p of component c.

A connector description consists of a set of initialisation statements followed by a set of rules. The initialisation statements define initial values of the variables U representing sets of components. The rules define sets of dynamic connectors. The format for the description is the same as for static connectors. The main difference is that the rules may involve guards and computation that modifies the sets of components.

The following example models a ring architecture composed of n elements

$$U := \{c_i : T, \underline{for}\ 0 \leq i < n\}, \tag{8}$$

$$r_i := (c_i.out, c_{(i+1)\%n}.in).[\mathbf{true} : X_{c_{(i+1)\%n}.in} := X_{c_i.out}], \underline{for}\ 0 \leq i < n. \tag{9}$$

Line (8) initialises a variable U with an array of component instances by using the iterator primitive $\underline{for}\ 0 \leq i < n$. Line (9) gives a set of n rules for specifying connectors transferring data from outputs to inputs.

The following example models a set of n components that must strongly synchronise through their port p, with the possibility of disconnecting a component when it detects a failure and the possibility to rejoin the group in case of recovery. The first line creates an array of n instances of components c of type T. The description uses two variables U and U_{act} representing sets of components. The former is used to record the universe of the created components and the latter to record the set of the active components.

The configurations are described by three rules. Rule (10) involves an interaction requiring the synchronisation of all the active components. The corresponding computation consists in assigning to the synchronised port variables the maximum of the exported values. Rule (11) describes disconnection of the i-th component c_i when it detects a failure. Rule (12) describes insertion of a component after recovery.

$$U := \{c_i : T, \; \underline{for} \; 0 \leq i < n\}, \quad U_{act} := U,$$

$$r := (c.p, \; \underline{for} \; c \in U_{act}).[\mathbf{true} : x_{c.p} := \max\{x_{c.p} \,|\, c \in U_{act}\}, \; \underline{for} \; c \in U_{act}], \tag{10}$$

$$r_c^{fail} := (c.fail).[\mathbf{true} : U_{act} := U_{act} - c], \; \underline{for} \; c \in U_{act}, \tag{11}$$

$$r_c^{join} := (c.join).[\mathbf{true} : U_{act} := U_{act} + c], \; \underline{for} \; c \in U \setminus U_{act}. \tag{12}$$

As a final illustration, consider the Master-Slave example presented in [19]. Systems are constructed from two types of components, respectively masters (M) and slaves (S). Every master m_i requests sequentially two distinct slaves s_j, s_k (rules 13, 14) and then interacts with both of them (rule 15 above). The rules are graphically depicted in Figure 5.

$$U := \{m_i : M, \; s_j : S, \; \underline{for} \; 0 \leq i < n, 0 \leq j < m\},$$

$$req_{ij}^1 := (m_i.req \; s_j.get)[x_{m_i.req} = \emptyset : x_{m_i.req} := x_{m_i.req} \cup s_j], \tag{13}$$
$$\underline{for} \; 0 \leq i < n, 0 \leq j < m$$

$$req_{ik}^2 := (m_i.req \; s_k.get)[s_k \notin x_{m_i.req} : x_{m_i.req} := x_{m_i.req} \cup s_k], \tag{14}$$
$$\underline{for} \; 0 \leq i < n, 0 \leq k < m$$

$$comp_{ijk} := (m_i.comp \; s_j.work \; s_k.work)[s_j, s_k \in x_{m_i.req} : x_{m_i.req} := \emptyset], \tag{15}$$
$$\underline{for} \; 0 \leq i < n, 0 \leq j, k < m$$

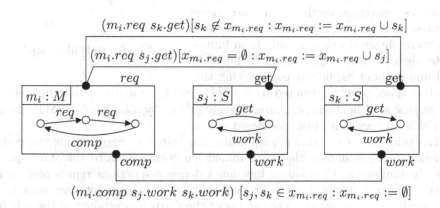

Fig. 5. Dynamic Connectors for the Master-Slave example

4   Achieving Correctness

We present two approaches for achieving correctness for component-based systems. The first is by compositional inference of global properties of a composite component from properties of its constituents and synchronisation constraints implied by composition operators. The second is by using and composing architectures that enforce specific coordination properties.

4.1   Compositional Verification

Compositional verification techniques are used to cope with state explosion in concurrent systems. The idea is to apply divide-and-conquer approaches to infer global properties of complex systems from properties of their components. Separate verification of components limits state explosion. Nonetheless, components mutually interact in a system and their behaviour and properties are inter-related. This is a major difficulty in designing compositional techniques. We developed for BIP a compositional verification method [11,10,9] for safety properties (invariants) based on the following rule:

$$\frac{\{C_i \models \Box \Phi_i\}_i \quad \Psi \in II(\gamma, (C_i)_i) \quad (\bigwedge_i \Phi_i) \wedge \Psi \Rightarrow \Phi}{\gamma((C_i)_i) \models \Box \Phi}. \tag{16}$$

This rule allows one to prove invariance of Φ for systems $\gamma((C_i)_i)$ constructed by using a parallel composition operation parameterised by a set of connectors γ on a set of components $(C_i)_i$. It relies on computing auxiliary invariants as the conjunction of component invariants Φ_i and an interaction invariant Ψ. Component invariants Φ_i are computed locally for components C_i, hence, they satisfy $C_i \models \Box \Phi_i$, for all is. Interaction invariants Ψ expresses constraints on the global state space induced by interactions between components. They are obtained automatically from finite-state abstractions of the system to be verified and without explicitly constructing the

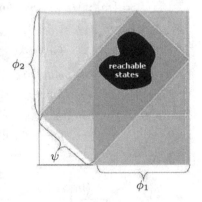

Fig. 6. Rule illustrated

product space, that is, denoted by $\Psi \in II(\gamma, (C_i)_i)$. Finally, if the implication $(\bigwedge_i \Phi_i) \wedge \Psi \Rightarrow \Phi$ holds, i.e. can be effectively proven by using a SAT/SMT solver, then Φ is an invariant of the composed system.

The principle of the rule is graphically illustrated in Figure 6 for two components C_1, C_2 assuming that each dimension corresponds to the state space of each component. Component invariants define restrictions represented as a vertical and a horizontal strip. The intersection of component invariants is a rectangular area including all the states of the Cartesian product of the sets of states meeting each invariant. The restriction induced by interaction invariants is an oblique strip that removes states of the rectangular area that are forbidden by the interactions.

As a concrete illustration, let us consider a simple benchmark example from [11]. The *Temperature Control System* models the control of the coolant temperature in a reactor tank by moving two independent refrigerating rods. The goal is to maintain the coolant between the temperatures $\theta_m = 100°C$ and $\theta_M = 1000°C$. When the temperature reaches its maximum value θ_M, the tank must be refrigerated with one of the rods. The temperature rises at a rate

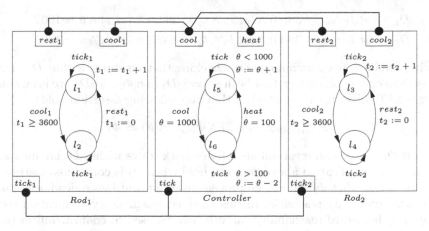

Fig. 7. Temperature Control System in BIP

$v_r = 1°C/s$ and decreases at rate $v_d = 2°C/s$. A rod can be moved again only if $T = 3600s$ has elapsed since the end of its previous movement. If the temperature of the coolant cannot decrease because there is no available rod, a complete shutdown is required. A discretised time model of the Temperature Control System in BIP is provided in Figure 7. The model consists of three atomic components, a *Controller* handling the temperature and two components Rod_1, Rod_2 modelling the rods. The variable θ within the *Controller* stores the temperature of the reactor. Its evolution depends on the state respectively, at l_5 (heating) it increases by one every time unit and at l_6 (cooling) it decreases by 2 every time unit. The transitions between states depend on the value of θ, as explained earlier. The $Rod_{1,2}$ components are identical. The $t_{1,2}$ variables are discrete clocks measuring the resting time. They increase by one every time unit. A rod can be used for cooling only when the resting time is greater than 3600. The *Controller* and the *Rods* are interconnected by five connectors $(tick\ tick_1\ tick_2)$, $(cool\ cool_1)$, $(cool\ cool_2)$, $(heat\ rest_1)$, $(heat\ rest_2)$ modelling respectively, the discrete time progress and the usage/releasing of the rods. In the BIP model, complete shutdown corresponds to a deadlock situation, henceforth, checking for functional correctness amounts to checking deadlock-freedom. The invariants computed on the BIP model are as follows:

$$\Phi_{Controller} = (at\_l_5 \land 100 \le \theta \le 1000) \lor (at\_l_6 \land 100 \le \theta \le 1000)$$
$$\Phi_{Rod1} = (at\_l_1 \land t_1 \ge 0) \lor (at\_l_2 \land t_1 \ge 3600)$$
$$\Phi_{Rod2} = (at\_l_3 \land t_2 \ge 0) \lor (at\_l_4 \land t_2 \ge 3600)$$
$$\Psi = (at\_l_2 \lor at\_l_4 \lor at\_l_5) \land (at\_l_1 \lor at\_l_3 \lor at\_l_6)$$

As explained in [11], deadlock-freedom of BIP models can be characterised as an invariant state property. For our example, potential deadlocks states include, e.g.

$$D_1 = (at\_l_1 \wedge t_1 < 3600) \wedge (at\_l_3 \wedge t_2 < 3600) \wedge (at\_l_6 \wedge \theta = 100)$$
$$D_2 = (at\_l_1 \wedge t_1 < 3600) \wedge (at\_l_3 \wedge t_2 < 3600) \wedge (at\_l_5 \wedge \theta = 1000)$$

Proving deadlock-freedom amounts to checking that no states within D_1 or D_2 are reachable, or equivalently, that both $\Phi_1 = \neg D_1$ and $\Phi_2 = \neg D_2$ are invariants. Using a SAT solver it can be checked that the following assertion holds

$$(\Phi_{Controller} \wedge \Phi_{Rod1} \wedge \Phi_{Rod2} \wedge \Psi) \Rightarrow \Phi_1$$

therefore Φ_1 is a system invariant and all deadlock states within D_1 are unreachable. But, the implication above does not hold when Φ_2 is considered instead of Φ_1. This means that Φ_2 cannot be proven invariant and hence deadlock states in D_2 are potentially reachable. In this case, complementary verification techniques, e.g. backward reachability analysis, can be used to confirm/infirm their reachability in the model.

Table 1 taken from [10] provides an overview of experimental results obtained for several benchmarks. For the columns: n is the number of BIP components in the example, q is the total number of control locations, x is the total number of boolean and integer variables, D provides, when possible, the estimated number of deadlock configurations, D_c (resp. D_{ci}) is the number of deadlock configurations remaining once component respectively interaction invariants are used and t is the total time for computing invariants and checking for satisfiability.

Table 1. Checking deadlock-freedom on classical benchmarks

example	n	q	x	D	D_c	D_{ci}	t
Temperature Control System (2 rods)	3	6	3	8	5	3	3s
Temperature Control System (4 rods)	5	10	5	32	17	15	6s
Readers-Writer (7000 readers)	7002	14006	1	-	-	0	17m27s
Readers-Writer (10000 readers)	10002	20006	1	-	-	0	36m10s
Gas station (100 pumps - 1000 customers)	1101	4302	0	-	-	0	9m14s
Philosophers (2000 Philos)	4000	10000	0	-	-	3	32m14s
Philosophers (3001 Philos)	6001	15005	0	-	-	1	54m34s

The original method from [11] has been extended in several directions. Incremental extensions, where invariants and properties are established along the model construction, have been studied in [8,7]. Moreover, it has been combined with backward reachability analysis and automatic strengthening of invariants for elimination of false positives [12]. More recently, the method has been extended to timed models and timed properties [3].

4.2   Property Enforcement—Architectures

Property enforcement consists in applying architectures to restrict the behaviour of a set of components so that the resulting behaviour meets a given property.

Depending on the expressiveness of the glue operators, it may be necessary to use additional components to achieve a coordination to satisfy the property.

Architectures depict design principles, paradigms that can be understood by all, allow thinking on a higher plane and avoiding low-level mistakes. They are a means for ensuring global properties characterising the coordination between components—correctness for free. Using architectures is key to ensuring trustworthiness and optimisation in networks, OS, middleware, HW devices etc.

System developers extensively use libraries of reference architectures ensuring both functional and non-functional properties, for example fault-tolerant architectures, architectures for resource management and QoS control, time-triggered architectures, security architectures and adaptive architectures. The proposed definition is general and can be applied not only to hardware or software architectures but also to protocols, distributed algorithms, schedulers, etc.

An architecture is a partial operator $A : \mathcal{C}^n \to \mathcal{C}$, imposing a characteristic property Φ and defined by a glue operator gl and a set of coordinating components $\mathcal{D}$, such that:

- A transforms a set of components $C_1, \ldots, C_n$ into a composite component $A[C_1, \ldots, C_n] = gl(C_1, \ldots, C_n, \mathcal{D})$;
- $A[C_1, \ldots, C_n]$ meets the characteristic property Φ.

An architecture is a solution to a coordination problem specified by Φ, using a particular set of interactions specified by gl. It is a partial operator, since the interactions of gl should match actions of the composed components.

Application and platform restrictions entail reduced expressiveness of the glue operator gl that must be compensated by using the additional set of components $\mathcal{D}$ for coordination. For instance, glue operators defined by connectors (cf. Sections 3.1–3.3) are memoryless. Hence, they can only be used to impose state properties. Imposing more complex safety properties requires additional coordination behaviour. Similarly, for distributed architectures, interactions are point-to-point by asynchronous message passing. Synchronisation among the components is achieved by stateful protocols.

The characteristic property assigns a meaning to the architecture that can be informally understood without the need for explicit formalisation (e.g. mutual exclusion, scheduling policy, clock synchronisation).

In addition to imposing the characteristic property, an architecture must preserve essential properties of the composed components. In particular, any invariant of a component C_i must be an invariant of $A[C_1, \ldots, C_n]$. In Section 4.3, we provide results about preservation of safety and liveness properties by architecture composition. Since there exists a unary identity architecture, which does not modify the behaviour of its operand, preservation of properties by architectures follows from that by architecture composition.

Architectures should, in principle, preserve deadlock-freedom: if components C_i are deadlock-free then $A[C_1, \ldots, C_n]$ should be deadlock-free too. However, in general, preservation of deadlock-freedom cannot be guaranteed by construction, since architectures restrict the behaviour of components they are applied to.

Instead, deadlock-freedom has to be verified a posteriori using techniques such as the one presented in Section 4.1.

4.3   Property Composability

In a design process it is often necessary to combine more than one architectural solution on a set of components to achieve a global property. System engineers use libraries of solutions to specific problems and they need methods for combining them without jeopardising their characteristic properties.

For example, a fault-tolerant architecture combines a set of features building protections against trustworthiness violations. These include 1) triple modular redundancy mechanisms ensuring continuous operation in case of single component failure; 2) hardware checks to be sure that programs use data only in their defined regions of memory, so that there is no possibility of interference; 3) default to least privilege (least sharing) to enforce file protection. Is it possible to obtain a single fault-tolerant architecture consistently combining these features? The key issue here is feature interaction in the integrated solution. Non-interaction of features is characterised below as property composability based on our concept of architecture.

Consider two architectures A_1, A_2, enforcing respectively properties Φ_1, Φ_2 on components $C_1, \ldots, C_n$. That is, $A_1[C_1, \ldots, C_n]$ and $A_2[C_1, \ldots, C_n]$ satisfy respectively the properties Φ_1, Φ_2. Is it possible to find an architecture $A[C_1, \ldots, C_n]$ that meets both properties? For instance, if A_1 ensures mutual exclusion and A_2 enforces a scheduling policy is it possible to find architectures on the same set of components that satisfies both properties?

A full, rigorous definition of the notions of architecture and property enforcement is provided in [4] alongside a constructive definition of an associative, commutative and idempotent architecture composition operator $\oplus$. An architecture is defined as a triple $A = (\mathcal{D}, P_A, \gamma)$, where $\mathcal{D}$ is a finite set of coordinating components, P_A is a set of ports and $\gamma \subseteq 2^{P_A}$ is an interaction model over P_A. Noticing that the interaction model γ can be represented by the corresponding characteristic predicate φ_γ on variables in P_A, the composition of two architectures $A_1 = (\mathcal{D}_1, P_{A_1}, \gamma_1)$ and $A_2 = (\mathcal{D}_2, P_{A_2}, \gamma_2)$ is defined by putting $A_1 \oplus A_2 \overset{def}{=} (\mathcal{D}_1 \cup \mathcal{D}_2, P_{A_1} \cup P_{A_2}, \gamma)$ where γ is such that $\varphi_\gamma = \varphi_{\gamma_1} \wedge \varphi_{\gamma_2}$. The properties of $\oplus$ are studied and applied for building correct-by-construction components incrementally. In particular $\oplus$ has a neutral element A_{id}, which is the most liberal architecture enforcing no coordination constraints.

When applying an architecture A to enforce a property Φ on components $C_1, \ldots, C_n$, the property Φ is expressed in terms of the states of $C_1, \ldots, C_n$. The states of the coordinating components $\mathcal{D}$ (see Section 4.2) are irrelevant. Therefore, we say that an architecture A enforces a property Φ on components $C_1, \ldots, C_n$ if the projection of every trace of $A[C_1, \ldots, C_n]$ onto the state space of $A_{id}[C_1, \ldots, C_n]$ satisfies Φ. In [4], we show that if two architectures A_1 and A_2 enforce the respective *safety* properties Φ_1 and Φ_2 on components $C_1, \ldots, C_n$, then $A_1 \oplus A_2$ enforces on these components the conjunction $\Phi_1 \wedge \Phi_2$ of the two properties.

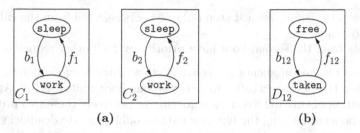

Fig. 8. Components (a) and coordinator (b) for Example 5

Example 5 (Mutual exclusion). Consider the components C_1 and C_2 in Figure 8a. In order to ensure mutual exclusion of their **work** states—$\Phi_{12} = (s_1 \neq$ **work** $\vee$ $s_2 \neq$ **work**$)$, where s_1 and s_2 are, respectively, state variables of C_1 and C_2—we apply the architecture A_{12} consisting of a coordinating component D_{12}, shown in Figure 8b, and the glue operator defined by the set of interactions and $\gamma_{12} = \{b_1b_{12}, b_2b_{12}, f_1f_{12}, f_2f_{12}\}$ (see Section 2.5).

Assuming that the initial states of C_1 and C_2 are **sleep**, and that of D_{12} is **free**, neither of the two states (**free, work, work**) and (**taken, work, work**) is reachable, i.e. the mutual exclusion property Φ_{12} holds in $A_{12}[C_1, C_2]$.

Let C_3 be a third component, similar to C_1 and C_2, with the set of ports $\{b_3, f_3\}$. We define two additional architectures A_{13} and A_{23} similar to A_{12}: they consist, respectively, of coordinating components D_{13} and D_{23}, which, up to the renaming of ports, are the same as D_{12} in Figure 8b, $\gamma_{13} = \{b_1b_{13}, b_3b_{13}, f_1f_{13}, f_3f_{13}\}$ and $\gamma_{23} = \{b_2b_{23}, b_3b_{23}, f_2f_{23}, f_3f_{23}\}$. As above, A_{13} and A_{23} enforce on $A_{13}[C_1, C_3]$ and $A_{23}[C_2, C_3]$, respectively, the mutual exclusion properties $\Phi_{13} = (s_1 \neq$ **work** $\vee$ $s_3 \neq$ **work**$)$ and $\Phi_{23} = (s_2 \neq$ **work** $\vee$ $s_3 \neq$ **work**$)$. The composition of the three architectures $A_{12} \oplus A_{13} \oplus A_{23}$, imposing the mutual exclusion property $\Phi_{12} \wedge \Phi_{13} \wedge \Phi_{23} = (s_1 \neq$ **work** $\wedge$ $s_2 \neq$ **work**$) \vee (s_2 \neq$ **work** $\wedge$ $s_3 \neq$ **work**$) \vee (s_1 \neq$ **work** $\wedge$ $s_3 \neq$ **work**$)$ on the three components C_1, C_2 and C_3, is given by the set of coordinating components $\{D_{12}, D_{13}, D_{23}\}$ and the set of interactions $\gamma = \{b_1b_{12}b_{13}, f_1f_{12}f_{13}, b_2b_{12}b_{23}, f_2f_{12}f_{23}, b_3b_{13}b_{23}, f_3f_{13}f_{23}\}$ (see [4] for details). □

One can define a canonical lattice on the set of architectures. The lattice is induced by the partial order relation $<$, defined by putting $A_1 < A_2$ if and only if $A_1 \oplus A_2 \cong A_1$. The neutral architecture A_{id} is the top element of the lattice; the bottom element is the "blocking" architecture, inhibiting all actions of the components, thus leading to a global deadlock.[3] The composition $A_1 \oplus A_2$ is then the greatest lower bound of A_1 and A_2 with respect to $<$. It represents the most liberal architecture enforcing both Φ_1 and Φ_2.

In the above setting, interfering features of a system are translated as contradictory properties. For example, the following two features can be required from an elevator cabin [23,37]:

---

[3] A deadlocked system trivially satisfies all safety properties.

1. If the elevator is full, it must stop only at floors selected from the cabin and ignore outside calls.
2. Requests from the second floor have priority over all other requests.

Clearly these two requirements are contradictory, since they cannot be jointly satisfied when the elevator is called from the second floor while it is full. Applying the composition of two architectures enforcing respectively these two properties on the components forming the elevator cabin would generate deadlocks.

Thus, although architecture composition $\oplus$ preserves safety properties, it does not preserve deadlock-freedom. Deadlock-freedom can be compositionally verified by techniques such as the one presented in Section 4.1.

The treatment of liveness properties is based on the idea that each coordinator must be "invoked sufficiently often" for the corresponding liveness properties to be imposed on the system as a whole. For each coordinator, one designates the set of its "idle states". It is then required that each coordinator be executed infinitely often, unless, from some point on, it remains forever in an idle state [4]. In [4], it is shown that this notion of liveness is preserved by the composition of architectures, provided that the composed system is deadlock-free and the composed architectures are pairwise non-interfering in the following sense. Architecture A_1 is *non-interfering* w.r.t. architecture A_2 and a set of components $C_1, \ldots, C_n$, if each path in $(A_1 \oplus A_2)[C_1, \ldots, C_n]$, which executes transitions of the coordinators of A_1 infinitely often, either executes transitions of the coordinators of A_2 or visits their idle states infinitely often.[4]

Example 6. Consider the system $(A_{12} \oplus A_{23} \oplus A_{13})[C_1, C_2, C_3]$, as in Example 5. Let each coordinator have a single idle state `free`. Consider the applications of each pair of coordinators, i.e. $(A_{12} \oplus A_{23})[C_1, C_2, C_3]$, $(A_{23} \oplus A_{13})[C_1, C_2, C_3]$ and $(A_{12} \oplus A_{13})[C_1, C_2, C_3]$. For $(A_{12} \oplus A_{23})[C_1, C_2, C_3]$, we observe that along any infinite path, either D_{12} executes infinitely often, or remains forever in its idle state after some point. Hence, A_{23} is non-interfering w.r.t. A_{12} and C_1, C_2, C_3. Likewise for the five other ordered pairs of coordinators. It can be verified that $(A_{12} \oplus A_{23} \oplus A_{13})[C_1, C_2, C_3]$ is deadlock-free. Hence, we conclude that $(A_{12} \oplus A_{23} \oplus A_{13})$ is live.   □

Thus, verifying liveness in a composed system is reduced to checking the deadlock-freedom and pairwise non-interference of architectures, both of which can be performed compositionally.

To put the above vision for correctness into practice, we need to develop a repository of reference architectures. The repository should classify existing architectures according to their characteristic properties. There exists a plethora of results on distributed algorithms, protocols, and scheduling algorithms. Most of these results focus on principles of solutions and discard essential operational details. Their correctness is usually established by assume/guarantee reasoning: a characteristic global property is implied from properties of the integrated components. This is enough to validate the principle but does not entail correctness

---

[4] Notice that the "non-interference w.r.t." relation is not commutative.

of particular implementations. Often, these principles of solutions do not specify concrete coordination mechanisms (e.g. in terms of operational semantics), and ignore physical resources such as time, memory and energy. The reference architectures included in the repository, should be

- described as executable models in the chosen component framework;
- proven correct with respect to their characteristic properties;
- characterised in terms of performance, efficiency and other essential non-functional properties.

For enhanced reuse, reference architectures should be classified according to their characteristic properties. A list of these properties can be established; for instance, architectures for mutual exclusion, time-triggered, security, fault-tolerance, clock synchronisation, adaptive, scheduling, etc. Is it possible to find a taxonomy induced by a hierarchy of characteristic properties? Moreover, is it possible to determine a minimal set of basic properties and corresponding architectural solutions from which more general properties and their corresponding architectures can be obtained?

The example of the decomposition of fault-tolerant architectures into basic features can be applied to other architectures. Time-triggered architectures usually combine a clock synchronisation algorithm and a leader election algorithm. Security architectures integrate a variety of mitigation mechanisms for intrusion detection, intrusion protection, sampling, embedded cryptography, integrity checking, etc. Communication protocols combine sets of algorithms for signalling, authentication and error detection/correction. Is it possible to obtain by incremental composition of features and their characteristic properties, architectural solutions that meet given global properties? This is an open problem whose solution would greatly enhance our capability to develop systems that are correct-by-construction and integrate only the features needed for a target characteristic property.

5   Architecture Specification

So far we have focused on modelling component-based systems and on methods for proving their behavioural correctness. In this section, we study logics for the specification of properties of architectures. Notice that the presented architecture modelling adopts an imperative description style: the coordination between components is given by a set of connectors. No interaction is allowed except the ones specified by connectors. In contrast, logics adopt a declarative style. A logical specification is the conjunction of formulas; its meaning is the set of the models belonging to the intersection of the meanings of the formulas. Consequently, logical specifications characterise not a single model but a set of models that may be empty. In the latter case, the specification is inconsistent.

Typically, an architecture defines a set of interactions between types of components. On the contrary, a class of architectures, what is usually called an architecture style, is represented by a set of congurations. We propose two types of logics for architectures: 1) Interaction logics to specify a particular architecture as the set of the allowed interactions; 2) Configuration logics to specify families of architectures as the set of the allowed configurations of interactions.

Configurations are defined as follows. Given a set of ports P an interaction a is a subset of P; there exist $2^{|P|}$ interactions on P. A configuration is a set of interactions $a_1, \ldots, a_n$ represented by a term of the form $a_1 + \cdots + a_n$ where $+$ is an associative commutative and idempotent operator. Notice that there exist $2^{2^{|P|}}$ configurations on the alphabet P. For instance, if $P = \{p, q\}$ then the set of non-empty interactions is $\{p, q, pq\}$ and the set of non-empty configurations is $\{p, q, pq, p + q, pq + p, pq + q, pq + p + q\}$.

For example, it is shown in the next subsection that the dynamic Master/Slave architecture presented in Section 3.3 can be specified in Interaction Logic. The class of Master/Slave architectures can be characterized by a formula of the configuration logic that specifies all the allowed configurations of interactions involving some master and slaves.

5.1   Interaction Logics

Let P be an alphabet of ports. The set of the formulas of the propositional interaction logic $PIL(P)$ is defined by the syntax:

$$f ::= \mathbf{true} \mid p \in P \mid f \wedge f \mid \overline{f}. \tag{17}$$

The models of the logic are interactions a on P. The semantics defined by the following satisfaction relation $\overset{i}{\models}$.

$$a \overset{i}{\models} \mathbf{true}, \quad \text{for any } a,$$

$$a \overset{i}{\models} p, \quad \text{if } p \in a,$$

$$a \overset{i}{\models} f_1 \wedge f_2, \quad \text{if } (a \overset{i}{\models} f_1) \wedge (a \overset{i}{\models} f_2),$$

$$a \overset{i}{\models} \overline{f}, \quad \text{if } (a \overset{i}{\models} f) \text{ does not hold.}$$

We use the logical connectives $\vee$ and $\Rightarrow$ with the usual meaning. Notice that the formulas of the logic can be put in the form of the disjunction of monomials $\bigwedge_{p \in I} p \wedge \bigwedge_{p \in J} \overline{p}$, such that $I \cap J = \emptyset$. An interaction a is characterised by the monomial $\bigwedge_{p \in a} p \wedge \bigwedge_{p \notin a} \overline{p}$. Propositional interaction logic has been extensively studied in [16] where it is shown that it can provide a basis for the efficient representation of connectors. For example, the interaction between p_1, p_2 and p_3 is defined by the formula $f_1 = (p_1 \Rightarrow p_2) \wedge (p_2 \Rightarrow p_3) \wedge (p_3 \Rightarrow p_1)$. Broadcast from a sending port s towards receiving ports r_1 and r_2 is defined by the formula $f_2 = (p_1 \Rightarrow s) \wedge (p_2 \Rightarrow s)$. Notice that the non-empty solutions are the interactions s, sp_1, sp_2, sp_1p_2.

In [19], we have shown that $PIL(P)$ can be extended into a first order logic to represent architectures built from arbitrary numbers of components, instantiating a finite number of component types. We present a slightly different version of this logic. As in [19], we assume that system specifications are built using arbitrary numbers of typed components. The type T of a component defines its set of ports and associated exported variables. Furthermore, we consider a set of component variables c_i with associated component types T. The fact that the component variable c_i is of type T is denoted by $c_i : T$. The syntax of the formulas of the first order interaction logic is defined by:

$$f ::= \text{true} \,|\, c.p \,|\, c = c' \,|\, f \wedge f \,|\, \overline{f} \,|\, \forall c{:}T.f, \tag{18}$$

where c and c' are component variables.

In this definition, T denotes a component type. Each component type represents a set of component instances with identical interface and behaviour. The variables c and c' range over component instances. They are strongly typed and, moreover, they can be tested for equality. The semantics of the logic can be derived from the semantics of the propositional logic as follows.

A formula of the logic defines the set of the interactions of a system built from known instances of typed components. Quantifiers can be eliminated by using the identity: $\forall c{:}T.F(c) \equiv F(t_1) \wedge \cdots \wedge F(t_k)$, where $t_1, \ldots, t_k$ are the instances of components of type T in the model. After quantifier elimination, we get a formula of the propositional logic. This logic can be used to specify dynamic architectures. For instance the formula $\forall c{:}\text{Sender}.\exists c'{:}\text{Receiver}.(c.send \wedge c'.receive)$, means that for any **Sender** there exists a **Receiver** such that their ports *send* and *receive*, respectively, interact. Relevant specification examples using this logic are provided in [19]. Furthermore, it is shown that for a given model the specified interactions can be computed efficiently by using a symbolic representation.

We provide logical specifications for the architecture of the Master-Slave example already seen in Section 3.3. Following the approach in [19], we introduce some additional notations that prove to be very useful for writing specifications:

$$Y.p \text{ requires } R.q \equiv \forall c : Y. \, \exists c' : R. \, (c.p \Rightarrow c'.q)$$

(every p port requires a q port for interaction)

$$Y.p \text{ accepts } R.q \equiv \forall c : Y. \bigwedge_{(T,r) \neq (R,q)} \forall c' : T.((c.p \neq c'.r) \Rightarrow \overline{c'.r})$$

(every p port can only interact with q ports)

$$unique \; Y.p \equiv \forall c : Y. \, \forall c' : Y.(c.p \wedge c'.p \Rightarrow c = c')$$

(no interaction between ports p)

Using the above abbreviations the architecture of the Master-Slave example is described by the following interaction logic formula:

$$(M.req \text{ requires } S.get) \wedge (M.req \text{ accepts } S.get) \wedge (unique \; S.get)$$
$$(S.get \text{ requires } M.req) \wedge (S.get \text{ accepts } M.req) \wedge (unique \; M.req)$$
$$(M.comp \text{ requires } S.work) \wedge (M.comp \text{ accepts } S.work)$$
$$(S.work \text{ requires } M.comp) \wedge (S.work \text{ accepts } M.comp) \wedge (unique \; M.comp)$$

Notice the difference in the description styles for the same example. When connectors are used, the style is imperative. The set of the interactions is constructed by enumerating connectors. When formulas are used, the style is declarative. The set of the interactions is in the intersection of the meanings of formulas which express constraints on the interactions required and accepted by each component. It has been shown that the two approaches are equivalent as long as we deal with interactions without data transfer. The association of computation and data transfer with formulas is not as natural as for connectors and raises methodological and technical issues.

The two styles correspond to two different approaches for eliciting architectural knowledge [22]. One is bottom-up and is adopted for building architectural models in various architecture description languages [28]. The other is top-down and is used to capture essential dependencies between features.

5.2 Configuration Logics

Let P be an alphabet on ports. The set of the formulas of the propositional configuration logic $PCL(P)$ is defined by the syntax:

$$f ::= \texttt{true} \mid m \in PIL(P) \mid f \wedge f \mid \neg f \mid f + f, \tag{19}$$

where m is a monomial of the interaction logic.

The models of the logic are configurations γ on P, of the form $\gamma = a_1 + \cdots + a_n$ where the a_i's are interactions on P. The semantics is defined by the satisfaction relation $\models$.

$$\gamma = a_1 + \cdots + a_n \models m, \qquad \text{if, for each } a_i, \, a_i \overset{i}{\models} m,$$
$$\gamma = a_1 + \cdots + a_n \models f_1 + f_2, \qquad \text{if, for each } a_i, \, (a_i \models f_1) \text{ or } (a_i \models f_2),$$

where m is a monomial of the interaction logic. For logical constants and connectives we take the standard meaning.

Notice the overloading of the $+$ operator. The meaning of the formula $f_1 + f_2$ is the set of the configurations obtained by combining some configuration satisfying f_1 with some configuration satisfying f_2. In particular, we have the property: $f_1 + (f_2 \vee f_3) = (f_1 + f_2) \vee (f_1 + f_3)$.

A simple example illustrates the expressive power of this logic. Let $P = \{p, q, r, s\}$ be an alphabet of ports. The monomial $p \wedge q \wedge \bar{r}$ specifies, in the interaction logic, the set of interactions pq and pqs. In the configuration logic, it specifies the set of configurations pq, pqs and $pq + pqs$. The formula $p \wedge q \wedge \bar{r} + \texttt{true}$ characterises all the configurations of the form $\gamma = \gamma_1 + \gamma_2$, where γ_1 satisfies $p \wedge q \wedge \bar{r}$ and γ_2 is an arbitrary configuration. Notice, in particular, that $\texttt{true}$ is not an absorbing element for $+$. Hence, γ_1 cannot be empty.

In general, a formula of the form $f + \texttt{true}$ characterises all the configurations comprising the configurations satisfying f. This type of formulas is particularly useful for writing specifications. We write $\sim f = f + \texttt{true}$ for any formula f of the logic. The operator $\sim$ is idempotent and satisfies the following property: $\sim f \wedge \sim g = \sim(f + g)$ for any formulas f and g.

We extend $PCL(P)$ into a second order logic. We assume that system models are built using arbitrary numbers of typed components. The type T of a component defines its set of ports and associated exported variables. We consider a set of component variables c_i with an associated component type T. The fact that the component variable c_i is of type T is denoted by $c_i : T$. Furthermore, we consider a set of variables U_i ranging over sets of components. This set includes a particular variable $\mathcal{U}$ representing the set of all the components of a model. We also adopt the notation $U_i : T$ to signify that all components in the set U_i are of type T.

The syntax of the second order configuration logic formulas is defined by:

$$f ::= \mathbf{true} \mid m \in PIL(P) \mid c = c' \mid c \in U \mid U \subseteq U' \mid$$
$$f \wedge f \mid \neg f \mid f + f \mid \forall U : T.f \mid \forall c : T.f, \quad (20)$$

where m is a monomial, c, c' are component variables and U, U' are variables over sets of components.

The semantics can be derived from the semantics of the propositional logic. For a given model $\gamma(C_1, \ldots, C_n)$, quantifiers can be eliminated in a formula to obtain a formula of the propositional logic.

The specification of a ring architecture composed of components $c : T$ having ports $c.in$ and $c.out$ is the conjunction of the following formulas:

$$\forall c : T. \exists c' : T \sim (c.out = c'.in) \wedge \forall c'' : T(c' \neq c''). \neg \sim (c.out = c''.in), \quad (21)$$
$$\forall c : T. \exists c' : T \sim (c.in = c'.out) \wedge \forall c'' : T(c' \neq c''). \neg \sim (c.in = c''.out), \quad (22)$$
$$\forall U' : T(U' \neq \mathcal{U}). \exists c \in U', c' \in \mathcal{U} \setminus U'. \sim (c.out = c'.in). \quad (23)$$

Formula (21) characterises all the configurations such that each output port $c.out$ of a component c is connected to some input port $c.in$ of some other component c' and explicitly excludes connections of $c.out$ with input ports of components other than c'. Formula (22) requires symmetrically connectivity of each input port to a single output port. The two formulas guarantee cyclical connectivity. Formula (23) requires that there exists a single (maximal) cycle. It says that any subset U' of components of the universal set $\mathcal{U}$ has a component that is connected to some component of its complement.

A comparison between the ring architecture model given in Section 3.3 and the above logical specification shows significant differences in both the style of expression (imperative vs. declarative) and the basic connectivity concepts. The model does not allow other configurations than the ones explicitly specified. Logical specifications characterise configurations that include token ring architectures without excluding other compatible connectivity properties.

6   Conclusion

The paper discusses research issues related to the design of component-based systems by distinguishing three main problems. The first problem is modelling

composite components as the composition of atomic components characterised
by their interface and behaviour. We propose a general framework for component
composition and study expressiveness of families of operators. For universal expressiveness, it is necessary to combine multiparty interaction and priorities. We
propose the concept of connector as a means for structuring interaction between
components. So far, static connectors and their properties have been thoroughly
studied. We present an extension for the description of dynamic connectors that
needs to be further studied and validated through application.

The second problem is achieving correctness of component-based systems by
application of scalable techniques. We identify two possible avenues. One relies on compositionality principles and proceeds by analysis of the composed
components and their coordination. The other relies on enforcement of specific
properties. A key problem in the application of this approach is composability:
how to obtain a system meeting a given global property by composing architectures meeting specific properties? Existing results limit both approaches to
particular classes of properties, e.g. deadlock-freedom and state invariants. We
believe that a significant research effort is needed to overcome these limitations.

The third problem is using logics to characterise architectures and their properties. We show that two types of logics are needed for this purpose. Interaction
logics characterise the possible interactions of a system, that is of a particular
architecture. These logics have been studied to a large extent and applied in
the BIP framework. In contrast, configuration logics can be used to characterise
families of architectures, e.g. architecture styles. They are languages used for a
feature-oriented analysis of architectures, such as OCL [27]. The relationships
between configuration logic and other approaches for the description of architectures styles [1,29,30,32] need to be investigated.

The paper clearly distinguishes between architecture models and two types
of logic-based specification formalisms. It also establishes links between the two
types of description through satisfaction relations. Table 2 depicts the main
characteristics of each formalism and significant differences.

Table 2. Architectures and Architectural Properties

Formalism features	Architecture Modeling Connectors (Imperative)	Architecture Modeling Interaction Logics (Declarative)	Architecture Styles Specification - Configuration Logics
Fixed set of components and connectors	Static connectors $I(P)$ $[g(X_P){:}X_P := f(X_P)]$	Propositional interaction logic, e.g. causality rules	Propositional configuration logic, e.g. connectivity primitives $\approx a$ and $\sim a$
Typed components; variables over components	Generic connectors	First-order interaction logic, e.g. Dy-BIP	First-order configuration logic
Variables over sets of components	Dynamic connectors	Second-order interaction logic	Second-order configuration logic

Interestingly, static models correspond to propositional logics, while dynamic models to higher order logics. Both dynamic models and higher order logics share the same basic concepts, e.g. they are defined on a set of typed components by using variables ranging over components and sets of components. Notice that component variables are needed to describe generic models and properties, while variables over sets of components are needed to describe dynamic creation/deletion and dynamic configurations. These similarities should allow a tight comparison of the three proposed formalisms, that needs to be further investigated.

References

1. Allen, R.B., Douence, R., Garlan, D.: Specifying and analyzing dynamic software architectures. In: Astesiano, E. (ed.) ETAPS 1998 and FASE 1998. LNCS, vol. 1382, pp. 21–37. Springer, Heidelberg (1998)
2. Arbab, F.: Reo: a channel-based coordination model for component composition. Mathematical Structures in Computer Science 14(3), 329–366 (2004)
3. Aştefănoaei, L., Ben Rayana, S., Bensalem, S., Bozga, M., Combaz, J.: Compositional invariant generation for timed systems. In: Ábrahám, E., Havelund, K. (eds.) TACAS 2014 (ETAPS). LNCS, vol. 8413, pp. 263–278. Springer, Heidelberg (2014)
4. Attie, P., Baranov, E., Bliudze, S., Jaber, M., Sifakis, J.: A general framework for architecture composability. In: Giannakopoulou, D., Salaün, G. (eds.) SEFM 2014. LNCS, vol. 8702, pp. 128–143. Springer, Heidelberg (2014)
5. Baranov, E., Bliudze, S.: Offer semantics: Achieving compositionality, flattening and full expressiveness for the glue operators in BIP. Technical Report EPFL-REPORT-203507, EPFL IC IIF RiSD (November 2014), http://infoscience.epfl.ch/record/203507.
6. Basu, A., Bozga, M., Sifakis, J.: Modeling heterogeneous real-time components in BIP. In: 4th IEEE International Conference on Software Engineering and Formal Methods (SEFM), pp. 3–12. IEEE Computer Society (2006)
7. Bensalem, S., Bozga, M., Boyer, B., Legay, A.: Incremental generation of linear invariants for component-based systems. In: 13th International Conference on Application of Concurrency to System Design (ACSD), pp. 80–89. IEEE (2013)
8. Bensalem, S., Bozga, M., Legay, A., Nguyen, T.-H., Sifakis, J., Yan, R.: Incremental component-based construction and verification using invariants. In: Bloem, R., Sharygina, N. (eds.) 10th International Conference on Formal Methods in Computer-Aided Design (FMCAD), pp. 257–256. IEEE (2010)
9. Bensalem, S., Bozga, M., Nguyen, T.-H., Sifakis, J.: D-finder: A tool for compositional deadlock detection and verification. In: Bouajjani, A., Maler, O. (eds.) CAV 2009. LNCS, vol. 5643, pp. 614–619. Springer, Heidelberg (2009)
10. Bensalem, S., Bozga, M., Nguyen, T.-H., Sifakis, J.: Compositional verification for component-based systems and application. IET Software 4(3), 181–193 (2010)
11. Bensalem, S., Bozga, M., Sifakis, J., Nguyen, T.-H.: Compositional verification for component-based systems and application. In: Cha, S(S.), Choi, J.-Y., Kim, M., Lee, I., Viswanathan, M. (eds.) ATVA 2008. LNCS, vol. 5311, pp. 64–79. Springer, Heidelberg (2008)

12. Bensalem, S., Griesmayer, A., Legay, A., Nguyen, T.-H., Peled, D.: Efficient dead-lock detection for concurrent systems. In: Singh, S., Jobstmann, B., Kishinevsky, M., Brandt, J. (eds.) 9th IEEE/ACM International Conference on Formal Methods and Models for Codesign (MEMOCODE), pp. 119–129. IEEE (2011)
13. Bliudze, S.: Towards a theory of glue. In: Carbone, M., Lanese, I., Silva, A., Sokolova, A. (eds.) 5th International Conference on Interaction and Concurrency Experience (ICE). EPTCS, vol. 104, pp. 48–66 (2012)
14. Bliudze, S., Sifakis, J.: The algebra of connectors — Structuring interaction in BIP. In: 7th ACM & IEEE International Conference on Embedded Software (EMSOFT), pp. 11–20. ACM SigBED (2007)
15. Bliudze, S., Sifakis, J.: A notion of glue expressiveness for component-based systems. In: van Breugel, F., Chechik, M. (eds.) CONCUR 2008. LNCS, vol. 5201, pp. 508–522. Springer, Heidelberg (2008)
16. Bliudze, S., Sifakis, J.: Causal semantics for the algebra of connectors. Formal Methods in System Design 36(2), 167–194 (2010)
17. Bliudze, S., Sifakis, J., Bozga, M., Jaber, M.: Architecture internalisation in BIP. In: Proceedings of The 17th International ACM Sigsoft Symposium on Component-Based Software Engineering (CBSE), pp. 169–178. ACM (July 2014)
18. Bonakdarpour, B., Bozga, M., Jaber, M., Quilbeuf, J., Sifakis, J.: From high-level component-based models to distributed implementations. In: 10th ACM International Conference on Embedded Software (EMSOFT), pp. 209–218. ACM, New York (2010)
19. Bozga, M., Jaber, M., Maris, N., Sifakis, J.: Modeling dynamic architectures using dy-BIP. In: Gschwind, T., De Paoli, F., Gruhn, V., Book, M. (eds.) SC 2012. LNCS, vol. 7306, pp. 1–16. Springer, Heidelberg (2012)
20. Bozga, M., Jaber, M., Sifakis, J.: Source-to-source architecture transformation for performance optimization in BIP. In: IEEE International Symposium on Industrial Embedded Systems (SIES), pp. 152–160 (July 2009)
21. Bruni, R., Melgratti, H., Montanari, U.: Behaviour, interaction and dynamics. In: Iida, S., Meseguer, J., Ogata, K. (eds.) Specification, Algebra, and Software. LNCS, vol. 8373, pp. 382–401. Springer, Heidelberg (2014)
22. Dhungana, D., Rabiser, R., Grünbacher, P., Prähofer, H., Federspiel, C., Lehner, K.: Architectural knowledge in product line engineering: An industrial case study. In: 32nd EUROMICRO Conference on Software Engineering and Advanced Applications (EUROMICRO-SEAA), pp. 186–197. IEEE (2006)
23. D'Souza, D., Gopinathan, M.: Conflict-tolerant features. In: Gupta, A., Malik, S. (eds.) CAV 2008. LNCS, vol. 5123, pp. 227–239. Springer, Heidelberg (2008)
24. Eker, J., Janneck, J., Lee, E., Liu, J., Liu, X., Ludvig, J., Neuendorffer, S., Sachs, S., Xiong, Y.: Taming heterogeneity—The Ptolemy approach. Proceedings of the IEEE 91(1), 127–144 (2003)
25. Fares, E., Bodeveix, J.-P., Filali, M.: Event algebra for transition systems composition - application to timed automata. In: Sánchez, C., Venable, K.B., Zimányi, E. (eds.) 20th International Symposium on Temporal Representation and Reasoning (TIME), pp. 125–132 (September 2013)
26. Hoare, C.A.R.: Communicating Sequential Processes. Prentice Hall International Series in Computer Science. Prentice Hall (April 1985)
27. ISO/IEC. Information technology – Object Management Group – Object Constraint Language (OCL). Technical Report ISO/IEC 19507, ISO, Object Management Group (2012)
28. ISO/IEC/IEEE. Systems and software engineering – Architecture description. Technical Report ISO/IEC/IEEE 42010, ISO (2011)

29. Koehler, C., Lazovik, A., Arbab, F.: Connector rewriting with high-level replacement systems. Electr. Notes Theor. Comput. Sci. 194(4), 77–92 (2008)
30. Kumar, A.: Software architecture styles a survey. International Journal of Computer Applications 87(9) (2014)
31. Lustig, Y., Vardi, M.: Synthesis from component libraries. International Journal on Software Tools for Technology Transfer 15(5-6), 603–618 (2013)
32. Metayer, D.L.: Describing software architecture styles using graph grammars. IEEE Trans. Software Eng. 24(7), 521–533 (1998)
33. Milner, R.: Calculi for synchrony and asynchrony. Theoretical Computer Science 25(3), 267–310 (1983)
34. Milner, R.: Communication and Concurrency. Prentice Hall International Series in Computer Science. Prentice-Hall (1989)
35. Milner, R.: Communicating and Mobile Systems: The π-calculus. Cambridge University Press (1999)
36. Papadopoulos, G.A., Arbab, F.: Configuration and dynamic reconfiguration of components using the coordination paradigm. Future Generation Computer Systems 17, 1023–1038 (2001)
37. Plath, M., Ryan, M.: Feature integration using a feature construct. Science of Computer Programming 41(1), 53–84 (2001)
38. Plotkin, G.D.: A structural approach to operational semantics. J. Log. Algebr. Program. 60-61, 17–139 (2004)

Effective and Efficient Model Clone Detection

Harald Störrle

Department of Applied Mathematics and Computer Science
Technical University of Denmark (DTU)
hsto@dtu.dk

Abstract. Code clones are a major source of software defects. Thus, it
is likely that model clones (i.e., duplicate fragments of models) have a
significant negative impact on model quality, and thus, on any software
created based on those models, irrespective of whether the software is
generated fully automatically ("MDD-style") or hand-crafted following
the blueprint defined by the model ("MBSD-style"). Unfortunately, however, model clones are much less well studied than code clones. In this
paper, we present a clone detection algorithm for UML domain models.
Our approach covers a much greater variety of model types than existing
approaches while providing high clone detection rates at high speed.

1   Introduction

Code clones (i.e., duplicate fragments of source code), have been identified as
"*a major source of faults, which means that cloning can be a substantial problem during development and maintenance*" (cf. [8, p. 494]). As a consequence, a
large body of research has been developed on how to prevent, or spot and eliminate code clones (see [12] and [21] for surveys). The problem with code clones
is that they are linked only by their similarity, i.e., implicitly rather than explicitly which makes it difficult to detect them. Therefore, changes like upgrades or
patches that are often meant to affect all clones in a similar way, are frequently
not applied to all of them uniformly. Therefore, code quality deteriorates, and
maintenance becomes more costly and/or error prone. Jürgens et al. report that
"*nearly every second unintentionally inconsistent change to a clone leads to a
fault*" (cf. [8, p. 494]). Experiences with large-scale models suggest that the phenomenon of clones arises in models in a very similar way to how it does in source
code. Deißenböck et al. even consider it "*obvious [that] the same [clone-related]
problems also occur [...] in model-based development*" (cf. [5, p. 57]). Consequently, the issue of clones has to be addressed for models, too: "*detecting clones
in models plays the same important role as in traditional software development*"
to use the words of Pham et al. [18, p. 276]. Observe that it is irrelevant whether
the models are used as the primary specification of a system, where production
quality code is to be generated from models only (as is frequently the case in
the automotive industry), or whether models are used in a more liberal way,
informing the software creation process rather than dictating it, as is the case
for more traditional domain models.

R. De Nicola and R. Hennicker (Eds.): Wirsing Festschrift, LNCS 8950, pp. 440–457, 2015.

1.1   Approach

In [23], we have studied the origins of model clones, derived a formal definition of model clones, and developed an algorithm for detecting them. Our approach was the first to address all of UML's 14 sub-languages rather than just a single model or diagram type, and so it is not surprising that it left room for improvement in terms of clone detection quality. In this article, we propose a modified algorithm and new similarity heuristics that improve on our previous results, while maintaining its generality. We also validate our approach far better, including 3 new case studies, and a field test.

1.2   Historical Background

As a young PhD-student under the tutelage of Martin, the author participated in the first UML-conference in Mulhouse. There was a great amount of enthusiasm about an important emerging topic, both in academia and industry, and the excitement spread over to Martin's chair, which of course was in a prime position to pick up the trend. Soon, many people at LMU worked on UML, and to this day, it is an important facet of the work done there.

One of the reasons why academia (and many formal-methods-inspired researchers in particular) picked up UML so readily is that it could be viewed as a visual front end to formal methods which had been less than popular with industry. UML, many researchers hoped, might be a way to bring formal methods to practice in a way that is easier to use. In fact, the author, in a fit of juvenile excitement, proclaimed that it had to be so easy as to push the proverbial button. While Martin was wise enough never to subscribe to the push-button benchmark, he was always keen on finding novel ways to improve software quality, one of them being presented here.

1.3   Paper Outline

The remainder of this article is structured as follows. In the next Section, we define the notion of model clone, and provide a taxonomy of clone types. In Section 3 we introduce an algorithm for clone detection and the model fragment similarity heuristics used at its core. In Section 5 we evaluate the effectiveness of our approach, and compare it to the related work in Section 6. Finally, we summarize our approach and draw conclusions.

2   Defining Model Clones

Probably the biggest problem in model clone detection is defining exactly what a model clone is—just as for code clones (cf. [9]). Fig. 1 shows a small part of a domain model of the "Library Management System" case study (LMS) which we use as our standard research object. The figure shows a part of the LMS information model with two Packages.[1] Fig. 1 shows two alternative views of the models: two class diagrams on the left, and the containment tree on the right. Most UML modeling tools today will allow several visual representations of the same model element, such as the Class "Reservation": it appears in both diagrams but exists only once in the containment tree. Thus, it is not a clone, but just one element appearing in two views. On the other hand, the Class "Book" occurs twice in the containment tree (highlighted by the red arrows). Looking closer, we analyze how similar the two model elements are. Assume that in this case, we find that they are identical in all but their internal identifier, so this model element is certainly a duplicate model fragment, i.e., a model clone. This kind of clone arises frequently in practical modeling, typically as a consequence of restructuring models, or from combining independent contributions that are not properly synchronized.

Requiring duplicate model fragments to be *identical* is clearly no adequate definition for the notion of "model clone". Instead, we propose to define a model clone as a set of model fragments each of which is closed under the containment-relationship and that have a high degree of similarity. Observe that this definition includes clones of all sizes, from individual elements via larger sets of model elements like a Property to large Packages containing entire subsystems. In order to refine this definition, we propose a taxonomy of model clone types. For code clone detection, there is a commonly accepted taxonomy of four types (see e.g. [12,21,26]). It can be generalized and adapted to accommodate our observations of natural model clones, as follows.

- **Type A: Exact model clones** are identical up to secondary notation and internal identifiers.
- **Type B: Modified model clones** may have small changes to names (e.g., typos) and other values, plus few additions/removals of parts.
- **Type C: Renamed model clones** may have any change to names, attributes, and parts, plus many additions/removals of attributes and parts.
- **Type D: Semantic model clones** are duplicates in content arising, e.g., from convergent modeling.

Formal definitions of the notions model, submodel, and clone are found in [23]. Orthogonal to the classification of the kind and degree of changes, model clones can also be classified in other ways.

- **Secondary clones** are pairs of duplicate model elements that satisfy the definition of a clone, but are each parts of larger model fragments, which in turn are clones of each other. For instance, the Class "Book" in the first example is a primary clone, and the Property "author" is a secondary clone.
- **Loophole clones** are duplicates introduced through idiosyncrasies of the modeling language. For instance, any two Activities that refer to the same data item will contain identical copies of a DataFlowNode, because the structure of the UML meta model forces these elements to be contained in an Activity rather than existing on their own. The modeler has no choice but to

---

[1] We adopt the UML convention of using CamelCaps for UML meta classes.

create such duplicates. In another modeling language (or in a future version of UML), they might not occur.

Both secondary and loophole clones will be among the detected clone candidates, and they may score substantially higher than actual clones, so they are presented before those clone candidates that, arguably, a modeler would expect to be presented first. Clearly, this depends on the similarity measure. For secondary clones, this is easily solved: out of a set of clones that can be (partially) ordered by containment, select only the largest one. But observe that loophole clones can be bigger than true clones. For instance, ActivityPartitions often contain many more elements than Properties, or even Classes. This is a substantial obstacle in similarity scoring, and thus in clone detection.

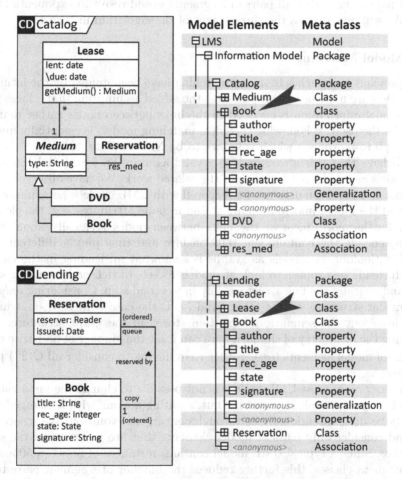

Fig. 1. Duplicate occurrence in diagrams does not constitute a clone (left, class "Reservation"); duplicates in the containment tree *may* be model clones (right, class "Book")

3   Detecting Model Clones

The starting point of the work reported here is the model clone detection algorithm N2 [23]. We now describe its shortcomings and how we overcome them, resulting in the new algorithm NWS. The improvements are based on (a) the detailed analysis of the algorithms' outputs for a great number of samples, and (b) the systematic exploration of a large number of alternative improvements and settings. We describe the various improvement steps from N2 to NWS.

The basic idea for detecting model clones is straightforward: (1) generate a set of (possibly) matching pairs of model fragments, (2) compute the similarity of each pair, and (3) select those pairs with the highest similarity. The problem with this approach is that, clearly, a model with n elements has up to 2^n fragments, so that naively matching all pairs of fragments would result in exponential runtime. We will now discuss the three stages of the algorithm in turn.

3.1   Model Matching

Many previous approaches to model matching have been guided by the intuition that models are more or less graphs, with the added assumption that a large part of the model information is encoded in the links between nodes rather than by the nodes themselves. Following this idea, matching models is essentially finding a subgraph isomorphism which is known to be NP-complete [3].

We believe that this idea is indeed a valid assumption for Matlab/Simulink flow models considered by much of the related work. We have observed, however, that this intuition does not fit very well with UML models: here, important aspects of the model information are stored in node attributes, e.g. the element names. Furthermore, most of the links between nodes (typically about 85%, see [23]) encode the containment relationship, and thus play a different role. Therefore, looking at models as graphs is somewhat misleading in the case of UML. Instead, we propose to look at models as sets of rich nodes owning small trees, and consider the link structure only in a second step. Considering *only* the containment structure, on the other hand (as is the case with XML-matching), would leave out the semantic information stored in the graph-structure. Also exploiting the symmetry of similarity, we can limit the number of pair-wise comparisons of model elements to $\frac{n^2}{2}$ rather than having to consider all $O(2^n)$ pairs of subgraphs.

Furthermore, in most UML tools it is not possible to change the meta class of a model element once it is created. Thus, creating a clone with a changed type can only be done intentionally or through convergent evolution. We ignore this case and consider only pairs of model elements that are instances of the same meta class. Since a typical UML model contains instances of between 50 and 60 different meta classes, this further reduces the number of fragment pairs to be considered from $\frac{n^2}{2}$ to around $\frac{1}{2}(\frac{n}{50...60})^2$ per element type on average.

Finally, the containment structure of UML models as defined by the UML standard implies that there are many model elements in a model that will typically not be considered as clones by a human modeler, i.e. the loophole clones described in the previous Section. We exclude instances of these meta classes up front, which typically account for more than half of all model elements in a UML model. Thus, the number of pairs to be considered is halved again. Together, these three assumptions drastically reduce the number of clone candidate pairs to be compared in our algorithm. These assumptions are realized in the first part of Algorithm 1.

3.2   Element Similarity (comparison and weighing)

In the second step, suitable pairs of elements are compared using different heuristics that are encapsulated in the *sim*-function used in step (2a) of Algorithm 1. The model element similarity function in N2 is based on similarities of the names of elements. We justified this by the observation that element names are very important in domain models. Of course, this notion of similarity is sensitive to renaming, a common operation in domain modeling. Thus, N2 also includes attributes other than the element name. Also, matching of neighbor elements is considered (by types and names).

While experimenting with this approach, we observed that the results were often skewed towards small fragments, because the degree of similarity computed by N2 is normalized by the number of potential similarities. Practically speaking, that means that a pair of fragments that coincide in 3 out of 5 possible ways are assigned a higher similarity measure than a pair of fragments that coincide in 30 of 51 possible ways. However, from a user's perspective, the latter is a more promising clone candidate by far: there is ten times as much evidence for the second pair being a clone than for the first one.

In order to account for this factor, we have implemented a new similarity heuristic in the NWS that includes the "weight" and "binding strength" of clone candidates. The weight which is computed as the number of elements and attributes of the elements contained in the clone candidates normalized by the binding strength. The contained elements are the transitive closure of a model element under UML's containment relationship (meta attribute "ownedMember"). This way, large clones with many small, slightly similar parts may take precedence over smaller clones with high similarity.

3.3   Candidate Selection

In practical modeling, clone detection very much resembles a web search: there are many potential hits, but modelers only ever explore a small fraction of them. So, the design goal of model clone detection is to provide the highest possible accuracy in a result set of a given (small) size. While weighing reduces the number of false positive clones, it is vulnerable against the phenomena of secondary and loophole clones we have explained in Section 2. In order to reduce these influences, NWS adds weighing and prioritizing to N2 (see stages 2b and the loop in stage 3 of Algorithm 1, respectively.

Clones of non-trivial size in UML domain models usually imply the existence of very similar sub-fragments, i.e., secondary clones. For instance in Fig. 1, a result

Algorithm 1. The NWS clone detection algorithm

Input:
- model M,
- result set size $k > 0$,
- threshold parameter *sensitivity*

Output:

- k clone candidates (pairs of elements of M)

1 - MATCH
$Elements \leftarrow \{e \in M \mid type(e) \in T\{Action, Actor, Class, \ldots\}\}$;
$Candidates \leftarrow \{\langle e_1, e_2\rangle \mid type(e_1) = type(e_2) \wedge e_1 \neq e_2 \wedge \{e_1, e_2\} \subseteq Elements\}$;

2a - COMPARE
$Comparisons \leftarrow \emptyset$;
forall the $\langle e_1, e_2\rangle \in Candidates$ **do**
  $E_1 \leftarrow$ transitive closure of e_1 wrt. `ownedMember`;
  $E_2 \leftarrow$ transitive closure of e_2 wrt. `ownedMember`;
  % *sim* **is a new heuristics for NWS**
  $s \leftarrow sim(E_1, E_2)$;
  if $sensitivity > 1/s$ **then**
    $\llcorner$ $Comparisons \leftarrow Comparisons \cup \langle E_1, E_2, s\rangle$

2b - WEIGH %new in NWS
$Results \leftarrow \emptyset$;
forall the $\langle E_1, E_2, s\rangle \in Comparisons$ **do**
  $s' \leftarrow s \cdot \frac{|E_1| + |E_2|}{binding(E_1, E_2, Comparisons)}$;
  $Result \leftarrow Result \cup \langle root(E_1), root(E_2), s'\rangle$;

3 - SELECT
sort *Results* by decreasing similarity;
$Selection \leftarrow \emptyset$;
%prefer primary over secondary clones
while $|Selection| < k$ **do**
  $Pick \leftarrow$ first element in *Results*;
  forall the $X \in Selection$ **do**
    if X *is contained in Pick* **then**
      $\llcorner$ $Selection \leftarrow Selection - X$
  $Selection \leftarrow Selection \cup \{Pick\}$;

return *Selection*;

Functions

type	:	type of model element (i.e. meta class)
sim	:	heuristic similarity of model elements, different for N2 and NWS
binding	:	binding strength between two fragments relative to a given set of similarities $binding(E_1, E_2, C) = \sum\{s \mid \langle E_1, E_2, s\rangle \in C\}$
root	:	root element of a fragment
$\|E\|$	:	number of model elements in a fragment

set might contain a reference to class "Book" as well as to the property "author" it contains. This can happen despite weighing due to the large variety of similarities and sizes of model clones: the secondary clones of one original may be both more similar and larger than the primary clones of another original. Human modelers usually have the insight to group together primary clones and secondary clones belonging to them, but this puts an extra burden on the modeler. In order to reduce this burden, we explicitly remove secondary clones from the result set (see the comment "case distinction in NWS only" in Algorithm 1). Loophole clones, on the other hand, are excluded by simply adding the respective meta classes to the list of types that are not considered when selecting comparison candidates (see parameter *sensitivity* in Algorithm 1).

4   Implementation

We have implemented our approach and integrated it into the MACH toolset [24]. MACH is available in various variants. First, there is stand-alone version with a textual user interface (called "Subsonic") which is available for download from the MACH homepage www.compute.dtu.dk/~hsto. Subsonic is also available in a pre-installed virtual machine that can be run remotely without installation or configuration on the SHARE platform http://fmt.cs.utwente.nl/redmine/projects/grabats/wiki, see the respective link at the MACH homepage.

Second, we have also provided a web-service based on MACH (called "Hypersonic", see [1]), where users simply upload a model in a web browser and receive a report on the most likely clone candidates. The implementation technology in all MACH variants (including the Hypersonic web server) is SWI Prolog (see swi-prolog.org). The web service is publicly available via the MACH homepage (http://www2.compute.dtu.dk/~hsto/tools/mach.html).

5   Evaluation

5.1   Samples

The work reported in this paper derives from the author's experience from two very large scale industrial projects. Due to legal and technical constraints, however, we could not use the models from these case studies directly for this paper. In order to evaluate the quality of our approach, we ran our implementation on four sample models created by students as part of their course work.

The first of these models, called LMS, has been created by a team of four students over 10 weeks; it contains 2,781 model elements (before clone seeding) and 74 diagrams. We used this model for exploration and experimenting with our approach. For the validation, we used three different case studies (called MMM, SBK, and HOS, respectively), created by teams of 5 to 6 students each over a period of 7 weeks. Table 1 presents some size metrics of these models. All of them were created using MagicDraw UML 16.9 (see www.magicdraw.com).

The LMS model was clone seeded by the author, the other models were clone seeded by their respective authors (i.e., teams of graduate students) as part of a challenge to create clones that our tool could not detect. Identification of seeded clones was achieved through a model difference. A typical example of a seeded Type A clone would be class "Book" in Fig. 1.

Table 1. The sizes of the sample models after seeding

Model	MMM	SBK	HOS	LMS	Sum
Elements	837	1,037	1,650	2,893	6,417
Attributes	2,097	2,915	10,493	17,196	32,701
Diagrams	26	54	33	74	191
Activity	10	27	9	36	82
Use Case	9	21	8	27	65
Class	4	4	7	7	22
Other	3	2	6	8	19
Diagram Types	6	5	8	6	

5.2   Method

As we have discussed in Section 1, there is no undisputed and precise definition of what is and is not a model clone. Relying on industrial models with natural clones, we have no control over the kinds and numbers of clones in them. Since our main objective is to develop algorithms, we resorted to manually seed models with clones. To do so, we randomly picked three typical examples of each of the meta classes UseCase, Class, and Activity in the sample model. We copied them (and their contained model elements), and changed them to emulate Type A, B, and C model clones. Then we marked both the nine original model fragments and the nine copied (and modified) model fragments manually as originals and clones, respectively. This resulted in 145 model elements being marked as clones and 155 being marked as originals, out of a total of 2893 model elements in the model after seeding, i.e., approx. 5.5% of the model elements were marked. A manual inspection of the LMS model did not reveal any natural model clones.

Our annotation allows automatic computation of precision and recall with respect to the seeded clones. The annotation was done by attaching comments to the elements. This way, the elements as such were not changed, as the connection between an element and its comments is established by a link in the comment, not in the commented element. Thus, we can exclude any influence on the clone detection by the annotation. Initially, we ran the clone detection algorithm without restricting the selection, thus yielding a very long list of clone candidates that contained a mixture of seeded clones, natural clones, and false positives. In order to identify the natural clone candidates, we manually reviewed them; almost all of them were loophole clones. We then annotated them so that they could be automatically classified by the test instrumentation of our tool. In order

Table 2. Measurements of clone detection quality: each box represents an individual seeded clone, a black box indicates detection within the respective constraints

HEURISTIC	N2				NWS			
RESULTS	@10	@20	@30	@100	@10	@20	@30	@100
PRECISION (SEEDED)	100.0%	54.5%	37.5%	16.7%	85.7%	53.8%	38.9%	13.3%
RECALL (SEEDED)	44.4%	66.7%	66.7%	66.7%	66.7%	77.8%	77.8%	88.9%
F MEASURE (SEEDED)	61.5%	60.0%	48.0%	26.7%	75.0%	63.6%	51.9%	23.1%
TYPE A CLONES	■■□	■■■	■■■	■■■	■■■	■■■	■■■	■■■
TYPE B CLONES	■■□	■■■	■■■	■■■	■■■	■■■	■■■	■■■
TYPE C CLONES	□□□	□□□	□□□	□□□	□□□	□■□	□■□	□■■

to control for bias originating from seeding by the experimenter, we conducted a second experiment. We challenged our students in a modeling class to seed their models with clones that our approach would not detect. This resulted in three clone-seeded models (SBK, HOS, MMM) which were comparable in terms of size and structure to the LMS model (see Table 1 for size metrics of these models). Subsequently, we ran the three detection algorithms on these models.

5.3   Data

Table 2 shows results for the heuristics N2 and NWS with varying result-set sizes. The first two lines show the precision and recall rates as percentages (based on seeded clones only). Since the LMS model did not contain natural clones prior to seeding, we compute recall and precision based on the seeded clones alone. The next three lines show the detection for different kinds of clones. Every box represents a particular seeded clone: the first box is a cloned UseCase, the second one is a cloned Class, and the third one is a cloned Activity. If a box is filled, the respective clone has been detected in the respective result set. So, for instance, □■□ in line "Type C" and column "NWS @30" means that neither the seeded UseCase nor Activity clones of type C were detected by algorithm NWS within the first 30 results, but the seeded Class clone was correctly identified. Similarly, ■■□ in row "Type A" and column "N2 @10" means that the N2 algorithm did not detect an identical copy of an Activity among the first ten results.

Table 3 shows the clone detection results in the models that were seeded by the students. We inspected the models manually to check detection results for accuracy. We also manually classified the clones according to our taxonomy; interestingly, the students' models also contained a number of natural clones that the students apparently were not aware of, but which our tool detected. See Table 3 for the detection rates.

5.4   Observations

Table 2 shows that precision decreases when recall increases, as is to be expected. Also, Type C clones are less often discovered than Type A and B clones. This is also no surprise since Type C clones have the greatest difference to the originals,

Table 3. Clone detection accuracy by case study and model type: N stands for natural clones, precision and recall are given relative to the first ten results, computed on seeded as well as natural clones

| Model | Detected/Seeded Clones | | | | NWS @10 | | |
	A	B	C	Natural	Precision	Recall	F-Measure
MMM	4/ 4	2/ 2	1/ 4	1/-	80.0%	88.9%	84.2%
SBK	6/ 6	2/ 2	0/ 2	2/-	100.0%	83.3%	90.9%
HOS	3/ 3	1/ 2	2/ 5	2/-	80.0%	80.0%	80.0%
All	13/13	5/ 6	3/11	5/-	86.7%	84.1%	85.4%

and thus the least similarity. The table also shows that NWS provides better detection rates than N2: among the first 10 hits, it covers more seeded Type A and Type B clones than N2. Among the first 20 hits, NWS yields fewer false positives. The same is true when extending the search focus to the first 30 hits. Then, most noticeably, NWS also finds the first Type C clone. Extending the search focus even further to the first 100 hits gives the same result. The increase in the number of false positives indicates that less duplicates are reported. The second Type C clone is reported among the first 100 hits.

Clearly, the results reported so far could have been achieved by tuning the algorithm to fit to the data, in particular to the seeding process. In order to ensure this is not biasing the results in a misleading way, we repeated the clone detection experiments with the models SBK, HOS, and MMM. They present a greater variety of models, and the seeding was done by students, not the author, with the specific instruction to try and break the approach. Even in these samples, however, we found the same differences in the detection rates of different clone types. Similar to the results obtained for the LMS model, Type A and B clones were detected reliably by NWS, that is, all seeded clones with no or little changes were among the first ten clone candidates. In the three models MMM, SBK, and HOS together, three out of eleven Type C clones were also correctly identified. Five natural (i.e., non-seeded) clones were identified, four of which were type A clones, and one of which was a type B clone.

In Fig. 2 (left), we show the first ten hits for each combination of the three algorithms and four models we have studied. We have sorted these ten reported clone suspects by the following four conditions: primary, secondary, duplicate, and false positive. Clearly, the goal is to have as many of the first kind in the result set as they will lead the modeler directly to a clone. Finding a secondary clone is second best, as it does lead the modeler to a clone, but only after having lead the modeler to some suspicious fragment of the clone first. Increasing either of these groups increases the detection precision and recall. Duplicate detections of clones do not add to the set of true positives, thus they do not increase precision and recall, though they still are, technically speaking, correctly identified clones. Finally, false positives are clearly the least desirable kind of reported clone candidates. The perfect score is to have ten primary clones among the first ten reported clone candidates.

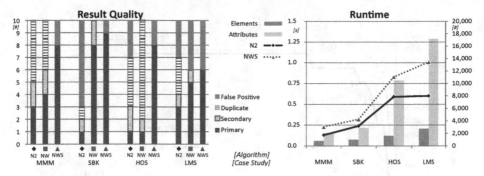

Fig. 2. Performance of three approaches to clone detection: a closer look at the first ten candidates (left); run-time vs. model size (right)

Obviously, the relative difference in clone detection accuracy between the three approaches that we have found in the previous experiment can be observed again in this sample: NWS outperforms N2 in all samples, if not in terms of precision then in terms of a higher rate of primary clones (case studies SBK and LMS). It is also clear, that the different case studies resulted in very different detection rates. Judging by these samples, our approach performs better on clone seeding done by other persons than the author.

Another important aspect of clone detection is the run-time. We have shown the measurements in Fig. 2 (right) by lines. We show the average of three subsequent runs to cancel out any effects due to garbage collection and similar factors. All of the experiments were conducted on a modest laptop computer (Intel i5-2520M 64bit processor at 2.5GHz with 8GB RAM running Windows 7). The run-time differed only insignificantly between NWS and N2 and seems to be independent from the size of the result set (see last row of Table 2). For N2, the run-time seems to slightly increase with the result size, but more detailed measurements would be required to support any stronger claims. The detection run-times are generally very low. To assess the relationship between run-times and model sizes, we have added the number of model elements and attributes in models as grey and blue bars, respectively. The measurements indicate that run-times of all algorithms are mildly polynomial in the model size. In fact, the polynomial appears to be so small, that for the model sizes at hand, it appears to be little more than linear, implying that the approach scales well and is applicable to real models.

5.5   Interpretation of Findings

The improvements of NWS over N2 come as no surprise: large duplicates are preferred over small duplicates with the same similarity. However, the details of the detection quality of NWS shown in Table 2 seem to be counter-intuitive: more false positives, and yet a higher coverage rate of seeded clones. This is entirely explained by the specific contribution of NWS, namely, the elimination

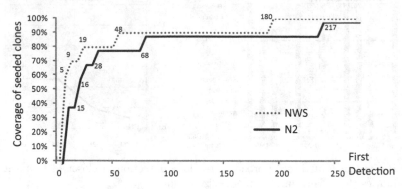

Fig. 3. Both heuristics find all seeded clones eventually, but NWS finds them faster than N2. The numbers in the graph indicate the rank of the last five detected seeded clones for NWS and N2, respectively.

of secondary clones. When there are indeed secondary clones for one primary clone in a given result set, removing all the secondary clones will promote the next batch of even less likely clone candidates into the result set. Sometimes, this batch contains another, true positive primary clone, but most of the time, there are just more false positives. And so, the precision drops. What NWS does in comparison to N2 is that it compresses the result set towards the top of the list, i.e., the quality of the first hits is improved. This can be seen quite clearly in Fig. 3, where we ran the three heuristics again and kept increasing the result set until all of them had perfect recall. We recorded the earliest position where each of the seeded clones was detected (x-axis) and plotted these against the number of detected clones in terms of the coverage (y-axis). It is easy to see how NWS consistently finds the seeded clones earlier than the other two heuristics.

Considering the run-time, it is at first sight surprising that the more elaborate heuristics in NWS would run faster than that of N2. However, recall that the largest part of the run-time is determined by model size, and that more selective similarity heuristics also imply an earlier elimination of potential solutions, reducing resource consumption. It is difficult to compare other approaches in terms of run-time: different settings may strongly influence the results. It does seem to be true, though, that competing approaches generally have higher run-times, that are either in the same order of magnitude (eScan), or one to three orders of magnitude larger (CloneDetective and aScan, respectively, see [18, p. 285]).

5.6 Threats to Validity

We have argued that code clones are actually occurring in practical settings, and that they are potentially damaging. However, most of our argument is only based on plausibility and subjective observations. Also, since this is a new area of research, there is not yet a large body of literature on this topic we can refer to support our point of view. Roy & Cordy described this as: *"more empirical*

studies with large scale industrial and open source software systems are required."
(cf. [21, p. 87]). However, it is very difficult to get access to industrial models,
and there are very few suitable freely available models, a problem that impedes
progress in this field (cf. the "Free Models Initiative", [25]).

The generalizability of our findings is limited by the number and the nature
of the models used to develop and validate our approach and the nature of the
clones in them: First, the model sample was not created in an industrial context,
but in an academic environment, so the models may not be representative. Second, the clones in the sample models are not natural but seeded, i.e. artificial,
so they may not be representative of the phenomena found in real models.

With regards to the first argument, consider that the related work in this area
has similar limitations: while they may use models of industrial origin, they use
very small sets of such models: e.g., the validations of [8], [6], and [18] are based
on five, one, and four different models, respectively. Clearly, such small samples
do not exhibit a higher level of representativeness than our models do. In the
absence of large scale representative field studies, using "real" models cannot
claim higher validity than using seeded models—only a large scale field study
will allow more general conclusions. However, in vitro work such as presented in
this paper is a necessary step towards such a large scale field study.

This observation applies to the second argument, too: seeded clones might
not be representative of real clones, but using such specimen is a necessary
stepping stone while better sample models are missing. Moreover, by seeding
the clones manually we can ensure that all kinds of clones are present in defined
quantities and qualities. In natural models, such properties are rarely found, and
any such selection would of course introduce undue bias, thus threatening the
representativeness of the model sample again. Since the primary purpose of the
work reported in this article is to develop algorithms, however, we think manual
seeding with full control over quantity and quality of clones across all categories
is not just acceptable, but actually essential. Developing our approach with the
models seeded by students would have been much more difficult, as the detection
results in Fig. 2 (left) suggest.

Still, one might object that it is unacceptable if the seeding is done by the
author himself; clearly, he is a potential source of bias. Therefore we also conducted the second experiment where we had no control over the models or the
clone seeding process. Surprisingly, the detection rates there are *better* than for
the models under the control of the authors, suggesting that the original benchmarks were biased, but no in favor of the algorithm under test, but against it.
As we have remarked, the resulting clone seedings were indeed different from
what we had expected, sometimes in quite surprising ways. However, our system
recognized 18 out of 18 seeded Type A and B clones, and 3 out of 11 seeded
Type C clones, within the very low threshold of just ten candidates. The seeded
clones that were not among the top ten candidates had undergone substantial
changes that made them hardly recognizable as clones, even to human observers
(in some cases, this included the students that created the respective clones).

5.7 End User Evaluation

The original implementation of our approach [23] had well over 100 parameters to be set manually. It required a deep understanding of the algorithms limiting the audience. Therefore, we have integrated our approach into the MACH model analysis and checking tool. We then deployed MACH to an undergraduate course on model based software development (41 students). After the course, we surveyed the students for their tool usage during the course (68% response rate), and found that students had some trouble installing MACH, and were unused to command line interfaces as such, but there were no negative remarks on the clone detection facilities. However, there were several positive remarks about this feature, e.g., students reported that it had helped them assess the quality of their models in unexpected ways. There were no problems in interpreting the results of clone detection either, although these results were not always perfect.

The field test clearly demonstrated, that it is possible to empower students with a very low level of qualification to routinely run an advanced clone detection algorithm without any additional support, without any noticeable problems. It is quite telling that the most negative comment on the clone detection was that "*at some point it reported clones that were actually not clones*" (i.e., false positives). We have since then used MACH in two more classes (48 and 54 students, respectively), without any problems.

6 Related Work

There is a large body of work on code clones: [12] provides a survey of the field, and [4] gives an overview of the state of the art. Clones in models, on the other hand, have received much less attention, only in the last few years have there been investigations into this topic. They can be divided broadly into four classes.

First, the CloneDetective system by Deißenböck et al. detects clones in Matlab/Simulink flow graph models [6,5]. This approach suffers from "*a large number of false positives*" (cf. [6, p. 609]), as the authors admit. It is also relatively slow (see [18]), since it effectively uses a graph isomorphism algorithm, Pham et al. [18] report run-times for CloneDetective in the range of a few hundreds of seconds for non-trivial models. Pham et al. then address this shortcoming with their ModelCD system using a hash-based clone detection algorithm. They achieve run-times roughly comparable to the ones we have presented above. Both CloneDetective and ModelCD are limited to Matlab/Simulink flow-models.

Second, there are various approaches dealing with matching of individual UML model types such as interactions [13,20] or state charts [17]. In contrast, our approach deals with all the UML's notations, including flow-like models such as activities, but also class models, use case models, interactions ("sequence diagrams"), and state machines.

Third, there have been approaches that have explored graphs and graph grammars as a generic underlying data structure for all types of models (cf. the PROGRESS system, [16,22]). These approaches have developed graph matching algorithms that might possibly be used for clone detection, but have not been studied under this angle. It does not seem like a promising avenue to explore, however, due to the fact that UML models do not store (much of) their semantic information in a graph structure. Rather than relatively dense and homogeneous networks of light-weight nodes, UML models are trees of heavy-weight nodes with some additional non-tree connections. Generic graph algorithms do not exploit this fact and thus miss a valuable opportunity (see [19] for a survey of graph- and tree-matching algorithms). In particular, consider Similarity Flooding (SF) [14], which is a fixed point computation that may take many iterations. Given the large number and size of potential mappings between duplicate fragments, such algorithms will not be applicable to clone detection for realistic models. To use the words of the inventors of Similarity Flooding: "*This approach [Similarity Flooding] is feasible for small schemas, but it does not scale to models with tens of thousands of concepts.*" (cf. [15, p. 3]). The heuristics we propose, however, appear to scale almost linearly. Moreover, Similarity Flooding depends on a reasonable initial seed value which is available for model matching in version control, but not for the kind of matching task we find in model clone detection.

Fourth, there are approaches that explore model matching for version control of models. Alanen and Porres [2] study set theory-inspired operators on models. Kolovos et al. on the other hand have proposed the Epsilon Merge Language ([11]) using a identifier-based matching process, while Kelter et al. [10] uses the Similarity Flooding algorithm in their SiDiff tool. Observe that in version control one can reasonably expect most model elements to have the same unchanged internal identifier in two subsequent model versions. Thus, it is easy to find a high-quality mapping to seed a matching algorithm. In clone detection, however, the problem is to efficiently find the mapping in the first place.

7 Conclusion

Model clones increasingly are a problem for model based development: there is "*strong evidence that inconsistent [code] clones constitute a major source of faults*" (cf. [8, p. 494]) and "*detecting clones in models plays the same important role as in traditional software development*" (cf. [18, p. 276]). However, there is currently not much published work on model clones, in particular on clones in UML models. In [23], we have developed a clone type taxonomy, and proposed an algorithm to detect clones. In this paper, we improved our earlier algorithm in terms of detection quality, and provide new front-ends to our implementation so that it can be used by non-experts. We also improved the scientific validity of our results by testing our approach with additional case studies that were clone seeded by independent parties, and a field test to assess the practical usability of our tool and approach.

The published data on approaches such as ModelCD and CloneDetective is somewhat incomplete making it difficult to compare them, though it seems that our approach is at least as good in terms of run-time and detection quality, while being applicable to a far wider range of model types: existing approaches cover only a single model type (e.g., UML State machines, or Matlab/Simulink models), while our approach applies to *all* of UML, and even DSLs.

Improving our previous work, the NWS algorithm provides much better detection rates, in particular with respect to improving the ranking of the first few clone candidates. Thus, from a modeler's point of view, the findings presented by NWS are of much higher quality. We have evaluated our approach, including also a field test with undergraduate students, underlining that clone detection is a practical tool rather than a mere research prototype. Reducing the number of false positives was made possible by understanding the structure of clones; these insights will likely be applicable in use cases of model similarity, too.

References

1. Acretoaie, V., Störrle, H.: Hypersonic - Model Analysis as a Service. In: Sauer, S., Wimmer, M., Genero, M., Qadeer, S. (eds.) Joint Proc. MODELS 2014 Poster Session and ACM Student Research Competition. CEUR, vol. 1258, pp. 1–5 (2014), http://ceur-ws.org/Vol-1258
2. Alanen, M., Porres, I.: Difference and union of models. In: Stevens, P., Whittle, J., Booch, G. (eds.) UML 2003. LNCS, vol. 2863, pp. 2–17. Springer, Heidelberg (2003)
3. Cook, S.A.: The complexity of theorem-proving procedures. In: Proc. 3rd Ann. ACM Symp. Theory of Computing, pp. 151–158. ACM (1971)
4. Cordy, J.R., Inoue, K., Koschke, R., Jarzabek, S. (eds.): Proc. 4th Intl. Ws. Software Clones (IWSC 2010). ACM (2010)
5. Deißenböck, F., Hummel, B., Juergens, E., Pfaehler, M., Schätz, B.: Model Clone Detection in Practice. In: Cordy, et al. (eds.) [4], pp. 57–64
6. Deißenböck, F., Hummel, B., Schaetz, B., Wagner, S., Girard, J., Teuchert, S.: Clone Detection in Automotive Model-Based Development. In: Proc. IEEE 30th Intl. Conf. Software Engineering (ICSE), pp. 603–612. IEEE Computer Society (2008)
7. Proc. IEEE 31st Intl. Conf. Software Engineering (ICSE). IEEE Computer Society (2009)
8. Juergens, E., Deißenböck, F., Hummel, B., Wagner, S.: Do code clones matter? In: ICSE 2009 [7], pp. 485–495
9. Kapser, C., Anderson, P., Godfrey, M., Koschke, R., Rieger, M., Van Rysselberghe, F., Weißgerber, P.: Subjectivity in clone judgment: Can we ever agree?. Tech. Rep. 06301, Internationales Begegnungs- und Forschungszentrum für Informatik Schloß Dagstuhl (2007)
10. Kelter, U., Wehren, J., Niere, J.: A Generic Difference Algorithm for UML Models. In: Proc. Natl. Germ. Conf. Software-Engineering (SE 2005). Lecture Notes in Informatics, GI e.V, vol. P-64, pp. 105–116 (2005)
11. Kolovos, D.S., Paige, R.F., Polack, F.A.C.: Merging Models with the Epsilon Merging Language (EML). In: Wang, J., Whittle, J., Harel, D., Reggio, G. (eds.) MoDELS 2006. LNCS, vol. 4199, pp. 215–229. Springer, Heidelberg (2006)
12. Koschke, R.: Survey of research on software clones. In: Walenstein, A., Koschke, R., Merlo, E. (eds.) Duplication, Redundancy, and Similarity in Software. Dagstuhl Seminar Proceedings, no. 06301, Intl. Conf. and Research Center for Computer Science, Dagstuhl Castle (2006)
13. Liu, H., Ma, Z., Zhang, L., Shao, W.: Detecting duplications in sequence diagrams based on suffix trees. In: 13th Asia Pacific Software Engineering Conf. (APSEC), pp. 269–276. IEEE CS (2006)

14. Melnik, S., Garcia-Molina, H., Rahm, E.: Similarity flooding: A versatile graph matching algorithm and its application to schema matching. In: Proc. 18th Intl. Conf. Data Engineering (ICDE 2002), pp. 117–128. IEEE (2002)
15. Mork, P., Bernstein, P.A.: Adapting a Generic Match Algorithm to Align Ontologies of Human Anatomy. In: Proc. 20th Intl. Conf. Data Engineering (ICDE 2004), pp. 787–791. IEEE Computer Society (2004)
16. Nagl, M., Schürr, A.: A Specification Environment for Graph Grammars. In: Ehrig, H., Kreowski, H.-J., Rozenberg, G. (eds.) Graph Grammars 1990. LNCS, vol. 532, pp. 599–609. Springer, Heidelberg (1991)
17. Nejati, S., Sabetzadeh, M., Chechik, M., Easterbrook, S., Zave, P.: Matching and merging of statecharts specifications. In: Proc. 29th Intl. Conf. Software Engineering (ICSE), pp. 54–64. IEEE Computer Society (2007)
18. Pham, N.H., Nguyen, H.A., Nguyen, T.T., Al-Kofahi, J.M., Nguyen, T.N.: Complete and accurate clone detection in graph-based models. In: ICSE 2009 [17], pp. 276–286
19. Rahm, E., Bernstein, P.A.: A Survey of Approaches to Automatic Schema Matching. VLDB Journal 10, 334–350 (2001)
20. Ren, S., Rui, K., Butler, G.: Refactoring the Scenario Specification: A Message Sequence Chart Approach. In: Masood, A., Léonard, M., Pigneur, Y., Patel, S. (eds.) OOIS 2003. LNCS, vol. 2817, pp. 294–298. Springer, Heidelberg (2003)
21. Roy, C.K., Cordy, J.R.: A Survey on Software Clone Detection. Tech. Rep. TR 541, Queen's University, School of Computing (2007)
22. Schürr, A.: Introduction to PROGRESS and an Attribute Graph Grammar Based Specification Language. In: Nagl, M. (ed.) WG 1989. LNCS, vol. 411, pp. 151–165. Springer, Heidelberg (1990)
23. Störrle, H.: Towards Clone Detection in UML Domain Models. J. Softw. Syst. Model 12(2), 307–329 (2013)
24. Störrle, H.: UML Model Analysis and Checking with MACH. In: van den Brand, M., Mens, K., Moreau, P.-E., Vinju, J. (eds.) 4th Intl. Ws. Academic Software Development Tools and Techniques (2013)
25. Störrle, H., Hebig, R., Knapp, A.: The Free Models Initative. In: Sauer, S., Wimmer, M., Genero, M., Qadeer, S. (eds.) Proc. MODELS 2014 Poster Session and ACM Student Research Competition, vol. 1258, pp. 36–40. CEUR (2014)
26. Tiarks, R., Koschke, R., Falke, R.: An Assessment of Type-3 Clones as Detected by State-of-the-Art Tools. In: Intl. Ws. Source Code Analysis and Manipulation, pp. 67–76. IEEE Computer Society (2009)

Living Modeling of IT Architectures: Challenges and Solutions

Thomas Trojer, Matthias Farwick, Martin Häusler, and Ruth Breu

Institute of Computer Science,
University of Innsbruck,
Innsbruck, Austria
{firstname.lastname}@uibk.ac.at

Abstract. Enterprise Architecture Models (EA Models) are documentations capturing the elements of an enterprise's IT infrastructure, setting these elements in relation to each other and setting them into the context of the business. EA Models are a crucial backbone for any IT management process and activities like analysing IT related risks and planning investments. The more companies depend on reliable IT services and use IT as innovation driver, the more high quality EA Models provide competitive advantage. In this paper we describe core challenges to the maintenance of EA Models based on previously conducted surveys and our longstanding experience in industrial collaborations. This is followed by a sketch of an innovative solution to solve these challenges.

1 Introduction

Enterprise Architecture Management (EAM) is an IT management process to describe, structure and plan complex IT systems in the context of the business. A core task within this process is to document the current state of business and IT infrastructure elements, e.g. business functions, software applications, servers, and to set these elements in relation to each other. The resulting *Enterprise Architecture Model* (EA Model) is usually very large in size, i.e. typically comprising several thousands of elements, and captures distributed knowledge of manifold stakeholders within the organization. There are a variety of tools for Enterprise Architecture Management off-the-shelf [22]. These tools typically support the documentation of architectural elements according to a given meta model and provide a set of representations, both of tree-like, graph-like or chart-like nature.

As we have shown in several surveys conducted with experts from industry [8,9], the quality of EA models in practice is an issue. Parts of this quality issue originate from organizational aspects, others stem from drawbacks of the available tools. One core drawback of available tools concerns the inflexibility of the EA Meta Model which does not adapt to grown terminology in organizations. A second drawback is deficiencies in the currentness of EA Models. EA Models which do not reflect the current state of the IT landscape may lead to wrong decisions on the management level. As two sources of this drawback we have been

R. De Nicola and R. Hennicker (Eds.): Wirsing Festschrift, LNCS 8950, pp. 458–474, 2015.

able to identify lacking automation capabilities and inappropriate user interfaces to maintain the model [7]. In addition, largely static visualizations of the EA Model in current tools are regularly mentioned to not adequately support the tasks of stakeholders like IT architects, operations staff and project managers.

In this paper we will start with a more thorough discussion of the challenges of tool support regarding EA models in the context of large IT infrastructures that are managed by geographically and organizationally distributed teams. These teams involve manifold stakeholders ranging from information officers, enterprise and IT architects to system administrators. This is followed by a presentation of possible corner stones for a solution to these challenges (see Section 3). Overall we call this modeling solution to be *living* in the respect that models and meta models can be maintained and visualized with a much higher degree of flexibility than in state of the art solutions.

We will demonstrate the materialization of the sketched solution within the novel EA modeling tool *Txture*[1] which has been developed by our team in the course of two industrial collaborations. Finally, we reference related work (see Section 4) and draw conclusions in Section 5.

2   Challenges

Typically IT management teams in enterprises have their own distinct terminology and levels of detail to document their IT systems and business functions. Hence, the need for flexible meta models is among the conclusions from conducted surveys. Flexibility means e.g. that the EA Meta Model which is underlying the architecture documentation needs to be customizable in order to fit the current information demand of an organization and its stakeholders. Over time these information demands usually change, e.g. due to the use of new technology or modified catalogues of provided business services. Hence, a properly usable EA Meta Model needs to adapt accordingly. This is in line with the work of Schweda [25], who also describes evolving organization-specific meta models as important and defines them as a requirement for successful EAM.

Once the EA Meta Model is aligned with the documentation requirements of an enterprise, a corresponding EA Model can be developed and describes the current state of the IT architecture and business assets. Modeling the EA is an incremental process and needs collaboration of a diverse set of stakeholders providing their knowledge about different enterprise aspects. While the enterprise transforms over time, the EA Model, in order to stay usable, needs to be adapted. Our experience has shown that enterprise stakeholders are often reluctant to keep the EA Model in-sync with reality, mostly because their documentation tools do not integrate well in their working environments. Recently we have described the use of text-based EA modeling [11], specifically tailored to support stakeholders with technical background. In general we argue that an EAM tool has to provide modeling support tailored towards the needs of its stakeholders. In particular this comprises consideration of both business-level

---

[1] See http://www.txture.org

stakeholders (preferring e.g. forms and charts) and technology-level stakeholders (preferring e.g. programming style or graphical representations).

Up-to-date EA Models are a prerequisite to EAM activities such as the analysis of current IT architectures and planning upcoming developments and projects. These analysis and planning steps require dedicated consideration and are commonly supported by a set of static visualizations providing specific views on the EA models [20]. Feedback received by experts from industry has shown that stakeholder-specific visualizations are to a large extent missing in current EAM tools. By stakeholder-specific visualizations we mean dynamic and navigable views, supporting an individual user to analyze the EA model. This is in line with trends in Business Intelligence, where such visualizations are also known and part of the *self-service* aspect[2].

Finally, an integral challenge to all of the aforementioned aspects is to maintain high computational performance of operations on top of EA Models. When dealing with large-scale EA Models optimized and automated adaptations based on a changed meta model, the browsing and querying of arbitrary EA Model elements and the creation of visualizations from the entire EA Model need to be accomplished in a timely manner. Otherwise, the usability of an EA modeling tool and the tool's acceptance by enterprise stakeholders may be heavily affected.

Overall, we summarize the EAM tool challenges we have outlined in this section as follows:

- Implementation of *flexible IT architecture modeling*
- Need for *stakeholder-centric modeling editors*
- Provision of *dynamic and navigable visualizations*
- *High performance of EAM operations* on top of large-scale EA Models

3   Solutions within the Living Modeling Environment Txture

In 2011 we started a consulting project with a banking data center and subsequently a research project with the data center of a large semiconductor manufacturer. The overall goal of both projects was to make the documentation of EA more efficient and effective. Enhanced flexibility as well as usability features and stakeholder orientation of the implemented tool were generally seen as important. In addition, requirements to support common EAM activities on top of an EA Model were considered.

The key features of the resulting modeling tool *Txture* are as follows:

- Modeling of the architecture via a form-based web-client to support less technically skilled users.
- Textual architecture modeling via a meta-model aware *Eclipse*-based text editor [11] provided to technical staff.
- Dynamic and flexible graph visualizations of EA Models.

---

[2] BI Survey '13, "The latest market trends", http://barc-research.com/bi-survey/

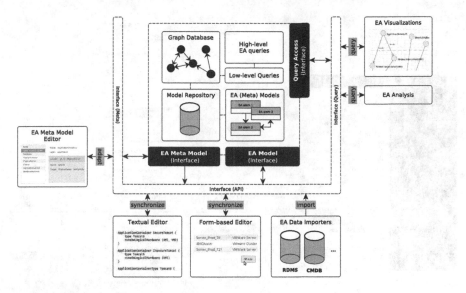

Fig. 1. The *Txture* environment showing the EA model persistence at its core and auxiliary components for EA management purposes

- High performance model queries via optimized persistence of models in a graph database.
- The ability to define and change the EA Meta Model at runtime.
- Configurable import mechanisms to automatically use architectural data contained in external sources such as in *Configuration Management Databases* (CMDB), *Excel* spreadsheets, source code or relational databases.

These key features are reflected in the architecture of the *Txture* modeling environment (see Figure 1).

Figure 2 depicts a graph-based architecture visualization (see top-most screenshot). There, relationships between *application containers*, an *application* and the underlying (clustered) hardware infrastructure are shown. Such visualization is used e.g. to perform impact and risk analysis of application deployments.

Several other key visualization features can be seen in the corresponding part of the figure:

- Architectural elements are assigned to *layers*, hence the visualization automatically shows an intuitive architectural stack.
- The visualization is *navigable* and *dynamic* via a set of modification operations (see the context menu depicted in the screenshot).
- Graph nodes are *styled* based on their type or other attributes, like mission-criticality (cf. the elements *VMWare Cluster* and *VMWare Server*).

Furthermore, Figure 2 shows the meta modeling capabilities via a form-based editor. This editor allows the user to change the EA Meta Model at runtime

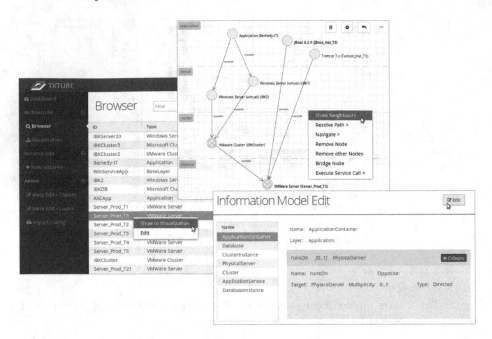

Fig. 2. The *Txture* environment showing the architecture browser (left screenshot), dynamic visualizations (top-most) and the ability to view and change the EA Meta Model (bottom-most)

which in turn directly influences the visualizations and the import configurations for mapping EA data of external data sources.

Finally, basic search and query functionality is implemented via an architecture browser and is indicated on the left side of Figure 2.

3.1   Modeling Framework

In this section we outline *Txture*'s employed modeling framework using a sample model (see Figure 3).

The EA Model in Figure 3 shows documented instances of IT system components. The example describes an application container instance "*JBoss_Inst_T3*" which "*runsOn*" a physical server named "*Server_Prod_T3*". As we have described in the previous section, such a model can be used e.g., to perform impact analysis ("What happens if the specific server crashes?") or to do infrastructure planning ("Is the specific server appropriately dimensioned to run such software?").

Additional to modeling IT component instances and their structural dependencies, a simple notion of *ontology* can be seen on the right side of the figure. Such ontological classifications are modeled as part of the documentation activity and allow responsible persons for EA elements to further describe and categorize their documented instances. In our example case, the application container instance is of *type* "*JBoss EAP 6.2.0*" which reflects a part of the enterprise's

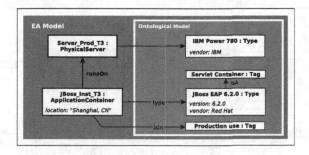

Fig. 3. A simple EA Model showing IT infrastructure elements

modeled ontology. Furthermore it is *tagged* with *"Servlet Container"* to indicate its relatedness (*"isA"*) to *Java servlet* technology. Ontologies in EA Models are established to introduce enterprise-specific terminology (e.g., by means of employed technology), but are also used in *Txture* to enhance browsing, search and filter functionality.

Figure 4 provides an extended view of our example model by including its corresponding meta-model hierarchy. On the EA Meta Model level, the expressiveness of the underlying EA Model is set. At this level the structure of a EA documentation that architects agreed upon is modeled.

The top-level artifact, the meta-meta model, defines all concepts that are needed to properly describe IT infrastructures. The meta-meta model defines the concepts of *class*, *association* (i.e. association classes) and *property* to develop the structure of an organization-specific architecture modeling language and the concepts *type*, *tag* and *mixin* that allow shaping the ontological model.

Classical Hierarchies to Separate Modeling Activities. One of the experiences we gained from modeling workshops with our industry partners is that modeling novices or software developers understand modeling best when using strict and limited hierarchies in which modeling concepts and their instantiations are described. In our case the modeling levels that users have to interact with are manifested by the EA Meta Model and the EA Model as its instantiation.

Besides understandability of concepts, having a clear cut between modeling levels also supports a permission and concern-oriented separation for managing the EA documentation and the meta model it relies on. This separation is important as different modeling activities are performed by individual stakeholders with potentially diverse domain expertise. This is further explained in Section 3.2.

Types to Mitigate Invasive Meta Model Changes. Another experience we made was that adapting the EA Meta Model is typically a recurring activity, triggered by frequent change requests from our partners and driven by adjustments, extensions and simplifications to modeled concepts.

It is common to any modeling activity, that changes to models may involve corresponding changes on dependent models, as part of re-establishing conformance in the model hierarchy. To minimize the efforts and consequences of such

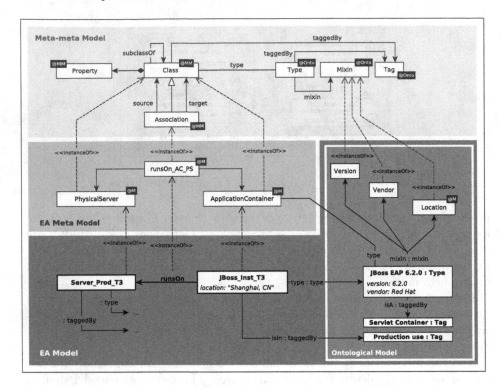

Fig. 4. The *Txture* modeling environment. Annotation boxes (black) reflect where a model element gets instantiated (@MM = EA Meta Model, @Onto = Ontological model and @M = EA Model)

changes, either well-defined automated model refactoring procedures are required or a meta model needs to be realized in a way such that the most common changes to it only minimally interfere.

For our industry partners a manual refactoring after changes to the EA Meta Model was out of question. This is why we settled on a modeling pattern similar to the one of *power types* [23] that allows for creating types at the EA Model level and therefore reduces the need to actually adapt the related meta model.

Our original modeling approach made heavy use of inheritance on the meta model level. For example we applied a deep inheritance structure to model different *Application Containers* according to their *vendor*, *software version* or required *runtime platform*. This rendered the meta model both large in size (i.e. number of model elements) and prone to frequent changes (e.g. on software version changes).

Using *types* greatly helped to reduce the size of the meta model and therefore maintaining comprehensibility and lowering the frequency in which changes to it needed to be applied. A modeling environment that allows types, can rely solely on generic meta model elements like *Physical Server* or *Application Container* and therefore provides stable modeling concepts that are *invariant* to an organization and all of its stakeholders. This means e.g. that no highly-specific vendor-based product terminology would be described within the EA Meta Model which would only be understood by a minority of the enterprise's stakeholders and which is likely to change over time (cf. *JBoss*-specific server software in the example of Figure 3).

Our understanding of types, as part of the ontological model, is that adjustments to them can be easily applied during the regular EA documentation processes. This is in line with Atkinson and Kühne [3], who describe the need for changes and newly added types that are possible while the system is running. Our type concept delivers a light-weight way for dynamic additions and proved to be intuitively usable in EA documentation practice.

In addition to types, we use *tags* to further categorize model elements. Tags are comparable to *UML stereotypes*[3] and can be applied to types and individual instances. In *Txture* both type and tag elements are modeled by responsible persons for EA elements and are part of the EA Model.

Multi-Level Instantiation to Support Dynamic Extensions. With the introduction of types on the EA Model level, we are able to limit the amount of changes that otherwise are applied to the meta model. While this is beneficial, maintaining an EA Meta Model of only generic concepts bares issues regarding the expressiveness of the documentation: Generic EA Meta Model concepts leave out detail and shift the specification of properties of model elements onto types.

Our documentation activities require that types and instances can be managed by the same stakeholders within the EA Model. For proper architecture documentation, types not only define properties to be instantiated by their related instances, but need to specify values for certain properties themselves.

Figure 4 shows that the *JBoss*-example type defines values for the properties *version* and *vendor*, whereas our example application container defines a text value reflecting its deployment *location* to be "Shanghai". In our example we assume this property to be dependent on the actual type, as e.g., not for all application containers the location is known or relevant to be documented. Because of this, we needed to realize a property-like concept, so called *mixins*, that can be instantiated on both the level of types and the level of documented instances. This is comparable to the concept of *deep instantiation* [2] or that of *intrinsic attributes* in the *MEMO* meta-modelling language [14].

The mixin concept aligns well with the flexible nature of our type concept and allows the documenting stakeholders to adapt the EA Model to cater for their particular documentation needs.

3.2   Stakeholder-Centric Editors

A key challenge in the context of EAM is to cater for the many different stakeholder types that are typically involved in editing the EA model. These range from database administrators and software developers to enterprise application architects, to process owners, project managers and even the CIO in some cases.

---

[3] cf. *UML 2.4.1* infrastructure specification, http://www.omg.org/spec/UML/2.4.1/

It is clear that each of these stakeholder types has different requirements when it comes to proper user interfaces. As we have described in our previous work [10], one problem in the EA management process is that users are often reluctant to enter data into an EA tool because of the time overhead involved. One reason for this problem are the potentially diverging conceptions between developers of an EA tool's features and its eventual users.

Following from this, we argue that adequate user interfaces for the different stakeholder groups can mitigate this problem by reducing the barriers for stakeholders to document the EA. Along this line we previously presented an approach to enter EA data in a textual way [11]. Our experience has shown that the textual editing approach generally works well for technical staff that is accustomed to work in text-based environments such as they are used for programming (e.g., via *Eclipse*[4]) or systems configuration (e.g., of databases or server applications). In other cases it might be more appropriate to let users enter data via simple form-based applications. Finally there are also users that commonly work with standard office applications like spreadsheets (most commonly *Microsoft Excel*).

In the following, we provide some detail on the different stakeholder-oriented editing functionality that we have implemented in *Txture*. The specific challenges that all EA model editors have in common is that they need to seamlessly cope with a changing underlying meta model and the multi-level modeling concepts like runtime-added types and attributes (cf. Section 3.1).

Textual Modeling Editor. While working with our first industry partner, we implemented textual editing of EA models. In a number of interviews with a variety of technologically educated stakeholders, we learned that text-based tools are commonly used by them. We decided to implement a textual editor for EA management in order to yield a high level of acceptance in this specific user group.

The editor (see Figure 5) was developed to be accessible within the *Eclipse* development environment and builds upon the textual modeling framework *Xtext*[5] in order to offer sophisticated textual editor functionality and user assistance out of the box. Visual support is provided via font- and color-based highlighting of known syntactical elements, including EA Meta Model classes, attribute names and types. The so called outline view (see the right part in the figure) delivers a navigable tree view that lists all described elements in a compact way. Besides the regular in-text search functionality, the outline view can be used to quickly overview the entire documentation and search for specific elements.

Beyond visual appeal and standard text editor functionality, our EA model editor also provides advanced features like automatic text completion for known syntax, error highlighting on failed model validations and the ability to insert placeholder text templates to help documenting new EA elements.

In a previous work [15] we have demonstrated textual modeling challenges, specifically by taking collaborative modeling efforts into account that involve the

---

[4] http://www.eclipse.org
[5] See http://www.xtext.org

Fig. 5. The textual editor as *Eclipse* plugin with file management, syntax highlighting, automatic text completion and outline support, developed with the *Xtext* framework

use of non-text based modeling editors as well. The main discrepancies between these two natures of editing are regarding the representation and persistence of EA model data. While models are commonly stored in a way so that only dedicated modeling tools can open and modify them (cf. XML-based persistence via e.g., *XML Metadata Interchange* (XMI)), any text editor can be used to work with a textual representation of models. Still, specific methods are required in order to manage the necessary file and folder based persistence of textual model parts and strategies which help to translate back and forth between text and other EA model representation formats. Considerations on e.g. the order of elements in text files or the storing of textual user comments had to be made and led to the requirement of maintaining *extensional information* about EA models.

Form-Based Modeling Editor. In addition to textual editing, *Txture* provides web-based forms to conveniently allow management of data by users with less technical background. There, the typical user interface elements like text fields and combo boxes are used to maintain attribute values of EA elements and cross-references between them.

Similar to the textual editor that provides syntactical keywords based on the currently employed EA Meta Model, the form-based editor is dynamically generated to reflect all available elements and their valid structure.

This type of editor is directly integrated as a web-based application within the *Txture* environment which we have shown in Figure 2.

Other Modeling Editors. To cover the entire range of stakeholder types for EA documentation, additional modeling editors can be considered for implementation. E.g. in a previous work [15] we have described our current efforts about an easy-to-use modeling extension for *Excel*. By now we have implemented a first prototype which renders documented EA elements together with their attributes and references into the cells of a spreadsheet. Such an editor is helpful to support business stakeholders and to integrate data that pre-exists in spreadsheet tables as external data sources.

Another current effort is to use *Java* code annotations to allow software developers to indicate a rough underlying software architecture. Such annotations get processed by a code analyzer and are fed into the EA documentation as well. The banking data center that we work together with, also operates a large software development department which established the use case of annotation-based modeling capabilities.

Our experience over the last years has shown the importance of first determining typical stakeholder tools and trying to adapt them, prior to making plans for custom tool developments. We have seen that users more easily accept and learn new functionality provided by familiar tools, as opposed to operating entirely new tools. Learning new tools, besides having to execute one's daily working activities, is often perceived as cumbersome and may in turn lead to an abandoned EA documentation.

3.3 Dynamic Architecture Visualizations

Architecture visualizations constitute a key reason why EA models are created. They are the means to reduce the architectural complexity and make potential problems visible to the persons responsible. The main challenge for EA visualizations is to present large models in a way that only the relevant information regarding a specific EA or IT architecture question are shown.

A typical approach is to allow users to pre-configure visualizations in a form-based manner and then generate graphical representations from this view-definition [24]. We argue that the roundtrip between configuration and the generation of the visualization presents a hurdle for the efficiency of creating adequate visualizations. In *Txture*, visualizations can be both created from a selection of EA elements or from a pre-defined view definition, but also edited dynamically from within a given visualization. Some of the editing functionality is shown within the top right screenshot in Figure 2, visible as the context menu that contains several options for editing the current visualization.

During the EA projects with our industry partners we gathered a number of requirements that useful architecture visualizations need to implement. Accordingly, visualizations should

- be able to represent EA model elements in different ways,
- be easily navigable in order to make the architecture's structure understandable,
- implement filter mechanisms to allow simplifications of the visualization and
- be visually extensible (e.g., via visual groups and separators derived from extensional EA model information), hence providing additional meaning to what is depicted.

The actual types of visualizations and the way EA model elements are represented are numerous and need to be adapted to the requirements of certain user groups. For instance, we interviewed system administrators who declared *treemap*-based visualizations as helpful in order to quickly determine *runs on* or *hosted by*-relationships between server applications and virtual systems that run on top of physical hardware. Software developers and IT systems architects felt comfortable with graph-based visualizations or a mixture of treemaps and graphs. With treemaps, the typical containment relationships are reflected, whereas a graph allowed them to determine system communication paths, e.g. implemented via services. By contrast, project managers and business-oriented stakeholders were interested in matrix or list-based representations of EA model elements. These stakeholder groups were mostly only interested in visualizing types that occur in an architecture, but no specific instances. We were told that this would allow them to get an overview of the employed technology stack or to make abstract business processes visible.

In the current version of *Txture*, navigation within visualizations is possible due to a number of operations. For example, the *show neighbours*-operation helps to explore the neighbourhood of a given model element by showing all of its directly related elements (via EA model cross-references). The *navigate*-operation allows to insert directly related model elements into the current visualization, by choosing a specific relationship of interest. Finally the *resolve path* functionality enables a user to resolve arbitrary dependencies of a selected model element to all elements of a specific type or class. This operation is intended to show transitive dependencies between EA elements. E.g. one could select a specific application and resolve all physical hardware that this application relies on.

Filter operations applied to current visualizations are a helpful tool to simplify what is depicted. E.g., we implemented the *removal, grouping* and *bridging* of EA model elements. The removal operation, as its name implies, deletes elements from the current visualization in order to simplify them if unnecessarily loaded. Grouped elements are visualized as a single node within the visualization. A label for the replacing group node is either automatically generated or can be defined manually. Groups can also be dissolved via an inverse *ungroup*-operation. Lastly, the bridging of nodes allows to transitively skip arbitrary model elements in the visualization. The skipped nodes are replaced by new relationships that are either labeled automatically or receive custom names. The purpose of bridging is to lower visual complexity by means of raising the abstraction level.

In order initiate new or extend current visualizations, an *adding*-operation enables a user to insert a selection of documented EA model elements. If requested, any direct dependencies to already visualized elements are shown as well.

Additional to these operations, other functionality is planned as well. Current efforts include the implementation of the aforementioned visual extensions by means of visual groups to mark arbitrary collections of elements. This will be done with the help of colors, separating boxes and custom labels.

One of the greatest challenges we encountered while implementing our visualization components was to keep the runtime performance of the described operations high. To us, this highlighted the need to establish an efficient, performance optimized model query framework.

3.4 Efficient Querying of Large EA Models

Querying EA models is especially important to perform analysis and to select EA model elements along with certain criteria. Results of such model queries are typically interpreted by enterprise stakeholders. Furthermore, query results are the basis of *Txture*'s visualizations.

Two main requirements guided our design decisions regarding a query framework. Namely, high performance in obtaining query results and access to a query expression language that is easy and intuitive to use.

In order to find out about the technology that best caters our requirements, we performed a number of benchmarks with different query frameworks. E.g., the *Object Constraint Language*[6] (OCL) and *EMF Model Query*[7] have been used. We were dissatisfied with all of the tested frameworks, regarding performance results or the high complexity as well as the low expressiveness of the query languages they offer.

We finally decided to create a query framework based on a graph persistence to store the structure of an EA model (cf. Figure 1, central part). Regarding performance, this decision reflects the choice of e.g. Barmpis and Kolovos [5], who evaluated graph database to be fastest for querying, out of a number of other model query and persistence approaches. Additionally, a regular indexed data container (in our case a relational database) is employed and holds the actual data of all model elements. As graph databases are typically capable of storing vertices and edges as well as properties for both of these entities, we found that these graphs are able to resemble the nature of EA models well.

The graph database we use is called *Titan*[8] and the query language it supports is *Gremlin*[9] . *Gremlin* is a highly sophisticated graph traversal language that is widely supported by current graph database systems. With it we were able to mitigate any performance issues while expressing queries. Nevertheless, its complexity would have not allowed any regular users of *Txture* to take advantage of its capabilities. Therefore we established an extensible set of high-level queries that build upon complex graph queries, but provide a simple interface to users. E.g., each of the visualization operations described in Section 3.3 is implemented as such a high-level query.

The graph-based mapping of EA models, low-level graph-based querying together with the layer containing the high-level queries is depicted as part of Figure 1 (see the right side of the core part of *Txture*'s architecture).

---

[6] See http://www.omg.org/spec/OCL/
[7] See http://www.eclipse.org/modeling/emf/?project=query
[8] See http://thinkaurelius.github.io/titan/
[9] See https://github.com/tinkerpop/gremlin/wiki

4   Related Work

This paper presents an overview of our experience in EAM, the *Txture* tool as well as a diverse set of challenges in the field. Accordingly, related work is similarily diverse. We start its discussion by naming advancements in three research fields that made the development of *Txture* possible. These are:

Advancements in Model-Driven Software Engineering. Runtime changes of the underlying EA Meta Model and the consecutive adaptation of an EA model is a complex problem. With the increased adoption of model-driven software development this problem has received considerable attention in research literature (see e.g. Favre [12]). In addition, allowing to model on multiple modeling layers, such as it is required in the context of EAM is another challenge. In particular, the work of Atkinson et al. [3] has helped in forming a better understanding of the problems of standard modeling languages such as the UML. Also, work on textual domain-specific languages (like *Xtext* is used for) has contributed to the development of the textual modeling editor of *Txture*.

Proliferation of Graph-databases. The already mentioned size of practical models in the EA context requires efficient methods for querying and storing models. Graph databases have recently gained much attention because of their utility for the use in social media applications and also other areas (an overview is given by Angles and Gutierrez [1]). Fortunately, this resulted in the development of several open-source, quality graph databases that are particularly useful for querying EA model element relationships.

Advancements in Web-Engineering for Visualizations. A key-factor for the utility of EA models are their visualizations. Building flexible client-side visualizations for web-applications was, until recently, limited by the lack of standards and accompanying technologies. With the adoption of new standards (like *HTML 5*[10]) by most modern browsers, major obstacles were removed, leading to sophisticated graphing and drawing libraries for the web.

In the context of EAM it is common that tools provide predefined EA Meta Models that can often only be adapted in a very limited way. For example, the EAM tool *iteraplan*[11] only allows for the extension of existing classes via attributes. As shown in the EAM tool survey by Matthes et al.[22] there exist some configurable tools, their technical foundation, however, is not clear. Other tools work with fixed EA Meta Models based on EA modeling standards such as *The Open Group Architecture Framework* [16] or *Archimate* [21]. We argue that these standards are inflexible as it is difficult to adapt them to the terminology used in an organization or to evolve. Schweda, on the other hand, presents a sophisticated approach to pattern-based creation of organization-specific meta

---

[10] cf. http://www.w3.org/TR/html5/

[11] http://www.iteraplan.de/en

models [25]. However, its practical applicability was not shown. With the *MEMO* meta-modeling language, Frank et al. [14] present a language and a tool suite for building modeling languages in the enterprise context. The tool is Eclipse-based and needs code generation steps in order to react on a changed meta model. The proposed language for IT infrastructure modeling, *ITML* [13], provides fixed concepts and can not support organization-specific meta models. Additionally, we found that some of the complex virtualization and clustering patterns that we have witnessed in practice cannot be modeled with this approach. In line with Kattenstroth [17], we conclude that although the need for organization-specific and evolving EA Meta Models has already been identified in literature [10,25], most related work focus on formulating generic and fixed meta models that cannot be adapted to the requirements of specific organizations.

Despite the existence of many commercial EA tools on the market, their capabilities for flexible visualizations are rather limited. A relatively recent development in the area of EA visualizations is to separate the model from the visualization unlike e.g. *Archimate* which makes use of a graphical modeling notation. This separation is suggested in several research works [24,18,6].

In the general model engineering community much groundwork has been laid. Recently, the multi-level modeling paradigm gained more attention due to the criticism of classical (two level) modeling, like done e.g. in the UML which only allows a model and an instantiation at the same time [4,19]. This paradigm has influenced the meta-modeling capabilities of *Txture*, in particular, by providing mechanisms to model types and mixins. Still, multi-level modeling mainly discusses requirements from software engineering and does not necessarily consider modeling techniques from other domains. Regarding our work on *Txture* we use a mixture of classical and multi-level modeling approaches and unified them in a novel way to contribute a usable EA documentation method.

5   Conclusion and Outlook

In this paper we have described the EA modeling framework underlying our research prototype *Txture*. It provides a unique feature set including classical meta-modeling, type-based modeling and mixins and tackles some of the pressing problems of EA and IT systems documentation.

As our research elicites requirements from practical experience, we believe that our work can be useful for other EA researchers as well, but also for vendors of existing EA tools.

Challenges we specifically discussed are:

1. The difficulty to adapt EA Meta Models at runtime which we tackle with a combination of multi-level modeling techniques and classical approaches like stereotyping and power typing.
2. Issues regarding dynamic and navigable visualizations that entail the problem of efficient queries over large EA Models. We solve this by using a graph-based model persistence together with a layer of high-level EA Model queries.

3. The requirement to be able to edit EA Models by considering preferences of different stakeholder groups. We solve this by implementing model editors that either extend existing tools or align custom editors with the requirements named by their prospective users.

In our future work we aim to further evaluate our approach in practice and conduct empirical studies that will assess to what extent our approach assists and motivates different stakeholder groups to contribute to EA documentation processes. So far, textual editing and dynamic visualizations have already shown their usefulness at work for both of our industry partners. In the banking data center enterprise architects, software developers and DevOps teams document their work in the EA model, without having to change tools. The semiconductor manufacturer uses pre-defined architecture visualizations as a starting point for impact analysis of systems in their data center. In discussions, users have confirmed the value for them to be able to define their own custom visualizations that support their daily working activities.

Recent developments in the fields of Model-driven Software Development, graph databases and web-engineering have made the development of the presented framework and prototypical tool implementation possible.

References

1. Angles, R., Gutierrez, C.: Survey of graph database models. ACM Computing Surveys (CSUR) 40(1) (2008)
2. Atkinson, C., Kühne, T.: The essence of multilevel metamodeling. The Unified Modeling Language. Modeling Languages, Concepts, and Tools (2001)
3. Atkinson, C., Kühne, T.: Model-driven development: a metamodeling foundation. IEEE Software 20(5) (2003)
4. Atkinson, C., Gerbig, R.: Harmonizing Textual and Graphical Visualizations of Domain Specific Models Categories and Subject Descriptors. In: Proceedings of the Second Workshop on Graphical Modeling Language Development. ACM (2013)
5. Barmpis, K., Kolovos, D.: Evaluation of contemporary graph databases for efficient persistence of large-scale models. Journal of Object Technology, JOT (2014)
6. Buckl, S., Ernst, A.M., Lankes, J.: Generating Visualizations of Enterprise Architectures using Model Transformations.. Enterprise Modelling and Information Systems Architectures 2(2) (2007)
7. Farwick, M.: A Situational Method for Semi-automated Enterprise Architecture Documentation. Ph.D. thesis, University of Innsbruck (2014)
8. Farwick, M., Berthold, A., Breu, R., Ryll, S., Voges, K., Hanschke, I.: Requirements for Automated Enterprise Architecture Model Maintenance. In: International Conference on Enterprise Information Systems (ICEIS). SciTePress (2011)
9. Farwick, M., Breu, R., Hauder, M., Roth, S., Matthes, F.: Enterprise Architecture Documentation: Empirical Analysis of Information Sources for Automation. In: Hawaii International Conference on System Sciences (HICSS). IEEE, Wailea (2013)
10. Farwick, M., Schweda, C.M., Breu, R., Hanschke, I.: A situational method for semi-automated Enterprise Architecture Documentation. SoSyM (2014)
11. Farwick, M., Trojer, T., Breu, M., Ginther, S., Kleinlercher, J., Doblander, A.: A Case Study on Textual Enterprise Architecture Modeling. In: Enterprise Distributed Object Computing Conference Workshops (EDOCW), IEEE (2013)

12. Favre, J.M.: Meta-model and model co-evolution within the 3d software space. In: Workshop on Evolution of Large-scale Industrial Software Applications (2003)
13. Frank, U., Heise, D., Kattenstroth, H., Ferguson, D.F., Hadar, E., Waschke, M.G.: ITML: A Domain-Specific Modeling Language for Supporting Business Driven IT Management. In: Proceedings of the 9th OOPSLA workshop on domain-specific modeling (DSM). ACM (2009)
14. Frank, U.: The MEMO meta modelling language (MML) and language architecture. 2nd Edition. Tech. rep., Institut für Informatik und Wirtschaftsinformatik (ICB) Universität Duisburg-Essen (2011)
15. Haeusler, M., Farwick, M., Trojer, T.: Combining textual and web-based modeling. Submitted to 16th IEEE/ACM MODELS (2014)
16. Haren, V.: TOGAF Version 9.1. Van Haren Publishing (2011)
17. Kattenstroth, H.: DSMLs for enterprise architecture management. In: Workshop on Domain-specific modeling (DSM). ACM Press (2012)
18. Kruse, S., Addicks, J.S., Postina, M., Steffens, U.: Decoupling models and visualisations for practical ea tooling. In: Service-Oriented Computing. ICSOC/ServiceWave 2009 Workshops (2010)
19. Kühne, T.: Matters of (Meta-) Modeling. SoSyM 5(4) (2006)
20. Lankes, J., Matthes, F., Wittenburg, A.: Softwarekartographie: Systematische darstellung von anwendungslandschaften. In: Wirtschaftsinformatik (2005)
21. Lankhorst, M.: Enterprise Architecture at Work, 3rd edn., vol. 36. Springer, Heidelberg (2012)
22. Matthes, F., Buckl, S., Leitel, J., Schweda, C.M.: Enterprise Architecture Management Tool Survey 2008. Tech. rep., Technische Universität München, Chair for Informatics 19, sebis (2008)
23. Odell, J.J.: Power Types. Journal of OO Programming (1994)
24. Roth, S., Hauder, M., Zec, M., Utz, A., Matthes, F.: Empowering Business Users to Analyze Enterprise Architectures: Structural Model Matching to Configure Visualizations. In: International Enterprise Distributed Object Computing Conference Workshops (EDOCW). IEEE (2013)
25. Schweda, C.M.: Development of Organization-Specific Enterprise Architecture Modeling Languages Using Building Blocks. Ph.D. thesis, Technical University of Munich (2011)

A Flow Analysis Approach
for Service-Oriented Architectures

Bernhard Bauer, Melanie Langermeier, and Christian Saad

Software Methodologies for Distributed Systems, University of Augsburg,
Augsburg, Germany
{bauer,langermeier,saad}@ds-lab.org

Abstract. The discipline of SOA (Service-oriented Architecture) provides concepts for designing the structural and behavioral aspects of application landscapes that rely on the interaction of self-contained services. To assess an architecture's quality and validate its conformance to behavioral requirements, those models must be subjected to sophisticated static analyses. We propose a comprehensive methodology that relies on data flow analysis for a context-sensitive evaluation of service-oriented system designs. The approach employs a model-based format for SOA artifacts which acts as a uniform basis for the specification and execution of various analyses. Using this methodology, we implement two analyses which reveal blocking calls and assess performance metrics. These applications are evaluated in the context of two case studies that have been developed in the SENSORIA and the ENVIROFI projects.

1 Introduction

The field of SOA is concerned with methods that enable the conceptual design of the relevant aspects of software ecosystems whose components interact in complex yet well-defined patterns to provide high-level services to consumers. This abstraction not only supports the task of documenting service landscapes in enterprises, the model-based formalization also facilitates automated code generation, following the principles of model-driven development (MDD). In this sense, SOA models represent integral artifacts of software development processes. Usually, the target system is first described at a higher level of abstraction with iterative refinements. To avoid the multiplication of errors in later stages, problems must be identified as early as possible. Analysis at the model level can also help in assessing the architecture's quality and in validating its conformance to functional and technical requirements before implementation begins.

Current approaches for the analysis of object-oriented models often focus on trivial metrics such as the number of classes, the number of methods per class or the number of sub/super classes [6]. Typically, the information aggregated by these methods only considers immediate neighbors [7]. For some use cases, canonical analysis techniques are not well-balanced with respect to their expressiveness and the resulting implementation effort: For context-sensitive measures and validation scenarios, methods such as the OCL are not sufficient while systems based on formal logic tend to introduce unnecessary complexity. The fact

R. De Nicola and R. Hennicker (Eds.): Wirsing Festschrift, LNCS 8950, pp. 475–489, 2015.

that business models are often incomplete or inconsistent further hinders the application of strict formal systems.

To close this gap, we establish a unified analysis methodology which relies on the principle of information propagation to enable a context-sensitive evaluation of SOA models. The motivation for this approach can therefore be summed up as follows: We intend to provide developers with a generic framework for implementing analyses in the SOA domain that do not necessitate the usage of formal semantics but, nevertheless, cannot be expressed using traditional constraint languages such as OCL due to their context-sensitive nature. The technique is therefore intended as an extension, rather than a replacement, for existing methods such as formal verification [22].

For this purpose, we employ a uniform model-based format which acts as a foundation for the specification and execution of analyses to abstract from the diversity found in canonical modeling languages for SOA. Based on this representation, we employ the model-based data flow analysis as a declarative "programming language" for the implementation of various analyses that depend on the computation of a fixed point (for approximating a system's run-time behavior) and/or the modeling of complex information flows through the designed architecture. We subsequently demonstrate how this methodology can be applied to compute performance metrics and check for potential blocking calls in contract and interface-based architectures. The approach is evaluated in the context of two case studies, that have been published by the SENSORIA [17] and the ENVIROFI project [8] respectively. We base our work on previous research, in which we applied a similar strategy to the field of enterprise architecture management (EAM) [12]. More specifically, the contributions of this paper comprise the adaptation of the methodology to the SOA domain, its evaluation in the context of existing case studies and the implementation of relevant analysis scenarios. Furthermore, the application to SOA is intended to emphasize the viability of the proposed methodology across different fields of research.

In the following section, we present an overview over related work and establish the link to the SENSORIA project. In section 3, we detail the different aspects of the analysis methodology, namely the flow-based analysis of models and the generic representation of SOA data. The next two sections describe two different analysis scenarios and their application to the use cases. The first one checks for blocking calls (section 4) while the second one derives performance measures (section 5). We conclude with a discussion of our method (section 6).

2   Related Work

Although service-oriented architectures have attracted much attention, the concept has often only been applied in an ad-hoc fashion. The SENSORIA project [17] defines a comprehensive approach for the design, formal analysis and automated deployment as well as the re-engineering of service-oriented applications [22]. SOA models are analyzed using formal methods such as process calculi, temporal logic and stochastic logic. Analyses are both qualitative and quantitative, e.g. conformance with contracts, deadlock freedom of compositions or the analysis of service properties like availability [22]. The formal foundation is tied to the UML4SOA [13] profile, a high-level domain specific language which incorporates behavioral aspects. This profile extends a previous version of the SoaML standard (to which the first author contributed) with concepts for modeling the behavior of services, service orchestrations, and service protocols. The current version of SoaML [3] (published in 2012) introduces two different architectural styles, based on interfaces and service-contracts respectively, and integrates UML sequence diagrams for the specification of communication protocols.

The Object Constraint Language (OCL) [2] is a widely used method for the specification of simple model analyses. For example, [6] provides a library for the extraction of metrics. OCL constraints enrich the abstract syntax of a modeling language, i.e. the meta model, with a definition of its static semantics. This means that analysis specifications are tightly integrated with the modeling ecosystem (i.e. canonical standards and tools) and therefore naturally support concepts such as generalization and instantiation. In contrast to the proposed flow-based method, OCL does however not support information propagation and fixed point convergence and is therefore restricted to basic validation scenarios.

In [12], we established a generic meta model (GMM) which encodes the structural composition of enterprise architectures in the form of a stereotyped graph. While we were able to redefine existing analyses using this unified representation, the lack of specific semantics has been identified as a challenge that must be addressed in future work.

3 Adaptive Analysis Methodology for SOA

This section describes an adaptive analysis methodology for the SOA domain which relies on static derivation of context-sensitive properties to validate an architecture's correctness and assess different types of quality attributes. The resulting approximation of the modeled system's runtime properties can provide valuable feedback, especially in early stages of the development process.

The design of an analysis methodology intended for use in the SOA domain poses different challenges: For one, architectures may be encoded in a variety of modeling languages, e.g. SoaML, UML4SOA or BPMN[1]. Furthermore, architectures may rely on different paradigms, such as contract- or interface-based styles. To avoid conceptual and technological gaps, the analysis technique should also be well-integrated with modeling standards such as the Meta Object Facility (MOF) and be capable of addressing a wide range of application scenarios.

We address these issues by combining a unified representation of SOA-specific (meta) model data with a framework for model-based flow analysis. Translation of the target SOA model into the unified SOA format can be achieved using canonical methods for model transformation such as Query/View/Transformation (QVT). Subsequently, the analyses can be executed. Figure 1 provides an overview of this process. This technique has already been successfully implemented for

---

[1] The Business Process Model and Notation (BPMN) can be used to specify behavioral aspects of services [16].

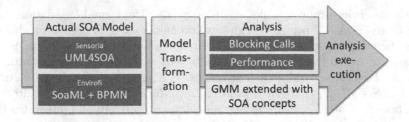

Fig. 1. Procedure of the data flow analysis approach for SOA

the EAM domain [12], a field which shares many of the described challenges, including the diversity of modeling standards and the fact that models may be incomplete or even inconsistent. To alleviate the problem of complex analysis specifications, we will subsequently extend the generic representation with domain-specific SOA concepts. Sections 4 and 5 exemplify the approach in the context of two case studies from the SENSORIA and the ENVIROFI project and two analysis scenarios, detection of blocking calls and computation of performance metrics.

3.1   Flow-Based Model Analysis

The technique of data flow analysis (DFA) is commonly employed in the area of compiler construction to analyze and optimize the control flow of programs by examining how information that is computed locally at the nodes (basic blocks) of a program control flow graph is disseminated. A canonical examples consists in the *reaching definitions* analysis, in which variable definitions generated inside basic blocks are propagated through the graph to determine the availability of variable assignments at subsequent instructions. By applying fixed point evaluation semantics, it is possible to compute with cyclic equation systems that result from the presence of loops in the control flow. Analyses are usually specified in a way that ensures that the result represents a conservative approximation of the program's run-time behavior.

The analysis specifications presented in the subsequent sections rely on the approach detailed in [15] which transfers the notion of data flow analysis to the modeling domain. Inspired by the related technique of attribute grammars [5], it supports the declaration of *data flow attributes* which can be assigned to classes in a target meta model. In some respects, this process can therefore be compared to the Object Constraint Language which is often used to formalize the static semantics of modeling languages by assigning constraints to meta model classes. However, each data flow attribute is connected to two *data flow equations*, which compute the attribute's initial value and its fixed point iteration result(s) respectively. Furthermore, to compute the result for a specific attribute, its data flow equation may access values of neighboring attributes, thereby inducing an information flow between the model's elements.

To execute the analysis, the *data flow solver* is supplied with the meta model, the data flow specification and the target model. In a first step, the attributes are instantiated for model elements of the respective types and initialized with their start value. Afterwards, the iteration values are computed by executing the associated equations. The solver monitors the propagation of data flow information between attribute instances and, if necessary, initiates the recomputation of unstable instances, until a fixed point has been reached.

This approach has multiple advantages: The method is fully integrated with the modeling domain, thus avoiding potential semantic gaps between different technological spaces. Furthermore, the declarative nature of the data flow specifications allows for an intuitive definition of analyses which rely on the (transitive) propagation of information along model paths. When computing the result for a concrete element in the model, it is therefore possible to take into account its overall context, that results from (transitive) connections to other elements. Finally, the fixed point semantics enable a conservative approximation of the run-time behavior of the modeled system.

3.2   Generic Meta Model

In the field of SOA, many competing standards and practices exist. It is therefore essential to provide a unified basis for analysis specifications to avoid the constant adaptation of existing analyses. Instead, the interpretation of language artifacts will be encoded in transformations for different source languages such as SoaML.

In previous work [12] we established a generic meta model (GMM) for enterprise architecture analysis. This format constitutes a high-level view on model data by abstracting from characteristics which may vary between different standards. In essence, it conforms to a stereotyped graph which incorporates model-oriented extensions such as properties and generalization relationships. It is important to note that a GMM instance represents both meta and model data. Case studies carried out in the field of enterprise architecture analysis have shown that this approach supports a wide variety of different modeling paradigms although the lack of domain-specific semantics tends to complicate analysis specification.

To provide better support for SOA-specific features, we extended the original GMM with concepts found in canonical ontologies, modeling languages and reference models from the SOA domain [10]. In their work, Kreger and Estefan examine different standards and conclude that the specifications agree on a set of core concepts. Based on this study, we established an abstract SOA model which incorporates features from The Open Group's SOA ontology [19] and Reference Architecture [20] as well as the OASIS Reference Model [14]. Figure 2 shows the resulting meta model with the essential classes and relationships.

The identified core concepts have been woven into the GMM as shown in figure 3. This representation can therefore be understood as a domain-specific language tailored to the specification of structural analyses in the SOA domain. While the right hand side encodes model data in the form of stereotyped *Nodes*, *Edges* and *Properties*, the left hand side represents the meta structure of the respective SOA language. Each specific concept inherits from the generic *MetaModelNode* while each relationship type is represented as a sub class of *MetaModelEdge*. Since they

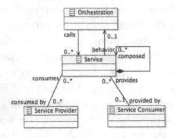

Fig. 2. Meta model capturing the core structure of service-oriented architectures

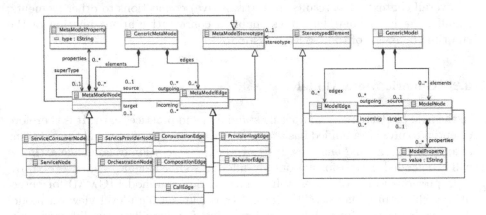

Fig. 3. Generic Meta Model [12] adapted for the SOA domain

are also specializations of the abstract class *StereotypedElement*, these concepts act as "data types" for model data.

The chosen layout allows for a certain degree of freedom when importing SOA models, as language-specific characteristics can be represented without modifications to the GMM, eliminating the need to adapt existing analyses. This generic approach is viable, since data flow analyses rely on information propagation and can therefore cope with extensive changes in the underlying language' structure.

The potential downside of this approach consists of increased complexity in the transformation logic. The benefits of the generic representation, namely the robustness of the analyses themselves, must therefore be weighed against the effort required for the translation of SOA models. If it can be expected that the underlying structure remains constant, it can therefore be beneficial to tie the data flow specifications directly to the target language's meta model.

3.3   Case Studies

The case studies, which form the basis for the evaluation of the proposed methodology, consist of two models that rely on different architectural styles. The first is an extended version of the automotive case study *On Road Assistance* from the SENSORIA [17,9] project. The second describes a *Personal Environmental Information System* (PEIS) and was developed in the ENVIROFI [8,11] project.

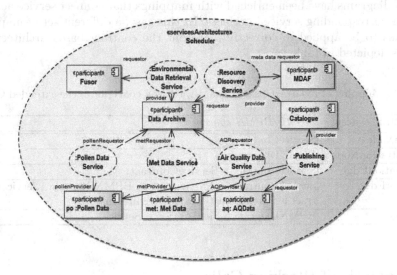

Fig. 4. Service Architecture for the participant *Scheduler* in the *PEIS* use case [11]

The *On Road Assistance* scenario supports the driver of a car if an engine failure makes it impossible to reach the planned destination. For this purpose, the SOA participant *OnRoadAssistant* invokes multiple services to find the "best" repair shops (garages) and rental car stations nearby, once the driver has made a security payment. The architecture uses the interface-based style of the SoaML specification [3] while behavioral aspects regarding service composition are modeled using the UML4SOA profile [13] developed by SENSORIA. We extended the definitions from [9] with a second participant *AssistanceStore* (excerpts can be seen in figure 5). The interactions between both participants form the basis for the analysis of blocking calls in section 4. Mappings between the UML4SOA/Activity Diagram and the extended GMM are shown in table 1.

The second scenario represents a *Personal Environmental Information System*, which generates personalized reports of pollen, air quality and meteoro-

Table 1. Mapping of UML4SOA concepts to the extended GMM

Ext. GMM concept	UML4SOA/Activity Diagram concept
ServiceNode	ServiceInterface
OrchestrationNode	ActivityDiagram
AggregationEdge	ServiceInterface ▷ Port
BehaviorEdge	Port ▷ LinkPin ▷ ActivityDiagramElement ▷ ActivityDiagram
UseEdge	ActivityDiagram ▷ ServiceSendAction ▷ LinkPin ▷ Port ▷ ServiceInterface

logical data depending on the current location of the user (cf. figure 4). The architecture relies on the contract-based SoaML approach [3]. Internal participant behavior is modeled using BPMN [1]. As proposed in [11] and [16], the BPMN diagrams have been enriched with mappings that connect service actions to their corresponding service interfaces. In this case, a different set of mapping rules has to be applied to correctly represent the contract based architectural style as depicted in table 2.

Table 2. Mapping of (contract-based) SoaML/BPMN concepts to the extended GMM

Ext. GMM concept	SoaML/BPMN concept
ServiceNode	ServiceContract
OrchestrationNode	BPMNDiagram
AggregationEdge	ServiceContract ▷ ServiceContract
BehaviorEdge	ServiceContract ▷ Participant ▷ BPMNDiagram, ServiceContract ▷ Participant ▷ ServiceArchitecture
UseEdge	BPMNDiagram ▷ SendAction ▷ Service

4   Analysis of Blocking Calls

Dependencies relating to the orchestration of services are an important aspect of service-oriented architectures. In larger systems, the call hierarchies (directly and indirectly invoked services) are often not obvious which may lead to blocking calls/deadlocks. In [4], Acciai et al. propose a type system to ensure deadlock freedom of the subsequent conversations after service invocation in well-typed CaSPiS processes. We implement a light-weight alternative to this approach based on a static approximation of the system's runtime behavior with the goal of detecting *potential* cyclic invocations.

In the general case, detecting blocking calls in an orchestrated architecture requires the identification of all the direct and indirect service calls that are required for the execution of a service. If this set contains the original service, the architectural design *may* result in a deadlocked system. Since orchestrations are typically described via process diagrams (e.g. UML Activity Diagrams, BPMN or BPEL models), the analysis has to focus both on the internal composition of a process and the (transitive) interactions between different orchestrations. By computing a fixed point of required service calls for each service, it is possible to either guarantee that the architecture will not result in blocking calls or to indicate potentially problematic situations to the user. In the following we will describe how this analysis can be specified and applied to both case studies.

4.1   Analysis Specification

To assess implicit service calls, we assign a data flow attribute *requiredServices* to the *ServiceNode* class in the architecture's GMM representation whose instances compute the sets of invoked services for each node. A second data flow attribute *serviceCalls* computes the set of called services for *OrchestrationNodes*. The respective data flow equation rules are shown in algorithms 1 and 2.

Algorithm 1. Data flow equation for the attribute *requiredServices*

```
1: DFA-EQUATION ServiceNode::requiredServices returns Set<ModelNode>

2:   Set<ModelNode> services = new Set<ModelNode>();

3:     // acquire values from composed services
4:     foreach (ModelEdge outgoingAggregation in self.outgoing)
5:       if (outgoingAggregation.target.stereotype is 'ServiceNode')
6:         services.addAll(outgoingAggregation.target.requiredServices());

7:     // acquire values from called services in the orchestration
8:     foreach (ModelEdge outgoingBehavior in self.outgoing)
9:       if (outgoingBehavior.target.stereotype is 'Orchestration')
10:        services.addAll(outgoingBehavior.target.serviceCalls());

11:  return services;
```

Algorithm 2. Data flow equation for the attribute *serviceCalls*

```
1: DFA-EQUATION OrchestrationNode::serviceCalls returns Set<ModelNode>

2:   Set<ModelNode> services = new Set<ModelNode>();

3:     // acquire values of called services from the orchestration
4:     foreach (ModelEdge outgoingCall in self.outgoing)
5:       if (outgoingCall.target.stereotype is 'ServiceNode')
6:         services.addAll(outgoingCall.target.requiredServices());

7:   return services;
```

The result set for the attribute *requiredServices* is first initialized with an empty call set (line 2). For aggregated services, the required calls of the substructures must be added as well. This is accomplished by requesting the value of *requiredServices* at those elements (which will implicitly trigger the data flow solver to recursively evaluate these dependencies) and adding them to the result (lines 4 - 6). To include behavior-related invocations, lines 8 - 10 process service calls of orchestrations (computed by *serviceCalls* for *OrchestrationNodes*).

The data flow solver will automatically terminate once a fixed point has been reached, i.e. no more elements are added to any result set. By examining the values computed by *requiredServices* for *ServiceNodes*, it is possible to detect whether a service may trigger its own invocation. If this is not the case for any service, the system will never execute a blocking call. Otherwise, a deadlock might exist, although not every execution necessarily results in that situation.

4.2 Case Study

The described analysis has been carried out for both use cases. For this purpose, the meta and model data has been transformed into the extended GMM format using the mappings from tables 1 and 2. For reasons of clarity, we will depict the results in the original representation rather than using the GMM concepts.

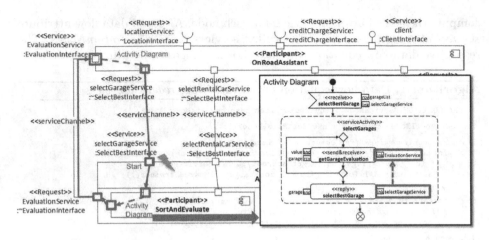

Fig. 5. Illustration of the blocking call in the use case *On Road Assistance*[9]

Figure 5 shows the identified potential deadlock for the *OnRoadAssistance* model. In this case, we assume that data flow analysis started with the *Service-Interface SelectGarageService*, which relies on the providing participant *AssistanceStore* (bottom). Its *ServicePoint* delegates to the internal component *SortAndEvaluate*, which has an associated Activity Diagram describing its internal behavior (right corner of figure 5). In this diagram, the *selectGarageService* is connected to the *ReplyAction selectBestGarage* via a *LinkPin*. Here, the set of preceding *SendActions* contains only the action *getGarageEvaluation*, which is linked to the *RequestPort EvaluationService*. This service, in turn, is connected to a *ServicePort* of the *OnRoadAssistance* participant.

Analysis of the component's behavior indicates that the *EvaluationService* may trigger the execution of the *selectGarageService* and the *selectRentalCarService*. As both implement *SelectBestInterface*, this element will be added to the result set. Subsequently, the algorithm determines the service calls of *selectRentalCarService*, which is provided by the *SortAndEvaluate* participant and uses the *EvaluationService*. Afterwards, the execution of the data flow rules terminates, as the analysis has converged in a fixed point. Because the call hierarchy of *SelectBestInterface* is cyclic, the absence of blocking behavior cannot be guaranteed for this architecture. The concrete result sets for all services are as follows[2]:

ClientInterface: { LocationService, creditChargeService, EvaluationService, SelectBestInterface, FindInterface }
EvaluationService: { SelectBestInterface, EvaluationService }
SelectBestInterface: { EvaluationService, SelectBestInterface }

For the PEIS example, the connection of BPMN actions to the used services is modeled via links as proposed by [16] and [11]. The call hierarchies for *Resource*

---

[2] Since the *LocationInterface*, the *CreditChargeInterface* and the *FindInterface* have no required service calls, they have been omitted from this representation.

Discovery Service and *Publishing Service* are empty since they have no required service calls. The result set for *Pollen Data Service*, *Meterological Data Service* and *Air Quality Data Service* consists only of the *Publishing Service*. Finally, the *Environmental Data Retrieval Service* may request the invocation of *Resource Discovery Service*, *Pollen Data Service*, *Meteorological Data Service*, *Air Quality Data Service* and *Publishing Service*. Since no result for the attribute *requiredServices* contains the associated service itself, we can conclude that the architecture of the *Scheduler* participant in the PEIS has no blocking calls. This is also evident from the structural overview shown in figure 4: Even without detailed knowledge about the inner structure of the participants, there exists no sequence of service calls that could potentially result in a cyclic invocation.

5 Performance Analysis

Performance aspects can be of vital importance in an SOA environment, especially if the architecture relies on a complex orchestration of many services. In this case, a static assessment of the run-time properties can provide valuable early feedback to the developer which can help in improving the system design to shorten response times for critical components. Examples for this kind of analysis include a method based on layered queuing networks for UML4SOA models that have been extended with MARTE (a UML profile for real-time systems) [21] or the use of *queuing network modeling* [18]. The latter proposal applies the analysis to a *distributed message passing* architecture with asynchronous message streams (messages are being queued at the components) where the response time of a system is defined as the *Population/Arrival Rate*. The latter denotes the number of incoming requests per time unit while the former describes the sum of currently processed and all waiting requests [18].

Transferring this method to the SOA domain necessitates some adaptations since the system's functionality is not only expressed by participants' internal components but also by service orchestrations. Furthermore, instead of having a single arrival rate for the whole system, each service may possess its own arrival rate which has to be based on the rates of all its requestors and an internal rate. The population of a service then depends on the internal population plus the population of all requested services during the provisioning.

It should be noted, that - in contrast to the blocking calls analysis - the evaluation of the performance metrics does not induce a fixed point computation. Instead, the declarative nature of data flow analysis specifications in combination with the information propagation principle is used to realize succinct and intuitive implementations of the recursive formulae.

5.1 Analysis Specification

Response time for (composite) services is computed by three data flow attributes:

- *arrivalRate* (r_s): the arrival rate for each service,
- *population* (p_s): the population for each service, and
- *responseTime* (t_s): the response time for each service

Furthermore, the SOA model must be enriched with additional data: *Services* require a property *service time* (s_s) which denotes the execution time for internal actions (excluding external service requests). A second property *local arrival rate* (r_s^l) specifies the number of local consumer requests not triggered by other services. Based on this information, the attribute *arrivalRate* can be computed using the data flow equation shown in algorithm 3.

Algorithm 3. Data flow equation for the attribute *arrivalRate*

```
1: DFA-EQUATION ServiceNode::arrivalRate returns Integer
2:   Integer rate = self.localArrivalRate;

3:   // for all calling services
4:   foreach (ModelEdge incomingCall in self.incoming)
5:     if (incomingCall.source.stereotype is 'Orchestration')
6:       rate += incomingCall.source.arrivalRate();

7:   return rate;
```

The arrival rate of a *Service* equals to the sum of the local arrival rate (line 2) and the arrival rates of all requesting services (lines 4 - 6). For this purpose, the latter part requests the *arrivalRate* result for the orchestration(s) from which the service is invoked, thereby computing the arrival rate from its service (and, if necessary, the compound services) recursively.

After the arrival rate has been determined, it is possible to calculate the internal and the composed population. The internal population is defined as $p_s^i = \frac{u_s}{1-u_s}$, with $u_s = r_s \cdot s_s$ representing the utilization of service s. The population of a composition is given as $p_s = p_s^i + \sum p_i$, where p_i are the populations of the requested services. The data flow equation is listed in algorithm 4.

Algorithm 4. Data flow equation for the attribute *population*

```
1: DFA-EQUATION ServiceNode::population returns Integer

2:   Integer utilization = self.arrivalRate() * self.serviceTime;
3:   Integer population = utilization / (1 - utilization); // internal population

4:   // add populations of all directly requested services
5:   foreach (ModelEdge outgoingEdge in self.outgoing)
6:     if (outgoingEdge.target.stereotype is 'Orchestration')

7:       foreach (ModelEdge outgoingCall in outgoingEdge.target.outgoing)
8:         if (outgoingCall.target.stereotype is 'ServiceNode')
9:           population += outgoingEdge.target.population();

10:  return population;
```

The internal population of a *Service* is computed using the model property *service time* and the data flow attribute *arrivalRate* (lines 2 - 3). For the overall population, this result is added to the populations of all *Services*, that are called in the respective *Orchestration* (lines 5 - 9). This process involves a recursive access to the *population* attribute (line 9) for which the data flow solver ensures that the indirectly required services are considered as well.

5.2   Case Study

We will now illustrate the performance analysis for the service *FindInterface* in the *OnRoadAssistance* model. The mappings of the meta model concepts are equal to those in the blocking calls scenario. In this case, we assume deadlock freedom and therefore will not consider the *EvaluationInterface* and its connections. The internal service times are given as $s_{FindInterface} = 0,03s$ and $s_{ClientInterface} = 0,05s$. The local arrival times are $r^l_{ClientInterface} = 10$ and $r^l_{findGaragesServices} = r^l_{findRentalCarStationsService} = 5$ requests/s. Analysis execution starts by evaluating the *FindInterface's population* which automatically triggers the computation of its *arrivalRate*. In addition to the arrival rates of the implementing service ports $r_{findGaragesService}$ and $r_{findRentalCarStationsService}$, the corresponding request ports are determined based on the behavior diagram of the *OnRoadAssistant* participant. The ports are used to provide the *client* service port, i.e. the set of *usingServicePorts* for both request ports, which contains only one element, the *client*. The arrival rate of the *client* service port is equal to its local arrival rate, because this port has no connections to other request ports. The arrival rate for the *FindInterface* is thus computed by:

$$R_{FindInterface} = r_{findGaragesService} + r_{client} + r_{findRentalCarStationsService}$$
$$+r_{client} = 5 + 10 + 5 + 10 = 30$$

The utilization is then calculated as $u_{FindInterface} = r_{FindInterface} \cdot s_{FindInterface}$ $= 30 \cdot 0,03 = 0,9$ and, consequently, the internal population yields:

$$p_{FindInterface} = \frac{u_{FindInterface}}{1 - u_{FindInterface}} = 9$$

Since no service calls are required for the provisioning of the *FindInterface*, its overall population is equal to the internal population and the analysis of this interface is finished. The results show that the *FindInterface* will have a utilization of 90%, with a population of 9. The application of the performance analysis for the *PEIS* use case can be carried out in an identical fashion.

6   Discussion and Conclusion

In this paper we presented a comprehensive analysis methodology for SOA models, which combines a generic representation of (meta) model data with an analysis technique that relies on information propagation and fixed point computation to enable a context-sensitive evaluation of model elements and the approximation of run-time behavior. We have demonstrated the viability of this methodology in the context of two use cases and two analysis scenarios, which implement a deadlock analysis and an evaluation of performance metrics respectively.

As shown in previous work, the unified representation has the benefit of providing a simple, yet concise foundation for the specification of flow sensitive analyses. To further improve the accessibility of this approach, we extended the generic structure of the GMM with SOA specific characteristics. It is thereby possible to base analyses on common SOA semantics while preserving the support for a wide range of different modeling languages and styles. By propagating locally computed information through the model, the data flow technique supports the implementation of context-sensitive analyses. As information is propagated across multiple (transitive) relationships, the specifications are invariant against a variety of structural changes in the underlying modeling language.

It should be noted that complications may arise if the concepts of the respective SOA language cannot be directly mapped to the analysis specification types. While it would generally be possible to implement the necessary adaptations in the transformation logic, a more generic solution for this problem would be advantageous. This could, for example, be realized through a sophisticated mapping technology which supports the translation of complex SOA concepts to suitable structures in the GMM representation. Possible implementations of this are for example graph transformations or semantic web technologies.

Dedication. We would like to thank the organizers for their hard work in coordinating this festschrift in honor of Martin Wirsing's emeritation and for the opportunity to contribute to it.

Personal Dedication of Bernhard Bauer: At the University of Passau, Martin teached me in Software Engineering and logic based specification methods. No other person influenced my research interests as profoundly as Martin did. I am deeply grateful to him for giving me the opportunity to conduct my first research steps at his chair in Passau and for always being open to my ideas. Apart from being a great researcher, Martin has also impressed me as a person. His helpful and friendly guidance as well as his professional expertise formed the motivation that made Software Engineering my passion and primary research interest.

Thank you very much for the many interesting and enjoyable years!

References

1. Business Process Modeling Notation (BPMN) 2.0 Specification (2011)
2. Object Constraint Language (OCL) 2.3.1 Specification (January 2012)
3. Service oriented architecture modeling language 1.0 specification. Tech. rep. (2012)
4. Acciai, L., Bodei, C., Boreale, M., Bruni, R., Vieira, H.T.: Static Analysis Techniques for Session-Oriented Calculi. In: Wirsing, M., Hölzl, M. (eds.) SENSORIA. LNCS, vol. 6582, pp. 214–231. Springer, Heidelberg (2011)
5. Babich, W.A., Jazayeri, M.: The Method of Attributes for Data flow Analysis. Acta Inf 10, 245–264 (1978)
6. El-Wakil, M., El-Bastawisi, A., Boshra, M., Fahmy, A.: Object-Oriented Design Quality Models - A Survey and Comparison. In: 2nd International Conference on Informatics and Systems (INFOS 2004) (2004)
7. Engelhardt, M., Hein, C., Ritter, T., Wagner, M.: Generation of Formal Model Metrics for MOF based Domain Specific Languages. ECEASST 24 (2009)
8. ENVIROFI: Environmental Observation Web and its Service Applications within the Future Internet - Environmental Usage Area, http://www.envirofi.eu
9. Koch, N., Heckel, R., Gönczy, L.: UML for Service-Oriented Systems (second version). Sensoria Deliverable D1.4b, http://pst.ifi.lmu.de/projekte/Sensoria/del_54/D1.4.b.pdf
10. Kreger, H., Estefan, J.: Navigating the SOA Open Standards Landscape Around Architecture. Whitepaper W096, The Open Group (2009)

11. Langermeier, M.: A model-driven approach for open distributed systems. Technical Report 2013-03, University of Augsburg (2013)
12. Langermeier, M., Saad, C., Bauer, B.: A unified Framework for Enterprise Architecture Analysis. In: Proceedings of the Enterprise Model Analysis Workshop in the Context of the 18th Enterprise Computing Conference, EDOC 2014 (2014)
13. Mayer, P., Koch, N., Schroeder, A., Knapp, A.: The UML4SOA Profile. Technical Report, LMU Muenchen Version 3.0 (2010)
14. Metz, R., McCabe, F., Laskey, K., MacKenzie, C.M., Brown, P.F.: Reference Model for Service Oriented Architecture 1.0. Official OASIS Standard (2006), http://docs.oasis-open.org/soa-rm/v1.0/
15. Saad, C., Bauer, B.: Data-Flow Based Model Analysis and Its Applications. In: Moreira, A., Schätz, B., Gray, J., Vallecillo, A., Clarke, P. (eds.) MODELS 2013. LNCS, vol. 8107, pp. 707–723. Springer, Heidelberg (2013)
16. Sadovykh, A., Desfray, P., Elvesæter, B., Berre, A.-J., Landre, E.: Enterprise architecture modeling with SoaML using BMM and BPMN - MDA approach in practice. In: 6th Central and Eastern European Software Engineering Conference, pp. 79–85. IEEE (2010)
17. SENSORIA: Software Engineering for Service-Oriented Overlay Computers (2010), http://www.sensoria-ist.eu
18. Spitznagel, B., Garlan, D.: Architecture-based performance analysis (1998)
19. The Open Group: Service-Oriented Architecture Ontology. Standard (2011)
20. The Open Group: SOA Reference Architecture. Standard (2011)
21. Tribastone, M., Mayer, P., Wirsing, M.: Performance prediction of service-oriented systems with layered queueing networks. In: Margaria, T., Steffen, B. (eds.) ISoLA 2010, Part II. LNCS, vol. 6416, pp. 51–65. Springer, Heidelberg (2010)
22. Wirsing, M., Hölzl, M., Koch, N., Mayer, P.: SENSORIA – software engineering for service-oriented overlay computers. In: Wirsing, M., Hölzl, M. (eds.) SENSORIA. LNCS, vol. 6582, pp. 1–14. Springer, Heidelberg (2011)

Service Composition
for Collective Adaptive Systems

Stephen Gilmore[1], Jane Hillston[1], and Mirco Tribastone[2]

[1] Laboratory for Foundations of Computer Science, University of Edinburgh,
Edinburgh, UK
[2] Electronics and Computer Science, University of Southampton,
Southampton, UK

Abstract. Collective adaptive systems are large-scale resource-sharing systems which adapt to the demands of their users by redistributing resources to balance load or provide alternative services where the current provision is perceived to be insufficient. Smart transport systems are a primary example where real-time location tracking systems record the location availability of assets such as cycles for hire, or fleet vehicles such as buses, trains and trams. We consider the problem of an informed user optimising his journey using a composition of services offered by different service providers.

1   Introduction

Flexible composition of services lies at the heart of collective adaptive systems (CAS) where the collective interaction of users of the system shapes future system behaviour because the system adapts to patterns of use. Adaptive systems such as these are subject to a continuous process of tuning based on measurement data collected by the system itself through integrated instrumentation. Use of the services provided by the system achieves goals which are important to the user (perhaps a goal as simple as travelling across the city to enjoy a social occasion with friends and colleagues) but it also alters the system so that user experience in the future will be affected by this use of this service, even if only very subtly. Service provision in the future depends on decisions made by transport system operators, based on perceived demand for services as determined by collective journey statistics.

CAS depend on real-time measurement and monitoring of their services coupled with the dissemination of service availability information, allowing users to make informed choices. The provision of real-time information makes it possible for users to interact intelligently with adaptive systems and to make informed decisions which are supported by vital, current information.

Investigation of such systems by the construction of formal models of their behaviour is a hugely productive activity. A formal model provides a compact representation of an important aspect of a complex system, throwing light on the most significant issues and giving us the intellectual tools to study them closely. In this paper we consider a formal model of a collective adaptive system

R. De Nicola and R. Hennicker (Eds.): Wirsing Festschrift, LNCS 8950, pp. 490–505, 2015.

which is composed of distributed services. In particular we study an integrated smart transport system which blends public transport and self-powered transport in an effort to solve the so-called *last mile* transport problem experienced in modern cities. This problem arises because although public transport can be used to transport a passenger close to their intended destination, a final stage of the journey (the "last mile") remains to be travelled in another way. The consequence of not addressing the last mile transport problem is that users become disenchanted with the service and resort to private transport, putting more cars on the road with negative consequences for road congestion and the environment.

Specifically, we consider the interaction between a real-time public-transport tracking service, a location-identification service, a transport-planning service, and a cycle-hire service, from the point-of-view of public transport passengers. These passengers also subscribe to a cycle-hire scheme and wish to optimise their journey to their destination. Subscribers in a cycle-hire scheme can borrow cycles from a cycle station when they need one, use the cycle for their allotted time, and then return the cycle to the cycle station nearest to their destination.

Authors' Note. Our interest in service composition, and the development of stochastic modelling techniques suitable for studying the performance of composed services, can be directly attributed to Martin. We had the great privilege of working with him on the SENSORIA project and we look forward to future opportunities to travel through Munich to enjoy a Maß with him, availing ourselves of smart transport services (such as those described in our scenario below).

2   Scenario: Travel in Munich

As our running example, we consider how the situation of users of an integrated smart transport system can be assisted by automated tools which allow them to make an optimal choice between alternative routes to reach a desired destination. If journey times were deterministic it would be possible to easily compute the shortest path. However, in reality all transport systems exhibit a great deal of uncertainty in journey times due their inherent stochasticity: a tram can break down, a bicycle tyre can go flat, traffic congestion may affect a bus journey, and so on. Our idea is to be able to compute an optimal path on-line using the current state of the system.

To be more concrete and to provide a familiar scenario, we set our example in Munich during Oktoberfest, and assume that the hard-working staff of the *Ludwig-Maximilians-Universität* at the LMU building in Oettingenstrasse wish to plan their journey to Theresienwiese for their well-earned *Maß*[1] after a long day in the office. Naturally they prefer to minimise their journey time. We assume that a user, hereby denoted by M, has a choice between the following three routes:

---

[1] Maß is the Bavarian for a mug of beer, equivalent to 1 litre.

1. Take the 54 bus from Hirschauer Strasse to Giselastrasse. We assume that a bike-sharing station is available at Giselastrasse. Thus M has three options: directly walk or cycle to Theresienwise, or change with the underground line U6 to Odeonsplatz. At Odeonsplatz is another bike-sharing station; now M has the choice to either walk or cycle to Theresienwise.
2. M may prefer to start the journey with a relaxing stroll through the English Gardens, and take the occasion to drop off a document at the LMU building in Leopoldstrasse. The journey can then continue by walking to nearby Universität U-Bahn station. There M will decide between continuing by bike to Theresienwise, or taking the U3 to Odeonsplatz, where he will choose between cycling or walking, as in Route 1.
3. Take the tram 18 to Lehel from Tivolistrasse, and change with the U4 to Hauptbahnhof. We assume the existence of a bike-sharing station at Lehel and Hauptbahnhof, thus M has always the choice to directly walk or cycle to Theresienwise.

We will refer to these as routes #1, #2 and #3.

3 Modelling

We may now represent this problem as a formal model with a network structure where the intermediate stops on the journey are represented as nodes in the network. We number the stops on each route to remind us of the journey. Thus route #1 has stops S_{10}, S_{11} and S_{12}. We can identify 12 nodes in the network. These are not all distinct and thus correspond to our 11 destinations of interest. The nodes and corresponding locations are given in Table 1.

Table 1. Nodes and locations in the network

Node	Location
S_0	Origin: The LMU building in Oettingenstrasse, at the end of the day
S_{10}	Hirschauer Strasse
S_{11}	Giselastrasse
S_{12}	Odeonsplatz
S_{20}	The English Gardens
S_{21}	The LMU building in Leopoldstrasse
S_{22}	Universität U-Bahn station
S_{23}	Odeonsplatz
S_{30}	Tivolistrasse
S_{31}	Lehel
S_{32}	Hauptbahnhof
D	Destination: Theresienwise, Oktoberfest, and a well-earned $Ma\beta$

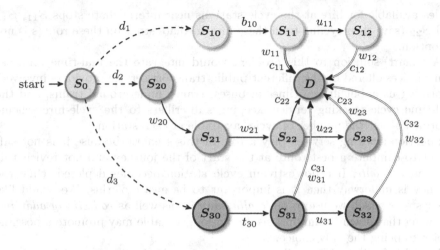

Fig. 1. Possible routes to the destination

Having named the nodes of interest we can now express the journey as a network such as the one illustrated in Figure 1 with our traveller M starting at the origin of the journey (S_0) with options to travel via routes #1, #2 or #3, each of which has intermediate stops along the way.

Every route eventually passes relatively close to their desired destination (D), but not so close that walking is the preferred option. Fortunately, cycle-hire stations are located at intermediate stops S_{11} and S_{12} on route #1, intermediate stops S_{22} and S_{23} on route #2, and intermediate stops S_{31} and S_{32} on route #3. The real-time public-transport tracking service predicts delays d_1, d_2 and d_3 for the public-transport services needed.

We write b_n and similarly for the average bus journey times from stop n. We write t_n for a tram journey from stop n and we use u_n to denote a journey by underground train. We write c_n for the average cycle journey time from stop n to the destination, and w_n for the average walking time. Journeys are always completed either by cycling or by walking, ending at the destination of Oktoberfest in our example (D).

In this scenario there are eleven possible journeys, depending on the route chosen, and where passenger M decides to alight in order to collect a cycle for the last stage of the journey.

$\bullet \xrightarrow{d_1} \bullet \xrightarrow{b_{10}} \bullet \xrightarrow{c_{11}} \bullet \qquad \bullet \xrightarrow{d_2} \bullet \xrightarrow{w_{20}} \bullet \xrightarrow{w_{21}} \bullet \xrightarrow{c_{22}} \bullet \qquad \bullet \xrightarrow{d_3} \bullet \xrightarrow{t_{30}} \bullet \xrightarrow{c_{31}} \bullet$

$\bullet \xrightarrow{d_1} \bullet \xrightarrow{b_{10}} \bullet \xrightarrow{w_{11}} \bullet \qquad \bullet \xrightarrow{d_2} \bullet \xrightarrow{w_{20}} \bullet \xrightarrow{w_{21}} \bullet \xrightarrow{u_{22}} \bullet \xrightarrow{c_{23}} \bullet \qquad \bullet \xrightarrow{d_3} \bullet \xrightarrow{t_{30}} \bullet \xrightarrow{w_{31}} \bullet$

$\bullet \xrightarrow{d_1} \bullet \xrightarrow{b_{10}} \bullet \xrightarrow{u_{11}} \bullet \xrightarrow{c_{12}} \bullet \qquad \bullet \xrightarrow{d_2} \bullet \xrightarrow{w_{20}} \bullet \xrightarrow{w_{21}} \bullet \xrightarrow{u_{22}} \bullet \xrightarrow{w_{23}} \bullet \qquad \bullet \xrightarrow{d_3} \bullet \xrightarrow{t_{30}} \bullet \xrightarrow{u_{31}} \bullet \xrightarrow{c_{32}} \bullet$

$\bullet \xrightarrow{d_1} \bullet \xrightarrow{b_{10}} \bullet \xrightarrow{u_{11}} \bullet \xrightarrow{w_{12}} \bullet \qquad \qquad \qquad \qquad \qquad \qquad \bullet \xrightarrow{d_3} \bullet \xrightarrow{t_{30}} \bullet \xrightarrow{u_{31}} \bullet \xrightarrow{w_{32}} \bullet$

Cycle stations can store only a limited number of cycles meaning that on a given day, some of these potential journeys might not be viable. If there are no cycles available for hire at the cycle stations near intermediate stops S_{11}, S_{12} and S_{22} (say) then cycling from these intermediate stops on these routes is not an option.

A 'smart' solution to this problem would integrate the real-time information services offered by the different public-transport service providers involved, informing us about arrival times of buses, trams, underground trains, and the real-time cycle tracking service, keeping subscribers to the cycle-hire scheme informed about the number of cycles available at each station.

Location-tracking services play a role in this scenario because it is not sufficient to compute a best route at the start of the journey and not revisit this decision *en route*. If a downstream cycle station becomes depleted while the journey is underway then it is important to be aware of this. We would like the systems which we use to be *locally adaptive* as well as *collectively adaptive*. Knowing that downstream options are no longer viable may promote a possible choice to being the only choice.

In order for it to be possible to compute results from our model, we must determine model parameters by estimating concrete values for journey times whether journeys are made by bus, tram, underground train, cycling or walking. Fortunately, in our data-rich times this information is readily available from a variety of web-based sources and we have been able to find all of the model parameters which we need for our example.

A more comprehensive treatment of all aspects of this scenario should also consider additional complications which we do not address here. As with all service-oriented computing, we should consider the possibility of lack-of-service for all of the services which the system depends upon. The actor in our story, M, may be unable to connect to the real-time bus information service because no 3G connection is available. Location-tracking services may be unavailable because of an occluded GPS signal. The cycle-hire tracking service may be unable to respond to our request for information because of excessive load on the server, software failures, network failures, a period of maintenance activity, or a host of other reasons. Failures are ubiquitous in distributed and service-oriented systems, so it is necessary to represent them in our models. We are aware that the model which we present in this paper misses many other sources of complexity in real-time-informed travel such as these.

We would also like our algorithm to prefer cycle stations where more cycles are available. It might at first seem that the number of cycles which are available should not play a role in the decision of which route to take: it is enough to know whether some are available, or none. However, there are at least two complicating factors. The first complication is that some of the cycles, although present, might not be usable because of flat tyres, missing saddles, damaged wheels, or other reasons. Cycle stands at cycle stations report whether a cycle is attached to the stand, but have no way of knowing whether or not the cycle is usable. The second complication is that CAS are *resource-sharing* systems. Other passengers, and other pedestrians, are also borrowing cycles concurrently, so a small supply of cycles might be depleted by the time that the bus, tram, or underground train has made its journey to the cycle station. For these, and other reasons, the *number* of cycles available is significant, not just the presence or absence of cycles.

Similarly, we should prefer those routes which offer more cycle stations, because this maximises the number of options which remain open to us once we have committed to a particular route, but we do not address this here.

4   Model

Our high-level representation of the system in Figure 1 is not yet in a form which is suitable for analysis. The reason for this is that although we have detailed durations and dependencies, we have not yet clarified the decision which the user has to make when they have to choose between cycling, or walking, or continuing to travel to the next cycle station (if there is a feasible cycle station further along the route).

If at the end of the route (say at stop S_{12}) then there is a two-way choice between cycling and walking. We can represent this choice by saying that the previous part-journey had two possible outcomes, leading to committing to cycling (S_{12}^c is reached with probability p_{12}^c) or committing to walking (S_{12}^w, reached with probability $p_{12}^w = (1 - p_{12}^c)$). Committing to cycling may incur a delay while waiting for a cycle to be returned by another user.

If instead there is another cycle station further along the route, then the user has a three-way choice, which we represent as being between states (for example S_{11}^c, S_{11}^u and S_{11}^w representing being at location S_{11}, having committed to travel the next part of the route by cycling, underground train, or walking respectively). These are reached with probabilities p_{11}^c, p_{11}^u and p_{11}^w, summing to 1. Figure 2 shows how these probabilities play a role in determining the journey to the destination.

Our next challenge in modelling arises from the fact that we have populations of users of the cycle-sharing scheme, and populations of cycles which can be borrowed. Cycle stations may vary from having the capacity to store as few as 10 cycles, or as many as 100. Without cycle stations having a finite capacity, and without a population of users concurrently borrowing cycles, the aspect of competition for resources which is a defining aspect of resource-sharing collective systems would not be captured in the model.

Cycle stations consist of an array of cycle stands, each of which is a simple process recording the presence or absence of a cycle at this stand, together with the activities which cause a change of state. Figure 3 illustrates the idea.

This modelling decision incorporates the simple but powerful abstraction that individuals in a population are identityless. One cycle in a cycle-sharing scheme is treated as being just like any other: each only represents the capacity to allow M to complete his journey more quickly than he would if he was walking. Similarly, the individual identities of the users of the cycle-hire scheme is not important in this modelling context. Each user just represents the potential to remove a cycle which was previously available for hire and hence possibly force

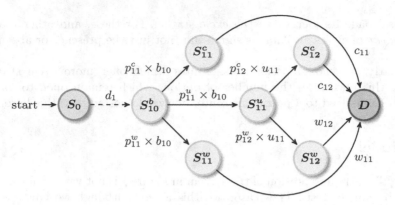

Fig. 2. Exploring route number #1 in greater detail

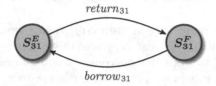

Fig. 3. A cycle station has several stands, each of which may be empty or full

the outcome that M must complete his journey by walking (if there are no cycles left to borrow at the chosen cycle station).

Appendix A presents the complete PEPA model for this scenario.

5   Analysis

We encoded our model in the stochastic process algebra PEPA [1] and analysed it with the PEPA Eclipse Plug-in [2], a modelling tool developed in the European project SENSORIA (Software Engineering for Service-Oriented Overlay Computers) and subsequently used in teaching and research internationally.

PEPA is a compact formal modelling language which provides the appropriate abstract language constructs to represent the model in our example. It has stochastically-timed activities which can be used to encode activities which take time to complete, such as travelling between intermediate stops in a journey and a probabilistic choice operator to express the likelihood of taking different routes. Different patterns of behaviour are encoded in recursive process definitions. Features such as these are found in many modelling formalisms [3] but a distinctive strength of the PEPA language is that populations of components, encoded as arrays of process instances, are both convenient to express in the language and efficiently supported by the dynamic analysis which reveals the collective behaviour which emerges from the interactions of the populations of components. The PEPA language has found application in many modelling problems such as scalable and quantitative analysis of web-services [4,5,6], comparing communications protocols [7], response-time analysis of safety-critical systems [8], software performance engineering with UML-based models [9,10], software patterns [11], software architecture [12], signalling pathways [13], model-driven development [14], and robot movement [15].

Many of these models would have been impossible to construct without an efficient method of analysing large-scale population-based models. A mapping from the PEPA language to systems of ordinary differential equations is presented in [16], making these analyses possible. A formal semantic account of the transformation is available [17], together with supporting theory enabling the definition of reward structures on top of the underlying fluid model [18].

These efficient analysis methods are implemented in the PEPA Eclipse Plug-in which provides an integrated modelling environment for PEPA. It incorporates a custom editor for PEPA models, model visualisation and static analysis tools, a model debugger, Markov chain analysis tools, stochastic simulation and discrete analysis tools, a model compiler which delivers a continuous representation of the system, efficient ODE-based solvers, and plotting functions for analysis results.

6   The Optimisation Problem

There are several possible optimisation problems which could be of interest to the traveller in our story, many of which depend heavily on the choice of which route to take at the outset of the journey because this makes a commitment to certain cycle stations.

Figure 4 depicts one aspect of the optimisation problem which we intend to solve. We assume that all model parameters except p_1, p_2, and p_3, are known. In practice, we may assume that these other parameters are inferred from measurements on the real system. Indeed, journey times were set using data collected from the Google Maps and the MVV (Munich's public transportation provider) websites. The probabilities related to traveller commitment were arbitrarily fixed. Here we present results with varying configurations of the cycle

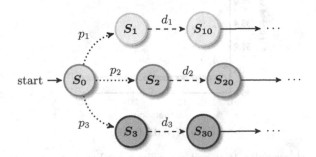

Fig. 4. The optimisation problem: choose p_1, p_2 and p_3 to minimise the time to travel to the destination

stations. Our problem is to find the optimal values of p_1, p_2, and p_3 to minimise the average journey time of a traveller wishing to start a journey at location S_0. We envisage this optimisation problem to be solved by a service provider which computes the optimal route, given the current conditions of the system. The solution can be interpreted as a *randomised algorithm*: for instance, p_1 represents the probability with which the service provider suggests to go to Hirschauer Strasse. This implicitly guarantees some balancing in the system — if all requests returned the same route, this would introduce contention for shared cycles along the route to which the traveller commits.

We solved the optimisation problem by means of genetic algorithms; in particular we used the implementation available in Matlab R2013b, with its default settings. Figure 5 shows the results of the optimisation problem for three different

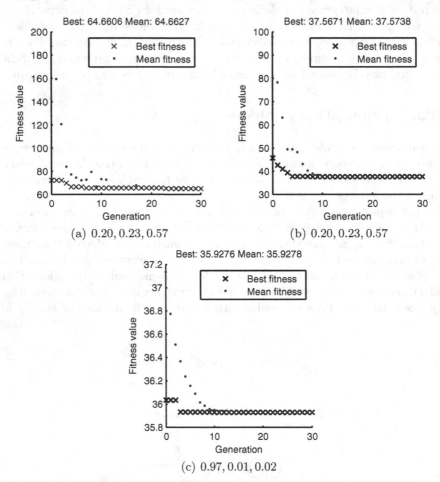

Fig. 5. Optimisation results. Best and mean fitness values (i.e., average journey time, measured in minutes) against generation for three different conditions of the bike sharing system. (a) 10 users per bike; (b) 5 users per bike; (c) 1 user per bike. Each caption shows the optimal configuration of p_1, p_2, and p_3, respectively.

load conditions on the cycle sharing system, characterised by the ratio between the number of users and the number of cycles available. For simplicity, we fixed the same capacity for all cycle stations.

Figure 5(a) plots the best and mean fitness values in the situation where the system has 10 users per available cycle. The optimal configuration suggests a preferential choice for route through Tivolistrasse, with probability 0.57. The average journey time is ca. 1 hour in this case.

Figure 5(b) shows the results for a less loaded cycle sharing system, where there are 5 users per available cycle. Although the optimal configuration is the same as in Figure 5(a), we observe that the average journey time is substantially reduced; this is explained by a lower contention for bikes at the cycle stations, leading to a higher probability that a traveller will find a cycle as soon as they arrive.

Finally, Figure 5(c) shows an ideal situation with no contention for bikes in the network. This leads to a slight improvement in the average journey time experienced by the user; more interestingly, the algorithm suggests a substantial preference for the route through S_{10}, unlike the previous cases.

7   Conclusions

Systems which are built as compositions of services are ubiquitous. The ability to consume services provided by others and to compose services from different sources plays a crucial role in the design and evolution of the systems of today. Services make systems work.

In part the impetus towards these kinds of service composition architectures has been fuelled by a change in attitude towards open systems and open data. Transport operators in particular have embraced the challenges of providing open access to their data about the state of their service, allowing others to build apps which give users access to information about journey times, disruptions, availability of cycles, and other key system descriptors. More recently apps and applications have been developed which aggregate disparate sources of data to give richer insights and open up new possibilities, as in the scenario considered here where bus and cycle services are integrated.

Possessing the ability to efficiently analyse such service-oriented systems is equally important. Advances in analysis tools and frameworks are needed to keep pace with the ever-increasing challenges which stem from the complex systems which surround us in our technology-dense lives.

Acknowledgements. This work is supported by the EU project QUANTICOL, 600708.

References

1. Hillston, J.: A Compositional Approach to Performance Modelling. Cambridge University Press (1996)
2. Tribastone, M., Duguid, A., Gilmore, S.: The PEPA Eclipse Plug-in. Performance Evaluation Review 36(4), 28–33 (2009)
3. Clark, A., Gilmore, S., Hillston, J., Tribastone, M.: Stochastic Process Algebras (chapter Stochastic Process Algebras). In: Bernardo, M., Hillston, J. (eds.) SFM 2007. LNCS, vol. 4486, pp. 132–179. Springer, Heidelberg (2007)
4. Gilmore, S., Tribastone, M.: Evaluating the scalability of a web service-based distributed e-learning and course management system. In: Bravetti, M., Núñez, M., Zavattaro, G. (eds.) WS-FM 2006. LNCS, vol. 4184, pp. 214–226. Springer, Heidelberg (2006)
5. Bravetti, M., Gilmore, S., Guidi, C., Tribastone, M.: Replicating web services for scalability. In: Barthe, G., Fournet, C. (eds.) TGC 2007. LNCS, vol. 4912, pp. 204–221. Springer, Heidelberg (2008)
6. Cappello, I., Clark, A., Gilmore, S., Latella, D., Loreti, M., Quaglia, P., Schivo, S.: Quantitative analysis of services. In: Wirsing, Hölzl (eds.) [19], pp. 522–540
7. Wang, H., Laurenson, D., Hillston, J.: Evaluation of RSVP and Mobility-aware RSVP Using Performance Evaluation Process Algebra. In: Proceedings of the IEEE International Conference on Communications, Beijing, China (May 2008)
8. Argent-Katwala, A., Clark, A., Foster, H., Gilmore, S., Mayer, P., Tribastone, M.: Safety and response-time analysis of an automotive accident assistance service. In: Margaria, Steffen (eds.) [20], pp. 191–205.
9. Tribastone, M., Gilmore, S.: Automatic extraction of PEPA performance models from UML activity diagrams annotated with the MARTE profile. In: Proceedings of the 7th International Workshop on Software and Performance (WOSP 2008), pp. 67–78. ACM Press, Princeton (2008)
10. Tribastone, M., Gilmore, S.: Automatic translation of UML sequence diagrams into PEPA models. In: 5th International Conference on the Quantitative Evaluation of SysTems (QEST 2008), pp. 205–214. IEEE Computer Society Press, St Malo (2008)
11. Wirsing, M., Hölzl, M., Acciai, L., Banti, F., Clark, A., Fantechi, A., Gilmore, S., Gnesi, S., Gönczy, L., Koch, N., Lapadula, A., Mayer, P., Mazzanti, F., Pugliese, R., Schroeder, A., Tiezzi, F., Tribastone, M., Varró, D.: SENSORIA patterns: Augmenting service engineering with formal analysis, transformation and dynamicity. In: Margaria, Steffen (eds.) [20], pp. 170–190
12. Knapp, A., Janisch, S., Hennicker, R., Clark, A., Gilmore, S., Hacklinger, F., Baumeister, H., Wirsing, M.: Modelling the coCoME with the JAVA/A component model. In: Rausch, A., Reussner, R., Mirandola, R., Plášil, F. (eds.) The Common Component Modeling Example. LNCS, vol. 5153, pp. 207–237. Springer, Heidelberg (2008)
13. Geisweiller, N., Hillston, J., Stenico, M.: Relating continuous and discrete PEPA models of signalling pathways. Theor. Comput. Sci. 404(1-2), 97–111 (2008)
14. Gilmore, S., Gönczy, L., Koch, N., Mayer, P., Tribastone, M., Varró, D.: Non-functional properties in the model-driven development of service-oriented systems. Software and System Modeling 10(3), 287–311 (2011)

15. Clark, A., Duguid, A., Gilmore, S.: Passage-end analysis for analysing robot movement. In: Wirsing, Hölzl (eds.) [19], pp. 506–521
16. Hillston, J.: Fluid flow approximation of PEPA models. In: Proceedings of the Second International Conference on the Quantitative Evaluation of Systems, Torino, Italy, pp. 33–43. IEEE Computer Society Press (September 2005)
17. Tribastone, M., Gilmore, S., Hillston, J.: Scalable differential analysis of process algebra models. IEEE Trans. Software Eng. 38(1), 205–219 (2012)
18. Tribastone, M., Ding, J., Gilmore, S., Hillston, J.: Fluid rewards for a stochastic process algebra. IEEE Trans. Software Eng. 38(4), 861–874 (2012)
19. Margaria, T., Steffen, B.: ISoLA 2008. CCIS, vol. 17. Springer, Heidelberg (2008)
20. Wirsing, M., Hölzl, M. (eds.): SENSORIA. LNCS, vol. 6582. Springer, Heidelberg (2011)

A   PEPA Model

This section contains the complete PEPA model for the scenario described in Section 4. It is presented with the syntax accepted by the PEPA Eclipse Plug-in.

```
 1  // Probabilities of choosing routes.
 2  p_1 = 0.20;
 3  p_2 = 0.23;
 4  p_3 = 0.57;
 5
 6  // Probabilities of cycling, walking or bussing from S11
 7  p_11_c = 0.45;
 8  p_11_w = 0.15;
 9  // Ensure p_11_c+p_11_w+p_11_b = 1
10  p_11_u = 1 - (p_11_c + p_11_w);
11
12  // Probabilities for S12
13  p_12_c = 0.385;
14  p_12_w = 1 - p_12_c;
15
16  // Probabilities for S22
17  p_22_c = 0.35;
18  p_22_u = 1 - p_22_c;
19
20  // Probabilities for S23
21  p_23_c = 0.3853232;
22  p_23_w = 1 - p_23_c;
23
24  // Probabilities for S31
25  p_31_c = 0.55;
26  p_31_w = 0.275;
27  p_31_b = 1 - (p_31_c + p_31_w);
28
29  // Probabilities for S32
30  p_32_c = 0.525;
31  p_32_w = 1 - p_32_c;
32
33  // Rate parameters: unit time is minutes
34
35  t = 1; // Think time
36
37  // Delays waiting for the buses
38  d_1 = 1/5;
39  d_2 = 1/8;
40  d_3 = 1/12;
41
42
43  b_10 = 1/17; // Bus time
44  t_30 = 1/10; // Tram time
45
46  // Cycle times
47  c_11 = 1/10;
48  c_12 = 1/7;
49  c_22 = 1/7;
50  c_23 = 1/9;
51  c_31 = 1/12;
52  c_32 = 1/15;
53
54  // Walking times are roughly twice the cycle times
55  w_11 = 1/20;
56  w_12 = 1/14;
57  w_20 = 1/6;
58  w_21 = 1/10;
59  w_23 = 1/18;
60  w_31 = 1/24;
61  w_32 = 1/30;
62
```

```
63  // Underground times
64  u_11 = 1/11;
65  u_22 = 1/14;
66  u_32 = 1/17;
67
68  // Return and borrow from S11
69  r_r_11 = 0.21431;
70  r_b_11 = 0.8239457;
71
72  // Return and borrow from S12
73  r_r_12 = 0.21431;
74  r_b_12 = 0.8239457;
75
76  // Return and borrow from S22
77  r_r_22 = 0.21242321;
78  r_b_22 = 0.2822223294527;
79
80  // Return and borrow from S23
81  r_r_23 = 0.212431;
82  r_b_23 = 0.8222329457;
83
84  // Return and borrow from S31
85  r_r_31 = 0.73453;
86  r_b_31 = 0.21348;
87
88  // Return and borrow from S32
89  r_r_32 = 0.37845;
90  r_b_32 = 0.13534;
91
92  // Return and borrow from D
93  r_r_D = 0.37845;
94  r_b_D = 0.13534;
95
96  // Work
97  w = 1;
98
99  User_0 = (choose, p_1/t). User_1
100        + (choose, p_2/t). User_2
101        + (choose, p_3/t). User_3;
102
103 // User taking the #1 route
104 User_1 = (delay_1, d_1). User_10;
105
106 User_10 = (bus_to_11, p_11_c*b_10). User_c_11
107         + (bus_to_11, p_11_w*b_10). User_w_11
108         + (bus_to_11, p_11_u*b_10). User_u_11;
109 User_c_11 = (borrow_11, r_b_11).(cycle_from_11, c_11).(return_D, r_r_D). User_W;
110 User_w_11 = (walk_from_11, w_11). User_W;
111 User_u_11 = (underground_to_12, p_12_c * u_11). User_c_12
112           + (underground_to_12, p_12_w * u_11). User_w_12;
113 User_c_12 = (borrow_12, r_b_12).(cycle_from_12, c_12).(return_D, r_r_D). User_W;
114 User_w_12 = (walk_from_12, w_12). User_W;
115
116 // User taking the #2 route
117 User_2 = (delay_2, d_2). User_20;
118
119 User_20 =  (walk_to_21, w_20). User_w_21;
120 User_w_21 = (walk_from_21, p_22_c * w_21). User_c_22
121           + (walk_from_21, p_22_u * w_21). User_u_22;
122 User_c_22 = (borrow_22, r_b_22).(cycle_from_22, c_22).(return_D, r_r_D). User_W;
123 User_u_22 = (underground_from_22, p_23_c * u_22). User_c_23
124           + (underground_from_22, p_23_w * u_22). User_w_23;
125 User_c_23 = (borrow_23, r_b_23).(cycle_from_23, c_23).(return_D, r_r_D). User_W;
126 User_w_23 = (walk_from_23, w_23). User_W;
127
128 // User taking the #3 route
129 User_3 = (delay_3, d_3). User_30;
130
```

```
131  User_30 = (tram_to_31, p_31_c * t_30). User_c_31
132          + (tram_to_31, p_31_w * t_30). User_w_31
133          + (tram_to_31, p_31_b * t_30). User_u_31;
134
135  User_c_31 = (borrow_31, r_b_31).(cycle_from_31, c_31).(return_D, r_r_D). User_W;
136  User_w_31 = (walk_from_31, w_31). User_W;
137  User_u_31 = (underground_to_32, p_32_c * u_32). User_c_32
138          + (underground_to_32, p_32_w * u_32). User_w_32;
139  User_c_32 = (borrow_32, r_b_32).(cycle_from_32, c_32).(return_D, r_r_D). User_W;
140  User_w_32 = (walk_from_32, w_32). User_W;
141
142  // User at work
143  User_W = (work, w). User_0;
144
145  // Definitions of stations
146  Station_11_Empty = (return_11, r_r_11). Station_11_Full;
147  Station_11_Full = (borrow_11, r_b_11). Station_11_Empty;
148
149  Station_12_Empty = (return_12, r_r_12). Station_12_Full;
150  Station_12_Full = (borrow_12, r_b_12). Station_12_Empty;
151
152  Station_22_Empty = (return_22, r_r_22). Station_22_Full;
153  Station_22_Full = (borrow_22, r_b_22). Station_22_Empty;
154
155  Station_23_Empty = (return_23, r_r_23). Station_23_Full;
156  Station_23_Full = (borrow_23, r_b_23). Station_23_Empty;
157
158  Station_31_Empty = (return_31, r_r_31). Station_31_Full;
159  Station_31_Full = (borrow_31, r_b_31). Station_31_Empty;
160
161  Station_32_Empty = (return_32, r_r_32). Station_32_Full;
162  Station_32_Full = (borrow_32, r_b_32). Station_32_Empty;
163
164  Station_D_Empty = (return_D, r_r_D). Station_D_Full;
165  Station_D_Full = (borrow_D, r_b_D). Station_D_Empty;
166
167  // Definitions for other users
168  User_11_Idle = (borrow_11, r_b_11). User_11_Busy;
169  User_11_Busy = (return_11, r_r_11). User_11_Idle;
170
171  User_12_Idle = (borrow_12, r_b_12). User_12_Busy;
172  User_12_Busy = (return_12, r_r_12). User_12_Idle;
173
174  User_21_Idle = (borrow_21, r_b_21). User_21_Busy;
175  User_21_Busy = (return_21, r_r_21). User_21_Idle;
176
177  User_22_Idle = (borrow_22, r_b_22). User_22_Busy;
178  User_22_Busy = (return_22, r_r_22). User_22_Idle;
179
180  User_23_Idle = (borrow_23, r_b_23). User_23_Busy;
181  User_23_Busy = (return_23, r_r_23). User_23_Idle;
182
183  User_31_Idle = (borrow_31, r_b_31). User_31_Busy;
184  User_31_Busy = (return_31, r_r_31). User_31_Idle;
185
186  User_32_Idle = (borrow_32, r_b_32). User_32_Busy;
187  User_32_Busy = (return_32, r_r_32). User_32_Idle;
188
189  User_D_Idle = (borrow_D, r_b_D). User_D_Busy;
190  User_D_Busy = (return_D, r_r_D). User_D_Idle;
191
192  (User_0[60]  <>  User_11_Idle[1]  <>  User_12_Idle[1]  <>
193    User_21_Idle[1]  <>  User_22_Idle[1]  <>  User_23_Idle[1]  <>
194      User_31_Idle[1]  <>  User_32_Idle[1]  <>  User_D_Idle[1]) <*> (
195        Station_11_Full[2]  <>  Station_12_Full[2]  <>
196          (Station_22_Full[2]  <>  Station_23_Full[2])  <>
197            (Station_31_Full[2]  <>  Station_32_Full[2]  <>  Station_D_Full[2]) )
```

Lines 2–4 define the probabilities of choosing routes. These are the variables in our optimisation problem; here they are set to the optimal values for the scenarios illustrated in Figures 5(a) and 5(b). Using the same notation as in the main text, lines 6–93 define all the other model parameters. Journey times were inferred from information available on the web, as discussed; the remaining parameters were arbitrarily fixed. Traveller behaviour is modelled in lines 98–142. The dynamics of a cycle station is characterised by a two-state automaton associated with each docking point, lines 145-164. We consider exogenous arrivals and departures to each cycle station by modelling further users, lines 1767–189. Finally, lines 191–296 defines the *system equation*, specifying the total population of users and the number of docking points for each cycle station. From [18], we compute the average journey time experienced by a user using Little's law as

$$\text{Average Journey Time} = \frac{60}{\text{User\_0} \times w},$$

where the numerator gives the total number of users of interest and User_0 gives the total number of users in the steady state which are about to start their journey.

The Evolution of Jolie
From Orchestrations to Adaptable Choreographies

Ivan Lanese[1], Fabrizio Montesi[2], and Gianluigi Zavattaro[1]

[1] Dep. of Computer Science and Engineering, INRIA FoCUS Team - Univ. Bologna
Mura A. Zamboni 7, 40127 Bologna, Italy
{lanese,zavattar}@cs.unibo.it
[2] Dep. of Mathematics and Computer Science, University of Southern Denmark
Campusvej 55, 5230 Odense, Denmark
fmontesi@imada.sdu.dk

Abstract. Jolie is an orchestration language conceived during Sensoria, an FP7 European project led by Martin Wirsing in the time frame 2005–2010. Jolie was designed having in mind both the novel –at project time– concepts related to Service-Oriented Computing and the traditional approach to the modelling of concurrency typical of process calculi. The foundational work done around Jolie during Sensoria has subsequently produced many concrete results. In this paper we focus on two distinct advancements, one aiming at the development of dynamically adaptable orchestrated systems and one focusing on global choreographic specifications. These works, more recently, contributed to the realisation of a framework for programming dynamically evolvable distributed Service-Oriented applications that are correct-by-construction.

1 Introduction

Sensoria (Software Engineering for Service-Oriented Overlay Computers)[1] is a research project funded by the European Commission under the 7-th Framework Programme in the time frame 2005–2010. Supervised by Martin Wirsing, the project has defined a novel approach for the engineering of advanced Service-Oriented applications. In fact, at project time, Service-Oriented Computing (SOC) was emerging as a novel and promising technology but, as frequently happens, the success of a promising technology requires the establishment of a mature methodology for the development of applications based on such technology. Easy-to-use tools are also needed to make the development methodology popular and largely diffused.

The success of Sensoria is demonstrated by the realisation of an integrated set of theoretical and concrete tools. In particular, UML-like visual languages have been developed for the high-level modelling of Service-Oriented applications (see, e.g., [18,7]), several process calculi have been designed to formally represent the operational aspects of such applications (see, e.g., [4,30,29,5]), analysis

---

[1] http://www.sensoria-ist.eu

R. De Nicola and R. Hennicker (Eds.): Wirsing Festschrift, LNCS 8950, pp. 506–521, 2015.
© Springer International Publishing Switzerland 2015

techniques have been developed to perform both qualitative and quantitative analysis on these formal models of the applications (see, e.g., [19,37,13]), and also runtime support for application deployment has been realised by providing some of the proposed calculi with an execution environment (see, e.g., [34,31]).

Among the implementations of process calculi, Jolie [34] was conceived as a fully fledged Service-Oriented programming language that, on the one hand, is based on a formally defined semantics and, on the other hand, turns out to be easy to integrate with state-of-the-art technologies (in particular those based on the Java platform). This marked technological flavour of the language is witnessed by the birth of the spin-off company *italianaSoftware s.r.l.*[2] whose mission is indeed the exploitation in industrial environments of Jolie and its related tools.

Beyond the initial development of Jolie within Sensoria, many advancements took place even after Sensoria ended. For instance, in [22] Jolie is extended with primitives for fault handling and compensations; in [15] linguistic primitives are proposed for easy realisation of software architectures including advanced connectors like proxies, wrappers, and load balancers; and in [21] Jolie is studied as a language for workflow management by showing how to implement the popular van der Aalst's workflow patterns [38].

In this paper, we narrate some of the extensions of Jolie in order to demonstrate how our experience in the development of an orchestration language during Sensoria provided us with valuable insights in related research lines.

We start by presenting two independent frameworks based on Jolie. The first one is JoRBA [27], a framework for the programming of service-oriented applications that can dynamically adapt to their execution context. JoRBA uses the code mobility mechanisms offered by Jolie to adapt the behaviour of services at runtime; the need for adaptation is decided by special rules given by programmers in a declarative way. The second one is Chor [11], a choreographic language allowing for the programming of distributed systems from a global viewpoint. Chor is equipped with a compiler that generates executable Jolie programs, which are guaranteed to be correct by construction from the originating global program. We finally present AIOCJ [16], a choreography language that combines the global approach of Chor to distributed programming with the adaptability features of JoRBA. The Jolie programs compiled by AIOCJ are guaranteed to be correct not only as far as the initial code is concerned, but also when the updates specified in AIOCJ are dynamically applied to the application endpoints.

Paper Structure. In Section 2 we recall the basics of the Jolie language. In Section 3 we discuss the importance of dynamic adaptation for modern applications and present JoRBA, an extension of Jolie that supports rule-based dynamic program updates. In Section 4 we discuss Chor, the Jolie based approach to the correct-by-construction realisation of communication-centred distributed applications. Finally, in Section 5 we present how in AIOCJ we have been able to combine the rule-based dynamic adaptation mechanisms explored with JoRBA

---

[2] http://www.italianasoftware.com

to the correct-by-construction approach characterising Chor. Related work is discussed in Section 6. We report some conclusive remarks in Section 7.

2 Service-Oriented Programming with Jolie

Jolie programs contain two parts related, respectively, to the *behaviour* of a service and to its *deployment*. Here, we describe in more details the basic primitives for programming the behavioural part of Jolie, while we simply mention that the deployment part is used to instantiate networking and lower-level communication aspects like the definition of the ports and of the communication protocols to be used.

Jolie combines message-passing and imperative programming style. Scopes, indicated by curly brackets { . . . }, are used to represent blocks and procedures. Procedures are labelled with the keyword define; the name of a procedure is unique within a service and the main procedure is the entry point of execution for each service. Traditional sequential programming constructs like conditions, loops, and sequence are standard. In addition, Jolie includes a *parallel* operator | that executes the left and right activities concurrently. Concerning communication, Jolie supports two kinds of message-passing operations, namely *One-Ways* (OWs) and *Request-Responses* (RRs). On the sender's side, the former operation sends a message and immediately passes the thread of control to the subsequent activity in the process, while the latter sends a request and keeps the thread of control until it receives a response. On the receiver's side, OWs receive a message and store it into a defined variable, whilst RRs receive a message, execute some internal code, and finally send the content of a second variable as response.

Jolie provides also an input-guarded choice $[\eta_1]\{B_1\} \ldots [\eta_n]\{B_n\}$, where η_i, $i \in \{1, \ldots, n\}$, is an input statement and B_i is the behaviour of the related branch. When a message on η_i is received, η_i is executed and all other branches are deactivated. Afterwards, B_i is executed. A static check enforces all the input choices to have different operations to avoid ambiguity.

Figure 1 reports a Jolie program taken from [21] including two services A and B. A sends in parallel the content of variables a and b through OW operations op1 and op2, respectively, at (@) B. When B receives a message on one of the corresponding OW operations, it stores the content of the message in the corresponding variable. After the completion of the scope at Lines 2-5, A proceeds with the subsequent RR operation op3, which sends the content of variable e and stores its response in h. The scope linked to op3, in Lines 6-8 of service B, is the activity executed before sending the response to A; as this activity assigns "Hello, world" to the return variable g, this string is returned to A, and thus A assigns it to its return variable h. The command at Line 8 of the service A sends the content of h to the println operation of the Console; in this way "Hello, world" is printed.

An interesting feature of Jolie is that it provides *dynamic embedding*. Dynamic embedding is a mechanism allowing to take the code of a Jolie service and dynamically run the service inside the current application. This mechanism is

```
1  //service A                  1  //service B
2  {                            2  {
3    op1@B( a )                 3    op1( c )
4    | op2@B( b )               4    | op2( d )
5  };                           5  };
6  op3@B( e )( h );             6  op3( f )( g ){
7  println@Console( h )()       7    g = "Hello, world"
                                8  }
```

Fig. 1. An example of composition and communication between services

used quite extensively when programming adaptive applications in Jolie, since it allows one to dynamically load new code to deal with unexpected needs.

3 Managing Dynamic Adaptation with JoRBA

Modern software applications change their behaviour, reconfigure their structure and evolve over time reacting to changes in the operating conditions, so to always meet users' expectations. This is fundamental since those applications live in distributed and mobile devices, such as mobile phones, PDAs, laptops, etc., thus their environment may change frequently. Also, user goals and needs may change dynamically, and applications should adapt accordingly, without intervention from technicians. We aim at *dynamic adaptation*, where the application is able to face unexpected adaptation needs. Dynamic adaptation is challenging since information on the update to be performed is not known when the application is designed, deployed, or even started.

JoRBA (Jolie Rule-Based Adaptation framework) [27] is a Jolie-based framework for programming adaptable applications, which is based on the separation between the application behaviour and the adaptation specification. An adaptable application should provide some *adaptation hooks*, i.e., information on part of its structure and its behaviour. The adaptation logic should be developed separately, for instance as a set of adaptation rules, by some adaptation engineer, and can be created/changed after the application has been deployed without affecting the running application. Adaptation should be enacted by an *adaptation middleware*, including an *adaptation manager* and some, possibly distributed, *adaptation servers*. The latter are services that act as repositories of adaptation rules. Running adaptation servers register themselves on the adaptation manager. The running application may interact with the adaptation manager to look for applicable adaptation rules. Whether a rule is applicable or not may depend on environment conditions (e.g., date, workload), including user preferences, and on properties of the current implementation (e.g., performance, code version, cost). The adaptation manager checks the available rules and returns one of them which can be applied, if it exists. The effect of an adaptation rule is to replace an activity with new code that answers a given adaptation need.

Table 1. List of possible (Travelling) domain activities

Activity	Functional Parameters			Non-functional Parameters	
Activity Name	Number	Source	Destination	Time	Cost
Take Train	IC2356	Bologna Train Station	Munich Train Station	7 h 41 m	80 euros
Take Bus	13	Munich Train Station	LMU	30 m	1 euro
Take Taxi	25	Munich Train Station	LMU	10 m	15 euros
Go To Meeting	-	Bob's House	LMU	9 h	100 euros

We describe now on a sample scenario the approach used in JoRBA to deal with dynamic adaptation.

Travelling Scenario. Consider Bob travelling from Bologna to LMU (Martin Wirsing's university) for a Sensoria meeting. He may have on his mobile phone an application instructing him about what to do, taking care of the related tasks. A set of possible tasks are in Table 1. For instance, the activity *Take Train* connects to the information system of Bologna train station to buy the train ticket. It also instructs Bob about how to take the train, and which one to take.

Assume that such an application has been developed for adaptation. This means that its *adaptation interface* specifies that some of the activities are adaptable. Each adaptable activity has a few parameters, e.g., *Number*, specifying the code of the train, bus or taxi to be taken, *Source* specifying the desired leaving place and *Destination* specifying the desired arrival place, all visible from the adaptation interface. Also, a few non-functional parameters for the activities may be specified as *Time* and *Cost*. We show now a couple of examples of adaptation.

Example 1. When Bob arrives to Bologna train station, its Travelling application connects to the adaptation server of the train station. Assume that a new "*Italo*" (Italian high speed train) connection has been activated from Bologna to Munich providing a connection with *Time=4 h 23 m* and *Cost=92 euros*. This is reflected by the existence of an adaptation rule specifying that all the applications providing an activity *Take Train* for a train for which the new connection is possible may be adapted. Adaptation may depend on Bob's preferences for comparing the old activity and the new one, or may be forced if, for instance, the old connection is no more available. If adaptation has to be performed, the new code for the activity is sent by the adaptation server to the application, where it becomes the new definition of activity *Take Train*. Note that the new code can be quite different from the old one, e.g., if the new trains are booked using a different communication protocol. Thus Bob can immediately exploit the new high speed connection, which was not expected when the application has been created.

Example 2. Suppose that the train from Bologna to Munich is one hour late. Bob mobile phone may have an adaptation server taking care of adapting all Bob's applications to changing environment conditions. The adaptation server will be notified about the train being late, and it may include an adaptation rule specifying that if Bob is late on his travel, he can take a taxi instead of arriving to LMU by bus. The adaptation rule thus replaces the activity *Take Bus* of the travelling application with a new activity *Take Taxi*. Again, this can be done even if different protocols and servers are used to buy bus tickets and to reserve a taxi.

A Rule-Based Approach to Dynamic Adaptation. Instead of presenting the syntax of JoRBA, we discuss its approach to dynamic adaptation which is general enough to be applied to applications developed using any other language, provided that (i) the application exposes the desired adaptation interface and (ii) the language is able to support the code mobility mechanism necessary for performing adaptation. At the end of this section we briefly show that Jolie supports both these features.

Thus we want to build an adaptable application using some language L and following the approach above to dynamic adaptation. The application must expose a set of *adaptable domain activities* (or, simply, activities) $\{A_i\}_{i \in I}$, together with some additional information. Activities A_i are the ones that may require to be updated to adapt the application to changes in the operating conditions. While it is necessary to guess where adaptation may be possible, it is not necessary to know at the application development time which actual conditions will trigger the adaptation, and which kind of adaptation should be performed.

The adaptable application will interact with an adaptation middleware providing the adaptation rules. The environment has full control over the set of rules, and may change them at any time, regardless of the state of the running application. Each such rule includes a description of the activity to be adapted, an applicability condition specifying when the rule is applicable, the new code of the activity, the set of variables required by the activity, and some information on the non-functional properties of the activity.

At runtime, the rule is matched against the application activity to find out whether adaptation is possible/required. In particular:

- the description of the activity to be adapted in the rule should be compatible with the description of the activity in the application;
- the applicability condition should evaluate to true; the applicability condition may refer to both variables of the environment (retrieved by the adaptation manager) and variables published by the adaptation interface of the application;
- the non-functional properties guaranteed by the new code provided by the adaptation rule should be better than the ones guaranteed by the old implementation, according to some user specified policy;
- the variables required by the new code should be a subset of the variables provided by the application for the activity.

If all these conditions are satisfied then adaptation can be performed, i.e. the new code of the activity should be sent by the adaptation manager to the application, and installed by the application replacing the old one. Since the update may also influence the state, we also allow the adaptation rule to specify a state update for the adaptable application.

More precisely, the following steps are executed:

1. the adaptation server sends the new code to the application, which replaces the old code of the activity;
2. the adaptation interface of the application is updated, with the new non-functional properties, e.g., *Time=4 h 23 m* and *Cost=92 euros*, replacing the old ones;
3. the state of the application is updated, e.g., by setting variable *Number* to *IT*82, the number of the "*Italo*" train.

The first step is the most tricky, since the new code needs to be sent from the adaptation server to the application and integrated with the rest of the application. For instance, it should be able to exploit the public variables of the application.

JoRBA is a proof-of-concept implementation of our adaptation mechanism based upon the Jolie language. Indeed, both the adaptation middleware, including the distributed adaptation servers, and the adaptable application are built as Jolie services. Thus, interactions between them are obtained using Jolie OWs and RRs communication primitives. The code inside adaptable activities is externalized from the main body of the application as a separate service. In this way adaptation is realized by disabling the service implementing the adaptable activity and replacing it with the new code coming from the adaptation manager, which is launched using Jolie dynamic embedding. Since both the main part of the application, the old service and the new one should share part of the state, this is externalized as a separate service accessible from all of them.

4   Correct-by-Construction Development with Chor

In the context of Service-Oriented Computing and, more in general, for the development of distributed communication-centred applications, the top-down approach based on *global* specifications that are automatically projected to *endpoint* code has recently emerged as a popular approach for the realisation of correct-by-construction applications [10,25,40,28,12]. Global specifications are expressed using so-called *choreography* languages: the message flow among the partners in the application is expressed from a global viewpoint as it happens, e.g., in Message Sequence Charts [23] or when security protocols are specified by using actions like, e.g., Alice $\rightarrow$ Bob : $\{M\}_k$ meaning that Alice sends to Bob the message M encrypted with the key k. These global specifications are guaranteed to be correct, in particular *deadlock- and race-free*, because only successful and completed communications among two interacting partners can be expressed. In other terms, it is not possible to specify an endpoint that remains blocked

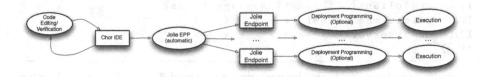

Fig. 2. Chor development methodology, from [11]

waiting indefinitely for a never arriving message. The actual communication behaviour of each single partner is in turn obtained by projection from the global specification: the obtained projected code is guaranteed to adhere to the global specification, thus correctness is preserved.

This popular approach has been also adapted to Jolie. In this case, the choreographic language is Chor [11]. Chor offers a programming language, based on choreographies, and an Integrated Development Environment (IDE) developed as an Eclipse plugin for the writing of programs. In the development methodology suggested with Chor, depicted in Figure 2, developers can first use the IDE to write protocol specifications and choreographies. The programmer is supported by on-the-fly verification which takes care of checking (i) the syntactic correctness of program terms and (ii) the type compliance of the choreography w.r.t. the protocol specifications, using a (behavioural) typing discipline.

Once the global program is completed, developers can automatically project it to an endpoint implementation. Endpoint implementations are given in Jolie. Nevertheless, Chor is designed to be extended to multiple endpoint languages: potentially, each process in a choreography could be implemented with a different endpoint technology.

Each Jolie endpoint program comes with its own deployment information, given as a term separated from the code implementing the behaviour of the projected process. This part can be optionally customised by the programmer to adapt to a specific communication technology. Finally, the Jolie endpoint programs can be executed; as expected, they will implement the originating choreography.

In order to give an idea of how global specifications can be expressed in Chor, we present a simple example.

Example 3 (Chor program example).

```
1  program simple;
2
3  protocol SimpleProtocol { C -> S: hi( string ) }
4
5  public a: SimpleProtocol
6
7  main
8  {
9    client[C] start server[S] : a( k );
```

```
10    ask@client( "[client] Message?", msg );
11    client.msg -> server.x : hi( k );
12    show@server( "[server] " + x )
13 }
```

Program `simple` above starts by declaring a protocol `SimpleProtocol`, in which role C (for client) sends a string to a role S (for server) through operation `hi`. In the choreography of the program, process `client` and a fresh service process `server` start a session k by synchronising on the public channel a.[3] Process `client` then asks the user for an input message and stores it in its local variable `msg`, which is then sent to process `server` through operation `hi` on session k, implementing protocol `SimpleProtocol`. Finally, process `server` displays the received message on screen.

As mentioned above, Chor has been equipped with an automatic endpoint projection (EPP) that generates Jolie code; the following example shows (part of) the result of the endpoint projection of the simple choreography presented above.

Example 4 (Endpoint Projection in Chor). We give an example of EPP by reporting a snippet of the code generated for process `server` from Example 3:

```
1  main
2  {
3    _start();
4    csets.tid = new;
5    _myRef.binding << global.inputPorts.MyInputPort;
6    _myRef.tid = csets.tid;
7    _start_S@a(_myRef)(_sessionDescriptor.k);
8    k_C << _sessionDescriptor.k.C.binding;
9    hi(x);
10   showMessageDialog@SwingUI("[server] " + x)()
11 }
```

The Jolie code above for process `server` waits to be started by receiving an input on operation `_start`. This starts the generation of the session k (Lines 4–8, that we do not comment in detail). Finally, in Lines 9–10, the `server` receives the message on operation `hi` from the client and displays it on screen as indicated by the choreography.

5   Correct-by-Construction Adaptive Applications

The JoRBA approach to adaptation and the use of choreographies to ensure that applications are deadlock- and race-free by construction can be combined.

---

[3] Session keys are necessary to keep track of the protocols: see, e.g., the presence of the session key k in Line 11 indicating that this interaction between `client` and `server` is part of the protocol started at Line 9.

We describe below AIOCJ [16][4], a framework to program adaptive choreographies. AIOCJ combines an Eclipse plugin to edit adaptable applications and generate code for each participant using a projection similar to the one of Chor, with an adaptation middleware similar to the one of JoRBA managing adaptation. The main point is that adaptation should be coordinated, so to ensure that no error occurs because of inconsistent updates.

We consider applications composed by processes deployed as services on different localities, including local state and computational resources. Each process has a specific duty in the choreography. As for JoRBA, adaptation is performed by interacting with an adaptation middleware storing adaptation rules. The main difference is that now a rule requires to update many participants of the choreography in a coordinated way. The parts of the choreography to be updated are syntactically delimited by *adaptation scopes*.

The language for programming AIOCJ applications relies on a set of roles that identify the processes in the choreography. Let us introduce the syntax of the language using an example where Bob invites Alice to see a film (Listing 1.1).

The code starts with some deployment information (Lines 1-9) that we discuss later on. The description of the behaviour starts at Line 11. The program is made by a loop where Bob first checks when Alice is available and then invites her to the cinema. Before starting the loop, Bob initialises the variable **end** to the boolean value **false** (Line 12). The variable is used to control the exit from the loop. Note the annotation @bob meaning that **end** is a local variable of Bob. The first instructions of the while loop are enclosed in an adaptation scope (Lines 14-18), meaning that this part of the program may be adapted in the future. The first operation within the adaptation scope is the call to the primitive function **getInput** that asks to Bob a day where he is free and stores this date into the local variable **free_day**. At Line 16 the content of **free_day** is sent to Alice via operation **proposal**. Alice stores it in its local variable **bob_free_day**. Then, at Line 17, Alice calls the external function **isFreeDay** that checks whether she is available on **bob_free_day**. If she is available (Line 19) then Bob sends to her the invitation to go to the cinema via the operation **proposal** (Line 21). Alice, reading from the input, accepts or refuses the invitation (Line 25). If Alice accepts the invitation then Bob first sets the variable **end** to **true** to end the loop. Then, he sends to the cinema the booking request via operation **book**. The cinema generates the tickets using the external function **getTicket** and sends them to Alice and Bob via operation **notify**. The two notifications are done in parallel using the parallel operator | (until now we composed statements using the sequential operator ;). Lines 20-32 are enclosed in a second adaptation scope with property N.scope_name = "event selection". If the agreement is not reached, Bob decides, reading from the input, if he wants to stop inviting Alice. If so, the program exits setting the variable **end** to **true**.

We remark the different possible meanings of annotations such as @bob and @alice. When prefixed by a variable, they identify the owner of the variable. Prefixed by the boolean guard of conditionals and loops, they identify the role

---

[4] http://www.cs.unibo.it/projects/jolie/aiocj.html

```
1   include isFreeDay from "calendar.org:80" with http
2   include getTicket from "cinema.org:8000" with soap
3
4   preamble {
5     starter: bob
6     location@bob = "socket://localhost:8000"
7     location@alice = "socket://alice.com:8000"
8     location@cinema = "socket://cinema.org:8001"
9   }
10
11  aioc{
12    end@bob = false;
13    while( ! end )@bob{
14      scope @bob {
15        free_day@bob = getInput( "Insert your free day" );
16        proposal: bob( free_day ) -> alice( bob_free_day );
17        is_free@alice = isFreeDay( bob_free_day );
18      } prop { N.scope_name = "matching day" };
19      if( is_free )@alice {
20        scope @bob {
21          proposal: bob( "cinema" ) -> alice( event );
22          agreement@alice = getInput( "Bob proposes " + event +
23                 ", do you agree?[y/n]");
24          if( agreement == "y" )@alice{
25            end@bob = true;
26            book: bob( bob_free_day ) -> cinema( book_day );
27            ticket@cinema = getTicket( book_day );
28            { notify: cinema( ticket ) -> bob( ticket )
29              | notify: cinema( ticket ) -> alice( ticket )
30            }
31          }
32        } prop { N.scope_name = "event selection" }
33      };
34      if( !end )@bob {
35        _r@bob = getInput( "Alice refused. Try another date?[y/n]" );
36        if( _r != "y" )@bob{ end@bob = true }
37      }
38    }
39  }
```

Listing 1.1. Appointment program

that evaluates the guard. Prefixed by the keyword **scope**, they identify the process coordinating the adaptation of that scope. An adaptation scope, besides the code, may also include some properties describing the current implementation. These can be specified using the keyword **prop** and are prefixed by N. For instance, each adaptation scope of the example includes the property **scope_name**, that can be used to find out its functionality.

AIOCJ can interact with external services, seen as functions. This allows both to interact with real services and to have easy access to libraries from other languages. To do that, one must specify the address and protocol used to interact with each service. For instance, the external function **isFreeDay** used in Line 17 is associated to the service deployed at the domain "calendar.org", reachable though port 80, and that uses http as serialisation protocol (Line 1). External functions are declared with the keyword **include**. To preserve deadlock freedom, external services must be non-blocking. After function declaration, in a **preamble** section, it is possible to declare the locations where processes are deployed. The keyword **starter** is mandatory and defines which process must be started first. The starter makes sure all other processes are ready before the execution of the choreography begins.

Now suppose that Bob, during summer, prefers to invite Alice to a picnic rather than to the cinema, provided that the weather forecasts are good. This can be obtained by adding the following adaptation rule to one of the adaptation servers. This may even be done while the application is running, e.g., while Bob is sending an invitation. In this case, if Bob first try is unsuccessful, in the second try he will propose a picnic.

```
1   rule {
2     include getWeather from "socket://localhost:8002"
3     on { N.scope_name == "event selection" and E.month > 5 and E.month < 10 }
4     do {
5       forecasts@bob = getWeather( free_day );
6       if( forecasts == "Clear" )@bob{
7         eventProposal: bob( "picnic" ) -> alice( event )
8       } else { eventProposal: bob( "cinema" ) -> alice( event ) };
9       agreement@alice = getInput( "Bob proposes " + event +
10        ", do you agree?[y/n]");
11      if( agreement == "y" )@alice {
12        end@bob = true |
13        if( event == "cinema" )@alice {
14          //cinema tickets purchase procedure
15        }
16      }
17    }
18  }
```

Listing 1.2. Event selection adaptation rule

A rule specifies its applicability condition and the new code to execute. In general, the applicability condition may depend only on properties of the adaptation scope, environment variables, and variables belonging to the coordinator of the adaptation scope. In this case, the condition, introduced by the keyword on (Line 3), makes the rule applicable to adaptation scopes having the property scope_name equal to the string "event selection" and only during summer. This last check relies on an environment variable month that contains the current month. Environment variables are prefixed by E.

The new code to execute if the rule is applied is defined using the keyword do (Line 4). The forecasts can be retrieved calling an external function getWeather (Line 5) that queries a weather forecasts service. This function is declared in Line 2. If the weather is clear, Bob proposes to Alice a picnic, otherwise he proposes the cinema. Booking (as in Listing 1.1, Lines 26-29) is needed only if Alice accepts the cinema proposal.

6 Related Work

Choreography-like methods for programming distributed systems have been applied for a long time, for example in MSC [26], security protocols [6,9,3] and automata theory [20]. Differently from Chor, these works were not intended as fully-fledged programming languages. For example, they do not deal with concrete data or different layers of abstraction (protocols and choreographies).

The development of Chor was partially inspired by the language WS-CDL [39] and the choreography fragment of BPMN [8]. Differently from those, Chor comes with a formal model defining its semantics and typing discipline. This model introduced a precise understanding of multiparty sessions and typical aspects of concurrency, such as asynchrony and parallelism, to choreographies [11]. The typing discipline is based on multiparty session types [25] (choreography-like protocols), bringing their benefits to choreographies; for example, Chor programs are statically guaranteed to follow their associated protocols (session fidelity, initially introduced in [24]). Remarkably, the development of Chor proved that the mixing of choreographies with multiparty session types yields more than just the sum of the parts. For example, it naturally supports a simple procedure for automatically inferring the protocols implemented by a choreography (type inference); and, it guarantees deadlock-freedom for a system even in the presence of arbitrary interleavings of session behaviours, without requiring additional machinery on top of types as is needed when dealing with processes instead of choreographies [2]. The theoretical model of Chor has been recently extended for supporting the reuse of external services in [35]. We refer the interested reader to [33] for a detailed explanation of these aspects and for an evaluation of Chor w.r.t. some concrete scenarios. Exploring a similar direction, Scribble is a choreography-like language for specifying communication protocols, based on multiparty session types [40]. Differently from Chor, Scribble protocols are not compiled to executable programs but to local abstract behaviours that are used to verify or monitor the concrete behaviour of endpoints in a distributed system (see, e.g., [36]).

Like choreographies, also adaptation is a lively research topic, as shown by the survey [32]. However, most of the approaches propose mechanisms for adaptation without any guarantee about the properties of the application after adaptation, as for JoRBA.

A few approaches try to apply multiparty session types to adaptation, obtaining some formal guarantee on the behaviour of the system. In this sense, they are different from Chor and AIOCJ, which are fully-fledged languages. For instance, [1] deals with dynamic software updates of systems which are concurrent, but not distributed. Furthermore, dynamic software updates are applied on demand, while enactment of adaptation depends on the environment and on the state of the running application. Another related approach is [14], which deals with monitoring of self-adaptive systems. There, all the possible behaviours are available since the very beginning, both at the level of types and of processes, and a fixed adaptation function is used to switch between them. This difference derives from the distinction between self-adaptive applications, as they discuss, and applications updated from the outside, as in our case. We also recall [17], which uses types to ensure no session is spoiled because of adaptation, and that needed services are not removed. However, [17] allows updates only when no session is active, while AIOCJ changes the behaviour of running interactions.

7   Conclusions

The aim of the European project Sensoria was to devise a methodology for the development of Service-Oriented applications, and realise the corresponding theoretical and practical tools. Most of the research effort of our research group in Bologna has been dedicated to the investigation of appropriate models and languages for specifying and programming such applications. The Service-Oriented programming language Jolie has been one of our main achievements. In this paper we have discussed how the activity initiated during the Sensoria project produced results far beyond our initial aims. In particular, we are still nowadays exploiting Jolie in the realisation of a framework for programming adaptable communication-centred applications that are correct-by-construction. Correctness is guaranteed because the updates are expressed from a global view-point, and then automatically projected and injected in the endpoints code. For instance, if in an application it is necessary to update a security protocol because of a detected flaw, the interacting partners need to be modified in order to replace the old protocol with a new one. Applying these dynamic unexpected updates is a critical task for modern applications. Our approach consists of describing the updates at the global level, generate the new endpoint code by projecting such updates on the affected partners, and then inject the new code to the endpoints in a coordinated manner.

A final remark is dedicated to Martin Wirsing, the coordinator of the Sensoria project. He did not limit his activity to the (hard) work of amalgamating the several heterogeneous partners of the Sensoria Integrated Project, but he continuously solicited the participants to conduct research that were innovative –in order to give to the project a long-term vision– as well as close to actual application needs –in order to avoid losing effort on abstract useless research. We consider the specific experience reported in this paper a concrete and relevant result of this enlightened Martin's approach to project coordination.

Acknowledgements. Montesi was supported by the Danish Council for Independent Research (Technology and Production), grant n. DFF–4005-00304.

References

1. Anderson, G., Rathke, J.: Dynamic software update for message passing programs. In: Jhala, R., Igarashi, A. (eds.) APLAS 2012. LNCS, vol. 7705, pp. 207–222. Springer, Heidelberg (2012)
2. Bettini, L., Coppo, M., D'Antoni, L., De Luca, M., Dezani-Ciancaglini, M., Yoshida, N.: Global progress in dynamically interleaved multiparty sessions. In: van Breugel, F., Chechik, M. (eds.) CONCUR 2008. LNCS, vol. 5201, pp. 418–433. Springer, Heidelberg (2008)
3. Bhargavan, K., Corin, R., Deniélou, P.-M., Fournet, C., Leifer, J.J.: Cryptographic protocol synthesis and verification for multiparty sessions. In: CSF, pp. 124–140. IEEE Computer Society (2009)
4. Boreale, M., et al.: SCC: A service centered calculus. In: Bravetti, M., Núñez, M., Zavattaro, G. (eds.) WS-FM 2006. LNCS, vol. 4184, pp. 38–57. Springer, Heidelberg (2006)

5. Boreale, M., Bruni, R., De Nicola, R., Loreti, M.: Sessions and pipelines for structured service programming. In: Barthe, G., de Boer, F.S. (eds.) FMOODS 2008. LNCS, vol. 5051, pp. 19–38. Springer, Heidelberg (2008)
6. Briais, S., Nestmann, U.: A formal semantics for protocol narrations. Theor. Comput. Sci. 389(3), 484–511 (2007)
7. Bruni, R., Hölzl, M., Koch, N., Lluch Lafuente, A., Mayer, P., Montanari, U., Schroeder, A., Wirsing, M.: A service-oriented UML profile with formal support. In: Baresi, L., Chi, C.-H., Suzuki, J. (eds.) ICSOC-ServiceWave 2009. LNCS, vol. 5900, pp. 455–469. Springer, Heidelberg (2009)
8. Business Process Model and Notation, http://www.omg.org/spec/BPMN/2.0/
9. Caleiro, C., Viganò, L., Basin, D.A.: On the semantics of Alice & Bob specifications of security protocols. Theor. Comput. Sci. 367(1-2), 88–122 (2006)
10. Carbone, M., Honda, K., Yoshida, N.: Structured communication-centered programming for web services. ACM Trans. Program. Lang. Syst. 34(2), 8 (2012)
11. Carbone, M., Montesi, F.: Deadlock-freedom-by-design: multiparty asynchronous global programming. In: Giacobazzi, R., Cousot, R. (eds.) POPL, pp. 263–274. ACM (2013)
12. Castagna, G., Dezani-Ciancaglini, M., Padovani, L.: On global types and multiparty session. Logical Methods in Computer Science 8(1) (2012)
13. Clark, A., Gilmore, S., Tribastone, M.: Quantitative analysis of web services using SRMC. In: Bernardo, M., Padovani, L., Zavattaro, G. (eds.) SFM 2009. LNCS, vol. 5569, pp. 296–339. Springer, Heidelberg (2009)
14. Coppo, M., Dezani-Ciancaglini, M., Venneri, B.: Self-adaptive monitors for multiparty sessions. In: PDP, pp. 688–696. IEEE Computer Society (2014)
15. Dalla Preda, M., Gabbrielli, M., Guidi, C., Mauro, J., Montesi, F.: Interface-based service composition with aggregation. In: De Paoli, F., Pimentel, E., Zavattaro, G. (eds.) ESOCC 2012. LNCS, vol. 7592, pp. 48–63. Springer, Heidelberg (2012)
16. Dalla Preda, M., Giallorenzo, S., Lanese, I., Mauro, J., Gabbrielli, M.: AIOCJ: A choreographic framework for safe adaptive distributed applications. In: Combemale, B., Pearce, D.J., Barais, O., Vinju, J.J. (eds.) SLE 2014. LNCS, vol. 8706, pp. 161–170. Springer, Heidelberg (2014)
17. Di Giusto, C., Pérez, J.A.: Disciplined structured communications with consistent runtime adaptation. In: Shin, S.Y., Maldonado, J.C. (eds.) SAC, pp. 1913–1918. ACM (2013)
18. Fiadeiro, J.L., Lopes, A., Bocchi, L.: A formal approach to service component architecture. In: Bravetti, M., Núñez, M., Zavattaro, G. (eds.) WS-FM 2006. LNCS, vol. 4184, pp. 193–213. Springer, Heidelberg (2006)
19. Foster, H., Uchitel, S., Magee, J., Kramer, J.: LTSA-WS: a tool for model-based verification of web service compositions and choreography. In: Osterweil, L.J., Rombach, H.D., Soffa, M.L. (eds.) ICSE, pp. 771–774. ACM (2006)
20. Fu, X., Bultan, T., Su, J.: Realizability of conversation protocols with message contents. International Journal on Web Service Res. 2(4), 68–93 (2005)
21. Gabbrielli, M., Giallorenzo, S., Montesi, F.: Service-oriented architectures: From design to production exploiting workflow patterns. In: Omatu, S., Bersini, H., Corchado Rodríguez, J.M., González, S.R., Pawlewski, P., Bucciarelli, E. (eds.) Distributed Computing and Artificial Intelligence 11th International Conference. AISC, vol. 290, pp. 131–139. Springer, Heidelberg (2014)
22. Guidi, C., Lanese, I., Montesi, F., Zavattaro, G.: Dynamic error handling in service oriented applications. Fundam. Inform. 95(1), 73–102 (2009)
23. Harel, D., Thiagarajan, P.: Message sequence charts. In: UML for real, pp. 77–105. Kluwer Academic Publishers (2003)

24. Honda, K., Vasconcelos, V.T., Kubo, M.: Language primitives and type discipline for structured communication-based programming. In: Hankin, C. (ed.) ESOP 1998. LNCS, vol. 1381, pp. 122–138. Springer, Heidelberg (1998)
25. Honda, K., Yoshida, N., Carbone, M.: Multiparty asynchronous session types. In: POPL, pp. 273–284. ACM (2008)
26. International Telecommunication Union. Recommendation Z.120: Message sequence chart (1996)
27. Lanese, I., Bucchiarone, A., Montesi, F.: A framework for rule-based dynamic adaptation. In: Wirsing, M., Hofmann, M., Rauschmayer, A. (eds.) TGC 2010, LNCS, vol. 6084, pp. 284–300. Springer, Heidelberg (2010)
28. Lanese, I., Guidi, C., Montesi, F., Zavattaro, G.: Bridging the gap between interaction- and process-oriented choreographies. In: SEFM, pp. 323–332. IEEE Computer Society (2008)
29. Lanese, I., Martins, F., Vasconcelos, V.T., Ravara, A.: Disciplining orchestration and conversation in service-oriented computing. In: SEFM, pp. 305–314. IEEE Computer Society (2007)
30. Lapadula, A., Pugliese, R., Tiezzi, F.: A calculus for orchestration of web services. In: De Nicola, R. (ed.) ESOP 2007. LNCS, vol. 4421, pp. 33–47. Springer, Heidelberg (2007)
31. Lapadula, A., Pugliese, R., Tiezzi, F.: Using formal methods to develop WS-BPEL applications. Sci. Comput. Program. 77(3), 189–213 (2012)
32. Leite, L.A.F., Oliva, G.A., Nogueira, G.M., Gerosa, M.A., Kon, F., Milojicic, D.S.: A systematic literature review of service choreography adaptation. Service Oriented Computing and Applications 7(3), 199–216 (2013)
33. Montesi, F.: Choreographic Programming. Ph.D. thesis, IT University of Copenhagen (2013), http://www.fabriziomontesi.com/files/m13_phdthesis.pdf
34. Montesi, F., Guidi, C., Zavattaro, G.: Composing Services with JOLIE. In: Proc. of ECOWS, pp. 13–22. IEEE Computer Society (2007)
35. Montesi, F., Yoshida, N.: Compositional choreographies. In: D'Argenio, P.R., Melgratti, H. (eds.) CONCUR 2013 – Concurrency Theory. LNCS, vol. 8052, pp. 425–439. Springer, Heidelberg (2013)
36. Neykova, R., Yoshida, N., Hu, R.: SPY: Local verification of global protocols. In: Legay, A., Bensalem, S. (eds.) RV 2013. LNCS, vol. 8174, pp. 358–363. Springer, Heidelberg (2013)
37. ter Beek, M.H., Fantechi, A., Gnesi, S., Mazzanti, F.: An action/State-based model-checking approach for the analysis of communication protocols for service-oriented applications. In: Leue, S., Merino, P. (eds.) FMICS 2007. LNCS, vol. 4916, pp. 133–148. Springer, Heidelberg (2008)
38. van der Aalst, W.M.P., ter Hofstede, A.H.M., Kiepuszewski, B., Barros, A.P.: Workflow patterns. Distributed and Parallel Databases 14(1), 5–51 (2003)
39. W3C WS-CDL Working Group. Web services choreography description language version 1.0 (2004), http://www.w3.org/TR/2004/WD-ws-cdl-10-20040427/
40. Yoshida, N., Hu, R., Neykova, R., Ng, N.: The scribble protocol language. In: Abadi, M., Lluch Lafuente, A. (eds.) TGC 2013. LNCS, vol. 8358, pp. 22–41. Springer, Heidelberg (2014)

Stochastic Model Checking
of the Stochastic Quality Calculus

Flemming Nielson, Hanne Riis Nielson, and Kebin Zeng

DTU Compute, Technical University of Denmark,
2800 Kgs. Lyngby, Denmark

Abstract. The Quality Calculus uses quality binders for input to express strategies for continuing the computation even when the desired input has not been received. The Stochastic Quality Calculus adds generally distributed delays for output actions and real-time constraints on the quality binders for input. This gives rise to Generalised Semi-Markov Decision Processes for which few analytical techniques are available.

We restrict delays on output actions to be exponentially distributed while still admitting real-time constraints on the quality binders. This facilitates developing analytical techniques based on stochastic model checking and we compute closed form solutions for a number of interesting scenarios. The analyses are applied to the design of an intelligent smart electrical meter of the kind to be installed in European households by 2020.

1 Introduction

Networked communication is the key for modern *distributed systems* – encompassing service-oriented systems as well as cyber-physical systems – and including systems that are essential for the infrastructure in the 21st century. The classical *"super-optimistic"* programming style of traditional software development no longer suffices – we need to take into account that the expected communications might not occur and that the systems still have to coordinate to the extent possible: we have to turn to a *"realistic-pessimistic"* programming style.

The Quality Calculus introduced in [15] is a first step towards a calculus supporting this change of paradigm; the communication paradigm is point-to-point (as in the π-calculus [12]) and is accompanied by a SAT-based analysis for checking whether the processes are vulnerable to unreliable communication. Probabilistic reasoning is added to the calculus in [14] in a setting where each input binder is annotated with a probability distribution indicating the trustworthiness of the inputs received with respect to a security lattice; a probabilistic trust analysis is then developed in order to identify the extent to which a robust programming style has been adhered to. Furthermore, a broadcast version of the calculus is developed in [17]; here it is additionally extended with cryptographic primitives and the focus is on the development of a rewriting semantics allowing us to reason – in a discrete setting – about unsolicited messages as well as the absence of expected communications.

R. De Nicola and R. Hennicker (Eds.): Wirsing Festschrift, LNCS 8950, pp. 522–537, 2015.

The Stochastic Quality Calculus (SQC) introduced in [20] is an extension of the previous works, and it differs in several aspects. It supports *truly concurrent broadcast communication* meaning that several processes may send messages at the same time (also over the same channel) and all processes that are ready to receive these messages must do so. Also *timing aspects* play a central role. The time for completing a communication depends on the hardware architecture and the communication protocols but also the cyber environment. Hence *real-time* considerations are relevant for those communications taking exact duration, and *stochastic time* considerations are relevant for those taking random time influenced by the cyber environment. In its most general form we allow general (not necessarily continuous) distributions, and processes give rise to Generalised Semi-Markov Decision Processes for which few analytical techniques are available.

In the present paper we restrict delays on output actions to be exponentially distributed while still admitting hard real-time constraints in the quality binders for input. We show that this facilitates developing analytical techniques based on stochastic model checking and we compute closed form solutions for a number of interesting scenarios. The analyses are applied to the design of an intelligent smart electrical meter of the kind to be installed in European households by 2020.

Related work studying the challenge of combining concurrency and stochasticity include PEPA [8] and IMC [5]; the challenge of combining concurrency, stochasticity and mobility have been addressed in the stochastic π-calculus [16] and StoKLAIM [7]; the challenge of combining concurrency and real-time have been addressed in timed CCS [19] and PerTiMo [6] as well as in [2–4]. Most stochastic calculi make use of exponential distributions to express random delay, and can then use classic techniques and tools for Markov chain analysis. However, the real-time (exact duration) delays are much less frequently incorporated in stochastic process calculi. This is the combination studied in the present paper.

The paper reviews the Stochastic Quality Calculus in Section 2, performs stochastic model checking on the exponential fragment in Section 3, applies the development to the Smart Meter example in Section 4, concludes in Section 5, and contains a dedication to Martin Wirsing in the Acknowledgements.

2   Stochastic Quality Calculus

In the Stochastic Quality Calculus [20] with exponential distributions (SQC_{exp}) we use exponentially distributed random variables to characterise communication delays. An output process has the form

$$c_1{}^{\ell,G}!c_2.P$$

Table 1. Syntax of the Stochastic Quality Calculus with exponential delays

---

$$P ::= (\nu c)\, P \;\mid\; 0 \;\mid\; t_1{}^{\ell,G}!t_2.P \;\mid\; b.P \;\mid\; \text{case } x \text{ of some}(y)\colon P_1 \text{ else } P_2$$
$$\quad\;\mid\; P_1 \| P_2 \;\mid\; A$$
$$b ::= t?x \;\mid\; \&_q^I(t_1?x_1, \cdots, t_n?x_n)$$
$$t ::= y \;\mid\; c \;\mid\; f(t)$$

---

specifying that the value c_2 should be communicated over the channel c_1 within some time determined by the exponential distribution G and where the channel c_1 has trust classification ℓ. We use intervals to indicate real-time constraints on when communication is allowed to happen. An input binder of the form

$$\&_q^{[a,a')}(c_1?x_1, \cdots, c_n?x_n).$$

specifies that the process is waiting for n inputs over the channels $c_1, \cdots, c_n$; it is waiting for at least a time units and at most a' time units, where $a < a'$, and within the time interval $[a, a')$ it will only progress if the quality predicate q determines that sufficient inputs have been obtained. The continuation process will then have to inspect which inputs have been received and take appropriate actions in each case – thereby enforcing the "realistic-pessimistic" programming style alluded to above.

The formal syntax consists of *processes* P, *binders* b, and *terms* t, and is given in Table 1. A *system* S consists a number of process definitions and a main process:

$$\text{define } A_1 \triangleq P_1$$
$$\vdots$$
$$A_n \triangleq P_n$$
$$\text{in} \quad P_*$$
$$\text{using } c_1, \cdots, c_m$$

Here A_i is the name of a process, P_i is its body, P_* is the initial main process and $c_1, \cdots, c_m$ is a list of channels.

Each output $t_1{}^{\ell,G}!t_2$ has a trust level ℓ and an exponential distribution G to express the delay of communications. To indicate the trust level, we use an element ℓ from a finite trust lattice $\mathcal{L}$ and we write $\leq$ for the ordering on $\mathcal{L}$. As an example, we might use $\mathcal{L} = (\{\text{L}, \text{M}, \text{H}\}, \leq)$ to denote that available channels are classified into low (L), medium (M) or high (H) trust and with the obvious linear ordering on these elements. The delay of communication is determined by the output, therefore *all the values communicated have the corresponding trust ℓ and stochasticity G*. We use *broadcast* transmission, so that all the receivers waiting on channel t_1 must receive the value t_2. All the channels used in a system are introduced either in the list $c_1, \cdots, c_m$ or using the syntax $(\nu c)\, P$ for introducing a new channel c to its scope P.

As a member of the quality calculus family, an *input process* is written $b.P$, where b is a *binder* specifying the desired inputs with real-time constraints to be satisfied before continuing with P. The simplest case of a binder is $t?x$ stating that some value should be received over channel t, and stored in variable x. A binder is in general of the form $\&_q^I(t_1?x_1, \cdots, t_n?x_n)$ indicating that n inputs are simultaneously active. A *time interval* I determines when the binder b may be passed; it can be $[0, a)$ meaning that the binder will wait at most until time a; it can be $[a, \infty)$ meaning that the binder has to wait at least until time a; it can be $[a, a')$ meaning that the binder has the minimum waiting time a and maximum waiting time a' (for $a < a'$); as a special case, it can be $[0, \infty)$ meaning that there is no time constraint. During the interval I the *quality predicate* q determines whether sufficient inputs have been received to continue before I has ended. The quality predicate q can be $\exists$ meaning that one input is required, or it can be $\forall$ meaning that all inputs are required; formally $\exists(x_1, \cdots, x_n) \Leftrightarrow x_1 \vee \cdots \vee x_n$ and $\forall(x_1, \cdots, x_n) \Leftrightarrow x_1 \wedge \cdots \wedge x_n$. For more expressiveness, we shall allow quality predicates as for example $[1 \vee (2 \wedge 3)](x_1, x_2, x_3) \Leftrightarrow x_1 \vee (x_2 \wedge x_3)$.

As an example, $\&_\exists^{[a,a')}(c_1?x_1, c_2?x_2) \parallel c_1^{\ell_1, G_1}!t_1 \parallel c_2^{\ell_2, G_2}!t_2$ expresses that both output processes are simultaneously active at time 0, and that we wait for their output to be performed. The quality predicate $\exists$ of the input process will be evaluated at time a for the first time, the process will continue if at least one of the two inputs has arrived. If not, the process will wait until one input arrives in the period $[a, a')$ but if no input arrives until time a', the process shall stop waiting and continue even though no input was received.

As a consequence of using $b.P$, some variables might not obtain proper values as the corresponding inputs are missing. To model this, let y denote *data variables* and x denote *optional data variables* like in the programming language Standard ML [11], and let some($\cdots$) express the presence of some data and none the absence of data. A *case construct* case x of some(y) : P_1 else P_2 has the following meaning: if x evaluates to some value some(c), bind c to y and continue with P_1; otherwise x evaluates to none and continue with P_2. The syntax of terms t make it clear that they can be data variables, constants or funtions applied to terms.

A process can also be a *recursive call* A to one of the defined processes. We require that recursion through parallel composition is not permitted, so that we ensure the resulting semantics to have a finite state space. We say $A \triangleq P$ has no recursion through parallel if the syntax tree for P does not contain any occurrence of the process name B in a descendant of a $\parallel$ construct, such that B might (perhaps indirectly) call A. We also require that the creation of a new channel in recursion is not permitted, so that we have a finite number of channels that can be used. We say $A \triangleq P$ has no creation of a new channel in recursion if the syntax tree for P does not contain any occurrence of a process name in a descendant of a (νc) construct.

3   Stochastic Model Checking

To show how to use Stochastic Model Checking to analyse a number of interesting scenarios in the Stochastic Quality Calculus with exponential distributions we need to review Continuous-Time Markov Chains (CTMC) and Continuous Stochastic Logic (CSL).

Continuous-Time Markov Chains. (CTMC) [1,9] are tuples (S, s^0, T, L) where S is a finite and nonempty set of states, $s^0 \in S$ is the initial state, $T : S \times S \to R_{\geq 0}$ is a mapping of pairs of states to a nonnegative rate of exponential distributions, $L : S \to \mathcal{P}(AP)$ is a function that labels each state with a set of atomic propositions drawn from the set AP. We interpret T in the following way: if $T(s, s') = 0$ then there is no transition from s to s' and if $T(s, s') > 0$ then there is a transition from s to s' with rate $T(s, s')$.

Continuous Stochastic Logic. (CSL) [1,9] has *path* formulae ϕ and *boolean state* formulae Φ defined as follows:

$$\Phi ::= \mathsf{true} \mid a \mid \neg\Phi \mid \Phi_1 \wedge \Phi_2 \mid \mathsf{P}[\phi] \bowtie p \mid \mathsf{S}[\Phi] \bowtie p$$
$$\phi ::= \mathsf{X}^I \Phi \mid \Phi_1 \mathsf{U}^I \Phi_2$$

Here $\mathsf{P}[\phi] \bowtie p$ indicates whether or not the probability of the event ϕ has the relation $\bowtie$ (chosen among $<, \leq, =, \neq, \geq$ and $>$) to the probability p; we shall feel free to use $\mathsf{P}[\phi]$ for the actual value (motivated by the notation of $\mathrm{CSL}_{\mathrm{MSR}}$ [13]). In a similar way $\mathsf{S}[\Phi] \bowtie p$ indicates whether or not the steady-state probability of satisfying Φ has the relation $\bowtie$ to p. The events are described by path formulae that essentially are LTL path formulae; the formula $\mathsf{X}^I \Phi$ indicates that Φ is true in the next state and that the transition to that state takes place at some time point in the interval I; and the formula $\Phi_1 \mathsf{U}^I \Phi_2$ indicates that Φ_1 holds until eventually Φ_2 holds at some time point in the interval I.

For completeness let us recall the formal definition of the semantics of CSL focussing only on the fragment needed for our development. Given a CTMC (S, s^0, T, L), a path η is an alternating sequence $s_0, t_0, s_1, t_1, \cdots$ of states s_i from S and positive real numbers t_i indicating time durations, subject to the following conditions: each $T(s_i, s_i + 1) > 0$, and the path is infinite unless the final state s_n is absorbing, meaning that $\forall s : T(s_n, s) = 0$. Write $\eta[i] = s_i$ to express the i'th state in the path and $\eta\langle i \rangle = t_i$ to denote the amount of time spent in the i'th state; for a finite path with final state s_n we informally set $\eta\langle n \rangle = \infty$. (With this definition we shall follow the usual convention of ignoring paths η for which $\Sigma_i \eta\langle i \rangle < \infty$ as their joint probability measure will be 0.) We then define $\eta@t$ to be the state $\eta[j]$ for the minimal value j such that $\Sigma_{i \leq j} \eta\langle i \rangle \geq t$ where t is a non-negative real number. The fact that a path η satisfies a path formula ϕ is written $\eta \models \phi$, and the fact that a state s satisfies a state formula Φ is written $s \models \Phi$, and they are defined by mutual recursion on the size of formulae as follows:

$$s \models \text{true} \Leftrightarrow \text{true}$$
$$s \models a \Leftrightarrow a \in L(s)$$
$$s \models \neg \Phi \Leftrightarrow \neg(s \models \Phi)$$
$$s \models \Phi_1 \wedge \Phi_2 \Leftrightarrow s \models \Phi_1 \wedge s \models \Phi_2$$
$$s \models \mathsf{P}[\phi] \bowtie p \Leftrightarrow \mathsf{Prob}_s(\{\eta \mid \eta \models \phi\}) \bowtie p$$
$$\eta \models \Phi_1 \ \mathsf{U}^I \ \Phi_2 \Leftrightarrow \exists t \in I : \eta@t \models \Phi_2 \wedge \forall t' < t : \eta@t' \models \Phi_1$$

where Prob_s denotes the probability measure on sets of measurable paths obtained via the cylinder set construction and assuming that s is the start state of the CTMC (referring to [1,9] for the details).

Our development will determine the probabilities that a process would need to survive the absence of desired data. For instance, how likely is it that the sufficient inputs specified by the binder $\&_q^I(c_1?x_1, \cdots, c_n?x_n)$ will become available in the desired period I? Such information should then be propagated through the process in order to argue that "undesirable" code fragments are only reached with an acceptably low probability. We performed such a development in [14], relying on the distribution π of probabilities on security levels arising from a binder b, and used the notation $\vdash b \blacktriangleright \pi$ to specify this. The development of [14] then propagated such probability distributions throughout the process of interest, wheras the development of the present paper shows how to obtain $\vdash b \blacktriangleright \pi$.

The remainder of this section considers four scenarios of processes waiting for inputs from external services:

1. The first is where we simply conduct a race between the stochastic external services as $\&_q(c_1?x_1, \cdots, c_n?x_n)$ without real-time constraints.
2. The other is when the race is subject to a minimum real waiting time a as $\&_q^{[a,\infty)}(c_1?x_1, \cdots, c_n?x_n)$.
3. The third is when the race is subject to a maximum real waiting time a as $\&_q^{[0,a)}(c_1?x_1, \cdots, c_n?x_n)$.
4. The last is when the race is subject to a minimum waiting time a as well as a maximum waiting time a', $\&_q^{[a,a')}(c_1?x_1, \cdots, c_n?x_n)$.

In each case the analysis is performed over CTMCs that are obtained by ignoring all the real-time constraints from the binders. Thereafter, we perform the desired numerical analysis on the CTMCs for all the disjoint time intervals given from the time interval of a binder.

The intuition for analysing the availability of a binder $\&_q^{[a,a')}(c_1?x_1, \cdots, c_n?x_n)$ is depicted in Fig 1. Part 1 illustrates the probability that sufficient inputs become available in the interval $[0, a)$; however, since a is the minimum waiting time, the process will have to wait until time a in order to proceed. Part 2 illustrates that sufficient inputs become available in the interval $[a, a')$ with the condition that they are not available in the interval $[0, a)$; the process is allowed

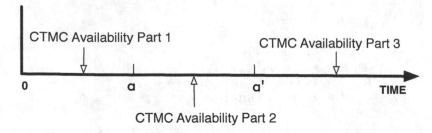

Fig. 1. Determine the availability of $\&_q^{[a,a')}(c_1?x_1, \cdots, c_n?x_n)$ using CTMCs

to proceed as soon as this happens. Part 3 illustrates the probability that sufficient inputs are not available in the interval $[0, a')$; at time a' the process is required to proceed nonetheless.

Scenario 1: Race between Stochastic Processes. Here n stochastic external services have started transmitting the outputs $c_1^{\ell_1, \lambda_1}!t_1, \cdots, c_n^{\ell_n, \lambda_n}!t_n$, and they then compete to provide the required input(s):

$$\&_q(c_1?x_1, \cdots, c_n?x_n).$$

As motivated by [14] and the above discussion, we intend to determine the relationship

$$\vdash \&_q(c_1?x_1, \cdots, c_n?x_n) \blacktriangleright \pi$$

between the binder $\&_q(c_1?x_1, \cdots, c_n?x_n)$ and a probability distribution $\pi \in \mathcal{D}(\{x_1, \cdots, x_n\} \to \mathcal{L}_\perp)$ indicating the probability of the various inputs having been received. Here $\perp$ denotes the absence of input and $\mathcal{L}_\perp$ is the lifted trust lattice obtained from $\mathcal{L}$ by adding the new element $\perp$ as the least element, i.e. $\mathcal{L}_\perp = (\{\perp, \text{L}, \text{M}, \text{H}\}, \leq)$.

We first consider the CTMC obtained from the exponential distributions of the outputs. Let the CTMC for the $c_i^{\ell_i, \lambda_i}$ be given by $(S_i = \{s_i^0, s_i^\star\}, s_i^0, T_i(s_i^0, s_i^\star) = \lambda_i, L_i(s_i^\star) = \{c_i\})$. We now construct the CTMC $(S_\otimes, s_\otimes^0, T_\otimes, L_\otimes)$ from the CTMCs $(S_i, s_i^0, T_i, L_i)_{i=1}^n$ by setting

- $S_\otimes = S_1 \times \cdots \times S_n,$
- $s_\otimes^0 = (s_1^0, \cdots, s_n^0),$
- $L_\otimes(s_1, \cdots, s_n) = L_1(s_1) \cup \cdots \cup L_n(s_n),$ and
- $T_\otimes((s_1, \cdots, s_n), (s_1', \cdots, s_n')) = \begin{cases} 0 & \text{if } |\{i \mid s_i \neq s_i'\}| \geq 2, \\ T_i(s_i, s_i') & \text{if } \{i \mid s_i \neq s_i'\} = \{i\}, \\ 0 & \text{if } \{i \mid s_i \neq s_i'\} = \emptyset, \end{cases}$

where $|X|$ denotes the size of the set X and $AP = \{c_1, \cdots, c_n\}$.

We now formulate the CSL query to be evaluated in the start state of $(S_\otimes, s_\otimes, T_\otimes, L_\otimes)$ for determining the probability distribution π resulting from the race $\&_q(c_1?x_1, \cdots, c_n?x_n)$. Let σ be a mapping from the variables $\{x_1, \cdots, x_n\}$ to elements of the lifted trust lattice $\mathcal{L}_\perp$. In the case where

$\exists i : \sigma(x_i) \notin \{\bot, \ell_i\}$ we set $\pi(\sigma) = 0$. In the case where $\forall i : \sigma(x_i) \in \{\bot, \ell_i\}$ we define the formulae

$$\Phi_{qn} = q(c_1, \cdots, c_n) \tag{1}$$

and

$$\Phi_\sigma = (\bigwedge_{\sigma(x_i)=\ell_i} c_i) \wedge (\bigwedge_{\sigma(x_i)=\bot} \neg c_i) \tag{2}$$

and we set

$$\pi(\sigma) = \mathsf{P} \left[(\neg \Phi_{qn}) \, \mathsf{U}^{[0,\infty)} \, (\Phi_{qn} \wedge \Phi_\sigma) \right]$$

This indicates the event that the quality predicate is satisfied and that input has been received as indicated by c_i and $\neg c_i$.

We can use a stochastic model checker as PRISM [10] to compute π numerically but it is worthwhile mentioning some special cases where the probabilities can be determined analytically. When the quality predicate q is $\forall$ we obtain

$$\pi(\sigma) = \begin{cases} 1 \text{ if } \forall i > 0 : \sigma(x_i) = \ell_i \\ 0 \text{ otherwise} \end{cases}$$

When the quality predicate q is $\exists$ we obtain

$$\pi(\sigma) = \begin{cases} \frac{\lambda_i}{\lambda_1 + \cdots + \lambda_n} \text{ if } \sigma(x_i) = \ell_i \wedge \forall j \neq i : \sigma(x_j) = \bot \\ 0 \qquad\qquad \text{otherwise.} \end{cases}$$

This correctly reflects that only one process can win the race, meaning that the other processes do not provide any data.

Scenario 2: Race between Stochastic Processes Subject to a Minimum Waiting Time. Here n stochastic external services have started transmitting the outputs $c_1^{\ell_1, \lambda_1}!t_1, \cdots, c_n^{\ell_n, \lambda_n}!t_n$, and they then compete to provide the required input(s), subject to a minimum waiting time given by a. It is helpful to imagine that $\&_q^{[a,\infty)}(c_1?x_1, \cdots, c_n?x_n)$ is transformed to $\&_{\dot{q}}(c_1?x_1, \cdots, c_n?x_n, c_a?x_a)$, where $\dot{q}(x_1, \cdots, x_n, x_a) = q(x_1, \cdots, x_n) \wedge x_a$ and where x_a indicates whether or not the minimum waiting time has been adhered to. This is motivated by the development in the full Stochastic Quality Calculus [20] where we would be able to model a "clock" a by means of an output $c_a^{\mathrm{H}, \delta_a}!\bullet$ where δ_a denotes the Dirac distribution that makes a transition exactly at time a. This also makes it clear that we regard the "clock" a as being highly trusted, giving it trust level H.

As in the previous scenario, we intend to determine the relationship

$$\vdash \&_{\dot{q}}(c_1?x_1, \cdots, c_n?x_n, c_a?x_a) \blacktriangleright \pi$$

between the transformed binder $\&_{\dot{q}}(c_1?x_1, \cdots, c_n?x_n, c_a?x_a)$ and the probability distribution $\pi \in \mathcal{D}(\{x_1, \cdots, x_n, x_a\} \to \mathcal{L}_\bot)$ indicating the probability of the various inputs having been received, subject to the minimum waiting time a.

This scenario involves calculating two contributions in Fig. 1: one is from the Part 1 and the other is from the merge of Part 2 and 3.

Unless otherwise specified, let i, j range over $1, \cdots, n$ and x_i, x_j range over $x_1, \cdots, x_n$. We now formulate the CSL query to be evaluated in the start state of the CTMC $(S_\otimes, s_\otimes, T_\otimes, L_\otimes)$ for determining the probability distribution π. Let σ be a mapping from variables $\{x_1, \cdots, x_n, x_a\}$ to elements of the lifted trust lattice $\mathcal{L}_\perp$. In the case where $\sigma(x_a) \neq \text{H} \vee \exists i : \sigma(x_i) \notin \{\perp, \ell_i\}$ we set $\pi(\sigma) = 0$. In the case where $\sigma(x_a) = \text{H} \wedge \forall i : \sigma(x_i) \in \{\perp, \ell_i\}$, taking Φ_{qn} from Formula (1) and Φ_σ from Formula (2) we set

$$\pi(\sigma) = \mathsf{P}\left[\text{true}\,\mathsf{U}^{[a,a]}\left(\Phi_{qn} \wedge \Phi_\sigma\right)\right] + \mathsf{P}\left[(\neg\Phi_{qn})\,\mathsf{U}^{[a,\infty)}\left(\Phi_{qn} \wedge \Phi_\sigma\right)\right]$$

where a is the minimum waiting time. This indicates the event that the quality predicate is satisfied and that input has been received as indicated by c_i and $\neg c_i$; the left summand takes care of the contribution from Part 1 (where it is acceptable that inputs arrive before time a but the system is not allowed to proceed until time a) and the right summand takes care of the contributions from Parts 2 and 3. Notice that, by the continuity of continuous distributions, the probability measure for the joint paths of the two contributions is strictly zero, i.e. $\mathsf{P}\left[(\neg\Phi_{qn})\,\mathsf{U}^{[a,a]}\left(\Phi_{qn} \wedge \Phi_\sigma\right)\right] = 0$.

Some special cases are worth mentioning. When q is $\forall$ we obtain

$$\pi(\sigma) = \begin{cases} 1 \text{ if } \sigma(x_a) = \text{H} \wedge \forall i : \sigma(x_i) = \ell_i \\ 0 \text{ otherwise} \end{cases}$$

When the quality predicate q is $\exists$, we may solve this analytically as follows. The first contribution $\pi_1 = \mathsf{P}\left[\text{true}\,\mathsf{U}^{[a,a]}\left(\Phi_{qn} \wedge \Phi_\sigma\right)\right]$ is given by

$$\pi_1(\sigma) = \left(\prod_{\sigma(x_i)=\perp} e^{-a\lambda_i}\right)\left(\prod_{\sigma(x_i)=\ell_i} (1 - e^{-a\lambda_i})\right)$$

if $\sigma(x_a) = \text{H} \wedge \forall j : \sigma(x_j) \in \{\ell_j, \perp\} \wedge \exists j : \sigma(x_j) = \ell_j$; otherwise $\pi_1(\sigma) = 0$. The $\pi_1(\sigma)$ expresses the probability of the events that one or more inputs have arrived by the time a. The second contribution $\pi_2 = \mathsf{P}\left[(\neg\Phi_{qn})\,\mathsf{U}^{[a,\infty)}\left(\Phi_{qn} \wedge \Phi_\sigma\right)\right]$ is given by

$$\pi_2(\sigma) = e^{-a(\lambda_1+\cdots+\lambda_n)}\frac{\lambda_i}{\lambda_1 + \cdots + \lambda_n}$$

if $\sigma(x_a) = \text{H} \wedge \exists i : \sigma(x_i) = \ell_i \wedge \forall j \neq i : \sigma(x_j) = \perp$; otherwise $\pi_2(\sigma) = 0$. The $\pi_2(\sigma)$ expresses the probability of the joint events that none of inputs has arrived by time a, corresponding to the part $e^{-a(\lambda_1+\cdots+\lambda_n)}$, and the input c_i wins the race, corresponding to the part $\frac{\lambda_i}{\lambda_1+\cdots+\lambda_n}$. We then get the overall contribution $\pi(\sigma) = \pi_1(\sigma) + \pi_2(\sigma)$ for the special case when q is $\exists$:

$$\pi(\sigma) = \begin{cases} \left(\prod_{\sigma(x_i)=\perp} e^{-a\lambda_i}\right)\left(\prod_{\sigma(x_i)=\ell_i}(1-e^{-a\lambda_i})\right) \\ \quad \text{if } \sigma(x_a) = \text{H} \wedge 1 < |\{j \mid \sigma(x_j) = \ell_j\}| \\[2mm] e^{-a(\lambda_1+\cdots+\lambda_n)}\left(e^{a\lambda_i} + \frac{\lambda_i}{\lambda_1+\cdots+\lambda_n} - 1\right) \\ \quad \text{if } \sigma(x_a) = \text{H} \wedge \sigma(x_i) = \ell_i \wedge 1 = |\{\sigma(x_j) = \ell_j\}| \\[2mm] 0 \quad \text{otherwise} \end{cases}$$

Scenario 3: Race between Stochastic Processes Subject to a Maximum Waiting Time. Here n stochastic external services have started transmitting the outputs $c_1^{\ell_1,\lambda_1}!t_1, \cdots, c_n^{\ell_n,\lambda_n}!t_n$, and they then compete to provide the required input(s), subject to a maximum waiting time given by the "clock" a. As in the previous case it is helpful to imagine that $\&_q^{[0,a)}(c_1?x_1, \cdots, c_n?x_n)$ is transformed to $\&_{\dot{q}}(c_1?x_1, \cdots, c_n?x_n, c_a?x_a)$, where $\dot{q}(x_1, \cdots, x_n, x_a) = q(x_1, \cdots, x_n) \vee x_a$ and where x_a indicates whether or not the maximum waiting time actually passed or not. We intend to determine the relationship

$$\vdash \&_{\dot{q}}(c_1?x_1, \cdots, c_n?x_n, c_a?x_a) \blacktriangleright \pi$$

between the transformed binder $\&_{\dot{q}}(c_1?x_1, \cdots, c_n?x_n, c_a?x_a)$ and the probability distribution $\pi \in \mathcal{D}(\{x_1, \cdots, x_n, x_a\} \to \mathcal{L}_\perp)$ indicating the probability of the various inputs having been received, subject to the maximum waiting time a. This scenario involves calculating two contributions in Fig. 1: one is from the merge of Part 1 and 2, and the other is Part 3.

We now formulate the CSL query to be evaluated in the start state of $(S_\otimes, s_\otimes, T_\otimes, L_\otimes)$ for determining the probability distribution π. Let σ be a mapping from variables $\{x_1, \cdots, x_n, x_a\}$ to elements of the lifted trust lattice $\mathcal{L}_\perp$. In the case where $\exists \sigma(x_i) \notin \{\perp, \ell_i\} \vee \sigma(x_a) \notin \{\perp, \text{H}\}$, we set $\pi(\sigma) = 0$. In the case where $\forall \sigma(x_i) \in \{\perp, \ell_i\} \wedge \sigma(x_a) \in \{\perp, \text{H}\}$, taking Φ_{qn} from Formula (1) and Φ_σ from Formula (2) we set

$$\pi(\sigma) = \begin{cases} \mathsf{P}\left[(\neg\Phi_{qn}) \, \mathsf{U}^{[0,a)} \, (\Phi_{qn} \wedge \Phi_\sigma)\right] & \text{if } \sigma(x_a) = \perp \\ \mathsf{P}\left[(\neg\Phi_{qn}) \, \mathsf{U}^{[a,a]} \, ((\neg\Phi_{qn}) \wedge \Phi_\sigma)\right] & \text{if } \sigma(x_a) = \text{H} \end{cases}$$

where a is the maximum waiting time. The case $\sigma(x_a) = \perp$ is when acceptable input has been received by time a and the case $\sigma(x_a) = \text{H}$ is when no acceptable input has been received by time a (at which time the real-time constraint terminates the race).

Some special cases are worth mentioning. When the quality predicate q is $\forall$, we may solve this analytically giving

$$\pi(\sigma) = \begin{cases} \prod_i (1 - e^{-a\lambda_i}) & \text{if } \sigma(x_a) = \perp \wedge \forall j : \sigma(x_j) = \ell_j \\[2mm] \left(\prod_{\sigma(x_i)=\perp} e^{-a\lambda_i}\right)\left(\prod_{\sigma(x_i)=\ell_i}(1-e^{-a\lambda_i})\right) \\ \quad \text{if } \sigma(x_a) = \text{H} \wedge \forall j : \sigma(x_j) \in \{l_j, \perp\} \wedge \exists j : \sigma(x_j) = \perp \\[2mm] 0 \quad \text{otherwise} \end{cases}$$

When the quality predicate q is $\exists$, we may solve this analytically giving

$$
\pi(\sigma) = \begin{cases}
(1 - e^{-a(\lambda_1 + \cdots + \lambda_n)}) \frac{\lambda_i}{\lambda_1 + \cdots + \lambda_n} \\
\quad \text{if } \sigma(x_a) = \bot \wedge \sigma(x_i) = \ell_i \wedge \forall j \neq i : \sigma(x_j) = \bot \\
e^{-a(\lambda_1 + \cdots + \lambda_n)} \quad \text{if } \sigma(x_a) = \text{H} \wedge \forall j : \sigma(x_j) = \bot \\
0 \quad \text{otherwise}
\end{cases}
$$

Scenario 4: Race between Stochastic Processes Subject to Both a Minimum and a Maximum Waiting Time. Here n stochastic external services have started transmitting the outputs $c_1^{\ell_1, \lambda_1} ! t_1, \cdots, c_n^{\ell_n, \lambda_n} ! t_n$, and they then compete to provide the required input(s), subject to both a minimum waiting time a and a maximum waiting time $a' > a$. As before, imagine that $\&_q^{[a,a']}(c_1?x_1, \cdots, c_n?x_n)$ is transformed to $\&_{\dot{q}}(c_1?x_1, \cdots, c_n?x_n, c_a?x_a, c_{a'}?x_{a'})$, where, $\dot{q}(x_1, \cdots, x_n, x_a, x_{a'}) = (q(x_1, \cdots, x_n) \wedge x_a) \vee x_{a'}$. We intend to determine the relationship

$$
\vdash \&_{\dot{q}}(c_1?x_1, \cdots, c_n?x_n, c_a?x_a, c_{a'}?x_{a'}) \blacktriangleright \pi
$$

between the transformed binder $\&_{\dot{q}}(c_1?x_1, \cdots, c_n?x_n, c_a?x_a, c_{a'}?x_{a'})$ and the probability distribution $\pi \in \mathcal{D}(\{x_1, \cdots, x_n, x_a, x_{a'}\} \to \mathcal{L}_\bot)$ indicating the probability of the various inputs having been received, subject to both the minimum waiting time a and the maximum waiting time a'. This scenario involves calculating three contributions corresponding to the three parts in Fig. 1.

We now formulate the CSL query to be evaluated in the start state of $(S_\otimes, s_\otimes, T_\otimes, L_\otimes)$ for determining the probability distribution π. Let σ be a mapping from variables $\{x_1, \cdots, x_n, x_a, x_{a'}\}$ to elements of the lifted trust lattice $\mathcal{L}_\bot$. In the case where $\exists \sigma(x_i) \notin \{\bot, \ell_i\} \vee \sigma(x_a) \neq \text{H} \vee \sigma(x_{a'}) \notin \{\bot, \text{H}\}$, we set $\pi(\sigma) = 0$. In the case where $\forall \sigma(x_i) \in \{\bot, \ell_i\} \wedge \sigma(x_a) = \text{H} \wedge \sigma(x_{a'}) \in \{\bot, \text{H}\}$, taking Φ_{qn} from Formula (1) and Φ_σ from Formula (2) we set

$$
\pi(\sigma) = \begin{cases}
\text{P} \left[\text{true } \text{U}^{[a,a]} (\Phi_{qn} \wedge \Phi_\sigma) \right] + \text{P} \left[(\neg \Phi_{qn}) \text{U}^{[a,a']} (\Phi_{qn} \wedge \Phi_\sigma) \right], \\
\quad \text{if } \sigma(x_a) = \text{H} \wedge \sigma(x_{a'}) = \bot, \\
\text{P} \left[(\neg \Phi_{qn}) \text{U}^{[a',a']} ((\neg \Phi_{qn}) \wedge \Phi_\sigma) \right] \\
\quad \text{if } \sigma(x_a) = \text{H} \wedge \sigma(x_{a'}) = \text{H},
\end{cases}
$$

where a is the minimum waiting time and a' is the maximum waiting time. In the case where $\sigma(x_a) = \text{H} \wedge \sigma(x_{a'}) = \bot$, there are two contributions: the probability that required inputs are satisfied before a, $\text{P} \left[\text{true } \text{U}^{[a,a]} (\Phi_{qn} \wedge \Phi_\sigma) \right]$, and the probability that required inputs are not satisfied before a but satisfied in the interval $[a,')$, $\text{P} \left[(\neg \Phi_{qn}) \text{U}^{[a,a']} (\Phi_{qn} \wedge \Phi_\sigma) \right]$. The case where $\sigma(x_a) = \text{H} \wedge \sigma(x_{a'}) = \text{H}$ expresses that the required inputs were not received by time a'.

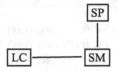

Fig. 2. The Smart Meter scenario

Some special cases are worth mentioning. When the quality predicate q is $\forall$, we may solve this analytically giving

$$
\pi(\sigma) = \begin{cases}
\prod_i \left(1 - e^{-a'\lambda_i}\right) \\
\quad \text{if } \sigma(x_a) = \text{H} \wedge \sigma(x_{a'}) = \bot \wedge \forall j : \sigma(x_j) = \ell_j \\[2mm]
\left(\prod_{\sigma(x_i)=\bot} e^{-a'\lambda_i}\right)\left(\prod_{\sigma(x_i)=\ell_i}(1 - e^{-a'\lambda_i})\right) \\
\quad \text{if } \sigma(x_a) = \text{H} \wedge \sigma(x_{a'}) = \text{H} \wedge \forall j : \sigma(x_j) \in \{\ell_j, \bot\} \wedge \exists j : \sigma(x_j) = \bot \\[2mm]
0 \quad \text{otherwise}
\end{cases}
$$

When the quality predicate q is $\exists$, we may solve this analytically giving

$$
\pi(\sigma) = \begin{cases}
\left(\prod_{\sigma(x_i)=\bot} e^{-a\lambda_i}\right)\left(\prod_{\sigma(x_i)=\ell_i}(1 - e^{-a\lambda_i})\right) \\
\quad \text{if } \sigma(x_a) = \text{H} \wedge \sigma(x_{a'}) = \bot \wedge 1 < |\{j \mid \sigma(x_j) = \ell_j\}|, \\[2mm]
e^{-a(\lambda_1+\cdots+\lambda_n)}(e^{a\lambda_i} - 1) + e^{-a(\lambda_1+\cdots+\lambda_n)}(1 - e^{-(a'-a)(\lambda_1+\cdots+\lambda_n)})\frac{\lambda_i}{\lambda_1+\cdots+\lambda_n} \\
\quad \text{if } \sigma(x_a) = \text{H} \wedge \sigma(x_{a'}) = \bot \wedge \sigma(x_i) = l_i \wedge |\{j \mid \sigma(x_j) = \ell_j\}| = 1, \\[2mm]
e^{-a'(\lambda_1+\cdots+\lambda_n)} \quad \text{if } \sigma(x_u) = \text{H} \wedge \sigma(x_{a'}) = \text{H} \wedge \forall j : \sigma(x_j) = \bot, \\[2mm]
0 \quad \text{otherwise}
\end{cases}
$$

4   Implementation of a Smart Meter

We now consider a scenario inspired by [18] where a smart meter SM of a household communicates with a service provider SP to obtain a schedule for operating a number of appliances taking pricing and availability of energy into account. Unfortunately, the SP is subject to denial of service attacks, therefore the SM is equipped with a local computer LC for computing a schedule to be used whenever the SP does not produce a schedule. The schedule computed by the SP is the preferred one, therefore only if no schedule is received from SP within some time period will the locally computed schedule be used. The overall scenario is illustrated in Fig. 2 and 3 and we shall now describe the individual processes in more detail. We shall feel free to use a polyadic version of the calculus when it eases the presentation, and we write (νd), global$(\cdot)$, local$(\cdot)$ for creating data d, performing functions global and local (taking data as input and returning

$$\begin{aligned}
\text{define } &\text{SP} \triangleq \cdots \text{ (see text) } \cdots \\
&\text{LC} \triangleq \cdots \text{ (see text) } \cdots \\
&\text{SM} \triangleq \cdots \text{ (see text) } \cdots \\
\text{in} \quad &\text{SP} \| \text{LC} \| \text{SM} \\
\text{using} \quad &\text{request}, \text{req}, \text{rep}_\text{L}
\end{aligned}$$

Fig. 3. The Smart Meter system

data and called f in the syntax in Table 1). We shall not further specify how the functions global and local compute schedules based on the data available to them.

The service provider SP is defined by:

$$\begin{aligned}
\text{SP} \triangleq \ &\&_\exists(\text{request}?(x_i\, x_r)). \\
&\text{case } x_i \text{ of some}(y_i): \\
&\quad \text{case } x_r \text{ of some}(y_r): \\
&\qquad y_i{}^{\text{M},\lambda_g}!(\text{global}(y_r)).\text{SP} \\
&\quad \text{else SP} \\
&\text{else SP}
\end{aligned}$$

The SP first obtains a request of x_r resources from a smart meter identifying itself as x_i. The next three lines express that SP computes a schedule using the function global and returns it to the smart meter before recursing. The case constructs ensure that the proper data is extracted and supplied to the function.

A local computer LC operates similarly to the service provider, but without checking identification:

$$\text{LC} \triangleq \&_\exists(\text{req}?(x_r)). \ \text{case } x_r \text{ of some}(y_r): \text{rep}_\text{L}{}^{\text{L},\lambda_l}!!\text{local}(y_r).\text{LC else LC}$$

It uses the function local to compute the schedule and uses the channel $\text{rep}_\text{L}{}^{\text{L},\lambda_l}$ to send the schedule; once more the case construct is used to extract the request.

Finally, let us consider the control process SM for a smart meter:

$$\begin{aligned}
\text{SM} \triangleq \ &(\nu\text{rep}_\text{G})\,(\nu d)\, \text{request}^{\text{H},\lambda_g}!(\text{rep}_\text{G}\, d). \ \text{req}^{\text{H},\lambda_l}!d. \\
&\&_\exists^{[5,\infty)}(\text{rep}_\text{G}?x_g, \text{rep}_\text{L}?x_l). \\
&\quad \text{case } x_g \text{ of some}(y_g): {}^1\text{install}(y_g).\text{SM} \\
&\qquad \text{else case } x_l \text{ of some}(y_l): {}^2\text{install}(y_l).\text{SM} \\
&\qquad \text{else } {}^3\text{warning}.\text{SM}
\end{aligned}$$

For later reference we have added labels to three subprocesses. The first line declares a response channel rep_G and a data d, then issues two requests, one to the SP and one to the LC. The binder of the second line expresses that the SM has to wait for 5 time units and that at least one schedule must have been received before continuing. As in the previous examples the case constructs are used to extract the required data: the third line will give priority to the global schedule (the process labelled 1), whereas in the absence of a global schedule the fourth line will install the local schedule before recursing (the process labelled 2), and the final else branch (labelled 3) corresponds to failure.

As an alternative we might replace the binder in the second line by

$$\&_{\forall}^{[5,8.7)}(\mathsf{rep_G}?x_g, \mathsf{rep_L}?x_l),$$

meaning that there is a maximum time bound for receiving schedules and that we prefer to wait for both schedules. If no schedule arrives by time 8.7, the SM will reach the final else branch (labelled 3).

Stochastic Model Checking of the Smart Meter. Let us consider the process SM and recall that the processes computing the global and local schedules are exponentially distributed with rates λ_g and λ_l, respectively. We want to determine a distribution π such that

$$\vdash \&_{\exists}^{[5,\infty)}(\mathsf{rep_G}?x_g, \mathsf{rep_L}?x_l) \blacktriangleright \pi$$

so we are in the special case described above. Let us assume that $\lambda_g = 0.2$ and $\lambda_l = 0.5$, Then we get

$$\pi([x_g \mapsto \mathrm{M}, \ x_l \mapsto \mathrm{L}, \ x_a \mapsto \mathrm{H}]) = 0.5802$$
$$\pi([x_g \mapsto \mathrm{M}, \ x_l \mapsto \bot, \ x_a \mapsto \mathrm{H}]) = 0.0605$$
$$\pi([x_g \mapsto \bot, \ x_l \mapsto \mathrm{L}, \ x_a \mapsto \mathrm{H}]) = 0.3593$$

and $\pi(\sigma) = 0$ in all other cases. It follows that there is no risk (or to be more pedantic, that the risk is 0%) that no schedules are received, and that there is a 35.93% risk that the global schedule is missing.

Now, let us consider the variant of SM using the binder

$$\vdash \&_{\forall}^{[5,8.7)}(\mathsf{rep_G}?x_g, \mathsf{rep_L}?x_l) \blacktriangleright \pi$$

gives rise to the following distribution using the same parameters as above:

$$\pi([x_g \mapsto \mathrm{M}, \ x_l \mapsto \mathrm{L}, \ x_a \mapsto \mathrm{H}, \ x_{a'} \mapsto \bot]) = 0.8138$$
$$\pi([x_g \mapsto \mathrm{M}, \ x_l \mapsto \bot, \ x_a \mapsto \mathrm{H}, \ x_{a'} \mapsto \mathrm{H}]) = 0.0106$$
$$\pi([x_g \mapsto \bot, \ x_l \mapsto \mathrm{L}, \ x_a \mapsto \mathrm{H}, \ x_{a'} \mapsto \mathrm{H}]) = 0.1733$$
$$\pi([x_g \mapsto \bot, \ x_l \mapsto \bot, \ x_a \mapsto \mathrm{H}, \ x_{a'} \mapsto \mathrm{H}]) = 0.0023$$

and $\pi(\sigma) = 0$ in all other cases. It follows that there is 0.23% risk both schedules are missing, 17.33% risk the global schedule is missing, and only 1.06% risk the local schedule is missing.

We have obtained the results reported above both by employing CSL model checking using PRISM and by our own implementation of the analytical formulae using MATLAB.

5   Conclusion

We believe future programming languages need to support a more robust ("pessimistic") programming style: What conceivably might go wrong, probably will go wrong. A major cause of disruption is due to the *networked communication* between distributed software components. The Quality Calculus [15] proposes a very robust way of programming distributed systems where default data should always be available to allow the system to continue its operation as best it can, rather than simply terminating with an error or getting stuck in an input operation. However, it does not contain any quantitative information about the robustness, typically showing how likely it is that the default data will be used due to a failure on receiving ideal data, which can eventually impact the system performance. This suggests extending the Quality Calculus to consider stochastic aspects.

This paper developed Stochastic Model Checking to determine the probability of a process surviving the absence of data in the exponential fragment of the Stochastic Quality Calculus (SQC). In the full Stochastic Quality Calculus [20], the communications had general distributed stochastic delay and were running concurrently and independently with clocks; here we allow only exponentially distributed delays in order to be able to apply model checking techniques. For the restricted Stochastic Quality Calculus with exponential distributions (SQC_{exp}), we showed how to perform numerical analysis by transforming real-timed delay into time boundaries, such that a probability measure on the availability of inputs is split into more than one availability query on Continuous-Time Markov Chains. The CTMC-based numerical analysis were performed both by means of stochastic model checking and by means of explicit analytical formulae. The whole development was demonstrated on the design of an intelligent smart electrical meter.

In our opinion, these analyses provide a foundation for supporting a new discipline of robust programming. We believe that with quantitative information on the robustness, it will be possible to better determine whether or not the software continues to deal appropriately with risks and threats as their application environment changes.

Acknowledgements. The research has been supported by IDEA4CPS studying the Foundations for Cyber Physical Systems and granted by the Danish Research Foundation for Basic Research (DNRF86-10). Cyber Physical Systems may be seen as an amalgamation of embedded systems and service-oriented systems, the latter being the topic of the European Integrated Project SENSORIA being led by Martin Wirsing and in which we participated. As in SENSORIA our focus is on identifying appropriate programming mechanisms for which also analysis methods can be developed.

References

[1] Aziz, A., Sanwal, K., Singhal, V., Brayton, R.K.: Verifying continuous time Markov chains. In: Alur, R., Henzinger, T.A. (eds.) CAV 1996. LNCS, vol. 1102, pp. 269–276. Springer, Heidelberg (1996)

[2] Bravetti, M.: An integrated approach for the specification and analysis of stochastic real-time systems. Electr. Notes Theor. Comput. Sci. 68(5), 34–64 (2002)

[3] Bravetti, M.: Stochastic and real time in process algebra: A conceptual overview. Electr. Notes Theor. Comput. Sci. 162, 113–119 (2006)

[4] Bravetti, M., D'Argenio, P.R.: Tutte le algebre insieme: Concepts, discussions and relations of stochastic process algebras with general distributions. In: Baier, C., Haverkort, B.R., Hermanns, H., Katoen, J.-P., Siegle, M. (eds.) Validation of Stochastic Systems. LNCS, vol. 2925, pp. 44–88. Springer, Heidelberg (2004)

[5] Brinksma, E., Hermanns, H.: Process Algebra and Markov Chains, pp. 183–231. Springer, Heidelberg (2001)

[6] Ciobanu, G., Koutny, M.: PerTiMo: A Model of Spatial Migration with Safe Access Permissions. Newcastle University, Computing Science (2011)

[7] De Nicola, R., Katoen, J.-P., Latella, D., Massink, M.: Stoklaim: A stochastic extension of klaim. CNR-ISTI Technical Report number ISTI-2006-TR-01 (2006)

[8] Hillston, J.: A compositional approach to performance modelling. Cambridge University Press, New York (1996)

[9] Kwiatkowska, M., Norman, G., Parker, D.: Stochastic model checking. In: Bernardo, M., Hillston, J. (eds.) SFM 2007. LNCS, vol. 4486, pp. 220–270. Springer, Heidelberg (2007)

[10] Kwiatkowska, M., Norman, G., Parker, D.: Prism: Probabilistic model checking for performance and reliability analysis. ACM SIGMETRICS Performance Evaluation Review 36(4), 40–45 (2009)

[11] Milner, R.: A proposal for Standard ML. In: Proceedings of the 1984 ACM Symposium on LISP and Functional Programming, pp. 184–197. ACM (1984)

[12] Milner, R.: Communicating and Mobile Systems: the Pi-Calculus. Cambridge University Press (1999)

[13] Nielsen, B.F., Nielson, F., Nielson, H.R.: Model checking multivariate state rewards. QEST 17, 7–16 (2010)

[14] Nielson, H.R., Nielson, F.: Probabilistic analysis of the quality calculus. In: Beyer, D., Boreale, M. (eds.) FORTE 2013 and FMOODS 2013. LNCS, vol. 7892, pp. 258–272. Springer, Heidelberg (2013)

[15] Nielson, H.R., Nielson, F., Vigo, R.: A calculus for quality. In: Păsăreanu, C.S., Salaün, G. (eds.) FACS 2012. LNCS, vol. 7684, pp. 188–204. Springer, Heidelberg (2013), http://dx.doi.org/10.1007/978-3-642-35861-6_12

[16] Priami, C.: Stochastic π-calculus. The Computer Journal 38(7), 578–589 (1995)

[17] Vigo, R., Nielson, F., Nielson, H.R.: Broadcast, denial-of-service, and secure communication. In: Johnsen, E.B., Petre, L. (eds.) IFM 2013. LNCS, vol. 7940, pp. 412–427. Springer, Heidelberg (2013)

[18] Wang, C., Groot, M.d.: Managing end-user preferences in the smart grid. In: Proceedings of the 1st International Conference on Energy-Efficient Computing and Networking, e-Energy 2010, pp. 105–114. ACM (2010)

[19] Yi, W.: CCS+time = an interleaving model for real time systems. In: Albert, J.L., Monien, B., Artalejo, M.R. (eds.) Automata, Languages and Programming. LNCS, vol. 510, pp. 217–228. Springer, Heidelberg (1991)

[20] Zeng, K., Nielson, F., Nielson, H.R.: The Stochastic Quality Calculus. In: Kühn, E., Pugliese, R. (eds.) COORDINATION 2014. LNCS, vol. 8459, pp. 179–193. Springer, Heidelberg (2014)

Software-Intensive Systems for Smart Cities: From Ensembles to Superorganisms

Nicola Bicocchi, Letizia Leonardi, and Franco Zambonelli

University of Modena and Reggio Emilia, Italy
name.surname@unimore.it

Abstract. Smart cities infrastructures can be considered as large-scale, software-intensive systems exhibiting close sinergies among ICT devices and humans. However, current deployments of smart city technologies rely on rather traditional technologies. This chapter introduces a novel perspective in which large-scale ensembles of software components, ICT devices, and humans, can be made working together in an orchestrated and self-organized way to achieve urban-level goals as if they were part of a single large-scale organism, i.e., a superorganism. Accordingly, we delineate our vision of urban superorganisms and overview related application areas. Finally, we identify the key challenges in engineering self-organizing systems that can work as a superorganism, and we introduce the reference architecture for an infrastructure capable of supporting our vision.

1 Introduction

The increasing diffusion of sensor networks, actuators, and computational resources is transforming urban environments [19,9]. In addition, social networks are promoting innovative models and tools to engage people in situated collaboration activities [28,20]. In smart city scenarios, these factors suggest integrating the complementary sensing, computing, and acting capabilities of ICT devices, software components, and of humans [36]. Further evolutions of this process could lead to large-scale, software-intensive systems [34,33] via which municipalities could continuously monitor their environment, and eventually control the system itself.

Unfortunately, the highly decentralized and open ended nature of this scenario (where it is impossible to exert control over each of its components, and definitely impossible to rely on their availability), make traditional approach to software composition inadequate [8]. Our vision comprises heterogeneous urban-scale ensemble of ICT devices, software components, and humans, becoming capable of spontaneously self-organize their collective activities to adaptively achieve specific urban-level goals as if they were part of a single organism. That is, what in biology is usually called a "superorganism" [15].

In this chapter, we start from the assessed biological perspective on superorganisms and sketch the future vision of urban superorganisms. In particular,

R. De Nicola and R. Hennicker (Eds.): Wirsing Festschrift, LNCS 8950, pp. 538–551, 2015.

we discuss how the urban superorganism *as a whole* will be able to: *(i)* combine a wide range of information sources (e.g., environmental data from sensor networks, mobility data and social network posts) [29,12]; *(ii)* perform advanced reasoning, identify patterns and situations, and plan actions [3,1,25]; *(iii)* engage in large-scale, coordinated tasks to achieve specific goals (e.g., optimise traffic flow in the city, make it more environmentally sustainable, etc.) [13]. Accordingly, we overview how such capabilities can be exploited to deploy applications and services, pushing the current smart city vision forward [19].

The road towards the full realization of this vision is plenty of challenging open research questions. These range from scientific questions (e.g., how can we enforce "by design" a specific self-organizing behavior?) to engineering (what coordination models and technologies better suit a large system of heterogeneous components?) and social ones (how can we made people willing to act as part of an urban superorganism?). This chapter analyzes the most prominent challenges and proposes a reference architecture aimed at supporting the deployment and execution of superorganisms services.

The rest of the chapter is organised as follows. Section 2 details our vision on urban superorganisms. Section 3 overviews innovative application areas for future urban superorganisms. Section 4 discusses the key research challenges. Section 5 proposes a general-purpose architecture addressing those challenges. Finally, section 6 draws conclusions.

2   From Ensembles to Urban Superorganisms

Very large ensembles of inter-connected components –humans, ICT devices and software components – can be potentially exploited to create dynamic, goal-oriented, collective entities usually defined in biology as superorganisms [15]. That is, large ensembles of individual organisms capable of behaving in a collectively orchestrated way to serve the good of the ensemble itself. In particular, closing the sensing, computing, and acting capabilities in a loop might lead to coherent collective behaviours, as it is observable in a number of natural situations [5].

2.1   Natural Superorganisms

A single ant, for example, has very limited sensing and acting capabilities, and little or no cognitive abilities. Yet, ants can indirectly coordinate their movements and activities, via spreading and sensing of pheromones in the environment, so as to exhibit, as a colony, very powerful collective behaviors.

This can occur because the pheromones mechanism induces coordinated activities that – by closing into a feedback loop – turns the limited individual capabilities of sensing, understanding and acting into collective ones [24,5]. More specifically:

- *Sensing*: To find food, an ant senses existing pheromone field gradients (if any, or wanders randomly otherwise). Such field gradients, if followed uphill,

eventually lead the ant to food. This makes the ant spreading pheromones in its turn and producing further paths that increase the chances for the ants of the colony to find food.
- *Understanding*: All that an individual ant has to do in terms of cognitive activities is computing the direction of the uphill gradient. However, the colony as a whole exhibits an incredible efficiency in finding food sources, in computing the shortest paths to food, and in adaptively reshaping the pheromone fields to account for contingencies.
- *Acting*: When an ant finds some food source, it starts spreading pheromones in the environment, thus creating a path that leads to food. The overall activities of the ants of the colony in spreading pheromones eventually shape a distributed field of pheromones that can be used to find food.

As ants behave as if they were a single superorganism, we envision that humans, along with software components and ICT devices, can be engaged in large-scale coordinated activities. All the involved entities from now on will be generally called *agents*. This would allow cities to become a sort of superorganism composed of heterogeneous agents.

2.2   From Individual to Collective Behaviors

Figure 1 illustrates the sensing-understanding-acting feedback loop that – as in ant colonies – can contribute leveraging individual capabilities into collective ones, and eventually make collective behaviours possible. More specifically:

- *Sensing* activities in which citizens, supported by ICT devices and services, get information about the current state of the environment (e.g., people location data) and can share such information (e.g., as already happens for mobile phone sport trackers).
- *Understanding* activities in which advanced forms of contextual information are derived from the sensed data (e.g., individual citizens mobility patterns), and possibly aggregated to evaluate the global properties of a city (e.g., the global mobility rhythms).
- *Acting* activities, in the form of seemingly goal-directed global coordinated tasks, supported by the extracted information, and put in actions by groups of agents (e.g., traffic steering on the basis of the identified mobility patterns, car sharing on the basis of people mobility routines, etc.).

To close the feedback loop, the results of acting activities clearly affect the overall state of the city and the individual state of citizens. Citizens can sense such changes at both the individual and collective levels, recognising the effects of their actions [23].

2.3   The Complementary Role of Humans Agents and ICT Agents

Citizens are increasingly equipped with smart phones that are very powerful in terms of battery life, sensing, computational power and connectivity. At the

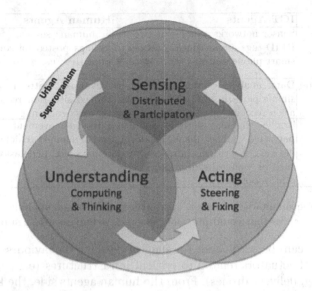

Fig. 1. Collaborative sensing, understanding and acting can be used to deploy advanced urban-level behaviours

same time, autonomous ICT infrastructures (sensor networks, security cameras, robots, etc.) are likely to pervade cities in the near future. Accordingly, the future urban environment is becoming a sort of dense digital ecosystem, whose components are characterised by heterogeneous and complementary sensing, understanding, and acting capabilities (Figure 2).

Sensing capabilities from the ICT agents side can be provided by: *(i)* mobile phones equipped with GPS, accelerometers and cameras; *(ii)* sensors networks and smart objects that follow the Internet of Things paradigm; *(iii)* tags that exploit the near field communication technologies (NFC, RFID and Bluetooth). From the human agents side, the five senses of humans can, in many situations, supply and be more accurate than ICT sensors (think about the possibility of sensing opinions and "moods", which sensors can hardly provide). Also, they can be easily put at work for the community, due to the possibility of continuous accessing to online social networks, where to express and make public the sensed information [29].

Understanding capabilities from the ICT agents side makes it possible to collect and digest very large amounts of urban data in a short time, and to perform some limited pattern analysis on such data. However, from the human agents side, one can effectively exploit the capability of recognising complex situations and patterns (so called human computation [35]), which machines can hardly tackle. Think, for example, of recognising a situation in which two friends pretend to fight just for joking and are not really hurting each other.

Acting capabilities from the ICT agents side can be provided by: *(i)* traffic controllers supporting control of vehicles movement (e.g., traffic lights); *(ii)* public

	ICT Agents	Human Agents
Sensing	Sensor networks, camera networks, RFID tags, opportunistic access to smart phone sensors	5 human senses, facts-opinions-feelings posted on social networks, proactive usage of smart phone sensors
Understanding	Data analysis, data aggregation, simple pattern analysis, basic situation recognition	Advanced pattern analysis, advanced situation recognition, emotion recognition
Acting	Traffic lights, digital signage, pervasive public displays, acting devices of critical infrastructures such as water distribution, energy grid, robots, etc.,	Physical movements of individuals and of manned vehicles, physical actions, social persuasion

Fig. 2. The table summarises sensing, computing, and acting capabilities of both humans and ICT devices that could mutually interact within an urban superorganism

displays that can be exploited to suggest specific behaviours to citizens; *(iii)* all kinds of actuators related to critical infrastructures (e.g., energy grid); *(iv)* robots (e.g. delivery drones). From the human agents side, the key elements involved are users themselves, which can perform a variety of actions related to moving items around or changing the properties of some physical entities. In addition, citizens could accomplish actions – such as social persuasion – based on their peculiar abilities. The goal-directed integration of the above capabilities and activities will allow to close the collective-awareness feedback loop, thus enabling large-scale coordinated behavior among humans and ICT devices and services.

3   Emerging Application Scenarios

Let us now introduce some exemplary application scenarios that could be enabled by the vision of self-organizing urban superorganisms, and by the defined collective feedback cycle.

3.1   Smart Mobility

Among many capabilities that future urban superorganisms will exhibit, the first that we expect to be in place, and for which we already observe embryonic examples around, will relate to urban mobility [16,13]. Specifically, it will relate to the capability of sensing, predicting, and affecting (i.e., steering) the movements of vehicles or pedestrians, thus improving overall efficiency of urban mobility, but also making it possible for citizens to dynamically satisfy at the best their mobility needs.

A variety of sensors already exist to detect the conditions of traffic or crowd in urban environments. In addition, users are increasingly given the possibility to contribute to such sensing activities by posting information on social networks or by opening access to their navigators and smart phone sensors. All this information can be used to understand how to improve traffic flow or how to avoid congestions. To this end: actuators such as traffic lights and digital traffic signs can be put at work for vehicles; public (wall mounted) displays [10] and private (smart phone) displays can be exploited to suggest directions to pedestrians.

However, one could push the capabilities of superorganisms much beyond [30]. For instance, one can think ofdynamically matching the similarity of the planned routes of vehicles, pedestrians, and merchandises to be delivered, in order to dynamically self-organize very flexible ride sharing and shipment services. In general, urban superorganisms induce a change in the dominant paradigm for the provisioning of mobility services: from sensing mobility patterns and adapting existing services to them, to dynamically collecting mobility needs and self-organizing the role and mobility patterns of vehicles accordingly.

3.2 Improved Sustainability

An additional example of how urban superorganisms can impact urban life is related to energy consumption [7]. Just imagine sensing energy consumption data to compute instantaneous carbon footprints for specific areas of the city or for specific groups of citizens.

Public displays can then be exploited to share this information and possibly some summaries of the factors contributing to it, and personal displays can be possibly exploited to let individual and groups become aware of their own contributions to the urban carbon footprint. Staring from these considerations, one could think of steering the behaviour of individual citizens towards more energy efficient behaviours. Also, one could engage groups of citizens in self-organized collaborative actions, with the aim of solving/improving specific energy problems in specific urban areas and thus supply the lack of actuators suitable to the purpose (e.g., detecting open windows and closing them).

3.3 Taking Care

Via similar means, it could be possible to dynamically involve citizens in proactively helping to take care of the city, e.g., to help keeping it cleaner or making it a safer place for everyone. For instance, one can think of dynamically engaging people to temporarily take care of children on their way to school, whenever the current activity and known habits of some persons suggests.

Ideally, in the presence of enough matching people and possibly of the necessary complementing sensors (e.g., cameras) and actuators (e.g., robots) already in place for that purpose, one could make sure that the whole path from home to school of every children in a city is properly covered and taken care of. Such a scenario is possibly a bit scary as of today, but a day will come when the idea of connected citizens and devices will become very common, and all related urban services will be perceived as highly trusted.

3.4 Feeling Part of It

Urban superorganisms, also, might show their advantages in the (not easily measurable) way by which they will improve our living. In particular, acting and moving around in a city by being given feedbacks on the effect of our own existence in it (and observing ourselves in relation with our environment and with the other citizens), can make most of our everyday actions inherently more pleasant and rewarding, and can promote a renewed and stronger sense of citizenship.

Indeed, there are already a variety of examples in which the adoption of social networks to exchange information and discuss problems within neighborhood of a city has helped promoting a renewed sense of citizenship. The so called "social streets" phenomena, in particular, help people understanding the fact that living in a specific part of the city implies belonging to a community and serving the community. We expect urban superorganisms will bring such understanding to a much wider scale.

4 Engineering Challenges

The vision of urban superorganisms raises challenges that can hardly be dealt by present networking and middleware architectures. In this section, and without the ambition of being exhaustive, we present several challenges and analyze how an infrastructure designed for urban superorganisms should address them.

4.1 Bringing Human and ICT Agents Together

The activities of urban superorganisms will involve a variety of heterogeneous agents: humans equipped with a mobile phone, ICT sensors and actuators, cameras, public displays, self-driving cars, different classes of robots [31]. Their capabilities are very different from each other: just think about how differently humans and artificial vision systems see and classify images [27], or at how differently robots and humans can assist people [31].

An infrastructure for future urban superorganisms should be able to support a general model for representing such different classes of agents and their specific features, as well as a general model to invoke them and properly collect their results. Also, the infrastructure should integrate a proper coordination model supporting the orchestration [21] of heterogeneous agents physically spread over an urban area.

4.2 Collective Situation Awareness

New types of sensors become available to sense information about environment, weather, presence or movements of different entities. Furthermore humans increasingly act as a kind of social sensor through mobile phones and social networks [29]. So, the availability of sensorial data is not an issue. The problems arise when trying to turn such large amounts of data into knowledge about situations [3].

In the past few years, there have been a notable progress in the identification of algorithms and data classification techniques for individual or homogeneous sensorial streams. The new challenge is to find ways of properly aggregate multiple streams from multiple and heterogeneous sources, so as to classify more complex and multifaceted situations. Early proposals towards advanced classification techniques exploiting multiple sensors can indeed be found in literature [4,14]. Yet, a general approach to sensor fusion and complex situation recognition, also accounting for global situations at urban scale are still missing, and so it is missing the identification of a proper infrastructure to support such a general approach.

4.3   Reconfiguration and Self-adaptivity

Reaching high-levels of awareness is necessary to understand what actions to undertake to achieve specific global level objectives. However, it is also necessary to continuously monitor – in a close feedback loop – the effect of the actions and to dynamically plan corrective actions if needed [8]. Such corrective actions may: *(i)* be caused by local effects and involve simply a change in how some individuals act; or *(ii)* be of a more global nature and involve a large number of individuals and their interaction schemes.

Accordingly, the general model for urban superorganisms should support dynamic discovery of components and dynamic reconfiguration (that is, the dynamic composition of agents and their involvement in different types of coordination patterns over time). And, clearly, this should take place in a self-adaptive way, without requiring human intervention.

4.4   Bottom Up Self-organization vs Top-Down Design

Due to their inherent decentralized nature and the lack of central control, the behaviours of urban superorganisms will have to be mostly based on bottom up self-organization. This means that the local activities and interactions of their components will have to make global patterns of behavior – serving specific urban-scale purposes – emerge despite the fact that such global behaviours will not be explicitly coded into any of the individual components [21,2].

However, engineering individual behaviors so as to achieve specific global goals is quite a challenge, and is mostly possible only by reverse engineering of known natural self-organizing phenomena [2]. Thus, a relevant thrust of research on adaptive and evolvable software systems is focussing on integrating adaptation in software systems according to the most assessed approaches of software engineering. This implies explicitly encoding global goals in a system that is designed and coordinated in a top-down way [8], and promoting adaptivity by having the system explicitly account for its awareness of the global situation.

The key question that arises in this context is how it is possible to define methodologies to smooth the tension between the two approaches, i.e., identifying how the two approaches can co-exist (and they will indeed have to) and possibly conflict in future urban superorganisms. The ultimate goal would be to tolerate development methodologies in which the bottom-up and self-adaptive endeavour of nature-inspired self-organizing systems can become part of a more traditional top-down approach to software engineering.

4.5   Predicting and Controlling Emergent Behaviors

Emergent bottom-up self-organization in natural systems, leading to self-adaptive properties, is by definition a non-deterministic and irreducible process. Although it is possible to design a self-organizing system that will probabilistically behave as desired, it is impossible to exactly predict its final configuration but by executing the system itself.

Probabilistic non-determinism may be satisfactory in some non-critical cases, e.g., in the diffusion of non-critical traffic information in a network of vehicles [17], where the existence of some vehicles not reached by the information is not critical. However, in other cases it may not be acceptable, e.g., in the exploration of an urban environment by a swarm of robots during a rescue operation [6], where one cannot tolerate the swarm to ignore some portion of the environment. Accordingly, a key issue is to compensate such unpredictability by defining tools to dynamically tune urban superorganisms if needed [11].

Some research in software engineering and distributed systems explicitly address this issue mostly with simulations for multi-agent systems or cellular automata [22]. Yet, a general understanding of how to control emergent behaviours in complex software systems is still to be reached. In our opinion, norm-based multi-agent systems and electronic institutions [26,18] can be an effective starting point towards achieving predictable and controllable urban superorganisms.

5   An Infrastructure for Urban Superorganisms

Let us now introduce the reference architecture for a general-purpose middleware infrastructure supporting urban superorganisms. The architecture relies on that developed in the context of the EU-funded SAPERE project (http://www.sapere-project.eu/). [38,37]. The reference architecture and its coordination laws can support coordination among heterogeneous agents, can express situation-awareness by integrating advanced classification techniques, and can support and control a variety of self-organizing coordination patterns.

5.1   Reference Architecture

The architecture (see Figure 3) supports the coordination of agents in an urban area by abstracting the urban environment itself in terms of a computational *spatial substrate*, in which the coordinated activities of urban agents take place. From the implementation viewpoint, such spatial substrate could be realized as a service in the cloud, or it also could be distributed across the actual pervasive ICT infrastructure, i.e., the dense connected system of heterogeneous ICT

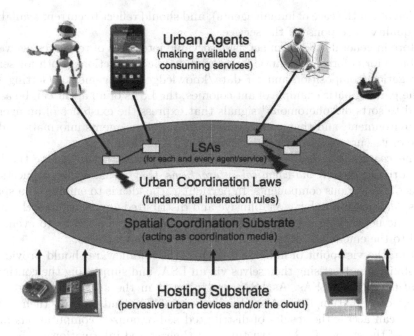

Fig. 3. A reference architecture for urban superorganisms infrastructures

devices that populate our urban environments (from smart phones to embedded sensors and actuators).

The spatial substrate acts as a sort of shared coordination media embedding the basic laws of coordination that rule the interactions between the urban agents. The agents include all those autonomous components providing (or can in turn request) resources and services to the overall urban environment. In the spatial substrate, agents can interact and combine with each other (in respect of the coordination laws and typically based on their spatial relationships), serving their own individual needs as well as those of the overall urban environment. Human agents, in particular, can access the urban environment in a decentralised way via their mobile phones (or any other portable devices that will be made available in the coming years) to use and consume data and services. They can also act as servers, to make available own human services.

For the heterogeneous urban agents living in the superorganisms, the architecture should adopt a common modelling and a common treatment. In particular, we propose this to be a semantic representation (which we call *Live Semantic Annotations*, or LSAs) associated to services and functionalities that the components of the superorganism can provide. An LSA is tightly associated to the agent it describes, and – unlike static service descriptions – must be capable of dynamically reflecting in their values the current situation and context of the services. In particular, the current situation should also account for the diverse means by which a service can be provided by different types of agents (e.g., whenever connected in the case of ICT devices, when available and willing to participate in the case of human agents), and should reflect to current availability and quality of response of the service.

More in general, LSAs can act as observable interfaces of resources, as well as the basis for enforcing semantic forms of dynamic interactions (both for service aggregation/composition and for data/knowledge management). Getting back to the paradigmatic example of ant colonies, the LSAs of an agent can be assimilated to sorts of "pheromone" signals that express the existence of an agent in an environment, and that make available to all other agents information about some of its current and/or past activities and knowledge.

The *coordination laws* integrated within the infrastructure define the basic laws driving virtual *bio-chemical interactions* that dynamically connects the LSAs of the various components. In particular, the idea is to enforce on a spatial basis, and possibly relying on diffusive and distributed aggregation mechanisms, dynamic networking and composition of data and services, so as to eventually head to the emergence of self-organized coordination patterns.

From the viewpoint of individual agents, the middleware should provide the possibility of advertising themselves via an LSA, and supporting the continuous updating of their LSAs. As LSAs are injected in the spatial substrate, they trigger coordination laws. Also, by accessing LSAs and reading their values, agents can access the results of distributed self-organized computations in the forms of the shape of LSAs structure and their stored information.

5.2   Addressing the Challenges

First, the LSA approach can be effective in representing both human and ICT components. In fact, being all LSAs residing in the same spatial substrate and being subject to the same coordination laws, this makes it possible to seamlessly involve in coordinated activities both human and ICT agents.

Second, concerning situation-awareness, at the local level LSAs can express local contextual information, and the connection to LSAs can provide for fusing information coming from heterogeneous sensors. In addition, the deployment of special classes of agents devoted to access LSAs containing raw sensorial information and of injecting back the results of pattern analysis and classification techniques, can be used to integrate advanced forms of situation-awareness in the overall activities of urban superorganisms.

Third, self-adaptivity and reconfiguration can be promoted not by the capability of individual components, but rather by the overall self-organizing dynamics of the superorganism. In particular, adaptivity is ensured by the fact that any change in the system will reflect in the firing of different coordination laws, thus possibly leading to the establishment of new connectors or in the breaking existing ones. Also, the proposed coordination laws make it possible to realise a wide variety of nature-inspired self-organized coordination patterns, from physically-inspired to chemically- and biologically-inspired ones, within the same infrastructure and with the same basic programming approach.

Fourth, to control emergent behaviours, one can think of deploying in the infrastructure special classes of agents that, by spreading "fake" LSAs that have the only goal of triggering some coordination-laws, eventually affecting the way coordination laws apply to LSAs of other agents [32]. The result could be in an overall adaptation of the behaviour of the superorganism, yet obtained in a fully decentralised way. In a similar way, special classes of agents capable of enforcing control could be used to properly mix the self-organized bottom-up behaviour of the urban superorganism with some forms of top-down behaviour, where such special classes of agents can explicitly encode the high-level goals to be achieved and act in a goal-oriented way.

6   Conclusion and Future Work

Innovative, large-scale, software-intensive services are emerging and dramatically changing the way we move, live, and work, in urban environments. However, to fully develop the superorganism vision we introduced, many research challenges still need to be addressed, and suitable models and infrastructures have to be developed. Nevertheless, we are aware that a number of additional scientific and social challenges – beside those we have identified – will emerge as the first instances of urban superorganisms will hit the ground. As future work, we plan to make use of the presented archicture and its coordination model to experiment with innovative university services within the campuses of our university.

Acknowledgements. Work supported by the ASCENS project (EU FP7-FET, Contract No. 257414).

References

1. Aiello, F., Bellifemine, F., Fortino, G., Galzarano, S., Gravina, R.: An agent-based signal processing in-node environment for real-time human activity monitoring based on wireless body sensor networks. Engineering Applications of Artificial Intelligence 24(7), 1147–1161 (2011)
2. Babaoglu, O., Canright, G., Deutsch, A., Di Caro, G.A., Ducatelle, F., Gambardella, L.M., Ganguly, N., Jelasity, M., Montemanni, R., Montresor, A., Urnes, T.: Design patterns from biology for distributed computing. ACM Transactions on Autonomous and Adaptive Systems 1(1), 26–66 (2006)
3. Bettini, C., Brdiczka, O., Henricksen, K., Indulska, J., Nicklas, D., Ranganathan, A., Riboni, D.: A survey of context modelling and reasoning techniques. Pervasive and Mobile Computing 6(2), 161–180 (2010)
4. Bicocchi, N., Castelli, G., Lasagni, M., Mamei, M., Zambonelli, F.: Experiences on sensor fusion with commonsense reasoning. In: IEEE Workshop on Context Modeling and Reasonings, Lugano, CH (2012)
5. Bonabeau, E., Dorigo, M., Theraulaz, G.: Swarm Intelligence: from Natural to Artificial Systems. Oxford University Press, London (1998)
6. Brambilla, M., Ferrante, E., Birattari, M., Dorigo, M.: Swarm robotics: a review from the swarm engineering perspective. Swarm Intelligence 7(1), 1–41 (2013)

7. Brenna, M., Falvo, M.C., Foiadelli, F., Martirano, L., Massaro, F., Poli, D., Vaccaro, A.: Challenges in energy systems for the smart-cities of the future. In: IEEE International Energy Conference and Exhibition, pp. 755–762 (September 2012)

8. Cheng, B.H.C., et al.: Software Engineering for Self-Adaptive Systems: A Research Roadmap. In: Cheng, B.H.C., de Lemos, R., Giese, H., Inverardi, P., Magee, J. (eds.) Software Engineering for Self-Adaptive Systems. LNCS, vol. 5525, pp. 1–26. Springer, Heidelberg (2009)

9. Chourabi, H., Nam, T., Walker, S., Ramon Gil-Garcia, J., Mellouli, S., Nahon, K., Pardo, T., Scholl, H.: Understanding smart cities: An integrative framework. In: IEEE Hawaii International Conference on System Sciences, Maui (HI), USA (2012)

10. Davies, N., Langheinrich, M., José, R., Schmidt, A.: Open display networks: A communications medium for the 21st century. IEEE Computer 45(5), 58–64 (2012)

11. Fernandez-Marquez, J.L., Di Marzo Serugendo, G., Stevenson, G., Ye, J., Dobson, S., Zambonelli, F.: Self-Managing and Self-Organising Mobile Computing Applications: a Separation of Concerns approach. In: Proceeding of the 29th Symposium on Applied Computing, SAC 2014 (2014)

12. Fortino, G., Li, X., Lin, X., Mayora, O., Natalizio, E., Yuce, M.: Wireless technology for pervasive healthcare. Mobile Networks and Applications 19(3), 273–275 (2014)

13. Harnie, D., D'Hondt, T., Gonzales Boix, E., De Meuter, W.: Programming urban-area applications for mobility services. ACM Transactions on Autonomous and Adaptive Systems 9(2) (2014)

14. Helaoui, R., Riboni, D., Stuckenschmidt, H.: A probabilistic ontological framework for the recognition of multilevel human activities. In: ACM International Joint Conference on Pervasive and Ubiquitous Computing, Zurich, CH (2013)

15. Holldobler, B., Wilson, O.: The Superorganism: the Beauty, Elegance, and Strangeness, of Insect Societies. W. W. Norton and Company, New York (2009)

16. Hu, X., Wang, W., Leung, V.: Vssa: A service-oriented vehicular social-networking platform for transportation efficiency. In: International Symposium on Design and Analysis of Intelligent Vehicular Networks and Applications, New York (NY), USA (2012)

17. Jelasity, M., Montresor, A., Babaoglu, Ö.: Gossip-based aggregation in large dynamic networks. ACM Transactions on Computer Systems 23(3), 219–252 (2005)

18. Jones, A.J.I., Artikis, A., Pitt, J.: The design of intelligent socio-technical systems. Artificil Intelicence Review 39(1), 5–20 (2013)

19. Kehoe, M., et al.: Understanding IBM Smart Cities. Redbook Series, IBM Corporation (2011)

20. Lathia, N., Pejovic, V., Rachuri, K.K., Mascolo, C., Musolesi, M., Rentfrow, P.J.: Smartphones for large-scale behavior change interventions. IEEE Pervasive Computing 12(3), 66–73 (2013)

21. Mamei, M., Menezes, R., Tolksdorf, R., Zambonelli, F.: Case studies for self-organization in computer science. Journal of Systems Architecture 52(8-9), 443–460 (2006)

22. Mamei, M., Roli, A., Zambonelli, F.: Emergence and control of macro-spatial structures in perturbed cellular automata, and implications for pervasive computing systems. IEEE Transactions on Systems, Man, and Cybernetics, Part A 35(3), 337–348 (2005)

23. Mitchell, M.: Self-awareness and control in decentralized systems. In: AAAI Spring Symposium: Meta-cognition in Computation, Palo Alto (CA), USA (2005)

24. Van Parunak, H.D.: Go to the ant: Engineering principles from natural multi-agent systems. Annals of Operations Research 75, 69–101 (1997)

25. Pitt, J., Bourazeri, A., Nowak, A., Roszczynska-Kurasinska, M., Rychwalska, A., Rodriguez Santiago, I., Lopez Sanchez, M., Florea, M., Sanduleac, M.: Transforming big data into collective awareness. Computer 46(6), 40–45 (2013)
26. Pitt, J., Schaumeier, J., Artikis, A.: Axiomatization of socio-economic principles for self-organizing institutions: Concepts, experiments and challenges. ACM Transactions on Autonomous and Adaptive Systems 7(4), 39 (2012)
27. Radu, A.-L., Ionescu, B., Menéndez, M., Stöttinger, J., Giunchiglia, F., De Angeli, A.: A hybrid machine-crowd approach to photo retrieval result diversification. In: Gurrin, C., Hopfgartner, F., Hurst, W., Johansen, H., Lee, H., O'Connor, N. (eds.) MMM 2014, Part I. LNCS, vol. 8325, pp. 25–36. Springer, Heidelberg (2014)
28. Rahwan, I., Dsouza, S., Rutherford, A., Naroditskiy, V., McInerney, J., Venanzi, M., Jennings, N., Cebrian, M.: Global manhunt pushes the limits of social mobilization. IEEE Computer 46(4), 68–75 (2010)
29. Rosi, A., Mamei, M., Zambonelli, F.: Integrating social sensors and pervasive services: approaches and perspectives. Journal of Pervasive Computing and Communications 9(4), 294–310 (2013)
30. Sassi, A., Zambonelli, F.: Towards an agent coordination framework for smart mobility services. In: 8th International workshop on agents in traffic and transportation (May 2014)
31. Scerri, P., Ma, Z., Chien, S.Y., Wang, H., Lee, P.-J., Lewis, M., Sycara, K.P.: An initial evaluation of approaches to building entry for large robot teams. Journal of Intelligent and Robotic Systems 64(2), 145–159 (2011)
32. Scheidler, A., Merkle, D., Middendorf, M.: Swarm controlled emergence for ant clustering. International Journal on Intelligent Computing and Cybernetics 6(1), 62–82 (2013)
33. Wirsing, M., Banâtre, J.-P., Hölzl, M., Rauschmayer, A. (eds.): Soft-Ware Intensive Systems. LNCS, vol. 5380. Springer, Heidelberg (2008)
34. Wirsing, M., Hölzl, M., Tribastone, M., Zambonelli, F.: ASCENS: Engineering Autonomic Service-Component Ensembles. In: Beckert, B., Damiani, F., de Boer, F.S., Bonsangue, M.M. (eds.) FMCO 2011. LNCS, vol. 7542, pp. 1–24. Springer, Heidelberg (2012)
35. Yuen, M., Chen, L., King, I.: A survey of human computation systems. In: International Conference on Computational Science and Engineering, Vancouver, Canada (2009)
36. Zambonelli, F.: Toward sociotechnical urban superorganisms. IEEE Computer 45(8), 76–78 (2012)
37. Zambonelli, F., Castelli, G., Mamei, M., Rosi, A.: Programming self-organizing pervasive applications with SAPERE. In: Zavoral, F., Jung, J.J., Badica, C. (eds.) IDC 2013. SCI, vol. 511, pp. 93–102. Springer, Heidelberg (2013)
38. Zambonelli, F., Viroli, M.: A survey on nature-inspired metaphors for pervasive service ecosystems. Journal of Pervasive Computing and Communications 7, 186–204 (2011)

A White Box Perspective
on Behavioural Adaptation[*]

Roberto Bruni[1], Andrea Corradini[1], Fabio Gadducci[1],
Alberto Lluch Lafuente[2], and Andrea Vandin[3]

[1] Department of Computer Science, University of Pisa, Italy
[2] DTU Compute, Technical University of Denmark, Denmark
[3] Electronics and Computer Science, University of Southampton, UK

Abstract. We present a white-box conceptual framework for adaptation developed in the context of the EU Project ASCENS coordinated by Martin Wirsing. We called it CoDA, for Control Data Adaptation, since it is based on the notion of *control data*. CoDA promotes a neat separation between application and adaptation logic through a clear identification of the set of data that is relevant for the latter. The framework provides an original perspective from which we survey a representative set of approaches to adaptation, ranging from programming languages and paradigms to computational models and architectural solutions.

Keywords: Adaptation, Self-*, Autonomic Computing, Programming Languages, Software Architectures, Computational Models, Computational Reflection.

1 Introduction

Self-adaptive systems have been widely studied in several disciplines like Biology, Engineering, Economy and Sociology. They have become a hot topic in Computer Science in the last decade as a convenient solution to the problem of mastering the complexity of modern software systems, networks and architectures. In particular, self-adaptation is considered a fundamental feature of *autonomic systems*, often realized by specialized self-* mechanisms like self-configuration, self-optimization, self-protection and self-healing, as discussed for example in [43].

The literature includes valuable works aimed at capturing the essentials of adaptation both in the most general sense (see, e.g., [52]) and more specifically fields such as software systems (see, e.g., [72,14,56,5,69]) providing in some cases very rich surveys and taxonomies. A prominent and interesting example is the taxonomy of concepts related to self-adaptation presented in [72], whose authors remark the highly interdisciplinary nature of the studies of such systems. Indeed, just restricting to the realm of Computer Science, active research on self-adaptive systems is carried out in Software Engineering, Artificial Intelligence, Control Theory, and Network and Distributed Computing, among others.

[*] Research supported by the European projects IP 257414 ASCENS and STReP 600708 QUANTICOL, and the Italian project PRIN 2010LHT4KM CINA.

R. De Nicola and R. Hennicker (Eds.): Wirsing Festschrift, LNCS 8950, pp. 552–581, 2015.

Despite all these classification efforts, there is no agreement on the *conceptual* notion of adaptation, neither in general nor for software systems. Lofti Zadeh noticed in [83] that *"it is very difficult—perhaps impossible—to find a way of characterizing in concrete terms the large variety of ways in which adaptive behavior can be realized"*. Zadeh's concerns were conceived in the field of Control Theory but as many authors agree (e.g., [69,72,5,52]), they are valid in Computer Science as well. One reason for Zadeh's lack of hope in a concrete unifying definition of adaptation is the attempt to subsume two aspects under the same hat: the *external* manifestations of adaptive systems, and the *internal* mechanisms by which adaptation is achieved. We shall refer to the first aspect as the *black-box* view on adaptation, and to the second aspect as the *white-box* one.[1]

Actually, in the realm of Software Engineering there are widely spread informal definitions, according to which a software system is called "self-adaptive" if it *"modifies its own behavior in response to changes in its operating environment"* [64], where such "environment" has to be understood in the widest possible way, including both the external environment and the internal state of the system itself. Typically, such changes are applied when the software system realizes that *"it is not accomplishing what the software is intended to do, or better functionality or performance is possible"* [50]. Such definitions can be exploited to measure what is often called the *degree of adaptivity*, i.e., to estimate the system robustness under some conditions. This approach can be traced back to Zadeh's proposal [83], but has been later adopted by many other authors (e.g., [62,41]).

The problem is that almost any software system can be considered self-adaptive according to the above definitions, as it can *modify its behaviour* (e.g., by redirecting the control flow) as a *reaction to a change in its context of execution* (like the change of variables). Thus, such definitions, concerned with the *observational* perspective only, are of difficult applicability for distinguishing adaptive systems from "non-adaptive" ones. Also, they are of little use for design purposes, where separation of concerns, modularization, reuse are crucial aspects.

The development and success of many emergent Computer Science paradigms is often strongly supported by the identification of key principles around which the theoretical aspects can be conveniently investigated and fully worked out. For example, in the case of distributed computing, there have been several efforts in studying the key primitives for communication, including mechanisms for passing communication means (name mobility) or entire processes (code mobility), which led to a widely understood theory of mobile process calculi. There is unfortunately no such agreement concerning (self-)adaptation, as it is not clear what are the characterizing structural features that distinguish such systems from plain ones.

Summarizing: (i) existing definitions of adaptation (and also *adaptivity* and *adaptability*) are not always useful in pinpointing adaptive systems, but they allow to discard many systems that certainly are not, and (ii) their focus is often more on the issue of *how much* a system adapts than *in which manner*.

---

[1] The black- and white-box *perspective* should not be confused with the white- and black-box component adaptation *techniques* as discussed, e.g., in [13], where *black* refers to exploiting the interface of a component and *white* to exploiting its internals.

Contributions and Structure. The paper presents a conceptual framework for adaptation by means of a simple structural criterion. This framework, introduced in Section 2, is called CoDa, Control Data Adaptation. Our contribution is a definition of adaptation that is applicable to most approaches in the literature, and in fact it is often coincident with them once it is instantiated to each approach. Also, we aim at a *separation of concerns* to distinguish changes of behaviour that are part of the application logic from those where they realize the adaptation logic, calling "adaptive" only those systems capable of the latter. More precisely, we propose concrete answers to basic questions like *"is a software system adaptive?"* or *"where is the adaptation logic in an adaptive system?"*. We take a *white-box* perspective that allows us to inspect, to some extent, the internal structure of a system. Moreover, we provide the designer with a criterion to specify where adaptation is located and, as a consequence, which parts of a system have to be adapted, by whom and how. Note that while adaptation can be concerned with a single component as well as with a whole system, we will not push this distinction and will address both situations in the paper: each time the case under consideration will be evident by the context.

The second part of the paper (Sections 3–5) is devoted to a *proof of concept*: we overview several approaches to adaptation and validate how the CoDa definition of adaptation is applied to them. This part of the paper is organized according to different pillars of Computer Science: *architectural* approaches (Section 3), *foundational* models (Section 4), and *programming* paradigms (Section 5). Approaches that cover more than one of such aspects are discussed only once.

It is worth remarking that it is not the programming paradigm, the architecture or the underlying foundational model what makes a system adaptive or not. For example, adaptive systems can be programmed in any language, exactly like object-oriented systems can in imperative languages, albeit with some effort. However, it is beyond the scope of this paper to discuss approaches that do not address adaptation in an explicit way, even if they might do so implicitly.

Section 6 overviews other surveys and taxonomies that address the same aim of our work. Finally, Section 7 concludes the paper and discusses future research.

Our work would not be the same without the support and insights from Martin Wirsing. It was indeed conceived in early meetings of the ASCENS project, coordinated by Martin. The main questions under discussion were the meaning of adaptation and its formalization. We presented some preliminary ideas essentially based on the use of logical reflection in algebraic specifications. Though sharing our passion for such disciplines and understanding our points, Martin warned us about the difficulties of meta-programming techniques and encouraged us to consider other approaches, including those proposed by other teams of the project. This lead us to investigate the essence of adaptation, and resulted first in the shorter, less inclusive version of this paper appeared as [21], and ultimately in the present work. We would like to express infinite gratitude to Martin, for his tenacious guidance, his calm patience and his pointed intuitions during all these beautiful years of fruitful research collaborations.

2   When Is a Software Component Adaptive?

The behavior of a software component is governed by a program, and, according to the traditional view (e.g., [82]), a program is made of *control* (i.e., algorithms) and *data*. This basic view of programs is sufficient for the sake of introducing our approach. CoDA requires to make explicit that the behaviour of a component depends on some *control data* that can be changed to *adapt* it. At this level of abstraction we are not concerned with the structure of control data, the way they influence the behaviour of the component, or the causes of their modification.

Our definition of adaptation is then very straight: *Given a component with a distinguished collection of control data, adaptation is the runtime modification of such control data.* From this definition we can easily derive several others. A component is *adaptable* if its control data may be modified at runtime, it is *adaptive* if its control data are actually modified at runtime in some execution, and it is *self-adaptive* if it modifies its own control data at runtime.

The CoDA point of view is in line with other white-box perspectives on adaptation as we discuss in Section 6. Our goal is to show that the conceptual view of CoDA enjoys two key properties: concreteness and generality.

Concreteness. Any definition of adaptation should face the problem that the judgement whether a system is adaptive or not is often subjective. From the CoDA perspective, this is captured by the fact that the collection of control data of a component can be defined, at least in principle, in an arbitrary way, ranging from the empty set ("the system is not adaptable") to the collection of all the data of the program ("any data modification is an adaptation"). As a concrete example, consider the following conditional statement:

if the_hill_is_too_steep then assemble_with_others else proceed_alone

Can it be interpreted as a form of adaptation? From a black-box perspective the answer is "it depends". Indeed, the above statement is typical of controllers for robots operating collectively as swarms and having to face environments with obstacles (see, e.g., [63]). As some authors observe [39] *"obstacle avoidance may count as adaptive behaviour if [...] obstacles appear rarely. [...] If the "normal" environment is [...] obstacle-rich, then avoidance becomes [...] normal behaviour rather than an adaptation".* In sum, the above conditional statement can be a form of adaptation in some contexts but not in others.

Now, suppose that the statement is part of the software controlling a robot, and that the_hill_is_too_steep is a boolean variable set according to the value returned by a sensor. Then, in our framework the change of behaviour caused by a modification of its value is considered as an adaptation or not depending on if the_hill_is_too_steep is considered as part of the control data or not.

Such a boolean variable is not in itself a datum obtained by a sensor: it is controlled by an adaptation logic that changes its value when a given threshold is reached in the information received by the sensors: thus, control data do not by necessity coincide with sensor data. In more general terms, the difference is going to be made explicit e.g. when we will instantiate our CoDA approach in the context of computational models that support meta-programming or reflective features, where a program-as-data paradigm holds: the issue is tackled in Section 4.2 and in the summary of forms assumed by control data in Fig. 1.

Summing up, the above question (*"can it be interpreted as a form of adaptation?"*) can be answered only after the identification of the control data. Thus, from the white-box perspective of CoDa the answer is still "it depends". With a fundamental difference: the responsibility of declaring which behaviours are part of the adaptation logic is passed from the observer to the designer. Ideally, a sensible collection of control data should enforce a separation of concerns, allowing to distinguish neatly the activities relevant to adaptation (those affecting the control data) from those relevant to the application logic only.

Generality. Any definition of adaptation should be general enough to capture the essence of the most relevant approaches to adaptation proposed in the literature. The generality of CoDa is witnessed by the discussion of Sections 3–5 where we overview several approaches to adaptation, pointing out for each of them what we consider the natural candidates for control data. More explicitly, the criterion that we shall use for determining such data is the following: *a system designed according to one of such approaches manifests an adaptation exactly when the corresponding control data are modified.*

Adaptive systems are realized by resorting to a variety of computational models and programming paradigms. The nature of control data can thus vary considerably: from simple configuration parameters to a complete representation of the program in execution that can be modified at runtime.

The variety of formalisms makes it hard to compare approaches with each other, unless one manages to map them into a unifying model of computation (which is far beyond the scope of this paper). However, for the sake of a brief discussion we enrich our intuitive view of a system as made of control, control data and ordinary data, with additional features such as the system's *architecture* (in a general sense, including the interconnection of components, communication stacks, workflows, etc.), and the *adaptation strategy* used to enact adaptation. Moreover we shall assume that the behavior of the system or component (i.e., its control) may be structured into sub-parts that we call *operation modes*.

Such simple perspective on adaptive systems helps us in classifying the main approaches surveyed in this paper as depicted in Figure 1. Symbol "*" is used to denote generic approaches that propose reference models where control data depends on concrete instances of the approach. The table also contains the control data as-it-is and the section where the approach is discussed.

Such classification has several advantages: (i) It provides a criterion that is orthogonal to those of the surveys and taxonomies discussed in Section 6 and to the classification by research areas along which we structure Sections 3–5. (ii) It allows to relate approaches presented independently and in different areas but sharing, essentially, the same category of control data. This is the case of the approaches based on modes of operation proposed by the Software Engineering community with paradigm-oriented approaches and by the Theoretical Computer Science community with automata and process-algebraic ones. (iii) It allows to

	CONTROL DATA (as-it-is)	CONTROL DATA (class)	Section
[42]	*	*	3.1
[25]	*	*	3.1
[81]	*	*	3.1
[45]	*	*	3.2
[66]	*	*	4.3
[11]	adaptation coordination strategies	adaptation strategy	4.1
[51]	adaptation rules	adaptation strategy	5.3
[16]	architecture	architecture	3.1
[49]	architecture	architecture	3.2
[64]	architecture	architecture	3.2
[70]	module stack	architecture	3.2
[23]	current workflow	architecture	3.2
[7]	connectors	architecture	3.2
[11]	architecture	architecture	4.1
[80]	effector channel	architecture	4.3
[51]	set of activities	architecture	5.3
[65]	entire programs	entire program	4.1
[59]	rewrite rules	entire program	4.2
[37]	processes	entire program	4.3
[32]	processes	entire program	4.3
[30]	features	operation mode	4.1
[57]	regions	operation mode	4.1
[87]	operation mode	operation mode	4.1
[1]	active configuration	operation mode	4.1
[76]	active configuration	operation mode	4.1
[20]	control proposition	operation mode	4.1
[86]	steady state programs	operation mode	4.1
[44]	state space zones	operation mode	4.1
[35]	graph rewrite rules	operation mode	4.2
[84]	base level Petri net	operation mode	4.3
[55]	adaptor processes	operation mode	4.3
[17]	adaptable (local) processes	operation mode	4.3
[73]	context stack	operation mode	5.1
[38]	advices	operation mode	5.2
[46]	policies	operation mode	5.3

Fig. 1. Summary of some of the control data forms discussed

compare approaches apparently similar (and falling in the same section) but based on different categories of control data. In some process-algebraic approaches the control data may e.g. reside in the communication topology or in the entire program. The classification depends on the envisioned conceptual computational formalisms where we map the approaches. We propose a simple one to illustrate a way of exploiting the notion of control data for comparison purposes.

3   Architectural Approaches to Adaptation

Several contributions to the literature describe architectural approaches to autonomic computing and self-adaptive software systems. In this section we survey some of such proposals, organizing the discussion around two main themes: reference models (Section 3.1) and reconfiguration-based approaches (Section 3.2).

3.1 Reference Models for Adaptation

In this section we review two influential reference models for adaptive systems: MAPE-K [42] and FORMS [81]. Both approaches propose general guidelines for the architecture of (self-)adaptive systems, the first one based on the presence of a control loop, the second one on the use of computational reflection. The identification of control data at this level of abstraction can only be generic, as concrete instances may realize the reference models in different ways.

The first reference model we consider is MAPE-K (Monitor, Analyse, Plan, Execute, Knowledge), introduced in the seminal [42]. A self-adaptive system is made of a component implementing the application logic, equipped with a control loop that monitors the execution through suitable sensors, analyses the collected data, plans an adaptation strategy, and finally executes the adaptation of the managed component through some effectors; all the phases of the control loop access a shared knowledge repository. The managed component is considered to be an adaptable component, and the system made of the component and the manager implementing the control loop is considered a self-adaptive component.

The conceptual role of the control loop in-duces a natural choice for the control data: while in the monitor phase a wide range of data from the managed component may be sensed, the control data are those that are modified by the execute phase of the control loop. Thus the control data of a managed component is (explicitly or implicitly) available via the interface it offers to its manager, which can use it to enact its control loop, as shown in Fig. 2. Clearly, the concrete structure of control data (e.g., variables, policies, ...) de-pends on the specific instance of the MAPE-K

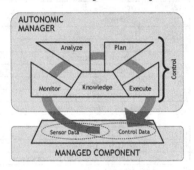

Fig. 2. Control data in MAPE-K

model and on the computational model or programming language used, as discussed in the next two sections. The construction can be iterated, as the manager itself can be an adaptable component.

Concrete instances of this scenario can be found, among others, in [11,51,24]. For example, in the latter, components follow plans to perform their tasks and re-planning is used to overcome unpredicted situations that may make current plans inefficient or impossible to realize. A component in this scenario can be adaptable, having a manager which devises new plans according to changes in the context or in the component's goals. In turn, this planning component might itself be adaptable, with another component that controls and adapts its planning strategy, e.g., on the basis of a tradeoff between optimality of the plans and computational cost of the

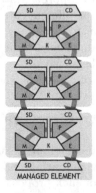

Fig. 3. Tower of adaptation

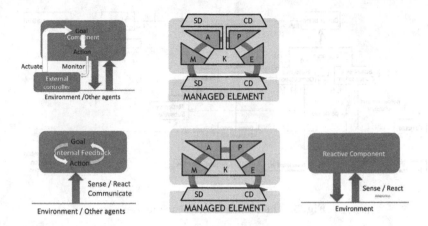

Fig. 4. External (top-left) and internal (bottom-left) control loop patterns and their presentation in terms of the MAPE-K model (center), and the reactive pattern (right)

planning algorithms. In this case, the planning component (that realizes the control loop of the base component) exposes some control data (conceptually part of its knowledge), thus enabling a hierarchical composition that allows building towers of adaptive components (Fig. 3).

The MAPE-K control loop is very influential in the autonomic computing community, but control loops in general have been proposed and extensively studied also by others as a key mechanism for achieving self-adaptation in software systems, also on the basis of the crucial role they play in engineering disciplines like Control Theory. An interesting survey of several types of control loops is presented in [19], which among others identifies the *Model Reference Adaptive Control loop*, where the control loop is fed with a model of the controlled component, and the *Model Identification Adaptive Control loop*, where the control loop tries to infer such a model directly from the behaviour of the component.

Typical control loop patterns are also proposed in [25], which presents a taxonomy of design patterns for adaptation (see Fig. 4). In the *internal control loop* pattern, the manager is a wrapper for the managed component and it is not adaptable. Instead, in the *external control loop* pattern, the manager is an adaptable component that is connected with the managed component. The distinction between external and internal control loops is also discussed in [72], where it is stressed that internal control loops offer poor scalability and maintainability due to the intertwining of the application and the adaptation logic. Indeed this contradicts the separation-of-concerns principle that the authors (and many others) promote as key feature of self-adaptive systems. Like for MAPE-K, also for these control-loop centered approaches to adaptivity a precise identification of control data is only possible in concrete instances.

The taxonomy of [25] includes a third pattern called *reactive pattern* that describes *reactive* components capable of modifying their behavior in reaction to an external event, without any control loop (or, equivalently, with a degenerate, "empty" control loop). In order to apply our definition of adaptation as

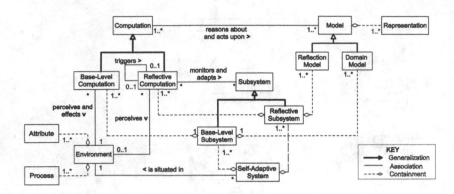

Fig. 5. The FORMS reference model

runtime modification of control data to a reactive system of this kind, one could simply identify as control data those data that, when modified by sensing the environment, cause an adaptation of the system. This is a good example of the generality of our definition of adaptation, which is applicable also to such quite extreme case.

The reference model in [6] promotes *computational reflection* as a necessary criterion for any self-adaptive software system. Reflection implies the presence, besides of base-level components and computations, of meta-level subsystems and meta-computations that act on a meta-model. Meta-computations inspect and modify the meta-model that is causally connected to the base-level system, so that changes in one are reflected in the other. The authors argue that most methodologies and frameworks for the design and development of self-adaptive systems rely on some form of reflection, even if not explicitly. Building on these considerations, they introduce the FOrmal Reference Model for Self-adaptation (FORMS) [81], providing basic modeling primitives, and relationships among them, for the design of self-adaptive systems (cf. Fig. 5), and making explicit the presence of reflective (meta-level) subsystems, computations and models.

The goals of [6] are not dissimilar from ours, as they try to capture the essence of self-adaptive systems, identifying it in computational reflection (one of the key features of self-adaptive systems according to [56] as well). The FORMS modeling primitives can be instantiated and composed in a variety of ways. For example, [81] provides one example that conforms to the MAPE-K reference model and another one that follows an application-specific design.

A precise identification of control data depends on the specific instance of the approach, and more precisely on the way modifications to the meta-level affect the base level, causing an adaptation. In instances featuring some kind of hot-linking from the meta- to the base-level component, the meta-level itself can be considered as control data. Otherwise, in general, control data will be identified at the boundary between the meta-level and the base-level components.

3.2   Reconfiguration-Based Approaches to Adaptation

Several approaches to the design of (self-)adaptive systems look at a system as a network of components, suitably arranged in a logical or physical topology that constraints the interactions or communications among components. Adaptations in this context are typically realized via *reconfigurations*, which can range from the replacement of a single component to local or even global changes to the interaction topology. Usually such reconfigurations do not modify the functionalities of the individual components, but only the way they are connected and/or interact with each other (see the survey [16], summarized in Section 6, and [49]). Therefore the control data in these approaches can be identified with the interconnection topology itself, which depending on the approaches can be made of channels, connectors, gates, protocol stacks, links, and so on.

A first example is the approach presented in [64], where dynamic software architecture has a dominant role. The proposed methodology combines an Adaptation Management loop, which is essentially a distributed, agent-based MAPE-K control loop, with an Evolution Management loop. In the latter, an architectural model is maintained at runtime, that describes the running implementation and that plays the role of our control data. In fact the architectural model, made of components and connectors, can be modified by the control loop, by adding or removing components or connectors or by changing the topology. An Architecture Evolution Manger mediates the changes of the architectural model and maintains the consistency between the model and the running implementation.

The Ensemble system [70] is a network protocol architecture conceived with the aim of facilitating the development of adaptive distributed applications. The main idea is that each component of the application relies on a reconfigurable stack made of simple micro-protocol modules, which implement different component-to-component communication features. The module stack imposes a layered structure to the communication infrastructure which is used to guide its adaptation. Adaptation can e.g. be triggered in a bottom-up way, when a layer n discovers some environmental changes that require an adaptation. Then the module at layer n may be adapted and, if not possible, the adaptation request is propagated to the upper layer $n + 1$. Such structure is also exploited when a coordinated, distributed adaptation is needed, which is tackled by the *Protocol Switching Protocol*, one the key features of the approach. The protocol is initiated by a global coordinator that sends the notification of the need of adaptation to each component. Within each component the notification is propagated through the protocol stack, so that each layer applies the necessary actions. Adaptation can happen at different points. In particular it may affect the components participating to the distributed application (or to groups within it) or the communication infrastructure (i.e., the module stack). Hence, generally speaking, the set of components, their state and the module stack form the control data of the adaptive application.

The authors of [45] discuss how to apply this model-based approach to Model-Integrated Computing to adaptive systems. Adaptation is mainly reconfiguration followed by automatic deployment, triggered at runtime by the user or by the system as a reaction to some events. In the proposed case study, a simple finite-state automaton determines the transitions from one behaviour to another: here, the natural choice of control data consists of the states of the automaton.

A life-cycle for service-based applications where adaptation is a first-class concern is defined in [23]. Such life-cycle continues during runtime to cope with dynamic requirements and the corresponding adaptations. In addition to the life-cycle, [23] focuses on the identification of a number of design principles and guidelines that are suitable for adaptable applications. Essentially, adaptation is understood as the modification of the workflow implementing a service-based application, from substituting individual services by equivalent ones, to recomposing a piece of the workflow to obtain an equivalent result. Therefore, roughly speaking, the current workflow is the control data of the service-based applications.

In the architectural approach of [7] a system specification has a two-layered architecture to enforce a separation between computation and coordination. The first layer includes the basic computational components and their interfaces, while the second one is made of connectors (called *coordination contracts*) that link the components to ensure the required system's functionalities. Adaptation in this context is obtained by reconfiguration, which consists of removal, addition or replacement of both base components and connectors among them. The possible reconfigurations of a system are described declaratively with suitable rules, grouped in *coordination contexts*: such rules can be either invoked explicitly, or triggered automatically when certain conditions are satisfied. In this approach, as adaptation is reconfiguration, the control data consist of the whole two-layered architecture, excluding the internal state of the computational components.

4   Computational Models for Adaptation

Computational reflection is widely accepted as one of the key instruments to build self-adaptive systems (cf. [56,33]). Indeed computational paradigms equipped with reflective, meta-level or higher-order features, allow one to represent programs as first-class citizens. In these cases adaptation emerges, according to our definitions, if the program in execution is represented in the control data of the system, and it is modified during execution. Prominent examples of such formalisms are, e.g., rewrite theories with logical reflection like rewriting logic [58] or process calculi with higher-order or meta-level aspects like HO π-calculus [75]. Systems represented within these paradigms can realize self-adaptation in a straightforward manner. Of course, computational reflection assumes different forms and, despite of being a very convenient mechanism, it is not strictly necessary: as we argued in Section 1 any programming language can be used to build a self-adaptive system.

We outline now some rules of thumb for the choice of control data within some well-known computational formalisms (deferring programming paradigms and languages to Section 5). In doing so, we restrict the attention to computational models that have been purposely introduced to represent adaptation and we point out how they can be used for modeling the behavior of self-adaptive systems. In addition, we survey a representative set of models that have been conceived with the purpose of modeling self-adaptive systems and supporting their formal analysis. We structure the presentation along three strands: automata-like computational models (Section 4.1), declarative, rule-based computational models (Section 4.2), and computational models from concurrency theory (Section 4.3).

4.1 Automata-Based Approaches to Adaptation

In many frameworks for the design of adaptive systems the base-level system has a fixed collection of possible behaviours (or behavioural models), and adaptation consists of passing from one behaviour to another. Some of the approaches discussed in this section achieve this by relying on a multi-layered structure reminiscent of hierarchical state machines and automata.

A first example of this tradition are the Adaptive Featured Transition Systems (A-FTS) of [30], which were introduced for the purpose of model checking adaptive software (with a focus on software product lines). A-FTSs are a sort of transition systems where states are composed by the local state of the system, its configuration (set of *active features*) and the configuration of the environment. Transitions are decorated with executability conditions that regard the valid configurations. Adaptation corresponds to reconfigurations (changing the system features). Hence, in terms of our white-box approach, reconfigurable system features play the role of control data. The authors introduce the notion of *resilience* as the ability of the system to satisfy properties despite of environmental changes (which essentially coincides with the notion of black-box adaptivity of [41]). Properties are expressed in AdaCTL, a variant of the computation-tree temporal logic CTL.

Another example of layered computational structures are S[B] systems [57], a model for adaptive systems based on 2-layered transitions systems. The base transition system B defines the ordinary behavior of the system, while S is the adaptation manager, which imposes some regions (subsets of states) and transitions between them (adaptations). Further constraints are imposed by S via adaptation invariants. Adaptations are triggered to change *region* (in case of local deadlock). Such regions, hence, form the control data of the system according to our white-box approach. The paper also formalizes notions of *weak* and *strong* adaptability, defined as the ability to conclude a triggered adaptation in some or all possible behaviors, respectively, and characterized by suitable CTL formulae.

Mode automata [53] have been also advocated as a suitable model for adaptive systems. For example, the approach of [87] represents adaptive systems with two layers: a *functional layer*, which implements the application logic and is represented by state machines called *adaptable automata*, and an *adaptation layer* that implements the adaptation logic and is represented with a mode automaton. Adaptation here is the change of mode, and these are the control data of this approach. The approach considers three kinds of specification properties: *local* (to be satisfied by the functional behavior of one particular mode, not involving adaptation), *adaptation* (to be satisfied by adaptation phases, i.e., transitions between modes), and *global* (to be satisfied by all behaviors). An extension of linear-time temporal logic (LTL) called $mLTL$ is used to express such properties.

Overlap adaptations [11] arise in long-running open and dynamic distributed applications where components can be removed, added or replaced with a certain frequency. Under these premises, it is clear that the set of components of the application corresponds to its control data. An overlap adaptation occurs when the execution of *old* components (i.e., components that need to be adapted) overlaps with the execution of *new* components (i.e., adapted components). This overlap introduces non-trivial issues but is required in order to adapt the whole application in a distributed manner without stopping it.

The authors identify several kinds of overlap adaptations which vary in the kind of allowed interactions between old and new components. The main concern of the approach is verifying the correctness of adaptations. For this purpose the approach relies on the concept of *transitional adaptation lattices*, roughly, diamond-shaped graphs whose nodes are automata and whose transitions correspond to atomic adaptation actions (cf. Fig. 6). Each automaton represents the behavior of the whole system in some state. The *top* automaton corresponds to the system before adaptation starts, while the *bottom* automaton corresponds to the system when adaptation ends. The diamond shape of the lattice implicitly imposes a confluent behavior of individual atomic adaptations.

Actually, the approach considers a finer granularity of components in terms of *fractions*, which are essentially the local instances of components in process locations, introducing a combinatorial explosion in the size of the lattices which has a negative impact in the effort required in their analysis. To mitigate this the authors propose a framework based on particular architectures and coordination protocols, where some specialized modules drive the adaptation phase through designated paths in the adaptation lattices. This implicitly introduces a higher-level adaptation since a system may vary the strategy of such modules according to various factors: the control data of the system correspond to such strategies.

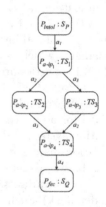

Fig. 6. Adaptation lattice

Another example of labelled transition system variant used for modeling self-adaptive systems are the *Synchronous Adaptive Systems* of MARS [1,76], where systems are modeled as sets of modules, each having a set of configurations. At runtime only one configuration is active. Adaptation consists on changing the active configuration, selected according to the configuration and environment status. Control data are thus those that determine the active configuration.

While the "programs-of-programs" spirit can raise scalability and complexity issues, the layered structure of some of the above models can be exploited to study adaptive systems compositionally. The authors of [86] propose a technique to verify properties of adaptive systems in a modular way. Adaptive programs are modeled with *n-plex adaptive programs* which are essentially sets of finite state machines, some of which representing *steady state programs* [4] and the rest representing adaptation transitions between those programs. The structure of an n-plex adaptive program makes explicit the separation of functional concerns (realized by steady state programs) and adaptation concerns (realized by adaptation transitions), which is exploited to reason about such systems in a modular way. Clearly, the separation of concerns coincides with the spirit of CoDA. In particular, control data here are the individual steady state programs.

This separation of concerns has its counterpart in the property specification language used, *Adapt-operator extended LTL* (A-LTL) [85]. A-LTL extends LTL with an operator that does not provide more expressive power but allows to express properties of adaptive systems more concisely. The modular verification phase exploits the separation of concerns and the assume/guarantee paradigm in order to avoid the state explosion problem, thus providing a more scalable solution. This allows the authors to tackle e.g. *transitional* properties of adaptation (graceful adaptation, hot-swapping adaptation, etc.) in an efficient manner.

Structuring the behavior of adaptive system is a major concern in [44]. The authors identify four main modes of operation (called *state space zones*) in an adaptive system: the *normal* behavior zone (the system operates as expected), the *undesired* behavior zone (the system has violated some constraint and needs to be adapted), the *invalid* behavior zone (the system has violated some constraint and cannot be adapted), and the *adaptation* behavior zone (the system is adapting to re-enter the normal behavior zone). The work is motivated by the necessity of shifting the focus to behavioral aspects of adaptation, as evidenced in previous experiences of the authors that were mainly concerned with architectural aspects [81]. In this approach, hence, the control data are those used to characterize the state space zones. The approach is validated with a case study of a decentralized adaptive traffic control system using timed automata and a timed extension of CTL. The authors distinguish two different adaptation capabilities (from the black-box perspective): *flexibility* (ability to adapt to changing environments, e.g., in order to improve performance) and *robustness* (ability to recover from failures).

Some of the above approaches rely on logical reasoning mechanisms to prove properties of adaptation. To this end, base steady programs are annotated with the properties they ensure (cf. the above discussed adaptation lattices [11]). This idea of specification-carrying programs is investigated in [65]. Suitable semantical domains aimed at capturing the essence of adaptation are identified. The behaviour of a system is formalized in terms of a category of specification-carrying programs (also called *contracts*), i.e., triples made of a program, a specification and a satisfaction relation among them; arrows between contracts are refinement relations. Contracts are equipped with a functorial semantics, and their adaptive version is obtained by indexing the semantics with respect to a set of *stages of adaptation*, yielding a coalgebraic presentation potentially useful for further generalizations. An adaptation is a transformation of a specification-carrying-program into another one, satisfying some properties. Therefore, the control data includes the entire program being executed.

Different in spirit is our proposal in [20] where we studied the consequences of making a particular choice of control data in Interface Automata [3], a foundational model of component-based systems. For this purpose we introduced Adaptable Transition Systems and their instantiation to Adaptable Interface Automata (AIA), an essential model of adaptive systems inspired by our white-box approach. The key feature of AIAs are control propositions, the formal counterpart of control data. The choice of such propositions is arbitrary, but it imposes a clear separation between ordinary behaviors and adaptive ones.

4.2 Rule-Based Models for Adaptation

Rule-based programming is an excellent example of a successful and widely adopted declarative paradigm, thanks to the solid foundations offered by rule-based theoretical frameworks like term and graph rewriting. As many other programming paradigms, several rule-based approaches have been tailored or directly applied to adaptive systems (e.g., graph transformation [35]). Typical solutions include dividing the set of rules into those that correspond to ordinary computations and those that implement adaptation mechanisms, or introducing context-dependent conditions in the rule applications (which essentially corresponds to the use of standard configuration variables). The control data are identified by the above mentioned separation of rules in the first case, and they correspond to the context-dependent conditions in the latter.

The situation is different when we consider rule-based approaches which enjoy higher-order or reflection mechanisms. A good example is *logical reflection*, a key feature of frameworks like rewriting logic [58]. At the ground level, a rewrite theory $\mathcal{R}$ (e.g., a software module) lets us infer a computation step $\mathcal{R} \vdash t \to t'$ from a term (e.g., a program state) t into t'. A universal theory $\mathcal{U}$ lets us infer the computation at the "meta-level", where theories and terms are meta-represented as terms: the above computation step can be expressed in $\mathcal{U}$ as $\mathcal{U} \vdash (\overline{\mathcal{R}}, \overline{t}) \to (\overline{\mathcal{R}}, \overline{t'})$; moreover, the rewrite theory $\mathcal{R}$ can be also rewritten by meta-level rewrite rules, like in $\mathcal{U} \vdash (\overline{\mathcal{R}}, \overline{t}) \to (\overline{\mathcal{R'}}, \overline{t'})$. Since $\mathcal{U}$ itself is a rewrite theory, the reflection mechanism can be iterated yielding what is called the *tower of reflection*, where not only terms $\overline{t}$, but also rewrite rules of the lower level can be accessed and modified at runtime. This mechanism is efficiently supported by Maude [28] and has given rise to many interesting meta-programming applications.

In particular, rewriting logic's reflection has been exploited in [59] to formalize a model for distributed object reflection, suitable for the specification of adaptive systems. Such model, called Reflective Russian Dolls (RRD), has a structure of layered configurations of objects, where each layer can control the execution of objects in the lower layer by accessing and

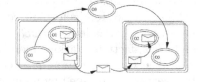

Fig. 7. RRD

executing their rules, possibly after modifying them, e.g., by injecting some specific adaptation logic in the wrapped components (cf. Fig. 7). The RRD model falls within our conceptual framework by identifying as control data for each layer the rules of its theory that are possibly modified by the upper layer. Note that, while the tower of reflection relies on a white-box architecture, the Russian Dolls approach can deal equally well with black-box components, because wrapped configurations can be managed by message passing. RRD has been further exploited for modeling policy-based coordination [77], for the design of PAGODA, a modular architecture for specifying autonomous systems [78], in the composite actors used in [34], and, by ourselves, in the design and analysis of self-assembly strategies for robot swarms [22].

4.3 Concurrency Models for Adaptation

Languages and models conceived in the area of concurrency theory are also good candidates for the specification and analysis of self-adaptive systems. We inspect some paradigmatic formalisms to see how the conceptual framework can help us in the identification of the adaptation logic within each model.

Petri nets are the most popular model of concurrency, based on a set of repositories (places), and a set of activities (transitions). The state of a Petri net is called a marking: a distribution of resources, called tokens, among the places of the net. A transition is an atomic action that consumes several tokens and produces fresh ones, possibly involving several repositories at once. In *coloured* Petri nets, tokens represent structured data and transitions can manipulate them.

The approach in [84] emphasizes the use of Petri nets to validate the development of adaptive systems. It represents the local behavioural models with coloured Petri nets, and the adaptation change from one local model to another with an additional Petri net transition labeled **adapt** (cf. Fig. 8). Such **adapt** transitions describe how to transform a state in the source Petri net into a state in the target one, thus providing a clean solution to the *state transfer problem* (i.e., the problem to consistently transfer the state of the system before and after the adaptation) common to these approaches. In this context, a natural choice of control data would be the Petri net that describes the current base-level computation, which is replaced during an adaptation.

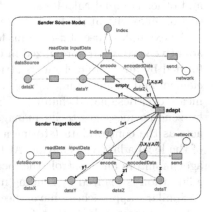

Fig. 8. Adaptive system's Petri net

Petri nets are used in [66] to formalize multi-layer adaptation in large scale applications spanning over heterogeneous organizations and technologies. Here the multi-layered architecture is motivated by the presence of different languages and technologies addressing their own concerns and views within the same application in a coherent manner and multi-layered adaptation must ensure that coherence between views is always maintained. For example, a three-layers architecture is typical of service-based applications: one layer for service specification (e.g., WSDL); one for behavior description (e.g., BPEL); and one for the organizational view that specifies the stakeholders involved in the business process.

Multi-layer adaptation is triggered by *adaptation events* that are raised by human stakeholders or by layer-specific monitors that discover, e.g., message-ordering mismatches (at the behavior level), or invocation mismatches (at the service layer). Application mismatches are organized along tree-based taxonomies that are put in correspondence with suitable adaptation templates. The main idea is that adaptation techniques that can tackle one application mismatch m can also be used to adapt mismatches that are "below" m in the taxonomy. Cross-layer adaptation is achieved by linking templates at different application layers: templates may trigger the executions of other templates both through direct invocation or by raising other adaptation events. Adaptation templates, the taxonomy navigation and the template-selection environment are modeled as Petri nets (they support the search of the templates starting from the more specific to the more general, w.r.t. the raised adaptation event). As the emphasis is the specification of a generic adaptation model for pervasive applications, the Petri net abstracts away from the execution of multi-layered applications and thus the identification of control data is only possible for concrete instances.

Classical process algebras (CCS, CSP, ACP) are tailored to the modeling of reactive systems and therefore their processes easily fall under the hat of the reactive pattern of adaptation. Instead, characterizing the control data and the adaptation logic is more difficult in this setting. The π-calculus, the join calculus and other nominal calculi can send and receive channels names, realizing some sort of reflexivity at the level of interaction: they transmit communication media.

An example of use of π-calculus for modeling autonomic systems is [80]. There, adaptive systems are organized in two-levels, local and global. The local level is formed by autonomic elements structured in the MAPE-K spirit as a managed element and an autonomic manager, defined by π-calculus processes that communicate over designated channels. The effector process enacts adaptation requests by sending messages to its managed element over the effector channel, which acts as the control data (storing a message in the channel triggers adaptation) of the local adaptive behavior. At the global level a centralized autonomic manager monitors and controls the locally distributed autonomic managers. Again, adaptation is realized by sending messages through suitable effector channels.

Similar approaches have been explored within process calculi that feature primitives adequate to model autonomic systems, including explicit locality aspects and code mobility. A paradigmatic example is KLAIM [31], which has been studied as a convenient language for modeling self-adaptive systems in [37]. The authors describe how to adopt in KLAIM three paradigms for adaptation: two that focus on

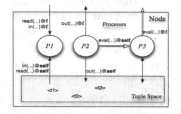

Fig. 9. A KLAIM node

the language-level, namely, context-oriented and aspect-oriented programming (cf. Sections 5.1 and 5.2, respectively), and one on the architectural-level (MAPE-K).

The main idea is to rely on *process tuples,* that is, tuples (the equivalent of messages in the tuple-space paradigm) that denote entire processes. Process tuples are sent by manager components (locations in KLAIM) to managed components, which can then install them via the *eval* primitive of KLAIM (cf. Fig. 9), i.e., adaptation is achieved by means of code mobility and code injection. The control data in this case amounts to the set of active processes in each location.

Stemming from this approach, the Service Component Ensemble Language (SCEL) has been proposed in [32] which realizes adaptation by combining different paradigms, i.e., policy-based programming (discussed in Section 5.3), tuple-space communication, and knowledge-based reasoning. In this case control data are spread among the policy rules, the process tuples and the knowledge facts.

In [55] the authors present a lightweight approach to service adaptation based on process algebraic techniques. As in [15], adaptation is achieved by the design-time synthesis of service adaptors that act as mediators for the communication between two services and allow to overcome signature and behaviour mismatches between their contracts. Differently from [15], an adaptor process is deployed that is itself adaptive, in the sense that its behaviour is initially distilled on the basis of adaptation contracts and then the adaptor is progressively refined at run-time exploiting the collected information about interaction failures. This is useful when service behavior may evolve at runtime due to changes of the environmental conditions in ways not foreseeable in the contract, e.g., depending on the current load of its server. The approach is lightweight because it introduces low overhead. Learning adaptors have been implemented and included in the Integrated Toolbox for Automatic Composition and Adaptation (ITACA) [26]. The control data of the approach are the adaptors themselves.

We conclude this section by mentioning the approach in [17], where the concept of *adaptable process* has been put forward to model dynamic process evolution patterns in process algebras. Adaptable processes are assigned a location and can be updated at runtime by executing an update prefix related to that location. Roughly, if P is an adaptable process running at location a, written $a[P]$, and U is a process context, called *update pattern,* then the execution of the update prefix $\tilde{a}\{U\}$ stops the execution of P within a (i.e., $a[P]$ is removed) and replaces it with $U(P)$. Note that location a is not necessarily preserved by the update, providing flexibility on the allowed update capabilities. For example, the prefix $\tilde{a}\{nil\}$ would just remove $a[P]$; the prefix $\tilde{a}\{a[Q]\}$ would replace $a[P]$ by $a[Q]$; the prefix $\tilde{a}\{b[\cdot]\}$ would move P from location a to the location b; and the prefix $\tilde{a}\{a[\cdot|\cdot]\}$ would spawn an extra copy of P within a. The authors exploit the formal model to study undecidability issues of two verification problems, called *bounded* and *eventual adaptation,* i.e., that there is a bound to the number of erroneous states that can be traversed and that whenever a state with errors is entered, then a state without errors will be eventually reached, respectively. The control data of [17] are the adaptable processes of the form $a[P]$.

5   Programming Paradigms for Adaptation

As we observed, the nature of control data can vary considerably depending both on the degree of adaptivity of the system and on the nature of the computational formalisms used to implement it. Examples of control data include configuration variables, rules and plans (in rule-based programming), code variations (in context-oriented programming), interactions (in connector-centered approaches), policies (in policy-driven languages), advices (in aspect-oriented languages), monads and effects (in functional languages), and even entire programs (in models of computation exhibiting higher-order or reflective features). Indeed, many programming languages that consider such forms of control data as first-class citizens have been promoted as suitable for programming adaptive systems (see the overviews of [36,74]). Just restricting to Java, technologies supporting adaptation include Jolie [61], ContextJ [8], JavAdaptor [68] and Chameleon [9]. This section surveys a representative set of such programming paradigms and explain their notion of adaptation in terms of CoDA. The approaches are organized according to three paradigms: context-oriented programming (Section 5.1), aspect-oriented programming (Section 5.2), and policy-oriented programming (Section 5.3).

5.1   Context-Oriented Programming for Adaptation

Context-oriented programing [40] (COP) has been designed as a convenient paradigm for programming autonomic systems [73]. The main idea is to rely on a pool of *code variations* chosen according to the program's *context*, i.e., the runtime environment under which the program is running. Under this paradigm the natural choice of control data is the current set of active code variations.

Many languages have been extended to adopt this paradigm. We mention among others Lisp, Python, Ruby, Smalltalk, Scheme, Java, and Erlang. The notion of context varies from approach to approach and it might refer to any computationally accessible information. Without giving any concrete reference, a typical example is the environmental data collected from sensors. In many cases the universe of all possible contexts is discretised in order to have a manageable, abstract set of fixed contexts. This is achieved, for instance by means of functions mapping the environmental data into the set of fixed contexts. Code fragments like methods or functions can then be specialized for each possible context. Such chunks of behaviours associated with contexts are called *variations*.

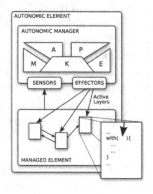

Fig. 10. MAPE-K architecture in COP

COP can be used to program autonomic systems by de/activating variations in reaction to context changes. The key mechanism is the dynamic dispatching of variations. When a piece of code is executed, a dispatcher examines the current context of the execution in order to decide which variation to invoke. Contexts thus act as some sort of possibly nested scopes. Indeed, often a stack is used to store the currently active contexts, and a variation can propagate the invocation to the variation of the enclosing context. To achieve adaptation along the lines of the MAPE-K framework, the manager controls the context stack and the managed component accesses it in a read-only manner. The points of the code in which the managed component queries the context stack are called *activation hooks* (*adaptation hooks* in [51] and in [37], see Sections 5.2 and 5.3, respectively).

Given our informal description, COP falls into CoDA assuming the context stack as control data. The only difference between the approach proposed in [73] (cf. Fig. 10) and our ideas is that the former suggests the context stack to reside within the manager (this may not be clear in the figure, and we refer to the example in [73]), while for us the control stack resides in the interface of the managed component, in order to identify such component as an adaptable one.

5.2 Aspect-Oriented Programming for Adaptation

Aspect-oriented programming [47] and, in particular, dynamic aspect-oriented programming [67] have been advocated as a convenient mechanism for developing self-adaptive software by many authors since the original proposal of [38]. The main idea is that the separation-of-concerns philosophy of aspects facilitates the addition of autonomic computing capabilities. Indeed, while early works [38] put the stress on monitoring as an aspect, subsequent works have generalized this idea to other capabilities. Adaptation can be realized through aspect weaving, i.e., the activation and deactivation of advices (the code to be executed at join points), possibly enacted by an autonomic manager. Advices, hence, can be understood as the control data of the aspect-based adaptation paradigm. Dynamic aspect oriented programming languages, equipped with dynamic aspect weaving mechanisms, thus facilitate the realization of dynamic adaptation.

5.3 Policy-Oriented Programming for Adaptation

As we have seen in Section 4.2, rule-based approaches have been advocated as a convenient mechanism for realizing self-adaptation. Another example of this tradition are policies. Generally speaking, policies are in fact rules that determine the behavior of an entity under specific conditions. Policies have been seen as mechanisms enjoying the flexibility required by self-* systems, and tackling the problem at the right (high-) level of abstraction. Quite naturally, adaptation can be realized by changing policies according to the program's current status. The natural choice of control data is then the current set of active policies.

A prominent example is the Policy-based Self-Adaptive Model (PobSAM) [46], a framework for modeling and analyzing self-adaptive systems which relies on policies as a high-level mechanism to realize adaptive behaviors. Building upon the authors experience in the PAGODA framework [78] (cf. Section 4.2), PobSAM combines the actor model of coordination [2] with process algebra machinery and shares the white-box spirit of separating application and adaptation concerns. The overall architecture of the system is composed by *managed actors*, which implement the functional behavior, and *autonomic manager (meta-)actors*, which control managed actors by enforcing policies. Thus, the adaptation logic is encoded in policies whose responsibility relies on well-identified components (i.e., the managers), and their configuration is determined by sets of policies which can vary dynamically. The currently active set of policies represents the control data. Adaptation is indeed the switch between active policies. Policies are rules that determine under which condition a specified subject must or must not do a certain action. PobSAM distinguishes between *governing* policies, which control the managed actors in their *stable* (cf. steady, normal) state and *adaptation* policies, which drive the actors in the transient states (cf. adaptation phases).

The authors of [51] propose a framework for dynamic adaptation based on the combination of *adaptation hooks*, which specify *where* to apply adaptation, and policies called *adaptation rules*, which specify *when* and *how* to apply it. An adaptable application exposes part of its states and the set of activities that it performs in an interface called *application interface*. Adaptation is enacted by managers that exploit the adaptation rules to introduce changes in the application through its interface. In particular, the rules define adaptations that may change the activities by instantiating new code or changing their configuration parameters and may change part of the application state. Thus, in this approach both the set of activities and the exposed application state are to be considered as control data in the basic adaptation layer. On top of this layer, *dynamic* adaptation can occur, which consists on modifying the adaptation rules at runtime. This makes adaptation managers adaptable as well. At this layer, hence, the control data are the adaptation rules, which determine the behavior of the adaptation managers.

The approach is instantiated in the Java Orchestration Language Interpreter Engine (Jolie) [61], a framework for rapid prototyping of service oriented applications. The approach is, however, language agnostic, as the authors identify the basic ingredients needed to implement their approach in other settings and a generic architecture to structure it. The former consists of mechanisms needed to implement the adaptation interface and its manipulation based on code mobility. At the architectural level applications are structured as *clients* which rely on an *activity manager* to run their activities. Adaptation is governed by *adaptation servers*, which are coordinated globally by an *adaptation manager service*.

6   Related Work

We have already discussed some of our sources of inspiration in the previous sections and spelled out how their underlying notion of adaptation can be recast in terms of our approach. This section discusses two kinds of related works. Section 6.1 is devoted to works that propose a definition of adaptation. Section 6.2 discusses works that provide a classification of approaches and techniques, guided by a set of dimensions or facets relevant to adaptive systems. Clearly, the references considered here represent only a fragment of the vast literature on adaptive systems: we refer the interested reader to the bibliography of the surveys discussed in this section for completing the picture.

6.1 On the Essence of Adaptation

This sections focuses on other approaches that aim to provide conceptual notions of adaptation. Several proposals follow a black-box perspective that, as discussed in the Introduction, focuses on the external observation of self-adaptive systems.

An interesting contribution is [52], which analyses the notion of adaptation in a general sense and identifies the main concepts around adaptation drawn from different disciplines, including evolution theory, biology, psychology, business, control theory and cybernetics. Furthermore it provides guidelines on the essential features of adaptive systems in order to support their design and understanding.

The author claims that *"in general, adaptation is a process about changing something, so that it would be more suitable or fit for some purpose that it would have not been otherwise"*. The term *adaptability* denotes the capacity of enacting adaptation, and *adaptivity* the degree or extent to which adaptation is enacted. This leads to the identification of four issues that typically play a role in adaptation: context, goals, time-frames, and granularity that are discussed in Section 6.2. The author concludes suggesting that *"due to the relativity of adaptation it does not really matter whether a system is adaptive or not (they all are, in some way or another), but with respect to what it is adaptive"*.

A formal black-box definition is proposed in [18]. If a system reacts differently to the same input stream at different times, then the system is considered to be adaptive, because ordinary systems should exhibit a deterministic behavior. Thus, a non-deterministic reaction is interpreted as an evidence of the fact that the system adapted its behaviour after an interaction with the environment. Despite its appeal and crispness, we believe that this and similar definitions of adaptation are based on too strong assumptions, restricting considerably its range of applicability. For example, a system where a change of behaviour is triggered by an interaction with the user would not be classified as adaptive.

As we argued in the Introduction, black-box approaches are useful for evaluating the system robustness under some conditions. However, they are of little use for design purposes where modularization and reuse are critical aspects. Therefore, we believe that a formal definition of adaptation should not be based on the observable behaviour of systems only. At the same time, we do believe that research efforts are needed to conciliate black-box and white-box perspectives. Ideally, the internal mechanisms and external manifestations of adaptive behavior should be coherent, so that, for instance, a black-box analysis can validate that the degree of adaptability is strongly dependent on the adaptation mechanisms.

A different perspective on adaptation, inspired by the seminal work of IBM on autonomic computing, has been adopted by many authors, e.g., [72]. The starting point is the observation that modern software can be seen as an open loop. Indeed, a software system is inevitably subject to continuous modifications, reparations and maintenance operations which require human intervention. Self-adaptation is seen as the solution to such openness by closing the loop with feedback from the software itself and its context of operation. In this view self-adaptation is seen as a complex feature built upon self-awareness and other self-* mechanisms. Control loops are seen as a fundamental process to achieve adaptive behaviors.

The kind of adaptation discussed so far is concerned essentially with individual components. However it may also happen that a complex system made of non-adaptive components exhibits a collective behavior which is considered to be adaptive (see, e.g., the discussion in [52]). Such *emergent adaptation*, typical of massively parallel and distributed systems such as *swarms*, results from the components' interactions. Often, emergent adaptation relies on decentralized coordination mechanisms (e.g., based on the spatial computing paradigm [79,10]). Interesting in this regard can be to shift the focus to *Singerian* forms of adaptation [71,14], where the subject of adaptation is the environment, as opposed to the *Darwinian* one we have focused on, where it is the system that adapts.

A conceptual framework for emergent adaptation would require to shift from a *local* notion of control data to a *global* one, where the control data of the individual components are treated as a whole, possibly requiring mechanisms to amalgamate them for the manager, and to project them back to the components.

6.2   The Facets of Adaptation

The literature on adaptive systems contains several interesting surveys and taxonomies based on the identification of the main facets of adaptation. The concept of control data provides one such facet that has been used in this paper to classify many proposals as discussed in Sections 3–5 and summarized in Fig. 1. In this section we relate control data with other facets proposed in the literature. In most cases these are orthogonal and provide complementary classification criteria. In a few cases they are closely related with control data, thus providing a more concrete perspective on the corresponding approaches.

The survey on self-adaptive software of [72] is one of the most comprehensive studies on the topic, including also approaches to adaptation from the fields of artificial intelligence, control theory and decision theory. It presents a taxonomy of adaptation concerns, surveys a wide set of representative approaches from many different areas, and identifies some key research challenges. The discussion is driven by the so-called six honest men issues in adaptation: (1) *Why* is adaptation required? Is the purpose of adaptation to meet some robustness criteria, to improve the system's performance or to satisfy some other goal? (2) *When* should adaptation be enacted? Should adaptation be applied reactively or proactively? (3) *Where* is the need to do an adaptation manifested? That is, which artifacts (sensors, variables, etc.) indicate that it is necessary to perform an adaptation? (4) *What* parts of the system should be adapted? That is, which artifacts (variables, components, connectors, interfaces, etc.) have to be modified in order to adapt? (5) *Who* should enact the adaptation? Which entity (e.g., human controller, autonomic manager) is in charge of each adaptation? (6) *How* should adaptation be applied? That is, which is the plan that establishes the order in which to apply the necessary adaptation actions?

Our conceptual framework fits well with this approach and is mainly devoted to the identification of the *where*, which facilitates finding the right characterization for the remaining *honest men* of the adaptation mechanism. In fact, in our view the *where* includes control data, since their manipulation forces a system to adapt. The taxonomy may distinguish between *weak* adaptation (e.g., modifying parameters) and *strong* adaptation (e.g., replacing entire components): the granularity of control data provides a finer spectrum between these two extremes.

The authors of [56] identify three technologies that enable the development of adaptive systems: component-based design, separation of concerns, and computational reflection. We remark that our aim is devoted to provide a common understanding of adaptation rather than promoting particular mechanisms. They argue that there are two main approaches to adaptation: *parameter* and *compositional* adaptation. In the former, control data can be identified in those program variables that affect the system behavior, and adaptation coincides with the modification of those variables. In the latter, control data can be identified in the system architecture, i.e., in the system components and interconnection, and adaptation coincides with architectural reconfiguration, from replacing whole components to modifying only parts of them. The authors pay attention to compositional adaptation and propose a taxonomy that focuses on three questions: the *when*, *how*, and *where* to compose. While our aim is centered around the conceptual forms of control data, the authors focus on concrete technological mechanisms and do not consider foundational models such as those in Section 4.

The authors of FORMS (cf. the discussion on [6,81] in Section 3) provide in [5] a classification of modeling facets for self-adaptive systems. The focus is on the underlying conceptual models rather than on the concrete technologies used to realize them. As a result, four main groups of facets are identified: those regarding the *goals* of adaptation, the *changes* that trigger it, the *mechanisms* that realize it, and its *effects*. Goal dimensions include flexibility, duration, and dependency of the system objectives. Change dimensions regard e.g. the source, the frequency, and the level of anticipation of the adaptation triggers. The mechanism-related dimensions range from the type to the level of autonomy, passing through scope, duration, and timeliness. Last, the dimensions concerning the effects of adaptation include criticality, predictability, and resilience. The proposed classes for each facet seem however orthogonal with respect to the choice of control data.

The authors exploit such classes to identify the research challenges of adaptation. They e.g. stress the need of mechanisms to conciliate conflicting goals of participants in open systems; of decentralized mechanisms for coordinating adaptation in distributed systems; and of verification, validation, and prediction mechanisms to ensure that self-adaptive systems behave correctly and predictably.

The survey [16] provides an overview of those approaches that support self-adaptation based on architectural reconfiguration. The authors consider that an architecture is *self-managed* if it can perform architectural changes at runtime by initiating, selecting, and assessing them by itself, without the assistance of an external entity. Contrary to other surveys on architectural reconfiguration (e.g., [29,60]) the focus is on formal models such as graphs, process algebras and logic.

The considered approaches are evaluated in terms of their support for basic re-configurations such as component or connector addition/removal and composite reconfiguration operations such as sequentialization, iteration and choices. With respect to our proposal, they clearly identify the software achitectures themselves as control data (cf. also the discussion in Section 3.2).

7   Conclusion

We presented CoDA, a white-box conceptual framework for adaptation that promotes a neat separation of the adaptation logic from the application logic through a clear identification of control data. To validate CoDA we described a representative set of approaches to (self-)adaptation ranging from architectural solutions (Section 3), to computational models (Section 4), and to programming languages and paradigms (Section 5). For each of them we highlighted the main distinguishing features and discussed the way they fit in CoDA. As a byproduct, our work provides an original perspective from which to survey Computer Science approaches to adaptive systems. We also discussed (Section 6) other surveys and taxonomies conceived with the aim to establish a common ground for fruitful research debates by clarifying and identifying the key features of adaptive systems.

The discussion of this paper helped us to identify many different forms of control data that can be found in the literature. Our position is that *the* best form of control data does not exist. However, we strongly believe that the choice of control data should adhere to the following three principles (cf. [56]): separation of concerns, component-based design and computational reflection.

Regarding the first two principles, we believe that the choice of control data should neatly separate the application logic from the adaptation logic, and should be clearly identified and encapsulated in a specific component of a suitable adaptation loop, in order to guarantee an understandable, modular design. For this purpose, sound design principles should be developed in order to ensure correctness-by-design, and guidelines for the development of adaptive systems conforming to well-understood patterns.

As for the third principle, we believe that higher-order forms of control data are to be preferred if computationally affordable, since they make it easy to carry the life-cycle of reliable adaptive systems to runtime, by providing runtime models that can be used to monitor, predict and modify the systems.

In Fig. 11 we recap how the (macro) classes of control data identified in Fig. 1 and discussed in Sections 3–5 (i.e., the rows of the table in Fig. 11) have been exploited for adaptation along three pillars of Computer Science (i.e., the columns of the table Fig. 11). Broadly speaking, the presence of blank cells in the table suggests us two main interesting and maybe surprising facts, which are concerned with: (i) the use of reflection in programming languages for adaptation; and (ii) the abstraction from operational aspects in architectural approaches.

While reflection offers a natural mechanism to implement adaptation, our analysis shows that it is more common to allow only a controlled form of reflection in languages designed for programming adaptive systems, as witnessed by the fact that the class "entire program" has no direct representative in the pillar

	Architectures		Models			Languages		
adaptation strategy			4.1				5.2	5.3
architecture	3.1	3.2	4.1		4.3			5.3
entire program			4.1	4.2	4.3			
operation mode			4.1	4.2	4.3	5.1	5.3	4.3

Fig. 11. Control data classes per pillars

"Languages". Our understanding is that reflection as-it-is does not offer a convenient abstraction to programmers: too powerful and too risky (i.e., error-prone).

Regarding the pillar "Architectures", it seems that the only class of control data exploited for adaptation is "architecture" itself (e.g., components and their connections), whereas operational aspects such as those related to the *how* and *why* are disregarded. While one can argue that both classes "entire program" and "operation mode" can be represented at the architecture level (e.g., the notion of component replacement can be instantiated to each class), we think that the same does not apply to the class "adaptation strategy". This remark was implicit in [16], where a lack in meta-levels for architectural formalisms was noted. To fill the gap, defining an architectural reference model of adaptation that has adaptation strategies as control data seems a topic worthy of further studies.

References

1. Adler, R., Schaefer, I., Schuele, T., Vecchié, E.: From model-based design to formal verification of adaptive embedded systems. In: Butler, M., Hinchey, M.G., Larrondo-Petrie, M.M. (eds.) ICFEM 2007. LNCS, vol. 4789, pp. 76–95. Springer, Heidelberg (2007)
2. Agha, G.: Actors: a model of concurrent computation in distributed systems. MIT Press (1986)
3. de Alfaro, L., Henzinger, T.A.: Interface automata. In: ESEC/FSE 2001. ACM SIGSOFT Software Engineering Notes, vol. 26(5), pp. 109–120. ACM (2001)
4. Allen, R.B., Douence, R., Garlan, D.: Specifying and analyzing dynamic software architectures. In: Astesiano, E. (ed.) FASE 1998. LNCS, vol. 1382, pp. 21–37. Springer, Heidelberg (1998)
5. Andersson, J., de Lemos, R., Malek, S., Weyns, D.: Modeling dimensions of self-adaptive software systems. In: Cheng, et al. (eds.) [27], pp. 27–47
6. Andersson, J., de Lemos, R., Malek, S., Weyns, D.: Reflecting on self-adaptive software systems. In: SEAMS 2009, pp. 38–47. IEEE Computer Society (2009)
7. Andrade, L.F., Fiadeiro, J.L.: An architectural approach to auto-adaptive systems. In: ICDCSW 2002, pp. 439–444. IEEE Computer Society (2002)
8. Appeltauer, M., Hirschfeld, R., Haupt, M., Masuhara, H.: ContextJ: Context-oriented programming with Java. Journal of the Japan Society for Software Science and Technology on Computer Software 28(1), 272–292 (2011)
9. Autili, M., Benedetto, P.D., Inverardi, P.: A programming model for adaptable java applications. In: Krall, A., Mössenböck, H. (eds.) PPPJ 2010, pp. 119–128. ACM (2010)
10. Beal, J., Cleveland, J., Usbeck, K.: Self-stabilizing robot team formation with proto: Ieee self-adaptive and self-organizing systems 2012 demo entry. In: SASO 2012, pp. 233–234. IEEE Computer Society (2012)

11. Biyani, K.N., Kulkarni, S.S.: Assurance of dynamic adaptation in distributed systems. Journal of Parallel and Distributed Computing 68(8), 1097–1112 (2008)
12. Boella, G., Dastani, M., Omicini, A., van der Torre, L.W., Cerna, I., Linden, I. (eds.): CoOrg 2006 & MTCoord 2006. ENTCS, vol. 181. Elsevier (2007)
13. Bosch, J.: Superimposition: a component adaptation technique. Information & Software Technology 41(5), 257–273 (1999)
14. Bouchachia, A., Nedjah, N.: Introduction to the special section on self-adaptive systems: Models and algorithms. ACM Transactions on Autonomous and Adaptive Systems 7(1), 13:1–13:4 (2012)
15. Bracciali, A., Brogi, A., Canal, C.: A formal approach to component adaptation. Journal of Systems and Software 74(1), 45–54 (2005)
16. Bradbury, J.S., Cordy, J.R., Dingel, J., Wermelinger, M.: A survey of self-management in dynamic software architecture specifications. In: Garlan, D., Kramer, J., Wolf, A.L. (eds.) WOSS 2004, pp. 28–33. ACM (2004)
17. Bravetti, M., Giusto, C.D., Pérez, J.A., Zavattaro, G.: Adaptable processes. Logical Methods in Computer Science 8(4), 13:1–13:71 (2012)
18. Broy, M., Leuxner, C., Sitou, W., Spanfelner, B., Winter, S.: Formalizing the notion of adaptive system behavior. In: Shin, S.Y., Ossowski, S. (eds.) SAC 2009, pp. 1029–1033. ACM (2009)
19. Brun, Y., Serugendo, G.D.M., Gacek, C., Giese, H., Kienle, H.M., Litoiu, M., Müller, H.A., Pezzè, M., Shaw, M.: Engineering self-adaptive systems through feedback loops. In: Cheng, et al. (eds.) [27], pp. 48–70
20. Bruni, R., Corradini, A., Gadducci, F., Lafuente, A.L., Vandin, A.: Adaptable transition systems. In: Martí-Oliet, Palomino (eds.) [54], pp. 95–110
21. Bruni, R., Corradini, A., Gadducci, F., Lluch Lafuente, A., Vandin, A.: A conceptual framework for adaptation. In: de Lara, J., Zisman, A. (eds.) FASE 2012. LNCS, vol. 7212, pp. 240–254. Springer, Heidelberg (2012)
22. Bruni, R., Corradini, A., Gadducci, F., Lluch Lafuente, A., Vandin, A.: Modelling and analyzing adaptive self-assembly strategies with Maude. In: Durán, F. (ed.) WRLA 2012. LNCS, vol. 7571, pp. 118–138. Springer, Heidelberg (2012)
23. Bucchiarone, A., Cappiello, C., Di Nitto, E., Kazhamiakin, R., Mazza, V., Pistore, M.: Design for adaptation of service-based applications: Main issues and requirements. In: Dan, A., Gittler, F., Toumani, F. (eds.) ICSOC/ServiceWave 2009. LNCS, vol. 6275, pp. 467–476. Springer, Heidelberg (2010)
24. Bucchiarone, A., Pistore, M., Raik, H., Kazhamiakin, R.: Adaptation of service-based business processes by context-aware replanning. In: Lin, K.J., Huemer, C., Blake, M.B., Benatallah, B. (eds.) SOCA 2011, pp. 1–8. IEEE Computer Society (2011)
25. Cabri, G., Puviani, M., Zambonelli, F.: Towards a taxonomy of adaptive agent-based collaboration patterns for autonomic service ensembles. In: Smari, W.W., Fox, G. (eds.) CTS 2011, pp. 508–515. IEEE Computer Society (2011)
26. Cámara, J., Martín, J.A., Salaün, G., Cubo, J., Ouederni, M., Canal, C., Pimentel, E.: Itaca: An integrated toolbox for the automatic composition and adaptation of web services. In: ICSE 2009, pp. 627–630. IEEE Computer Society (2009)
27. Cheng, B.H.C., de Lemos, R., Giese, H., Inverardi, P., Magee, J. (eds.): Software Engineering for Self-Adaptive Systems. LNCS, vol. 5525. Springer, Heidelberg (2009)
28. Clavel, M., Durán, F., Eker, S., Lincoln, P., Martí-Oliet, N., Meseguer, J., Talcott, C.: All About Maude - A High-Performance Logical Framework. LNCS, vol. 4350. Springer, Heidelberg (2007)
29. Clements, P.: A survey of architecture description languages. In: IWSSD 1996, pp. 16–25. IEEE Computer Society (1996)

30. Cordy, M., Classen, A., Heymans, P., Legay, A., Schobbens, P.-Y.: Model checking adaptive software with featured transition systems. In: Cámara, J., de Lemos, R., Ghezzi, C., Lopes, A. (eds.) Assurances for Self-Adaptive Systems. LNCS, vol. 7740, pp. 1–29. Springer, Heidelberg (2013)
31. De Nicola, R., Ferrari, G.L., Pugliese, R.: Klaim: A kernel language for agents interaction and mobility. IEEE Transactions on Software Engineering 24(5), 315–330 (1998)
32. De Nicola, R., Loreti, M., Pugliese, R., Tiezzi, F.: A formal approach to autonomic systems programming: The SCEL language. ACM Transactions on Autonomous and Adaptive Systems 9(2), 7:1–7:29 (2014)
33. Dowling, J., Schäfer, T., Cahill, V., Haraszti, P., Redmond, B.: Using reflection to support dynamic adaptation of system software: A case study driven evaluation. In: Cazzola, W., Houmb, S.H., Tisato, F. (eds.) Reflection and Software Engineering. LNCS, vol. 1826, pp. 169–188. Springer, Heidelberg (2000)
34. Eckhardt, J., Mühlbauer, T., Meseguer, J., Wirsing, M.: Statistical model-checking for composite actor systems. In: Martí-Oliet, Palomino (eds.) [54], pp. 143–160
35. Ehrig, H., Ermel, C., Runge, O., Bucchiarone, A., Pelliccione, P.: Formal analysis and verification of self-healing systems. In: Rosenblum, D.S., Taentzer, G. (eds.) FASE 2010. LNCS, vol. 6013, pp. 139–153. Springer, Heidelberg (2010)
36. Ghezzi, C., Pradella, M., Salvaneschi, G.: An evaluation of the adaptation capabilities in programming languages. In: Giese, H., Cheng, B.H.C. (eds.) SEAMS 2011, pp. 50–59. ACM (2011)
37. Gjondrekaj, E., Loreti, M., Pugliese, R., Tiezzi, F.: Modeling adaptation with a tuple-based coordination language. In: Ossowski, S., Lecca, P. (eds.) SAC 2012, pp. 1522–1527. ACM (2012)
38. Greenwood, P., Blair, L.: Using dynamic aspect-oriented programming to implement an autonomic system. In: DAW 2004, pp. 76–88. RIACS (2004)
39. Harvey, I., Paolo, E.A.D., Wood, R., Quinn, M., Tuci, E.: Evolutionary robotics: A new scientific tool for studying cognition. Artificial Life 11(1-2), 79–98 (2005)
40. Hirschfeld, R., Costanza, P., Nierstrasz, O.: Context-oriented programming. Journal of Object Technology 7(3), 125–151 (2008)
41. Hölzl, M., Wirsing, M.: Towards a system model for ensembles. In: Agha, G., Danvy, O., Meseguer, J. (eds.) Formal Modeling: Actors, Open Systems, Biological Systems. LNCS, vol. 7000, pp. 241–261. Springer, Heidelberg (2011)
42. Horn, P.: Autonomic computing: IBM's perspective on the state of information technology. IBM (2001)
43. IBM Corporation: An architectural blueprint for autonomic computing. IBM (2005)
44. Iftikhar, M.U., Weyns, D.: A case study on formal verification of self-adaptive behaviors in a decentralized system. In: Kokash, Ravara (eds.) [48], pp. 45–62
45. Karsai, G., Sztipanovits, J.: A model-based approach to self-adaptive software. Intelligent Systems and their Applications 14(3), 46–53 (1999)
46. Khakpour, N., Jalili, S., Talcott, C., Sirjani, M., Mousavi, M.: Formal modeling of evolving self-adaptive systems. Science of Computer Programming 78(1), 3–26 (2012)
47. Kiczales, G., Lamping, J., Mendhekar, A., Maeda, C., Lopes, C., Loingtier, J., Irwin, J.: Aspect-oriented programming. In: Akşit, M., Matsuoka, S. (eds.) ECOOP 1997. LNCS, vol. 1241, pp. 220–242. Springer, Heidelberg (1997)
48. Kokash, N., Ravara, A. (eds.): FOCLASA 2012. EPTCS, vol. 91. EPTCS (2012)

49. Kramer, J., Magee, J.: A rigorous architectural approach to adaptive software engineering. Journal of Computer Science and Technology 24(2), 183–188 (2009)
50. Laddaga, R.: Self-adaptive software: BAA 98-12 proposer information pamphlet. DARPA (1997)
51. Lanese, I., Bucchiarone, A., Montesi, F.: A framework for rule-based dynamic adaptation. In: Wirsing, M., Hofmann, M., Rauschmayer, A. (eds.) TGC 2010. LNCS, vol. 6084, pp. 284–300. Springer, Heidelberg (2010)
52. Lints, T.: The essentials in defining adaptation. IEEE Aerospace and Electronic Systems Magazine 1(27), 37–41 (2012)
53. Maraninchi, F., Rémond, Y.: Mode-automata: About modes and states for reactive systems. In: Hankin, C. (ed.) ESOP 1998. LNCS, vol. 1381, pp. 185–199. Springer, Heidelberg (1998)
54. Martí-Oliet, N., Palomino, M. (eds.): WADT 2012. LNCS, vol. 7841. Springer, Heidelberg (2013)
55. Martín, J.A., Brogi, A., Pimentel, E.: Learning from failures: A lightweight approach to run-time behavioural adaptation. In: Arbab, F., Ölveczky, P.C. (eds.) FACS 2011. LNCS, vol. 7253, pp. 259–277. Springer, Heidelberg (2012)
56. McKinley, P.K., Sadjadi, S.M., Kasten, E.P., Cheng, B.H.C.: Composing adaptive software. IEEE Computer 37(7), 56–64 (2004)
57. Merelli, E., Paoletti, N., Tesei, L.: A multi-level model for self-adaptive systems. In: Kokash, Ravara (eds.) [48], pp. 112–126
58. Meseguer, J.: Conditional rewriting logic as a unified model of concurrency. Theoretical Computer Science 96(1), 73–155 (1992)
59. Meseguer, J., Talcott, C.: Semantic models for distributed object reflection. In: Magnusson, B. (ed.) ECOOP 2002. LNCS, vol. 2374, pp. 1–36. Springer, Heidelberg (2002)
60. Mikic-Rakic, M., Medvidovic, N.: A classification of disconnected operation techniques. In: SEAA 2006, pp. 144–151. IEEE Computer Society (2006)
61. Montesi, F., Guidi, C., Lucchi, R., Zavattaro, G.: JOLIE: a Java orchestration language interpreter engine. In: Boella, et al. (eds.) [12], pp. 19–33
62. Mühl, G., Werner, M., Jaeger, M., Herrmann, K., Parzyjegla, H.: On the definitions of self-managing and self-organizing systems. In: KiVS 2007. IEEE Computer Society (2007)
63. O'Grady, R., Groß, R., Christensen, A.L., Dorigo, M.: Self-assembly strategies in a group of autonomous mobile robots. Autonomous Robots 28(4), 439–455 (2010)
64. Oreizy, P., Gorlick, M.M., Taylor, R.N., Heimbigner, D., Johnson, G., Medvidovic, N., Quilici, A., Rosenblum, D.S., Wolf, A.L.: An architecture-based approach to self-adaptive software. Intelligent Systems and their Applications 14(3), 54–62 (1999)
65. Pavlovic, D.: Towards semantics of self-adaptive software. In: Robertson, P., Shrobe, H.E., Laddaga, R. (eds.) IWSAS 2000. LNCS, vol. 1936, pp. 50–64. Springer, Heidelberg (2001)
66. Popescu, R., Staikopoulos, A., Brogi, A., Liu, P., Clarke, S.: A formalized, taxonomy-driven approach to cross-layer application adaptation. ACM Transactions on Autonomous and Adaptive Systems 7(1), 7:1–7:30 (2012)
67. Popovici, A., Alonso, G., Gross, T.R.: Just-in-time aspects: efficient dynamic weaving for Java. In: AOSD 2003, pp. 100–109. ACM (2003)
68. Pukall, M., Kästner, C., Cazzola, W., Götz, S., Grebhahn, A., Schröter, R., Saake, G.: Javadaptor - flexible runtime updates of Java applications. Software, Practice and Experience 43(2), 153–185 (2013)
69. Raibulet, C.: Facets of adaptivity. In: Morrison, R., Balasubramaniam, D., Falkner, K. (eds.) ECSA 2008. LNCS, vol. 5292, pp. 342–345. Springer, Heidelberg (2008)

70. van Renesse, R., Birman, K.P., Hayden, M., Vaysburd, A., Karr, D.A.: Building adaptive systems using ensemble. Software, Practice and Experience 28(9), 963–979 (1998)
71. Sagasti, F.: A conceptual and taxonomic framework for the analysis of adaptive behavior. General Systems XV, 151–160 (1970)
72. Salehie, M., Tahvildari, L.: Self-adaptive software: Landscape and research challenges. ACM Transactions on Autonomous and Adaptive Systems 4(2), 14:1–14:42 (2009)
73. Salvaneschi, G., Ghezzi, C., Pradella, M.: Context-oriented programming: A programming paradigm for autonomic systems. Tech. Rep. abs/1105.0069, CoRR (2011)
74. Salvaneschi, G., Ghezzi, C., Pradella, M.: Towards language-level support for self-adaptive software. ACM Transactions on Autonomous and Adaptive Systems (to appear, 2014)
75. Sangiorgi, D.: Expressing Mobility in Process Algebras: First-Order and Higher-Order Paradigms. Ph.D. thesis, University of Edinburgh (1992)
76. Schaefer, I., Poetzsch-Heffter, A.: Using abstraction in modular verification of synchronous adaptive systems. In: Autexier, S., Merz, S., van der Torre, L.W.N., Wilhelm, R., Wolper, P. (eds.) Trustworthy Software. OASICS, vol. 3. IBFI, Schloss Dagstuhl, Germany (2006)
77. Talcott, C.L.: Coordination models based on a formal model of distributed object reflection. In: Brim, L., Linden, I. (eds.) MTCoord 2005. ENTCS, vol. 150(1), pp. 143–157. Elsevier (2006)
78. Talcott, C.L.: Policy-based coordination in PAGODA: A case study. In: Boella, et al. (eds.) [12], pp. 97–112
79. Viroli, M., Casadei, M., Montagna, S., Zambonelli, F.: Spatial coordination of pervasive services through chemical-inspired tuple spaces. ACM Transactions on Autonomous and Adaptive Systems 6(2), 14:1–14:24 (2011)
80. Wang, H., Lv, H., Feng, G.: A self-reflection model for autonomic computing systems based on π-calculus. In: Xiang, Y., Lopez, J., Wang, H., Zhou, W. (eds.) NSS 2009, pp. 310–315. IEEE Computer Society (2009)
81. Weyns, D., Malek, S., Andersson, J.: FORMS: Unifying reference model for formal specification of distributed self-adaptive systems. ACM Transactions on Autonomous and Adaptive Systems 7(1), 8:1–8:61 (2012)
82. Wirth, N.: Algorithms + Data Structures = Programs. Prentice-Hall (1976)
83. Zadeh, L.A.: On the definition of adaptivity. Proceedings of the IEEE 3(51), 469–470 (1963)
84. Zhang, J., Cheng, B.H.C.: Model-based development of dynamically adaptive software. In: Osterweil, L.J., Rombach, H.D., Soffa, M.L. (eds.) ICSE 2006, pp. 371–380. ACM (2006)
85. Zhang, J., Cheng, B.H.C.: Using temporal logic to specify adaptive program semantics. Journal of Systems and Software 79(10), 1361–1369 (2006)
86. Zhang, J., Goldsby, H., Cheng, B.H.C.: Modular verification of dynamically adaptive systems. In: Sullivan, K.J., Moreira, A., Schwanninger, C., Gray, J. (eds.) AOSD 2009, pp. 161–172. ACM (2009)
87. Zhao, Y., Ma, D., Li, J., Li, Z.: Model checking of adaptive programs with mode-extended linear temporal logic. In: EASe 2011, pp. 40–48. IEEE Computer Society (2011)

Rule-Based Modeling and Static Analysis
of Self-adaptive Systems
by Graph Transformation

Antonio Bucchiarone[1], Hartmut Ehrig[2],
Claudia Ermel[2], Patrizio Pelliccione[3], and Olga Runge[2]

[1] Fondazione Bruno Kessler, Trento, Italy
bucchiarone@fbk.eu
[2] Technische Universität Berlin, Germany
firstname.lastname@tu-berlin.de
[3] Chalmers University of Technology and University of Gothenburg, Sweden
patrizio.pelliccione@gu.se

Abstract. Software systems nowadays require continuous operation despite changes both in user needs and in their operational environments. Self-adaptive systems are typically instrumented with tools to autonomously perform adaptation to these changes while maintaining some desired properties. In this paper we model and analyze self-adaptive systems by means of typed, attributed graph grammars. The interplay of different grammars representing the application and the adaptation logic is realized by an adaption manager. Within this formal framework we define consistency and operational properties that are maintained despite adaptations and we give static conditions for their verification. The overall approach is supported by the AGG tool for modeling, simulating, and analyzing graph transformation systems. A case study modeling a business process that adapts to changing environment conditions is used to demonstrate and validate the formal framework.

1 Introduction

Self-adaptive systems are systems that autonomously decide (e.g., without or with minimal interference) how to adapt at runtime according to the internal reconfiguration and optimization requirements or to environment (context) changes and threats [1]. Thus, a self-adaptive system should be able to *monitor* itself and its context, to *detect* context changes that require system adaptations, to *decide* how to react and *act* to execute such decisions [2].

On their common basis of self-awareness, self-monitoring and context-awareness, self-adaptive systems are further classified by their characteristics, known as *self-* *properties* [3,4]. The initial four self-* properties of self-adaptive systems are self-configuration, self-healing[1], self-optimization, and self-protection [3]. Self-configuration comprises components installation and configuration based on some

---

[1] Following [5] we consider self-healing and self-repair as synonyms.

R. De Nicola and R. Hennicker (Eds.): Wirsing Festschrift, LNCS 8950, pp. 582–601, 2015.

high-level policies. Self-healing deals with automatic discovery of system failures, and with techniques to recover from them. Self-optimization monitors the system status and adjusts parameters to increase performance when possible. Finally, self-protection aims to detect external threats and to mitigate their effects [6].

In previous work [7,8], the authors modeled and verified dynamic software architectures and self-healing systems by means of graph transformation systems, and proposed a formal approach to prove consistency and operational properties. In this paper, we extend the work in [8] by formally modeling, simulating and validating self-adaptive systems based on the framework of algebraic graph transformation. Our modeling and validation framework is supposed to be used off-line to evaluate and evolve a self-adaptive system: the framework helps the developer to decide which adaptation solutions used and logged in the past have desired properties and should become part of the final system model.

Self-adaptive systems are modeled in our approach as a set of typed graph grammars where three kinds of system rules are distinguished: normal, context, and adaptation rules. Normal rules define the normal and ideal behavior of the system. Context rules define context flags (also called adaptation hooks) that trigger adaptation rules. Different sets of adaptation rules define the adaptation logic. The choice of the "right" set of adaptation rules is performed manually by an adaptation manager, while the adaptation itself is executed automatically.

Based on the formal model, we specify and analyse operational properties of self-adaptive systems. Such properties concern overall conflicts and dependencies of normal system behavior and adaptations. Hence, the analysis is not tailored to specific desired properties concerning e.g., security aspects in self-protective systems or performance analysis of self-optimization. Operational properties define (i) when a system in an adaptation state can be adapted in a system-*enhancing* way to be in a normal state again, (ii) if the nature of the adaptation is *corrective*, i.e., the system state before adaptation can be recovered completely. Operational properties can be checked statically for the given system rules in an automatic way using the AGG[2] modeling and analysis tool for typed attributed graph transformation systems. The theory is presented by use of a running example, a car logistics scenario in a seaport terminal. Please note that not all formal background definitions concerning the theory of graph transformation can be reviewed in this paper due to lack of space. We refer the interested reader to [9,10].

The paper is organized as follows. Sec. 2 presents our running example. Sec. 3 introduces the framework for modeling and analyzing self-adaptive systems. Sec. 4 models the car logistics scenario by using the algebraic graph transformation framework. Sec. 5 describes how to formally verify desirable consistency and operational properties of self-adaptive systems. In Sec. 6, we compare the approach proposed in this paper with related work, and we conclude the paper in Sec. 7. For full proofs of the technical theorems and all details of our case study, the reader is referred to our technical report [10].

---

[2] AGG (Attributed Graph Grammars): http://www.tfs.tu-berlin.de/agg

2 Running Example

In this section we describe the *Car Logistics System (CLS)* scenario that will be used throughout the paper to explain the approach. At the automobile terminal of the Bremerhaven sea port [11], nearly 2 million of new vehicles are handled each year; the business goal is *to deliver them from the manufacturer to the dealer.* Several intermediate business activities are involved, to unload and store cars from a ship, apply treatments to them to meet the customer's requirements and to distribute them to the retailers. The CLS must implement the business process depicted in Fig. 1 by invoking and orchestrating the set of available services in a proper way. Each business activity of the process is executed invoking a set of available services (i.e., Car Check Service, Unloading Service, etc.) that can be atomic or composite (i.e., Store Car Service). Additional services, i.e., services that are not directly attached to the business process, are defined and they may be used during the application execution. For example, the Car Repair Service may be invoked during the application execution according to a context in which the vehicle under consideration is damaged and needs to be repaired.

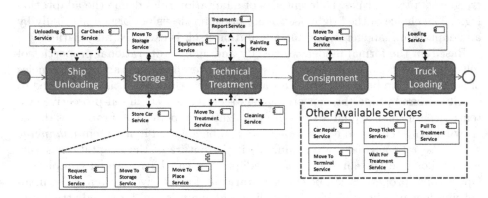

Fig. 1. Business Process and Services of the Car Logistics Scenario

The CLS executes the business process for each vehicle under the following assumptions: (i) each business activity is executed in the defined order; (ii) the context in which the business process is executed can evolve in time.

Yet, there may occur situations in which the business process cannot proceed according to the defined CLS execution. The main reasons for that are: (i) some specific business process variants have not been specified at design time (e.g., due to some error) and (ii) it is not possible to predict a priori which variants should be followed (due to lack of information on the execution contexts). Assume, for instance, the following case that might happen at run-time:

– *Severe Vehicle Damage:* A vehicle has been unloaded from the ship and has requested a ticket (using the Request Ticket Service) to park in the storage area. It receives a ticket and starts to move to the storage (using the Move To Storage Service). While moving, the vehicle is severely damaged.

In this case, the business process should not proceed as planned. A system adaptation is required. In the next section we present a framework for rule-based dynamic adaptation to model and analyze systems that exhibit the aforementioned characteristics and problems.

3 Framework for Rule-Based Dynamic Adaptation

The framework manages the dynamic adaptation by specifying when and how adaptation is triggered, how the choice among the possible adaptations is performed, and, finally, how the nature of adaptations can be characterized.

Requirements: To be able to execute system behaviour also in case of unexpected situations, an adaptation framework needs to address the following problems:

- *Context-Awareness:* To relate the application execution to the context, the application must be context-aware, i.e., during the execution information on the underlying environment can be obtained (e.g., relevant information on entities involved, status of the business process execution, human activities, etc.). To be adaptable, an application should provide adaptation hooks, i.e., context information on parts of the application's structure and behavior. The adaptation hooks should be used to select the most suitable adaptation strategy.

- *Separation of Concerns:* The adaptation logic should be developed separately from the application logic, which can be created and/or changed after the application has been deployed without modifying the running application. At runtime, the context (adaptation hooks) should be checked to control whether any adaptations are required; if this is the case, the system should be adapted in the best suitable way.

Components: Our adaptation framework (AF) is composed of three fundamental components as shown by Fig. 2: the *Context Monitor* describes properties on the application operational environment and how they evolve (by *context rules* and *adaptation hooks*), the *Application Logic* describes how the application evolves (by *application rules*). The *Adaptation Manager* specifies how a system is adapted in case of adaptation needs (using *adaptation rules*).

According to the scenario in Sec. 2, the considered self-adaptive system is the Car Logistics application. Its application logic describes what are the different activities that can be executed (i.e., Ship Unloading, Storage, Technical Treatment, Consignment, and Truck Loading), the set of available services that can be used to realize such activities (i.e., Store Car Service, Move To Treatment Service, Cleaning Service, etc.) and the assumed behavior of the overall application. The behavior describes the order of the activities a car must execute. For each activity, a number of services must be used (in arbitrary order).

The *Context Monitor* models the addition of *adaptation hooks* to the system to trigger the adaptation process. If one or more adaptation hooks are found, an *adaptation problem* is reported to the *Adaptation Manager*. In response, the *Adaptation Manager* (manually) selects a suitable set of adaptation rules and applies them, thereby doing its best to "recover" the system, so that the blocked activity can be executed and the main process can continue. The recovered system state is returned as *adaptation solution* to the application logic.

Formalization: The formal model of a self-adaptive system is a set of graph grammars typed over the same type graph. A main system grammar consists of *system rules* modeling normal behavior (the *Application Logic*) and *context rules* modeling

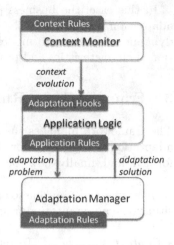

Fig. 2. AF Components

changes that require adaptation by generating adaptation hooks. *Context Monitoring* is modeled by context constraints in the main system grammar that are violated in the presence of adaptation hooks and trigger the (semi-automatic) selection of a corresponding adaptation grammar (the *Adaptation Logic*). An *adaptation grammar* contains *adaptation rules* modeling reactions to the detection of context changes. The interplay of the different grammars representing the adaptation logic is realized manually by the *Adaptation Manager*.

Ordering Adaptations: Different adaptations may be applicable during the system execution. The choice of which adaptation to apply may influence the final result. In our framework, adaptations are selected manually by the adaptation manager.

Nature of Adaptations: We consider two classes of adaptations that can be applied and treated in different ways [12,13], in particular:

- *Corrective Adaptations* take care of adapting the application when the current implementation instance cannot proceed with the execution in the current context (i.e., a car is damaged). The main objective is to recover the application and hence focuses on the *self-healing* property. The adaptation starts from the actual context state and performs the necessary changes to bring the application and its context to the expected state where it can be executed again. In our framework, an adaptation is *corrective* if each adaptation state can be *repaired*, i.e., the normal state before the adaptation became necessary is reestablished.
- *Enhancing Adaptations* expand existing services of the application; this may for instance change the non-functional properties of the service, or provide new services with the same or augmented functionalities. In our framework, an adaptation is *enhancing* if each adaptation state can become a normal state, possibly by adding new functionalities and services. The adaptation solution is *not necessarily* identic with the normal state before the adaptation became necessary.

4 Modeling SA Systems by Graph Transformation

In this section, we show how to model self-adaptive (SA-) systems in the formal framework of algebraic graph transformation (AGT) [9]. Specifically, typed graphs, introduced in Def. 1, are used to model the static part of the system. Typed graphs are enriched with constraints that SA-systems have to satisfy even during adaptation. Moreover, we model the behavior and the adaptation of SA-systems by means of graph grammars, introduced in Def. 2.

Definition 1 (Typed Graphs). *A graph $G = (N, E, s, t)$ consists of a set of nodes N, a set of edges E and functions $s, t : E \to N$ assigning to each edge $e \in E$ the source $s(e) \in N$ and target $t(e) \in N$. A graph morphism $f : G \to G'$ is given by a pair of functions $f = (f_N : N \to N', f_E : E \to E')$ which is compatible with source and target functions, i.e., $f_N \circ s = s' \circ f_E$, and $f_N \circ t = t' \circ f_E$. A type graph TG is a graph where nodes and edges are considered as node and edge types, respectively. A TG-typed graph $\overline{G} = (G, t)$ consists of a graph G and a graph morphism $t : G \to TG$, called typing morphism of G. Morphisms $f : \overline{G} \to \overline{G'}$ of typed graphs are graph morphisms $f : G \to G'$ which are compatible with the typing morphisms $t : G \to TG$ and $t' : G' \to TG$, i.e., $t' \circ f = t$.*

For simplicity, we abbreviate $\overline{G} = (G, t)$ by G in the following. Moreover, the approach is also valid for *attributed* and *typed attributed graphs* where nodes and edges can have data type attributes [9], as used in our running example. Note that we also use the extended concept of type graphs with inheritance and multiplicities, stemming from object-oriented (meta) modeling. Typed attributed graphs with inheritance enable an elegant, formal description of hierarchy [9,14]. Formally, a *type graph with inheritance* consists of a type graph according to Def. 1 and an inheritance graph. The type graph consists of all nodes and the arrows with filled arrowheads. The inheritance graph consists of all nodes and the arrows with empty arrowheads. Abstract nodes are marked by {}-brackets. In addition, our type graph may contain multiplicity constraints on edge types that constrain how many objects may be connected by an instance of a certain edge type. A node type may have a multiplicity constraint, restricting the number of instances of this node type [9].

Example 1 (CLS Type Graph and Initial State). Fig. 3 shows the type graph with inheritance for the Car Logistics System, which contains types used for modeling the "normal" aspects of the car logistics scenario, as well as the context types used for adaptation, e.g., the adaptation hooks (context flags) that trigger the adaptation rules.

In the integrated type graph, we have the following types for normal behavior:

- Start, End and BusinessActivity are the main business activities (the colored nodes in Fig. 1). They all inherit from (are subtypes of) the abstract type Activity, hence, their instances may be linked by next edges. The source and target multiplicities of the next edge type are "0..1", meaning that each business activity node is the source [target] of at most one next edge. Node

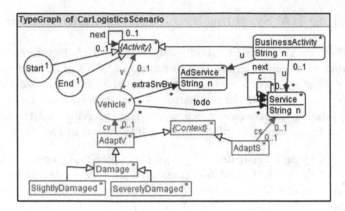

Fig. 3. Type Graph of the Car Logistics Case Study

types Start, End have "1" as multiplicities, denoting that exactly one instance of each of these types must occur in a valid typed graph; type BusinessActivity has multiplicity "*", meaning that we allow arbitrary many instances.

- Service is a service station belonging (linked) to a BusinessActivity. A service may be a composite service. Then it contains other services which are ordered (linked by next arcs). Containment of sub-services in a composite service is modeled by c edges from the sub-services to its composite service.
- Vehicle is a car running through the business process. At the beginning it will be linked (by a v link) to the Start activity and is ready to enter a service. Note that the v link in the type graph links the Vehicle type to the abstract Activity type, meaning that vehicle instances may be linked to instances of arbitrary subtypes of Activity. A todo link between a vehicle and each service of each BusinessActivity is generated when a Vehicle starts the business process. The successful processing of a service leads to the deletion of the corresponding todo link. When all services belonging to the business process have been processed (all todo links are removed), the Vehicle arrives at the End activity as a completed product ready to be delivered to a retailer.

For adaptation handling we have the following types:

- Context is the super-type for all possible context signals, including adaptation hooks. These hooks are used for triggering the adaptation grammars. We specify two main context types AdaptV and AdaptS.
- AdaptV with refinement Damage denotes that a car is damaged and needs to be repaired (SlightlyDamaged) or disposed (SeverelyDamaged).
- AdaptS is the super-type for all possible Service context signals. An edge of type extraSrvBy connects a Vehicle to an adaptation service.
- AdService is an adaptation service not directly attached to a BusinessActivity. Such additional services are used during the business process execution according to an adaptation scenario.

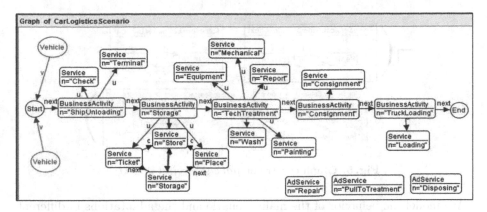

Fig. 4. Initial State Graph of the Car Logistics Case Study

Fig. 4 shows the initial state graph of a scenario with two vehicles.

In order to model consistency and adaptation constraints of a self-adaptive system, we use (TG-typed) graph constraints [10]. Graph constraints denote graph patterns (invariants) that are required or forbidden in each reachable state. A *graph constraint* is given by an injective graph morphism $c : P \to C$ (where P is called *premise* and C *conclusion*). Constraint $c : P \to C$ is *satisfied by a graph G*, written $G \models c$, if the existence of an injective graph morphism $p : P \to G$ implies the existence of an injective graph morphism $q : C \to G$, such that $q \circ c = p$. Graph constraints can be negated or combined by logical connectors (e.g., $\neg c$). If P is empty, only the existence of C is required.

Example 2 (Graph constraints for the Car Logistics system). The set $C_{consist} = \{noFalseServiceConnect, sameBAforComp, noEqualContextFlags\}$ contains some consistency constraints, i.e. structural system requirements that cannot be expressed directly by the type graph and have to be satisfied throughout all states of the car logistics model. For example, the constraint *noFalseService-Connect*, shown in Fig. 5, means that there must be no next or containment loops, a vehicle must not be served (todo edge) by a service which is a container of other services, and a subservice must not be a composite service.

The constraint *sameBAforComp* (not depicted) means that all subservices belonging to the same composite service are linked to the same BusinessActivity and to the same composite service node. Constraint *noEqualContextFlags* (not depicted) requires that the same element (vehicle or service) is not marked by more than one adaptation hook of the same type.

Apart from consistency constraints, we have the set $C_{adapt} = \{Damage\}$ of adaptation constraints (not depicted), containing the adaptation hooks that are required for certain adaptations to occur, i.e., a node of type SlightlyDamaged or SeverelyDamaged connected to a vehicle.

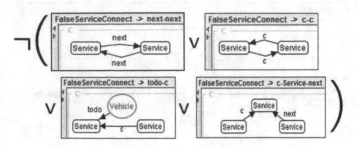

Fig. 5. Graph constraint *noFalseServiceConnect*

We model the behavior of the main scenario and the adaptations in different graph grammars. Whenever an adaptation becomes necessary, the respective adaptation rules are loaded manually into the main case study grammar.

Definition 2 (Typed Graph Grammar). *A typed graph grammar GG = $(TG, G_{init}, Rules)$ consists of a type graph TG, a TG-typed initial graph G_{init} and a set of graph transformation rules ($Rules$). Each rule $r \in Rules$ is given by a span $(L \leftarrow I \rightarrow R)$, where L, I and R are TG-typed graphs, called* left-hand side, interface *and* right-hand side, *respectively. Moreover, $I \rightarrow L$, $I \rightarrow R$ are injective typed graph morphisms where in most cases I can be considered as the intersection of L and R. A rule $r \in Rules$ is applied to a TG-typed graph G by a match morphism $m : L \rightarrow G$ leading to a direct transformation $G \xLongrightarrow{r,m} H$ via (r, m) in two steps: first, we delete the match $m(L)$ without $m(I)$ from G to obtain a context graph D, and then, we glue together D with R along I, i.e., we construct a union of D and R with the intersection graph I, leading to a TG-typed graph H. This gluing construction is represented in the diagram below, where square (1) (resp. (2)) corresponds to gluing G of L and D along I (resp. to gluing H of R and D along I). Note that square (1) in step 1 only exists if the match m leads to a well-defined TG-*

$$N \xleftarrow{nac} L \xleftarrow{l} I \xrightarrow{r} R$$
$$q \searrow \quad m\downarrow \quad (1) \quad \downarrow \quad (2) \quad \downarrow m^*$$
$$G \longleftarrow D \longrightarrow H$$

typed graph D, leaving no dangling edges[3]. Moreover, rules are allowed to have one or more Negative Application Conditions *(NACs). A NAC is a negative graph constraint $nac : L \rightarrow N$. A rule r with a NAC can only be applied at match $m : L \rightarrow G$ if this match satisfies the negative constraint, i.e., there is no injective morphism $q : N \rightarrow G$ with $q \circ nac = m$. This means intuitively that r cannot be applied to G if graph N occurs in G. A transformation $G_0 \xLongrightarrow{*} G_n$ via Rules in GG consists of $n \geq 0$ direct transformations $G_0 \Rightarrow G_1 \Rightarrow ... \Rightarrow G_n$ via rules $r \in Rules$. For $n \geq 1$ we write $G_0 \xLongrightarrow{+} G_n$.*

For transformations of typed attributed graphs with inheritance, abstract nodes and edges may be used in the rules. By matching, they are instantiated

---

[3] Formally, (1) and (2) are *pushouts* in the category **Graphs**$_{TG}$ of TG-typed graphs.

to concrete nodes and edges in the model whose types must be subtypes of the abstract types used in the rules.

Example 3 (Normal behavior rules for the Car Logistics system).   Fig. 6 shows as example the normal behavior rule ServiceToDo[4]. It models the first step for each vehicle, i.e. entering the business process by creating todo edges between the vehicle and each service not yet marked. Three NACs ensure that a todo edge is created only if there is not already a todo edge between the vehicle and the service (NAC ServiceNotDone), that the vehicle is not marked by an adaptation hook (NAC NoAdaptV) and that it is not linked to a composite service (NAC NoSubService). Note that the NAC containing the adaptation hook realizes a priority of adaptation rules over normal rules: normal behavior is blocked at places where adaptation hooks have been placed. Other normal behavior rules move Vehicles to the next BusinessActivity (rules EnterBP, NextBA), process services of the current BusinessActivity by removing todo edges (rules DoService, DoSubService), and finish the business process (rule FinishBP).

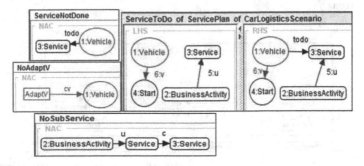

Fig. 6. The normal behavior rule ServiceToDo

In addition to the *normal behavior* rules, the main grammar contains *context rules* that are applicable at any time simulate unforeseen system changes by creating adaptation hooks.

Example 4 (Context rules for the Car Logistics system).   In the CLS, context rules mark vehicles or services with an adaptation hook, i.e., they create a node of one of the context node types AdaptV or AdaptS, respectively. For example, if a car is slightly damaged, rule SlightlyDamage marks it by an adaptation hook of type SlightlyDamaged as shown in Fig. 7. Analogously, rule SeverelyDamaged marks a severely damaged car.

The adaptation hooks trigger the adaptation logic, modeled by adaptation grammars.

---

[4] The rule interface I is not shown by our tool. Equal numbers at graph objects denote mappings in rule and NAC morphisms. An object that is numbered by the same number in L and in R does also occur in I and is hence preserved by the rule.

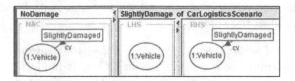

Fig. 7. The context rule SlightlyDamage

Example 5 (Adaptation rules for the Car Logistics system). We may have different adaptation grammars that are suitable for the same adaptation hook. For instance, if a damaged car is in the midst of a composite service, first a rollback adaptation has to be performed and then a repair adaptation (see Fig. 8). In a rollback-adaptation, the already finished sub-services are "rolled back" by applying rule RollBack as long as possible before the vehicle is moved to the treatment area to be repaired. When repair is needed, two additional services are evoked, i.e., the Vehicle is linked to them, one after the other. Rule TakePullToTreatmentService in Fig. 8 uses an extra service to pull up the damaged Vehicle to the treatment area.

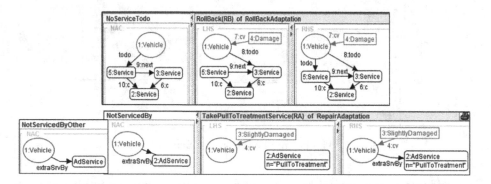

Fig. 8. The rollback-adaptation rule RollBack and the repair-adaptation rule TakePull-ToTreatmentService

Rule TakeRepairService (not depicted) allocates an extra repair service for the slightly damaged Vehicle. After repair, the Vehicle should continue its normal behavior. The composite service it left before (and which has rolled back by applying the rollback-adaptation) may now start again from the beginning. Note that the Vehicle does not forget which services have been done already and which are still to do. Severely damaged cars are picked up by a disposing service applying rule TakeDisposingService. Before the vehicle can be disposed of, its todo links and all flags of kind SlightlyDamaged or SeverelyDamaged are removed by applying rules RemoveToDo and RemoveDamageFlag. Finally, the vehicle is disposed of by rule DisposeVehicle.

An SA-system is defined in Def. 3 by a typed graph grammar where system rules can be partitioned into *normal, context* and *adaptation* rules. Moreover, we have two kinds of constraints, namely *consistency* and *adaptation* constraints.

Definition 3 (Self-Adaptive system in AGT-framework). *A self-adaptive system (SA-system) is given by $SAS = (GG, C_{sys})$, where:*

- $GG = (TG, G_{init}, R_{sys})$ *is a typed graph grammar with type graph TG, a TG-typed initial graph G_{init}, a set of TG-typed rules R_{sys} (system rules), defined by $R_{sys} = R_{norm} \cup R_{cont} \cup R_{adapt}$, where R_{norm} (normal rules), R_{cont} (context rules) and R_{adapt} (adaptation rules) are pairwise disjoint.*
- C_{sys} *is a set of TG-typed graph constraints, called* system constraints, *with $C_{sys} = C_{consist} \cup C_{adapt}$, where $C_{consist}$ (called* consistency constraints*) and C_{adapt} (called* adaptation constraints*) are pairwise disjoint.*

We distinguish reachable, adaptation *and* normal *states, where reachable states are partitioned into normal and adaptation states.*

- $Reach(SAS) = \{G \mid G_{init} \stackrel{*}{\Longrightarrow} G$ *via* $R_{sys}\}$, *i.e., all states reachable via system rules,*
- $Adapt(SAS) = \{G \mid G \in Reach(SAS) \wedge \exists C \in C_{adapt} : G \vDash C\}$, *the adaptation states, i.e., all reachable states satisfying some adaptation constraints,*
- $Norm(SAS) = \{G \mid G \in Reach(SAS) \wedge \forall C \in C_{adapt} : G \nvDash C\}$, *the normal states, i.e., reachable states not satisfying any adaptation constraints.*

For SA-systems, we require that

1. *each pair of a context and a normal rule $(p, r) \in R_{cont} \times R_{norm}$ is sequentially independent [9] (i.e., if there exists a sequence where a context rule is applied first, and a normal rule is applied afterwards (to a different part of the system), then the two rule applications may be swapped),*
2. *SAS is* system consistent: *all reachable states are consistent, i.e., they fulfill the consistency constraints: $\forall G \in Reach(SAS), \forall C \in C_{consist} : G \vDash C$,*
3. *SAS is* normal-state consistent, *i.e., normal rules must not create adaptation hooks: the initial state is normal and all normal rules preserve and reflect normal states: $G_{init} \in Norm(SAS)$ and $\forall G_0 \stackrel{r}{\Longrightarrow} G_1$ via $r \in R_{norm}$ $[G_0 \in Norm(SAS) \Leftrightarrow G_1 \in Norm(SAS)]$*
4. *The set of adaptation rules R_{adapt} is confluent and terminating, i.e., adaptation results are unique and do not depend on the order or location of the adaptation rule applications.*

The requirements of SA-systems can be checked in a static way by inspecting the corresponding rules. This means e.g. that we do not need to check the consistency of all states reachable via system rules; instead, we only check G_{init} for consistency and then check the system rules whether they preserve consistent states. In particular, we can check statically that different adaptations do not interfere with each other, i.e., they are confluent and terminating (see requirement 4). This property is interesting, if more than one set of adaptation rules have to be used to adapt a given state, which is a highly relevant practical problem.

Example 6 (Car Logistics System as SA-system). We define the Car Logistics SA-system $CLS = (GG, C_{sys})$ by the type graph TG in Fig. 3, the initial state G_{init} in Fig. 4, and the sets of rules and constraints (previously explained in Examples 2 to 5):

- R_{norm} = { ServiceToDo, EnterBP, DoService, DoSubService, NextBA, FinishBP },
- R_{cont} = { SlightlyDamage, SeverelyDamage },
- $R_{adapt} = R_{adapt}^1 \cup R_{adapt}^2 \cup R_{adapt}^3$ with
- R_{adapt}^1 = { Rollback },
- R_{adapt}^2 = { TakePullToTreatmentService, TakeRepairService, RepairVehicle }
- R_{adapt}^3 = { TakePullToTreatmentService, TakeRepairService, TakeDisposingService, RemoveTodo, RemoveDamageFlag, DisposeVehicle }
- $C_{consist}$ = { noFalseServiceConnect, sameBAforComp, noEqualContextFlags },
- C_{adapt} = { Damage }

It is shown in [10] that the requirements for SA-systems in Def. 3 are satisfied for the Car Logistics System.

5   Static Analysis of Self-adaptive Systems

In this section, we define desirable operational properties of SA-systems and propose static analysis techniques to verify them. With the *enhancing*-adaptation property below, we require that a system in an adaptation state is eventually adapted, i.e., transformed again to a normal state, by adding new functionalities to the system. *Corrective* self-adaptation means that the system will be repaired leading to the normal state before the adaptation hook was created. In the following, we write $G \Rightarrow^! G'$ to denote a transformation where the rules are applied as long as possible; we write $G \Rightarrow^* G'$ to denote a transformation where the rules are applied arbitrarily often, and the transformation $G \Rightarrow^+ G'$ consists of at least one rule application.

Definition 4 (Self-Adaptation Classes). *An SA-System SAS is called*

1. enhancing, *if each adaptation state is adapted to become a normal state, possibly by adding or by removing functionalities and services:*
   $\forall G_{init} \Rightarrow^* G$ *via* $(R_{norm} \cup R_{cont})$ *with* $G \in Adapt(SAS) \; \exists \; G \Rightarrow^! G'$ *via* R_{adapt} *with* $G' \in Norm(SAS)$.
2. corrective, *if each adaptation state is adapted in a corrective way (repaired):*
   $\forall G_{init} \Rightarrow^* G$ *via* $(q_1 \dots q_n) \in (R_{norm} \cup R_{cont})^*$ *with* $G \in Adapt(SAS) \; \exists \; G \Rightarrow^! G'$ *via* R_{adapt} *with* $G' \in Norm(SAS)$ *and* $\exists G_{init} \Rightarrow^* G'$ *via* $(r_1 \dots r_m) \in R_{norm}^*$, *where* $(r_1 \dots r_m)$ *is the subsequence of all normal rules in* $(q_1 \dots q_n)$.

Remark 1. - By definition, each *corrective* SA system is also *enhancing*, but not vice versa. In corrective SA systems, state G' obtained after adaptation is not only normal but can be generated by all normal rules in the given mixed sequence $(q_1 \dots q_n)$ of normal and context rules, as if no context rule had been applied.

In Def. 5, we define adaptation properties, which imply that the SA-system is corrective/enhancing under suitable conditions, stated in Thm. 1. We want to ensure that for each context rule that adds an adaptation hook, there are suitable adaptation rules leading again to a state without this adaptation hook, even if they are not applied immediately after the hook was set but later when the context monitor reveals that the adaptation must be invoked. This means that other normal and context rules may have been applied before the occurrence of the adaptation hook is monitored.

Definition 5 (Self-Adaptation (SA) Properties). *Let SAS be an SA-system and $G_0 \in Reach(SAS)$. SAS has the*

1. direct adaptation property, *if the adaptation can be performed directly, i.e.,*
   $\forall G_0 \xRightarrow{p} G_1$ *via* $p \in R_{cont} \; \exists \; G_1 \Rightarrow^* G_0$ *via* R_{adapt}*;*
2. normal adaptation property, *if the adaptation can be performed up to normal transformations leading to a possibly different normal state that is reachable from the state before the adaptation hook was set, i.e.,* $\forall G_0 \xRightarrow{p} G_1$ *via* $p \in R_{cont} \; \exists \; G_1 \Rightarrow^+ G_2$ *via* R_{adapt} *s.t.* $\exists \; G_0 \Rightarrow^* G_2$ *via* R_{norm}*;*
3. rollback adaptation property, *if the adaptation can be performed up to normal transformations leading to a possibly different normal state from which the state before the adaptation hook was set is reachable, i.e.,* $\forall G_0 \xRightarrow{p} G_1$ *via* $p \in R_{cont} \; \exists \; G_1 \Rightarrow^+ G_2$ *via* R_{adapt} *s.t.* $\exists \; G_2 \Rightarrow^* G_0$ *via* R_{norm}*.*

Theorem 1 (Self-Adaptation Classes and their SA Properties)
An SA-System SAS is
I. *corrective, if we have property 1 below*
II. *enhancing, if we have a) property 2, or b) properties 3 and 4 below.*

1. *SAS has the direct adaptation property.*
2. *SAS has the normal adaptation property.*
3. *SAS has the rollback adaptation property,*
4. *each pair $(r, q) \in R_{norm} \times R_{adapt}$ is sequentially independent.*

Proof Sketch. (For a complete proof, see [10].)
I. Given $G_{init} \Rightarrow^* G$ via $(q_1, \ldots q_n) \in (R_{norm} \cup R_{cont})^*$ with $G \in Adapt(SAS)$ we have $n \geq 1$, because $G_{init} \in Norm(SAS)$ since SAS is normal-state consistent. By sequential independence we can switch the order of $(q_1, \ldots q_n)$, s.t. first all normal rules $r_i \in R_{norm}$ and then all context rules $p_i \in R_{cont}$ are applied. As example let us consider $G_{init} \Rightarrow^+ G$ via $(r_1, p_1, r_2, p_2, r_3)$ with $r_i \in R_{norm}$ and $p_j \in R_{cont}$. Then sequential independence leads by the Local Church-Rosser theorem to equivalent sequences in subdiagram (1), (2), (3) respectively.

$$G_{init} \xRightarrow{r_1} G_1 \xRightarrow{p_1} G_2 \xRightarrow{r_2} G_3 \xRightarrow{p_2} G_4 \xRightarrow{r_3} G$$

By the direct adaptation property 1, we have $G'_4 \Rightarrow^* G'_3$ and $G \Rightarrow^* G'_4$ via R^*_{adapt}. With $G' = G'_3$ we have $G \Rightarrow^+ G'$ via R^*_{adapt} and $G_{init} \Rightarrow^* G'$ via $(r_1, r_2, r_3) \in R^*_{norm}$ where (r_1, r_2, r_3) is the subsequence $(r_1, p_1, r_2, p_2, r_3)$ which consists of only normal rules, and normal-state consistency implies $G_{init}, G' \in Norm(SAS)$. Note that in the adaptation sequence $G \Rightarrow^+ G'$ the (possible) adaptations due to the adaptation hooks caused by $p_1, p_2 \in R_{cont}$ are performed in opposite order. In general, the sequence $(q_1, \ldots q_n)$ $(n \geq 1)$ contains at least one rule in R_{cont}, because otherwise $G \notin Adapt(SAS)$ (due to normal-state consistency), which is a contradiction to the assumption $G \in Adapt(SAS)$. This implies that we have an adaptation sequence $G \Rightarrow^+ G'$ via R_{adapt}. Since adaptation rules are confluent and terminating, all possible adaptation transformations $G \Rightarrow^+ \overline{G}$ lead to the same result $\overline{G} \cong G'$. Hence SAS is corrective.

II. The second part of the proof works analogously, by arguing that rules can be switched due to independence, leading to the required normal rule sequences in an enhancing SAS.   □

Remark 2. Note that our sufficient conditions for Thm. 1 are also necessary in case that the context rules are sequentially independent. It is advisable to model the set of context rules in this way because usually the need for adaptation may arise in any possible states from independent sources of disturbances issued by the environment. In our example, the context rules are all independent, i.e. if they are applicable in a sequence, their order can be swapped.

In Thm. 2 we give static conditions for the direct, normal and rollback adaptation properties. In part 1 of Thm. 2 we require that for each context rule p the *inverse rule* $p^{-1} = (R \leftarrow I \rightarrow L)$ is *SAS-equivalent* to the *concurrent rule* q^* constructed from an adaptation rule sequence $(q_1, \ldots, q_n) \in R_{adapt}$. Two rules r_1, r_2 are *SAS*-equivalent (written $r_1 \simeq r_2$) if they model the same possible system changes, i.e., $(\exists G \xrightarrow{r_1} G') \Longleftrightarrow (\exists G \xrightarrow{r_2} G')$ with $G \in Reach(SAS)$. A concurrent rule summarizes a given rule sequence in one equivalent rule [9]. A concurrent rule $p *_E q$ is constructed from two rules p and q that may be sequentially dependent via an overlapping graph E by modeling all deletions and creations of elements that are modeled either in p or in q.

In Thm. 2.1, we require that each context rule p has a corresponding adaptation sequence $(q_1 * \ldots * q_n) \in R_{adapt}$, which is not necessarily inverse to p. In Thm. 2.2, it is sufficient to require for the normal adaptation property that we can construct a concurrent rule $p *_{E_0} (q_1, \ldots, q_n)_E$ which is *SAS*-equivalent to a concurrent rule r constructed from a normal rule sequence $(r_1, \ldots, r_m) \in R_{norm}$. Analogously, for the rollback adaptation property we require that $p *_{E_0} (q_1, \ldots, q_n)_E$ is *SAS*-equivalent to an inverse concurrent normal rule r^{-1}.

Theorem 2 (Verification of Self-Adaptation Properties)
   Let SAS be an SA-system and G a reachable system state. SAS has

   1. *the* direct adaptation property, *if for each context rule p there is an adaptation rule sequence that directly reverses the effect of the context rule i.e.,*

$\forall p \in R_{cont} \exists q = (q_1 * \ldots * q_n)_E$ via $E = (E_1, \ldots, E_{n-1})$ and $n \geq 1, q_i \in R_{adapt}$ with $q \simeq p^{-1}$.

2. the normal (resp. rollback) adaptation property, if for each context rule p there is an adaptation rule sequence that reverses the effect of the context rule up to normal rule applications, i.e., $\forall p \in R_{cont}$ we have

   (a) $\exists q = (q_1 * \ldots * q_n)_E$ via $E = (E_1, \ldots, E_{n-1})$ and $n \geq 1, q_i \in R_{adapt}$, and q is applicable after p has been applied,

   (b) $\forall$ overlappings E_0 of p and q leading to a concurrent rule $p *_{E_0} q \exists r = (r_1 * \ldots * r_m)_{E'}$ with $m \geq 1$ via $E' = (E_1', \ldots, E_{m-1}')$ with $r_i \in R_{norm}$ such that $p *_{E_0} q \simeq r$ (resp. $p *_{E_0} q \simeq r^{-1}$ in case of rollback).

Proof. See [10].

In Ex. 7, we verify the SA properties for one variant of our Car Logistics System *CLS*. More examples are elaborated in [10], including a counterexample, where the self-adaptation properties do not hold. In Ex. 7, we have the normal rules $R_{norm} = \{$ServiceToDo, EnterBP, DoService, DoSubService, NextBA, FinishBP$\}$ and the context rule $R_{cont} = \{$SlightlyDamage$\}$ of *CLS*. Hence, we have sequential independence of context rules and normal rules, and, since *CLS* is normal-state consistent, also CLS_{Repair} is normal-state consistent.

Example 7 (SA-System CLS_{Repair} is corrective).
CLS_{Repair} contains one context rule $R_{cont} = \{$SlightlyDamage$\}$ (Fig. 7), and the set of adaptation rules $R_{adapt} = R_{adapt}^2 = \{$TakePullToTreatmentService, TakeRepairService, RepairVehicle$\}$. Moreover, $C_{adapt} = \{Damage\}$ is the set of adaptation constraints.

According to Thm. 1, we have to show that CLS_{Repair} has the direct adaptation property. According to Thm. 2, CLS_{Repair} has the direct adaptation property if for $p = $ SlightlyDamage we have $(q_1, \ldots, q_n) \in R_{adapt}$ with $q = (q_1 * \ldots * q_n)_E \simeq p^{-1}$, where q is the concurrent rule of the adaptation rule sequence $(q_1, \ldots, q_n)$. This means, we have to find an adaptation rule sequence that results in a concurrent rule q which is *SAS*-equivalent to the inverse context rule $p = $ SlightlyDamage (i.e., it removes the SlightlyDamaged flag).

We consider the adaptation rule sequence $s = \{$TakePullToTreatmentService, TakeRepairService, RepairVehicle$\}$ together with suitable dependencies (overlapping) of the right-hand side of q_i and the left-hand side of q_{i+1}, and construct a concurrent rule from this sequence in an iterated way[5]. For our sequence, we get the concurrent adaptation rule q shown in Fig. 9, which is *SAS*-equivalent to the inverse context rule $p = $ SlightlyDamage due to the following argumentation: The additional elements in rule q wrt. rule p (the PullToTreatment and Repair nodes) are preserved by rule q, and are always there in all possible states, since no system rule ever adds or deletes PullToTreatment and Repair nodes.

Hence, CLS_{Repair} has the direct adaptation property, and due to Thm. 1, we can conclude that CLS_{Repair} is corrective.

---

[5] In AGG, concurrent rules can be computed from rule sequences automatically.

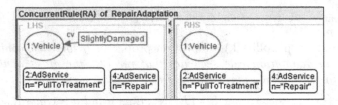

Fig. 9. Concurrent Adaptation Rule q constructed from sequence s in CLS_{Repair}

6   Related Work

A conceptual framework for adaptation is presented in [15]. Adaptation is defined as the run-time modification of the control data. Our approach is compatible with this framework, in the sense that the control data can be identified by the different rule sets that correspond to ordinary computations and to adaptations.

Software Architectures: There is a wealth of Architecture Description Languages (ADLs) and architectural notations which provide support for dynamic software architectures analysis [16]. The *Genie* approach [17] offers management of structural variability of adaptive systems. Genie can be considered as an ADL with generative capabilities to reconfigure from one system structure to another according to changes in the environment and to decide what kind of structural reconfiguration has to be performed. The main limit of this approach is the absence of a way to guarantee desired properties of the systems after each adaptation execution; from the modeling point of view, the approach is specifically architectural, whereas we propose a general approach that can be used at different levels of abstraction. The SA-framework *Rainbow* [18] uses external mechanisms and an SA model to monitor a managed system, detect problems, determine a course of action, and carry out adaptation actions at explicit customization points. In our approach, we do not rely on pre-defined customization points to manage the adaptation, but we monitor context properties to adapt the system. Becker and Giese [19] present a graph transformation based approach to model SA-systems on a high level of abstraction. The correctness of the modeled SA-systems is checked by using simulation and invariant checking techniques to verify that a given set of graph transformations will never reach a forbidden state. The limitation of this approach is that a unique model is used for application and adaptation logics. This means that when a new adaptation case is added, the overall model must be refined. In our approach, the adaptation logic is developed separately from the application logic in terms of adaptation rules.

Service-Oriented Computing (SOC): In the SOC community, various approaches supporting self-healing have been defined, e.g., triggering repair strategies as a consequence of a requirement violation [20], and optimizing QoS of service-based applications [21],Repair strategies usually are specified by means of policies to manage the dynamism of the execution environment [22,23]. The goals of the strategies proposed by the aforementioned approaches range from service selection to rebinding and application reconfiguration [24]. Some techniques enable the definition of various adaptation strategies but they all lack a coherent design approach to support designers in this complex task.

Summarizing, our approach abstracts from particular languages and notations[6] and can be applied at different levels of granularity. In our framework, the system can be modeled together with adaptation strategies and mechanisms, and their properties can be verified in a semi-automatic way using static analysis.

7   Conclusion and Future Work

In [7,8], we already modeled self-healing (SH) systems using algebraic graph transformation and formulated preliminary sufficient conditions allowing for a static analysis of self-healing system properties. In this paper, we built on these preliminary results and generalised the approach to the class of adaptive systems that is identified in Sec. 2 and that includes *corrective* and *enhancing* adaptive systems, i.e., systems that need rollback adaptations or adaptations that extend existing services of the application.

We classified SA-systems by their operational properties and defined adaptation properties concerning the behavior of adaptations w.r.t. their influence on the normal system behavior. The classification helps to reason about system behavior, where e.g., systems with the rollback adaptation property may be more in danger of repeated failures than systems with normal adaptation property, since states that preceded failures are reached again after the adaptation. Note that the operational properties concern *all* reachable system states, whereas they are checked in our approach in a static way by inspecting only the rules without producing all reachable states explicitly.

Our main results concerning operational properties are summarized in Fig. 10, where most of the static conditions in Thm. 1 and Thm. 2 can be automatically checked by AGG. We needed some manual effort to show termination and *SAS*-equivalence of rules, but it was always possible to perform the analysis statically. Although static conditions lead to over-approximating systems, we found

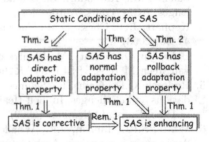

Fig. 10. Static SAS analysis

that the conditions to be checked were reasonable to be expected in SA-systems and did not restrict our intuitive notion of SA-system properties. Exemplarily, the different properties have been verified for different adaptations of our car logistics system in a seaport terminal [10].

Work is in progress to evaluate the usability of our approach by larger case studies, and to further automate the checks currently needing manual effort with AGG. Finally, we plan an integration of our formal framework with a real process engine like JBoss jBPM [25]. The idea is to use our framework as an analysis tool to guarantee the system consistency when each adaptation is executed.

---

[6] Several other related SA-modeling approaches are discussed in [10].

Acknowledgement. This paper is dedicated to Martin Wirsing as one of the pioneers of algebraic specification and data types in the early 1980ies in Germany. As member of the famous CIP-group in Munich he influenced the development of algebraic specification languages, especially ASL [26], which is based on loose semantics with hierarchy constraints. In contrast to the CIP-group, the TFS-group of Hartmut Ehrig in Berlin followed the ADJ-approach based on initial algebra semantics leading to the algebraic specification language ACT ONE [27]. Actually there was a fruitful cooperation between these and other European groups leading to the European project COMPASS [28] and later on to the algebraic specification language CASL[7]. In the European project SENSORIA[8], that was coordinated by Martin Wirsing, these foundational theories, techniques and methods were integrated in a pragmatic software engineering approach. One of the authors, Antonio Bucchiarone, was working for SENSORIA in Lucca, and got his PhD when Martin was PhD school board member of the IMT Institute for Advanced Studies. Today, algebraic specifications and data types are integrated in several other software development concepts and languages. Especially in this paper, we demonstrated the use of attributed graph transformations, which combine algebraic specification with graph transformation.

References

1. Brun, Y., Marzo Serugendo, G., Gacek, C., Giese, H., Kienle, H., Litoiu, M., Müller, H., Pezzè, M., Shaw, M.: Engineering self-adaptive systems through feedback loops. Software Engineering for Self-Adaptive Systems, 48–70 (2009)
2. Salehie, M., Tahvildari, L.: Self-adaptive software: Landscape and research challenges. ACM Trans. Auton. 4(2), 14:1–14:42 (2009)
3. Kephart, J.O., Chess, D.M.: The vision of autonomic computing. Computer 36(1), 41–50 (2003)
4. Babaoğlu, Ö., Jelasity, M., Montresor, A., Fetzer, C., Leonardi, S., van Moorsel, A., van Steen, M. (eds.): SELF-STAR 2004. LNCS, vol. 3460. Springer, Heidelberg (2005)
5. Rodosek, G.D., Geihs, K., Schmeck, H., Burkhard, S.: Self-healing systems: Foundations and challenges. In: Self-Healing and Self-Adaptive Systems. Number 09201 in Proc. Dagstuhl Seminar (2009)
6. White, S.R., Hanson, J.E., Whalley, I., Chess, D.M., Segal, A., Kephart, J.O.: Autonomic computing: Architectural approach and prototype. Integr. Comput.-Aided Eng. 13(2), 173–188 (2006)
7. Bucchiarone, A., Pelliccione, P., Vattani, C., Runge, O.: Self-repairing systems modeling and verification using AGG. In: IEEE Joint Working IEEE/IFIP Conference on Software Architecture (WICSA 2009), pp. 181–190 (2009)
8. Ehrig, H., Ermel, C., Runge, O., Bucchiarone, A., Pelliccione, P.: Formal analysis and verification of self-healing systems. In: Rosenblum, D.S., Taentzer, G. (eds.) FASE 2010. LNCS, vol. 6013, pp. 139–153. Springer, Heidelberg (2010)
9. Ehrig, H., Ehrig, K., Prange, U., Taentzer, G.: Fundamentals of Algebraic Graph Transformation. In: EATCS Monographs in Theor. Comp. Science. Springer (2006)

---

[7] http://en.wikipedia.org/wiki/Common_Algebraic_
   Specification_Language
[8] http://www.sensoria-ist.eu

10. Bucchiarone, A., Ehrig, H., Ermel, C., Pelliccione, P., Runge, O.: Modeling and analysis of self-adaptive systems based on graph transformation. Technical Report 2013/03, TU Berlin (2013), http://www.eecs.tu-berlin.de/menue/forschung/forschungsberichte/2013

11. Böse, F., Piotrowski, J., Scholz-Reiter, B.: Autonomously controlled storage management in vehicle logistics - applications of RFID and mobile computing systems. Int. Journal of RT Technologies: Research an Application 1(1), 57–76 (2009)

12. Chapin, N., Hale, J.E., Kham, K.M., Ramil, J.F., Tan, W.G.: Types of software evolution and software maintenance. Software Maintenance 13(1), 3–30 (2001)

13. Lanese, I., Bucchiarone, A., Montesi, F.: A framework for rule-based dynamic adaptation. In: Wirsing, M., Hofmann, M., Rauschmayer, A. (eds.) TGC 2010, LNCS, vol. 6084, pp. 284–300. Springer, Heidelberg (2010)

14. Golas, U., Lambers, L., Ehrig, H., Orejas, F.: Attributed graph transformation with inheritance: Efficient conflict detection and local confluence analysis using abstract critical pairs. Theor. Comput. Sci. 424, 46–68 (2012)

15. Bruni, R., Corradini, A., Gadducci, F., Lluch Lafuente, A., Vandin, A.: A conceptual framework for adaptation. In: de Lara, J., Zisman, A. (eds.) Fundamental Approaches to Software Engineering. LNCS, vol. 7212, pp. 240–254. Springer, Heidelberg (2012)

16. Bradbury, J.S., Cordy, J.R., Dingel, J., Wermelinger, M.: A survey of self-management in dynamic software architecture specifications. In: Proc. 1st ACM SIG-SOFT Workshop on Self-Managed Systems (WOSS 2004), pp. 28–33. ACM (2004)

17. Bencomo, N., Blair, G.S.: Using architecture models to support the generation and operation of component-based adaptive systems. Software Engineering for Self-Adaptive Systems, 183–200 (2009)

18. Garlan, D., Cheng, S.W., Huang, A.C., Schmerl, B., Steenkiste, P.: Rainbow: Architecture-based self-adaptation with reusable infrastructure. Computer 37(10), 46–54 (2004)

19. Becker, B., Giese, H.: Modeling of correct self-adaptive systems: A graph transformation system based approach. In: Soft Computing as Transdisciplinary Science and Technology (CSTST 2008), pp. 508–516. ACM Press (2008)

20. Spanoudakis, G., Zisman, A., Kozlenkov, A.: A service discovery framework for service centric systems. In: Proc. Int. Conf. on Services Computing, pp. 251–259 (2005)

21. Canfora, G., Penta, M.D., Esposito, R., Villani, M.L.: An approach for QoS-aware service composition based on genetic algorithms. In: Proc. Conf. on Genetic and Evolutionary Computation (GECO 2005), pp. 1069–1075 (2005)

22. Baresi, L., Guinea, S., Pasquale, L.: Self-healing BPEL processes with Dynamo and the JBoss rule engine. In: ESSPE 2007, pp. 11–20. ACM (2007)

23. Colombo, M., Di Nitto, E., Mauri, M.: SCENE: A service composition execution environment supporting dynamic changes disciplined through rules. In: Dan, A., Lamersdorf, W. (eds.) ICSOC 2006. LNCS, vol. 4294, pp. 191–202. Springer, Heidelberg (2006)

24. Pfeffer, H., Linner, D., Steglich, S.: Dynamic adaptation of workflow based service compositions. In: Huang, D.-S., Wunsch II, D.C., Levine, D.S., Jo, K.-H. (eds.) ICIC 2008. LNCS, vol. 5226, pp. 763–774. Springer, Heidelberg (2008)

25. JBoss: jBPM Engine, http://www.jboss.org/jbpm

26. Wirsing, M.: Structured algebraic specifications: A kernel language. Theor. Comput. Sci., 123–249 (1986)

27. Ehrig, H., Mahr, B.: Fundamentals of Algebraic Specification 1: Equations and Initial Semantics, Berlin. EATCS Monographs on Theoretical Computer Science, vol. 6 (1985)

28. Krieg-Brückner, B.: Seven years of COMPASS. In: COMPASS/ADT, pp. 1–13 (1995)

Formalization of Invariant Patterns
for the Invariant Refinement Method

Tomáš Bureš, Ilias Gerostathopoulos, Jaroslav Keznikl,
František Plášil, and Petr Tůma

Charles University in Prague
Faculty of Mathematics and Physics
Prague, Czech Republic
{bures,iliasg,keznikl,plasil,tuma}@d3s.mff.cuni.cz

Abstract. Refining high-level system invariants into lower-level software obligations has been successfully employed in the design of ensemble-based systems. In order to obtain guarantees of design correctness, it is necessary to formalize the invariants in a form amenable to mathematical analysis. This paper provides such a formalization and demonstrates it in the context of the Invariant Refinement Method. The formalization is used to formally define invariant patterns at different levels of abstraction and with respect to different (soft) real-time constraints, and to provide proofs of theorems related to refinement among these patterns.

Keywords: architecture refinement, requirements, assume-guarantee.

1 Introduction

Invariant-based design is advantageous for designing adaptive self-organizing systems formed by ensembles of autonomic components [7–9] – see e.g. SOTA [1] – as it explicitly captures the valid states of the system, i.e., the invariant properties of a correct system. Such ensemble-based systems [2] operate autonomously in an open-ended environment, and invariants are well-suited for capturing the properties of a component with respect to its environment.

The problem of invariant refinement is that the requirements of a system are typically described in a much higher level of abstraction than the properties (invariants) of the individual constituents of system architecture (components, component processes, ensembles). The transition from high-level obligations to low-level constraints includes a number of design choices without firm borders and guidelines, and thus is prone to errors.

In our work we have proposed to bridge this gap by gradual step-wise refinement (decomposition) of invariants, which ends up with detailed specification of the behavior of the involved architectural elements – ensembles, components. We call this approach *Invariant Refinement Method – IRM* [2, 10]. IRM however requires the steps of the refinement to be well-defined (ideally formally), so that the refinement itself represents a proof of the correctness of the design. *In*

R. De Nicola and R. Hennicker (Eds.): Wirsing Festschrift, LNCS 8950, pp. 602–618, 2015.
© Springer International Publishing Switzerland 2015

other words, it is necessary to have (formal) means allowing for deciding upon the correctness of the refinement.

Having a formal framework that formalizes these relations allows for (i) design-time guarantees of design correctness, i.e., guarantees that the system design truly addresses the high-level requirements, and (ii) runtime monitoring, i.e., detection of discrepancies in system design during execution.

In this paper we provide such a formal framework, and also provide mathematical proofs of "correctness by construction", as a continuation of the work presented in [10]. To do so, we first describe and formalize the invariant concept and invariant refinement in the light of our running example (Section 2). We then provide a formal account of the invariant patterns that can guide the IRM design (Section 3), and provide the main contribution of the paper, i.e., the set of theorems and lemmas that formally ground the relations between the invariant patterns (Section 4). Finally, we discuss some of the implications of our approach and conclude (Section 5).

Personal Note: Ideas presented in this paper have been inspired by the work of Martin Wirsing in the field of formal software engineering of autonomous service-components. We have known Martin for a long time, and we have been able to stay up-to-date with the advancements of his research group at LMU, as one of the authors has been a visiting professor at LMU for the past years. We have also had the opportunity to work with him and his colleagues from his department in the ASCENS project, which he was coordinating. Cooperating with Martin is always both enjoyable and inspiring, not only because of his firm knowledge and fresh ideas, but also because of his kind and welcoming personality.

1.1   Running Example

To illustrate the IRM-based design, we use a running example from the ASCENS e-mobility case study [14]. In this case study, electric vehicles (e-vehicles) have to coordinate in order to reach particular places of interest (POIs) within certain time constraints specifying the expected POI arrival and departure times, as prescribed by the drivers' daily schedules (calendars). At the same time, e-vehicles compete for stopovers in limited energy charging stations (CSs) along their route. Specifically, each e-vehicle has to plan its individual trip according to the driver's calendar and the (perceived) available time slots for charging at each relevant charging station. This results in a fully decentralized – and thus scalable – system.

To simplify the presentation of our approach, we assume for the running example that each vehicle has a single driver and a single destination POI. This results in the scenario where the goal of every vehicle is to reach its POI in time, while visiting charging stations during the trip if necessary. The charging stations may however become unavailable at any time and thus it is necessary to introduce monitoring of charging stations and potential re-planning.

2   Background

2.1   Invariant Refinement

In principle, IRM employs *invariants* to describe a desired state of the system-to-be at every time instant; i.e., to describe the *operational normalcy* of the system-to-be, essential for its continuous operation. When using IRM to design ensemble-based systems, the objective is to refine the overall system goal(s) in an iterative way and end up with the invariants that concern the individual constituents of system architecture – components, component processes, and ensembles.

The refinement is performed by decomposing a higher-level invariant into a set of lower-level sub-invariants (AND-decomposition). In order for the decomposition of a parent I_p into the children $I_{s1}, \ldots, I_{sn}$ to be an actual refinement, the *conjunction* of the children have to *entail* the parent, i.e., it has to hold:

$$I_{s1} \wedge \ldots \wedge I_{sn} \Rightarrow I_p \quad (entailment)$$
$$I_{s1} \wedge \ldots \wedge I_{sn} \nRightarrow false \ (consistency)$$

This type of decomposition is applied iteratively, starting from the high-level invariants that reflect system-level goals and ending with low-level ones that refer to a single component or an ensemble of components. The outcome is a graph capturing the structural elaborations and design decisions at different abstraction levels. Since each decomposition step may involve a design decision, it is important to ensure that this decision complies with the entailment and consistency conditions.

Invariant Refinement of the Running Example. An invariant-based design of a system targeting the running example is presented in Figure 1. A description of each individual invariant follows.

(1) This is the main goal of the scenario.
(2) This expresses a specific requirement on the designed system and the vehicle's planner input in particular. In this context, a plan is a black-box giving for each time instance the expected position of the vehicle at that time.
(3) This reflects the assumption that the plan is always realistic (i.e., that it is actually possible to follow it given the traffic and car characteristics), and that the driver would follow it precisely.
(4) This expresses the assumption that charging station availability does not change too quickly and that the initial set-up of the environment is "planning-friendly".
(5) A specific system requirement that constrains the input and timing of the planner. In particular, we assume read consistency with respect to the belief (i.e., new plan is always based on the *same or newer* belief than the previous plan). Moreover, (5) and (6) together represent the design decision of dividing the activity of computing the plan from remote data into two activities of (i) creating a local belief of the remote data and (ii) computing the plan from the local belief.

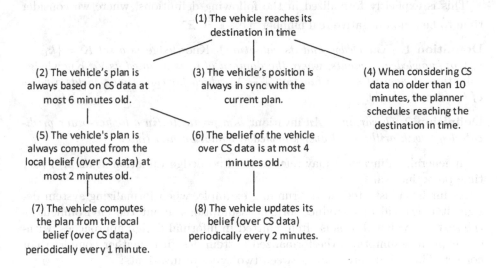

Fig. 1. Invariant refinement of the running example

(6) A specific system requirement that constrains the timing of charging station monitoring and belief updating.

(7) A specific system requirement precisely determining the input and timing of the planner. In particular, we assume real-time periodic computation.

(8) A specific system requirement precisely determining the timing of CS monitoring. In particular, we assume (distributed) real-time periodic monitoring.

Note that the invariant-based design such as the one presented in Figure 1 is hardly ever a product of a top-down design process. In practice, a mixed top-down/bottom-up process is followed, where sub-invariants are identified by asking "*how* can this invariant be satisfied" and parent invariants are identified by asking "*why* should this invariant(s) be satisfied".

2.2   Invariant Formalization

In general, the goal of invariant-based system design is to formally capture properties of a valid system. Thus, we will first discuss the necessary characteristics of such formalization (i.e., characteristics implied by the domain).

In the domain of (soft) real-time component ensembles, the way of expressing properties of a valid system is, as indicated by the running example, to capture a valid evolution of knowledge values in time. To do that, the underlying formalism has to provide means for referring to knowledge values at arbitrary time instants. When generalized, we can say the formalism needs to refer to timed sequences of knowledge values (i.e., timed streams of data), which provide a complete view on the knowledge value evolution in time.

This is explicitly formalized in the following definitions, where we consider time to be a non-negative real number, i.e., $\mathbb{T} \stackrel{\text{def}}{=} \mathbb{R}_0^+$.

Definition 1. *(Knowledge and its valuation)* Knowledge *is a set* $K = \{k_1, \dots k_n\}$ *of knowledge elements, where the domain of* k_i *is denoted as* V_i. *Knowledge valuation of element* k_i *is a function* $\mathbb{T} \to V_i$ *which for each time* t *yields a value of* k_i *(denoted* $k_i[t]$*).*

Definition 2. *(Invariant)* An invariant *is a predicate (in a higher-order predicate logic with arithmetic) over knowledge valuation and time.*

In general, an invariant may refer to the knowledge valuation at an arbitrary time point/interval.

As further illustrated by the running example, when formalizing system design, it is critical to introduce formal assumptions about the environment of the system. Although this is often omitted in informal design approaches, without explicit assumptions the formalized system design is neither complete nor correct. Thus we differentiate between two types of invariants:

- *System invariants* reflect properties of the individual architectural elements of the system. Their validity is to be ensured by the implementation of the system.
- *Assumptions* reflect the properties of the system's environment assumed by system invariants. Validity of these invariants is usually out of control of the designer and is necessary for correct operation of the implementation.

For example, invariant (2) from the running example is a system invariant while invariant (4) is an assumption.

3   Invariant Patterns

In general, the form of invariants is not explicitly restricted. However, at particular levels of abstraction (when describing architectural elements) there are several patterns virtually omnipresent in any invariant-based design [10]. It is thus beneficial to have means for concise and consistent representation of such invariant patterns.

General Invariants. At the highest abstraction level, *general invariants* relate to system-level goals. They capture the operational normalcy of a system by relating the past and current knowledge valuations to future knowledge valuations. Therefore, a general invariant can have an arbitrary internal structure.

Present-past Invariants. At a lower abstraction level, the invariants express that some knowledge is based on other knowledge, which, at the same time, is no older than a particular time interval – *lag*. This reflects the fact (abstracted by general invariants) that software systems cannot employ future knowledge to maintain their operational normalcy, but have to depend on present and/or past knowledge instead.

In this case, such invariants typically capture that there is a particular relation (frequently capturing a post-condition P of a computation) between current knowledge and knowledge no older than the lag L. In the idealized case where all components have always up-to-date beliefs and their actions are instant the lag is equal to zero. In general, though, the lag is inversely proportional to the observed precision (assuming that precision depends on the oldness of observed data) and robustness (as in the case of real-time software control systems).

Definition 3. *(Present-past invariants) For a predicate P capturing the relation between valuation of knowledge elements $I_1, \ldots, I_n$ and $O_1, \ldots, O_m$, and the lag L, the expression $P_{p-p}^{L}[I_1, \ldots, I_n][O_1, \ldots, O_m]$ denotes the following present-past invariant:*

$$\forall t \in \mathbb{T}, \exists t_1, \ldots, t_n : 0 \leq t - t_i \leq L, i \in 1..n :$$
$$P(I_1[t_1], \ldots, I_n[t_n], O_1[t], \ldots, O_m[t])$$

In this context, we call $I_1, \ldots, I_n$ "input" variables and $O_1, \ldots, O_m$ "output" variables of the invariant so as to denote the correspondence of these variables to the inputs/outputs of the computation that is responsible for maintaining the invariant.

During refinement of a general invariant into (a conjunction of) present-past invariants, it is necessary to introduce assumptions to guarantee that maintaining the operational normalcy based on the current and/or past knowledge valuation will eventually result in reaching the operational normalcy based on a future knowledge valuation – e.g. assumption (4) in Figure 1.

Activity Invariants. Another frequent form of timed invariants, used at a lower level of abstraction, closely reflects properties of a (soft) real-time activity while assuming read consistency with respect to the input knowledge of this activity, i.e., that each output knowledge valuation is based on the same or newer input knowledge valuation than the previous one. This is illustrated in Figure 2.

In this case, an *activity invariant* captures that the output knowledge valuation changes only as a result of performing the activity. Moreover, although reading the input knowledge of the activity, as well as computing and writing the output knowledge, takes some time, it never (altogether) exceeds the corresponding time limit (i.e., lag).

More rigorously, at any time the output knowledge valuation corresponds to the outcome of the activity applied on input knowledge valuation not older than the lag. Moreover, each output is based on same or newer inputs than the previous output.

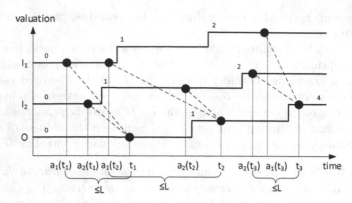

Fig. 2. Illustration of a valid knowledge valuation with respect to an activity where the output O represents sum of inputs I_1 and I_2, while meeting lag L

Definition 4. *(Activity invariant) For a predicate P reflecting the post-condition of an activity with inputs $I_1, \ldots, I_n$ and outputs $O_1, \ldots, O_m$, and for lag L, the expression $P_{act}^{L}[I_1, \ldots, I_n][O_1, \ldots, O_m]$ denotes the following activity invariant:*

$$\exists a_1, \ldots, a_n : \mathbb{T} \to \mathbb{T}, \forall t \in \mathbb{T}, 0 \le t - a_i(t) \le L, a_i \text{ non-decreasing, } i \in 1..n :$$
$$P(I_1[a_1(t)], \ldots, I_n[a_n(t)], O_1[t], \ldots, O_m[t])$$

where the non-decreasing function a_i gives for each time t the corresponding time t' such that the valuation of I_i at t' was "used to compute" the valuation of $O_1, \ldots, O_m$ at t, as shown in Figure 2.

Process Invariants. At the lowest level of abstraction (i.e., in the leaves of the invariant decomposition), an activity invariant that captures local computation (i.e., with no distributed knowledge involved) while assuming read consistency is refined into an invariant capturing a periodic real-time component process – a *process invariant*.

Compared to activity invariants, process invariants introduce the additional constraint that the activity is performed exactly once in every *period*. The period thus becomes an elaboration of the activity lag, and the output knowledge evaluation is determined by the release time (time at which a task becomes ready for execution) and finish time in each period [3].

Specifically, such an invariant captures that if the current time is before the finish time of the process in the current period, then the outputs are the same as in the previous period (i.e., they correspond to the inputs used in the previous period). Otherwise, the outputs correspond to the inputs at the release time of the process in this period.

Definition 5. *(Process invariant) For a predicate P reflecting the post-condition of a periodic real-time process with inputs $I_1, \ldots, I_n$, outputs $O_1, \ldots, O_m$, and* *period L, the expression $P^L_{proc}[I_1, \ldots, I_n][O_1, \ldots, O_m]$ denotes the following process invariant:*

$$\exists R, F : \mathbb{N} \to \mathbb{T} : E(x-1) \leq R(x) < F(x) < E(x) \; \forall x \in \mathbb{N},$$
$$\forall p \in \mathbb{N}, \forall t \in \langle E(p-1), E(p)) :$$
$$t < F(p) \Rightarrow P(I_1[R(p-1)], \ldots, I_n[R(p-1)], O_1[t], \ldots, O_m[t])$$
$$t \geq F(p) \Rightarrow P(I_1[R(p)], \ldots, I_n[R(p)], O_1[t], \ldots, O_m[t])$$

where $E(n) : \mathbb{N}_0 \to \mathbb{T} = n \cdot L$, i.e., the end of the n-th period. $R(n)$ and $F(n)$ denote the release and finish time of the real-time process in the n-th period.

Note that unlike activity invariants, there is the same R for each I, reflecting that at the release time the process reads all the inputs atomically.

Exchange Invariants. Similar to a process invariant, an activity invariant at the lowest level of abstraction that captures establishment of a belief (that can be addressed by ensemble knowledge exchange) while assuming distributed read consistency is refined into an invariant capturing periodic knowledge exchange of an ensemble – an *exchange invariant*.

Contrary to process invariants, exchange invariants assume that the input values might have been read at different times, since the inputs are potentially distributed (however, the times have to fit into the same period). Another difference is that exchange invariants consider also the knowledge propagation delays stemming e.g. from delays in data transfer over the network. An exchange invariant thus models a composite activity consisting of (i) knowledge transfer (with an upper bound on its duration), and (ii) periodic evaluation of the membership condition and knowledge exchange.

An important assumption is that each component executes the incoming knowledge exchange (i.e., knowledge exchange that updates the local component's knowledge) on its own, while the other components asynchronously send the required input knowledge. These composite activities may be partially overlapping to cater for situations where the knowledge transfer time is larger than the knowledge exchange period.

Definition 6. *(Exchange invariant) Let P be a predicate reflecting the postcondition of a periodic knowledge exchange with inputs $I_1, \ldots, I_n$, outputs $O_1, \ldots, O_m$, and period L. Provided that it takes at most T for the knowledge to become available at the component executing the knowledge exchange, the expression $P^{L,T}_{exc}[I_1, \ldots, I_n][O_1, \ldots, O_m]$ denotes the following exchange invariant:*

$$\exists a_1, \ldots, a_n : \mathbb{T} \to \mathbb{T}, \forall t \in \mathbb{T}, 0 \leq t - a_i(t) \leq T, a_i \text{ non-decreasing}, i \in 1..n :$$
$$\exists R, F : \mathbb{N} \to \mathbb{T} : E(x-1) \leq R(x) < F(x) < E(x) \; \forall x \in \mathbb{N},$$
$$\forall p \in \mathbb{N}, \forall t \in \langle E(p-1), E(p)) :$$
$$t < F(p) \Rightarrow P(I_1[a_1(R(p-1))], \ldots, I_n[a_n(R(p-1))], O_1[t], \ldots, O_m[t])$$
$$t \geq F(p) \Rightarrow P(I_1[a_1(R(p))], \ldots, I_n[a_n(R(p))], O_1[t], \ldots, O_m[t])$$

where $E(n) : \mathbb{N}_0 \to \mathbb{T} = n \cdot L$, *i.e., the end of the n-th period. $R(n)$ and $F(n)$ denote the release and finish time of the real-time knowledge exchange in the n-th period. Finally, a_i gives for each time t the corresponding time t' such that the valuation of I_i that was available to the component executing the knowledge exchange at t was sent to the component at t'.*

Note, that there is a (potentially) different a_i for each I_i, reflecting that the inputs can be sent to the component executing the knowledge exchange at different times. Moreover, there is the same t for each O_i, which corresponds to the assumption, that knowledge exchange is unidirectional, i.e., it writes only into the knowledge of one component, and thus the writes can be atomic.

3.1   Illustration of Invariant Patterns on the Running Example

Using the above-defined invariant patterns, the case-study invariants can be formalized as follows. Note that the patterns are not applicable for invariants 1 and 3, and are only partially applicable for invariant 4 (only for the left hand side of the implication), since 1 is a general invariant and 3 and 4 are assumptions.

(1) *The vehicle reaches its destination in time:*

$$\exists t \in \mathbb{T}, t \leq DEADLINE : v.pos[t] = DEST$$

(2) *The vehicle's plan is always based on CS data at most 6 minutes old:*

$$Plan_{p-p}^{6min}[t, v.pos, v.charge, CS_1, \ldots, CS_n][v.plan]$$

where the *Plan* predicate denotes the post-condition of the planning algorithm given the current time, current position, current charge, and CS data.

(3) *The vehicle's position is always in sync with the current plan:*

$$\forall t \in \mathbb{T} : v.pos[t] = v.plan[t](t)$$

(4) *When considering CS data no older than 10 minutes, the planner schedules reaching the destination in time.*

$$Plan_{p-p}^{10min}[t, v.pos, v.charge, CS_1, \ldots, CS_n][v.plan]$$
$$\Rightarrow \exists t' \in \mathbb{T}, t' \leq DEADLINE : v.plan[t](t') = DEST$$

(5) *The vehicle's plan is always computed from the local belief (over CS data) at most 2 minutes old.*

$$Plan_{act}^{2min}[t, v.pos, v.charge, v.belief][v.plan]$$

(6) *The belief of the vehicle over CS data is at most 4 seconds old.*

$$Belief_{p-p}^{4min}[CS_1, \ldots, CS_n][v.belief]$$

where the *Belief* predicate denotes the condition of the vehicle's belief being equal to the CS data.

(7) *The vehicle computes the plan from the local belief (over CS data) periodically every 1 minute.*

$$Plan_{proc}^{1min}[t, v.pos, v.charge, v.belief][v.plan]$$

(8) *The vehicle updates its belief (over CS data) periodically every 2 minutes.*

$$Belief_{exc}^{2min}[CS_1, \ldots, CS_n][v.belief]$$

Naturally, the usage of invariant patterns particularly simplifies the lower-level, more technical invariants that capture computation activities. This allows for more concise and consistent invariant-based design.

4 Correctness by Construction

A simplification of invariant-based design is not the only benefit of using the invariant patterns during invariant-based design. The main advantage is the ability of formal reasoning on the level of patterns instead of reasoning on the level of predicate logic upon knowledge valuations (since state-of-the-art theorem provers for such complex logics still do not have the necessary performance).

Thus, we propose a formal framework allowing for formal reasoning on the level of invariant patterns.

4.1 Basic Pattern Relations

First, we elaborate on the basic relations of the invariant patterns which correspond to the natural relations among the related software concepts of activity/activity with read consistency/process/ensemble.

A straightforward observation for a present-past invariant is that, given a particular knowledge valuation, if the outputs are always based on inputs within the given time limit, increasing the limit maintains this property. A similar observation holds for activity invariants. This is formalized in the following theorem.

Theorem 1. *(Maximal lag refinement) For $K \leq L$:*

$$P_{p-p}^K[I_1, \ldots, I_n][O_1, \ldots, O_m] \Rightarrow P_{p-p}^L[I_1, \ldots, I_n][O_1, \ldots, O_m]$$
$$P_{act}^K[I_1, \ldots, I_n][O_1, \ldots, O_m] \Rightarrow P_{act}^L[I_1, \ldots, I_n][O_1, \ldots, O_m]$$

Proof. A direct corollary of the lag/activity invariant definition. In particular, the existence of t_i such that $0 < t - t_i \leq K$ in $P_{p-p}^K[I_1, \ldots, I_n][O_1, \ldots, O_m]$ guarantees the existence of t_i such that $0 < t - t_i \leq L$ in $P_{p-p}^L[I_1, \ldots, I_n][O_1, \ldots, O_m]$ (similarly for a_i and $0 < x - a_i(x) \leq L$). $\qquad\square$

One can also observe that the requirement of read consistency of inputs in addition to the time limit (in activity invariants) is a stronger requirement than the time limit only (in present-past invariants); this is formalized in the following theorem.

Theorem 2. *(Activity invariant implies present-past invariant) Assuming that* $I = I_1, \ldots, I_n$ *and* $O = O_1, \ldots, O_m$, *it holds:*

$$P_{act}^L[I][O] \Rightarrow P_{p-p}^L[I][O]$$

Proof. The existence of $t_1, \ldots, t_n$ for $P_{p-p}^L[I][O]$ is given by $a_1, \ldots, a_n$ of $P_{act}^L[I][O]$. In particular, $\forall t$ we set $t_i = a_i(t)$. □

A similar theorem can be formulated for the process and activity invariants. Here, the idea is that, in reality, a periodic process is actually a strict refinement of an activity with read consistency and time limit on input data. However, instead of considering the same time limit for both invariants as in previous cases, the activity invariant needs twice the time limit of the process invariant. This also complies with the well-known fact in the area of real-time scheduling: in order to achieve a particular end-to-end response time with a real-time periodic process, the period needs to be at most half of the desired response time [3]. For our invariant patterns, this fact is formalized in the following theorem.

Theorem 3. *(Process invariant implies activity invariant) Assuming that* $I = I_1, \ldots, I_n$ *and* $O = O_1, \ldots, O_m$, *it holds:*

$$P_{proc}^L[I][O] \Rightarrow P_{act}^{2L}[I][O]$$

Proof. Without loss of generality let us assume that $|I| = |O| = 1$. Given $t \in \mathbb{T}$ let $p = \lceil \frac{t}{L} \rceil$. The required $a : \mathbb{T} \to \mathbb{T}$ for $P_{act}^{2L}[I][O]$ is given by R and F from $P_{proc}^L[I][O]$ as follows:

$$a(t) = \begin{cases} R(p-1) & \text{if } t < F(p) \\ R(p) & \text{if } t \geq F(p) \end{cases}$$

First, we prove that $0 < t - a(t) \leq 2L$. Since $p = \lceil \frac{t}{L} \rceil$, then also $(p-1) \cdot L \leq t \leq p \cdot L$. According to Definition 5, $E(p-1) \leq R(p) < F(p) \leq E(p)$, where $E(p) = p \cdot L$. Therefore, given the properties of R, F, and $a(t)$, we have $E(p-2) \leq R(p-1) \leq a(t)$ and $a(t) < t$. Together, we have $(p-2) \cdot L \leq a(t) < t \leq p \cdot L$. Therefore, $0 < t - a(t) \leq 2L$.

Further, a is non-decreasing since R and F are non-decreasing. Thus, from $P_{proc}^L[I][O]$ we get $P_{act}^{2L}[I][O]$. □

Similarly, it holds that the exchange invariant pattern is a refinement of the activity invariant pattern with lag equal twice the period of the exchange invariant pattern plus the time for distributed transfer of the knowledge, as formulated by the following theorem.

Theorem 4. *(Exchange invariant implies activity invariant) Assuming that* $I = I_1, \ldots, I_n$ *and* $O = O_1, \ldots, O_m$, *it holds:*

$$P_{exc}^{L,T}[I][O] \Rightarrow P_{act}^{2L+T}[I][O]$$

Proof. The proof is similar to Theorem 3, differing only in the part relevant to knowledge transfer over network. For the purpose of the proof, we denote $R_i(p) = a_i(R(p)), \forall p \in \mathbb{N}$ for R and a_i from $P_{exc}^{L,T}[I][O]$.

Given $t \in \mathbb{T}$ let $p = \lceil \frac{t}{L} \rceil$. The required $a_i : \mathbb{T} \to \mathbb{T}$ for $P_{act}^{2L+T}[I][O]$ is given by R_i and F from $P_{exc}^{L,T}[I][O]$ as follows:

$$a_i : (t) = \begin{cases} R_i(p-1) & \text{if } t < F(p) \\ R_i(p) & \text{if } t \geq F(p) \end{cases}$$

First, we prove that $0 < t - a_i(t) \leq 2L + T$. Since $p = \lceil \frac{t}{L} \rceil$, then also $(p-1) \cdot L \leq t \leq p \cdot L$. According to Definition 6, $E(p-1) - T \leq R(p) - T \leq R_i(p) < F(p) \leq E(p)$, where $E(p) = p \cdot L$ (recall that $x - a_i^{ens}(x) \leq T$). Therefore, given the properties of R_i, F, and $a(t)$, we have $E(p-2) - T \leq R_i(p-1) \leq a(t)$ and $a(t) < t$. Together, we have $(p-2) \cdot L - T \leq a(t) < t \leq p \cdot L$. Therefore, $0 < t - a(t) \leq 2L + T$.

Further, a_i is non-decreasing since R_i and F are non-decreasing. Thus, from $P_{exc}^{L,T}[I][O]$ we get $P_{act}^{2L+T}[I][O]$. □

4.2 Pipeline Decomposition

Here, we present a logical framework that would enable for formal reasoning about refinement in a particular form of decomposition – *pipeline decomposition*, which due to its relative generality covers most practical cases of invariant decomposition. Specifically, we focus on the level of activity invariants, as they represent a suitable level of abstraction, generalizing both process and exchange invariants.

As an important observation, the fact that a decomposition is actually a refinement of the parent invariant is, with respect to time, largely affected by sharing of invariant variables among the child invariants. Thus, we introduce the concept of *dependency chain*. A vector of activity invariants forms a dependency chain if some of the output variables of an invariant in the vector are among the input variables of the next invariant in the vector. This is formalized in the following definition.

For brevity, we introduce the following notation. Given an activity (or process/exchange) invariant $P_{act}^L[I_1, \ldots, I_n][O_1, \ldots, O_m]$, $In(P)$ denotes the set $\{I_1, \ldots, I_n\}$, while $Out(P)$ denotes the set $\{O_1, \ldots, O_m\}$.

Definition 7. *(Dependency chain) Each vector* $\left(P_{1act}^{L_1}, \ldots, P_{pact}^{L_p} \right)$ *of invariants forms a* dependency chain *iff:*

$$\forall i \in \{1, \ldots, p-1\} \exists O, I :$$
$$O \in Out(P_i) \wedge I \in In(P_{i+1}) \wedge O = I$$

In a pipeline decomposition the children reflect simple pipeline-like flows among the corresponding activities that refine the parent activity. A formal interpretation is given in the following definition.

Definition 8. *(Pipeline decomposition)* *Having a parent invariant P_{act}^L, a set of child invariants $\left\{ P_{iact}^{L_i}, i = 1..p \right\}$ forms a pipeline decomposition of P_{act}^L iff:*

(i) each input variable of the parent is an input variable of exactly one child:

$$\forall I \in In(P) \; \exists! j \in \{1, \ldots, p\} : I \in In(P_j)$$

(ii) each output variable of the parent is an output variable of exactly one child:

$$\forall O \in Out(P) \; \exists! j \in \{1, \ldots, p\} : O \in Out(P_j)$$

(iii) the decomposition includes only such dependency chains, in which (a) all input variables of the first invariant are input variables of the parent, (b) all output variables of the last invariant are output variables of the parent, (c) for each two consecutive invariants within the dependency chain, the output variables of the former are exactly the input variables of the latter:

$$\forall \mathcal{C} = \left(P_{i_1 act}^{L_{i_1}}, \ldots, P_{i_q act}^{L_{i_q}} \right), \{i_1, \ldots, i_q\} \subseteq \{1, \ldots, p\}, \mathcal{C} \text{ dependency chain:}$$

$$In(P_{i_1}) \subseteq In(P) \wedge Out(P_{i_q}) \subseteq Out(P)$$

$$\wedge \; \forall j = i_1..i_{q-1} \; Out(P_j) = In(P_{j+1})$$

(iv) the decomposition includes only such dependency chains that do not share input/output variables:

$$\forall \mathcal{C}_1 = \left(P_{i_1 act}^{L_{i_1}}, \ldots, P_{i_q act}^{L_{i_q}} \right), \{i_1, \ldots, i_q\} \subseteq \{1, \ldots, p\}, \mathcal{C}_1 \text{ dependency chain,}$$

$$\forall \mathcal{C}_2 = \left(P_{j_1 act}^{L_{j_1}}, \ldots, P_{j_r act}^{L_{j_r}} \right), \{j_1, \ldots, j_r\} \subseteq \{1, \ldots, p\}, \mathcal{C}_2 \text{ dependency chain,}$$

$$\forall P_{k act}^{L_k} \in \mathcal{C}_1, \forall P_{l act}^{L_l} \in \mathcal{C}_2 :$$

$$\mathcal{C}_1 \neq \mathcal{C}_2 \Rightarrow \left(In(P_{k act}^{L_k}) \cup Out(P_{k act}^{L_k}) \right) \cap \left(In(P_{l act}^{L_l}) \cup Out(P_{l act}^{L_l}) \right) = \emptyset$$

An example is the decomposition of (2) into (5) and (6) in the running example.

Intuitively, the definition of pipeline decomposition requires the children to reflect simple parallel pipeline-like flows (dependency chains) among the corresponding activities that refine the parent activity.

For pipeline decomposition, a straightforward rule for determining refinement can be formulated. In a correct refinement, provided that the decomposition is logically consistent with the parent invariant when not considering time, the lag of the parent invariant should be at least the sum of the lags of the invariants in the longest (in terms of time) pipeline (i.e., dependency chain) of the decomposition. Indeed, this intuitive observation was confirmed in our invariant-based formalism as demonstrated in the following theorem.

Theorem 5. *(Activity invariant pipeline refinement)* *Having invariant P_{act}^L $[I_1, \ldots, I_n][O_1, \ldots, O_m]$ and its pipeline decomposition $\mathcal{D} = \left\{ P_{1act}^{L_1}, \ldots, P_{Pact}^{L_p} \right\}$, the decomposition is a refinement of the parent, i.e., it holds that $P_{1act}^{L_1} \wedge \cdots \wedge P_{Pact}^{L_p} \Rightarrow P_{act}^L$, if:*

(i) $P_1 \wedge \cdots \wedge P_p \Rightarrow P$, i.e., the decomposition is logically consistent without considering time

(ii) for each dependency chain $\mathcal{C} = \left(P_{i_1\,act}^{L_{i_1}}, \ldots, P_{i_q\,act}^{L_{i_q}} \right)$ in $\mathcal{D}$ it holds that $\sum_{j=i_1}^{i_q} L_j \leq L$, i.e., the lag of the parent invariant is at least the sum of the lags of the longest (in terms of time) dependency chain among the child invariants.

Proof. To prove the above theorem, we need to prove that given $\mathcal{D}$, P, and the assumptions (i) and (ii), the following lemma holds:

$$P_{1\,act}^{L_1} \wedge \cdots \wedge P_{p\,act}^{L_p} \Rightarrow (P_1 \wedge \cdots \wedge P_p)_{act}^L$$

Then, the correctness of the theorem is an immediate result of this lemma and the assumption (i). To prove the lemma, let $Q_{act}^L \overset{\text{def}}{=} (P_1 \wedge \cdots \wedge P_p)_{act}^L$.

Without loss of generality, let us assume that each dependency chain $\mathcal{C} = \left(P_{i_1\,act}^{L_{i_1}}, \ldots, P_{i_q\,act}^{L_{i_q}} \right)$ in $\mathcal{D}$, its first invariant $P_{i_1\,act}^{L_{i_1}}$ in particular, has only one input variable (i.e., $I_\mathcal{C}$). Also, let us assume that $\mathcal{C}$, its last invariant $P_{i_q\,act}^{L_{i_q}}$ in particular, has only one output variable (i.e., $O_\mathcal{C}$). Similarly, we assume that all the intermediate invariants within $\mathcal{C}$ have exactly one input and one output variable. This assumption is safe since the multiple input/output variables can be merged into one as they are referred exactly from one other invariant (which is also in $\mathcal{C}$).

For the variable $I_\mathcal{C}$, we define the $a_\mathcal{C} : \mathbb{T} \to \mathbb{T}$ required for Q_{act}^L (according to the Definition 4) as follows:

$$a_\mathcal{C}(t) \overset{\text{def}}{=} a_{i_1}\left(a_{i_2}\left(\ldots a_{i_q}(t) \ldots \right) \right)$$

where $a_{i_1}, \ldots, a_{i_q}$ are taken from to $P_{i_1\,act}^{L_{i_1}}, \ldots, P_{i_q\,act}^{L_{i_q}}$.

Because $\sum_{j=i_1}^{i_q} L_j \leq L$ and $0 < x - a_{i_1}(x) \leq L_{i_1}, \ldots, 0 < x - a_{i_q}(x) \leq L_{i_q}$, it holds that $0 < x - a_\mathcal{C} \leq L$.

The assumption of the above lemma (i.e., $P_{1\,act}^{L_1} \wedge \cdots \wedge P_{p\,act}^{L_p}$) and the properties of the dependency chain $\mathcal{C} = \left(P_{i_1\,act}^{L_{i_1}}, \ldots, P_{i_q\,act}^{L_{i_q}} \right)$ as a part of the pipeline decomposition $\mathcal{D}$ give us the following corollary:

$$P_{i_1}(I_\mathcal{C}[a_{i_1}(a_{i_2}(\ldots a_{i_q}(t) \ldots))], O_{i_1}[a_{i_2}(\ldots a_{i_q}(t) \ldots)]) \wedge O_{i_1} = I_{i_2} \wedge$$
$$P_{i_2}(I_{i_2}[a_{i_2}(a_{i_3}(\ldots a_{i_q}(t) \ldots))], O_{i_2}[a_{i_3}(\ldots a_{i_q}(t) \ldots)]) \wedge O_{i_2} = I_{i_3} \wedge$$
$$\vdots$$
$$P_{i_q}(I_{i_q}[a_{i_q}(t)], O_\mathcal{C}[t])$$

By combining these corollaries for each dependency chain in the pipeline decomposition $\mathcal{D}$ of Q (i.e., each input and output variable of Q), we get:

$$Q\left(I_1\left[a_1(t)\right], \ldots, I_n\left[a_n(t)\right], O_1[t], \ldots O_n[t]\right)$$

where I_i, O_i, and a_i correspond to the dependency chain $\mathcal{C}_i$ in $\mathcal{D}$.

By combining all the above facts, we get: $P_{1\,act}^{L_1} \wedge \cdots \wedge P_{p\,act}^{L_p} \Rightarrow Q_{act}^L$ $\square$

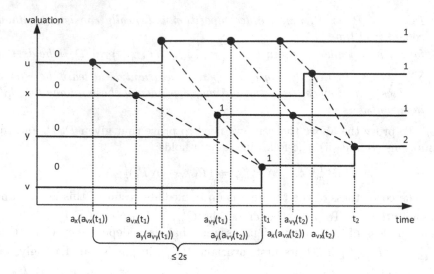

Fig. 3. A counterexample illustrating the importance of the pipeline refinement assumption in Theorem 5

4.3   More Complex Types of Refinement

The assumption of pipeline decomposition in Theorem 5 is essential for its correctness. This means that in the case of a decomposition that does not respect all four points of Definition 8, applying Theorem 5 can lead to the wrong results. To support this claim and highlight the importance of strictly following the above-mentioned definition, we present the following counterexample to the relaxed Theorem 5 (where the assumption of pipeline decomposition is lifted).

Counterexample to relaxed Theorem 5. Consider the parent invariant $P_p \stackrel{\text{def}}{=} (v = 2u)^{2s}_{act}[u][v]$, that is decomposed into three sub-invariants:

$$P_\alpha \stackrel{\text{def}}{=} (x = u)^{1s}_{act}[u][x], \quad P_\beta \stackrel{\text{def}}{=} (y = u)^{1s}_{act}[u][y], \quad P_\gamma \stackrel{\text{def}}{=} (v = x + y)^{1s}_{act}[x, y][v].$$

This decomposition is not a pipeline decomposition, because the input variable of the parent (variable u) is input of more than one children in the decomposition (both P_α and P_β), thus invalidating the first point of Definition 8. The relaxed Theorem 5 would ensure that this decomposition is a refinement. However, if we consider the trace illustrated in Figure 3, it is obvious that although the trace is valid for all the sub-invariants P_α, P_β, and P_γ, it is not valid for the parent invariant P_p, as there cannot be an $a_p(t)$ such that $v[t_1] = 1 = 2 * u[a_p(t_1)]$. $\square$

The reason why the relaxed Theorem 5 does not work for the counterexample is that while the parent works with the valuation of a at a single time instant, the decomposition employs the valuation of a at two different time instants (by aliasing to x and y). This observation applies in general. Moreover, for some decompositions it appears that it is not possible to formulate similar theorems.

5   Discussion and Conclusions

The choice of the proposed formalization of invariants and invariant patterns in higher-order predicate logic was driven by the practical reason of being able to formulate and prove the relevant theorems that hold in different invariant refinements. Other forms of formalization would have been more appropriate when different goals are pursued by the formalization task. For example, the use of a real-time temporal logic [12] would have been a sensible choice if we would like to use IRM model fragments as input for model-checking purposes.

Indeed, formalization of goals in goal models in real-time LTL has already been pursued in the context of both KAOS [13] and Tropos [6] (e.g., Formal Tropos [5]), two of the most prominent requirements engineering frameworks. Our invariant refinement patterns can be compared to the goal refinement patterns à la KAOS [4], which encode known refinement tactics. The difference is that KAOS patterns can be formally checked with a theorem prover, while our patterns have to be manually proven, as state-of-the-art theorem provers cannot cope with the complexity of our expressive logic.

The invariant decomposition in IRM is inspired by the decomposition of system-level goals into sub-goals, assumptions and domain properties in KAOS. A similar approach is also pursued within Tropos, where goals, soft-goals, tasks, and dependencies and identified and iteratively decomposed from the perspective of the individual agents. The differences lie in that (i) neither KAOS nor Tropos provide a direct translation to the implementation-level concepts of autonomic components and ensembles; (ii) the objective of IRM is not to produce requirements documents (like KAOS), but software architectures; (iii) IRM invariants do not focus on future states (like goals in Tropos), but on knowledge valuation at every time instant, fitting better the design of feedback-based systems.

The diagrams used to illustrate the knowledge valuation in time in IRM (e.g., Fig. 2 and 3) are reminiscent of timed UML 2 interaction diagrams [11], as they capture the system behavior over time in a declarative way. However, UML 2 activity diagrams focus on the message exchange between predefined instances, whereas IRM invariants capture the evolution in the knowledge of distributed components (which could be implemented by exchange of messages among them) that is necessary in order for certain system-level requirements to be met.

To conclude, in this paper we have provided a formal framework for invariant refinement in the context of the Invariant Refinement Method (IRM). Our approach is modeling the invariants in higher-order predicate logic and identifying common invariant types (patterns) at different levels of abstraction. Some of the refinement relations between different patterns have also been formally proven (via mathematical theorems): present-past to activity invariants, activity to process/exchange invariants, and pipeline decomposition of activity/process/exchange invariants. More complex types of refinement have to be investigated separately in order to be able to formulate similar theorems. This is the focus of our future work.

Another element of future work is to test the proposed design method in a real-scale case study with real system designers.

Acknowledgements. This work was partially supported by the EU project ASCENS 257414 and by Charles University institutional funding SVV-2014-260100. The research leading to these results has received funding from the European Union Seventh Framework Programme FP7-PEOPLE-2010-ITN under grant agreement n°264840.

References

1. Abeywickrama, D.B., Bicocchi, N., Zambonelli, F.: SOTA: Towards a General Model for Self-Adaptive Systems. In: Proc. of WETICE, pp. 48–53. IEEE (2012)
2. Bures, T., Gerostathopoulos, I., Hnetynka, P., Keznikl, J., Kit, M., Plasil, F.: DEECo — an Ensemble-Based Component System. In: Proc. of CBSE 2013, Vancouver, Canada, pp. 81–90. ACM (June 2013)
3. Buttazzo, G.C.: Hard Real-Time Computing Systems: Predictable Scheduling Algorithms and Applications, 3rd edn. Springer (2011)
4. Darimont, R., van Lamsweerde, A.: Formal Refinement Patterns for Goal-Driven Requirements Elaboration. In: Gollmann, D. (ed.) FSE 1996. LNCS, vol. 1039, pp. 179–190. Springer, Heidelberg (1996)
5. Fuxman, A., Pistore, M., Mylopoulos, J., Traverso, P.: Model Checking Early Requirements Specifications in Tropos. In: Proc. of RE 2001, Toronto, ON, Canada, pp. 174–181. IEEE (August 2001)
6. Giorgini, P., Kolp, M., Mylopoulos, J., Pistore, M.: The Tropos Methodology: An Overview. In: Methodologies and Software Engineering For Agent Systems, pp. 89–106. Kluwer Academic Publishers (2004)
7. Hölz, M., Wirsing, M.: Towards a System Model for Ensembles. In: Formal modeling, pp. 241–261. Springer (2012)
8. Hölzl, M., et al.: Engineering Ensembles: A White Paper of the ASCENS Project. ASCENS Deliverable JD1.1 (2011), http://www.ascens-ist.eu/whitepapers
9. Hölzl, M., Rauschmayer, A., Wirsing, M.: Software engineering for ensembles. In: Wirsing, M., Banâtre, J.-P., Hölzl, M., Rauschmayer, A. (eds.) Soft-Ware Intensive Systems. LNCS, vol. 5380, pp. 45–63. Springer, Heidelberg (2008)
10. Keznikl, J., Bures, T., Plasil, F., Gerostathopoulos, I., Hnetynka, P., Hoch, N.: Design of Ensemble-Based Component Systems by Invariant Refinement. In: Proc. of CBSE 2013, Vancouver, Canada, pp. 91–100. ACM (June 2013)
11. Knapp, A., Störrle, H.: Efficient Representation of Timed UML 2 Interactions. In: Amyot, D., Fonseca i Casas, P., Mussbacher, G. (eds.) SAM 2014. LNCS, vol. 8769, pp. 110–125. Springer, Heidelberg (2014)
12. Koymans, R. (ed.): Specifying Message Passing and Time-Critical Systems with Temporal Logic. LNCS, vol. 651. Springer, Heidelberg (1992)
13. Lamsweerde, A.V.: Requirements engineering in the year 00: a research perspective. In: Proceedings of ICSE 2000, Limerick, Ireland, pp. 5–19. ACM (June 2000)
14. Serbedzija, N., Reiter, S., Ahrens, M., Velasco, J., Pinciroli, C., Hoch, N., Werther, B.: Requirement Specification and Scenario Description of the ASCENS Case Studies. Deliverable D7.1 (2011), http://www.ascens-ist.eu/deliverables

On StocS: A Stochastic Extension of SCEL[*]

Diego Latella[1], Michele Loreti[2], Mieke Massink[1], and Valerio Senni[3]

[1] Istituto di Scienza e Tecnologia dell'Informazione 'A. Faedo', CNR, Italy
[2] Università di Firenze, Italy
[3] IMT-Lucca, Italy

Abstract. Predicate-based communication allows components of a system to send messages and requests to ensembles of components that are determined at execution time through the evaluation of a predicate, in a multicast fashion. Predicate-based communication can greatly simplify the programming of autonomous and adaptive systems. We present a stochastically timed extension of the Software Component Ensemble Language (SCEL) that was introduced in previous work. Such an extension allows for quantitative modelling and analysis of system behaviour (e.g. performance) but rises a number of non-trivial design and formal semantics issues with different options as possible solutions at different levels of abstraction.

1   Introduction

SCEL (Software Component Ensemble Language) [5,8], is a kernel language that is equipped with programming abstractions for the specification of system models within the framework of the *autonomic computing* paradigm, and for programming such systems. These abstractions are specifically designed for representing behaviours, knowledge, and aggregations according to specific policies, and to support programming context-awareness, self-awareness, and adaptation.

The main focus of the SCEL language is on supporting the development of autonomous, loosely-coupled, component-based software systems. For this purpose, a number of underlying assumptions are made on the kind of peculiarities of these software systems, among which adaptivity, open-endedness, ensemble-orientedness, high ability of reconfiguration, and support for heterogeneity. Two novel key aspects of SCEL, that distinguish it from other languages, are designed to support these peculiarities: predicate-based communication and the role of the component knowledge-base. Predicate-based communication allows to send messages to *ensembles* of components that are not predetermined at modeling time, but are defined at execution time, depending on how the communication predicate evaluates w.r.t. the destination interface. The component knowledge-base allows to realise various adaptation patterns, by explicit separation of adaptation data in the spirit of [3], and to model components view

---

[*] This research has been partially funded by the EU projects ASCENS (nr. 257414) and QUANTICOL (nr. 600708), and the IT MIUR project CINA.

R. De Nicola and R. Hennicker (Eds.): Wirsing Festschrift, LNCS 8950, pp. 619–640, 2015.

on (and awareness of) the environment. SCEL has been developed in the EU ASCENS project[1] and it has been used to specify many scenarios related to the project case studies [12,10,14,13]. These specifications witness how SCEL primitives simplify the programming of autonomous and adaptive systems.

In [11] we addressed the problem of enriching SCEL with information about action durations, which results in a stochastic semantics for the language. In fact, our goal is to provide a formal, language based, framework for quantitative (e.g. performance) modelling and analysis of autonomic computing systems. Even if there exist various stochastic process languages, including some which incorporate notions of spatial distribution (see [4,9] and references therein) and frameworks that support the systematic development of stochastic languages (see [7] and references therein), the main challenge in developing a stochastic semantics for SCEL is in making appropriate modeling choices, both taking into account the specific application needs and allowing to manage model complexity and size. Our contribution in [11] was the proposal of four variants of STOCS, a Markovian extension of a significant fragment of SCEL. These variants adopt *the same syntax* of SCEL but denote different underlying stochastic models, having a different level of granularity.

STOCS, and its support framework extend SCEL by providing the system modeller with means for characterising relevant delays—related to the execution of SCEL actions—modelling them as random variables (RVs) with negative exponential distributions. The resulting models are continuous time Markov chains (CTMCs).

In the design of STOCS, we deliberately omit to incorporate certain advanced features of SCEL, such as the presence and role of policies.

In this book we focus on the *network oriented* variant of STOCS briefly introduced in [11]. The semantics of this variant entails that actions are *non-atomic*. Indeed, they are executed through several intermediate steps, each of which requires appropriate time duration.

The work we present in this book is only the latest step of a long journey started more than ten years ago with the AGILE EU project, and carried on first within the SENSORIA EU project and later within the ASCENS EU project. The collaboration with Martin Wirsing, who acted as Coordinator of all these projects, gave us the possibility to study the specific formal tools to use for providing stochastic semantics of domain specific languages as well as to investigate general issues concerning such tools. We would like to thank Martin for the many stimulating discussions we had and for his excellent coordination work. Thank you Martin.

The outline of this chapter is as follows. Section 2 discusses the intuitions behind the stochastic extension of SCEL which is presented in 4 after some preliminary definitions are recalled in Section 3. In Section 5 we present a simple case study to illustrate the use of the various language primitives of STOCS.

Concluding remarks and lines for possible future research are presented in Section 6.

---

[1] http://www.ascens-ist.eu/

Table 1. STOCS syntax (KNOWLEDGE K, TEMPLATES T, and ITEMS t are parameters)

SYSTEMS:	S	$::=$	$C \mid S \parallel S$
COMPONENTS:	C	$::=$	$I[K, P]$
PROCESSES:	P	$::=$	$\mathbf{nil} \mid a.P \mid P + P \mid P \mid P \mid X \mid A(\bar{p})$
ACTIONS:	a	$::=$	$\mathbf{get}(T)@c \mid \mathbf{qry}(T)@c \mid \mathbf{put}(t)@c$
TARGETS:	c	$::=$	$\mathsf{self} \mid \mathsf{p}$
ENSEMBLE PREDICATES:	p	$::=$	$tt \mid e \bowtie e \mid \neg\mathsf{p} \mid \mathsf{p} \wedge \mathsf{p}$ with $\bowtie \in \{<, \leq, >, \geq\}$
EXPRESSIONS:	e	$::=$	$v \mid x \mid a \mid \cdots$

2 StocS: A Stochastic Extension of SCEL

In this section we present the main features of STOCS. We start by illustrating its main syntactic ingredients. Then, we discuss the stochastically timed semantics we present in this chapter.

2.1 Syntax

The syntax of STOCS is presented in Table 1. The basic category defines PROCESSES that are used to specify the order in which ACTIONS can be performed. Sets of processes are used to define the behavior of COMPONENTS, that in turn are used to define SYSTEMS. ACTIONS operate on local or remote knowledge-bases and have a TARGET to determine which other components are involved in the action. As we mentioned in the Introduction, for the sake of simplicity, in this version of STOCS we do not include POLICIES, whereas, like SCEL, STOCS is parametric w.r.t. KNOWLEDGE, TEMPLATES and ITEMS.

We define the following domains for variables and for defining functions signature: $\mathbb{A}$ is the a of attribute names (which include the constant id used to indicate the component identifier), $\mathbb{V}$ is a set of values, $\mathbb{K}$ is a set of possible knowledge states, $\mathbb{I}$ is a set of knowledge items, $\mathbb{T}$ is a set of knowledge templates. So, in Table 1, $a \in \mathbb{A}$, $v \in \mathbb{V}$, $K \in \mathbb{K}$, $t \in \mathbb{I}$, $T \in \mathbb{T}$.

Example 1 (Items and Templates as Tuples and Patterns). Consider a signature $(\mathcal{V}, \mathcal{F})$ where $\mathcal{V}$ is a set of variables and $\mathcal{F}$ is a set of function symbols with arity (we indicate by f/n a function symbol f with arity n) such that $\langle\rangle/i \in \mathcal{F}$ for $i = 0, 1, 2, \ldots$. We denote by $Terms(\mathcal{V}, \mathcal{F})$ the set of all possible finite terms on the given signature (i.e. the terms with variables, constructed respecting function symbols arities) and by $Terms(\mathcal{F})$ the set of all possible finite ground terms. A *pattern* is a term of the form $\langle t_1, \ldots, t_n \rangle$, with $t_i \in Terms(\mathcal{V}, \mathcal{F})$ for $i = 1, \ldots, n$. A *tuple* is a term of the form $\langle t_1, \ldots, t_n \rangle$, with $t_i \in Terms(\mathcal{F})$ for $i = 1, \ldots, n$. In this example we have defined the set of Templates $\mathbb{T}$ as the set of patterns and the set of Items $\mathbb{I}$ as the set of tuples.

Systems and Components. We let Sys, ranged over by $S, S_1, \ldots, S' \ldots$ denote the set of systems defined by the syntax in Table 1. A system S consists of an aggregation of COMPONENTS obtained via the (parallel) *composition* operator $\_ \| \_$. A component $I[K, P]$ consists of:

1. An *interface*, which is a function $I : \mathbb{K} \to (\mathbb{A} \to \mathbb{V})$ used for publishing information about the component's state in the form of attribute values. Among the possible attributes, id is mandatory and is bound to the name of the component. Component names are not required to be unique, so that replicated service components can be modelled. The *evaluation* of an interface I in a knowledge state K is denoted as $I(K)$. The set of possible interface evaluations is denoted by $\mathbb{E}$.
2. A *knowledge repository* K, managing both application data and awareness data (following the approach of [3]), together with the specific handling mechanism.
3. A *process* P, together with a set of process definitions. Processes may execute local computations, coordinate local and remote interaction with a knowledge repository, or perform adaptation and reconfiguration.

Processes. PROCESSES are the active computational units. Each process is built up from the *inert* process **nil** via *action prefixing* ($a.P$), *nondeterministic choice* ($P_1 + P_2$), *parallel composition* ($P_1|P_2$), *process variable* (X), and *parameterised process invocation* ($A(\bar{p})$). We feel free to omit trailing occurrences of **nil**, writing e.g. a instead of $a.\textbf{nil}$, whenever there is no confusion arising. Process variables can be used in templates so that processes can also be stored in / retrieved from knowledge repositories.

We assume that A ranges over a set of parameterised *process identifiers* that are used in recursive process definitions. We also assume that each process identifier A has a *single* definition of the form $A(\bar{f}) \triangleq P$ where all free variables in P are contained in $\bar{f}$ and all occurrences of process identifiers in P are within the scope of an action prefixing. $\bar{p}$ and $\bar{f}$ denote lists of actual and formal parameters, respectively. In the sequel we will use *Proc* to denote the set of processes, ranged over by variables $P, Q, \ldots, P_1, Q_1 \ldots, P', Q', \ldots$.

Actions and Targets. Processes can perform three different kinds of ACTIONS: $\textbf{get}(T)@c$, $\textbf{qry}(T)@c$ and $\textbf{put}(t)@c$, used to act over shared knowledge repositories by, respectively, withdrawing, retrieving, and adding information items from/to the knowledge repository identified by c.

These actions exploit templates T as patterns to select knowledge items t in the repositories. The precise syntax of templates and knowledge items depends on the specific instance of *knowledge repository* that is used. Indeed, in Example 1 we provided the syntax for items ($\mathbb{I}$) and templates ($\mathbb{T}$) for one possible instance of the repository. In the next section we show how STOCS is in fact parametric with respect to different types of *knowledge repository*.

For the sake of simplicity, in this book we restrict targets c to the distinguished variable self, that is used by processes to refer to the component hosting it, and to component *predicates* p, i.e. formulas on component attributes. A component $I[K, P]$ is *identified* by a predicate p if $I(K) \models$ p, that is, the interpretation defined by the evaluation of I in the knowledge state K is a model of the formula p. Note that here we are assuming a fixed interpretation for functions and predicate symbols that are not within the attributes ($\mathbb{A}$). E.g. *battery* < 3 is a possible predicate, where $<$ and 3 have a fixed interpretation, while the value of *battery* depends on the specific component addressed.

The informal, abstract, semantics of the actions is the following:

- **put**(t)@c is non-blocking, its execution causes knowledge item t be added to the knowledge repository of *all* the components (the interface of which is) identified by c, *if any*;
- **get**(T)@c (**qry**(T)@c, respectively) is blocking, it causes a knowledge item t matching pattern T be withdrawn (retrieved, respectively) from the knowledge repository of *any of* the components (the interface of which is) identified by c, *if any*. If no such component/item is available, the process executing it is *blocked* in a waiting state. The two actions differ for the fact that **get** removes the requested item from the knowledge repository while **qry** leaves the target repository unchanged.

The set of components satisfying a given target c of a communication action can be considered as the *ensemble* with which the process performing the action intends to interact.

Knowledge Behavior. Since STocS is parametric w.r.t. the specific knowledge repository used in a specification, we provide no specific syntax/semantics for knowledge repositories. We only require that a *knowledge repository type* is completely described by a tuple $(\mathbb{K}, \mathbb{I}, \mathbb{T}, \oplus, \ominus, \vdash)$ where $\mathbb{K}$ is the set of possible *knowledge states* (the variables K, K_1, ..., K', ... range over $\mathbb{K}$), $\mathbb{I}$ is the set of *knowledge items* (the variables t, $t_1,\ldots,t',\ldots$ range over $\mathbb{I}$) and $\mathbb{T}$ is the set of *knowledge templates* (the variables T, $T_1,\ldots,$ $T',\ldots$ range over $\mathbb{T}$). Knowledge items have no variable, while knowledge templates have. We assume to have a partial function match : $\mathbb{T} \times \mathbb{I} \to$ Subst$(\mathbb{I})$ (where Subst(X) is the set of substitutions with range in X) and we denote as match$(T, t) = \vartheta$ the substitution obtained by matching the pattern T against the item t, if any. By a small abuse of notation, we write $\neg$match(T, t) to denote that match(T, t) is undefined.

The operators $\oplus, \ominus, \vdash$ are used to add, withdraw, and infer knowledge items to/from knowledge repositories in $\mathbb{K}$, respectively. These functions have the following signature, where Dist(X) denotes the class of probability distributions on set X with finite support:

- $\oplus : \mathbb{K} \times \mathbb{I} \to$ Dist$(\mathbb{K})$.
- $\ominus : \mathbb{K} \times \mathbb{T} \hookrightarrow$ Dist$(\mathbb{K} \times \mathbb{I})$;
- $\vdash : \mathbb{K} \times \mathbb{T} \hookrightarrow$ Dist$(\mathbb{I})$;

Function $\oplus$ is *total* and defines how a knowledge item can be inserted into a knowledge repository: $K \oplus t = \pi$ is the probability distribution over knowledge states obtained as the effect of adding t. If the item addition operation is modelled in a deterministic way, then the distribution π is a Dirac function. One advantage of allowing a probabilistic item addition operation is, for example, the ability of modeling possible.

Function $\ominus$ is *partial* and computes the result of withdrawing a template from a knowledge state in terms of a probability distribution $K \ominus T$ over the set of pairs $(K, t) \in (\mathbb{K} \times \mathbb{I})$ such that the item t matches the template T. Intuitively, if $K \ominus T = \pi$ and $\pi(K', t) = p$ then, when one tries to remove an item matching template T from K, with probability p item t is obtained and the resulting knowledge state is K'. If a tuple matching template T is not found in K then $K \ominus T$ is undefined, which is indicated by $K \ominus T = \bot$.

Function $\vdash$ is *partial* and computes (similarly to $\ominus$) a probability distribution over the possible knowledge items matching template T that can be inferred from K. Thus, if $K \vdash T = \pi$ and $\pi(t) = p$ then the probability of inferring t when one tries to infer from K a tuple matching T is p. If no tuple matching T can be inferred from K then $K \vdash T$ is undefined, which is indicated by $K \vdash T = \bot$.

2.2   Informal Timed Semantics

The semantics of SCEL does not consider any time related aspect of computation. More specifically, the execution of an action of the form $\mathbf{act}(T)@c \, . \, P$ (for $\mathbf{put}/\mathbf{get}/\mathbf{qry}$ actions) is described by a *single* transition of the underlying SCEL Labelled Transition System (LTS) semantics. In the system state reached by such a transition it is guaranteed that the process which executed the action is in its local state P and that the knowledge repositories of all components involved in the action execution have been modified accordingly. In particular, SCEL abstracts away details concerning:

1. when the execution of the action starts;
2. if c is a predicate p, when the possible destination components are required to satisfy p;
3. when the process executing the action resumes execution (i.e. becomes P);

and their consequent time relationship. If we want to extend SCEL with an explicit notion of (stochastic) time, we need to take into account the time-related issues mentioned above. These issues can be addressed at different levels of abstraction, reflecting a different choice of details that are considered in modeling SCEL actions.

In the following, the process/component initiating an action will be often called the *source* of the action execution, while the other components involved in the execution will be the *destinations*.

Point (1) above does not require particular comments. Point (2) requires to define *when* a component satisfies p with respect to a process executing an action, when time and possibly space are taken into consideration. We assume that source components are not aware of which are the components satisfying predicate p. Therefore, we define the notion of *observation* of the component by the process, the result of which allows to establish whether the component satisfies the predicate or not. In the context of distributed systems this is often realised by means of a message, called an *envelope*, carrying the actual data item, sent by the process to the other components. According to this view, the check whether a component satisfies predicate p is performed *when the message reaches it*. This means that, as e.g. in PALOMA [9], a STOCS action may require broadcast communication to be executed, even if its effect involves a few and possibly no components. In distributed systems different components may have different response times depending on different network conditions.

Finally, point (3) rises the issue on when source component execution is to be resumed. In particular, it is necessary to identify how the source component is made aware that its role in the communication has been completed. Get/query actions are blocking and they terminate when the source receives a knowledge item from any component. A reasonable choice is that further responses received are ignored. We assume appropriate mechanisms that ensure no confusion arises between distinct actions and corresponding messages. Put actions are non-blocking, so it is sufficient that the source component is aware that all reachable components are involved in the evaluation of the predicate. A possible choice is to set-up the transmission of one request of predicate evaluation for each component and then terminate the execution on the source side immediately. On the destination side, it is necessary to model the reception time as well as subsequent evaluation and corresponding knowledge repository modification.

In this book, we assume a *network-oriented* (NET-OR) view on the system, i.e. the execution of the various phases sketched above is explicitly modelled in detail by the operational semantics, which entails that actions are *non-atomic*. Indeed, they are executed through several intermediate steps, each of which requires appropriate time duration modelling. This kind of semantics is appropriate for models with spatial aspects, where distribution is a sensible aspect influencing the duration of communications on the basis of the location of components.

In order to obtain an underlying CTMC semantics, in STOCS relevant delays—related to the execution of SCEL actions—are modelled as random RVs with negative exponential distributions. Therefore, in the following, whenever we associate a rate λ with a duration, the duration is exponentially distributed with rate λ. Non-determinism in process behaviour gives raise to race-conditions.

2.3   Explanatory Example

Let us consider three components (see Fig. 1): $C_1 = I_1 [K_1, P_1], C_2 = I_2 [K_2, P_2]$, and $C_3 = I_3 [K_3, P_3]$ and let us assume process P_1 is defined as $\mathbf{put}(t)@\mathsf{p}.Q$.[2] Note that different components may be in different locations.

The execution of $\mathbf{put}(t)@\mathsf{p}$ starts in C_1 with the first phase in which one copy of the envelope message $\{t@\mathsf{p}\}$ is sent, on behalf of P_1, *to each* other component

---

[2] For the sake of notational simplicity, in this book we assume that predicate p in process actions implicitly refers only to the *other* components, excluding the one where the process is in execution.

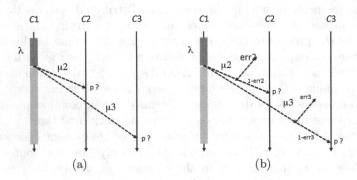

Fig. 1. Dynamics of the **put** action

of the system[3]. In our example two copies are created/sent, one for/to C_2 and one for/to C_3. The time required for this phase (denoted in grey in Fig. 1 (a)) is modelled by a RV with rate λ: this value is computed as a function of several factors, among which is (the size of) t. Each envelope travels in the system and reaches the component it is associated with. Different envelopes may experience different transmission delays; therefore, *distinct* rates μ_2 and μ_3 are associated to each target (in Fig. 1 (a) this is illustrated by two arrows) and each rate may depend on t as well as other parameters like the distance between C_1 and the destination component. After message creation, P_1 can proceed—since **put** actions are non-blocking—behaving like Q; the light-grey stripe in Fig. 1 (a) illustrates the resumed execution of P_1 in C_1. The evaluation of predicate p is performed in each destination component C_j *when the message arrives at* C_j, and appropriate actions are taken on K_j. For example, it may happen that C_2 satisfies p *at the time the message reaches* C_2, which causes item t to be added to K_2—while C_3 does not satisfy p *at the time the message reaches* C_3—so that K_3 is left unchanged.

In practice, one can be interested in modeling also the event of failed delivery of the envelopes. This is interesting for instance for producing more realistic models with unreliable network communication. Furthermore, the inclusion of additional branches for failure modelling helps reducing discontinuities, which may facilitate the application of advanced analysis techniques based on fluid approximation [2], such as fluid model-checking [1]. Therefore, we add an error probability to the envelopes delivery, which we indicate as p_{err} (or simply err, in the figure). This more detailed semantics of the **put**(t)@p action is illustrated in Fig. 1 (b).

---

[3] In an implementation of SCEL, this corresponds to a *request* sent either via a *broadcast*, that is not really efficient, or via a *multicast* to all the components potentially involved in the operation. jRESP, the *runtime-environment* of SCEL, provides both of these communication mechanisms [8].

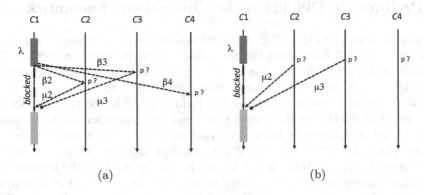

Fig. 2. Dynamics of the **get** action

Let us now consider a scenario with four components $C_1 = I_1[K_1, P_1]$, $C_2 = I_2[K_2, P_2]$, $C_3 = I_3[K_3, P_3]$, and $C_4 = I_4[K_4, P_4]$ with P_1 of the form $\mathbf{get}(T)@\mathsf{p}.Q$ (or $\mathbf{qry}(T)@\mathsf{p}.Q$).

Similarly to the execution of $\mathbf{put}(t)@\mathsf{p}$, the first phase consists in the creation of the envelope messages—with rate λ; this is represented by the grey stripe in Fig. 2 (a). Since the **get** (resp. **qry**) action is blocking, P_1 is then put into a waiting state (denoted by a dashed line in the figure). Each copy of the message is sent to the corresponding component C_j, with transmission rate β_j. Upon envelope arrival, each component checks for satisfaction of predicate p and availability of an item t matching template T. Those components for which such a check gives a positive result, say C_2 and C_3, are eligible to answer the request with item t_2 and t_3 respectively, and a race condition takes place, so that *only one* component, say C_2, succeeds in providing the item, as required by SCEL semantics. Once the item (t_2) reaches C_1, P_1 can restart its execution from $Q\vartheta$, with a suitable variable binding $\mathsf{match}(T, t) = \vartheta$; when the other item (t_3) will reach C_1 it will be disregarded. Transmission rate from C_2 (C_3 respectively) is μ_2 (μ_3).

In order to simplify the semantics of the **get/qry** actions and to make it more similar to the two-steps semantics of the **put** action, we decided to model the two phases of envelope delivery and response collection as a single one. So, on message creation, the source (P_1) is blocked on waiting for some destination to synchronise with it on the exchange of the retrieved item t matching the template T, as illustrated in Fig. 2 (b). During this synchronization, the predicate p is also checked, on the side of the destination, and the knowledge is changed accordingly. The synchronization attempt of all other candidates (C_3, in the example) is simply lost. In terms of the underlying stochastic model, we are replacing a phase-type distribution, consisting of the sequence of two exponential RVs, with an exponential RV. This choice is also convenient for simplifying the definition of the formal semantics, since it avoids the need of giving a unique id to envelope messages, to be used in the subsequent response collection phase.

3   Preliminary Definitions for Operational Semantics

In this section we provide preliminary notions to support the presentation of the semantics of STOCS formalising the ideas described in the previous section. The semantics definition is given in the FuTSs style [7] and, in particular, using its Rate Transition Systems (RTS) instantiation [6].

In RTSs, a transition is a triple of the form $(P, \alpha, \mathscr{P})$, the first and second components of which are the source state and the transition label, as usual, and the third component $\mathscr{P}$ is the *continuation function*[4] that associates a real non-negative value with each state P'. A non-zero value represents the rate of the exponential distribution characterising the time needed for the execution of the action represented by α, necessary to reach P' from P via the transition. Whenever $\mathscr{P} P' = 0$, this means that P' is not reachable from P via α. RTS continuation functions are equipped with a rich set of operations that help to define these functions over sets of processes, components, and systems. Below we show the definition of those functions that we use in this chapter, after having recalled some basic notation, and we define them in an abstract way, with respect to a generic sets $X, X_1, X_2, \dots$

Let $\mathbf{TF}(X, \mathbb{R}_{\geq 0})$ denote the set of *total* functions from X to $\mathbb{R}_{\geq 0}$, and $\mathscr{F}$, $\mathscr{P}$, $\mathscr{Q}$, $\mathscr{R}$, … range over it. We define $\mathbf{FTF}(X, \mathbb{R}_{\geq 0})$ as the subset of $\mathbf{TF}(X, \mathbb{R}_{\geq 0})$ containing only functions with *finite support*: $\mathscr{F}$ is an element of $\mathbf{FTF}(X, \mathbb{R}_{\geq 0})$ if and only if there exist $\{d_1, \dots, d_m\} \subseteq X$, the *support* of $\mathscr{F}$, such that $\mathscr{F} d_i \neq 0$ for $i = 1 \dots m$ and $\mathscr{F} d = 0$ for all $d \in X \setminus \{d_1, \dots, d_m\}$. We equip $\mathbf{FTF}(X, \mathbb{R}_{\geq 0})$ with the operators defined below. The resulting *algebraic structure* of the set of finite support functions will be crucial for the compositional features of our approach.

Definition 1

1. *For elements $d_1, \dots, d_m \in X$ and $\gamma_1, \dots, \gamma_m \in \mathbb{R}_{\geq 0}$ we use the notation $[d_1 \mapsto \gamma_1, \dots, d_m \mapsto \gamma_m]$ for denoting the following function:*

$$[d_1 \mapsto \gamma_1, \dots, d_m \mapsto \gamma_m] d =_{\mathrm{def}} \begin{cases} \gamma_i & \text{if } d = d_i \in \{d_1, \dots, d_m\}, \\ 0 & \text{otherwise.} \end{cases}$$

   the 0 constant function in $\mathbf{FTF}(X, \mathbb{R}_{\geq 0})$ is denoted by $[]$;
2. *We define addition on $\mathbf{FTF}(X, \mathbb{R}_{\geq 0})$ as the point-wise extension of $+$ on $\mathbb{R}$, i.e. $(\mathscr{F}_1 + \mathscr{F}_2) d =_{\mathrm{def}} (\mathscr{F}_1 d) + (\mathscr{F}_2 d)$;*
3. *For any injective binary operator $\bullet : X_1 \times X_2 \to X$ we define its lifting to $\mathbf{FTF}(X_1, \mathbb{R}_{\geq 0}) \times \mathbf{FTF}(X_2, \mathbb{R}_{\geq 0}) \to \mathbf{FTF}(X, \mathbb{R}_{\geq 0})$ by letting*

$$(\mathscr{F}_1 \bullet \mathscr{F}_2) d =_{\mathrm{def}} \begin{cases} (\mathscr{F}_1 d_1) \cdot (\mathscr{F}_2 d_2) & \text{if } \exists d_1 \in X_1, d_2 \in X_2.\ d = d_1 \bullet d_2, \\ 0 & \text{otherwise.} \end{cases}$$

4. *We use the characteristic function $\mathcal{X}$ on X with $\mathcal{X} : X \to \mathbf{FTF}(X, \mathbb{R}_{\geq 0})$ such that $\mathcal{X} d =_{\mathrm{def}} [d \mapsto 1]$*

---

[4] In the sequel, Currying will be used for continuation function application.

Definition 2. *An A-RTS is a tuple* $(S, A, \mathbb{R}_{\geq 0}, \rightarrowtail)$ *where* S *and* A *are countable, non-empty, sets of* states *and transition* labels, *respectively, and relation* $\rightarrowtail \subseteq S \times A \times \mathbf{FTF}(S, \mathbb{R}_{\geq 0})$ *is the A-labelled* transition relation.

In order to distinguish and identify the rules of the semantics definition, we label them by unique names. Note that a rule with name r may have one or more associated blocking rules r_B which have the role of allowing the execution of no actions other than those explicitly allowed by existing inference rules. These B-rules will not be further commented in the following sections.

4   Network-Oriented Operational Semantics

We recall that the *evaluation* of an interface I in a knowledge state K is denoted as $I(K)$. The set of possible interface evaluations is denoted by $\mathbb{E}$. Interface evaluations are used within the so-called *rate function* $\mathcal{R} : \mathbb{E} \times Act \times \mathbb{E} \to \mathbb{R}_{\geq 0}$, which defines the rates of actions depending on the interface evaluation of the *source* of the action, the action itself (where Act denotes the set of possible actions), and the interface evaluation of the *destination*. For this purpose, interface evaluations will be embedded within the transition labels to exchange information about source/destination components in a synchronisation action. The rate function is not fixed but it is a parameter of the language. Considering interface evaluations in the rate functions, together with the executed action, allows us to take into account, in the computation of actions rates, various aspects depending on the component state such as the position/distance, as well as other time-dependent parameters. We also assume to have a *loss probability function* $f_{\mathrm{err}} : \mathbb{E} \times Act \times \mathbb{E} \to [0, 1]$ computing the probability of an error in message delivery. In the semantics, we distinguish between output actions (those issued by a source component) and input actions (those accepted by a destination component). To simplify the synchronisation of input and output actions, we assume input actions are *probabilistic*, and output actions are *stochastic*, therefore their composition is directly performed through multiplication.

In order to realise this semantics we extend the set of labels of actions performed by processes and systems as described in the following.

4.1   Operational Semantics of Processes

The NET-OR semantics of STOCS processes is the RTS $(Proc, Act_{Proc}, \mathbb{R}_{\geq 0}, \rightarrow_e)$. $Proc$ is the set of process terms defined according to the syntax of STOCS given in Table 1 Act_{Proc} is the set of labels defined according to the grammar below (where $t \in \mathbb{I}$, $T \in \mathbb{T}$, $\mathbf{gq} \in \{\mathbf{get}, \mathbf{qry}\}$, c is a TARGET, and e is the evaluation of an interface) and it is ranged over by $\alpha, \alpha', \ldots$:

$$Act_{Proc} \quad ::= \quad \tau \quad | \quad \overline{\{t@\mathsf{p}\}} \quad | \quad \overline{e : \mathbf{put}(t)@c} \quad | \quad \overline{e : \mathbf{gq}(T : t)@c}$$

The transition relation $\rightarrow \subseteq Proc \times Act_{Proc} \times \mathbf{FTF}(Proc, \mathbb{R}_{\geq 0})$ is the least relation satisfying the rules of Table 2. $\rightarrow_e$ is parametrized by e, which is the interface

Table 2. Operational semantics of STOCS processes

Inactive process and envelopes:

$$\frac{}{\mathbf{nil} \xrightarrow{\alpha} []} \;(\text{NIL}) \qquad \frac{}{\{t@p\}_\mu \xrightarrow{\overline{\{t@p\}}} [\mathbf{nil} \mapsto \mu]} \;(\text{ENV}) \qquad \frac{\alpha \neq \overline{\{t@p\}}}{\{t@p\}_\mu \xrightarrow{\alpha} []} \;(\text{ENV}_\text{B})$$

Actions (where, $\mathbf{gq} \in \{\mathbf{get}, \mathbf{qry}\}$, c is a TARGET, and p is a PREDICATE):

$$\frac{\lambda = \mathcal{R}(\sigma, \mathbf{put}(t)@c, \_)}{\mathbf{put}(t)@c\,.\,P \xrightarrow{\overline{\mathbf{put}(t)@c}}_\sigma [P \mapsto \lambda]} \;(\text{PUT}) \qquad \frac{\alpha \neq \overline{\mathbf{put}(t)@c}}{\mathbf{put}(t)@c.P \xrightarrow{\alpha} []} \;(\text{PUT}_\text{B})$$

$$\frac{\mathsf{match}(T,t) = \vartheta \quad \lambda = \mathcal{R}(\sigma, \mathbf{gq}(T:t)@\mathsf{self}, \_)}{\mathbf{gq}(T)@\mathsf{self}.P \xrightarrow{\sigma\,:\,\mathbf{gq}(T:t)@\mathsf{self}}_\sigma [P\vartheta \mapsto \lambda]} \;(\text{GQL})$$

$$\frac{\neg\mathsf{match}(T,t)}{\mathbf{gq}(T)@\mathsf{self}.P \xrightarrow{\_\,:\,\mathbf{gq}(T:t)@\mathsf{self}} []} \;(\text{GQL}_\text{B1}) \qquad \frac{\alpha \neq \overline{\_\,:\,\mathbf{gq}(T:t)@\mathsf{self}}}{\mathbf{gq}(T)@\mathsf{self}.P \xrightarrow{\alpha} []} \;(\text{GQL}_\text{B2})$$

$$\frac{\lambda = \mathcal{R}(\sigma, \mathbf{gq}(T:\_)@p, \_)}{\mathbf{gq}(T)@p.P \xrightarrow{\tau}_\sigma [\{\mathbf{gq}(T)@p\}.P \mapsto \lambda]} \;(\text{GQW}) \qquad \frac{\alpha \neq \tau}{\mathbf{gq}(T)@p.P \xrightarrow{\alpha} []} \;(\text{GQW}_\text{B})$$

$$\frac{\mathsf{match}(T,t) = \vartheta \quad \beta = \mathcal{R}(\sigma, \{\mathbf{gq}(T:t)@p\}, \delta)}{\{\mathbf{gq}(T)@p\}.P \xrightarrow{\delta\,:\,\{\mathbf{gq}(T:t)@p\}}_\sigma [P\vartheta \mapsto \beta]} \;(\text{GQD})$$

$$\frac{\neg\mathsf{match}(T,t)}{\{\mathbf{gq}(T)@p\}.P \xrightarrow{\_\,:\,\{\mathbf{gq}(T:t)@p\}} []} \;(\text{GQD}_\text{B1}) \qquad \frac{\alpha \neq \overline{\_\,:\,\{\mathbf{gq}(T:t)@p\}}}{\{\mathbf{gq}(T)@p\}.P \xrightarrow{\alpha} []} \;(\text{GQD}_\text{B2})$$

Choice, definition, and parallel composition:

$$\frac{P \xrightarrow{\alpha}_e \mathscr{P} \quad Q \xrightarrow{\alpha}_e \mathscr{Q}}{P + Q \xrightarrow{\alpha}_e \mathscr{P} + \mathscr{Q}} \;(\text{CHO}) \qquad \frac{A(\vec{x}) \stackrel{def}{=} P \quad P[\vec{v}/\vec{x}] \xrightarrow{\alpha}_e \mathscr{P}}{A(\vec{v}) \xrightarrow{\alpha}_e \mathscr{P}} \;(\text{DEF})$$

$$\frac{P \xrightarrow{\alpha}_e \mathscr{P} \quad Q \xrightarrow{\alpha}_e \mathscr{Q}}{P \mid Q \xrightarrow{\alpha}_e \mathscr{P} \mid (\mathcal{X}\,Q) + (\mathcal{X}\,P) \mid \mathscr{Q}} \;(\text{PAR})$$

---

evaluation of the component in which the process resides: we feel free to omit the parameter, if not used in the rule.

We now briefly illustrate the rules of Table 2. We assume to have additional syntactical terms (not available at the user syntax level) which we call *envelopes*. They are of the form $\{t@p\}_\mu$, can be put in parallel with processes, and denote messages that are currently traveling towards targets. A second syntactical construct we introduce is $\{\mathbf{get}(T)@\mathsf{p}\}$ ($\{\mathbf{qry}(T)@\mathsf{p}\}$, respectively) which denotes a *waiting* state of the process and it is treated as an action.

(NIL) **nil** is the terminated process, since no process is reachable from it via any action;

(ENV) allows to complete envelope delivery with duration specified by μ;

(PUT)/(PUT$_B$) describe possible transitions of a process of the form $\mathbf{put}(t)@c.P$. The first rule states that $\mathbf{put}(t)@c.P$ evolves with rate λ to P after a transition labeled $\overline{\mathbf{put}(t)@c}$. This rate is computed by using rate function $\mathcal{R}$. The execution of a $\mathbf{put}(t)@c$ action depends on the source component and *all* the other components in the system, which are involved as potential destinations. Consequently, the execution rate λ can be seen as a function of the action and of the source component (interface evaluation) only; in particular, the action rate *does not* depend on (the interface evaluation of) a specific (destination) component; this is represented by using the symbol $\_$ in the destination argument of $\mathcal{R}$. On the contrary, rule (PUT$_B$) states that $\mathbf{put}(t)@c.P$ cannot reach any process after a transition with a label that is different from $\overline{\mathbf{put}(t)@c}$.

(GQL) allows a process to issue a **get** (**qry**, respectively) action over the local knowledge repository (i.e. with target self). The rule models the execution of action $\mathbf{get}(T)@\mathsf{self}$ ($\mathbf{qry}(T)@\mathsf{self}$, respectively) by process $\mathbf{get}(T)@\mathsf{self}.P$ ($\mathbf{qry}(T)@\mathsf{self}.P$, respectively). The duration of this action is described by a rate λ computed using the function $\mathcal{R}$ depending on the interface evaluation of the source σ (i.e. the container component) and on the action; the continuation associates λ with $P\vartheta$, i.e. the process obtained by applying to P the substitution ϑ resulting from match-ing template T against item t;

(GQW) realises the first step of a **get** (**qry**, respectively) action over a remote knowledge in a component satisfying a predicate p, which consists in preparing an envelope $\{\mathbf{get}(T)@\mathsf{p}\}$ ($\{\mathbf{qry}(T)@\mathsf{p}\}$, respectively), which takes a time interval exponentially distributed with rate λ, and brings process P to a *wait* state $\{\mathbf{get}(T)@\mathsf{p}\}.P$ ($\{\mathbf{qry}(T)@\mathsf{p}\}.P$, respectively). Recall that **get**/**qry** actions are *blocking* and the execution of P is resumed only when a counterpart satisfying p has a knowledge item t matching T available and the delivery of t is completed. The duration of this first step is described by a rate λ computed using the function $\mathcal{R}$ depending only on the interface evaluation of the source σ (i.e. the container component) and the sent template T;

(GQD) realises the second step of a **get** (**qry**, respectively) action, which consists in the *delivery* of the knowledge item t matching T and has a duration described by a rate β computed by the function $\mathcal{R}$. Note that in this case the function $\mathcal{R}$ is computed considering interface evaluation of the source σ and the destination δ, as well as the sent item t, which means that this rate can be made dependent (for example) on the distance of the two parties.

(CHO) cumulates the relevant rates by means of the application of the *choice* operator $+$ on the continuation of P ($\mathscr{P}$) and that of Q ($\mathscr{Q}$), thus conforming to the race condition principle of CTMCs;

Table 3. Operational semantics of STOCS components (Part 1)

---

put actions:

$$\dfrac{\sigma = I(K) \quad P \xrightarrow{\overline{\mathsf{put}(t)@\mathsf{self}}}_\sigma \mathscr{P} \quad K \oplus t = \pi}{I\,[\,K,\,P\,] \xrightarrow{\overleftrightarrow{\sigma:\mathsf{put}(t)@\mathsf{self}}} I[\pi,\mathscr{P}]} \quad \text{(C-PUTL)}$$

$$\dfrac{\sigma = I(K) \quad P \xrightarrow{\overline{\mathsf{put}(t)@\mathsf{p}}}_\sigma \mathscr{P}}{I\,[\,K,\,P\,] \xrightarrow{\sigma\,:\,\mathsf{put}(t)@\mathsf{p}} I[(\mathcal{X}K),\mathscr{P}]} \quad \text{(C-PUTO)}$$

$$\dfrac{\delta = I(K) \quad \mu = \mathcal{R}(\sigma,\{t@\mathsf{p}\},\delta) \quad p_{\mathsf{err}} = f_{\mathsf{err}}(\sigma,\{t@\mathsf{p}\},\delta)}{I\,[\,K,\,P\,] \xrightarrow{\sigma\,:\,\mathsf{put}(t)@\mathsf{p}} [\,I\,[\,K,\,P\,] \mapsto p_{\mathsf{err}},\ I[K,P|\{t@\mathsf{p}\}_\mu] \mapsto (1 - p_{\mathsf{err}})\,]} \quad \text{(C-PUTI)}$$

$$\dfrac{P \xrightarrow{\overline{\{t@\mathsf{p}\}}} \mathscr{P} \quad I(K) \models \mathsf{p} \quad K \oplus t = \pi}{I\,[\,K,\,P\,] \xrightarrow{\overline{\{t@\mathsf{p}\}}} I[\pi,\mathscr{P}]} \quad \text{(C-ENVA)}$$

$$\dfrac{P \xrightarrow{\overline{\{t@\mathsf{p}\}}} \mathscr{P} \quad I(K) \not\models \mathsf{p}}{I\,[\,K,\,P\,] \xrightarrow{\overline{\{t@\mathsf{p}\}}} I[(\mathcal{X}K),\mathscr{P}]} \quad \text{(C-ENVR)}$$

(DEF) is the rule for process instantiation;

(PAR) realises process parallel composition $P \mid Q$ and uses Def. 1, item (3) applied to the process parallel composition syntactic constructor $\mid$ (which is obviously injective). Therefore, given two functions $\mathscr{R}_1$ and $\mathscr{R}_2$, the function $\mathscr{R}_1 \mid \mathscr{R}_2$ applied to process term R returns the product $(\mathscr{R}_1\,R_1) \cdot (\mathscr{R}_2\,R_2)$, whenever R is of the form $R_1 \mid R_2$, for some terms R_1 and R_2, and 0 otherwise. In the rule, also the characteristic function $\mathcal{X}$ is used. Function $\mathscr{P} \mid (\mathcal{X}Q)$ applied to R returns $\mathscr{P}\,R'$ if $R = R' \mid Q$ for some R' and 0 otherwise; i.e. the function behaves as the continuation of P $(\mathscr{P})$ for terms where Q does not progress (for one step). In conclusion, $\mathscr{P} \mid (\mathcal{X}\,Q) + (\mathcal{X}\,P) \mid \mathscr{Q}$ correctly represents process interleaving, keeping track of the relevant rates.

4.2 Operational Semantics of Components and Systems

The NET-OR semantics of STOCS systems is the RTS $(Sys, Act_{Sys}, \mathbb{R}_{\geq 0}, \rightarrow)$. Sys is the set of system terms defined according to the syntax of STOCS given in Table 1. Set Act_{Sys} of labels is defined according to the grammar below (where $\mathbf{gq} \in \{\mathbf{get}, \mathbf{qry}\}$, $t \in \mathbb{I}$, $T \in \mathbb{T}$, p is a PREDICATE, and e is the evaluation of an interface):

Table 4. Operational semantics of STOCS components (Part 2)

---

get/qry actions (where, $gq \in \{get, qry\}$):

$$\frac{\sigma = I(K) \quad P \xrightarrow{\overline{\sigma : get(T:t)@self}}_\sigma \mathscr{P} \quad K \ominus T = \pi}{I[K, P] \xrightarrow{\overleftarrow{\sigma : get(T:t)@self}} I[\pi(t), \mathscr{P}]} \quad (\text{C-GETL})$$

$$\frac{\sigma = I(K) \quad P \xrightarrow{\overline{\sigma : qry(T:t)@self}}_\sigma \mathscr{P} \quad K \vdash T = \pi}{I[K, P] \xrightarrow{\overleftarrow{\sigma : qry(T:t)@self}} I[(\mathcal{X}K) \cdot \pi(t), \mathscr{P}]} \quad (\text{C-QRYL})$$

$$\frac{K \ominus T = \bot}{I[K, P] \xrightarrow{\overleftarrow{\sigma : get(T:t)@self}} []} \quad (\text{C-GETL}_{\text{B}}) \qquad \frac{K \vdash T = \bot}{I[K, P] \xrightarrow{\overleftarrow{\sigma : qry(T:t)@self}} []} \quad (\text{C-QRYL}_{\text{B}})$$

$$\frac{\sigma = I(K) \quad P \xrightarrow{\overline{\delta : \{gq(T:t)@p\}}}_\sigma \mathscr{P}}{I[K, P] \xrightarrow{\delta : \{gq(T:t)@p\}} I[(\mathcal{X}K), \mathscr{P}]} \quad (\text{C-GQO})$$

$$\frac{\delta = I(K) \quad \delta \models p \quad K \ominus T = \pi}{I[K, P] \xrightarrow{\delta : \{get(T:t)@p\}} I[\pi(t), (\mathcal{X}P)]} \quad (\text{C-GETI})$$

$$\frac{\delta \neq I(K) \quad \vee \quad I(K) \not\models p \quad \vee \quad K \ominus T = \bot}{I[K, P] \xrightarrow{- : \{get(T:t)@p\}} []} \quad (\text{C-GETI}_{\text{B}})$$

$$\frac{\delta = I(K) \quad \delta \models p \quad K \vdash T = \pi}{I[K, P] \xrightarrow{\delta : \{qry(T:t)@p\}} [I[K, P] \mapsto \pi(t)]} \quad (\text{C-QRYI})$$

$$\frac{\delta \neq I(K) \quad \vee \quad I(K) \not\models p \quad \vee \quad K \vdash T = \bot}{I[K, P] \xrightarrow{- : \{qry(T:t)@p\}} []} \quad (\text{C-QRYI}_{\text{B}})$$

τ actions:
$$\frac{\rho = I(K) \quad P \xrightarrow{\tau}_\rho \mathscr{P}}{I[K, P] \xrightarrow{\tau} I[(\mathcal{X}K), \mathscr{P}]} \quad (\text{C-TAU})$$

$$Act_{Sys} \quad ::= \quad e : \mathbf{put}(t)@\mathsf{p} \quad | \quad e : \{\mathbf{gq}(T:t)@\mathsf{p}\} \quad | \quad \text{(input actions)}$$

$$\overline{e : \mathbf{put}(t)@\mathsf{p}} \quad | \quad \overline{e : \{\mathbf{gq}(T:t)@\mathsf{p}\}} \quad | \quad \text{(output actions)}$$

$$\tau \quad | \quad \overleftrightarrow{e : \{\mathbf{gq}(T:t)@\mathsf{p}\}} \quad | \qquad \text{(synchronisations)}$$

$$\overline{\{t@\mathsf{p}\}} \qquad\qquad\qquad\qquad\qquad \text{(envelopes)}$$

The transition relation $\rightarrow \subseteq Sys \times Act_{Sys} \times \mathbf{FTF}(Sys, \mathbb{R}_{\geq 0})$ is the least relation satisfying the rules of Tables 3, 4 and 5, where the process relation defined in Table 2 is also used.

Table 5. Operational semantics of STOCS systems

---

put synchronization:

$$\dfrac{S_1 \xrightarrow{\sigma\,:\,\mathbf{put}(t)@\mathsf{p}} \mathscr{S}_1^o \quad S_1 \xrightarrow{\sigma\,:\,\mathbf{put}(t)@\mathsf{p}} \mathscr{S}_1^i \quad S_2 \xrightarrow{\sigma\,:\,\mathbf{put}(t)@\mathsf{p}} \mathscr{S}_2^o \quad S_2 \xrightarrow{\sigma\,:\,\mathbf{put}(t)@\mathsf{p}} \mathscr{S}_2^i}{S_1 \parallel S_2 \xrightarrow{\sigma\,:\,\mathbf{put}(t)@\mathsf{p}} \mathscr{S}_1^o \parallel \mathscr{S}_2^i + \mathscr{S}_1^i \parallel \mathscr{S}_2^o} \quad \text{(S-PO)}$$

$$\dfrac{S_1 \xrightarrow{\sigma\,:\,\mathbf{put}(t)@\mathsf{p}} \mathscr{S}_1 \quad S_2 \xrightarrow{\sigma\,:\,\mathbf{put}(t)@\mathsf{p}} \mathscr{S}_2}{S_1 \parallel S_2 \xrightarrow{\sigma\,:\,\mathbf{put}(t)@\mathsf{p}} \mathscr{S}_1 \parallel \mathscr{S}_2} \quad \text{(S-PI)}$$

---

get/qry synchronization $(\mathbf{gq} \in \{\mathbf{get}, \mathbf{qry}\})$:

$$\dfrac{\begin{array}{c} S_1 \xrightarrow{\overleftrightarrow{\delta\,:\,\{\mathbf{gq}(T:t)@\mathsf{p}\}}} \mathscr{S}_1^s \quad S_1 \xrightarrow{\overline{\delta\,:\,\{\mathbf{gq}(T:t)@\mathsf{p}\}}} \mathscr{S}_1^o \quad S_1 \xrightarrow{\delta\,:\,\{\mathbf{gq}(T:t)@\mathsf{p}\}} \mathscr{S}_1^i \\ S_2 \xrightarrow{\overleftrightarrow{\delta\,:\,\{\mathbf{gq}(T:t)@\mathsf{p}\}}} \mathscr{S}_2^s \quad S_2 \xrightarrow{\overline{\delta\,:\,\{\mathbf{gq}(T:t)@\mathsf{p}\}}} \mathscr{S}_2^o \quad S_2 \xrightarrow{\delta\,:\,\{\mathbf{gq}(T:t)@\mathsf{p}\}} \mathscr{S}_2^i \end{array}}{S_1 \parallel S_2 \xrightarrow{\overleftrightarrow{\delta\,:\,\{\mathbf{gq}(T:t)@\mathsf{p}\}}} \mathscr{S}_1^s \parallel (\mathcal{X} S_2) + \mathscr{S}_1^o \parallel \mathscr{S}_2^i + \mathscr{S}_1^i \parallel \mathscr{S}_2^o + (\mathcal{X} S_1) \parallel \mathscr{S}_2^s} \quad \text{(S-GQS)}$$

$$\dfrac{S_1 \xrightarrow{\delta\,:\,\{\mathbf{gq}(T:t)@\mathsf{p}\}} \mathscr{S}_1 \quad S_2 \xrightarrow{\delta\,:\,\{\mathbf{gq}(T:t)@\mathsf{p}\}} \mathscr{S}_2}{S_1 \parallel S_2 \xrightarrow{\delta\,:\,\{\mathbf{gq}(T:t)@\mathsf{p}\}} \mathscr{S}_1 \parallel (\mathcal{X} S_2) + (\mathcal{X} S_1) \parallel \mathscr{S}_2} \quad \text{(S-GQI)}$$

Internal actions, for $\alpha \in \{\tau, \overleftrightarrow{e : \mathbf{put}(t)@\mathsf{self}}, \overleftrightarrow{e : \mathbf{gq}(T:t)@\mathsf{self}}, \overline{\{t@\mathsf{p}\}}\}$:

$$\dfrac{S_1 \xrightarrow{\alpha} \mathscr{S}_1 \quad S_2 \xrightarrow{\alpha} \mathscr{S}_2}{S_1 \parallel S_2 \xrightarrow{\alpha} \mathscr{S}_1 \parallel (\mathcal{X} S_2) + (\mathcal{X} S_1) \parallel \mathscr{S}_2} \quad \text{(S-SPL)}$$

The definition of the semantics of system parallel composition $S_1 \parallel S_2$ uses Def. 1, item (3) applied to the system parallel composition constructor $\parallel$, which is injective. As usual, interleaving is modelled as a combination of lifted $\parallel$, $+$ on functions and the characteristic function. In the rules, we also use Def. 1, item (3) applied to the component syntactic constructors $I[\cdot, \cdot]$, which is injective.

In Table 3 and Table 4, rules are grouped to illustrate how the various action types are realised.

(C-PUTL) describes the execution of **put** actions operating at self. Let $I[K, P]$ be a component; this rule states that P executes action **put**(t)@self with local interface evaluation $\sigma = I(K)$ and evolves to $\mathscr{P}$, then a local execution of the action can occur and the entire component evolves with label $\overleftarrow{\sigma} : \overrightarrow{\textbf{put}(t)\text{@self}}$ to $I[\pi, \mathscr{P}]$, where $\pi = K \oplus t$ is a probability distribution over the possible knowledge states obtained from K by adding the knowledge item t, while $I[\pi, \mathscr{P}]$ is the function which maps any term of the form $I[K, P]$ to $(\pi K) \cdot (\mathscr{P}P)$ and any other term to 0.

(C-PUTO) this rule is used when the target of a **put** is not self but a predicate p; the rule simply lifts an output **put** action from the process level to the component level and transmits to its counterpart its current interface evaluation σ by including it in the transition label.

(C-PUTI) models the *initiation* of the execution of action **put**(t)@c, which requires several steps to complete, it allows the reception of a **put** action, and it is responsible for the creation of the envelope (carrying the incoming message) in parallel to the local process of a component, thus modeling its travel towards that component in terms of the time necessary to reach it, parametrized by rate μ (the fact that the envelope is in parallel with the process of the potential receiver component by no means should be interpreted as the representation of the fact that the message reached the component; simply, the association between the message and the component is represented by means of a parallel composition term; in other words, the fact that a specific message is 'addressed' to a component is represented syntactically by such a parallel composition); this action is executed with rate λ, computed using the function $\mathcal{R}$ depending on the interface evaluation of the source σ (i.e. the container component) and the sent item t; this is postulated by the rule (PUT) and realised at system level by the broadcast rules of Table 5.

(C-ENVA)/(C-ENVR) realise envelope delivery by specifying the conditions under which a component *accepts* or *refuses*, respectively, an arriving envelope;

(C-GETL)/(C-QRYL) realise the local **get** (**qry**) action retrieving an item $t \in \mathbb{I}$ matching the pattern T, if possible, in the execution of process P (in the label of the process action we include the item t and we include the interface evaluation σ of the component for computing the action rate) and, since the **get** (**qry**) action may result in several distinct knowledge bases, these need to be summed together considering all possibilities: π is a distribution over pairs (knowledge base and knowledge item) and the possible components in the continuation are weighted by using π;

(C-GQO) realises an output **get**/**qry** action as in the ACT-OR semantics, but with a different label ($\{\ldots\}$) which denotes the synchronization on a *waiting state*;

(C-GETI)/(C-QRYI) realise an input **get/qry** action, again as in the ACT-OR
semantics, but with a different label ({...});

(C-TAU) allows a component to make a τ whenever its process makes such an
action.

Finally, we discuss the rules in Table 5:

(S-PO)/(S-PI) realise the broadcast communication of **put**: (S-PO) ensures that
if any subsystem executes an output **put** action (i.e. it executes a transition
with label $\sigma : \mathbf{put}(t)@\mathsf{p}$), then the remaining subsystem must execute the
corresponding input **put** action (i.e. it should execute a $\sigma : \mathbf{put}(t)@\mathsf{p}$ labeled transition); the composed system does not exhibit a synchronization
label, but it rather propagates the output $\sigma : \mathbf{put}(t)@\mathsf{p}$ to allow further synchronization with all the other components in parallel; in the computation
of the final rate it is necessary to consider output on the left sub-system
and input on the right as well as the symmetric case; while (S-PI) allows an
input **put** action forcing *all* of the components of a sub-system to perform
that action;

(S-GQS) realises one-to-one synchronization of **get/qry** actions (which are not
broadcast), denoted by a $\overleftrightarrow{e : \mathbf{gq}(T : t)@\mathsf{p}}$ label, and performs aggregation of:
(1) the synchronization rate of the left (right) sub-system, with the right
(resp. left) subsystem that must not progress (this is realised using the $\mathcal{X}$
characteristic function), and (2) output rates of the left sub-system and input
rates of the right subsystem (as well as the symmetric case), combined with
the $\|$ operator;

(S-GQI) realises the input **get** (resp. **qry**) action for systems in which *one* component, among those satisfying the target predicate and having a matching
knowledge item, can answer;

(S-SPL/S-SGQL) allow a system to execute an internal action and exposes the
label denoting the type of action to allow appropriate aggregation of the
observed rates.

5   StocS at Work

In this section we use a simple example to show how STOCS can be used to
specify and verify quantitative properties of adaptive systems. We consider a
cloud scenario where users can execute their task in a distributed environment.
A *QoS* profile is associated to each user. Possible profiles are: *basic, standard,
premium* and *super premium*. Our system has two main requirements. First, we
have to reduce the number of tasks submitted by *premium* and *super premium*
users that are waiting for the execution. Moreover, we have to minimise the
number of computational resources allocated for the execution of tasks.

In STOCS both *users* and *computational resources* can be rendered via *components*. We refer to the first group of components as *user components*, while
the components in the second group are referred as *computational components*.

Components associated to users publish in the interface the user QoS level. Moreover, users communicate the need to execute a task via their knowledge. Computational components retrieve the corresponding knowledge element. The following process, executed at users components, models this behaviour:

$$\text{UTask}() \stackrel{def}{=} \text{put}(\text{"}TASK\text{"})@\text{self.UTask}()$$

We assume that tasks requests arrive at a rate $\lambda_{tr} = 50.0$. We also assume that 40% of the requests come from *basic* users; 35% come from *standard* users while 15% and 10% arrive from *premium* and *super premium* users respectively.

Computational resources can execute at most k tasks at the same time (in the following we consider $k = 15$). This value corresponds to the number of ServiceAgents that are executed at each computational component. These processes retrieve and execute tasks. We can vary the method used by ServiceAgent to retrieve pending tasks from users to obtain different kinds of specifications. In particular, we consider three possible approaches: *static allocation*, *progressive allocation* and *dynamic allocation*. When *static allocation* is used, each computational component only handles tasks from users of a given level. In the *progressive allocation*, like in the previous case, each computational component is associated with a QoS level. However, differently from the *static allocation*, each process is able to handle tasks from users with a QoS level that is equal or higher than the associated one. Finally, in the *dynamic allocation*, the class of users that a component can handle depends on the *computation load*: the higher is the number of executed tasks in a component, the higher is the QoS level that the same component can handle.

Process ServiceAgent is defined as follows:

$$\text{ServiceAgent}() \stackrel{def}{=} \text{get}(\text{"}TASK\text{"})@c.$$
$$\text{put}(\text{"}EXECUTE\text{"})@\text{self.}$$
$$\text{ServiceAgent}()$$

The **get** action is activated with rate $\lambda = 1$ that is also the rate of data transmission. The execution time of action **put**($\text{"}EXECUTE\text{"}$)@self mimics the task execution time and it is exponentially distributed with rate $\lambda_e = \frac{1}{3}$. All the above mentioned rates do not appear explicitly in the syntax of the specifications. These are obtained via the appropriate rate function $\mathcal{R}$ according to the kind of action performed, the data transmitted and the interfaces of the involved components, provides the actual action rate. Due to lack of space we omit the explicit definition of function $\mathcal{R}$ that can be easily inferred from the informal description.

Note that in process ServiceAgent, the term c varies according to the considered *allocation method*:

static allocation

$$\text{this.}level == \mathcal{I}.level$$

progressive allocation

$$\text{this.}level <= \mathcal{I}.level$$

dynamic allocation

$$((\text{this}.load <= 50\%) \wedge \mathcal{I}.level >= \text{base}) \vee$$
$$((\text{this}.load <= 66\%) \wedge \mathcal{I}.level >= \text{standard}) \vee$$
$$((\text{this}.load <= 88\%) \wedge \mathcal{I}.level >= \text{premium}) \vee$$
$$(\mathcal{I}.level == \text{superpremium})$$

The formulas listed above identifies the specific predicates used by ServiceAgent to retrieve requests from *user components*. Above, this is used to refer to the interface of the local component (i.e. the *computational component* executing a ServiceAgent) while $\mathcal{I}$ refers to the target interface, i.e. the component from which the request is retrieved. Two attributes are used in the considered predicates: level and load. These identify the user QoS level and the workload of a component, respectively.

Note that in the case of *dynamic allocation, self-awareness* is rendered directly in the target predicated used to retrieve user requests. A ServiceAgent handles base (resp. standard, premium) users only when the component's load is under 50% (resp. 66%, 88%), while super premium users are always executed. The actual value of attribute *load* is transparently published on the component interface and dynamically computed according to the number of executed tasks.

To perform analyses of the considered system we use jRESP [5]. This is a Java environment that provides a simulation environment that, while implementing

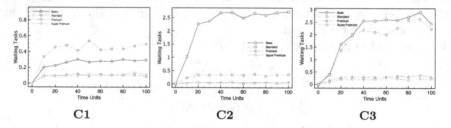

C1	C2	C3

Fig. 3. Simulation results: Number of waiting tasks

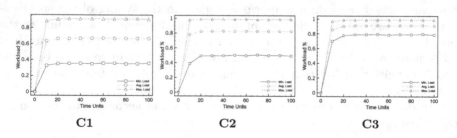

C1	C2	C3

Fig. 4. Simulation results: Workload

---

[5] http://jresp.sourceforge.org

the stochastic semantics presented in Section 4, can be used to analyse STOCS specifications.

We consider three configurations:

C1 *static allocation* with 16 components: 6 for *base*, 5 *standard*, 3 *premium* and 2 *super premium*;

C2 *progressive allocation* with 13 components: 7 for *base*, 4 *standard*, 2 *premium*;

C3 *dynamic allocation* with 12 components.

The results of simulations are reported in Figure 3 and Figure 4. If we compare the three configurations with respect to the average number of waiting tasks, the model **C1** is the one guaranteeing better quality of service (see Figure 3). However, if we consider the workload, **C3** is the one that, by using a less number of computational resources, guarantees a well balanced use of resources (see Figure 4).

6   Conclusions and Future Work

We have introduced STOCS, a stochastic extension of SCEL, for the modeling and analysis of performance aspects of ensemble based autonomous systems. One of the original features of the language is the use of stochastic predicate based multi-cast communication which poses particular challenges concerning stochastically timed semantics. The proposed semantics models the execution STOCS actions through several intermediate steps modelling the behaviour of an underling framework providing the machinery for realising the STOCS communication primitives. A case study concerning an abstract model of a cloud system was presented to illustrate the use of the various language primitives of STOCS. As a future work we plan to develop fluid semantics of STOCS together with the related verification techniques that can be used to address the analysis of large scale collective systems along the lines of work in [1,2].

References

1. Bortolussi, L., Hillston, J.: Fluid model checking. In: Koutny, M., Ulidowski, I. (eds.) CONCUR 2012. LNCS, vol. 7454, pp. 333–347. Springer, Heidelberg (2012)
2. Bortolussi, L., Hillston, J., Latella, D., Massink, M.: Continuous approximation of collective system behaviour: A tutorial. Perform. Eval. 70(5), 317–349 (2013)
3. Bruni, R., Corradini, A., Gadducci, F., Lluch Lafuente, A., Vandin, A.: A conceptual framework for adaptation. In: de Lara, J., Zisman, A. (eds.) Fundamental Approaches to Software Engineering. LNCS, vol. 7212, pp. 240–254. Springer, Heidelberg (2012)
4. De Nicola, R., Katoen, J.-P., Latella, D., Loreti, M., Massink, M.: Model Checking Mobile Stochastic Logic. Theoretical Computer 382(1), 42–70 (2007), http://dx.doi.org/10.1016/j.tcs.2007.05.008, doi:10.1016/j.tcs.2007.05.008.
5. De Nicola, R., Ferrari, G., Loreti, M., Pugliese, R.: A language-based approach to autonomic computing. In: Beckert, B., Damiani, F., de Boer, F.S., Bonsangue, M.M. (eds.) FMCO 2011. LNCS, vol. 7542, pp. 25–48. Springer, Heidelberg (2012)

6. De Nicola, R., Latella, D., Loreti, M., Massink, M.: Rate-based transition systems for stochastic process calculi. In: Albers, S., Marchetti-Spaccamela, A., Matias, Y., Nikoletseas, S., Thomas, W. (eds.) ICALP 2009, Part II. LNCS, vol. 5556, pp. 435–446. Springer, Heidelberg (2009)

7. Nicola, R.D., Latella, D., Loreti, M., Massink, M.: A uniform definition of stochastic process calculi. ACM Comput. Surv. 46(1), 5:1–5:35 (2013)

8. Nicola, R.D., Loreti, M., Pugliese, R., Tiezzi, F.: A formal approach to autonomic systems programming: The SCEL language. TAAS 9(2), 7 (2014)

9. Feng, C., Hillston, J.: PALOMA: A process algebra for located markovian agents. In: Norman, G., Sanders, W. (eds.) QEST 2014. LNCS, vol. 8657, pp. 265–280. Springer, Heidelberg (2014)

10. N. Koch, M. Hölzl, A. Klarl, P. Mayer, T. Bures, J. Combaz, A.L. Lafuente, R.D. Nicola, S. Sebastio, F. Tiezzi, A. Vandin, F. Gadducci, V. Monreale, U. Montanari, M. Loreti, C. Pinciroli, M. Puviani, F. Zambonelli, N. Šerbedžija, E. Vassev.: JD3.2: Software engineering for self-aware SCEs. ASCENS Deliverable JD3.2 (2013)

11. Latella, D., Loreti, M., Massink, M., Senni, V.: Stochastically timed predicate-based communication primitives for autonomic computing. In: Bertrand, N., Bortolussi, L. (eds.) Proceedings Twelfth International Workshop on Quantitative Aspects of Programming Languages and Systems, QAPL 2014, Grenoble, France, April 12-13. EPTCS, vol. 154, pp. 1–16 (2014)

12. Nicola, R.D., Hölzl, M., Loreti, M., Lafuente, A.L., Montanari, U., Vassev, E., Zambonelli, F.: JD2.1: Languages and knowledge models for self-awareness and self-expression. ASCENS Deliverable JD2.1 (2012)

13. Šerbedžija, N., Hoch, N., Pinciroli, C., Kit, M., Bures, T., Monreale, V., Montanari, U., Mayer, P., Velasco, J.: D7.3: Third report on wp7 - integration and simulation report for the ascens case studies, ASCENS Deliverable D7.3 (2013)

14. Šerbedžija, N., Massink, M., Pinciroli, C., Brambilla, M., Latella, D., Dorigo, M., Birattari, M., Mayer, P., Velasco, J.A., Hoch, N., Bensler, H.P., Abeywickrama, D., Keznikl, J., Gerostathopoulos, I., Bures, T., Nicola, R.D., Loreti, M.: D7.2: Second report on wp7 - integration and simulation report for the ascens case studies. ASCENS Deliverable D7.2 (2012)

Programming Autonomic Systems
with Multiple Constraint Stores*

Ugo Montanari[1], Rosario Pugliese[2], and Francesco Tiezzi[3]

[1] Università di Pisa, Italy
ugo@di.unipi.it
[2] Università degli Studi di Firenze, Italy
rosario.pugliese@unifi.it
[3] IMT Institute for Advanced Studies, Lucca, Italy
francesco.tiezzi@imtlucca.it

Abstract. Developing autonomic systems is a major challenge due to their distributed nature, large dimension, high dynamism, open-endedness, and need of adaptation. In this paper, we tackle this challenge by proposing a language, called CCSCEL, that combines abstractions and primitives specifically devised for programming autonomic systems by also using constraints and operations on them. We show that constraints permit addressing issues related to the programming of autonomic systems, since they are suitable means to deal with, e.g., partial knowledge, multi-criteria optimisation, preferences, uncertainty. We also present an advanced form of interaction that is particularly convenient in this setting. It allows a component of a system to access the constraint-based knowledge of all components checking its consistency and implications.

1 Introduction

Developing massively distributed and highly dynamic computing systems which interact with and control the physical world is a major challenge in software engineering [17]. Many difficulties arise from the fact that large-scale distributed systems are open-ended and dynamic, meaning that their components may freely appear and disappear as well as change their interaction partners. Other difficulties arise from the fact that the external environment can be non-deterministic and subject to unpredictable changes. Hence, hardware and software systems operating in these settings should be *autonomic* [11], that is they should feature a certain degree of self-awareness and self-adaptability for achieving desired behaviour while at the same time hiding intrinsic complexity to users.

Ensembles of components is a promising way of building autonomic systems which is being pursued by the EU project ASCENS. Contrary to classical component-based software engineering, it features important, related concepts of knowledge and ensembles. The *knowledge* of a component is a set of facts with

---

* This work has been partially sponsored by the EU project ASCENS (257414) and by the Italian MIUR PRIN project CINA (2010LHT4KM).

R. De Nicola and R. Hennicker (Eds.): Wirsing Festschrift, LNCS 8950, pp. 641–661, 2015.

well-defined relations. The facts in the knowledge change at runtime to reflect the state of the component and its belief about the environment, thus effectively addressing the self-awareness of the component. *Ensembles* are interaction groups of several, possibly heterogeneous, components, formed on demand to reflect intentions of components relatively to the current state of their environment. This way, ensembles address the dynamicity and self-adaptivity of components.

Ensembles are often required to solve complex problems of real life, even situations in which the level of interaction between humans and components of the ensemble is strongly limited or absent. Therefore, their components usually collaborate with each other in order to achieve a common goal. This calls for further features, such as self-configuration, self-optimisation, self-healing and self-protection, that increase the self-management capability of the systems.

With the goal of developing a coherent, integrated set of linguistic primitives specifically devised to model and program ensembles, in previous work we have proposed the language SCEL (Software Component Ensemble Language, [8]). In SCEL, autonomic components are entities with dedicated knowledge repositories and resources that can cooperate while playing different roles. Knowledge repositories also enable components to store and retrieve information about their working environment, and to use it for redirecting and adapting their behavior. Each component is equipped with an interface, consisting of a collection of attributes, such as provided functionalities, spatial coordinates, group memberships, trust level, response time, etc. Attributes are used by the components to dynamically organize themselves into ensembles. The way sets of partners are selected for interaction, and thus how ensembles are formed, is one of the main novelties of SCEL. In fact, individual components can not only single out interaction partners by using their identities, but they can also select partners by exploiting the attributes in the interfaces of the individual components. Predicates over such attributes are used to specify the targets of interaction actions, thus providing a sort of attribute-based interaction. In this way, the formation rule of ensembles is endogenous to components: members of an ensemble are connected by the interdependency relations defined through predicates. An ensemble is therefore not a rigid fixed network, but rather a highly dynamic structure where components linkages are dynamically established.

SCEL has proven to be suitable to model many different autonomic systems scenarios [8,5,6,13,14,3,12,9,7]. In the context of intelligent navigation of electric vehicles (e-Mobility), in [3] we have complemented the SCEL specification of the system with an approach based on *soft constraint programming* specifically targeting intuitive specification of *optimization problems* that frequently appear in autonomic systems. The interplay of the two approaches has turned out to be very useful for describing mutually related activities of interaction and coordination among vehicles combined with finding a tradeoff between local-global optima (reflecting both the complexity of a globally optimal policy and the need of harmonizing the selfish and cooperative concerns of vehicles).

In this paper we further push forward the integration of soft constraints with SCEL. Technically, we exploit the fact that the SCEL language definition abstracts from a few ingredients of the language and we appropriately specialize these parameters of the language so that constraints and operations on them are smoothly incorporated in SCEL. We obtain in this way a dialect of SCEL, that we call ccSCEL, specifically devised for enabling soft concurrent constraint programming (SCCP) [2] via the interaction primitives of SCEL. We demonstrate that using constraints as a form of knowledge of SCEL components can bring benefits to address issues related to ensembles of components. Constraints are indeed suitable to represent partial knowledge, to deal with multi-criteria optimization, to express preferences, fuzziness, and uncertainty[1].

The contribution of this work is twofold. On the one hand, we define a fully-specified dialect of SCEL for programming autonomic systems in terms of both tuple-based and constraint-based coordination. Both coordination approaches are supported by a common set of primitives and are hence formalised by means of a uniform semantics. This permits using ccSCEL for programming a wide range of relevant autonomic systems, since one can deal at once with such issues as constraint-driven decision making, achievement of service-level agreements, coordination of asynchronous interactions, concurrent activities, resource usage, self-awareness and adaptation, in a distributed, open-ended setting. From the constraint programming point of view, we present a novel distributed variant of the SCCP paradigm, where constraints are stored in the local stores of the components of an ensemble but, when specifically required by a component, they may be involved in a global check of consistency at ensemble level.

More specifically, in ccSCEL each component is equipped with a local store which is a multiset of constraints. This store is independent from the stores of the other components since the variables occurring in the constraints stored locally are private to the component and are thus distinct from the variables used in the other stores. Processes running at components can operate on (possibly non local) stores by inserting, entailing and withdrawing constraints. The language semantics ensures that when such an operation is performed, the consistency of the target store is preserved. ccSCEL also provides policies for regulating the behaviour of components. In case of remote insertion of a constraint, some of these policies require to check the consistency of multiple stores temporarily related through constraints equating variables of the different components. Similarly, in case of remote retrieval of a constraint, these policies require to check the entailment of a constraint by the multiset of constraints obtained by temporarily relating different stores. This sort of 'global' consistency, unlike the 'local' consistency of a single store, is however not guaranteed to be preserved while the computation progresses: it surely holds when a constraint is inserted (as it is a necessary condition for the insertion), afterwards it could be violated because of, e.g., local insertion of constraints.

We also present an extension of the ccSCEL dialect enabling a form of ensemble-wide interaction. By resorting to this kind of interaction, a component can access the knowledge of the components of an ensemble as a whole. In particular, it can send a constraint to the ensemble components and check for

---

[1] Additional details and motivations on the use of constraints can be found in [1,16].

consistency of the multiset of all their constraints. Similarly, it can check if a constraint is entailed from the multiset of all ensemble components' constraints.

It is worth noticing that there is neither automatic generation and propagation of entailed constraints, nor automatic saturation of constraint stores. This design choice enables (syntactic) constraints withdrawal and is in line with the highly dynamic and open-ended nature of the systems under consideration. Of course, enrichment of stores with some of the constraints entailed at a certain point of the computation can be explicitly programmed. These constraints may represent knowledge that is acquired also thanks to the contribution of other members of an ensemble, whose knowledge might thus be only temporarily available (i.e. as long as the component is part of the ensemble). In this way, CCSCEL turns out to be flexible enough for adequately modelling both 'memory-full' scenarios, where it might be useful to preserve the knowledge acquired during the computation, and 'memoryless' scenarios, where only the knowledge that can be inferred at each computation step is taken into account.

We also want to remark that an important design aspect of programming languages is about the delicate tradeoff between expressiveness of constructs and their conceptual and implementation complexity. In our case, CCSCEL does not require any extension of SCEL, but only a specialisation. Also, the logical independence of the constraint stores of the various components allows for smaller complexity (checking for constraint satisfaction is NP-complete even in the simplest cases) and for different deduction approaches, e.g. monotonic increase in a component and retract capability in another. Conversely, the CCSCEL extension enabling to check for global consistency is a powerful, expressive feature which could be very useful in the design phase, and possibly implemented in an approximated way in the refined implementation.

The rest of the paper is structured as follows. In Section 2, we provide the background notions on (soft) constraints used in Section 3 to define the CCSCEL dialect. Section 4 shows CCSCEL at work on a Web hosting example. Section 5 presents the extension of the language to support the ensemble-wide interaction. Finally, Section 6 concludes by touching upon comparisons with related work and directions for future work. To save space, we refer the interested reader to [15] for the complete definitions of the semantics of CCSCEL and its extension.

During the last twelve years the authors had the chance to collaborate with Professor Martin Wirsing in several occasions, especially in the context of the European projects he recently coordinated: Agile, Sensoria and Ascens. He has been a source of inspiration and enrichment, from both a scientific and a human point of view. In particular, this paper proposes an integration of autonomic systems programming and soft constraint programming, two key topics of Ascens Martin significantly contributed to. Many thanks Martin, this paper is dedicated to you on the occasion of your Emeritation!

2   Semiring-Based Constraints

In this section, we report some basic definitions concerning the concept of (soft) constraints.

Among the many available formalizations, hereafter we refer to the one based on *c-semirings* [1,16], which generalizes many of the others. Intuitively, a constraint is a relation that gives information on the possible values that the variables of a specified set may assume. We adopt a functional formulation. Hence, given a set V of variables and a domain D of values that the variables may assume, assignments and constraints are defined as follows.

Definition 1. *An assignment η of values to variables is a function $\eta : V \to D$.*

Definition 2. *A constraint χ is a function $\chi : (V \to D) \to \{\mathbf{true}, \mathbf{false}\}$.*

A constraint is then represented as a function that, given an assignment η, returns a truth value indicating if the constraint is satisfied by η. An assignment that satisfies a constraint is called a *solution*.

In CCSCEL, V is the set of *constraint variables* and D is the set of SCEL *basic values* (e.g., integers and strings). Constraint variables are written as pairs of names of the form $n@n'$ (e.g., *cost@client* and *battery_level@robot*), where n is the variable name and n' the name of the component that *owns* the variable. Notably, different components may own variables with the same name; such variables are distinct and may thus store different values.

When convenient, we will denote an assignment as a collection of pairs of the form $n@n' \mapsto v$, where $n@n'$ and v range over variables and values, respectively. Such pairs explicitly specify the associations for only the variables relevant for the considered constraint; these variables form the so-called *support* [2] of the constraint, which is supposed to be finite. For example, given the constraints *cost@client* ≥ 350 and *cost@client* $=$ *bw@client* $\cdot\, 0.05$, the assignment $\{$*cost@client* $\mapsto 500,$ *bw@client* $\mapsto 8000\}$ satisfies the first constraint (i.e., returns **true**) but does not satisfy the second one (i.e., returns **false**).

The constraints introduced above are called *crisp* in the literature, because they can only be either satisfied or violated. A more general notion is represented by *soft constraints*. These constraints, given an assignment, return an element of an arbitrary constraint semiring (*c-semiring* [1]). C-semirings are partially ordered sets of 'preference' values equipped with two suitable operations for comparison $(+)$ and combination $(\times)$ of (tuples of) values and constraints.

Definition 3. *A c-semiring is an algebraic structure $\langle S, +, \times, 0, 1 \rangle$ such that: S is a set and $0, 1 \in S$; $+$ is a binary operation on S that is commutative, associative, idempotent, 0 is its unit element and 1 is its absorbing element; $\times$ is a binary operation on S that is commutative, associative, distributes over $+$, 1 is its unit element and 0 is its absorbing element. Operation $+$ induces a partial order $\leq$ on S defined by $a \leq b$ iff $a + b = b$, which means that a is more constrained than b or, equivalently, that b is better than a. The minimal element is thus 0 and the maximal 1.*

Definition 4. *Let $\langle S, +, \times, 0, 1 \rangle$ be a c-semiring. A soft constraint χ is a function $\chi : (V \to D) \to S$.*

In particular, crisp constraints can be understood as soft constraints on the c-semiring $\langle \{\mathbf{true}, \mathbf{false}\}, \vee, \wedge, \mathbf{false}, \mathbf{true} \rangle$.

By lifting the c-semiring operators to constraints, we get the operators

$$(\chi_1 + \chi_2)(\eta) \;=\; \chi_1(\eta) + \chi_2(\eta) \qquad\qquad (\chi_1 \times \chi_2)(\eta) \;=\; \chi_1(\eta) \times \chi_2(\eta)$$

(their n-ary extensions are straightforward). We can formally define the notions of consistency and entailment. The *consistency* condition $\chi \neq 0$ stands for

$$\exists \eta \;:\; \chi(\eta) \neq 0$$

i.e. a constraint is consistent if it has at least one solution; the *entailment* condition $\chi_1 \leq \chi_2$ stands for

$$\forall \eta, \; \chi_1(\eta) \leq \chi_2(\eta) \,.$$

3   The ccSCEL Dialect

SCEL is a kernel language for programming autonomic computing systems in terms of Behaviours, Knowledge and Aggregations, according to specific Policies. *Behaviours* describe how computations progress and are modelled as processes executing actions. *Knowledge* is represented through items containing either application data enabling the progress of components' computations, or awareness data providing information about the environment in which the components are running (e.g., monitored data from sensors) or about the status of a component (e.g., its current location). *Aggregations* describe how different entities are brought together to form components and ensembles. In particular, components result from a form of syntax-based aggregation that puts together a knowledge repository, a set of policies and a set of behaviours, by wrapping them in an interface providing a set of *attributes*, i.e. names referring to information stored in the knowledge repository. Components' composition and interaction are implemented by relying on *predicates* over the attributes exposed in components' interfaces. This semantics-based aggregation of components permits defining ensembles, representing social or technical networks of components, and configuring them to dynamically adapt to changes in the environment. Finally, *policies* control and adapt the actions of the different components for guaranteeing accomplishment of specific tasks or satisfaction of specific properties.

In the design of SCEL, some ingredients of the language have been intentionally left unspecified in order to fit different paradigms and application domains. Different dialects can thus be derived by simply instantiating the SCEL's parameters without modifying the semantics. These parameters are

1. the languages for representing knowledge *items* and the *templates* to be used to retrieve these items from the repositories;
2. the language for representing *knowledge* repositories, together with the three *operations*, i.e. withdrawal, retrieval and insertion, that each knowledge repository's handling mechanism must provide;
3. *interaction predicate* and *authorisation predicate*;
4. the language for expressing *policies*.

Table 1. CCSCEL syntax

SYSTEMS: $S ::= C \mid S_1 \parallel S_2 \mid (\nu n)S$	COMPONENTS: $C ::= \mathcal{I}[\mathcal{K}, \Pi, P]$
PROCESSES: $P ::= \textbf{nil} \mid a.P \mid P_1 + P_2 \mid P_1 \mid P_2 \mid X \mid A(\bar{p})$	
ACTIONS: $a ::= \textbf{get}(T)@c \mid \textbf{qry}(T)@c \mid \textbf{put}(t)@c \mid \textbf{fresh}(n) \mid \textbf{new}(\mathcal{I}, \mathcal{K}, \Pi, P)$	
TARGETS: $c ::= n \mid x \mid \textsf{self} \mid \mathcal{P} \mid p$	

KNOWLEDGE: $\mathcal{K} ::= \emptyset \mid t \parallel \mathcal{K}$	POLICIES: $\Pi ::= \Pi_{1store} \mid \Pi_{2store} \mid \Pi_N$
ITEMS: $t ::= \chi \mid \langle f \rangle$	TEMPLATES: $T ::= \chi \mid \langle F \rangle$
DATA TUPLE FIELDS: $f ::= e \mid c \mid P \mid f_1, f_2$	DATA TEMPLATE FIELDS: $F ::= e \mid c \mid ?x \mid ?X \mid F_1, F_2$

We introduce the syntax and (a sketch of the) semantics of the CCSCEL dialect, which enables (soft concurrent) constraint programming via the interaction primitives of SCEL[2]. To define CCSCEL, the SCEL parameters are instantiated as follows: 1. items are *constraints* and *data tuples*, while templates are constraints and data templates; 2. knowledge repositories behave as constraint stores and tuple spaces, i.e., according to the considered kind of knowledge, the withdrawal, retrieval and insertion operations act as the SCCP actions **tell**, **ask** and **retract** or as the tuple-based actions **out**, **read** and **in**, respectively; 3. the interaction predicate is defined so that the different kinds of knowledge items are appropriately taken into account (e.g., pattern-matching is used to pick a tuple matching a given template out of a repository) and evaluated; similarly, the authorisation predicate is defined so that the different policies are appropriately enforced (e.g., the insertion of a constraint is always allowed if it occurs locally, otherwise consistency of the combination of the constraint to be added with the remote and local constraint repositories is required); 4. the policy language is very basic and only includes three elementary policies which only differ for the requirements about consistency in case of constraint insertion and entailment.

3.1 Syntax

The syntax of CCSCEL is illustrated in Table 1. The grammar definitions in the upper part of the table are directly borrowed from SCEL without any change. Thus, the basic syntactic category is the one defining PROCESSES that are used

---

[2] We refer the interested reader to [8] for a full account of the SCEL language.

to build up COMPONENTS that in turn are used to define SYSTEMS. PROCESSES specify the flow of the ACTIONS that can be performed. ACTIONS can have a TARGET to determine the other components that are involved in that action. In particular, there are five different kinds of actions: **get**, **qry** and **put** are used to withdraw/retrieve/add information items from/to knowledge repositories; **fresh** generates fresh names; **new** creates new components. The grammar definitions in the lower part of the table are specific to the notion of knowledge considered in CCSCEL which is the topic of the rest of this section.

A knowledge repository $\mathcal{K}$ can contain two kinds of items: *constraints* χ and data *tuples* $\langle f \rangle$. Thus, a repository can play the role of both a constraint store[3] and a tuple space.

Constraints stored in knowledge repositories are as introduced in Section 2, while constraints used as action arguments may only involve process variables and *underspecified* constraint variables. These latter ones are constraint variables lacking the name of the owner component and thus ending with the symbol @, as e.g. *cost*@, which permits to distinguish them from process variables. The owner of such a variable is the component target of the action. Its name will be automatically added to the variable name at the time of the insertion of the constraint in the target store (see Section 3.2). The restriction of using only underspecified constraint variables in action arguments ensures that all the constraints stored in the same repository only involve variables owned by the same component, which is the owner of the repository. Thus, for example, it will never happen that the *client*'s repository stores a constraint like *cost@provider* < 100.

A data tuple is a sequence of actual fields, while a data template $\langle F \rangle$ is a sequence of actual and formal fields. Actual fields can either be expressions or targets. We assume that expressions contain boolean, integer, float, and string values and variables, together with the corresponding standard operators. Targets can be (component) names or variables, the distinguished variable self, predicates or predicate names. Formal fields, written as $?x$ or $?X$, are used to bind variables to values or to processes, respectively. More precisely, actions **get**$(\langle F \rangle)$@c and **qry**$(\langle F \rangle)$@c bind the variables occurring in the data template $\langle F \rangle$. Action **fresh**(n) is a binder for the name n which is ensured to be different from any other name previously used. For all these three action binders, the scope is the process P syntactically following the action in a prefix form $a.P$. Instead, the restriction operator $(\nu n)_-$ binds the name n in the scope $_-$.

CCSCEL also relies on three policies regulating the behaviour of components. They only differ for the requirements in case of constraints insertion and entailment. Indeed, when the insertion is local to the component performing the action, only the consistency of the local store is checked, no matter what the policy is. Otherwise, policy Π_{1store} prescribes to combine (by means of operation $\times$) and check for consistency only the constraints within the remote store. Policy Π_{2store} prescribes to combine, and check for consistency, the constraints within

---

[3] In the rest of the paper, we will use the term 'repository' to refer to a generic container of knowledge items and the term 'store' to refer to (the part of) a container storing constraints.

the remote and local stores. The two stores are temporarily related through some constraints equating all the homonymous variables owned by the two components. Entailment is handled similarly. Notice that if a variable in a store has no counterpart in the other store no problem arises, simply no equation is generated. The consistency/entailment check over the combined store is performed when at least one between the component performing the action and the target one is exposing the Π_{2store} policy. Policy Π_N is similar to Π_{2store}, but for the fact that only variables in the set of names N are equated.

3.2 Semantics

In CCSCEL, arguments of actions can either be constraints or data tuples; therefore, their semantics is specialized as follows. When the argument of actions **put**, **qry** and **get** is a constraint, they play the role of actions **tell**, **ask** and **retract**, respectively, commonly used in the SCCP paradigm to add a constraint to a store, to check entailment of a constraint by a store and to remove a constraint from a store. Instead, when the argument of actions **put**, **qry** and **get** is a data tuple, they play the role of actions **out**, **read** and **in**, respectively, commonly used in the tuple-based coordination paradigm [10] to add, read and withdraw tuples to/from a tuple space via pattern-matching.

Constraints used as action arguments are evaluated in order to assign a component owner to each underspecified constraint variable occurring in the constraints. The use of underspecified constraint variables is just a shorthand for the corresponding constraint variables in case of point-to-point interaction (i.e., when the target of the action is a specific component), while it has a key role in case of group-oriented interaction (i.e., when the target of the action is an ensemble predicate), because in this latter case the involved components are dynamically determined. For example, the action **put**$(cost@ < 100)@provider$ executed by the *client* component adds the constraint $(cost@provider < 100)$ to the *provider*'s store. Similarly, the action **put**$(cost@ < 100)@\mathcal{P}$, where $\mathcal{P}$ is a predicate identifying at runtime an ensemble of two components, say $provider_1$ and $provider_2$, adds the constraint $(cost@provider_1 < 100)$ to $provider_1$'s store and $(cost@provider_2 < 100)$ to $provider_2$'s store.

According to SCEL's operational semantics, processes interact with knowledge repositories by means of the following operations that each knowledge repository's handling mechanism must provide:

- $\mathcal{K} \ominus t = \mathcal{K}'$: the *withdrawal* of item t from the repository $\mathcal{K}$ returns $\mathcal{K}'$;
- $\mathcal{K} \vdash t$: the *retrieval* of item t from the repository $\mathcal{K}$ is possible;
- $\mathcal{K} \oplus t = \mathcal{K}'$: the *insertion* of item t into the repository $\mathcal{K}$ returns $\mathcal{K}'$.

In CCSCEL, the three operations above are defined in two different ways, depending on whether the item t is a data tuple (rules in the upper part of Table 2) or a constraint (rules in the lower part of Table 2). Given a repository $\mathcal{K}$, we use $\mathcal{K}_{tuples}$ (resp. $\mathcal{K}_{const}$) to denote the knowledge corresponding to all data tuples (resp. constraints) within $\mathcal{K}$; in other words, each CCSCEL repository $\mathcal{K}$ can

Table 2. Knowledge repository operations

$$\mathcal{K} \ominus_n \langle f \rangle = \mathcal{K}' \ if\ \mathcal{K} \equiv \mathcal{K}' \parallel \langle f \rangle \qquad \mathcal{K} \vdash_n \langle f \rangle \ if\ \mathcal{K} \equiv \mathcal{K}' \parallel \langle f \rangle \qquad \mathcal{K} \oplus_n \langle f \rangle = \mathcal{K} \parallel \langle f \rangle$$

$$\mathcal{K} \ominus_n \chi = \begin{cases} \mathcal{K}' \ if\ \mathcal{K} \equiv \mathcal{K}' \parallel \chi @ n \\ \mathcal{K} \ otherwise \end{cases}$$

$$\mathcal{K} \vdash_n \chi \qquad\qquad if\ \mathcal{K} \equiv (\mathcal{K}_{tuples} \parallel \chi_1 \parallel \dots \parallel \chi_m)\ and\ (\chi_1 \times \dots \times \chi_m) \le \chi @ n$$

$$\mathcal{K} \oplus_n \chi = \mathcal{K} \parallel \chi @ n \quad if\ \mathcal{K} \equiv (\mathcal{K}_{tuples} \parallel \chi_1 \parallel \dots \parallel \chi_m)\ and\ (\chi_1 \times \dots \times \chi_m \times \chi @ n) \ne 0$$

be seen as the composition $\mathcal{K}_{tuples} \parallel \mathcal{K}_{const}$ of two repositories, where $\mathcal{K}_{tuples}$ is of the form $\langle f_1 \rangle \parallel \dots \parallel \langle f_n \rangle$ and $\mathcal{K}_{const}$ is of the form $\chi_1 \parallel \dots \parallel \chi_m$. We use $\mathcal{K}_1 \equiv \mathcal{K}_2$ to denote that $\mathcal{K}_1$ and $\mathcal{K}_2$ are equal up to commutation of items and addition/removal of the unit element $\emptyset$. Operation $\ominus$ (resp. $\vdash$, resp. $\oplus$) takes as a further parameter a component identifier n, used to fill the underspecified constraint variables occurring in the constraint to be retracted (resp. entailed, resp. added). Notation $\chi @ n$ indicates the constraint obtained from χ by completing each underspecified constraint variable occurring therein by using the identifier n. In the definition of $\mathcal{K} \vdash_n \chi$ and $\mathcal{K} \oplus_n \chi$, if the constraint store is empty (i.e. $m = 0$), then it suffices to verify that χ is a tautology (i.e., it is a constant function returning the c-semiring value 1 for any assignment) and that $\chi @ n$ has at least one solution (i.e., it differs from the c-semiring value 0), resp.

Another parameter that we need to instantiate for defining the ccSCEL dialect is the *interaction predicate* $\Pi, \mathcal{I} : \alpha \succ \lambda, \sigma, \Pi'$. It is used to evaluate the parameters of the action α which is going to be performed by a process running at a component with policy Π and interface $\mathcal{I}$. This evaluation returns the label λ corresponding to the action actually performed and the effects of its execution: the substitution σ (i.e. a partial function from variables to values) associates values to the variables possibly occurring in the formal fields of α and is used to capture the changes induced by interaction; the policy Π' is in force after the transition (in principle, it may differ from that in force before the transition, but in ccSCEL it remains unchanged). The predicate is defined by a set of inference rules an excerpt of which is shown in Table 3 (the full definition is reported in [15]). We only show the rules for action **qry**, whose corresponding system label is $\mathcal{I} : t \blacktriangleleft \gamma$ denoting the intention of component $\mathcal{I}$ to retrieve item t from the repository at γ. Rules for actions **get** and **put** are similar. For each of these actions, we have two rules[4] to separately deal with two different kinds of arguments: in case of a data template, the pattern-matching with a data tuple is checked and a substitution is generated (by means of the function *match*, whose definition is straightforward and can be found in [15]); in case of a constraint, no pattern-matching evaluation is needed and the empty

---

[4] Instead, for each of the actions **new** and **fresh**, we have only one straightforward rule.

Table 3. The interaction predicate $\Pi, \mathcal{I} : \alpha \succ \lambda, \sigma, \Pi'$ (excerpt of rules)

$$\frac{\mathcal{E}[\![\langle F \rangle]\!]_{\mathcal{I}} = \langle F' \rangle \quad \mathcal{E}[\![c]\!]_{\mathcal{I}} = \gamma \quad match(F', f) = \sigma}{\Pi, \mathcal{I} : \mathbf{qry}(\langle F \rangle)@c \succ \mathcal{I} : \langle f \rangle \blacktriangleleft \gamma, \sigma, \Pi} \qquad \frac{\mathcal{E}[\![\chi]\!]_{\mathcal{I}} = \chi' \quad \mathcal{E}[\![c]\!]_{\mathcal{I}} = \gamma}{\Pi, \mathcal{I} : \mathbf{qry}(\chi)@c \succ \mathcal{I} : \chi' \blacktriangleleft \gamma, \{\}, \Pi}$$

substitution (denoted by $\{\}$) is returned. Moreover, the parameters of the action are evaluated with respect to the interface of the component performing the action through the auxiliary function $\mathcal{E}[\![\_]\!]_{\_}$. Specifically, $\mathcal{E}[\![T]\!]_{\mathcal{I}}$ ($\mathcal{E}[\![c]\!]_{\mathcal{I}}$, resp.) denotes the evaluation of the data template T (target c, resp.) with respect to interface $\mathcal{I}$, where the attributes occurring in T (c, resp.) are replaced by the corresponding values in the interface $\mathcal{I}$; in particular, the target self is replaced by the component name (which is bound to $\mathcal{I}.id$). Instead, the predicates possibly occurring in targets are left unchanged. For example, if a process executes the action $\mathbf{put}(resources@\mathsf{self} = res)@\mathsf{self}$ and its component interface $\mathcal{I}$ specifies the attributes $(id, provider)$ and $(res, 15)$, then the constraint to be added to the local store is $\mathcal{E}[\![resources@\mathsf{self} = res]\!]_{\mathcal{I}} = (resources@provider = 15)$.

The last parameter that we need to instantiate for completing the definition of the CCSCEL dialect is the *interaction predicate* $\Pi \vdash \lambda, \Pi'$. It means that under policy Π, the label λ (which can be thought of as an *authorisation request*) is allowed and the policy Π' is produced. The predicate is defined by the set of inference rules shown in Table 4. These rules enforce the policies Π_{1store} and Π_{2store} informally described in Section 3.1 (the rules for constraint entailment in case of policy Π_{2store} and all rules for policy Π_N can be found in [15]). In the table, $\mathcal{K}_{\mathcal{I}}$ and $\mathcal{K}_{\mathcal{J}}$ stand for the knowledge repository of the components with interface $\mathcal{I}$ and $\mathcal{J}$, respectively. The first rule authorises any action different from the acceptance of a **put** action having a constraint as argument; such an action is authorised by the second rule provided that the store resulting from the addition of the constraint is consistent. The third rule is similar to the first one, it also does not authorises the acceptance of a **qry** action having a constraint as argument. The fourth rule authorises the local insertion of a constraint (indeed, the target component $\mathcal{J}$ coincides with the component executing the action) provided that the store resulting from the addition of the constraint is consistent. The case of a remote **put** action is covered by the last rule that, when the policy is Π_{2store}, checks the consistency of the (temporary) combination of the constraint to be added with the remote and local stores. This combination is further enriched with some constraints equating *all* homonymous constraint variables occurring in the stores of the two components. To generate these constraints we use the function

$$eq(\mathcal{K}_{\mathcal{I}}, \mathcal{K}_{\mathcal{J}}) = \prod_{n@n_1 \in v(\mathcal{K}_{\mathcal{I}}), n@n_2 \in v(\mathcal{K}_{\mathcal{J}})} n@n_1 = n@n_2$$

where function $v(\mathcal{K})$ returns the set $\{n@n' \in cv(\chi) \mid \mathcal{K} \equiv (\mathcal{K}' \parallel \chi)\}$ of constraint variables used in $\mathcal{K}$, while $cv(\chi)$ returns the set of constraint variables used in χ. The (omitted) rules for Π_N are like the three rules for Π_{2store}, but for the last rule where the eq function is replaced by

$$eq_N(\mathcal{K}_{\mathcal{I}}, \mathcal{K}_{\mathcal{J}}) = \prod_{n@n_1 \in v(\mathcal{K}_{\mathcal{I}}), n@n_2 \in v(\mathcal{K}_{\mathcal{J}}), n \in N} n@n_1 = n@n_2$$

Table 4. The authorisation predicate $\Pi \vdash \lambda, \Pi'$ (for policies Π_{1store} and Π_{2store})

$$\frac{\lambda \notin \{\mathcal{I} : \chi \triangleright \mathcal{J}\}}{\Pi_{1store} \vdash \lambda, \Pi_{1store}} \qquad\qquad \frac{\mathcal{K}_{\mathcal{J}} \oplus_{\mathcal{J}.id} \chi}{\Pi_{1store} \vdash \mathcal{I} : \chi \triangleright \mathcal{J}, \Pi_{1store}}$$

$$\frac{\lambda \notin \{\mathcal{I} : \chi \triangleright \mathcal{J}, \mathcal{I} : \chi \blacktriangleleft \mathcal{J}\}}{\Pi_{2store} \vdash \lambda, \Pi_{2store}} \qquad\qquad \frac{\mathcal{K}_{\mathcal{J}} \oplus_{\mathcal{J}.id} \chi}{\Pi_{2store} \vdash \mathcal{J} : \chi \triangleright \mathcal{J}, \Pi_{2store}}$$

$$\frac{\mathcal{I} \neq \mathcal{J} \qquad (\mathcal{K}_{\mathcal{I}} \parallel \mathcal{K}_{\mathcal{J}} \parallel eq(\mathcal{K}_{\mathcal{I}}, \mathcal{K}_{\mathcal{J}})) \oplus_{\mathcal{J}.id} \chi}{\Pi_{2store} \vdash \mathcal{I} : \chi \triangleright \mathcal{J}, \Pi_{2store}}$$

Thus, only the constraint variables whose names are in the set N are equated.

4 ccSCEL at Work

In this section, we show an application of ccSCEL to a Web hosting example, where the involved parties behave in an autonomic fashion in order to optimize their goals and utility functions. In particular, in our scenario, there is a client that aims at identifying in its working environment a service provider offering a Web hosting solution at an affordable price. On the other hand, there could be many providers offering different solutions, varying in cost and in bandwidth, and possibly relying on third party services. Providers act in a dual way with respect to the client: they aim at selling their services at the highest price. Constraint-based programming is used here as a suitable means for allowing the parties to autonomously interact in order to negotiate the service provision and possibly achieve a Service Level Agreement (SLA).

Firstly, consider a scenario including a client $\mathcal{C}$ and a single service provider $\mathcal{P}$. Before the execution of the service, $\mathcal{C}$ and $\mathcal{P}$ want to sign a SLA contract. For the sake of simplicity, in this example we assume the constraint system to be based on crisp constraints. The scenario can be rendered in ccSCEL as follows:

$$\mathcal{I}_{\mathcal{C}}[\emptyset, \Pi_{\mathcal{C}}, P_{\mathcal{C}}] \parallel \mathcal{I}_{\mathcal{P}}[\emptyset, \Pi_{\mathcal{P}}, P_{\mathcal{P}}]$$

where $\mathcal{I}_{\mathcal{C}}.id = \mathcal{C}$ and $\mathcal{I}_{\mathcal{P}}.id = \mathcal{P}$. The repositories of the two components initially contain no constraints. Concerning policies and processes of the components, we show below different modelling approaches.

4.1 Point-to-point Interaction

According to the policies $\Pi_{\mathcal{C}}$ and $\Pi_{\mathcal{P}}$ exhibited by $\mathcal{C}$ and $\mathcal{P}$ to regulate the consistency checking of their stores, the behaviour of the two components may be specified in different ways in order to achieve the desired SLA.

Let us first consider the case $\Pi_{\mathcal{C}} = \Pi_{\mathcal{P}} = \Pi_{1store}$, where no combination between constraints stored by components $\mathcal{C}$ and $\mathcal{P}$ is performed during the consistency evaluation. The process $P_{\mathcal{P}}$ running in the provider component, in charge of negotiating the SLA with the client, is as follows:

$$P_{\mathcal{P}} \triangleq \mathbf{put}(price@ \geqslant 50)@\mathsf{self}.\ P'_{\mathcal{P}}$$

By performing the **put** action, the provider imposes the minimum price of 50 Euros for the service by adding the constraint $price@\mathcal{P} \geqslant 50$ to its store. Instead, the process $P_{\mathcal{C}}$ running in the client component is defined as follows:

$$P_{\mathcal{C}} \triangleq \mathbf{put}(price@ \leqslant 100)@\mathcal{P}$$

The client's constraint specifies the maximum cost 100 Euros the client is willing to pay for the service. In particular, by means of the **put** action, which tries to add the constraint $price@\mathcal{P} \leqslant 100$ to the provider store, the client process activates the consistency check of this constraint with respect to the constraint imposed by the provider. If the constraint $price@\mathcal{P} \leqslant 100$ is successfully added to the provider store, then the SLA is achieved, and the resulting contract is the combination (the logical conjunction, in this case) between the two constraints. This means that there exists a price between the minimum and the maximum price required by the provider and the client, respectively.

It is worth noticing that in this case the execution order of the **put** actions performed by provider and client does not matter, since the values 50 and 100 permit achieving a SLA. Instead, if the SLA could not be achieved, the process performing the first **put** action would proceed, while the other would be blocked. When necessary, such situations can be handled by means of explicit coordination mechanisms (e.g., via tuple-based synchronisation, as in the example in Section 4.4) or specific policies (which, e.g., authorise external access to the repositories only after the writing of local constraints is terminated).

Now, let us suppose that at least one between $\Pi_{\mathcal{C}}$ and $\Pi_{\mathcal{P}}$ is set to Π_{2store}. In this case, the consistency of the local constraints of the provider is evaluated in combination with the local constraints of the client. Of course, the processes described in the previous case can be used also in this setting. However, for increasing loose-coupling among components, a different approach can be applied in this case: the client sets locally its constraint about the maximum price and, then, interacts with the provider to negotiate the SLA. In this way, if the SLA is not achieved, the client could exploit the stored constraint for other negotiations.

While process $P_{\mathcal{P}}$ remains the same as before, this time process $P_{\mathcal{C}}$ is defined as follows:

$$P_{\mathcal{C}} \triangleq \mathbf{put}(price@ \leqslant 100)@\mathsf{self}.\ \mathbf{put}(\mathbf{true})@\mathcal{P}$$

The client fixes the maximum price it can pay for the service, using the first **put** action that acts locally. Then, with the second **put** action, it requests a consistency check of the combination of its local constraint with the provider's one. The two constraints are put in relation by means of the temporary constraint $price@\mathcal{P} = price@\mathcal{C}$ automatically generated when controlling authorisation with respect to policy Π_{2store}. If the check succeeds, then the SLA is achieved. Notably, the constraints composing the contract are distributed among the stores of the client and the provider, but the consistency of the contract is verified globally.

4.2   Constraint Variables with Restricted Access

We discuss here two approaches for restricting the access to given constraint variables from other components.

The first approach relies on the use of fresh names. If we assume that constraint variables are names, they can be dynamically generated by means of the **fresh** action and are subject to scope restriction as all other names in CCSCEL. For example, in the Web hosting scenario, the client could make private its variable $price@\mathcal{C}$, and the involved constraint, by means of the following process:

$$P_{\mathcal{C}} \triangleq \mathbf{fresh}(price).\,\mathbf{put}(price@ \leqslant 100)@\mathsf{self}.\ P'_{\mathcal{C}}$$

Now, the action **fresh** produces a restriction $(\nu\,price)$, at system level, whose scope is the client component. This means that the name $price$, as well as the corresponding variable $price@\mathcal{C}$ occurring in the local constraint generated by the **put** action, are only visible from within the client component. Therefore, all other components cannot refer to this variable in their actions **get**, **qry** and **put**, unless the name $price$ has been previously exchanged in interactions (as part of a data tuple). In fact, as in the π-calculus, when a name is sent via a message, its scope is extruded; this enables the receiving process to access the corresponding remote variable. In the considered example, in order to share the name, the client could perform the action $\mathbf{put}(\langle\text{"share\_var"}, price\rangle)@\mathcal{P}$ while the provider could then read the name and bind it to variable x by means of action $\mathbf{get}(\langle\text{"share\_var"}, ?x\rangle)@\mathsf{self}$.

Another way to prevent unauthorised access to constraint variables can be achieved by using *access control* policies (we refer to [13] for their definition and integration with SCEL). This kind of policies permit denying access to the repository of a component to other components. Suppose that, e.g., a component with identifier n has attached the following policy:

$$\langle\,\mathsf{permit\text{-}unless\text{-}deny}$$
$$\mathsf{rules}:(\mathsf{deny}\ \ \mathsf{target}:\mathsf{subset}(\{price\}, action/item.vars)$$
$$\wedge\ \mathsf{equal}(n, object/id)\,)\,\rangle$$

Intuitively, the policy states that all actions are allowed (algorithm permit-unless-deny) except those involving a constraint variable with name $price$ at n. Indeed, attribute $action/item.vars$ is used here to retrieve the names of all constraint variables occurring in the item argument of the action under authorisation evaluation. Thus, if this item is a constraint involving $price$ and if the target of the action (retrieved by means of attribute $object/id$) is the component n, then the inner rule returns deny. This leads to an unsuccessful evaluation of the authorisation predicate, which thus blocks the action execution.

4.3   Group-Oriented Interaction

In the previous examples, only a form of point-to-point interaction has been used by the components in order to enact dyadic interactions. We show here how the group-oriented interaction primitives provided by CCSCEL can be used for a convenient form of negotiation in an autonomic system where more parties can be dynamically involved at the same time.

Consider again the Web hosting scenario, where now the client will contact an *ensemble* of providers offering the same service. The client is not interested in interacting with a specific provider or knowing its identity, but it wants to achieve a SLA concerning the service price with as many providers in the ensemble as possible, because it is acting as a broker that intends to resell the services.

This scenario can be rendered in CCSCEL as follows:

$$\mathcal{I}_C[\mathcal{K}_C, \Pi_{1store}, P_C] \parallel \mathcal{I}_{\mathcal{P}1}[\mathcal{K}_{\mathcal{P}1}, \Pi_{1store}, P_{\mathcal{P}1}] \parallel \ldots \parallel \mathcal{I}_{\mathcal{P}n}[\mathcal{K}_{\mathcal{P}n}, \Pi_{1store}, P_{\mathcal{P}n}]$$

where, for all $j \in J$ with $J \subseteq \{1..n\}$, we have that $\mathcal{I}_{\mathcal{P}j}.srvType = webHosting$ and $\mathcal{K}_{\mathcal{P}j}$ contains a constraint of the form $(price@\mathcal{P}_j \geqslant v_j)$. Notably, both the client and all providers enforce the policy Π_{1store}.

Now, in order to interact with the ensemble of providers, the client uses the predicate *Pred* defined as $(srvType = webHosting)$, which identifies all components that offers a Web hosting solution as a service type. In particular, the process P_C running in the client component is defined as follows:

$$P_C \triangleq \mathbf{put}(price@ \leqslant 100)@\mathit{Pred}.\ \mathbf{qry}(price@ \leqslant 100)@\mathit{Pred}.\ P_C'$$

In this way, the client tries to send its constraint about the maximum price it is willing to pay to any provider within the ensemble; for each involved $\mathcal{P}_j$, the client's constraint $(price@\mathcal{P}_j \leqslant 100)$ will be stored or not in the provider repository depending on the minimum price v_j specified by the provider. Indeed, the execution of a **put** for group-oriented communication is non-blocking, i.e. it is performed regardless of whether there are components in the system that do not satisfy the ensemble predicate or do not authorise the action. The latter case includes the situation where the insertion of the constraint to the repository of a target component would make it inconsistent. Afterwards, the client checks if the agreement has been achieved with at least a provider of the ensemble, by resorting again to a group-oriented interaction, and in the positive case proceeds as P_C'. Indeed, the semantics of the group-oriented **qry** action prescribes that it can be successfully executed only if the client's constraint has been added to at least a provider, regardless of its identity.

4.4   Towards Multiparty Negotiation

Now, let us extend the considered scenario by adding another actor: a third party $\mathcal{T}$ that provides bandwidth services to $\mathcal{P}$. Thus, the success of the SLA negotiation also depends on the services provided by $\mathcal{T}$ and, hence, on the constraints this actor imposes. The new scenario can be rendered in CCSCEL as follows:

$$\mathcal{I}_C[\mathcal{K}_C, \Pi_{\{price\}}, P_C] \parallel \mathcal{I}_{\mathcal{P}}[\mathcal{K}_{\mathcal{P}}, \Pi_{\{price\}}, P_{\mathcal{P}}] \parallel \mathcal{I}_{\mathcal{T}}[\mathcal{K}_{\mathcal{T}}, \Pi_{1store}, P_{\mathcal{T}}]$$

where $\mathcal{I}_{\mathcal{T}}.id = \mathcal{T}$ and actors $\mathcal{C}$ and $\mathcal{P}$ exhibit the policy $\Pi_{\{price\}}$.

The process P_T running in the third party component is as follows:

$$P_T \triangleq \mathbf{put}(bw@ \leqslant v_{max\_bw})@\mathcal{P}.\,\mathbf{put}(\langle\text{``}max\_bandwidth\_fixed\text{''}\rangle)@\mathcal{P}$$

The third party fixes the maximum bandwidth v_{max_bw} that it can supply, by adding a constraint to the provider's store. Then, it notifies the provider by adding the tuple $\langle\text{``}max\_bandwidth\_fixed\text{''}\rangle$ to the provider's repository.

The process $P_\mathcal{P}$ running in the provider component is as follows:

$$P_\mathcal{P} \triangleq \mathbf{put}(price@ \geqslant v_{min\_price})@\mathsf{self}.\,\mathbf{put}(price@ = bw@ \cdot 25)@\mathsf{self}.$$
$$\mathbf{get}(\langle\text{``}max\_bandwidth\_fixed\text{''}\rangle)@\mathsf{self}.\,\mathbf{put}(\langle\text{``}ready\_for\_negotiation\text{''}\rangle)@\mathsf{self}$$

The provider specifies the minimum price v_{min_price} for the service and the price per unit of bandwidth. Then, after the third party has fixed the maximum bandwidth (this is guaranteed by the execution of the $\mathbf{get}$ action), it notifies the clients that it is ready to negotiate, by locally adding the tuple $\langle\text{``}ready\_for\_negotiation\text{''}\rangle$.

The process $P_\mathcal{C}$ running in the client component is as follows:

$$P_\mathcal{C} \triangleq \mathbf{put}(price@ \leqslant v_{max\_cost})@\mathsf{self}.\,\mathbf{get}(\langle\text{``}ready\_for\_negotiation\text{''}\rangle)@\mathcal{P}.$$
$$\mathbf{put}(\mathbf{true})@\mathcal{P}$$

Now, the second $\mathbf{put}$ action can be performed only after the provider has notified that it is ready for negotiation. This action activates the consistency check of the combination of the client and provider stores, by also taking into account the temporary constraint $price@\mathcal{P} = price@\mathcal{C}$. Notice that policy $\Pi_{\{price\}}$ allows the generation of only this equation, while other variables of $\mathcal{K}_\mathcal{C}$ and $\mathcal{K}_\mathcal{P}$ not involved in this negotiation are kept apart. If the check is successful, then the SLA is achieved.

It is worth noticing that, although the negotiation involves three parties, only dyadic interactions are performed. Thus, to avoid inconsistency, such interactions are coordinated via tuple-based synchronisation (see the use of tuples $\langle\text{``}max\_bandwidth\_fixed\text{''}\rangle$ and $\langle\text{``}ready\_for\_negotiation\text{''}\rangle$). This coordination protocol uses a sort of dynamic programming technique to distribute the computation between the locations, similarly to the example shown in Section 7 in [2]. Moreover, since according to policy Π_N only the stores of the interacting components are combined while the stores of the others are ignored, the third party has to add its constraint about the maximum bandwidth to the provider store, rather than storing it locally and then putting it in relationship with the provider constraints.

Also resorting to the group-oriented interaction, by defining the three components as an ensemble identified by a predicate, the problem above is not solved. Indeed, the stores of all components of an ensemble do not represent a distributed store of the ensemble, since their global consistency[5] is never checked (only a form of dyadic consistency can be checked when a constraint is added to the

---

[5] Of course, the same problem occurs in case of entailment.

repositories of the ensemble components). This need of a global consistency/entailment check at ensemble level has motivated the extension of the language presented in the next section.

On the other hand, existing algorithms for distributed constraint satisfaction (see e.g. [16, Chapter 20]) operate in a way similar to the example above. While the computation proceeds, the global constraint is internalised more and more in the local constraints of the components, until either an inconsistency is found, or, in the worst case, the whole global constraint is reconstructed inside a component and fully checked. Therefore, the ensemble-wide interaction described in the next section could be programmed in CCSCEL using the above algorithms.

5 Extending ccSCEL with Ensemble-Wide Interaction

We consider now an extension of the language with a form of ensemble-wide interaction, where a component can add a constraint to the store of the components that are part of a given ensemble, or check the entailment of a constraint, by involving in the consistency check the constraints stored in every ensemble component. In this section, we present the extensions which are necessary to enable this form of interaction.

Firstly, we extend the syntactic category TARGETS with ek : $\mathcal{P}$. The idea is that the new form of interaction is triggered by using the keyword ek (which stands for *ensemble knowledge*) in addition to the predicate $\mathcal{P}$ identifying the target ensemble.

A component can specify which constraints generated by ensemble-wide interactions it is interested to accept in its store. This can be achieved by means of an interface attribute, called *voi* (*variables of interest*), whose value is a list of variable names relevant for the component. Thus, only constraints containing at least one variable whose name is in this list are considered for insertion in the component store. To perform this check we will use the auxiliary function $v(\chi)$, which returns the set of names $\{n \mid n@n' \in cv(\chi) \lor n@ \in ucv(\chi)\}$, where function $ucv(\chi)$ returns the set of underspecified constraint variables used in χ.

The (operational) semantics of extended CCSCEL is defined by a set of inference rules: those specific to the ensemble-wide **put** action are reported in Table 5, while, due to lack of space, the remaining ones can be found in [15]. For enabling the ensemble-wide interaction, a labelled transition relation $\xrightarrow[\mathcal{K}]{\lambda}$ is introduced, where λ describes the action performed by the component, while $\mathcal{K}$ is a partial computation, performed while the inference of the transition proceeds, of the knowledge involved in the interaction. In particular, the labels λ considered here are as follows: $\mathcal{I} : \chi \triangleright \text{ek} : \mathcal{P}$ denotes the intention of component $\mathcal{I}$ to synchronise with the stores of the components that are part of the ensemble identified by $\mathcal{P}$ in order to check the insertion of constraint χ; $\mathcal{I} : \chi \bar{\triangleright} \mathcal{J}$ indicates that component $\mathcal{I}$ is allowed to add constraint χ to the store of component $\mathcal{J}$. Below, we comment on the operational rules.

Rule *(pr-sysputens)* generates the appropriate label λ corresponding to an ensemble-wide **put** action, and registers the knowledge $\mathcal{K}$ of the local store in

Table 5. Additional rules for ensemble-wide interaction (via **put** action)

$$\frac{P \downarrow_{\mathbf{put}(\chi')@\mathsf{ek}:\mathcal{P}} P' \quad \Pi,\mathcal{I}:\mathbf{put}(\chi')@\mathsf{ek}:\mathcal{P} \succ \mathcal{I}:\chi \triangleright \mathsf{ek}:\mathcal{P},\{\},\Pi' \quad \mathcal{I} \models \mathcal{P}}{\mathcal{I}[\mathcal{K},\Pi,P] \xrightarrow[\mathcal{K}]{\mathcal{I}:\chi \triangleright \mathsf{ek}:\mathcal{P}} \mathcal{I}[\mathcal{K},\Pi',P']} \;(pr\text{-}sysputens)$$

$$\frac{\Pi \vdash \mathcal{I}:\chi \bar{\triangleright} \mathcal{J},\Pi' \quad \mathcal{K} \oplus_{\mathcal{J}.id} \chi = \mathcal{K}' \quad v(\chi) \cap \mathcal{J}.voi \neq \emptyset}{\mathcal{J}[\mathcal{K},\Pi,P] \xrightarrow[\mathcal{K}']{\mathcal{I}:\chi \bar{\triangleright} \mathcal{J}} \mathcal{J}[\mathcal{K}',\Pi',P]} \;(accputens\text{-}p)$$

$$\frac{\Pi \vdash \mathcal{I}:\chi \bar{\triangleright} \mathcal{J},\Pi' \quad v(\chi) \cap \mathcal{J}.voi = \emptyset}{\mathcal{J}[\mathcal{K},\Pi,P] \xrightarrow[\mathcal{K}]{\mathcal{I}:\chi \bar{\triangleright} \mathcal{J}} \mathcal{J}[\mathcal{K},\Pi',P]} \;(accputens\text{-}d)$$

$$\frac{S_1 \xrightarrow[\mathcal{K}_1]{\mathcal{I}:\chi \triangleright \mathsf{ek}:\mathcal{P}} S_1' \quad S_2 \xrightarrow[\mathcal{K}_2]{\mathcal{I}:\chi \bar{\triangleright} \mathcal{J}} S_2' \quad \mathcal{K}_1 \oplus \mathcal{K}_2 = \mathcal{K} \quad \mathcal{J} \models \mathcal{P} \quad \mathcal{I}.\pi \vdash \mathcal{I}:\chi \bar{\triangleright} \mathcal{J},\Pi'}{S_1 \parallel S_2 \xrightarrow[\mathcal{K}]{\mathcal{I}:\chi \triangleright \mathsf{ek}:\mathcal{P}} S_1'[\mathcal{I}.\pi := \Pi'] \parallel S_2'} \;(syncputens)$$

$$\frac{S_1 \xrightarrow[\mathcal{K}]{\mathcal{I}:\chi \triangleright \mathsf{ek}:\mathcal{P}} S_1' \quad (\mathcal{J} \not\models \mathcal{P} \;\vee\; \Pi \not\vdash \mathcal{I}:\chi \bar{\triangleright} \mathcal{J},\Pi')}{S_1 \parallel \mathcal{J}[\mathcal{K},\Pi,P] \xrightarrow[\mathcal{K}]{\mathcal{I}:\chi \triangleright \mathsf{ek}:\mathcal{P}} S_1' \parallel \mathcal{J}[\mathcal{K},\Pi,P]} \;(asyncputens)$$

the produced transition. Differently from standard group-oriented interaction, the rule applies only if the acting component $\mathcal{I}$ belongs to the ensemble defined by $\mathcal{P}$ (i.e., $\mathcal{I} \models \mathcal{P}$). Notably, the interaction predicate extends naturally to the actions (hence, the labels) using the keyword ek.

Rules *(accputens-p)* and *(accputens-d)* are applied when component $\mathcal{J}$ is ready to participate in the ensemble-wide consistency check triggered by the insertion of the constraint χ by $\mathcal{I}$. In particular, the first rule checks that the store of the component $\mathcal{J}$, enriched with the new constraint χ (whose underspecified constraint variables are properly filled), is consistent; if this holds, the local store of the component is updated and the knowledge of the local store enriched with the new constraint is registered in the label of the produced transition. This rule is applied only if the constraint χ involves some variable of interest for $\mathcal{J}$ (i.e., $v(\chi) \cap \mathcal{J}.voi \neq \emptyset$); otherwise the second rule is used to register the local knowledge of the component $\mathcal{J}$ in the transition label without performing any constraint insertion. Notably, in case of ensemble-wide interaction, the policies do not play any role. Therefore, the authorization predicate $\Pi \vdash \mathcal{I}:\chi \bar{\triangleright} \mathcal{J},\Pi'$ is always satisfied regardless of whether Π is either Π_{1store}, Π_{2store} or Π_N. Anyway, the authorization predicate is still used in the rules in Table 5 in order to keep the possibility of exploiting other kinds of policies in CCSCEL.

Rule *(syncputens)* deals with the interaction among components willing to take part in it. The rule broadcasts the **put** action to any component of the ensemble identified by $\mathcal{P}$ by spreading the label $\mathcal{I}:\chi \triangleright \mathsf{ek}:\mathcal{P}$ into the whole system, together with the partial knowledge $\mathcal{K}$ (resulting from the composition of the partial knowledge $\mathcal{K}_1$ previously computed along the inference and the local knowledge $\mathcal{K}_2$ of the accepting component). Formally, the composition $\mathcal{K}_1 \oplus \mathcal{K}_2$ is defined as follows:

$$\mathcal{K}_1 \oplus \mathcal{K}_2 = \mathcal{K}_1 \parallel \mathcal{K}_2 \parallel eq(\mathcal{K}_1, \mathcal{K}_2) \quad if \ \mathcal{K}_1 \equiv (\mathcal{K}^1_{tuples} \parallel \chi^1_1 \parallel \cdots \parallel \chi^1_m) \ and$$
$$\mathcal{K}_2 \equiv (\mathcal{K}^2_{tuples} \parallel \chi^2_1 \parallel \cdots \parallel \chi^2_l) \ and$$
$$eq(\mathcal{K}_1, \mathcal{K}_2) \equiv (\chi^3_1 \parallel \cdots \parallel \chi^3_h) \ and$$
$$(\chi^1_1 \times \cdots \times \chi^1_m \times \chi^2_1 \times \cdots \times \chi^2_l \times \chi^3_1 \times \cdots \times \chi^3_h) \neq 0$$

Thus, the consistency is evaluated by also taking into account all constraints equating constraint variables that are homonymous in $\mathcal{K}_1$ and $\mathcal{K}_2$. Such equation constraints are also returned in the composed knowledge and, hence, they will be registered in the transition label.

Rule *(asyncputens)* prevents involving in the interaction those components that do not authorise the interaction or do not belong to the ensemble.

We conclude this section by revisiting the Web hosting example introduced in Section 4.4 in order to demonstrate how to take advantage of the ensemble-wide interaction mechanism just introduced.

Now, the three participants expose the attribute $(srvType, webHosting)$ in their interfaces, and exhibit the policy $\Pi_{\{price, bw\}}$. Moreover, we let $\mathcal{I}_T.voi = \{bw\}$ and $\mathcal{I}_P.voi = \{bw, price\}$.

The third party and the provider set their constraints locally:

$$P_T \triangleq \mathbf{put}(bw@ \leqslant v_{max\_bw})@\mathsf{self}$$

$$P_P \triangleq \mathbf{put}(price@ \geqslant v_{min\_price})@\mathsf{self}.\,\mathbf{put}(price@ = bw@ \cdot 25)@\mathsf{self}$$

Notably, the values of the two variables with name bw will be connected by a temporary equation. This will permit to take into account the constraint concerning the maximum bandwidth posed by the third party during the evaluation of the constraints from the client and the provider. Afterwards, the client can check the consistency of its requirement with respect to the ensemble knowledge by simply performing the following action:

$$P_C \triangleq \mathbf{put}(price@ \leqslant v_{max\_cost})@\mathsf{ek} : (srvType = webHosting)$$

This action triggers the evaluation of the stores consistency at ensemble-level, by also including the temporary constraint $bw@\mathcal{T} = bw@\mathcal{P}$. If the action execution succeeds, the store of $\mathcal{C}$ is unchanged, while the stores of $\mathcal{P}$ and $\mathcal{T}$ become:

$$\mathcal{K}'_\mathcal{P} \stackrel{def}{=} \mathcal{K}_\mathcal{P} \parallel price@\mathcal{P} \geqslant v_{min\_price} \parallel price@\mathcal{P} = bw@\mathcal{P} \cdot 25 \parallel price@\mathcal{P} \leqslant v_{max\_cost}$$

$$\mathcal{K}'_\mathcal{T} \stackrel{def}{=} \mathcal{K}_\mathcal{T} \parallel bw@\mathcal{T} \leqslant v_{max\_bw}$$

Notice that the constraint $price@\mathcal{T} \leqslant v_{max\_cost}$ is not added to the store of the third party, because $price$ is not one of its variables of interest.

6   Concluding Remarks

We have introduced CCSCEL (and a mild extension), a formal language providing interaction primitives for programming distributed autonomic systems in terms of *(i)* constraints manipulation (i.e., generation, retraction, check of consistency and entailment), both at component and ensemble level; and *(ii)* tuple-based coordination, via pattern-matching over multiple tuple spaces. This combined approach permits dealing in a convenient way with the design and development of systems featuring self-adaptation, self-awareness and self-optimisation.

CCSCEL is a novel distributed variant of the SCCP paradigm, where knowledge (i.e., variables and constraints) is distributed among the stores of the interacting ensemble components but, when specifically required by a component, it can be involved in a global check of consistency at ensemble level. Our setting supports in a natural way the implementation of distributed solutions to constraint satisfaction problems. It is thus particularly suitable for autonomic computing systems, where knowledge cannot be centralised for different reasons, such as e.g. dynamicity and open-endedness, system partitioning, complexity of constraint formalisation, security/privacy issues.

Our main concern was the development of a coherent, integrated set of linguistic primitives to model and program ensembles. Many techniques have been proposed in the literature for constraint satisfaction and optimisation in distributed settings. For an overview we refer the reader to [16, Chapter 20].

In this paper, we have shown how to incorporate basic (soft) concurrent constraint programming features in SCEL. We intend to continue this programme by transporting more advanced SCCP functionalities, borrowed from [2], in our language. For example, when soft constraints are used, it is also natural to exploit interaction primitives that explicitly deal with the c-semiring levels. This requires to extend the constraint items used in CCSCEL with a further parameter representing a *consistency threshold*, which is used to determine the success of the corresponding interaction actions. Another possibility is to use soft semiring extensions, as shown in [4], to enrich ask and tell actions with *priorities*. Among the enabled actions, a dynamic (partial) ordering is established, where only those actions in the top position are actually (nondeterministically) executed. It may also be useful to have the possibility of tuning the consistency of the store of each component with respect to its *best level of consistency*. Finally, in an ensemble-wide interaction, each component that is part of the ensemble currently contributes to the global knowledge with all constraints in its store. However, for the sake of efficiency (and privacy), each component should have the possibility of specifying the knowledge it would like to share with the other members of the ensemble. This could be achieved by resorting to suitable *projection functions*.

References

1. Bistarelli, S., Montanari, U., Rossi, F.: Semiring-based constraint satisfaction and optimization. J. ACM 44(2), 201–236 (1997)
2. Bistarelli, S., Montanari, U., Rossi, F.: Soft concurrent constraint programming. ACM Trans. Comput. Log. 7(3), 563–589 (2006)
3. Bures, T., De Nicola, R., Gerostathopoulos, I., Hoch, N., Kit, M., Koch, N., Monreale, G., Montanari, U., Pugliese, R., Serbedzija, N., Wirsing, M., Zambonelli, F.: A Life Cycle for the Development of Autonomic Systems: The e-mobility showcase. In: SASOW, pp. 71–76. IEEE (2013)
4. Buscemi, M.G., Montanari, U.: QoS negotiation in service composition. J. Log. Algebr. Program. 80(1), 13–24 (2011)
5. Cesari, L., De Nicola, R., Pugliese, R., Puviani, M., Tiezzi, F., Zambonelli, F.: Formalising adaptation patterns for autonomic ensembles. In: Fiadeiro, J.L., Liu, Z., Xue, J. (eds.) FACS 2013. LNCS, vol. 8348, pp. 100–118. Springer, Heidelberg (2014)
6. De Nicola, R., Ferrari, G., Loreti, M., Pugliese, R.: A language-based approach to autonomic computing. In: Beckert, B., Damiani, F., de Boer, F.S., Bonsangue, M.M. (eds.) FMCO 2011. LNCS, vol. 7542, pp. 25–48. Springer, Heidelberg (2012)
7. De Nicola, R., Lluch Lafuente, A., Loreti, M., Morichetta, A., Pugliese, R., Senni, V., Tiezzi, F.: Programming and verifying component ensembles. In: Bensalem, S., Lakhneck, Y., Legay, A. (eds.) From Programs to Systems. LNCS, vol. 8415, pp. 69–83. Springer, Heidelberg (2014)
8. De Nicola, R., Loreti, M., Pugliese, R., Tiezzi, F.: A formal approach to autonomic systems programming: The SCEL language. ACM Transactions on Autonomous and Adaptive Systems 9(2), 7:1–7:29 (2014)
9. Cabri, G., Capodieci, N., Cesari, L., De Nicola, R., Pugliese, R., Tiezzi, F., Zambonelli, F.: Self-expression and Dynamic Attribute-Based Ensembles in SCEL. In: Margaria, T., Steffen, B. (eds.) ISoLA 2014, Part I. LNCS, vol. 8802, pp. 147–163. Springer, Heidelberg (2014)
10. Gelernter, D.: Generative Communication in Linda. ACM Trans. Program. Lang. Syst. 7(1), 80–112 (1985)
11. Kephart, J.O., Chess, D.M.: The Vision of Autonomic Computing. Computer 36, 41–50 (2003)
12. Loreti, M., Margheri, A., Pugliese, R., Tiezzi, F.: On Programming and Policing Autonomic Computing Systems. In: Margaria, T., Steffen, B. (eds.) ISoLA 2014, Part I. LNCS, vol. 8802, pp. 164–183. Springer, Heidelberg (2014)
13. Margheri, A., Pugliese, R., Tiezzi, F.: Linguistic abstractions for programming and policing autonomic computing systems. In: UIC/ATC, pp. 404–409. IEEE (2013)
14. Mayer, P., Klarl, A., Hennicker, R., Puviani, M., Tiezzi, F., Pugliese, R., Keznikl, J., Bures, T.: The Autonomic Cloud: A vision of voluntary, peer-2-peer cloud computing. In: SASOW, pp. 89–94. IEEE (2013)
15. Montanari, U., Pugliese, R., Tiezzi, F.: Programming autonomic systems with multiple constraint stores. Technical Report (2014), http://rap.dsi.unifi.it/scel/
16. Rossi, F., Beek, P.v., Walsh, T.: Handbook of Constraint Programming. Elsevier (2006)
17. Sommerville, I., Cliff, D., Calinescu, R., Keen, J., Kelly, T., Kwiatkowska, M., Mcdermid, J., Paige, R.: Large-scale Complex IT Systems. Commun. ACM 55(7), 71–77 (2012)

Adaptive and Autonomous Systems and Their Impact on Us

Nikola Šerbedžija

Fraunhofer FOKUS, Berlin, Germany

Abstract. With technology becoming increasingly ubiquitous and through a wide use of interconnected "smart devices", the impacts these advanced products have on us is gaining in significance. As technology providers, we are very proud to share the tribute for creating new infrastructures that bring benefits to individuals and society and make life easier. But we may also be held responsible for the possible detrimental impacts that new technology brought about. Especially, if we ignore the threatening consequences and fail to offer some protective solutions. Up to now, there has been some attention paid to privacy issues and security of commercial transactions, but the negative influence of "smart" technology on human behavior has been widely neglected. This paper considers the effects that adaptive and autonomous technologies have on their users. As the impacts can best be observed in practice, a number of application scenarios are taken into account, illustrating both the technical aspects and their possible effects on us.

1 Introduction

As a field initially derived from mathematics and electrical engineering, computer science in its early days performed mostly numeric and data processing in various application domains. Gradually, a number of other disciplines merged into the field, extending digital paradigm with principles taken from physics, chemistry, biology, psychology and social sciences. The application domain also spread to almost all aspects of our activities, making computers unavoidable in industry, administration, commerce and entertainment. Furthermore, present cyber-physical systems are bridging the gap between virtual and real worlds, placing humans directly in the processing loop, increasing the impact the technology has on us. We are not anymore just users that exploit the benefits of the technology, we ourselves are becoming a part of the computation and thus exposed to possible manipulation. More and more often, we rely on computers and do what they instruct us to do. We are guided by the rules imposed by technical systems, modifying our behavior accordingly. Mostly it is done with the user consent, but not rarely the changes in our behavior happen unconsciously.

This paper focuses on adaptive and autonomous systems as an important segment of technology advances and investigates the effects that practical deployments may have on us. Engineering the natural phenomena like awareness,

R. De Nicola and R. Hennicker (Eds.): Wirsing Festschrift, LNCS 8950, pp. 662–675, 2015.

adaptation and autonomy does include a human in the processing loop affecting and controlling personal behavior, causing impacts that may go beyond our ethical norms. Having in mind that artificial adaptation and autonomy are not the same as the natural ones, the challenges, difficulties and solutions for development and deployment of adaptive and autonomous systems are explored. The reasoning described here stems from two concrete methodologies and their applications. The two approaches are presented rather descriptive, focusing on a general strategy necessary to explore technology impacts.

Further references for the detailed technical solutions could be found at [1, 3]. One case study is specially highlighted: the cyber-race, where our autonomous robot competes with a human and wins. The example helps in better framing the rationale of use, indicating in which domains we should or should not apply autonomous systems and to what extent we are sacrificing our own autonomy when using autonomous systems.

The paper is structured in six sections. After introduction, the section 2 considers technology advances and their possible influence on people and society. Then, the two approaches for adaptive (section 3) and autonomous (section 4) systems are presented together with a number of concrete use cases. A representative deployment scenario of autonomous system is given in more details (section 5) and the concluding remarks (section 6) highlight major conclusions and trace further work.

2 Technology Impacts: A Digital Storm

Brainstorming is a popular phrase among scientists. It denotes an intense exchange of ideas on a specific research challenge. But brainstorming our brain in order to understand it and engineer something similar, is like going through a labyrinth of *controversy*. Neural networks, artificial intelligence, psychological and evolutionary computing are examples of the domains with numerous breakthroughs, but no real "silver bullet". In a way, this is understandable since we are dealing with extremely hard problem. If our brain were simpler, we would be simpler too, and it would be even more difficult for us to comprehend how it functions and engineer something similar. Even when a natural characteristic is successfully re-created, its deployment often brings dual effects. For example, reasoning about autonomous systems and their impacts, brings us in a dilemma: "should we use the autonomous systems, and if yes, in which domains". Namely, if we define autonomy as "acting according to own rules", a question arises: are we autonomous when we use autonomous system? Obviously a use of autonomous systems requires giving up a part of the own autonomy. Considering a wider arena of smart technology, one could observe a resembling situation in today market: there are numerous advertisement of a kind: "be smart use smart systems" luring people to purchase some smart product. Mostly the people who do not doubt their own reasoning fall in the trap. Sometimes, an artificial achievements may weaken its natural counterpart, not intentionally, but rather as a side effect. It seems that brainstorming the natural phenomena resulted in a digital storm, characterized by a wide and premature acceptance of digital technology, where we cannot be only proud of its positive impacts but also held responsible for some of its negative consequences.

Many technical breakthroughs stem from imitating the nature and its spectacular wonders. But how can it be, that imitating something so harmonious can result in controversy? Probably, it is our inappropriate interference with nature that creates puzzling situation. Concentrated on a specific engineering goal, we often overlook the wide spectrum of the problem, solving one aspect and neglecting the others that constitute the natural harmony. It seems that we are impatient: we try to solve the problem before we truly understood it. For example in the artificial intelligence or neural networks domain an engineer interferes with something, not fully understood even by neuro-experts. It seems that we are dealing with multifaceted assignments, appealing but hard, maybe Sisyphus's. The controversy often occurs when advanced computing model includes humans into the processing loop creating obvious benefits and hidden harms. Especially when interfering with subtle subjective experiences like senses, feelings or (sub) consciousness. Essentially, we are all very skeptical in submitting our autonomy, privacy and habits to the others (especially machines). Practically, however, we have been guided, data minded and exposed to commercialization to the point that we do not see the obvious anymore.

Since 1995, the famous Weiser's statement on disappearing computers [4] has been inspiring the work in ubiquitous computing domain. It envisages that "computers will be disappearing i.e. they will be miniaturized and integrated in fabrics of everyday life, omni-present and invisible". In 2005, Streitz and Nixon further elaborated: "The rate at which computers disappear will be matched by the rate at which information technology will increasingly permeate our environment and determine our lives" [6]. The man-computer interaction will intensify to such an extent that even absence of interaction will gain an interaction significance (scaring but true). In another words you cannot not communicate in inevitably ubiquitous environment (the statement known as the first of five /sometimes paradoxical/ axioms of communication, from Watzlawick [6]). It seems the better we are in our technical achievements, the controversial it gets. Yet another paradoxical situation could be observed on the Internet arena. Once conceptualized as a highly distributed network, World Wide Web is being more and more controlled. Some of the leading Web2.0 players are squeezing the Web into an almost centralized system with millions of thin clients communicating with a few major sites, that collect and process data (often silently and without user consent) for commercial purposes.

Being aware of promises and threats that modern technology has brought about we should strive to enhance the benefits, reduce (collateral) damages and avoid controversy. Otherwise we have not learned much from the past. Back in 1818, M. Shelley[7] frightened the generation to come with her gothic Frankenstein tale about curse of man using technology to "play God". Today, modern "Smart-kensteins" are devouring our privacy, social spirits, and physicality, according to Huxleys [8] nightmarish observation on how control can be achieved by giving people what they want. We are stunned, but instead of adapting our high-tech products to us (our norms and practices) we are changing our behavior according to the technical systems rules: we are re-defining our ethics and conducts (e.g. often we hear that privacy is not that important as traditionally thought; virtual contacts are as important as physical; etc,), letting our wash-prone brain to adapt to a new situation. And being so naturally adaptive it will continue to do so.

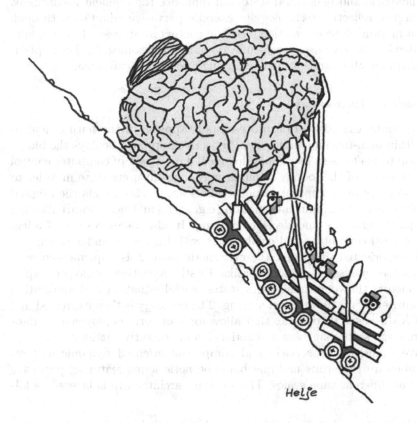

Fig. 1. Smart Sisyphus

Aware that a success in engineering a natural phenomenon may be a Pyrrhic victory for humanity, especially when carelessly mass-applied on individuals and society, we should try to explore both the principles of adaptive and autonomous systems and possible impacts of their use, thus maximizing the benefits and minimizing drawbacks and paradoxical traps. Not to repeat the mistakes from more mature Internet domains where the impacts are being discovered a *posteriori*, here the possible drawbacks are considered in time, hoping that they could be avoided.

3 Adaptive Systems

One approach to construct a user-centric adaptive systems is the reflective technology [1]. It is an interdisciplinary endeavor aiming to construct smart environments with pervasive adaptive control. A general purpose assistance should enrich control systems with implicit man-machine interaction sensitive to cognitive, emotional and/or physical state of the user. The ultimate goal of such reflective assistance is to observe people in a specific real-life situation, diagnose their psychological and behavioral state and influence the ambient accordingly. The system uses reflective technology to exercise pervasive adaptation through non explicit man-machine interaction based on context awareness. Recent results demonstrates its effective use in vehicular domain and promise further applications in environmental, ambient assisted living and health care areas [1].

3.1 Reflective Technology

In effort to mimic the adaptation process, as it appears in the nature, and to apply it within man-machine interaction, reflective approach deploys the biocybernetic loop to make users psychophysiological data a part of computer control logic. The function of the loop is to monitor changes in users state in order to initiate an appropriate computer response. This approach extends the original concept to a wider set of input information (e.g. social and behavioral) allowing for a composite analyses and decision making. It also takes results of affective/physiological computing and combines it with high level understanding of social and goaloriented situations. Bio-cybernetic loop [2] is implemented with the help of sense-analyse-react control troika. Firstly, reflective ontology classifies numerous factors that determine users states, social situation and application goals, defining elements for decision making. The ontology is then expressed in a number of XML-based taxonomies that allow for a uniform deployment in data acquisition, users state diagnoses and activation of corrective actions.

Reflective framework is service- and component-oriented dynamic and reactive middleware that runs multiple bio-cybernetic loops featuring pervasive adaptation at different time scales. The software architecture is layered as follows:

- Tangible layer - a low-level subsystem that controls sensor and actuator devices. It offers its services (sensor measurements/actuator controls) to the rest of the system.
- Reflective layer - a core of the system that combines tangible services with users profile and scenario descriptions to perform diagnoses of users state and provoke system (re-) action relative to the situation and the application goals.
- Application layer - a high level part of the system that defines application scenario and system goals. By combining low and high level services and components from other layers, application layer runs and controls the whole system.

The reflective framework has been developed using the software components paradigm and implemented in the Java programming language on top of OSGI environment.

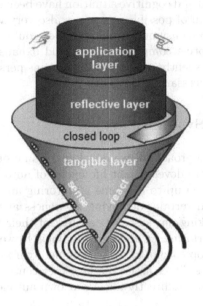

Fig. 2. System architecture

Figure 2 illustrates the reflective software architecture with three major stages, exercising different bio-cybernetic loops at tangible, reflective and application level. The control loop (initialized with users profile and scenario settings denoted by human hand on the top of Figure 2) starts by sampling the psycho-physiological measurements, continues with their analyses and finishes by adaptive system reaction (denoted by a "digital hand" on top of Figure 2). In a next iteration the system influence (caused by the reaction) can also be sensed and further tuned.

3.2 Reflective Use Cases

The developed reflective system is able to grasp and influence human mental and physical state. Together with psychologists [2] and bio-engineers [1], we implemented a personal advertiser that could tailor advertising content to the mental reaction of the viewer; a mood player that selects the music to comfort the listeners emotional state; a computer game that adapts its difficulty level according to mental effort of the player, a smart seat that recognizes how comfortable it is for a person and re-shape accordingly. Putting some of the stated results together, we prototyped a "vehicle as co-driver" [1] system with a capability to configure and dynamically modify vehicles settings and performance according to emotional, cognitive and physical drivers condition. When deployed, a reflective system is personalized and its reactions are tuned to the person being observed. In a number of case studies a positive impact in terms of comforting users physical emotional and cognitive situation have been experimentally proved [1]. However, a spectrum of possible misuses is also very wide. An adaptive advertiser could mislead a consumer, a mood player could manipulate emotional state of a person, adaptive computer game could exhaust a passionate player and a wary "co-driver" silently collects and maintains personal information that the driver would not necessarily share with others.

4   Autonomous Systems

Within the ASCENS approach [3] we developed numerous tools and methods that support one or more development life cycles of autonomous systems, from requirements specification up to run-time monitoring and verification. Here we choose ethically neutral terrain, deploying awareness and autonomic behavior purely in software, making our systems "aware" of their functional and operational requirements, performance and surroundings. However, keeping a human out of the processing loop has not saved us completely from the ethical concerns. The impact there is less direct as in affective user-centric systems, but relying on system autonomy does indirectly affect our own autonomy.

4.1   ASCENS Technology

ASCENS approach explores awareness, adaptation and self-organization offering high-level methods and practical tools for developing autonomous systems. Under the motto simplifying complexity, the technological challenge is in controlling the dynamics of inherently distributed environments while harmonizing and optimizing individual and collective goals. Trail examples are on: how to organize a rescue operation with self-aware and self-healing robot swarms; how to build a scientific cloud platform that turns a huge number of voluntary computing devices into a super computer; and how to optimally control mobility with electric vehicles taking into account energy restrictions, multiple itineraries, parking availability and traffic conditions.

To behave autonomously, a control system needs to maintain knowledge about itself (particular objectives, capabilities, execution state and restrictions) and about its environment. Such collection of facts yields awareness of own functionality and effects it has on the environment which further allows for adaptive performance. Being capable of operating according to these three principles (knowledge, awareness, adaptation), the system is able to re-configure, re-tune and act appropriately thus behaving in autonomous manner.

The approach breaks up a complex control problem into its elementary constituents. It deals with complications at a bottom level, solving issues at a lower scale and then harmonizing these solutions with more global ones. Localization and de-centralization is the fourth major principle of our approach. Service components with clearly defined elementary objectives are basic system elements. They gather in larger symbiosis called ensembles in order to fulfill collective goals. As the controlled situation changes, i.e. goals are (partially) fulfilled, regrouping takes place and the symbiosis re-structures. The criteria to construct an ensemble of service-components is some joint interest which can be expressed as a logical sentence, e.g. "connect all robots that can carry up to 4kg and are in the radius of 100m with the aim to cooperatively transport 25kg heavy object" or "select all free parking lots in the radius of 300m that have a charging plug". That makes the communication implicit and predicate-based. The connections are established at run-time, depending on the live situation at particular time. These logical rules for highly dynamic grouping are further used for formal reasoning on optimization and coordination among distributed elements.

The overall system development life cycle consists of the following phases: rigorous design (requirement specification, modelling and validation/verification), deployment (programming) and run-time monitoring (live examination of awareness, adaptation and autonomous behavior). A number of tools have been made [3] that support the development process at each step, thus guiding and facilitating the whole development process.

Requirement specification is a phase where the dissection of the problem to be solved takes place. Each system element is separately defined both functionally (what to do) and non-functionally (how to do) yielding a set of goals that embrace the terms of functioning and description of environment. The knowledge required for system awareness and adaptation is used as a major attribute repository for system construction. The SCEL (service-component ensembles language) [9] has been developed for high-level system modelling with service components and their ensembles. Both service-components and ensembles have local knowledge used to express their goals. Knowledge is represented by ontologies that contain hierarchical and meaningful description of system properties and system goals. The goals are described as rules i.e. logical expressions with system properties.

The adaptation phenomenon is formally modeled as a progress in a multi-dimensional space where each axis represents one orthogonal aspect of system awareness (facts about its own functional, operational, or any other necessities defined within requirement specification phase). Adaptation actually happens when the system state moves from one to another position within the space according to the pre and post- condition on each of its awareness- dimensions. Adaptation is a continuous process where a system acts appropriately i.e. in harmony with own capabilities and the observed environment. The adaptation model called SOTA (State of the Affairs) [10] is used to extract major application requirements and offer appropriate adaptation patterns that effectively control system dynamics with numerous feedback-loops.

In order to guarantee correct and timely behavior in such demanding and highly dynamic circumstances this approach relies on formal methods. The major safety and liveness properties are formally proved using SCEL process algebra (e.g. prove that two e-vehicles will never block each other while competing for a free charging station, or prove that the foraging algorithm of a robot converges in a given time). Further validation and verification of specific optimization algorithms are performed in order to guarantee correct system behavior in early design phase (e.g. prove that the optimization method will deliver the most energy-efficient route for a given multi-routing problem). Once the system is rigorously modelled and validated, the actual deployment may take place sewing the system together. The jRESP[3] and jDEECO [3] deployment tools offer direct Java programming support for the SCEL and SOTA models. Due to a seamless functioning of autonomous systems, where system changes are means for "appropriate" behavior, possible malfunctions are difficult to discover. Therefore, a number of tools have been developed for run-time monitoring where internal system knowledge and topology (ensemble construction) as well as awareness and adaptive characteristics are observed. For example, the monitoring tools can visualize how the robots, close to the target and with enough battery-charge are grouped into ensemble to perform joint transport of a heavy object. Once the task is performed, the ensembles are dismantled freeing robots for another assignment. Monitoring inspects and displays major system principles: knowledge, awareness and adaptation, offering a visualization of dynamic ensemble building criteria, thus directly observing autonomous behavior. If some malfunctioning is discovered at run-time, a system modification is considered going back to modelling and design system development phases.

4.2   ASCENS Use Cases

Pragmatic orientation means building technical systems that perform concrete tasks, like autonomous robot swarms performing rescue operation, autonomous cloud platforms transforming numerous small computers into a super computing environment or autonomous e-mobility support that ensures energy-aware transportation services. These are highly dynamic environments where physical and social context, operational and functional requirements and workloads are constantly changing. Through practical deployments we want to show that our approach behaves autonomously and at the same time it integrates smoothly into our ethical codex. Since autonomous behavior means functioning without human intervention, we need to ensure that rules driving system autonomy does not collide with our own independence.

By design our robots know their own functionality, battery state, position, and the location of nearby robots, so they indeed perform actions according to that knowledge. The collective knowledge is constructed dynamically based on the contextual situation, making the whole system highly cooperative, self-healing and autonomous. In the cloud computing scenario, the system knowledge is based on the computing capabilities of voluntary computers that join the cloud. Most of the control functions are exercised at ensemble level featuring self-monitoring, self-organized and distributed deployment and execution. The control system for e-mobility takes into account on-going information about routing, vehicle energy states, traffic conditions and parking/charging availabilities and calculates optimal routing. The system is highly dynamic with ensembles, representing different system goals, being continuously (re-)organized offering alternatives for optimized control (like ensembles of near-by parking places, ensembles of vehicles travelling in same directions, etc.). In a live system, adaptive behavior is crucial as sudden changes in real settings require re-optimization and re-allocation of resources.

The autonomy model we are using is based on presupposed knowledge and real-time awareness and adaptation. Contrary to natural autonomy which is based on learning, experience and evolution, here, the autonomy is much more rigid, based on prior system knowledge and corresponding rules and policies. It is restricted to our understanding of the control environment, without support of (artificial) intelligence, learning, or similar strategies that would ensure skillful handling of unknown problems. Such systems should be used only where human control is not possible due to different dangers, heavy tasks, compute intense calculations, etc. or when delegating a task to a machine is a genuine benefit for people. The application area should comprise well known domains where problems to be solved can be predicted or their solution depends on huge number of factors that is overwhelming for us (e.g. traffic conditions, multi-route optimization, scientific computing, etc.). Further application domains include operations in places dangerous for humans (emergency situations), or assisting by disabilities (medical assistance systems), or even doing boring tasks for us.

Fig. 3. Digital clouds

The cases where autonomous systems may interfere with our own autonomy should be considered carefully. In general, where a person is a part of the control loop, possibilities of negative impacts are higher: the autonomous system may pursuit the goals which are not necessarily the same as those the person using autonomous system wants to follow.

5   Cyber Race

The challenges of controlling the robot behavior in performing certain task can best be understood if seen from the robot perspective. The complexity does not primarily come from the task itself, but rather from the interaction that goes on between the robot sensory system, environment and self-directed robot performance. To illustrate that, we set an exhibition at well attended ICT conference [11] where our autonomous robot competes with a human-controlled robot. The task is to find building blocks in a closed area, grab them (one by one), and carry them to the place where a wall should be constructed. The robot is operated by a joystick which can move the robot left/right; forward/backwards and instruct it to grab/release the building blocks. The task seems trivial, so most of the competitors believe our robot does not stand a chance. That proved to be wrong. Most people lost, only a couple of young, joystick-virtuous competitors won. Then, we imposed a "fair-play" rule: since the robots sensory system is less sophisticated than ours, we reduced the vision of the human competitor to the visual system of the robot, giving the competitors equal chances. When both competitors have exactly the same information about environment, our robot performed much better. That shows how seemingly simple assignment (from our point of view) is actually complex for a fully autonomous robot. Taking into account relatively primitive robot sensory system, the robot performance is quite good and reliable, especially well-suited for the kind of tasks that we do not want to participate in (like removing objects in a poisoned/radiated/high temperature areas, carrying heavy objects, underwater operations, etc.) [12].

6   Conclusion: Sunshine Breaks through Digital Fog

The illustrations presented summarize the approach in dissecting and sewing adaptive and autonomous behavior. The first figure shows a swarm of autonomous robots rolling the human brain up the hill, a task too difficult to complete. It illustrates the way out of one of the hardest and most controversial assignments men can get. Instead of doing the task ourselves, we can assign it to a multi-robot system. Metaphorically, the figure also expresses our belief that overthrowing human brain is a Sisyphus task. The second figure illustrates reflective approach to create a personal assistant that adapts to physical and mental state of a user. Iterative and ubiquitous nature of the system is metaphorically presented by a spinning top that sense, diagnose and react in each of its rounds (being driven by measurement and computer generated actions). A dazzling

Fig. 4. Cyber runners

character of the approach that may influence person involved, both positively and negatively, is illustrated by "magic circles" casted by the spinning top.

The third figure illustrates our approach to decompose a complex system into simple elements, structure them in digital symbioses (depicted as clouds) and use them to control swarm of robots, electrical vehicles transportation or to manage the cloud computation itself. These are all ethically non problematic practices, delegating a part of tasks we are either not willing to get involved in, or not capable to solve, to a technical system. In this case: (1) rescue operation in presence of dangerous material, (2) optimization of multi-route problems in presence of energy restrictions and (3) performing scientific calculations on a cloud platform. The whole approach features de-centralization, symbiotic grouping and implicit communication. The resulting system behavior is autonomous based on local/global knowledge, awareness and adaptation. The absence of central control is crucial for our approach and in all cases the application scenarios run in a truly distributed manner.

The fourth figure metaphorically shows our competition arena [11] where an autonomous robot wins the race against its human rival. The cyber runner experiment places the human competitor into "the robot perspective" and demonstrates how a cyber-vision may reduce our skills. Often, cyber glasses are advertised as something that "extend" our perception which is not necessarily always the case. Besides offering extra information, they can also decline our concentration, sometime mislead and in general weaken our performance.

The times of paradoxical "centralized network" may be passing as we are adding more and more smart devices into the network that cannot be effectively managed centrally, but is rather self-organized and performs in an ad hoc manner. Evolving cyber-physical systems are melting man-machine interaction into a man-machine confluence where protecting human virtues and ethical codices could be imbedded into system requirements level and more effectively supported in all development phases. The near future technology may bring new generation of simple and highly de-centralized autonomous devices that self-assemble (disassemble) in fulfilling a temporal goal. Businesses may look for new methods of technical symbioses with dynamic grouping and dismantling, which would perform tasks autonomously and much more efficiently. Big data mining and collecting everything about anything may lose its significance, because new generation of systems will work much more effectively if bypassing the overloaded and busy Internet, concentrating rather on qualitative then on quantitative data analyses. Re-gaining our privacy and social norms may be a collateral benefit, coming as a sunshine through the digital clouds.

Acknowledgements. All the credits for the work described here goes to the REFLECT [1] and ASCENS [3] project teams. However, if there is a single person to be highlighted as a pillar of the research being conducted, then it is Martin Wirsing [13]. He and his LMU team inspired and contributed to the two projects significantly. Working with Martin was like balancing at the pinnacle of the computer science breakthroughs, both fascinating and provocative at the same time. The more successful we were the more controversial it got. This paper recalled some joint achievements, thoughts and afterthoughts steaming from our collaboration and is dedicated to Martin Wirsing. The tribute for the cartoons on figures 1, 3 and 4 go to Jens-Helge Dahmen (Fraunhofer FOKUS Berlin), who designed them for the purpose of this paper.

References

[1] REFLECT project - Responsive Flexible Collaborating Ambient, http://reflect.pst.ifi.lmu.de/
[2] Serbedzija, N., Fairclough, S.: Reflective Pervasive Systems. ACM Transactions on Autonomous and Adaptive Systems (TAAS) 7(1) (April 2012)
[3] ASCENS Project - Autonomic Service-Component Ensembles, http://www.ascens-ist.eu/
[4] Weiser, M.: The computer for the 21st century. Scientific American, 94–104 (September 1991)
[5] Streitz, Nixon: The Disappearing Computer. Communications of the ACM 8(3) (2005)
[6] Watzlawick, P., Beavin-Bavelas, J., Jackson, D.: Some Tentative Axioms of Communication. In: Pragmatics of Human Communication - A Study of Interactional Patterns, Pathologies and Paradoxes. W.W. Norton, New York (1967)

[7] Shelley, M., Frankenstein, E.J.M., Smith, J.M.: The first edition of Frankenstein; or, The Modern Prometheus was published anonymously in three volumes by Lackington, Hughes, Harding, Mavor and Jones on January 1, 1818. St. Martins, Boston (1992)

[8] Huxley, A.: Brave New World. Harper and Bros, New York (1946)

[9] De Nicola, R., Loreti, M., Pugliese, R., Tiezzi, F.: A formal approach to autonomic systems programming: the SCEL Language. ACM Transactions on Autonomous and Adaptive Systems, 1–29 (in press, 2014) ISSN 1556-4665

[10] Abeywickrama, D.B., Bicocchi, N., Zambonelli, F.: SOTA: Towards a General Model for Self-Adaptive Systems. In: IEEE 21st International Workshop on Enabling Technologies: Infrastructure for Collaborative Enterprises, WETICE, pp. 48–53 (2012)

[11] Serbedzija, N.: The beauty is in the eye of the beholder, blog, http://blog.ascens-ist.eu/2013/11/beauty-is-in-the-eye-of-the-beholder/

[12] Soleymani, T., Trianni, V., Bonani, M., Mondada, F., Dorigo, M.: Autonomous Construction with Compliant Building Material. In: Proc. 13th International Conference on Intelligent Autonomous Systems, IAS-13. AISC, vol. 301. Springer (2014)

[13] Wirsing, M., http://www.pst.ifi.lmu.de/people/staff/wirsing/

The KnowLang Approach to Self-adaptation

Emil Vassev and Mike Hinchey

Lero–The Irish Software Engineering Research Centre,
University of Limerick, Limerick, Ireland
{emil.vassev,mike.hinchey}@lero.ie

Abstract. Self-adaptive systems autonomously monitor their behavior and eventually modify that behavior according to changes in the operational environment or in the system itself. In this entry, we present an approach to implementing self-adaptation capabilities with KnowLang, a special framework for knowledge representation and reasoning. KnowLang provides for a special knowledge context and a special reasoner operating in that context. The approach is formal and demonstrates how knowledge representation and reasoning help to establish the vital connection between knowledge, perception, and actions that realize self-adaptive behavior. Knowledge is used against the perception of the world to generate appropriate actions in compliance with some set of goals and beliefs.

1 Introduction

There are many advantages to self-adaptation. Among the most promising are the fact that self-adaptation enables software-intensive systems to become more versatile, flexible, resilient, dependable, robust, energy-efficient, recoverable, customizable, configurable, and self-optimizing by adapting to changing operational contexts, environments or system characteristics. Prof. Wirsing's work on developing *large software-intensive systems with self-adaptive capabilities* [1] has revealed a new niche in this extremely challenging domain of computer science and software engineering. Here, it is important to mention the personal contribution of Prof. Wirsing in defining the concept of autonomic ensembles. Being a group leader in the ICT-FET project InterLink [2], his contribution helped that project to coin the term *ensemble* for a particular kind of system: *Ensembles are software-intensive systems with massive numbers of nodes or complex interactions between nodes, operating in open and non-deterministic environments in which they have to interact with humans or other software-intensive systems in elaborate ways.* Therefore, ensembles have to dynamically adapt to new requirements, technologies or environmental conditions without redeployment and without interruption of the system's functionality, thereby blurring the *distinction between design-time and runtime*.

One of the key challenges of developing autonomic ensembles is the problem of Knowledge Representation and Reasoning (KR&R) for awareness and self-adaptive behavior. In this entry, we present KnowLang, an approach to knowledge representation for self-adaptive behavior and awareness based on the methodology discussed above. KnowLang [3–5] is an initiative undertaken by Lero–the Irish Software Engineering Research Center within Lero's mandate in the ASCENS Project [6]. Autonomic

R. De Nicola and R. Hennicker (Eds.): Wirsing Festschrift, LNCS 8950, pp. 676–692, 2015.
© Springer International Publishing Switzerland 2015

Service-Component ENSembles (ASCENS)[1] is an FP7 (Seventh Framework Program) project targeting the development of a coherent and integrated set of methods and tools providing a comprehensive approach to developing ensembles (or swarms) of *intelligent, self-aware* and *adaptive* service components. One of the main scientific contributions that we expect to achieve with ASCENS is related to KR&R. Note that it is of major importance for an ASCENS system to acquire and structure comprehensive knowledge in such a way that it can be effectively and efficiently processed, so such a system becomes aware of itself and its environment. Moreover, ASCENS is an AI project tackling self-adaptation of systems operating in open-ended environments, e.g., our physical world. Such systems need to be developed with initial knowledge and learning capabilities based on knowledge processing and awareness. How the system knowledge is both structured and modeled is very important to providing the essence of self-adaptation.

The rest of this entry is organized as follows. Section 2 introduces a running example intended to assist the reader in uderstanding the concept of self-adaptation. Section 3 presents KnowLang as a formal specification language for knowledge representation in self-adaptive systems. In Section 4, we present a proof-of-concept case study where KnowLang is used to build a KR model for the running example presented in Section 2. Section 5 presents related work and finally, Section 6 presents a brief conclusion and future work.

2   eMobility: A Case Study of Self-adaptation

To better understand the concept of self-adaptive systems, in this section, we present a running example, based on the ASCENS eMobility [6] case study. Note that this example is further used as a case study presenting the KnowLang approach to KR&R for self-adaptive systems.

An eMobility system [7, 8] needs to thematically, temporally and spatially coordinate mobility entities where the system must be modeled as a heterogeneous system composed of intelligent and self-aware nodes, which are cross-connected by information and communication technology. In such a system, e-vehicles are competing for infrastructure resources of the traffic environment where the infrastructure resources are constrained. For example, roads, parking lots and charging stations have a limited capacity. The cost for a e-vehicle to use the infrastructure capacity is variable and changes with time and location. Situations occur in which the availability of infrastructure resources does not match the demand.

eMobility brings most of the challenges that the theories and methodologies developed for self-adaptive systems are striving to solve. Hence, self-adaptation has emerged as an important paradigm making eMobility capable of modifying the system behavior and/or structure in response to increasing workload demands and service failures. A common characteristic of self-adaptive eMobility is to emphasize the self-adaptations required to ensure that services will be provided in a fail-safe manner and under consideration of system goals.

---

[1] The ASCENS Project (2010-2014) was coordinated by Prof. Martin Wirsing.

In eMobility, vehicles move according to a schedule defined by a driver [7, 8]. Every e-vehicle component is responsible for driving along the optimal route, meeting time constraints imposed by the driver's schedule and reserving spaces at a particular Point of Interest (POI). Vehicles are competing for infrastructure resources of the traffic environment and a set of locally optimal solutions should be computed for each individual driver. Each e-vehicle is equipped with a Vehicle Planning Utility (Route Planner) that plans travel, including a set of alternative routes. Traffic routes are composed of multiple driving locations, e.g., POIs. A set of locally optimal solutions is computed for each individual user. This set is negotiated at a global level in order to satisfy the global perspective. The set of locally optimal solutions guarantees a minimum quality for each individual driver. The global optimization scheme guarantees optimal resource distribution within the local constraints. The size of the set of locally optimal solutions determines the cooperative nature of the individual driver. The smaller the set, the more competitive the driver is. The larger the set, the more cooperative the driver is. The process of Route Selection (RouteSAM) advises on a route choice, which is made from a set of alternative routes generated by the route planner. The RouteSAM considers road capacity and traffic levels. It optimizes overall throughput of the roads by balancing the route assignments of the vehicles. From a local vehicle perspective, the journey time is minimized; from a global perspective, congestion levels are minimized. The route selection process strives to satisfy global optimality criteria of road capacity. Once a vehicle is in the close vicinity of a destination, it computes a set of locally optimal parking lots. Again, the process of selecting parking lots satisfies global optimality criteria of parking capacity.

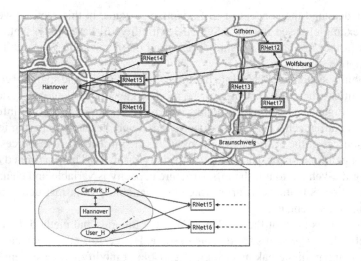

Fig. 1. eMobility Example [8]

Figure 1 shows a formal Petri net representation of a real example scenario that considers four destinations (Wolfsburg, Gifhorn, Braunschweig, and Hannover), the road network between the destinations and the processes which are taking place at the destination locations [8]. The road network is described by several transition framed subnets (e.g., RNet15). It is assumed that the journeys between destinations contain a limited set of variants. Typically three alternative routes and three alternative driving styles are considered, generating a maximal set of nine variants. Each destination is represented by a transition framed subnet (e.g., Hannover), which models both the vehicle charging process (e.g., CarPark H) and user specific processes (e.g., User H) such as appointments. The charging stations that are connected to the car parks support three different charging modes (normal, fast and ultra-fast charging). In this constraint environment, self-adaption is required in situations that occur when the availability of infrastructure resources does not match the demand - not enough capacity, or environment constraints (e.g., speed limit, or delay due to high traffic) hinder the e-vehicle goals. eMobility considers five different levels of self-adaptation [9]:

- *Level-1*: A vehicle computes a set of alternative routes for its current destination. This operation is performed locally by use of the vehicle's planning utility.
- *Level-2*: A vehicle chooses the best option from those alternatives that are computed in the previous level. The vehicle observes the situation and adapts by triggering a new adaptation cycle, starting at Level-1 to the changes in the environment. This operation may require central planning and reasoning at group (ensemble) level.
- *Level-3*: A vehicle computes a set of parking lots near the current destination. This operation is local and is performed by the vehicle's planning utility.
- *Level-4*: A central parking lot planner (PLCSSAM) chooses the best option from those alternatives that are provided by the vehicle in the previous level. As a result, vehicles are assigned an optimal or near-optimal parking lot reservation. At the same time, a "near-optimal parking lot" load-balancing is established.
- *Level-5*: A vehicle issues a reservation request for the selected parking lot. As a result the parking space at that parking lot is booked. Both the vehicle and the parking lot monitor the situation. If required, a new adaptation cycle is triggered.

3   KnowLang

A key feature of KnowLang [5] is a formal language with a multi-tier knowledge specification model allowing for integration of ontologies together with rules and Bayesian networks [10]. The language aims at efficient and comprehensive knowledge structuring and awareness based on logical and statistical reasoning. It helps us tackle: 1) explicit representation of domain concepts and relationships; 2) explicit representation of particular and general factual knowledge, in terms of predicates, names, connectives, quantifiers and identity; and 3) uncertain knowledge in which additive probabilities are used to represent degrees of belief [3]. Other noteworthy features are related to knowledge cleaning (allowing for efficient reasoning) [3, 5] and knowledge representation for autonomic behavior [4, 5]. By applying the KnowLang's multi-tier specification model (see Figure 2) we build a Knowledge Base (KB) structured in three main tiers [5, 3]: 1) *Knowledge Corpuses*; 2) *KB Operators*; and 3) *Inference Primitives*. The tier of Knowledge Corpuses is used to specify KR structures. The tier of KB Operators provides access to Knowledge Corpuses via special classes of *ASK* and *TELL Operators*, where ASK Operators are dedicated to knowledge querying and retrieval and TELL Operators allow for knowledge update. When we specify knowledge with KnowLang,

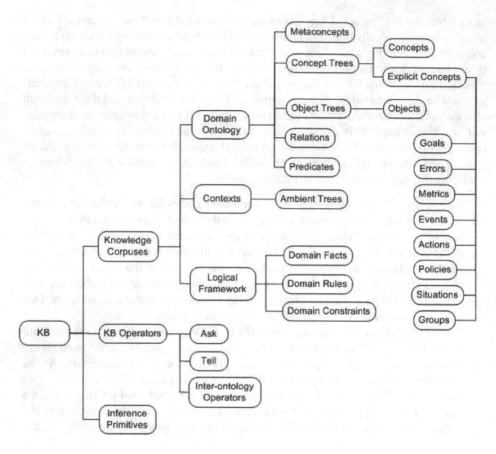

Fig. 2. KnowLang Specification Model

we build a KB with a variety of knowledge structures such as *ontologies, facts, rules* and *constraints* where we need to specify the ontologies first in order to provide the "vocabulary" for the other knowledge structures. A KnowLang ontology is specified over *concept trees, object trees, relations* and *predicates*. Concepts are specific domain terms, e.g., in the eMobility case study, some good candidates for domain concepts are *vehicle, journey*, and *route* (see Section 2). Each concept is specified with special properties and functionalities and is hierarchically linked to other concepts through *PARENTS* and *CHILDREN* relationships. For reasoning purposes every concept specified with KnowLang has an intrinsic *STATE* attribute that may be associated with a set of possible *state values* these concept instances may be in. Concept instances are considered as objects and are structured in object trees — a conceptualization of how objects existing in the world of interest are related to each other. The relationships in an object tree are based on the principle that objects have properties, where the value of a property is another object, which in turn also has properties. Moreover, concepts and objects may be connected via *relations*. Relations are binary and may have probability-distribution attributes (e.g., over time, over situations, over concepts' properties, etc.).

Probability distribution is provided to support probabilistic reasoning and by specifying relations with probability distributions we actually specify Bayesian networks connecting the concepts and objects of an ontology. Figure 3 shows a KnowLang specification sample demonstrating both the language syntax [11] and its visual counterpart — a concept map based on interrelations with no probability distributions. Modeling knowledge with KnowLang requires a number of phases:

- Initial knowledge gathering – involves domain experts to determine the basic notions, relations and functions (operations) of the domain of interest.
- Behavior definition – identifies situations and behavior policies as "control data" helping to identify important self-adaptive scenarios.
- Knowledge structuring – encapsulates domain entities, situations and behavior into KnowLang structures such as concepts, objects, relations, facts and rules.

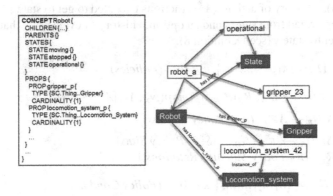

Fig. 3. KnowLang Specification Sample

3.1   Modeling Self-adaptive Behavior

KnowLang employs special knowledge structures and a reasoning mechanism for modeling autonomic self-adaptive behavior [4]. In eMobility, self-adaptive behavior is exhibited by the five levels of self-adaptation (see Section 2). Such a behavior can be expressed via KnowLang *policies*, *events*, *actions*, *situations* and *relations* between policies and situations (see Definitions 1 through 10). Policies (Π) are at the core of autonomic behavior. A policy π has a *goal* (g), *policy situations* (Si_π), *policy-situation relations* (R_π), and *policy conditions* (N_π) mapped to *policy actions* (A_π) where the evaluation of N_π may eventually (with some degree of probability) imply the evaluation of actions (denoted $N_\pi \xrightarrow{[Z]} A_\pi$) (see Definition 2). A condition is a Boolean expression over an ontology (see Definition 4), e.g., the occurrence of a certain event.

   Policy situations Si_π are situations (see Definition 7) that may trigger (or imply) a policy π, in compliance with the policy-situations relations R_π(denoted by $Si_\pi \xrightarrow{[R_\pi]} \pi$), thus implying the evaluation of the policy conditions N_π(denoted by $\pi \rightarrow N_\pi$)(see Definition 2). Therefore, the optional policy-situation relations (R_π) justify the relationships between a policy and the associated situations (see Definition 10). Note that in order to allow for self-adaptive behavior, *relations* must be specified to connect policies with situations over an optional probability distribution (Z) where a policy might be related to multiple situations and vice versa. Probability distribution is provided to support probabilistic reasoning and to help the reasoner to choose the most probable situation-policy "pair". Thus, we may specify a few relations connecting a specific situation to different policies to be undertaken when the system is in that particular situation and the probability distribution over these relations (involving the same situation) should help the reasoner decide which policy to choose (denoted by $si \xrightarrow{[Z]} \pi$ – see Definition 10). Hence, the presence of *probabilistic beliefs* in both mappings and policy relations justifies the probability of policy execution, which may vary with time. A goal g is a desirable transition to a state, or from a specific state to another state, (denoted by $s \Rightarrow s'$) (see Definition 5). A state s is a Boolean expression over ontology ($be(O)$)(see Definition 6), e.g., "a specific property of an object must hold a specific value". A situation is expressed with a state (s), a history of actions ($A \overleftarrow{si}$) (actions executed to get to state s), actions A_{si} that can be performed from state s and an optional history of events $E \overleftarrow{si}$ that eventually occurred to get to state s (see Definition 8).

Definition 1. $\Pi := \{\pi_1, \pi_2, ..., \pi_n\}, n \geq 0$ *(Policies)*

Definition 2. $\pi :=< g, Si_\pi, [R_\pi], N_\pi, A_\pi, map(N_\pi, A_\pi, [Z]) >$
$\quad A_\pi \subset A, N_\pi \xrightarrow{[Z]} A_\pi \quad (A_\pi$ - *Policy Actions)*
$\quad Si_\pi \subset Si, Si_\pi \xrightarrow{[R_\pi]} \pi \to N_\pi \quad (Si_\pi$ - *Policy Sitns)*
$\quad R_\pi \subset R \quad (R_\pi$-*Policy-Situation Relations)*

Definition 3. $N_\pi := \{n_1, n_2, ..., n_k\}, k \geq 0 \quad$ *(Policy Condtns)*

Definition 4. $n := be(O) \quad$ *(Boolean Expression over Ontology)*

Definition 5. $g := \langle \Rightarrow s' \rangle | \langle s \Rightarrow s' \rangle \quad$ *(Goal)*

Definition 6. $s := be(O) \quad$ *(State)*

Definition 7. $Si := \{si_1, si_2, ..., si_n\}, n \geq 0 \quad$ *(Situations)*

Definition 8. $si :=< s, A \overleftarrow{si}, [E \overleftarrow{si}], A_{si} > \quad$ *(Situation)*
$\quad A \overleftarrow{si} \subset A \quad (A \overleftarrow{si}$ - *Executed Actions)*
$\quad A_{si} \subset A \quad (A_{si}$ - *Possible Actions)*
$\quad E \overleftarrow{si} \subset E \quad (E \overleftarrow{si}$ - *Situation Events)*

Definition 9. $R := \{r_1, r_2, ..., r_n\}, n \geq 0 \quad$ *(Relations)*

Definition 10. $r :=< \pi, [rn], [Z], si > \quad$ *(rn - Relation Name)*
$\quad si \in Si, \pi \in \Pi, si \xrightarrow{[Z]} \pi$

Ideally, KnowLang policies are specified to handle specific situations, which may trigger the application of policies. A policy exhibits a behavior via actions generated in the environment or in the system itself. Specific conditions determine, which specific actions (among the actions associated with that policy – see Definition 2) shall be executed. These conditions are often generic and may differ from the situations triggering the policy. Thus, the behavior not only depends on the specific situations a policy is specified to handle, but also depends on additional conditions. Such conditions might be organized in a way allowing for synchronization of different situations on the same policy. When a policy is applied, it checks what particular conditions are met and performs the mapped actions ($map(N_\pi, A_\pi, [Z])$ – see Definition 2). An optional probability distribution may additionally restrict the action execution. Although specified initially, the probability distribution at both mapping and relation levels is recomputed after the execution of any involved action. The re-computation is based on the consequences of the action execution, which allows for *reinforcement learning*.

3.2 Converting Sensory Data to KR

One of the biggest challenges is *"how to map sensory raw data to KR symbols"*. Our approach to this problem is to specify special explicit concepts called *METRICS*. In general, a self-adaptive system has sensors that connect it to the real world and eventually help it listen to its internal components. These sensors generate raw data that represent the physical characteristics of the world. The problem is that these low-level data streams must be: 1) converted to programming variables or more complex data structures that represent collections of sensory data; 2) those programming data structures must be labeled with KR Symbols. Hence, it is required to relate encoded data structures with KR concepts and objects used for reasoning purposes. KnowLang assumes that each sensor is controlled by a software driver where appropriate methods are used to control the sensor and read data from it. Considering the eMobility case study, good candidates for metrics are the sensors used to measure the vehicle speed and the battery level (see Section 2). Both the *sensory data* and *sensors* should be represented in the KB by using *METRIC* explicit concepts and instantiate objects of these concepts. By specifying a METRIC concept we introduce a *class of sensors* to the KB and by specifying objects, instances of that class, we give the actual KR of a real sensor. KnowLang allows the specification of four different types of metrics [11, 5]:

- RESOURCE – measure resources like capacity;
- QUALITY – measure qualities like performance, response time, etc.;
- ENVIRONMENT – measure environment qualities and resources;
- ENSEMBLE – measure complex qualities and resources; might be a function of multiple metrics both of RESOURCE and QUALITY type.

3.3 KnowLang Reasoner

A very challenging task is the R&D of the inference mechanism providing for *knowledge reasoning and awareness*. In order to support reasoning about self-adaptive

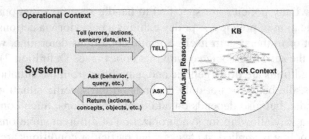

Fig. 4. KnowLang Reasoner

behavior and to provide a KR gateway for communication with the KB, we have developed a special KnowLang Reasoner. The reasoner communicates with the system and operates in the KR Context, a context formed by the represented knowledge (see Figure 4).

The KnowLang Reasoner should be supplied as a component hosted by the system and, thus, it runs in the system's Operational Context as any other system's component. However, it operates in the KR Context and on the KR symbols (represented knowledge). The system talks to the reasoner via special ASK and TELL Operators allowing for knowledge queries and knowledge updates (See Figure 4). Upon demand, the KnowLang Reasoner can also build up and return a self-adaptive behavior model - a chain of actions to be realized in the environment or in the system.

4   Knowledge Representation for eMobility with KnowLang

In order to specify a KR model for eMobility, the first step is to specify a knowledge base (KB) representing the eMobility system, i.e., e-vehicles, parking lots, routes, traffic lights, etc. To do so, we need to specify an ontology structuring the knowledge domains of eMobility. Note that these domains are described via domain-relevant concepts and objects (concept instances) related through relations. To handle explicit concepts like situations, goals, and policies, we grant some of the domain concepts explicit state expressions where a state expression is a Boolean expression over the ontology (see Definition 6 in Section 3.1).

Figure 5 depicts a graphical representation of the eMobility ontology relating most of the domain concepts within an eMobility system. Note that the relationships within a concept tree are "is-a" (inheritance), e.g., the RoadElement concept is a TraficEntity and the Action concept is a Knowledge and subsequently Phenomenon. The following is a sample of the KnowLang specification representing three important concepts: *Vehicle*, *Journey*, and *Route*. As specified, the concepts in a concept tree might have properties of other concepts, functionalities (actions associated with that concept), states (Boolean expressions validating a specific state), etc. For example, the Vehicle's *IsMoving* state holds when the vehicle speed (the VehicleSpeed property) is greater than 0.

```
// e-Vehicle
CONCEPT Vehicle {
  PARENTS {eMobility.eCars.CONCEPT_TREES.Entity}
  CHILDREN {     }
```

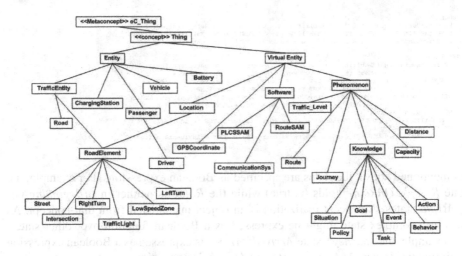

Fig. 5. eMobility Ontology Specified with KnowLang

```
PROPS {
  PROP carDriver {
    TYPE {eMobility.eCars.CONCEPT_TREES.Driver} CARDINALITY {1} }
  PROP carPassengers {
    TYPE {eMobility.eCars.CONCEPT_TREES.Passenger} CARDINALITY {*} }
  PROP carBattery {
    TYPE {eMobility.eCars.CONCEPT_TREES.Battery} CARDINALITY {1} }
}
FUNCS {
  FUNC startEngine {TYPE {eMobility.eCars.CONCEPT_TREES.StartEngine}}
  FUNC stopEngine {TYPE {eMobility.eCars.CONCEPT_TREES.StopEngine}}
  FUNC accelerate {TYPE {eMobility.eCars.CONCEPT_TREES.Accelerate}}
  FUNC slowDown {TYPE {eMobility.eCars.CONCEPT_TREES.SlowDown}}
  FUNC startDriving {TYPE {eMobility.eCars.CONCEPT_TREES.StartDriving}}
  FUNC stopDriving {TYPE {eMobility.eCars.CONCEPT_TREES.StopDriving}}
}
STATES {
  STATE IsOperational{
NOT eMobility.eCars.CONCEPT_TREES.Vehicle.PROPS.carBattery.STATES.batteryLow }
  STATE IsMoving{ eMobility.eCars.CONCEPT_TREES.VehicleSpeed > 0 }
}
}


CONCEPT Journey {
  PARENTS {eMobility.eCars.CONCEPT_TREES.Phenomenon}
  CHILDREN {}
  PROPS {
    PROP journeyRoute {TYPE {eMobility.eCars.CONCEPT_TREES.Route} CARDINALITY {1}}
    PROP journeyTime {TYPE {DATETIME} CARDINALITY {1}}
    PROP journeyCars {TYPE {eMobility.eCars.CONCEPT_TREES.Vehicle} CARDINALITY {*}}
  }
  STATES
  {
    STATE InSufficientBattery {/* to specify */}
    STATE InNotSufficientBattery {
      NOT eMobility.eCars.CONCEPT_TREES.Journey.STATES.InSufficientBattery}
    STATE Arrived {eMobility.eCars.CONCEPT_TREES.Journey.PROPS.journeyRoute.STATES.AtEnd}
    STATE ArrivedOnTime { eMobility.eCars.CONCEPT_TREES.Journey.STATES.Arrived AND
                         (eMobility.eCars.CONCEPT_TREES.JourneyTime <=
                          eMobility.eCars.CONCEPT_TREES.Journey.PROPS.journeyTime)
                        }
  }
}

CONCEPT Route {
  PARENTS {eMobility.eCars.CONCEPT_TREES.Phenomenon}
  CHILDREN {}
  PROPS {
    PROP locationA {TYPE {eMobility.eCars.CONCEPT_TREES.Location} CARDINALITY {1}}
    PROP locationB {TYPE {eMobility.eCars.CONCEPT_TREES.Location} CARDINALITY {1}}
    PROP intermediateStops {TYPE {eMobility.eCars.CONCEPT_TREES.Location} CARDINALITY {*}}
    PROP currentRoad {TYPE {eMobility.eCars.CONCEPT_TREES.Road} CARDINALITY {1}}
    PROP alternativeRoads {TYPE {eMobility.eCars.CONCEPT_TREES.Road} CARDINALITY {*}}
  }
```

```
FUNCS {
  FUNC getCurrentLocation {TYPE {eMobility.eCars.CONCEPT_TREES.GetCurrentLocation}}
  FUNC takeAlternativeRoad {TYPE {eMobility.eCars.CONCEPT_TREES.TakeAlternativeRoad}}
  FUNC recomputeRoads {TYPE {eMobility.eCars.CONCEPT_TREES.RecomputeRoads}}
}
STATES {
  STATE AtBeginning {eMobility.eCars.CONCEPT_TREES.Route.FUNCS.getCurrentLocation =
                     eMobility.eCars.CONCEPT_TREES.Route.PROPS.locationA}
  STATE AtEnd {eMobility.eCars.CONCEPT_TREES.Route.FUNCS.getCurrentLocation =
               eMobility.eCars.CONCEPT_TREES.Route.PROPS.locationB}
  STATE OnRoute { NOT eMobility.eCars.CONCEPT_TREES.Route.STATES.AtBeginning AND
                  NOT eMobility.eCars.CONCEPT_TREES.Route.STATES.AtEnd}
  STATE InHighTraffic {
    eMobility.eCars.CONCEPT_TREES.Route.PROPS.currentRoad.STATES.InHighTraffic}
  STATE InLowTraffic {
    eMobility.eCars.CONCEPT_TREES.Route.PROPS.currentRoad.STATES.InFluentTraffic}
}
}
```

As mentioned above, the states are specified as Boolean expressions. For example, the state *Route*'s *OnRoute* holds (is true) while the *Route* is neither in *AtBeginning* nor at *AtEnd* states. A concept realization is an object instantiated from that concept. As shown, a complex state might be expressed as a Boolean function over other states. For example, the *Journey*'s state *ArrivedOnTime* is expressed as a Boolean expression involving the *Journey*'s *Arrived* state and *Journey*'s properties.

Note that *states* are extremely important for the specification of *goals* (objectives), *situations*, and *policies*. For example, states help the KnowLang Reasoner determine at runtime whether the system is in a particular situation or a particular goal (objective) has been achieved.

4.1 Specifying Self-adaptive Behavior

To specify self-* objectives with KnowLang, we use *goals*, *policies*, and *situations*. These are defined as explicit concepts in KnowLang, and for the eMobility Ontology we specified them under the concepts *Virtual_entity→Phenomenon→Knowledge* (see Figure 5). Figure 6, depicts a concept tree representing the specified eMobility goals. Recall that KnowLang specifies goals as functions of states where any combination of

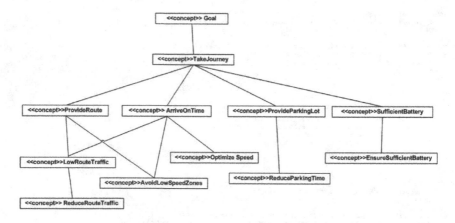

Fig. 6. eMobility Ontology: eMobility Goal Concept Tree

states can be involved (see Section 3.1). A goal has an arriving state (Boolean function of states) and an optional departing state (another Boolean function of states) (see Definition 5 in Section 3.1). A goal with a departing state is more restrictive; i.e., it can be achieved only if the system departs from the specific goal's departing state.

The following code samples present the specification of two simple goals. Usually, goals' arriving and departing states can be either single states or sequences of states. Note that the states used to specify the goals below are specified as part of both *Journey* and *Route* concepts.

```
//
//==== eMobility Goals =============================================
//
CONCEPT_GOAL ArriveOnTime {
  CHILDREN {eMobility.eCars.CONCEPT_TREES.Goal}
  PARENTS {}
  SPEC {
    DEPART { eMobility.eCars.CONCEPT_TREES.Journey.PROPS.journeyRoute.STATES.AtEnd }
    ARRIVE { eMobility.eCars.CONCEPT_TREES.Journey.STATES.ArrivedOnTime }
  }
}
CONCEPT_GOAL LowRouteTraffic {
  CHILDREN {eMobility.eCars.CONCEPT_TREES.Goal}
  PARENTS {}
  SPEC {
    DEPART { eMobility.eCars.CONCEPT_TREES.Route.STATES.InHighTraffic }
    ARRIVE { eMobility.eCars.CONCEPT_TREES.Route.STATES.InLowTraffic }
  }
}
```

The following is a specification sample showing an eMobility policy called *Reduce-RouteTraffic* – as the name says, this policy is intended to reduce the route traffic. As shown, the policy is specified to handle the goal *LowRouteTraffic* and is triggered by the situation *RouteTrafficIncreased*. Further, the policy conditionally triggers via its *MAPPING* sections (e.g., there is a *CONDITONS* directive that requires the *Route*'s state *OnRoute* to be hold) the execution of a sequence of actions. When the conditions are the same, we specify a probability distribution among the *MAPPING* sections involving same conditions (e.g., *PROBABILITY* 0.7), which represents our initial belief in action choice.

```
CONCEPT_POLICY ReduceRouteTraffic {
  CHILDREN {}
  PARENTS {eMobility.eCars.CONCEPT_TREES.Policy}
  SPEC {
    POLICY_GOAL {eMobility.eCars.CONCEPT_TREES.LowRouteTraffic}
    POLICY_SITUATIONS {eMobility.eCars.CONCEPT_TREES.RouteTrafficIncreased}
    POLICY_RELATIONS {eMobility.eCars.RELATIONS.Situation_Policy_1}
    POLICY_ACTIONS {eMobility.eCars.CONCEPT_TREES.TakeAlternativeRoad,
                    eMobility.eCars.CONCEPT_TREES.RecomputeRoads}
    POLICY_MAPPINGS {
      MAPPING {
        CONDITIONS {eMobility.eCars.CONCEPT_TREES.Route.STATES.OnRoute}
        DO_ACTIONS {eMobility.eCars.CONCEPT_TREES.Route.FUNCS.takeAlternativeRoad}
        PROBABILITY {0.7}
      }
      MAPPING {
        CONDITIONS { eMobility.eCars.CONCEPT_TREES.Route.STATES.OnRoute}
        DO_ACTIONS { eMobility.eCars.CONCEPT_TREES.Route.FUNCS.recomputeRoads,
                     eMobility.eCars.CONCEPT_TREES.Route.FUNCS.takeAlternativeRoad}
        PROBABILITY {0.3}
      }
      MAPPING {
        CONDITIONS { eMobility.eCars.CONCEPT_TREES.Route.STATES.AtBeginning}
        DO_ACTIONS { eMobility.eCars.CONCEPT_TREES.Route.FUNCS.recomputeRoads,
                     eMobility.eCars.CONCEPT_TREES.Route.FUNCS.takeAlternativeRoad}
      }
    }
  }
}
```

As specified, the probability distribution gives the initial designer's preference about what actions should be executed if the system ends up in running the *ReduceRouteTraffic* policy. Note that at runtime, the KnowLang Reasoner maintains a record of all the action executions and re-computes the probability rates every time when a policy has been applied and subsequently, actions have been executed. Thus, although initially the system will execute the function *takeAlternativeRoad* (it has the higher probability rate of 0.7), if that policy cannot achieve its goal with this action, then the probability distribution will be shifted in favor of the function sequence *recomputeRoads, takeAlternativeRoad*, which might be executed the next time when the system will try to apply the same policy. Therefore, probabilities are recomputed after every action execution, and thus the behavior changes accordingly.

Moreover, to increase goal-oriented autonomicity [12] in policy specification, we may use a special operator implemented in KnowLang called *GENERATE_NEXT_ACTIONS*. This operator will automatically generate the most appropriate actions to be undertaken by eMobility. The action generation is based on the computations performed by a special *reward function* implemented by the KnowLang Reasoner. The *KnowLang Reward Function* (KLRF) observes the outcome of the actions to compute the possible successor states of every possible action execution and grants the actions with a special reward number considering the current system state (or states, if the current state is a composite state) and goals. KLRF is based on past experience and uses Discrete Time Markov Chains [13] for probability assessment after action executions [5].

Note that when generating actions, the *GENERATE_NEXT_ACTIONS* operator follows a sequential decision-making algorithm where actions are selected to maximize the total reward. This means that the immediate reward for the execution of the first action, or the generated list of actions, might not be the highest one, but the overall reward of executing all the generated actions will be the highest possible one. Moreover, note that, the generated actions are selected from the predefined set of actions (e.g., the implemented eMobility actions). The principle of the decision-making algorithm used to select actions is as follows:

1. The average cumulative reward of the reinforcement learning system is calculated.
2. For each policy-action mapping, the KnowLang Reasoner learns the value function, which is relative to the sum of average rewards.
3. According to the value function and *Bellman optimality principle*[2], the optimal sequence of actions is generated.

As mentioned above, policies are triggered by situations. Therefore, while specifying policies handling eMobility objectives, we need to think of important situations that may trigger those policies. These situations will eventually be outlined by scenarios. A single policy is required to be associated with (related to) at least one situation (see Section 3.1), but for polices handling self-* objectives we eventually need more situations. Actually, because the policy-situation relation is bidirectional, it is maybe more accurate to say that a single situation may need more policies, those providing alternative behaviors or execution paths out of that situation. The following code represents the specification of the situation *RouteTrafficIncreased*, used for the specification of the *ReduceRouteTraffic* policy.

---

[2] The Bellman optimality principle: If a given state-action sequence is optimal, and we were to remove the first state and action, the remaining sequence is also optimal (with the second state of the original sequence now acting as initial state).

```
CONCEPT_SITUATION RouteTrafficIncreased {
   CHILDREN {}
   PARENTS {eMobility.eCars.CONCEPT_TREES.Situation}
   SPEC {
      SITUATION_STATES {eMobility.eCars.CONCEPT_TREES.Route.STATES.InHighTraffic}
      SITUATION_ACTIONS {eMobility.eCars.CONCEPT_TREES.TakeAlternativeRoad}
   }
}
```

As shown, the situation is specified with *SITUATION_STATES* (e.g., *InHighTraffic*) and *SITUATION_ACTIONS* (e.g., *TakeAlternativeRoad*). To consider a situation effective (i.e., the system is currently in that situation), the situation states must be effective (evaluated as true). For example, the situation *RouteTrafficIncreased* is effective if the *Route*'s state *InHighTraffic* is effective (is hold). The possible actions define what actions can be undertaken once the system falls into a particular situation. For example, the *RouteTrafficIncreased* situation has one possible action: *TakeAlternativeRoad*.

Recall that situations are related to policies via relations (see Definition 2 in Section 3.1). The following code demonstrates how we related the situation *RouteTrafficIncreased* to the policy *ReduceRouteTraffic* .

```
RELATION Situation_Policy_1{
   RELATION_PAIR {
      eMobility.eCars.CONCEPT_TREES.RouteTrafficIncreased,
      eMobility.eCars.CONCEPT_TREES.ReduceRouteTraffic}
   }
}
```

Recall that the representation of monitoring sensors in KnowLang is handled via the explicit *Metric concept* (see Section 3.2). The following is a specification of metrics mainly used to assist the specification of states in the specification of the eMobility concept (see Section 6).

```
// metrics
CONCEPT_METRIC RoadTrafficLevel {
   CHILDREN {}
   PARENTS {eMobility.eCars.CONCEPT_TREES.Metric}
   SPEC {
      METRIC_TYPE { ENVIRONMENT }
      METRIC_SOURCE {      "ECarClass.GetRoadTrafficLevel" }
      DATA_TYPE { NUMBER }
   }
}
CONCEPT_METRIC BatteryEnergyLevel {
   CHILDREN {}
   PARENTS {eMobility.eCars.CONCEPT_TREES.Metric}
   SPEC {
      METRIC_TYPE { RESOURCE }
      METRIC_SOURCE {      "ECarClass.GetBatteryEnergyLevel" }
      DATA_TYPE { NUMBER }
   }
}
CONCEPT_METRIC VehicleSpeed {
   CHILDREN {}
   PARENTS {eMobility.eCars.CONCEPT_TREES.Metric}
   SPEC {
      METRIC_TYPE { RESOURCE }
      METRIC_SOURCE {      "ECarClass.GetVehicleSpeed" }
      DATA_TYPE { NUMBER }
   }
}
CONCEPT_METRIC JourneyTime {
   CHILDREN {}
   PARENTS {eMobility.eCars.CONCEPT_TREES.Metric}
   SPEC {
      METRIC_TYPE { RESOURCE }
      METRIC_SOURCE {      "ECarClass.GetJourneyTime" }
      DATA_TYPE { DATETIME }
   }
}
```

5 Related Work

Developing self-adaptive systems with KR&R has been an increasingly interesting topic for years. Examples are found in semantic mapping [14], improving planning and control aspects [15], and most notably in human-robotic interaction (HRI) systems [16, 17]. Overall, KR&R aims to solve complex problems where the operational environment is non-deterministic and a system needs to reason at runtime to find missing answers. Decision-making is a complex process that is often based on more than logical conclusions. Probability and statistics may provide for the so-called probabilistic and statistical reasoning intended to capture uncertain knowledge in which additive probabilities are used to represent degrees of belief of rational agents in the truth of statements. For example, the purpose of a statistical inference might be to draw conclusions about a population based on data obtained from a sample of that population. Probability theory and Baye's theorem [18] lay the basis for such reasoning where Bayesian networks [10] are used to represent belief probability distributions, which actually summarize a potentially infinite set of possible circumstances. The key point is that nodes in a Bayesian network have direct influence on other nodes; given values for some nodes, it is possible to infer the probability distribution for values of other nodes.

Knowledge representation for self-adaptive systems is a wide-open research area with only a limited number of approaches yet considered. The work that is most similar in spirit to our own is that on developing cognitive robots relying on *deliberative controllers*. Architectures for autonomous control in robotic systems require concurrent embedded real-time performance, and are typically too complex to be developed and operated using conventional programming techniques. The core of an autonomous controller is an execution system that executes commands and monitors the environment [19]. Execution systems with deliberative controllers are based on knowledge that contains an explicitly represented symbolic model of the world. Deliberation is the explicit consideration of alternative behaviors (courses of actions).

In [20], an agent programming language called Goal is used to program a cognitive robot control architecture that combines low-level sub-symbolic control with high-level symbolic control. The Goal language helps to realize a cognitive layer where low-level execution control and processing of sensor data are delegated to components in other layers. Similar to KnowLang, Goal supports the goal-oriented behavior and decomposition of complex behavior by means of modules that can focus their attention on relevant sub-goals. However, KnowLang is far more expressive than Goal, especially at the level of modeling self-adaptive behavior, which is not supported by Goal. The integration of situations, goals, policies, and actions with a Bayesian network probability distribution allows for self-adaptation based on both logical and statistical reasoning.

In [21], the high-level language Golog is used for robot programming. Golog supports writing control programs in a high-level logical language, and provides an interpreter that, given a logical axiomatization of a domain, will determine a plan. Similar to KnowLang, Golog also supports actions and situations (actually the language incorporates the Situation Calculus), but again, KnowLang is far more expressive with its Ontology-logical framework knowledge structuring. Moreover, Golog does not provide a means for self-adaptive KR, which is provided by KnowLang.

All known approaches to KR&R pay scant attention to the problem of self-adaptation in software-intensive systems. To the best of our knowledge, KnowLang is unique by its capabilities to handle KR&R for self-adaptive behavior. Through special knowledge constructs and mechanisms, such as probability distribution at different levels of KR, KnowLang allows for the specification of self-adaptive behavior and reasoning on the same. As a result, systems implementing the KnowLang Reasoner can query the KB at runtime for behavior, expressed as sequence of actions that will help the system to transit from an undesirable state to a desirable one.

6 Conclusion and Future Work

In this entry, we have presented the KnowLang Framework as an approach to KR&R allowing for self-adaptive behavior in software-intensive systems. The ultimate goal is to structure computerized knowledge so that a computerized system can effectively process it and gain awareness capabilities and eventually derive its own behavior. The approach allows for efficient and comprehensive knowledge structuring and awareness based on logical and statistical reasoning. The KnowLang Reasoner provides for a mechanism for self-adaptive behavior where KR&R help to establish the vital connection between knowledge, perception, and actions realizing self-adaptive behavior. The knowledge is used against the perception of the world to generate appropriate actions in compliance to some goals and beliefs. The mechanism incorporates special ASK and TELL operators used by the system to talk to the KnowLang Reasoner.

KnowLang adds to Prof. Wirsing's work on defining the concept of autonomic ensembles by introducing KR&R to it. So far, KnowLang has been successfully used to specify and implement knowledge representation for self-adaptive behavior for four different case studies: swarm robotics, scientific clouds, eMobility (all provided by the ASCENS Project), and BepiColombo (as part of a joint project between Lero and ESA). At the time of writing this entry, KnowLang was being finalized as part of the AS-CENS Project. In addition, our plans for future work and further KnowLang extensions include: 1) to continue enhancing the reasoner, especially its ability for state evaluation, and probability distribution needed by reinforcement learning; and 2) to develop an additional KnowLang toolset for knowledge validation and verification (currently KnowLang provides automated tools for syntax and consistency checking only). This will help us verify and validate the specification models before integrating them into the targeted systems.

Acknowledgments. This work was supported by the European Union FP7 Integrated Project Autonomic Service-Component Ensembles (ASCENS) and by Science Foundation Ireland grant 03/CE2/I303_1 to Lero–the Irish Software Engineering Research Centre.

References

1. Hölzl, M., Rauschmayer, A., Wirsing, M.: Engineering of software-intensive systems: State of the art and research challenges. In: Wirsing, M., Banâtre, J.-P., Hölzl, M., Rauschmayer, A. (eds.) Soft-Ware Intensive Systems. LNCS, vol. 5380, pp. 1–44. Springer, Heidelberg (2008)

2. InterLink Project, `http://interlink.ics.forth.gr/central.aspx` (last accessed: November 7, 2014)
3. Vassev, E., Hinchey, M.: Knowledge representation for cognitive robotic systems. In: Proceedings of the 15th IEEE International Symposium on Object/Component/Service-oriented Real-time Distributed Computing Workshops (ISCORCW 2012), pp. 156–163. IEEE Computer Society (2012)
4. Vassev, E., Hinchey, M., Gaudin, B.: Knowledge representation for self-adaptive behavior. In: Proceedings of C* Conference on Computer Science & Software Engineering (C3S2E 2012), pp. 113–117. ACM (2012)
5. Vassev, E., Hinchey, M., Montanari, U., Bicocchi, N., Zambonelli, F., Wirsing, M.: D3.2: Second Report on WP3: The KnowLang Framework for Knowledge Modeling for SCE Systems. ASCENS Deliverable (2012)
6. ASCENS: ASCENS - Autonomic Service-Component Ensembles (2012), `http://www.ascens-ist.eu/`
7. Serbedzija, N., Massink, M., Pinciroli, C., Brambilla, M., Latella, D., Dorigo, M., Birattari, M., Mayer, P., Velasco, J., Hoch, N., Bensler, H.P., Abeywickrama, D., Keznikl, J., Gerostathopoulos, I., Bures, T., Nicola, R.D., Loreti, M.: D7.2: Second Report on WP7 Ensemble Model Syntheses with Robot, Cloud Computing and e-Mobility, ASCENS Deliverable (2012)
8. Serbedzija, N., Reiter, S., Ahrens, M., Velasco, J., Pinciroli, C., Hoch, N., Werther, B.: D7.1: First Report on WP7 Requirement Specification and Scenario Description of the ASCENS Case Studies, ASCENS Deliverable (2011)
9. Serbedzija, N., Hoch, N., Pinciroli, C., Kit, M., Bures, T., Monreale, G., Montanari, U., Mayer, P., Velasco, J.: D7.3: Third Report on WP7 Integration and Simulation Report for the ASCENS Case Studies, ASCENS Deliverable (2013)
10. Neapolitan, R.: Learning Bayesian Networks. Prentice Hall (2003)
11. Vassev, E.: KnowLang Grammar in BNF. Technical Report Lero-TR-2012-04, Lero, University of Limerick, Ireland (2012)
12. Vassev, E., Hinchey, M.: Autonomy Requirements Engineering for Space Missions. NASA Monographs in Systems and Software Engineering. Springer (2014)
13. Ewens, W., Grant, G.: Stochastic processes (i): Poison processes and Markov chains. In: Statistical Methods in Bioinformatics, 2nd edn., Springer, New York (2005)
14. Galindo, C., Fernandez-Madrigal, J., Gonzalez, J., Saffiotti, A.: Robot task planning using semantic maps. Robotics and Autonomous Systems 56(11), 955–966 (2008)
15. Mozos, O., Jensfelt, P., Zender, H., Kruijff, G.J.M., Burgard, W.: An integrated system for conceptual spatial representations of indoor environments for mobile robots. In: Proceedings of the IROS 2007 Workshop: From Sensors to Human Spatial Concepts (FS2HSC), pp. 25–32 (2007)
16. Holzapfel, H., Neubig, D., Waibel, A.: A dialogue approach to learning object descriptions and semantic categories. Robotics and Autonomous Systems 56(11), 1004–1013 (2008)
17. Kruijff, G.J.M., Lison, P., Benjamin, T., Jacobsson, H., Hawes, N.: Incremental, multi-level processing for comprehending situated dialogue in human-robot interaction. In: Proceedings of the Symposium on Language and Robots (2007)
18. Robinson, P., Bauer, S.: Introduction to Bio-Ontologies. CRC Press (2011)
19. Ocón, J., et al.: Autonomous controller - survey of the state of the art, ver. 1.3. Technical Report GOAC, GMV-GOAC-TN01, Contract No. 22361/09/NL/RA, October 31, ESTEC (2011)
20. Wei, C., Hindriks, K.V.: An agent-based cognitive robot architecture. In: Programming Multi-Agent Systems (ProMAS) Workshop Affiliated with AAMAS 2012, Valencia, Spain, pp. 55–68 (2012)
21. Soutchanski, M.: High-level robot programming and program execution. In: Proceedings of the ICAPS 2003 Workshop on Plan Execution. AAAI Press (2003)

Author Index

Anders, Gerrit   115
Arbab, Farhad   273
Areces, Carlos   30
Astesiano, Egidio   377
Autexier, Serge   355

Batory, Don   291
Bauer, Bernhard   475
Baumeister, Hubert   134
Beek, Maurice H. ter   312
Bensalem, Saddek   409
Bergstra, Jan A.   46
Bettaz, Mohamed   134
Bicocchi, Nicola   538
Bliudze, Simon   409
Bozga, Marius   409
Breu, Ruth   458
Broy, Manfred   329
Bruni, Roberto   552
Bucchiarone, Antonio   582
Bureš, Tomáš ·   602

Cengarle, María Victoria   193
Choppy, Christine   377
Corradini, Andrea   552

De Nicola, Rocco   1

Ehrig, Hartmut   582
Ermel, Claudia   582

Farwick, Matthias   458
Fiadeiro, José Luiz   155
Fontaine, Pascal   30
Futatsugi, Kokichi   171

Gadducci, Fabio   552
Gerostathopoulos, Ilias   602
Ghomsi Nokam, Sidoine   355
Gilmore, Stephen   490
Gnesi, Stefania   312

Häusler, Martin   458
Hennicker, Rolf   1

Hesse, Wolfgang   24
Hillston, Jane   490
Hinchey, Mike   676
Hofmann, Martin   62
Höfner, Peter   291
Hölzl, Matthias   13
Hussmann, Heinrich   27

Keznikl, Jaroslav   602
Knapp, Alexander   115, 193, 215
Koch, Nora   13
Köppl, Dominik   291
Krieg-Brückner, Bernd   355
Kurz, Alexander   75

Lanese, Ivan   506
Langermeier, Melanie   475
Latella, Diego   619
Leonardi, Letizia   538
Liu, Si   231
Lluch Lafuente, Alberto   552
Loreti, Michele   619
Lucas, Salvador   91

Maouche, Mourad   134
Massink, Mieke   619
Mayer, Philip   13
Mazzanti, Franco   312
Merz, Stephan   30
Meseguer, José   91, 231
Milius, Stefan   75
Möller, Bernhard   291
Montanari, Ugo   641
Montesi, Fabrizio   506
Mossakowski, Till   215
Mosteghanemi, M'hamed   134

Nielson, Flemming   522
Nielson, Hanne Riis   522

Ölveczky, Peter Csaba   231
Orejas, Fernando   155

Pattinson, Dirk   75
Pelliccione, Patrizio   582

Plášil, František   602
Ponse, Alban   46
Pugliese, Rosario   641

Reggio, Gianna   377
Reif, Wolfgang   115
Rink, Martin   355
Roggenbach, Markus   215
Runge, Olga   582

Saad, Christian   475
Sannella, Donald   253
Schiendorfer, Alexander   115
Schröder, Lutz   75
Schroeder, Andreas   13
Senni, Valerio   619
Šerbedžija, Nikola   662
Siefert, Florian   115
Sifakis, Joseph   409

Steghöfer, Jan-Philipp   115
Störrle, Harald   440

Talcott, Carolyn   273
Tarlecki, Andrzej   253
Tiezzi, Francesco   641
Tribastone, Mirco   490
Trojer, Thomas   458
Tůma, Petr   602

Vandin, Andrea   552
Vassev, Emil   676

Yadav, Maneesh   273

Zambonelli, Franco   538
Zavattaro, Gianluigi   506
Zelend, Andreas   291
Zeng, Kebin   522